# NIALS LAWS OF NIGERIA

(ANNOTATED)

# COMPANIES AND ALLIED MATTERS ACT

First Published in 2013
By
Nigerian Institute of Advanced Legal Studies,
P.M.B. 12820,
University of Lagos Campus,
Lagos,
Nigeria

**ISBN : 978-978-8407-95-9**

**TABLE OF CONTENTS**

*GENERAL EDITOR*

**PROFESSOR EPIPHANY AZINGE, *SAN, Ph.D., LLD.***

*EDITOR*

**PROFESSOR DAKAS C.J. DAKAS**

## THE PROJECT EDITORIAL TEAM

| | | |
|---|---|---|
| 1. | Professor Epiphany Azinge, *SAN, Ph.D, LLD* | - General Editor |
| 2. | Professor Dakas C.J. Dakas | - Editor |
| 3. | Dr. Chinyere Ani | - Project Coordinator |
| 4. | Osatohanmwen Eruaga | - Asst. Project Coordinator |

### Contributing Academic Staff

1. Osatohanmwen Eruaga
2. Emeka Odum
3. Chizoba Ada
4. Enuma Muoneke
5. Gloria Nwamu
6. T.I. Iber
7. Ogor Mgbakogu
8. Adejoke Adediran
9. Ebele Gloria Ogwuda
10. Esther Hatsiwa
11. Temidayo Idowu
12. Prudence Okparavero
13. Ijeoma Anozie
14. Awele L. Ikobi-Anyali
15. Ijeoma Okonkwo
16. Okechukwu Emmanuel Effoduh
17. Kelechukwu Mbajiorgu
18. Fedilia Obiora.
19. Ann-Sophie Udoh

### Honorary Editorial Advisers

1. Hon. Justice M. L. Uwais *GCON. CJN* 1995- 2006
2. Hon. Justice S. M. A. Belgore, *GCON, CJN* 2006-2007
3. Hon. Justice Kayode Eso, *CON, JSC*
4. Hon. Justice G. A. Oguntade, *CON, JSC*

## The Pioneer Project Editorial Committee (1991- 1995)

1. Professor M. A. Ajomo - General Editor
2. Professor C. O. Okonkwo
3. Professor Akintunde Emiola
4. Professor Oluwole Akanle - Project Coordinator
5. Bolaji Owasanoye - Asst. Project Coordinator

## The Pioneer Contributing Editors (1991- 1995)

Members of the Project Committee as well as the following:

1. Mrs. Bola Adewale
2. Dr. Wale Ajai
3. Dr. Epiphany Azinge
4. P. K. Fogam
5. Mike Ikhariale
6. Ademola Popoola
7. Ameze Guobadia
8. Adedeji Adekunle
9. I. O. Smith
10. Bola Ogunsanwo
11. Tokunbo Akomolafe

## The Honorary Editorial Advisers (1991- 1995)

1. The late Sir Adetokunbo Ademola
2. The late Judge Taslim Elias
3. The late Justice Mohammed Bello
4. The late Justice Atanda Fatayi- Williams
5. The late Justice G. S. Sowemimo
6. The late Justice G. A. Irikefe

## INTRODUCTION TO THE NIALS' LAWS OF NIGERIA

### *(COMPANIES AND ALLIED MATTERS ACT ANNOTATED)*

The NIALS' Laws of Nigeria (Annotated) series was inspired by acknowledged annotated works as Halsbury's Law of England and the US Code Annotated. As stated in the first NIALS Laws of Nigeria - Annotated Criminal Administration of Justice, the main objective of producing annotated Statutes was and remains providing a one-stop source containing annotations and updates of the provisions of the Statute with cross references to relevant subjects and sections.

Following the successful annotation of the Criminal Administration of Justice, Matrimonial Causes and Banking Statute, the Institute felt it imperative to undertake next, the annotation of the Six-Hundred and twelve sectioned Companies and Allied Matters Act (CAMA), which is the primary legislation that governs the formation and functioning of Companies in Nigeria. The provisions of the Act are still very much similar to the old English Companies Act and references are still made in indigenous scholarly works on the subject matter of company law, to English cases. Thus, the Research team deemed it important that only Nigerian cases that are relevant to the Statute are included in the Annotation. This accounts for the paucity of case law annotation in some sections of the Act. In addition to case law annotation, Company Law texts and scholarly publications were widely consulted and relevant references to same have been included in order to enrich the content.

This Annotation of the Company and Allied Matters, the fourth in the Annotation of Statutes remains unique in the manner of presentation and details, making it a must have for all legal practitioners, judges, law lecturers and all those interested in the practice of Company Law.

**Professor Epiphany Azinge, *SAN***
**General Editor**

## FOREWORD

It is with great delight that I write a foreword to the Laws of Nigeria (Company Law Annotated) published by the Nigerian Institute of Advanced Legal Studies.

The publication, which is the fourth in the series of NIALS' Laws of Nigeria (Annotated), is aimed at providing easy access to Company Law applicable in Nigeria, referring to relevant case law. By providing a section-by-section annotation of the Company and Allied Matters Act, in the form of definitions, case law annotation, cross-referencing with other relevant statute and further reading, the publication adequately simplifies the provisions of the Act as it is applied in Nigeria.

The importance of this Company Law Statute (Annotated) cannot be emphasised when one considers that many persons, educated and uneducated, citizens and foreigners alike are engaged in the process of formation of companies for doing business in Nigeria. This annotated version of the Companies and Allied Matters Act, is geared towards enriching and simplifying the study of corporate activities of companies, organisations and businesses registered under the Act. Legal practitioners and Students will thus find this publication a very handy guide to understanding the provisions of the sections of the Act.

I must not fail at this point to commend the dogged effort of the present Director- General of the Institute, Professor Epiphany Azinge SAN, who had worked tirelessly on this and other projects of the Institute.

I recommend the COMPANIES AND ALLIED MATTERS ACT (ANNOTATED) to all and sundry

**Hon. Justice S.M.A Belgore**
Former Chief Justice of Nigeria.

# COMPANIES AND ALLIED MATTERS ACT

# Table of Cases

**Nigerian Cases**

**Foreign Cases**

## Table of Statutes

# COMPANIES AND ALLIED MATTERS ACT 1990

## ARRANGEMENT OF SECTIONS

**SECTION**

PART A
*Companies*

PART I
*Corporate Affairs Commission*



PART II
*Incorporation of Companies and Incidental Matters*

CHAPTER 1

*Formation of company*

CHAPTER 2

*Conversion and re-registration of companies*



CHAPTER 3
*Foreign companies*



CHAPTER 4
*Promoters*



PART III
*Acts by or on Behalf of the Company*

*Exercise of company's powers*



*Liability for acts of the company*



*Constructive notice of registered documents*

## PART V
### *Share Capital*

*Minimum share capital*



*Alteration of share capital*



*Reduction of share capital*



*Miscellaneous matters relating to capital*



## PART VI
### *Shares*

*Nature of shares*



*Issue of shares*

*Transfer and transmission*



*Transactions by company in respect of its own shares*



PART VII
*Debentures*

*Creation of debenture and debenture stock*



*Types of debentures*



*Fixed and floating charges*

*General meeting*



*Extraordinary general meeting*



*Notice of meetings*



*Voting*



*Resolutions*



*Miscellaneous matters relating to meetings and proceedings*

PART IX

*Directors and secretaries of the company*

CHAPTER 1
*Directors*

*Action by or against the company*



*Relief on the grounds of unfairly prejudicial and oppressive conduct*



*Investigation of companies and their affairs*



PART XI
*Financial statements and audit*

CHAPTER 1
*Financial statements*

*Accounting records*



*Directors' reports*



*Procedure on completion of financial statements*



*Modified financial statements*



*Publication of financial statements*



*Supplementary*



CHAPTER 2
*Audit*

PART XII
*Annual returns*



PART XIII
*Dividends and profits*



PART XIV
*Receivers and managers*

*Appointment of receivers and managers*

*Committee of inspection, special manager, etc.*



*General powers of court in case of winding up by court*



*Enforcement of and appeals from orders*



CHAPTER 3
*Voluntary winding up*

*Resolutions for and commencement of voluntary winding up*



*Consequences of voluntary winding up*

PART C

*Incorporated trustees*



PART D
*Short Title*

# SCHEDULES

FIRST SCHEDULE
*Tables A, B, C and D*

SECOND SCHEDULE
*Form and content of companies financial statements*

THIRD SCHEDULE
*Miscellaneous matters to be disclosed in notes to company financial statements*

FOURTH SCHEDULE
*Particulars in company financial statements of loan and other transactions favouring directors and officers*

FIFTH SCHEDULE
*Matters to be dealt with in director's report*

SIXTH SCHEDULE
*Matters to be expressly stated in auditors report*

SEVENTH SCHEDULE
*Modified financial statements of companies qualifying as small companies*

EIGHTH SCHEDULE
*Contents and form of annual returns of a company having shares other than a small company*

NINTH SCHEDULE
*Annual return of a small company*

TENTH SCHEDULE
*Annual return of a company limited by guarantee*

ELEVENTH SCHEDULE
*Powers of receivers and managers of the whole or substantially the whole of the company's property*

TWELFTH SCHEDULE

*Provisions not applicable on winding up under supervision of court*

THIRTEENTH SCHEDULE
*Provision of this Act applying to unregistered companies*

FOURTEENTH SCHEDULE
*Forms of statement to be published by banking and insurance companies and deposit, provident or benefit societies*

FIFTEENTH SCHEDULE
*Fees to be paid for matters under Part A of the Act*

PART A

# COMPANIES

## PART I

### 1. Corporate Affairs Commission

Establishment of the Corporate Affairs Commission

(1) There is hereby established under this Act, a body to be known as the Corporate Affairs Commission (in this Act referred to as "the Commission").

(2) The Commission[1] shall be-

(a) A body corporate with perpetual succession[2] and a common seal[3];

(b) Capable of suing and being sued in its corporate name[4]; and

(c) Capable of acquiring, holding or disposing of any property, movable or immovable, for the purpose of carrying out its functions.

(3) The headquarters of the Commission[1] shall be situated in the Federal Capital Territory, Abuja, and there shall be established an office of the Commission[1] in each State of the Federation.

---

**Notes**

**Section 1(2)**

1. "Commission" means the Corporate Affairs Commission established under section 1 of this Act. See **Section 567 CAMA Cap. C20, LFN 2004.**
2. "Perpetual succession" means the continuation of a corporation's legal status despite changes in ownership or management. See **Garner. B. (ed) Black's Law Dictionary 8th ed.**
3. "Common Seal" means a piece of wax, a wafer, or some other substance affixed to the paper or other material on which a promise or release, or conveyance is written together with recital or expression of intention by which the promisor, releasor, or grantor manifest that a piece of wax, wafer, or other substance is a seal. See **Garner. B. (ed.) Black's Law Dictionary 8th ed.**
4. "Corporate Name" means the registered name under which a corporation conducts legal affairs See **Garner. B. (ed) Black's Law Dictionary 8th ed.**

**Cross Reference**

For a complete list of all the States that makes the Federation, see **schedule 1, Constitution of the Federal Republic of Nigeria, 1999 Constitution.**

On the obligation of a company to keep a common seal and use of the company's common seal, see **Section 74 CAMA Cap. C20, LFN 2004**

---

2. The Commission[1] shall consist of the following members, [2] that is-

(a) a chairman[3] who shall be appointed by the President on the recommendation of the Minister, [4] being a person who by reason of his ability, experience or specialized knowledge of corporate, industrial, commercial, financial or economic matters or of business or professional attainments would in his opinion be capable of making outstanding contributions to the work of the Commission [1];

(b) one representative of the business community, appointed by the Minister[4] on the recommendation of the Nigerian Association of Chambers of Commerce, Industries, Mines and Agriculture;

(c) one representative of the legal profession, appointed by the Minister[4] on the recommendation of the Nigerian Bar Association;

(d) one representative of the accountancy profession, appointed by the Minister[4] on the recommendation of the Institute of Chartered Accountants of Nigeria;

(e) one representative of the Manufacturers Association of Nigeria, appointed by the Minister [4] on the recommendation of the Association;

(f) one representative of the Securities and Exchange Commission not below the grade of Director or its equivalent;

(g) one representative of each of the following Federal Ministries, that is-

(i) Commerce;

(ii) Justice;

(iii) Industry, and

(h) the Registrar-General[5] of the Commission[1].

---

**Notes**
**Section 2(1)**

1. "Commission" means the Corporate Affairs Commission established under section 1 of this Act. See **Section 567 CAMA Cap. C20, LFN 2004.**
2. "Member" means any member of the Commission1 including the chairman. See **section 17 CAMA Cap. C20 LFN 2004**
3. "Chairman" means a person who is in charge of a meeting. See **Oxford Advanced Learner's Dictionary 6th ed.**
   "Chairman" means the chairman of the Commission. See **section 17 CAMA Cap. C20, LFN 2004**
4. "Minister" means the Minister charged with responsibility for trade; and "Ministry" shall be constituted accordingly. See **Section 567 CAMA Cap. C20, LFN 2004.**
5. "Registrar-General" means the Registrar-general appointed under section 8. **See part 1 of the first schedule of CAMA, Cap. C20 LFN 2004.**

Cross Reference

On the establishment of the Office of the President of Nigeria, See **Section 130 of the Constitution of the Federal Republic of Nigeria 1999 as amended.**

On the appointment of Ministers, See **Section 147 of the Constitution of the Federal Republic of Nigeria 1999 as amended.**

On the establishment of the Institute of Chartered Accounts of Nigeria, See **Section 1 of the Institute of Chartered Accountants of Nigeria Act, Cap. I11, LFN, 2004.**

On the Legal Profession, see the **Legal Practitioner's Act, Cap. L11, LFN, 2004**

On the establishment of the Securities and Exchange Commission, see Section 1 of the **Investments and Securities Act, 2007.**

---

**Cases**

The Corporate Affairs Commission is conferred with the responsibility of registering companies operating in Nigeria by Statute, and under the said statute it can prohibit and restrict certain names to be registered. See ***Mustapha v. CAC (2009)*** **Vol. 43 W.R.N. 1-171 pg 156.**

**For Further Reading**

On Corporate Affairs Commission, Incorporation of Companies, Membership of a company, and Share Capital, see:

Orojo, J. Ola **Company Law and Practice in Nigeria** 3rd Edition, Mbeyi & Associates (Lagos, Nigeria) 1992.

Ogbuanya C.S. Nelson **Essentials of Corporate Law Practice in Nigeria** Novena Publishers Limited 2012

Sasegbon Deji & Co **Companies and Allied Matters Law and Practice** (NCAMLP) DSC Publications Ltd 2006

## 3. Tenure of Office

(1) Subject to the provisions of subsection (2) of this section, a person appointed as a member [1] of the Commission [2] (not being an ex-officio member)[3] shall hold office for three years and shall be eligible for re-appointment for one further term of three years.

(2) The Minister [4] may, with the approval of the President at any time remove any member [1] of the Commission [2] from office if the Minister[4] is of the opinion that it is not in the interest of the Commission[2] for the member [1] to continue in office and shall notify the member[1] in writing to that effect.

(3) The members [1] of the Commission [2] except the Registrar-General[5] shall be part-time members [1] of the Commission. [2]

(4) Any member [1] of the Commission [2] shall cease to hold office if-

(a) he becomes of unsound mind or is incapable of carrying out his duties;

(b) he becomes bankrupt [6] or has made arrangement with his creditors[7];

(c) he is convicted of a felony or any offence involving dishonesty;

(d) he is guilty of serious misconduct relating to his duties; or

(e) in the case of a person possessed of professional qualifications, he is disqualified or suspended (other than at his own request) from practicing his profession in any part of Nigeria by the order of any competent authority made in respect of him personally.

---

**Notes**

**Section 3 (1)**

1. "Member" means any member of the Commission including the Chairman. See **Section 17 CAMA Cap. C20, LFN, 2004.**
2. "Commission" means the Corporate Affairs Commission established under section 1 of this Act. See **section 567 CAMA Cap. C20 LFN 2004**
3. "Ex –officio member" means, a member whose membership will pass to his or her successor. See **Garner B. (ed) Black's Law Dictionary 8th ed.**

**Section 3 (2)**

4. "Minister" means the Minister charged with responsibility for trade; and "Ministry" shall be constituted accordingly. See **Section 567 CAMA Cap. C20, LFN 2004**

**Section 3 (3)**

5. "Registrar-General" means the Registrar-general appointed under section 8. **See part 1 of the first schedule of CAMA, CAP C20 LFN 2004.**
6. "Bankrupt" means a person who cannot meet current financial obligations; an insolvent person. See **Garner B. (ed) Black's Law Dictionary 8th ed.**
7. "Creditor" means one to whom a debt is owed whether contractual or otherwise. See **Garner B. (ed.) Black's Law Dictionary 8 th ed.**

Cross Reference

On the meaning of a felony, see **section 3 Criminal Code, Cap. C38, LFN 2004**

**On the meaning of offence, see section 2 Criminal Code Cap. C38 LFN 2004**

On the appointment of Ministers, See **section 147 of the Constitution of the Federal Republic of Nigeria 1999 (as amended.)**

On the establishment of the Office of the President of Nigeria, See **section 130 of the Constitution of the Federal Republic of Nigeria 1999 (as amended).**

---

## 4. Remuneration and allowance

Members[1] of the Commission[2] appointed under section 2 (a), (b), (c), (d), (e), (f), (g) and (h) shall be paid such remuneration[3] and allowances as the President may, from time to time, direct.

---

**Notes**

**Section 4**

1. "Member" means any member of the Commission including the Chairman. See **Section 17 of the Companies and Allied Matters Act, CAP C20, LFN, 2004**
2. "Commission" means the Corporate Affairs Commission established under section 1 of this Act. See **section 567 CAMA Cap. C20 LFN 2004**
3. "Remuneration" means payment; compensation. **Garner B. (ed) Black's Law Dictionary 8th ed.**

Cross Reference

On the establishment of the Office of the President of Nigeria, See **section 130 of the Constitution of the Federal Republic of Nigeria 1999 as amended.**

---

**For Further Reading**

On Corporate Affairs Commission, Incorporation of Companies, Membership of a company, and Share Capital, see:

Orojo, J. Ola **Company Law and Practice in Nigeria** 3rd Edition, Mbeyi & Associates (Lagos, Nigeria) 1992.
Ogbuanya C.S. Nelson **Essentials of Corporate Law Practice in Nigeria** Novena Publishers Limited 2012
Sasegbon Deji & Co **Companies and Allied Matters Law and Practice** (NCAMLP) DSC Publications Ltd 2006

## 5. Proceedings of the Commission

(1) Subject to this section and section 27 of the Interpretation Act, the Commission [1] may make standing orders regulating its proceedings.

(2) The chairman [2] shall preside at every meeting [3] of the Commission[1] but, in his absence, the members [4] present shall elect one of their number present to preside at the meeting. [3]

(3) The quorum [5] for meetings[3] of the Commission [1] shall be five.

(4) The Commission [1] may appoint any of its officers to act as secretary at any of its meetings. [4]

---

**Notes**

**Section 5(1)**

1. "Commission" means the Corporate Affairs Commission established under section 1 of this Act. See **section 567 CAMA Cap C20 LFN 2004**

**Section 5(2)**

2. "Chairman" means a person who is in charge of a meeting. See **Oxford Advanced Learner's Dictionary 6th ed.**
   "Chairman" means the chairman of the Commission. See **section 17, CAMA Cap C38, LFN 2004**
3. "Meetings" means the gathering of people to discuss or act on matters in which they have a common interest. See **Garner, B. (ed) Black's Law Dictionary, 8th ed.**
4. "Member" means any member of the Commission including the Chairman. See **Section 17 CAMA, Cap C20, LFN, 2004**

**Section 5(3)**

5. "Quorum" means the minimum number of members who must be present for a deliberative assembly. See **Garner B. (ed) Black's Law Dictionary 8th ed.**

**Cross Reference**

On special provisions as to the acts of certain statutory bodies, see **section 27, Interpretation Act Cap. I23 LFN 2004**

---

**For Further Reading**

On Corporate Affairs Commission, Incorporation of Companies, Membership of a company, and Share Capital. See:

Orojo, J. Ola **Company Law and Practice in Nigeria** 3rd Edition, Mbeyi & Associates (Lagos, Nigeria) 1992.
Ogbuanya C.S. Nelson **Essentials of Corporate Law Practice in Nigeria** Novena Publishers Limited 2012
Sasegbon Deji & Co **Companies and Allied Matters Law and Practice** (NCAMLP) DSC Publications Ltd 2006

## 6. Disclosure of interest

(1) A member [1] of the Commission [2] who is directly interested in any company [3] or enterprise, the affairs of. which are being deliberated upon by the Commission [2], or is interested in any contract made or proposed to be made by the Commission [2] shall, as soon as possible after the relevant facts have come to his knowledge, disclose the nature of his interest at a meeting [4] of the Commission.[2]

(2) A disclosure, under subsection (1) of this section, shall be recorded in the minutes of the Commission, [2] and the member shall-

(a) not take part after such disclosure in any deliberation or decision of the Commission [2] with regard to the subject matter in respect of which his interest is thus disclosed;

(b) be excluded for the purpose of constituting a quorum [5] of the Commission[2] for any such deliberation or decision.

---

**Notes**

**Section 6(1)**

1. "Member" means any member of the Commission including the Chairman. See **Section 17 CAMA, Cap. C20, LFN, 2004**
2. "Commission" means the Corporate Affairs Commission established under section 1 of this Act . **See section 567 Cap. C20, LFN, 2004.**
3. "Company" means a company formed and registered under this Act or, as the case may be, formed and registered in Nigeria before and in existence on the commencement of this Act, **Companies and Applied Matters Act, Cap. C20, LFN, 2004.**
4. "Meeting" means the gathering of people to discuss or act on matters in which they have a common interest. **See Garner B. (ed) Black's Law Dictionary, 8th ed.**

**Section 6(2)**

5. "Quorum" means the minimum number of members who must be present for a deliberative assembly. See **Garner B. (ed) Black's Law Dictionary 8th ed.**

---

**Cases**

The definition of a company in Section 650 of Companies and Allied Matters Act puts the matter beyond doubt. It defines a 'company' or 'existing' to mean....a company formed and registered in Nigeria before and in existence on the commencement of this Act. ***Agro Allied Dev. Ent. Ltd v Reefer* (2009) Vol. 31 W.R.N 1-185 at pg 7**

**For Further Reading**
On Corporate Affairs Commission, Incorporation of Companies, Membership of a company, and Share Capital. See:
Orojo, J. Ola **Company Law and Practice in Nigeria** 3rd Edition, Mbeyi & Associates (Lagos, Nigeria) 1992.
Ogbuanya C.S. Nelson **Essentials of Corporate Law Practice in Nigeria** Novena Publishers Limited 2012
Sasegbon Deji & Co. **Companies and Allied Matters Law and Practice** (NCAMLP) DSC Publications Ltd 2006

## 7. Functions

(1) The functions of the Commission [1] shall be to-

(a) subject to section 541 of this Act, administer this Act including the regulation and supervision of the formation, incorporation[2], registration, management, and winding up[3] of companies[4] under or pursuant to this Act;

(b) establish and maintain a company's [4] registry and offices in all the States of the Federation suitably and adequately equipped to discharge its functions under this Act or any other law in respect of which it is charged with responsibility;

(c) arrange or conduct an investigation into the affairs of any company[4] where the interests of the shareholders [5] and the public so demand;

(d) perform such other functions as may be specified by any Act or enactment; and

(e) undertake such other activities as are necessary or expedient for giving full effect to the provisions of this Act.

(2) Nothing in this section shall affect the powers, duties or jurisdiction of the Securities and Exchange Commission under the Investments and Securities Act.

---

**Notes**
**Section 7(1)**

1. "Commission" means the Corporate Affairs Commission established under section 1 of this Act. See **Section 567 CAMA, Cap. C20, LFN, 2004.**
2. "Incorporation" means the formation of a legal corporation. See **Garner B. (ed ) Black's Law Dictionary 8th ed.**
3. "Winding up" means means the process of settling accounts and liquidating assets in anticipation of a partnership's or corporation's dissolution. See **Garner B. (ed) Black's Law Dictionary, 8th ed**
4. "Company" means a company formed and registered under this Act or, as the case may be, formed and registered in Nigeria before and in existence on the commencement of this Act. See **Section 567 CAMA, Cap. C20, LFN, 2004.**

**Cross Reference**

On modes of winding up companies, see **section 401 CAMA Cap. C20 LFN 2004**

For a complete list of all the States that makes the Federation, see **schedule 1, Constitution of the Federal Republic of Nigeria, 1999 Constitution.**

On the establishment of the Securities and Exchange Commission, see **section 1 of the Investments and Securities Act, 2007**

---

**Cases**

The Corporate Affairs Commission is conferred with the responsibility of registering companies operating in Nigeria by Statute. See ***Mustapha v. CAC*** **(2009) Vol. 43 W.R.N. 1-171 pg 156.**

**For Further Reading**

For further reading on Corporate Affairs Commission, Incorporation of Companies, Membership of a company, and Share Capital see:

Orojo, J. Ola **Company Law and Practice in Nigeria** 3rd Edition, Mbeyi & Associates (Lagos, Nigeria) 1992. Ogbuanya C.S. Nelson **Essentials of Corporate Law Practice in Nigeria** Novena Publishers Limited 2012

Sasegbon Deji & Co **Companies and Allied Matters Law and Practice** (NCAMLP) DSC Publications Ltd 2006

## 8. Appointment of Registrar-General

(1) There shall be appointed by the Commission [1] a Registrar-General[2] who shall be qualified to practice as a legal practitioner [3] in Nigeria and has been so qualified for not less than 10 years and in addition, has had experience in company law practice or administration for not less than 8 years.

(2) The Registrar-General [2] shall be the chief executive of the Commission[1] and shall be subject to the directives of the Commission[1] and shall hold office on such terms and conditions as may be specified in his letter of appointment and on such other

terms and conditions as may be determined, from time to time, by the Commission[1] with the approval of the President.

(3) The Registrar-General [2] shall be the accounting officer for the purpose of controlling and disbursing amounts from the fund established pursuant to section 12 of this Act.

---

**Notes**
**Section 8(1)**

1. "Commission" means the Corporate Affairs Commission established under section 1 of this Act. See **Section 567 CAMA, Cap. C20, LFN, 2004.**
2. "Registrar-General" means the Registrar-general appointed under section 8 of this Act. See **Section 567 CAMA, Cap. C20, LFN, 2004.**
3. "Legal practitioner" has the meaning assigned to it by the Legal Practitioners Act. See **section 567 CAMA, Cap. C20, LFN 2004.**

**Cross Reference**

On meaning of Legal Practitioner, **see section 24 of the Legal Practitioners Act, Cap. L11 LFN 2004**

On the establishment of the Office of the President of Nigeria, See **section 130 of the Constitution of the Federal Republic of Nigeria 1999 as amended.**

---

**For Further Reading**

On Corporate Affairs Commission, Incorporation of Companies, Membership of a company, and Share Capital. See:

Orojo, J. Ola **Company Law and Practice in Nigeria** 3rd Edition, Mbeyi & Associates (Lagos, Nigeria) 1992.

Ogbuanya C.S. Nelson **Essentials of Corporate Law Practice in Nigeria** Novena Publishers Limited 2012

Sasegbon Deji & Co **Companies and Allied Matters Law and Practice** (NCAMLP) DSC Publications Ltd 2006

## 9. Appointment of staff

The Commission[1] may appoint such other staff[2] as it may deem necessary for the efficient performance of the functions of the Commission[1] under or pursuant to this Act.

---

**Notes**
**Section 9**

1. "Commission" means the Corporate Affairs Commission established under section 1 of this Act. See **section 567 CAMA, Cap. C20, LFN, 2004.**

2. "Staff" means all the workers employed in an organization considered as a group. **See Oxford Advanced Learner's Dictionary of Current English, 6[th] ed.**

Cross Reference

For functions of the Commission, see **Section 7 of CAMA, Cap. C20, LFN, 2004.**

---

**For Further Reading**

On Corporate Affairs Commission, Incorporation of Companies, Membership of a company, and Share Capital. See:

Orojo, J. Ola **Company Law and Practice in Nigeria** 3[rd] Edition, Mbeyi & Associates (Lagos, Nigeria) 1992.

Ogbuanya C. S. Nelson **Essentials of Corporate Law Practice in Nigeria** Novena Publishers Limited 2012

Sasegbon Deji & Co **Companies and Allied Matters Law and Practice** (NCAMLP) DSC Publications Ltd 2006.

## 10. Right to appear in court

Notwithstanding the provisions of any enactment to the contrary, a person appointed to the office of Registrar-General [1] under section 8 of this Act or a person appointed under section 9 of this Act who is a legal practitioner [2] shall, while so appointed, be entitled to represent the Commission [3] as a legal practitioner [3] for the purpose and in the course of his employment.

---

**Notes**

**Section 10**

1. "Registrar-General" means the Registrar-general appointed under Section 8 of this Act. See **Section 567 CAMA, Cap C20, LFN, 2004.**
2. "Legal practitioner" has the meaning assigned to it by the Legal Practitioners Act. See **section 567 CAMA, Cap. C20, LFN 2004.**
3. "Commission" means the Corporate Affairs Commission established under section 1 of this Act See **Section 567 CAMA, Cap. C20, LFN, 2004.**

Cross Reference

On meaning of Legal Practitioner, **see section 24 of the Legal Practitioners Act, CAP L11 LFN 2004.**

---

**For Further Reading**

On Corporate Affairs Commission, Incorporation of Companies, Membership of a company, and Share Capital. See:

Orojo, J. Ola **Company Law and Practice in Nigeria** 3[rd] Edition, Mbeyi & Associates (Lagos, Nigeria) 1992.

Ogbuanya C.S. Nelson **Essentials of Corporate Law Practice in Nigeria** Novena Publishers Limited 2012
Sasegbon Deji & Co **Companies and Allied Matters Law and Practice** (NCAMLP) DSC Publications Ltd 2006

## 11. Service in the Commission to be pensionable

Service in the Commission [1] shall be approved service for the purpose of the Pensions Act and accordingly, officers and other persons employed in the Commission [1] shall in respect of their service in the Commission [1] be entitled to pensions [2], gratuities and other retirement benefits enjoyed by persons holding equivalent grades in the public service of the Federation, so however that nothing in this Act shall prevent the appointment of a person to any office on terms which preclude the grant of a pension [2] and gratuity in respect of that office.

---

**Notes**
**Section 11**

1. "Commission" means the Corporate Affairs Commission established under Section 1 of this Act. See **Section 567 CAMA, CAP C20, LFN, 2004.**
2. "Pension" means an amount of money paid regularly by a government or company to somebody who is considered too old or too ill to work. See **Oxford Advanced Learner's Dictionary of Current English. 6 th ed.**

**Cross Reference**

On the establishment of acontributory scheme for employees in the public and private sector and the establishment of the Pension Commission, **see generally Pension Reform Act Cap. P4 LFN 2004**

Public service of the Federation is as defined in **section 318 of the Constitution of the Federal Republic of Nigeria, 1999(as amended)**

On meaning of public officers for the purpose of the application of the code of conduct bureau, see **Part II, Fifth Schedule, Constitution of the Federal Republic of Nigeria, 1999( as amended).**

---

## 12. Fund of the Commission

The Commission [1] shall establish a fund [2] which shall consist of such sums as may be allocated to it by the Federal Government and such other funds as may accrue to it in the discharge of its functions.

---

**Notes**
**Section 12**

1. "Commission" means the Corporate Affairs Commission established under section 1 of this Act. See **Section 567 CAMA, Cap C20, LFN, 2004.**
2. "Fund" means an amount of money that has been saved or has been made available for a particular purpose. See Oxford **Advanced Learner's Dictionary of Current English. 6 th ed.**

**For Further Reading**
On Corporate Affairs Commission, Incorporation of Companies, Membership of a company, and Share Capital see:
Orojo J. Ola **Company Law and Practice in Nigeria** 3rd Edition, Mbeyi & Associates (Lagos, Nigeria) 1992.
Ogbuanya C.S. Nelson **Essentials of Corporate Law Practice in Nigeria** Novena Publishers Limited 2012
Sasegbon Deji & Co **Companies and Allied Matters Law and Practice** (NCAMLP) DSC Publications Ltd 2006.

## 13. Expenditure of the Commission

The Commission[1] may, from time to time, apply the proceeds of the fund established in pursuance of section 12 of this Act-

(a) to the cost of administration of the Commission [1];
(b) for re-imbursing members [2] of the Commission[1] or any Committee set up by the Commission [1] for such expenses as may be authorised or approved by the Commission, [1] in accordance with the rate approved in that behalf by the President;
(c) to the payment of salaries, fees or other remuneration or allowances, pensions[3] and gratuities payable to the employees of the Commission[1];
(d) for the maintenance of any property acquired or vested in the Commission[1]; and
(e) for, and in connection with, all or any of the functions of the Commission[1] under this Act.

**Notes**
**Section 13**

1. "Commission" means the Corporate Affairs Commission established under section 1 of this Act. See **Section 567 CAMA, Cap. C20, LFN, 2004.**

2. "Member" means any member of the Commission including the Chairman. See **Section 17 CAMA, Cap. C20, LFN, 2004**
3. "Pension" means an amount of money paid regularly by a government or company to somebody who is considered too old or too ill to work. See **Oxford Advanced Learner's Dictionary of Current English. 6 [th]ed.**

Cross Reference

On establishment of the Fund of the Commission, see **section 12 CAMA Cap. C20, LFN 2004**

On the establishment of the Office of the President of Nigeria, See **section 130 of the Constitution of the Federal Republic of Nigeria 1999 as amended.**

---

**For Further Reading**

On Corporate Affairs Commission, Incorporation of Companies, Membership of a company, and Share Capital see:

Orojo, J. Ola **Company Law and Practice in Nigeria** 3[rd] Edition, Mbeyi & Associates (Lagos, Nigeria) 1992.

Ogbuanya C.S. Nelson **Essentials of Corporate Law Practice in Nigeria** Novena Publishers Limited 2012

Sasegbon Deji & Co. **Companies and Allied Matters Law and Practice** (NCAMLP) DSC Publications Ltd 2006

## 14. Annual accounts, audit and estimates

(1) The Commission [1] shall keep proper accounts and proper records in relation thereto and shall prepare in respect of each year a statement of accounts in such form as the President may direct.

(2) The accounts of the Commission [1] shall be audited not later than six months after the end of the year by auditors [2] appointed by the Commission [1] from the list and in accordance with guidelines supplied by the Auditor-General for the Federation; and the fees of the auditors [2] and the expenses of the audit generally shall be paid from the funds of the Commission. [1]

(3) The Commission [1] shall cause to be prepared, not later than 30 September in each year, an estimate of the expenditure and income of the Commission [1] during the next succeeding year and when prepared they shall be submitted through the Minister [3] to the President.

---

**Notes**

**Section 14(1)**

1. "Commission" means the Corporate Affairs Commission established under Section 1 of this Act. See **Section 567 CAMA, Cap. C20, LFN, 2004.**

**Section 14(2)**

2. "Auditor" means one who checks the accuracy, fairness and general acceptability of accounting records and statements and then attests to them. See **Garner .B (ed) Black's Law Dictionary, 8 [th]ed**

**Section 14(3)**

3. "Minister" means the Minister charged with responsibility for trade; and "Ministry" shall be constituted accordingly. See **Section 567 CAMA Cap. C20, LFN 2004**

**Cross Reference**

On the establishment of the Office of the President of Nigeria, See **section 130 of the Constitution of the Federal Republic of Nigeria 1999 as amended.**

On the appointment of the Auditor- General, see **section 86, Constitution of the Federal Republic of Nigeria**

On the obligation of the Auditor –General to provide a list of qualified auditors from which statutoty bodies shall appoint externa auditors, see **section 85(3) Constitution of the Federal Republic of Nigeria**

On the appointment of Ministers, See **section 147 of the Constitution of the Federal Republic of Nigeria 1999 as amended.**

---

**For Further Reading**

On Corporate Affairs Commission, Incorporation of Companies, Membership of a company, and Share Capital. See:

Orojo, J. Ola **Company Law and Practice in Nigeria** 3[rd] Edition, Mbeyi & Associates (Lagos, Nigeria) 1992.

Ogbuanya C.S. Nelson **Essentials of Corporate Law Practice in Nigeria** Novena Publishers Limited 2012

Sasegbon Deji & Co **Companies and Allied Matters Law and Practice** (NCAMLP) DSC Publications Ltd 2006.

## 15. Annual report

The Commission[1] shall, not later than 30 June in each year, submit to the President a report on the activities of the Commission [1] during the immediate preceding year, and shall include in such report the audited accounts of the Commission [1].

---

**Notes**

**Section 15**

1. "Commission" means the Corporate Affairs Commission established under Section 1 of this Act. See **Section 567 CAMA, Cap. C20, LFN, 2004.**

**Cross Reference**

On the establishment of the Office of the President of Nigeria, see **section 130 of the Constitution of the Federal Republic of Nigeria 1999 as amended.**

On obligation on the Commission to audit its account annually , see **section 14 CAMA, Cap. C20, LFN, 2004.**

---

**For Further Reading**

On Corporate Affairs Commission, Incorporation of Companies, Membership of a company, and Share Capital. See:

Orojo, J. Ola **Company Law and Practice in Nigeria** 3rd Edition, Mbeyi & Associates (Lagos, Nigeria) 1992.

Ogbuanya C.S. Nelson **Essentials of Corporate Law Practice in Nigeria** Novena Publishers Limited 2012

Sasegbon Deji & Co. **Companies and Allied Matters Law and Practice** (NCAMLP) DSC Publications Ltd 2006.

## 16. Regulations

The Minister[1] may, with the approval of the President, make regulations[2] generally for the purpose of this Act and in particular, without prejudice to the generality of the foregoing provisions, make regulations[2]-

(a) prescribing the forms and returns and other information required under this Act;

(b) prescribing the procedure for obtaining any information required under this Act;

(c) requiring returns to be made within the period specified therein by any company[3] or enterprise to which this Act applies; and

(d) prescribing any fees payable under this Part, that is, Part A of this Act.

---

**Notes**

**Section 16**

1. "Minister" means the Minister charged with responsibility for trade; and "Ministry" shall be constituted accordingly. See **Section 567 CAMA Cap. C20, LFN 2004**
2. "Regulations" means having power to control an area of business or industry and makes sure it is operating fairly. **See Oxford Advanced Learner's Dictionary of Current English, 6 th ed.**
3. "Company" means a company formed and registered under this Act or, as the case may be, formed and registered in Nigeria before and in existence on the commencement of this Act, See **Section 567 CAMA, Cap.C20, LFN, 2004.**

Cross Reference

On the establishment of the Office of the President of Nigeria, See **section 130 of the Constitution of the Federal Republic of Nigeria 1999 as amended.**

---

**Cases**

The definition of a company in section 650 of Companies and Allied Matters Act puts the matter beyond doubt. It defines a 'company' or 'existing' to mean....a company formed and registered in Nigeria before and in existence on the commencement of this Act. ***Agro Allied Dev. Ent. Ltd. v. Reefer (2009) vol.31 W.R.N 1-185 at pg 7.***

The Company is distinct from its promoters or directors and a director is an agent of the company. Consequently, where a director enters into a contract in the name of or purporting to bind the company, it is the company, as principal that is liable, not the director . ***Dansa Foods (Nig.) Ltd v. Isong (2011) ALL F.W.L.R. part 596 404-600 at p.595***

## 17. Meaning of certain words used in this Part

In this Part of this Act-

"**chairman**" means the chairman of the Commission [1]; and

"**member**" means any member of the Commission [1] including the chairman.

---

**Notes**

**Section 17**

1. "Commission"means the Corporate Affairs Commission established under section 1 of this Act. See **Section 567 CAMA, Cap. C20 LFN, 2004**

Cross Reference

On tenure of officers appointed to the Commission, see **section 6 CAMA Cap. C20, LFN 2004**

---

**Cases**

In the performance of their duties, section 677(1) of CAMA gives the respondents absolute discretion. The community reading of section 32(1) and section 677(1) confirm the absolute discretion given to the Commission in the Registration of proposed names. See ***Benard Amasike v. R.G Corporate Affairs Commission & Anor. (2010) LPELR-SC.204/2005***

PART II

***Incorporation of companies and incidental matters***

*Chapter 1*

*Formation of Company*

## 18. Right to form a company

As from the commencement of this Act, any two or more persons may form and incorporate a company [1] by complying with the requirements of this Act in respect of registration of such company.[1]

---

**Notes**

**Section 18**

1. "Company" means a company formed and registered under this Act or, as the case may be, formed and registered in Nigeria before and in existence on the commencement of this Act, See **Section 567 CAMA, Cap. C20, LFN, 2004.**

**Cross Reference**

On the documents required for the incporporation of companies, see **section 35 CAMA Cap. C20 LFN 2004.**

---

**Cases**

The definition of a company in section 650 of Companies and Allied Matters Act puts the matter beyond doubt. It defines a 'company' or 'existing' to mean….a company formed and registered in Nigeria before and in existence on the commencement of this Act. ***Agro Allied Dev. Ent. Ltd. v. Reefer (2009) vol.31 W.R.N 1-185 at pg 7.***

The Company is distinct from its promoters or directors and a director is an agent of the company. Consequently, where a director enters into a contract in the name of or purporting to bind the company, it is the company, as principal that is liable, not the director . ***Dansa Foods (Nig.) Ltd v. Isong (2011) ALL F.W.L.R. part 596 404-600 at p. 595***

## 19. Partnership, etc., of more than 20 members when permitted

(1) No company, [1] association, or partnership [2] consisting of more than 20 persons shall be formed for the purpose of carrying on any business for profit or gain by the company, [1] association, or

partnership[2], or by the individual members [3] thereof, unless it is registered as a company [1] under this Act, or is formed in pursuance of some other enactment in force in Nigeria.

(2) Nothing in this section shall apply to-

(a) any co-operative society registered under the provisions of any enactment in force in Nigeria; or

(b) any partnership [2] for the purpose of carrying on practice-

(i) as legal practitioners, [4] by persons each of whom is a legal practitioner[4]; or

(ii) as accountants by persons each of whom is entitled by law to practice as an accountant.

(3) If at any time the number of members [3] of a company, [1] association or partnership [2] exceeds 20 in contravention of this section and it carries on business for more than 14 days while the contravention continues, every person who is a member [3] of the company[1], association or partnership [2] during the time that it so carries on business after those 14 days shall be liable to a fine of N25 for every day during which the default continues.

---

**Notes**

**Section 19(1)**

1. "Company" means a company formed and registered under this Act or, as the case may be, formed and registered in Nigeria before and in existence on the commencement of this Act. See **Section 567 CAMA, CAP C20, LFN, 2004.**
2. "Partnership" means a voluntary association of two or more persons who jointly own and carry on a business for profit. See **Garner .B, (ed)Black's Law Dictionary, 8 [th]ed**
3. "Members" includes the heir, executor, administrator, or other personal representatives, as the case may be, of the member. See **Section 567 Companies and Allied Matters Act Cap. C20, LFN 2004**

**Section 19(2)**

4. "Legal practitioner" has the meaning assigned to it by the Legal Practitioners Act. See **section 567 CAMA Cap. C20, LFN 2004.**
   "Legal practitioner" means a person entitled in accordance with the provisions of this Act to practise as a barrister or as a barrister and solicitor, either generally or for the purposes of any particular office or proceedings. See **section 24 Legal Practitioners Act Cap. L11, LFN 2004.**

**Cross Reference**

On the establishment of the Institute of Chartered Accountant and its functions, see generally **Institute of Chartered Accountant Act Cap. I 11 LFN 2004**

On the requirements for practice as a legal practitioner, see generally, **Legal Practitioners Act Cap. L11, LFN 2004**

---

**Cases**

The definition of a company in section 650 of Companies and Allied Matters Act puts the matter beyond doubt. It defines a 'company' or 'existing' to mean….a company formed and registered in Nigeria before and in existence on the commencement of this Act. ***Agro Allied Dev. Ent. Ltd. v. Reefer (2009) vol.31 W.R.N 1-185 at pg 7***

The Company is distinct from its promoters or directors and a director is an agent of the company. Consequently, where a director enters into a contract in the name of or purporting to bind the company, it is the company, as principal that is liable, not the director . ***Dansa Foods (Nig.) Ltd v. Isong (2011) ALL F.W.L.R. part 596 404-600 at p. 595***

## 20. Capacity of individual to form company

(1) Subject to subsection (2) of this section, an individual shall not join in the formation of a company [1] under this Act if-

(a) he is less than 18 years of age; or

(b) he is of unsound mind [2] and has been so found by a court [3] in Nigeria or elsewhere; or

(c) he is an undischarged bankrupt [4]; or

(d) he is disqualified under section 254 of this Act from being a director[5] of a company [1].

(2) A person shall not be disqualified under paragraph (a) of subsection (1) of this section, if two other persons not disqualified under that subsection have subscribed to the memorandum. [6]

(3) A corporate body in liquidation shall not join in the formation of a company [1] under this Act.

(4) Subject to the provisions of any enactment regulating the rights and capacity of aliens [7] to undertake or participate in trade or business, an alien [7] or a foreign company [8] may join in forming a company.[1]

---

**Notes**

**Section 20(1)**

1. "Company" means a company formed and registered under this Act or, as the case may be, formed and registered in Nigeria before and in existence on the commencement of this Act. See **Section 567 CAMA, Cap. C20, LFN, 2004.**

2. "Unsound mind" means not responsible for your actions because of mental illness or condition. See **Oxford Advanced Learner's Dictionary of Current English. 6 [th]ed.**
3. "Court" used in relation to a company, means the Federal High Court, and to the extent to which application may be made to it as; court includes the Court of Appeal and the Supreme Court of Nigeria. See **Section 567 CAMA, Cap. C20 , LFN 2004**
4. "Undischarged bankrupt" means a person who has been officially stated to be bankrupt by a court of law but who still pay his or her debt. See **Oxford Advanced Learner's Dictionary of Current English. 6 [th]ed.**
5. "Director" means persons duly appointed by the company to direct and manage the business of the company. See **Garner B. (ed), Black's Law Dictionary, 8 [th]ed**

   Director includes any person occupying the position of director by whatever name called, and includes any person in accordance with whose directions or instructions the directors are accustomed to act. See **Section 567 CAMA, Cap. C20, LFN 2004**

**Section 20(2)**

6. "Memorandum" means the memorandum of association of a company as originally framed or as altered in pursuance of any enactment. See **Section 567 CAMA, Cap. C20, LFN 2004** .

   "Memorandum of Association" means a legal document, setting up a corporation, either with or without limited liability, and including the company's name, purpose, and duration. **See Garner B. (ed) Black's Law Dictionary, 8th ed.**

**Section 20(4)**

7. "Alien" means a person or association, whether corporate or unincorporated, other than a Nigerian citizen or association. See **Section 567 CAMA, Cap. C20, LFN 2004**
8. 8. "Foreign company" means a company incorporated elsewhere than in Nigeria. See **Section 567 CAMA, Cap. C20, LFN 2004**

**Cross Reference**

On the documents required for the incporporation of companies, see **section 35 CAMA Cap. C20 LFN 2004**

On establishment and jurisdiction of the Federal High Court, see **section 249 & 251, Constitution of the Federal Republic of Nigeria, 1999 (as amended).**

---

## Cases

The definition of a company in section 650 of Companies and Allied Matters Act puts the matter beyond doubt. It defines a 'company' or 'existing' to mean….a company formed and registered in Nigeria before and in existence on the commencement of this Act. ***Agro Allied Dev. Ent. Ltd. v. Reefer (2009) vol.31 W.R.N 1-185 at pg 7.***

The Company is distinct from its promoters or directors and a director is an agent of the company. Consequently, where a director enters into a contract in the name of or purporting to bind the company, it is the company, as principal that is liable, not the director . ***Dansa Foods (Nig.) Ltd v. Isong (2011) ALL F.W.L.R. part 596 404-600 at p.595***

**For Further Reading**

On Corporate Affairs Commission, Incorporation of Companies, Membership of a company, and Share Capital see:

Orojo J. Ola **Company Law and Practice in Nigeria** 3rd Edition, Mbeyi & Associates (Lagos, Nigeria) 1992.

Ogbuanya C.S. Nelson **Essentials of Corporate Law Practice in Nigeria** Novena Publishers Limited 2012

Sasegbon Deji & Co **Companies and Allied Matters Law and Practice** (NCAMLP) DSC Publications Ltd 2006

On participation of aliens/foreigners in the formation of companies, see *"Akpotaire, v., The Nigerian Indigenization Laws as Disincentives to Foreign Investments:* The End of an Era" **(2005) 3 Business Law Review 62**.

Ogowewo T. I. "The Shift to the Classical Theory of Foreign Investment: Opening up the Nigerian Market" **(1995) 44 The International and Comparative Law Quarterly 915**.

Ikeyi N. "The Export Processing Zones and Foreign Investment Promotion in Nigeria: A Note on Recent Legislation" **(1998) 42 Journal of African Law 223.**

## 21. Types of companies

(1) An incorporated company [1] may be a company [1]-

(a) having the liability of its members [2] limited by the memorandum[3] to the amount, if any, unpaid on the shares[4] respectively held by them (in this Act termed "a company limited by shares" [5]); or

(b) having the liability of its members [2] limited by the memorandum[3] to such amount as the members [2] may respectively thereby undertake to contribute to the assets of the company[1] in the event of its being wound up [6] (in this Act termed "a company limited by guarantee" [7]); or

(c) not having any limit on the liability of its members [2] (in this Act termed "an unlimited company" [8]).

(2) A company[1] of any of the foregoing types may either be a private company[9] or a public company. [10]

---

**Notes**

**Section 21 (1)**

1. "Company" means a company formed and registered under this Act or, as the case may be, formed and registered in Nigeria before and in existence on the commencement of this Act. See **Section 567 CAMA, Cap. C20, LFN, 2004.**
2. "Members" includes the heir, executor, administrator, or other personal representatives, as the case may be, of the member. See **Section 567 CAMA Cap. C20, LFN 2004**
3. "Memorandum" means the memorandum of association of a company as originally framed or as altered in pursuance of any enactment. See **Section 567 CAMA, Cap. C20, LFN 2004** .
   "Memorandum of Association" means a legal document, setting up a corporation, either with or without limited liability, and including the company's name, purpose, and duration. **See Garner B. (ed) Black's Law Dictionary, 8th ed**
4. "Shares" means the interest in a company's share capital of a member who is entitled to share in the capital or income of such company. See **Section 567 CAMA, Cap. C20, LFN, 2004**
5. "Company limited by shares" has the meaning assigned by section 21 of this Act. See **section 567 CAMA Cap. C20, LFN 2004**
6. "Wound up" see "winding up." It means means the process of settling accounts and liquidating assets in anticipation of a partnership's or corporation's dissolution. See **Garner B. (ed) Black's Law Dictionary, 8th ed**
7. "Company limited by guarantee" has the meaning assigned by section 21 of this Act. See **section 567 CAMA Cap. C20, LFN 2004**
8. "Unlimited company" has the meaning assigned to it by section 21 (1) of this Act. See **section 567 CAMA Cap. C20, LFN 2004**

**Section 21(2)**

9. "Private company" is one which is stated in its memorandum to be a private company. See **Section 22 CAMA Cap. C20 LFN 2004**
10. "Public company" any company other than a private company is a public company. See **Section 24 CAMA Cap. C20 LFN 2004**

**Cross Reference**

On the documents required for the incporporation of companies, see **section 35 CAMA Cap. C20 LFN 2004**

On modes of winding up companies, see **section 401 CAMA Cap. C20 LFN 2004**

---

**Cases**

A limited liability Company is separate and apart from its members and officers. This decision was further magnified in the case of ***H. L. Bolton Co. v. T. J. Graham*** **(1956) 3 ALL E.R 624 at 630** when Denning L. J. said: A Company may in many ways be likened to a human body. They have a brain and a nerve center which controls what they do. They also have hands which hold the tools and act in accordance with direction from the center. Some of the people in a company are mere servants and agents who are nothing more than hands to the work and cannot be said to represent the mind or will. Others are directors and managers who represent the directing mind and will of the company and control what they do. The state of the mind of these managers is the state of mind of the company and it is treated by the Law as such. So you will find in cases where the Law requires personal fault as a condition of liability in tort, the fault of the managers will be the personal fault of the company. See ***Chartered Brains Ltd. V Intercity Bank Plc.*** **(2009) Vol.49 W.R.N. 1-182 at pg 116**.

Corporate personality presupposes that a company assumes a separate and distinct personality from its members from the moment of incorporation. **Habib Nig. Bank Ltd v. Ochete (2001) F.W.L.R (pt. 54) 384.** See also ***Bebeji Oil Allied Prod. Ltd. v. Pancosta Ltd.*** **(2007) (vol. 31) WRN 163**

**For Further Reading**

For further reading on Corporate Affairs Commission, Incorporation of Companies, Membership of a company, and share capital see:

Orojo J. Ola **Company Law and Practice in Nigeria** 3rd Edition, Mbeyi & Associates (Lagos, Nigeria) 1992.

Ogbuanya C.S. Nelson **Essentials of Corporate Law Practice in Nigeria Novena Publishers Limited 2012**

Sasegbon Deji& Co **Companies and Allied Matters Law and Practice (NCAMLP) DSC Publications Ltd 2006.**

## 22. Private company

(1) A private company is one which is stated in its memorandum[1] to be a private company.

(2) Every private company shall by its articles [2] restrict the transfer of its shares. [3]

(3) The total number of members [4] of a private company shall not exceed 50, not including persons who are bona fide in the employment of the company,[5] or were while in that employment and have continued after the determination of that employment to be, members [4] of the company. [5]

(4) Where two or more persons hold one or more shares [3] in a company[5] jointly, they shall for the purpose of subsection (3) of this section be treated as a single member. [4]

(5) A private company shall not, unless authorized by law, invite the public to-

(a) subscribe for any shares [3] or debentures [6] of the company [5]; or

(b) deposit money for fixed periods or payable at call, whether or not bearing interest.

---

**Notes**

**Section 22(1)**

1. "Memorandum" means the memorandum of association of a company as originally framed or as altered in pursuance of any enactment. See **Section 567 CAMA, Cap. C20, LFN 2004** .

   "Memorandum of Association" means a legal document, setting up a corporation, either with or without limited liability, and including the company's name, purpose, and duration. **See Garner B. (ed) Black's Law Dictionary, 8th ed.**

**Section 22(2)**

2. "Articles" means the articles of association of a company, as originally framed or as altered by special resolution. See **Section 567 Companies and Allied Matters Act Cap. C20, LFN 2004**
3. "Shares" see "share". It means the interest in a company's share capital of a member who is entitled to share in the capital or income of such company and except where a distinction between stock and shares is expressed or implied, includes stock. See **Section 567 Companies and Allied Matters Act Cap. C20, LFN 2004**

**Section 22(3)**

4. "Members" includes the heir, executor, administrator, or other personal representatives, as the case may be, of the member. See **Section 567 Companies and Allied Matters Act Cap. C20, LFN 2004**
5. 5. "Company" means a company formed and registered under this Act or, as the case may be, formed and registered in Nigeria before and in existence on the commencement of this Act. See **Section 567 CAMA, Cap. C20, LFN, 2004.**

**Section 22(5)**

6. "Debentures" means a written acknowledgment of indebtedness by the company setting out terms and conditions of the indebtedness, and includes debenture stock, bonds and other securities of a company whether constituting a charge on the assets of the company or not. See **Section 567 CAMA, Cap. C20, LFN, 2004**

**Cross Reference**

On how shares are transferred, see **section 151, CAMA Cap. C20 LFN 2004**

On delivery of the Memorandum of Association as part of documents for incorporation, see **section 35(2) CAMA Cap. C20 LFN 2004**

---

**Cases**

By the provisions of Companies and Allied Matters Act, Section 115, shares are in the nature of personal estate and freely transferable but subject to statutory restrictions and the articles of the company. Members in a company have a right to transfer shares belonging to them therein and this right is unfettered unless there is an express restriction to that effect in the articles or constitution of the company. ***N.R.I. Ltd v. Oranusi*** **[2011] ALL F.W.L.R part 577.625-824 at p.765** .

**For Further Reading**
On shares, debentures, memorandum, see Orojo, J. Ola **Company Law and Practice in Nigeria** 3rd Edition, Mbeyi & Associates (Lagos, Nigeria) 1992.

## 23. Consequences of default in complying with conditions constituting a private company

(1) Subject to subsection (2) of this section, where default is made in complying with any of the provisions of section 22 of this Act in respect of a private company, [1] the company[2] shall cease to be entitled to the privileges and exemptions conferred on private companies[1] by or under this Act and this Act shall apply to the company[2] as if it were not a private company. [1]

(2) If a court, [3] on the application of the company [2] or any other person interested, is satisfied that the failure to comply with the provisions of section 22 of this Act was accidental or due to inadvertence or to some other sufficient cause, or that on other grounds it is just and equitable to grant relief, the court [3] may, on such terms and conditions as may seem to it to be just and expedient, order that the company [2] be relieved from the consequences mentioned in subsection (1) of this section.

---

**Notes**
**Section 23(1)**

1. "Private company" is one which is stated in its memorandum to be a private company. See **Section 22 CAMA, Cap. C20, LFN 2004**
2. "Company" means a company formed and registered under this Act or as the case may be, formed and registered in Nigeria before and in existence on the commencement of this Act. See **Section 567 CAMA, Cap. C20 LFN 2004**
3. "Court" used in relation to a company, means the Federal High Court, and to the extent to which application may be made to it as; court includes the Court of Appeal and the Supreme Court of Nigeria; See **Section 567 CAMA, Cap. C20 , LFN 2004**

**Cross Reference**
On establishment and jurisdiction of the Federal High Court, see **section 249 & 251, Constitution of the Federal Republic of Nigeria, 1999 (as amended).**

**Cases**

The definition of a company in section 650 of Companies and Allied Matters Act puts the matter beyond doubt. It defines a 'company' or 'existing' to mean....a company formed and registered in Nigeria before and in existence on the commencement of this Act . ***Agro Allied Dev. Ent. Ltd. v. Reefer (2009)*** **vol.31 W.R.N 1-185 at pg 7**

The Company is distinct from its promoters or directors and a director is an agent of the company. Consequently, where a director enters into a contract in the name of or purporting to bind the company, it is the company, as principal that is liable, not the director. ***Dansa Foods (Nig.) Ltd v. Isong*** **(2011) ALL F.W.L.R. part 596 404-600 at p.595**

## 24. Public company

Any company[1] other than a private company [2] shall be a public company[3] and its memorandum[4] shall state that it is a public company.[3]

---

**Notes**

**Section 24**

1. "Company" means a company formed and registered under this Act or as the case may be, formed and registered in Nigeria before and in existence on the commencement of this Act. See **Section 567 CAMA, Cap. C20, LFN 2004** .
2. "Private company" means one which is stated in its memorandum to be a private company. See **Section 22CAMA, Cap. C20, LFN 2004.**
3. "Public company" means any other company other than a private company. See **Section 24 CAMA, Cap. C20, LFN 2004.**
4. "Memorandum" means the memorandum of association of a company as originally framed or as altered in pursuance of any enactment. See **Section 567 CAMA, Cap. C20, LFN 2004** .

   "Memorandum of Association" means a legal document, setting up a corporation, either with or without limited liability, and including the company's name, purpose, and duration. **See Garner B. (ed) Black's Law Dictionary, 8th ed.**

**Cross Reference**

On delivery of the Memorandum of Association as part of documents for incorporation, see **section 35(2) CAMA Cap. C20 LFN 2004.**

---

**Cases**

The definition of a company in section 650 of Companies and Allied Matters Act puts the matter beyond doubt. It defines a 'company' or 'existing' to mean....a company formed and registered in Nigeria before and in existence on the commencement of this Act. ***Agro Allied Dev. Ent. Ltd. v. Reefer*** **(2009) vol.31 W.R.N 1-185 at pg 7.**

**For Further Reading**

For further reading on Corporate Affairs Commission, Incorporation of Companies, Membership of a company, and Share Capital see:

Orojo, J. Ola **Company Law and Practice in Nigeria** 3rd Edition, Mbeyi & Associates (Lagos, Nigeria) 1992.

Ogbuanya C.S. Nelson **Essentials of Corporate Law Practice in Nigeria** Novena Publishers Limited 2012

Sasegbon Deji & Co **Companies and Allied Matters Law and Practice** (NCAMLP) DSC Publications Ltd 2006

## 25. Unlimited company to have share capital

As from the commencement of this Act, an unlimited company[1] shall be registered with a share capital [2]; and where an existing unlimited company[1] is not registered with a share capital, [2] it shall, not later than the appointed day [3], alter its memorandum [4] so that it becomes an unlimited company [1] having a share capital[2] not below the minimum share capital[2] permitted under section 99 of this Act.

---

**Notes**

**Section 25**

1. "Company" means a company formed and registered under this Act or as the case may be, formed and registered in Nigeria before and in existence on the commencement of this Act. See section 567 **CAMA Cap. C20, LFN 2004**
2. "Share capital" See capital, means a fund representing the nominal value of shares issued by a registered company. See **Martins E. (ed.) Oxford Dictionary of Law 4th ed.**
3. "Appointed day" means a period of one year from the commencement of this Act. See **section 567 CAMA Cap. C20, LFN 2004**
4. "Memorandum" means the memorandum of association of a company as originally framed or as altered in pursuance of any enactment. See **Section 567 CAMA, Cap. C20, LFN 2004** .

**Cross Reference**

On delivery of the Memorandum of Association as part of documents for incorporation, see **section 35(2) CAMA Cap. C20 LFN 2004**

On authorized minimum share capital of companies with share capital, see **section 99 CAMA Cap. C20, LFN 2004**

**Cases**

The definition of a company in section 650 of Companies and Allied Matters Act puts the matter beyond doubt. It defines a 'company' or 'existing' to mean....a company formed and registered in Nigeria before and in existence on the commencement of this Act. See ***Agro Allied Dev. Ent. Ltd. v. Reefer* (2009) vol.31 W.R.N 1-185 at pg 7**

**For Further Reading**

On membership, proxy, share capital and company generally, see Sofowora, M.O **Modern Nigerian Company Law** Soft Associates, 2[nd] Edition 2002. Pages 13, 304, 405,

## 26. Company limited by guarantee

(1) Where a company[1] is to be formed for promoting commerce, art, science, religion, sports, culture, education, research, charity or other similar objects, and the income and property of the company[1] are to be applied solely towards the promotion of its objects and no portion thereof is to be paid or transferred directly or indirectly to the members[2] of the company[1] except as permitted by this Act, the company[1] shall not be registered as a company limited by shares,[3] but may be registered as a company limited by guarantee.[4]

(2) As from the commencement of this Act, a company limited by guarantee[4] shall not be registered with a share capital[5] and every existing company limited by guarantee[4] and having a share capital[5] shall, not later than the appointed day, alter its memorandum[6] so that it becomes a company limited by guarantee[4] and not having a share capital[5].

(3) In the case of a company limited by guarantee,[4] every provision in the memorandum[6] or articles[7] or in any resolution[8] of the company[1] purporting to give any person a right to participate in the divisible profits of the company[1] otherwise than as a member[2] or purporting to divide the company's[1] undertaking into shares[9] or interests shall be void.

(4) A company limited by guarantee[4] shall not be incorporated with the object of carrying on business for the purpose of making profits for distribution to members.[2]

(5) The memorandum[6] of a company limited by guarantee[4] shall not be registered without the authority of the Attorney-General of the Federation.

(6) If any company limited by guarantee [4] carries on business for the purpose of distributing profits, all officers [10] and members[2] thereof who are cognisant of the fact that it is so carrying on business shall be jointly and severally liable for the payment and discharge of all the debts and liabilities of the company [1] incurred in carrying on such business, and the company [1] and every such officer[10] and member[2] shall be liable to a fine not exceeding N100 for every day during which it carries on such business.

(7) The total liability of the members [2]of a company limited by guarantee[4] to contribute to the assets of the company [1] in the event of its being wound up [11] shall not at any time be less than N10,000.

(8) Subject to compliance with subsection (6) of this section, the articles of association[7] of a company limited by guarantee [4] may provide that members[2] can retire or be excluded from membership of the company[1].

(9) If, in breach of subsection (6) of this section, the total liability of the members[2] of any company limited by guarantee [4] shall at any time be less than Nl0,000, every director [12] and member[2] of the company[1] who is cognisant of the breach shall be liable to a fine of N50 for every day during which the default continues.

(10) If, upon the winding up [11] of a company limited by guarantee[4], there remains after the discharge of all its debts and liabilities any property of the company, [1] the same shall not be distributed among the members[2] but shall be transferred to some other company limited by guarantee[4] having objects similar to the objects of the company[1] or applied to some charitable object and such other company[1] or charity shall be determined by the members[2] prior to the dissolution of the company. [1]

---

**Notes**
**Section 26(1)**

1. "Company" means a company formed and registered under this Act or as the case may be, formed and registered in Nigeria before and in existence on the commencement of this Act. See **Section 567 CAMA Cap. C20 LFN, 2004.**
2. "Members" includes the heir, executor, administrator, or other personal representatives, as the case may be, of the member. See **Section 567 CAMA Cap. C20, LFN 2004.**
3. "Company limited by shares" means a company having the liability of its members limited by the memorandum to the amount if any, unpaid on

the shares respectively held by them. See **Section 21 CAMA Cap. C20, LFN 2004.**

4. "Company limited by guarantee" means a company having the liability of its members limited by the memorandum to such amount as the members may respectively thereby undertake to contribute to the assets of the company, in the event of its being wound up. See **Garner. B. (ed) Black's Law Dictionary 8th ed.**

   "Company limited by guarantee" has the meanings assigned to it by section 21 of this Act. See **section 567 CAMA Cap C20, LFN 2004**

**Section 26(2)**

5. "Share capital" See capital, means a fund representing the nominal value of shares issued by a registered company. See **Martins E. (ed.) Oxford Dictionary of Law 4th ed.**
6. "Memorandum" means the memorandum of association of a company as originally framed or as altered in pursuance of any enactment. See **Section 567 CAMA, Cap. C20, LFN 2004** .

   "Memorandum of Association" means a legal document, setting up a corporation, either with or without limited liability, and including the company's name, purpose, and duration. **See Garner B. (ed) Black's Law Dictionary, 8th ed.**

**Section 26(3)**

7. "Articles" means the articles of association of a company, as originally framed or as altered by special resolution. See **Section 567 CAMA, Cap C20, LFN 2004.**
8. "Resolution" means a main motion that formally expresses the sense, will or action of a deliberative assembly. See **Garner B. (ed) Black's Law Dictionary 8th ed.**
9. "Shares" means the interest in a company's share capital of a member who is entitled to share in the capital or income of such company; and except where a distinction between stock and shares is expressed or implied, includes stock. See **section 567 CAMA Cap C20, LFN 2004**

**Section 26(6)**

10. "Officer" in relation to a body corporate includes a director, manager or secretary. See **section 567 CAMA Cap. C20, LFN 2004**

**Section 26(7)**

11. "Wound up" see "winding up." It means means the process of settling accounts and liquidating assets in anticipation of a partnership's or corporation's dissolution. See **Garner B. (ed) Black's Law Dictionary, 8th ed**

**Section 26(9)**

12. "Director" means a person duly appointed by the company to direct and manage the business of the company. **See Garner B. (ed) Black's Law Dictionary, 8th ed.**

    "Director" includes any person occupying the position of director by whatever name called; and includes any person in accordance with whose directions or instructions the directors of the company are accustomed to act. See **section 567 CAMA Cap. C20 LFN 2004**

**Cross Reference**

On dissolution of Company after winding up, see **section 454 CAMA Cap. C20 LFN 2004**
On the appointment of and the powers of the the Attorney General of the Federation, see **section 150 & 174, Constitution of the Federal Republic of Nigeria, 1999 (as amended).**

**Cases**
The rule of a corporation is well stated in the case of ***Trenco (Nig.) Ltd. v. African Real Estate*** **(1978) 7 Law Reports of Nig page 146 at 153** as follows: "But a company, although a legal person is an artificial one which can only act through its human agents and officers. Viscount Huldane L.C. in Lennard's ***Carrying Co. vs. Asiatic Petroleum Co. Ltd. (1915) AC 705*** stated: My lords, a corporation is an abstraction. It has a body of its own. It is active and directing will must consequently be sought in the person of somebody who for some purpose may be called an agent; but who is really the directing mind and will of the corporation." This human personification of a company was clearly brought out by Denning L.J ***In Bolton (Engineering Co. Ltd v. Graham & Sons (1975) 1 Q.B. Page 159 at 172*** where he said: "A company may in many ways be likened to a human body. It has a brain and nerve centre which controls what it does. It also has hands which hold the tools and act in accordance with the directions from the centre. Some of the people in the company are mere servants and agents who are nothing more than hands to do work and cannot be said to represent the mind or will. Others are directors and managers who represent the directing mind and will of the company and is treated by law as such." It follows that a company, although having corporate personality is deemed to have human personality through its officers and agents and will therefore speaking generally, contract like an individual, the veil of incorporation ought to be lifted in the interest of justice in the circumstance of this case. ***Aminu Musa Oyebanji v.The State (2011) LPELR-CA/I/199/02***

**For Further Reading**
On Corporate Affairs Commission, Incorporation of Companies, Membership of a company, and Share Capital see:
Orojo, J. Ola **Company Law and Practice in Nigeria** 3rd Edition, Mbeyi & Associates (Lagos, Nigeria) 1992.
Ogbuanya C.S. Nelson **Essentials of Corporate Law Practice in Nigeria** Novena Publishers Limited 2012.
Sasegbon Deji & Co **Companies and Allied Matters Law and Practice** (NCAMLP) DSC Publications Ltd 2006

*Memorandum of association*

**27. Requirements with respect to the memorandum of a company**

(1) The memorandum [1] of every company [2] shall state-

(a) the name of the company [2];

(b) that the registered office [3] of the company [2] shall be situated in Nigeria;

(c) the nature of the business or businesses which the company [2] is authorised to carry on, or, if the company [2] is not formed for the purpose of carrying on business, the nature of the object or objects for which it is established;

(d) the restriction, if any, on the powers of the company [2];

(e) that the company [2] is a private [4] or public company, [5] as the case may be;

(f) that the liability of its members [6] is limited by shares [7] or by guarantee [8] or is unlimited [9], as the case may be.

(2) If the company has a share capital [10]-

(a) the memorandum [1] shall also state the amount of authorised share capital, [10] not being less than Nl0,000 in the case of a private company [4] and N500,000 in the case of a public company, [5] with which the company [2] proposed to be registered, and the division thereof into shares [11] of a fixed amount;

(b) the subscribers [12] of the memorandum [1] shall take among them a total number of shares [11] of a value of not less than 25 per cent of the authorized share capital [10]; and

(c) each subscriber [12] shall write opposite to his name the number of shares he takes.

(3) A subscriber [12] of the memorandum [1] who holds the whole or any part of the shares [11] subscribed by him in trust for any other person shall disclose in the memorandum [1] that fact and the name of the beneficiary.

(4) The memorandum [1] of a company [2] limited by guarantee [8] shall also state that-

(a) the income and property of the company [2] shall be applied solely towards the promotion of its objects, and that no portion thereof shall be paid or transferred directly or indirectly to the members [6] of the company [2] except as permitted by or under this Act; and

(b) each member[6] undertakes to contribute to the assets of the company[2] in the event of its being wound up [13] while he is a member[6] or within one year after he ceases to be a member[6] for payment of debts and liabilities of the company[2], and of the costs of winding up, [13] such amount as may be required not exceeding a specified amount and the total of which shall not be less than Nl0, 000

(5) The memorandum [1] shall be signed by each subscriber [12] in the presence of at least one witness who shall attest the signature.

(6) The memorandum [1] shall be stamped as a deed. [14]

---

**Notes**
**Section 27(1)**

1. "Memorandum" means the memorandum of association of a company as originally framed or as altered in pursuance of any enactment. See **Section 567 CAMA, Cap. C20, LFN 2004** .
   "Memorandum of Association" means a legal document, setting up a corporation, either with or without limited liability, and including the company's name, purpose, and duration. **See Garner B. (ed) Black's Law Dictionary, 8th ed.**
2. "Company" means a company formed and registered under this Act or as the case may be, formed and registered in Nigeria before and in existence on the commencement of this Act. **See Section 567 CAMA, Cap. C20, LFN, 2004**
3. "Registered office" means the official address of a registered company. It must be notified to the Companies Registry before registration of the company and it must appear on company letter-head and order forms. Documents may be served to a company's registered office and various registers and records may be inspected there. **See Martins E. (ed.) Oxford Dictionary of Law 4 th ed**
4. "Private Company" means one which is stated in its memorandum to be a private company. See **Section 22 CAMA, Cap C20, LFN 2004.**
5. "Public Company" means any other company other than a private company. See **Section 24 CAMA, Cap. C20, LFN 2004.**
6. "Members" includes the heir, executor, administrator, or other personal representatives, as the case may be, of the member. **See section 567 CAMA Cap. C 20 LFN 2004**
7. "Company limited by shares" means a company having the liability of its members limited by the memorandum to the amount if any, unpaid on the shares respectively held by them. **See Section 21 CAMA, Cap. C20. LFN, 2004**
8. "Company limited by guarantee" a company having the liability of its members limited by the memorandum to such amount as the members may respectively thereby undertake to contribute to the assets of the

company, in the event of its being wound up. **See Section 21 CAMA, Cap. C20. LFN, 2004**

9. "Unlimited Company" means a company not having any limit on the liability of its members. **See Section 21 CAMA, Cap. C20 LFN 2004.**

**Section 27(2)**

10. "Share capital" any of the units of equal value into which a company is divided and sold to raise money. See **Oxford Advanced Learner's Dictionary of Current English. 6th ed**
11. "Shares" means the interest in a company's share capital of a member who is entitled to share in the capital or income of such company. See **Section 567 CAMA, Cap. C20, LFN, 2004**
12. "Subscriber" means a person who by agreement contributes a sum of money or property to a specific person or for a specific purpose. **See Garner B. (ed) Black's Law Dictionary, 8th ed.**

**Section 27(4)**

13. "Wound up" see "winding up. " It means the process of settling accounts and liquidation of assets in anticipation of a partnership's or a corporation dissolution. . **See Garner B. (ed) Black's Law Dictionary, 8th ed.**

**Section 27(6)**

14. "Deed" means any written instrument that is signed, sealed and delivered and that conveys some interest in property. **See Garner B. (ed) Black's Law Dictionary, 8th ed.**

**Cross Reference**

On obligation to provide registered address during process of incorporation see **section 35 CAMA Cap C20, LFN 2004**

On change of registered office address see **section 547 CAMA Cap C20, LFN 2004**

On instruments on which stamp duties are paid, see generally, **Stamp Duties Act Cap. S8 LFN 2004**

---

**Cases**

A just and equitable ground is one of the grounds upon which a court having jurisdiction can rely to make an order for winding up a company. See Section 408(e) of the Companies and Allied Matters Act, cap 59, Laws of the Federation of Nigeria 1990. Section 408(e) of same law contained in cap c20 of Laws of the Federation of Nigeria 2004. A just and equitable ground for winding up a company is a remedy most suitable for contributories. Where a contributory brings a petition under this head as was found by the trial court and where the trial court is of the opinion that the petitioner is entitled to the order of winding up, it must make the order unless it appears to the court that some other remedy is available to the petitioner and that he is acting unreasonably in seeking a winding up order instead of pursuing that other remedy. ***Ado Ibrahim & Company Ltd v. Bendel Cement Company Ltd*** **(2007) S.C. 284/2001.**

**For Further Reading**

On company, winding up, membership, see Asomugha E. Maduelosi **Company law in Nigeria under the Companies and Allied Matters Act.** E. M. Asomugha (Lagos) 1994.

On Company and Types of companies, See Kiser Barnes **Cases and Materials on Nigeria Company Law** (1992) Obafemi Awolowo University Press Ltd, Ile-Ife, Nigeria.

## 28. Form of memorandum

Subject to the provisions of section 27 of this Act, the form of a memorandum of association[1] of-

(a) a company limited by shares [2];

(b) a company limited by guarantee [3]; and

(c) an unlimited company, [4]

shall be as specified in Tables B, C and D respectively in the First Schedule to this Act, or as near that form as circumstances admit.

---

**Notes**

**Section 28**

1. "Memorandum of association" see "memorandum" means the memorandum of association of a company as originally framed or as altered in pursuance of any enactment. See **Section 567 CAMA, Cap. C20, LFN 2004**.
   "Memorandum of Association" means a legal document, setting up a corporation, either with or without limited liability, and including the company's name, purpose, and duration. **See Garner B. (ed) Black's Law Dictionary, 8th ed**
2. "Company limited by shares" means a company having the liability of its members limited by the memorandum to the amount if any, unpaid on the shares respectively held by them. See **Section 21 CAMA, Cap. C20 LFN 2004**
3. "Company limited by guarantee" means a company having the liability of its members limited by the memorandum to such amount as the members may respectively thereby undertake to contribute to the assets of the company, in the event of its being wound up. See **Section 21 CAMA, Cap. C20 LFN 2004.**
4. "Unlimited Company" means a company not having any limit on the liability of its members. See **Section 21 CAMA, Cap. C20 LFN 2004.**

---

**For Further Reading**

On company and types of companies, see Kiser Barnes **Cases and Materials on Nigeria Company Law** (1992) Obafemi Awolowo University press Ltd, Ile-Ife, Nigeria.

*Name of company*

## 29. Name as stated in the memorandum[1]

(1) The name of a private company [2] limited by shares [3] shall end with the word "Limited".

(2) The name of a public company [4] limited by shares [3] shall end with the words "Public Limited Company."

(3) The name of a company limited by guarantee [5] shall end with the words "(Limited by Guarantee)" in brackets.

(4) The name of an unlimited company [6] shall end with the word "Unlimited".

(5) A company may use the abbreviations "Ltd," "PLC" "(Ltd/Gte)" and "Ultd" for the words "Limited," "Public Limited Company," "(Limited by Guarantee)" and "Unlimited" respectively in the name of the company.

---

**Notes**
**Section 29**

1. "Memorandum" means the memorandum of association of a company as originally framed or as altered in pursuance of any enactment. See **Section 567 CAMA, Cap. C20, LFN 2004** .
   "Memorandum of Association" means a legal document, setting up a corporation, either with or without limited liability, and including the company's name, purpose, and duration. **See Garner B. (ed) Black's Law Dictionary, 8th ed.**
2. "Private company" means one which is stated in its memorandum to be a private company. See **Section 22 CAMA, Cap C20, LFN 2004.**
3. "Company limited by shares" means a company having the liability of its members limited by the memorandum to the amount if any, unpaid on the shares respectively held by them. See **Section 21 CAMA, Cap. C20, LFN 2004.**
4. "Public company" means any other company other than a private company. See **Section 24 CAMA, Cap. C20, LFN 2004.**
5. "Company limited by guarantee" means a company having the liability of its members limited by the memorandum to such amount as the members may respectively thereby undertake to contribute to the assets of the company, in the event of its being wound up. See **Section 21 CAMA, Cap. C20, LFN 2004.**
6. "Unlimited company" means a company not having any limit on the liability of its members. **See Section 567 CAMA, Cap C20, LFN 2004**

---

**For Further Reading**
Oon Memorandum, Companies and their Types, see Ephraim Madeueulosi Asomugha **Company law in Nigeria under the companies and Allied Matters Act,** (1994) E.M. Asumugha, Lagos

For further reading on Company and Types of companies, See Kiser Barnes **Cases and Materials on Nigeria Company Law** (1992) Obafemi Awolowo University Press Ltd, Ile-Ife, Nigeria.

## 30. Prohibited and restricted names

(1) No company [1] shall be registered under this Act by a name which-

(a) is identical with that by which a company [1] in existence is already registered, or so nearly resembles that name as to be calculated to deceive, except where the company [1] in existence is in the course of being dissolved and signifies its consent in such manner as the Commission [2] requires; or

(b) contains the words "Chamber of Commerce" unless it is a company limited by guarantee [3]; or

(c) in the opinion of the Commission [2] is capable of misleading as to the nature or extent of its activities or is undesirable, offensive or otherwise contrary to public policy; or

(d) in the opinion of the Commission [2] would violate any existing trade mark [4] or business name [5] registered in Nigeria unless the consent of the owner of the trade mark [4] or business name [5] has been obtained.

(2) Except with the consent of the Commission, [2] no company shall be registered by a name which-

(a) includes the word "Federal," "National," "Regional", "State", "Government," or any other word which in the opinion of the Commission [2] suggests or is calculated to suggest that it enjoys the patronage of the Government of the Federation or the Government of a State in Nigeria, as the case may be, or any Ministry or Department of Government; or

(b) contains the word "Municipal" or "Chartered" or in the opinion of the Commission [2] suggests, or is calculated to suggest, connection with any municipality or other local authority; or

(c) contains the word "Co-operative" or the words "Building Society"; or

(d) contains the word "Group" or "Holding."

---

**Notes**
**Section 30**

1. "Company" means a company formed and registered under this Act or as the case may be, formed and registered in Nigeria before and in existence on the commencement of this Act. See **Section 567 CAMA, Cap. C20, LFN, 2004**
2. "Commission" means the Corporate Affairs Commission established under Section 1 of this Act. **See section 567 CAMA, Cap. C20, LFN, 2004**
3. "Company limited by guarantee" means a company having the liability of its members limited by the memorandum to such amount as the members may respectively thereby undertake to contribute to the assets of the company, in the event of its being wound up. See **Section 21 CAMA, Cap. C20, LFN 2004.**
4. "Trade mark" is a word or logo used by a company or manufacturer to distinguish its product from those of others . See **Garner B. (ed) Black's Law Dictionary, 8th ed.**
5. "Business name" means the name or style under which any business is carried on whether in partnership or otherwise. See **section 588(1) CAMA Cap. C20, LFN 2004**

**Cross Reference**

For requirement for registering Trade Marks, see **Copy Rights Act Cap. C28, LFN 2004**

On the effect of non-registration of trademarks, see **section 3, Trademarks Act, Cap. T13, LFN 2004**

For requirements for registering Business Name, see **Part B of CAMA, Cap. C20, LFN, 2004.**

On dissolution of Company after winding up, see **section 454 CAMA Cap. C20 LFN 2004.**

---

**Cases**

The definition of a company in section 650 of Companies and Allied Matters Act puts the matter beyond doubt. It defines a 'company' or 'existing' to mean….a company formed and registered in Nigeria before and in existence on the commencement of this Act. ***Agro Allied Dev. Ent. Ltd. v. Reefer* (2009)] vol.31 W.R.N 1-185 at pg 7**

The Company is distinct from its promoters or directors and a director is an agent of the company. Consequently, where a director enters into a contract in the name of or purporting to bind the company, it is the company, as principal that is liable, not the director. ***Dansa Foods (Nig.) Ltd v. Isong* (2011) ALL F.W.L.R. part 596 404-600 at p.595**

**For Further Reading**

On Corporate Affairs Commission, Incorporation of Companies, Membership of a company, and Share Capital see:

Orojo, J. Ola **Company Law and Practice in Nigeria** 3rd Edition, Mbeyi & Associates (Lagos, Nigeria) 1992.

Ogbuanya C.S. Nelson **Essentials of Corporate Law Practice in Nigeria** Novena Publishers Limited 2012
Sasegbon Deji & Co. **Companies and Allied Matters Law and Practice** (NCAMLP) DSC Publications Ltd 2006

### 31. Change of name of company

(1) If a company, [1] through inadvertence or otherwise, on its first registration or on its registration by a new name, is registered under a name identical with that by which a company [1] in existence is previously registered, or so nearly resembling it as to be likely to deceive, the first-mentioned company [1] may, with the approval of the Commission[2], change its name; and if the Commission [2] so directs, within six months of its being registered under that name, the company[1] concerned shall change its name within a period of six weeks from the date of the direction or such longer period as the Commission[2] may allow.

(2) If a company [1] makes default in complying with a direction under subsection (1) of this section, it shall be liable to a fine of N25 for every day during which the default continues.

(3) Any company[1] may, by special resolution [3] and with the approval of the Commission [2] signified in writing, change its name: Provided that no such approval shall be required where the only change in the name of a company [1] is the substitution of the words "Public Limited Company" [4] for the word "Limited" or vice versa on the conversion of a private company [5] into a public company[4] or a public company[4] into a private company [5] in accordance with the provisions of this Act.

(4) Nothing in this Act shall preclude the Commission [2] from requiring a company[1] to change its name if it is discovered that such a name conflicts with an existing trade mark [6] or business name[7] registered in Nigeria prior to the registration of the company[1] and the consent of the owner of the trade mark [6] or business name[7] was not obtained.

(5) Where a company [1] changes its name, the Commission [2] shall enter the new name on the register in place of the former name, and issue a certificate of incorporation [8] altered to meet the circumstances of the case.

(6) The change of name shall not affect any rights or obligations of the company[1], or render defective any legal proceedings by or against the company [1], and any legal proceedings

that could have been continued or commenced against it or by it in its former name may be continued or commenced against or by it in its new name.

(7) Any alteration made in the name under this section shall be published by the Commission [2] in the Gazette. [8]

(8) A certificate or publication in the Gazette [8] under this section shall be evidence of the alteration to which it relates.

---

**Notes**

**Section 31(1)**

1. "Company "means a company formed and registered under this Act or as the case may be, formed and registered in Nigeria before and in existence on the commencement of this Act. See **Section 567 CAMA, Cap. C20, LFN, 2004**
2. "Commission" means the Corporate Affairs Commission established under section 1 of this Act. See **Section 567 CAMA, Cap. C20, LFN, 2004**

**Section 31(3)**

3. "Special resolution" means a resolution passed by not less than three fourths of the votes cast by such members of the company as, being entitled to do so, vote in person or by proxy at a general meeting of which 21 days' notice, specifying the intention to propose the resolution as a special resolution, has been duly given. See **Section 233(2) CAMA, Cap. C20, LFN, 2004** .
4. "Public limited company" see" public company," It means any other company other than a private company. See **Section 24 CAMA, Cap C20, LFN 2004.**
5. "Private company" means one which is stated in its memorandum to be a private company. See **Section 22 CAMA, Cap C20, LFN 2004**

**Section 31(4)**

6. "Trade mark" is a word or logo used by a company or manufacturer to distinguish its product from those of others . See **Garner B. (ed) Black's Law Dictionary, 8th ed.**
7. "Business name" means the name or style under which any business is carried on whether in partnership or otherwise. See **section 588(1) CAMA Cap. C20, LFN 2004**

**Section 31(5)**

8. "Certificate of Incorporation" means a document issued by a state authority granting a corporation its legal existence and the right to function as a corporation. **See Garner B. (ed) Black's Law Dictionary, 8th ed.**

**Section 31(8)**

9. "Gazette" means an official newspaper of the government in which acts of the government and other legal matters are reported. See **Garner B. (ed) Black's Law Dictionary, 8 th ed.**

Gazette means the official *Gazette* of the Federation. See **section 567 CAMA Cap. C20 LFN 2004**

Cross Reference

On requirements for registration of companies, see **section 32 CAMA Cap. C20 LFN 2004**

---

**Cases**

The definition of a company in section 650 of Companies and Allied Matters Act puts the matter beyond doubt. It defines a 'company' or 'existing' to mean....a company formed and registered in Nigeria before and in existence on the commencement of this Act. ***Agro Allied Dev. Ent. Ltd. v. Reefer*** **(2009) vol.31 W.R.N 1-185 at pg 7**

**For Further Reading**

On Corporate Affairs Commission, Incorporation of Companies, Membership of a company, and Share Capital see:

Orojo, J. Ola **Company Law and Practice in Nigeria** 3rd Edition, Mbeyi & Associates (Lagos, Nigeria) 1992.

Ogbuanya C.S. Nelson **Essentials of Corporate Law Practice in Nigeria** Novena Publishers Limited 2012

Sasegbon Deji & Co **Companies and Allied Matters Law and Practice** (NCAMLP) DSC Publications Ltd 2006

On company change of name see, Orojo J. Ola **Company Law and Practice in Nigeria** 3rd Edition, Mbeyi & Associates (Lagos, Nigeria) 1992.

## 32. Reservation of name

(1) The Commission[1] may on written application and on payment of the prescribed fee reserve [2] a name pending registration of a company[3] or a change of name by a company. [3]

(2) Such reservation[2] as is mentioned in subsection (1) of this section shall be for such period as the Commission [1] shall think fit not exceeding 60 days, and during the period of reservation [2] no other company[3] shall be registered under the reserved name or under any other name which in the opinion of the Commission [1] bears too close a resemblance to the reserved name.

---

**Notes**

**Section 32**

1. "Commission" means the Corporate Affairs Commission established under section 1 of this Act. See **Section 567 CAMA, Cap. C20, LFN, 2004.**

2. "Reserved" means something retained or stored for future use. **See Garner .B. (ed) Black's Law Dictionary, 8th ed** .
3. "Company" means a company formed and registered under this Act or as the case may be, formed and registered in Nigeria before and in existence on the commencement of this Act. See **Section 567 CAMA, Cap. C20, LFN, 2004.**

**Cross Reference**

On requirements for registration of companies, see **section 32 CAMA Cap. C20 LFN 2004.**

---

**Cases**

The definition of a company in section 650 of Companies and Allied Matters Act puts the matter beyond doubt. It defines a 'company' or 'existing' to mean….a company formed and registered in Nigeria before and in existence on the commencement of this Act. ***Agro Allied Dev. Ent. Ltd. v. Reefer* (2009) vol. 31 W.R.N 1-185 at pg 7**

The Corporate Affairs Commission is conferred with the responsibility of registering companies operating in Nigeria by Statute, and under the said statute it can prohibit and restrict certain names to be registered. See ***Mustapha v. CAC (2009)* Vol. 43 W.R.N. 1-171 pg 156.**

*Articles of association*

## 33. Articles for regulating companies

There shall be registered, with the memorandum [1] of association, articles[2] of association signed by the subscribers [3] to the memorandum[1] of association, and prescribing regulations for the company.[4]

---

**Notes**

**Section 33**

1. "Memorandum" means the memorandum of association of a company as originally framed or as altered in pursuance of any enactment. See **Section 567 CAMA, Cap. C20, LFN 2004** .

   "Memorandum of Association" means a legal document, setting up a corporation, either with or without limited liability, and including the company's name, purpose, and duration. **See Garner B. (ed) Black's Law Dictionary, 8th ed.**
2. "Articles" means the articles of association of a company, as originally framed or as altered by special resolution. See **Section 567 CAMA, Cap. C20, LFN 2004** .

3. "Subscriber" means a person who by agreement contributes a sum of money or property to a specific person or for a specific purpose. **See Garner B. (ed) Black's Law Dictionary, 8 th ed.**
4. "Company" means a company formed and registered under this Act or as the case may be, formed and registered in Nigeria before and in existence on the commencement of this Act. See **Section 567 CAMA, Cap. C20, LFN, 2004** .

**Cross Reference**

On requirements for registration of companies, see **section 32 CAMA Cap. C20 LFN 2004**

---

**Cases**

A study of the article of association of a company leaves me in no doubt that they contain the rules and regulations by which the internal affairs of a company are governed....articles of association when registered therefore, become a contract between the company and its members and officers and between the members officers themselves. ***Ladejobi v. Odutola Ltd*** **[2002] 3 N.W.LR. 121 at 152-153** .

The definition of a company in section 650 of Companies and Allied Matters Act puts the matter beyond doubt. It defines a 'company' or 'existing' to mean....a company formed and registered in Nigeria before and in existence on the commencement of this Act. ***Agro Allied Dev. Ent. Ltd. v. Reefer*** **(2009)] vol.31 W.R.N 1-185 at pg 7**

**For Further Reading**

On company, memorandum and articles of association, see Ayua, I.A **Nigerian Company Law** G. Burn (Leighton Buzzard, Bedfordshire, United Kingdom) 1984

## 34. Form and contents of articles

(1) The form and contents of the articles [1] of association of a public company[2] having a share capital [3], a private company [4] having a share capital [3], a company limited by guarantee [5] and an unlimited company[6] shall be as in Parts I, II, III and IV respectively, of Table A in the First Schedule to this Act with such additions, omissions or alterations as may be required in the circumstances.

[First Schedule Parts I, II, III and IV. Table A.]

(2) In the case of a company limited by guarantee, [5] the articles of association [1] shall state the number of members [7] with

which the company[8] proposes to be registered for the purpose of enabling the Commission[9] to determine the fees payable on registration.

(3) The articles [1] of association shall-

(a) be printed;

(b) be divided into paragraphs numbered consecutively; and

(c) be signed by each subscriber [10] of the memorandum [11] of association in the presence of at least one witness who shall attest the signature.

(4) The articles [1] shall bear the same stamp duty as if they were contained in a deed [12].

---

**Notes**

**Section 34(1)**

1. "Articles" means the articles of association of a company, as originally framed or as altered by special resolution. **See Section 567 CAMA, Cap. C20 LFN**.
2. "Public company" means any other company other than a private company. See **Section 24 CAMA, Cap C20, LFN 2004.**
3. "Share Capital" means any of the units of equal value into which a company is divided and sold to raise money. See **Oxford Advanced Learner's Dictionary of Current English. 6th ed.**
4. "Private company" means one which is stated in its memorandum to be a private company. See **Section 22 CAMA, Cap C20, LFN 2004**
5. "Company Limited by Guarantee" means a company having the liability of its members limited by the memorandum to such amount as the members may respectively thereby undertake to contribute to the assets of the company, in the event of its being wound up. **See Section 21 CAMA, Cap C20, LFN 2004.**
6. "Unlimited company" means a company not having any limit on the liability of its members. See **Section 21 CAMA Cap. C20 LFN 2004**

**Section 34(2)**

7. "Members" see "member". It includes the heir, executor, administrator, or other personal representatives , as the case may be, of the member. **Garner. B. (ed) Black's Law Dictionary, 8th ed.**
8. "Company" means a company formed and registered under this Act or as the case may be, formed and registered in Nigeria before and in existence on the commencement of this Act. See **Section 567 CAMA, Cap. C20, LFN, 2004**
9. "Commission" means the Corporate Affairs Commission established under section 1 of this Act. See **Section 567 CAMA, Cap. C20, LFN, 2004**

**Section 34(3)**

10. "Subscriber" means a person who by agreement contributes a sum of money or property to a specific person or for a specific purpose. **See Garner B. (ed) Black's Law Dictionary, 8 th ed.**

11. "Memorandum" means the memorandum of association of a company as originally framed or as altered in pursuance of any enactment. See **Section 567 CAMA, Cap. C20, LFN 2004** .
"Memorandum of Association" means a legal document, setting up a corporation, either with or without limited liability, and including the company's name, purpose, and duration. **See Garner B. (ed) Black's Law Dictionary, 8th ed**
12. "Deed" means any written instrument that is signed, sealed and delivered and that conveys small interest in property. **See Garner B. (ed) Black's Law Dictionary 8th ed**

**Cross Reference**

On competent authority to impose, charge and collect duties on instruments related to matters executed between a company and an individual , group or body of individuals, See **section 3, Stamp Duties Act, Cap. S8, LFN 2004**

---

**Cases**

A study of the article of association of a company leaves me in no doubt that they contain the rules and regulations by which the internal affairs of a company are governed....articles of association when registered therefore, become a contract between the company and its members and officers and between the members officers themselves. ***Ladejobi v. Odutola Ltd* (2002) 3 N.W.LR. 121 at 152-153** .

**For Further Reading**

On company, Memorandum and Articles of association, see Ayua, I.A *Nigerian Company Law* G. Burn (Leighton Buzzard, Bedfordshire, United Kingdom) 1984.

*Registration of companies*

## 35. Documents of incorporation

(1) As from the commencement of this Act, a company [1] shall be formed in the manner set out in this section.

(2) There shall be delivered to the Commission [2]-

(a) the memorandum[3] of association and articles[4] of association complying with the provisions of this Part of this Act;

(b) the notice of the address of the registered office [5] of the company[1] and the head office if different from the registered office[5]:

Provided that a postal box address or a private bag address shall not be accepted by the Commission [2] as the registered office[5];

(c) a statement in the prescribed form containing the list and particulars together with the consent of the persons who are to be the first directors [6] of the company [1];

(d) a statement of the authorised share capital [7] signed by at least one director [6]; and

(e) any other document required by the Commission [2] to satisfy the requirements of any law relating to the formation of a company [1].

(3) A statutory declaration [8] in the prescribed form by a legal practitioner that those requirements of this Act for the registration of a company [1] have been complied with shall be produced to the Commission [2], and it may accept such a declaration as sufficient evidence of compliance:

Provided that where the Commission [2] refuses a declaration, [8] it shall within 30 days of the date of receipt of the declaration [8] send to the declarant a notice of its refusal giving the grounds of such refusal.

---

**Notes**

**Section 35(1)**

1. "Company" means a company formed and registered under this Act or as the case may be, formed and registered in Nigeria before and in existence on the commencement of this Act. See **Section 567 CAMA, Cap. C20, LFN, 2004**
2. "Commission" means the Corporate Affairs Commission established under section 1 of this Act. See **CAMA, Section 567 Cap. C20, LFN, 2004**

**Section 35(2)**

3. "Memorandum" means the memorandum of association of a company as originally framed or as altered in pursuance of any enactment. See **Section 567 CAMA, Cap. C20, LFN 2004** .
   "Memorandum of Association" means a legal document, setting up a corporation, either with or without limited liability, and including the company's name, purpose, and duration. **See Garner B. (ed) Black's Law Dictionary, 8th ed**
4. "Articles" means the articles of association of a company, as originally framed or as altered by special resolution. **See Section 567 CAMA, Cap. C20 LFN**.
5. "Registered office" means the official address of a registered company. It must be notified to the Companies Registry before registration of the company and it must appear on company letter-head and order forms. Documents may be served to a company's registered office and various registers and records may be inspected there. See **Martins E. (ed.) Oxford Dictionary of Law 4 th ed**

6. "Directors" see "director". "Director" means a person duly appointed by the company to direct and manage the business of the company. See **Garner .B, (ed) Black's Law Dictionary, 8 [th]ed**
Director includes any person occupying the position of director by whatever name called, and includes any person in accordance with whose directions or instructions the directors are accustomed to act. See **Section 567 CAMA, Cap. C20, LFN 2004**
7. "Authorised share capital" means the share capital of a company at any given time. See **Section 567 CAMA, Cap. C20, LFN 2004**

**Section 35(3)**

8. "Statutory declaration" means a declaration voluntarily made under the Oaths Act 1963 and in Nigeria includes one so made under any other enactment or law providing for the taking of voluntary declaration. See **Section 567 CAMA, Cap. C20, LFN 2004**

---

**Cases**

A study of the article of association of a company leaves me in no doubt that they contain the rules and regulations by which the internal affairs of a company are governed....articles of association when registered therefore, become a contract between the company and its members and officers and between the members officers themselves. ***Ladejobi v. Odutola Ltd*** **(2002) 3 N.W.LR. 121 at 152-153** .

**For Further Reading**

On Corporate Affairs Commission, Incorporation of Companies, Membership of a company, and Share Capital see:
Orojo, J. Ola **Company Law and Practice in Nigeria** 3[rd] Edition, Mbeyi & Associates (Lagos, Nigeria) 1992.
Ogbuanya C.S. Nelson **Essentials of Corporate Law Practice in Nigeria** Novena Publishers Limited 2012
Sasegbon Deji & Co. **Companies and Allied Matters Law and Practice** (NCAMLP) DSC Publications Ltd 2006
On company, memorandum, articles, shares, see Orojo, J. Ola **Company Law and Practice in Nigeria** 3[rd] Edition, Mbeyi & Associates (Lagos, Nigeria) 1992.
Olufemi Amao and Kenneth Amaeshi "Galvanizing Shareholder Activism: A Prerequisite for Effective Corporate Governance and Accountability in Nigeria" (2008) 82 **Journal of Business Ethics** 119-130.

36. Registration

(1) The Commission[1] shall register the memorandum[2] and articles[3] unless in its opinion-

(a) they do not comply with the provisions of this Act; or

(b) the business which the company [4] is to carry on, or the objects for which it is formed, or any of them, are illegal; or
(c) any of the subscribers [5] to the memorandum [2] is incompetent or disqualified in accordance with section 20 of this Act; or
(d) there is non-compliance with the requirement of any other law as to registration and incorporation of a company; or
(e) the proposed name conflicts with or is likely to conflict with an existing trade mark [6] or business name [7] registered in Nigeria.

(2) Any person aggrieved by the decision of the Commission [1] under subsection (1) of this section, may give notice to the Commission [1] requiring it to apply to the court [8] for directions and the Commission [1] shall within 21 days of the receipt of such notice apply to the court [8] for the directions.

(3) The Commission [1] may, in order to satisfy itself as provided in subsection (1) (c) of this section, by instrument in writing require a person subscribing to the memorandum [2] to make and lodge with the Commission[1], a statutory declaration [9] to the effect that he is not disqualified under section 20 of this Act from joining in forming a company[4].

(4) Steps to be taken under this Act to incorporate a company [4] shall not include any invitation to subscribe for shares [10] or otherwise howsoever on the basis of a prospectus [11].

(5) Upon registration of the memorandum [2] and articles[3], the Commission[1] shall certify under its seal-

(a) that the company [4] is incorporated;
(b) in the case of a limited company [12], that the liability of the members [13] is limited by shares [10] or by guarantee [14]; or
(c) in the case of an unlimited company [15], that the liability of the members[13] is unlimited; and
(d) that the company [4] is a private [16] or public company [17], as the case may be.

(6) The certificate of incorporation [18] shall be prima facie evidence that all the requirements of this Act in respect of registration and of matters precedent and incidental to it have been complied with and that the Association is a company [4] authorised to be registered and duly registered under this Act.

---

**Notes**

**Section 36(1)**

1. "Commission" means the Corporate Affairs Commission established under section 1 of this Act. See **Section 567 CAMA, Cap. C20, LFN, 2004**

2. "Memorandum" means the memorandum of association of a company as originally framed or as altered in pursuance of any enactment. See **Section 567 CAMA, Cap. C20, LFN 2004** .
"Memorandum of Association" means a legal document, setting up a corporation, either with or without limited liability, and including the company's name, purpose, and duration. **See Garner B. (ed) Black's Law Dictionary, 8th ed.**
3. "Articles" means the articles of association of a company, as originally framed or as altered by special resolution. **See Section 567 CAMA, Cap. C20 LFN 2004.**
4. "Company" means a company formed and registered under this Act or as the case may be, formed and registered in Nigeria before and in existence on the commencement of this Act. See **Section 567 CAMA, Cap. C20, LFN, 2004** .
5. "Subscriber" means a person who by agreement contributes a sum of money or property to a specific person or for a specific purpose. **See Garner B. (ed) Black's Law Dictionary, 8th ed.**
6. "Trade mark" is a word or logo used by a company or manufacturer to distinguish its product from those of others . See **Garner B. (ed) Black's Law Dictionary, 8th ed.**
7. "Business name" means the name or style under which any business is carried on whether in partnership or otherwise. See **section 588(1) CAMA Cap. C20, LFN 2004**

**Section 36(2)**

8. "Court" means the Federal High Court, and to the extent to which application may be made to it as: court includes the Court of Appeal, and the Supreme Court of Nigeria. See **Section 567 CAMA Cap. C20, LFN 2004**

**Section 36(3)**

9. "Statutory declaration" means a declaration voluntarily made under the Oaths Act 1963 and in Nigeria includes one so made under any other enactment or law providing for the taking of voluntary declaration. See **Section 567 CAMA, Cap. C20, LFN 2004**
"Statutory declaration" means a formal statement, proclamation, one embodied in an instrument. See **Garner .B. (ed) Black's Law Dictionary, 8th ed.**

**Section 36(4)**

10. "Shares" means the interest in a company's share capital of a member who is entitled to share in the capital or income of such company. See **Section 567 CAMA, Cap. C20, LFN, 2004.**
11. "Prospectus" means any prospectus, notice, circular, advertisement, or other invitation, offering to the public for subscription or purchase any shares or debentures of a company and includes any documents which save to the extent that it offers securities for a consideration other than cash is a prospectus. See **Section 567 CAMA, Cap. C20, LFN, 2004**
It also means a document that gives information about a company's shares before they are offered for sale. See **Oxford Advanced Learner's Dictionary of Current English. 6 th ed.**

**Section 36(5)**

12. "Limited company" see "Company". It means a company in which the liability of each shareholder is limited to the amount individually invested. See **Garner .B. (ed) Black's Law Dictionary, 8th ed.**
13. "Members" includes the heir, executor, administrator or other personal representative, as the case maybe, of the member. See **Section 567 CAMA, Cap. C20, LFN, 2004**
14. "Limited by guarantee" has the meaning assigned by section 21 of this Act. See **Section 567 CAMA, Cap. C20, LFN, 2004.**
15. "Unlimited company" means a company not having any limit on the liability of its members. See **Section 21 CAMA Cap. C20 LFN 2004.**
16. "Private company" means one which is stated in its memorandum to be a private company. See **Section 22 CAMA, Cap C20, LFN 2004**
17. "Public company" means any company other than a private company is a public company. See **Section 24 CAMA Cap. C20 LFN 2004.**

**Section 36(6)**

18. "Certificate of Incorporation" means a document issued by a state authority granting a corporation its legal existence and the right to function as a corporation **.See Garner B. (ed) Black's Law Dictionary, 8th ed**

**Cross Reference**

On the establishment and jurisdiction of the Federal High Court, see **sections 259& 251 Constitution of the Federal Republic of Nigeria, 1999(as amended)**

---

**Cases**

A study of the article of association of a company leaves me no doubt that they contain the rules and regulations by which the internal affairs of a company are governed.......articles of association when registered therefore, become a contract between the company and its members and officers and between the members officers themselves.... ***Ladejobi v. Odutola Ltd*** **[2002] 3 N.W.LR. 121 at 152-153** .

A Court is duty bound to confine its decisions to issues raised by the parties. The Court has no power to formulate cases for the parties or to speculate on the evidence parties ought to proffer otherwise it might find itself covered by the dust of conflict. ***Anambra State Envi. Sani.Auth. v. Ekwenem*** **(2009) Vol. 45 W.R.N. 1-175 at p.12**

**For Further Reading**

On Company, Articles, Shareholders/subscribers. See Sofowora, M.O **Modern Nigerian Company Law Soft Associates**, 2nd Edition 2002 Pages 13, 304, 405,

## 37. Effect of Registration

As from the date of incorporation mentioned in the certificate of incorporation,[1] the subscriber[2] of the memorandum[3] together with such other persons as may, from time to time, become members[4] of the company,[5] shall be a body corporate by the name contained in the memorandum,[3] capable forthwith of exercising all the powers and functions of an incorporated company[5] including the power to hold land, and having perpetual succession[6] and a common seal[7] but with such liability on the part of the members[4] to contribute to the assets[8] of the company[5] in the event of its being wound up as is mentioned in this Act.

---

**Notes**
**Section 37**

1. "Certificate of Incorporation" means a document issued by a state authority granting a corporation its legal existence and the right to function as a corporation **.See Garner B. (ed) Black's Law Dictionary, 8th ed**
2. "Subscriber" means a person who by agreement contributes a sum of money or property to a specific person or for a specific purpose. See **Garner B. (ed) Black's Law Dictionary, 8th ed.**
3. "Memorandum" means the memorandum of association of a company as originally framed or as altered in pursuance of any enactment. See **Section 567 CAMA, Cap. C20, LFN 2004** .
   "Memorandum of Association" means a legal document, setting up a corporation, either with or without limited liability, and including the company's name, purpose, and duration. **See Garner B. (ed) Black's Law Dictionary, 8th ed**
4. "Members" includes the heir, executor, administrator, or other personal representatives, as the case may be, of the member. **Garner. B. (ed) Black's Law Dictionary, 8th ed.**
5. "Company" means a company formed and registered under this Act or as the case may be, formed and registered in Nigeria before and in existence on the commencement of this Act. **CAMA, Cap. C20, LFN, 2004**.
6. "Perpetual succession" means the continuation of a corporation's legal status despite changes in ownership or management. See **Garner B. (ed) Black's Law Dictionary, 8th ed.**
7. "Common seal" means to authenticate or execute a document by use of a seal .See **Garner. B. (ed) Black's Law Dictionary, 8th ed.**
8. "Asset(s)" means an item that is owned and has value. **See Garner B. Ed. Black's Law Dictionary, 8 th ed.**
9. An asset is a thing of value, especially property, that a person or company owns, and which can be used or sold to pay debts. See **Oxford Advanced learners Dictionary, 6 th ed**

Cross Reference

On effect of use of common seal, see **section 604 CAMA Cap. C20, LFN 2004**.

---

**Cases**

Corporate personality presupposes that a company assumes a separate and distinct personality from its members from the moment of incorporation. ***Habib Nig. Bank Ltd. v. Ochete*** **(2001) F.W.L.R (pt.54) 384.**

**For Further Reading**

On Company Membership, see Orojo, J. Ola **Company Law and Practice in Nigeria** 3rd Edition, Mbeyi & Associates (Lagos, Nigeria) 1992.

## 38. Powers of companies

(1) Except to the extent that the company's [1] memorandum[2] or any enactment otherwise provides, every company [1] shall, for the furtherance of its authorised business or objects, have all the powers of a natural person of full capacity.

(2) A company[1] shall not have or exercise power either directly or indirectly to make a donation or gift of any of its property or funds to a political party or political association, or for any political purpose; and if any company [1], in breach of this subsection makes any donation or gift of its property to a political party or political association, or for any political purpose, the officers[3] in default and any member [4] who voted for the breach shall be jointly and severally liable to refund to the company [1] the sum or value of the donation or gift and in addition, the company [1] and every such officer[3] or member[4] shall be guilty of an offence and liable to a fine equal to the amount or value of the donation or gift.

---

**Notes**

**Section 38**

1. "Company" means a company formed and registered under this Act or as the case may be, formed and registered in Nigeria before and in existence on the commencement of this Act. See **Section 567 CAMA, Cap. C20, LFN, 2004.**
2. "Memorandum" means the memorandum of association of a company as originally framed or as altered in pursuance of any enactment. See **Section 567 CAMA, Cap. C20, LFN 2004** .

   "Memorandum of Association" means a legal document, setting up a corporation, either with or without limited liability, and including the company's name, purpose, and duration. **See Garner B. (ed) Black's Law Dictionary, 8th ed**

3. "Officer" in relation to a body corporate, includes a director, manager or secretary. See **Section 567 CAMA, Cap. C20, LFN 2004**
4. "Members" includes the heir, executor, administrator, or other personal representatives, as the case may be, of the member. See **Garner .B. (ed) Black's Law Dictionary, 8th ed.**

Cross Reference

On meaning of offence, see **section 2 Criminal Code Cap. C38, LFN 2004**
On prohibition of political activities by certain associations, see **221 Constitution of the Federal Republic of Nigeria, 1999(as amended)**
On meaning of political party, see **section 229, Constitution of the Federal Republic of Nigeria, 1999(as amended)**

**Cases**
Corporate personality presupposes that a company assumes a separate and distinct personality from its members from the moment of incorporation. ***Habib Nig. Bank Ltd. v. Ochete*** **(2001) F.W.L.R (pt.54) 384.**

**For Further Reading**
A Political party starts as and is basically an Association . **See *INEC v. Balarabe Musa (2002-2003) 2 LLRN 822-896***
On Corporate Affairs Commission, Incorporation of Companies, Membership of a company, and Share Capital see:
Orojo, J. Ola **Company Law and Practice in Nigeria** 3rd Edition, Mbeyi & Associates (Lagos, Nigeria) 1992.
Ogbuanya C.S. Nelson **Essentials of Corporate Law Practice in Nigeria** Novena Publishers Limited 2012
Sasegbon Deji & Co. **Companies and Allied Matters Law and Practice** (NCAMLP) DSC Publications Ltd 2006

## 39. Effect of ultra vires acts

(1) A company[1] shall not carry on any business not authorized by its memorandum[2] and shall not exceed the powers conferred upon it by its memorandum [2] or this Act.

(2) A breach of subsection (1) of this section, may be asserted in any proceedings under sections 300 to 313 of this Act or under subsection (4) of this section.

(3) Notwithstanding the provisions of subsection (1) of this section, no act of a company [1] and no conveyance or transfer of property to or by a company [1] shall be invalid by reason of the fact that such act, conveyance or transfer was not done or made for the furtherance of any of the authorised business of the company [1] or that the company[1] was otherwise exceeding its objects or powers.

(4) On the application of-

(a) any member [3] of the company [1]; or

(b) the holder of any debenture [4] secured by a floating charge [5] over all or any of the company's property or by the trustee of the holders of any such debentures, [4]

the court[6] may prohibit, by injunction, the doing of any act or the conveyance or transfer of any property in breach of subsection (1) of this section.

(5) If the transactions sought to be prohibited in any proceeding under subsection (4) of this section are being, or are to be performed or made pursuant to any contract to which the company[1] is a party, the court [6] may, if it deems the same to be equitable and if all the parties to the contract are parties to the proceedings, set aside and prohibit the performance of such contract, and may allow to the company [1] or to the other parties to the contract compensation for any loss or damage sustained by them by reason of the setting aside or prohibition of the performance of such contract but no compensation shall be allowed for loss of anticipated profits to be derived from the performance of such contract.

---

**Notes**

**Section 39(1)**

1. "Company" means a company formed and registered under this Act or as the case may be, formed and registered in Nigeria before and in existence on the commencement of this Act. See **Section 567 CAMA, Cap. C20, LFN, 2004**
2. "Memorandum" means the memorandum of association of a company as originally framed or as altered in pursuance of any enactment. See **Section 567 CAMA, Cap. C20, LFN 2004** .
   "Memorandum of Association" means a legal document, setting up a corporation, either with or without limited liability, and including the company's name, purpose, and duration. **See Garner B. (ed) Black's Law Dictionary, 8th ed**

**Section 36(4)**

3. "Member" includes the heir, executor, administrator, or other personal representatives, as the case may be, of the member. See **Section 567 CAMA, Cap. C20, LFN, 2004**
4. "Debenture" means a written acknowledgment of indebtedness by the company setting out terms and conditions of the indebtedness, and includes debenture stock, bonds and other securities of a company

whether constituting a charge on the assets of the company or not. See **Section 567 CAMA, Cap. C20, LFN, 2004**

5. "Floating charge" means a lien that continues to exist even when the collateral changes in character, classification, or location. See **Garner B. (ed) Black's Law Dictionary, 8th ed.**
6. "Court" means the Federal High Court, and to the extent to which application may be made to it as: court includes the court of Appeal, and the Supreme Court of Nigeria. See **567 CAMA, Cap. C20, LFN, 2004**

**Cases**

Where a resolution was ultra vires the Trade Union Constitution, the Court held that the plaintiffs were entitled to sue in spite of the fact that they participated in the meeting at which the resolution was passed. ***Benson Oduduro and Anor v. National Union of Hotels and Personal Services Workers and Others*** **(Unreported) Suit No. FCA/L/226/83.**

**For Further Reading**

On illegal or ultra vires acts of the company, See P. Ehi Oshio,'The True Ambit of Majority Rule under the Companies and Allied Matters Act 1990 revisited" **Modern Practice Journal of Finance and Investment Law, Lagos, Vol.** (University of Benin Press)

## 40. Effect of reliance on restrictions in the memorandum

(1) Where there is provision in the memorandum [1] of association of a company[2] restricting the powers and capacity of the company [2] to carry on its authorized business or object, the restriction may be relied on and have effect only for the purpose of-

(a) proceedings against the company [2] by a director [3] or member [4] of the company[2], or where the company [2] has issued debentures [5] secured by a floating charge [6] over all or any of the company's property, by the holder of any of the debentures [5] or the trustee for the holders of the debentures [5]; or

(b) proceedings by the company [2] or a member [4] of the company [2] against the present or former officers [7] of the company [2] for failure to observe any such restriction; or

(c) proceedings by the Commission [8] or a member [4] of the company [2] to wind up the company [2]; or

(d) proceedings for the purpose of restraining the company [2] or other person from acting in breach of the memorandum [1] or directing the company [2] or such person to comply with the same.

(2) A person may not in proceedings referred to in subsection (1) (a), (b) or (c), of this section, rely on a restriction of the power or capacity of the company [2] contained in the memorandum [1] in any case

where he voted in favor of, or otherwise expressly or by conduct agreed to the doing of an act by the company [2] or the conveyance by or to the company[2] of property which, it is alleged in the proceedings, was or would be contrary to such a restriction.

---

**Notes**
**Section 40**

1. "Memorandum" means the memorandum of association of a company as originally framed or as altered in pursuance of any enactment. See **Section 567 CAMA, Cap. C20, LFN 2004** .
   "Memorandum of Association" means a legal document, setting up a corporation, either with or without limited liability, and including the company's name, purpose, and duration. **See Garner B. (ed) Black's Law Dictionary, 8th ed**
2. "Company" means a company formed and registered under this Act or as the case may be, formed and registered in Nigeria before and in existence on the commencement of this Act. See **Section 567 CAMA, Cap. C20, LFN, 2004.**
3. "Director" means a person duly appointed by the company to direct and manage the business of the company. See **Garner B, (ed)Black's Law Dictionary, 8th ed**
   Director includes any person occupying the position of director by whatever name called, and includes any person in accordance with whose directions or instructions the directors are accustomed to act. See **Section 567 CAMA, Cap. C20, LFN 2004** .
4. "Member" includes the heir, executor, administrator, or other personal representatives, as the case may be, of the member. See **Section 567 CAMA, Cap. C20, LFN, 2004.**
5. "Debenture" means a written acknowledgment of indebtedness by the company setting out terms and conditions of the indebtedness, and includes debenture stock, bonds and other securities of a company whether constituting a charge on the assets of the company or not. See **Section 567 CAMA, Cap. C20, LFN, 2004**
6. "Floating charge" means a lien that continues to exist even when the collateral changes in character, classification, or location. See **Garner B. (ed) Black's Law Dictionary, 8th ed** .
7. "Officer" in relation to a body corporate, includes a director, manager or secretary. See **Section 567 CAMA, Cap. C20, LFN, 2004.**
8. "Commission" means the Corporate Affairs Commission established under section 1 of this Act. See **Section 567 CAMA, Cap. C20, LFN, 2004.**

---

**For Further Reading**
On memorandum, directors, company, see Kiser Barnes, **Cases and Materials on Nigeria Company Law** (1992) Obafemi Awolowo University press Ltd, Ile-Ife, Nigeria

*Effect of memorandum and articles*

## 41. Effect of memorandum and articles

(1) Subject to the provisions of this Act, the memorandum [1] and articles,[2] when registered, shall have the effect of a contract under seal between the company [3] and its members [4] and officers [5] and between the members [4] and officers [5] themselves whereby they agree to observe and perform the provisions of the memorandum [1] and articles[2], as altered from time to time in so far as they relate to the company[3], members [4], or officers [5] as such.

(2) All money payable by any member [4] to the company [3] under the memorandum [1] or articles [2] shall be a debt due from him to the company and shall be of the nature of a specialty debt.

(3) Where the memorandum [1] or articles [2] empower any person to appoint or remove any director [6] or other officer of the company [3], such power shall be enforceable by that person not withstanding that he is not a member [4] or officer [5] of the company [3].

(4) In any action by any member [4] or officer [5] to enforce any obligation owed under the memorandum [1] or articles [2] to him and any other member [4] or officer [5], such member [4] or officer [5] may, if any other member [4] or officer [5] is affected by the alleged breach of such obligation, with his consent, sue in a representative capacity [7] on behalf of himself and all other members [4] or officers [5] who may be affected other than any who are defendants and the provisions of Part XI of this Act shall apply.

**Notes**

**Section 41(1)**

1. "Memorandum" means the memorandum of association of a company as originally framed or as altered in pursuance of any enactment. See **Section 567 CAMA, Cap. C20, LFN 2004** .

   "Memorandum of Association" means a legal document, setting up a corporation, either with or without limited liability, and including the company's name, purpose, and duration. **See Garner B. (ed) Black's Law Dictionary, 8th ed**
2. "Articles" means the articles of association of a company, as originally framed or as altered by special resolution. **See Section 567 CAMA, Cap. C20 LFN 2004.**
3. "Company" means a company formed and registered under this Act or as the case may be, formed and registered in Nigeria before and in existence on the commencement of this Act. See **Section 567 CAMA, Cap. C20, LFN, 2004.**

4. "Member" includes the heir, executor, administrator, or other personal representatives, as the case may be, of the member. See **Section 567 CAMA, Cap. C20, LFN, 2004**
5. "Officer" in relation to a body corporate, includes a director, manager or secretary. See **Section 567 CAMA, Cap. C20, LFN, 2004**

**Section 41(3)**

6. "Director" means a person duly appointed by the company to direct and manage the business of the company. See **Garner B. (ed) Black's Law Dictionary, 8th ed**

   Director includes any person occupying the position of director by whatever name called, and includes any person in accordance with whose directions or instructions the directors are accustomed to act. See **Section 567 CAMA, Cap. C20, LFN 2004** .

**Section 41(4)**

7. "Representative capacity" means one who stands for or acts on behalf of another. See **Garner, B. (ed) Black's Law Dictionary, 8th ed** .

---

**Cases**

The entire Law of Contract is founded on the "Consensus" or "will" theory of contract, which asserts that contractual obligations are by definition self imposed and in terms of the function of the courts, finds expression in the idea that the exclusive task of a court in contract cases is to discover what the parties have agreed and give effect to it except in cases of mistake, duress and illegality. ***Coop. Dev. Bank Plc v. Ekanem* (2009) 16 N.W.L.R. part 1168 443-658 at pg.588.**

A study of the article of association of a company leaves me no doubt that they contain the rules and regulations by which the internal affairs of a company are governed...articles of association when registered therefore, become a contract between the company and its members and officers and between the members officers themselves:. ***Ladejobi v. Odutola Ltd* (2002) 3 N.W.LR. 121 at 152-153.**

*Member's right to copy of memorandum and articles*

## 42. Member's right to copies of memorandum, etc.

(1) A company[1] shall, on being so required by any member [2], send to him a copy of the memorandum[3] and of the articles[4], if any, and a copy of any enactment which alters the memorandum[3], subject to payment, in the case of a copy of the memorandum[3] and of the articles[4], of N20 or such less sum as the company[1] may prescribe and in the case of a copy of an enactment of such sum not exceeding the published price thereof as the company[1] may require.

(2) If a company[1] makes default in complying with this section, the company[1] and every officer[5] of the company[1] who is in default shall be liable for each offence to a fine not exceeding N25.

---

**Notes**

**Section 42(1)**

1. "Company" means a company formed and registered under this Act or as the case may be, formed and registered in Nigeria before and in existence on the commencement of this Act. See **Section 567 CAMA, Cap. C20, LFN, 2004** .
2. "Member" includes the heir, executor, administrator, or other personal representatives, as the case may be, of the member. See **Section 567 CAMA, Cap. C20, LFN, 2004** .
3. "Memorandum" means the memorandum of association of a company as originally framed or as altered in pursuance of any enactment. See **Section 567 CAMA, Cap. C20, LFN 2004** .
   "Memorandum of Association" means a legal document, setting up a corporation, either with or without limited liability, and including the company's name, purpose, and duration. **See Garner B. (ed) Black's Law Dictionary, 8th ed.**
4. "Articles" means the articles of association of a company, as originally framed or as altered by special resolution. **See Section 567 CAMA, Cap. C20 LFN 2004.**

**Section 42(2)**

5. "Officer" in relation to a body corporate, includes a director, manager or secretary. See **Section 567 CAMA, Cap. C20, LFN 2004** .

Cross Reference

On meaning of offence, see **section 2 Criminal Code Cap. C38, LFN 2004**

---

**Cases**

A study of the article of association of a company leaves me no doubt that they contain the rules and regulations by which the internal affairs of a company are governed...articles of association when registered therefore, become a contract between the company and its members and officers and between the members officers themselves....... ***Ladejobi v. Odutola Ltd* (2002) 3 N.W.LR. 121 at 152-153.**

**For Further Reading**

On memorandum and articles of Association, see Ephraim Madeueulosi Asomugha, **Company law in Nigeria under the companies and Allied Matters Act,** (1994) E.M. Asumughai Lagos.

## 43. Copies of memorandum issued to embody alterations

(1) Where an alteration is made in the memorandum [1] of a company[2] every copy of the memorandum [3] issued after the date of the alteration shall be in accordance with the alteration.

(2) If, where any such alteration has been made, the company [2] at any time after the date of the alteration issues any copies of the memorandum[1] which are not in accordance with the alteration, it shall be liable to a fine not exceeding N25 for each copy so issued, and every officer[3] of the company[2] who is in default shall be liable to the like penalty.

---

**Notes**
**Section 43(1)**

1. "Memorandum" means the memorandum of association of a company as originally framed or as altered in pursuance of any enactment. See **Section 567 CAMA, Cap. C20, LFN 2004** .
   "Memorandum of Association" means a legal document, setting up a corporation, either with or without limited liability, and including the company's name, purpose, and duration. **See Garner B. (ed) Black's Law Dictionary, 8th ed.**
2. "Company" means a company formed and registered under this Act or as the case may be, formed and registered in Nigeria before and in existence on the commencement of this Act. See **Section 567 CAMA, Cap. 20, LFN, 2004** .

**Section 43(2)**

3. "Officer" in relation to a body corporate, includes a director, manager or secretary. See **Section 567 CAMA, Cap. 20, LFN, 2004.**

---

**For Further Reading**
On company, memorandum, articles, see Ayua, I.A **Nigerian Company Law** G. Burn (Leighton Buzzard, Bedfordshire, United Kingdom) 1984

*Alteration of memorandum and articles*

## 44. Restriction on alteration of memorandum

(1) A company[1] may not alter the conditions contained in its memorandum[2] except in the cases and in the manner and to the extent for which express provision is made in this Act.

(2) Only those provisions which are required by section 27 of this Act or by any other specific provision contained in this Act, to be stated in the memorandum[2] of the company[1] concerned, shall be deemed to be conditions contained in its memorandum[2].

---

**Notes**
**Section 44**

1. "Company" means a company formed and registered under this Act or as the case may be, formed and registered in Nigeria before and in existence on the commencement of this Act. See **Section 567 CAMA Cap.20 LFN, 2004** .
2. "Memorandum" means the memorandum of association of a company as originally framed or as altered in pursuance of any enactment. See **Section 567 CAMA, Cap. C20, LFN 2004** .

   "Memorandum of Association" means a legal document, setting up a corporation, either with or without limited liability, and including the company's name, purpose, and duration. **See Garner B. (ed) Black's Law Dictionary, 8th ed.**

**Cross reference**

For contents of a Memorandum of association, see **section. 27 CAMA, Cap. C20, LFN, 2004.**

## 45. Alteration of memorandum

(1) The name of the company [1] shall not be altered except with the consent of the Commission[2] in accordance with section 31 of this Act.

(2) The business which the company [1] is authorized to carryon or, if the company [1] is not formed for the purpose of carrying on business, the objects for which it is established, may be altered or added to in accordance with the provisions of section 46 or of Part XV of this Act.

(3) Any restriction on the powers of the company [1] may be altered in the same way as the business or object of the company [1].

(4) The share capital [3] of the company[1] may be altered in accordance with the provisions of sections 100 to 111 of this Act, but not otherwise.

(5) Subject to section 49 of this Act, any other provision of the memorandum[4] may be altered in accordance with section 46 of this Act, or as otherwise provided in this Act.

**Notes**
**Section 45(1)**

1. "Company" means a company formed and registered under this Act or as the case may be, formed and registered in Nigeria before and in existence on the commencement of this Act. **See Section 567 CAMA Cap. 20 LFN 2004.**

2. "Commission" means the Corporate Affairs Commission established under section 1 of this Act. See **Section 567 CAMA, Cap.20, LFN, 2004.**

**Section 45(4)**

3. "Share capital" means one of the definite numbers of equal parts into which the capital stock of a corporation or joint stock company is divided. See **Garner B. (ed) Black's Law Dictionary, 8th ed.**

**Section 45(5)**

4. "Memorandum" means the memorandum of association of a company as originally framed or as altered in pursuance of any enactment. See **Section 567 CAMA, Cap. C20, LFN 2004** .

   "Memorandum of Association" means a legal document, setting up a corporation, either with or without limited liability, and including the company's name, purpose, and duration. **See Garner B. (ed) Black's Law Dictionary, 8th ed**

**Cross Reference**

On procedure for change of name of a company, see **section 31 CAMA Cap. C20, LFN 2004**

On mode of altering the business or objects of a company, see **section 46 CAMA Cap. C20, LFN 2004.**

On limitation of liability of members to contribute where the memorandum and articles of association of a company is altered, see **section 49 CAMA Cap. C20 LFN 2004**

On alteration of the share capital of a company, see **sections 100 -111 CAMA Cap. C20, LFN 2004**

---

**For Further Reading**

On company, business, see Owolabi, N.B. and Badmus, M.A. (Eds) (2003) **Nigerian Business and & co-operative law** (Printouts limited, Lagos)

## 46. Mode of alteration of business or objects

(1) A company [1] may, at a meeting [2] of which notice in writing has been duly given to all members [3] (whether or not otherwise entitled thereto), by special resolution [4] alter the provisions of its memorandum[5] with respect to the business or objects of the company[1]:

Provided that if an application is made to the court [6] in accordance with this section for the alteration to be cancelled, it shall not have effect except in so far as it is confirmed by the court [6].

(2) An application under this section may be made to the court[6]-

(a) by the holders of not less in the aggregate than 15 per cent in nominal value of the company's [1] issued share capital [7] or any class thereof or, if the company [1] is not limited by shares[8], not less than 15 per cent of the company's [1] members[3]; or

(b) by the holders of not less than 15 per cent of the company's[1] debentures[8] entitling the holders to object to alterations of its objects:

Provided that any such application shall not be made by any person who has consented to or voted in favour of the alteration.

(3) An application under this section shall be made not later than 28 days after the date on which the resolution [4] altering the company's[1] business or objects was passed, and may be made on behalf of the persons entitled to make the application by such one or more of their number as they may appoint in writing for the purpose.

(4) On an application under this section, the court [6] may make an order confirming the alteration either wholly or in part and on such terms and conditions as it thinks fit, and may adjourn the proceedings in order that an arrangement may be made to the satisfaction of the court[6] for the purchase of the interest of dissenting members[3], and the court [6] may give such directions and make such orders as it thinks expedient for facilitating or carrying into effect any such arrangement:

Provided that no part of the capital of the company [1] shall be expended in any purchase.

(5) The debentures[9] entitling the holders to object to alterations of a company's [1] business or objects shall be any debentures[9] secured by a floating charge. [10]

(6) The special resolution[4] altering a company's [1] business or objects shall require the same notice to the holders of any such debentures [9] as to members [3] of the company[1]; and in default of any provisions regulating the giving of notice to any such debenture holders [11], the provisions of the company's [1] articles[12] regulating the giving of notice to members [3] shall apply.

(7) Where a company [1] passes a resolution[4] altering its business or objects and-

(a) application is thereafter made to the court [6] for its confirmation under this section, the company [1] shall forthwith give notice to the Commission [13] of the making of the application, and thereafter there shall be delivered to the Commission[13] within 15 days from the date of its making-

(i) a certified true copy of the order in the case of refusal to confirm the resolution [4]; and

(ii) a certified true copy of the order in the case of confirmation of the resolution[4] together with a printed copy of the memorandum [5] as thereby altered;

(b) no application is made with respect thereto to a court [6] under this section, the company [1] shall within 15 days from the end of the period for making such an application deliver to the Commission [13] a copy of the resolution[4] as passed.

(8) f the Commission [13]-

(a) is satisfied, a printed copy of the memorandum [5] as altered by the resolution[4] shall forthwith thereafter be delivered to it;

(b) is not satisfied, it shall give notice in writing to the company[1] of its decision and an appeal from its decision shall thereafter lie to the court [6] at the suit of any person aggrieved, if made within 21 days from the date of the receipt by the company [1] of the notice of the rejection, or within such extended time as the court [6] may allow.

(9) The court[6] may at any time extend the time for the delivery of documents to the Commission [13] under paragraph (a) of subsection (7) of this section for such period as the court [6] may think proper.

(10) If a company [1] makes default in giving notice or delivering any document to the Commission [13] as required by subsection (6) of this section, the company [1] and every officer [14] of the company[1] who is in default shall be liable to a fine of N50.

(11) The validity of an alteration of the provision of a company's [1] memorandum[5] with respect to the business or objects of the company[1] shall not be questioned on the ground that it was not authorised by subsection (1) of this section except in proceedings taken for the purpose (whether under this section or otherwise) before the expiration of 21 days after the date of the resolution [4] in that behalf; and where any such proceedings are taken otherwise than under this section, subsections (6), (7), (8) and (9) of this section shall apply in relation thereto as if they had been taken

under this section, and as if any order declaring the alteration invalid were an order cancelling it and as if any order dismissing the proceedings were an order confirming the alteration.

(12) In this section "member [3]" includes any person financially interested in the company. [1]

**Notes**

**Section 46(1)**

1. "Company" means a company formed and registered under this Act or as the case may be, formed and registered in Nigeria before and in existence on the commencement of this Act. See **Section 567 CAMA, Cap. C20, LFN, 2004.**
2. "Meeting" means the gathering of people to discuss or act on matters in which they have a common interest. See **Garner B. (ed) Black's Law Dictionary, 8th ed.**
3. "Member" includes the heir, executor, administrator, or other personal representatives, as the case may be, of the member. **See Section 567 CAMA, Cap. C20, LFN, 2004**
4. "Special resolution" means a resolution passed by not less than three fourths of the votes cast by such members of the company as, being entitled to do so, vote in person or by proxy at a general meeting of which 21 days' notice, specifying the intention to propose the resolution as a special resolution, has been duly given. See **Section 233(2) CAMA, Cap. C20, LFN, 2004**
5. "Memorandum" means the memorandum of association of a company as originally framed or as altered in pursuance of any enactment. See **Section 567 CAMA, Cap. C20, LFN 2004** .

   "Memorandum of Association" means a legal document, setting up a corporation, either with or without limited liability, and including the company's name, purpose, and duration. **See Garner B. (ed) Black's Law Dictionary, 8th ed**
6. "Court" means the Federal High Court, and to the extent to which application may be made to it as: court includes the court of Appeal, and the Supreme Court of Nigeria. See **Constitution of the Federal Republic of Nigeria, Cap. C23 LFN, 2004**

**Section 46(2)**

7. "Issued share capital" in relation to any reduction has the meaning assigned to it by section 105(2) of this Act , See **Section 567 CAMA, Cap. C20, LFN 2004.**
8. "Shares" means the interest in a company's share capital of a member who is entitled to share in the capital or income of such company. See **Section 567 CAMA, Cap. C20, LFN, 2004**
9. "Debenture" means a written acknowledgment of indebtedness by the company setting out terms and conditions of the indebtedness, and includes debenture stock, bonds and other securities of a company whether constituting a charge on the assets of the company or not. See **.Section 567 CAMA, Cap. C20, LFN 2004**

**Section 46(5)**

10. Floating charge" means a lien that continues to exist even when the collateral changes in character, classification, or location. See **Garner B. (ed) Black's Law Dictionary, 8th ed.**
11. "Debenture holders" see "debenture" and "holder. Debenture means a written acknowledgement of indebtedness by the company, setting out the terms and conditions of the indebtedness and includes debenture stock, bonds and any other securities of any company whether constituting a charge on the assets of the company or not. See **Section 567 CAMA Cap. C20 LFN, 2004.** "Holder" is one who has legal possession of a negotiable instrument and is entitled to receive payment on it. A holder is a person who has legal possession of a document of title or an investment security. See **Garner B. (ed.) Black's Law Dictionary, 8th ed.**

**Section 46(6)**

12. "Articles" means the articles of association of a company, as originally framed or as altered by special resolution. See **Section 567 Companies and Allied Matters Act Cap. C20, LFN 2004**

**Section 46(7)**

13. "Commission" means the Corporate Affairs Commission established under section 1 of this Act. See **Section 567 CAMA, Cap. C20, LFN, 2004.**

**Section 46(10)**

14. "Officer" in relation to a body corporate includes a director, manager or secretary. See **Section 567 CAMA Cap. C20, LFN 2004 .**

---

**Cases**

Generally companies speak or express their decisions through resolutions, which must be validly passed. No member of a company has a right to unilaterally commit the company on any matter without its consent and approval. Let me emphatically say that no member of a company is allowed to wake up one morning and sell off the company. ***New Resources Int'l Ltd. &Anor.v. Ejike Oranusi*** **(2010) LPELR-CA/L/461/08.**

**For Further Reading**

On Corporate Affairs Commission, Incorporation of Companies, Membership of a company, and Share Capital see:

Orojo, J. Ola **Company Law and Practice in Nigeria** 3rd Edition, Mbeyi & Associates (Lagos, Nigeria) 1992.

Ogbuanya C.S. Nelson **Essentials of Corporate Law Practice in Nigeria** Novena Publishers Limited 2012

Sasegbon Deji & Co. **Companies and Allied Matters Law and Practice** (NCAMLP) DSC Publications Ltd 2006.

## 47. Power to alter provisions in the memorandum in certain cases

(1) Subject to the provisions of section 44 of this Act and of this section and of any part of Part A of this Act (which preserves the rights of minorities in certain cases) any provision in a company's[1] memorandum[2], which might lawfully have been in articles[3] of association instead of in the memorandum, [2] may be altered by the company[1] by special resolution[4]; but if an application is made to the court[5] for the alteration to be cancelled, the alteration shall not have effect except in so far as it is confirmed by the court.

(2) This section shall not apply where the memorandum [2] itself provides for or prohibits the alteration of all or any of the said provisions, and shall not authorize any variation or abrogation of the special rights of any class of members [6].

(3) Subsections (2), (3), (4), (7), (8) and (9) of section 46 of this Act (which relate to mode of alteration of business or objects) except paragraph (b) of subsection (2) thereof, shall apply in relation to any alteration and to any application made under this section as they apply in relation to alterations and to applications made under that section.

(4) This section shall apply to a company's [1] memorandum[2], whether registered before or after the commencement of this Act.

**Notes**

**Section 47(1)**

1. "Company" means a company formed and registered under this Act or as the case may be, formed and registered in Nigeria before and in existence on the commencement of this Act. See **Section 567 CAMA, Cap. C20, LFN 2004.**
2. "Memorandum" means the memorandum of association of a company as originally framed or as altered in pursuance of any enactment. See **Section 567 CAMA, Cap. C20, LFN 2004** .
   "Memorandum of Association" means a legal document, setting up a corporation, either with or without limited liability, and including the company's name, purpose, and duration. **See Garner B. (ed) Black's Law Dictionary, 8th ed**
3. "Articles" means the articles of association of a company, as originally framed or as altered by special resolution. See **Section 567 Companies and Allied Matters Act Cap. C20, LFN 2004**
4. "Special resolution" means a resolution passed by not less than three fourths of the votes cast by such members of the company as, being entitled to do so, vote in person or by proxy at a general meeting of which 21 days' notice, specifying the intention to propose the resolution

as a special resolution, has been duly given. See **Section 233(2) CAMA, Cap. C20, LFN, 2004**

5. "Court" means the Federal High Court, and to the extent to which application may be made to it as: court includes the court of Appeal, and the Supreme Court of Nigeria. See **Constitution of the Federal Republic of Nigeria, Cap. C23, LFN, 2004.**
6. "Members" see "member" It means one of the individuals of whom a deliberative assembly consists and who enjoys the full rights of participating in the organization-including the rights of making, debating and voting on motions- except to the extent that the organization reserves those rights to certain classes of membership. See **Garner B.** (ed.) Black's Law Dictionary 8th ed.
   It includes the heir, executor, administrator or other personal representative as the case may be, of the member. **See Section 567 of CAMA Cap C20 LFN, 2004**

**Cross Reference**

For the definition, capacity of, rights and obligations of Members of a Company, see **Part IV of CAMA, Cap C20, LFN, 2004.**

---

**Cases**

The definition of a company in section 650 of Companies and Allied Matters Act puts the matter beyond doubt. It defines a 'company' or 'existing' to mean....a company formed and registered in Nigeria before and in existence on the commencement of this Act. ***Agro Allied Dev. Ent. Ltd. v. Reefer (2009) Vol.31 W.R.N 1-185 at pg 7.***

The Company is distinct from its promoters or directors and a director is an agent of the company. Consequently, where a director enters into a contract in the name of or purporting to bind the company, it is the company, as principal that is liable, not the director . ***Dansa Foods (Nig.) Ltd v. Isong (2011) ALL F.W.L.R. part 596 404-600 at p.595***

**For Further Reading**

On company, memorandum, articles; See Orojo J. Ola **Company Law and Practice in Nigeria** 3rd Edition, Mbeyi & Associates (Lagos, Nigeria) 1992.

## 48. Alteration of articles

(1) Subject to the provisions of this Act and to the conditions or other provisions contained in its memorandum, [1] a company[2] may by special resolution[3] alter or add to its articles. [4]

(2) Any alteration or addition so made in the articles [4] shall, subject to the provisions of this Act, be as valid as if originally

contained therein and be subject, in like manner, to alteration by special resolution.[3]

---

**Notes**

**Section 48(1)**

1. "Memorandum" means the memorandum of association of a company as originally framed or as altered in pursuance of any enactment. See **Section 567 CAMA, Cap. C20, LFN 2004** .
   "Memorandum of Association" means a legal document, setting up a corporation, either with or without limited liability, and including the company's name, purpose, and duration. **See Garner B. (ed) Black's Law Dictionary, 8th ed**
2. "Company" means a company formed and registered under this Act or as the case may be, formed and registered in Nigeria before and in existence on the commencement of this Act. See **Section 567 CAMA, Cap. C20, LFN, 2004** .
3. "Special resolution" means a resolution passed by not less than three fourths of the votes cast by such members of the company as, being entitled to do so, vote in person or by proxy at a general meeting of which 21 days' notice, specifying the intention to propose the resolution as a special resolution, has been duly given. See **Section 233(2) CAMA, Cap. C20, LFN, 2004**

**Section 48(2)**

4. "Articles" means the articles of association of a company, as originally framed or as altered by special resolution. See **Section 567 Companies and Allied Matters Act Cap. C20, LFN 2004**

---

**Cases**

A study of the article of association of a company leaves me no doubt that they contain the rules and regulations by which the internal affairs of a company are governed...articles of association when registered therefore, become a contract between the company and its members and officers and between the members officers themselves: ***Ladejobi v. Odutola Ltd*** **(2002) 3 N.W.LR. 121 at 152-153.**

**For Further Reading**

On Corporate Affairs Commission, Incorporation of Companies, Membership of a company, and Share Capital see:

Orojo, J. Ola **Company Law and Practice in Nigeria** 3rd Edition, Mbeyi & Associates (Lagos, Nigeria) 1992.

Ogbuanya C.S. Nelson **Essentials of Corporate Law Practice in Nigeria**, Novena Publishers Limited 2012.

Sasegbon Deji & Co. **Companies and Allied Matters Law and Practice** (NCAMLP) DSC Publications Ltd 2006.

## 49. Limitation of liability to contribute to share capital if memorandum, etc., altered

Save to the extent to which a member [1] of a company[2] agrees in writing at any time to be bound thereby, and anything to the contrary in the memorandum[3] or articles[4] notwithstanding, the member[1] shall not be bound by any alteration made in the memorandum[3] or articles[4] of the company[2] requiring him on or after the date of the alteration to-

(a) take or subscribe for more shares [5] than he held at the date on which he became a member [1]; or

(b) increase his liability to contribute to the share capital [6] of the company[2]; or

(c) pay money by any other means to the company. [2]

---

**Notes**
**Section 49**

1. "Member" includes the heir, executor, administrator, or other personal representatives, as the case may be, of the member. See **Section 567 CAMA, Cap. C20, LFN, 2004**
2. "Company" means a company formed and registered under this Act or as the case may be, formed and registered in Nigeria before and in existence on the commencement of this Act. See **Section 567 CAMA, Cap. C20, LFN, 2004.**
3. "Memorandum" means the memorandum of association of a company as originally framed or as altered in pursuance of any enactment. See **Section 567 CAMA, Cap. C20, LFN 2004** .
   "Memorandum of Association" means a legal document, setting up a corporation, either with or without limited liability, and including the company's name, purpose, and duration. **See Garner B. (ed) Black's Law Dictionary, 8th ed**
4. "Articles" means the articles of association of a company, as originally framed or as altered by special resolution. See **Section 567 Companies and Allied Matters Act Cap. C20, LFN 2004**
5. "Shares" see "share". It means the interest in a company's share capital of a member who is entitled to share in the capital or income of such company. See **Section 567 CAMA, Cap. C20, LFN, 2004**
6. "Share capital" means one of the definite numbers of equal parts into which the capital stock of a corporation or joint stock company is divided. **See Garner B. (ed) Black's Law Dictionary, 8th ed.**

**Cases**

By the provisions of Companies and Allied Matters Act, Section 115, shares are in the nature of personal estate and freely transferable but subject to statutory restrictions and the articles of the company. Members in a company have a right to transfer shares belonging to them therein and this right is unfettered unless there is an express restriction to that effect in the articles or constitution of the company ***N.R.I. Ltd v. Oranusi*** **(2011) AllL F.W.L.R part 577.625-824 at p.765** .

**For Further Reading**

On memorandum, shareholder, membership, see Orojo, J. Ola **Company Law and Practice in Nigeria** 3rd Edition, Mbeyi & Associates (Lagos, Nigeria) 1992.

Olufemi Amao and Kenneth Amaeshi "Galvanizing Shareholder Activism: A Prerequisite for Effective Corporate Governance and Accountability in Nigeria" (2008) 82 **Journal of Business Ethics** 119-130.

*CHAPTER 2*

*Conversion and re-registration of companies*

## 50. Re-registration of private company as public

(1) Subject to this section, a private company [1] having a share capital[2] may be re-registered as a public company [3] if-

(a) a special resolution[4] that it should be so re-registered is passed; and

(b) an application for re-registration is delivered to the Commission[5] together with the documents prescribed in subsection (3) of this section.

(2) The special resolution [4] shall-

(a) alter the company's [6] memorandum[7] so that it states that the company[6] is to be a public company [3]; and

(b) make such other alterations in the memorandum [7] as are necessary to bring it in-to conformity with the requirements of this Act with respect to the memorandum [7] of a public company[3] in accordance with section 27 of this Act; and

(c) make such alterations in the company's articles [8] as are requisite in the circumstances.

(3) The application shall be made to the Commission [5] in the prescribed form and be signed by at least one director [9] and the

secretary[10] of the company[6]; and the documents to be delivered with it are the following-

(a) a printed copy of the memorandum[7] and articles[8] as altered in pursuance of the resolution; and

(b) a copy of a written statement by the directors[9] and the secretary[10] certified on oath by them, and showing that the paid up capital[11] of the company[6] as at the date of the application is not less than 25 per cent of the authorised share capital[12] as at that date; and

(c) a copy of the balance sheet of the company[6] as at the date of the resolution[4] or the preceding 6 months, whichever is later; and

(d) a statutory declaration[13] in the prescribed form by a director[9] and the secretary[10] of the company[6]-

(i) that the special resolution[4] required under this section has been passed; and

(ii) that the company's net assets are not less than the aggregate of the paid up share capital[12] and undistributable reserves; and

(e) a copy of any prospectus or statement in lieu of prospectus[14] delivered within the preceding 12 months to the Securities and Exchange Commission established under the Investments and Securities Act.

[Cap. 124.]

(4) If the Commission[5] is satisfied that a company[6] has complied with the provisions of this section and may be re-registered as a public company[3], it shall-

(a) retain the application and other documents delivered to it under this section;

(b) register the application and other documents; and

(c) issue to the company a certificate of incorporation,[15] stating that the company[6] is a public company.[3]

(5) Upon the issue to a company[6] of the certificate of incorporation[15] under this section-

(a) the company[6] shall by virtue of the issue of that certificate become a public company[3]; and

(b) any alterations in the memorandum[7] and articles[8] set out in the resolution[4] shall take effect accordingly.

(6) The certificate shall be prima facie evidence that-

(a) the requirements of this Act in respect of re-registration and of matters precedent and incidental thereto have been complied with; and

(b) the company[6] is a public company.[3]

(7) A company[6] shall not be re-registered under this section if it has previously been re-registered as an unlimited company.[16]

---

**Notes**

**Section 50(1)**

1. "Private company" is one which is stated in its memorandum to be a private company. See **Section 22 CAMA Cap. C20 LFN 2004**
2. "Share capital" means one of the definite numbers of equal parts into which the capital stock of a corporation or joint stock company is divided. See **Garner, B. (ed) Black's Law Dictionary, 8th ed.**
3. "Public company" means any company other than a private company is a public company. See **Section 24 CAMA Cap. C20 LFN 2004.**
4. "Special resolution" means a resolution passed by not less than three fourths of the votes cast by such members of the company as, being entitled to do so, vote in person or by proxy at a general meeting of which 21 days' notice, specifying the intention to propose the resolution as a special resolution, has been duly given. See **Section 233(2) CAMA, Cap. C20, LFN, 2004**
5. "Commission" means the Corporate Affairs Commission established under section 1 of this Act. See **Section 567 CAMA Cap. C20, LFN 2004.**

**Section 50(2)**

6. "Company" means a company formed and registered under this Act or as the case may be, formed and registered in Nigeria before and in existence on the commencement of this Act. See **Section 567 CAMA, Cap. C20, LFN, 2004.**
7. "Memorandum" means the memorandum of association of a company as originally framed or as altered in pursuance of any enactment. See **Section 567 CAMA, Cap. C20, LFN 2004** .

   "Memorandum of Association" means a legal document, setting up a corporation, either with or without limited liability, and including the company's name, purpose, and duration. **See Garner B. (ed) Black's Law Dictionary, 8th ed**
8. "Articles" means the articles of association of a company, as originally framed or as altered by special resolution. See **Section 567 Companies and Allied Matters Act Cap. C20, LFN 2004**

**Section 50(3)**

9. "Director" means persons duly appointed by the company to direct and manage the business of the company. See **Garner B. (ed)Black's Law Dictionary, 8th ed**

   Director includes any person occupying the position of director by whatever name called, and includes any person in accordance with whose

directions or instructions the directors are accustomed to act. See **Section 567 CAMA, Cap. C20, LFN 2004**

10. "Secretary" means (1) an administrative assistant (2) a corporate officer in charge of official correspondence, minutes of board meetings, and records of stock ownership and transfer(3) an officer charged with recording a deliberative assembly's proceedings. **Garner B. (ed) Black's Law Dictionary 8th ed**
11. "Paid up capital" means that portion of the issued share capital of a company that has been paid for in cash or valuable consideration other than cash. See **Garner, B. (ed) Black's Law Dictionary, 8th ed.**
12. "Authorized share capital" means the share capital of a company at any given time. See **Section 567 CAMA, Cap. C20 LFN, 2004**
13. "Statutory declaration" means a declaration voluntarily made under the Oaths Act 1963 and in Nigeria includes one so made under any other enactment or law providing for the taking of voluntary declaration. See **Section 567 CAMA, Cap. C20, LFN 2004**

    "Statutory declaration" means a formal statement, proclamation, one embodied in an instrument. See **Garner B. (ed) Black's Law Dictionary, 8th ed.**
14. "Prospectus" means any prospectus, notice, circular, advertisement, or other invitation, offering to the public for subscription or purchase any shares or debentures of a company and includes any documents which save to the extent that it offers securities for a consideration other than cash is a prospectus. See **Section 567 CAMA, Cap. C20, LFN, 2004**

    It also means a document that gives information about a company's shares before they are offered for sale. See **Oxford Advanced Learner's Dictionary of Current English. 6 th ed.**

**Section 50(4)**

15. "Certificate of Incorporation" means a document issued by a state authority granting a corporation its legal existence and the right to function as a corporation. See **Garner B. (ed) Black's Law Dictionary, 8th ed.**

**Section 50(7)**

16. Unlimited company" means a company not having any limit on the liability of its members. See **Section 21 CAMA Cap. C20 LFN 2004.**

Cross Reference

For establishment, composition, functions and powers of the **Securities and Exchange Commission, see the Investment and Securities Act 2007**

---

**For Further Reading**

On company and types of company, see Kiser Barnes **Cases and Materials on Nigeria Company Law** (1992) ObafemiAwolowo University press Ltd, Ile-Ife, Nigeria

**Cases**

The only admissible evidence of legal capacity of a body corporate is the certificate of incorporation and no other and not even an admission of incorporation by an adverse partyorally, by document or admission in pleadings would be admitted as proof of legal capacity. See ***Ndoma-Egba v. Chukwugor (2004) 26 NWLR (Pt 869) 32*** **, see also** ***NNPC v. Lutin Investment Ltd (2006) CLRN 1***

### 51. Re-registration of company limited by shares as unlimited

(1) Subject as follows, a company [1] which is registered as limited by shares [2] may be re-registered as unlimited in pursuance of an application in that behalf complying with the requirements of this section.

(2) A company [1] shall be precluded from re-registering under this section if it is limited by virtue of re-registration under section 52 of this Act.

(3) A public company [3] or a company [1] which has previously been re-registered as an unlimited company [4] shall not be registered under this section.

(4) An application under this section shall be in the prescribed form and signed by a director [5] and the secretary [6] of the company[1], and be lodged with the Commission [7] together with the documents specified in subsection (6) of this section.

(5) The application shall set out such alterations in the company's memorandum [8] and articles [9] as are requisite to bring it into conformity with the requirements of this Act with respect to the memorandum [8] and articles [9] of a company [1] to be formed as an unlimited company.[4]

(6) The documents to be lodged with the Commission [7] are as follows-

(a) the prescribed form of assent to the company [1] being registered as unlimited, subscribed by or on behalf of all the members [10] of the company [1];

(b) a statutory declaration [11] made by the directors [5] of the company[1]-

(i) that the persons by whom or on whose behalf the form of assent is subscribed constitute the whole membership of the company [1]; and

(ii) if any of the members [10] have not subscribed that form themselves, that the directors [5] have taken all reasonable steps to satisfy themselves that each person who subscribed to it on behalf of a member [10] was lawfully empowered to do so; and

(c) a printed copy of the memorandum [8] and the articles [9] incorporating the alterations set out in the application.

(7) If the Commission [7] is satisfied that the company [1] be registered under this section as an unlimited company, [4] it shall retain the application and other documents [12] lodged with it under this section and-

(a) register the application and other documents [12]; and

(b) issue to the company [1] a certificate of incorporation [13] appropriate to the status to be assumed by virtue of this section.

(8) On the issue of the certificate-

(a) the status of the company, [1] by virtue of the issue, shall be changed from limited to unlimited; and

(b) the alterations in the memorandum [8] set out in the application and any alteration in the articles [9] so set out shall take effect as if duly made by resolution [14] of the company[1]; and

(c) the provisions of this Act shall apply accordingly to the memorandum[8] and articles [9] as altered.

(9) The certificate [13] shall be prima facie evidence that the requirements of this section in respect of the re-registration and of matters precedent and incidental to it have been complied with, and that the company [1] was authorised to be re-registered under this Act in pursuance of this section and was duly so re-registered.

---

**Notes**

**Section 51(1)**

1. "Company" means a company formed and registered under this Act or, as the case may be, formed and registered in Nigeria before and in existence on the commencement of this Act. See **Section 567 CAMA, Cap. C20, LFN, 2004.**
2. "Shares" see "share". It means the interest in a company's share capital of a member who is entitled to share in the capital or income of such company. See **Section 567 CAMA, Cap. C20, LFN, 2004**

**Section 51(3)**

3. "Public company" means any company other than a private company is a public company. See **Section 24 CAMA Cap. C20 LFN 2004.**
4. "Unlimited Company" means a company not having any limit on the liability of its members. **See Section 21 CAMA, Cap. C20 LFN 2004.**

**Section 51(4)**

5. "Director" means a person duly appointed by the company to direct and manage the business of the company. See **Garner B. (ed) Black's Law Dictionary, 8th ed.**
   Director includes any person occupying the position of director by whatever name called, and includes any person in accordance with whose directions or instructions the directors are accustomed to act. See **Section 567 CAMA, Cap. C20, LFN 2004**
6. "Secretary" means a corporate officer in charge of official correspondence, minutes of board meetings, and records of stock ownership and transfer (3) an officer charged with recording a deliberative assembly's proceedings. **See Garner B, (ed) Black's Law Dictionary 8th ed**
7. "Commission" means the Corporate Affairs Commission established under section 1 of this Act. See **Section 567 CAMA Cap. C20, LFN 2004**

**Section 51(5)**

8. "Memorandum" means the memorandum of association of a company as originally framed or as altered in pursuance of any enactment. See **Section 567 CAMA, Cap. C20, LFN 2004** .
   "Memorandum of Association" means a legal document, setting up a corporation, either with or without limited liability, and including the company's name, purpose, and duration. **See Garner B. (ed) Black's Law Dictionary, 8th ed**
9. "Articles" means the articles of association of a company, as originally framed or as altered by special resolution. See **Section 567 CAMA, Cap. C20, LFN 2004** .

**Section 51(6)**

10. "Members" see "member". It includes the heir, executor, administrator, or other personal representatives, as the case may be, of the member. See **Section 567 CAMA, Cap. C20, LFN 2004 .Section 51(7)**
11. "Statutory declaration" means a declaration voluntarily made under the Oaths Act 1963 and in Nigeria includes one so made under any other enactment or law providing for the taking of voluntary declaration. See **Section 567 CAMA, Cap. C20, LFN 2004**
12. "Documents" see "document". It includes summons, notice, order and other legal process, and register. See **Section 567 CAMA, Cap. C20 LFN 2004.**
13. "Certificate of Incorporation" means a document issued by a state authority granting a corporation its legal existence and the right to function as a corporation. **See Garner, B. (ed) Black's Law Dictionary, 8th ed.**

**Section 51(8)**

14. "Resolution" means a main motion that formally expresses the sense, will or action of a deliberative assembly. See **Garner B. (ed) Black's Law Dictionary, 8th ed.**

Cross Reference

On Re-registration of private company as public, see **section 50 CAMA Cap. C20, LFN 2004**

On Re-registration of unlimited as limited by shares, see **section 52 CAMA Cap. C20, LFN 2004**

---

**Cases**

The definition of a company in section 650 of Companies and Allied Matters Act puts the matter beyond doubt. It defines a 'company' or 'existing' to mean....a company formed and registered in Nigeria before and in existence on the commencement of this Act. ***Agro Allied Dev. Ent. Ltd. v. Reefer (2009) vol.31 W.R.N 1-185 at pg 7.***

The Corporate Affairs Commission is conferred with the responsibility of registering companies operating in Nigeria by Statute, and under the said statute it can prohibit and restrict certain names to be registered. See ***Mustapha v. CAC (2009)*** **Vol. 43 W.R.N. 1-171 pg 156.**

**For Further Reading**

On Corporate Affairs Commission, Incorporation of Companies, Membership of a company, and Share Capital. See:

Orojo, J. Ola **Company Law and Practice in Nigeria** 3rd Edition, Mbeyi & Associates (Lagos, Nigeria) 1992.

Ogbuanya C.S. Nelson **Essentials of Corporate Law Practice in Nigeria** Novena Publishers Limited 2012

Sasegbon Deji& Co **Companies and Allied Matters Law and Practice** (NCAMLP) DSC Publications Ltd 2006

## 52. Re-registration of unlimited as limited by shares

(1) Subject as follows, a company [1] which is registered as unlimited may be re-registered as limited by shares [2] if a special resolution[3] that it should be so registered is passed, and the requirements of this section are complied with in respect of the resolution[3] and otherwise.

(2) A company[1] shall not under this section be re-registered as a public company[4] or company limited by guarantee [5]; and a company[1] shall be precluded from registering under it if it is unlimited by virtue of re-registration under section 51 of this Act.

(3) The special resolution [3] shall state the proposed authorised share capital[6] and provide for the making of such alterations in the

memorandum[7] as are necessary to bring it into conformity with the requirements of this Act with respect to the memorandum [7] of a company[1] so limited, and such alterations in the articles [8] as are requisite in the circumstances.

(4) An application in the prescribed form for the company [1] to be re-registered as limited signed by a director [9] and the secretary [10] of the company[1] shall be lodged with the Commission [11] together with the necessary documents [12] not earlier than the day on which the resolution[3] was filed under section 237 of this Act.

(5) The documents [12] to be lodged with the Commission [11] shall be a printed copy of the-

(a) memorandum[7] as altered in pursuance of the resolution [3]; and

(b) articles[8] as so altered.

(6) If the Commission [11] is satisfied that the company [1] be re-registered under this section as a company limited by shares, [2] it shall retain the application and other documents [12] lodged with it under this section and register them, and it shall issue to the company[1] a certificate of incorporation [13] appropriate to the status to be assumed by the company [1] by virtue of this section.

(7) On the issue of the certificate-

(a) the status of the company [1] shall, by virtue of the issue, change from unlimited to limited; and

(b) the alterations in the memorandum [7] specified in the resolution and the alterations in, and additions to, the articles[8] so specified shall take effect accordingly.

(8) The certificate [13] shall be prima facie evidence that the requirements of this section in respect of re-registration and of matters precedent and incidental to it have been complied with, and that the company[1] was authorised to be re-registered in pursuance of this section and was duly so re-registered.

(9) The re-registration of an unlimited company [14] as a limited company[15] shall not affect the rights and liabilities of the company [1] in respect of any debt or obligation incurred, or any contract entered into, by, to, with, or on behalf of the company [1] before the re-registration, and those rights or liabilities may be enforced in the manner provided by Part III of this Act as in the case of a company[1] registered pursuant to Part II of this Act.

**Notes**

**Section 52(1)**

1. "Company" means a company formed and registered under this Act or, as the case may be, formed and registered in Nigeria before and in existence on the commencement of this Act, See **Section 567 CAMA, Cap. C20, LFN, 2004.**
2. "Shares" see "share". It means the interest in a company's share capital of a member who is entitled to share in the capital or income of such company. See **Section 567 CAMA, Cap. C20, LFN, 2004**
3. "Special resolution" means a resolution passed by not less than three fourths of the votes cast by such members of the company as, being entitled to do so, vote in person or by proxy at a general meeting of which 21 days' notice, specifying the intention to propose the resolution as a special resolution, has been duly given. See **Section 233(2) CAMA, Cap. C20, LFN, 2004** .

**Section 52(2)**

4. "Public company" means any company other than a private company is a public company. See **Section 24 CAMA Cap. C20 LFN 2004.**
5. "Company Limited by Guarantee" means a company having the liability of its members limited by the memorandum to such amount as the members may respectively thereby undertake to contribute to the assets of the company, in the event of its being wound up. **See Section 21 CAMA, Cap C20, LFN 2004.**

**Section 52(3)**

6. "Authorised share capital" means the share capital of a company at any given time. See **Section 567 CAMA, Cap. C20, LFN 2004.**
7. "Memorandum" means the memorandum of association of a company as originally framed or as altered in pursuance of any enactment. See **Section 567 CAMA, Cap. C20, LFN 2004**
   "Memorandum of Association" means a legal document, setting up a corporation, either with or without limited liability, and including the company's name, purpose, and duration. **See Garner B. (ed) Black's Law Dictionary, 8th ed**
8. "Articles" means the articles of association of a company, as originally framed or as altered by special resolution. See **Section 567 Companies and Allied Matters Act Cap. C20, LFN 2004**

**Section 52(4)**

9. "Director" means a person duly appointed by the company to direct and manage the business of the company. See **Garner B, (ed) Black's Law Dictionary, 8$^{th}$ed.**
   Director includes any person occupying the position of director by whatever name called, and includes any person in accordance with whose directions or instructions the directors are accustomed to act. See **Section 567 CAMA, Cap. C20, LFN 2004**
10. "Secretary" means a corporate officer in charge of official correspondence, minutes of board meetings, and records of stock ownership and transfer (3) an officer charged with recording a deliberative assembly's proceedings. **Garner B, (ed) Black's Law Dictionary 8$^{th}$ ed**.

11. "Documents" see "document". It includes summons, notice, order and other legal process, and register. See **Section 567 CAMA, Cap. C20 LFN 2004.**
12. "Commission" means the Corporate Affairs Commission established under section 1 of this Act. See **Section 567 CAMA Cap. C20, LFN 2004**

**Section 52(6)**

13. "Certificate of Incorporation" means a document issued by a state authority granting a corporation its legal existence and the right to function as a corporation. **See Garner, B. (ed) Black's Law Dictionary, 8th ed.**

**Section 52(9)**

14. "Unlimited Company" means a company not having any limit on the liability of its members. **See Section 21 CAMA, Cap. C20 LFN 2004**
15. "Limited Company" means a company having its liability of its members limited by the memorandum to the amount, if any, unpaid on the shares respectively held by them (referred to a company limited by shares) or, having the liability of its members limited by the memorandum to such amount as the members may have respectively thereby undertake to contribute to the assets of the company in the event of being wound-up (referred to a company limited by guarantee). See **section 21(a) & (b), CAMA Cap. C20 LFN, 2004**

**Cross Reference**

On Re-registration of private company as public, see **section 50 CAMA Cap. C20, LFN 2004**

On re-registration of a public company as a private company, see **section 53, CAMA Cap. C20, LFN 2004**

---

**Cases**

The Corporate Affairs Commission is conferred with the responsibility of registering companies operating in Nigeria by Statute, and under the said statute it can prohibit and restrict certain names to be registered. See *Mustapha v. CAC ([2009)* **Vol. 43 W.R.N. 1-171 pg 156.**

**For Further Reading**

On Membership, Proxy, Share capital and Company generally; see Sofowora, M.O *Modern* **Nigerian Company Law** Soft Associates, 2[nd] Edition 2002. Pages 13, 304, 405.

## 53. Re-registration of public company as private

(1) A public company[1] may be re-registered as a private company[2] if-

(a) a special resolution[3] complying with subsection (2) of this section that it should be so re-registered is passed and has not been cancelled by the court[4] under this section;

(b) an application for the purpose in the prescribed form and signed by a director [5] and the secretary [6] of the company [7] is delivered to the Commission [8] together with a printed copy of the memorandum [9] and articles [10] of the company [7] as altered by the resolution [3]; and

(c) either-

(i) the period during which an application for the cancellation of the resolution [3] under this section may be made has expired without any such application having been made; or

(ii) where such an application has been made, the application has been withdrawn or an order has been made confirming the resolution and a copy of that order has been delivered to the Commission [8].

(2) The special resolution [3] shall alter the company's memorandum [9] so that it states that the company [7] is a private company [3] and shall make such other alterations in the company's memorandum [9] and articles [10] as are requisite in the circumstances.

(3) Where the special resolution [3] is passed, an application may be made to the court [4] for the cancellation of the resolution, [3] and such application may be made by-

(a) the holders of not less in the aggregate than five per cent in nominal value of the company's issued share capital, [11] or any class thereof; or

(b) not less than five per cent of the company's members [12];

but not by a person who has consented to or voted in favour of the resolution. [3]

(4) The application shall be made within 28 days after the passing of the resolution [3] and the applicant shall forthwith give notice of the application in the prescribed form to the Commission [8] and to the company. [7]

(5) On the hearing of the application, the court [4] shall make an order either cancelling or confirming the resolution and may make all such orders or give such directions as it may think expedient under the circumstances.

(6) The company [7] shall, within 15 days from the making of the court's [4] order, or with-in such other period as the court [4] may by order direct, deliver to the Commission [8] a certified true copy of the order.

(7) If a company[7] fails to deliver to the Commission[8] a certified true copy of the order as required in subsection (6) of this section, the company[7] and any officer of it who is in default, shall be guilty of an offence and liable to a fine of NI00 and for continued contravention, to a daily default fine of N25.

(8) If the Commission[8] is satisfied that a company may be re-registered under this section, it shall-

(a) retain the application and other documents[13] delivered to it under this section;

(b) register the application and other documents[13]; and

(c) issue the company[7] with a certificate of incorporation[14] as a private company[2].

(9) On the issue of the certificate[14]-

(a) the company[7] shall become a private company[2]; and

(b) the alteration in the memorandum[9] and articles[10] set out in the resolution shall take effect accordingly.

(10) The certificate[14] shall be prima facie evidence that-

(a) the requirements of this section in respect of re-registration and of matters precedent and incidental to it have been complied with; and

(b) the company[7] is a private company.[2]

---

**Notes**

**Section 53(1)**

1. "Public company" means any company other than a private company is a public company. See **Section 24 CAMA Cap. C20 LFN 2004.**
2. "Private company" is one which is stated in its memorandum to be a private company. See **Section 22 CAMA Cap. C20 LFN 2004**
3. "Special resolution" means a resolution passed by not less than three fourths of the votes cast by such members of the company as, being entitled to do so, vote in person or by proxy at a general meeting of which 21 days' notice, specifying the intention to propose the resolution as a special resolution, has been duly given. See **Section 233(2) CAMA, Cap. C20, LFN, 2004**
4. "Court" used in relation to a company, means the Federal High Court, and to the extent to which application may be made to it as; court includes the Court of Appeal and the Supreme Court of Nigeria; See **Section 567 CAMA, Cap. C20 , LFN 2004**
5. "Director" means a person duly appointed by the company to direct and manage the business of the company. See **Garner B. (ed) Black's Law Dictionary, 8$^{th}$ed.**

   Director includes any person occupying the position of director by whatever name called, and includes any person in accordance with whose

directions or instructions the directors are accustomed to act. See **Section 567 CAMA, Cap. C20, LFN 2004**

6. "Secretary" means (1) an administrative assistant (2) a corporate officer in charge of official correspondence, minutes of board meetings, and records of stock ownership and transfer (3) an officer charged with recording a deliberative assembly's proceedings. **See Garner B. (ed) Black's Law Dictionary 8th ed.**
7. "Company" means a company formed and registered under this Act or, as the case may be, formed and registered in Nigeria before and in existence on the commencement of this Act, See **Section 567 CAMA, Cap. C20, LFN, 2004.**
8. "Commission" means the Corporate Affairs Commission established under section 1 of this Act. See **Section 567 CAMA Cap. C20, LFN 2004**
9. "Memorandum" means the memorandum of association of a company as originally framed or as altered in pursuance of any enactment. See **Section 567 CAMA, Cap. C20, LFN 2004** .

   "Memorandum of Association" means a legal document, setting up a corporation, either with or without limited liability, and including the company's name, purpose, and duration. **See Garner B. (ed) Black's Law Dictionary, 8th ed.**
10. "Articles" means the articles of association of a company, as originally framed or as altered by special resolution. See **Section 567 Companies and Allied Matters Act Cap. C20, LFN 2004.**

**Section 53(3)**

11. "Share capital" See capital, means a fund representing the nominal value of shares issued by a registered company. See **Martins E. (ed.) Oxford Dictionary of Law 4th ed.**
12. "Members" see "member." It includes the heir, executor, administrator, or other personal representatives, as the case may be, of the member. See **Section 567 CAMA Cap. C20, LFN 2004.**

**Section 53(8)**

13. "Documents" see "document." It includes summons, notice, order and other legal process, and register. See **Section 567 CAMA, Cap. C20 LFN 2004.**
14. "Certificate of Incorporation" means a document issued by a state authority granting a corporation its legal existence and the right to function as a corporation**. See Garner, B. (ed) Black's Law Dictionary, 8th ed.**

Cross Reference

On Re-registration of private company as public, see **section 50 CAMA Cap. C20, LFN 2004**

On Re-registration of unlimited as limited by shares, see **section 52 CAMA Cap. C20, LFN 2004**

---

**Cases**

The Corporate Affairs Commission is conferred with the responsibility of registering companies operating in Nigeria by Statute, and under the said statute it can prohibit and restrict certain names to be registered. See ***Mustapha v. CAC [2009]*** **Vol. 43 W.R.N. 1-171 pg 156**

**For Further Reading**
On Membership, Proxy, Share capital and Company generally; see Sofowora, M.O *Modern* **Nigerian Company Law** Soft Associates, 2[nd] Edition 2002. Pages 13, 304, 405.

## *CHAPTER 3*

### *Foreign companies*

### 54. Foreign companies intending to carryon business in Nigeria

(1) Subject to sections 56 to 59 of this Act, every foreign company[1] which before or after the commencement of this Act was incorporated outside Nigeria, and having the intention of carrying on business in Nigeria, shall take all steps necessary to obtain incorporation[2] as a separate entity in Nigeria for that purpose, but until so incorporated, the foreign company [1] shall not carryon business in Nigeria or exercise any of the powers of a registered company[3] and shall not have a place of business or an address for service of documents[4] or processes[5] in Nigeria for any purpose other than the receipt of notices and other documents, [4] as matters preliminary to incorporation [2] under this Act.

(2) Any act of the company [1] in contravention of subsection (1) of this section shall be void.

(3) Nothing in this section shall affect the status of-

(a) any foreign company [1] which before the commencement of this Act was granted exemption from compliance with Part X of the Companies Act 1968;

(b) any foreign companies [1] exempted under any treaty to which Nigeria is a party.

---

**Notes**
**Section 54**

1. "Foreign company" means a company incorporated elsewhere than in Nigeria. See **Section 567 CAMA Cap. C20, LFN 2004**

2. "Incorporation" means the formation of a legal corporation. See **Garner, B. (ed) Black's Law Dictionary, 8th ed.**
3. "Registered company" means a company incorporated or deemed to be incorporated under this Act. See **Section 567 CAMA, Cap. C20, LFN, 2004.**
4. "Documents" includes summons, notice, order and other legal process and register. See **Section 567 CAMA Cap. C20, LFN 2004**
5. "Processes" means the proceeding in any action or prosecution. See **Garner, B. (ed) Black's Law Dictionary, 8th ed.**

**Cases**

Our courts will not enforce contracts by an unregistered company without exemption as they are void ab initio . See ***Solanke v. Abed (1962) 1, ANLR 230.***

The relevant law to my understanding is that a foreign company which has not been registered in Nigeria under the Act, cannot carry on business in Nigeria, unless and until it has taken steps to incorporate same. Failure to do so, some punishments have been stipulated in the same chapter, ie. Chapter 3. I must state clearly that whatever happens "carry on business cannot be the same as capacity to sue and be sued. Section 54 is concerned with "carry on business". ***Ritz WKG v. Techno Ltd.(1999) 4 NWLR (Pt 598)***

**For Further Reading**

On foreign companies, see Ogowewo, T.I., "The Shift to the Classical Theory of Foreign Investment: Opening up the Nigerian Market" (1995) 44 **The International and Comparative Law Quarterly 915.**

Ikeyi, N., "The Export Processing Zones and Foreign Investment Promotion in Nigeria: A Note on Recent Legislation" **(1998) 42 Journal of African Law 223.**

## 55. Penalties

If any foreign company [1] fails to comply with the requirements of section 54 of this Act in so far as they may apply to the company[1], the company [1] shall be guilty of an offence and liable on conviction to a fine of not less than N2,500; and every officer [2] or agent of the company[1] who knowingly and willfully authorizes or permits the default or failure to comply shall, whether or not the company[1] is also convicted of any offence, be liable on conviction to a fine of not less than N250 and where the offence is a continuing one to a further fine of N25 for every day during which the default continues.

**Notes**

**Section 55**

1. "Foreign company" means a company incorporated elsewhere than in Nigeria. See **Section 567 CAMA, Cap. C20, LFN, 2004.**
2. "Officer" in relation to a body corporate includes a director, manager or secretary. See **section 567 CAMA Cap. C20, LFN 2004**

**Cross Reference**

On the need of a foreign company to first be incorporated in Nigeria before carrying on business in Nigeria, see **section 54, CAMA Cap. C20, LFN 2004**

On power of the President to exempt foreign companies from the obligation to be incorporated in Nigeria before carrying on business, see **section 56 CAMA Cap. C20, LFN 2004**

**Cases**

Our courts will not enforce contracts by an unregistered company without exemption as they are void ab initio .***Solanke v. Abed (1962) 1, ANLR 230.***

The relevant law to my understanding is that a foreign company which has not been registered in Nigeria under the Act, cannot carry on business in Nigeria, unless and until it has taken steps to incorporate same. Failure to do so, some punishments have ben stipulated in the same chapter, ie. Chapter 3. I must state clearly that whatever happens "carry on business cannot be the same as capacity to sue and be sued. Section 54 is concerned with "carry on business". ***Ritz WKG v. Techno Ltd. (1999) 4 NWLR (Pt 598)***

**For Further Reading**

On foreign companies, see Ogowewo, T.I., "The Shift to the Classical Theory of Foreign Investment: Opening up the Nigerian Market" ( **1995) 44 The International and Comparative Law Quarterly 915.**

Ikeyi, N. "The Export Processing Zones and Foreign Investment Promotion in Nigeria: A Note on Recent Legislation" **(1998) 42 Journal of African Law 223.**

## 56. Power to exempt foreign companies

(1) A foreign company[1] may apply to the President for exemption from the provisions of section 54 of this Act if that

foreign company[1] belongs to one of the following categories, that is-

(a) foreign companies[1] (other than those specified in paragraph (d) of this subsection) invited to Nigeria by or with the approval of the Federal Government to execute any specified individual project;

(b) foreign companies[1] which are in Nigeria for the execution of specific individual loan projects on behalf of a donor country or international organisation;

(c) foreign government-owned companies engaged solely in export promotion activities; and

(d) engineering consultants and technical experts engaged on any individual specialist project under contract with any of the governments in the Federation or any of their agencies or with any other body or person, where such contract has been approved by the Federal Government.

(2) An application for exemption under this section shall be in writing addressed to the Secretary to the Government of the Federation and shall set out-

(a) the name and place of business of the foreign company [1] outside Nigeria;

(b) the name and place of business or the proposed name and place of business of the foreign company [1] in Nigeria;

(c) the name and address of each director, [2] partner or other principal officer[3] of the foreign company [1];

(d) a certified copy of the charter, statutes, or memorandum [4] and articles[5] of association of the company, [1] or other instrument constituting or defining the constitution of the company[1] and if the instrument is not written in the English language, a certified translation thereof;

(e) the names and addresses of some one or more persons resident in Nigeria authorised to accept on behalf of the foreign company[1] services of process[6] and any notices required to be served on the company [1];

(f) the business or proposed business in Nigeria of the foreign company[1] and the duration of such business;

(g) particulars of any project previously carried out by the company[1] as an exempted foreign company [1]; and

(h) such other particulars as may be required by the Secretary to the Federal Government.

(3) Where the President upon the receipt of an application for exemption is of the opinion that the circumstances are such as to render it expedient that such an exemption should be granted, the President may, subject to such conditions as it may prescribe, exempt the foreign company[1] from the obligations imposed by or under this Act.

(4) Every exemption granted in pursuance of this section shall specify the period or, as the case may be, the project or series of projects, for which it is granted and shall lapse at the end of such period or upon the completion of such project or series of projects.

(5) The President may at any time revoke any exemption granted to any company[1] if it is of the opinion that the company[1] has contravened any provision of this Act or has failed to fulfil any condition contained in the exemption order or for any other good or sufficient reason.

(6) The President shall cause to be published in the Gazette[7] the name of any company-

(a) to which an exemption has been granted and the period or, as the case may be, the project or series of projects for which the exemption is granted;

(b) whose exemption has been revoked and the effective date of such revocation.

---

**Notes**

**Section 56(1)**

1. "Foreign company" means a company incorporated elsewhere than in Nigeria. See **Section 567 CAMA, Cap. C20, LFN, 2004.**

**Section 56(2)**

2. "Director" means a person duly appointed by the company to direct and manage the business of the company. See **Garner B. (ed) Black's Law Dictionary, 8th ed.**
   Director includes any person occupying the position of director by whatever name called, and includes any person in accordance with whose directions or instructions the directors are accustomed to act. See **Section 567 CAMA, Cap. C20, LFN 2004**
3. "Principal Officer" means an officer with the most authority of the officers being considered for some purpose. **See Garner, B. (ed) Black's Law Dictionary, 8th ed.**
4. "Memorandum" means the memorandum of association of a company as originally framed or as altered in pursuance of any enactment. See **Section 567 CAMA, Cap. C20, LFN 2004** .
   "Memorandum of Association" means a legal document, setting up a corporation, either with or without limited liability, and including the

company's name, purpose, and duration. **See Garner B. (ed) Black's Law Dictionary, 8th ed.**

5. "Articles" means the articles of association of a company, as originally framed or as altered by special resolution. See **Section 567 Companies and Allied Matters Act Cap. C20, LFN 2004.**
6. "Processes" means the proceeding in any action or prosecution. See **Garner, B. (ed) Black's Law Dictionary, 8th ed.**

**Section 56(6)**

7. "Gazette" means the official gazette of the Federation. See **Section 567 CAMA, Cap. C20, LFN, 2004.**

**Cross Reference**

On the need of a foreign company to first be incorporated in Nigeria before carrying on business in Nigeria, see **section 54, CAMA Cap. C20, LFN 2004**

On the establishment of the Office of the President of Nigeria, See **Section 130 of the Constitution of the Federal Republic of Nigeria 1999 as amended.**

On the establishment of the Civil service of the Federation and the right of the President to appoint the Secretary to the Government of the Federation, see **Sections 169-171, Constitution of the Federal Republic of Nigeria 1999 as amended.**

---

**Cases**

The relevant law to my understanding is that a foreign company which has not been registered in Nigeria under the Act, cannot carry on business in Nigeria, unless and until it has taken steps to incorporate same. Failure to do so, some punishments have been stipulated in the same chapter, ie. Chapter 3. I must state clearly that whatever happens "carry on business cannot be the same as capacity to sue and be sued. Section 54 is concerned with "carry on business". ***Ritz WKG v. Techno Ltd. (1999) 4 NWLR (Pt 598)***

**For Further Reading**

On Corporate Affairs Commission, Incorporation of Companies, Membership of a company, and Share Capital, see:

Orojo, J. Ola **Company Law and Practice in Nigeria** 3rd Edition, Mbeyi & Associates (Lagos, Nigeria) 1992,

Ogbuanya C.S. Nelson **Essentials of Corporate Law Practice in Nigeri** *a* Novena Publishers Limited 2012

Sasegbon Deji & Co **Companies and Allied Matters Law and Practice** (NCAMLP) DSC Publications Ltd 2006

## 57. Annual report

Every exempted foreign company [1] shall deliver to the Commission,[2] every calendar year, a report in the form prescribed by the Commission.[2]

---

**Notes**
**Section 57**

1. "Foreign company" means a company incorporated elsewhere than in Nigeria. See **Section 567 CAMA, Cap. C20, LFN, 2004**
2. Commission" means the Corporate Affairs Commission established under section 1 of this Act. See **Section 567 CAMA, Cap. C20, LFN, 2004.**

**Cross Reference**

On the need of a foreign company to first be incorporated in Nigeria before carrying on business in Nigeria, see **section 54, CAMA Cap. C20, LFN 2004**

On power of the President to exempt foreign companies from the obligation to be incorporated in Nigeria before carrying on business, see **section 56 CAMA Cap. C20, LFN 2004**

---

**Cases**

Our courts will not enforce contracts by an unregistered company without exemption as they are void ab initio . ***Solanke v. Abed (1962) 1, ANLR 230.***

The relevant law to my understanding is that a foreign company which has not been registered in Nigeria under the Act, cannot carry on business in Nigeria, unless and until it has taken steps to incorporate same. Failure to do so, some punishments have ben stipulated in the same chapter, ie. Chapter 3. I must state clearly that whatever happens "carry on business cannot be the same as capacity to sue and be sued. Section 54 is concerned with "carry on business". ***Ritz WKG v. Techno Ltd.(1999) 4 NWLR (Pt 598)***

## 58. Exempted foreign company to have status of unregistered company

Subject to this Act and save as may be stated in the instrument of exemption, a foreign company [1] exempted pursuant to this Act shall have the status of an unregistered company [2] and accordingly, the provisions of this Act applicable to an unregistered company [2] shall apply in relation to such an exempted company as they apply in relation to an unregistered company [2] under this Act.

---

**Notes**
**Section 58**

1. "Foreign company" means a company incorporated elsewhere than in Nigeria. See **Section 567, CAMA, Cap. C20, LFN 2004.**
2. "Unregistered company" means and includes any partnership, association or company with the following exceptions- (a) a company and any existing company registered under this Act; and (b) a partnership, association or company which consists of less than eight members and is not a foreign partnership, association or company. See **section 567 CAMA, Cap. C20 , LFN 2004.Cases**

**Cross Reference**

On the need of a foreign company to first be incorporated in Nigeria before carrying on business in Nigeria, see **section 54, CAMA Cap. C20, LFN 2004**

On power of the President to exempt foreign companies from the obligation to be incorporated in Nigeria before carrying on business, see **section 56 CAMA Cap. C20, LFN 2004**

---

**Cases**

The relevant law to my understanding is that a foreign company which has not been registered in Nigeria under the Act, cannot carry on business in Nigeria, unless and until it has taken steps to incorporate same. Failure to do so, some punishments have been stipulated in the same chapter, ie. Chapter 3. I must state clearly that whatever happens "carry on business cannot be the same as capacity to sue and be sued. Section 54 is concerned with "carry on business". ***Ritz WKG v. Techno Ltd.(1999) 4 NWLR (Pt 598)***

## 59. Penalties for false information

(1) Any person who for the purpose of obtaining an exemption or of complying with any of the provisions of section 56 of this Act, makes any statement or presents any instrument [1] which is false in a material particular shall be guilty of an offence unless he proves that he has taken all reasonable steps to ascertain the truth of the statement made or contained in the instrument [1] so presented.
(2) Any person who is guilty of an offence under this section shall be liable on conviction to a fine of N5,000 or imprisonment for a term of three years.

---

**Notes**
**Section 59**

1. "Instrument" means a written legal document that defines rights, duties, entitlements, or liabilities. See **Garner, B. (ed) Black's Law Dictionary, 8th ed.**

Cross Reference

On the need of a foreign company to first be incorporated in Nigeria before carrying on business in Nigeria, see **section 54, CAMA Cap. C20, LFN 2004**

On power of the President to exempt foreign companies from the obligation to be incorporated in Nigeria before carrying on business, see **section 56 CAMA Cap. C20, LFN 2004**

On meaning of offence, see **section 2, Criminal Code Act, Cap. C38, LFN 2004**

---

**Cases**

The relevant law to my understanding is that a foreign company which has not been registered in Nigeria under the Act, cannot carry on business in Nigeria, unless and until it has taken steps to incorporate same. Failure to do so, some punishments have been stipulated in the same chapter, i.e. Chapter 3. I must state clearly that whatever happens "carry on business cannot be the same as capacity to sue and be sued. Section 54 is concerned with "carry on business". ***Ritz WKG v. Techno Ltd.(1999) 4 NWLR (Pt 598)***

**For Further Reading**

On criminal liability of companies/persons see, Okoli, C., "Criminal Liability of Corporations in Nigeria: A Current Perspective" **(1994) 38 Journal of African Law 35.**

## 60. Application of certain sections to foreign companies

For the avoidance of doubt, it is hereby declared that-

(a) save as provided in sections 55, 56, 57 and 58 of this Act, nothing in this Act shall be construed as authorizing the disregard by any exempted foreign company [1] of any enactment or rule of law; and

(b) nothing in this Chapter shall be construed as affecting the rights or liability of a foreign company [1] to sue or be sued in its name or in the name of its agent.

---

**Note**

**Section 60**

1. "Foreign company" means a company incorporated elsewhere than in Nigeria. See **Section 567, CAMA, Cap. C20, LFN, 2004** .

Cross Reference

On the need of a foreign company to first be incorporated in Nigeria before carrying on business in Nigeria, see **section 54, CAMA Cap. C20, LFN 2004**

On power of the President to exempt foreign companies from the obligation to be incorporated in Nigeria before carrying on business, see **section 56 CAMA Cap. C20, LFN 2004**

**Cases**

The relevant law to my understanding is that a foreign company which has not been registered in Nigeria under the Act, cannot carry on business in Nigeria, unless and until it has taken steps to incorporate same. Failure to do so, some punishments have been stipulated in the same chapter, ie. Chapter 3. I must state clearly that whatever happens "carry on business cannot be the same as capacity to sue and be sued. Section 54 is concerned with "carry on business". ***Ritz WKG v. Techno Ltd.(1999) 4 NWLR (Pt 598)***

**For Further Reading**

On foreign companies, investment in Nigeria see, Ogowewo, T.I. "The Shift to the Classical Theory of Foreign Investment: Opening up the Nigerian Market" **(1995) 44 The International and Comparative Law Quarterly 915.**

*CHAPTER 4*

*Promoters*

## 61. Persons promoting a company

Any person who undertakes to take part in forming a company [1] with reference to a given project and to set it going and who takes the necessary steps to accomplish that purpose, or who, with regard to a proposed or newly formed company [1], undertakes a part in raising capital[2] for it, shall prima facie be deemed a promoter of the company:[1]

Provided that a person acting in a professional capacity for persons engaged in pro-curing the formation of the company [1] shall not thereby be deemed to be a promoter.

**Notes**

**Section 61**

1. "Company" means a company formed and registered under this Act or as the case may be, formed and registered in Nigeria before and in existence on the commencement of this Act. **See Section 567 CAMA, Cap. C20, LFN, 2004.**

2. "Capital" means money or assets invested, or available for investments, in a business; the total amount or value of a Corporation's stock. See **Garner B. (ed) Black's Law Dictionary 8 th ed**

Cross Reference

On duties and liabilities of a promoter, see **section 62 CAMA Cap. C20, LFN 2004**

---

**Cases**

The Company is distinct from its promoters or directors and a director is an agent of the company. Consequently, where a director enters into a contract in the name of or purporting to bind the company, it is the company, as principal that is liable, not the director . ***Dansa Foods (Nig.) Ltd v. Isong*** **(2011) All F.W.L.R. part 596 404-600 at p.595**

The Court set up a test of determining who is a promoter, thus "A promoter is one who undertakes to form a company with reference to a given object and set it going and who takes necessary steps to accomplish that purpose. ***Garba v. Sheba International (Nig) ltd*** **(2002) 1 NWLR Pt. 748, 372 at 401 para D-E**

## 62. Duties and liabilities of a promoter

(1) A promoter[1] stands in a fiduciary[2] relationship to the company[3] and shall observe the utmost good faith towards the company[3] in any transaction with it or on its behalf and shall compensate the company[3] for any loss suffered by reason of his failure so to do.

(2) A promoter[1] who acquired any property or information in circumstances in which it was his duty as a fiduciary[2] to acquire it on behalf of the company[3] shall account to the company[3] for such property and for any profit which he may have made from the use of such property or information.

(3) Any transaction between a promoter[1] and the company[3] may be rescinded by the company[3] unless, after full disclosure of all material facts known to the promoter[1], such transaction shall have been entered into or ratified on behalf of the company[3]-

(a) by the company's board of directors[4] independent of the promoter[1]; or

(b) by all the members[5] of the company[3]; or

(c) by the company[3] at a general meeting[6] at which neither the promoter[1] nor the holders of any shares[7] in which he is beneficially interested shall vote on the resolution[8] to enter into or ratify that transaction.

(4) No period of limitation shall apply to any proceedings brought by the company[3] to enforce any of its rights under this section but in any such proceedings the court[9] may relieve a promoter[1] in whole or in part and on such terms as it thinks fit from liability here-under if in all the circumstances, including lapse of time, the court[9] thinks it equitable to do so.

---

**Notes**

**Section 62(1)**

1. "Promoter" means any person who undertakes to take part in forming a company with reference to a given project and to set it going and who takes the necessary steps to accomplish that purpose, or who, with regard to a proposed or newly formed company, undertakes a part in raising capital for it. See **section 61 CAMA, Cap. C20 LFN 2004**
2. "Fiduciary" means a person who is required to act for the benefit of another person on all matters within the scope of their relationship. See **Garner. B. (ed) Black's Law Dictionary 8 th ed.**
3. "Company" means a company formed and registered under this Act or as the case may be, formed and registered in Nigeria before and in existence on the commencement of this Act. **See Section 567 CAMA, Cap. C20, LFN, 2004.**

**Section 62(3)**

4. "Board of directors" mean persons duly appointed by the company to direct and manage the business of the company. See **Garner. B. (ed) Black's Law Dictionary 8th ed.**
5. "Members" see "member". It includes the heir, executor, administrator, or other personal representatives, as the case may be, of the member. See **Section 567 CAMA, Cap. C20, LFN, 2004.**
6. "General meeting" means a meeting of company members whose decisions can bind the company. See **Martin, E., (ed.) Oxford Dictionary of Law, 4 th ed.**
7. "Shares" see "share". It means the interest in a company's share capital of a member who is entitled to share in the capital or income of such company. See **Section 567 CAMA, Cap. C20, LFN, 2004**
8. "Resolution" means a main motion that formally expresses the sense, will, or action of a deliberative assembly. See **Garner. B. (ed) Black's Law Dictionary 8th ed.**

**Section 62(4)**

9. "Court" used in relation to a company, means the Federal High Court, and to the extent to which application may be made to it as; court includes the Court of Appeal and the Supreme Court of Nigeria; See **Section 567 CAMA, Cap. C20 , LFN 2004**

**Cross Reference**

On the establishment and jurisdiction of the Federal High Court, see **sections 249 & 251 Constitution of the Federal Republic of Nigeria, 1999** (as amended)

---

**Cases**

A company is not bound by any agreement purportedly made on its behalf by the promoters before its formation ***Orhobo v. Tarka*** **(1976) 1 F.N.L.R.208.**

The Company is distinct from its promoters or directors and a director is an agent of the company. Consequently, where a director enters into a contract in the name of or purporting to bind the company, it is the company, as principal that is liable, not the director . ***Dansa Foods (Nig.) Ltd v. Isong*** **(2011) All F.W.L.R. part 596 404-600 at p.595**

The Court set up a test of determining who is a promoter, thus "A promoter is one who undertakes to form a company with reference to a given object and set it going and who takes necessary steps to accomplish that purpose.***Garba v. Sheba International (Nig) ltd (2002) 1 NWLR PT 748, 372 at 401 para D-E***

*PART III*

*Acts by or on behalf of the company*

*Exercise of company's powers*

## 63. Division of powers between general meeting and board of directors

(1) A company[1] shall act through its members[2] in general meeting[3] or its board of directors[4] or through officers[5] or agents[6], appointed by, or under authority derived from, the members[2] in general meeting[3] or the board of directors[4].

(2) Subject to the provisions of this Act, the respective powers of the members[2] in general meeting[3] and the board of directors[4] shall be determined by the company's articles[7].

(3) Except as otherwise provided in the company's articles[7], the business of the company[1] shall be managed by the board of directors[4] who may exercise all such powers of the company as are not by this Act or the articles[7] required to be exercised by the members[2] in general meeting[3].

(4) Unless the articles[7] shall otherwise provide, the board of directors,[4] when acting within the powers conferred upon them by

this Act or the articles [7], shall not be bound to obey the directions or instructions of the members [2] in general meeting: [3]
Provided that the directors acted in good faith and with due diligence.

(5) Notwithstanding the provisions of subsection (3) of this section, the members [2] in general meeting [3] may-

(a) act in any matter if the members [2] of the board of directors[4] are disqualified or are unable to act because of a deadlock on the board or otherwise;

(b) institute legal proceedings in the name and on behalf of the company[1], if the board of directors [4] refuse or neglect to do so;

(c) ratify or confirm any action taken by the board of directors[4]; or

(d) make recommendations to the board of directors [4] regarding action to be taken by the board.

(6) No alteration of the articles [7] shall invalidate any prior act of the board of directors [4] which would have been valid if that alteration had not been made.

---

**Notes**

**Section 63(1)**

1. "Company" means a company formed and registered under this Act or as the case may be, formed and registered in Nigeria before and in existence on the commencement of this Act. **See Section 567 CAMA, Cap. C20, LFN, 2004.**
2. "Members" see "member". It includes the heir, executor, administrator, or other personal representatives, as the case may be, of the member. See **Section 567 CAMA, Cap. C20, LFN, 2004.**
3. "General meeting" means a meeting of company members whose decisions can bind the company. See **Martin, E. (ed.) Oxford Dictionary of Law, 4th ed.**
4. "Board of directors" means persons duly appointed by the company to direct and manage the business of the company. See **Garner. B. (ed) Black's Law Dictionary 8th ed**
5. "Officers" see "officer". In relation to a body corporate, officer includes a director, manager or secretary. See **Section 567 CAMA, Cap. C20, LFN, 2004.**
6. "Agents" does not include a legal practitioner acting as counsel for any person. See **Section 567 CAMA, Cap. C20, LFN, 2004.**

**Section 63(3)**

7. "Articles" means the articles of association of a company, as originally framed or as altered by special resolution. See **Section 567 CAMA Cap. C20, LFN 2004**

---

**Cases**

The Supreme Court held that a director of the company is in the eye of the law an agent of the company, such that when a director enters into a contract for a company, it is the company, the principal which is liable on it and not the Directors. ***Okolo v. Union Bank of Nigeria Plc. (2004) 3 NWLR (859) SC 87***.

It is not the act of every officer that binds the company, those whose acts binds the company are the alter ego: those whose position are the directing mind and will of the company. ***Orji v. Anyaso (2000) 2 NWLR (Pt. 643).*** See also ***Delta Steel Nigeria ltd v. American Computer Tech Inc. (1999) 4 NWLR Pt. 597*** – The Court held that since the Directors and Managers control what the company does, the state of the mind of this special class of employees is the state of mind of the company and thus the company is bound by the acts of its Directors and managers

## 64. Delegation to committees and managing directors

Unless otherwise provided in this Act or in the articles [1], the board of directors [2] may-

(a) exercise their powers through committees consisting of such members[3] of the body as they think fit; or

(b) from time to time, appoint one or more of their body to the office of managing director [4] and may delegate all or any of their powers to such managing director [4].

---

**Notes**

**Section 64**

1. "Articles" means the articles of association of a company, as originally framed or as altered by special resolution. See **Section 567 CAMA Cap. C20, LFN 2004**
2. "Board of directors" means the governing body of a corporation elected by shareholders to establish corporate policy, appoint executive officers and make major business and financial decisions. See **Garner. B. (ed) Black's Law Dictionary 8th ed.**
3. "Members" see "member". It includes the heir, executor, administrator, or other personal representatives, as the case may be, of the member. See **Section 567 CAMA Cap. C20, LFN 2004**
4. "Managing director" means the person who is in charge of a business. See **Oxford Advanced Learners Dictionary of current English. 6 th ed.**

**Cross Reference**

On division of powers between general meeting and board of directors, see **section 63 CAMA Cap. C20, LFN 2004**

On acts in a general meeting, board of directors, or of managing directors to be treated as acts of the company, see **section 65 CAMA Cap. C20, LFN 2004**

---

**Cases**

Directors have sometimes been called trustees, or commercial trustees, and sometimes they have been called managing partners. It does not matter what you call them so long as you understand what their true position is, which is that they are really commercial when managing a trading concern for the benefit of themselves and all other shareholders in it. ***Iwuchukwu vs. Nwizu*** **(1994) 7 N.W.L.R (part 357) 379 at 396**

A limited liability company or an incorporated company is a different legal entity from its management, it has a separate and distinct life and existence, in other words, the officers and members of an incorporated company are covered by the company's veil of incorporation and that veil cannot be lifted for the purpose of attaching legal responsibility or liability to its officers who are carrying on usual business of the company. ***C.B Ltd v. Intercity Bank Plc. (2009) 15 NWLR Pt. 1165 C A 445 at 462 A-H:***

*Liability for the acts of the company*

## 65. Acts of general meeting, board of directors, or of managing directors

Any act of the members [1] in general meeting [2], the board of directors, [3] or of a managing director [4] while carrying on in the usual way the business of the company, [5] shall be treated as the act of the company [5] itself and the company [5] shall be criminally and civilly liable therefore to the same extent as if it were a natural person: Provided that-

(a) the company [5] shall not incur civil liability to any person if that person had actual knowledge at the time of the transaction in question that the general meeting, [2] board of directors, [3] or managing director, [4] as the case may be, had no power to act in the matter or had acted in an irregular manner or if, having regard to his position with or relationship to the company, [5] he ought to have known of the absence of such power or of the irregularity;

(b) if in fact a business is being carried on by the company, [5] the company[5] shall not escape liability for acts undertaken in connection with that business merely because the business in question was not among the business authorised by the company's [5] memorandum.[6]

---

**Notes**
**Section 65**

1. "Members" see "member." It **includes** the heir, executor, administrator, or other personal representatives, as the case may be, of the member. See **Section 567 CAMA Cap. C20, LFN 2004**
2. "General meeting" means a meeting of company members whose decisions can bind the company. See **Martin, E. (ed.) Oxford Dictionary of Law, 4th ed.**
3. "Board of directors" means the governing body of a corporation elected by shareholders to establish corporate policy, appoint executive officers and make major business and financial decisions. See **Garner. B. (ed) Black's Law Dictionary 8th ed.**
4. "Managing director" means the person who is in charge of a business. **Oxford Advanced Learners Dictionary of current English. 6th ed.**
5. "Company" means a company formed and registered under this Act or as the case may be, formed and registered in Nigeria before and in existence on the commencement of this Act. See **Section 567 CAMA, Cap. C20, LFN. 2004.**
6. "Memorandum" means the memorandum of association of a company as originally framed or as altered in pursuance of any enactment. See **Section 567 CAMA, Cap. C20, LFN 2004** .
   "Memorandum of Association" means a legal document, setting up a corporation, either with or without limited liability, and including the company's name, purpose, and duration. **See Garner B. (ed) Black's Law Dictionary, 8th ed**

**Cross Reference**

On division of powers between general meeting and board of directors, see **section 63 CAMA Cap. C20, LFN 2004**

On power of the board of directors to delegate to committees, see section **64 CAMA Cap. C20, LFN 2004**

On acts in a general meeting, board of directors, or of managing directors to be treated as acts of the company, see **section 65 CAMA Cap. C20, LFN 2004**

---

**Cases**

A limited liability Company is separate and apart from it's members and officers. This decision was further magnified in the case of ***H.L. Bolton Co. v. T.J.Graham (1956) 3 ALL E.R 624 at 630*** when Denning L.J. said: A Company may in many ways be likened to a human body. They have a brain and a nerve center which controls what they do. They also have hands which hold the tools and act in accordance with direction from the center. Some of the people in a company are mere servants and agents who are nothing more than hands to the work and cannot be said to represent the mind or will. Others are directors and managers who represent the directing mind and will of the company and control what they do. The state of the mind of these managers is the state of mind of the company and it is treated by the Law as such. So you will find in cases where the Law requires personal fault as a condition of liability in tort, the fault of the managers will be the personal fault of the company. ***Chartered Brains Ltd. v. Intercity Bank Plc.*** **(2009) Vol. 49 W.R.N. 1-182 at pg 116**

## 66. Acts of officers or agents

(1) Except as provided in section 65 of this Act, the acts of any officer[1] or agent[2] of a company[3] shall not be deemed to be acts of the company[3], unless-

(a) the company,[3] acting through its members[4] in general meeting[5], board of directors,[6] or managing director,[7] shall have expressly or impliedly authorised such officer[1] or agent[2] to act in the matter; or

(b) the company,[3] acting as mentioned in paragraph (a) of this subsection, shall have represented the officer[1] or agent[2] as having its authority to act in the matter, in which event the company[3] shall be civilly liable to any person who has entered into the transaction in reliance on such representation unless such person had actual knowledge that the officer[1] or agent[2] had no authority or unless having regard to his position with or relationship to the company,[3] he ought to have known of such absence of authority.

(2) The authority of an officer [1]or agent[2] of the company[3] may be conferred prior to any action by him or by subsequent ratification, and knowledge of such action by the officer[1] or agent[2] and acquiescence therein by all the members[4] of the company[3] or by the directors[6] for the time being, or by the managing director[7] for the time being, shall be equivalent to ratification by the members[4] in general meeting,[5] board of directors,[6] or managing director,[7] as the case may be.

(3) Nothing in this section shall derogate from the vicarious liability[8] of the company[3] for the acts of its servants while acting within the scope of their employment.

---

**Notes**
**Section 66**

1. "Officer" in relation to a body corporate, officer includes a director, manager or secretary. See **Section 567 CAMA, Cap. C20, LFN, 2004.**
2. "Agent" means one who is authorized to act for in place of another. See **Garner. B. (ed) Black's Law Dictionary 8 th ed.**
   "Agent" does not include a legal practitioner acting as counsel for any person. See **Section 567 CAMA, Cap. C20, LFN, 2004.**
3. "Company" means a company formed and registered under this Act or as the case may be, formed and registered in Nigeria before and in existence on the commencement of this Act. See **Section 567 CAMA, Cap. C20, LFN. 2004.**
4. "Members" see "member". It includes the heir, executor, administrator, or other personal representatives, as the case may be, of the member . See **Section 567 CAMA, Cap. C20, LFN, 2004.**
5. "General meeting" means a meeting of company members whose decisions can bind the company. See **Martin, E. (ed.) Oxford Dictionary of Law, 4 th ed.**
6. "Board of directors" means the governing body of a corporation, elected by shareholders to establish corporate policy, appoint executive officers and make major business and financial decision. See **Garner B. (ed) Black's Law Dictionary 8th ed**
7. "Managing director" means the person who is in charge of a business, **Oxford Learners Dictionary of current English 6 th ed.**
8. "Vicarious liability" means liability the supervisory party such as an employer bears for actionable conduct of a subordinate or associate such as an employee based on the relationship between the two parties. See **Garner. B. (ed) Black's Law Dictionary 8 th ed.**

**Cross Reference**

On division of powers between general meeting and board of directors, see **section 63 CAMA Cap. C20, LFN 2004**

On power of the board of directors to delegate to committees, see section **64 CAMA Cap. C20, LFN 2004**

On acts in a general meeting, board of directors, or of managing directors to be treated as acts of the company, see **section 65 CAMA Cap. C20, LFN 2004**

---

**Cases**

Unless an employer could otherwise explain his non-liability, he as employer of the servant is vicariously liable for the negligence of his servant in the performance of his duty, where such negligence occurred in the normal course of his business. See ***Nwabuokei v Iwenjiwe (1978) SC 61.***

**For Further Reading**

On acts of agents, directors of the company, see Bakibinga, D. J. "Directors' Duty to Act Bona Fide in the Interest of the Company" **(1990) 39 (2) The International and Comparative Law Quarterly 451.**

## 67. When provision exempting, etc., officer from liability to the company is void

(1) Any provision, whether contained in the articles [1] of the company[2] or in any contract with a company [2] or otherwise, for exempting any officer[3] of the company[3] or any person (whether an officer[3] of the company[2] or not) employed by the company [2] as auditor[4] from, or indemnifying him against any liability which by virtue of any rule of law would otherwise attach to him in respect of any negligence, default, or breach of trust of which he may be guilty in relation to the company [3], shall be void.

(2) Notwithstanding the provisions of subsection (1) of this section-

(a) a person shall not be deprived of any exemption or right to be indemnified in respect of anything done or omitted to be done by him while any such provision as mentioned in that subsection was in force; and

(b) a company[2] may, in pursuance of any such provision as mentioned in subsection (1) of this section, indemnify any such officer[3] or auditor[4] against any liability incurred by him in defending any proceedings, whether civil or criminal, in which judgment is given in his favour or in which he is acquitted or in connection with any application under section 641 of this Act in which relief is granted to him by the court.

---

**Notes**

**Section 67(1)**

1. "Articles" means the articles of association of a company, as originally framed or as altered by special resolution, including so far as they apply to the regulations contained in Table A in the First Schedules of the Companies Act, 1922 or in that Table as altered by any subsequent enactment or reprint of the laws, or in Table A in the First Schedule to this Act. See **Section 567 CAMA Cap. C20, LFN 2004**

2. "Company" means a company formed and registered under this Act or as the case may be, formed and registered in Nigeria before and in existence on the commencement of this Act. See **Section 567 CAMA Cap. C20, LFN 2004**
3. "Officer" in relation to a body corporate, includes a director, manager or secretary. See **Section 567 CAMA, Cap. C20, LFN 2004**

**Section 67(2)**

4. "Auditor" means a person or firm or an accounting firm or an accountant, which formally examines an individual or entity's record. See **Garner. B. (ed) Black's Law Dictionary 8 th ed.**

**Cross Reference**

On division of powers between general meeting and board of directors, see **section 63 CAMA Cap. C20, LFN 2004**

On power of the board of directors to delegate to committees, see section **64 CAMA Cap. C20, LFN 2004**

On acts in a general meeting, board of directors, or of managing directors to be treated as acts of the company, see **section 65 CAMA Cap. C20, LFN 2004**

---

**Cases**

A limited liability Company is separate and apart from it's members and officers. This decision was further magnified in the case of ***H.L. Bolton Co. v. T. J. Graham*** **(1956) 3 ALL E.R 624 at 630** when Denning L.J. said: A Company may in many ways be likened to a human body. They have a brain and a nerve center which controls what they do. They also have hands which hold the tools and act in accordance with direction from the center. Some of the people in a company are mere servants and agents who are nothing more than hands to the work and cannot be said to represent the mind or will. Others are directors and managers who represent the directing mind and will of the company and control what they do. The state of the mind of these managers is the state of mind of the company and it is treated by the Law as such. So you will find in cases where the Law requires personal fault as a condition of liability in tort, the fault of the managers will be the personal fault of the company. ***Chartered Brains Ltd. v. Intercity Bank Plc.*** **(2009) Vol.49 W.R.N. 1-182 at pg 116**

**For Further Reading**

On acts of agents, directors of the company, see Bakibinga, D.J., "Directors' Duty to Act Bona Fide in the Interest of the Company" (1990) 39 (2) **The International and Comparative Law Quarterly 451.**

For further reading on companies, officers and their acts see, Kiser Barnes *Cases and Materials on Nigeria Company Law* (1992) Obafemi Awolowo University press Ltd, Ile-Ife, Nigeria

*Constructive notice of registered documents*

## 68. Abolition of constructive notice of registered documents

Except as mentioned in section 197 of this Act, regarding particulars in the register of particulars of charges, a person shall not be deemed to have knowledge of the contents of the memorandum[1] and articles[2] of a company[3] or of any other particulars, documents[4] or the contents of documents[4] merely because such particulars or documents[4] are registered by the Commission[5] or referred to in any particulars or documents[4] so registered, or are available for inspection at an office of the company.[3]

---

**Notes**
**Section 68**

1. "Memorandum" means the memorandum of association of a company as originally framed or as altered in pursuance of any enactment. See **Section 567 CAMA, Cap. C20, LFN 2004** .
   "Memorandum of Association" means a legal document, setting up a corporation, either with or without limited liability, and including the company's name, purpose, and duration. **See Garner B. (ed) Black's Law Dictionary, 8th ed**
2. "Articles" means the articles of association of a company, as originally framed or as altered by special resolution, including so far as they apply to the regulations contained in Table A in the First Schedules of the Companies Act, 1922 or in that Table as altered by any subsequent enactment or reprint of the laws, or in Table A in the First Schedule to this Act. See **Section 567 CAMA Cap. C20, LFN 2004**
3. "Company" means a company formed and registered under this Act or as the case may be, formed and registered in Nigeria before and in existence on the commencement of this Act, See **Section 567 CAMA, Cap. C20, LFN, 2004** .
4. "Documents" see "document." It includes summons, notices, order and other legal processes and register. See **Garner. B. (ed) Black's Law Dictionary 8th ed.**
5. "Commission" means the Corporate Affairs Commission established under section 1 of this Act, See **Section 567 CAMA, Cap. C20, LFN, 2004.**

**Cross Reference**

On division of powers between general meeting and board of directors, see **section 63 CAMA Cap. C20, LFN 2004**

On power of the board of directors to delegate to committees, see section **64 CAMA Cap. C20, LFN 2004**

On acts in a general meeting, board of directors, or of managing directors to be treated as acts of the company, see **section 65 CAMA Cap. C20, LFN 2004**

**Cases**

A person dealing with a company is entitled to assume, in the absence of facts putting him on inquiry that there has been due compliance with all matters of internal management and procedure required to by the articles, and is not required to inquire into the internal workings of the company. ***Metalimpex v. A.G. Leventis and Co. (Nig.) Ltd*** **(1976) 2 S.C. 91.**

**For Further Reading**

On companies, officers and their acts see, Kiser Barnes **Cases and Materials on Nigeria Company Law** (1992) Obafemi Awolowo University press Ltd, Ile-Ife, Nigeria

## 69. Presumptions of regularity

Any person having dealings with a company [1] or with someone deriving title under the company [1], shall be entitled to make the following assumptions and the company [1] and those deriving title under it shall be estopped from denying their truth that-

(a) the company's [1] memorandum[2] and articles[3] have been duly complied with;

(b) every person described in the particulars filed with the Commission[4] pursuant to sections 35 and 292 of this Act as a director,[5] managing director[6] or secretary[7] of the company,[1] or represented by the company,[1] acting through its members[8] in general meeting,[9] board of directors,[10] or managing director,[6] as an officer[11] or agent[12] of the company,[1] has been duly appointed and has authority to exercise the powers and perform the duties customarily exercised or performed by a director,[6] managing director,[7] or secretary of a company[8] carrying on business of the type carried on by the company[1] or customarily exercised or performed by an officer[11] or agent[12] of the type concerned;

(c) the secretary[7] of the company,[1] and every officer[11] or agent[12] of the company[1] having authority to issue documents[13] or certified copies of documents[13] on behalf of the company[1], has authority to warrant the genuineness of the documents[13] or the accuracy of the copies so issued;

(d) a document[13] has been duly sealed by the company[1] if it bears what purports to be the seal of the company[1] attested by what purports to be the signatures of two persons who, in accordance with paragraph (b) of this section, can be assumed to be a director[5] and the secretary[7] of the company[1]:

Provided that-

(i) a person shall not be entitled to make such assumptions as aforesaid, if he had actual knowledge to the contrary or if, having regard to his position with or relationship to the company,[1] he ought to have known the contrary;

(ii) a person shall not be entitled to assume that anyone or more of the directors[5] of the company[1] have been appointed to act as a committee of the board of directors[10] or that an officer[11] or agent[12] of the company[1] has the company's[1] authority merely because the company's[1] articles[3] provided that authority to act in the matter may be delegated to a committee or to an officer[11] or agent.[12]

---

**Notes**

**Section 69**

1. "Company" means a company formed and registered under this Act or as the case may be, formed and registered in Nigeria before and in existence on the commencement of this Act, See **Section 567 CAMA, Cap. C20, LFN, 2004.**
2. "Memorandum" means the memorandum of association of a company as originally framed or as altered in pursuance of any enactment. See **Section 567 CAMA, Cap. C20, LFN 2004** .
   "Memorandum of Association" means a legal document, setting up a corporation, either with or without limited liability, and including the company's name, purpose, and duration. **See Garner B. (ed) Black's Law Dictionary, 8th ed**
3. "Articles" means the articles of association of a company, as originally framed or as altered by special resolution, including so far as they apply to the regulations contained in Table A in the First Schedules of the Companies Act, 1922 or in that Table as altered by any subsequent enactment or reprint of the laws, or in Table A in the First Schedule to this Act. See **Section 567 CAMA Cap. C20, LFN 2004**
4. "Commission" means the Corporate Affairs Commission established under section 1 of this Act, See **Section 567 CAMA, Cap. C20, LFN, 2004.**

5. "Director" includes any person occupying the position of director by whatever name called; and includes any person in accordance with whose directions or instructions the directors of the company are accustomed to act. See **Section 567 CAMA Cap. C20, LFN 2004**
6. "Managing director" means the person who is in charge of a business. See **Oxford Learners Dictionary of Current English 6th ed.**
7. "Secretary" means (1) an administrative assistant (2) a corporate officer in charge of official correspondence, minutes of board meetings, and records of stock ownership and transfer (3) an officer charged with recording a deliberative assembly's proceedings. **See Garner B, (ed) Black's Law Dictionary 8th ed**
8. "Members" see "member." It includes the heir, executor, administrator, or other personal representatives, as the case may be, of the member. See **Section 567 CAMA Cap. C20, LFN 2004**
9. "General meeting" means a meeting of company members whose decisions can bind the company. See **Martin, E. (ed.) Oxford Dictionary of Law, 4th ed.**
10. "Board of directors" means the governing body of a corporation, elected by shareholders to establish corporate policy, appoint executive officers and make major business and financial decision. **See Garner B, (ed) Black's Law Dictionary 8th ed**
11. "Officer" in relation to a body corporate includes a director, manager or secretary. See **Section 567 CAMA Cap. C20, LFN 2004.**
12. "Agent" means one who is authorized to act for in place of another. See **Garner. B. (ed) Black's Law Dictionary 8 th ed.**
    "Agent" does not include a legal practitioner acting as counsel for any person. See **Section 567 CAMA, Cap. C20, LFN, 2004.**
13. "Documents" see "document". It includes summons, notices, order and other legal processes and register. See **Garner. B. (ed) Black's Law Dictionary 8th ed.**

**Cross Reference**

On division of powers between general meeting and board of directors, see **section 63 CAMA Cap. C20, LFN 2004**

On power of the board of directors to delegate to committees, see section **64 CAMA Cap. C20, LFN 2004**

On acts in a general meeting, board of directors, or of managing directors to be treated as acts of the company, see **section 65 CAMA Cap. C20, LFN 2004**

---

**Cases**

A person dealing with a company is entitled to assume, in the absence of facts putting him on inquiry that there has been due compliance with all matters of internal management and procedure required to by the articles, and is not required to inquire into the internal workings of the company. ***Metalimpex v. A.G. Leventis and Co. (Nig.) Ltd*** **(1976) 2 S.C. 91.**

**For Further Reading**

On companies, officers and their acts see, Kiser Barnes **Cases and Materials on Nigeria Company Law** (1992) Obafemi Awolowo University press Ltd, Ile-Ife, Nigeria

## 70. Liability of company not affected by fraud or forgery of officer

Where, in accordance with sections 65 to 69 of this Act, a company[1] would be liable to a third party for the acts of any officer[2] or agent,[3] the company[1] shall, except where there is collusion between the officer[2] or agent[3] and the third party, be liable notwithstanding that the officer[2] or agent[3] has acted fraudulently or forged a document[4] purporting to be sealed by or signed on behalf of the company.[1]

---

**Notes**

**Section 70**

1. "Company" means a company formed and registered under this Act or as the case may be, formed and registered in Nigeria before and in existence on the commencement of this Act, See **Section 567 CAMA, Cap. C20, LFN, 2004.**
2. "Officer" in relation to a body corporate, includes a director, manager or secretary. See **Section 567 CAMA, Cap. C20, LFN 2004.**
3. "Agent" means one who is authorized to act for in place of another. **See Garner B. (ed) Black's Law Dictionary, 8th ed**
   "Agent" does not include a legal practitioner acting as counsel for any person. See **Section 567 CAMA, Cap. C20, LFN, 2004.**
4. "Document" includes summons, notices, order and other legal processes and register. **See Garner B. (ed) Black's Law Dictionary, 8th ed.**

**Cross Reference**

On acts in a general meeting, board of directors, or of managing directors to be treated as acts of the company, see **section 65 CAMA Cap. C20, LFN 2004**

On acts of the officers and agents of a company being the acts of the company, see **section 66 CAMA Cap. C20, LFN 2004**

When provision exempting, etc., officer from liability to the company is void see, **section 67 CAMA Cap. C20, LFN 2004**

Abolition of constructive notice of registered documents see **section 68 CAMA Cap. C20, LFN 2004**

On Presumption of regularity, see **section 69 CAMA Cap. C20, LFN 2004**

On effect of use of company seal, see **section 604 CAMA Cap. C20, LFN 2004.**

**Cases**
A person dealing with a company is entitled to assume, in the absence of facts putting him on inquiry that there has been due compliance with all matters of internal management and procedure required to by the articles, and is not required to inquire into the internal workings of the company.***Metalimpex v. A.G. Leventis and Co. (Nig.) Ltd*** **(1976) 2 S.C. 91.**

**For Further Reading**
on companies, officers and their acts see, Kiser Barnes **Cases and Materials on Nigeria Company Law** (1992) Obafemi Awolowo University press Ltd, Ile-Ife, Nigeria.

*Company's contracts*

## 71. Form of contract

(1) Contracts on behalf of a company [1] may be made, varied or discharged as follows-

(a) any contract which if made between individuals would be by law required to be in writing under seal, or which would be varied, or discharged only by writing under seal, may be made, varied or discharged, as the case may be, in writing under the common seal [2] of the company [1];

(b) any contract which if made between individuals would be by law required to be in writing, signed by the parties to be charged therewith, or which could be varied or discharged only by writing or written evidence signed by the parties to be charged, may be made, varied or discharged, as the case may be, in writing signed in the name or on behalf of the company[1]; and

(c) any contract which if made between individuals would be valid although made by parol only and not reduced into writing or which could be varied or discharged by parol, may be made varied or discharged, as the case may be, by parol on behalf of the company.[1]

(2) A contract made according to this section shall be effectual in law, and shall bind the company [1] and its successors and all other parties thereto, their heirs, executors or administrators, as the case may be; and may be varied or discharged in the same manner in which it is authorised by this section to be made.

**Notes**

**Section 71(1)**

1. "Company" means a company formed and registered under this Act or as the case may be, formed and registered in Nigeria before and in existence on the commencement of this Act, See **Section 567 CAMA, Cap. C20, LFN, 2004.**
2. "Common Seal" means a piece of wax, a wafer, or some other substance affixed to the paper or other material on which a promise or release , or conveyance is written together with recital or expression of intention by which the promisor, releasor, or grantor manifest that a piece of wax, wafer , or other substance is a seal. See **Garner. B. (ed) Black's Law Dictionary 8th ed.**

**Cross Reference**

On effect of use of company seal, see **section 604 CAMA Cap. C20, LFN 2004.**

---

**Cases**

The court held that after incorporation the company is ready to do business by itself unless otherwise required in any case, a company contracts in the same way as an individual, accordingly a contract may be made, varied or discharged under seal, in writing or by parole i.e. not reduced into writing, if such forms would be proper in similar contracts between individuals. Thus what determines the manner in which a company can enter its contract is the nature of the transaction and legal requirement for its valid execution by an individual. ***Trenco (Nig) v. A.R.E.I co ltd 1979 11 NSCC 220***

The court held that in order to establish a legal relationship with an artificial legal entity it takes more than a common discussion between a party and an officer of the company in order that it may be bound by the officers representation. See also ***Nigeria Dynamics ltd v. Maimuda Ibrahim (2002) 8 NWLR (768) C A 63 at 103***

## 72. Pre-incorporation contracts

(1) Any contract or other transaction purporting to be entered into by the company[1] or by any person on behalf of the company [1] prior to its formation may be ratified by the company [1] after its formation and thereupon the company [1] shall become bound by and entitled to the benefit thereof as if it has been in existence at the date of such contract or other transaction and had been a party thereto

(2) Prior to ratification by the company, [1] the person who purported to act in the name of or on behalf of the company [1] shall,

in the absence of express agreement to the contrary, be personally bound by the contract[1] or other transaction and entitled to the benefit thereof.

**Notes**

**Section 72**

1. "Company" means a company formed and registered under this Act or as the case may be, formed and registered in Nigeria before and in existence on the commencement of this Act. **See Section 567 CAMA, Cap. C20 LFN, 2004.**

**Cross Reference**

On persons promoting a company, their duties and liabilities, see **sections 61 & 62 CAMA Cap. C20, LFN 2004**

**Cases**

The rigid legal status of pre-incorporation contract at common law has been modified in Nigeria to the extent that the pre incorporation contract can be ratified by the company upon incorporation See ***Societe Generale Bank (Nig) Ltd v. Societe Generale Favouriser etc (1995) 3 NWLR Pt.384, 497 (CA); (1997) 4 NWLR (pt. 497) 8 (SC)***

A company is not bound by any agreement purportedly made on its behalf by the promoters before its formation. ***Orhobo v. Tarka*** **(1976) 1 F.N.L.R.208.**

## 73. Bills of exchange and promissory note.

(1) A bill of exchange[1] or promissory note[2] shall be deemed to have been made, accepted, or endorsed on behalf of a company[3] if made, or expressed to be made, accepted, or endorsed in the name of the company,[3] or if expressed to be made, accepted or endorsed on behalf or on account of the company[3] by a person acting under its authority.

(2) The company[3] and its successors shall be bound thereby if the company[3] is, in accordance with sections 65 to 67 of this Act, liable for the acts of those who made, accepted or endorsed it in its name or on its behalf or account, and a signature by a director[4] or the secretary[5] on behalf of the company[3] shall not be deemed to be a signature by procuration for the purposes of section 25 of the Bills of Exchange Act.

**Notes**

**Section 73(1)**

1. "Bill of exchange" means an unconditional written order in writing, addressed by one person to another, signed by the person giving it, requiring the person whom it is addressed to pay on demand or at a fixed or determinable future time a sum certain in money or to the order of a specified person, or to bearer. See **section 3, Bills of Exchange Act, Cap. B8, LFN 2004**
2. "Promissory note" means an unconditional promise in writing, made by one person to another, signed by the maker, engaging to pay, on demand or at a fixed determinable future time, the sum certain in money, or to the order of, a specified person or to bearer. See section 85(1) **Bills of Exchange Act, Cap. B8, LFN 2004**
3. "Company" means a company formed and registered under this Act or as the case may be, formed and registered in Nigeria before and in existence on the commencement of this Act. See **Section 567 CAMA, Cap. C20, LFN, 2004.**

**Section 73(2)**

4. "Director" includes any person occupying the position of director by whatever name called; and includes any person in accordance with whose directions or instructions the directors of the company are accustomed to act. See **Section 567 CAMA Cap. C20, LFN 2004**
5. "Secretary" means (1) an administrative assistant (2) a corporate officer in charge of official correspondence, minutes of board meetings, and records of stock ownership and transfer (3) an officer charged with recording a deliberative assembly's proceedings. **See Garner B, (ed) Black's Law Dictionary 8th ed**

**Cross Reference**

On nature of promissory note, see **section 86 Bills of Exchange Act, Cap. B8, LFN 2004**

---

## 74. Common seal of the company

A company[1] shall have a common seal,[2] the use of which shall be regulated by the articles.[3]

---

**Notes**

**Section 74**

1. "Company" means a company formed and registered under this Act or as the case may be, formed and registered in Nigeria before and in existence on the commencement of this Act. See **Section 567 CAMA Cap C20, LFN 2004**
2. "Common seal" means a design embossed or stamped on paper to authenticate, confirm, or attest; an impression or sign that has legal consequence when applied to an instrument. The purpose of a seal is to secure or prove authenticity. See **Garner, B. (ed.) Black's Law Dictionary, 8th ed**

3. "Articles" means the articles of association of a company, as originally framed or as altered by special resolution. See **Section 567 CAMA Cap C20, LFN 2004**

Cross Reference

On the obligation of a company to keep a common seal and use of the company's common seal, see **Section 74 CAMA Cap. C20, LFN 2004**

**Cases**

Failure to use the common seal when necessary renders the Agreement ineffectual. ***African Development Corp Ltd v. L.E.D.B (1966) NCLR 438***

"The Articles of Association is the contract governing the relationship between shareholders and any infraction of such articles may confer on the shareholder adversely affected a right of action" ***Attorney General of Lagos State v Eko Hotel Ltd &Oha Ltd*** **(2001)] FWLR Page 1996** at **2000**

## 75. Official seal for use abroad

(1) A company[1] whose objects require or compromise the transaction of business in foreign countries may, if authorised by its articles[2], have for use in any territory, district, or place outside Nigeria, an official seal, which shall be a facsimile of the common seal[3] of the company,[1] with the addition on its face of the name of every territory, distract, or place where it is to be used.

(2) A company[1] having such an official seal may, by writing under its common seal,[3] authorize any person appointed for the purpose in any territory, district, or place outside Nigeria, to affix the same to any deed[4] or other document[5] to which the company[1] is party in that territory, district, or place.

(3) The Authority of any such agent[6] shall, as between the company[1] and any person dealing with the agent,[6] continue during the period, if any, mentioned in the instrument conferring the authority, or if no period is there mentioned, then until notice of the revocation or determination of the agent's authority has been given to the person dealing with him.

(4) The person affixing any such official seal shall, by writing under his hand, on the deed[4] or other document[5] to which the seal[3] is affixed, certify the date on which and place at which it is affixed.

(5) A deed[4] or other document[5] to which an official seal is duly affixed shall bind the company[1] as if it has been sealed with the common seal[3] of the company[1].

**Notes**

**Section 75(1)**

1. "Company" means a company formed and registered under this Act or as the case may be, formed and registered in Nigeria before and in existence on the commencement of this Act. See **Section 567 CAMA Cap C20, LFN 2004**
2. "Articles" means the articles of association of a company, as originally framed or as altered by special resolution. See **Section 567 CAMA Cap. C20 LFN 2004**
3. "Common seal" means a design embossed or stamped on paper to authenticate, confirm, or attest; an impression or sign that has legal consequence when applied to an instrument. The purpose of a seal is to secure or prove authenticity. See **Garner, B. (ed.) Black's Law Dictionary, 8th ed**

**Section 75(2)**

4. "Deed" means any written instrument that is signed, sealed and delivered and that conveys some interest in property. **See Garner B. (ed) Black's Law Dictionary, 8th ed.**
5. "Document" includes summons, notices, order and other legal processes and register. See **Garner .B. (ed) Black's Law Dictionary, 8 th ed.**

**Section 75(3)**

6. "Agent" means one who is authorized to act for in place of another. **See Garner B. (ed) Black's Law Dictionary, 8th ed**

   "Agent" does not include a legal practitioner acting as counsel for any person. See **Section 567 CAMA, Cap. C20, LFN, 2004.**

**Cross Reference**

On the obligation of a company to keep a common seal and use of the company's common seal, see **Section 74 CAMA Cap. C20, LFN 2004**

**Cases**

Failure to use the common seal when necessary renders the Agreement ineffectual. ***African Development Corp Ltd v. L.E.D.B (1966) NCLR 438***

"The Articles of Association is the contract governing the relationship between shareholders and any infraction of such articles may confer on the shareholder adversely affected a right of action" ***Attorney General of Lagos State v Eko Hotel Ltd & Oha Ltd (2001) FWLR Page 1996** at **2000***

## 76. Powers of attorney

(1) A company[1] may, by writing under seal, empower any person, either generally or in respect of any specified matter, as its

attorney[2], to execute deeds[3] on its behalf in any place within or outside Nigeria.

(2) A deed[3] signed by a person empowered as provided in subsection (1) of this section shall bind the company[1] and have the same effect as it would have if it were under the company's common seal[4].

**Notes**

**Section 76(1)**

1. "Company" means a company formed and registered under this Act or as the case may be, formed and registered in Nigeria before and in existence on the commencement of this Act. See **section 567 CAMA, Cap. C20, LFN, 2004.**
2. "Attorney" see "Power of Attorney". It means an instrument granting someone to act as agent or attorney in fact for the grantor. See **Garner .B. (ed) Black's Law Dictionary, 8th ed.**
3. "Deed" means any written instrument that is signed, sealed and delivered and that conveys some interest in property. **See Garner B. (ed) Black's Law Dictionary, 8th ed.**

**Section 76(2)**

4. "Common seal" means a design embossed or stamped on paper to authenticate, confirm, or attest; an impression or sign that has legal consequence when applied to an instrument. The purpose of a seal is to secure or prove authenticity. See **Garner, B. (ed.) Black's Law Dictionary, 8th ed**

**Cross Reference**

On the obligation of a company to keep a common seal and use of the company's common seal, see **Section 74 CAMA Cap. C20, LFN 2004**
On official use of seal abroad, see **section 75 CAMA Cap. C20, LFN 2004**

**Cases**

Failure to use the common seal when necessary renders the Agreement ineffectual. ***African Development Corp Ltd V L.E.D.B (1966) NCLR 438***

"The Articles of Association is the contract governing the relationship between shareholders and any infraction of such articles may confer on the shareholder adversely affected a right of action" ***Attorney General of Lagos State v Eko Hotel Ltd &Oha Ltd*** **(2001) FWLR Page 1996** at **2000**

The Company is distinct from its promoters or directors and a director is an agent of the company. Consequently, where a director enters into a contract in the name of or purporting to bind the company, it is the company, as principal that is liable, not the director. ***Dansa Foods (Nig.) Ltd v. Isong*** **(2011) All F.W.L.R. part 596 404-600 at p.595**

*Authentication and service of documents*

## 77. Authentication of documents

A document[1] or proceeding requiring authentication [2] by a company[3] may be signed by a director, [4] secretary, [5] or other authorised officer[6] of the company, [3] and need not be under its common seal[7] unless otherwise so required in this Part of this Act.

---

**Notes**
**Section 77**

1. "Document" includes summons, notices, order and other legal processes and register. See See **section 567 CAMA, Cap. C20, LFN, 2004.**
2. "Authentication" means the act of proving that something (as a document) is true or genuine. See **Garner B. (ed) Black's Law Dictionary, 8th ed.**
3. "Company" means a company formed and registered under this Act or as the case may be, formed and registered in Nigeria before and in existence on the commencement of this Act. See **Section 567 CAMA, Cap. C20, LFN, 2004.**
4. "Director" means a person duly appointed by the company to direct and manage the business of the company. See **Garner B, (ed) Black's Law Dictionary, 8thed**
   Director includes any person occupying the position of director by whatever name called, and includes any person in accordance with whose directions or instructions the directors are accustomed to act. See **Section 567 CAMA, Cap. C20, LFN 2004**
5. "Secretary" means (1) an administrative assistant (2) a corporate officer in charge of official correspondence, minutes of board meetings, and records of stock ownership and transfer (3) an officer charged with recording a deliberative assembly's proceedings. **See Garner B, (ed) Black's Law Dictionary 8th ed**
6. "Officer" in relation to a body corporate, includes a director, manager or secretary. See **Section 567 CAMA, Cap. C20, LFN 2004**
7. "Common seal" means a design embossed or stamped on paper to authenticate, confirm, or attest; an impression or sign that has legal consequence when applied to an instrument. The purpose of a seal is to secure or prove authenticity. See **Garner, B. (ed.) Black's Law Dictionary, 8th ed**

**Cross Reference**

On the obligation of a company to keep a common seal and use of the company's common seal, see **Section 74 CAMA Cap. C20, LFN 2004**
On official use of seal abroad, see **section 75 CAMA Cap. C20, LFN 2004**

---

**Cases**

The court in interpreting section 77 of CA M A held that: "if a document is signed by the alter ego of a company, sealing is no longer a sine qua non to the validity of the same since its purpose is to ensure that the right person entered into an agreement on behalf of the company. See ***S P D C (Nig) ltd v. Allaputa (2005) 9 NWLR (Pt.931) 475 at 545***

## 78. Service of documents on companies

A court[1] process shall be served on a company [2] in the manner provided by the Rules of Court and any other document [3] may be served[2] on a company[3] by leaving it at, or sending it by post to, the registered office[4] or head office of the company. [3]

---

**Notes**
**Section 78**

1. "Court" used in relation to a company, means the Federal High Court, and to the extent to which application may be made to it as; court includes the Court of Appeal and the Supreme Court of Nigeria; See **Section 567 CAMA, Cap. C20 , LFN 2004**
2. "Company" means a company formed and registered under this Act or as the case may be, formed and registered in Nigeria before and in existence on the commencement of this Act, See **Section 567 CAMA, Cap. C20, LFN, 2004.**
3. "Document" includes summons, notices, order and other legal processes and register. **Garner. B. (ed) Black's Law Dictionary, 8 th ed.**
4. "Registered office" means the official address of a registered company. It must be notified to the Companies Registry before registration of the company and it must appear on company letter-head and order forms. Documents may be served to a company's registered office and various registers and records may be inspected there. **Martins E. (ed.) Oxford Dictionary of Law 4 th ed**

Cross Reference

On the power of the various courts to make rules of court, see **sections 236, 248, 254,259, 246,269,274, 279 and 284, Constitution of the Federal Republic of Nigeria, 1999 (as amended)**

*PART IV*

*Membership of the company*

## 79. Definition of member

(1) The subscribers [1] of the memorandum [2] of a company [3] shall be deemed to have agreed to become members [4] of the company [3], and on its registration shall be entered as members [4] in its register of members[4].

(2) Every other person who agrees in writing to become a member[4] of a company [3], and whose name is entered in its register of members,[4] shall be a member [4] of the company. [3]

(3) In the case of a company [3] having a share capital, [5] each member[4] shall be a shareholder [6] of the company and shall hold at least one share. [7]

---

**Notes**

**Section 79(1)**

1. "Subscriber" means a person who by agreement contributes a sum of money or property to a specific person or for a specific purpose. **See Garner B. (ed) Black's Law Dictionary, 8th ed.**
2. "Memorandum" means the memorandum of association of a company as originally framed or as altered in pursuance of any enactment. See **Section 567 CAMA, Cap. C20, LFN 2004** .
   "Memorandum of Association" means a legal document, setting up a corporation, either with or without limited liability, and including the company's name, purpose, and duration. **See Garner B. (ed) Black's Law Dictionary, 8th ed**
3. "Company" means a company formed and registered under this Act or as the case may be, formed and registered in Nigeria before and in existence on the commencement of this Act. See section 567 **CAMA, Cap. C20, LFN, 2004.**
4. "Members" see "member". It means one of the individuals of whom an organisation or a deliberative assembly consist, and who enjoys the full rights of participation in the organization including the right of making, debating, and voting on motions. **See Garner. B. (ed) Black's Law Dictionary 8th ed.**
   It includes the heir, executor, administrator, or other personal representatives, as the case may be, of the member. See **Section 567 CAMA Cap. C20, LFN 2004**

**Section 79(3)**

5. "Share Capital" means one of the definite numbers of equal parts into which the capital stock of a corporation or joint stock company is divided. **See Garner. B. (ed) Black's Law Dictionary, 8th ed.**
6. "Shareholder" means one who owns or holds a share or shares in a company. See **Garner .B. (ed) Black's Law Dictionary, 8th ed.**
7. "Share" means the interest in a company's share capital of a member who is entitled to share in the capital or income of such company. See **Garner .B. (ed) Black's Law Dictionary 8 th ed.**

**Cross Reference**

On rights of members to attend meeting, see **section 81 CAMA Cap. C20, LFN 2004**

On register of members, see **section 83 CAMA Cap. C20, LFN 2004**

---

**Cases**

The court held that upon registration, the subscribers are deemed to have agreed to become members and their names must be put in the register of members. ***Ezeonwu v. Onyechi (1996) 2 SCNJ 250***

**For Further Reading**

Olufemi Amao and Kenneth Amaeshi "Galvanizing Shareholder Activism: A Prerequisite for Effective Corporate Governance and Accountability in Nigeria" **(2008) 82 Journal of Business Ethics 119-130.**

Akaki, J.O, **Essays on Company Law,** University of Lagos Press, 1992

Ola, C.S. **Company Law in Nigeria,** Heunemann Educational Books (Nig), 1999

Adeogun, A.A, "Membership of a Company," **Essays on Company Law** Pages 73 - 75

## 80. Capacity to be a member

(1) As from the commencement of this Act, an individual shall not be capable of becoming a member [1] of a company [2] if-

(a) he is of unsound mind [3] and has been so found by a court [4] in Nigeria or elsewhere; or

(b) he is an undischarged bankrupt. [5]

(2) A person under the age of 18 years shall not be counted for the purpose of determining the legal minimum number of members [1] of a company [2].

(3) A corporate body [6] in liquidation [7] shall not be capable of becoming a member [1] of a company. [2]

(4) Where at the commencement of this Act, any person falling within the provisions of subsection (1) of this section is a

member[1] of a company[2] by reason of being a shareholder [8] of the company,[2] his share[9] shall vest in his committee or trustee, [10] as the case may be.

(5) Where after the commencement [1] of this Act, any shareholder[8] purports to transfer any shares [9] to a person falling within the provisions of subsection (1) of this section, the purported transfer shall not vest the title in the shares [9] in that person, but the title shall remain in the purported transferor or his personal representative[11] who shall hold the shares [9] in trust for that person during the period of his incapacity.

---

**Notes**

**Section 80(1)**

1. "Member" includes the heir, executor, administrator or other personal representative, as the case may be, of the member. See **Section 567 CAMA, Cap. C20, LFN 2004**
2. "Company" means a company formed and registered under this Act or, as the case may be, formed and registered in Nigeria before and in existence on the commencement of this Act. See **Section 567 CAMA, Cap. C20, LFN 2004**
3. "Unsound mind" means not responsible for your actions because of a mental illness or condition. **See Oxford Advanced Learners Dictionary, 6th ed.**
4. "Court" means the Federal High Court, and to the extent to which application may be made to it as: court includes the court of Appeal, and the Supreme Court of Nigeria. See **Section 567 CAMA, Cap. C20, LFN 2004**
5. "Undischarged bankrupt" means a person who has been officially stated to be bankrupt by a court of law but who still pay his or her debt. See **Oxford Advanced Learner's Dictionary of Current English. 6 th ed.**

**Section 80(3)**

6. "Corporate" means an entity having authority under law to act as a single person distinct from the shareholders who own it and having rights to issue stock and exist indefinitely. See **Garner B. (ed) Black's Law Dictionary, 8th ed.**
7. "Liquidation" means the act of settling a debt by payment or other satisfaction. See **Garner B. (ed) Black's Law Dictionary, 8th ed.**

**Section 80(4)**

8. "Shareholder" means one who owns or holds a share or shares in a company. **See Garner B. (ed) Black's Law Dictionary, 8 th ed.**
9. "Shares" see "share" It means the interest in a company's share capital of a member who is entitled to share in the capital or income of such company. See **Section 567 CAMA, Cap. C20, LFN, 2004**

10. "Personal representative" means a person who manages the legal affairs of another because of incapacity or death, such as the executor of an estate. See **Garner B. (ed) Black's Law Dictionary, 8th ed** .

Cross Reference

On rights of members to attend meeting, see **section 81 CAMA Cap. C20, LFN 2004**

On register of members, see **section 83 CAMA Cap. C20, LFN 2004**

---

**Cases**

The court held that upon registration, the subscribers are deemed to have agreed to become members and their names must be put in the register of members. ***Ezeonwu v. Onyechi (1996) 2 SCNJ 250***

Corporate personality presupposes that a company assumes a separate and distinct personality from its members from the moment of incorporation. ***Habib Nig. Bank Ltd. v. Ochete*** **(2001) F.W.L.R (pt.54) 384.**

**For For Further Reading**

Akaki, J.O, **Essays on Company Law,** University of Lagos Press, 1992

Irukwu, J.O, **The Company, The Shareholder, The Director and The Law**, Fourth Dimension Publishing Co. Ltd 1994

Ola, C.S. **Company Law in Nigeria,** Heunemann Educational Books (Nig), 1999

Adeogun, A.A, "Membership of a Company," **Essays on Company Law** Pages 73 - 75

## 81. Right of member to attend meetings and vote

Every member[1] shall notwithstanding any provision in the articles [2], have a right to attend any general meeting [3] of the company[4] and to speak and vote on any resolution [5] before the meeting[3]:

Provided that the articles[2] may provide that a member [1] shall not be entitled to attend and vote unless all calls or other sums payable by him in respect of shares [6] in the company[4] have been paid.

---

**Notes**

**Section 81**

1. "Members" see "member". It means one of the individuals of whom an organization or a deliberative assembly consist, and who enjoys the full rights of participation in the organization including the right of making, debating, and voting on motions. See **Garner. B, (ed) Black's Law Dictionary, 8th ed**

   "Member" includes heirs, executor, administrator or other personal representatives as the case may be, of the member. See **Section 567 CAMA, Cap. C23, LFN 2004**

2. "Articles" means the articles of association of a company, as originally framed or as altered by special resolution. See **Section 567 CAMA, Cap. C20, LFN 2004** .
3. "Meeting" means the gathering of people to discuss or act on matters in which they have a common interest. See **Garner, B. (ed) Black's Law Dictionary, 8th ed.**
4. "Company" means a company formed and registered under this Act or, as the case may be, formed and registered in Nigeria before and in existence on the commencement of this Act. See **Section 567 CAMA, Cap. C20, LFN 2004**
5. "Resolution" means a main motion that formally expresses the sense, will or action of a deliberative assembly. See **Garner, B. (ed) Black's Law Dictionary, 8th ed.**
6. "Shares" means the interest in a company's share capital of a member who is entitled to share in the capital or income of such company. See **Section 567 CAMA, Cap. C20, LFN, 2004**

**Cross Reference**

On definition of members, see **section 79 CAMA Cap. C20, LFN 2004**
On capacity of members, see **section 80 CAMA Cap. C20, LFN 2004**
On the creation of the register of members, see **section 83 CAMA Cap. C20, LFN 2004**

---

**Cases**

Generally companies speak or express their decisions through resolutions, which must be validly passed. No member of a company has a right to unilaterally commit the company on any matter without its consent and approval. Let me emphatically say that no member of a company is allowed to wake up one morning and sell off the company. ***New Resources Int'l Ltd. & Anor.v. EjikeOranusi*** **(2010) LPELR-CA/L/461/08**

**For Further Reading**

Olufemi Amao and Kenneth Amaeshi "Galvanizing Shareholder Activism: A Prerequisite for Effective Corporate Governance and Accountability in Nigeria" (2008) 82 Journal of Business Ethics 119-130.

## 82. Personating of members

If any person falsely and deceitfully personates any member [1] of a company[2] and thereby obtains or endeavours to obtain any benefit due to any such member, [2] he shall be guilty of an offence and be liable on conviction to imprisonment for a term of not more than 7 years or a fine of not more than N2,500.

---

**Notes**
**Section 82**

1. "Members" means one of the individuals of whom an organization or a deliberative assembly consist, and who enjoys the full rights of participation in the organization including the right of making, debating, and voting on motions. See **Garner. B. (ed) Black's Law Dictionary, 8th ed**
"Members" includes heirs, executor, administrator or other personal representatives as the case may be, of the member. See **Section 567 CAMA, Cap. C23, LFN 2004**
2. "Company" means a company formed and registered under this Act or, as the case may be, formed and registered in Nigeria before and in existence on the commencement of this Act. See **Section 567 CAMA, Cap. C20, LFN 2004**

Cross Reference

On definition of members, see **section 79 CAMA Cap. C20, LFN 2004**
On capacity of members, see **section 80 CAMA Cap. C20, LFN 2004**
On the creation of the register of members, see **section 83 CAMA Cap. C20, LFN 2004**
On meaning of offence, see **section 2, Criminal Code Act, C38, LFN 2004**

---

**For Further Reading**
On Memorandum, Shareholder, membership, see Orojo, J. Ola **Company Law and Practice in Nigeria** 3rd Edition, Mbeyi & Associates (Lagos, Nigeria) 1992.

*Register of members*

## 83. Register of members

(1) Every company [1] shall keep a register of its members [2] and enter in it the following particulars-

(a) the names and addresses of the members, [2] and in the case of a company[1] having a share capital, [3] a statement of the shares[4] and class of shares, [4] if any, held by each member,[2] distinguishing each share[4] by its number so long as the share[4] has a number, and of the amount paid or agreed to be considered as paid on the shares [4] of each member[2];

(b) the date on which each person was registered as a member[2]; and

(c) the date on which any person ceased to be a member [2]:

Provided that, where the company [1] has converted any of its shares[4] into stock and given notice of the conversion to the Commission,[5] the register shall show the amount of stock[6] held by each member[2] instead of the amount of shares[4] and the particulars relating to shares [4] specified in paragraph (a) of this subsection.

(2) The entry required under paragraph (a) or (b) of subsection (1) of this section, shall be made within 28 days of the conclusion of the agreement with the company [1] to become a member[2] or, in the case of a subscriber [7] of the memorandum,[8] within 28 days of the registration of the company. [1]

(3) The entry required under paragraph (c) of subsection (1) of this section, shall be made within 28 days of the date on which the person concerned ceased to be a member, [2] or if he ceased to be a member[2] otherwise than as a result of action by the company [1], within 28 days of production to the company [1] of evidence satisfactory to the company [1] of the occurrence of the event whereby he ceased to be a member. [2]

(4) Where a company [1] makes default in complying with the provisions of this section, the company [1] and every officer [9] of the company[1] who is in default shall be liable to a fine of N25 and a daily default fine of N5.

(5) Liability incurred by a company [1] from the making or deletion of an entry in its register of members, [2] or from a failure to make or delete any such entry, shall not be enforceable after the expiration of 20 years from the date on which the entry was made or deleted or, in the case of any such failure, from the date on which the failure first occurred.

---

**Notes**
**Section 83(1)**

1. "Company" means a company formed and registered under this Act or, as the case may be, formed and registered in Nigeria before and in existence on the commencement of this Act. See **Section 567 CAMA, Cap. C20, LFN 2004**
2. "Members" see "member". It means one of the individuals of whom an organization or a deliberative assembly consist, and who enjoys the full rights of participation in the organization including the right of making, debating, and voting on motions. See **Garner. B. (ed) Black's Law Dictionary, 8th ed**

"Members" includes heirs, executor, administrator or other personal representatives as the case may be, of the member. See **Section 567 CAMA, Cap. C23, LFN 2004**

3. "Share capital" means one of the definite numbers of equal parts into which the capital stock of a corporation or joint stock company is divided. See **Garner, B. (ed) Black's Law Dictionary, 8th ed.**
4. "Shares" means the interest in a company's share capital of a member who is entitled to share in the capital or income of such company. See **Section 567 CAMA, Cap. C20, LFN, 2004**
5. "Commission" means the Corporate Affairs Commission established under Section 1 of this Act. See **Section 567 CAMA, Cap. C23, LFN 2004.**

**Section 83(2)**

6. "Subscriber" means a person who by agreement contributes a sum of money or property to a specific person or for a specific purpose. **See Garner B. (ed) Black's Law Dictionary, 8th ed.**
7. "Memorandum" means the memorandum of association of a company as originally framed or as altered in pursuance of any enactment. See **Section 567 CAMA, Cap. C20, LFN 2004** .

   "Memorandum of Association" means a legal document, setting up a corporation, either with or without limited liability, and including the company's name, purpose, and duration. **See Garner B. (ed) Black's Law Dictionary, 8th ed.**

**Section 83(3)**

8. "Officer" in relation to a body corporate, includes a director, manager or secretary. See **Section 567 CAMA, Cap. C20, LFN 2004**

Cross Reference

On the location of the register of members, see **section 84 CAMA Cap. C20, LFn 2004**

On capacity of members, see **section 80 CAMA Cap. C20, LFN 2004**

On the creation of the register of members, see **section 83 CAMA Cap. C20, LFN 2004**

On meaning of offence, see **section 2, Criminal Code Act, C38, LFN 2004**

---

**Cases**

A registered holder of shares in a company becomes entitled to certain rights, benefits and privileges. Except as otherwise provided by the Law and the provisions of the memorandum and Articles of Association of the company, he has the right to sell, mortgage or otherwise dispose of the shares. He is entitled to receive dividends on the shares registered in his name and to keep the dividends so received for his own use. In other words, the essence of being registered as an owner or a holder of shares in a company is that one is inter alia, entitled to enjoy in one's right the foregoing rights, benefits and privileges. ***Kotoye vs. Saraki*** **(1994) 7 N.W.L.R (part 357) 414** .

**For Further Reading**

For further reading on Memorandum, Shareholder, membership, see Orojo, J. Ola **Company Law and Practice in Nigeria** 3rd Edition, Mbeyi & Associates (Lagos, Nigeria) 1992

## 84. Location of register

(1) The register of members [1] shall be kept at the registered office[2] of the company, [3] except that if-

(a) the work of making it up is done at another office of the company,[3] it may be kept at that other office; and

(b) the company[3] arranges with some other person for the making up of the register to be undertaken on behalf of the company [3] by that person, it may be kept at the office of that other person at which the work is done, but the register shall not be kept in the case of a company[3] registered in Nigeria at a place outside Nigeria.

(2) Every company[3] shall send notice to the Commission[4] of the place where the register is kept and of any change of that place.

(3) A company[3] shall not be bound to send notice under this subsection where the register has, at all times since it came into existence or, in the case of a register in existence at the commencement of this Act, at all times since then, been kept at the registered office[2] of the company.[3]

(4) If a company[3] makes default for 28 days in complying with subsection (2) of this section, the company and every one of its officers[5] who is in default shall be liable to a fine of N10 and, for continued contravention, to a daily default fine of N5.

---

**Notes**

**Section 84(1)**

1. "Members" see "member". It means one of the individuals of whom an organization or a deliberative assembly consist, and who enjoys the full rights of participation in the organization including the right of making, debating, and voting on motions. See **Garner. B. (ed) Black's Law Dictionary, 8th ed**

   "Member" includes heirs, executor, administrator or other personal representatives as the case may be, of the member. See **Section 567 CAMA, Cap. C20, LFN 2004**

2. "Registered office" means the official address of a registered company. It must be notified to the Companies Registry before registration of the company and it must appear on company letter-head and order forms.

Documents may be served to a company's registered office and various registers and records may be inspected there. See **Martins E. (ed.) Oxford Dictionary of Law 4th ed**

3. "Company" means a company formed and registered under this Act or, as the case may be, formed and registered in Nigeria before and in existence on the commencement of this Act. See **Section 567 CAMA, Cap. C20, LFN 2004.**

**Section 82(2)**

4. "Commission" means the Corporate Affairs Commission established under Section 1 of this Act. See **Section 567 CAMA, Cap. C20, LFN 2004.**
5. "Officer" in relation to a body corporate includes a director, manager or secretary. See **section 567 CAMA, Cap C20, LFN 2004**

**Cross Reference**

On the rights of members to attend meeting and vote, see **section 81 CAMA Cap. C20, LFn 2004**

On capacity of members, see **section 80 CAMA Cap. C20, LFN 2004**

On the creation of the register of members, see **section 83 CAMA Cap. C20, LFN 2004**

---

**Cases**

A registered holder of shares in a company becomes entitled to certain rights, benefits and privileges. Except as otherwise provided by the Law and the provisions of the memorandum and Articles of Association of the company, he has the right to sell, mortgage or otherwise dispose of the shares. He is entitled to receive dividends on the shares registered in his name and to keep the dividends so received for his own use. In other words, the essence of being registered as an owner or a holder of shares in a company is that one is inter alia, entitled to enjoy in one's right the foregoing rights, benefits and privileges. ***Kotoye vs. Saraki*** **(1994) 7 N.W.L.R. (part 357) 414** .

**For Further Reading**

For further reading on Memorandum, Shareholder, membership, see Orojo, J. Ola **Company Law and Practice in Nigeria** 3rd Edition, Mbeyi & Associates (Lagos, Nigeria) 1992

## 85. Index of members to be kept

(1) Every company [1] having more than 50 members [2] shall, unless the register of members [2] is in such a form as to constitute in itself an index, keep an index of the names of the members [2] of the company[1] and shall, within 14 days after the date on which any alteration is made in the register of members, [2] make any necessary alteration in the index.

(2) The index shall in respect of each member [2] contain sufficient indication to enable the account of that member [2] in the register to be readily found.

(3) The index shall, at all times, be kept at the same place as the register of members. [2]

(4) If default is made in complying with the provisions of this section, the company [1] and every officer [3] of the company [1] who is in default shall be liable to a fine of N50.

---

**Notes**

**Section 85(1)**

1. "Company" means a company formed and registered under this Act or, as the case may be, formed and registered in Nigeria before and in existence on the commencement of this Act. See **Section 567 CAMA, Cap. C20, LFN 2004.**
2. "Members" see "member". It means one of the individuals of whom an organization or a deliberative assembly consist, and who enjoys the full rights of participation in the organization including the right of making, debating, and voting on motions. See **Garner. B, (ed) Black's Law Dictionary, 8th ed**

   "Members" includes heirs, executor, administrator or other personal representatives as the case may be, of the member. See **Section 567 CAMA, Cap. C23, LFN 2004**

**Section 85(4)**

3. "Officer" in relation to a body corporate, includes a director, manager or secretary. See **Section 567 CAMA, Cap. C20, LFN 2004**

**Cross Reference**

On the rights of members to attend meeting and vote, see **section 81 CAMA Cap. C20, LFn 2004**

On capacity of members, see **section 80 CAMA Cap. C20, LFN 2004**

On the creation of the register of members, see **section 83 CAMA Cap. C20, LFN 2004**

---

**Cases**

A registered holder of shares in a company becomes entitled to certain rights, benefits and privileges. Except as otherwise provided by the Law and the provisions of the memorandum and Articles of Association of the company, he has the right to sell, mortgage or otherwise dispose of the shares. He is entitled to receive dividends on the shares registered in his name and to keep the dividends so received for his own use. In other words, the essence of being registered as an owner or a holder of shares in a company is that one is inter alia, entitled to enjoy in one's right the foregoing rights, benefits and privileges. ***Kotoye v. Saraki* (1994) 7 N.W.L.R (part 357) 414** .

**For Further Reading**

On Memorandum, Shareholder, membership, see Orojo, J. Ola ***Company Law and Practice in Nigeria*** 3rd Edition, Mbeyi & Associates (Lagos, Nigeria) 1992

## 86. Entry of trusts prohibited

No notice of any trust, express, implied or constructive, shall be entered on the register of members [1] or be receivable by the Commission[2].

---

**Notes**

**Section 86**

1. "Members" see "member" It means one of the individuals of whom an organization or a deliberative assembly consist, and who enjoys the full rights of participation in the organization including the right of making, debating, and voting on motions. See **Garner. B, (ed) Black's Law Dictionary, 8th ed**

   **"Members"** includes heirs, executor, administrator or other personal representatives as the case may be, of the member. See **Section 567 CAMA, Cap. C23, LFN 2004**
2. "Commission" means the Corporate Affairs Commission established under Section 1 of this Act. See **Section 567 CAMA, Cap. C23, LFN 2004.**

**Cross Reference**

On definition of member, see **section 79 CAMA Cap. C20, LFN 2004**

On the rights of members to attend meeting and vote, see **section 81 CAMA Cap. C20, LFn 2004**

On capacity of members, see **section 80 CAMA Cap. C20, LFN 2004**

On the creation of the register of members, see **section 83 CAMA Cap. C20, LFN 2004**

---

**For Further Reading**

On Memorandum, Shareholder, membership, see Orojo, J. Ola **Company Law and Practice in Nigeria** 3rd Edition, Mbeyi & Associates (Lagos, Nigeria) 1992

## 87. Inspection of register and index

(1) Except when the register of members [1] is closed under the provisions of this Act, the register and the index of members' [1] names shall be open during business hours (subject to such reasonable restrictions as the company [2] in general meeting [3] may impose, so however, that not less than 2 hours in each day shall be

allowed for inspection) to the inspection of any member [1] of the company[2] without charge, and with the permission of the company [2] to any other person on payment of N1 or any less sum as the company[2] may prescribe for each inspection.

(2) Any member [1] or, with the permission of the company [2], any other person may require a copy of the register, or of any part thereof, on payment of 50 kobo, or such less sum as the company [2] may prescribe, for every 100 words or fractional part thereof required to be copied; and the company [2] shall cause any copy so required by any person to be sent to that person within a period of 10 days commencing on the day next after the day on which the requirement is received by the company. [2]

(3) In the case of a member [1], if any inspection required under this section is refused or if any copy required under this section is not sent within the prescribed period, the company [2] and every officer[4] of the company who is in default shall be liable in respect of each offence to a fine of N10.

(4) In the case of any such refusal or default in the case of a member,[1] the court[5] may by order compel an immediate inspection of the register and index or direct that the copies required shall be sent to the persons requiring them.

**Notes**

**Section 87(1)**

1. "Members" see "member." It means one of the individuals of whom an organization or a deliberative assembly consist, and who enjoys the full rights of participation in the organization including the right of making, debating, and voting on motions. See **Garner. B. (ed) Black's Law Dictionary, 8th ed**

   "Member" includes heirs, executor, administrator or other personal representatives as the case may be, of the member. See **Section 567 CAMA, Cap. C20, LFN 2004**
2. "Company" means a company formed and registered under this Act or, as the case may be, formed and registered in Nigeria before and in existence on the commencement of this Act. See **Section 567 CAMA, Cap. C20, LFN 2004.**
3. "Meeting" means the gathering of people to discuss or act on matters in which they have a common interest. See **Garner, B. (ed) Black's Law Dictionary, 8th ed.**

**Section 87(3)**

4. "Officer" in relation to a body corporate, includes a director, manager or secretary. See **Section 567 CAMA, Cap. C20, LFN 2004**

**Section 87(4)**

5. "Court" used in relation to a company, means the Federal High Court, and to the extent to which application may be made to it as a court includes Appeal and Supreme Court of Nigeria. See **Section 567 CAMA, Cap. C20, LFN 2004**

**Cross Reference**

On definition of member, see section 79 CAMA Cap. C20, LFN 2004

On the rights of members to attend meeting and vote, see **section 81 CAMA Cap. C20, LFn 2004**

On capacity of members, see **section 80 CAMA Cap. C20, LFN 2004**

On the creation of the register of members, see **section 83 CAMA Cap. C20, LFN 2004**

On establishment and jurisdiction of the Federal High Court, see **sections 249 &251, Constitution of the Federal Republic of Nigeria, 1999 (as amended)**

On meaning of offence, see **section 2, Criminal Code, Cap. C38, LFN 2004**

**For Further Reading**

For further reading on Memorandum, Shareholder, membership, see Orojo, J. Ola **Company Law and Practice in Nigeria** 3rd Edition, Mbeyi & Associates (Lagos, Nigeria) 1992

## 88. Consequences of failure by agents' default to keep register

Where, by virtue of paragraph (b) of subsection (1) of section 84 of this Act, the register of members [1] is kept at the office of some person other than the company [2], and by reason of any default of his, the company [2] fails to comply with subsection (1) or (2) of section 84 of this Act, or with any requirements of this Act as to the production of the register, that other person shall be liable to the same penalties as if he were an officer [3] of the company who was in default, and the power of the court [4] under subsection (4) of section 87 of this Act shall extend to the making of orders against that other person and his officers [3] and servants.

---

**Notes**
**Section 88**

1. "Members" means one of the individuals of whom an organization or a deliberative assembly consist, and who enjoys the full rights of participation in the organization including the right of making, debating, and voting on motions. See **Garner B, (ed) Black's Law Dictionary, 8th ed**

   "Members" includes heirs, executor, administrator or other personal representatives as the case may be, of the member. See **Section 567 CAMA, Cap. C20, LFN 2004.**
2. "Company" means a company formed and registered under this Act or, as the case may be, formed and registered in Nigeria before and in existence on the commencement of this Act. See **Section 567 CAMA, Cap. C20, LFN 2004.**
3. "Officer" in relation to a body corporate, includes a director, manager or secretary. See **Section 567 CAMA, Cap. C20, LFN 2004**
4. "Court" used in relation to a company, means the Federal High Court, and to the extent to which application may be made to it as a court includes Appeal and Supreme Court of Nigeria. See **Section 567 CAMA, Cap. C20, LFN 2004.**

**Cross Reference**

On definition of member, see **section 79 CAMA Cap. C20, LFN 2004**

On the rights of members to attend meeting and vote, see **section 81 CAMA Cap. C20, LFn 2004**

On capacity of members, see **section 80 CAMA Cap. C20, LFN 2004**

On the creation of the register of members, see **section 83 CAMA Cap. C20, LFN 2004**

On establishment and jurisdiction of the Federal High Court, see **sections 249 &251, Constitution of the Federal Republic of Nigeria, 1999** (as amended)

---

**Cases**

A registered holder of shares in a company becomes entitled to certain rights, benefits and privileges. Except as otherwise provided by the Law and the provisions of the memorandum and Articles of Association of the company, he has the right to sell, mortgage or otherwise dispose of the shares. He is entitled to receive dividends on the shares registered in his name and to keep the dividends so received for his own use. In other words, the essence of being registered as an owner or a holder of shares in a company is that one is inter alia, entitled to enjoy in one's right the foregoing rights, benefits and privileges. ***Kotoye v. Saraki* (1994) 7 N.W.L.R (part 357) 414** .

## 89. Power to close register

A company[1] may, on giving notice by advertisement in a daily newspaper circulating in the district in which the registered office [2] of the company[1] is situated, close the register of members [3] or any part of it for any time or times not exceeding on the whole 30 days in each year.

---

**Notes**
**Section 89**

1. "Company" means a company formed and registered under this Act or, as the case may be, formed and registered in Nigeria before and in existence on the commencement of this Act. See **Section 567 CAMA, Cap. C20, LFN 2004**
2. "Registered office" means the official address of a registered company. It must be notified to the Companies Registry before registration of the company and it must appear on company letter-head and order forms. Documents may be served to a company's registered office and various registers and records may be inspected there. See **Martins E. (ed.) Oxford Dictionary of Law 4th ed**
3. "Members" see "member". It means one of the individuals of whom an organization or a deliberative assembly consist, and who enjoys the full rights of participation in the organization including the right of making, debating, and voting on motions. See **Garner. B. (ed) Black's Law Dictionary, 8th ed**

   "Members" includes heirs, executor, administrator or other personal representatives as the case may be, of the member. See **Section 567 CAMA, Cap. C20, LFN 2004**

Cross Reference

On definition of member, see **section 79 CAMA Cap. C20, LFN 2004**

On the rights of members to attend meeting and vote, see **section 81 CAMA Cap. C20, LFN 2004**

On capacity of members, see **section 80 CAMA Cap. C20, LFN 2004**

On the creation of the register of members, see **section 83 CAMA Cap. C20, LFN 2004**

**Cases**

A registered holder of shares in a company becomes entitled to certain rights, benefits and privileges. Except as otherwise provided by the Law and the provisions of the memorandum and Articles of Association of the company, he has the right to sell, mortgage or otherwise dispose of the shares. He is entitled to receive dividends on the shares registered in his name and to keep the dividends so received for his own use. In other words, the essence of being registered as an owner or a holder of shares in a company is that one is inter alia, entitled to enjoy in one's right the foregoing rights, benefits and privileges. ***Kotoye vs. Saraki* (1994) 7 N.W.L.R (part 357) 414**

## 90. Power of court to rectify register

(1) If-

(a) the name of any person is, without sufficient cause, entered in or omitted from the register of members [1] of a company[2]; or

(b) default is made or unnecessary delay takes place in entering on the register the fact of any person having ceased to be a member, [1]

the person aggrieved, or any member [1] of the company, [2] or the company, [2] may apply to the court [3] for rectification of the register.

(2) The court [3] may refuse the application, or order rectification of the register and payment by the company [2] of any damages sustained by the party aggrieved.

(3) On an application under this section, the court [3] may decide any question relating to the title of any person [1] who is a party to the application to have his name entered in or omitted from the register, whether the question arises between members [1] or alleged members, [1] or between members [1] and alleged members [1] on the one hand and the company [2] on the other hand, and generally may decide any question necessary or expedient to be decided for rectification of the register.

(4) In the case of a company [2] required by this Act to send a list of its members [1] to the Commission, [4] the court, [3] when making an order for rectification of the register shall, by its order, direct notice of the rectification to be given to the Commission. [4]

**Notes**

**Section 90(1)**

1. "Members" see "member". It includes heirs, executor, administrator or other personal representatives as the case may be, of the member. See **Section 567 CAMA, Cap. C20, LFN 2004**
2. "Company" means a company formed and registered under this Act or, as the case may be, formed and registered in Nigeria before and in existence on the commencement of this Act. See **Section 567 CAMA, Cap. C20, LFN 2004**
3. "Court" used in relation to a company, means the Federal High Court, and to the extent to which application may be made to it as a court includes Appeal and Supreme Court of Nigeria. See **Section 567 CAMA, Cap. C20, LFN 2004**

**Section 90(4)**

4. "Commission" means the Corporate Affairs Commission established under Section 1 of this Act. See **Section 567 CAMA, Cap. C20, LFN 2004**

**Cross Reference**

For Jurisdiction of Federal High Court, **See Section 251, Constitution of the Federal Republic of Nigeria, 1999** (as amended).

On the creation of the register of members, see **section 83 CAMA Cap. C20, LFN 2004**

**Cases**

A registered holder of shares in a company becomes entitled to certain rights, benefits and privileges. Except as otherwise provided by the Law and the provisions of the memorandum and Articles of Association of the company, he has the right to sell, mortgage or otherwise dispose of the shares. He is entitled to receive dividends on the shares registered in his name and to keep the dividends so received for his own use. In other words, the essence of being registered as an owner or a holder of shares in a company is that one is inter alia, entitled to enjoy in one's right the foregoing rights, benefits and privileges. ***Kotoye vs. Saraki*** **(1994) 7 N.W.L.R (part 357) 414** .

**For Further Reading**

On company, winding up, membership, see Asomugha, E. Maduelosi: **Company Law in Nigeria under the Companies and Allied Matters Act** E.M. Asomugha (Lagos) 1994.

On Company and Types of companies, See Kiser Barnes **Cases and Materials on Nigeria Company Law** (1992) Obafemi Awolowo University Press Ltd, Ile-Ife, Nigeria.

## 91. Register to be evidence

The register of members [1] shall be prima facie evidence of matters which are by this Act directed or authorised to be inserted in it.

---

**Notes**

**Section 91**

1. "Members" see "member". It means one of the individuals of whom an organization or a deliberative assembly consist, and who enjoys the full rights of participation in the organization including the right of making, debating, and voting on motions. See **Garner. B, (ed) Black's Law Dictionary, 8th ed**

   "Member" includes heirs, executor, administrator or other personal representatives as the case may be, of the member. See **Section 567 CAMA, Cap. C20, LFN 2004**

**Cross Reference**

On definition of member, see section **79 CAMA Cap. C20, LFN 2004**

On capacity of members, see **section 80 CAMA Cap. C20, LFN 2004**

On the creation of the register of members, see **section 83 CAMA Cap. C20, LFN 2004**

On power of court to rectify register of members, see **section 90 CAMA Cap. C20, LFN 2004**

---

**Cases**

A registered holder of shares in a company becomes entitled to certain rights, benefits and privileges. Except as otherwise provided by the Law and the provisions of the memorandum and Articles of Association of the company, he has the right to sell, mortgage or otherwise dispose of the shares. He is entitled to receive dividends on the shares registered in his name and to keep the dividends so received for his own use. In other words, the essence of being registered as an owner or a holder of shares in a company is that one is inter alia, entitled to enjoy in one's right the foregoing rights, benefits and privileges. ***Kotoye v. Saraki* (1994) 7 N.W.L.R (part 357) 414**

## 92. Liability of members

(1) Prior to the winding up [1] of a company [2], a member [3] of the company [2] with shares [4] shall be liable to contribute the balance, if any, of the amount payable in respect of the shares held by him in accordance with the terms of the agreement under which the shares [4] were issued or in accordance with a call validly made by the company [2] pursuant to its articles. [5]

(2) Where any contribution has become due and payable by reason of a call validly made by the company [2] pursuant to the articles[5] or where, under the terms of any agreement with the company[2], a member [3] has undertaken personal liability to make future payments in respect of shares [4] issued to him, the liability of the member[3] shall continue notwithstanding that the shares [4] held by him are subsequently transferred or forfeited under a provision to that effect in the articles [5], but his liability shall cease if and when the company[2] shall have received payment in full of all such moneys in respect of the shares. [4]

(3) Subject to subsections (1) and (2) of this section, no membe[3] or past member [3] shall be liable to contribute to the assets of the company, [2] except in the event of its being wound up. [1]

(4) In the event of a company [2] being wound up, [1] every present or past member [3] shall be liable to contribute to the assets of the company [1]to an amount sufficient for payment of its debts and liabilities and for the costs, charges and expenses of the winding up[1] and for the adjustment of the rights of the members [3] and past members[3] among themselves, but subject to the following qualifications-

(a) a past member [3] shall not be liable to contribute if he has ceased to be a member [3] for a period of 1 year or upwards before the commencement of the winding up [1];

(b) a past member [3] shall not be liable to contribute unless it appears to the court [6] that the existing members [3] are unable to satisfy the contributions required to be made by them in pursuance of this section;

(c) in the case of a company limited by shares, [7] no contribution shall be required from any member [3] or past member[3] exceeding the amount, if any, unpaid on the shares in respect of which he is liable as a present or past member[3];

(d) in the case of a company limited by guarantee, [8] no contribution shall be required from any member [3] or past member[3] exceeding the amount undertaken to be contributed by him to the assets of the company [2] in the event of its being wound up; and

(e) any sum due from the company [2] to a member [3] or past member, in his capacity as member, [3] by way of dividends or otherwise shall not be set-off against the amount for which he is liable to contribute in accordance with this section but any such sum shall be taken into account for the purposes of final adjustment of the rights of the members[3] and past members amongst themselves.

(5) For the purposes of this section, the expression "past member" includes the estate of a deceased member and where any person[8] dies after becoming liable as a member [3]or past member, such liability shall be enforceable against his estate.

(6) Except as contained in this section, a member or past member shall not be liable as a member or past member for any of the debts and liabilities of the company. [2]

---

**Notes**

**Section 92(1)**

1. "Winding up" means the process of settling accounts and liquidation of assets in anticipation of a partnership's or a corporation dissolution. See **Garner. B, (ed) Black's Law Dictionary, 8 th ed.**
2. "Company" means a company formed and registered under this Act or, as the case may be, formed and registered in Nigeria before and in existence on the commencement of this Act. See **Section 567 CAMA, Cap. C20, LFN 2004**
3. "Member" includes heirs, executor, administrator or other personal representatives as the case may be, of the member. See **Section 567 CAMA, Cap. C20, LFN 2004**
4. "Shares" see "share". It means the interest in a company's share capital of a member who is entitled to share in the capital or income of such company. See **Section 567 CAMA, Cap. C20, LFN 2004**
5. "Articles" means the articles of association of a company, as originally framed or as altered by special resolution. See **Section 567 CAMA, Cap. C20, LFN 2004** .

**Section 92(4)**

6. "Court" used in relation to a company, means the Federal High Court, and to the extent to which application may be made to it as a court includes Appeal and Supreme Court of Nigeria. See **Section 567 CAMA, Cap. C20, LFN 2004**
7. "Company limited by shares" means a company having the liability of its members limited by the memorandum to the amount if any, unpaid on the shares respectively held by them. See **Section 21 CAMA, Cap. C20 LFN 2004**
8. "Company limited by guarantee" means a company having the liability of its members limited by the memorandum to such amount as the members may respectively thereby undertake to contribute to the assets of the company, in the event of its being wound up. See **Section 21 CAMA, Cap. C20 LFN 2004.**

Cross Reference

On definition of member, see **section 79 CAMA Cap. C20, LFN 2004**

On capacity of members, see **section 80 CAMA Cap. C20, LFN 2004**

On the creation of the register of members, see **section 83 CAMA Cap. C20, LFN 2004**

On power of court to rectify register of members, see **section 90 CAMA Cap. C20, LFN 2004**

For Jurisdiction of Federal High Court, **See Section 251, Constitution of the Federal Republic of Nigeria, 1999** as amended.

---

**For Further Reading**

On company, winding up, membership, see Asomugha, E. Maduelosi: **Company Law in Nigeria under the Companies and Allied Matters Act** E.M. Asomugha (Lagos) 1994.

On Company and Types of companies, See Kiser Barnes **Cases and Materials on Nigeria Company Law** (1992) Obafemi Awolowo University Press Ltd, Ile-Ife, Nigeria.

For further reading on Membership, Shares, Company, see Sofowora, M.O **Modern Nigerian Company Law** Soft Associates, 2nd Edition 2002.Pages 13, 304, 405,

## 93. Liability for company debts where membership is below legal minimum

If a company[1] carries on business without having at least two members[2] and does so for more than 6 months, every director [3] or officer[4] of the company[1] during the time that it so carries on business with only one or no member [2] shall be liable jointly and severally with the company[1] for the debts of the company[1] contracted during that period.

---

**Notes**
**Section 93**

1. "Company" means a company formed and registered under this Act or, as the case may be, formed and registered in Nigeria before and in existence on the commencement of this Act. See **Section 567 CAMA, Cap. C20, LFN 2004**
2. "Members" see "member". It includes heirs, executor, administrator or other personal representatives as the case may be, of the member. **See Section 567 CAMA, Cap. C20, LFN 2004**
3. "Director" means persons duly appointed by the company to direct and manage the business of the company. See **Garner B. (ed) Black's Law Dictionary, 8thed**
   Director includes any person occupying the position of director by whatever name called, and includes any person in accordance with whose

directions or instructions the directors are accustomed to act. See **Section 567 CAMA, Cap. C20, LFN 2004**

4. "Officer" in relation to a body corporate, includes a director, manager or secretary. See **Section 567 CAMA, Cap. C20, LFN 2004**

Cross Reference

On definition of member, see section 79 CAMA Cap. C20, LFN 2004

On capacity of members, see **section 80 CAMA Cap. C20, LFN 2004**

On the creation of the register of members, see **section 83 CAMA Cap. C20, LFN 2004**

On liability of members of a company, see **section 92 CAMA Cap. C20, LFN 2004**

---

## 94. Power of company to require disclosure

(1) Notwithstanding the provisions of section 95 of this Act, a public company[1] may, by notice in writing, require any member [2] of the company[1], within such reasonable time as is specified in the notice-

(a) to indicate in writing the capacity in which he holds any shares[3] in the company[1]; and

(b) if he holds them other than as beneficial owner, to indicate in writing the particulars of the identity of persons interested in the shares [3] in question and whether persons interested in the same shares [3] are parties to any agreement or arrangement relating to the exercise of any rights conferred by the holding of the shares [3].

(2) Where a company [1] is formed in pursuance of a notice given to any person under subsection (1) of this section, or under this subsection, that any other person has an interest in any shares [3] in the company[1], the company [1] may, by notice in writing, require that other person within such reasonable time as is specified in the notice-

(a) to indicate in writing the capacity in which he holds that interest; and

(b) if he holds it otherwise than as beneficial owner, to indicate in writing, so far as it lies within his knowledge, the persons who have any interests in them (either by name and address or by other particulars sufficient to enable them to be identified) and the nature of their interests.

(3) Whenever a company [1] receives information from a person in pursuance of a requirement imposed on him under this section

with respect to shares [3] held by a member [2] of the company, [1] it shall be under an obligation to inscribe against the name of the member [2] in the register of members [2]-

(a) the fact that the requirement was imposed; and

(b) the information received in pursuance of the requirement.

(4) Subject to subsection (5) of this section, any person who-

(a) fails to comply with a notice under this section; or

(b) in purported compliance with such a notice makes any statement which he knows to be false in a material particular or recklessly makes any statement which is false in a material particular,

shall be guilty of an offence and liable to imprisonment for six months or to a fine of N25 for every day during which the default continues.

(5) A person shall not be guilty of an offence under subsection (4) (a) of this section, if he proves that the information in question was already in the possession of the company [1] or that the requirement to give it was for any other reason frivolous or vexatious.

---

**Notes**

**Section 94(1)**

1. "Public company" means any company other than a private company is a public company. See **Section 24 CAMA Cap. C20 LFN 2004**
2. "Member" includes heirs, executor, administrator or other personal representatives as the case may be, of the member. See **Section 567, CAMA, Cap. C20, LFN 2004**
3. "Shares" see "share". It means the interests in a company's share capital of a member who is entitled to share in the capital or income of such company; and except where a distinction between stock and shares is expressed or implied, includes stock. See **Section 567 CAMA, Cap. C20, LFN, 2004.**

Cross Reference

On the creation of the register of members, see **section 84, CAMA Cap. C20, LFN 2004**

---

**For Further Reading**

On shareholders see, Olufemi Amao and Kenneth Amaeshi "Galvanizing Shareholder Activism: A Prerequisite for Effective Corporate Governance and Accountability in Nigeria" ( **2008) 82 Journal of Business Ethics 119-130.**

**Cases**

A registered holder of shares in a company becomes entitled to certain rights, benefits and privileges. Except as otherwise provided by the Law and the provisions of the memorandum and Articles of Association of the company, he has the right to sell, mortgage or otherwise dispose of the shares. He is entitled to receive dividends on the shares registered in his name and to keep the dividends so received for his own use. In other words, the essence of being registered as an owner or a holder of shares in a company is that one is inter alia, entitled to enjoy in one's right the foregoing rights, benefits and privileges. ***Kotoye v. Saraki* (1994) 7 N.W.L.R (part 357) 414** .

## 95. Obligation of disclosure by substantial shareholder in public company

(1) A person who is a substantial shareholder [1] in a public company[2] shall give notice in writing to the company [2] stating his name and address and giving full particulars of the shares [3] held by him or his nominee (naming the nominee) by virtue of which he is a substantial shareholder[1].

(2) A person is a substantial shareholder [1] in a public company [2]if he holds himself or by his nominee, shares [3] in the company[4] which entitle him to exercise at least 10 per cent of the unrestricted voting rights at any general meeting [5] of the company[4].

(3) A person required to give a notice under subsection (1) of this section, shall do so within 14 days after that person [1] becomes aware that he is a substantial shareholder. [1]

(4) The notice shall be so given notwithstanding that the person[1] has ceased to be a substantial shareholder [1] before the expiration of the period referred to in subsection (3) of this section.

(5) A person who fails to comply with the provisions of this section shall be liable to a fine of N50 for every day during which the default continues.

---

**Notes**

**Section 95(1)**

1. "Shareholder" means one who owns or holds a share or shares in a company. See **Garner. B. (ed) Black's Law Dictionary, 8 th ed.**
2. "Public company" means any company other than a private company is a public company. See **Section 24 CAMA Cap. C20 LFN 2004**

3. "Shares" means the interests in a company's share capital of a member who is entitled to share in the capital or income of such company; and except where a distinction between stock and shares is expressed or implied, includes stock. See **Section 567 CAMA, Cap. C20, LFN, 2004.**
4. "Company" means a company formed and registered under this Act or, as the case may be, formed and registered in Nigeria before and in existence on the commencement other Companies and Allied Matters Act. See **section 567 CAMA Cap. C20, LFN 2004**

**Section 95(2)**

5. "Meeting" means the gathering of people to discuss or act on matters in which they have a common interest. See **Garner B. (ed) Black's Law Dictionary, 8th ed.**

---

**For Further Reading**

On shareholders see, Olufemi Amao and Kenneth Amaeshi "Galvanizing Shareholder Activism: A Prerequisite for Effective Corporate Governance and Accountability in Nigeria" **(2008) 82 Journal of Business Ethics 119-130**.

**Cases**

A registered holder of shares in a company becomes entitled to certain rights, benefits and privileges. Except as otherwise provided by the Law and the provisions of the memorandum and Articles of Association of the company, he has the right to sell, mortgage or otherwise dispose of the shares. He is entitled to receive dividends on the shares registered in his name and to keep the dividends so received for his own use. In other words, the essence of being registered as an owner or a holder of shares in a company is that one is inter alia, entitled to enjoy in one's right the foregoing rights, benefits and privileges. ***Kotoye v. Saraki* (1994) 7 N.W.L.R (part 357) 414** .

## 96. Person ceasing to be a substantial shareholder to notify company

(1) A person who ceases to be a substantial shareholder [1] in a public company[2] shall give notice in writing to the company [2] stating his name and the date on which he ceased to be a substantial shareholder[1] and giving full particulars of the circumstances by reason of which he ceased to be substantial shareholder. [1]

(2) A person required to give notice under subsection (1) of this section, shall do so within 14 days after he becomes aware that he has ceased to be substantial shareholder. [1]

---

**Notes**
**Section 96**

1. "Shareholder" means one who owns or holds a share or shares in a company. See **Garner. B. (ed) Black's Law Dictionary, 8 th ed.**
2. "Public company" means any company other than a private company is a public company. See **Section 24 CAMA Cap. C20 LFN 2004**

**Cross Reference**

On creation of register of members, see **section 84 CAMA Cap. C20, LFN 2004**

On obligation of disclosure of substantial interest in a public company, see **section 95 CAMA Cap. C20, LFN 2004**

---

**Cases**

A registered holder of shares in a company becomes entitled to certain rights, benefits and privileges. Except as otherwise provided by the Law and the provisions of the memorandum and Articles of Association of the company, he has the right to sell, mortgage or otherwise dispose of the shares. He is entitled to receive dividends on the shares registered in his name and to keep the dividends so received for his own use. In other words, the essence of being registered as an owner or a holder of shares in a company is that one is inter alia, entitled to enjoy in one's right the foregoing rights, benefits and privileges. ***Kotoye v. Saraki* (1994) 7 N.W.L.R (part 357) 414** .

**For Further Reading**

On shareholders see, Olufemi Amao and Kenneth Amaeshi "Galvanizing Shareholder Activism: A Prerequisite for Effective Corporate Governance and Accountability in Nigeria" in the ( **2008) 82 Journal of Business Ethics 119-130.**

## 97. Register of interests in shares

(1) A public company[1] shall keep a register in which it shall enter-

(a) in alphabetical order, the names of persons from whom it has received a notice under section 95 of this Act; and

(b) against each name so entered, the information given in the notice, and where it receives a notice under section 95 of this Act, the information given in that notice.

(2) The register shall be kept at the place where the register of members[2] required to be kept under section 84 of this Act is kept and subject to the same right of inspection as the register of members.[2]

(3) The Commission[3] may, at any time, in writing, require the company[1] to furnish it with a copy of the register or any part of the register and the company[1] shall furnish the copy within 14 days after the day on which the requirement is received by the company[1].

(4) If the company[1] ceases to be public company,[1] it shall continue to keep the register until the end of the period of six years beginning with the day next following that on which it ceases to be such a company[1].

(5) A company[1] shall not, by reason of anything done for the purposes of this section, be affected with notice of, or put on enquiry as to, a right of a person to or in relation to a share[4] in the company.[1]

(6) If default is made in complying with this section, the company[1] and every officer[5] of the company[1] who is in default shall be liable to a fine of N25 and a daily default fine of N5.

**Notes**
**Section 97**

1. "Public company" means any company other than a private company is a public company. See **Section 24 CAMA Cap. C20 LFN 2004**
2. "Members" see "member" It includes the heir, executor, administrator, or other personal representatives, as the case may be, of the member. See **Section 567 CAMA Cap. C20 LFN 2004**
3. "Commission" means the Corporate Affairs Commission established under section 1 of this Act. See **Section 567 CAMA Cap. C20, LFN 2004**
4. "Shares" see "share". It means the interests in a company's share capital of a member who is entitled to share in the capital or income of such company; and except where a distinction between stock and shares is expressed or implied, includes stock. See **Section 567 CAMA, Cap. C20, LFN, 2004.**
5. "Officer" in relation to a body corporate, includes a director, manager or secretary. See **Section 567 CAMA Cap. C20 LFN 2004**

**Cross Reference**

On creation of register of members, see **section 84 CAMA Cap. C20, LFN 2004**

On obligation of disclosure of substantial interest in a public company, see **section 95 CAMA Cap. C20, LFN 2004**

**Cases**

The Corporate Affairs Commission is conferred with the responsibility of registering companies operating in Nigeria by Statute, and under the said statute it can prohibit and restrict certain names to be registered. ***Mustapha v. CAC* (2009) Vol. 43 W.R.N. 1-171 pg 156**

**For Further Reading**

On shareholders see, Olufemi Amao and Kenneth Amaeshi "Galvanizing Shareholder Activism: A Prerequisite for Effective Corporate Governance and Accountability in Nigeria" ( **2008) 82 Journal of Business Ethics 119-130.**

## 98. Registration of interests to be disclosed

The matter relating to beneficial interests in shares [1] required by section 94 of this Act shall be entered in a different part of the register of interests which shall be so made up that the entries inscribed in it appear in chronological order.

**Notes**
**Section 98**

1. "Shares" means the interests in a company's share capital of a member who is entitled to share in the capital or income of such company; and except where a distinction between stock and shares is expressed or implied, includes stock. See **Section 567 CAMA, Cap. C20, LFN, 2004.**

Cross Reference

On power of company to require disclosure of interest, see **section 94 CAMA Cap. C20, LFN 2004**

On creation of register of interest, see **section 97 CAMA Cap. C20 LFN 2004**

---

*PART V*

*Share capital*

*Minimum share capital*

## 99. Authorised minimum share capital

(1) Where, after the commencement of this Act, a memorandum[1] delivered to the Commission[2] under section 35 of this Act states that the association to be registered is to be registered with shares[3], the amount of the share capital[4] stated in the memorandum[1] to be registered shall not be less than the authorised minimum share capital[5] and not less than 25 per cent of that capital shall be taken by the subscribers of the memorandum.[1]

(2) No company[6] having a share capital[4] shall, after the commencement of this Act, be registered with an authorised share capital[5] less than the authorised minimum share capital.[5]

(3) Where, at the commencement of this Act, the authorised share capital[5] of an existing company[6] is less than the authorised minimum share capital[5], the company[6] shall, not later than 30 days after the appointed day, increase the share capital[4] to an amount not less than the authorised minimum share capital[5] of which not less than 25 per cent shall be issued.

(4) Subject to subsection (3) of this section and to section 103 of this Act, where a company[6] is registered with shares,[3] its issued capital[7] shall not at any time be less than 25 per cent of the authorised share capital.[5]

(5) Where a company[6] to which subsections (3) and (4) of this section apply fails to comply with the applicable subsection, it shall be liable to a fine of N2,500, and every officer[8] who is in default

shall be liable to a fine ofN50 for every day during which the default continues.

---

**Notes**
**Section 99**

1. "Memorandum" means the memorandum of association of a company as originally framed or as altered in pursuance of any enactment. See **Section 567 CAMA, Cap. C20, LFN 2004** .
   "Memorandum of Association" means a legal document, setting up a corporation, either with or without limited liability, and including the company's name, purpose, and duration. **See Garner B. (ed) Black's Law Dictionary, 8th ed**
2. "Commission" means the Corporate Affairs Commission established under section 1 of this Act. See **Section 567 CAMA Cap. C20, LFN 2004**
3. "Shares" see "share." It means the interest in a company's share capital of a member who is entitled to share in the capital or income of such company. See **Section 567 CAMA, Cap. C20, LFN, 2003.**
4. "Share capital" means one of the definite numbers of equal parts into which the capital stock of a corporation or joint stock company is divided. **See Garner, B. (ed) Black's Law Dictionary, 8th ed.**
5. "Authorised share capital" means the share capital of a company at any given time. **See Section 567 CAMA, Cap. C20, LFN, 20043.Section 99(2).** " Authorised minimum share capital" means N10,000 in the case of a private company and N500,00 in the case of a public company. See **Section 567 CAMA, Cap. C20, LFN, 2004.**
6. "Company" means a company formed and registered under this Act or, as the case may be, formed and registered in Nigeria before and in existence on the commencement of this Act. See **Section 567 CAMA, Cap. C20, LFN, 2004.**
7. "Issued share capital" in relation to any reduction has the meaning assigned to it by section 105(2) of this Act , See **Section 567 CAMA, Cap. C20, LFN 2004.**
8. "Officer" in relation to a body corporate, includes a director, manager or secretary. See **Section 567 CAMA, Cap. C20, LFN 2004.**

---

**Cases**

Shares are in the nature of personal estate and freely transferable but subject to statutory restrictions and the articles of the company. Members in a company have a right to transfer shares belonging to them therein and this right is unfettered unless there is an express restriction to that effect in the articles or constitution of the company. ***N.R.I. Ltd v. Oranusi*** **[2011] ALL F.W.L.R part 577, 625-824 at p.765**

**For Further Reading**

On share capital, company, See Sofowora, M.O **Modern Nigerian Company Law** Soft Associates, 2[nd] Edition 2002. Pages 13, 304, 405, On Corporate Affairs Commission, Incorporation of Companies, Membership of a company, and Share Capital see:
Ogbuanya C.S. Nelson **Essentials of Corporate Law Practice in Nigeria** Novena Publishers Limited 2012
Sasegbon Deji & Co **Companies and Allied Matters Law and Practice** (NCAMLP) DSC Publications Ltd 2006

## 100. Alteration of share capital by consolidation, etc.

(1) A company[1] having a share capital[2] may in general meeting[3] and not otherwise alter the conditions of its memorandum[4] to the following extent, that is to say, it may-

(a) consolidate and divide all or any part of its share capital[2] into shares[5] of larger amount than its existing shares[5];

(b) convert all or any of its paid-up shares[5] into stock,[6] and re-convert that stock[6] into paid-up shares[5] of any denomination;

(c) subdivide its shares[5] or any of them, into shares[5] of smaller amount than is fixed by the memorandum,[4] so however, that in the subdivision the proportion between the amount paid and the amount, if any, unpaid on each reduced share[5] shall be the same as it was in the case of the share[5] from which the reduced share[5] is derived;

(d) cancel shares[5] which, at the date of the passing of the resolution[7] in that behalf, have not been taken or agreed to be taken by any person, and diminish the amount of its share capital[2] by the amount of the shares[5] so cancelled.

(2) Cancellation of shares[5] made in pursuance of this section shall not be deemed to be a reduction of share capital[2] within the meaning of this Act.

---

**Notes**
**Section 100(1)**

1. "Company" means a company formed and registered under this Act or, as the case may be, formed and registered in Nigeria before and in existence on the commencement of this Act. See **Section 567 CAMA, Cap. C20, LFN, 2004.**
2. "Share capital" means one of the definite numbers of equal parts into which the capital stock of a corporation or joint stock company is divided.. **See Garner, B. (ed) Black's Law Dictionary, 8th ed.**

3. "Meeting" means the gathering of people to discuss or act on matters in which they have a common interest. See **Garner B. (ed) Black's Law Dictionary, 8th ed.**
4. "Memorandum" means the memorandum of association of a company as originally framed or as altered in pursuance of any enactment. See **Section 567 CAMA, Cap. C20, LFN 2004** .

   "Memorandum of Association" means a legal document, setting up a corporation, either with or without limited liability, and including the company's name, purpose, and duration. **See Garner B. (ed) Black's Law Dictionary, 8th ed**
5. "Shares" means the interest in a company's share capital of a member who is entitled to share in the capital or income of such company. See **Section 567 CAMA, Cap. C20, LFN, 2004**
6. "Stock" means the value of the shares in a company that has been sold. **See Oxford Advanced Learner's Dictionary 6th edition**
7. "Resolution" means a main motion that formally expresses the sense, will or action of a deliberative assembly. See **Garner B. (ed) Black's Law Dictionary, 8th ed.**

Cross Reference

On minimum authorized share capital of a company, see **section 99, CAMA Cap. C20, LFN 2004**

---

**Cases**

Shares are in the nature of personal estate and freely transferable but subject to statutory restrictions and the articles of the company. Members in a company have a right to transfer shares belonging to them therein and this right is unfettered unless there is an express restriction to that effect in the articles or constitution of the company. ***N.R.I. Ltd v. Oranusi*** **[2011] ALL F.W.L.R part 577, 625-824 at p.765**

**For Further Reading**

On share capital, company, See Sofowora, M.O **Modern Nigerian Company Law** Soft Associates, 2nd Edition 2002. Pages 13, 304, 405,

## 101. Notice required where shares and stock consolidated, etc.

(1) If a company [1] having share capital [2] has-

(a) consolidated and divided its share capital [2] into shares [3] of larger amount than its existing shares [3]; or

(b) converted any shares [3] into stock [4]; or

(c) re-converted stock [4] into shares [3]; or

(d) subdivided its shares [3] or any of them; or

(e) cancelled any shares, [3] otherwise than in connection with a reduction of share capital [2] under section 105 of this Act, it shall within one month after so doing, give notice of it to the Commission[5] specifying, as the case may be, the shares[3] consolidated, divided, converted, subdivided, cancelled, or the stock [4] re-converted.

(2) If default is made in complying with this section, the company[1] and every officer [6] of the company [1] who is in default shall be liable to a fine of N50 for every day during which the default continues.

---

**Notes**
**Section 101(1)**

1. "Company" means a company formed and registered under this Act or, as the case may be, formed and registered in Nigeria before and in existence on the commencement of this Act. See **Section 567 CAMA, Cap. C20, LFN, 2004.**
2. "Share capital" means one of the definite numbers of equal parts into which the capital stock of a corporation or joint stock company is divided. **See Garner, B. (ed) Black's Law Dictionary, 8th ed.**
3. "Shares" means the interest in a company's share capital of a member who is entitled to share in the capital or income of such company. See **Section 567 CAMA, Cap. C20, LFN, 2004**
4. "Stock" means the value of the shares in a company that has been sold. **See Oxford Advanced Learner's Dictionary 6 th edition**
5. "Commission" means the Corporate Affairs Commission established under section 1 of this Act. See **Section 567 CAMA Cap. C20, LFN 2004**

Cross Reference

On minimum authorized share capital of a company, see **section 99, CAMA Cap. C20, LFN 2004**

---

**Cases**

Shares are in the nature of personal estate and freely transferable but subject to statutory restrictions and the articles of the company. Members in a company have a right to transfer shares belonging to them therein and this right is unfettered unless there is an express restriction to that effect in the articles or constitution of the company. ***N.R.I. Ltd v. Oranusi*** **[2011] ALL F.W.L.R part 577, 625-824 at p.765**

**For Further Reading**

On share capital, company, See Sofowora, M.O **Modern Nigerian Company** *Law* Soft Associates, 2 nd Edition 2002. Pages 13, 304, 405
Akaki, J.O, **Essays on Company Law,** University of Lagos Press, 1992
Irukwu, J.O, **The Company, The Shareholder, The Director and The Law,** Fourth Dimension Publishing Co. Ltd 1994

Ola, C.S. **Company Law in Nigeria,** Heinemann Educational Books (Nig), 1999
Adeogun, A.A, "Membership of a Company," ***Essays on Company Law*** Pages 73 - 75

## 102. Increase of share capital and notice of increase

(1) A company [1] having a share capital, [2] whether or not the shares[3] have been converted into stock [4], may in general meeting [5] and not otherwise, increase its share capital [2] by new shares [3] of such amount as it thinks expedient.

(2) Where a company [1] has increased its share capital [2] it shall, within 15 days after the passing of the resolution [6] authorising the increase, give to the Commission [7] notice of the increase and the Commission[7] shall record the increase.

(3) Where, in connection with the increase of shares, [3] any approval is required to be obtained under any enactment other than this Act, the Commission [7] may on application by a company [1] extend the time within which to give notice of the increase to the Commission.[7]

(4) The notice to be given under this section shall include any particulars prescribed with respect to the classes of shares [3] affected and the condition subject to which the new shares [3] have been or are to be issued and the notice shall be accompanied by a printed copy of the resolution [6] authorising the increase.

(5) If default is made in complying with the provisions of this section, the company [1] in default shall be liable to a fine ofN50 for every day during which the default continues.

---

**Notes**

**Section 102(1)**

1. "Company" means a company formed and registered under this Act or, as the case may be, formed and registered in Nigeria before and in existence on the commencement of this Act. See **Section 567 CAMA, Cap. C20, LFN, 2004.**
2. "Share capital" means one of the definite numbers of equal parts into which the capital stock of a corporation or joint stock company is divided. **See Garner, B. (ed) Black's Law Dictionary, 8th ed.**
3. "Shares" see "share". It means the interest in a company's share capital of a member who is entitled to share in the capital or income of such company. See **Section 567 CAMA, Cap. C20, LFN, 2004**
4. "Stock" means the value of the shares in a company that has been sold. **See Oxford Advanced Learner's Dictionary 6th edition**

5. "Meeting" means the gathering of people to discuss or act on matters in which they have a common interest. See **Garner B. (ed) Black's Law Dictionary, 8th ed.**

**Section 102(2)**

6. "Resolution" means a main motion that formally expresses the sense, will or action of a deliberative assembly. See **Garner, B. (ed) Black's Law Dictionary, 8th ed.**
7. "Commission" means the Corporate Affairs Commission established under section 1 of this Act. See **Section 567 CAMA Cap. C20, LFN 2004**
8. "Officer" in relation to a body corporate, officer includes a director, manager or secretary **. See Section 567 CAMA, Cap. C20, LFN 2004**

**Cross Reference**

On minimum authorized share capital of a company, see **section 99, CAMA Cap. C20, LFN 2004**

On types of resolutions, **see section 233 CAMA Cap. C20, LFN 2004**

---

**Cases**

Generally companies speak or express their decisions through resolutions, which must be validly passed. No member of a company has a right to unilaterally commit the company on any matter without its consent and approval. Let me emphatically say that no member of a company is allowed to wake up one morning and sell off the company. ***New Resources Int'l Ltd. & Anor.v. EjikeOranusi*** **(2010) LPELR-CA/L/461/08**

By the provisions of Companies and Allied Matters Act, Section 115, shares are in the nature of personal estate and freely transferable but subject to statutory restrictions and the articles of the company. Members in a company have a right to transfer shares belonging to them therein and this right is unfettered unless there is an express restriction to that effect in the articles or constitution of the company. ***N.R.I. Ltd v. Oranusi*** **(2011) ALL F.W.L.R part 577.625-824 at p.765** .

**For Further Reading**

On Corporate Affairs Commission, Incorporation of Companies, Membership of a company, and Share Capital see:

Orojo, J. Ola **Company Law and Practice in Nigeria** 3rd Edition, Mbeyi & Associates (Lagos, Nigeria) 1992.

Ogbuanya C.S. Nelson **Essentials of Corporate Law Practice in Nigeria** Novena Publishers Limited 2012

Sasegbon Deji & Co **Companies and Allied Matters Law and Practice** (NCAMLP) DSC Publications Ltd 2006

## 103. Increase of paid-up capital on increase of shares

Where a company [1] passes a resolution [2] increasing its authorised share capital, [3] the increase shall not take effect unless-

(a) within six months of giving notice of the increase to the Commission[4] not less than 25 per cent of the share capital [5] including the increase has been issued; and

(b) the directors [6] have delivered to the Commission [4] a statutory declaration[7] verifying that fact.

---

**Notes**

**Section 103**

1. "Company" means a company formed and registered under this Act or, as the case may be, formed and registered in Nigeria before and in existence on the commencement of this Act. See **Section 567 CAMA, Cap. C20, LFN, 2004.**
2. "Resolution" means a main motion that formally expresses the sense, will or action of a deliberative assembly. See **Garner B. (ed) Black's Law Dictionary, 8th ed.**
3. "Authorised share capital" means the share capital of a company at any given time. **See Garner B. (ed) Black's Law Dictionary, 8th ed.**
4. "Commission" means the Corporate Affairs Commission established under section 1 of this Act. See **Section 567 CAMA Cap. C20, LFN 2004**
5. "Share capital" means one of the definite numbers of equal parts into which the capital stock of a corporation or joint stock company is divided. **See Garner, B. (ed) Black's Law Dictionary, 8th ed.**
6. "Director" mean persons duly appointed by the company to direct and manage the business of the company. See **Garner B. (ed) Black's Law Dictionary, 8th ed**

   Director includes any person occupying the position of director by whatever name called, and includes any person in accordance with whose directions or instructions the directors are accustomed to act. See **Section 567 CAMA, Cap. C20, LFN 2004**
7. "Statutory declaration" means a declaration voluntarily made under the Oaths Act 1963 and in Nigeria includes one so made under any other enactment or law providing for the taking of voluntary declaration. See **Section 567 CAMA, Cap. C20, LFN 2004**

**Cross Reference**

On minimum authorized share capital of a company, see **section 99, CAMA Cap. C20, LFN 2004**

On types of resolution, see **section 233 CAMA Cap. C20, LFN 2004**

---

**Cases**

Generally companies speak or express their decisions through resolutions, which must be validly passed. No member of a company has a right to unilaterally commit the company on any matter without its consent and approval. Let me emphatically say that no member of a company is allowed to wake up one morning and sell off the company. ***New Resources Int'l Ltd. & Anor. v. Ejike Oranusi*** **(2010) LPELR-CA/L/461/08**

By the provisions of Companies and Allied Matters Act, Section 115, shares are in the nature of personal estate and freely transferable but subject to statutory restrictions and the articles of the company. Members in a company have a right to transfer shares belonging to them therein and this right is unfettered unless there is an express restriction to that effect in the articles or constitution of the company. ***N.R.I. Ltd v. Oranusi*** **(2011) ALL F.W.L.R part 577.625-824 at p.765** .

**For Further Reading**

On Corporate Affairs Commission, Incorporation of Companies, Membership of a company, and Share Capital see:

Orojo, J. Ola **Company Law and Practice in Nigeria** 3rd Edition, Mbeyi & Associates (Lagos, Nigeria) 1992.

Ogbuanya C.S. Nelson **Essentials of Corporate Law Practice in Nigeria** Novena Publishers Limited 2012

Sasegbon Deji & Co **Companies and Allied Matters Law and Practice** (NCAMLP) DSC Publications Ltd 2006

## 104. Power for unlimited company to provide reserve share capital on re-registration

If an unlimited company[1] resolves to be registered as a limited company[2] under this Act, it may-

(a) increase the nominal amount of its share capital [3] by increasing the nominal amount of each of its shares, [4] but subject to the condition that no part of the increased capital[5] shall be capable of being called up except in the event and for the purpose of the company [2] being wound up[6]; or

(b) provide that a specified portion of its uncalled share capital[3] shall not be capable of being called up except in the event and for the purposes of the company [2] being wound up.[6]

---

**Notes**
**Section 104**

1. Unlimited company" means a company not having any limit on the liability of its members. See **Section 21 CAMA Cap. C20 LFN 2004.**
2. "Company" means a company formed and registered under this Act or, as the case may be, formed and registered in Nigeria before and in existence on the commencement of this Act. See **Section 567 CAMA, Cap. C20, LFN, 2004.**
3. "Share capital" means a fund representing the nominal value of shares issued by a registered company. See **Martins E. (ed.) Oxford Dictionary of Law 4th ed.**
   "Shares" see "share. It means the interests in a company's share capital of a member who is entitled to share in the capital or income of such company; and except where a distinction between stock and shares is expressed or implied, includes stock; See **Section 567 CAMA, Cap. C20, LFN, 2004.**
4. "Capital" means money or assets invested, or available for investments, in a business; the total amount or value of a Corporation's stock. See **Garner B. (ed) Black's Law Dictionary 8 th ed.**
5. "Wound up" see "winding up." It means the process of settling accounts and liquidating assets in anticipation of a partnership's or corporation's dissolution. See **Garner B. (ed) Black's Law Dictionary, 8th ed**

**Cross Reference**

On minimum authorized share capital of a company, see **section 99, CAMA Cap. C20, LFN 2004**

On modes of winding up a company, see **section 400 CAMA Cap. C20, LFn 2004**

**For Further Reading**

On Corporate Affairs Commission, Incorporation of Companies, Membership of a company, and Share Capital see:

Ogbuanya C.S. Nelson Essentials of Corporate Law Practice in Nigeria Novena Publishers Limited 2012

Sasegbon Deji & Co **Companies and Allied Matters Law and Practice** (NCAMLP) DSC Publications Ltd 2006

On Company, Winding up, Membership, See Asomugha, E. Maduelosi **Company Law in Nigeria under the Companies and Allied Matters Act**

*Reduction of share capital*

## 105.Restriction on reduction of issued share capital

(1) Except as authorised by this Act, a company [1] having a share capital[2] shall not reduce its issued share capital. [2]

(2) For the purposes of this and other sections relating to reduction of share capital[2], any issue of share capital [2] shall include

the share premium account [3] and any capital [4] redemption reserve account[5] of a company, [1] and "issued share capital" [6] shall be construed accordingly.

**Notes**
**Section 105**

1. "Company": means a company formed and registered under this Act or, as the case may be, formed and registered in Nigeria before and in existence on the commencement of this Act. See **Section 567 CAMA, Cap. C20, LFN 2004.**
2. "Share Capital": See "Capital". It means a fund representing the nominal value of shares issued by a registered company . See **Martins E. (ed) Oxford Dictionary of Law 7 th ed.**
3. "Share Premium account" means the account where a sum equal to the aggregate amount or value of the premium from shares issued at a premium by a company is transferred. See **section 120 (2) CAMA, Cap. C20, LFN 2004.**
4. "Capital" means money or assets invested, or available for investments, in a business; the total amount or value of a Corporation's stock. See **Garner B. (ed) Black's Law Dictionary 8 th ed.**
5. "Reserve Account": See" Impound Account". It means an account of accumulated funds held by a lender for payments of taxed, insurance or other periodic debts against real property. **Garner B. (ed.) Black's Law Dictionary 8th ed.**

**Cross Reference**

On powers of the Company to issue shares up to the total number authorized in its memorandum of association, see **section 117 CAMA Cap. C20, LFN 2004**

**Cases**

The definition of a company in section 650 of Companies and Allied Matters Act puts the matter beyond doubt. It defines a 'company' or 'existing' to mean....a company formed and registered in Nigeria before and in existence on the commencement of this Act. ***Agro Allied Dev. Ent. Ltd. v. Reefer*** **(2009) vol. 31 W.R.N 1-185 at pg 7** .

## 106. Special resolution for reduction of share capital

(1) Subject to confirmation by the court, [1] a company[2] having share capital[3] may, if so authorised by its articles, [4] by special resolution[5] reduce its share capital [3] in any way.

(2) In particular, and without prejudice to subsection (1) of this section, the company [2] may-

(a) extinguish or reduce the liability on any of its shares [6] in respect of share capital [3] not paid up; or

(b) either with or without extinguishing or reducing liability on any of its shares, [6] cancel any paid-up share capital [3] which is lost or unrepresented by available assets [7]; or

(c) either with or without extinguishing or reducing liability on any of its shares [6], cancel any paid-up share capital [3] which is in excess of the company's [2] wants,

and the company [2] may, if and so far as is necessary, alter its memorandum[8] by reducing the amount of its share capital[3] and of its shares [6] accordingly.

(3) A special resolution [4] under this section shall in this Act be referred to as "a resolution for reducing share capital."

---

**Notes**
**Section 106**

1. "Court" the Court used in relation to a company, means the Federal High Court, and to the extent to which application may be made to it as; court includes the Court of Appeal and the Supreme Court of Nigeria. See **Section 567 CAMA, Cap C2O, LFN 2004.**
2. "Company" means a company formed and registered under this Act or, as the case may be, formed and registered in Nigeria before and in existence on the commencement of this Act. **See Section 567 CAMA, Cap C2O, LFN 2004**
3. "Share capital" see "Capital." It means a fund representing the nominal value of shares issued by a registered company. See **Martins E. (ed) Oxford Dictionary of Law 7 th ed.**
4. "Special resolution": A resolution shall be a special resolution when it has been passed by not less than three fourths of the votes cast by such members of the company as, being entitled to do so, vote in person or by proxy at a general meeting of which 21 days' notice, specifying the intention to propose the resolution as a special resolution, has been duly given: **See Section 233 CAMA, Cap C20, LFN 2004.**
5. "Articles" means the articles of association of a company, as originally framed or as altered by special resolution including so far as they apply to the regulations contained in table A in the first schedules of the companies Act, 1922 or in that table as altered by any subsequent enactment or reprint of the laws, or in table A in schedule 1 to this Act. See **section 567 of CAMA Cap C20 LFN, 2004**
6. "Shares" means the interests in a company's share capital of a member who is entitled to share in the capital or income of such company; and except where a distinction between stock and shares is expressed or implied, includes stock See **Section 567 CAMA, Cap C2O, LFN 2004.**
7. "Assets" means an item that is owned and has value. See

**Garner B (ed.) Black's Law Dictionary 8th ed.**

8. "Memorandum" means the memorandum of association of a company as originally framed or as altered in pursuance of any enactment. See **Section 567 CAMA, Cap C2O, LFN 2004.**

Cross Reference

Special Resolution is passed by not less than three fourths of the votes cast by such members of the company as, being entitled to do so, vote in person or by proxy at a general meeting of which 21 days' notice, specifying the intention to propose the resolution as a special resolution, has been duly given: **see section 223 (2) of this Act.**

---

**Cases**

Generally companies speak or express their decisions through resolutions, which must be validly passed. No member of a company has a right to unilaterally commit the company on any matter without its consent and approval. Let me emphatically say that no member of a company is allowed to wake up one morning and sell off the company. ***New Resources Int'l Ltd. & Anor. v. Ejike Oranusi (2010) LPELR-CA/L/461/08.***

For further reading on resolutions, company, share capital see, Sofowora, M.O *Modern Nigerian Company Law* Soft Associates, 2[nd] Edition 2002.

## 107. Application to court for order of confirmation

(1) Where a company [1] has passed a resolution [2] for reducing share capital,[3] it may apply to the court [4] for an order confirming the reduction.

(2) If the proposed reduction of share capital [3] involves either-

(a) diminution of liability in respect of unpaid share capital [3]; or

(b) subject to subsection (6) of this section, the payment to a shareholder[5] of any paid-up share capital, [3]

and in any other case if the court [4] so directs, subsection (3), (4) and (5) of this section shall have effect.

(3) Every creditor [6] of the company [1] who at the date fixed by the court[4] is entitled to any debt [7] or claim which, if that date were the commencement of the winding up [8] of the company, [1] would be admissible in proof against the company, [1] shall be entitled to object to the reduction of capital [9].

(4) The court [4] shall settle a list of creditors [6] entitled to object, and for that purpose-

(a) shall ascertain, as far as possible without requiring an application from any creditor, [6] the names of those creditors[6] and the nature and amount of the debts [7] or claims;

(b) may publish notices fixing a day or days within which creditors[6] not entered on the list are to claim to be so entered or are to be excluded from the right of objecting to the reduction of capital. [9]

(5) If a creditor [6] entered on the list whose debt [7] or claim is not discharged or has not been determined does not consent to the reduction, the court [4] may, if it thinks fit, dispense with the consent of that creditor, [6] on the company [1] securing payment of his debt [7] or claim by appropriating (as the court [4] may direct) the following amount if-

(a) the company [1] admits the full amount of the debt [7] or claim or, though not admitting it, is willing to provide for it, then the full amount of the debt [7] or claim;

(b) the company [1] does not admit, and is not willing to provide for, the full amount of the debt [7] or claim, or if the amount is contingent or not ascertained, then an amount fixed by the court[4] after the like enquiry and adjudication as if the company[1] were being wound up [8] by the court. [4]

(6) If a proposed reduction of share capital [3] involves either the diminution of any liability [4] in respect of unpaid share capital [3] or the payment to any shareholder [5] of any paid-up share capital, [3] the court[7] may, if having regard to any special circumstances of the case it thinks proper to do so, direct that subsections (3) to (5) of this section shall not apply as regards any class or any classes of creditors. [6]

---

**Notes**
**Section 107**

1. "Company" means a company formed and registered under this Act or, as the case may be, formed and registered in Nigeria before and in existence on the commencement of this Act. **See section 567, CAMA, Cap C20, LFN 2004**
2. "Resolution": A main motion that formally expresses the sense, will or action of a deliberative assembly. See **Garner B. (ed) Black's Law Dictionary, 8th ed.**
3. "Share capital": See Capital; means a fund representing the nominal value of shares issued by a registered company. **See Martins E. (ed) Oxford Dictoionary of Law 7th ed.**

4. "Liability" means the quality or state of being legally obligated or accountable; legal responsibility to another or to society, enforceable by civil remedy or criminal punishment. **Garner B. (ed) Black's Law Dictionary, 8th ed.**
5. "Shareholder": one who owns or holds a share or shares in a company especially a corporation. **Garner B. (ed) Black's Law Dictionary, 8 th ed.**
6. "Creditor" means one to whom a debt is owed; one who gives credit for money or goods. **Garner B. (ed) Black's Law Dictionary, 8 th ed.**
7. "Court" or "the Court" used in relation to a company, means the Federal High Court, and to the extent to which application may be made to it as; court includes the Court of Appeal and the Supreme Court of Nigeria See **Section 567 CAMA, Cap C2O, LFN 2004.**
8. "Debt" means the aggregate of all existing claims against a person, entity or state See **Garner B. (ed) Black's Law Dictionary, 9 th ed.**
9. "Winding up" means the process of settling accounts and liquidating assets in anticipation of a partnership's or a corporation's dissolution . **Garner, B. (ed) Black's Law Dictionary, 8 th ed.**

**Cross Reference**

On Winding up of Companies, see generally Part XV **CAMA, Cap. C20, LFN 2004**

---

**Case**

A Court is duty bound to confine its decisions to issues raised by the parties. The Court has no power to formulate cases for the parties or to speculate on the evidence parties ought to proffer otherwise it might find itself covered by the dust of conflict. See ***Anambra State Envi. Sani. Auth. v. Ekwenem*** **(2009) Vol. 45 W.R.N. 1-175 at p.12**

**108.Court order confirming reduction (1) The court, if satisfied-**

(a) with respect to every creditor [1] of the company[2] who under section 107 of this Act is entitled to object to the reduction of capital[3], that either-

(i) his consent to the reduction has been obtained; or

(ii) his debt[4] or claim has been discharged or has determined, or has been secured; and

(b) that the share capital [3] does not by this reduction fall below the authorised mini-mum share capital, [4]

may make an order confirming the reduction on such terms and conditions as it thinks fit.

(2) Where the Court [4] so orders, it may also-

(a) if for any special reason it thinks it proper to do so, make an order directing that the company [2] shall, during such period (commencing on or at any time after the date of the order) as is specified in the order, add to its name as its last words "and reduced";

(b) make an order requiring the company [2] to publish (as the court[4] directs) the reasons for reduction of capital [3] or such other information in regard to it as the court [4] thinks expedient with a view to giving proper information to the public and (if the court [4] thinks fit) the causes which led to the reduction.

(3) Where the company [2] is ordered to add to its name the words "and reduced", those words shall, until the expiration of the period specified in the order, be deemed to be part of the company's [2] name.

---

**Notes**
**Section108**

1. "Creditor" means one to whom a debt is owed; one who gives credit for money or goods. See **Garner, B. (ed) Black's Law Dictionary, 8 th ed.**
2. "Company" means a company formed and registered under this Act or, as the case may be, formed and registered in Nigeria before and in existence on the commencement of this Act. See **Section 567 CAMA, CAP C2O, LFN 2004.**
3. "Capital" means Money or assets invested, or available for investments, in a business; the total amount or value of a Corporation's stock, **Garner, B. (ed) Black's Law Dictionary 9 th ed.**
4. "Court" " or "the Court" used in relation to a company, means the Federal High Court, and to the extent to which application may be made to it as; court includes the Court of Appeal and the Supreme Court of Nigeria. See **Section 567 CAMA, CAP C2O, LFN 2004.**

---

## 109. Registration of order and minutes of reduction

(1) The Commission [1], on production to it of the order of the court[2] confirming the reduction of a company's [3] share capital [4], and the delivery to it of a copy of the order and of minutes of the meeting[5] of the company[3] (approved by the court) showing, with respect to the company's [3] share capital [4] as altered by the order-

(a) the amount of the share capital [4];

(b) the number of shares [6] into which it is to be divided, and the amount of each share, [6] and

(c) the amount (if any) at the date of the registration deemed to be paid up on each share, [6] shall register the order and minutes.

(2) On the registration of the order and minutes, and not before, the resolution [7] for reducing share capital [4] as confirmed by the order so registered shall take effect.

(3) A notice of the registration shall be published in such manner as the court [2] may direct.

(4) The Commission [1] shall certify the registration of the order and minutes; and the certificate-

(a) may be either signed by the Registrar-General [8] or authenticated by its official seal;

(b) shall be prima facie evidence that all the requirements of this Act with respect to the reduction of share capital [4] have been complied with, and that the company's [3] share capital[4] is as stated in the minutes.

(5) The minutes, when registered, shall be deemed to be substituted for the corresponding part of the company's [3] memorandum[9], and valid and alterable as if it had been originally contained in it.

(6) The substitution of such minutes for part of the company's memorandum[8] shall be deemed an alteration of the memorandum [9].

---

**Notes**

**Section 109**

1. "Commission" Commission means Corporate Affairs Commission. See **Section 567 CAMA, Cap. C20, LFN 2004.**
2. "Court Order" is as a decision that is made in a Court of Law about what must happen in a particular situation. see **Oxford Advanced Learner's Dictionary 6th ed.**
3. "Company": means a company formed and registered under this Act or, as the case may be, formed and registered in Nigeria before and in existence on the commencement of this Act. See **Section 567 CAMA, Cap. C2O, LFN 2004.**
4. "Share Capital" means any of the units of equal value into which a company is divided and sold to raise money. People who owns shares receives part of the company profit. See **Oxford Advanced Learners Dictionary, New 7th Edition** "Share Capital": See Capital; means a fund representing the nominal value of shares issued by a registered company. See **Martins E. (ed) Oxford Dictionary of Law 7 th ed.**
5. "Meeting" means the gathering of people to discuss or act on matters in which they have a common interest. See **Garner B. (ed) Black's Law Dictionary, 8th ed.**

6. "Shares" see "share". It means the interests in a company's share capital of a member who is entitled to share in the capital or income of such company; and except where a distinction between stock and shares is expressed or implied, includes stock. See **Section 567 CAMA, Cap C2O, LFN 2004.**
7. "Resolution": A main motion that formally expresses the sense, will or action of a deliberative assembly. See **Garner B. (ed) Black's Law Dictionary, 8th ed.**
8. **"Registrar-General"** means the Registrar-general appointed under section 8. **See part 1 of the first schedule of CAMA, Cap C20, LFN, 2004.**
9. "Memorandum" of association as a legal document, setting up a corporation, either with or without limited liability, and including the company's name, purpose, and duration. **Garner B. (ed) Black's Law Dictionary, 8th ed.** "Memorandum" means the memorandum of association of a company as originally framed or as altered in pursuance of any enactment. See **section 567 CAMA Cap C20 LFN 2004**

Cross Reference

On the issue of and effect of certificate of incorporation, see **section 36(6) CAMA, Cap C20 LFN 2004**

---

**For Further Reading**

On meetings, minutes, company and share capital see, Orojo, J. Ola **Company Law and Practice in Nigeria** 3rd Edition, Mbeyi & Associates (Lagos, Nigeria) 1992

## 110. Liability of members on reduced shares

(1) Where a company's [1] share capital[2] is reduced, a member [3] of the company[1] (past or present) shall not be liable in respect of any share[4] to any call or contribution exceeding in amount the difference (if any) between the amount of the share [4] as fixed by the minutes and the amount paid on the share [4] or the reduced amount (if any), which is deemed to have been paid on it, as the case may be.

(2) Subsections (3) and (4) of this section shall apply if-

(a) a creditor[5], entitled in respect of a debt [6] or claim to object to the reduction of share capital [2], by reason of his ignorance of the proceedings for reduction of share capital[2], or of their nature and effect with respect to his claim, is not entered on the list of creditors [5]; and

(b) after the reduction of capital [2], the company [1] is unable (within the meaning of section 409 of this Act) to pay the amount of his debt[6] or claim.

(3) Every person who was a member [3] of the company [1] at the date of the registration of the order for reduction and minutes, shall be liable to contribute for the payment of the debt [6] or claim in question an amount not exceeding that which he would have been liable to contribute if the company [1] had commenced to be wound up[7] on the day before that date.

(4) If the company [1] is wound up, [7] the Court, [8] on application of the creditor [5] in question and proof of ignorance referred to in subsection (2) (a), of this section, may (if it thinks fit), settle accordingly a list of persons so liable to contribute, and make and enforce calls and orders on the contributories [9] settled on the list, as if they were ordinary contributories [9] in a winding up. [7]

(5) Nothing in this section shall affect the rights of the contributories[9] among themselves.

---

**Notes**
**Section 110**

1. Company" means a company formed and registered under this Act or, as the case may be, formed and registered in Nigeria before and in existence on the commencement of this Act. See **Section 567 CAMA, Cap C20, LFN 2004.**
2. "Share Capital": See Capital; means a fund representing the nominal value of shares issued by a registered company. See **Martins E. (ed) Oxford Dictionary of Law 7 th ed.**
3. "Member" includes the heir, executor, administrator or other personal representative, as the case may be, of the member. See **Section 567 CAMA, Cap C20, LFN 2004**
4. "Share": means the interests in a company's share capital of a member who is entitled to share in the capital or income of such company; and except where a distinction between stock and shares is expressed or implied, includes stock. See **Section 567 CAMA, Cap C20, LFN 2004.**
5. "Creditor" means one to whom a debt is owed; one who gives credit for money or goods. **See Garner B. (ed) Black's Law Dictionary, 8 th ed.**
6. "Debt" means the aggregate of all existing claims against a person, entity or state. See **Garner B. (ed) Black's Law Dictionary, 8 th ed.**
7. "Wound up" see "winding up". It means the process of settling accounts and liquidating assets in anticipation of a partnership's or a corporation's dissolution. **See Garner B. (ed) Black's Law Dictionary, 8 th ed.**
8. "Court" or "the Court" used in relation to a company, means the Federal High Court, and to the extent to which application may be made to it as; court includes the Court of Appeal and the Supreme Court of Nigeria see **Section 567 CAMA, Cap C20, LFN2004**
9. "Contributories": See ''Contributory" which means every person liable to contribute to the assets of a company in the event of its being wound up

and for the purposes of all proceedings for determining, and all proceedings prior to the final determination of, the persons who are to be deemed contributories, the expression includes any person alleged to be contributory. See **Section 567 CAMA, Cap. C20, LFN 2004.**

Cross Reference

On duty of a company to keep Minutes of proceedings and the effect, see **section 241, CAMA CAP C20, LFN 2004**

On definition of contributories, liabilities of contributories as past and present members and on death of a member, see **sections 402-406, CAMA CAP C20, LFN 2004**

---

**Cases**

It does not matter if the company's shares are owned substantially by one of the shareholders with only a very small fraction held by one or Few of others. ***Dunlop Nigerian Industries Ltd vs. Forward Nigerian Enterprises Ltd & Fafore*** **(1976) (1) A.L.R.**

## 111. Penalty for concealing name of creditor, etc.

If an officer [1] of the company [2]-

(a) wilfully conceals the name of a creditor [3] entitled to object to the reduction of capital [4]; or

(b) wilfully misrepresents the nature or amount of the debt [5] or claim of any creditor [3]; or

(c) aids, abets or is privy to any such concealment or misrepresentation as is mentioned above,

he shall be guilty of an offence and liable on conviction to a fine of N500

---

**Notes**

**Section 111**

1. "Officer" means a person who holds an office of trust, authority or command. See **Garner, B. (ed) Black's Law Dictionary 8 th ed.**
2. "Company" means a company formed and registered under this Act or, as the case may be, formed and registered in Nigeria before and in existence on the commencement of this Act. **See Section 567 CAMA, Cap C20, LFN 2004.**
3. "Creditor" means one to whom a debt is owed; one who gives credit for money or goods also termed debtee. See **Garner B. (ed) Black's Law Dictionary, 8th ed.**
4. "Capital": Money or assets invested, or available for investments, in a business; the total amount or value of a Corporation's stock. See **Garner, B. (ed) Black's Law Dictionary 8 th ed.**
5. "Debt": means the aggregate of all existing claims against a person, entity or state. See **Garner B. (ed) Black's Law Dictionary, 8 th ed.**

Cross Reference

On on the reduction of share capital, see generally **sections 105-110 CAMA CAP C20, LFN 2004**

On definition of Offence, see **section 2 Criminal Code, CAP C38 LFN 2004**

---

**For Further Reading**

On company, creditors, see Ayua, I.A **Nigerian Company Law** G. Burn (Leighton Buzzard, Bedfordshire, United Kingdom) 1984.

*Miscellaneous matters relating to capital*

## 112. Duty of directors on serious loss of capital

(1) Where the net assets [1] of a public company [2] are half or less of its called-up share capital, [3] the directors [4] shall, not later than 30 days from the earliest day on which that fact is known to a director [4] of the company, [2] duly convene an extraordinary general meeting [5] of the company, [2] for a day not later than 60 days from that day for the purpose of considering whether any, and if so, what steps should be taken to deal with the situation.

(2) If there is a failure to convene an general meeting [5] as required by subsection (1) of this section, each of the directors [4] of the company[2] who-

(a) knowingly and wilfully authorises or permits the failure; or

(b) after the expiry of the period during which that meeting [5] should have been convened, knowingly and wilfully authorises or permits the failure to continue, shall be liable to a fine of N500

(3) Nothing in this section shall authorise the consideration, at a meeting[5] convened in pursuance of subsection (1) of this section, of any matter which could have been considered at that meeting [5] apart from this section.

---

**Notes**
**Section 112**

1. "Assets" means an item that is owned and has value. See **Garner B. (ed.) Black's Law Dictionary, 8 th ed.**
2. "Company" means a company formed and registered under this Act or, as the case may be, formed and registered in Nigeria before and in existence on the commencement of this Act. See **Section 567 CAMA, Cap C20, LFN 2004.**
3. Share Capital" means any of the units of equal value into which a company is divided and sold to raise money. People who owns shares receives part of the company profit. See **Oxford Advanced Learners Dictionary New 7th Edition.** "Share Capital": See Capital; means a fund representing the nominal value of shares issued by a registered company. See **Martins, E. (ed) Oxford Dictionary of Law 7 th ed.**
4. "Director" means any person occupying the position of director by whatever name called; and includes any person in accordance with

whose directions or instructions the directors of the company are accustomed to act. See **Section 567 CAMA, Cap C20, LFN 2004.**

5. "Meeting" means the gathering of people to discuss or act on matters in which they have a common interest. See **Garner B. (ed) Black's Law Dictionary 8th ed.**

Cross Reference

On types of General meeting to be held by a Company, see **sections 211, 213 and 215 CAMA Cap C20 LFN 2004**

On the conduct of extraordinary general meetings, see **section 215 CAMA Cap C20 LFN 2004**

---

**Cases**

A director is a person appointed or elected according to Law, authorized to manage and direct the affairs of a corporation or company. ***Olufosoye v. Fakorede*** **(1993) 1 N.W.L.R 947.** See also ***Longe v. First Bank Nigeria Plc*** **(2006) 3 N.W.L.R 228 at 270.**

**For Further Reading**

On directors see, Bakibinga, D. J. "Directors' Duty to Act Bona Fide in the Interest of the Company" (1990) 39 (2) **The International and Comparative Law Quarterly** 451.

## 113. Power to pay interest out of capital in certain cases

Where any shares [1] of a company [2] are issued for the purposes of raising money to defray the expenses of the construction of any works or buildings or the provision of any plant which cannot be made profitable for a long period, the company [2] may pay interest [3] on so much of that share capital [4] as if for the time being paid up for the period and subject to the conditions and restrictions mentioned in this section, and may charge the same to capital [4] as part of the cost of construction of the work or building or the provision of plant:

Provided that-

(a) no such payment shall be made unless it is authorised by the articles [5] or by special resolution [6];

(b) no such payment, whether authorised by the articles [5] or by special resolution [6], shall be made without the previous sanction of the Commission [7];

(c) before sanctioning any such payment the Commission [7] may, at the expense of the company, [2] appoint a person to inquire and report to it as to the circumstances of the case, and may, before making the appointment, require the company[2] to give security for the payment of the costs of the inquiry;

(d) the payment shall be made only for such period as may be determined by the Commission[7] which shall in no case extend beyond the close of six months after the half year [8] during which the works or buildings have been actually completed or the plant provided;

(e) the rate of interest [3] shall not exceed the current bank rate;

(f) the payment of the interest [3] shall not operate as a reduction of the amount paid up on the shares [1] in respect of which it is paid.

**Notes**
**Section 113**

1. "Shares" means the interests in a company's share capital of a member who is entitled to share in the capital or income of such company; and except where a distinction between stock and shares is expressed or implied, includes stock. See **Section 567 CAMA, Cap C20,LFN 2004.**
2. "Company" means a company formed and registered under this Act or, as the case may be, formed and registered in Nigeria before and in existence on the commencement of this Act. See **Section 567, CAMA, Cap C20, LFN 2004.**
3. "Interest" means the object of any human desire, esp.; advantage or profit of a financial nature. See **Garner B. (ed) Black's Law Dictionary, 8 th ed.**
4. "Capital" means money or assets invested, or available for investments, in a business; the total amount or value of a Corporation's stock **. See Garner, B. (ed) Black's Law Dictionary 8 th ed.**
5. "Articles" means the articles of association of a company, as originally framed or as altered by special resolution, including so far as they apply to the regulations contained in Table A in the First Schedules of the Companies Act, 1922 or in that Table as altered by any subsequent enactment or reprint of the laws, or in Table A in the First Schedule to this Act. See **Section 567, CAMA, Cap C20, LFN 2004.**
6. "Special Resolution" is a resolution that has been passed by not less than three fourths of the votes cast by such members of the company as, being entitled to do so, vote in person or by proxy at a general meeting of which 21 days' notice, specifying the intention to propose the resolution as a special resolution, has been duly given. See **Section 233 CAMA, Cap C20, LFN 2004.**
7. "Commission" Commission means Corporate Affairs Commission. See **Section 567, CAMA, Cap C20, LFN 2004.**
8. "Year" means a period of twelve months. See **section 18 Interpretation Act Cap I23 LFN 2004**

Cross Refernece

On the form and content of the Articles of Association of a Company , see **section 34, CAMA, Cap C20, LFN 2004.**
On types of resolutions see **section 233 CAMA, Cap C20, LFN 2004.**

---

**Cases**
It does not matter if the company's shares are owned substantially by one of the shareholders with only a very small fraction held by one or Few of others. See ***Dunlop Nigerian Industries Ltd vs. Forward Nigerian Enterprises Ltd & Fafore*** **(1976) (1) A.L.R.**

*PART VI*

*Shares*

*Nature of shares*

## 114. Rights and liabilities attached to shares

Subject to the provisions of this Act, the rights [1] and liabilities[2] attaching to the shares[3] of a company[4] shall-

(a) be dependent on the terms of issue and of the company's [4] articles[5]; and

(b) not withstanding anything to the contrary in the terms or the articles[5], include the right to attend any general meeting[6] of the company[4] and vote at such a meeting. [6]

---

**Notes**
**Section 114**

1. "Rights" see "right". It means a legally enforceable claim that another will do or will not do a given act; a recognized and protected interest, the violation of which is wrong. See **Garner B. (ed) Black's Law Dictionary, 8th ed.**
2. "Liabilities" see "liability". It means the quality or state of being legally obligated or accountable; legal responsibility to another or to society, enforceable by civil remedy or criminal punishment. See **Garner B. (ed) Black's Law Dictionary, 8th ed.**
3. "Shares" means the interests in a company's share capital of a member who is entitled to share in the capital or income of such company; and except where a distinction between stock and shares is expressed or implied, includes stock. See **Section 567 CAMA, Cap C20, LFN 2004.**
4. "Company" means a company formed and registered under this Act or, as the case may be, formed and registered in Nigeria before and in

existence on the commencement of this Act. See **section 567, CAMA Cap C20, LFN 2004.**

5. "Articles" means the articles of association of a company, as originally framed or as altered by special resolution, including so far as they apply to the regulations contained in Table A in the First Schedules of the Companies Act, 1922 or in that Table as altered by any subsequent enactment or reprint of the laws, or in Table A in the First Schedule to this Act; See **section 567, CAMA Cap C20, LFN 2004.**
6. "Meeting" means the gathering of people to discuss or act on matters in which they have a common interest. See **Garner B. (ed) Black's Law Dictionary 8th ed.**

**Cross Reference**

On types of General meeting to be held by a Company, see **sections 211, 213 and 215 CAMA Cap C20 LFN 2004**

On the conduct of extraordinary general meetings, see **section 215 CAMA Cap C20 LFN 2004**

---

## 115. Shares as transferable property

The shares[1] or other interests[2] of a member[3] in a company[4] shall be property transferable in the manner provided in articles of association[5] of the company.[4]

---

**Notes**

**Section 115**

1. "Shares" means the interests in a company's share capital of a member who is entitled to share in the capital or income of such company; and except where a distinction between stock and shares is expressed or implied, includes stock. See **Section 567 CAMA, Cap C20, LFN 2004.**
2. "Interests" see "interest". It means the object of any human desire, esp.; advantage or profit of a financial nature. See **Garner B. (ed) Black's Law Dictionary, 8th ed.**
3. "Member": includes the heir, executor, administrator or other personal representative, as the case may be, of the member. See **Section 567 CAMA, Cap C20, LFN 2004.**
4. "Company." means a company formed and registered under this Act or, as the case may be, formed and registered in Nigeria before and in existence on the commencement of this Act. See **Section 567 CAMA, Cap C20, LFN 2004.**
5. "Articles of Association" means the articles of association of a company, as originally framed or as altered by special resolution, including so far as they apply to the regulations contained in Table A in the First Schedules of the Companies Act, 1922 or in that Table as altered by any subsequent enactment or reprint of the laws, or in Table A in the First Schedule to this Act. See **Section 567, CAMA, Cap C20, LFN 2004.**

**Cross Reference**

On form and content of the Articles of Association of a company, see **section 34 CAMA, Cap C20, LFN 2004**
On manner by which shares of a company can be transferred, see **section 151 CAMA, Cap C20, LFN 2004**

---

**Cases**
By the provisions of Companies and Allied Matters Act, Section 115, shares are in the nature of personal estate and freely transferable but subject to statutory restrictions and the articles of the company. Members in a company have a right to transfer shares belonging to them therein and this right is unfettered unless there is an express restriction to that effect in the articles or constitution of the company. ***See N.R.I. Ltd v. Oranusi* [2011] ALL F.W.L.R part 577. 625-824 at p.765** .
**For Further Reading**
On shares, company, articles of Association, see Sofowora, M.O **Modern Nigerian Company Law** Soft Associates, 2nd Edition 2002.

## 116. Prohibition of non-voting and weighted shares

(1) Unless otherwise provided by any other enactment-

(a) any share[1] issued by a company[2] after the date of commencement of this Act, shall carry the right on a poll at a general meeting[3] of the company[2] to one vote in respect of each share[1] and no company[2] may by its articles[4] or otherwise authorise the issue of shares[1] which carry more than one vote in respect of each share[1] or which do not carry any right to vote; and

(b) where, at the commencement of this Act, any share of a company[2] carries more than one vote or does not carry any vote at a general meeting[3] of the company,[2] such a share[1] shall be deemed, as from the appointed day, to carry one vote only.

(2) If a company[2] contravenes any of the provisions of this section, the company[2] and any officer[5] in default shall be liable to a daily default fine of N50 and any resolution[6] passed in contravention of this section shall be void.

(3) Nothing in this section shall affect any right attached to a preference share[7] under section 143 of this Act.

---

**Notes**
**Section 116**

1. "Share" means the interests in a company's share capital of a member who is entitled to share in the capital or income of such company; and except where a distinction between stock and shares is expressed or implied, includes stock. See **Section 567, CAMA, Cap C20, LFN 2004.**
2. "Company" means a company formed and registered under this Act or, as the case may be, formed and registered in Nigeria before and in existence on the commencement of this Act. See **Section 567, CAMA, Cap C20, LFN 2004.**
3. "Meeting" means the gathering of people to discuss or act on matters in which they have a common interest. See **Garner B. (ed) Black's Law Dictionary 8th ed.**
4. "Articles" means the articles of association of a company, as originally framed or as altered by special resolution, including so far as they apply to the regulations contained in Table A in the First Schedules of the Companies Act, 1922 or in that Table as altered by any subsequent enactment or reprint of the laws, or in Table A in the First Schedule to this Act. See **Section 567, CAMA, Cap C20, LFN 2004.**
5. "Officer" in relation to a body corporate, includes a director, manager or secretary. See **Section 567, CAMA, Cap C20, LFN 2004.**
6. "Resolution" means main motion that formally expresses the sense, will or action of a deliberative assembly. See **Garner B. (ed) Black's Law Dictionary, 8th ed.**
7. "Preference Share" means a share, by whatever name designated, which does not entitle the holder of it to any right to participate beyond a specified amount in any distribution whether by way of dividend or on redemption, in a winding up, or otherwise. See **Section 567, CAMA, Cap C20, LFN 2004.**

**Cross Reference**

On form and content of the Articles of Association of a Company, see **section 34, CAMA Cap C20, LFN 2004.**

On types of general meeting held by a company, see **sections 211, 213 and 215 CAMA Cap C20, LFN 2004.**

On voting procedure at meetings, see **section 224, CAMA Cap C20, LFN 2004**

---

*Issue of shares*

## 117. Power of companies to issue shares

Subject to any limitation in the articles [1] of a company [2] with respect to the number of shares [3] which may be issued, and any pre-emptive rights[4] prescribed in the articles [1] in relation to the shares, [3] a company[2] shall have the power, at such times and for such consideration as it shall determine, to issue shares [3] up to the total number authorised in the memorandum. [5]

---

**Notes**
**Section 117**

1. "Articles" means the articles of association of a company, as originally framed or as altered by special resolution, including so far as they apply to the regulations contained in Table A in the First Schedules of the Companies Act, 1922 or in that Table as altered by any subsequent enactment or reprint of the laws, or in Table A in the First Schedule to this Act. See **Section 567, CAMA, Cap C20, LFN 2004.**
2. "Company" "means a company formed and registered under this Act or, as the case may be, formed and registered in Nigeria before and in existence on the commencement of this Act. See **section 567 CAMA, Cap C20, LFN, 2004**
3. "Shares" see "share". It means the interests in a company's share capital of a member who is entitled to share in the capital or income of such company; and except where a distinction between stock and shares is expressed or implied, includes stock. See **section 567 CAMA, Cap C20, LFN, 2004**
4. "Pre-emptive rights" means the privilege to purchase newly issued stock, before the shares are offered to the public, in an amount proportionate to the shareholder's current holdings in order to prevent dilution of the shareholder's ownership interest. This right must be exercised within a fixed period, usually 30 to 60 days, also termed subscription privilege. **See Garner B. (ed) Black's Law Dictionary, 8th ed.**
5. "Memorandum" means the memorandum of association of a company as originally framed or as altered in pursuance of any enactment; See **section 567 CAMA, Cap C20, LFN, 2004**

**Cross Reference**

On requirements with respect to the Memorandum of a Company, see **section 27 CAMA, Cap C20, LFN, 2004.**

On form and content of the Articles of Association of a Company, see **section 34, CAMA Cap C20, LFN 2004.**

---

**Cases**

"A study of the article of association of a company leaves me no doubt that they contain the rules and regulations by which the internal affairs of a company are governed...articles of association when registered therefore, become a contract between the company and its members and officers and between the members officers themselves..."See ***Ladejobi v. Odutola Ltd*** **(2002) 3 N.W.LR. 121 at 152-153** .

## 118. Issue of classes of shares

(1) A company[1] may, where so authorised by its articles, [2] issue classes of shares. [3]

(2) Shares[3] shall not be treated as being of the same class unless they rank equally for all purposes.

---

**Notes**
**Section 118**

1. "Company" means a company formed and registered under this Act or, as the case may be, formed and
registered in Nigeria before and in existence on the commencement of this Act. See **section 567 CAMA, Cap C20, LFN, 2004.**
2. "Articles": means the articles of association of a company, as originally framed or as altered by special resolution, including so far as they apply to the regulations contained in Table A in the First Schedules of the Companies Act, 1922 or in that Table as altered by any subsequent enactment or reprint of the laws, or in Table A in the First Schedule to this Act. **See section 567 CAMA, Cap C20, LFN, 2004**
3. "Shares" see "share". It means the interests in a company's share capital of a member who is entitled to share in the capital or income of such company; and except where a distinction between stock and shares is expressed or implied, includes stock. See **section 567 CAMA, Cap C20, LFN, 2004**

**Cross Reference**

On form and content of the Articles of Association of a Company, see **section 34, CAMA Cap C20, LFN 2004.**

---

**Cases**

It does not matter if the company's shares are owned substantially by one of the shareholders with only a very small fraction held by one or few of others. ***See Dunlop Nigerian Industries Ltd vs. Forward Nigerian Enterprises Ltd & Fafore*** **(1976) (1) A.L.R.**

## 119. Issue with rights attached

Without prejudice to any special rights [1] previously conferred on the holders of any existing shares or class of shares, [2] any share[2] in a company[3] may be issued with such preferred, deferred or other special rights or such restrictions, whether with regard to dividend [4], return of capital[5] or otherwise, as the company [3] may, from time to time, determine by ordinary resolution. [6]

---

**Notes**
**Section 119**

1. "Rights" see "right". It means a legally enforceable claim that another will do or will not do a given act; a recognized and protected interest, the violation of which is wrong. See **Garner B. (ed) Black's Law Dictionary, 8th ed.**
2. "Shares" see "share". It means the interests in a company's share capital of a member who is entitled to share in the capital or income of such company; and except where a distinction between stock and shares is expressed or implied, includes stock. See **section 567 CAMA, Cap C20, LFN, 2004**
3. "Company" means a company formed and registered under this Act or, as the case may be, formed and registered in Nigeria before and in existence on the commencement of this Act. See **section 567, CAMA Cap C20, LFN, 2004**
4. "Dividend" means a proportion of the distributed profits of the company which may be a fixed annual percentage, as in the case of preference shares, or it may be variable according to the prosperity or other circumstances of the company, as in the case of equity shares; See **section 567, CAMA Cap C20, LFN, 2004**
5. "Capital" means money or assets invested, or available for investments, in a business; the total amount or value of a Corporation's stock. See **Garner B. (ed) Black's Law Dictionary 8th ed** .
6. "Ordinary Resolution" is a resolution passed by a simple majority of votes cast by such members of the company as, being entitled to do so, vote in person or by proxy at a general meeting. See **section 233(1), CAMA Cap C20, LFN, 2004**

**Cross Reference**

On declaration of Dividends and payment of interim dividends, see **section 379 CAMA Cap C20, LFN, 2004**

On types of resolutions, see **section 233 CAMA Cap C20, LFN, 2004**

---

**Cases**

***Kotoye vs. Saraki*** **(1994) 7 N.W.L.R (part 357) 414** . A registered holder of shares in a company becomes entitled to certain rights, benefits and privileges. Except as otherwise provided by the Law and the provisions of the memorandum and Articles of Association of the company, he has the right to sell, mortgage or otherwise dispose of the shares. He is entitled to receive dividends on the shares registered in his name and to keep the dividends so received for his own use. In other words, the essence of being registered as an owner or a holder of shares in a company is that one is inter alia, entitled to enjoy in one's right the foregoing rights, benefits and privileges.

**For Further Reading**

On dividends see, Deji Sasegbon, *Nigerian Companies And Allied Matters Law & Practice*, Dsc. Publications, Lagos (1 st Ed,1992)

## 120. Issue of shares at a premium

(1) Shares [1] of a company [2] may be issued at a premium. [3]

(2) Where a company [2] issues shares [1] at a premium, [3] whether for cash or otherwise, a sum equal to the aggregate amount or value of the premium [3] on those shares [1] shall be transferred to an account, to be called "the share premium account," and the provisions of this Act relating to the reduction of the share capital [4] of a company [2] shall, except as provided in this section, apply as if the share premium account were paid-up share capital [4] of the company [2].

(3) Notwithstanding, anything to the contrary in subsection (2) of this section, the share premium account may be applied by the company [2] in paying up unissued shares of the company [2] to be issued to members [5] of the company [2] as fully-paid bonus shares, [6] in writing off-

(a) the preliminary expenses of the company [2]; or

(b) the expenses of, or the commission paid or discount allowed on, any issue of shares [1] of the company [2]; or in providing for the premium [3] payable on redemption of any redeemable share [7] of the company. [2]

(4) Where a company [2] has before the commencement of this Act issued any shares [1] at a premium, [3] this section shall apply as if the shares [1] had been issued after the commencement of this Act: Provided that any part of the premium [3] which has been so applied that it does not at the commencement of this Act form an identifiable part of the company's [2] reserves within the meaning of the Second Schedule to this Act, shall be disregarded in determining the sum to be included in the share premium account.

---

**Notes**

**Section 120**

1. "Shares" see "share". It means the interests in a company's share capital of a member who is entitled to share in the capital or income of such company; and except where a distinction between stock and shares is

expressed or implied, includes stock. See **section 567 CAMA, Cap C20, LFN, 2004**

2. "Company" means a company formed and registered under this Act or, as the case may be, formed and registered in Nigeria before and in existence on the commencement of this Act. See **section 567 CAMA, Cap C20, LFN, 2004**
3. "Premium" means he sum of money paid in addition to a regular price, salary or other amount; a bonus. See Garner B. (ed) Black's Law Dictionary, 8 th ed.
4. Share Capital" see "capital". It means a fund representing the nominal value of shares issued by a registered company. **See Martin E. (ed.) Oxford Dictionary of Law 4 th ed.**
5. "Members" :includes the heir, executor, administrator or other personal representative, as the case may be, of the member See **section 567 CAMA, Cap C20, LFN, 2004**
6. "Bonus Shares" see bonus issue". It a method of increasing a company's issued capital by issuing further shares to existing company members. These shares are paid for out of undistributed profits of the company and made in proportion of their shareholding. See **Martin E. (ed.) Oxford Dictionary of Law 4 th ed.**
7. "Redeemable Shares" are issued subject to the provisio that they will or may be bought back (at the option of the shareholder or the company) by the company. They cannot be bought back unless fully paid –up and then, only out of profit. See **Martin E. (ed.) Oxford Dictionary of Law 4th ed.**

**Cross Reference**

On authority of Company to issue classes of shares, see **section 118, CAMA Cap C20, LFN 2004**

---

**For Further Reading**

On shares, types of shares, see, Orojo, J. Ola **Company Law and Practice in Nigeria** 3rd Edition, Mbeyi & Associates (Lagos, Nigeria) 1992.

## 121. Issue of shares at a discount

(1) Subject to the provisions of this section, it shall be lawful for a company[1] to issue at a discount shares[2] in the company[1] of a class of shares[2] already issued:

Provided that-

(a) the issue of the shares[2] at a discount is authorised by resolution[3] passed in general meeting[4] of the company[1], and thereafter is sanctioned by the court[5];

(b) the resolution[3] specifies the maximum rate of discount[6] at which the shares[2] are to be issued; and

(c) the shares[2] to be issued at a discount are issued within the month after the date on which the issue is sanctioned by the court[5] or within such extended time as the court [5] may allow.

(2) Where a company [1] has passed a resolution [3] authorising the issue of shares [2] at a discount, it may apply to the court [5] for an order sanctioning the issue, and on any such application the court, [5] having regard to all the circumstances of the case, and if it thinks fit so to do on such terms and conditions as it may impose, may make an order sanctioning the issue.

(3) Every prospectus [6] relating to the issue of the shares, [2] shall contain particulars of the discount allowed on the issue of the shares[2] or of so much of that discount as has not been written off at the date of the issue of the prospectus. [6]

(4) If default is made in complying with subsection (3) of this section, the company [1] and every officer [7] of the company [1] who is in default shall be liable to a fine of N50 for every day during which the default continues.

Subject to the provisions of section 158 of this Act, a company[1] limited by shares [8] may, if so authorised by its articles, [9] issue preference shares [10] which shall, or at the option of the company,[1] be liable to be redeemed.

---

**Notes**
**Section 121**

1. "Company" means a company formed and registered under this Act or, as the case may be, formed and registered in Nigeria before and in existence on the commencement of this Act. See **section 567, CAMA Cap C20, LFN, 2004.**
2. "Shares" see "share". It means the interests in a company's share capital of a member who is entitled to share in the capital or income of such company; and except where a distinction between stock and shares is expressed or implied, includes stock. See **section 567 CAMA, Cap C20, LFN, 2004**
3. "Resolution" means main motion that formally expresses the sense, will or action of a deliberative assembly. See **Garner B. (ed) Black's Law Dictionary, 8th ed.**
4. "Meeting" means the gathering of people to discuss or act on matters in which they have a common interest. See **Garner B. (ed) Black's Law Dictionary 8th ed.**
5. "Court" used in relation to a company, means the Federal High Court, and to the extent to which application may be made to it as; court

includes the Court of Appeal and the Supreme Court of Nigeria. See **section 567, CAMA Cap. C20, LFN, 2004.**

6. "Prospectus" means any prospectus, notice, circular, advertisement, or other invitation, offering to the public for subscription or purchase any shares or debentures of a company and includes any document which, save to the extent that it offers securities for a consideration other than cash, is a prospectus. See **section 567, CAMA Cap. C20, LFN, 2004.**
7. "Officer" in relation to a body corporate, includes a director, manager or secretary. See **Section 567 CAMA, Cap. C20 , LFN 2004**
8. "Company limited by shares" is a company having the liability of its members limited by the memorandum to the amount if any, unpaid on the shares respectively held by them. **See Garner B. (ed) Black's Law Dictionary, 8th ed.**
9. "Company limited by shares" have the meanings assigned to them respectively by section 21 of this Act. See **Section 567 CAMA, Cap. C20, LFN 2004**
10. "Articles" means the articles of association of a company, as originally framed or as altered by special resolution, including so far as they apply to the regulations contained in Table A in the First Schedules of the Companies Act, 1922 or in that Table as altered by any subsequent enactment or reprint of the laws, or in Table A in the First Schedule to this Act. See **Section 567 CAMA, Cap. C20, LFN 2004.**
11. "Preference Shares" means a share, by whatever name designated, which does not entitle the holder of it to any right to participate beyond a specified amount in any distribution whether by way of dividend or on redemption, in a winding up, or otherwise. See **Section 567 CAMA, Cap. C20, LFN 2004.**

**Cross Reference**

On form and content of the Article of Association of a company, **see section 34 CAMA Cap. C20, LFN 2004**

On authority of Company to issue classes of shares, see **section 118, CAMA Cap. C20, LFN 2004**

On types of general meeting held by a company, see **section 211, 213 and 215 CAMA Cap. C20, LFN 2004**

On types of resolutions **see section 233 CAMA Cap. C20, LFN 2004**

---

**Cases**

The definition of a company in section 650 of Companies and Allied Matters Act puts the matter beyond doubt. It defines a 'company' or 'existing' to mean...a company formed and registered in Nigeria before and in existence on the commencement of this Act. ***Agro Allied Dev. Ent. Ltd. v. Reefer* (2009) vol.31 W.R.N 1-185 at pg 7** .

## 123. Validation of improperly issued shares

(1) Where a company [1] has purported to issue or allot shares [2] and the creation, issue or allotment of those shares [2] was invalid by

reason of any provision of this Act or any other enactment or of the articles[3] of the company[1] or otherwise, or the terms of issue or allotment were inconsistent with or unauthorised by any such provision, the court[4] may upon application made by the company[1] or by a holder or mortgagee[5] of those shares[2] or by a creditor[6] of the company,[1] and upon being satisfied that in all the circumstances it is just and equitable to do so, validate the issue or allotment of those shares[2] or confirm the terms of the issue and allotment, as the case may be.

(2) In every case where the court[4] validates an issue or allotment of shares[2] or confirms the terms of an issue or allotment in accordance with subsection (1) of this section, it shall make, upon payment of the prescribed fees, an order which shall be proof of the validation or confirmation and upon the issue of the order, those shares[2] shall be deemed to have been issued or allotted upon the relevant terms of issue or allotment.

---

**Notes**
**Section 123**

1. "Company" means a company formed and registered under this Act or, as the case may be, formed and registered in Nigeria before and in existence on the commencement of this Act. See **section 567, CAMA Cap. C20, LFN, 2004.**
2. Shares" see "share". It means the interests in a company's share capital of a member who is entitled to share in the capital or income of such company; and except where a distinction between stock and shares is expressed or implied, includes stock. See **section 567 CAMA, Cap. C20, LFN, 2004**
3. "Articles" means the articles of association of a company, as originally framed or as altered by special resolution, including so far as they apply to the regulations contained in Table A in the First Schedules of the Companies Act, 1922 or in that Table as altered by any subsequent enactment or reprint of the laws, or in Table A in the First Schedule to this Act. See **section 567 CAMA, Cap. C20, LFN, 2004**
4. "Court" used in relation to a company, means the Federal High Court, and to the extent to which application may be made to it as; court includes the Court of Appeal and the Supreme Court of Nigeria. See **section 567 CAMA, Cap. C20, LFN, 2004**
5. "Mortgagee" is one to whom property is mortgaged, the mortgage creditor or lender. See **Garner B. (ed) Black's Law Dictionary, 8 th ed.**
6. "Creditor": means one to whom a debt is owed; one who gives credit for money or goods. **See Garner B. (ed) Black's Law Dictionary, 8 th ed.**

Cross Reference

On issue of classes of shares by a Company, see **section 118 CAMA, Cap. C20, LFN, 2004**

On authority to allot shares by a company, see **section 124 CAMA, Cap. C20, LFN, 2004**

---

*Allotment of shares*

## 124. Authority to allot shares

Subject to the provisions of the Investment and Securities Act, the power to allot shares [1] shall be vested in the company, [2] which may delegate it to the directors [3], subject to any conditions or directions that may be imposed in the articles [4] or from time to time by the company[2] in general meeting. [5]

---

**Notes**

Section 124

1. "Shares" see "share". It means the interests in a company's share capital of a member who is entitled to share in the capital or income of such company; and except where a distinction between stock and shares is expressed or implied, includes stock. See **section 567 CAMA, Cap. C20, LFN, 2004.**
2. "Company" means a company formed and registered under this Act or, as the case may be, formed and registered in Nigeria before and in existence on the commencement of this Act. See **section 567 CAMA, Cap. C20, LFN, 2004.**
3. "Director" means any person occupying the position of director by whatever name called; and includes any person in accordance with whose directions or instructions the directors of the company are accustomed to act; See **section 567 CAMA, Cap. C20, LFN, 2004.**
4. "Articles" means the articles of association of a company, as originally framed or as altered by special resolution, including so far as they apply to the regulations contained in Table A in the First Schedules of the Companies Act, 1922 or in that Table as altered by any subsequent enactment or reprint of the laws, or in Table A in the First Schedule to this Act; See **section 567 CAMA, Cap. C20, LFN, 2004.**
5. "General Meeting" means the gathering of people to discuss or act on matters in which they have a common interest. See **Garner B. (ed) Black's Law Dictionary 8th ed.**

Cross Reference

On the powers of the Securities and Exchange Commission over the capital market, see **section 13, Investment and Securities Act, 2007**

On types of general meeting, see **sections 211, 213 and 215 CAMA, Cap. C20, LFN, 2004 .**

**Cases**

A director is a person appointed or elected according to Law, authorized to manage and direct the affairs of a corporation or company. ***Olufosoye v. Fakorede*** **(1993) 1 N.W.L.R 947.**

## 125. Method of application and allotment

Without prejudice to the provisions of sections 566 to 574 of this Act, the following provisions shall apply in respect of an application for an allotment of issued shares [1] of a company [2]-

(a) in the case of a private company [3] or a public company [4] where the issue of shares [1] is not public, there shall be submitted to the company [2] a written application signed by the person wishing to purchase shares [1] and indicating the number of shares [1] required;

(b) in the case of a public company, [4] subject to any conditions imposed by the Securities and Exchange Commission where the issue of shares [1] is public, there shall be returned to the company [2] a form of application as prescribed in the company's [2] articles, [5] duly completed and signed by the person wishing to purchase shares [1];

(c) upon the receipt of an application, a company [1] shall, where it wholly or partially accepts the application, make an allotment to the applicant and within 42 days after the allotment notify the applicant of the fact of allotment and the number of shares [1] allotted to him;

(d) an applicant under this section shall have the right at any time before allotment, to withdraw his application by written notice to the company [2]

**Notes**

**Section 125**

1. "Shares" see "share". It means the interests in a company's share capital of a member who is entitled to share in the capital or income of such company; and except where a distinction between stock and shares is expressed or implied, includes stock. See **section 567 CAMA Cap. C20, LFN 2004**.
2. "Company" means a company formed and registered under this Act or, as the case may be, formed and registered in Nigeria before and in

existence on the commencement of this Act. See **section 567 CAMA Cap. C20, LFN 2004.**

3. "Private Company" has the meaning as described in section 22 of this Act. See **section 567 CAMA Cap. C20, LFN 2004.**
4. "Public Company" is any company other than a private company and its memorandum states that it is a public company. See **section 24 CAMA Cap. C20, LFN 2004.**
5. "Articles" means the articles of association of a company, as originally framed or as altered by special resolution, including so far as they apply to the regulations contained in Table A in the First Schedules of the Companies Act, 1922 or in that Table as altered by any subsequent enactment or reprint of the laws, or in Table A in the First Schedule to this Act. See **section 567 CAMA Cap. C20, LFN 2004.**

Cross Reference

On the establishment and functions of the Securities and Exchange Commission, see **section 1 and 13, Investment and Securities Act, 2007**

On powers of a company to allot shares, see **section 124 CAMA Cap. C20, LFN 2004.**

---

## 126. Allotment as acceptance of contract

An allotment of shares[1] made and notified to an applicant in accordance with section 125 of this Act shall be an acceptance by the company[2] of the offer by the applicant to purchase its shares [1] and the contract takes effect on the date on which the allotment is made by the company.[2]

---

**Notes**

**Section 126**

1. Shares" see "share." It means the interests in a company's share capital of a member who is entitled to share in the capital or income of such company; and except where a distinction between stock and shares is expressed or implied, includes stock. See **section 567 CAMA Cap. C20, LFN 2004** .
2. "Company" means a company formed and registered under this Act or, as the case may be, formed and registered in Nigeria before and in existence on the commencement of this Act. See **section 567 CAMA Cap. C20, LFN 2004.**

Cross Reference

On powers of a company to allot shares, see **section 124 CAMA Cap. C20, LFN 2004.**

---

**Cases**

The entire Law of Contract is founded on the "Consensus" or "will" theory of contract, which asserts that contractual obligations are by definition self imposed and in terms of the function of the of the courts, finds expression in the idea that the exclusive task of a court in contract cases is to discover what the parties have agreed and give effect to it except in cases of mistake, duress and illegality. ***Coop. Dev. Bank Plc v. Ekanem*** **(2009) 16 N.W.L.R. part 1168 443-658 at pg.588.**

## 127. Payment on allotment

Subject to the provisions of sections 135 to 138 of this Act, a company[1] may, in its articles, [2] make provision with respect to payments on allotment of its shares. [3]

Notes

1. "Company" means a company formed and registered under this Act or, as the case may be, formed and registered in Nigeria before and in existence on the commencement of this Act. See **section 567 CAMA Cap. C20, LFN 2004.**
2. "Articles" means the articles of association of a company, as originally framed or as altered by special resolution, including so far as they apply to the regulations contained in Table A in the First Schedules of the Companies Act, 1922 or in that Table as altered by any subsequent enactment or reprint of the laws, or in Table A in the First Schedule to this Act. See **section 567 CAMA Cap. C20, LFN 2004.**
3. "Shares" see "share". It means the interests in a company's share capital of a member who is entitled to share in the capital or income of such company; and except where a distinction between stock and shares is expressed or implied, includes stock. See **section 567 CAMA Cap. C20, LFN 2004**.

**Cross Reference**

On form and content of the Article of Association of a company, **see section 34 CAMA Cap. C20, LFN 2004.**

On powers of a company to allot shares, see **section 124 CAMA Cap. C20, LFN 2004.**

**Cases**

A study of the article of association of a company leaves me no doubt that they contain the rules and regulations by which the internal affairs of a company are governed....articles of association when registered therefore, become a contract between the company and its members and officers and between the members officers themselves. See ***Ladejobi v. Odutola Ltd*** **(2002) 3 N.W.LR. 121 at 152-153** .

## 128. Effect of irregular allotment

(1) An allotment made by a company [1] before the holding of the statutory meeting[2] to an applicant in contravention of the provisions of this Act, shall be voidable [3] at the instance of the applicant within one month after the holding of the statutory meeting[2] of the company[1] and not later, or where the allotment is made after the holding of the statutory meeting, [2] within one month after the date of the allotment, and not later, and the allotment shall be so voidable[3] notwithstanding that the company[1] is in the course of being wound up.[4]

(2) If any director [5] of a company[1] knowingly contravenes or permits or authorises the contravention of any of the provisions of this Act with respect to allotment, he shall be liable to compensate the company[1] and the allottee[6] respectively for any loss, damages or costs which the company or the allottee [6] may have sustained or incurred thereby:

Provided that proceedings to recover any such loss, damages, or costs shall not be commenced after the expiration of two years from the date of the allotment.

---

**Notes**

**Section 128**

1. "Company" means a company formed and registered under this Act or, as the case may be, formed and registered in Nigeria before and in existence on the commencement of this Act. See **Section 567 CAMA, Cap. C20, LFN 2004.**
2. "Statutory Meeting" means the meeting required to be held by section 211 (1) of this Act. See **Section 567 CAMA, Cap. C20, LFN 2004.**
3. "Voidable" means valid until annulled (of a contract) capable of being affirmed or rejected at the option of one of the parties. This term describes a valid act that may be voided rather than an invalid act that may be ratified. **See Garner, B. (ed) Black's Law Dictionary, 8 th ed.**
4. "Wound up" see "winding up". It means the process of settling accounts and liquidating assets in anticipation of a partnership's or a corporation's dissolution. **Garner B. (ed) Black's law dictionary 8th ed.**
5. "Director" means any person occupying the position of director by whatever name called; and includes any person in accordance with whose directions or instructions the directors of the company are accustomed to act. See **Section 567 CAMA, Cap. C20, LFN 2004.**
6. "Allottee" means one to whom an allotment is made; a recipient of an allotment. See **Garner B. (ed) Black's Law Dictionary, 8 th ed.**

**Cross Reference**

On powers of a company to allot shares, see **section 124 CAMA Cap. C20, LFN 2004.**
On the period within which a public company on incorporation shall hold its statutory meeting, see **section 211, CAMA Cap. C20 LFN 2004**

---

**Cases**
A director is a person appointed or elected according to Law, authorized to manage and direct the affairs of a corporation or company. ***Olufosoye v. Fakorede*** **(1993) 1 N.W.L.R 947.**

## 129. Return as to allotment

(1) Whenever a company limited by shares [1] makes any allotment of its shares [2], the company [1] shall within one month thereafter deliver to the Commission [3] for registration-

(a) a return of the allotments, stating the number and nominal amount of the shares [2] comprised in the allotment, the names, addresses and description of the allottees, [4] and the amount, if any, paid or due and payable on each share [2]; and

(b) in the case of shares [2] allotted as fully or partly paid up otherwise than in cash-

(i) a contract in writing, constituting the title of the allottee[4] to the allotment together with any contract of sale, or for services or other consideration in respect of which that allotment was made, such contracts being duly stamped;

(ii) a return stating the number and nominal amount of shares[2] so allotted, the extent to which they are to be treated as paid up, and the consideration for which they have been allotted; and

(iii) particulars of the valuation of the consideration in accordance with section 137 of this Act, if any.

(2) If default is made in complying with this section, every officer[5] of the company [1] who is in default shall be liable to a fine of N50 for every day during which the default continues:
Provided that, in case of default in delivering to the Commission [3] within one month after the allotment any document [6] required to be delivered by this section, the company [1] or any officer [5] liable for the default, may apply to the court [7] for relief, and the court, [7] if satisfied that the omission to deliver the document [6] was accidental

or due to inadvertence or that it is just and equitable to grant relief, may make an order extending the time for the delivery of the document[6] for such period as the court [7] may think proper.

---

**Notes**
**Section 129**

1. "Company limited by shares" is a company having the liability of its members limited by the memorandum to the amount if any, unpaid on the shares respectively held by them. **See Garner B. (ed) Black's Law Dictionary, 8th ed.**
   "Company limited by shares" have the meanings assigned to them respectively by section 21 of this Act. See **Section 567 CAMA, Cap. C20, LFN 2004.**
2. "Shares" see "share." It means the interests in a company's share capital of a member who is entitled to share in the capital or income of such company; and except where a distinction between stock and shares is expressed or implied, includes stock. See **section 567 CAMA Cap. C20, LFN 2004** .
3. "Commission" means Corporate Affairs Commission, established under section 1 of this Act. See **Section 567 CAMA, Cap. C20, LFN 2004.**
4. "Allottees" see "allotteee". It means one to whom an allotment is made; a recipient of an allotment. See **Garner B. (ed) Black's Law Dictionary, 8th ed.**
5. "Officer" in relation to a body corporate, includes a director, manager or secretary. See **Section 567 CAMA, Cap. C20, LFN 2004.**
6. "Document" includes summons, notice, order and other legal process, and register. **Section 567 CAMA, Cap. C20, LFN 2004.**
7. "Court" used in relation to a company, means the Federal High Court, and to the extent to which application may be made to it as; court includes the Court of Appeal and the Supreme Court of Nigeria. See **Section 567 CAMA Cap. C20, LFN, 2004.**

Cross Reference

On Jurisdiction of the Federal High Court, see **section 251 of the 1999 Constitution.**

---

**Cases**

The Corporate Affairs Commission is conferred with the responsibility of registering companies operating in Nigeria by Statute, and under the said statute it can prohibit and restrict certain names to be registered. ***Mustapha v. CAC*** **(2009) Vol. 43 W.R.N. 1-171 pg 156.**

## 130. Prohibition of payments of commissions, discounts out of shares and capital

(1) Except as provided in section 131 of this Act, no company[1] shall apply any of its shares [2] or capital money either directly or indirectly in payment of any commission, discount or allowance to any person in consideration of his subscribing [4] or agreeing to subscribe[3], whether absolutely or conditionally, for any shares[2] in the company[1], or procuring or agreeing to procure subscriptions, whether absolute or conditional, for any shares [2] in the company,[1] whether the shares[2] or capital money are so applied by being added to the purchase money of any property acquired by the company[1] or to the contract price of any work to be executed for the company[1] or any such money is paid out of the nominal purchase money or contract price, or otherwise.

(2) Nothing in this section shall affect the payment of any brokerage[4] as is usual for a company to pay.

(3) A vendor[5] to, promoter [6] of or other person who receives payment in money or shares [2] from a company, [1] shall have and shall be deemed always to have had power to apply any part of the money or shares[2] so received in payment of any commission, the payment of which, if made directly by the company, [1] would have been legal under this section.

---

**Notes**
**Section 130**

1. "Company" means a company formed and registered under this Act or, as the case may be, formed and registered in Nigeria before and in existence on the commencement of this Act. See **Section 567 CAMA, Cap. C20, LFN 2004.**
2. "Shares" see "share". It means the interests in a company's share capital of a member who is entitled to share in the capital or income of such company; and except where a distinction between stock and shares is expressed or implied, includes stock. See **Section 567 CAMA, Cap. C20, LFN, 2004.**
3. "Subscribe" see "subscription". It means the act of signing one's name on a document; the signature so affixed. See **Garner B. (ed) Black's Law Dictionary, 8th ed.**
4. "Brokerage" means the business or office of a broker. See **Garner B. (ed) Black's Law Dictionary, 8th ed.**
5. "Vendor "means a seller, usually of real property. See **Garner B. (ed) Black's Law Dictionary, 8th ed.**
6. "Promoter" is a founder or organiser of a corporation or business venture, one who takes the entrepreneurial initiative in founding or organising a business or enterprise. See **Garner, B. (ed) Black's Law Dictionary, 8th ed.**

"Promoter" means any person who undertakes to take part in forming a company with reference to a given project and to set it going and who takes the necessary steps to accomplish that purpose, or who, with regard to a proposed or newly formed company, undertakes a part in raising capital for it. See **section 61 CAMA, Cap. C20 LFN 2004**

Cross Reference

On duties and liabilities of promoters, see **section 62 CAMA, Cap. C20 LFN 2004**

## 131. Power to pay commission in certain cases

(1) It shall be lawful for a company [1] to pay a commission to any person in consideration of his subscribing [2] or agreeing to subscribe,[2] whether absolutely or conditionally, for any shares [3] in the company[1] or procuring or agreeing to procure subscription, [2] whether absolute or conditional, for any shares [3] in the company [1] if-

(a) the payment of the commission is authorised by the articles[4]; and

(b) the commission paid or agreed to be paid does not exceed ten per cent of the price at which the shares [3] are issued or the amount or rate authorised by the articles, [4] whichever is the lesser;

(c) the amount or rate per cent of the commission paid or agreed to be paid is-

(i) in the case of shares [3] offered to the public for subscription[2] disclosed in the prospectus [5]; or

(ii) in the case of shares [3] not offered to the public for subscription,[2] disclosed in the statement in lieu of prospectus,[5] or in a statement in the prescribed form signed in like manner as a statement in lieu of prospectus,[5] and delivered before the payment of the commission to the Commission [6] for registration, and where a circular or notice, not being a prospectus [5] inviting subscription[2] for the shares [3] is issued, also disclosed in that circular or notice; and

(d) the number of shares [3] which persons have agreed for a commission to subscribe[2] absolutely is disclosed in the manner specified in this section.

(2) If default is made in delivering to the Commission [6] any document[7] required to be delivered to the Commission [6] under this

section, the company [1] and every officer [8] in default shall be liable to a fine of N250.

---

**Notes**
**Section 131**

1. "Company" means a company formed and registered under this Act or, as the case may be, formed and registered in Nigeria before and in existence on the commencement of this Act. See **Section 567 CAMA, Cap. C20, LFN 2004.**
2. "Subscribe" see "subscription". It means the act of signing one's name on a document; the signature so affixed. See **Garner, B. (ed) Black's Law Dictionary, 8th ed.**
3. "Shares" see "share." It means is the interests in a company's share capital of a member who is entitled to share in the capital or income of such company; and except where a distinction between stock and shares is expressed or implied, includes stock. See **Section 567 CAMA, Cap. C20, LFN, 2004.**
4. "Articles" means the articles of association of a company, as originally framed or as altered by special resolution, including so far as they apply to the regulations contained in Table A in the First Schedules of the Companies Act, 1922 or in that Table as altered by any subsequent enactment or reprint of the laws, or in Table A in the First Schedule to this Act. See **Section 567 CAMA, Cap. C20, LFN 2004.**
5. "Prospectus" means any prospectus, notice, circular, advertisement, or other invitation, offering to the public for subscription or purchase any shares or debentures of a company and includes any document which, save to the extent that it offers securities for a consideration other than cash, is a prospectus. See **Section 567 CAMA, Cap. C20, LFN 2004.**
6. "Commission" means Corporate Affairs Commission, established under section 1 of this Act. See **Section 567 CAMA, Cap. C20, LFN 2004.**
7. "Documents" includes summons, notice, order and other legal process, and register. See **Section 567 CAMA, Cap. C20 LFN 2004.**
8. "Officer" in relation to a body corporate, includes a director, manager or secretary. See **Section 567 CAMA Cap. C20 LFN 2004**

**Cross Reference**

On amount of shares subscribers must take up in a company at incorporation, see section 37(2) **CAMA Cap. C20 LFN 2004**

---

**For Further Reading**

On companies, officers and their acts see, Kiser Barnes **Cases and Materials on Nigeria Company Law** (1992) Obafemi Awolowo University press Ltd, Ile-Ife, Nigeria

## 132. Statement in balance sheet as to commission

(1) Where a company[1] has paid any sum by way of commission in respect of any shares[2] in the company[1], the amount so paid or so much of it as has not been written off, shall be stated in every balance sheet[3] of the company[1] until the whole amount has been written off.

(2) If default is made in complying with this section, the company[1] and every officer[4] of the company[1] in default is guilty of an offence and liable to a fine of N50 for every day during which the default continues.

---

**Notes**
**Section 132**

1. "Company" means a company formed and registered under this Act or, as the case may be, formed and registered in Nigeria before and in existence on the commencement of this Act. See **Section 567 CAMA, Cap. C20, LFN 2004.**
2. "Shares" see "share". It means is the interests in a company's share capital of a member who is entitled to share in the capital or income of such company; and except where a distinction between stock and shares is expressed or implied, includes stock. See **Section 567 CAMA, Cap. C20, LFN, 2004.**
3. "Balance Sheet "is a statement of an entity's current financial position, disclosing the value of the entity's assets, liabilities, and owners' equity. See **Garner, B (ed) Black's Law Dictionary, 8 th ed.**
4. "Officer" A person who holds an office of trust, authority or command. See **Garner B, (ed) Black's Law Dictionary, 8 th ed.** "Officer" in relation to a body corporate, includes a director, manager or secretary. See **Section 567 CAMA Cap. C20 LFN 2004.**

Cross Reference

On definition of offence, see **section 2 Criminal Code Cap. C38, LFN 2004**

---

*Call on and payment for shares*

## 133. Call on shares

(1) Subject to the terms of the issue of the shares[1] and of the articles[2], the directors[3] may from time to time make calls upon the members[4] in respect of any moneys unpaid on their shares[1] (whether on account of the nominal value of the shares[1] or by way of premium[5]) and not by the conditions of allotment of the shares[1] made payable at fixed times:

Provided that no call shall exceed one fourth of the nominal value of the share[1] or be payable at less than one month from the date fixed for the payment of the last preceding call, and each member [4] shall (subject to receiving at least 14 days' notice specifying the time or times and place of payment) pay to the company [6] at the time or times and place so specified the amount called on his shares[1], so however that a call may be revoked or postponed as the directors[3] may determine.

(2) A call shall be deemed to have been made at the time when the resolution[7] of the directors [3] authorising the call was passed, and may be required to be paid by instalments.

(3) The joint holders of a share [1] shall be jointly and severally liable to pay all calls in respect of the share. [1]

(4) If a sum called in respect of a share [1] is not paid before or on the day appointed for payment, the person from whom the sum is due shall pay interest on the sum from the day appointed for payment to the time of actual payment at such rate not exceeding the current bank rate per annum, as the directors [3] may determine, but the directors[3] shall be at liberty to waive payment of such interest wholly or in part.

(5) Any sum which by the terms of issue of a share [1] becomes payable on allotment or at any fixed date, whether on account of the nominal value of the shares [1] or by way of premium [5] shall, for the purposes of these provisions, be deemed to be a call duly made and payable on the date on which by the terms of issue the same becomes payable, and in case of non-payment, all the relevant provisions of this Act as to payment of interest and expenses, forfeiture or otherwise shall apply as if such sum had become payable by virtue of a call duly made and notified.

(6) The directors [3] may, if they think fit, receive from any member[4] willing to advance the same, all or any part of the moneys uncalled and unpaid upon any shares [1] held by him; and upon all or any of the moneys

---

**Notes**
**Section 133**

1. "Shares" see "share". It means is the interests in a company's share capital of a member who is entitled to share in the capital or income of such company; and except where a distinction between stock and shares

is expressed or implied, includes stock. See **section 567 CAMA, Cap. C20, LFN, 2004.**

2. "Articles" means the articles of association of a company, as originally framed or as altered by special resolution, including so far as they apply to the regulations contained in Table A in the First Schedules of the Companies Act, 1922 or in that Table as altered by any subsequent enactment or reprint of the laws, or in Table A in the First Schedule to this Act. See **section 567 CAMA, Cap. C20, LFN, 2004.**
3. "Director" means any person occupying the position of director by whatever name called; and includes any person in accordance with whose directions or instructions the directors of the company are accustomed to act. See **section 567 CAMA, Cap. C20, LFN, 2004.**
4. "Members" includes the heir, executor, administrator or other personal representative, as the case may be, of the member. See **section 567 CAMA, Cap. C20, LFN, 2004.**
5. "Premium" means the sum of money paid in addition to a regular price, salary or other amount; a bonus. See **Garner B. (ed) Black's Law Dictionary, 8th ed.**
6. "Company" means a company formed and registered under this Act or, as the case may be, formed and registered in Nigeria before and in existence on the commencement of this Act. See **section 567 CAMA, Cap. C20, LFN, 2004.**
7. "Resolution" is a main motion that formally expresses the sense, will or action of a deliberative assembly. See **Garner B. (ed) Black's Law Dictionary, 8th ed.**

**Cross Reference**

On form and content of the Articles of Association of a company, see **section 34 CAMA, Cap. C20, LFN, 2004.**

On rights and liabilities attached to shares, see **section 114 CAMA, Cap. C20, LFN, 2004.**

---

**Cases**

Where two or more persons make joint and several promises to another, each of the promisors incurs both a joint and a several liability. All or any of the promisors may be sued, at the option of the promise, in respect of a joint and several liability, and separate actions may be brought against each. See ***Ogida v. Oliha (1986) 1 NWLR (Pt.19)786***

Shares are in the nature of personal estate and freely transferable but subject to statutory restrictions and the articles of the company. Members in a company have a right to transfer shares belonging to them therein and this right is unfettered unless there is an express restriction to that effect in the articles or constitution of the company. See ***N.R.I. Ltd v. Oranusi (2011) ALL F.W.L.R part 577. 625-824 at p.765.*** A director is a person appointed or elected according to Law, authorized to manage and direct the affairs of a corporation or company. ***Olufosoye v. Fakorede* (1993) 1 N.W.L.R 947.**

**For Further Reading**

On shares, articles, directors, members see, Asomugha, E. Maduelosi **Company law in Nigeria under the Companies and Allied Matters Act** E.M. Asomugha (Lagos) 1994.

Irukwu, J.O, **The Company, The Shareholder, The Director and The Law,** Fourth Dimension Publishing Co. Ltd 1994

## 134. Reserve liability of company having share capital

A company limited by shares [1] may by special resolution [2] determine that any portion of its share capital [3] which has not been already called up shall not be capable of being called up except in the event and for the purposes of the company [4] being wound up[5]; and thereupon that portion of its share capital [3] shall not be capable of being called up, except in the event and for the purposes specified in this section.

---

**Notes**

**Section 134**

1. "Company limited by Shares" means a company having the liability of its members limited by the memorandum to the amount if any, unpaid on the shares respectively held by them. **See Garner B. (ed) Black's Law Dictionary, 8th ed.**

   "Company limited by shares" have the meaning assigned by section 21 of this Act. See **section 567 CAMA, Cap. C20, LFN 2004.**
2. "Special Resolution" is a resolution that has been passed by not less than three fourths of the votes cast by such members of the company as, being entitled to do so, vote in person or by proxy at a general meeting of which 21 days' notice, specifying the intention to propose the resolution as a special resolution, has been duly given. See **section 233 CAMA, Cap. C20, LFN 2004.**
3. Share Capital" means any of the units of equal value into which a company is divided and sold to raise money. People who owns shares receives part of the company profit. See **Oxford Advanced Learners Dictionary ,New 7[th] Edition**

   "Share Capital" see "capital". It means a fund representing the nominal value of shares issued by a registered company. See **Martins E. (ed) Oxford Dictoionary of Law 7[th] ed.**
4. "Company" means a company formed and registered under this Act or, as the case may be, formed and registered in Nigeria before and in existence on the commencement of this Act. See **section 567 CAMA, Cap. C20, LFN 2004.**
5. "Wound up" see "winding up". It means the process of settling accounts and liquidating assets in anticipation of a partnership's or a corporation's dissolution. See **Garner B. (ed) Black's Law Dictionary, 8 [th] ed.**

Cross Reference

On authority of directors to call on shares of the Company, see **section 133 CAMA, Cap. C20, LFN 2004.**

On Winding-up of companies, see Part XV **CAMA, Cap. C20, LFN 2004.**

---

**Cases**

The definition of a company in section 650 of Companies and Allied Matters Act puts the matter beyond doubt. It defines a 'company' or 'existing' to mean....a company formed and registered in Nigeria before and in existence on the commencement of this Act. ***Agro Allied Dev. Ent. Ltd. v. Reefer*** **[2009] vol.31 W.R.N 1-185 at pg 7**

## 135. Payment for shares

Subject to the provisions of sections 136 and 137 of this Act, the shares[1] of a company[2] and any premium[3] on them shall be paid up in cash, or where the articles [4] so permit, by a valuable consideration other than cash or partly in cash and partly by a valuable consideration[5] other than cash.

---

**Notes**
**Section 135**

1. "Shares" see "share." It means is the interests in a company's share capital of a member who is entitled to share in the capital or income of such company; and except where a distinction between stock and shares is expressed or implied, includes stock. See **section 567 CAMA, Cap. C20, LFN, 2004.**
2. "Company" means a company formed and registered under this Act or, as the case may be, formed and registered in Nigeria before and in existence on the commencement of this Act. See **section 567 CAMA, Cap. C20, LFN 2004.**
3. "Premium" means the sum of money paid in addition to a regular price, salary or other amount; a bonus. See **Garner B. (ed) Black's Law Dictionary, 8th ed.**
4. "Articles" means the articles of association of a company, as originally framed or as altered by special resolution, including so far as they apply to the regulations contained in Table A in the First Schedules of the Companies Act, 1922 or in that Table as altered by any subsequent enactment or reprint of the laws, or in Table A in the First Schedule to this Act. See **section 567 CAMA, Cap. C20, LFN, 2004.**

Cross Reference

On form and content of Articles of Association of a company, see **section 34 CAMA, Cap. C20, LFN, 2004.**

On rights and liabilities attached to shares, see section 114 **CAMA, Cap. C20, LFN, 2004.**

On meaning of payment for shares in cash, see section 136 **CAMA, Cap. C20, LFN, 2004.**
On meaning of payment for shares for valuable consideration, see section 137 **CAMA, Cap. C20, LFN, 2004.**

**Cases**

Shares are in the nature of personal estate and freely transferable but subject to statutory restrictions and the articles of the company. Members in a company have a right to transfer shares belonging to them therein and this right is unfettered unless there is an express restriction to that effect in the articles or constitution of the company. See ***N.R.I. Ltd v. Oranusi [2011] ALL F.W.L.R part 577. 625-824 at p.765***

## 136. Meaning of payment in cash

Shares[1] shall not be deemed to have been paid for in cash except to the extent that the company[2] shall actually have received cash for them at the time of, or subsequently to, the agreement to issue the shares[1], and where shares[1] are issued to a person who has sold or agreed to sell property or rendered or agreed to render services to the company[2] or to persons nominated by him, the amount of any payment made for the property or services shall be deducted from the amount of any cash payment made for the shares[1] and only the balance (if any) shall be treated as having been paid in cash for such shares[1] notwithstanding any exchange of cheques[3] or other securities[4] for money.

---

**Notes**

**Section 136**

1. "Shares" see "share." It means is the interests in a company's share capital of a member who is entitled to share in the capital or income of such company; and except where a distinction between stock and shares is expressed or implied, includes stock. See **section 567 CAMA, Cap. C20, LFN, 2004.**
2. "Company" means a company formed and registered under this Act or, as the case may be, formed and registered in Nigeria before and in existence on the commencement of this Act. See **section 567 CAMA, Cap. C20, LFN 2004.**
3. "Cheque" means a draft signed by a maker or drawer, drawn on a bank, payable on demand and unlimited in negotiability. See **Garner B. (ed) Black's Law Dictionary, 8th ed.**
4. "Securities" includes shares, debentures, debenture stock, bonds, notes (other than promissory notes) and units under a unit trust scheme. See **section 567 CAMA, Cap. C20, LFN, 2004.**

**Cross Reference**

On rights and liabilities attached to shares, see section 114 **CAMA, Cap. C20, LFN, 2004.**

On payment of shares generally, see section **135 CAMA, Cap. C20, LFN, 2004.**

---

**Cases**

Shares are in the nature of personal estate and freely transferable but subject to statutory restrictions and the articles of the company. Members in a company have a right to transfer shares belonging to them therein and this right is unfettered unless there is an express restriction to that effect in the articles or constitution of the company. See ***N.R.I. Ltd v. Oranusi [2011] ALL F.W.L.R part 577. 625-824 at p.765***

## 137. Payment other than in cash

(1) Where a company[1] agrees to accept payment for its shares[2] otherwise than wholly in cash, it shall appoint an independent valuer[3] who shall determine the true value of the consideration[4] other than cash and prepare and submit to the company[1] a report on the value of the consideration.[4]

(2) The valuer[3] shall be entitled to require from the officers[5] of the company[1] such information and explanation as he thinks necessary to enable him to carry out the valuation or make the report under subsection (3) of this section.

(3) The company[1] shall, not more than three days after the receipt by it of the valuer's[3] report, send a copy of it to the proposed purchaser of shares,[2] and indicate to the proposed purchaser whether or not it intends to accept the consideration[4] as payment or part-payment for its shares[2].

(4) A company[1] shall not accept as payment or part-payment for its shares[2] consideration[4] other than cash unless the cash value of the consideration[4] as determined by the valuer[3] is worth at least as much as may be credited as paid up in respect of the shares[2] allowed to the proposed purchaser.

(5) A valuer[3] who, in his report or otherwise, knowingly or recklessly makes a statement which is misleading, false or deceptive in a material particular, shall be guilty of an offence and liable to imprisonment for 12 months or to a fine of N 1,000 or both such imprisonment and fine.

(6) For the purposes of this section "valuer"[3] means an auditor, a valuer,[3] a surveyor or engineer or an accountant not

being a person in the employment of the company [1] nor an agent [5] or associate of the company [1] or any of its directors [6] or officers. [7]

---

**Notes**
**Section 137**

1. "Company" means a company formed and registered under this Act or, as the case may be, formed and registered in Nigeria before and in existence on the commencement of this Act. See **section 567 CAMA, Cap. C20, LFN 2004.**
2. "Shares" see "share." It means is the interests in a company's share capital of a member who is entitled to share in the capital or income of such company; and except where a distinction between stock and shares is expressed or implied, includes stock. See **section 567 CAMA, Cap. C20, LFN, 2004.**
3. "Valuer" see "appraiser." It means an impartial person who estimates the value of something, such as real estate, jewelry or rare books. See **Garner B. (ed) Black's Law Dictionary, 8 th ed.**
4. "Consideration" means something, (such as an act, a forebearance, or a return promise) bargained for and received by a promisor from a promisee; that which motivates a person to do something, especially to engage in a legal act. See **Garner B. (ed) Black's Law Dictionary, 8 th ed.**
5. "Agent" is one who is authorized to act for or in place of another; a representative. See **Garner B. (ed) Black's Law Dictionary, 8 th ed.**
6. "Director" means any person occupying the position of director by whatever name called; and includes any person in accordance with whose directions or instructions the directors of the company are accustomed to act. See **section 567 CAMA, Cap. C20, LFN, 2004.**
7. "Officer" in relation to a body corporate, includes a director, manager or secretary. See **Garner B. (ed) Black's Law Dictionary, 8th ed.**

**Cross Reference**

On rights and liabilities attached to shares, see section 114 **CAMA, Cap. C20, LFN, 2004.**

On payment of shares generally, see section **135 CAMA, Cap. C20, LFN, 2004.**

---

**Cases**

Shares are in the nature of personal estate and freely transferable but subject to statutory restrictions and the articles of the company. Members in a company have a right to transfer shares belonging to them therein and this right is unfettered unless there is an express restriction to that effect in the articles or constitution of the company. See ***N.R.I. Ltd v. Oranusi (2011) All F.W.L.R part 577. 625-824 at p.765***

A director is a person appointed or elected according to Law, authorized to manage and direct the affairs of a corporation or company. ***Olufosoye v. Fakorede*** **(1993) 1 N.W.L.R 947.**

## 138. Power to pay different amounts on shares

To the extent to which it is so authorised by its articles [1], a company[2] may-

(a) make arrangements on the issue of shares [3] for a difference between the shareholders[4] in the amounts and times of payment of calls on their shares [3];

(b) accept from any member [5] the whole or a part of the amount remaining unpaid on any shares [3] held by him, although no part of that amount has been called up;

(c) pay dividend[6] in proportion to the amount paid up on each share[3] where a larger amount is paid up on some shares [3] than on others.

---

**Notes**
**Section 138**

1. "Articles" means the articles of association of a company, as originally framed or as altered by special resolution, including so far as they apply to the regulations contained in Table A in the First Schedules of the Companies Act, 1922 or in that Table as altered by any subsequent enactment or reprint of the laws, or in Table A in the First Schedule to this Act. See **section 567 CAMA, Cap. C20, LFN, 2004.**
2. "Company" means a company formed and registered under this Act or, as the case may be, formed and registered in Nigeria before and in existence on the commencement of this Act. See **section 567 CAMA, Cap. C20, LFN 2004.**
3. "Shares" see "share." It means is the interests in a company's share capital of a member who is entitled to share in the capital or income of such company; and except where a distinction between stock and shares is expressed or implied, includes stock. See **section 567 CAMA, Cap. C20, LFN, 2004.**
4. "Shareholder" means one who owns or holds a share or shares in a company. See **Garner B. (ed) Black's Law Dictionary, 8th ed.**
5. "Member" includes the heir, executor, administrator or other personal representative, as the case maybe, of the member. See **section 567 CAMA, Cap. C20, LFN, 2004.**
6. "Dividend" means a portion of the distributed profit of the company which may be a fixed annual percentage, as in the case of preference share, or it may be variable according to the prosperity or other

circumstances of the company, as in the case of equity shares . **Section 567 of CAMA, Cap. C20, LFN 2004.**

Cross Reference

On rights and liabilities attached to shares, see section 114 **CAMA, Cap. C20, LFN, 2004.**

On call on shares of a company, see **section 133 CAMA Cap. C20, LFN 2004**

On payment of shares generally, see section **135 CAMA, Cap. C20, LFN, 2004.**

---

**Cases**

"The Articles of Association is the contract governing the relationship between shareholders and any infraction of such articles may confer on the shareholder adversely affected a right of action" ***Attorney General of Lagos State v Eko Hotel Ltd & Oha Ltd (2001) FWLR page 1996*** *at 2000*

For Further reading on shareholders, see Olufemi Amao and Kenneth Amaeshi "Galvanizing Shareholder Activism: A Prerequisite for Effective Corporate Governance and Accountability in Nigeria" (2008) 82 Journal of Business Ethics 119-130

*Lien and forfeiture of shares*

## 139. Lien on shares

(1) A company[1] shall have a first and paramount lien[2] on every share,[3] (not being a fully paid share[3] for all moneys (whether currently payable or not) called or payable at a fixed time in respect of that share,[3] and the company[1] shall also have a first and paramount lien[2] on all shares[3] (other than fully paid shares[3]) standing registered in the name of a single person for all moneys presently payable by him or his estate to the company[1]; but the directors[4] may at any time declare any share to be wholly or in part exempt from the provisions of this subsection.

(2) A company's lien,[2] if any, on a share[4] shall extend to all dividends[5] payable on it.

(3) A company[1] may sell, in such manner as the directors[4] think fit, any shares[3] on which the company[1] has a lien,[2] but no sale shall be made unless a sum in respect of which the lien[2] exists is currently payable, nor until the expiration of 14 days after a notice in writing, stating and demanding payment of such part of the amount in respect of which the lien[2] exists as is currently payable, has been given to the registered holder for the time being of the

shares,[3] or the person entitled to them by reason of his death or bankruptcy.[6]

(4) For the purpose of giving effect to any such sale, the directors[4] may authorise some person to transfer the shares [3] sold to the purchaser of the shares [3] and the purchaser shall be registered as the holder of the shares [3] comprised in any such transfer.

(5) The purchaser shall not be bound to see to the application of the purchase money and his title to the shares [3] shall not be affected by any irregularity or invalidity in the proceedings in reference to the sale.

---

**Notes**
**Section 139**

1. "Company" means a company formed and registered under this Act or, as the case may be, formed and registered in Nigeria before and in existence on the commencement of this Act. See **section 567 CAMA, Cap. C20, LFN 2004.**
2. "Lien" is a legal right or interest that a creditor has in another's property, lasting usually until a debt or duty that it secures is satisfied. Typically, the creditor does not take possession of the property on which the lien has been obtained. See **Garner B. (ed) Black's Law Dictionary, 8th ed.**
3. "Shares" see "share." It means is the interests in a company's share capital of a member who is entitled to share in the capital or income of such company; and except where a distinction between stock and shares is expressed or implied, includes stock. See **section 567 CAMA, Cap. C20, LFN, 2004.**
4. "Director" means any person occupying the position of director by whatever name called; and includes any person in accordance with whose directions or instructions the directors of the company are accustomed to act. See **section 567 CAMA, Cap. C20, LFN, 2004.**
5. "Dividends" means a portion of the distributed profit of the company which may be a fixed annual percentage, as in the case of preference share, or it may be variable according to the prosperity or other circumstances of the company, as in the case of equity shares **. See section 567 of CAMA, Cap. C20, LFN 2004.**
6. "Bankruptcy" means astatutory procedure by which a (usually insolvent) debtor obtains financial relief and undergoes a judicially supervised reorganization or liquidation of a debtor's assets for the benefit of ceditors. See **Garner B. (ed) Black's Law Dictionary, 8 [8h] ed.**

**Cross Reference**

As to when a debtor commits an act of bankruptcy, see **section 1, Bankruptcy Act Cap. B2 LFN 2004**

**Cases**
A registered holder of shares in a company becomes entitled to certain rights, benefits and privileges. Except as otherwise provided by the Law and the provisions of the memorandum and Articles of Association of the company, he has the right to sell, mortgage or otherwise dispose of the shares. He is entitled to receive dividends on the shares registered in his name and to keep the dividends so received for his own use. In other words, the essence of being registered as an owner or a holder of shares in a company is that one is inter alia, entitled to enjoy in one's right the foregoing rights, benefits and privileges. ***Kotoye vs. Saraki*** **(1994) 7 N.W.L.R (part 357) 414**

**For Further Reading**
On company, shares and directors, see, Ayua, I.A **Nigerian Company Law** G. Burn ( Bedfordshire, United Kingdom 1984)

## 140. Forfeiture of shares

(1) If a member [1] fails to pay any call or instalment of a call on the day appointed for payment, the directors [2] may, at any time thereafter during such time as any part of the call or instalment remains unpaid, serve a notice on him requiring payment of so much of the call or instalment as is unpaid, together with any interest[3] which may have accrued.

(2) The notice shall name a further day (not earlier than the expiration of 14 days from the date of service of the notice) on or before which the payment required by the notice is to be made, and it shall state that in the event of non-payment at or before the time appointed, the shares [4] in respect of which the call was made shall be liable to be forfeited.

(3) If the requirements of any such notice as is mentioned in subsections (1) and (2) of this section are not complied with, any share[4] in respect of which notice has been given may at any time thereafter, before the payment required by the notice has been made, be forfeited by a resolution [5] of the directors [2] to that effect.

(4) A forfeited share [4] may be sold or otherwise disposed of on such terms and in such manner as the directors [2] think fit, and at any time before a sale or disposition, the forfeiture may be cancelled on such terms as the directors [2] think fit.

(5) A person whose shares [4] have been forfeited shall cease to be a member[1] in respect of the forfeited shares [4], but shall, notwithstanding, remain liable to pay to the company [7] all moneys which, at the date of forfeiture, were payable by him to the company[6] in respect of the shares [4], but his liability shall cease if and when the company[7] receives payment in full of all such moneys in respect of the shares [4].

(6) A statutory declaration [7] that the declarant is a director [2] or the secretary [8]of the company[6], and that a share [4] in the company[6] has been duly forfeited on a date stated in the declarations, [7] shall be prima facie evidence of the facts stated in it as against all persons claiming to be entitled to the shares. [4]

(7) The company[6] may receive the consideration, if any, given for the share [4] on any sale or disposition of it and may execute a transfer of the share in favour of the person to whom the share [4] is sold or disposed of, and he shall thereupon be registered as the holder of the share, [4] and shall not be bound to see to the application of the purchase money, if any, nor shall his title to the share [4] be affected by any irregularity or invalidity in the proceedings in reference to the forfeiture, sale or disposal of the share. [4]

(8) The provisions of this section as to forfeiture shall apply in the case of non-payment of any sum which, by the terms of issue of a share[4], becomes payable at a fixed time, whether on account of the nominal value of the share or by way of premium [9], as if the same had been payable by virtue of a call duly made and notified.

---

**Notes**
**Section 140**

1. "Member" includes the heir, executor, administrator or other personal representative, as the case maybe, of the member. See **section 567 CAMA, Cap. C20, LFN, 2004.**
2. "Director" means any person occupying the position of director by whatever name called; and includes any person in accordance with whose directions or instructions the directors of the company are accustomed to act. See **section 567 CAMA, Cap. C20, LFN 2004.**
3. "Interest" means the object of any human desire, especially advantage or profit of a financial nature. See **Garner B. (ed) Black's Law Dictionary, 8th ed.**
4. "Shares" see "share". It means is the interests in a company's share capital of a member who is entitled to share in the capital or income of such company; and except where a distinction between stock and shares

is expressed or implied, includes stock. See **section 567 CAMA, Cap. C20, LFN, 2004.**

5. "Resolution" is main motion that formally expresses the sense, will or action of a deliberative assembly. See **Garner B. (ed) Black's Law Dictionary, 8th ed.**
6. "Company" means a company formed and registered under this Act or, as the case may be, formed and registered in Nigeria before and in existence on the commencement of this Act. See **section 567 CAMA, Cap. C20, LFN 2004.**
7. "Statutory declaration" means a declaration voluntarily made under the Oaths Act and in Nigeria includes one so made under any other enactment or law providing for the taking of a voluntary declaration. See **section 567 CAMA, Cap. C20, LFN 2004.**
8. "Secretary "means a corporate officer in charge of official correspondence, minutes of board meetings and records of stock ownership and transfer. See **Garner B. (ed) Black's Law Dictionary, 8th ed.**
9. "Premium" means the sum of money paid in addition to a regular price, salary or other amount; a bonus. See **Garner B. (ed) Black's Law Dictionary, 8th ed.**

**Cross Reference**

On powers of a the director to call for shares on behalf of the company, see **section 133 CAMA, Cap. C20, LFN, 2004.**

On rights and liabilities attached to shares, see section 114 **CAMA, Cap. C20, LFN, 2004.**

On payment of shares generally, see section **135 CAMA, Cap. C20, LFN, 2004.**

On the qualifications of a secretary, see **section 295 CAMA, Cap. C20, LFN, 2004.**

On the duties of a Secretary see **section 298 CAMA, Cap. C20, LFN, 2004.**

---

**Cases**

By the provisions of Companies and Allied Matters Act, Section 115, shares are in the nature of personal estate and freely transferable but subject to statutory restrictions and the articles of the company. Members in a company have a right to transfer shares belonging to them therein and this right is unfettered unless there is an express restriction to that effect in the articles or constitution of the company. ***N.R.I. Ltd v. Oranusi*** **(2011) All F.W.L.R part 577. 625-824 at p. 765** .

## 140. Forfeiture of shares

(1) If a member[1] fails to pay any call or installment of a call on the day appointed for payment, the directors may, at any time thereafter during such time as any part of the call or instalment

remains unpaid, serve a notice on him requiring payment of so much of the call or instalment as is unpaid, together with any interest which may have accrued.

(2) The notice shall name a further day (not earlier than the expiration of 14 days from the date of service of the notice) on or before which the payment required by the notice is to be made, and it shall state that in the event of non-payment at or before the time appointed, the shares [2] in respect of which the call was made shall be liable to be forfeited.

(3) If the requirements of any such notice as is mentioned in subsections (1) and (2) of this section are not complied with, any share[2] in respect of which notice has been given may at any time thereafter, before the payment required by the notice has been made, be forfeited by a resolution [3] of the directors [4] to that effect.

(4) A forfeited share [2] may be sold or otherwise disposed of on such terms and in such manner as the directors [4] think fit, and at any time before a sale or disposition, the forfeiture may be cancelled on such terms as the directors [4] think fit.

(5) A person whose shares [2] have been forfeited shall cease to be a member[1] in respect of the forfeited shares, [2] but shall, notwithstanding, remain liable to pay to the company [5] all moneys which, at the date of forfeiture, were payable by him to the company[5] in respect of the shares [2], but his liability shall cease if and when the company[5] receives payment in full of all such moneys in respect of the shares [2].

(6) A statutory declaration [6] that the declarant is a director [4] or the secretary of the company, [5] and that a share [2] in the company has been duly forfeited on a date stated in the declarations, [6] shall be prima facie evidence of the facts stated in it as against all persons claiming to be entitled to the shares. [2]

(7) The company [5] may receive the consideration, if any, given for the share [2] on any sale or disposition of it and may execute a transfer of the share [2] in favour of the person to whom the share is sold or disposed of, and he shall thereupon be registered as the holder of the share [2], and shall not be bound to see to the application of the purchase money, if any, nor shall his title to the share [2] be affected by any irregularity or invalidity in the proceedings in reference to the forfeiture, sale or disposal of the share. [2]

(8) The provisions of this section as to forfeiture shall apply in the case of non-payment of any sum which, by the terms of issue

of a share, [2] becomes payable at a fixed time, whether on account of the nominal value of the share [2] or by way of premium, [7] as if the same had been payable by virtue of a call duly made and notified.

---

**Notes**
**Section 140**

1. "Member" means the heir, executor, administrator or other personal representative, as the case may be, of the member. **See section 567 CAMA Cap. C20 LFN 2004**
2. "Share" means the interests in a company's shares capital of a member who is entitled to share in the Capital or income of such company and except where a distinction between stock and shares is expressed or implied, includes stock. **See section 567 of CAMA Cap C20 LFN, 2004**
3. "Resolution" means a main motion that formally expresses the sense, will or action of a deliberative assembly. **See Garner, B. (ed) Black's Law Dictionary, 8th ed.**
4. "Director" means any person occupying the position of director by whatever name called; and includes any person in accordance with whose directions or instructions the directors of the company are accustomed to act. See **section 567 CAMA, Cap. C20, LFN, 2004.**
5. "Company" means a company formed and registered under this Act or as the case may be, formed and registered in Nigeria before and in existence on the commencement of this Act **See section 567 CAMA, Cap. C20, LFN, 2004.**
6. "Statutory declaration" means a declaration voluntarily made under the Oaths Act and in Nigeria includes one so made under any other enactment or law providing for the taking of a voluntary declaration. See **section 567 of CAMA Cap C20 LFN, 2004**
7. "Premium" means the sum of money paid in addition to a regular price, salary or other amount; a bonus. See **Garner. (ed) Black's Law Dictionary, 8th ed.**

**Cross Reference**

On powers of a the director to call for shares on behalf of the company, see **section 133 CAMA, Cap. C20, LFN, 2004.**

On rights and liabilities attached to shares, see section 114 **CAMA, Cap. C20, LFN, 2004.**

On payment of shares generally, see section **135 CAMA, Cap. C20, LFN, 2004.**

---

**For Further Reading**

On Shares, Lien and Forfeiture of shares, Classes of Shares, Numbering of Shares, Share Certificates and Conversion of Shares see:

Orojo, J. Ola **Company Law and Practice in Nigeria** 3rd Edition, Mbeyi & Associates (Lagos, Nigeria) 1992.

Ogbuanya C.S. Nelson **Essentials of Corporate Law Practice in Nigeria** Novena Publishers Limited 2012

## 141. Power to vary rights

(1) If at any time the share capital [1] of a company[2] is divided into different classes of shares[3] under section 118 of this Act, the rights attached to any class (unless otherwise provided by the terms of issue of the shares of that class) may, whether or not the company[2] is being wound up[4], be varied with the consent, in writing, of the holders of three-quarters of the issued shares [3] of that class, or with the sanction of a special resolution [5] passed at a separate general meeting[6] of the holders of the shares [3] of the class.

(2) To every such separate general meeting [6] as is mentioned in subsection (1) of this section, the provisions of this Act relating to general meetings[6] shall apply, so however that the necessary quorum[7] shall be two persons at least holding or representing by proxy one-third of the issued shares of the class and that any holder of shares of the class present in person or by proxy may demand a poll.

(3) The rights conferred upon the holders of the shares [3] of any class issued with preferred or other rights shall not, unless otherwise expressly provided by the terms of issue of the shares [3] of that class, be deemed to be varied by the creation or issue of further shares ranking pari passu with them.

A resolution[8] shall be a special resolution [5] when it has been passed by not less than three fourths of the votes cast by such members [9] of the company[2]as, being entitled to do so, vote in person or by proxy at a general meeting[6] of which 21 days' notice, specifying the intention to propose the resolution [8] as a special resolution,[5] has been duly given: (see S. 223 (2) CAMA)

---

**Notes**

**Section 141**

1. "Share Capital" means one of the definite numbers of equal parts into which the capital stock of a corporation or joint stock company is divided. **See Garner, B. (ed) Black's Law Dictionary, 8th ed.**
2. "Company" means a company formed and registered under this Act or as the case may be, formed and registered in Nigeria before and in existence on the commencement of this Act **See section 567 CAMA, Cap. C20, LFN, 2004.**
3. "Shares" see "share". It means the interests in a company's shares capital of a member who is entitled to share in the Capital or income of such company and except where a distinction between stock and shares is

expressed or implied, includes stock. **Section 567 of CAMA Cap C20 LFN, 2004**

4. "Wound up" see "winding up". It means the process of settling accounts and liquidation of assets in anticipation of a partnership's or a corporation dissolution. . **See Garner B. (ed) Black's Law Dictionary, 8th ed.**
5. "Special resolution" is a resolution that has been passed by not less than three fourths of the votes cast by such members of the company as, being entitled to do so, vote in person or by proxy at a general meeting of which 21 days' notice, specifying the intention to propose the resolution as a special resolution, has been duly given. See **section 233 CAMA, Cap. C20, LFN 2004.**
6. "Meeting" means a gathering of people to discuss or act on matters in which they have common interest esp. a deliberative assembly to transact business. See **Garner, B. (ed) Black's Law Dictionary, 8 th ed.**
7. "Quorum" means the minimum number of members who must be present for a deliberative assembly. See **Garner B. (ed) Black's Law Dictionary 8th ed.**
8. "Resolution" means a main motion that formally expresses the sense, will or action of a deliberative assembly. **See Garner, B. (ed) Black's Law Dictionary, 8th ed.**
9. "Members" see "member". It means one of the individuals of whom a deliberative assembly consists and who enjoys the full rights of participating in the organization-including the rights of making, debating and voting on motions- except to the extent that the organization reserves those rights to certain classes of membership. See **Garner B. (ed.) Black's Law Dictionary 8th ed.**

   "Member" includes the heir, executor, administrator or other personal representative as the case may be, of the member. See **section 567 of CAMA Cap C20 LFN, 2004**

**Cross Reference**

On Winding-up of companies, see Part XV **CAMA, Cap. C20, LFN 2004.**

On types of resolution, see **section 233 CAMA Cap. C20, LFN 2004**

---

## 142. Application for cancellation of variation

(1) Where in pursuance of section 141 of this Act, the rights attached to any class of shares [1] are at any time varied, the holder of not less in the aggregate than fifteen per cent of the issued shares [1] of that class, being persons who did not consent to or vote in favour of the resolution[2] for the variation, may apply to the court [3] to have the variation cancelled, and, where any such application is made, the variation shall not have effect, unless and until it is confirmed by the court.[3]

(2) An application to the court [3] under this section shall, in a proper case, be made within 21 days after the date on which the

consent was given or the resolution [2] was passed, as the case may be, and may be made on behalf of the shareholders [4] entitled to make the application or by such one or more of their number as they may appoint in writing for the purpose.

(3) If on any such application the court, [3] after hearing the applicant and any other persons applying to it to be heard and appearing to be interested in the application, is satisfied that the variation would unfairly prejudice the shareholders [4] of the class represented by the applicant, the court, [3] having regard to all the circumstances of the case, may disallow the variation, and shall, if not satisfied, confirm the variation.

(4) The decision of the court [3] on any such application shall be final.

(5) The company [5] shall, within 15 days after the making of an order by the court [3] on an application to it under this section, forward a copy of the order to the Commission [6] and if default is made in complying with the provisions of this subsection, the company[5] and every officer [7] of the company [5] who is in default shall be liable to a fine of N50 for every day during which the default continues.

(6) In this section, "variation" includes abrogation and cognate expressions shall be constructed accordingly.

---

**Notes**
**Section 142**

1. Shares" see "share." It means the interest in a company's share capital of a member who is entitled to share in the capital or income of such company. See sect**ion 567 CAMA Cap. C20 LFN 2004**
2. "Resolution" means a main motion that formally expresses the sense, will or action of a deliberative assembly. **See Garner, B. (ed) Black's Law Dictionary, 8th ed.**
3. "Court" means the Federal High Court, and to the extent to which application may be made to it as: court includes the court of Appeal, and the Supreme Court of Nigeria. **See section 567 CAMA, Cap. C20, LFN, 2004.**
4. "Shareholders" see "shareholder". It means one who owns or holds a share or shares in a company. See **Garner B. (ed) Black's Law Dictionary, 8th ed.**
5. "Company" means a company formed and registered under this Act or as the case may be, formed and registered in Nigeria before and in existence on the commencement of this Act **See section 567 CAMA, Cap. C20, LFN, 2004.**

6. "Commission" means the Corporate Affairs Commission established under section 1 of this Act. **See section 567 CAMA, Cap. C20, LFN, 2004.**

Cross Reference

On types of resolution, see **section 233 CAMC Cap. C20, LFN 2004**

On the establishment and jurisdiction of the Federal High Court, **see section 249 & 251 of Constitution of the Federal Republic of Nigeria, 1999(as amended)**

**For Further Reading**

On Shares, Lien and Forfeiture of shares, Classes of Shares, Numbering of Shares, Share Certificates and Conversion of Shares see:

Orojo, J. Ola **Company Law and Practice in Nigeria** 3rd Edition, Mbeyi & Associates (Lagos, Nigeria) 1992.

Ogbuanya C.S. Nelson **Essentials of Corporate Law Practice in Nigeria** Novena Publishers Limited 2012

## 143. Right of a preference share to more than one vote

(1) Notwithstanding the provisions of section 116 of this Act, the articles[1] may provide that preference shares [2] issued after the commencement of this Act shall carry the rights to attend general meetings[3] and on a poll at the meetings, [3] to more than one vote per share[4] in the following circumstances, but not otherwise, that is to say-

(a) upon any resolution [5] during such period as the preferential dividend[6] or any part of it remains in arrears and unpaid, such period starting from a date not more than 12 months or such lesser period as the articles [1] may provide, after the due date of the dividend [6]; or

(b) upon any resolution [5] which varies the rights attached to such shares[4]; or

(c) upon any resolution [5] to remove an auditor [7] of the company[8] or to appoint another person in place of such auditor;[7] or

(d) upon any resolution [5] for the winding up [9] of the company [8] or during the winding up [9] of the company. [8]

(2) Notwithstanding the provisions of section 116 of this Act, any special resolution [10] of a company [8] increasing the number of shares[4] of any class, may validly resolve that any existing class of preference shares [2] shall carry the right to such votes additional to

one vote per share[4] as shall be necessary in order to preserve the existing ratio which the votes exercisable by the holders of such preference shares[3] at a general meeting[3] of the company[8] bear to the total votes exercisable at the meeting.[3]

(3) For the purposes of subsection (2) of this section, a dividend[6] shall be deemed to be due on the date appointed in the articles[1] for the payment of the dividend[6] for any year or other period, or if no such date is appointed, upon the day immediately following the expiration of the year or other period, and whether or not such dividend[6] shall have been earned or declared.

A resolution[5] shall be a special resolution[10] when it has been passed by not less than three fourths of the votes cast by such members[7] of the company[8] as, being entitled to do so, vote in person or by proxy at a general meeting[3] of which 21 days' notice, specifying the intention to propose the resolution[5] as a special resolution,[10] has been duly given: (see S. 223 (2) CAMA)

---

**Notes**
**Section 143**

1. "Articles" means the articles of association of a company, as originally framed or as altered by special resolution, including so far as they apply to the regulations contained in Table A in the First Schedules of the Companies Act, 1922 or in that Table as altered by any subsequent enactment or reprint of the laws, or in Table A in the First Schedule to this Act. See **section 567 CAMA, Cap. C20, LFN, 2004.**
2. "Preference shares" means a share, by whatever name designated, which does not entitle the holder of it to any right to participate beyond a specified amount in any distribution whether by way of dividend or on redemption, in a winding up, or otherwise. See **Section 567 CAMA, Cap. C20 , LFN 2004.**
3. "General Meeting" means the gathering of people to discuss or act on matters in which they have a common interest. See **Garner B. (ed) Black's Law Dictionary 8th ed.**
4. "Share" means the interests in a company's shares capital of a member who is entitled to share in the Capital or income of such company and except where a distinction between stock and shares is expressed or implied, includes stock. See **section 567 of CAMA Cap C20 LFN, 2004**
5. "Resolution" means a main motion that formally expresses the sense, will or action of a deliberative assembly. **See Garner, B. (ed) Black's Law Dictionary, 8th ed.**
6. "Dividend" means a proportion of the distributed profits of the company which may be a fixed annual percentage, as in the case of preference shares, or it may be variable according to the prosperity or other

circumstances of the company, as in the case of equity shares. See section**567 CAMA Cap. C20 LFN 2004**

7. "Auditor" means a person or firm, usually an accountant that formally examines an individual or an entity's financial records or status. See **Garner B. (ed.) Black's Law Dictionary8th ed.**
8. "Company" means a company formed and registered under this Act or as the case may be, formed and registered in Nigeria before and in existence on the commencement of this Act **See section 567 CAMA, Cap. C20, LFN, 2004.**
9. "Winding up" means the process of settling accounts and liquidation of assets in anticipation of a partnership's or a corporation dissolution. . **See Garner B. (ed) Black's Law Dictionary, 8th ed.**
10. "Special resolution" is a resolution that has been passed by not less than three fourths of the votes cast by such members of the company as, being entitled to do so, vote in person or by proxy at a general meeting of which 21 days' notice, specifying the intention to propose the resolution as a special resolution, has been duly given. See **section 233 CAMA, Cap. C20, LFN 2004.**

**For Further Reading**

On Shares, Lien and Forfeiture of shares, Classes of Shares, Numbering of Shares, Share Certificates and Conversion of Shares see:

Orojo, J. Ola **Company Law and Practice in Nigeria** 3rd Edition, Mbeyi & Associates (Lagos, Nigeria) 1992.

Ogbuanya C.S. Nelson **Essentials of Corporate Law Practice in Nigeria** Novena Publishers Limited 2012

---

## 144. Construction of class rights

In construing the provisions of a company's [1] articles[2] in respect of the rights attached to shares[3], the following rules of construction shall be observed-

(a) unless the contrary intention appears, no dividend [4] shall be payable on any shares[3] unless the company[5] shall resolve to declare such dividend[4];

(b) unless the contrary intention appears, a fixed preferential dividend[4] payable on any class of shares [3]is cumulative, that is to say, no dividend [4]shall be payable on any shares[3] ranking subsequent to them until all the arrears of the fixed dividend[4] have been paid;

(c) unless the contrary intention appears, in a winding up [5] arrears of any cumulative preferential dividend, [4] whether earned or declared or not, are payable up to the date of actual payment in the winding up[5];

(d) if any class of shares [3] is expressed to have a right to a preferential dividend[4], then, unless the contrary intention appears, such class has no further right to participate in dividends[4];

(e) if any class of shares [3] is expressed to have preferential rights to payment out of the assets of the company [2] in the event of winding up[5], then unless the contrary intention appears, such class has no further right to participate in the distribution of assets in the winding up [5];

(f) in determining the rights of the various classes to share in the distribution of the company's [1] property on a winding up,[5] no regard shall be paid, unless the contrary intention appears, to whether or not such property represents accumulated profits or surplus which would have been available for dividend[4] while the company[1] remained a going concern;

(g) subject to this section, all shares [3] rank equally in all respects unless the contrary intention appears in the company's [1] articles. [2]

---

**Notes**
**Section 144**

1. "Company" means a company formed and registered under this Act or as the case may be, formed and registered in Nigeria before and in existence on the commencement of this Act **See section 567 CAMA, Cap. C20, LFN, 2004.**
2. "Articles" means the articles of association of a company, as originally framed or as altered by special resolution, including so far as they apply to the regulations contained in Table A in the First Schedules of the Companies Act, 1922 or in that Table as altered by any subsequent enactment or reprint of the laws, or in Table A in the First Schedule to this Act. See **section 567 CAMA, Cap. C20, LFN, 2004.**
3. "Shares" see "share". It means the interest in a company's share capital of a member who is entitled to share in the capital or income of such company. **See section 567 CAMA, Cap. C20, LFN, 2004.**
4. "Dividend" means a proportion of the distributed profits of the company which may be a fixed annual percentage, as in the case of preference shares, or it may be variable according to the prosperity or other circumstances of the company, as in the case of equity shares. See section**567 CAMA Cap. C20 LFN 2004**
5. "Winding up" means the process of settling accounts and liquidation of assets in anticipation of a partnership's or a corporation dissolution. . **See Garner B. (ed) Black's Law Dictionary, 8th ed.**

**For Further Reading**

On Shares, Lien and Forfeiture of shares, Classes of Shares, Numbering of Shares, Share Certificates and Conversion of Shares see:

Orojo, J. Ola **Company Law and Practice in Nigeria** 3rd Edition, Mbeyi & Associates (Lagos, Nigeria) 1992.

Ogbuanya C.S. Nelson **Essentials of Corporate Law Practice in Nigeria Novena** Publishers Limited 2012

## 145. Shares to be numbered

Each share[1] in a company[2] having a share capital[3] shall be distinguished by its appropriate number:

Provided that, if at any time all the issued shares [1] in a company,[2] or all of its issued shares [1]of a particular class, are fully paid up and rank pari passu for all purposes, none of those shares [1] need thereafter have a distinguishing number so long as it remains fully paid up and ranks pari passu for all purposes with all shares [1] of the same class for the time being issued and fully paid up.

**Notes**

**Section 145**

1. "Shares" see "share". it means the interests in a company's shares capital of a member who is entitled to share in the Capital or income of such company and except where a distinction between stock and shares is expressed or implied, includes stock. **Section 567 of CAMA Cap C20 LFN, 2004**
2. "Company" means a company formed and registered under this Act or as the case may be, formed and registered in Nigeria before and in existence on the commencement of this Act. **See section 567 CAMA, Cap. C20, LFN, 2004.**
3. "Share capital" means one of the definite numbers of equal parts into which the capital stock of a corporation or joint stock company is divided. **See Garner B. (ed) Black's Law Dictionary, 8th ed.**

**For Further Reading**

On Shares, Lien and Forfeiture of shares, Classes of Shares, Numbering of Shares, Share Certificates and Conversion of Shares see:

Orojo, J. Ola **Company Law and Practice in Nigeria** 3rd Edition, Mbeyi & Associates (Lagos, Nigeria) 1992.

Ogbuanya C.S. Nelson **Essentials of Corporate Law Practice in Nigeria** Novena Publishers Limited 2012

*Share certificates*

**146. Issue of share certificates**

(1) Every company [1] shall, within two months after the allotment of any of its shares [2] and within three months after the date on which a transfer of any such shares is lodged with the company[1], complete and have ready for delivery the certificates [3] of all shares[2] allotted or transferred, unless the conditions of issue of the shares[2] otherwise provide.

(2) Every person whose name is entered as a member [4] in the register of members [4] shall be entitled, without payment, to receive within three months of allotment or lodgement of transfer or within such other period as the conditions of issue shall provide, one certificate[3] for all his shares [2]or several certificates [3] each for one or more of his shares [2] upon payment of a fee as the directors [5] shall, from time to time, determine.

(3) Every certificate issued by a company shall be under the company's [1] seal[6] and shall specify the shares [2] to which it relates and the amount paid up on them:
Provided that in respect of shares [2] held jointly by several persons [3], the company[1] shall not be bound to issue more than one certificate, and delivery of a certificate [3] for shares [2] to one of several joint holders shall be sufficient delivery to all such holders.

(4) If a share certificate [3] is defaced, lost or destroyed, it may be replaced on such terms (if any), as to evidence and indemnity and the payment of out-of-pocket expenses of the company [1] of investigating evidence as the directors [5] think fit.

(5) If any company [1] on which a notice has been served requiring it to make good any default in complying with the provisions of subsection (1) of this section, fails to make good the default within 10 days after the service of the notice, the court [6] may, on the application of the person entitled to have the certificate[3] delivered to him, make an order directing the company [1]and any officer [7] of the company [1] to make good the default within such time as may be specified in the order, and any such order may provide that all costs of and incidental to the application shall be borne by the company [1] or by any officer [7] of the company [1] responsible for the default.

(6) If default is made in complying with this section, the company[1] and every officer [7] of the company [1] who is in default,

shall be liable to a fine of N50 for every day during which the default continues.

(7) In this section, "transfer" means a transfer duly stamped and otherwise valid, but does not include a transfer which under this Act a company[1] is for any reason entitled to refuse to, and does not, register.

---

**Notes**
**Section 146**

1. "Company" "means" a company formed and registered under this Act or as the case may be, formed and registered in Nigeria before and in existence on the commencement of this Act. **See section 567 CAMA, Cap. C20, LFN, 2004.**
2. "Shares" see "share." It means the interests in a company's shares capital of a member who is entitled to share in the Capital or income of such company and except where a distinction between stock and shares is expressed or implied, includes stock. **Section 567 CAMA Cap C20 LFN, 2004**
3. "Certificate" see "share certificate." It means an instrument evidencing ownership of a bond or shares of stock. See **Garner B. (ed.) Black's Law Dictionary 8th ed.**
4. "Members" "see "member." It means one of the individuals of whom a deliberative assembly consists and who enjoys the full rights of participating in the organization-including the rights of making, debating and voting on motions- except to the extent that the organization reserves those rights to certain classes of membership. See **Garner B. (ed.) Black's Law Dictionary 8th ed.** "Member" includes the heir, executor, administrator or other personal representative as the case may be, of the member. See **section 567 CAMA Cap C20 LFN, 2004**
5. "Director" means any person occupying the position of director by whatever name called; and includes any person in accordance with whose directions or instructions the directors of the company are accustomed to act. See **section 567 CAMA, Cap. C20, LFN, 2004.**
6. "Court" when used in relation to a company, means the federal High court, and to the extent to which application may be made to it as; court includes the court of appeal and the supreme court of Nigeria. See **section 567 CAMA, Cap. C20, LFN 2004.**
7. "Officer" means in relation to a body corporate includes a director, manager or secretary. See **Section 567 CAMA Cap. C20, LFN 2004.**

**Cross Reference**

On the establishment and jurisdiction of the Federal High Court, **see section 249 & 251 of Constitution of the Federal Republic of Nigeria, 1999(as amended)**

---

**For Further Reading**

On Shares, Lien and Forfeiture of shares, Classes of Shares, Numbering of Shares, Share Certificates and Conversion of Shares see:

Orojo, J. Ola **Company Law and Practice in Nigeria** 3rd Edition, Mbeyi & Associates (Lagos, Nigeria) 1992.

Ogbuanya C.S. Nelson **Essentials of Corporate Law Practice in Nigeria** Novena Publishers Limited 2012

## 147. Effect of share certificate

(1) A certificate [1], under the common seal [2] of the company [3], specifying any shares [4] held by any member, [5] shall be prima facie evidence of the title of the member [5] to the shares. [4]

(2) If any person changes his position to his detriment in good faith on the continued accuracy of the statements made in a certificate, the company [3] shall be estopped from denying the continued accuracy of such statements and shall compensate the person for any loss suffered by him in reliance on them and which he would not have suffered had the statements been or continued to be accurate.

(3) Nothing contained in subsection (2) of this section shall derogate from any right the company [2] may have to be indemnified by any other person.

---

**Notes**

**Section 147**

1. "Certificate" see "share certificate" means an instrument evidencing ownership of a bond or shares of stock. See **Garner B. (ed.) Black's Law Dictionary 8th ed.**
2. "Common Seal" "means a seal adopted by a company for authenticating and executing its corporate and legal instruments. **See Garner B. (ed). Black's Law Dictionary, 8th ed.**
3. "Company" " means a company formed and registered under this Act or as the case may be, formed and registered in Nigeria before and in existence on the commencement of this Act. **See section 567 CAMA, Cap. C20, LFN, 2004**
4. "Members" see "member". It means one of the individuals of whom a deliberative assembly consists and who enjoys the full rights of participating in the organization-including the rights of making, debating and voting on motions- except to the extent that the organization reserves those rights to certain classes of membership. See **Garner B. (ed.) Black's Law Dictionary 8th ed.**

"Member" includes the heir, executor, administrator or other personal representative as the case may be, of the member. See **section 567 CAMA Cap C20 LFN, 2004**

5. "Shares" see "share". It means the interests in a company's shares capital of a member who is entitled to share in the Capital or income of such company and except where a distinction between stock and shares is expressed or implied, includes stock. **See section 567 CAMA Cap C20 LFN, 2004**

Cross Reference

On obligation of the company to have and use common seal, see **section 74 CAMA, Cap. C20, LFN 2004**

**Cases**

Failure to use the common seal when necessary renders the Agreement ineffectual. See ***African Development Corp Ltd V L.E.D.B (1966) NCLR 438***

**For Further Reading**

On Shares, Lien and Forfeiture of shares, Classes of Shares, Numbering of Shares, Share Certificates and Conversion of Shares see:

Orojo, J. Ola **Company Law and Practice in Nigeria** 3rd Edition, Mbeyi & Associates (Lagos, Nigeria) 1992.

Ogbuanya C.S. Nelson **Essentials of Corporate Law Practice in Nigeria** Novena Publishers Limited 2012

## 148. Probate, etc., as evidence of grant

The production to a company[1] of any document[2] which is by law sufficient evidence of probate of the will, or letters of administration of the estate, or confirmation as executor, of a deceased person having been granted to some person, shall be accepted by the company[1] as sufficient evidence of the grant, notwithstanding anything in its articles[3] to the contrary.

**Notes**

**Section 148**

1. "Company" means a company formed and registered under this Act or as the case may be, formed and registered in Nigeria before and in existence on the commencement of this Act. **See section 567CAMA, Cap. C20, LFN, 2004**
2. "Document" includes summons, notices, order and other legal processes and register. See **Garner B. (ed) Blacks's Law Dictionary, 8th ed.**
3. "Articles" means the articles of association of a company, as originally framed or as altered by special resolution, including so far as they apply

to the regulations contained in Table A in the First Schedules of the Companies Act, 1922 or in that Table as altered by any subsequent enactment or reprint of the laws, or in Table A in the First Schedule to this Act. See **section 567 CAMA, Cap. C20, LFN, 2004.**

---

## 149. Abolition of share warrants

(1) As from the date of commencement of this Act, no company[1] shall have the power to issue warrants. [2]

(2) Every company [1] shall within a period of 30 days from the date of commencement of this Act, cancel any share warrants [2] previously issued by it which are still valid on that date and enter in its register of members [3] the names and relevant particulars of the bearers of the share warrants [3].

(3) A person whose name is entered in a company's [2] register of members[3] by virtue of subsection (2) of this section, shall be deemed to be a member [3] of the company [1] with effect from the date on which

---

**Notes**
**Section 149**

1. "Company" means a company formed and registered under this Act or as the case may be, formed and registered in Nigeria before and in existence on the commencement of this Act. **See section 567 CAMA, Cap. C20, LFN, 2004**
2. "Warrants" see "warrant". It means a document conferring authority, especially to pay or receive money. See **Garner B. (ed.) Black's Law Dictionary 8th ed.**
3. "Members" see "member". It means one of the individuals of whom a deliberative assembly consists and who enjoys the full rights of participating in the organization-including the rights of making, debating and voting on motions- except to the extent that the organization reserves those rights to certain classes of membership. See **Garner B., (ed.) Black's Law Dictionary 8th ed.**
   "Member" includes the heir, executor, administrator or other personal representative as the case may be, of the member. **See section 567 CAMA Cap C20 LFN, 2004**

---

### *Conversion of shares into stock*

**Section 150**

(1) The provisions of this section shall apply with respect to the conversion of all or any of the shares [1] of a company[2]

into stock and the re-conversion of such stock into shares [1] under the provisions of section 100 of this Act.

(2) The conversion of any paid-up shares [1] into stock and the re-conversion of any stock into paid-up shares [1] shall be by ordinary resolution [3] of the company at a general meeting. [4]

(3) The holders of stock may transfer the same, or any part of it, in the same manner and subject to the same conditions, as and subject to which the shares [1] from which the stock arose might, previous to the conversion, have been transferred, or as near to it as circumstances admit; and the directors [5] may, from time to time, fix the minimum amount of stock transferable, so however that such minimum shall not exceed the nominal amount of the shares from which the stock arose.

(4) The holders of stock shall, according to the amount of stock held by them, have the same rights, privileges and advantages as regards dividends [6], voting at meetings [4] of the company[2] and other matters as if they held the shares [1] from which the stock arose, but no such privilege or advantage (except participation in the dividends [5] and profit of the company [2] and in the assets on winding up [7]) shall be conferred by an amount of stock which would not, if existing in shares, have conferred that privilege or advantage.

(5) Such of the articles [8] of the company [2] as are applicable to paid-up shares[1] shall apply to stock, and the words "shares" [1] and "shareholder" [9] in those articles shall include "stock" and "stockholder."

---

**Notes**

**Section 150**

1. "Shares" see "share." It means the interests in a company's shares capital of a member who is entitled to share in the Capital or income of such company and except where a distinction between stock and shares is expressed or implied, includes stock. **Section 567 of CAMA Cap C20 LFN, 2004**
2. "Company" " means a company formed and registered under this Act or, as the case may be, formed and registered in Nigeria before and in existence on the commencement of this Act. See section 567 **CAMA, Cap. C20, LFN, 2004.**

3. "Ordinary resolution" is a resolution reached when it has been passed by a simple majority of votes cast by such members of the company as, being entitled to do so, vote in person or by proxy at a general meeting. See **section 233(1) CAMA Cap. C20, LFN 2004**
"Ordinary resolution" means a decision reached by a simple majority (i.e. of more than 50%) of company members voting in person or by proxy. It is appropriate where no other type of resolution is expressly required by the Companies Acts or the articles of association. See **Martins E. (ed.) Oxford Dictionary of Law 4 th ed.**
4. "Meeting" means the gathering of people to discuss or act on matters in which they have a common interest. See **Garner B. (ed) Black's Law Dictionary 8th ed.**
5. "Director" means any person occupying the position of director by whatever name called; and includes any person in accordance with whose directions or instructions the directors of the company are accustomed to act. See **section 567 CAMA, Cap. C20, LFN, 2004.**
6. "Dividend" means a proportion of the distributed profits of the company which may be a fixed annual percentage, as in the case of preference shares, or it may be variable according to the prosperity or other circumstances of the company, as in the case of equity shares. See section**567 CAMA Cap. C20 LFN 2004**
7. "Articles" means the articles of association of a company, as originally framed or as altered by special resolution, including so far as they apply to the regulations contained in Table A in the First Schedules of the Companies Act, 1922 or in that Table as altered by any subsequent enactment or reprint of the laws, or in Table A in the First Schedule to this Act. See **section 567 CAMA, Cap. C20, LFN, 2004.**
8. "Shareholder" means one who owns or holds a share or shares in a company. See **Garner B. (ed) Black's Law Dictionary, 8th ed.**

---

**For Further Reading**

On Shares, Lien and Forfeiture of shares, Classes of Shares, Numbering of Shares, Share Certificates and Conversion of Shares see:

Orojo, J. Ola **Company Law and Practice in Nigeria** 3rd Edition, Mbeyi & Associates (Lagos, Nigeria) 1992.

Ogbuanya C.S. Nelson **Essentials of Corporate Law Practice in Nigeria** Novena Publishers Limited 2012

## 151. Transfer of shares

(1) The transfer of a company's [1] shares[2] shall be by instrument of transfer and except as expressly provided in the articles,[3] transfer of shares [2] shall be without restrictions.

(2) Notwithstanding anything in the articles [3] of a company, [1] it shall not be lawful for the company [1] to register a transfer of shares [2]

in the company,[1] unless a proper instrument of transfer has been delivered to the company [1]
Provided that nothing in this section shall prejudice any power of the company[1] to register as shareholder, [4] any person to whom the right to any shares[2] in the company[1] has been transmitted by operation of law.

(3) The instrument of transfer of any share [2] shall be executed by or on behalf of the transferor and transferee, and the transferor shall be deemed to remain a holder of the share [2] until the name of the transferee is entered in the register of members [5] in respect of the share,[2]

(4) Subject to such of the restrictions of a company [1]'s articles[3] as may be applicable, any member [5] may transfer all or any of his shares[2] by instrument in writing in any usual or common form or any other form which the directors [6] may approve.

---

**Notes**
**Section 151**

1. "Company" means a company formed and registered under this Act or, as the case may be, formed and registered in Nigeria before and in existence on the commencement of this Act. See **section 567 CAMA, Cap. C20, LFN, 2004**
2. "Shares" see "share". It means the interests in a company's shares capital of a member who is entitled to share in the Capital or income of such company and except where a distinction between stock and shares is expressed or implied, includes stock. **Section 567 of CAMA Cap C20 LFN, 2004**
3. "Articles" means the articles of association of a company, as originally framed or as altered by special resolution, including so far as they apply to the regulations contained in Table A in the First Schedules of the Companies Act, 1922 or in that Table as altered by any subsequent enactment or reprint of the laws, or in Table A in the First Schedule to this Act. See **section 567 CAMA Cap. C20 LFN 2004**
4. "Shareholder" is one who owns or holds a share or shares in a company especially a corporation. **See Garner B. (ed) Black's Law Dictionary, 8th ed.**
5. "Members" see "member." It means one of the individuals of whom a deliberative assembly consists and who enjoys the full rights of participating in the organization-including the rights of making, debating and voting on motions- except to the extent that the organization reserves those rights to certain classes of membership. See Garner B., (ed.) Black's Law Dictionary 8th ed.
"Member" includes the heir, executor, administrator or other personal representative as the case may be, of the member. See section 567 of CAMA Cap C20 LFN, 2004

6. "Directors" see "director". It includes any person occupying the position of director by whatever name called; and includes any person in accordance with whose directions or instructions the directors of the company are accustomed to act. See **Section. 567 CAMA, Cap. C20 , LFN 2004**

Cross Reference

On obligation of a Company to enter names of members in the register of members, see **section 79 CAMA Cap. C20 LFN 2004**

**Cases**

Upon registration, the subscribers are deemed to have agreed to become members and their names must be put in the register of members. See ***Ezeonwu v. Onyechi (1996) 2 SCNJ 250***

By the provisions of Companies and Allied Matters Act, Section 115, shares are in the nature of personal estate and freely transferable but subject to statutory restrictions and the articles of the company. Members in a company have a right to transfer shares belonging to them therein and this right is unfettered unless there is an express restriction to that effect in the articles or constitution of the company. ***N.R.I. Ltd v. Oranusi*** **(2011) All F.W.L.R part 577. 625-824 at p.765** .

**For Further Reading**

On transfer of shares, company, see, Sofowora, M.O **Modern Nigerian Company Law** (Soft Associates, 2nd Edition 2002).

## 152. Entry in register of transfers

(1) On the application of the transferor of any share [1] or interest in a company[2], the company[2] shall enter in its register of members[3], the name of the transferee in the same conditions as if the application for the entry were made by the transferee.

(2) Until the name of the transferee is entered in the register of members[3] in respect of the transferred shares [1], the transferor shall, so far as concerns the company, [2] be deemed to remain the holder of the shares [1].

(3) The company[2] may refuse to register the transfer of a share[1] (not being a fully paid share [1]) to a person of whom they do not approve, and may also refuse to register the transfer of a share [1] on which the company[2] has a lien.[4]

(4) The company[2] may refuse to recognise any instrument of transfer unless-

(a) a fee as the company [2] may, from time to time, determine is paid to the company [2] in respect of the instrument [5]; and

(b) the instrument[5] of transfer is accompanied by the certificate of the shares[1] to which it relates and such other evidence as the directors[6] may reasonably require to show the right of the transferor to make the transfer; and

(c) the instrument[5] of transfer is in respect of only one class of shares.[1]

---

**Notes**
**Section 152**

1. "Shares" see share. It means the interests in a company's shares capital of a member who is entitled to share in the Capital or income of such company and except where a distinction between stock and shares is expressed or implied, includes stock. **Section 567 of CAMA Cap C20 LFN, 2004**
2. "Company" means a company formed and registered under this Act or, as the case may be, formed and registered in Nigeria before and in existence on the commencement of this Act. See **section 567 CAMA, Cap. C20, LFN, 2004**
3. "Members" see "member." It means one of the individuals of whom a deliberative assembly consists and who enjoys the full rights of participating in the organization-including the rights of making, debating and voting on motions- except to the extent that the organization reserves those rights to certain classes of membership. **See Garner B. (ed.) Black's Law Dictionary 8th ed.**
   "Member" includes the heir, executor, administrator or other personal representative as the case may be, of the member. **See section 567 of CAMA Cap C20 LFN, 2004**
4. **"Lien"**
5. "Instrument" is a written legal document that defines rights, duties, entitlements, or liabilities, such as a contract, will, promissory note, or share certificate. See **Garner B. (ed) Black's Law Dictionary, 8th ed.**
6. "Director" includes any person occupying the position of director by whatever name called; and includes any person in accordance with whose directions or instructions the directors of the company are accustomed to act. See **Section. 567 CAMA, Cap. C20 , LFN 2004**

**Cross Reference**

On obligation of a Company to enter names of members in the register of members, see **section 79 CAMA Cap. C20 LFN 2004**

---

**Cases**

The definition of a company in section 650 of Companies and Allied Matters Act puts the matter beyond doubt. It defines a 'company' or 'existing' to mean....a company formed and registered in Nigeria before and in existence on the commencement of this Act. ***Agro Allied Dev. Ent. Ltd. v. Reefer*** **(2009) Vol.31 W.R.N 1-185 at pg 7** .

**For Further Reading**

Oon company, register of transfer of shares, see, Ayua, I.A *Nigerian Company Law* G. Burn (Leighton Buzzard, Bedfordshire, United Kingdom) 1984.

## 153. Notice of refusal to register

(1) If a company [1] refuses to register a transfer of any shares [2] it shall, within two months after the date on which the transfer was lodged with it, send notice of the refusal to the transferee.

(2) If default is made in complying with this section, the company and every officer [3]of the company who is in default shall be liable to a fine of N 200.

---

**Notes**

**Section 153**

1. "Company" means a company formed and registered under this Act or, as the case may be, formed and registered in Nigeria before and in existence on the commencement of this Act. See **section 567 CAMA, Cap. C20, LFN, 2004**
2. "Shares" see "share". It means the interests in a company's shares capital of a member who is entitled to share in the Capital or income of such company and except where a distinction between stock and shares is expressed or implied, includes stock. **Section 567 of CAMA Cap C20 LFN, 2004**
3. "Officer" in relation to a body corporate includes a director, manager or secretary. See **section 567 CAMA Cap. C20, LFN 2004**

**Cross Reference**

On transfer of shares, see **section 151 CAMA Cap. C20 LFN 2004**

---

## 154. Transfer by personal representative

A transfer of the share [1] or other interest of a deceased member[2] of a company[3] made by his personal representative [4] shall, although the personal representative[4] is not himself a member[2] of the company,[3] be as valid as if he had been such a member [2] at the time of the execution of the instrument [5] of transfer.

---

**Notes**

1. "Share" means the interests in a company's shares capital of a member who is entitled to share in the Capital or income of such company and except where a distinction between stock and shares is expressed or implied, includes stock. See **Section 567 of CAMA Cap C20 LFN, 2004**
2. "Member" means one of the individuals of whom a deliberative assembly consists and who enjoys the full rights of participating in the organization-including the rights of making, debating and voting on motions- except to the extent that the organization reserves those rights to certain classes of membership. See **Garner B.** (ed.) Black's Law Dictionary 8th ed.
   "Member" includes the heir, executor, administrator or other personal representative as the case may be, of the member. See **section 567 of CAMA Cap C20 LFN, 2004**
3. "Company" means a company formed and registered under this Act or, as the case may be, formed and registered in Nigeria before and in existence on the commencement of this Act. See **section 567 CAMA, Cap. C20, LFN, 2004**
4. "Personal Representative" means a person who manages the legal affairs of another because of incapacity or death, such as the executor of an estate. See **Garner, B. (ed) Black's Law Dictionary, 8th ed.**
   "personal representative" where customary law is applicable, includes successors appointed in respect of deceased contributories. See **section 567 CAMA Cap. C20, LFN 2004**
5. "Instrument" is a written legal document that defines rights, duties, entitlements, or liabilities, such as a contract, will, promissory note, or share certificate. See **Garner B. (ed) Black's Law Dictionary, 8th ed.**

---

**Cases**

Entry in the register of the company is another method of proof of being a shareholder, but it is not the only method nor can the absence of that method of proof invalidate other methods. ***Ponmile v. Sparks Electrics (Nig) Ltd*** **(1986) 2 N.W.L.R pg 519.**

## 155. Transmission of shares

(1) In case of the death of a member [1], the survivor or survivors where the deceased was a joint holder, or the legal personal representative[2] of the deceased where he was a sole holder, shall be the only persons recognised by the company [3] as having any title to his interest in the shares [4]; but nothing in this

section shall release the estate of a deceased joint holder from any liability in respect of any share [4] which had been jointly held by him with other persons.

(2) Any person becoming entitled to a share [4] in consequence of the death or bankruptcy [5] of a member may, upon such evidence being produced as may, from time to time, properly be required by the directors [6] and subject as hereafter provided in this section, elect either to be registered himself as holder of the share [4], or to have some person nominated by him registered as the transferee of the share[4]; but the company [3] shall, in either case, have the same right to decline or suspend registration as they would have had in the case of a transfer of the share [4] by that member [1] before his death or bankruptcy[5], as the case may be.

(3) If the person so becoming entitled elects to be registered himself, he shall deliver or send to the company [3] a notice in writing signed by him stating that he so elects and if he elects to have another person registered, he shall testify his election by executing to that person a transfer of the share. [4]

(4) All the limitations, restrictions and provisions of this Act and the company's [3] articles[7] relating to the rights to transfer and the registration of transfers of share [4], shall be applicable to any such notice or transfer as mentioned in subsection (3) of this section as if the death or bankruptcy [5] of the member [1] had not occurred and the notice or transfer were a transfer signed by that member [1].

(5) A person becoming entitled to a share [4] by reason of the death or bankruptcy [5] of the holder, shall be entitled to the same dividends[8] and other advantages to which he would be entitled if he were the registered holder of the share, [4] except that he shall not, unless the articles [7] otherwise provide, before being registered as a member[1] in respect of the share, [4] be entitled in respect of it to exercise any right conferred by membership in relation to meetings [9] of the company[3]:
Provided that the directors [6] may at any time give notice requiring any such person to elect either to be registered himself or to transfer the share [4], and if the notice is not complied with within 90 days the directors [6] may thereafter withhold payment of all dividends[8], bonuses or other moneys payable in respect of the share until the requirements of the notice have been complied with.

**Notes**

**Section 155**

1. "Member" means one of the individuals of whom a deliberative assembly consists and who enjoys the full rights of participating in the organization-including the rights of making, debating and voting on motions- except to the extent that the organization reserves those rights to certain classes of membership. See **Garner B. (ed.) Black's Law Dictionary 8th ed.**
   "Member" includes the heir, executor, administrator or other personal representative as the case may be, of the member. See **section 567 of CAMA Cap C20 LFN, 2004**
2. "Personal representative" means a person who manages the legal affairs of another because of incapacity or death, such as the executor of an estate. **See Garner, B. (ed) Black's Law Dictionary, 8th ed.**
   "Personal representative" where customary law is applicable, includes successors appointed in respect of deceased contributories. **See section 567 CAMA Cap. C20, LFN 2004**
3. "Company" means a company formed and registered under this Act or, as the case may be, formed and registered in Nigeria before and in existence on the commencement of this Act. See **section 567 CAMA, Cap. C20, LFN, 2004**
4. "Share" means the interests in a company's shares capital of a member who is entitled to share in the Capital or income of such company and except where a distinction between stock and shares is expressed or implied, includes stock. **Section 567 of CAMA Cap C20 LFN, 2004**
5. "Bankruptcy" is a statutory procedure by which an insolvent debtor obtains financial relief and undergoes a judicially supervised reorganisation or liquidation of the debtors' assets for the benefit of creditors. See **Garner B. (ed) Black's Law Dictionary, 8th ed** .
6. "Director" includes any person occupying the position of director by whatever name called; and includes any person in accordance with whose directions or instructions the directors of the company are accustomed to act. See **Section. 567 CAMA, Cap. C20 , LFN 2004**
7. "Articles" means the articles of association of a company, as originally framed or as altered by special resolution, including so far as they apply to the regulations contained in Table A in the First Schedules of the Companies Act, 1922 or in that Table as altered by any subsequent enactment or reprint of the laws, or in Table A in the First Schedule to this Act. See **section 567 CAMA Cap. C20 LFN 2004**
8. "Dividend" means a proportion of the distributed profits of the company which may be a fixed annual percentage, as in the case of preference shares, or it may be variable according to the prosperity or other circumstances of the company, as in the case of equity shares. See section**567 CAMA Cap. C20 LFN 2004**
9. "Meetings" see "meeting". It means the gathering of people to discuss or act on matters in which they have a common interest; especially the convening of a deliberative assembly to transact business. **See Garner B., Ed. Black's Law Dictionary**

**Cross Reference**

On obligation of a Company to enter names of members in the register of members, see **section 79 CAMA Cap. C20 LFN 2004**
On the nature of shares, see **section 115 CAMA Cap. C20, LFN 2004**
On transfer of shares, see **section 151 CAMA Cap. C20 LFN 2004**

**Cases**
By the provisions of Companies and Allied Matters Act, Section 115, shares are in the nature of personal estate and freely transferable but subject to statutory restrictions and the articles of the company. Members in a company have a right to transfer shares belonging to them therein and this right is unfettered unless there is an express restriction to that effect in the articles or constitution of the company. See ***N.R.I. Ltd v. Oranusi* [2011] ALL F.W.L.R part 577. 625-824 at p.765** .

## 156. Protection of beneficiaries

(1) Any person claiming to be interested in any shares [1] or the dividends[2] or interest on them, may protect his interest by serving on the company[3] concerned a notice and affidavit[4] of interest.

(2) Notwithstanding the provisions of section 86 of this Act, the company[3] shall enter on the register of members, [4] the fact that such notice has been served and shall not register any transfer or make any payment or return in respect of the shares [1] contrary to the terms of the notice until the expiration of 42 days' notice to the claimant of the proposed transfer or payment.

(3) In the event of any default by the company [3] in complying with this section, the company [3] shall compensate any person injured by the default.

**Notes**
**Section 156**

1. "Share" means the interests in a company's shares capital of a member who is entitled to share in the Capital or income of such company and except where a distinction between stock and shares is expressed or implied, includes stock. **Section 567 of CAMA Cap C20 LFN, 2004**
2. "Dividends" see "dividend". It means a proportion of the distributed profits of the company which may be a fixed annual percentage, as in the case of preference shares, or it may be variable according to the prosperity or other circumstances of the company, as in the case of equity shares. See section **567 CAMA Cap. C20 LFN 2004**
3. "Company" means a company formed and registered under this Act or, as the case may be, formed and registered in Nigeria before and in existence on the commencement of this Act. See **section 567 CAMA, Cap. C20, LFN, 2004**

4. "Affidavit" means a voluntary declaration of facts written down and sworn to by the declarant before an officer authorized to administer oaths, such as a notary public. See **Garner B. (ed) Black's Law Dictionary, 8th ed.**

5."Member" means one of the individuals of whom a deliberative assembly consists and who enjoys the full rights of participating in the organization-including the rights of making, debating and voting on motions- except to the extent that the organization reserves those rights to certain classes of membership. See **Garner B. (ed.) Black's Law Dictionary 8th ed.**

"Member" includes the heir, executor, administrator or other personal representative as the case may be, of the member. See **section 567 of CAMA Cap C20 LFN, 2004**

**Cross Reference**

On obligation of a Company to enter names of members in the register of members, see **section 79 CAMA Cap. C20 LFN 2004**

On the nature of shares, see **section 115 CAMA Cap. C20, LFN 2004**

On transfer of shares, see **section 151 CAMA Cap. C20 LFN 2004**

On contents of an affidavit admissible in court, see **section 115 Evidence Act 2011**

On declaration of Dividends and payment of interim dividends, see **section 379 CAMA Cap. C20, LFN, 2004**

---

**Cases**

The definition of a company in section 650 of Companies and Allied Matters Act puts the matter beyond doubt. It defines a 'company' or 'existing' to mean....a company formed and registered in Nigeria before and in existence on the commencement of this Act. ***Agro Allied Dev. Ent. Ltd. v. Reefer*** **[2009] vol.31 W.R.N 1-185 at pg 7** .

**For Further Reading**

On shares, company, interest, dividend, see, Kiser Barnes **Cases and Materials on Nigeria Company Law** (1992) Obafemi Awolowo University press Ltd, Ile-Ife, Nigeria

## 157. Certification of transfers

(1) When the holder [1] of any shares [2] of a company [3] wishes to transfer to any person only a part of the shares [2] represented by one or more certificates [4], the instrument of transfer together with the relevant certificates [4] shall be delivered to the company [3] with a request that the instrument of transfer be recognised and registered.

(2) A company [3] to which a request is made under subsection (1) of this section, may recognise the instrument of transfer by

endorsing on it the words "certificate lodged" or words to the like effect.

(3) The recognition by a company [3] of any instrument of transfer of shares [2] in the company [3] shall be taken as a representation by the company [3] to any person acting on the faith of the recognition that there have been produced to the company [3] such documents [5] as on the face of them show a prime facie title to the shares [2] in the transferor named in the instrument of transfer, but not as a representation that the transferor has any title to the shares. [2]

(4) Where any person acts on the faith of a false recognition by a company [3] made negligently, the company [3] shall be under the same liability to that person as if the recognition has been made fraudulently.

(5) For the purposes of this section-

(a) an instrument of transfer shall be deemed to be recognised if it bears the words "certificate lodged" or words to the like effect;

(b) the recognition of an instrument of transfer shall deemed to be made by a company [3] if-

(i) the person issuing the instrument is a person authorised to issue certificated instruments of transfers on the company's [3] behalf; and

(ii) the recognition is signed by a person authorised to recognise transfers of shares [2] on the company's [3] behalf or by any officer [6] or servant either of the company [3] or of a body corporate [7] so authorised;

(c) a recognition shall be deemed to be signed by any person if-

(i) it purports to be authenticated by his signature or initials (whether handwritten or not); and

(ii) it is not shown that the signature or initials was or were placed there by any person other than him or a person authorised to use the signature or initials for the purpose of transfers on the company's [3] behalf.

**Notes**
**Section 157**

1. "Holder" is a person who has legal possession of a document of title or an investment security. See **Garner B., (ed.) Black's Law Dictionary 8th ed.**

2. "Shares" see "share". It means the interests in a company's share capital of a member who is entitled to share in the capital or income of such company; and except where a distinction between stock and shares is expressed or implied, includes stock. See **section 567, CAMA Cap. C20 LFN, 2004**
3. "Company" means a corporation - or, less commonly, an association, partnership, or union that carries on a commercial or industrial enterprise**. See Garner B, (ed) Black's Law Dictionary 8th ed.**
   "Company" means a company formed and registered under this Act or, as the case may be, formed and registered in Nigeria before and in existence on the commencement of this Act. See **Section 567 CAMA, Cap. C20, LFN 2004**
4. "Certificates" see "share certificate". It means a document issued by a company evidencing that a named person is a company member and stating the number of all shares registered in his nameand the extent of which they are paid up. See **Martin E. (ed.) Oxford Dictionary of Law 4 th ed.**
5. "Documents" this includes summons, notice, order and other legal process and registers. See **Section 567 CAMA C20 LFN 2004.**
6. "Officer" means in relation to a body corporate includes a director, manager or secretary; **Section 567 CAMA, Cap. C20, LFN 2004.**
7. "Body Corporate" see corporation. It means an entity (usually a business) having authority under law to act as a single person distinct from the shareholders who own it and having rights to issue stock and exist indefinitely; a group or succession of persons established in accordance with legal rules into a legal or juristic person that has a legal personality distinct from the natural persons who make it up, exists indefinitely apart from them, and has the legal powers that its constitution gives it. See **Garner B. (ed) Black's Law Dictionary 8th ed.**

---

**Cases**

A limited liability Company is separate and apart from it's members and officers. This decision was further magnified in the case of ***H.L. Bolton Co. v. T.J.Graham*** **(1956) 3 ALL E.R 624 at 630** when Denning L.J. said: A Company may in many ways be likened to a human body. They have a brain and a nerve center which controls what they do. They also have hands which hold the tools and act in accordance with direction from the center. Some of the people in a company are mere servants and agents who are nothing more than hands to the work and cannot be said to represent the mind or will. Others are directors and managers who represent the directing mind and will of the company and control what they do. The state of the mind of these managers is the state of mind of the company and it is treated by the Law as such. So you will find in cases where the Law requires personal fault as a condition of liability in tort, the

fault of the managers will be the personal fault of the company. ***Chartered Brains Ltd. v. Intercity Bank Plc.* (2009) Vol.49 W.R.N. 1-182 at pg 116.**
A registered holder of shares in a company becomes entitled to certain rights, benefits and privileges. Except as otherwise provided by the Law and the provisions of the memorandum and Articles of Association of the company, he has the right to sell, mortgage or otherwise dispose of the shares. He is entitled to receive dividends on the shares registered in his name and to keep the dividends so received for his own use. In other words, the essence of being registered as an owner or a holder of shares in a company is that one is inter alia, entitled to enjoy in one's right the foregoing rights, benefits and privileges. ***Kotoye vs. Saraki* (1994) 7 N.W.L.R (part 357) 414**

*Transactions by company in respect of its own shares*

## 158. Redemption of redeemable preference shares

(1) The provisions of this section shall apply with respect to the redemption by a company [1] of any redeemable preference shares[2] issued by it under section 122 of this Act.

(2) The shares [3] shall not be redeemed unless they are fully paid, and redemption shall be made only out of-

(a) profits of the company [1] which would otherwise be available for dividend; [4] or

(b) the proceeds of a fresh issue of shares [3] made for the purposes of the redemption.

(3) Before the shares [3] are redeemed, the premium, [5] if any, payable on redemption, shall be provided for out of the profits of the company[1] or out of the company's [1] share premium account. [6]

(4) Where shares [3] are redeemed otherwise than out of the proceeds of a fresh issue, there shall, out of profits which would otherwise have been available for dividend, [4] be transferred to a reserve fund, to be called "the capital redemption reserve fund", a sum equal to the nominal amount of the shares [3] redeemed, and the provisions of this Act relating to the reduction of the share capital [7] of a company[1] shall, except as provided in this section, apply as if the capital redemption reserve fund were paid-up share capital [7] of the company.[1]

(5) Subject to the provisions of this section, the redemption of preference shares [2] there under may be effected on such terms and in such manner as are provided by the articles [8] of the company. [1]

(6) The redemption of preference shares [2] under this section by a company[1] shall not be taken as reducing the amount of the company's [1] authorised share capital. [7]

(7) Where, in pursuance of this section, a company [1] has redeemed or is about to redeem any preference shares, [2] it shall have power to issue shares [3] up to the nominal amount of the shares [3] redeemed or to be redeemed as if those shares [1] had never been issued, and accordingly, the share capital [7] of the company[1] shall not, for the purposes of any enactments relating to stamp duty, be deemed to be increased by the issue of shares [3] in pursuance of this subsection:

Provided that, where new shares [3] are issued before the redemption of the old shares,[3] the new shares[3] shall not, so far as relates to stamp duty, be deemed to have been issued in pursuance of this subsection, unless the old shares [3] are redeemed within one month after the issue of the new shares. [3]

(8) The capital redemption reserve fund may, notwithstanding anything in this section, be applied by the company [1] in paying up unissued shares of the company[1] to be issued to members [9] of the company[1] as fully paid bonus shares. [10]

---

**Notes**
**Section 158**

1. "Company" means a corporation - or, less commonly, an association, partnership, or union that carries on a commercial or industrial enterprise. **See Garner B. (ed) Black's Law Dictionary 8th ed.**
   "Company" means a company formed and registered under this Act or, as the case may be, formed and registered in Nigeria before and in existence on the commencement of this Act. See **Section 567 CAMA, Cap. C20, LFN 2004**
2. "Preference shares" means a share, by whatever name designated, which does not entitle the holder of it to any right to participate beyond a specified amount in any distribution whether by way of dividend or on redemption, in a winding up, or otherwise. See **Section 567 CAMA, Cap. C20, LFN 2004.**
3. "Shares" see "share". it means the interests in a company's share capital of a member who is entitled to share in the capital or income of such company; and except where a distinction between stock and shares is expressed or implied, includes stock. See s **ection 567 CAMA, Cap. C20, LFN 2004.**
4. "Dividend" means a portion of the distributed profit of the company which may be a fixed annual percentage, as in the case of preference share, or it may be variable according to the prosperity or other

circumstances of the company, as in the case of equity shares. See **section 567 CAMA, Cap. C20, LFN 2004.**

5. "Premium" means the sum of money paid in addition to a regular price, salary or other amount; a bonus. See **Garner. (ed) Black's Law Dictionary, 8$^{th}$ ed.**
6. "Share premium account" means the amount paid by shareholders to a company on the purchase of the company's shares which is in excess of the nominal value of the shares, reflecting the market values of the shares. It is paid into the company's share premium account. See **Sheila B Osborne Concise Law Dictionary 9$^{th}$ ed**
   "Share premium account" means the account where a sum equal to the aggregate amount or value of the premium from shares issued at a premium by a company is transferred. See **section 120 (2) CAMA, Cap. C20, LFN 2004.**
7. "Share capital" see "Capital". It means a fund representing the nominal value of shares issued by a registered company. See **Martins E. (ed) Oxford Dictionary of Law 7th ed.**
8. "Articles" means the articles of association of a company, as originally framed or as altered by special resolution, including so far as they apply to the regulations contained in Table A in the First Schedules of the Companies Act, 1992 or in that Table as altered by any subsequent enactment or reprint of the Laws, or in Table A in Schedule 1 to this Act. **See Section 567 CAMA, Cap. C20, LFN 2004**
9. "Members" see "member". It includes the heir, executor, administrator or other personal representative, as the case may be, of the member . **Section 567 CAMA, Cap. C20, LFN 2004.**
10. "Bonus share" see" bonus issue". It a method of increasing a company's issued capital by issuing further shares to existing company members. These shares are paid for out of undistributed profits of the company and made in proportion of their shareholding. See **Martin E. (ed.) Oxford Dictionary of Law 4$^{th}$ ed.**

**Cross Reference**

On form and content of the Articles of Association of a Company, see **section 34, CAMA Cap. C20, LFN 2004.**

On competent authority to impose, charge and collect duties on instruments related to matters executed between a company and an individual , group or body of individuals, See **section 3, Stamp Duties Act, Cap. S8, LFN 2004**

---

**Cases**

It does not matter if the company's shares are owned substantially by one of the shareholders with only a very small fraction held by one or Few of others. ***Dunlop Nigerian Industries Ltd vs. Forward Nigerian Enterprises Ltd & Fafore*** **(1976) (1) A.L.R.**

---

**Section 159**

---

**Prohibition of financial assistance by company for acquisition of its shares**

(1) In this section, financial assistance includes a gift, guarantee[1], security [2]or indemnity[3], loan, any form of credit and any financial assistance given by a company[4] the net assets[5] of which are thereby reduced to a material extent or which has no net assets [5].

(2) Subject to the provisions of this section-

(a) where a person is acquiring or is proposing to acquire shares[6] in a company,[4] it shall not be lawful for the company[4] or any of its subsidiaries[7] to give financial assistance directly or indirectly for the purpose of that acquisition before or at the same time as the acquisition takes place; and

(b) where a person has acquired shares[6] in a company[4] and any liability has been incurred (by that or any other person), for the purpose of this acquisition, it shall not be lawful for the company[4] or any of its subsidiaries[7] to give financial assistance directly or indirectly for the purpose of reducing or discharging the liability so incurred.

(3) Nothing in subsection (1) of this section shall be taken to prohibit-

(a) the lending of money by the company[4] in the ordinary course of its business, where the lending of money is part of the ordinary business of a company;[4]

(b) the provision by a company,[4] in accordance with any scheme for the time being in force, of money for the purchase of, or subscription for, fully-paid shares in the company[4] or its holding company[8], being a purchase or subscription by trustees[9] of or for shares[6] to be held by or for the benefit of employees of the company,[4] including any director[10] holding a salaried employment or office in the company;4

(c) the making by a company[4] of loans to persons, other than directors,[10] bona fide in the employment of the company[4] with a view to enabling those persons to purchase or subscribe for fully-paid shares[6] in the company[4] or its holding company,[8] to be held themselves by way of beneficial ownership;

(d) any act or transaction otherwise authorised by law.

(4) If a company[3] acts in contravention of this section, the company[4] and every officer[11] of the company[4] who is in default shall be liable to a fine not exceeding N500.

---

**Notes**
**Section 159**

1. "Guarantee" means to assume a suretyship obligation; to agree to answer for a debt or default. 2.See **Garner B. Ed. Black's Law Dictionary 8th ed**
2. "Security" means collateral given or pledged to guarantee the fulfilment of an obligation; especially the assurance that a creditor will be repaid(usu. with interest) any money or credit extended to a debtor. See **Garner B. Ed. Black's Law Dictionary 8th ed**
3. "Indemnity" means protection against damage or loss, especially in the form of a promise to pay for any that happens. See **Oxford Advanced Learner's Dictionary 6th ed.**
4. "Company" means a corporation - or, less commonly, an association, partnership, or union that carries on a commercial or industrial enterprise. **See Garner B. (ed) Black's Law Dictionary 8th ed.**
   "Company" means a company formed and registered under this Act or, as the case may be, formed and registered in Nigeria before and in existence on the commencement of this Act. See **Section 567 CAMA, Cap. C20, LFN 2004**
5. "Assets" means an item that is owned and has value **. See Garner B. Ed. Black's Law Dictionary 8th ed.**
6. "Share" means the interest in a company's share capital of a member who is entitled to share in the capital or income of such company; and except where a distinction between stock and shares is expressed or implied, includes stock. **See section 567, CAMA Cap C20 LFN, 2004**
7. "Subsidiaries" see "subsidiary". It means, in relation to a body corporate, a subsidiary as defined by section 338 of this Act. See **section 567 CAMA, Cap. C20, LFN 2004.**
8. "Holding Company" means a holding company as defined by section 338**. See section 567 CAMA, Cap. C20, LFN 2004.**
9. "Trustee" means one who, having legal title to property holds it in trust for the benefit of another and owes a fiduciary duty to that beneficiary. See **Garner, B. (ed.) Black's Law Dictionary 8 th ed.**
10. "Directors" means (1) one who manages, guides, or orders; a chief administrator (2) a person appointed or elected to sit on a board that manages the affairs of a corporation or other organisation by electing and exercising control over its officer. See **Garner B. (ed) Black's Law Dictionary 8th ed.**
    "Director" includes any person occupying the position of director by whatever name called; and includes any person in accordance with whose directions or instructions the directors of the company are accustomed to act. **Section 567 CAMA, Cap. C20, LFN 2004**

11. "Officer" in relation to a body corporate, includes a director, manager, or secretary. See **Section 567 CAMA C 20 LFN 2004**

Cross Reference

On meaning of "holding company", "subsidiary" and "wholly-owned subsidiary", see **section 338 CAMA Cap. C20, LFN 2004**

---

**Cases**

A director is a person appointed or elected according to Law, authorized to manage and direct the affairs of a corporation or company. ***Olufosoye v. Fakorede*** **(1993) 1 N.W.L.R 947.** See also ***Longe v. First Bank Nigeria Plc*** **(2006) 3 N.W.L.R 228 at 270.**

**For Further Reading**

On holding company and its subsidiaries, directors, Oserheimen A. Osunbor "**The Agent-Only Subsidiary Company and The Control of Multinational Groups", The International and Comparative Law Quaterly**, Vol. 38, No. 2 (Apr; 1989), pp 377 –

**387 Published by Cambridge university press**

Iruchukwu, J.O. **The Company, The Shareholder, The Director and the Law,** (Fourth Dimension Publishing Co. Ltd. 1994).

## 160. Acquisition by a company of its own shares

(1) Subject to the provisions of subsection (2) of this section and its articles[1], a company[2] may not purchase or otherwise acquire shares[3] issued by it.

(2) A company[2] may acquire its own shares[3] for the purpose of-

(a) settling or compromising a debt or claim asserted by or against the company[2]; or

(b) eliminating fractional shares;[3] or

(c) fulfilling the terms of a non-assignable agreement under which the company[2] has an option or is obliged to purchase shares[3] owned by an officer[4] or an employee of the company[2]; or

(d) satisfying the claim of a dissenting shareholder;[5] or

(e) complying with a court[6] order.

(3) A company[2] may accept from any shareholder,[5] a share[3] in the company[2] surrendered to it as a gift, but may not extinguish or

reduce a liability in respect of an amount unpaid on any such share,[3] except in accordance with section 106 of this Act.

---

**Notes**

**Section 160**

1. "Articles" means the articles of association of a company, as originally framed or as altered by special resolution, including so far as they apply to the regulations contained in Table A in the First Schedules of the Companies Act, 1992 or in that Table as altered by any subsequent enactment or reprint of the Laws, or in Table A in Schedule 1 to this Act. See **section 567 CAMA, Cap. C20, LFN 2004.**
2. "Company" means a corporation - or, less commonly, an association, partnership, or union that carries on a commercial or industrial enterprise. See **Garner B. (ed) Black's Law Dictionary 8th ed.** "Company" means a company formed and registered under this Act or, as the case may be, formed and registered in Nigeria before and in existence on the commencement of this Act; **Section 567 CAMA, Cap. C20, LFN 2004.**
3. "Share" means the interests in a company's share capital of a member who is entitled to share in the capital or income of such company; and except where a distinction between stock and shares is expressed or implied, includes stock. See **section 567, CAMA Cap C20 LFN, 2004.**
4. "Officer" means in relation to a body corporate includes a director, manager or secretary. See **Section 567 CAMA Cap. C20, LFN 2004.**
5. "Shareholder" It means one who owns or holds a share or shares in a company. **Garner B. ed. Black's Law Dictionary 8th ed.**
6. "Court" when used in relation to a company, means the federal High court, and to the extent to which application may be made to it as; court includes the court of appeal and the supreme court of Nigeria. See **section 567 CAMA, Cap. C20, LFN 2004.**

**Cross Reference**

On special resolution for reducing share capital of a company, see **section 106 CAMA Cap. C20 LFN 2004**

On the establishment and jurisdiction of the Federal High Court, see **sections 249 &251 Constitution of the Federal Republic of Nigeria, 1999 (as amended)**

---

**Cases**

A registered holder of shares in a company becomes entitled to certain rights, benefits and privileges. Except as otherwise provided by the Law and the provisions of the memorandum and Articles of Association of the company, he has the right to sell, mortgage or otherwise dispose of the shares. He is entitled to receive dividends on the shares registered in his name and to keep the dividends so received for his own use. In other words, the essence of being registered as an owner or a holder of shares in a company is that one is inter alia, entitled to enjoy in one's right the foregoing rights, benefits and privileges. See ***Kotoye vs. Saraki*** **(1994) 7 N.W.L.R (part 357) 414** .

## 161. Conditions for purchase by a company of its own shares.

Notwithstanding any provision in the articles, [1] a company[2] shall not purchase any of its own shares [3]except on compliance with the following conditions, that is-

(a) shares[3] shall only be purchased out of profits of the company[2] which would otherwise be available for dividend[4] or the proceeds of a fresh issue of shares [3] made for the purpose of the purchase;

(b) redeemable shares[3] shall not be purchased at a price greater than the lowest price at which they are redeemable or shall be redeemable at the next date thereafter at which they are due or liable to be redeemed;

(c) no purchase shall be made in breach of section 162 of this Act.

---

**Notes**

**Section 161**

1. "Articles" means the articles of association of a company, as originally framed or as altered by special resolution, including so far as they apply to the regulations contained in Table A in the First Schedules of the Companies Act, 1992 or in that Table as altered by any subsequent enactment or reprint of the Laws, or in Table A in Schedule 1 to this Act. See **section 567 CAMA, Cap. C20, LFN 2004.**
2. "Company" means a corporation - or, less commonly, an association, partnership, or union that carries on a commercial or industrial enterprise. **Garner B. (ed) Black's Law Dictionary 8th ed.**
   "Company" or "existing company" means a company formed and registered under this Act or, as the case may be, formed and registered in Nigeria before and in existence on the commencement of this Act. **See section 567 CAMA, Cap. C20, LFN 2004**
3. "Share" means the interests in a company's share capital of a member who is entitled to share in the capital or income of such company; and except where a distinction between stock and shares is expressed or implied, includes stock. **See section 567, CAMA Cap C20 LFN, 2004**
4. "Dividend" means a portion of the distributed profit of the company which may be a fixed annual percentage, as in the case of preference share, or it may be variable according to the prosperity or other circumstances of the company, as in the case of equity shares. See **section 567 CAMA, Cap. C20, LFN 2004.**

**Cross Reference**

On acquisition of its shares by a company, see **section 160 CAMA Cap. C20, LFN 2004**

**Cases**

A study of the article of association of a company leaves me no doubt that they contain the rules and regulations by which the internal affairs of a company are governed....articles of association when registered therefore, become a contract between the company and its members and officers and between the members officers themselves: ***Ladejobi v. Odutola Ltd*** **[2002] 3 N.W.LR. 121 at 152-153** .

## 162. Limit on number of shares acquired

No transaction shall be entered into by or on behalf of a company[1] whereby the total number of its shares, [2] or of its shares [2] of anyone class, held by persons other than the company [1] or its nominees[3] becomes less than 85 per cent of the total number of shares,[2] or of shares [2] of that class, which have been issued:
Provided that-

(a) redeemable shares [2] shall be disregarded for the purposes of this section; and

(b) where, after shares [2] of any class have been issued, the number of such shares [3] has been reduced, this section shall apply as if the number originally issued (including shares of that class cancelled before the reduction took effect) has been the number as so reduced.

---

**Notes**

**Section 162**

1. "Company" means a corporation - or, less commonly, an association, partnership, or union that carries on a commercial or industrial enterprise. See **Garner B. (ed) Black's Law Dictionary 8th ed.** "Company" or "existing company" means a company formed and registered under this Act or, as the case may be, formed and registered in Nigeria before and in existence on the commencement of this Act. See **section 567 CAMA, Cap. C20, LFN 2004**
2. "Shares" see "share". It means the interests in a company's share capital of a member who is entitled to share in the capital or income of such company; and except where a distinction between stock and shares is expressed or implied, includes stock. **See section 567, CAMA Cap C20 LFN, 2004**

Cross Reference

On authorization of a company to create classes of shares, see **section 118 CAMA Cap. C20 LFN 2004**

---

**For Further Reading**

On company, shares, see, Ephraim Madeueulosi ***Asomugha Company law in Nigeria under the companies and Allied Matters Act,*** (1994) E.M. Asumughai Lagos

## 163. Enforceability of contract to acquire shares

(1) A contract with a company [1] providing for the acquisition by the company[1] of shares[2] in the company[1] is specifically enforceable against the company,[1] except to the extent that the company[1] cannot perform the contract without thereby being a breach of the provisions of section 160 of this Act.

(2) In any action brought on a contract referred to in subsection (1) of this section, the company [1] shall have the burden of proving that performance of the contract is prevented by the provisions of section 160 of this Act.

---

**Notes**
**Section 163**

1. "Company" means a corporation - or, less commonly, an association, partnership, or union that carries on a commercial or industrial enterprise. See **Garner B, (ed) Black's Law Dictionary 8th ed.** "Company" means a company formed and registered under this Act or, as the case may be, formed and registered in Nigeria before and in existence on the commencement of this Act. See **Section 567 CAMA, Cap. C20, LFN 2004**
2. "Share" means the interests in a company's share capital of a member who is entitled to share in the capital or income of such company; and except where a distinction between stock and shares is expressed or implied, includes stock. **See section 567, CAMA Cap C20 LFN, 2004**

---

### Cases

The entire Law of Contract is founded on the "Consensus" or "will" theory of contract, which asserts that contractual obligations are by definition self imposed and in terms of the function of the of the courts, finds expression in the idea that the exclusive task of a court in contract cases is to discover what the parties have agreed and give effect to it except in cases of mistake, duress and illegality. ***Coop. Dev. Bank Plc v. Ekanem* (2009) 16 N.W.L.R. part 1168 443-658 at pg.588.**

## 164. Re-issue of shares acquired

Where shares [1] in a company[2] are redeemed, purchased, acquired or forfeited, such shares [1] shall, unless the company [2] by alteration of its articles of association [3] cancels the shares [1], be available for re-issue by the company. [2]

---

**Notes**
**Section 164**

1. "Share" means the interests in a company's share capital of a member who is entitled to share in the capital or income of such company; and except where a distinction between stock and shares is expressed or implied, includes stock. **See section 567, CAMA Cap C20 LFN, 2004**
2. "Company" means a corporation - or, less commonly, an association, partnership, or union that carries on a commercial or industrial enterprise. See **Garner B, (ed) Black's Law Dictionary 8th ed.** "Company" means a company formed and registered under this Act or, as the case may be, formed and registered in Nigeria before and in existence on the commencement of this Act. See **Section 567 CAMA, Cap. C20, LFN 2004**
3. "Articles of association" means the articles of association of a company, as originally framed or as altered by special resolution, including so far as they apply to the regulations contained in Table A in the First Schedules of the Companies Act, 1992 or in that Table as altered by any subsequent enactment or reprint of the Laws, or in Table A in Schedule 1 to this Act. See **section 567 CAMA, Cap. C20, LFN 2004.**

---

**Cases**

The Articles of Association is the contract governing the relationship between shareholders and any infraction of such articles may confer on the shareholder adversely affected a right of action" See ***Attorney General of Lagos State v Eko Hotel Ltd & Oha Ltd(2001) FWLR page 1996 at 2000***

## 165. Acquisition of shares of holding company

(1) A company [1] which is a subsidiary [2] may acquire shares[3] in its holding company[4] where the subsidiary [2] company[1] is concerned as personal representative [5] or trustee [6], unless the holding company [4] or any subsidiary [2] of it is beneficially interested otherwise than by way of security[7] for the purposes of a transaction entered into by it in the ordinary course of a business which includes the lending of money.

(2) A subsidiary [2] which is, at the commencement of this Act, a holder[8] of shares [3] of its holding company [4] or a subsidiary [2] which acquired shares[3] in its holding company [4] before it became a subsidiary[2] of that holding company [4], may continue to hold such shares[3] but, subject to subsection (1) of this section, shall have no

right to vote at meetings[9] of the holding company[4] or any class of shareholders[10] of the holding company[4] and shall not acquire any future shares[3] in it except on a capitalisation issue.

---

**Notes**
**Section 165**

1. "Company" means a corporation - or, less commonly, an association, partnership, or union that carries on a commercial or industrial enterprise. See **Garner B, (ed) Black's Law Dictionary 8th ed.** "Company" means a company formed and registered under this Act or, as the case may be, formed and registered in Nigeria before and in existence on the commencement of this Act. See **Section 567 CAMA, Cap. C20, LFN 2004**
2. "Subsidiary" means, in relation to a body corporate, a subsidiary as defined by section 338 of this Act. **See section 567 CAMA, Cap. C20, LFN 2004.**
3. "Shares" see "share". It means the interests in a company's share capital of a member who is entitled to share in the capital or income of such company; and except where a distinction between stock and shares is expressed or implied, includes stock. See **section 567 CAMA Cap. C20, LFN 2004**
4. "Holding Company" means a holding company as defined by section 338**. See section 567 CAMA, Cap. C20, LFN 2004.**
5. "Personal Representative" means a person who manages the legal affairs of another because of incapacity or death, such as the executor of an estate. See **Garner. (ed.) Black's Law Dictionary, 8 th ed.** "Personal representative" where customary law is applicable, includes successors appointed in respect of deceased contributories. See **section 567 CAMA Cap. C20, LFN 2004**
6. "Trustee" means one who having legal title to property, holds it in trust for the benefit of another and owes a fiduciary duty to that beneficiary. See **Garner, B. (ed) Black's Law Dictionary, 8 th ed.**
7. "Security" means collateral given or pledged to guarantee the fulfilment of an obligation. See **Garner, B. (ed) Black's Law Dictionary, 8 th ed.**
8. "Holder" means a person who has legal possession of a negotiable instrument and is entitled to receive payment on it. See **Garner, B. (ed) Black's Law Dictionary, 8 th ed.**
9. "Meetings" means a gathering of people to discuss or act on matters in which they have common interest esp. a deliberative assembly to transact business. See **Garner, B. (ed) Black's Law Dictionary, 8 th ed.**
10. "Shareholders" see "shareholder." It means one who owns or holds a share or shares in a company especially a corporation. See **Garner, B. (ed) Black's Law Dictionary, 8 th ed.**

---

**For Further Reading**

On holding company and its subsidiary, see, Oserheimen A. Osunbor "The Agent-Only Subsidiary Company and The Control of Multinational Groups", **The International and Comparative law Quarterly**, Vol. 38, No. 2 (Apr; 1989), pp 377 -387 published by Cambridge University Press.

*PART VII*

*Debentures*

*Creation of debenture and debenture stock*

## 166.Power to borrow money, to charge property and to issue debentures

A company[1] may borrow money for the purpose of its business or objects and may mortgage[2] or charge[3] its undertaking, property and uncalled capital[4], or any part thereof, and issue debentures[5], debenture stock[6] and other securities[7] whether outright or as security[8] for any debt, liability or obligation of the company[1] or of any third party.

---

**Notes**
**Section 166**

1. "Company" means a corporation - or, less commonly, an association, partnership, or union that carries on a commercial or industrial enterprise. See **Garner B. (ed) Black's Law Dictionary 8th ed.**
   "Company" means a company formed and registered under this Act or, as the case may be, formed and registered in Nigeria before and in existence on the commencement of this Act. See **Section 567 CAMA, Cap. C20, LFN 2004**
2. "Mortgage" means a conveyance of title to property that is given as security for the payment of a debt or the performance of a duty and that will become void upon payment or performance according to the stipulated terms. See **Garner, B. (ed) Black's Law Dictionary, 8th ed.**
3. "Charge" means an encumbrance, lien or claim. See **Garner, B. (ed) Black's Law Dictionary, 8th ed.**
4. "Capital" means money or assets invested, or available for investments, in a business; the total amount or value of a Corporation's stock. See **Garner, B. (ed) Black's Law Dictionary, 8th ed.**
5. "Debentures" see "debenture". It means a written acknowledgement of indebtedness by the company, setting out the terms and conditions of the indebtedness and includes debenture stock, bonds and any other securities of any company whether constituting a charge on the assets of the company or not. See **Section 567 CAMA, Cap. C20, LFN 2004.**

6. "Debenture stock" means stock that is issued under a contract providing for periodic fixed payment. See **Garner B. (ed) Black's Law Dictionary, 8th ed.**
7. "Securities" includes shares, debentures, debenture stock, bonds, notes (other than promissory notes) and units under a unit trust scheme. See **Section 567 CAMA, Cap. C20, LFN 2004.**
8. "Security" means \collateral given or pledged to guarantee the fulfillment of an obligation, esp. the assurance that a creditor will be repaid. See **Garner, B. (ed) Black's Law Dictionary, 8 th ed.**

Cross Reference

For the situations under which debentures shall belong to different classes, see **section 183(4) and (5), CAMA Cap. C20 LFN, 2004**

---

**Cases**

"A debenture consists of a debt owed by a company to another secured by a deed which prescribes the condition of the realization of the debt, and it may be created over the fixed or floating assets of the company " **See *UBN v. Tropics Foods (1992) 3NWLR (Pt 228) 231***

The definition of a company in section 650 of Companies and Allied Matters Act puts the matter beyond doubt. It defines a 'company' or 'existing' to mean....a company formed and registered in Nigeria before and in existence on the commencement of this Act. ***Agro Allied Dev. Ent. Ltd. v. Reefer* (2009) vol.31 W.R.N 1-185 at pg 7** .

## 167. Documents of title to debentures or certificate of debenture stock

(1) Every company [1] shall, within 60 days after the allotment [2] of any of its debentures [3] or after the registration of the transfer of any debentures,[3] deliver to the registered holder [4] thereof, the debenture[3] or a certificate of the debenture stock [5] under the common seal[6] of the company [1].

(2) If a debenture [3] or debenture stock [5] certificate is defaced, lost or destroyed, the company, [1] at the request of the registered holder[4] of the debenture,[3] shall issue a certified copy of the debenture[3] or renew the debenture stock [5] certificate on payment of a fee not exceeding N5 and on such terms as to evidence and indemnity and the payment of the company's [1] out-of-pocket expenses of investigating evidence, as the company [1] may reasonably require.

(3) If default is made in complying with this section, the company[1] and any officer [7] of the company [1] who is in default, shall be liable to a fine not exceeding N25; and on application by any

person entitled to have the debentures[3] or debenture stock[5] certificate delivered to him, the court[8] may order the company[1] to deliver the debenture[3] or debenture stock[5] certificate and may require the company[1] and any such officer[7] to bear all the costs of and incidental to the application.

---

**Notes**

Section 167

1. "Company" means a corporation - or, less commonly, an association, partnership, or union that carries on a commercial or industrial enterprise. See **Garner B, (ed) Black's Law Dictionary 8th ed.** "Company" means a company formed and registered under this Act or, as the case may be, formed and registered in Nigeria before and in existence on the commencement of this Act. See **Section 567 CAMA, Cap. C20, LFN 2004**
2. "Allotment" means a share or portion of something, such as property previously held in common or shares in a corporation. See **Garner, B. (ed.) Black's Law Dictionary, 8 th ed.**
3. "Debentures" see "debenture". It means a written acknowledgement of indebtedness by the company, setting out the terms and conditions of the indebtedness and includes debenture stock, bonds and any other securities of any company whether constituting a charge on the assets of the company or not. "holder" is one who has legal possession of a negotiable instrument and is entitled to receive payment on it. **See section 567 CAMA, Cap. C20, LFN 2004.**
4. "Holder" means a person who has legal possession of a negotiable instrument and is entitled to receive payment on it. See **Garner, B. (ed) Black's Law Dictionary, 8 th ed.**
5. "Debenture stock" means stock that is issued under a contract providing for periodic fixed payment. See **Garner B. (ed) Black's Law Dictionary, 8th ed.**
6. "Common seal" means a design embossed or stamped on paper to authenticate, confirm, or attest; an impression or sign that has legal consequence when applied to an instrument. The purpose of a seal is to secure or prove authenticity. See **Garner B. (ed.) Black's Law Dictionary, 8th ed.**
7. "Officer" in relation to a body corporate, includes a director, manager or secretary. See **Section 567 CAMA, Cap. C20, LFN 2004**
8. "Court" used in relation to a company, means the Federal High Court, and to the extent to which application may be made to it as; court includes the Court of Appeal and the Supreme Court of Nigeria. See **Section 567 CAMA, Cap. C20, LFN 2004**

**Cross Reference**

On obligation of the company to have and use common seal, see **section 74 CAMA, Cap. C20, LFN 2004**

On establishment of and the jurisdiction of the Federal High Court, see **section 249 &251 of the Constitution of the Federal Republic of Nigeria, 1999(as amended)**

---

**Cases**

"A debenture is a document which either creates or acknowledges a debt...This obligation is in most casesat the present day, accompanied by some charge or security " ***Fasakin v. Fasakin (1994) 4 N.W.L.R Pt. 340; pg.620 par. C-E***

For Further reading see generally, **Sofowora M. O. Modern Nigerian Company Law 2nd ed. (2002) Soft Associates, Pages 334**

## 168. Statements to be included in debentures

Every debenture[1] shall include a statement on the following matters, that is-

(a) the principal amount borrowed;

(b) the maximum discount which may be allowed on the issue or re-issue of the debentures[1], and the maximum premium[2] at which the debentures[1] may be made redeemable;

(c) the rate of and the dates on which interest on the debentures[1] issued shall be paid and the manner in which payment shall be made;

(d) the date on which the principal amount shall be repaid or the manner in which redemption shall be effected, whether by the payment of instalments of principal or otherwise;

(e) in the case of convertible debentures, [1] the date and terms on which the debentures[1] may be converted into shares [3] and the amounts which may be credited as paid up on those shares[3], and the dates and terms on which the holders[4] may exercise any right to subscribe for shares [3] in respect of the debentures[1] held by them;

(f) the charges[5] securing the debenture[1] and the conditions subject to which the debenture[1] shall take effect.

---

**Notes**

**Section 168**

**1.** "Debentures" see "debenture." It means a written acknowledgement of indebtedness by the company, setting out the terms and conditions of the indebtedness, and includes debenture stock, bonds and any other securities of a company whether constituting a charge on the assets of the company or not. See **Section 567 of CAMA Cap C20 LFN, 2004**

2. "Premium" means sum of money paid in addition to a regular price, salary or other amount; a bonus. See Garner **B. (ed) Black's Law Dictionary 8th ed.**
3. "Shares" see "share." It means the interests in a company's share capital of a member who is entitled to share in the capital or income of such company; and except where a distinction between stock and shares is expressed or implied, includes stock. See **Section 567 CAMA, Cap. C20, LFN 2004**
4. "Holders" see "holder." It means a person who has legal possession of a negotiable instrument and is entitled to receive payment on it. See Garner **B. (ed) Black's Law Dictionary 8th ed.**
5. "Charges" see" charge." It means an encumbrance, lien or claim. See Garner **B. (ed) Black's Law Dictionary 8th ed**

---

**Cases**

A debenture consists of a debt owed by a company to another secured by a deed which prescribes the condition of the realization of the debt, and it may be created over the fixed or floating assets of the company **" See *UBN v. Tropics Foods (1992) 3NWLR (Pt 228) 231***

**For further reading on debentures,**

see, Orojo, J. Ola **Company Law and Practice in Nigeri***a* 3rd Edition, Mbeyi & Associates (Lagos, Nigeria) 1992.

## 169. Effect of statements in debentures

(1) Statements made in debenture[1] or debenture stock[2] certificates shall be prima facie evidence of the title to the debentures[1] of the person named therein as the registered holder[3] and of the amounts secured thereby.

(2) If any person shall change his position to his detriment in reliance in good faith on the continued accuracy of any statements made in the debenture[1] or debenture stock[2] certificate, the company[4] shall be estopped in favour of such person from denying the continued accuracy of such statements and shall compensate such person for any loss suffered by him in reliance thereon and which he would not have suffered had the statement been or continued to be accurate:

Provided that nothing in this subsection shall derogate from any right the company[4] may have to be indemnified by any other person.

**Notes**

Section 169

1. "Debentures" see "debenture." It means a written acknowledgement of indebtedness by the company, setting out the terms and conditions of the indebtedness, and includes debenture stock, bonds and any other securities of a company whether constituting a charge on the assets of the company or not. See **Section 567 of CAMA Cap C20 LFN, 2004**
2. "Debenture stock" means stock that is issued under a contract providing for periodic fixed payment. See **Garner B. (ed) Black's Law Dictionary, 8$^{th}$ ed.**
3. "Holder" means a person who has legal possession of a negotiable instrument and is entitled to receive payment on it. See Garner **B. (ed) Black's Law Dictionary 8th ed.**
4. "Company" means a company formed and registered under this Act or, as the case may be, formed and registered in Nigeria before and in existence on the commencement of this Act. See **Section 567 CAMA Cap C20 LFN, 2004**

Cross Reference

On power of a company to redeem debentures, see **section 174, CAMA CAP C20, LFN 2004.**

## 170. Enforcement of contracts relating to debentures

A contract with a company[1] to take up and pay for any debentures[2] of the company[1] may be enforced by an order for specific performance.

**Notes**

**Section 170**

1. "Company" means a company formed and registered under this Act or, as the case may be, formed and registered in Nigeria before and in existence on the commencement of this Act. **See section 567 of CAMA Cap C20 LFN, 2004**

Cross Reference

On the power of a company to create debentures and debenture stock, see **section 166 CAMA CAP C20 LFN 2004**

On power of a company to redeem debentures, see **section 174, CAMA CAP C20, LFN 2004.**

On remedies available to a debenture holder, see **section 209 CAMA CAP C20 LFN 2004**

**Cases**

The entire Law of Contract is founded on the "Consensus" or "will" theory of contract, which asserts that contractual obligations are by definition self imposed and in terms of the function of the of the courts, finds expression in the idea that the exclusive task of a court in contract cases is to discover what the parties have agreed and give effect to it except in cases of mistake, duress and illegality. ***Coop. Dev. Bank Plc v. Ekanem*** **(2009) 16 N.W.L.R. part 1168 443-658 at pg.588.**

*Types of debentures*

## 171. Perpetual debentures

A company[1] may issue perpetual debentures, [2] and a condition contained in any debentures[3], or in any deed [4] for securing any debentures,[3] shall not be invalid by reason only that the debentures [3] are made irredeemable or redeemable only on the happening of a contingency, however remote, or on the expiration of a period, however long, any rule of equity to the contrary notwithstanding.

---

**Notes**
**Section 171**

1. "Company" means a company formed and registered under this Act or, as the case may be, formed and registered in Nigeria before and in existence on the commencement of this Act. **Section 567 of CAMA Cap C20 LFN, 2004**
2. "Perpetual Debenture": are made irredeemable or redeemable only in the happening of a contingency however remote. See **section 171 CAMA CAP C20 LFN 2004**
3. "Debenture" means a written acknowledgement of indebtedness by the company, setting out the terms and conditions of the indebtedness, and includes debenture stock, bonds and any other securities of a company whether constituting a charge on the assets of the company or not. See **Section 567 of CAMA Cap C20 LFN, 2004**
4. "Deed" means any written instrument that is signed, sealed and delivered and that conveys small interest in property. **See Garner B. (ed) Black's Law Dictionary 8th ed**

Cross Reference

On the power of a company to create debentures and debenture stock, see **section 166 CAMA CAP C20 LFN 2004**

On power of a company to redeem debentures, see **section 174, CAMA Cap. C20, LFN 2004**

## 172. Convertible debentures

Debentures[1] may be issued upon the terms that in lieu of redemption or repayment, they may, at the option of the holder [2] or the company[3], be converted into shares [4] in the company[3] upon such terms as may be stated in the debentures [1].

**Notes**

**Section172**

1. "Debenture" means a written acknowledgement of indebtedness by the company, setting out the terms and conditions of the indebtedness, and includes debenture stock, bonds and any other securities of a company whether constituting a charge on the assets of the company or not. See **Section 567 CAMA Cap C20 LFN, 2004**
2. "Holder" means a person who has legal possession of a negotiable instrument and is entitled to receive payment on it. See **Garner B. (ed) Black's Law Dictionary 8th ed.**
3. "Company" means a company formed and registered under this Act or, as the case may be, formed and registered in Nigeria before and in existence on the commencement of this Act. **See section 567 CAMA Cap C20 LFN, 2004**

Cross Reference

On the power of a company to create debentures and debenture stock, see **section 166 CAMA CAP C20 LFN 2004**

On power of a company to redeem debentures, see **section 174, CAMA Cap C20, LFN 2004**

**Cases**

A registered holder of shares in a company becomes entitled to certain rights, benefits and privileges. Except as otherwise provided by the Law and the provisions of the memorandum and Articles of Association of the company, he has the right to sell, mortgage or otherwise dispose of the shares. He is entitled to receive dividends on the shares registered in his name and to keep the dividends so received for his own use. In other words, the essence of being registered as an owner or a holder of shares in a company is that one is inter alia, entitled to enjoy in one's right the foregoing rights, benefits and privileges. ***Kotoye vs. Saraki* (1994) 7 N.W.L.R (part 357) 414** .

"A debenture is a document which either creates or acknowledges a debt....This obligation is in most casesat the present day, accompanied by some charge or security" ***Fasakin v. Fasakin (1994) 4 N.W.L.R Pt. 340; pg.620 par. C-E***

**For Further Reading**

See generally, **Sofowora M. O. Modern Nigerian Company Law 2nd ed., (2002) Soft Associates, Pages.334**

## 173. Secured or naked debentures

(1) Debentures[1] may either be secured by a charge [2] over the company's[3] property or may be unsecured by any charge [2].

(2) Debentures[1] may be secured by a fixed charge [4] on certain of the company's[3] property or a floating charge [5] over the whole or a specified part of the company's [3] undertaking and assets, or by both a fixed charge[4] on certain property and a floating charge [5].

(3) A charge[2] securing debentures[1] shall become enforceable on the occurrence of the events specified in the debentures [1] or the deed[6] securing the same.

(4) Where any legal proceedings are brought by a debenture holder[7] to enforce the security [8] of a series of debentures [1] of which he holds part, the debenture holder [7] shall sue in a representative capacity on behalf of himself and all other debenture holders [7] of that series.

---

**Notes**

**Section 173**

1. "Debenture" means a written acknowledgement of indebtedness by the company, setting out the terms and conditions of the indebtedness, and includes debenture stock, bonds and any other securities of a company whether constituting a charge on the assets of the company or not. See **Section 567 CAMA Cap C20 LFN, 2004**
2. "Charge" means an encumbrance, lien or claim. **See Garner B. (ed) Black's Law Dictionary, 8th ed.**
3. "Company" means a company formed and registered under this Act or, as the case may be, formed and registered in Nigeria before and in existence on the commencement of this Act. **Section 567 CAMA Cap C20 LFN, 2004**
4. "Fixed Charge" also termed "fixed cost". It means a cost whose value does not fluctuate with changes in output or business activity. See **Garner B. ed. Black's Law Dictionary 8th ed.**

5. "Floating Charge" means an equitable charge over the whole or a specified part of the company's undertakings and assets, including cash and uncalled capital of the company both present and future. **See section 178(1),CAMA CAP C20, LFN 2004**
5. "Deed" means any written instrument that is signed, sealed and delivered and that conveys small interest in property. **See Garner B. (ed) Black's Law Dictionary 8[th] ed**
6. "Debenture Holder" see "debenture" and "holder". Debenture means a written acknowledgement of indebtedness by the company, setting out the terms and conditions of the indebtedness and includes debenture stock, bonds and any other securities of any company whether constituting a charge on the assets of the company or not. See **Section 567 CAMA Cap C20 LFN, 2004.** "Holder" is one who has legal possession of a negotiable instrument and is entitled to receive payment on it. A holder is a person who has legal possession of a document of title or an investment security. See **Garner B. (ed.) Black's Law Dictionary.**

**For Further Reading**

On Company, debenture, types of Debenture, see, Orojo, J. Ola **Company Law and Practice in Nigeria** 3[rd] Edition, Mbeyi & Associates (Lagos, Nigeria) 1992.

## 174. Redeemable debentures

A company[1] limited by shares[2] may issue[3] debentures[4] which are, or at the option of the company [1] are to be liable, to be redeemed.

---

Notes

Section 174

1. "Company" It means a company formed and registered under this Act or, as the case may be, formed and registered in Nigeria before and in existence on the commencement of this Act. **Section 567 of CAMA Cap C20 LFN, 2004**
2. Shares" see "share". It means the interests in a company's share capital of a member who is entitled to share in the capital or income of such company; and except where a distinction between stock and shares is expressed or implied, includes stock. See **Section 567 of CAMA Cap C20 LFN, 2004**
3. "Issue" means a class or series of securities that are simultaneously offered for sale. See **Garner B. (ed.) Black's Law Dictionary 8th ed.**
4. "Debentures" see "debenture". It means a written acknowledgement of indebtedness by the company, setting out the terms and conditions of the indebtedness, and includes debenture stock, bonds and any other securities of a company whether constituting a charge on the assets of the company or not. See **Section 567 CAMA Cap C20 LFN, 2004**

Cross Reference

On companies limited by shares, see **section 21, CAMA, Cap C 20 , LFN 2004**

**Cases**

A debenture consists of a debt owed by a company to another secured by a deed which prescribes the condition of the realization of the debt, and it may be created over the fixed or floating assets of the company " **See *UBN v. Tropics Foods (1992) 3NWLR (Pt 228) 231***

**For Further Reading**

On debentures, see, Orojo, J. Ola **Company Law and Practice in Nigeria** 3rd Edition, Mbeyi & Associates (Lagos, Nigeria) 1992.

### 175. Power to re-issue redeemed debentures in certain cases

(1) Where either before or after the commencement of this Act, a company [1] has redeemed any debentures [2] previously issued[3], then unless-

(a) any provision, express or implied, to the contrary is contained in the articles[4] or in any contract entered into by the company[1]; or

(b) the company[1] has, by passing a resolution [5] to that effect or by some other act, manifested its intention that the debentures shall be cancelled, the company [1] shall have, and shall be deemed always to have had, power to re-issue[6] the debentures,[3] either by re-issuing[6] the same debentures[2] or by issuing[3] other debentures[2] in their place.

(2) On a re-issue[6] of redeemed debentures[2] the person entitled to the debentures,[2] shall have, and shall be deemed always to have had, the same priorities as if the debentures [2]had never been redeemed.

(3) Where a company[1] has, either before or after the commencement of this Act, deposited any of its debentures[2] to secure advances, from time to time, on current account or otherwise, the debenture [3] shall not be deemed to have been redeemed by reason only of the account of the company[1] having ceased to be in debit, whilst the debentures[2] remained so deposited.

(4) The re-issue[6] of a debenture[2] or the issue[3] of another debenture[2] in its place under the power given by this

section to or deemed to have been possessed by a company,[1] whether the re-issue[6] or issue[3] was made before or after the commencement of this Act, shall be treated as the issue[3] of a new debenture[2] for the purposes of a stamp duty, but it shall not be so treated for the purposes of any provision limiting the amount or number of debentures[2] to be issued[3]:

Provided that any person lending money on the security[7] of a debenture[2] re-issued[6] under this section which appears to be duly stamped, may give the debenture[2] in evidence in any proceedings for enforcing his security[7] without payment of the stamp duty or any penalty in respect thereof, unless he had notice or, but for his negligence, might have discovered, that the debenture[2] was not duly stamped, but in any such case the company[1] shall be liable to pay the proper stamp duty and penalty.

(5) Nothing in this section shall prejudice any power to issue debentures[2] in place of any debentures[2] paid off or otherwise satisfied or extinguished which, by its debentures[2] or the securities[7] for the same, is reserved to a company.

---

**Notes**

Section 175

1. "Company" means a company formed and registered under this Act or, as the case may be, formed and registered in Nigeria before and in existence on the commencement of this Act. See **Section 567 CAMA Cap C20 LFN, 2004**
2. "debentures" see "debenture." It means a written acknowledgement of indebtedness by the company, setting out the terms and conditions of the indebtedness, and includes debenture stock, bonds and any other securities of a company whether constituting a charge on the assets of the company or not. See **Section 567 CAMA Cap C20 LFN, 2004**
3. "issued" see "issue." It means a class or series of securities that are simultaneously offered for sale. See **Garner B. (ed.) Black's Law Dictionary 8th ed.**
4. "Articles" means the articles of association of a company, as originally framed or as altered by special resolution, including so far as they apply to the regulations contained in Table A in the First Schedules of the Companies Act, 1922 or in that Table as altered by any subsequent enactment or reprint of the laws, or in Table A in the First Schedule to this Act. See Section **567 of CAMA Cap C20 LFN, 2004**

5. "resolution" means a main motion that formally expresses the sense, will, or action of a deliberative assembly. See **Garner B. (ed.) Black's Law Dictionary 8th ed.**
6. "re-issue" means to issue something again, especially something that has not been available for some time. See **Oxford advanced Learners Dictionary 6th ed.**
7. "security" means collateral given or pledged to guarantee the fulfilment of an obligation; especially the assurance that a creditor will be repaid. See **Garner B. (ed.) Black's Law Dictionary 8 th ed.**
"securities" includes shares, debentures, debenture stock, bonds, notes (other than promissory notes) and units under a unit trust scheme. See Section **567 CAMA Cap C20 LFN, 2004**

Cross Reference

On the charge of duties on several instruments, including re-issued redeemed debentures, see **section 3, Stamp Duties Act, Cap 8S LFN 2004**
On power of a company to redeem debentures, see **section 174, CAMA Cap C20, LFN 2004.**

---

**Cases**

A debenture is a document which either creates or acknowledges a debt....This obligation is in most cases at the present day, accompanied by some charge or security" ***Fasakin v. Fasakin (1994) 4 N.W.L.R Pt. 340; pg.620 par. C-E***

**For Further Reading**

See generally, **Sofowora M.O; Modern Nigerian Company Law 2nd ed. (2002) Soft Associates, Pages. 334**

## 176. Rights of debenture holders

(1) The trustee[1] of a debenture[2] trust deed[3] shall hold all contracts, stipulations and undertakings given to him and all mortgages,[4] charges[5] and securities[6] vested in him in connection with the debentures[2] covered by the deed[3], or some of those debentures[2], exclusively for the benefit of the debenture holders[7] concerned (except in so far as the deed otherwise provides) and the trustee[1] shall exercise due diligence in respect of the enforcement of those contracts, stipulations, undertakings, mortgages,[4] charges[5] and securities[6] and the fulfilment of his functions generally.

(2) A debenture holder[7] may sue-

(a) the company[8] which issued the debentures[2] he holds for payment of any amount payable to him in respect of the debentures[2]; or

(b) the trustee[1] of the debenture[2] trust deed[3] covering the debentures[2] he holds for compensation for any breach of the duties which the trustee[1] owes him, and in any such action, it shall not be necessary for any other debenture holders[2] of the same class, or if the action is brought against the company,[8] the trustee[1] of the covering trust deed[3], to be joined as a party.

(3) This section shall apply notwithstanding anything contained in a debenture[2] or trust deed[3] or other instrument, but a provision in a debenture[2] or trust deed[3] shall be valid and binding on all the debenture holders[7] of the class concerned in so far as it enables a meeting[9] of the debenture holders[7] by a resolution[10] supported by the votes of the holders[7] of at least three quarters in value of the debentures[2] of that class in respect of which votes are cast on the resolution[10] to-

(a) release any trustee[1] from liability for any breach of his duties to the debenture holders[7] which he has already committed, or generally from liability for all such breaches (without necessarily specifying them) upon his ceasing to be trustee[1];

(b) consent to the alteration or abrogation of any of the rights, powers or remedies of the debenture holders[7] and the trustee[1] of the debenture[2] trust deed[3] covering their debentures[2] (except the powers and remedies under section 209 of this Act); or

(c) consent to the substitution for the debentures[2] of a different class issued by the company[8] or any other company[8] or corporation, or the cancellation of the debentures[2] in consideration of the issue to the debenture holders[7] of shares[11] credited as fully paid in the company[8] or any other company.[8]

---

**Notes**
**Section 176**

1. "Trustee" means one who, having legal title to property holds it in trust for the benefit of another and owes a fiduciary duty to that beneficiary. See **Garner B. (ed.) Black's Law Dictionary 8 th ed.**
2. "Debenture" means a written acknowledgement of indebtedness by the company, setting out the terms and conditions of the indebtedness, and includes debenture stock, bonds and any other securities of a company whether constituting a charge on the assets of the company or not. See **Section 567 CAMA Cap C20 LFN, 2004**

3. "Trust deed" see declaration of trust. It means the instrument that creates a trust. See **Garner B (ed.) Black's Law Dictionary 8th ed.**
4. "Mortgages" see "mortgage". It means a conveyance of title to property that is given as security for the payment of a debt or the performance of a duty and that will become void upon payment or performance according to the stipulated terms. See **Garner B. (ed) Black's Law Dictionary 8th edition**
5. "Charges" see charge. It means an encumbrance, lien or claim. See **Garner B. (ed.) Black's Law Dictionary 8th ed.**
6. "Securities" see "security". It means collateral given or pledged to guarantee the fulfilment of an obligation; especially the assurance that a creditor will be repaid. **Garner B. (ed.) Black's Law Dictionary 8 th ed.** "Securities" includes shares, debentures, debenture stock, bonds, notes (other than promissory notes) and units under a unit trust scheme. See Section **567 CAMA Cap C20 LFN, 2004**
7. "Debenture holders" see "debenture" and "holder." Debenture means a written acknowledgement of indebtedness by the company, setting out the terms and conditions of the indebtedness and includes debenture stock, bonds and any other securities of any company whether constituting a charge on the assets of the company or not. See **Section 567 CAMA Cap C20 LFN, 2004.** "Holder" is one who has legal possession of a negotiable instrument and is entitled to receive payment on it. A holder is a person who has legal possession of a document of title or an investment security. See **Garner B. (ed.) Black's Law Dictionary**
8. "Company" means a company formed and registered under this Act or, as the case may be, formed and registered in Nigeria before and in existence on the commencement of this Act. See **Section 567 CAMA Cap C20 LFN, 2004**
9. "Meeting" means the gathering of people to discuss or act on matters in which they have a common interest. See **Garner B. (ed.) Black's Law Dictionary 8th ed.**
10. "Resolution" means a main motion that formally expresses the sense, will or action of a deliberative assembly. See **Garner B. (ed.) Black's Law Dictionary 8th ed.**
11. "Shares" see "share". It means one of the definite number of equal parts into which the capital stock of a corporation or joint stock company is divided. See **Garner B. (ed.) Black's Law Dictionary 8th ed.** "Share" means the interest in a company's share capital of a member who is entitled to share in the capital or income of such company; and except where a distinction between stock and shares is expressed or implied, includes stock. **Section 567 of the CAMA, Cap C20 LFN, 2004**

**Cross Reference**

On the power of a company to create debentures and debenture stock, see **section 166 CAMA CAP C20 LFN 2004**

On remedies available to a debenture holder, see **section 209 CAMA Cap C20 LFN 2004**

## 177. Meetings of debenture holders

(1) The terms of any debentures [1] or trust deed [2] may provide for the convening of general meetings [3] of the debenture holders [4] and for the passing, at such meetings, [3] of a resolution [5] binding on all the holders [4] of the debentures [1] of the same class. [6]

(2) Whether or not the debentures [1] or trust deed [2] contain such provisions as are referred to in subsection (1) of this section, the Commission[8] may at any time direct a meeting [3] of the debenture holders[4] of any class[6] to be h conducted in such manner as the Commission[7] thinks fit to consider ancillary or consequential direction as it shall think fit.

(3) Notwithstanding anything contained in a debenture [1] trust deed[2], or in any debenture [1] or contract or instrument, the trustee [8] of a debenture[1] deed[2] shall, on the requisition of persons holding, at the date of the deposit of the acquisition debentures [1] covered by the trust deed[2] which carry not less than one tenth of the total voting rights attached to all the issued and outstanding debentures [1] of that class, forthwith, proceed duly to convene a meeting [4] of that class of debenture holders. [4]

---

**Notes**

**Section 177(1)**

1. "Debentures" see "debenture" means a written acknowledgement of indebtedness by the company, setting out the terms and conditions of the indebtedness and includes debenture stock, bonds and any other securities of any company whether constituting a charge on the assets of the company or not. **See section 567, CAMA Cap C20, LFN 2004**
2. "Trust deed" see declaration of trust. It means the instrument that creates a trust. **See Garner B ed. Black's Law Dictionary 8 th Ed.**
3. "General Meeting" see "general" and "meeting." "General means affecting all or most people" **(See Oxford Advanced Learner's Dictionary)**. "Meeting" means the gathering of people to discuss or act on matters in which they have a common interest. (See **Garner B. ed. Black's Law Dictionary, 8 th Ed.**)
4. Debenture holders" see "debenture" and "holder." Debenture means a written acknowledgement of indebtedness by the company, setting out the terms and conditions of the indebtedness and includes debenture stock, bonds and any other securities of any company whether constituting a charge on the assets of the company or not. ( **See section 567 CAMA LFN 2004**). "Holder" is one who has legal possession of a negotiable instrument and is entitled to receive payment on it. (See **Garner B. ed. Black's Law Dictionary, 8 th Ed**

5. Resolution" means a decision reached by a majority of the m embers at a company meeting. **Martins E. (ed.) Oxford Dictionary of Law 4 th ed.** (2). A main motion that formally expresses the sense, will or action of a deliberative assembly. **See Garner B ed. Black's Law Dictionary 8th ed.**
6. "Class" means a group of people, things, qualities or activities that have common characteristics or attributes. **See Garner B ed. Black's Law Dictionary 8th ed. Section 177(2)**
7. "Commission" means Corporate Affairs Commission, established under s.1 of the Companies and Allied Matters Act. **See section 567, CAMA LFN 2004**
8. "Trustee" means one who, having legal title to property holds it in trust for the benefit of another and owes a fiduciary duty to that beneficiary. **See Garner B. (ed.) Black's Law Dictionary 8th ed.**

Cross Reference

For the rights of debenture holders see **section 176, Company and Allied Matters Act, Cap LFN 2004**

No debenture trust deed may cover more than one class of debenture . **See section 183(1), CAMA. LFN 2004**

For the situations under which debentures shall belong to different classes, **see section 183(4) and (5), CAMA LFN 2004**

---

**Cases**

"A debenture is a company's security for a monetary loan. The security usually creates a charge on the company's stock or property " **See *NIDB v. Olalomi Ind. Ltd. (2002) 5 N.W.L.R (pt 761)532***

"A debenture consists of a debt owed by a company to another secured by a deed which prescribes the condition of the realization of the debt, and it may be created over the fixed or floating assets of the company " **See *UBN v. Tropics Foods (1992) 3NWLR (Pt 228) 231***

"A debenture is a document which either creates or acknowledges a debt....This obligation is in most casesat the present day, accompanied by some charge or security " ***Fasakin v. Fasakin (1994) 4 N.W.L.R Pt. 340; pg.620 par. C-E***

**For Further Reading**

See generally, Sofowora M.O; **Modern Nigerian Company Law 2nd ed., (2002) Soft Associates, Pages. 334**

*Fixed and floating charges*

## 178. Meaning of "floating" and "fixed" charges

(1) A "floating charge [1]" means an equitable charge [1] over the whole or a specified part of the company's [2] undertakings and

assets,[3] including cash and uncalled capital[4] of the company[2] both present and future, but so that the charge [1] shall not preclude the company[2] from dealing with such assets [3] until-

(a) the security[5] becomes enforceable and the holder [6] thereof, pursuant to a power in that behalf in the debenture [7] or the deed securing the same, appoints a receiver [8] or manager[9] or enters into possession of such assets[3]; or

(b) the court [10] appoints a receiver[8] or manager[9] of such assets[3] on the application of the holder [6]; or

(c) the company[2] goes into liquidation[11]

(2) On the happening of any of the events mentioned in subsection (1) of this section, the charge [1] shall be deemed to crystallise and to become a fixed equitable charge [1] on such of the company's[2] assets[3] as are subject to the charge, [1] and if a receiver[8] or manager[9] is withdrawn with the consent of the chargee, or the chargee withdraws from possession before the charge [1] has been fully discharged, the charge [1] shall thereupon be deemed to cease to be a fixed charge[1] and again to become a floating charge. [1]

---

**Notes.**
**Section 178 (1)**

1. "Charge" means an encumbrance, lien or claim. See **Garner B ed. Black's Law Dictionary 8th ed.**
2. "Company" means a company formed and registered under this Act or as the case may be, formed and registered in Nigeria before and in existence on the commencement of this Act. See **section 567, CAMA Cap. C20, LFN 2004**
3. "Assets" see "Asset". It means an item that is owned and has value. See **Garner B. (ed) Black's Law Dictionary, 8 th ed**.
4. "Capital" means of or relating to economic or financial capital. Money or assets invested or available for investment. See **Garner B. (ed) Blacks' law dictionary 8th ed**.
5. "Security" means collateral given or pledged to guarantee the fulfilment of an obligation; especially the assurance that a creditor will be repaid. See **Garner B., (ed.) Black's Law Dictionary 8 th ed.**
   "Securities" includes shares, debentures, debenture stock, bonds, notes (other than promissory notes) and units under a unit trust scheme. See Section **567 of CAMA Cap C20 LFN, 2004**
6. "Holder" is one who has legal possession of a negotiable instrument and is entitled to receive payment on it. A holder is a person who has legal possession of a document of title or an investment security. See **Garner B. (ed.) Black's Law Dictionary**
7. "Debentures" see "debenture". It means a written acknowledgement of indebtedness by the company, setting out the terms and conditions of the

indebtedness and includes debenture stock, bonds and any other securities of any company whether constituting a charge on the assets of the company or not. **See s. 567, CAMA, Cap. C20, LFN 2004**

8. "Receiver" means a disinterested person appointed by a court, or by a corporation or other person, for the protection or collection of property that is subject of diverse claims. See **Garner B. ed. Black's Law Dictionary 8th ed. page 1296**
   Receiver includes a manager. **See section 567, CAMA Cap. C20, LFN 2004**
9. "Manager" means one who is in charge or corporation and control of its business. **Garner, B. (ed.) Black's Law Dictionary 8 th ed.**
10. "Court" means the Federal High Court and to the extent to which application may be made to it as; court includes the Court of Appeal and the Supreme Court. **See section 567, CAMA Cap. C20, LFN 2004**
11. Liquidation" means the act of settling a debt by payment or other satisfaction. See Garner Black's Law Dictionary, 8 th ed.
    "Liquidation" see "winding up". It means a procedure by which a company can be dissolved. It may be instigated by members or creditors of the company or by order of the court. In both cases the process involves the appointment of a liquidator to assume control of the company from its directors. He collects the assets, pays debts, and distributes any surplus to company members in accordance with their rights. **See Martins E. (ed.) Oxford Dictionary of Law 4 th ed.**

**Cross Reference**

For the provision that confers jurisdiction on Federal High Court, see **section 251 of the Constitution of the Federal Republic of Nigeria, 1999(as amended)**

---

**Cases**

"A receiver is defined as a disinterested person, appointed by the court or by a corporation or other persons for the protection or collection of property that is the subject of diverse claims, for example, because it belongs to a bankrupt or is otherwise being litigated ." **See *Dagazu v. Bokir (2011) 14 N.W.L.R Pt 1267, p261at 345***

A receiver has duty to stop business, collect the debts and release the assets. But a manager has power to continue a business or a going concern: ***Ponson Enterprise Nig. Ltd v. Njigha (2001) FWLR pt. 61 p. 3***

## 179. Priority of fixed over floating charge

A fixed charge[1] on any property shall have priority [2] over a floating charge[3] affecting that property, unless the terms on which the floating charge[3] was granted prohibited the company [4] from granting any later charge[5] having priority over the floating charge [3] and the person in whose favour such later charge [5] was granted had actual notice[6] of that prohibition at the time when the charge [5] was granted to him.

---

**Notes**
**Section 179**

1. "Fixed Charge" also termed "fixed cost". It means a cost whose value does not fluctuate with changes in output or business activity. See **Garner B. ed. Black's Law Dictionary 8th ed.**
2. "Priority" means (1) the status of being earlier in time or higher in degree or rank. (2)An established right to precedence especially a Creditor's right to have a claim paid before other creditors of the same debtors receive payment. See **Garner B. ed. Black's Law Dictionary 8th ed.**
3. "Floating Charge" means an equitable charge over the whole or a specified part of the company's undertakings and assets, including cash and uncalled capital of the company both present and future. **See section 178(1), CAMA Cap. C20, LFN 2004**
4. "Company" means a company formed and registered under this Act or as the case may be, formed and registered in Nigeria before and in existence on the commencement of this Act. See **section 567, CAMA Cap. C20, LFN 2004**
5. "Charge" means an encumbrance, lien or claim. See **Garner B ed. Black's Law Dictionary 8th ed.**
6. "Actual Notice" means notice given directly to, or received personally by a party. See **Garner B ed. Black's Law Dictionary 8 th ed.**

## 180. Powers of the court

(1) Whenever a fixed [1] or floating charge [2] has become enforceable, the court [3] shall have power to appoint a receiver [4] and in the case of a floating charge, [2] a receiver [4] and manager [5] of the assets [6] subject to the charge. [7]

(2) In the case of a floating charge [2], the court [3] may, notwithstanding that the charge [7] has not become enforceable, appoint a receiver [4] or manager [5] if satisfied that the security [8] of the debenture holder [9] is in jeopardy; and the security [8] of the debenture holder [9] shall be deemed to be in jeopardy if the court [3] is satisfied that events have occurred or are about to occur which render it unreasonable in the interests of the debenture holder [9] that the company [10] should retain power to dispose of its assets. [6]

(3) A receiver [4] or manager [5] shall not be appointed as a means of enforcing debentures [11] not secured by any charge [7].

**Notes**
**Section 180**

1. "Fixed charge" also termed "fixed cost". It means a cost whose value does not fluctuate with changes in output or business activity. See **Garner B ed. Black's Law Dictionary 8 th ed.**
2. "Floating Charge" see floating lien. It means a charge that continues to exist even when the collateral changes in character, classification or location. **Garner B ed. Black's Law Dictionary 8 th ed.**
   It means an equitable charge over the whole or a specified part of the company's undertakings and assets, including cash and uncalled capital of the company both present and future. **See section 178(1), CAMA Cap. C20, LFN 2004**
3. "Court" means the Federal High Court and to the extent to which application may be made to it as; court includes the Court of Appeal and the Supreme Court. See section **567, CAMA Cap. C20, LFN 2004**
4. "Receiver" means a disinterested person appointed by a court, or by a corporation or other person, for the protection or collection of property that is subject of diverse claims. See **Garner B. ed. Black's Law Dictionary 8th ed.**
5. Receiver includes a manager. See section **567, CAMA Cap. C20, LFN 2004.**
6. "Manager" means one who is in charge or corporation and control of its business **See Garner, B.(ed.) Black's Law Dictionary 8 th ed.**
7. **"Assets"** see "Asset". It means an item that is owned and has value. See **Garner B. (ed) Black's Law Dictionary, 8 th ed.**

8. "Charge" means an encumbrance, lien or claim. See **Garner B. (ed.) Black's Law Dictionary 8th ed.**
9. "Security" means collateral given or pledged to guarantee the fulfilment of an obligation; especially the assurance that a creditor will be repaid. **Garner B., (ed.) Black's Law Dictionary 8 th ed.**
   "Securities" includes shares, debentures, debenture stock, bonds, notes (other than promissory notes) and units under a unit trust scheme. See Section See section **567, CAMA Cap. C20, LFN 2004**
10. "Debenture holder" see "debenture" and "holder." Debenture means a written acknowledgement of indebtedness by the company, setting out the terms and conditions of the indebtedness and includes debenture stock, bonds and any other securities of any company whether constituting a charge on the assets of the company or not. See **Section 567 CAMA Cap. C20 LFN, 2004.** "Holder" is one who has legal possession of a negotiable instrument and is entitled to receive payment on it. A holder is a person who has legal possession of a document of title or an investment security. See **Garner B., (ed.) Black's Law Dictionary**
11. "Company" means a company formed and registered under this Act or, as the case may be, formed and registered in Nigeria before and in existence on the commencement of this Act. **Section 567 of CAMA Cap C20 LFN, 2004**
12. "Debentures" see "debenture". It means a written acknowledgement of indebtedness by the company, setting out the terms and conditions of the indebtedness, and includes debenture stock, bonds and any other securities of a company whether constituting a charge on the assets of the company or not. See **Section 567 of CAMA Cap C20 LFN, 2004**

**Cross Reference**

For the provision that confers jurisdiction on Federal High Court, see **section 251 of the 1999 Constitution of the Federal Republic of Nigeria, 1999(as amended)**

For the rights of debenture holders see **section 176, Company and Allied Matters Act, Cap. LFN 2004**

---

**Cases**

On distinction between a receiver and manager:

"Indeed in ***Inter contractors Nig. Ltd v. N.P.F.M.B (1988) 2 NWLR (Pt 76)*** 208 Oputa JSC (as he then was) explained the subtle distinction between the two offices. According to the distinguished jurist, a receiver's duty is only to realize the debenture holder's security. Thus, it is not his duty to manage the affairs of the company for its benefit, citing Re B. Johnson & CO.(Builders)ltd (1995) Ch. 634. Where on the other hand it is necessary for the receiver to carry on the business of the company, the court usually appointed the receiver as both receiver and manager. Above all, a manager is not generally appointed except to carry on the business for the purpose of selling it as a going concern, citing ***Marshall v. South***

***Staffordshire Tramways Co. (1895)2 Ch 36" See P.I.P ltd v. Trade Bank Nig. Plc (2009) All FWLR Pt 495 p.1678 @1722***

## 181.Advertisement of appointment of receiver and manager

Where a receiver [1] or a receiver [1] and manager[2] is appointed[3] by the court[4], advertisement to this effect shall be made by the receiver[1] or the receiver [1] and manager[2] in the Gazette[5] and in two daily newspapers.

---

**Notes**
**Section 181**

1. "Receiver" means a disinterested person appointed by a court, or by a corporation or other person, for the protection or collection of property that is subject of diverse claims. See **Garner B. ed. Black's Law Dictionary 8th ed.**
   "Receiver" includes a manager. See **section 567 CAMA Cap. C20, LFN 2004**
2. "Manager" means one who has charge of corporation and control of its business, or of its branch establishments, divisions, or departments . **See Garner B., (ed.) Black's Law Dictionary 8 th ed.**
3. "Appointed". See appoint. It means to choose someone for a job or responsibility. See **Garner B. ed. Black's Law Dictionary**
4. "Court" means the Federal High Court and to the extent to which application may be made to it as; court includes the Court of Appeal and the Supreme Court. See **section 567 CAMA Cap. C20, LFN 2004**
5. "Gazette" means the official gazette of the Federation. See **section 567 CAMA Cap. C20, LFN 2004**

**Cross Reference**

On the establishment and jurisdiction of the Federal High Court, see **sections 249& 251 of the Constitution of the Federal Republic of Nigeria, 1999(as amended)**

---

**Cases**

On the Statutory powers to appoint a receiver

"The Statutory powers to appoint a receiver and or manager of a company incorporated under CAMA are contained in sections 209 and 389 of the Act. A receiver may be appointed out of court pursuant to section 209(1)(a)-(d) of the Act or by the court pursuant to section 389(1)(a) and (b) thereof. In respect of debentures, a receiver may be appointed out of court...Where a receiver is appointed out of court he may pursuant to section 391 of CAMA, apply to the court for directions in relation to any particular matter arising in connection with the performance of his function" See ***Nashtex International Limited v. Habib Nigeria Bank Limited*** **(2009)All FWLR PT 466 1974 at1989**

**For Further Reading**
On Receivers, Managers and Debenture Trust Deed see: Orojo, J. Ola **Company Law and Practice in Nigeria** 3rd Edition, Mbeyi & Associates (Lagos, Nigeria) 1992.
Ogbuanya C.S. Nelson **Essentials of Corporate Law Practice in Nigeria** Novena Publishers Limited 2012;
Sasegbon Deji & Co *Companies and Allied Matters Law and Practice* (NCAMLP) DSC Publications Ltd 2006

## 182. Preferential payment to debenture holders in certain cases

(1) Where a receiver [1] is appointed[2] on behalf of the holders of any debentures[3] of a registered company [4] secured by a floating charge[5], or possession is taken by, or on behalf of those debenture holders[6] of any property comprising or subject to the charge, [5] then if the company[4] is not at the time in course of being wound up, [7] the debts which in every winding up [7] are under the provisions relating to preferential payments [8] in Part XV of this Act to be paid in priority to all other debts, shall be paid out of any assets coming to the hands of the receiver [1] or other person taking possession as aforesaid in priority to any claim for principal or interest in respect of the debentures [3].

(2) In the application of the provisions relating to preferential payments[8]-

(a) section 494 of this Act shall be construed as if the provision for payment of accrued holiday remuneration [9] becoming payable on the termination of employment before or by the effect of the winding-up [7] order or resolution,[10] were a provision for payment of such remuneration[9] becoming payable on the termination of employment before or by the effect of appointment of the receiver[1] or possession being taken as aforesaid; and

(b) the periods of time mentioned therein shall be reckoned from the date of the appointment of the receiver [1] or of possession being taken as aforesaid, as the case may be, and if such date occurred before the commencement of this Act, the provisions relating to preferential payments [8] which would have applied but for this Act, shall be deemed to remain in full force.

(3) Any payments made under this section, shall be recouped as far as may be out of the assets of the company [4] available for payment of general creditors. [11]

---

**Notes**

**Section 182(1)**

1. "Receiver" means a disinterested person appointed by a court, or by a corporation or other person, for the protection or collection of property that is subject of diverse claims. **Garner B. ed. Black's Law Dictionary 8th ed.**
   Receiver includes a manager. See **section 567 CAMA Cap. C20, LFN 2004**
2. "Appointed" appoint It means to choose someone for a job or responsibility. See **Garner B. (ed.) Black's Law Dictionary 8 th ed.**
3. "Debentures" "debenture" means a written acknowledgement of indebtedness by the company, setting out the terms and conditions of the indebtedness and includes debenture stock, bonds and any other securities of any company whether constituting a charge on the assets of the company or not. See **section 567 CAMA Cap. C20, LFN 2004**
4. "Registered company" means a company incorporated or deemed to be incorporated under CAMA. See **section 567 CAMA Cap. C20, LFN 2004**
5. "Floating Charge" see floating lien. It means a charge that continues to exist even when the collateral changes in character, classification or location. See **Garner B. ed. Black's Law Dictionary 8 th ed.**
6. "Debenture holders" see "debenture" and "holder." Debenture means a written acknowledgement of indebtedness by the company, setting out the terms and conditions of the indebtedness and includes debenture stock, bonds and any other securities of any company whether constituting a charge on the assets of the company or not.( See **section 567 CAMA Cap. C20, LFN 2004).** "Holder" is one who has legal possession of a negotiable instrument and is entitled to receive payment on it. See **Garner B. ed. Black's Law Dictionary 8 th ed.**
7. "Winding up" means the process of settling accounts and liquidating assets in anticipation of a partnership or a company dissolution. See **Garner B. ed. Black's Law Dictionary 8 th ed.**
8. "Preferential payment" For the meaning of preferential payment, **see section 494, CAMA Cap. C20, LFN 2004**
9. "Remuneration" means amount of money paid for work done before. See **Oxford Advanced Learner's Dictionary, 6 th ed.**

**Section 182(2)**

10. "Resolution" means a main motion that formally expresses the sense, will or action of a deliberative assembly. **See Garner B. (ed.) Black's Law Dictionary 8th ed.**

**Section 182(3)**

11. "Creditors" means one to whom a debt is owed whether contractual or otherwise. See **Garner B. (ed.) Black's Law Dictionary 8 th ed.**

**Cross Reference**

For the requirements for incorporating a company and the effect of incorporation under CAMA, **see sections 35-37 CAMA Cap. C20, LFN 2004**

On preferential payments, see **section 494 CAMA Cap. C20 LFN 2004**

On Winding up of a Company, generally **Part XV, CAMA Cap. C20 LFN 2004**

---

**For Further Reading**

On Receivers, Managers and Debenture Trust Deed see: Orojo, J. Ola **Company Law and Practice in Nigeria** 3rd Edition, Mbeyi & Associates (Lagos, Nigeria) 1992; Ogbuanya C.S. Nelson **Essentials of Corporate Law Practice in Nigeria** Novena Publishers Limited 2012; Sasegbon Deji & Co. **Companies and Allied Matters Law and Practice** (NCAMLP) DSC Publications Ltd 2006

*Debenture trust deed*

## 183. Execution of debenture trust deed

(1) Every company [1] which offers debentures [2] to the public for subscription[3] or purchase shall, before issuing any of the debentures,[2] execute a debenture trust deed [4] in respect of them and procure the execution of the deed [4] by the trustee [5] for the debenture holders[6] appointed by the deed. [4]

(2) No debenture trust deed [4] shall cover more than one class of debentures,[2] whether or not the trust deed [4] is required by this section to be executed.

(3) Where a trust deed [4] is required to be executed by this section but has not been executed, the court, [7] on the application of a debenture holder [6] concerned, may-

(a) Order the company [1] to execute a trust deed [4];

(b) Direct that a person nominated by the court [7] shall be appointed to be trustee [5]; and

(c) Give such consequential directions as it thinks fit, as to the contents of the trust deed [4] and its execution by the trustee[5] thereof.

(4) For the purposes of this Act, debentures [2] shall belong to different classes if different rights attach to them in respect of-

(a) The rate of, or dates for payment of interest;

(b) the dates when, or the installments by which, the principal of the debenture[2] shall be repaid, unless the difference is solely that the class of debentures [2] shall be repaid during a stated period of time and particular debentures [2] may be repaid at different dates during that period according to selections made by the company[1] or by drawings, ballot or otherwise;

(c) any right to subscribe for or convert the debentures [2] into shares[8] in, or other debentures [2] of, the company [1] or any other company[1]; or

(d) the powers of the debenture holders [6] to realize any security.[9]

(5) Debentures[2] further belong to different classes, if they do not rank equally for payment when any security [9] invested in the debenture holders[6] under any trust deed [4] is realised or when the company[1] is wound up, [10] that is to say, if, in the circumstances mentioned in subsection (4) of this section the subject matter of any such security[9] or the proceeds thereof, or any assets available to satisfy the debentures,[2] is or are not to be applied in satisfying the debentures[2] strictly in proportion to the amount of principal, premiums[11] and arrears of interest to which the holders of them are respectively entitled.

(6) A debenture[2] is covered by a trust deed [4] if-

(a) the holder of the debenture [2] is entitled to participate in any money payable by the company [1]under the deed[4]; or

(b) is entitled to the benefit of any mortgage, [12] charge[13] or security[9]created by the deed[4], whether alone or together with other persons.

(7) If a company [1] issues debentures[2] in circumstances in which this section requires a debenture trust deed [4] to be executed, without such a deed having been executed in compliance with this section, or if the company [1] issues debentures[2] under a trust deed [4] which covers two or more classes of debentures, [2] the directors [14] of the company[1] who are in default are guilty of an offence and liable on conviction to a fine of N 5,000 jointly or severally.

---

**Notes**

**Section 183(1)**

1. "Company" means a company formed and registered under this Act or, as the case may be, formed and registered in Nigeria before and in

existence on the commencement of this Act. **See section 567 CAMC Cap. C20, LFN 2004**

2. "Debentures" see "debenture." It means a written acknowledgement of indebtedness by the company, setting out the terms and conditions of the indebtedness and includes debenture stock, bonds and any other securities of any company whether constituting a charge on the assets of the company or not. **See section 567 CAMC Cap. C20, LFN 2004**
3. "Subscription" means a written contract to purchase newly issued shares of stocks or bonds. See **Garner B. Black's Law Dictionary, 8th ed.**
4. "Debenture trust deed see "deed of trust" It means a deed conveying title to real property to a trustee as security until the grantor repays a loan. See **Garner B. ed. Black's Law Dictionary, 8th ed.**
5. "Trustee" means one who, having legal title to property, holds it in trust for the benefit of another and owes a fiduciary duty to that beneficiary. See **Garner B. ed. Black's Law Dictionary, 8th ed.**
6. "Debenture holders" see debenture holder. See "debenture" and "holder." Debenture means a written acknowledgement of indebtedness by the company, setting out the terms and conditions of the indebtedness and includes debenture stock, bonds and any other securities of any company whether constituting a charge on the assets of the company or not.( s. **section 567, CAMA** . )"Holder" is one who has legal possession of a negotiable instrument and is entitled to receive payment on it.
7. "Court" in relation to a Company, means the Federal High Court and to the extent to which application may be made to it as; court includes the Court of Appeal and the Supreme Court of Nigeria. See s **ection 567 of CAMA Cap. C20, LFN 2004**
8. "Shares" means an equity or ownership interest in the corporation or Joint Stock Company. See **Garner B. ed. Black's Law Dictionary 8 th ed.**

   It means the interests in a company's shares capital of a member who is entitled to share in the Capital or income of such company and except where a distinction between stock and shares is expressed or implied, includes stock. See **section 567 of CAMA Cap. C20 LFN 2004**
9. "Security" means an instrument that evidences the holder's ownership rights in a firm. See **Garner B. ed. Black's Law Dictionary 8 th ed.** See Securities. It includes shares, debentures, debenture stock, bonds, notes (other than promissory notes) and units under a unit trust scheme. See section 567 of CAMA

**Section 183(5)**

10. "Wound-up" see winding-up. It means the process of settling accounts and liquidating assets in anticipation of a corporation's dissolution. See **Garner B. ed. Black's Law Dictionary 8 th ed.**
11. "Premium" means the amount by which a security's market value exceeds its face value. See **Garner B. (ed.) Black's Law Dictionary, 8th ed. Section 183(6)**
12. "Mortgage" means a lien against a property that is granted to secure an obligation such as a debt and that is extinguished upon payment or performance according to stipulated terms. See **Garner B, (ed.) Black's Law Dictionary 8th ed.**

13. "Charge" means an encumbrance, lien or claim. See **Garner B. ed. Black's Law Dictionary 8th ed. Section 183(7)**
14. "Directors" See Director. It means a person appointed or elected to sit on a board that manages the affairs of a corporation or other organization by electing and exercising control over its officers. **Garner B. ed. Black's Law Dictionary**
    It includes any person occupying the position of director by whatever name called; and includes any person in accordance with whose directions or instructions the directors of the company are accustomed to act. See **section 567 CAMA Cap. C20, LFN 2004**

Cross Reference

For nature, rights and liabilities accruing to shares, **generally Part VI, CAMA**

On allotment of shares, **generally section 124-129 CAMA**

**Cases**

On the use of the word "shall:"

In the interpretation of Statute, the word shall has various meanings. It may be used as implying futurity or implying a mandate. It imports that a thing must be done… It is a form of a command or mandate See ***Nigerian LNG Limited v. African Development Insurance Co. Ltd. (1995)8 NWLR (Pt. 416) 677.*** Generally, when the word "shall is used in a Statute, it is not permissive. It is mandatory. See ***Col. KalielRtd. v. AlhajiAilero (1999) 4NWLR (Pt. 597) 139.*** The word shall in its ordinary meaning is a word of command which is normally given a compulsory meaning because it is intended to denote obligation. As contended…, it is sometimes intended to be directory only and in that case it is equivalent to "may" and will be construed as being merely permissive. See Amokeodo v. Inspector General of Police (1999) 6 NWLR (Pt. 607)467. See ***Ugwu v. Ararume (2007) 31 WRN 1, 65 line 30-45***

**For Further Reading**

On Receivers, Managers and Debenture Trust Deed see: Orojo, J. Ola *Company Law and Practice in Nigeria* 3rd Edition, Mbeyi & Associates (Lagos, Nigeria) 1992; Ogbuanya C. S. Nelson **Essentials of Corporate Law Practice in Nigeria** Novena Publishers Limited 2012; Sasegbon Deji & Co **Companies and Allied Matters Law and Practice** (NCAMLP) DSC Publications Ltd 2006

## 184. Contents of debenture trust deed

(1) Every debenture [1] trust deed [2], whether required by section 183 of this Act or not, shall state-

(a) the maximum sum which the company [3] may raise by issuing debentures [1] of the same class;

(b) the maximum discount which may be allowed on the issue or re-issue of the debentures, [1] and the maximum premium[4] at which the debentures[1] may be made redeemable;

(c) the nature of any assets [5] over which a mortgage, [6] charge[7] or security[8] is created by the trust deed [2] in favor of the trustee[9] for the benefit of the debenture holders [10] equally, and except where such a charge [7] is a floating charge [11] or a general floating charge, [11] the identity of the assets subject to it;

(d) the nature of any assets [5] over which a mortgage, [6] charge[7] or security[8] has been or will be created in favor of any person other than the trustee [9] for the benefit of the debenture holders[10] equally, and except where such a charge[7] is a floating charge[11] or a general floating charge,[11] the identity of the assets subject to it;

(e) Whether the company[3] has created or will create any mortgage,[6] charge[7] or security[8] for the benefit of some, but not all, of the holders of debentures [10] issued under the trust deed[2];

(f) any prohibition or restriction on the power of the company[3] to issue debentures[1] or to create mortgages [6], charges[7] or any security [8] on any of its assets ranking in priority to, or equally with the debentures [1] issued under the trust deed[2];

(g) Whether the company[3] shall have power to acquire debentures[1] issued under the trust deed [2] before the date of their redemption and to re-issue the debentures [1];

(h) The rate of and the dates on which interest on the debentures[1] issued under the trust deed [2] shall be paid and the manner in which payment may be made;

(i) the date or dates on which the principal or the debentures [1] issued under the trust deed [2] shall be repaid, and unless the whole principal is to be repaid to all the debenture holders[10] at the same time, the manner in which redemption shall be effected, whether by the payment of equal installments of principal in respect of each debenture[1], or by the selection of debentures [1] for redemption by the company[3], or by drawing, ballot, or otherwise;

(j) in the case of convertible debentures, [12] the dates and terms on which the debentures [3] may be converted into shares[13] and the amounts which may be credited as paid up on those shares [13] in right of the debentures [3] held by them;

(k) the circumstances in which the debenture holders [10] shall be entitled to realise any mortgage, [6] charge[7] or security[8] invested in the trustee[9] or any other person for their benefit (other than the circumstances in which they are entitled to do so by this Act);

(I) the powers of the company [3] and the truste[9] to call meetings[14] of the debenture holders [10] and the rights of debenture holders [10] to require the company [3] or the trustee [9] to call such meetings [14];

(m) Whether the rights of debenture holders [10] may be altered or abrogated and if so, the conditions which must be fulfilled, and the procedure which must be followed, to effect such an alteration or abrogation; and

(n) The amount or rate of remuneration to be paid to the trustee[9] and the period for which it shall be paid, and whether it shall be paid in priority to the principal, interest and costs in respect of debentures [1] issued under the trust deed[2].

(2) If debentures [1] are issued without a covering debenture [1] trust deed[2] being executed, the statements required by subsection (1) of his section shall be included in each debenture [1] or in a note forming part of the same document or endorsed thereon, and in applying that subsection references therein to "the debenture trust deed" shall be construed as references to all or any of the debentures[1] of the same class.

(3) Subsection (2) of this section shall not apply if the debenture[1] is the only debenture of the class to which it belongs which has been or may be issued, and the rights of the debenture holder[10] may not be altered or abrogated without his consent.

(4) Any director [15] who issues a debenture [1] in violation of the provisions of this section shall be guilty of an offence.

**Notes**

**Section 184(1)**

1. "Debenture" means a written acknowledgement of indebtedness by the company, setting out the terms and conditions of the indebtedness and includes debenture stock, bonds and any other securities of any company whether constituting a charge on the assets of the company or not. **See section 567, CAMA Cap. C20 LFN 2004.**
2. "Trust deed" see "deed of trust". It means a deed conveying title to real property to a trustee as security until the grantor repays a loan. **See Garner B. ed. Black's Law Dictionary, 8 th ed.**
3. "Company" means a company formed and registered under this Act or, as the case may be, formed and registered in Nigeria before and in existence on the commencement of this Act. **See section 567, CAMA Cap. C20, LFN 2004**
4. "Premium" means a sum paid in addition to a regular price or amount; a bonus. See **Garner B., (ed.) Black's Law Dictionary 8 th ed.**
5. "Asset" means an item that is owned and has value. See **Garner B. (ed.) Black's Law Dictionary 8th ed.**
6. "Mortgage" means a lien against property that is granted to secure an obligation and that is extinguished upon payment or performance according to stipulated terms. See **Garner B. (ed.) Black's Law Dictionary 8th ed.**
7. "Charge" means an encumbrance, lien or claim. See **Garner B. (ed.) Black's Law Dictionary 8th ed.**
8. "Security" means an instrument that evidences the holder's ownership rights in a firm. **See Garner B. ed. Black's Law Dictionary 8 th ed.**
9. "Trustee" means one who, having legal title to property holds it in trust for the benefit of another and owes a fiduciary duty to that beneficiary. See **Garner B. (ed.) Black's Law Dictionary 8 th ed.**
10. "Debenture holders" see "debenture" and "holder". Debenture means a written acknowledgement of indebtedness by the company, setting out the terms and conditions of the indebtedness and includes debenture stock, bonds and any other securities of any company whether constituting a charge on the assets of the company or not. **See section 567, CAMA Cap. C20 LFN 2004.** "Holder" is one who has legal possession of a negotiable instrument and is entitled to receive payment on it. See **Garner B. (ed.) Black's Law Dictionary 8 th ed.**
11. "Floating charge" means an equitable charge over the whole or a specified part of the company's undertakings and assets, including cash and uncalled capital of the company both present and future. **See section 178(1), CAMA Cap. C20, LFN 2004**
12. "Convertible debentures" are debentures issued upon the terms that in lieu of redemption or repayment, they may, at the option of the holder or the company, be converted into shares in the company upon such terms as may be stated in the debentures. See **section 172 CAMA Cap. C20, LFN 2004**
13. "Shares" means an equity or ownership interest in the corporation or Joint Stock Company. **See Garner B. ed. Black's Law Dictionary 8th ed.**

It means the interests in a company's shares capital of a member who is entitled to share in the Capital or income of such company and except where a distinction between stock and shares is expressed or implied, includes stock. See **section 567 of CAMA Cap. C20, LFN 2004**

14. "Meeting" means the gathering of people to discuss or act on matters in which they have a common interest; especially the convening of a deliberative assembly to transact business. **See Garner B. (ed.) Black's Law Dictionary 8th ed. Section 184(4)**
15. "Director" See Director. It means a person appointed or elected to sit on a board that manages the affairs of a corporation or other organization by electing and exercising control over its officers. **See Garner B, Ed. Black's Law Dictionary**
    It includes any person occupying the position of director by whatever name called; and includes any person in accordance with whose directions or instructions the directors of the company are accustomed to act . See **section 567 CAMA Cap. C20 LFN 2004**

**Cross Reference**

On the power of a company to create debentures and debenture stock, see **section 166 CAMA Cap. C20 LFN 2004**

On power of a company to redeem debentures, see **section 174, CAMA Cap. C20, LFN 2004**

On meaning of offence, see **section 2 Criminal Code, Cap. C38, LFN 2004**

---

**Cases**

"A debenture is a document which either creates or acknowledges a debt...This obligation is in most casesat the present day, accompanied by some charge or security " ***Fasakin v. Fasakin (1994) 4 N.W.L.R Pt. 340; pg.620 par. C-E***

In the interpretation of Statute, the word shall has various meanings. It may be used as implying futurity or implying a mandate. It imports that a thing must be done... It is a form of a command or mandate Se ***e Nigerian LNG Limited v. African Development Insurance Co. Ltd.*** **(1995)8 NWLR (Pt. 416) 677.** Generally, when the word "shall is used in a Statute, it is not permissive. It is mandatory. See Col. ***Kaliel Rtd. v. AlhajiAilero*** **(1999) 4NWLR (Pt. 597) 139.** The word shall in its ordinary meaning is a word of command which is normally given a compulsory meaning because it is intended to denote obligation. As contended..., it is sometimes intended to be directory only and in that case it is equivalent to "may" and will be construed as being merely permissive. See ***Amokeodo v. Inspector General of Police*** **(1999) 6 NWLR (Pt. 607) 467. See** ***Ugwu v. Ararume*** **(2007) 31 WRN 1, 65 line 30-45**

## 185. Contents of debenture covered by trust deed

(1) Every debenture [1] covered by a debenture [1] trust deed [2] shall state, either in the body thereof or in a note forming part of the same document or endorsed thereon-

(a) the matters required to be stated in a debenture [1] trust deed[2] by paragraphs (a), (b), (f), (h), (i), (j), (I) and (m) of subsection (1) of section 184 of this Act;

(b) whether the trustee [3] of the covering debenture [1] trust deed [2] holds the mortgages [3], charges [4] and securities [5] vested in him by the trust deed [2] in trust for the debenture holders [6] equally, or in trust for some only of the debenture holders[6], and if so, which debenture holders [6]; and

(c) whether the debenture [1] is secured by a general floating charge[7] vested in the trustee [3] of the covering debenture [1] trust deed[2] or in the debenture holders. [6]

(2) A debenture [1] issued by a company [8] shall state on its face in clearly legible print, that it is unsecured if no mortgage, [3] charge [4] or security [5] is vested in the holder of the debenture [1] or in any other person for his benefit as security [5] for payment of principal or interest.

(3) Any director [9] of a company [8] who issues a debenture [1] in violation of the provisions of subsections (1) and (2) of this section shall be guilty of an offence.

---

**Notes**
**Section 185(1)**

1. "Debenture" means a written acknowledgement of indebtedness by the company, setting out the terms and conditions of the indebtedness and includes debenture stock, bonds and any other securities of any company whether constituting a charge on the assets of the company or not. **See section 567, CAMA Cap. C20 LFN 2004.**
2. "Trust deed" see "deed of trust". It means a deed conveying title to real property to a trustee as security until the grantor repays a loan. See Garner B. ed. Black's Law Dictionary, 8th ed.
3. "Mortgages" see "mortgage." It means a lien against property that is granted to secure an obligation and that is extinguished upon payment or performance according to stipulated terms. See **Garner B. (ed.) Black's Law Dictionary 8th ed.**
4. "Charges" see charge. It means an encumbrance, lien or claim. See **Garner B. (ed.) Black's Law Dictionary 8 th ed.**
5. "Securities" includes shares, debentures, debenture stock, bonds, notes (other than promissory notes) and units under a unit trust scheme. See Section **567 of CAMA Cap C20 LFN, 2004**

6. "Debenture holders" see "debenture" and "holder." Debenture means a written acknowledgement of indebtedness by the company, setting out the terms and conditions of the indebtedness and includes debenture stock, bonds and any other securities of any company whether constituting a charge on the assets of the company or not. **See section 567, CAMA Cap. C20 LFN 2004.** "Holder" is one who has legal possession of a negotiable instrument and is entitled to receive payment on it. See **Garner B. (ed.) Black's Law Dictionary 8 th ed.**
7. "Floating charge" means an equitable charge over the whole or a specified part of the company's undertakings and assets, including cash and uncalled capital of the company both present and future. **See section 178(1), CAMA Cap. C20, LFN 2004**
8. "Trustee" means one who, having legal title to property holds it in trust for the benefit of another and owes a fiduciary duty to that beneficiary. See **Garner B. (ed.) Black's Law Dictionary 8 th ed.**

**Section 185(2)**

9. "Company" means a company formed and registered under this Act or, as the case may be, formed and registered in Nigeria before and in existence on the commencement of this Act. **See section 567, CAMA Cap. C20, LFN 2004**

**Section 185(3)**

10. "Director" means a person appointed or elected to sit on a board that manages the affairs of a corporation or other organization by electing and exercising control over its officers. See **Garner B. (ed.) Black's Law Dictionary 8th ed.**
11. It includes any person occupying the position of director by whatever name called; and includes any person in accordance with whose directions or instructions the directors of the company are accustomed to act. **See section 567, CAMA Cap. C20, LFN 2004**

**Cross Reference**

For contents of a debenture trust deed, see section 184 **CAMA Cap. C20, LFN 2004**

On meaning of Offence, see **section 2 Criminal Code, Cap. C38, LFN 2004**

---

**For Further Reading**

On Receivers, Managers and Debenture Trust Deed see: Orojo, J. Ola **Company Law and Practice in Nigeria** 3rd Edition, Mbeyi & Associates (Lagos, Nigeria) 1992; Ogbuanya C.S. Nelson **Essentials of Corporate Law Practice in Nigeria** Novena Publishers Limited 2012; Sasegbon Deji & Co **Companies and Allied Matters Law and Practice** (NCAMLP) DSC Publications Ltd 2006

## 186. Trustees for debenture holders

(1) Whether or not a debenture [1] is secured by a charge [2] over the company's [3] property, it may be secured by a trust deed [4] appointing trustees[5] for the debenture holders. [6]

(2) It shall be the duty of such trustees [5] to safeguard the rights of the debenture holders [6] and, on behalf of and for the benefit of the debenture holders [6], to exercise the rights, powers and discretions conferred upon them by the trust deed. [4]

(3) Charges [2] securing the debentures [1] may be created in favour of the debenture holders [6] by vesting them in the trustees [5].

(4) Any provision contained in a trust deed [4] or in any contract with the holders of debentures [1] secured by a trust deed [4] shall be void in so far as it would have the effect of exempting a trustee [5] thereof from, or indemnifying him against, liability for any breach of trust or failure to show the degree of care and diligence required of him as trustee [5] having regard to the powers, authorities or discretions conferred on him by the trust deed: [4]
Provided that nothing herein contained shall be deemed to invalidate any release otherwise validly given in respect of anything done or omitted to be done by a trustee [5] on the agreement to such release of a majority of not less than three quarters in value of the debenture holders [6] present in person, or where proxies [7] are permitted, by proxy [7] at a meeting [8] summoned for the purpose.

(5) Notwithstanding any provisions contained in the debentures[1] or trust deed [4], the court [9] may, on the application of any debenture holder[6] or of the Commission [10] remove any trustee [5] and appoint another in his place if satisfied that such trustee [5] has interests which conflict or may conflict with those of the debenture holders[6] or that for any reason it is undesirable that such trustee [5] should continue to act:
Provided that where any such application is made by a debenture holder[6], the court [9] if it thinks fit, may order the applicant to give security for the payment of the costs of the trustee [5] and may direct that the application shall be heard in Chambers.

---

**Notes**
**Section 186(1)**

1. "Debenture" means a written acknowledgement of indebtedness by the company, setting out the terms and conditions of the indebtedness and includes debenture stock, bonds and any other securities of any

company whether constituting a charge on the assets of the company or not. **See section 567, CAMA Cap. C20 LFN 2004.**

2. "Charge" means an encumbrance, lien or claim. **See Garner B. (ed.) Black's Law Dictionary 8th ed.**
3. "Company" means a company formed and registered under this Act or, as the case may be, formed and registered in Nigeria before and in existence on the commencement of this Act. **See section 567 CAMA Cap. C20, LFN 2004**
4. "Trust deed" see "deed of trust". It means a deed conveying title to real property to a trustee as security until the grantor repays a loan. See **Garner B. ed. Black's Law Dictionary, 8th ed.**
5. "Trustee" means one who, having legal title to property holds it in trust for the benefit of another and owes a fiduciary duty to that beneficiary. See **Garner B. ed. Black's Law Dictionary, 8th ed.**
6. "Debenture holders" see debenture holder. see "debenture" and "holder". Debenture means a written acknowledgement of indebtedness by the company, setting out the terms and conditions of the indebtedness and includes debenture stock, bonds and any other securities of any company whether constituting a charge on the assets of the company or not. **See section 567 CAMA Cap. C20, LFN 2004.** "Holder" is one who has legal possession of a negotiable instrument and is entitled to receive payment on it. See **Garner B. ed. Black's Law Dictionary, 8th ed.**

**Section 186(4)**

7. "Proxy" means one who is authorized to act as a substitute for another; a person who is authorized to vote another's stock shares. **See Garner B. (ed.) Black's Law Dictionary 8 th ed.**
8. "Meeting" means the gathering of people to discuss or act on matters in which they have a common interest; especially the convening of a deliberative assembly to transact business. **See Garner B. (ed.) Black's Law Dictionary 8th ed.**

**Section 186(5)**

9. "Court" in relation to a Company, means the Federal High Court and to the extent to which application may be made to it as; court includes the Court of Appeal and the Supreme Court of Nigeria **See section 567 CAMA Cap. C20, LFN 2004.**
10. "Commission" means the Corporate Affairs Commission established under section 1 of this Act. **See section 567 CAMA Cap. C20, LFN 2004**

**Cross Reference**

On entitlement of member of company to attend and vote at meetings, see **Section 230, CAMA Cap. C20, LFN 2004**

On establishment and jurisdiction of the Federal High Court, see **section 249 & 251, Constitution of the Federal Republic of Nigeria, 1999(as amended)**

## 187. Disqualification for appointment as trustee of debenture trust deed

(1) A person is not qualified for appointment as a trustee [1] of a debenture[2] trust deed[3] if he is-

(a) an officer[4] or an employee of the company [5] which issues debentures[2] covered by the trust deed [3]or of a company [5] in the same group of companies [5] as the company [5] so issuing debentures[2];

(b) less than 18 years of age;

(c) of unsound mind[6] and has been so found by a court [7] in Nigeria or elsewhere;

(d) an undischarged bankrupt [8];

(e) disqualified under section 257 of this Act from being appointed as a director [9] of a company [5];

(f) a substantial shareholder [10] (as defined in section 95 of this Act) of the company [5].

(2) If a trustee [1] becomes subject to any of the disqualifications mentioned in subsection (1) of this section after he has been appointed, he shall immediately cease to be qualified to act as a trustee [1] of the debenture [2] trust deed [3].

(3) Any person who acts as a trustee [1] of a debenture [2] trust deed[3] shall be guilty of an offence, if his appointment is invalid under subsection (1) of this section or if he is disqualified from acting under subsection (2) of this section.

---

**Notes**

**Section 187(1)**

1. "Trustee" means one who, having legal title to property holds it in trust for the benefit of another and owes a fiduciary duty to that beneficiary. **See Garner B. (ed.) Black's Law Dictionary 8 th ed.**
2. "Debenture" means a written acknowledgement of indebtedness by the company, setting out the terms and conditions of the indebtedness and includes debenture stock, bonds and any other securities of any company whether constituting a charge on the assets of the company or not. **See section 567, CAMA Cap. C20 LFN 2004.**
3. "Trust" deed "see "deed of trust". It means a deed conveying title to real property to a trustee as security until the grantor repays a loan. See **Garner B. ed. Black's Law Dictionary, 8th ed.**
4. "Officer" means a person who holds an office of trust, authority or command. See **Garner B., (ed.) Black's Law Dictionary 8 th ed.**
   In relation to a body corporate, officer includes a director, manager or secretary. **Section 567 of CAMA Cap C20 LFN, 2004**

5. "Company" means a company formed and registered under this Act or, as the case may be, formed and registered in Nigeria before and in existence on the commencement of this Act. **See section 567 CAMA Cap. C20, LFN 2004**
6. "Unsound mind" means not mentally well. See **Garner B., (ed.) Black's Law Dictionary 8th ed.**
7. "Court" used in relation to a company, means the Federal High Court , and to the extent to which application may be made to it as; court includes the Court of Appeal and the Supreme court of Nigeria
8. "Undischarged bankrupt" means a person who has been officially stated to be bankrupt by a court of law but who still pay his or her debt. See **Oxford Advanced Learner's Dictionary of Current English. 6 th ed.**
9. "Director" means a person appointed or elected to sit on a board that manages the affairs of a corporation or other organization by electing and exercising control over its officers. **See Garner B, Ed. Black's Law Dictionary 8th ed**

   It includes any person occupying the position of director by whatever name called; and includes any person in accordance with whose directions or instructions the directors of the company are accustomed to act. See **section 567 CAMA Cap. C20, LFN 2004**
10. "Shareholders" see shareholder. It means one who owns or holds a share or shares in a company. **See Garner B., ed. Black's Law Dictionary 8th ed**
11. "Offence" means a violation of the law. **Garner B., ed. Black's Law Dictionary**

**Cross Reference**

On persons disqualified from being appointed as a director under CAMA, see Section 257, CAMA Cap. C 20, LFN 2004

As to when a debtor commits an act of bankruptcy, see **section 1, Bankruptcy Act Cap. B2 LFN 2004**

---

## 188. Liability of trustees for debenture holders

(1) Subject to the provisions of this section, anything contained in a trust deed[1] for securing an issue of debentures, [2] or in any contract with the holders[3] of debentures[2] secured by a trust deed[1], shall be void in so far as it would have the effect of exempting a trustee[4] thereof from or indemnifying him against liability for breach of trust, where he fails to show the degree of care and diligence required of him as trustee,[4] having regard to the provisions of the trust deed[1] conferring on him any powers, authorities or discretions.

(2) Subsection (1) of this section shall not invalidate-

(a) any release[5] otherwise validly given in respect of anything done or omitted to be done by a trustee [4] before the giving of the release[5]; or

(b) Any provision enabling such a release [5] to be given-

(i) on the agreement thereto of a majority of not less than three quarters in value of the debenture holders [3] present and voting in person or, where proxies [6] are permitted, by proxy [6] at a meeting[7] summoned for the purpose; and

(ii) either with respect to specific acts or omissions or on the trustee[4] dying or ceasing to act.

(3) Subsection (1) of this section shall not operate to-

(a) invalidate any provision in force at the commencement of this Act in any such trust deed [1] or contract, so long as any person entitled to the benefit of that provision, or afterwards given the benefit thereof under subsection (4) of this section, remains a trustee [4] of the trust deed[1] in question; or

(b) deprive any person of any exemption or right to be indemnified in respect of anything done or omitted to be done by him, while any such provision was in force.

(4) While any trustee[4] of a trust deed[1] remains entitled to the benefit of a provision saved by subsection (3) of this section, the benefit of that provision may be given-

(a) to all trustees[4] of the deed, present and future; or

(b) to any named trustees[4] or proposed trustees[4] thereof,

by a resolution,[8] passed by a majority of not less than three quarters in value of the debenture holders [3] present in person or, where proxies [6] are permitted by proxy [6] at a meeting[7] summoned for the purpose in accordance with the provisions of the trust deed[1] or, if the trust deed [1] makes no provision for summoning meetings, [7] a meeting[7] summoned for the purpose in any manner approved by the court.[9]

---

**Notes**

**Section 188(1)**

1. "Trust deed" see "deed of trust". It means a deed conveying title to real property to a trustee as security until the grantor repays a loan. See **Garner B. ed. Black's Law Dictionary, 8th ed.**

2. "Debenture" means a written acknowledgement of indebtedness by the company, setting out the terms and conditions of the indebtedness and includes debenture stock, bonds and any other securities of any company whether constituting a charge on the assets of the company or not. **See section 567, CAMA Cap. C20 LFN 2004.**
3. "Debenture holders" see debenture holder. see "debenture" and "holder." Debenture means a written acknowledgement of indebtedness by the company, setting out the terms and conditions of the indebtedness and includes debenture stock, bonds and any other securities of any company whether constituting a charge on the assets of the company or not. **See section 567 CAMA Cap. C20, LFN 2004.** "Holder" is one who has legal possession of a negotiable instrument and is entitled to receive payment on it. See **Garner B. (ed.) Black's Law Dictionary, 8th ed.**
4. "Trustee" means one who, having legal title to property holds it in trust for the benefit of another and owes a fiduciary duty to that beneficiary. See **Garner B. ed. Black's Law Dictionary, 8th ed.**

**Section 188(2)**

5. "Release" means liberation from an obligation, duty or demand; the act of giving up a right or claim to the person against whom it could have been enforced. See **Garner B, (ed.) Black's Law Dictionary 8th ed**.
6. "Proxies" see "proxy." It means one who is authorized to act as a substitute for another; a person who is authorized to vote another's stock shares. See **Garner B, (ed.) Black's Law Dictionary 8 th ed**.
7. "Meeting" means the gathering of people to discuss or act on matters in which they have a common interest; especially the convening of a deliberative assembly to transact business. See **Garner B, (ed.) Black's Law Dictionary 8 th ed**.

**Section 188(4)**

8. "Resolution" means a main motion that formally expresses the sense, will or action of a deliberative assembly. **See Garner B., (ed.) Black's Law Dictionary 8 th ed.**
9. "Court" means the Federal High Court and to the extent to which application may be made to it as; court includes the Court of Appeal and the Supreme Court. **See section 567, CAMA Cap. C20 LFN 2004.**

**Cross Reference**

On entitlement of member of company to attend and vote at meetings, see **Section 230, CAMA Cap. C20, LFN 2004**

On establishment and jurisdiction of the Federal High Court, see **section 249 & 251, Constitution of the Federal Republic of Nigeria, 1999(as amended)**

---

**For Further Reading**

On Receivers, Managers and Debenture Trust Deed see: Orojo, J. Ola **Company Law and Practice in Nigeria** 3rd Edition, Mbeyi & Associates (Lagos, Nigeria) 1992; Ogbuanya C.S. Nelson **Essentials of Corporate Law Practice in Nigeria** Novena Publishers Limited 2012; Sasegbon Deji & Co **Companies and Allied Matters Law and Practice** (NCAMLP) DSC Publications Ltd 2006

## 189. Restrictions on transferability of debentures

(1) Except as expressly provided in the terms of any debentures,[1] debentures[1] shall be transferable[2] without restriction by a written transfer in common form and so that the transferee[3] shall be entitled to the debenture[1] and to the moneys secured[4] thereby without regard to any equities, set-off,[5] or cross-claim[6] between the company[7] and the original or any intermediate holder.

(2) The terms of any debenture[1] may impose restrictions of any nature whatsoever on the transferability[2] of debentures[1], including power for the company[7] to refuse to register any transfer[2] and provisions for compulsory acquisition[8] or rights of first refusal[9] in favour of other debenture holders,[10] or members[11] or officers[12] of the company:[7]
Provided that if any restriction is imposed on the right to transfer[2] any debenture[1], notice of the restriction shall be endorsed on the face of the debenture[1] or debenture[1] stock certificate and in the absence of such endorsement, the restriction shall be ineffective as regards any transferee[3] for value, whether or not he has notice of the restriction.

---

**Notes**
**Section 189(1)**

1. "Debentures" see "debenture". It means a written acknowledgement of indebtedness by the company, setting out the terms and conditions of the indebtedness and includes debenture stock, bonds and any other securities of any company whether constituting a charge on the assets of the company or not. See **Section 567, CAMA Cap. C20 LFN, 2004**
2. "Transferable" means capable of being transferred, together with all rights of the original holder. See **Garner B. (ed.) Black's Law Dictionary 8th ed.**
3. "Transferee" means one to whom property interest is conveyed. See **Garner B. (ed.) Black's Law Dictionary 8 th ed.**
4. "Secured" means supported or backed by security or collateral. See **Garner B. (ed.) Black's Law Dictionary 8 th ed.**

5. "Set-off" means a defendant's counter-demand against the plaintiff arising out of a transaction independent of the plaintiff's claim. See **Garner B., (ed.) Black's Law Dictionary 8 th ed.**
6. "Cross-claim" means a claim asserted between codefendants or coplaintiffs in a case and that relates to the subject of the original claim or counter claim. See **Garner B., (ed.) Black's Law Dictionary 8 th ed.**
7. "Company" means a company formed and registered under this Act or, as the case may be, formed and registered in Nigeria before and in existence on the commencement of this Act. See **Section 567, CAMA Cap. C20 LFN, 2004**

**Section 189(2)**

8. "Acquisition" means the gaining of possession or control over something. See **Garner B. (ed.) Black's Law Dictionary 8 th ed.**
9. "Right of first refusal" means a potential buyer's contractual right to meet the terms of a third party's higher offer. See **Garner B., (ed.) Black's Law Dictionary 8th ed.**
10. "Debenture holders" see "debenture" and "holder". Debenture means a written acknowledgement of indebtedness by the company, setting out the terms and conditions of the indebtedness and includes debenture stock, bonds and any other securities of any company whether constituting a charge on the assets of the company or not. **Section 567 CAMA Cap C20 LFN, 2004.** "Holder" is one who has legal possession of a negotiable instrument and is entitled to receive payment on it. A holder is a person who has legal possession of a document of title or an investment security. See **Garner B. (ed.) Black's Law Dictionary 8 th ed.**
11. "Members" see "member". It means one of the individuals of whom a deliberative assembly consists and who enjoys the full rights of participating in the organization-including the rights of making, debating and voting on motions- except to the extent that the organization reserves those rights to certain classes of membership. See **Garner B. (ed.) Black's Law Dictionary 8th ed.**

    It includes the heir, executor, administrator or other personal representative as the case may be, of the member. See **Section 567 of CAMA Cap C20 LFN, 2004**
12. "Officers" see officer. It means a person who holds an office of trust, authority or command. **Garner B. (ed.) Black's Law Dictionary 8 th ed.** In relation to a body corporate, officer includes a director, manager or secretary. **Section 567 of CAMA Cap C20 LFN, 2004**

**Cross Reference**

For the definition, capacity of, rights and obligations of Members of a Company, see **Part IV of CAMA, Cap C20, LFN, 2004**

On the power of a company to create debentures and debenture stock, see **section 166 CAMA Cap. C20 LFN 2004**

On power of a company to redeem debentures, see **section 174, CAMA Cap. C20, LFN 2004**

**Cases**

"A debenture is a company's security for a monetary loan. The security usually creates a charge on the company's stock or property " **See *NIDB v. Olalomi Ind. Ltd. (2002) 5 N.W.L.R (pt 761)532***

**For Further Reading**

On debentures, see, Orojo, J. Ola **Company Law and Practice in Nigeria** 3rd Edition, Mbeyi & Associates (Lagos, Nigeria) 1992.

*Provisions as to company's register of charges, debenture holders and as to copies of instruments creating charges*

## 190. Company to keep copies of instruments creating charges

Every company[1] shall cause a copy of every instrument[2] creating any charge[3] requiring registration under this Part of this Act to be kept at the registered office of the company[1]:

Provided that, in the case of a series of uniform debenture[4], a copy of one debenture[4] of the series shall be sufficient.

---

**Notes**

**Section 190**

1. "Company" means a company formed and registered under this Act or, as the case may be, formed and registered in Nigeria before and in existence on the commencement of this Act. See **Section 567, CAMA Cap. C20 LFN, 2004**
2. "Instrument" means a written legal document that defines rights, duties, entitlements or liabilities, such as a contract, will, promissory note or share certificate. See **Garner B. (ed.) Black's Law Dictionary 8th ed.**
3. "Charge" means an encumbrance, lien or claim. **See Garner B. (ed.) Black's Law Dictionary 8th ed.**
4. "Debenture" means a written acknowledgement of indebtedness by the company, setting out the terms and conditions of the indebtedness and includes debenture stock, bonds and any other securities of any company whether constituting a charge on the assets of the company or not. **Section 567 CAMA Cap. C20 LFN, 2004.**

**Cross Reference**

On the need to deliver to the Corporate Affairs Commission a notice of the registered address of a Company as part of Incorporation documents, see **section 35 CAMA Cap C20 LFN, 2004.**

On obligation of a Compnay to keep a register of charges, see **section 191 CAMA Cap C20 LFN, 2004.**

For definition of debentures in Investment and Securities Act, see **section 315, Investment ans Securities Act, Cap. I 15, LFN 2004**

---

**Cases**

A debenture consists of a debt owed by the company to another secured by a deed which prescribes the condition of the realization of the debt. ***Intercontractors Nig Ltd v N.P.F.M.B* (1988) 2 NWLR (Pt 76) page 280.** This definition has been adopted in the cases of ***U.B.N. v Tropic Foods* (1992) 3 NWLR (Pt 228) page 231** and ***NIDB v Olalomi Ind Ltd.*(2002) 5 NWLR (Pt761) page 532**

## 191. Company's register of charges

(1) Every limited company [1] shall keep at the registered office of the company[2], a register of charges and enter therein all charges [3] specifically affecting property of the company [2] and all floating charges[4] on the undertaking or any property of the company [2], giving in each case a short description of the property charged, the amount of the charge[3], and, except in the case of securities to bearer[5], the names of the persons entitled thereto.

(2) If any officer [6] of the company[2] knowingly and willfully authorizes or permits the omission of any entry required to be made in pursuance of this section, he shall be guilty of an offence and liable on conviction to a fine not exceeding N250.

---

**Notes**

**Section 191(1)**

1. "Limited Company" means a company having its liability of its members limited by the memorandum to the amount, if any, unpaid on the shares respectively held by them (referred to a company limited by shares) or, having the liability of its members limited by the memorandum to such amount as the members may have respectively thereby undertake to contribute to the assets of the company in the event of being wound-up (referred to a company limited by guarantee). See **section 21(a) & (b), CAMA Cap. C20 LFN, 2004**
2. "Company" means a company formed and registered under this Act or, as the case may be, formed and registered in Nigeria before and in existence on the commencement of this Act. See **section 567, CAMA Cap. C20 LFN, 2004**
3. "Charges" see charge. It means an encumbrance, lien or claim. See **Garner B. (ed.) Black's Law Dictionary 8th ed.**
4. "Floating charges" see floating lien. It means a charge that continues to exist even when the collateral changes in character, classification or location. See **Garner B. (ed.) Black's Law Dictionary 8th ed.**

A "floating charge" means an equitable charge over the whole or a specified part of the company's undertakings and assets, including cash and uncalled capital of the company both present and future, but so that the charge shall not preclude the company from dealing with such assets until- (a) the security becomes enforceable and the holder thereof, pursuant to a power in that behalf in the debenture or the deed securing the same, appoints a receiver or manager or enters into possession of such assets; or (b) the court appoints a receiver or manager of such assets on the application of the holder; or (c) the company goes into liquidation. See section 178 **CAMA Cap. C20 LFN, 2004**

5. "Securities to bearer" see bearer security. It means an unregistered security payable to the holder. See **Garner B. (ed.) Black's Law Dictionary 8th ed.**

**Section 191(2)**

6. "Officer" means a person who holds an office of trust, authority or command. See **Garner B. (ed.) Black's Law Dictionary 8th ed.**
   In relation to a body corporate, it includes a director, manager or secretary. See **Section 567 of CAMA Cap. C20 LFN, 2004**

Cross Reference

On the need to deliver to the Corporate Affairs Commission a notice of the registered address of a Company as part of Incorporation documents, see **section 35 CAMA Cap. C20 LFN, 2004.**

On effect of a floating charge, see section 498 **CAMA Cap. C20 LFN, 2004.**

On meaning of offence, see **section 2, Criminal Code C38, LFN 2004**

---

## 192. Inspection of register and copies of instruments

(1) The copies of instruments [1] creating any charge [2] requiring registration under this Part of this Act with the Commission [3] and the register of charges [2] kept in pursuance of section 191 of this Act, shall be open during business hours (but subject to such reasonable restrictions as the company [4] in general meeting [5] may impose, so that not less than two hours in each day shall be allowed for inspection) to inspection by any creditor [6] or member [7] of the company [4] without fee and the register of charges [2] shall also be open to inspection by any other person on payment of such fee, not exceeding N5 for each inspection, as the company [4] may prescribe.

(2) If inspection of copies of instruments [1] creating charges [2] or of the register is refused, every officer [8] of the company [4] who is in default shall be guilty of an offence and liable to a fine not exceeding N10 for every day during which the refusal continues.

(3) If any such refusal occurs in relation to a company [4] registered in Nigeria or, in so far as a foreign company [9] has an established place of business within Nigeria and an instrument [1]

creates a charge[2] over any of its property in Nigeria and the refusal relates to that charge,[2] the court[11] may by order compel an immediate inspection of the copies of instruments[1] or register.

---

**Notes**

**Section 192(1)**

1. "Instruments" see "instrument". It means a written legal document that defines rights, duties, entitlements or liabilities such as a contract, will, promissory note or share certificate. See **Garner B. (ed). Black's Law Dictionary 8th ed.**
2. "Charge" means an encumbrance, lien or claim. See **Garner B. (ed.) Black's Law Dictionary 8th ed.**
3. "Commission" means the Corporate Affairs Commission established under section 1 of this Act. **See section 567, CAMA Cap. C20 LFN, 2004**
4. "Company" means a company formed and registered under this Act or, as the case may be, formed and registered in Nigeria before and in existence on the commencement of this Act. **See section 567, CAMA Cap. C20 LFN, 2004**
5. "General meeting" means the gathering of people to discuss or act on matters in which they have a common interest. See **Garner B. (ed) Black's Law Dictionary 8th ed.**
6. "Creditor" means one to whom a debt is owed whether contractual or otherwise.See **Garner B. (ed.) Black's Law Dictionary 8 th ed.**
7. "Member" means one of the individuals of whom a deliberative assembly consists and who enjoys the full rights of participating in the organization-including the rights of making, debating and voting on motions- except to the extent that the organization reserves those rights to certain classes of membership. See **Garner B. (ed.) Black's Law Dictionary 8th ed.**

   It includes the heir, executor, administrator or other personal representative as the case may be, of the member. See **section 567 CAMA Cap. C20 LFN, 2004**

**Section 192(2)**

7. "Officer" means a person who holds an office of trust, authority or command**. See Garner B., (ed.) Black's Law Dictionary 8th ed.**

   In relation to a body corporate, it includes a director, manager or secretary. See s**ection 567 CAMA Cap. C20 LFN, 2004**

**Section 192(3)**

8. "Foreign company" means a company incorporated elsewhere than in Nigeria. **See section 567, CAMA Cap C20 LFN, 2004.**
9. "Court" means the Federal High Court and to the extent to which application may be made to it as; court includes the Court of Appeal and the Supreme Court. See **Section 567 CAMA Cap. C20 LFN, 2004**

**Cross Reference**

On obligation of a company to keep a register of charges, see section 191 **CAMA Cap. C20 LFN, 2004**

On obligation of Corporate Affairs Commission to keep a register of charges for each company, see **section 198 CAMA Cap. C20 LFN, 2004**
On meaning of offence, see **section 2, Criminal Code C38, LFN 2004**

---

## 193. Register of debenture holders

(1) A company [1] which issues [2] or has issued [2] debentures [3] shall maintain a register of the holders [4] thereof.

(2) The register shall contain the following information that is-

(a) the names and addresses of the debenture holders [4];
(b) the principal of the debentures [3] held by each of them;
(c) the amount or the highest amount of any premium [5] payable on redemption of the debentures [3];
(d) the issue [2] price of the debenture [3] and the amount paid up on the issue [2] price;
(e) the date on which the name of each person was entered on the register as a debenture holder [4]; and
(f) the date on which each person ceased to be a debenture holder [4].

(3) The entry required under this section shall be made within 30 days of the conclusion of the agreement with the company [1] to become a debenture holder [4] or within 30 days of the date at which he ceases to be one.

---

**Notes**
**Section 193(1)**

1. "Company" means a company formed and registered under this Act or, as the case may be, formed and registered in Nigeria before and in existence on the commencement of this Act. See **Section 567, CAMA Cap. C20 LFN, 2004**
2. "Issues" see "issue." It means a class or series of securities that are simultaneously offered for sale. See **Garner B. (ed.) Black's Law Dictionary 8th ed.**
3. "Debentures" see "debenture" It means a written acknowledgement of indebtedness by the company, setting out the terms and conditions of the indebtedness and includes debenture stock, bonds and any other securities of any company whether constituting a charge on the assets of the company or not. See **Section 567, CAMA Cap. C20 LFN, 2004**
4. "Holders" see "holder". A holder is a person who has legal possession of a document of title or an investment security. **Garner B. (ed.) Black's Law Dictionary 8th ed.**

**Section 193(2)**

5. "Premium" means a sum paid in addition to a regular price or amount; a bonus. See **Garner B., (ed.) Black's Law Dictionary 8 th ed.**

Cross Reference

For types of debentures, see **Section 171-174, CAMA Cap. C20 LFN, 2004.**

---

**Cases**

On meaning of Debenture:

"A debenture is a company's security for a monetary loan. The security usually creates a charge on the company's stock or property" ***NIDB v. Olalomi Ind. Ltd.*** **(2002) 5 N.W.L.R (pt. 761)532**

"A debenture consists of a debt owed by a company to another secured by a deed which prescribes the condition of the realization of the debt, and it may be created over the fixed or floating assets of the company" ***UBN v. Tropics Foods*** **(1992) 3NWLR (Pt. 228) 231**

"A debenture is a document which either creates or acknowledges a debt....This obligation is in most cases at the present day, accompanied by some charge or security" ***Fasakin v. Fasakin*** **(1994) 4 N.W.L.R Pt. 340; pg.620 par. C-E**

## 194. Inspection of register of debentures, etc.

(1) Every register of holders [1] of debentures [2] of a company [3] shall, except when duly closed (but subject to such reasonable restrictions as the company [3] may in general meeting [4] impose, so that not less than two hours in each day shall be allowed for inspection), be open to the inspection of the registered holder [1] of any such debentures [2] or any holder [1] of shares [5] in the company [3] without fee, and of any other person on payment of a fee of N 1 or such less sum as may be prescribed by the company. [3]

(2) Any such registered holder [1] of debentures [2] as aforesaid or any other person may require a copy of the register of the holders [1] of debentures [2] of the company [3] or any part thereof on payment of 50 kobo for every 100 words required to be copied.

(3) A copy of any trust deed [6] for securing any issue [7] of debentures [2] shall be forwarded to every holder [1] of any such debentures [2] at his request on payment in the case of a printed trust deed, [6] of the sum of N 1 or such less sum as may be prescribed by the company, [3] or, where the trust deed [6] has not been printed, on payment of 50 kobo for every 100 words required to be copied.

(4) If inspection is refused, or a copy is refused or not forwarded, the company [3] and every officer [8] of the company [4] who is in default shall be guilty of an offence and liable to a fine not

exceeding N50 and in case of a continuing default, to a further fine of N10 for every day during which the default continues.

(5) Where a company [3] is in default as aforesaid, the court [9] convicting may by order compel an immediate inspection of the register or direct that the copies required shall be sent to the person requiring them.

(6) For the purposes of this section, a register shall be deemed to be duly closed in accordance with provisions contained in the articles [10] or in the debentures [2] or, in the case of debenture stock, [11] in the stock certificates, or in the trust deed [6] or other document [12] securing the debentures [2] or debenture stock, [11] during such periods, not exceeding in the whole 30 days in any year, as may be therein specified.

---

**Notes**

**Section 194(1)**

1. "Holder" means a person who has legal possession of a document of title or an investment security. See **Garner B. (ed.) Black's Law Dictionary 8th ed.**
2. "Debenture" means a written acknowledgement of indebtedness by the company, setting out the terms and conditions of the indebtedness and includes debenture stock, bonds and any other securities of any company whether constituting a charge on the assets of the company or not. See **Section 567, CAMA Cap. C20 LFN, 2004**
3. "Company" means a company formed and registered under this Act or, as the case may be, formed and registered in Nigeria before and in existence on the commencement of this Act. See **Section 567, CAMA Cap. C20 LFN, 2004**
4. "General meeting" means the gathering of people to discuss or act on matters in which they have a common interest. See **Garner. B. (ed) Black's Law Dictionary 8th ed.**
5. "Shares" means an equity or ownership interest in the corporation or Joint Stock Company. See **Garner B. (ed.) Black's Law Dictionary 8th ed.**

   It means the interests in a company's shares capital of a member who is entitled to share in the Capital or income of such company and except where a distinction between stock and shares is expressed or implied, includes stock. See **Section 567 of CAMA Cap. C20 LFN, 2004**

**Section 194(3)**

6. "Trust deed" see declaration of trust. It means the instrument that creates a trust. See **Garner B (ed.) Black's Law Dictionary 8th ed**
7. "Issue" means a class or series of securities that are simultaneously offered for sale. See **Garner B. (ed.) Black's Law Dictionary, 8 th ed**

**Section 194(4)**

8. "Officer" means a person who holds an office of trust, authority or command. **Garner B., (ed.) Black's Law Dictionary 8th ed.**
In relation to a body corporate, it includes a director, manager or secretary. **Section 567 of CAMA Cap. C20 LFN, 2004**

**Section 194(5)**

9. "Court" means the Federal High Court and to the extent to which application may be made to it as; court includes, the Court of Appeal and the Supreme Court. See **Section 567 of CAMA Cap. C20 LFN, 2004**

**Section 194(6)**

10. "Articles" means the articles of association of a company, as originally framed or as altered by special resolution including so far as they apply to the regulations contained in table A in the first schedules of the companies Act, 1922 or in that table as altered by any subsequent enactment or reprint of the laws, or in table A in schedule 1 to this Act. See **Section 567 of CAMA Cap. C20 LFN, 2004**
11. "Debenture stock" means a type of bond representing money borrowed by a company using its property or other fixed assets as security. See **Garner B., (ed.) Black's Law Dictionary 8th ed.**
12. "Document" includes summons, notice, order and other legal process and registers. See **Section 567 of CAMA Cap. C20 LFN, 2004**

**Cross Reference**

On jurisdiction of the Federal High Court, see **section 251 of the Constitution of the Federal Republic of Nigeria, 1999 (as amended)**

---

## 195. Entry in register of transfer

On the application[1] of the transferor[2] of any debenture[3] in a company[4], the company[4] shall enter in its register of debenture holders[5], the name of the transferee[6] in the same manner and subject to the same conditions as if the application[1] for the entry were made by the transferee[6].

---

**Notes**

**Section 195**

1. "Application" means a request or petition. See **Garner B., (ed.) Black's Law Dictionary 8th ed.**
2. "Transferor" means one who conveys an interest in property. See **Garner B. (ed.) Black's law Dictionary 8th ed.**
3. "Debenture" means a written acknowledgement of indebtedness by the company, setting out the terms and conditions of the indebtedness and includes debenture stock, bonds and any other securities of any company whether constituting a charge on the assets of the company or not. See **section 567 of CAMA Cap C20 LFN, 2004**
4. "Company" means a company formed and registered under this Act or, as the case may be, formed and registered in Nigeria before and in

existence on the commencement of this Act. See **section 567 of CAMA Cap C20 LFN, 2004**

5. "Debenture holders" see "debenture" and "holder". Debenture means a written acknowledgement of indebtedness by the company, setting out the terms and conditions of the indebtedness and includes debenture stock, bonds and any other securities of any company whether constituting a charge on the assets of the company or not. See s **ection 567 CAMA Cap C20 LFN, 2004** .

   "Holder" is one who has legal possession of a negotiable instrument and is entitled to receive payment on it. A holder is a person who has legal possession of a document of title or an investment security. See **Garner B., (ed.) Black's Law Dictionary 8 th ed.**

6. "Transferee" means one to whom a property interest is conveyed. See **Garner B., (ed.) Black's Law Dictionary 8 th ed.**

**Cross Reference**

On obligation of a company to keep a register of charges, see section 191 **CAMA Cap. C20 LFN, 2004**

On obligation of Corporate Affairs Commission to keep a register of charges for each company, see **section 198 CAMA Cap. C20 LFN, 2004**

## 196. Notice of refusal to register

(1) If a company[1] refuses to register a transfer[2] of any debentures,[3] the company[1] shall, within two months after the date on which the transfer[2] was lodged with the company,[1] send to the transferee[4] notice of the refusal.

(2) If any default is made in complying with the provisions of this section, the company[1] and every officer[5] of the company[1] who is in default shall be guilty of an offence and liable to a fine of N500.

**Notes**

**Section 196(1)**

1. "Company" means a company formed and registered under this Act or, as the case may be, formed and registered in Nigeria before and in existence on the commencement of this Act. See **section 567 CAMA Cap C20 LFN, 2004**
2. "Transfer" means any mode of disposing of or parting with an asset or an interest in an asset. See **Garner B. (ed.) Black's Law Dictionary 8 th ed.**
3. "Debentures" see "debenture." It means a written acknowledgement of indebtedness by the company, setting out the terms and conditions of the indebtedness and includes debenture stock, bonds and any other securities of any company whether constituting a charge on the assets of the company or not. See **section 567 of CAMA Cap C20 LFN, 2004**

4. "Transferee" means one to whom a property interest is conveyed. See **Garner B. (ed.) Black's law Dictionary 8 th ed.**

**Section 196(2)**

5. "Officer" means a person who holds an office of trust, authority or command. See **Garner B. (ed.) Black's Law Dictionary 8th ed.** In relation to a body corporate, it includes a director, manager or secretary. **Section 567 of CAMA Cap C20 LFN, 2004.**

**Cross Reference**

On obligation of a company to keep a register of charges, see section 191 **CAMA Cap. C20 LFN, 2004**

On obligation of Corporate Affairs Commission to keep a register of charges for each company, see **section 198 CAMA Cap. C20 LFN, 2004**

On meaning of offence, see **section 2, Criminal Code C38, LFN 2004**

---

## 197. Registration of charges created by companies

(1) Subject to the provisions of this Part of this Act, every charge[1] created by a company,[2] being a charge[1] to which this section applies, shall so far as any security[3] on the company's[2] property or undertaking is conferred, be void against the liquidator[4] and any creditor[5] of the company[2], unless the prescribed particulars of the charge[1] together with the instrument,[6] if any, by which the charge[1] is created or evidenced, have been or are delivered to or received by the Commission[7] for registration in the manner required by this Act or by any enactment repealed by this Act within 90 days after the date of its creation, but without prejudice to any contract or obligation for repayment of the money thereby secured, and when a charge[1] becomes void under this section, the money thereby secured shall immediately become payable.

(2) The provisions of this section shall apply to the following charges[1] that is-

(a) a charge[1] for the purpose of securing any issue of debentures[8];

(b) a charge[1] on uncalled share capital[9] of the company[2];

(c) a charge[1] created or evidenced by an instrument[6] which if executed by an individual would require registration as a bill of sale[10];

(d) a charge[1] on land, wherever situate, or any interest therein, but not including a charge[1] for rent or other periodical sum issuing out of land;

(e) a charge[1] on book debts of the company[2];

(f) a floating charge [11] on the undertaking or property of the company[2];

(g) a charge [1] on calls made but not paid;

(h) a charge [1] on a ship or aircraft or any share in a ship;

(i) a charge [1] on goodwill, [12] on a patent [13] or a licence under a patent,[3] on trademark [14] or on a copyright [15] or a licence [17] under a copyright [15].

(3) Where a charge [1] affects or relates to property situated in Nigeria and in addition to registration under subsection (1) of this section, registration elsewhere in Nigeria is necessary to make the charge[1] valid or effectual, it shall, subject to this subsection, be sufficient evidence of compliance with the requirements of subsection (1) of this section, if, instead of delivery of the original instrument[6] creating or evidencing the charge, [1] there is delivered to and received by the Commission [7] within the prescribed period of 90 days, or such extended time as the court [16] may allow, a true copy of it duly certified as such by the secretary [17] to the company. [2]

(4) A reference in any enactment to the date of execution of an instrument[6] for the purposes of computation of time within which registration is to be effected with or without penalty, shall be construed as a reference to the date of presentation of a copy of the instrument[6] to the Commission[7] under this Act, and time shall be computed accordingly; and if a certified copy is delivered to the Commission[7] under this subsection, the original of it shall be produced to it for inspection and comparison, if the Commission [7] so requires.

(5) In the case of a charge [1] created out of Nigeria, affecting or in relation to property situate outside Nigeria, the delivery to and the receipt by the Commission [7] of a copy verified in the prescribed manner of the instrument [6] by which the charge [1] is created or evidenced, shall have the same effect for the purposes of this section as the delivery and receipt of the instrument itself, and 90 days after the date on which the instrument [6] or copy could, in due course of post, and if dispatched with diligence, have been received in Nigeria shall be substituted for 90 days after the date of the creation of the charges [1] as the time within which the particulars and instrument or copy are to be delivered to the Commission. [7]

(6) Where a charge [1] is created in Nigeria but affects or relates to property outside Nigeria, the instrument [6] creating or purporting to create the charge [1] may be sent for registration under

this section, notwithstanding that further proceedings may be necessary to make the charge [1] valid or effectual according to the law of the country in which the property is situate.

(7) Where a negotiable instrument [18] has been given to secure the payment of any book debts of a company, [2] the deposit of the instrument[6] for the purpose of securing an advance to the company [2] shall not, for the purposes of this section, be treated as a charge [1] on those book debts.

(8) The holding of debentures [8] entitling the holder [19] to a charge[1] on land shall not, for the purposes of this section, be deemed to be an interest in land.

(9) Where a series of debentures [8] containing, or giving by reference to any other instrument, [6] any charge[1] to the benefit of which the debenture holders [19] of that series are entitled paripassu is created by a company, [2] it shall, for the purposes of this section, be sufficient if there are delivered to or received by the Commission [7] within 90 days after the execution of the deed [19] containing the charge[1] or, if there is no such deed, after the execution of any debentures[8] of the series, the following particulars-

(a) the total amount secured by the whole series; and

(b) the dates of the resolutions [20] authorising the issues of the series and the date of the covering deed, if any, by which the security is created or defined; and

(c) a general description of the property charged [1]; and

(d) the names of the trustees, [21] if any, for the debenture holders[19]; together with the deed containing the charge [1], or, if there is no such deed, one of the debentures [8] of the series:

Provided that, where more than one issue is made of debentures [8] in the series, there shall be sent to the Commission [7] for entry in the register particulars of the date and amount of each issue, but an omission to do this shall not affect the validity of the debentures [8] issued.

(10) Where any commission, allowance or discount has been paid or made either directly or indirectly by a company [2] to any person in consideration of his subscribing or agreeing to subscribe, whether absolutely or conditionally, for any debentures [8] of the company,[2] or procuring or agreeing to procure subscriptions, whether absolute or conditional, for any such debentures, [8] the particulars required to be sent for registration under this section

shall include particulars as to the amount or rate per cent of commission, discount or allowance so paid or made, but an omission to do this shall not affect the validity of the debentures [8] issued:

Provided that the deposit of any debentures [8] as security [3] for any debt of the company [2] shall not, for the purposes of this subsection, be treated as the issue of the debentures [8] at a discount.

(11) In this Part of this Act, "charge" [1] includes mortgage. [22]

---

**Notes**

**Section 197(1)**

1. "Charge" means an encumbrance, lien or claim. See **Garner B. (ed.) Black's Law Dictionary 8th ed.**
2. "Company" means a company formed and registered under this Act or, as the case may be, formed and registered in Nigeria before and in existence on the commencement of this Act. See s **ection 567 CAMA Cap. C20 LFN, 2004**
3. "Security" means collateral given or pledged to guarantee the fulfillment of an obligation; especially the assurance that a creditor will be repaid. See **Garner B. (ed.) Black's Law Dictionary 8 th ed.**
4. "Liquidator" means a person appointed to wind up a business's affairs especially by selling off its assets. See **Garner B. (ed.) Black's Law Dictionary 8th ed.**
5. "Creditor" means one to whom a debt is owed whether contractual or otherwise. See **Garner B. ed. Black's Law Dictionary 8 th ed.**
6. "Instrument" means a written legal document that defines rights, duties, entitlements or liabilities. See **Garner B. (ed.) Black's Law Dictionary 8th ed.**
7. "Commission" means Corporate Affairs Commission, established under Section 1 of the **Companies and Allied Matters Act Cap C20 LFN, 2004**.See **Section 567 CAMA Cap. C20 LFN, 2004**

**Section 197(2)**

8. "Debenture" means It means a written acknowledgement of indebtedness by the company, setting out the terms and conditions of the indebtedness and includes debenture stock, bonds and any other securities of any company whether constituting a charge on the assets of the company or not. **Section 567 CAMA Cap. C20 LFN, 2004**
9. "Share capital" see "share" and "capital". Share represents an equity or ownership interest in the corporation. Capital means money or assets available for investment in a business See **Garner B. (ed.) Black's Law Dictionary 8th ed.**
10. "Bill of sale" means an instrument for conveying title to personal property, absolutely or by way of security. **Garner B. (ed.) Black's Law Dictionary 8th ed.**
11. "Floating charge" see "floating lien." It means (i) a charge that continues to exist even when the collateral changes in character,

classification or location. See **Garner B. (ed.) Black's Law Dictionary 8th ed.**

A "floating charge" means an equitable charge over the whole or a specified part of the company's undertakings and assets, including cash and uncalled capital of the company both present and future, but so that the charge shall not preclude the company from dealing with such assets until- (a) the security becomes enforceable and the holder thereof, pursuant to a power in that behalf in the debenture or the deed securing the same, appoints a receiver or manager or enters into possession of such assets; or (b) the court appoints a receiver or manager of such assets on the application of the holder; or (c) the company goes into liquidation. See section 178 **CAMA Cap. C20 LFN, 2004**

12. "Goodwill" means a business's reputation, patronage and other intangible asset that are considered when appraising the business especially for purchase. See **Garner B. (ed.) Black's Law Dictionary 8th ed.**
13. "Patent" means the right to exclude other from making, using marketing, selling, offering for sale or importing as invention for a specified period. See **Garner B. (ed.) Black's Law Dictionary 8 th ed.**
14. "Trademark" means a word, phrase, logo or other graphic symbol used by a manufacturer or seller to distinguish its product from those of others. See **Garner B. (ed.) Black's Law Dictionary 8 th ed.**
15. "Copyright" means the right to copy; specifically a property right in an original work of authorship fixed in any tangible medium of expression, giving the holder the exclusive right to reproduce, adapt, distribute, perform and display the work. See **Garner B. (ed.) Black Law's Dictionary 8th ed**

**Section 197(3)**

16. "Court" means the Federal High Court and to the extent to which application may be made to it as; court includes the Court of Appeal and the Supreme Court. **Section 567 CAMA Cap. C20 LFN, 2004**
17. "Secretary" means a corporate officer in charge of official correspondence, minutes of board meetings and records of stock ownership and transfer. See **Garner B. (ed) Black's Law Dictionary, 8th ed.**

**Section 197(7)**

18. "Negotiable instrument" means a written instrument that is signed by the maker or drawer, with an unconditional promise or order to pay a specified sum payable on demand or at a specified time to order or to the bearer. **Garner B., (ed.) Black's Law Dictionary 8 th ed.**

**Section 197(8)**

19. "Debenture holders" see "debenture" and "holder." Debenture means a written acknowledgement of indebtedness by the company, setting out the terms and conditions of the indebtedness and includes debenture stock, bonds and any other securities of any company whether constituting a charge on the assets of the company or not. See section 567 **CAMA Cap C20 LFN, 2004.**

    "Holder" is one who has legal possession of a negotiable instrument and is entitled to receive payment on it. A holder is a person who has legal possession of a document of title or an investment security. See Garner B., (ed.) Black's Law Dictionary 8th ed.

**Section 197(9)**

20. "Resolution" means a main motion that formally expresses the sense, will or action of a deliberative assembly. See **Garner B. (ed.) Black's Law Dictionary 8th ed.**
21. "Trustee" means one who, having legal title to property holds it in trust for the benefit of another and owes a fiduciary duty to that beneficiary. See **Garner B. (ed.) Black's Law Dictionary 8 th ed.**

**Section 197(11)**

22. "Mortgage" means a conveyance of title to property that is given as security for payment of a debt or the performance of a duty and that will become void upon payment or performance according to stipulated terms. **Garner B. ed. Black's Law Dictionary 8 th ed.**

Cross Reference

On nature of shares generally see **Part VI, CAMA Cap C20 LFN, 2004**

On registration of trademarks, see **section 22, Trademarks Act, Cap. T13, LFN 2004**

On works eligible for copy right and general nature of copyright, see **section 1&6, Copy Rights Act, Cap. C28, LFN 2004**

On obligation of a Company to maintain a register of charges, see **section 191 CAMA Cap. C20, LFN 2004**

On types of Resolutions, see **section 233 CAMA Cap. C20, LFN 2004**

On how a liquidator is appointed, see **section 473, CAMA Cap. C20 LFN, 2004.**

Effect of a Floating Charge, see **section 498 CAMA Cap. C20 LFN, 2004.**

---

**Cases**

A Liquidator owes a duty to the whole body of creditors and shareholders and to the court to make himself thoroughly acquainted with the affairs of the company and suppress or conceal anything coming to his knowledge in the course of his investigation which is material. See ***Re J.A. Balogun* (1977) FRCR 122**

## 198. Register of particulars of charges

(1) The Commission[1] shall keep with respect to each company,[2] a register in the prescribed form of all the charges [3] requiring registration under this Part of this Act, and shall, on payment of such fee as may be specified by regulations made by the Commission[1], enter in the register with respect to such charges [3] the following particulars-

(a) in the case of a charge [3] to the benefit of which the holders[4] of a series of debentures [5] are entitled, such particulars as are specified in section 197 (9) of this Act;

(b) in the case of any other charge [3]-

(i) if the charge [3] is a charge [3] created by the company [2], the date of its creation, and if the charge [3] was a charge [3] existing on property acquired by the company [2], the date of its creation and the date of the acquisition of the property;

(ii) the amount secured by the charge [3];

(iii) short particulars of the property; and

(iv) he persons entitled to the charge [3].

(2) Where a charge [3] is registered under this Part of this Act, the Commission [1] shall issue a registration certificate setting out the parties to the charge [3], the amount thereby secured, with such other particulars as the Commission [1] may consider necessary; and the certificate shall be prima facie evidence of due compliance with the requirements as to registration under this Part of his Act.

(3) The register kept in pursuance of this section shall be open to inspection by any person on payment of such fee, not exceeding N 1 for each inspection as may be specified by regulations made by the Commission [1].

---

**Notes**

**Section 198(1)**

1. "Commission" means Corporate Affairs Commission, established under Section 1 of the Companies and Allied Matters Act. See **section 567 of CAMA Cap C20 LFN, 2004**
2. "Company" means a company formed and registered under this Act or, as the case may be, formed and registered in Nigeria before and in existence on the commencement of this Act. See **section 567 of CAMA Cap C20 LFN, 2004**
3. "Charge" means an encumbrance, lien or claim. See **Garner B., (ed.) Black's Law Dictionary 8th ed.**
4. "Holders" A holder is a person who has legal possession of a document of title or an investment security. See **Garner B. (ed.) Black's Law Dictionary 8th ed.**
5. "Debenture" It means a written acknowledgement of indebtedness by the company, setting out the terms and conditions of the indebtedness and includes debenture stock, bonds and any other securities of any company whether constituting a charge on the assets of the company or not. See **section 567 of CAMA Cap C20 LFN, 2004**

Cross Reference

On effect of non-registration of charges on Liquidator, a company or creditor, see **section 197 CAMA Cap. C20, LFN 2004**

## 199. Duty of company to register charges

(1) It shall be the duty of a company [1] to send to the Commission[2] for registration, the particulars of every charge [3] created by the company [1] and of the issues of debentures [4] of a series requiring registration under section 197 of this Act, but registration of any such charge [3] may be effected on the application of any person interested therein.

(2) Where registration is effected on the application of some person other than the company, [1] that person shall be entitled to recover from the company [1] the amount of any fees properly paid by him to the Commission [2] on the registration.

(3) If any company [1] makes default in sending to the Commission[2] for registration, the particulars of any charge [3] created by the company[1] or of the issues of debentures [4] of a series requiring registration as aforesaid, then, unless the registration has been effected on the application of some other person, the company [1] and every officer[5] of the company[1] who is in default shall be guilty of an offence[6] and liable to a fine of N500.

**Notes**

**Section 199(1)**

1. "Company" means a company formed and registered under this Act or, as the case may be, formed and registered in Nigeria before and in existence on the commencement of this Act. **See section 567 of CAMA Cap C20 LFN, 2004**
2. "Commission" means Corporate Affairs Commission, established under Section 1 of the Companies and Allied Matters Act. See **section 567 of CAMA Cap C20 LFN, 2004**
3. "Charge" means an encumbrance, lien or claim. See **Garner B., (ed.) Black's Law Dictionary 8th ed.**
4. "Debenture" means a written acknowledgement of indebtedness by the company, setting out the terms and conditions of the indebtedness and includes debenture stock, bonds and any other securities of any company whether constituting a charge on the assets of the company or not. See **section 567 of CAMA Cap C20 LFN, 2004**

**Section 199(2)**

5. "Officer" means a person who holds an office of trust, authority or command. See **Garner B. (ed.) Black's Law Dictionary 8th ed.**

In relation to a body corporate, it includes a director, manager or secretary. See **section 567 of CAMA Cap C20 LFN, 2004**

Cross Reference

On meaning of offence, see **section 2, Criminal Code C38, LFN 2004**

On obligation of a Company to keep a register of charges at its registered office, see **section 191 CAMA Cap. C20, LFN 2004**

---

## 200. Duty of company acquiring property to register subsisting charges

(1) Where a company [1] acquires any property which is subject to a charge[2] of any such kind as would, if it has been created by the company[1] after the acquisition of the property, have been required to be registered under this Part of this Act, the company [1] shall cause the prescribed particulars of the charge, [2] together with a copy (certified in the prescribed manner to be a correct copy) of the instrument,[3] if any, by which the charge [2] was created or is evidenced, to be delivered to the Commission [4] for registration in the manner required by this Act within 90 days after the date on which acquisition is completed:

Provided that, if the property is situated and the charge [2] was created outside Nigeria, 90 days after the date on which the copy of the instrument[3] could in due course of post, and if dispatched with due diligence, have been received in Nigeria shall be substituted for 90 days after the completion of the acquisition, as the time within which the particulars and the copy of the instrument [3] are to be delivered to the Commission. [4]

(2) If default is made in complying with this section, the company[1] and every officer [5] of the company [1] who is in default shall be guilty of an offence and liable to a fine of N250.

(3) It shall be sufficient compliance with this section in any case affecting land registered under any enactment in a State, where the charge[2] is registered thereunder before the land is acquired by the company[1], if a true copy of the charge duly certified by the Registrar of Land is delivered to the Commission [4] within the time prescribed by this section.

---

**Notes**

**Section 200(1)**

1. "Company" means a company formed and registered under this Act or, as the case may be, formed and registered in Nigeria before and in

existence on the commencement of this Act. **See section 567 of CAMA Cap. C20 LFN, 2004**

2. "Charge" means an encumbrance, lien or claim. See **Garner B. (ed.) Black's Law Dictionary 8th ed.**
3. "Instrument" means a written legal document that defines rights, duties, entitlements or liabilities. See **Garner B. (ed.) Black's Law Dictionary 8th ed.**
4. "Commission" means Corporate Affairs Commission, established under Section 1 of the Companies and Allied Matters Act. See **section 567 of CAMA Cap. C20 LFN, 2004**

**Section 200(2)**

5. "Officer" means a person who holds an office of trust, authority or command. See **Garner B., (ed.) Black's Law Dictionary 8th ed.**
   In relation to a body corporate, it includes a director, manager or secretary. See **section 567 of CAMA Cap C20 LFN, 2004**

**Cross Reference**

On meaning of offence, see **section 2, Criminal Code C38, LFN 2004**

On rights of holder of a statutory right of occupany to transfer, assign or mortgage any improvement on land, see **section 15, Land Use Act Cap. L5 LFN 2004**

On registration of charges on Land, **see Registration of Instrument Law of the various states. (For example, Registration of Titles Law, Cap. R4, Laws of Lagos State, 2003)**

On obligation of a Company to keep a register of charges at its registered office, see **section 191 CAMA Cap. C20, LFN 2004.**

**Cases**

An unregistered land instrument must not be pleaded in court as it is inadmissible. Where it is wrongly pleaded in evidence, it will be expunged. See ***Akinduro v. Alaya (2007) 15 NWLR (Pt.1057) 312***

A purchaser of land or a lessee in active possession of land by virtue of an unregistered land instrument acquires an equitable interest in the land which equitable interest can only be defeated by another purchaser for value without notice of the prior unregistered equity. See ***Nsiegbe v. Mgbemena (2007) 10 NWLR (Pt. 1042) 364***

## 201. Existing charges

(1) Where, at the date of commencement of this Act, a company[1] has property on which there is a charge, [2] particulars of which would require registration if it had been created by the company[1] after the date of such commencement, then, unless the charge[2] has been discharged[3] or the property has ceased to be held by the company[1] prior to the expiration of six months from the date of such commencement, the company [1] shall, within that time, cause

particulars of the charge [2] as prescribed by section 197 of this Act to be delivered to the Commission [4] for registration together with the document, if any, by which the charge [2] was created or a copy thereof, certified as required by that section.

(2) Every existing company [5] shall, prior to the expiration of six months from the commencement of this Act, deliver to the Commission[4] for registration a statutory declaration [6] made by a director[7] and the secretary [8] of the company [1] stating whether or not there are any charges [2] on the company's [1] property of which particulars require to be registered under this section and confirming that particulars of any such charges [2] have been duly delivered to the Commission [3] for registration.

(3) In the event of default in complying with subsection (2) of this section, the company [1] and every officer [9] of the company [1] who is in default shall be guilty of an offence and liable to a fine not exceeding N50 for every day during which the default continues.

(4) Failure to comply with the provisions of this section shall not affect the validity of the charge. [2]

---

**Notes**

**Section 201(1)**

1. "Company" means a company formed and registered under this Act or, as the case may be, formed and registered in Nigeria before and in existence on the commencement of this Act. See **section 567 of CAMA Cap C20 LFN, 2004**
2. "Charge" means an encumbrance, lien or claim. See **Garner B. (ed.) Black's Law Dictionary 8th ed.**
3. "Discharged" means any method by which a legal debt is extinguished especially the payment of a debt or satisfaction of some other obligation. See **Garner B. (ed.) Black's Law Dictionary 8 th ed.**
4. "Commission" means Corporate Affairs Commission, established under s.1 of the Companies and Allied Matters Act. See **section 567 of CAMA Cap C20 LFN, 2004**

**Section 201(2)**

5. "Existing company" means a company formed and registered under this Act or, as the case may be, formed and registered in Nigeria before and in existence on the commencement of this Act. See **section 567 of CAMA Cap C20 LFN, 2004**
6. "Statutory declaration" means a declaration voluntarily made under the Oaths Act and in Nigeria includes one so made under any other enactment or law providing for the taking of a voluntary declaration. See **section 567 of CAMA Cap C20 LFN, 2004**

7. "Director" includes any person occupying the position of director by whatever name called; and includes any person in accordance with whose directions or instructions the directors of the company are accustomed to act. See s**ection 567 of CAMA Cap C20 LFN, 2004**
8. "Secretary" means a corporate officer in charge of official correspondence, minutes of board meetings and records of stock ownership and transfer. See **Garner. B. (ed) Black's Law Dictionary, 8th ed.** Section 201(3)
9. "Officer" means a person who holds an office of trust, authority or command. **Garner B. (ed.) Black's Law Dictionary 8th ed.**
   In relation to a body corporate, it includes a director, manager or secretary. **Section 567 CAMA Cap C20 LFN, 2004**

**Cross Reference**

On meaning of offence, see **section 2, Criminal Code C38, LFN 2004**

On the qualifications of a secretary, see **section 295 CAMA, Cap. C20, LFN, 2004.**

On the duties of a Secretary see **section 298 CAMA, Cap. C20, LFN,2004.**

## 202. Charges to secure fluctuating amounts

Where a charge,[1] particulars of which require registration under section 197 of this Act, is expressed to secure all sums due or to become due or some other uncertain or fluctuating amount, the particulars required under paragraph (a) of subsection (9) of section 197 of this Act shall state the maximum sum deemed to be secured by such charge[1] (being the maximum sum covered by the stamp duty paid thereon) and such charge shall be void [2], so far as any security[3] on the company's [4] property is thereby conferred, as respects any excess over the stated maximum:

Provided that, if-

(a) additional stamp duty[5] is subsequently paid on such charge[1]; and

(b) at any time thereafter prior to the commencement of the winding up[6] of the company,[4] amended particulars of the said charge[1] stating the increased maximum sum deemed to be secured thereby (together with the original instrument by which the charge [1] was created or evidenced) are delivered to the Commission [7] for registration, then, as from the date of such delivery, the charge, [1] if otherwise valid, shall be effective to the extent of such increased maximum sum except as regards any person who, prior to the date of such delivery, has acquired any proprietary rights [8] in, or a fixed [9] or floating charge [10] on, the property subject to the charge. [1]

**Notes**

**Section 202**

1. "Charge" means an encumbrance, lien or claim. See **Garner B. (ed.) Black's Law Dictionary 8th ed.**
2. "Void" means of no legal effect. See **Garner B. ed. Black's Law Dictionary 8th ed.**
3. "Security" means collateral given or pledged to guarantee the fulfillment of an obligation; especially the assurance that a creditor will be repaid. See **Garner B. (ed.) Black's Law Dictionary 8 th ed.**
4. "Company" means a company formed and registered under this Act or, as the case may be, formed and registered in Nigeria before and in existence on the commencement of this Act. See **section 567 CAMA Cap. C20 LFN, 2004**
5. "Stamp duty" means a tax raised by requiring stamps sold by the government to be affixed to designated documents, thus forming part of the perpetual revenue. See **Garner B., (ed.) Black's Law Dictionary 8 th ed.**
6. "Winding-up" means the process of settling accounts and liquidating assets in anticipation of dissolution. See **Garner B. ed. Black's Dictionary 8th ed.**
7. "Commission" means Corporate Affairs Commission, established under Section 1 of the Companies and Allied Matters Act. See **section 567 CAMA Cap. C20 LFN, 2004**
8. "Proprietary rights" see proprietary right. It means a right that is part of a person's estate, assets, or property, as opposed to a right arising from the person's legal status. See **Garner B. (ed.) Black's Law Dictionary 8th ed.**
9. "Fixed charge" means a charge over the whole or a specified part of the company's undertakings and assets, including cash and uncalled capital of the company both present and future, which precludes the company from dealing with such assets after (a) the security becomes enforceable and the holder thereof, pursuant to a power in that behalf in the debenture or the deed securing the same, appoints a receiver or manager or enters into possession of such assets; or (b) the court appoints a receiver or manager of such assets on the application of the holder; or (c) the company goes into liquidation. See **section 178(2) CAMA Cap. C20 LFN, 2004**
10. "Floating charge" see "floating lien." It means (i) a charge that continues to exist even when the collateral changes in character, classification or location. See **Garner B.(ed.) Black's Law Dictionary 8th ed. page. 942** .

    (ii) It means an equitable charge over the whole or a specified part of the company's undertakings and assets, including cash and uncalled capital of the company both present and future, which does not preclude the company from dealing with such assets. See **Section 178(1), CAMA Cap. C20 LFN, 2004**

Cross Reference

On priority of fixed charge over floating charge, see **section 179 CAMA Cap. C20 LFN, 2004**
On competent authority to impose, charge and collect duties on instruments related to matters executed between a company and an individual, group or body of induvuduals, See **section 3, Stamp Duties Act, Cap. S8, LFN 2004**

---

## 203. Endorsement of certificate of registration on debentures

(1) The company[1] shall cause a copy of every certificate of registration given under section 198 of this Act to be endorsed on every debenture[2] or certificate of debenture stock[3] which is issued by the company[1] and the payment of which is secured by the charge[4] so registered:
Provided that nothing in this subsection shall be construed as requiring a company[1] to cause a certificate of registration of any charge[4] so given to be enforced on any debenture[2] or certificate of debenture stock[3] issued by the company[1] before the charge[4] was created.

(2) If any person knowingly and willfully authorizes or permits the delivery of any debenture[2] or certificate of debenture stock[3] which under the provisions of this section is required to have endorsed on it a copy of a certificate of registration without the copy being so endorsed upon it, he shall, without prejudice to any other liability[5], be guilty of an offence and liable to a fine not exceeding N500.

---

**Notes**
**Section 203(1)**

1. "Company" means a company formed and registered under this Act or, as the case may be, formed and registered in Nigeria before and in existence on the commencement of this Act. See **Section 567 CAMA Cap. C20 LFN, 2004**
2. "Debenture" means a written acknowledgement of indebtedness by the company, setting out the terms and conditions of the indebtedness and includes debenture stock, bonds and any other securities of any company whether constituting a charge on the assets of the company or not. See **Section 567 CAMA Cap. C20 LFN, 2004**
3. "Debenture stock" means a type of bond representing money borrowed by a company by using its property or other fixed assets as security. See **Garner B. (ed.) Black's Law Dictionary 8 th ed.**
4. "Charge" means an encumbrance, lien or claim. See **Garner B. (ed.) Black's Law Dictionary 8th ed.**

**Section 203(2)**

5. "Liability" means the quality or state of being legally obligated or accountable. **Garner B. (ed.) Black's law Dictionary 8 th ed.**
   The state of being legally responsible for something. **Oxford Advanced learners Dictionary.6th ed.**

Cross Reference

On meaning of offence, see **section 2, Criminal Code C38, LFN 2004**
On obligation of a Company to keep a register of charges at its registered office, see **section 191 CAMA Cap. C20, LFN 2004.**
On the obligation on Corporate Affairs Commission to issue a certificate of registration upon the registration of charges, see **section 198 CAMA Cap. C20 LFN, 2004.**

---

## 204. Entries of satisfaction of charges

If the Commission[1] is satisfied with respect to any registered charge[2] that-

(a) the debt[3] for which the charge[2] was given has been paid or satisfied in whole or in part; or

(b) part of the property or undertaking charged has been released[4] from the charge[2] or has ceased to form part of the company's[5] property or undertaking, it may enter on the register a memorandum of satisfaction[6] to the extent necessary to give effect thereto and, where it enters a memorandum of satisfaction[6] it shall, if required, furnish the company[5] with a copy of the entry, and any such entry shall have effect, subject to the requirement of any other enactment as to registration.

---

**Notes**

**Section 204**

1. "Commission" means Corporate Affairs Commission, established under Section 1 of the Companies and Allied Matters Act. See **section 567 CAMA Cap C20 LFN, 2004**
2. "Charge" means an encumbrance, lien or claim. See **Garner B. (ed.) Black's Law Dictionary 8th ed.**
3. "Debt" means liability on a claim; a specific sum of money due by agreement or otherwise. See **Garner B. (ed.) Black's Law Dictionary, 8th ed.**
4. "Released" see "release". It means liberation from an obligation, duty or demand; the act of giving up a right or claim to the person against whom it could have been enforced. See **Garner B. (ed.) Black's Law Dictionary, 8th ed.**

5. "Company" means a company formed and registered under this Act or, as the case may be, formed and registered in Nigeria before and in existence on the commencement of this Act. See **section 567 CAMA Cap. C20 LFN, 2004**
6. "Satisfaction" means the giving of something with the intention, express or implied that it is to extinguish some existing legal or moral obligation. See **Garner B., (ed.) Black's Law Dictionary 8 th ed**.

**Cross Reference**

On obligation of a Company to keep a register of charges at its registered office, see **section 191 CAMA Cap. C20, LFN 2004.**

On the obligation on Corporate Affairs Commission to issue a certificate of registration upon the registration of charges, see **section 198 CAMA Cap. C20 LFN, 2004**

---

## 205. Rectification of register

The court,[1] on being satisfied that the omission to register a charge [2] within the time required by this Act or that the omission or misstatement of any particular with respect to any such charge [2] or in a memorandum of satisfaction[3] was accidental, or due to inadvertence or to some other sufficient cause, or is not of a nature to prejudice the position of creditors [4] or shareholders[5] of the company,[6] or that on other grounds it is just and equitable to grant relief, may, on the application [7] of the company[6] or any person interested and on such terms and conditions as seems to the court [1] just and expedient, order that the time for registration shall be extended or, as the case may be, that the omission or misstatement shall be rectified.

---

**Notes**

**Section 205**

1. "Court" means the Federal High Court and to the extent to which application may be made to it as; court includes the Court of Appeal and the Supreme Court. **Section 567 CAMA Cap. C20 LFN, 2004**
2. "Charge" means an encumbrance, lien or claim. See **Garner B. (ed.) Black's Law Dictionary 8th ed.**
3. "Satisfaction" means the giving of something with the intention, express or implied that it is to extinguish some existing legal or moral obligation. See **Garner B., (ed.) Black's Law Dictionary 8 th ed**.
4. "Creditors" means one to whom a debt is owed whether contractual or otherwise. See **Garner B., (ed.) Black's Law Dictionary 8 th ed.**
5. "Shareholders" see "shareholder." It means one who owns or holds a share or shares in a company, especially a corporation. See **Garner B., (ed.) Black's Law Dictionary 8 th ed.**

6. "Company" means a company formed and registered under this Act or, as the case may be, formed and registered in Nigeria before and in existence on the commencement of this Act. See **Section 567 CAMA Cap. C20 LFN, 2004**
7. "Application" means a request or petition. **Garner B. (ed.) Black's Law Dictionary 8th ed.**

Cross Reference

On the powers and jurisdiction of the Federal High Court, see **Section 251 of the Constitution of the Federal Republic of Nigeria, 1999.**

---

**Cases**

"The Articles of Association is the contract governing the relationship between shareholders and any infraction of such articles may confer on the shareholder adversely affected a right of action . See ***Attorney General of Lagos State v Eko Hotel Ltd &Oha Ltd (2001) FWLR page 1996 at 2000***

**For Further Reading**

On shareholders, see Olufemi Amao and Kenneth Amaeshi "Galvanizing Shareholder Activism: A Prerequisite for Effective Corporate Governance and Accountability in Nigeria" **(2008) 82 Journal of Business Ethics 119-130**

## 206. Registration of appointment order, etc.

(1) If any person obtains an order for the appointment [1] of a receiver[2] or manager[3] of the property of a company, [4] or appoints[1] such a receiver[2] or manager[3] under any powers contained in any instrument,[5] he shall, within seven days from the date of the order or the appointment[1] under the said powers, give notice of the fact to the Commission[6] and the Commission[6] shall, on payment of such fee as may be specified by regulations [7] made under this Act, enter the fact in the register of charges. [8]

(2) Where any person appointed [1] receiver[2] or manager[3] of the property of a company[4] under the powers contained in any instrument[5], ceases to act as such receiver [2] or manager,[3] he shall, on so ceasing, give the Commission [6] notice to that effect, and the Commission[6] shall enter the notice in the register of charges. [8]

(3) If any person makes default in complying with the requirements of this section, he shall be guilty of an offence and liable to a fine not exceeding N 50 for every day during which the default continues.

---

**Notes**

**Section 206(1)**

1. "Appointed" see "appoint." It means to choose someone for a job or responsibility. See **Garner B. (ed.) Black's Law Dictionary 8 th ed.**
2. "Receiver" means a disinterested person appointed by a court, or by a corporation or other person, for the protection or collection of property that is subject of diverse claims. See **Garner B. (ed.) Black's Law Dictionary 8th ed.**

   Receiver includes a manager. See **Section 567 of CAMA Cap. C20 LFN, 2004**
3. "Manager" means one who has charge of corporation and control of its business, or of its branch establishments, divisions, or departments . **See Garner B. (ed.) Black's Law Dictionary 8 th ed.**
4. "Company" means a company formed and registered under this Act or, as the case may be, formed and registered in Nigeria before and in existence on the commencement of this Act. See **Section 567 CAMA Cap. C20 LFN, 2004**
5. "Instrument" means a written legal document that defines rights, duties, entitlements, or liabilities. See **Garner B. (ed.) Black's Law Dictionary 8th ed.**
6. "Commission" means Corporate Affairs Commission, established under Section 1 of the Companies and Allied Matters Act. See **Section 567 CAMA Cap. C20 LFN, 2004**
7. "Regulation" means the act or process of controlling by rule or restriction. See **Garner B. (ed.) Black's Law Dictionary 8 th ed.**

**Section 206(2)**

8. "Charges" see "charge." It means an encumbrance, lien or claim. See **Garner B. (ed.) Black's Law Dictionary 8 th ed.**

**Cross Reference**

On meaning of offence, see **section 2, Criminal Code C38, LFN 2004**

On duty of company to register Charges with the Corporate Affairs Commission, see **section 191 CAMA Cap. C20 LFN, 2004**

On power of Court to rectify the Register of charges, see **section 205 CAMA Cap. C20 LFN, 2004**

---

**Cases**

Where a receiver or manager is appointed for the whole o substantially the whole of a company's property, the powers conferred on him by the debentures by virtue of which he was appointed, shall be deemed to include, except in so far as they are with any of these debentures, the powers specified in the eleventh schedule to the Act: ***See Onafowokan & 2 Ors v. Wema Bank & 2 Ors 88/2004 SC delivered 13/05/2010.***

Whilst receivership and manager open exclusively dominate the company affairs and dealings with the outside world, it does not affect the internal domestic structure of the company ***: See Unibiz (Nig.) Ltd. v. Commercial***

***Bank Credit Lyonnais Nig. Ltd.(for and on behalf of Babington Ashaye (2001) 7NWLR (pt 713) 534.***

## 207. Inspection of register and copies of instruments

(1) The copies of instruments [1] creating any charge [2] requiring registration under this Part of this Act with the Commission [3] and the register of charges [2] kept in pursuance of section 198 of this Act, shall be open during business hours (but subject to such reasonable restrictions as the company [4] in general meeting [5] may impose, so that not less than two hours in each day shall be allowed for inspection) to inspection by any creditor [6] or member [7] of the company [4] without fee, and the register of charges [2] shall also be open to inspection by any other person on payment of such fee, not exceeding N10 for each inspection, as the company [4] may prescribe.

(2) If inspection of copies of instruments [1] creating charges [2] or of the register is refused, every officer [8] of the company [4] who is in default shall be guilty of an offence and liable to a fine not exceeding N50 for every day during which the refusal continues.

(3) If any such refusal occurs in relation to a company [4] registered in Nigeria or, in so far as a foreign company [9] has an established place of business within Nigeria and an instrument [1] creates a charge [2] over any of its property in Nigeria and the refusal relates to that charge [2], the court [10] may by order compel an immediate inspection of the copies or register.

---

**Notes**

**Section 207(1)**

1. "Instruments" see "instrument." It means a written legal document that defines rights, duties, entitlements, or liabilities. See **Garner B. (ed.) Black's Law Dictionary 8th ed.**
2. "Charge." It means an encumbrance, lien or claim. See **Garner B. (ed.) Black's Law Dictionary 8th ed.**
3. "Commission" means Corporate Affairs Commission, established under Section 1 of the Companies and Allied Matters Act. See **Section 567 CAMA Cap. C20 LFN, 2004**
4. "Company." It means a company formed and registered under this Act or, as the case may be, formed and registered in Nigeria before and in existence on the commencement of this Act. See **Section 567 CAMA Cap. C20 LFN, 2004**
5. "General meeting" means the gathering of people to discuss or act on matters in which they have a common interest. See **Garner. B. (ed) Black's Law Dictionary 8th ed.**

6. "Creditor" means one to whom a debt is owed whether contractual or otherwise. See **Garner B. (ed.) Black's Law Dictionary 8 th ed.**
7. "Member" means one of the individuals of whom a deliberative assembly consists and who enjoys the full rights of participating in the organization-including the rights of making, debating and voting on motions- except to the extent that the organization reserves those rights to certain classes of membership. See **Garner B. (ed.) Black's Law Dictionary 8th ed.**

   It includes the heir, executor, administrator or other personal representative as the case may be, of the member. See **section 567 CAMA Cap. C20 LFN, 2004**

**Section 207(2)**

8. "Officer" means a person who holds an office of trust, authority or command. **Garner B., (ed.) Black's Law Dictionary 8 th ed.**

   In relation to a body corporate, it includes a director, manager or secretary. **Section 567 CAMA Cap. C20 LFN, 2004**

**Section 207(3)**

9. "Foreign company" means a company incorporated elsewhere than in Nigeria. See **Section 567 CAMA Cap. C20 LFN, 2004.**
10. "Court" means the Federal High Court and to the extent to which application may be made to it as; court includes the Court of Appeal and the Supreme Court. **Section 567 of CAMA Cap C20 LFN, 2004.**

**Cross Reference**

On meaning of offence, see **section 2, Criminal Code C38, LFN 2004.**

On the powers and jurisdiction of the Federal High Court, see **Section 251 of the Constitution of the Federal Republic of Nigeria, 1999.**

---

*Realisation of security*

## 208. Realisation of debenture holder's security

(1) A debenture holder [1] shall be entitled to realize any security[2] vested in him or in any other person for his benefit if-

(a) the company[3] fails to pay any instalment [4] of interest [5], or the whole or part of the principal [6] or any premium,[7] owing under the debenture [8] or the debenture[8] trust deed[9] covering the debenture, [8] within one month after it becomes due; or

(b) the company[3] fails to fulfil any of the obligations imposed on it by the debentures [8] or the debenture [8] trust deed[9];

(c) any circumstances occur which by the terms of the debentures[8] or debenture [8] trust deed[9] entitled the holder[1] of the debenture [8] to realise his security [2]; or

(d) the company[3] is wound up. [10]

(2) A debenture holder[1] whose debenture[8] is secured[11] by a general floating charge[12] vested in him or the trustee[13] of the covering debenture[8] trust deed,[9] or any other person, shall additionally be entitled to realise his security[2] if-

(a) any creditor[14] of the company[3] issues a process of execution against any of its assets[15] or commences proceedings for winding up[10] of the company[3] by order of any court[16] of competent jurisdiction; or

(b) the company[3] ceases to pay its debts[17] as they fall due; or

(c) the company[3] ceases to carry on business[18]; or

(d) the company[3] suffers, after the issue[19] of debentures[8] of the class concerned, losses or diminutions in the value of its assets[16] which in the aggregate amount to more than one half of the total amount owing in respect of debentures[8] of the class held by the debenture holder[1] who seeks to enforce his security[2] and debentures[8] whose holder[1] ranks before him for payment of principal[6] or interest[5]; or

(e) any circumstances occur which entitles a debenture holder[1] who ranks for payment of principal[6] or interest[5] in priority[20] to the debentures[8] secured[11] by the general floating charges[12] to realise his security.[2]

---

**Notes**

**Section 208(1)**

1. "Debenture holder" see "debenture" and "holder." Debenture means a written acknowledgement of indebtedness by the company, setting out the terms and conditions of the indebtedness and includes debenture stock, bonds and any other securities of any company whether constituting a charge on the assets of the company or not. See **Section 567 CAMA Cap. C20 LFN, 2004**. "Holder" is one who has legal possession of a negotiable instrument and is entitled to receive payment on it. See **Garner B. (ed.) Black's Law Dictionary 8th ed.**
2. "Security" means collateral given or pledged to guarantee the fulfillment of an obligation; especially the assurance that a creditor will be repaid. See **Garner B. (ed.) Black's Law Dictionary 8th ed.**
3. "Company" It means a company formed and registered under this Act or, as the case may be, formed and registered in Nigeria before and in existence on the commencement of this Act. See **Section 567 CAMA Cap. C20 LFN, 2004**

4. "Instalment" means a periodic payment of a debt. See **Oxford Advanced Learner's Dictionary**
5. "Interest" means advantage or profit, esp. of a financial nature. See **Oxford Advanced Learner's Dictionary**
6. "Principal" means an amount of money that you lend to somebody or invest to earn interest. See **Oxford Advanced Learner's Dictionary**
7. "Premium" means the sum of money paid in addition to a regular price, salary or other amount; a bonus. See **Garner B. (ed) Black's Law Dictionary, 8th ed.**
8. "Debenture" means a written acknowledgement of indebtedness by the company, setting out the terms and conditions of the indebtedness and includes debenture stock, bonds and any other securities of any company whether constituting a charge on the assets of the company or not. See **Section 567 CAMA Cap. C20 LFN, 2004**
9. "Trust deed" see declaration of trust. 2. The instrument that creates a trust. See **Garner B., (ed.) Black's Law Dictionary 8 th ed.**
10. "Wound up" see "winding up." It means the process of settling accounts and liquidating assets in anticipation of a partnership or dissolution. See **Garner B. (ed.) Black's Law Dictionary 8 th ed.**

**Section 208(2)**

11. "Secured" means supported or backed by security or collateral. See **Garner B., (ed.) Black's Law Dictionary 8 th ed.**
12. "Floating charge" see floating lien. It means a charge that continues to exist even when the collateral changes in character, classification or location. See **Garner B (ed.) Black's Law Dictionary 8th ed.**
    A "floating charge" means an equitable charge over the whole or a specified part of the company's undertakings and assets, including cash and uncalled capital of the company both present and future, but so that the charge shall not preclude the company from dealing with such assets until- (a) the security becomes enforceable and the holder thereof, pursuant to a power in that behalf in the debenture or the deed securing the same, appoints a receiver or manager or enters into possession of such assets; or (b) the court appoints a receiver or manager of such assets on the application of the holder; or (c) the company goes into liquidation. See section 178 **CAMA Cap. C20 LFN, 2004**
13. "Trustee" means one who, having legal title to property holds it in trust for the benefit of another and owes a fiduciary duty to that beneficiary. See **Garner B. (ed.) Black's Law Dictionary 8 th ed**.
14. "Creditor" means one to whom a debt is owed whether contractual or otherwise. See **Garner B. (ed.) Black's Law Dictionary 8 th ed.**
15. "Assets" means an item that is owned and has value. See **Garner B. (ed.) Black's Law Dictionary 8 th ed.**
16. "Court" means the Federal High Court and to the extent to which application may be made to it as; court includes the Court of Appeal and the Supreme Court. See **Section 567 CAMA Cap. C20 LFN, 2004**
17. "Debt" means liability on a claim; a specific sum of money due by agreement or otherwise. **Garner B. (ed.) Black's Law Dictionary, 8 th ed.**

18. "Business" means includes any trade, industry and profession and any occupation carried on for profit. See **588 CAMA Cap. C20 LFN, 2004**
19. "Issue" It means a class or series of securities that are simultaneously offered for sale. **Garner B. (ed.) Black's Law Dictionary 8 th ed.**
20. "Priority" means (1) the status of being earlier in time or higher in degree or rank. (2)An established right to precedence especially a Creditor's right to have a claim paid before other creditors of the same debtors receive payment. See **Garner B. (ed.) Black's Law Dictionary 8th ed.**

**Cross Reference**

On the Jurisdiction of the Federal High Court, see **section 251, Constitution of the Federal Republic of Nigeria, 1999**

---

**Cases**

"A debenture consists of a debt owed by a company to another secured by a deed which prescribes the condition of the realization of the debt, and it may be created over the fixed or floating assets of the company" ***UBN v. Tropics Foods* (1992) 3NWLR (Pt. 228) 231**

"A debenture is a document which either creates or acknowledges a debt....This obligation is in most cases at the present day, accompanied by some charge or security" ***Fasakin v. Fasakin* (1994) 4 N.W.L.R Pt. 340; pg.620 par. C-E**

On a court of competent jurisdiction:

In ***Madukolu v. Nkemdilim (1962)2 NSCC 374 at 379-380***, this court stated that "a court is properly constituted as regards the number and qualification of its members on the bench , and no member is disqualified for one reason or the other and the subject matter of the case is within the jurisdiction and there is no feature in the case which prevents the court from exercising its jurisdiction and the case coming up before the court was initiated by due process of law and upon fufilment if any condition precedent to the exercise of jurisdiction." See ***SLB Consortium v. Nigerin National Peroleum Corporation (NNPC) SC 180/2008 delivered 15/04/11***

## 209. Remedies available to debenture holders

(1) At any time after a debenture holder [1] or a class [2] of debenture holders[1] becomes entitled to realise his or their security [3], a receiver[4] of any assets[5] subject to a mortgage, [6] charge[7] or security[3] in favour of the class [2] of debenture holders [1] or the trustee [8] of the covering trust deed [9], or any other person, may be appointed by-

(a) that trustee[8];

(b) the holders of debentures [1] of the same class [2] containing power to appoint; or

(c) debenture holders [1] having more than one half of the total amount owing in respect of all the debentures [9] of the same class[2]; or

(d) the court [10] on the application of the trustee [8].

(2) Subject to any conditions imposed in the debenture or debenture trust deed [9], a debenture holder [1], or a trustee [8] in the case of a trust deed [9], may-

(a) bring an action in a representative capacity against the company[11] for payment and enforcement of the security [3]; or

(b) realise his security [3] by-

(i) bringing a foreclosure action; or

(ii) commencing a winding-up [12] proceeding.

(3) A receiver [4] appointed under this section shall have, subject to the order made by the court [1,0] power to take possession of the assets[5] subject to the mortgage, [6] charge[7] or security [3]and to sell those assets[5] and, if the mortgage, [6] charge[7] or security [3] extends to such property, to collect debts owed to the property, to enforce claims vested in the company, [11] to compromise, settle and enter into arrangements [13] in respect of claims by or against the company,[11] on the company's [11] business with a view to selling it on the most favourable terms, to grant or accept leases of land and licences in respect of patents, designs, copyright or trademarks, and to recover any instalment unpaid on the company's [11] issued shares. [14]

(4) Where a representative action is being brought under paragraph (a) of subsection (2) of this section, the approval of the court[10] shall be obtained where the company [11] is being wound up. [12]

(5) The remedies given by this section shall be in addition to, and not in substitution for, any other powers and remedies conferred on the trustee [8] of the debenture trust deed [9] or on the debenture holders[1] by the debentures or debenture trust deed, [9] and any power or remedy which is expressed in any instrument [15] to be exercisable if the debenture holders [1] become entitled to realise their security[3] is exercisable on the occurrence of any of the events specified in subsection (1) of section 208 of this Act or in the case of a general charge in subsections (1) and (2) of section 208 of this Act; but a manager [16] of the business or of any of the assets [5] of a company[11] may not be appointed for the benefit of debenture

holders[1] unless a receiver[4] has also been appointed and has not ceased to act.

(6) The provisions of sections 387 to 400 of this Act shall apply to receivers[4] and managers[16] under this Part of this Act.

(7) No provision in any instrument[15] which purports to exclude or restrict the remedies given by this section shall be valid.

---

**Notes**

**Section 209(1)**

4. "Debenture holders" see "debenture" and "holder." Debenture means a written acknowledgement of indebtedness by the company, setting out the terms and conditions of the indebtedness and includes debenture stock, bonds and any other securities of any company whether constituting a charge on the assets of the company or not. **Section 567 of CAMA Cap C20 LFN, 2004**. "Holder" is one who has legal possession of a negotiable instrument and is entitled to receive payment on it.
5. "Class" means 1. A group of people, things, qualities or activities that have common characteristics or attributes. **Garner B. (ed.) Black's Law Dictionary 8th ed.**
6. "Security" means an instrument that evidences the holder's ownership rights in a firm. **Garner B., (ed.) Black's Law Dictionary 8th ed.** See Securities. It includes shares, debentures, debenture stock, bonds, notes (other than promissory notes) and units under a unit trust scheme. **Section 567 of CAMA Cap C20 LFN, 2004**
7. "Receiver" means a disinterested person appointed by a court, or by a corporation or other person, for the protection or collection of property that is subject of diverse claims. **Garner B. (ed.) Black's Law Dictionary 8th ed.** Receiver includes a manager. **Section 567 of CAMA Cap C20 LFN, 2004**
8. "Assets" means an item that is owned and has value. **Garner B. (ed.) Black's Law Dictionary 8th ed.**
9. "Mortgage" means a lien against a property that is granted to secure an obligation such as a debt and that is extinguished upon payment or performance according to stipulated terms **Garner B. (ed.) Black's Law Dictionary 8th ed.**
10. "Charge" It means an encumbrance, lien or claim. **Garner B. (ed.) Black's Law Dictionary 8th ed.**
11. "Trustee" means one who, having legal title to property holds it in trust for the benefit of another and owes a fiduciary duty to that beneficiary. **Garner B. (ed.) Black's Law Dictionary 8th ed.**

**Section 209(2)**

12. "Trust deed" see declaration of trust. 2. The instrument that creates a trust. **Garner B (ed.) Black's Law Dictionary 8th ed.**

13. "Court" means the Federal High Court and to the extent to which application may be made to it as; court includes the Court of Appeal and the Supreme Court. **Section 567 of CAMA Cap C20 LFN, 2004**
14. "Company" It means a company formed and registered under this Act or, as the case may be, formed and registered in Nigeria before and in existence on the commencement of this Act. **Section 567 of CAMA Cap C20 LFN, 2004**
15. "Winding-up" means the process of settling accounts and liquidating assets in anticipation of a partnership or company dissolution. **Garner B. (ed.) Black's Law Dictionary 8 th ed.**

**Section 209(3)**

16. "Arrangement" means any change in the rights or liabilities of members, debenture holders or creditors of a company or any class of them in the regulation of a company, other than a change effected under any other provision of this Act or by the unanimous agreement of all parties affected thereby. **Section 537, CAMA Cap C20 LFN, 2004**
17. "Shares" see "share." It means the interests in a company's share capital of a member who is entitled to share in the capital or income of such company; and except where a distinction between stock and shares is expressed or implied, includes stock. See **section 567 CAMA Cap. C20 LFN, 2004**

**Section 209(5)**

18. "Instrument" means a written legal document that defines rights, duties, entitlements, or liabilities. See **Garner B. (ed.) Black's Law Dictionary 8th ed.**
19. "Manager" means one who has charge of corporation and control of its business, or of its branch establishments, divisions, or departments . **Garner B. (ed.) Black's Law Dictionary 8 th ed.**

**Cross Reference**

On inventions that are patentable, see **section 1, Patent and Designs Act, Cap. P2 LFN 2004**

On works eligible for copyright, see **section 1, Copyrights Act**

On appointment and renumeration of a Liquidator, see **section 422 CAMA Cap. C20, LFN 2004**

On the Power to appoint a Liquidator, see **section 464 CAMA Cap. C20, LFN 2004**

No debenture trust deed may cover more than one class of debenture. See **section 183(1), CAMA Cap. C20 LFN, 2004**

For the situations under which debentures shall belong to different classes, see **section 183(4) and (5), CAMA Cap. C20 LFN, 2004**

---

**Cases**

On the Statutory powers to appoint a receiver

"The Statutory powers to appoint a receiver and or manager of a company incorporated under CAMA are contained in sections 209 and 389 of the Act. A receiver may be appointed out of court pursuant to section 209(1)(a)-(d) of the Act or by the court pursuant to section 389(1)(a) and

(b) thereof. In respect of debentures, a receiver may be appointed out of court....Where a receiver is appointed out of court he may pursuant to section 391 of CAMA, apply to the court for directions in relation to any particular matter arising in connection with the performance of his function" See ***Nashtex International Limited v. Habib Nigeria Bank Limited*** **(2009)All FWLR Pt 466 1974 at1989**

"Section 209 of the Act relates to an aspect of the operations and management of a company by providing for the appointment of a receiver which allows a debenture holder realize his security or preserve his assets in the company" See ***Nashtex International Limited v. Habib Nigeria Bank Limited*** **(2009) All FWLR Pt 466 1974 at 1990**

## 210. Application of certain sections

Subject to the provisions of this Part of this Act and unless the context otherwise admits, the provisions of sections 146, 147, 151, 153, 156 and 157 of this Act relating to share certificates [1] and transfer[2] of shares[3] shall apply in respect of shares[3] as if "debentures[4]" were substituted for "shares" [3] and "debenture holders"[5] for "shareholders. [6]"

---

**Notes**
**Section 210**

1. "Certificates" see "certificate." It means a document in which a fact is formally attested. See **Garner B. (ed.) Black's Law Dictionary 8 th ed.**
2. "Transfers" see transfer. It means any mode of disposing of or parting with an asset or an interest in an asset. See **Garner B. (ed.) Black's Law Dictionary 8th ed.**
3. "Shares" see "share." It means the interests in a company's share capital of a member who is entitled to share in the capital or income of such company; and except where a distinction between stock and shares is expressed or implied, includes stock. See **Section 567, CAMA Cap. C20 LFN, 2004**
   It means an equity or ownership interest in the corporation or Joint Stock Company. See **Garner B. (ed.) Black's Law Dictionary 8 th ed.**
4. "Debentures" see "debenture." It means a written acknowledgement of indebtedness by the company, setting out the terms and conditions of the indebtedness and includes debenture stock, bonds and any other securities of any company whether constituting a charge on the assets of the company or not. See **Section 567, CAMA Cap. C20 LFN, 2004**
   "Debenture holders" see "debenture" and "holder." Debenture means a written acknowledgement of indebtedness by the company, setting out the terms and conditions of the indebtedness and includes debenture stock, bonds and any other securities of any company whether constituting a charge on the assets of the company or not. **See Section**

**567, CAMA Cap. C20 LFN, 2004** . "Holder" is one who has legal possession of a negotiable instrument and is entitled to receive payment on it. See **Garner B. (ed.) Black's Law Dictionary 8 th ed.**

5. "Shareholders" see "shareholder". It means one who owns or holds a share or shares in a company, especially a corporation. See **Garner B. (ed.) Black's Law Dictionary 8 th ed.**

Cross Reference

On issue of Share certificates, see **section 146, CAMC Cap. C20 LFN 2004**

On the effect of issued share certificates see section 147, **CAMA Cap. C20 LFN, 2004**

On transfer of shares, see section 151, **CAMA Cap. C20 LFN, 2004**

On notice of refusal to register shares transferred, see section 153, **CAMA Cap. C20 LFN, 2004**

On protection of beneficiaries of shares, see section 156, **CAMA Cap. C20 LFN, 2004**

On the issuance of certificate of Corporate Affairs Commission, see section 157, **CAMA Cap. C20 LFN, 2004**

---

**Cases**

On meaning of debenture

"A debenture consists of a debt owed by a company to another secured by a deed which prescribes the condition of the realization of the debt, and it may be created over the fixed or floating assets of the company" See ***UBN v. Tropics Foods*** **(1992) 3NWLR (Pt. 228) 231**

"A debenture is a document which either creates or acknowledges a debt...This obligation is in most cases at the present day, accompanied by some charge or security" See ***Fasakin v. Fasakin*** **(1994) 4 N.W.L.R Pt. 340; pg.620 par. C-E**

---

*PART VIII*

*Meetings and proceedings of companies*

*Statutory meeting*

## 211. Statutory meeting

(1) Every public company[1] shall, within a period of six months from the date of its incorporation[2], hold a general meeting[3] of the members[4] of the company[5] (in this Act referred to as "the statutory meeting.[6]")

(2) The directors[7] shall, at least 21 days before the day on which the statutory meeting[6] is held, forward to every member[4] of the company[5] a copy of the statutory report.[8]

(3) The statutory report[8] shall be certified by not less than two directors[7] or by a director[7] and the secretary[9] of the company[5] and shall state-

(a) the total number of shares[10] allotted, distinguishing shares[10] allotted as fully or partly paid-up otherwise than in cash, and stating in the case of shares[10] partly paid-up, the extent to which they are so paid up, and in either case the consideration for which they have been allotted;

(b) the total amount of cash received by the company[5] in respect of all the shares[10] allotted, distinguished as aforesaid;

(c) the names, addresses and descriptions of the directors[7], auditors,[11] managers,[12] if any, and secretary[9] of the company[5];

(d) the particulars of any pre-incorporation contract together with the particulars of any modification or proposed modification thereon;

(e) any underwriting contract that has not been carried out and the reasons therefor;

(f) the arrears, if any, due on calls from every director;

(g) the particulars of any commission[13] or brokerage[14] paid or to be paid in connection with the issue or sale of shares[10] or debentures[15] to any director[7] or to the manager.[12]

(4) The report shall also contain an abstract of the receipts of the company[5] and of the payments made from them up to a date within seven days of the date of the report, exhibiting under distinctive headings the receipts of the company[5] from shares[10] and debentures[15] and other sources, the payments made from such receipts and particulars concerning the balance remaining in hand, and an account or estimate of the preliminary expenses of the company.[5]

(5) The statutory report[9] shall, so far as it relates to the shares[10] allotted by the company,[5] and to the cash received in respect of such shares[10] and to the receipts and payments of the company[5] on capital account, be certified as correct by the auditors.[11]

(6) The directors [7] shall cause a copy of the statutory report, [9] certified as required by this section, to be delivered to the Commission[16] for registration forthwith after the sending of copies to the members[4] of the company. [5]

(7) The directors [7] shall cause a list, showing the names, descriptions and addresses of the members [4] of the company[5] and the number of shares [10] held by them respectively, to be produced at the commencement of the meeting[17] and to remain open and accessible to any member[4] of the company[5] during the continuance of the statutory meeting. [6]

(8) The members [4] of the company[5] present at the statutory meeting[6] shall be at liberty to discuss any matter relating to the formation of the company, [5] and its commencement of business or arising out of the statutory report. [9]

(9) Any member [14] who wishes a resolution [18] to be passed on any matter arising out of the statutory report [9] shall give further 21 days notice from the date on which the statutory report [9] was received to the company[5] of his intention to propose such a resolution. [18]

(10) The statutory meeting [6] may adjourn from time to time, and at any adjourned meeting [17] any resolution[18] of which notice has been given in accordance with the articles, [19] either before or subsequently to the former meeting, [17] may be passed, and the adjourned meeting[17] shall have the same powers as an original meeting. [17]

---

**Notes**
**Section 211(1)**

1. "Public Company" means any company other than a private company and its memorandum shall state it is a public company. See **Section 24 CAMA Cap. C20 LFN, 2004**
2. "Incorporation" means the formation of a legal corporation. See **Garner B. (ed.) Black's Law Dictionary 8 th ed.**
3. "General meeting" see "Annual meeting" – a yearly meeting to elect or install officers or directors and to conduct other routine organizational business. **Garner B, (ed.) Black's Law Dictionary 8 th ed.**
4. "Members" see "member". It means one of the individuals of whom a deliberative assembly consists and who enjoys the full rights of participating in the organization-including the rights of making, debating and voting on motions- except to the extent that the organization reserves those rights to certain classes of membership. **Garner B. (ed.) Black's Law Dictionary 8th ed.**

It includes the heir, executor, administrator or other personal representative as the case may be, of the member. See **section 567 CAMA Cap. C20 LFN, 2004**

5. "Company" It means a company formed and registered under this Act or, as the case may be, formed and registered in Nigeria before and in existence on the commencement of this Act. See **Section 567, CAMA Cap. C20 LFN, 2004**
6. "Statutory Meeting" means the meeting required to be held by section 211(1) of CAMA. See **Section 567 CAMA Cap. C20 LFN, 2004**

**Section 212(2)**

7. "Directors" See Director. It means a person appointed or elected to sit on a board that manages the affairs of a corporation or other organization by electing and exercising control over its officers. **Garner B, (ed.) Black's Law Dictionary 8th ed.**
   "Director" includes any person occupying the position of director by whatever name called; and includes any person in accordance with whose directions or instructions the directors of the company are accustomed to act. See **Section 567 CAMA Cap. C20 LFN, 2004**
8. "Statutory report" has the meaning assigned to it by section 211(2) of CAMA. **Section 567 CAMA Cap. C20 LFN, 2004**
9. "Secretary" means a corporate officer in charge of official correspondence, minutes of board meetings and records of stock ownership and transfer. See **Garner. B. (ed) Black's Law Dictionary, 8th ed.**

**Section 201(3)**

10. "Shares" see "share." It means the interests in a company's share capital of a member who is entitled to share in the capital or income of such company; and except where a distinction between stock and shares is expressed or implied, includes stock. **Section 567 CAMA Cap. C20 LFN, 2004**
11. "Auditor" means a person or firm, usually an accountant that formally examines an individual or an entity's financial records or status. See **Garner B. (ed.) Black's Law Dictionary 8th ed.**
12. "Manager" means one who has charge of corporation and control of its business, or of its branch establishments, divisions, or departments . **See Garner B. (ed.) Black's Law Dictionary 8 th ed.**
13. "Commission" means a fee paid to an agent or employee for a particular transaction usually as a percentage of the money received from the transaction. See **Garner B., (ed.) Black's Law Dictionary 8 th ed.**
14. "Brokage" means the fee paid to a broker. See **Garner B. (ed.) Black's Law Dictionary 8th ed.**
15. "Debentures" see "debenture" It means a written acknowledgement of indebtedness by the company, setting out the terms and conditions of the indebtedness and includes debenture stock, bonds and any other securities of any company whether constituting a charge on the assets of the company or not. See **Section 567, CAMA Cap. C20 LFN, 2004**
16. "Commission" means Corporate Affairs Commission, established under Section 1 of the Companies and Allied Matters Act. **Section 567, CAMA Cap. C20 LFN, 2004**

17. "Meeting" means the gathering of people to discuss or act on matters in which they have a common interest. See **Garner B., (ed.) Black's Law Dictionary 8th ed.**
18. "Resolution" means a main motion that formally expresses the sense, will or action of a deliberative assembly. **Garner B. (ed.) Black's Law Dictionary 8th ed.**
19. "Articles" means the articles of association of a company, as originally framed or as altered by special resolution including so far as they apply to the regulations contained in table A in the first schedules of the companies Act, 1922 or in that table as altered by any subsequent enactment or reprint of the laws, or in table A in schedule 1 to this Act. See **section 567 CAMA Cap. C20 LFN, 2004**

**Cross Reference**

For the name of company as stated in the memorandum, see **section 29, CAMA Cap. C20 LFN, 2004**

For the provisions relating to the incorporation of companies and incidental matters, see generally **Part II, Chapter 1, CAMA Cap. C20 LFN, 2004.**

For types of general meeting see **Section 213 & Section 215, CAMA Cap. C20 LFN, 2004**

For types of resolution, see **section 233 CAMA Cap. C20 LFN, 2004**

On the appointment of auditors, see **section 357 CAMA Cap. C20 LFN, 2004**

---

**Cases**

"Statutory report deals mainly with the allotment and payment for shares in the company, names and addresses of directors, auditors, managers and the company secretary, particulars of pre-incorporation contract, particulars of brokeage and commission paid, abstracts of receipts and payments made. It is this statutory report together with matters relating to the formation of the company and its commencement of business that the company is expected to discuss at its statutory meeting under section 211(8-9)" See **Agbo JCA, *G.E.B Plc v. Odukwu* (2009) All FWLR Pt. 491 page. 924 at943 D-F**

On the status of pre-incorporation contracts:

The rigid legal status of pre-incorporation contract at common law has been modified in Nigeria to the extent that the pre incorporation contract can be ratified by the company upon incorporation ***See Societe Generale Bank (Nig) Ltd V Societe Generale Favouriser etc (1995) 3 NWLR Pt.384, 497 (CA); (1997) 4 NWLR (pt. 497) 8 (SC)***

The Articles of Association is the contract governing the relationship between shareholders and any infraction of such articles may confer on the shareholder adversely affected a right of action" See ***Attorney General of Lagos State v Eko Hotel Ltd &Oha Ltd ([2001) FWLR page 1996*** *at 2000*

## 212. Non-compliance and penalty

Without prejudice to the provisions of section 408 of this Act, if a company[1] fails to comply with the requirements of section 211 of this Act, the company[1] and any officer[2] in default shall be guilty of an offence and liable to a fine of N50 for every day during which the default continues.

---

**Notes**
**Section 212**

1. "Company" means Corporate Affairs Commission, established under s.1 of the Companies and Allied Matters Act. See **Section 567, CAMA Cap. C20 LFN, 2004**
2. "Officer" means a person who holds an office of trust, authority or command. **Garner B. (ed.) Black's Law Dictionary 8th ed.**
   In relation to a body corporate, it includes a director, manager or secretary. **Section 567 CAMA Cap. C20 LFN, 2004**

Cross Reference
On meaning of offence, see **section 2, Criminal Code C38, LFN 2004.**

---

*General meeting*

## 213. Annual general meeting

(1) Every company[1] shall in each year hold a general meeting[2] as its annual general meeting[2] in addition to any other meetings[3] in that year, and shall specify the meeting[3] as such in the notices calling it; and not more than 15 months shall elapse between the date of one annual general meeting[2] of a company[1] and that of the next:

Provided that-

(a) so long as a company[1] holds its first annual general meeting[2] within 18 months of its incorporation[4] it need not hold it in that year or in the following year;

(b) except for the first annual general meeting[2], the Commission[5] shall have power to extend the time within which any annual general meeting[2] shall be held, by a period not exceeding three months.

(2) If default is made in holding a meeting[3] of a company[1] in accordance with subsection (1) of this section, the Commission,[5] may, on the application of any member[6] of the company[1] call, or direct the calling of, a general meeting[2] of the company[1] and give

such ancillary or consequential directions as the Commission [5] thinks expedient, including directions modifying or supplementing, in relation to the calling, holding and conducting of the meeting, [3] the operation of the company's [1] articles; and it is hereby declared that the directions that may be given under this subsection shall include a direction that one member [6] of the company [1] present in person or by proxy [7] may apply to the court for an order to take a decision which shall bind all the members.

(3) A general meeting [2] held in pursuance of subsection (2) of this section shall, subject to any directions of the Commission, [5] be deemed to be an annual general meeting [2] of the company [1]; but, where a meeting [3] so held is not held in the year in which the default in holding the company's annual general meeting [2] occurred, the meeting so held shall not be treated as the annual general meeting [2] for the year in which it is held unless at that meeting [3] the company [1] resolves that it shall be so treated.

(4) Where a company [1] resolves that a meeting [3] shall be treated as its annual general meeting [2], a copy of the resolution [8] shall, within 15 days after the passing thereof, be filed with the Commission[5].

(5) If default is made in holding a meeting [2] of the company [1] in accordance with subsection (1) of this section, or in complying with any directions of the Commission [5] under subsection (2) thereof, the company [1] and every officer [9] of the company [1] who is in default, shall be guilty of an offence and be liable to a fine of N 500, and if default is made in complying with subsection (4) of this section, the company [1] and every officer [9] of the company [1] who is in default shall be liable to a fine of N25.

---

**Notes**
**Section 213**

1. "Company" means a company formed and registered under this Act or as the case may be, formed and registered in Nigeria before and in existence on the commencement of this Act. See **Section 567, CAMA Cap. C20 LFN, 2004**
2. "General meeting" see "Annual meeting" – a yearly meeting to elect or install officers or directors and to conduct other routine organizational business. **See Garner B. (ed.) Black's Law Dictionary 8 th ed.**

3. "Meeting" means the gathering of people to discuss or act on matters in which they have a common interest. See **Garner B. (ed.) Black's Law Dictionary 8th ed.**
4. "Incorporation" means the formation of a legal corporation. See **Garner B. (ed.) Black's Law Dictionary 8 th ed.**
5. "Commission" means Corporate Affairs Commission, established under Section 1 of the Companies and Allied Matters Act. See **section 567, CAMA Cap. C20 LFN, 2004**
6. "Member" means one of the individuals of whom a deliberative assembly consists and who enjoys the full rights of participating in the organization-including the rights of making, debating and voting on motions- except to the extent that the organization reserves those rights to certain classes of membership. See **Garner B. (ed.) Black's Law Dictionary 8th ed.**
   "Member" includes the heir, executor, administrator or other personal representative, as the case maybe, of the member. See **section 567 CAMA, Cap. C20, LFN,2004.**
7. "Proxy" means one who is authorized to act as a substitute for another; a person who is authorized to vote another's stock shares. See **Garner B. (ed.) Black's Law Dictionary 8 th ed.**
8. "Resolution" means a main motion that formally expresses the sense, will or action of a deliberative assembly. See **Garner B. (ed.) Black's Law Dictionary 8th ed.**
9. "Officer" means a person who holds an office of trust, authority or command. **Garner B. (ed.) Black's Law Dictionary 8 th ed.**
   In relation to a body corporate, officer includes a director, manager or secretary. **Section 567 of CAMA Cap C20 LFN, 2004**

Cross Reference

For types of general meeting see **Section 213 & Section 215, CAMA Cap C20 LFN, 2004**

On entitlement of member of company to attend and vote at meetings, see **Section 230, CAMA Cap. C20, LFN 2004**

---

**Cases**

The decisions of a company are generally taken at the meeting of its members which constitutes its primary organ. But if all the members agree, a decision may be taken even though no formal meeting is held. ***Okeowo v. Migliore (1979) 11 S.C.138.***

**For Further Reading**

On meetings of companies, see, Orojo, J. Ola **Company Law and Practice in Nigeria** 3rd Edition, Mbeyi & Associates (Lagos, Nigeria) 1992. Pp. 273-293.

## 214. Businesses transacted at annual general meeting

All businesses transacted at annual general meetings [1] shall be deemed special business, except declaring a dividend, [2] the presentation of the financial statements and the reports of the directors[3] and auditors, [4] the election of directors [3] in the place of those retiring, the appointment, and the fixing of the remuneration of the auditors[4] and the appointment of the members of the audit committee, which shall be ordinary business.

---

**Notes**
**Section 214**

1. "General meetings" see "Annual meeting" – a yearly meeting to elect or install officers or directors and to conduct other routine organizational business. See **Garner B, (ed.) Black's Law Dictionary 8th ed.**
2. "Dividend" means a portion of a company's earnings or profits distributed pro rata to its shareholders usually in cash or in the form of additional shares. See **Garner B. (ed.) Black's Law Dictionary 8 th ed.**
   It means a proportion of the distributed profits of the company which may be a fixed annual percentage, as in the case of preference shares, or it may be variable according to the prosperity or other circumstances of the company, as in the case of equity shares; See **section 567 CAMA, Cap. C20, LFN 2004.**
3. "Directors" See Director. It means a person appointed or elected to sit on a board that manages the affairs of a corporation or other organization by electing and exercising control over its officers. **Garner B, (ed.) Black's Law Dictionary 8 th ed.**
   "Director" means any person occupying the position of director by whatever name called; and includes any person in accordance with whose directions or instructions the directors of the company are accustomed to act. See **Section 567 CAMA, Cap. C20, LFN 2004.**
4. "Auditors" means a person or firm usually an accountant or an accounting firm that formally examines an individual's or entity's financial records or status. See **Garner B. (ed.) Black's Law Dictionary 8th ed.**

Cross Reference

For types of general meeting see **Section 213 & Section 215, CAMA Cap C20 LFN, 2004**

On declaration of dividends, see **section 379 CAMA Cap. C20 LFN 2004**

---

**Cases**

Generally companies speak or express their decisions through resolutions, which must be validly passed. No member of a company has a right to unilaterally commit the company on any matter without its consent and approval. Let me emphatically say that no member of a company is allowed to wake up one morning and sell off the company. ***New Resources Int'l Ltd. & Anor. v. Ejike Oranusi (2010) LPELR-CA/L/461/08.***

Dividends are the payment made out of profits to shareholders of a company from time to time. See ***Kotoye v. Saraki (1994) 7 NWLR. 357, 414***

*Extraordinary general meeting*

## 215. Extraordinary general meeting

(1) The board of directors [1] may convene an extraordinary general meeting[2] whenever they deem fit, and if at any time there are not within Nigeria sufficient directors [3] capable of acting to form a quorum, any director [3] may convene an extraordinary general meeting.[2]

(2) An extraordinary general meeting [2] of a company[4] may be requisitioned by any member[5] or members[5] of the company[4] holding at the date of the requisition not less than one tenth of the paid up capital[6] of the company[4] as at the date of the deposit carrying the right of voting, or in the case of a company [4] not having a share capital,[7] members[5] of the company[4] representing not less than one tenth of the total voting rights of all the members [5] having at the said date a right to vote[7] at general meetings[2] of the company,[4] and the directors[1] shall on receipt of the requisition forthwith proceed duly to convene an extraordinary general meeting [1] of the company[4], notwithstanding anything in its articles[8]

(3) The requisition shall state the objects of the meeting [9], and be signed by the requisitionists and deposited at the registered office of the company[4], and the requisition may consist of several documents in like form each signed by one or more requisitionists.

(4) If the directors [3] do not within 21 days from the date of the deposit of the requisition proceed duly to convene a meeting [9], the requisitionists, or anyone or more of them representing more than one half of the total voting[7] rights of all of them, may themselves convene a meeting:[10]

Provided that any meeting[9] so convened shall not be held after the expiration of three months from that date.

(5) A meeting[9] convened under this section by a requisitionist or requisitionists shall be convened in the same manner, as nearly

as possible, as that in which meetings [10] are to be convened by directors.[3]

(6) Any reasonable expenses incurred by the requisitionist or requisitionists by reason of the failure of the directors [3] duly to convene a meeting[9], shall be repaid to the requisitionists by the company,[4]

(7) For the purpose of this section the directors [3] shall, in the case of a meeting[9] at which a resolution [10] is to be proposed as a special resolution[11], be deemed not to have duly convened the meeting if they do not give such notice as is required by section 217 of this Act.

(8) All businesses transacted at an extraordinary general meeting[2] shall be deemed special.

---

**Notes**
**Section 215**

1. "Board of directors" mean persons duly appointed by the company to direct and manage the business of the company. See **Garner. B. (ed) Black's Law Dictionary 8th ed.**
2. "Extraordinary General Meeting" means a meeting that is not a regular meeting. A meeting called for a special purpose. See **Garner B, (ed) Black's Law Dictionary 8th ed**
3. "Directors" see "director." Director means any person occupying the position of director by whatever name called; and includes any person in accordance with whose directions or instructions the directors of the company are accustomed to act. See **Section 567 CAMA, Cap. C20, LFN 2004.**
4. "Company" means a company formed and registered under this Act or, as the case may be, formed and registered in Nigeria before and in existence on the commencement of this Act. See section **567 CAMA, Cap. C20, LFN 2004.**
5. "Member" means one of the individuals of whom a deliberative assembly consists and who enjoys the full rights of participating in the organization-including the rights of making, debating and voting on motions- except to the extent that the organization reserves those rights to certain classes of membership. See **Garner B. (ed.) Black's Law Dictionary 8th ed.**
   "Member" includes the heir, executor, administrator or other personal representative, as the case maybe, of the member. See **section 567 CAMA, Cap. C20, LFN, 2004.**
6. "Paid up Capital" means that portion of the issued share capital of a company that has been paid for in cash or valuable consideration other than cash. See **Garner, B. (ed) Black's Law Dictionary, 8th ed.**

7. "Share Capital" means any of the units of equal value into which a company is divided and sold to raise money. People who owns shares receives part of the company profit. See **Oxford Advanced Learners Dictionary, 6th Edition**
"Share Capital:" See Capital; means a fund representing the nominal value of shares issued by a registered company . **See Martins, E. (ed) Oxford Dictionary of Law 4th ed.**
8. "Articles" means the articles of association of a company, as originally framed or as altered by special resolution, including so far as they apply to the regulations contained in Table A in the First Schedules of the Companies Act, 1922 or in that Table as altered by any subsequent enactment or reprint of the laws, or in Table A in the First Schedule to this Act. See **Section 567, CAMA, Cap. C20, LFN 2004.**
9. "Meeting" means the gathering of people to discuss or act on matters in which they have a common interest. See **Garner B. (ed.) Black's Law Dictionary 8th ed.**
10. "Resolution" means a main motion that formally expresses the sense, will or action of a deliberative assembly. See **Garner B. (ed.) Black's Law Dictionary 8th ed.**
11. "Special resolution" is a resolution that has been passed by not less than three fourths of the votes cast by such members of the company as, being entitled to do so, vote in person or by proxy at a general meeting of which 21 days' notice, specifying the intention to propose the resolution as a special resolution, has been duly given. See **Section 233 CAMA, Cap. C20, LFN 2004.**

**Cross Reference**

On the requirement that the registered office of a company be situate in Nigeria, see **section 27 CAMA, Cap. C 20, LFN 2004**

On types of General meeting to be held by a Company, see **sections 211, 213 and 215 CAMA Cap. C20 LFN 2004**

On the conduct of extraordinary general meetings, see **section 215 CAMA Cap. C20 LFN 2004**

On the form and content of the Articles of Association of a Company , see **section 34, CAMA, Cap. C20, LFN 2004.**

On length of notice required for meetings, see **section 217 CAMA, Cap. C20, LFN 2004**

On types of resolution, see **section 233 CAMA, Cap. C20, LFN 2004.**

On quorum of directors see **section 264 CAMA, Cap. C20, LFN 2004.**

---

**Cases**

A director is a person appointed or elected according to Law, authorized to manage and direct the affairs of a corporation or company. ***Olufosoye v. Fakorede*** **(1993) 1 N.W.L.R 947.** See also ***Longe v. First Bank Nigeria Plc*** **(2006) 3 N.W.L.R 228 at 270.**

**For Further Reading** on General meeting, Extraordinary general meeting, Notice of meetings, Voting and Resolutions, see, Orojo, J. Ola **Company Law and Practice in Nigeria** 3rd Edition, Mbeyi & Associates (Lagos, Nigeria) 1992, Ogbuanya C.S. Nelson **Essentials of Corporate Law Practice in Nigeria** Novena Publishers Limited 2012

## 216. Place of meeting

All statutory[1] and annual general meetings[2] shall be held in Nigeria.

---

**Notes**
**Section 216**

1. "Statutory Meeting" means the meeting required to be held by section 211(1) of CAMA. See **Section 567 CAMA Cap. C20 LFN, 2004.**
2. "Annual general meeting" means a yearly meeting to elect or install officers or directors and to conduct other routine organizational business. **See Garner B, (ed) Black's Law Dictionary 8 th ed.**
   "Annual general meeting" means a general meeting held yearly and specified as such. See **section 213 CAMA Cap. C20 LFN, 2004.**

**Cross Reference**
On types of General meeting to be held by a Company, see **sections 211, 213 and 215 CAMA Cap. C20 LFN 2004**

---

*Notice of meetings*

## 217. Length of notice for calling meetings

(1) The notice required for all types of general meetings [1] from the commencement of this Act shall be 21 days from the date on which the notice was sent out.

(2) A general meeting[1] of a company[2] shall, notwithstanding that it is called by a shorter notice than that specified in subsection (1) of this section, be deemed to have been duly called if it is so agreed in the case of-

(a) a meeting[1] called as the annual general meeting [3], by all the members[4] entitled to attend and vote thereat; and

(b) any other general meeting [1], by a majority in number of the members[4] having a right to attend and vote at the meeting[1], being a majority together holding not less than 95 per cent in nominal value of the shares [5] giving a right to attend and vote at the meeting [1] or, in the case of a company[2] not having a share capital [6], together representing not less than 95 per cent of the total voting rights at that meeting [1] of all the members [4].

---

**Notes**

**Section 217(1)**

1. "Meeting(s)" means an assembling of a number of persons for the purpose of discussing and acting upon some matter or matters in which they have a common interest. See **Garner B. (ed) Black's Law Dictionary 8th ed**

**Section 217(2)**

2. "Company" means a corporation - or, less commonly, an association, partnership, or union that carries on a commercial or industrial enterprise. **See Garner B, (ed) Black's Law Dictionary 8 th ed.**
   "Company" means a company formed and registered under this Act or, as the case may be, formed and registered in Nigeria before and in existence on the commencement of this Act. See **section 567 CAMA, Cap. C20, LFN 2004**
3. "Annual general meeting" means a yearly meeting to elect or install officers or directors and to conduct other routine organizational business. **Garner B. (ed) Black's Law Dictionary 8 th ed.**
   "Annual general meeting" means a general meeting held yearly and specified as such. See **section 213 CAMA Cap. C20 LFN, 2004.**
4. "Member" means one of the individuals of whom a deliberative assembly consists and who enjoys the full rights of participating in the organization-including the rights of making, debating and voting on motions- except to the extent that the organization reserves those rights to certain classes of membership. See **Garner B. (ed.) Black's Law Dictionary 8th ed.**
   "Member" includes the heir, executor, administrator or other personal representative, as the case may be, of the member. See **Section 567 CAMA Cap. C20, LFN 2004.**
5. "Shares" means the interests in a company's share capital of a member who is entitled to share in the capital or income of such company; and except where a distinction between stock and shares is expressed or implied, includes stock. See **section 567 CAMA, Cap. C20, LFN 2004**
6. "Share Capital" See "capital." It means a fund representing the nominal value of shares issued by a registered company. See **Martins E. (ed.) Oxford Dictionary of Law 4th ed.**

Cross Reference

On types of General meeting to be held by a Company, see **sections 211, 213 and 215 CAMA Cap. C20 LFN 2004**

On procedure of voting at general meetings see **section 224 CAMA Cap. C20 LFN 2004**

---

**For Further Reading**

On General meeting, Extraordinary general meeting, Notice of meetings, Voting and Resolutions, see, Orojo, J. Ola **Company Law and Practice in Nigeria** 3rd Edition, Mbeyi & Associates (Lagos, Nigeria) 1992, Ogbuanya C.S. Nelson **Essentials of Corporate Law Practice in Nigeria** Novena Publishers Limited 2012

## 218. Contents of Notice

(1) The notice of a meeting [1] shall specify the place, date and time of the meeting[1], and the general nature of the business to be transacted thereat in sufficient detail to enable those to whom it is given to decide whether to attend or not, and where the meeting [1] is to consider a special resolution [2], shall set out the terms of the resolution[3].

(2) In the case of notice of an annual general meeting [4], a statement that the purpose is to transact the ordinary business of an annual general meeting[4] shall be deemed to be a sufficient specification that the business is for the declaration of dividends [5], presentation of the financial statements, reports of the directors [6] and auditors[7], the election of directors [6] in the place of those retiring, the fixing of the remuneration of the auditors [7] and, if the requirements of sections 362 and 363 of this Act are duly complied with, the removal and election of auditors [7] and directors [6].

(3) No business may be transacted at any general meeting [1] unless notice of it has been duly given.

(4) In every case in which a member [8] is entitled, pursuant to section 230 of this Act, to appoint a proxy [9] to attend and vote instead of him, the notice shall contain with reasonable prominence, a statement that the member[8] has the right to appoint a proxy [9] to attend and vote instead of him and that the proxy [9] need not be a member[8] of the company [10], and if default is made in complying with this subsection as respects any meeting [1], every officer [11] of the company[10] who is in default shall be guilty of an offence and liable to a fine not exceeding N500.

(5) An error or omission in a notice with respect to the place, date, time or general nature of the business of a meeting [1] shall not invalidate the meeting,[1] unless the officer[11] of the company [10] responsible for the error or omission acted in bad faith or failed to exercise due care and diligence:

Provided that in the case of accidental error or omission, the officer[11] responsible shall effect the necessary correction either before or during the meeting [1].

---

**Notes**

**Section 218(1)**

1. "Meeting" means an assembling of a number of persons for the purpose of discussing and acting upon some matter or matters in which they have a common interest. See **Garner B. (ed) Black's Law Dictionary 8 th ed.**
2. "Special resolution" means resolution passed by not less than three-fourths of the votes by such members of the company as being entitled to do so, vote by person or in proxy at a general meeting of which 21days notice, specifying the intention to propose the resolution is a special resolution, has been duly given. See **Section 233(2) CAMA, Cap. C20, LFN 2004**
3. "Resolution" means a formal expression of the opinion or will of an official body or a public assembly, adopted by vote as a legislative resolution. See **Garner .B. (ed) Black's Law Dictionary, 8 th ed.**
4. "Annual general meeting" means a yearly meeting to elect or install officers or directors and to conduct other routine organizational business. See **Garner B, (ed) Black's Law Dictionary 8 th ed.**
5. "Dividend" means a portion of a company's earnings or profits distributed prorate to its shareholders, usually in the form of cash or additional shares **Garner B. (ed) Black's Law Dictionary 8 th ed**.
   It means a proportion of the distributed profits of the company which may be a fixed annual percentage, as in the case of preference shares, or it may be variable according to the prosperity or other circumstances of the company, as in the case of equity shares; See s **ection 567 CAMA, Cap. C20, LFN 2004.**
6. "Director" includes any person occupying the position of director by whatever name called; and includes any person in accordance with whose directions or instructions the directors of the company are accustomed to act. See **section 567 CAMA, Cap. C20, LFN 2004.**
7. "Auditor" means a person or firm, usually an accountant that formally examines an individual or an entity's financial records or status. See **Garner B. (ed) Black's Law Dictionary 8 th ed.**

**Section 218(4)**

8. "Member" includes the heir, executor, administrator or other personal representative, as the case may be, of the member. See **section 567 CAMA Cap. C20, LFN 2004.**
9. "Proxy" means one who is authorized to act as a substitute for another; a person who is authorized to vote another's stock shares. See **Garner B. ed. Black's Law Dictionary 8th Ed** .
10. "Company" means a corporation - or, less commonly, an association, partnership, or union that carries on a commercial or industrial enterprise. See **Garner B, (ed) Black's Law Dictionary 8 th ed.**

"Company" means a company formed and registered under this Act or, as the case may be, formed and registered in Nigeria before and in existence on the commencement of this Act. See **section 567 CAMA, Cap. C20, LFN 2004.**

11. "Officer" means a person who holds an office of trust, authority or command. **See Garner B. (ed) Black's Law Dictionary, 8 th ed.** "Officer" in relation to a body corporate, includes a director, manager or secretary; **Section 567 CAMA, Cap. C20, LFN 2004.**

Cross Reference

On types of General meeting to be held by a Company, see **sections 211, 213 and 215 CAMA Cap. C20 LFN 2004**

On meaning of Offence, see **section 2, Criminal Code C38, LFN 2004.**

On declaration of dividends, see **section 379 CAMA Cap. C20 LFN 2004**

**Cases**

Dividends are the payment made out of profits to shareholders of a company from time to time. See ***Kotoye v. Saraki (1994) 7 NWLR. 357, 414***

**For Further Reading**

On General meeting, Extraordinary general meeting, Notice of meetings, Voting and Resolutions, see, Orojo, J. Ola **Company Law and Practice in Nigeria** 3rd Edition, Mbeyi & Associates (Lagos, Nigeria) 1992.
Ogbuanya C.S. Nelson **Essentials of Corporate Law Practice in Nigeria** Novena Publishers Limited 2012

## 219. Persons entitled to notice

(1) The following persons shall be entitled to receive notice of a general meeting [1]-

(a) every member [2];

(b) every person upon whom the ownership of a share [3] devolves by reason of his being a legal representative, receiver[4] or a trustee [5] in bankruptcy[6] of a member [2];

(c) every director [7] of the company [8];

(d) every auditor [9] for the time being of the company [8]; and

(e) the secretary [10].

(2) No other person shall be entitled to receive notices of general meetings[1].

**Notes**
**Section 219**

1. "Meeting" means an assembling of a number of persons for the purpose of discussing and acting upon some matter or matters in which they have a common interest. **See Garner B, (ed) Black's Law Dictionary 8 th ed.**
2. "Member" includes the heir, executor, administrator or other personal representative, as the case may be, of the member. See **Section 567 CAMA Cap. C20, LFN 2004.**
3. "Shares" means the interests in a company's share capital of a member who is entitled to share in the capital or income of such company; and except where a distinction between stock and shares is expressed or implied, includes stock. See **Section 567 CAMA, Cap. C20, LFN 2004**
4. "Receiver" means a disinterested person appointed by a court, or by a corporation or other person, for the protection or collection of property that is the subject of diverse claims. See **Garner B, (ed) Black's Law Dictionary 8th ed.**

   A receiver includes a manager. See **section 567 CAMA Cap. C20, LFN 2004.**
5. "Trustee" means one who having legal title to property holds it in trust for the benefit of another and owes a fiduciary duty to that beneficiary. See **Garner B, (ed) Black's Law Dictionary 8 th ed.**
6. "Bankruptcy" means a statutory procedure by which a (usu. Insolvent) debtor obtains financial relief and undergoes judicially supervised reorganization or liquidation of the debtors assets for the benefit of the creditor. See **Garner B, (ed) Black's Law Dictionary 8 th ed**.
7. "Director" includes any person occupying the position of director by whatever name called; and includes any person in accordance with whose directions or instructions the directors of the company are accustomed to act. See **Section 567 CAMA, Cap. C20, LFN 2004.**
8. "Company" means a corporation - or, less commonly, an association, partnership, or union that carries on a commercial or industrial enterprise. **Garner B (ed) Black's Law Dictionary 8 th ed.**

   "Company" or "existing company" means a company formed and registered under this Act or, as the case may be, formed and registered in Nigeria before and in existence on the commencement of this Act. **Section 567 CAMA, Cap. C20, LFN 2004.**
9. "Auditor" means a person or firm, usually an accountant that formally examines an individual or an entity's financial records or status. See **Garner B, (ed) Black's Law Dictionary 8 th ed.**
10. "Secretary" means an officer charged with the direction and management of that part of the business of the company which is concerned with keeping records, the official correspondence, with giving and receiving notices, countersigning documents, e.t.c. See **Garner B. (ed) Black's Law Dictionary 8th ed**

Cross Reference

On types of General meeting to be held by a Company, see **sections 211, 213 and 215 CAMA Cap. C20 LFN 2004**

**Cases**

A receiver has duty to stop business, collect the debts and release the assets. But a manager has power to continue a business or a going concern: ***Ponson Enterprise Nig. Ltd v. Njigha (2001) FWLR pt. 61 p. 3***

**For Further Reading**
On General meeting, Extraordinary general meeting, Notice of meetings, Voting and Resolutions, see, Orojo, J. Ola **Company Law and Practice in Nigeria** 3rd Edition, Mbeyi & Associates (Lagos, Nigeria) 1992.
Ogbuanya C.S. Nelson **Essentials of Corporate Law Practice in Nigeria** Novena Publishers Limited 2012

## 220. Service of Notice

(1) A notice may be given by the company [1] to any member [2] either personally or by sending it by post to him or to his registered address, or (if he has no registered address within Nigeria) to the address, if any, supplied by him to the company [1] for the giving of notice to him.

(2) Where a notice is sent by post, service of the notice shall be deemed to be effected by properly addressing, prepaying, and posting a letter containing the notice, and to have been effected in the case of a notice of a meeting at the expiration of seven days after the letter containing the same is posted, and in any other case at the time at which the letter would be delivered in the ordinary course of post.

(3) A notice may be given by the company [1] to the joint holders of a share [3] by giving the notice to the joint holder first named in the register of members [2] in respect of the share [3].

(4) A notice may be given by the company [1] to the persons entitled to a share [3] in consequence of the death or bankruptcy [4] of a member[2] by sending it through the post in a prepaid letter addressed to them by name, or by the title of representatives of the deceased, or trustee[5] of the bankrupt[4], or by any like description, at the address, if any, within Nigeria supplied for the purpose by the person claiming to be so entitled, or (until such an address has been so supplied) by giving the notice in any manner in which the same might have been given if the death or bankruptcy [4] had not occurred.

(5) "Registered address" means, in the case of a member [2], any address supplied by him to the company [1] for the giving of notice to him.

**Notes**

**Section 220(1)**

1. "Company" means a corporation - or, less commonly, an association, partnership, or union that carries on a commercial or industrial enterprise. **See Garner B (ed) Black's Law Dictionary 8 th ed.** "Company" or "existing company" means a company formed and registered under this Act or, as the case may be, formed and registered in Nigeria before and in existence on the commencement of this Act. See **Section 567 CAMA, Cap. C20, LFN 2004.**
2. "Member" includes the heir, executor, administrator or other personal representative, as the case may be, of the member. Se **Section 567 CAMA Cap. C20, LFN 2004.**
3. "Shares" means the interests in a company's share capital of a member who is entitled to share in the capital or income of such company; and except where a distinction between stock and shares is expressed or implied, includes stock. See **Section 567 CAMA, Cap. C20, LFN 2004.**

**Section 220(3)**

4. "Bankruptcy" means a statutory procedure by which a (usually Insolvent) debtor obtains financial relief and undergoes judicially supervised reorganization or liquidation of the debtors assets for the benefit of the creditor. See **Garner B, (ed) Black's Law Dictionary 8 th ed.**
5. "Trustee" means one who having legal title to property holds it in trust for the benefit of another and owes a fiduciary duty to that beneficiary. See **Garner B, (ed) Black's Law Dictionary 8 th ed.**

**Cross Reference**

On obligation of a company to maintain a register of members, see **section 83 CAMA Cap. C20, LFN 2004**

As to when a debtor commits an act of bankruptcy, see **section 1, Bankruptcy Act Cap. B2 LFN 2004**

**Cases**

Upon registration, the subscribers are deemed to have agreed to become members and their names must be put in the register of members.See ***Ezeonwu V Onyechi (1996) 2 SCNJ 250***

**For Further Reading**

On General meeting, Extraordinary general meeting, Notice of meetings, Voting and Resolutions, see, Orojo, J. Ola **Company Law and Practice in Nigeria** 3rd Edition, Mbeyi & Associates (Lagos, Nigeria) 1992.

Ogbuanya C.S. Nelson **Essentials of Corporate Law Practice in Nigeria** Novena Publishers Limited 2012

## 221. Failure to give notice

(1) Failure to give notice of any meeting [1] to a person entitled to receive it shall invalidate the meeting [1] unless such failure is an

accidental omission on the part of the person or persons giving the notice.

(2) Failure to give notice to a person entitled to it due to a misrepresentation or misinterpretation of the provisions of this Act, or of the articles [2], shall not amount to an accidental omission for the purposes of the foregoing subsection.

---

**Notes**
**Section 221(1)**

1. "Meeting(s)" means an assembling of a number of persons for the purpose of discussing and acting upon some matter or matters in which they have a common interest. See **Garner B (ed) Black's Law Dictionary 8th ed**
2. **Section 221(2)**"Articles" means the articles of association of a company, as originally framed or as altered by special resolution including so far as they apply to the regulations contained in Table A I the First Schedules of the Companies Act 1922 or in that Table as altered by any subsequent enactment or reprint of the laws, or in Table A in Schedule 1. See **section 567 CAMA Cap. C20, LFN 2004**

**Cross Reference**

On Content of a Notice for meetings, see **section 218 CAMA Cap. C20, LFN 2004**

---

**For Further Reading**

On General meeting, Extraordinary general meeting, Notice of meetings, Voting and Resolutions, see, Orojo, J. Ola **Company Law and Practice in Nigeria** 3rd Edition, Mbeyi & Associates (Lagos, Nigeria) 1992, Ogbuanya C.S. Nelson **Essentials of Corporate Law Practice in Nigeria** Novena Publishers Limited 2012_

## 222. Additional notice

In addition to the notice required to be given to those entitled to receive it in accordance with the provisions of this Act, every public company[1] shall, at least 21 days before any general meeting [2], advertise a notice of such meeting [2] in at least two daily newspapers.

---

**Notes**
**Section 222**

1. "Public Company" is any company other than a private company and its memorandum states that it is a public company. See **section 24 CAMA Cap. C20, LFN 2004.**

2. "Meeting(s)" means an assembling of a number of persons for the purpose of discussing and acting upon some matter or matters in which they have a common interest. See **Garner B. (ed) Black's Law Dictionary 8th ed**

Cross Reference

On types of meeting to be held by a Company, see **sections 211, 213 and 215 CAMA Cap. C20 LFN 2004**

---

**For Further Reading**

On General meeting, Extraordinary general meeting, Notice of meetings, Voting and Resolutions, see, Orojo, J. Ola **Company Law and Practice in Nigeria** 3rd Edition, Mbeyi & Associates (Lagos, Nigeria) 1992.

Ogbuanya C.S. Nelson **Essentials of Corporate Law Practice in Nigeria** Novena Publishers Limited 2012

## 223. Power of court to order meetings

(1) If for any reason it is impracticable to call a meeting [1] of a company[2] or of the board of directors [3] in any manner in which meetings[1] of that company[2] or board[3] may be called, or to conduct the meeting[1] of the company[2] or board[3] in the manner prescribed by the articles[4] or this Act, the court [5] may, either of its own motion or on the application of any director[6] of the company[2] or of any member[7] of the company[2] who would be entitled to vote at the meeting,[1] in the case of the meeting [1] of the company[2], and of any director[6] of the company[2], in case of the meeting [1] of the board[3], order a meeting[1] of the company[2] or board[3], as the case may be, to be called, held and conducted in such manner as the court [5] thinks fit, and where any such order is made, may give such ancillary or consequential directions as it thinks expedient.

(2) It is hereby declared that the directions that may be given under subsection (1) of this section shall include a direction that one member[7] of the company[2] present in person or by proxy [8] in the case of a meeting[1] of the company[2], and one director [6] in the case of the board[3] may, apply to the court [5] for an order to take a decision which shall bind all the members [7].

(3) Any meeting[1] called, held and conducted in accordance with an order under subsection (1) of this section, shall for all purposes be deemed to be a meeting [1] of the company[2] or of the board of directors [3] duly called, held and conducted.

---

**Notes**

**Section 223(1)**

1. "Meeting" means an assembling of a number of persons for the purpose of discussing and acting upon some matter or matters in which they have a common interest. See **Garner B. (ed) Black's Law Dictionary 8 th ed.**
2. "Company" means a corporation - or, less commonly, an association, partnership, or union that carries on a commercial or industrial enterprise. **Garner B, (ed) Black's Law Dictionary 8 th ed.** "Company" or "existing company" means a company formed and registered under this Act or, as the case may be, formed and registered in Nigeria before and in existence on the commencement of this Act. **Section 567 CAMA, Cap. C20, LFN 2004.**
3. "Board of directors" means persons duly appointed by the company to direct and manage the business of the company. See **Garner. B. (ed) Black's Law Dictionary 8th ed.**
4. "Articles" means the articles of association of a company, as originally framed or as altered by special resolution including so far as they apply to the regulations contained in Table A I the First Schedules of the Companies Act 1922 or in that Table as altered by any subsequent enactment or reprint of the laws, or in Table A in Schedule 1. See **section 567 CAMA Cap. C20, LFN 2004.**
5. "Court" used in relation to a company, means the Federal High Court, and to the extent to which application may be made to it as; court includes the Court of Appeal and the Supreme Court of Nigeria. See **Section 567 CAMA Cap. C20, LFN 2004.**
6. "Director" includes any person occupying the position of director by whatever name called; and includes any person in accordance with whose directions or instructions the directors of the company are accustomed to act. See **Section 567 CAMA, Cap. C20, LFN 2004.**
7. "Member" includes the heir, executor, administrator or other personal representative, as the case may be, of the member; **Section 567 CAMA Cap. C20, LFN 2004**

**Cross Reference**

On types of meeting to be held by a Company, see **sections 211, 213 and 215 CAMA Cap. C20 LFN 2004**

On establishment and jurisdiction of the Federal High Court, see **sections 249&251, Constitution of the Federal Republic of Nigeria, 199(as amended).**

---

**For Further Reading**

On General meeting, Extraordinary general meeting, Notice of meetings, Voting and Resolutions, see, Orojo, J. Ola **Company Law and Practice in Nigeria** 3rd Edition, Mbeyi & Associates (Lagos, Nigeria) 1992, Ogbuanya C.S. Nelson **Essentials of Corporate Law Practice in Nigeria** Novena Publishers Limited 2012

*Voting*

## 224. Procedure of voting

(1) At any general meeting [1], a resolution [2] put to the vote shall be decided on a show of hands,
unless a poll is (before or on the declaration of the result of the show of hands) demanded by-

(a) the chairman [3], where he is a shareholder [4] or a proxy [5];
(b) at least three members [6] present in person or by proxy [5];
(c) any member [6] or members [6] present in person or by proxy [5] and representing not less than one tenth of the total voting rights of all the members [6] having the right to vote at the meeting [7]; or
(d) any member [6] or members [6] holding shares [8] in the company [9] conferring a right to vote at the meeting [7] being shares [8] on which an aggregate sum has been paid up equal to not less than one tenth of the total sum paid up on all the shares [8] conferring that right.

(2) Unless a poll is so demanded, a declaration by the chairman [3] that a resolution [2] has on a show of hands been carried or carried unanimously, or by a particular majority, or lost, and an entry to that effect in the book containing the minutes [10] of the proceedings of the company [9], shall be conclusive evidence of the fact, without proof of the number or proportion of the votes recorded in favour of, or against, the resolution [2].

---

**Notes**
**Section 224(1)**

1. "Meeting" means an assembling of a number of persons for the purpose of discussing and acting upon some matter or matters in which they have a common interest.See **Garner B, (ed) Black's Law Dictionary 8 th ed.**
2. "Resolution" means a formal expression of the opinion or will of an official body or a public assembly, adopted by vote as a legislative resolution. See **Garner .B,(ed) Black's Law Dictionary, 8 th ed.**
3. "Chairman" means a deliberative assembly's presiding officer. See **Garner .B,(ed) Black's Law Dictionary, 8 th ed.**
4. "Shareholder" means one who owns or holds a share or shares in a company especially a corporation. **Garner .B,(ed) Black's Law Dictionary, 8 th ed.**
5. "Proxy" means one who is authorized to act as a substitute for another; a person who is authorized to vote another's stock shares. See **Garner B. ed. Black's Law Dictionary 8th Ed.**
6. "Member" includes the heir, executor, administrator or other personal representative, as the case may be, of the member. See **section 567 CAMA Cap. C20, LFN 2004.**

7. "Meeting(s)" means an assembling of a number of persons for the purpose of discussing and acting upon some matter or matters in which they have a common interest. See **Garner B, (ed) Black's Law Dictionary 8th ed.**
8. "Share" means the interests in a company's share capital of a member who is entitled to share in the capital or income of such company; and except where a distinction between stock and shares is expressed or implied, includes stock. See **Section 567 CAMA Cap. C20, LFN 2004.**
9. "Company" means a corporation - or, less commonly, an association, partnership, or union that carries on a commercial or industrial enterprise. See **Garner B, (ed) Black's Law Dictionary 8 th ed.**
"Company" or "existing company" means a company formed and registered under this Act or, as the case may be, formed and registered in Nigeria before and in existence on the commencement of this Act. See **Section 567 CAMA, Cap. C20, LFN 2004.**

**Section 224(2)**

10. "Minutes" means notes or records of business transacted at a meeting. See **Sheila Bone, (ed) Osborn's Concise Law Dictionary, 9 th ed.**

**Cross Reference**

On types of meeting to be held by a Company, see **sections 211, 213 and 215 CAMA Cap. C20 LFN 2004**

On Powers and duties of a chairman at the general meeting, see **section 240 CAMA Cap. C20, LFN 2004**

For the definition, capacity of, rights and obligations of Members of a Company, see **Part IV of CAMA, Cap C20, LFN, 2004**

---

**For Further Reading**

On General meeting, Extraordinary general meeting, Notice of meetings, Voting and Resolutions, see, Orojo, J. Ola Company Law and Practice in Nigeria 3rd Edition, Mbeyi & Associates (Lagos, Nigeria) 1992, Ogbuanya C.S. Nelson **Essentials of Corporate Law Practice in Nigeria** Novena Publishers Limited 2012

## 225. Right to demand poll

(1) Any provision contained in a company [1]'s articles [2] shall be void in so far as it would have the effect either of-

(a) excluding the right to demand a poll [3] at a general meeting [4] on any question other than the election of the chairman [5] of the meeting[4] or the adjournment of the meeting [4]; or

(b) making ineffective a demand for a poll [3] on any such question which is made by any of the persons mentioned in section 224 of this Act.

(2) The instrument appointing a proxy [6] to vote at a meeting [4] of a company[1] shall be deemed also to confer authority to demand

or join in demanding a poll, [3] and for the purposes of subsection (1) of this section, a demand by a person as proxy [6] for a member [7] shall be the same as a demand by the member. [7]

(3) Notwithstanding section 224 of this Act and subsections (1) and (2) of this section, there shall be no right to demand a poll [3] on the election of members [7] of the audit committee [8] under section 359 of this Act.

**Notes**

**Section 225(1)**

1. "Company" means a corporation - or, less commonly, an association, partnership, or union that carries on a commercial or industrial enterprise. See **Garner B, (ed) Black's Law Dictionary 8 th ed.**"Company" or "existing company" means a company formed and registered under this Act or, as the case may be, formed and registered in Nigeria before and in existence on the commencement of this Act. **Section 567 CAMA Cap. C20, LFN 2004**
2. "Articles" means the articles of association of a company, as originally framed or as altered by special resolution including so far as they apply to the regulations contained in Table A I the First Schedules of the Companies Act 1922 or in that Table as altered by any subsequent enactment or reprint of the laws, or in Table A in Schedule 1. See **section 567 CAMA Cap. C20, LFN 2004.**
3. "Poll" means taking a vote on election or on a motion. See **Sheila Bone, (ed) Osborn's Concise Law Dictionary, 9 th ed.**
4. "Meeting" means an assembling of a number of persons for the purpose of discussing and acting upon some matter or matters in which they have a common interest. **Garner B. (ed) Black's Law Dictionary 8 th ed.**
5. "Chairman" means a deliberative assembly's presiding officer **Garner B. (ed) Black's Law Dictionary, 8 th ed.**

**Section 225(2)**

6. "Proxy" means one who is authorized to act as a substitute for another; a person who is authorized to vote another's stock shares. **Garner B. ed. Black's Law Dictionary 8th ed**.
7. "Member" includes the heir, executor, administrator or other personal representative, as the case may be, of the member; **Section 567 CAMA Cap. C20, LFN 2004.**

**Section 225(3)**

8. "Audit Committee" means a committee appointed by the board of an organization especially a corporation to oversee the financial reporting process, select an independent auditor and receive the audit. See **Garner B. (ed) Black's Law Dictionary 8 th ed.**

**Cross Reference**

On types of meeting to be held by a Company, see **sections 211, 213 and 215 CAMA Cap. C20 LFN 2004**

On Powers and duties of a chairman at the general meeting, see **section 240 CAMA Cap. C20, LFN 2004**

For the definition, capacity of, rights and obligations of Members of a Company, see **Part IV of CAMA, Cap C20, LFN, 2004**

**For Further Reading**

On General meeting, Extraordinary general meeting, Notice of meetings, Voting and Resolutions, see, Orojo, J. Ola **Company Law and Practice in Nigeria** 3rd Edition, Mbeyi & Associates (Lagos, Nigeria) 1992, Ogbuanya C.S. Nelson **Essentials of Corporate Law Practice in Nigeria** Novena Publishers Limited 2012

## 226. Voting on a poll

(1) On a poll [1] taken at a meeting [2] of a company [3], or a meeting [2] of any class of members [4] of a company [3], a member [4] entitled to more than one vote need not, if he votes, use all his votes or cast all the votes he uses in the same way.

(2) Except as provided in subsection (4) of this section, if a poll [1] is duly demanded, it shall be taken in such manner as the chairman [5] directs, and the result of the poll shall be deemed to be the resolution [6] of the meeting [2] at which the poll [1] was demanded.

(3) In the case of an equality of votes, whether on a show of hands or on a poll [1], the chairman [5] of the meeting [2] at which the show of hands takes place or at which the poll [1] is demanded, shall be entitled to a second or casting vote.

(4) A poll [1] demanded on the election of a chairman [5] or on a question of adjournment shall be taken forthwith, and on any other question shall be taken at such time as the chairman [5] of the meeting [2] directs, and any business other than that upon which a poll [1] has been demanded may be proceeded with pending the taking of the poll [1].

**Notes**

**Section 226(1)**

1. "Poll" means taking a vote on election or on a motion. See **Sheila Bone, (ed) Osborn's Concise Law Dictionary, 9th ed.**
2. "Meeting" means an assembling of a number of persons for the purpose of discussing and acting upon some matter or matters in which they have a common interest. See **Garner B, (ed) Black's Law Dictionary 8th ed.**
3. "Company" means a corporation - or, less commonly, an association, partnership, or union that carries on a commercial or industrial enterprise. See **Garner B. (ed) Black's Law Dictionary 8th ed.** "Company" or "existing company" means a company formed and

registered under this Act or, as the case may be, formed and registered in Nigeria before and in existence on the commencement of this Act. See **Section 567 CAMA, Cap. C20, LFN 2004**

4. "Member" includes the heir, executor, administrator or other personal representative, as the case may be, of the member. See **Section 567 CAMA Cap. C20, LFN 2004**

**Section 226(2)**

5. "Chairman" means a deliberative assembly's presiding officer. See **Garner B, (ed) Black's Law Dictionary, 8 th ed.**
6. "Resolution" means a formal expression of the opinion or will of an official body or a public assembly, adopted by vote as a legislative resolution. See **Garner B,(ed) Black's Law Dictionary, 8th ed**

Cross Reference

On types of meeting to be held by a Company, see **sections 211, 213 and 215 CAMA Cap. C20 LFN 2004**

On Powers and duties of a chairman at the general meeting, see **section 240 CAMA Cap. C20, LFN 2004**

---

## 227. Right of attendance at general meeting

(1) Subject to section 228 of this Act, every member [1] shall have a right to attend any general meeting [2] of the company[3] in accordance with the provisions of section 81 of this Act.

(2) In the case of joint holders, the vote of the senior joint holder who tenders a vote, whether in person or by proxy [4], shall be accepted to the exclusion of the votes of the other joint holders; and for this purpose seniority shall be determined by the order in which the names stand in the register of members [1].

(3) A member[1] of unsound mind, or in respect of whom an order has been made by any court [5] having jurisdiction in lunacy, may vote, whether on a show of hands or on a poll [6], by his committee, receiver[7], curator bonis [9], or other person in the nature of a committee, receiver [7] or curator bonis [8] appointed by that court [5], and any such committee, receiver [7], curator bonis [8] or other person may vote by proxy[4].

---

**Notes**

**Section 227(1)**

1. "Member" includes the heir, executor, administrator or other personal representative, as the case may be, of the member. See **Section 567 CAMA Cap. C20, LFN 2004.**

2. "Meeting" means an assembling of a number of persons for the purpose of discussing and acting upon some matter or matters in which they have a common interest. See **Garner B (ed) Black's Law Dictionary 8 th ed.**
3. "Company" means a corporation - or, less commonly, an association, partnership, or union that carries on a commercial or industrial enterprise. See **Garner B. (ed) Black's Law Dictionary 8 th ed.** "Company" or "existing company" means a company formed and registered under this Act or, as the case may be, formed and registered in Nigeria before and in existence on the commencement of this Act. See **Section 567 CAMA, Cap. C20, LFN 2004**

**Section 227(2)**

4. "Proxy" means one who is authorized to act as a substitute for another; a person who is authorized to vote another's stock shares. See **Garner B. ed. Black's Law Dictionary 8th Ed.**

**Section 227(3)**

5. "Court" used in relation to a company, means the Federal High Court, and to the extent to which application may be made to it as; court includes the Court of Appeal and the Supreme Court of Nigeria. See **Section 567 CAMA Cap. C20, LFN 2004.**
6. "Poll" means taking a vote on election or on a motion; **Sheila Bone, (ed) Osborn's Concise Law Dictionary, 9 th ed**
7. "Receiver" means a disinterested person appointed by a court, or by a corporation or other person, for the protection or collection of property that is the subject of diverse claims. See **Garner B. (ed) Black's Law Dictionary 8th ed.**
8. "Curator bonis" means (1) A guardian appointed to care for property, especially for the benefit of creditors. (2) A person appointed by a court to manage an estate, especially of a minor or an insane person See **Garner B. (ed) Black's Law Dictionary 8 th ed.**

**Cross Reference**

On types of meeting to be held by a Company, see **sections 211, 213 and 215 CAMA Cap. C20 LFN 2004**

On rights of members of a company to attend meetings and vote, see **section 81, CAMA Cap. C20, LFN 2004**

On Jurisdiction of the Federal High Court, see **section 251 of the Constitution of the Federal Republic of Nigeria, 1999(as amended)**

---

## Cases

A receiver has duty to stop business, collect the debts and release the assets. But a manager has power to continue a business or a going concern: See ***Ponson Enterprise Nig. Ltd v. Njigha (2001) FWLR pt. 61 p. 3***

## For Further Reading

On General meeting, Extraordinary general meeting, Notice of meetings, Voting and Resolutions, see, Orojo, J. Ola **Company Law and Practice in Nigeria** 3rd Edition, Mbeyi & Associates (Lagos, Nigeria) 1992,

Ogbuanya C.S. Nelson **Essentials of Corporate Law Practice in Nigeria** Novena Publishers Limited 2012

## 228. Attendance at meetings

Every person who is entitled to receive notice of a general meeting[1] of the company[2] as provided by section 227 of this Act, shall be entitled to attend such a meeting [1].

---

**Notes**
**Section 228**

1. "Meeting" means an assembling of a number of persons for the purpose of discussing and acting upon some matter or matters in which they have a common interest. See **Garner B, (ed) Black's Law Dictionary 8 th ed.**
2. "Company" means a corporation - or, less commonly, an association, partnership, or union that carries on a commercial or industrial enterprise. See **Garner B, (ed) Black's Law Dictionary 8 th ed.**
   "Company" or "existing company" means a company formed and registered under this Act or, as the case may be, formed and registered in Nigeria before and in existence on the commencement of this Act. See **Section 567 CAMA, Cap. C20, LFN 2004**

Cross Reference

On types of meeting to be held by a Company, see **sections 211, 213 and 215 CAMA Cap. C20 LFN 2004**

On length of notice required for general meetings, see **section 217, CAMA Cap. C20 LFN 2004**

---

**For Further Reading**

On General meeting, Extraordinary general meeting, Notice of meetings, Voting and Resolutions, see, Orojo, J. Ola **Company Law and Practice in Nigeria** 3rd Edition, Mbeyi & Associates (Lagos, Nigeria) 1992, Ogbuanya C.S. Nelson **Essentials of Corporate Law Practice in Nigeria** Novena Publishers Limited 2012

## 229. Objections as to qualification to vote

No objections shall be raised to the qualification of any voter except at the meeting[1] or adjourned meeting[1] at which the vote objected to is given or tendered, and every vote not disallowed at such meeting[1] shall be valid for all purposes and any such objection made in due time shall be referred to the chairman [2] of the meeting[1], whose decision shall be final and conclusive.

---

**Notes**
**Section 229**

1. "Meeting" means an assembling of a number of persons for the purpose of discussing and acting upon some matter or matters in which they have a common interest. See **Garner B (ed) Black's Law Dictionary 8th ed.**
2. "Chairman" means a deliberative assembly's presiding officer **Garner B, (ed) Black's Law Dictionary, 8 th ed**

**Cross Reference**

On Powers and duties of a chairman at the general meeting, see **section 240 CAMA Cap. C20, LFN 2004**

---

## 230. Proxies

(1) Any member[1] of a company[2] entitled to attend and vote at a meeting[3] of the company[2] shall be entitled to appoint another person (whether a member or not) as his proxy [4] to attend and vote instead of him, and a proxy [4] appointed to attend and vote instead of a member[1] shall also have the same right as the member [1] to speak at the meeting[3]:

Provided that, unless the articles [5] otherwise provide, this section shall not apply in the case of a company [2] not having a share capital[6].

(2) In every notice calling a meeting [3] of a company[2] having a share capital[6], there shall appear with reasonable prominence a statement that a member[1] entitled to attend and vote is entitled to appoint a proxy[4] or, where that is allowed, two or more proxies [4], to attend and vote instead of him, and that a proxy [4] need not be a member[1] and if default is made in complying with this subsection as respects any meeting[3], every officer[7] of the company[2] who is in default shall be guilty of an offence and liable to a fine of N250.

(3) Any provision contained in a company's [2] articles[5] shall be void in so far as it would have the effect of requiring the instrument appointing a proxy[4] or any other document necessary to show the validity of or otherwise relating to the appointment of a proxy [4], to be received by the company[2] or any other person more than 48 hours before a meeting[2] or adjourned meeting[3] in order that the appointment may be effective at the meeting [3].

(4) If, for the purpose of any meeting [3] of a company[2], invitations to appoint as proxy[4] a person or one of a number of persons specified in the invitations are issued at the company's [2] expense to some only of the members [1] entitled to be sent notice of

the meeting[3] and to vote by proxy[4] at the meeting[3], every officer[7] of the company[2] who knowingly and wilfully authorises or permits their issue as aforesaid shall be guilty of an offence and liable to a fine of N500:
Provided that an officer[7] shall not be liable under this subsection by reason only of the issue to a member[1] at his request in writing of a form of appointment naming the proxy[4] or of a list of persons willing to act as proxy[4] if the form or list is available on request in writing to every member[1] entitled to vote at the meeting[3] by proxy[4].

(5) A vote given in accordance with the terms of an instrument of proxy[4] shall be valid notwithstanding the previous death or insanity of the principal or revocation of the proxy[4] or of the authority under which the proxy[4] was executed, or the transfer[8] of the share[9] in respect of which the proxy[4] is given:
Provided that no intimation in writing of such death, insanity, revocation or transfer[8] as aforesaid has been received by the company[2] before the commencement of the meeting[3] or adjourned meeting[3] at which the proxy[4] is used.

(6) The instrument appointing a proxy[4] shall be in writing, under the hand of the appointer or of his attorney duly authorised in writing or, if the appointer is a corporation, either under seal, or under the hand of an officer[7] or attorney duly authorised.

(7) The instrument appointing a proxy[4] and the power of attorney[10] or other authority, if any, under which it is signed or a certified copy of that power or authority shall be deposited at the registered office[11] or head office of the company[2] or at such other place within Nigeria as is specified for that purpose in the notice convening the meeting[3], not less than 48 hours before the time for holding the meeting[3] or adjourned meeting[3], at which the person named in the instrument proposes to vote, or, in the case of a poll[12], not less than 24 hours before the time appointed for the taking of the poll[12]; and in default, the instrument of proxy[4] shall not be treated as valid.

(8) This section shall apply to meetings[3] of any class of members[1] of a company[2] as it applies to general meetings[3] of the company[2].

---

**Notes**

**Section 230(1)**

1. "Member" includes the heir, executor, administrator or other personal representative, as the case may be, of the member. See **Section 567 CAMA Cap. C20, LFN 2004.**

2. "Company" means a corporation - or, less commonly, an association, partnership, or union that carries on a commercial or industrial enterprise. See **Garner B, (ed) Black's Law Dictionary 8 th ed.**
"Company" or "existing company" means a company formed and registered under this Act or, as the case may be, formed and registered in Nigeria before and in existence on the commencement of this Act. See **section 567 CAMA, Cap. C20, LFN 2004.**
3. "Meeting" means an assembling of a number of persons for the purpose of discussing and acting upon some matter or matters in which they have a common interest. See **Garner B, (ed) Black's Law Dictionary 8 th ed.**
4. "Proxy" means one who is authorized to act as a substitute for another; a person who is authorized to vote another's stock shares. See **Garner B. ed. Black's Law Dictionary 8th ed.**
5. "Articles" means the articles of association of a company, as originally framed or as altered by special resolution, including so far as they apply to the regulations contained in Table A in the First Schedules of the Companies Act, 1922 or in that Table as altered by any subsequent enactment or reprint of the laws, or in Table A in the First Schedule to this Act. See **section 567 CAMA, Cap. C20, LFN 2004.**
6. "Share capital" means any of the units of equal value into which a company is divided and sold to raise money. People who owns shares receives part of the company profit. See Oxford Advanced Learners Dictionary ,New 7th Edition
"Share Capital": See Capital; means a fund representing the nominal value of shares issued by a registered company. See Martins, E. (ed) Oxford Dictionary of Law 7th ed.

**Section 230(2)**

7. "Officer" in relation to a body corporate, includes a director, manager or secretary. See **section 567 CAMA, Cap. C20, LFN 2004.**

**Section 230(5)**

8. Transfer" means to move from one place to another; to move something or somebody from one place to another. See Oxford Advanced Learner's Dictionary 6th ed.
9. "Share" means the interests in a company's share capital of a member who is entitled to share in the capital or income of such company; and except where a distinction between stock and shares is expressed or implied, includes stock. See **Section 567 CAMA Cap. C20, LFN 2004**

**Section 230(6)**

10. "Power of Attorney" means an instrument granting someone to act as agent or attorney in fact for the grantor. See **Garner .B. (ed) Black's Law Dictionary, 8th ed.**

**Section 230(7)**

11. "Registered Office" means the official address of a registered company. It must be notified to the Companies Registry before registration of the company and it must appear on company letter-head and order forms. Documents may be served to a company's registered office and various registers and records may be inspected there. **See Martins E. (ed.) Oxford Dictionary of Law 4 th ed.**

12. "Poll" means taking a vote on election or on a motion. See **Sheila Bone, (ed) Osborn's Concise Law Dictionary, 9 th ed.**

Cross Reference

On the requirement that the registered office of a company be situate in Nigeria, see **section 27 CAMA, Cap. C 20, LFN 2004**

On obligation of every registered company to have a common seal, and use of the seal, see **section 74 CAMA, Cap. C 20, LFN 2004**

On transfer of shares of a company, see **section 151 CAMA, Cap. C 20, LFN 2004**

On length of notice required for meetings, see **section 217 CAMA, Cap. C 20, LFN 2004**

On persons entitled to notice of meeting, see **section 219 CAMA, Cap. C 20, LFN 2004**

On meaning of offence, see **section 2 Criminal Code Cap. C38 LFN 2004**

---

**For Further Reading**

On General meeting, Extraordinary general meeting, Notice of meetings, Voting and Resolutions, see, Orojo, J. Ola **Company Law and Practice in Nigeria** 3rd Edition, Mbeyi & Associates (Lagos, Nigeria) 1992, Ogbuanya C.S. Nelson **Essentials of Corporate Law Practice in Nigeria** Novena Publishers Limited 2012.

## 231.Corporation representation at meetings of companies, etc.

(1) A corporation, whether a company [1] within the meaning of this Act or not, may if it is-

(a) a member[2] of another corporation, being a company [1] within the meaning of this Act, by resolution [3] of its directors[4] or other governing body, authorise such person as it thinks fit to act as its representative at any meeting [5] of the company[1] or at any meeting[5] of any class of members[2] of the company[1];

(b) a creditor[6] (including a holder of debentures [7]) of another corporation, being a company [1] within the meaning of this Act, by resolution[3] of its directors[4] or other governing body, authorise such person as it thinks fit to act as its representative at any meeting[5] of any creditors[6] of the company[1] held in pursuance of this Act or of any rules made thereunder or in pursuance of the provisions contained in any debenture[7] or trust deed[8], as the case may be.

(2) A person authorised as provided in subsection (1) of this section, shall be entitled to exercise the same powers on behalf of the corporation which he represents as that corporation might exercise if it were an individual shareholder [9], creditor [6] or holder of debentures[7] of that other company [1].

---

**Notes**

**Section 231(1)**

1. "Company" means a corporation - or, less commonly, an association, partnership, or union that carries on a commercial or industrial enterprise. See **Garner B, (ed) Black's Law Dictionary 8 th ed.** "Company" or "existing company" means a company formed and registered under this Act or, as the case may be, formed and registered in Nigeria before and in existence on the commencement of this Act. See **section 567 CAMA, Cap. C20, LFN 2004.**
2. "Member" includes the heir, executor, administrator or other personal representative, as the case may be, of the member See s **ection 567 CAMA Cap. C20, LFN 2004.**
3. "Resolution" means a formal expression of the opinion or will of an official body or a public assembly, adopted by vote as a legislative resolution. See **Garner .B,(ed) Black's Law Dictionary, 8 th ed.**
4. "Director" includes any person occupying the position of director by whatever name called; and includes any person in accordance with whose directions or instructions the directors of the company are accustomed to act. See **section 567 CAMA, Cap. C20, LFN 2004.**
5. "Meeting" means an assembling of a number of persons for the purpose of discussing and acting upon some matter or matters in which they have a common interest. See **Garner B, (ed) Black's Law Dictionary 8 th ed.**
6. "Creditor" means one to whom a debt is owed. **See Garner B.,(ed.) Black's Law Dictionary Eight Edition)**
7. "Debenture" means a written acknowledgement of indebtedness by the company, setting out the terms and conditions of the indebtedness, and includes debenture stock, bonds and any other securities of a company whether constituting a charge on the assets of the company or not. See **Section 567 CAMA Cap. C20, LFN 2004.**
8. "Trust deed", see "deed of trust". It means a deed conveying title to real property to a trustee as security until the grantor repays a loan. See **Garner B. ed. Black's Law Dictionary, 8th ed.**

**Section 231(2)**

9. "Shareholder" means one who owns or holds a share or shares in a company especially a corporation. See **Garner .B,(ed) Black's Law Dictionary, 8 th ed**

Cross Reference

On types of resolutions, see **section 233 CAMA Cap. C20, LFN, 2004**

---

**For Further Reading**
On General meeting, Extraordinary general meeting, Notice of meetings, Voting and Resolutions, see, Orojo, J. Ola **Company Law and Practice in Nigeria** 3rd Edition, Mbeyi & Associates (Lagos, Nigeria) 1992, Ogbuanya C.S. Nelson **Essentials of Corporate Law Practice in Nigeria** Novena Publishers Limited 2012

## 232. Quorum

(1) Unless otherwise provided in the articles [1], no business shall be transacted at any general meeting [2] unless a quorum [3] of members[4] is present at the time when the meeting [2] proceeds to business and throughout the meeting [2].

(2) Unless otherwise provided in the articles [1], the quorum [3] for the meeting[2] of a company[5] shall be one third of the total number of members [4] of the company [5] or 25 members [4] (whichever is less) present in person or by proxy [6]:
Provided that where the number of members [4] is not a multiple of three, then the number nearest to one third, and where the number of members[4] is six or less, the quorum [3], shall be two members [4].

(3) For the purpose of determining a quorum [3], all members [4] or their proxies [6] shall be counted.

(4) Where a member or members [4] withdraw from the meeting[2] for what appears to the chairman [7] to be insufficient reasons and for the purpose of reducing the quorum [3], and in fact the quorum[3] is no longer present, the meeting [2] may continue with the number present, and their decision shall bind all the shareholders[8] and where there is only one member [4], he may seek direction of the court [9] to take a decision.

(5) Where there is a quorum [3] at the beginning, but no quorum[3] later due to some share-holders [8] leaving for what appears to the chairman[7] to be sufficient reasons, the meeting [2] shall be adjourned to the same place, and time, in a week's time, and if there is no quorum [3] still at the adjourned meeting [2], the members [4] present shall then be the quorum [3] and their decision shall bind all shareholders[8] and where only one member [4] is present, he may seek direction of the court [9] to take a decision.

---

**Notes**
**Section 232(1)**

1. "Articles" means the articles of association of a company, as originally framed or as altered by special resolution, including so far as they apply

to the regulations contained in Table A in the First Schedules of the Companies Act, 1922 or in that Table as altered by any subsequent enactment or reprint of the laws, or in Table A in the First Schedule to this Act. See **section 567 CAMA, Cap. C20, LFN 2004.**

2. "Meeting" means an assembling of a number of persons for the purpose of discussing and acting upon some matter or matters in which they have a common interest. See **Garner B, (ed) Black's Law Dictionary 8 th ed.**
3. "Quorum" means the minimum number of members who must be present for a deliberative assembly. See **Garner B (ed.), Blacks' Law Dictionary 8th ed.**
4. "Member" includes the heir, executor, administrator or other personal representative, as the case may be, of the member. See **Section 567 CAMA Cap. C20, LFN 2004.**

**Section 232(2)**

5. "Company" means a corporation - or, less commonly, an association, partnership, or union that carries on a commercial or industrial enterprise. See **Garner B, (ed) Black's Law Dictionary 8 th ed.**
   "Company" or "existing company" means a company formed and registered under this Act or, as the case may be, formed and registered in Nigeria before and in existence on the commencement of this Act. **Section 567 CAMA, Cap. C20, LFN 2004.**
6. "Proxy" means one who is authorized to act as a substitute for another; a person who is authorized to vote another's stock shares. See **Garner B. ed. Black's Law Dictionary 8th Ed**

**Section 232 (4)**

7. "Chairman" means a deliberative assembly's presiding officer. See **Garner .B,(ed) Black's Law Dictionary, 8 th ed.**
8. "Shareholder" means one who owns or holds a share or shares in a company especially a corporation. See **Garner .B,(ed) Black's Law Dictionary, 8 th ed**

**Section 232 (5)**

9. "Court" used in relation to a company, means the Federal High Court, and to the extent to which application may be made to it as; court includes the Court of Appeal and the Supreme Court of Nigeria. See **Section 567 CAMA Cap. C20, LFN 2004.**

**Cross Reference**

On Powers and duties of a chairman at the general meeting, see **section 240 CAMA Cap. C20, LFN 2004**

On types of meeting to be held by a Company, see **sections 211, 213 and 215 CAMA Cap. C20 LFN 2004**

On Jurisdiction of the Federal High Court, see **section 251 of the Constitution of the Federal Republic of Nigeria, 1999** (as amended)

---

*Resolutions*

## 233. Resolutions

(1) A resolution [1] shall be an ordinary resolution [2] when it has been passed by a simple majority of votes cast by such members [3] of

the company[4] as, being entitled to do so, vote in person or by proxy[5] at a general meeting [6].

(2) A resolution [1] shall be a special resolution [7] when it has been passed by not less than three fourths of the votes cast by such members[3] of the company[4] as, being entitled to do so, vote in person or by proxy [5] at a general meeting [6] of which 21 days' notice, specifying the intention to propose the resolution [1] as a special resolution[7], has been duly given:

Provided that, if it is so agreed by majority in number of the members[3] having the right to attend and vote at any such meeting [6], being a majority together holding not less than 95 per cent in nominal value of the shares [8] giving that right or, in the case of a company[4] not having a share capital [9] together representing not less than 95 per cent of the total voting rights at that meeting [6] of all the members[3], a resolution [1] may be proposed and passed as a special resolution[7] at a meeting[6] of which less than 21 days' notice has been given.

(3) At any meeting[6] at which a special resolution [7] is submitted to be passed, a declaration of the chairman [10] that the resolution [1] is carried shall, unless a poll [11] is demanded, be conclusive evidence of the fact without proof of the number or proportion of the votes recorded in favour of or against the resolution [1].

(4) In computing the majority of a poll [11] demanded on the question that a special resolution [7] be passed, reference shall be had to the number of votes cast for and against the resolution [1].

(5) For the purposes of this section, notice of a meeting [6] shall be deemed to be duly given and the meeting [6] to be duly held when the notice[8] is given and the meeting [6] held in the manner provided by this Act or the articles [12].

(6) A company [4] may, by its articles [12], provide that any matter not required by the articles [12] or by this Act to be passed by a special resolution[7], shall be passed by an ordinary resolution [2].

**Notes**

**Section 233(1)**

1. "Resolution" means a formal expression of the opinion or will of an official body or a public assembly, adopted by vote as a legislative resolution. See **Garner .B,(ed) Black's Law Dictionary, 8 th ed.**
2. "Ordinary resolution" means a decision reached by a simple majority (i.e. of more than 50%) of company members voting in person or by proxy. It is appropriate where no other type of resolution is expressly

required by the Companies Acts or the articles of association. See **Martins E. (ed.) Oxford Dictionary of Law 4 th ed.**

3. "Member" includes the heir, executor, administrator or other personal representative, as the case may be, of the member. See **Section 567 CAMA Cap. C20, LFN 2004.**
4. "Company" means a corporation - or, less commonly, an association, partnership, or union that carries on a commercial or industrial enterprise. **See Garner B. (ed) Black's Law Dictionary 8 th ed.**
   "Company" or "existing company" means a company formed and registered under this Act or, as the case may be, formed and registered in Nigeria before and in existence on the commencement of this Act. **See section 567 CAMA, Cap. C20, LFN 2004.**
5. "Proxy" means one who is authorized to act as a substitute for another; a person who is authorized to vote another's stock shares. See **Garner B. ed. Black's Law Dictionary 8th ed.**
6. "Meeting" means an assembling of a number of persons for the purpose of discussing and acting upon some matter or matters in which they have a common interest. **See Garner B, (ed) Black's Law Dictionary 8 th ed**

**Section 233 (2)**

7. "Special resolution" means a resolution passed by not less than three fourths of the votes cast by such members of the company as, being entitled to do so, vote in person or by proxy at a general meeting of which 21 days' notice, specifying the intention to propose the resolution as a special resolution, has been duly given. See **Section 233(2)CAMA CAP C20, LFN,2004** .
8. "Shares" means the interests in a company's share capital of a member who is entitled to share in the capital or income of such company; and except where a distinction between stock and shares is expressed or implied, includes stock. See **Section 567 CAMA, Cap. C20, LFN 2004.**
9. "Share capital" means any of the units of equal value into which a company is divided and sold to raise money. People who owns shares receives part of the company profit. See Oxford Advanced Learners Dictionary ,New 7th Edition
   "Share Capital": See Capital; means a fund representing the nominal value of shares issued by a registered company. See **Martins, E. (ed) Oxford Dictionary of Law 4th ed.**
10. **Section 233 (3)**
11. "Chairman" means a deliberative assembly's presiding officer. See **Garner .B,(ed) Black's Law Dictionary, 8 th ed.**
12. "Poll" means taking a vote on election or on a motion; **Sheila Bone, (ed) Osborn's Concise Law Dictionary, 9 th ed.**

**Section 233 (6)**

13. "Articles" means the articles of association of a company, as originally framed or as altered by special resolution, including so far as they apply to the regulations contained in Table A in the First Schedules of the Companies Act, 1922 or in that Table as altered by any subsequent enactment or reprint of the laws, or in Table A in the First Schedule to this Act. See **Section 567, CAMA, Cap. C20, LFN 2004.**

Cross Reference

On the form and content of the Articles of Association of a Company , see **section 34, CAMA, Cap. C20, LFN 2004.**
On Powers and duties of a chairman at the general meeting, see **section 240 CAMA Cap. C20, LFN 2004**
On types of meeting to be held by a Company, see **sections 211, 213 and 215 CAMA Cap. C20 LFN 2004**

**For Further Reading**
On General meeting, Extraordinary general meeting, Notice of meetings, Voting and Resolutions, see, Orojo, J. Ola **Company Law and Practice in Nigeria** 3rd Edition, Mbeyi & Associates (Lagos, Nigeria) 1992, Ogbuanya C.S. Nelson **Essentials of Corporate Law Practice in Nigeria** Novena Publishers Limited 2012

## 234. Written resolutions

All resolutions[1] shall be passed at general meetings [2] and shall not be effective unless so passed:
Provided that in the case of a private company [3] a written resolution signed by all the members entitled to attend and vote [4] shall be as valid and effective as if passed in a general meeting.

**Notes**
**Section 234**
1. "Resolution" means a main motion that formally expresses the sense, will, or action of a deliberative assembly **Garner B., (ed.) Black's Law Dictionary 8th ed.**
2. "General Meeting" see "Annual meeting" – a yearly meeting to elect or install officers or directors and to conduct other routine organizational business. See **Garner B, (ed.) Black's Law Dictionary 8 th ed.**
3. "Private company" has the meaning assigned to it by **section 22 (1) CAMA Cap C20 LFN, 2004**
4. "Vote" means the expression of one's preference or opinion in a meeting or election by ballot, show of hands, or other type of communication. See **Garner B., (ed.) Black's Law Dictionary 8 th ed.**

**Cases**
Where the provisions of the Act and the articles regarding such matters as notice of meetings, quorum, proceedings at and conduct of meetings, are not strictly complied with, any resolution passed at such meetings will be a nullity. Obikoya v. Ezenwani (1964) 2 All NLR 133.

**For Further Reading**
On resolutions see, Ayua, I.A **Nigerian Company Law** G. Burn (Leighton Buzzard, Bedfordshire, United Kingdom) 1984

## 235. Circulation of members' resolutions

(1) Subject to the following provisions of this section, it shall be the duty of a company [1], on the requisition in writing of such number of members [2] as is hereinafter specified and (unless the company[1] otherwise resolves) at the expense of the company [1] to-

(a) give to members [2] of the company [1] entitled to receive notice of the next annual general meeting [3] notice of any resolution[4] submitted by a member [2] which may properly be moved and is intended to be moved at that meeting [3];

(b) circulate to members [3] entitled to have notice of any general meeting[3] sent to them, any statement of not more than 1,000 words with respect to the matter referred to in any proposed resolution [4] or the business to be dealt with at that meeting[3], and where the statement has more than 1,000 words to circulate a summary of it.

(2) The number of members [2] necessary for a requisition under subsection (1) of this section shall be-

(a) nyone or more members [2] representing not less than one twentieth of the total voting rights of all the members having at the date of the requisition a right to vote at the meeting[3] to which the requisition relates; or

(b) not less than one hundred members [2] holding shares [5] in the company[1] on which there has been paid up an average sum, per member[2], of not less than N500.

(3) Notice of any such resolution [4] shall be given, and any such statement shall be circulated, to members [2] of the company [1] entitled to have notice of the meeting [3] sent to them, by serving a copy of the resolution [4] or statement on each such member [2] in any manner permitted for service of notice of the meeting [3], and notice of any such resolution [4] shall be given to any other member [2] of the company[1] by giving notice of the general effect of the resolution [4] in any manner permitted for giving notice of meetings [3] of the company[1]:

Provided that the copy shall be served, or notice of the effect of the resolution[4] shall be given, as the case may be, in the same manner and so far as practicable, at the same time as notice of the meeting [3] and, where it is not practicable for it to be served or given at that time, it shall be served or given as soon as practicable thereafter.

(4) A company [1] shall not be bound under this section to give notice of any resolution [4] or to circulate any statement unless-

(a) a copy of the requisition [4] signed by the requisitionists [6] (or two or more copies which between them contain the signatures of all the requisitionists [6]) is deposited at the registered office of the company [1]-

(i) in the case of a requisition requiring notice of a resolution[4], not less than six weeks before the meeting[3]; and

(ii) in the case of any other requisition, not less than one week before the meeting [3]; and

(b) there is deposited or tendered with the requisition, a sum reasonably sufficient to meet the company's [1] expenses in giving effect thereto:

Provided that if, after a copy of a requisition requiring notice of a resolution [4] has been deposited at the registered office of the company [1], an annual general meeting [3] is called for a date six weeks or less after the copy has been deposited, the copy, though not deposited within the time required by this subsection, shall be deemed to have been properly deposited for the purposes thereof.

(5) The company [1] shall also not be bound under this section to circulate any statement if, on the application either of the company[1] or of any other person who claims to be aggrieved, the court[7] is satisfied that the rights conferred by this section are being abused to secure needless publicity for defamatory matter; and the court may order the company's [1] costs on an application under this section to be paid in whole or in part by the requisitionist [6], notwithstanding that the requistionist [6] is not party to the application.

(6) Notwithstanding anything in the company's [1] articles [8], the business which may be dealt with at an annual general meeting shall include any resolution of which notice is given in accordance with this section and for the purposes of this subsection, notice shall be deemed to have been so given, notwithstanding the accidental omission in giving it to one or more members.

(7) In the event of any default in complying with the provisions of this section, every officer [9] of the company who is in default shall be guilty of an offence and liable to a fine of N500.

**Notes**

**Section 235**

1. "Company" means a company formed and registered under this Act or, as the case may be, formed and registered in Nigeria before and in existence on the commencement of this Act. **See section 567 CAMA, Cap. C20, LFN 2004.**
2. "Member" means one of the individuals of whom a deliberative assembly consists and who enjoys the full rights of participating in the organization-including the rights of making, debating and voting on motions- except to the extent that the organization reserves those rights to certain classes of membership. See **Garner B. (ed.) Black's Law Dictionary 8th ed.**
   "Member" includes the heir, executor, administrator or other personal representative, as the case maybe, of the member. See **section 567 CAMA, Cap. C20, LFN, 2004.**
3. "General meeting" see "Annual meeting" – a yearly meeting to elect or install officers or directors and to conduct other routine organizational business. See **Garner B, (ed.) Black's Law Dictionary 8 th ed.**
4. "Resolution" means a main motion that formally expresses the sense, will, or action of a deliberative assembly See **Garner B. (ed.) Black's Law Dictionary 8th ed.**
5. "Shares" see "share." It means the interests in a company's share capital of a member who is entitled to share in the capital or income of such company; and except where a distinction between stock and shares is expressed or implied, includes stock. See **Section 567 CAMA, Cap. C20, LFN 2004.**
6. "Requisitionists" see "requisitionist." It means one who makes demand for the performance of an obligation. See **Garner B. (ed.) Black's Law Dictionary 8th ed.**
7. "Court" used in relation to a company, means the Federal High Court, and to the extent to which application may be made to it as; court includes the Court of Appeal and the Supreme Court of Nigeria. See **Section 567 CAMA Cap. C20, LFN 2004.**
8. "Articles" means the articles of association of a company, as originally framed or as altered by special resolution, including so far as they apply to the regulations contained in Table A in the First Schedules of the Companies Act, 1922 or in that Table as altered by any subsequent enactment or reprint of the laws, or in Table A in the First Schedule to this Act. See **Section 567, CAMA, Cap. C20, LFN 2004.**
9. "Officer in relation to a body corporate, includes a director, manager or secretary. See **Section 567, CAMA Cap. C20 LFN, 2004.**

**Cross Reference**

On types of general meeting, see **section 215 CAMA Cap. C20 LFN 2004**

On types of resolution, see **section 233 CAMA Cap. C20 LFN 2004**

On length of notice required for meetings, see **section 217 CAMA Cap. C20, LFN 2004**

On establishment of and jurisdiction of the Federal High Court, see **section 249& 251 Constitution of the Federal Reublic of Nigeria, 1999(as amended)**

---

**Case law**
The Articles of Association is the contract governing the relationship between shareholders and any infraction of such articles may confer on the shareholder adversely affected a right of action." ***Attorney General of Lagos State v Eko Hotel Ltd & Oha Ltd*** **(2001) FWLR page. 1996 at 2000**.

## 236. Resolutions requiring special notice

Where by any provision contained in this Act, special notice is required of a resolution,[1] the resolution[1] shall not be effective unless notice of the intention to move it has been given to the company[2] not less than 28 days before the meeting [3]at which it is to be moved, and the company[2] shall give its members[4] notice of any such resolution[1] at the same time and in the same manner as it gives notice of the meeting[3], or if that is not practicable, shall give them notice thereof, either by advertisement in a newspaper having an appropriate circulation, or in any other mode allowed by the articles[5], not less than 21 days before the meeting:[3]
Provided that if, after notice of the intention to move such a resolution[1] has been given to the company[2], a meeting[3] is called for a date 28 days or less after the notice has been given, the notice, though not given within the time required by this section, shall be deemed to have been properly given for purposes thereof.

---

**Notes**
**Section 236**

1. "Resolution" means a main motion that formally expresses the sense, will, or action of a deliberative assembly. See **Garner B. (ed.) Black's Law Dictionary 8th ed.**
2. "Company" means a company formed and registered under this Act or, as the case may be, formed and registered in Nigeria before and in existence on the commencement of this Act. See **Section 567 CAMA Cap. C20 LFN, 2004**
3. "Meeting" means an assembling of a number of persons for the purpose of discussing and acting upon some matter or matters in which they have a common interest. **See Garner B, (ed) Black's Law Dictionary 8 th ed**
4. "Members" includes the heir, executor, administrator, or other personal representatives, as the case may be, of the member. See **section 567 CAMA Cap. C20 LFN 2004**
5. "Articles" means the articles of association of a company, as originally framed or as altered by special resolution, including so far as they apply

to the regulations contained in Table A in the First Schedules of the Companies Act, 1922 or in that Table as altered by any subsequent enactment or reprint of the laws, or in Table A in the First Schedule to this Act. See **Section 567, CAMA, Cap. C20, LFN 2004.**

Cross Reference

On types of general meeting, see **section 215 CAMA Cap. C20 LFN 2004**

On types of resolution, see **section 233 CAMA Cap. C20 LFN 2004**

On length of notice required for meetings, see **section 217 CAMA Cap. C20, LFN 2004**

---

**Cases**

"The Articles of Association is the contract governing the relationship between shareholders and any infraction of such articles may confer on the shareholder adversely affected a right of action." ***Attorney General of Lagos State v Eko Hotel Ltd &Oha Ltd*** **(2001) FWLR page 1996 at 2000.**

## 237. Registration and copies of certain resolutions

(1) Subject to subsection (7) (b) of section 46 of this Act, a printed copy of every resolution [1] or agreement to which this section applies shall, within 15 days after the passing or making of the resolution[1] or agreement, as the case may be, be forwarded to the Commission[2].

(2) Where, pursuant to the provisions of sections 44 to 47 of this Act, a company [3] by special resolution [4] alters the provisions of its memorandum[5]and the Commission[2] is satisfied that the alteration is not in compliance with the applicable provisions of those sections, it may refuse to file a copy of the resolution [1] in its records and shall notify the company [3] accordingly and any person aggrieved by the refusal may appeal to the court [6] within 21 days from the receipt of the notification.

(3) A copy of every such resolution [1] or agreement for the time being in force shall be embodied in or annexed to every copy of the articles[7] issued after the passing of the resolution [1] or the making of the agreement.

(4) This section shall apply to-

(a) special resolutions [4];

(b) resolutions [1] which have been agreed to by all the members[7] of a company [3], but which, if not so agreed to, would not have been effective for their purpose, unless, as the case may be, they had been passed as special resolution[4]; or

(c) resolutions[1] or agreements which have been agreed to by all the members[7] of any class of shareholders[8] but which, if not so agreed to, would not have been effective for their purpose, unless they had been passed by some particular majority or otherwise in some particular manner, and all resolutions[1] or agreements which effectively bind all the members[7] of any class of shareholders[8] though not agreed to by all those members[7]; and

(d) resolutions[1] requiring a company[3] to be wound up voluntarily[9], passed under paragraph (a) of section 457 of this Act.

(5) If a company[3] fails to comply with subsection (1) of this section, the company[3] and every officer[10] of the company[3] who is in default shall be guilty of an offence and liable to a fine of N50.

(6) If a company[3] fails to comply with subsection (3) of this section, the company[3] and every officer[10] of the company[3] who is in default shall be guilty of an offence and liable to a fine of N5 for each copy in respect of which default is made.

(7) For the purposes of subsections (5) and (6) of this section, a liquidator[11] of the company[3] shall be deemed to be an officer[10] of the company.[3]

---

**Notes**
**Section 237**

1. "Resolution" means a main motion that formally expresses the sense, will, or action of a deliberative assembly **Garner B. (ed.) Black's Law Dictionary 8th ed.**
2. "Commission" means the Corporate Affairs Commission established under section 1. **See section 567 CAMA Cap. C20 LFN 2004.**

**Section 237 (2)**

3. "Company" means a company formed and registered under this Act or, as the case may be, formed and registered in Nigeria before and in existence on the commencement of this Act. See **Section 567 CAMA Cap. C20 LFN, 2004.**
4. "Special resolution" means a resolution passed by not less than three fourths of the votes cast by such members of the company as, being entitled to do so, vote in person or by proxy at a general meeting of which 21 days' notice, specifying the intention to propose the resolution as a special resolution, has been duly given. See **Section 233(2) CAMA Cap. C20, LFN, 2004** .

5. "Memorandum" means the memorandum of association of a company as originally framed or as altered in pursuance of any enactment. See **section 567 CAMA Cap. C20, LFN 2004**
6. "Court" used in relation to a company, means the Federal High Court, and to the extent to which application may be made to it as; court includes the Court of Appeal and the Supreme Court of Nigeria. See **Section 567 CAMA Cap. C20, LFN** 2004.

**Section 237(4)**

7. "Members" see "member." It includes the heir, executor, administrator, or other personal representatives, as the case may be, of the member. See **section 567 CAMA Cap. C20 LFN 2004**
8. "Articles" means the articles of association of a company, as originally framed or as altered by special resolution, including so far as they apply to the regulations contained in Table A in the First Schedules of the Companies Act, 1922 or in that Table as altered by any subsequent enactment or reprint of the laws, or in Table A in the First Schedule to this Act. See **Section 567, CAMA, Cap. C20, LFN 2004.**
9. "Wound up voluntarily" see "voluntary winding up." It has the meaning assigned to it by **section 462(4) CAMA Cap. C20 LFN 2004**

**Section 237(7)**

10. "Officer" in relation to a body corporate, includes a director, manager or secretary. **Section 567, CAMA Cap. C20 LFN, 2004.**
11. "Liquidator" means a person appointed to wind up a business' affairs, especially by selling off its assets. **Garner B. (ed.) Black's Law Dictionary 8th ed.**

Cross Reference

On types of resolutions, see **section 233 CAMA Cap. C20, LFN 2004**

On types of meeting, see **section 215 CAMA Cap. C20 LFN 2004**

On appointment and renumeration of a Liquidator, see **section 422 CAMA Cap. C20, LFN 2004**

On the Power to appoint a Liquidator, see **section 464 CAMA Cap. C20, LFN 2004**

On establishment of and jurisdiction of the Federal High Court, see **section 249& 251 Constitution of the Federal Reublic of Nigeria, 1999(as amended)**

On the creation of classes of chares by a Company, see **section 118 CAMA Cap. C20, LFN 2004**

---

## 238. Effect of resolutions passed at adjourned meetings

Where a resolution[1] is passed at an adjourned meeting of-

(a) a company[3];

(b) the holders of any class of shares [5] in a company[3]; or

(c) the directors[5] of a company,[3]

the resolution[1] shall for all purposes be treated as having been passed on the date on which it was in

---

fact passed, and shall not be deemed to have been passed on any earlier date.

---

**Notes**
**Section 238**

1. "Resolution" means a main motion that formally expresses the sense, will, or action of a deliberative assembly. See **Garner B. (ed.) Black's Law Dictionary 8 th ed.**
2. "Meeting" means the gathering of people to discuss or act on matters in which they have a common interest; esp. the convening of a deliberate assembly to transact business. See **Garner B. (ed.) Black's Law Dictionary 8th ed.**
3. "Company" means a company formed and registered under this Act or, as the case may be, formed and registered in Nigeria before and in existence on the commencement of this Act. See **Section 567 CAMA Cap. C20 LFN, 2004.**
4. "Shares" see "share". It means one of the definite number of equal parts into which the capital stock of a corporation or joint stock company is divided. See **Garner B. (ed.) Black's Law Dictionary 8th ed.**
   "Share" means the interests in a company's share capital of a member who is entitled to share in the capital or income of such company; and except where a distinction between stock and shares is expressed or implied, includes stock. See **Section 567 CAMA Cap. C20 LFN, 2004**
5. "Director" means (1) one who manages, guides, or orders; a chief administrator (2) a person appointed or elected to sit on a board that manages the affairs of a corporation or other organisation by electing and exercising control over its officers. **Garner B. (ed.) Black's Law Dictionary 8th ed.**
   "Director" includes any person occupying the position of director by whatever name called; and includes any person in accordance with whose directions or instructions the directors of the company are accustomed to act. See **Section 567 CAMA Cap. C20 LFN, 2004**

Cross Reference

On types of resolutions, see **section 233 CAMA Cap. C20, LFN 2004**
On the creation of classes of chares by a Company, see **section 118 CAMA Cap. C20, LFN 2004**

---

*Miscellaneous matters relating to meetings and proceedings*

## 239. Adjournment

(1) The chairman[1] may, with the consent of any meeting [2]at which a quorum[3]is present (and shall if so directed by the

meeting[2]), adjourn the meeting [2] from time to time and from place to place, but no business shall be transacted at any adjourned meeting [2] other than the business left unfinished at the meeting [2] from which the adjournment took place.

(2) When a meeting [2] is adjourned for 30 days or more, notice of the adjourned meeting [2] shall be given as in the case of an original meeting[2]; but otherwise it shall not be necessary to give any notice of an adjournment or of the business to be transacted at an adjourned meeting [2].

(3) If within one hour from the time appointed for the meeting[2] a quorum [3] is not present, the meeting [2] if convened upon the requisition[4] of members [5] shall be dissolved, but in any other case, it shall stand adjourned to the same day in the next week, at the same time and place or to such other day and at such other time and place as the chairman [1], and in his absence the directors [6], may direct.

(4) If a meeting [2] stands adjourned under subsection (3) of this section any two or more members [5] present at the place and time to which it so stands adjourned shall form a quorum [3] and their decision shall bind all shareholders [7], and where only one member [5] is present, he may seek the direction of the court [8] to take a decision.

---

**Notes**

**Section 239(1)**

1. "Chairman" means a deliberative assembly's presiding officer. See **Garner B. (ed.) Black's Law Dictionary 8 th ed.**
2. "Meeting" "means the gathering of people to discuss or act on matters in which they have a common interest; esp. the convening of a deliberate assembly to transact business. See **Garner B. (ed.) Black's Law Dictionary 8th ed.**
3. "Quorum" means the minimum number of members (usually a majority of all the members) who must be present for a deliberative assembly to legally transact business. See **Garner B. (ed.) Black's Law Dictionary 8th ed.**

**Section 239 (3)**

4. "Requisition" means an authoritative formal demand. See **Garner B. (ed.) Black's Law Dictionary 8 th ed.**
5. "Members" see "member" It includes the heir, executor, administrator, or other personal representatives, as the case may be, of the member. See **section 567 CAMA Cap. C20 LFN 2004**

6. "Directors" see "director." t means (1) one who manages, guides, or orders; a chief administrator (2) a person appointed or elected to sit on a board that manages the affairs of a corporation or other organisation by electing and exercising control over its officers. **Garner B. (ed.) Black's Law Dictionary 8th ed.**
"Director" includes any person occupying the position of director by whatever name called; and includes any person in accordance with whose directions or instructions the directors of the company are accustomed to act. See **Section 567 CAMA Cap. C20 LFN, 2004**
6. "Shareholders" see "shareholder". It means one who owns or holds a share or shares in a company, especially a corporation. See **Garner B. (ed.) Black's Law Dictionary 8 th ed.**
7. "Court" used in relation to a company, means the Federal High Court, and to the extent to which application may be made to it as; court includes the Court of Appeal and the Supreme Court of Nigeria. See **Section 567 CAMA Cap. C20, LFN 2004.**

Cross Reference

On duties of a chairman at a meeting, see **section 240 CAMA Cap. C20, LFN 2004**

---

**For Further Reading**

On meetings, types, minutes, adjournment, see, Orojo, J. Ola **Company Law and Practice in Nigeria** 3rd Edition, Mbeyi & Associates (Lagos, Nigeria) 1992. p. 273-293

## 240. Powers and duties of the chairman of the general meeting

(1) The chairman, [1] if any, of the board of directors [2] shall preside as chairman [1] at every general meeting [3] of the company, [4] or if there is no such chairman [1], or if he is not present within one hour after the time appointed for the holding of the meeting [3] or is unwilling to act, the directors [5] present shall elect one of their number to be chairman [1] of the meeting. [3]

(2) If at any meeting [3] no director [5] is willing to act as chairman [1] or if no director [5] is present within one hour after the time appointed for holding the meeting, [3] the members [6] present shall choose one of their members [6] to be chairman [1] of the meeting. [3]

(3) The duties and powers of the chairman [1] shall include a duty to-

(a) preserve order and powers to take such measures as are reasonably necessary to do so;

(b) see that proceedings are conducted in a regular manner;

(c) ensure that the true intention of the meeting [3] is carried out in resolving any issue that arises before it;

(d) ensure that all questions that arise are promptly decided; and

(e) act bonafide in the interest of the company [4]

(4) The chairman [1] shall cast his vote bonafide in the interest of the company[4] as a whole, provided that if he is also a shareholder[7], he may cast it in his own interest.

(5) The chairman [1] shall have power to adjourn a meeting [3] in accordance with section 239 (1) of this Act.

---

**Notes**

**Section 240(1)**

1. "Chairman" means a deliberative assembly's presiding officer. See **Garner B. (ed.) Black's Law Dictionary 8 th ed.**
2. "Board of Directors" means the governing body of a corporation, elected by the shareholders to establish corporate policy, appoint executive officers, and make major business and financial decisions. See **Garner B. (ed.) Black's Law Dictionary 8 th ed.**
3. "Meeting" means the gathering of people to discuss or act on matters in which they have a common interest; esp. the convening of a deliberate assembly to transact business. See **Garner B. (ed.) Black's Law Dictionary 8th ed.**
4. "Company" means a corporation - or, less commonly, an association, partnership, or union that carries on a commercial or industrial enterprise
   "Company" means a company formed and registered under this Act or, as the case may be, formed and registered in Nigeria before and in existence on the commencement of this Act; **Section 567 CAMA Cap C20 LFN, 2004**
5. "Director" includes any person occupying the position of director by whatever name called; and includes any person in accordance with whose directions or instructions the directors of the company are accustomed to act. See **section 567 CAMA Cap. C20 LFN 2004**
   Directors of the company registered under the Act are persons duly appointed by the company to direct and manage the business of the company. See **Garner B. (ed.) Black's Law Dictionary 8 th ed.**
6. "Members" see "member." It includes the heir, executor, administrator or other personal representative, as the case maybe, of the member. See **Section 567 CAMA Cap C20 LFN, 2004**
7. "Shareholder" see "shareholder." It means one who owns or holds a share or shares in a company especially a corporation. See **Garner B. (ed.) Black's Law Dictionary 8 th ed.**

**Cross Reference**

On obligation to hold general meeting, see section **213 CAMA Cap C20 LFN, 2004**
On meaning of directors, appointment of and removal, see **part 1X, CAMA Cap C20 LFN**, 2004

---

**For Further Reading**
On directors and their meetings, see, Bakibinga, D. J. "Directors' Duty to Act Bona Fide in the Interest of the Company" (1990) 39 (2) **The International and Comparative Law Quarterly 451.**

## 241. Minutes of proceedings and effect

(1) Every company[1] shall cause minutes[2] of-
(a) all proceedings of general meetings;[3]
(b) all proceedings at meetings[4] of its directors[5]; and
(c) where there are managers,[6] all proceedings at meetings[4] of its managers[6], to be entered in books kept for that purpose.

(2) Any such minute[2] if purporting to be signed by the chairman[7] of the meeting[4] at which the proceedings were held, or by the chairman[7] of the next succeeding meeting[4], shall be prima facie evidence of the proceedings.

(3) Where minutes[2] have been made, in accordance with the provisions of this section, of the proceedings at any general meeting[3] of the company[1] or meeting[4] of directors[5] or managers[6], then, until the contrary is proved, the meeting[4] shall be deemed to have been duly held and convened, and all proceedings had at the meeting[4] to have been duly had, and all appointments of directors[5], managers[6] or liquidators[8] shall be deemed to be valid.

(4) If a company[1] fails to comply with the provisions of subsection (1) of this section, the company[1] and every officer[9] of the company[1] who is in default shall be guilty of an offence and liable to a fine of N500.

---

**Notes**
**Section 241**

1. "Company" means a corporation or, less commonly, an association, partnership, or union that carries on a commercial or industrial enterprise

"Company" or "existing company" means a company formed and registered under this Act or, as the case may be, formed and registered in Nigeria before and in existence on the commencement of this Act. See **Section 567 CAMA Cap C20 LFN, 2004**

2. "Minutes" means memoranda or notes of a transaction or proceeding. See **Garner B. (ed.) Black's Law Dictionary 8 th ed.**
3. "General Meeting" see "Annual meeting" – a yearly meeting to elect or install officers or directors and to conduct other routine organisational business. See **Garner B., (ed.) Black's Law Dictionary 8 th ed.**
4. "Meeting" means the gathering of people to discuss or act on matters in which they have a common interest; esp. the convening of a deliberate assembly to transact business. See **Garner B. (ed.) Black's Law Dictionary 8th ed.**
5. "Directors" see "director". It means a person appointed or elected to sit on a board that manages the affairs of a corporation or other organisation by electing and exercising control over its officers. See **Garner B. (ed.) Black's Law Dictionary 8th ed.**
   "Director" includes any person occupying the position of director by whatever name called; and includes any person in accordance with whose directions or instructions the directors of the company are accustomed to act. See **section 567 CAMA Cap. C20 LFN 2004**
6. "Manager" means a person who administer or supervises the affairs of a business, office, or other organization, including authority over other managers. See **Garner B., (ed.) Black's Law Dictionary 8 th ed.**
7. "Chairman" means a deliberative assembly's presiding officer. See **Garner B. (ed.) Black's Law Dictionary 8 th ed.**
8. "Liquidator" means a person appointed to wind up a business's affairs, especially by selling off its assets. **See Garner B. (ed.) Black's Law Dictionary 8th ed.**
9. "Officer" in relation to a body corporate, includes a director, manager or secretary. **Section 567 CAMA Cap. C20 LFN, 2004**

**Cross Reference**

On obligation to keep minutes book and keep it open for inspection without charge, see **section 242, CAMA Cap C20 LFN, 2004.**

On powers and duties of a chairman in a general meeting, see **section 240 CAMA Cap. C20, LFN 2004**

On appointment of liquidator and cesser of director's powers, see **section 473 CAMA Cap. C20, LFN 2004**

On meaning of offence, see **section 2, Criminal Code, Cap. C38 LFN 2004**

**Cases**

In accordance with sections 241(2) and (3), where minutes are signed by the chairman of the meeting at which the proceedings were had or by the chairman of the next succeeding meeting, they will be evidence of the proceedings and until the contrary is proved, the meeting will be prima facie deemed to have been duly held. ***Tung v. Nigeria Carton and***

*Packaging Manufacturing Co. Ltd.* **Suit No. FRC/L/M. 82/78, (unreported).**

**For Further Reading** On minutes of meetings, see, Orojo, J. Ola **Company Law and Practice in Nigeria** 3rd Edition, Mbeyi & Associates (Lagos, Nigeria) 1992. P.293.

## 242. Inspection of minute books and copies

(1) The books containing the minutes [1] of proceedings of any general meeting[2] of a company[3] held on or after the commencement of this Act, shall be kept at the registered office [4] of the company[3], and shall during business hours (subject to such reasonable restrictions as the company[3] may by its articles[5] or in general meeting[2] impose, but so that no less than six hours in each day be allowed for inspection) be open to inspection by members [6] without charge.

(2) Any member[6] shall be entitled to be furnished within seven days after receipt of his request in that behalf to the company[3], with a copy of any such minutes [1] certified by the secretary[7] at a charge not exceeding 10 kobo for every hundred words.

(3) If any inspection required under this section is refused or if any copy required under this section is not sent within the proper time, the company[3] and every officer [8] of the company[3] who is in default shall be guilty of an offence and liable in respect of each offence to a fine of N25.

(4) In the case of any such refusal or default, the court [9] may by order compel an immediate inspection of the books in respect of all proceedings of general meetings,[2] or direct that the copies required shall be sent to the person requiring them.

---

**Notes**
**Section 242**

1. "Minutes" means memoranda or notes of a transaction or proceeding. See **Garner B. (ed.) Black's Law Dictionary 8th ed.**
2. "Meeting" means the gathering of people to discuss or act on matters in which they have a common interest; esp. the convening of a deliberate assembly to transact business. See **Garner B., (ed.) Black's Law Dictionary 8th ed.**

3. "Company" means a corporation or, less commonly, an association, partnership, or union that carries on a commercial or industrial enterprise. See **Garner B. (ed.) Black's Law Dictionary 8 th ed.** "Company" means a company formed and registered under this Act or, as the case may be, formed and registered in Nigeria before and in existence on the commencement of this Act. See **Section 567 CAMA Cap C20 LFN, 2004**
4. "Registered office" means the official address of a registered company; It must be notified to the Companies Registry before registration of the company and it must appear on company letter-head and order forms. Documents may be served to a company's registered office and various registers and records may be inspected there. See **Martins E. (ed.) Oxford Dictionary of Law 4 th ed.**
5. "Articles" means the articles of association of a company, as originally framed or as altered by special resolution, including so far as they apply to the regulations contained in Table A in the First Schedules of the Companies Act, 1922 or in that Table as altered by any subsequent enactment or reprint of the laws, or in Table A in the First Schedule to this Act. See **Section 567 CAMA Cap C20 LFN, 2004**
6. "Members" see "member". It includes the heir, executor, administrator or other personal representative, as the case maybe, of the member. See **Section 567 CAMA Cap C20 LFN, 2004**
7. "Secretary" an officer charged with recording a deliberative assembly's proceedings. See **Garner B, (ed) Black's Law Dictionary 8 th ed.**
8. "Officer" means in relation to a body corporate, includes a director, manager or secretary. See **Section 567 CAMA Cap. C20 LFN, 2004**
9. "Court" means the Federal High Court and to the extent to which application may be made to it as; court includes the Court of Appeal and the Supreme Court. **See Section 567, CAMA Cap. C20 LFN, 2004**

---

**Cases**

In accordance with sections 241(2) and (3), where minutes are signed by the chairman of the meeting at which the proceedings were had or by the chairman of the next succeeding meeting, they will be evidence of the proceedings and until the contrary is proved, the meeting will be prima facie deemed to have been duly held. ***Tung v. Nigeria Carton and Packaging Manufacturing Co. Ltd.*** **Suit No. FRC/L/M. 82/78, unreported.**

**243. The provisions of the foregoing sections shall apply to any class meetings except where expressly excluded by this Act.**

---

**Notes**
**Section 243**

1. "Meeting" means the gathering of people to discuss or act on matters in which they have a common interest; esp. the convening of a deliberate assembly to transact business. See **Garner B. (ed.) Black's Law Dictionary 8th ed.**

Cross Reference

On rights of companies to divide shares into classes **see section 118 CAMA CAP C20, LFN 2004**

---

*PART IX*

*Directors and secretaries of the company*

*Chapter 1 - Director*

## 244. Meaning of "directors"

(1) Directors [1]of a company[2] registered under this Act are persons duly appointed by the company[2] to direct and manage the business[3] of the company[2].

(2) In favour of any person dealing with the company [2] there shall be a rebuttable presumption[4] that all persons who are described by the company[2] as directors[1], whether as executive or otherwise, have been duly appointed.

(3) Where a person not duly appointed acts or holds himself out as a director[1], he shall be guilty of an offence, and on conviction shall be liable to imprisonment for two years or to a fine of N100 for each day he so acts or holds out himself as a director [1], or to both such imprisonment and fine and shall be restrained by the company[2].

(4) If it is the company [2] that holds him out as a director [1], it shall be liable to a fine of Nl,000 each day it holds him out, and he and the company[2] may be restrained by any member [5] from so acting unless or until he is duly appointed.

---

**Notes**

**Section 244(1)**

1. "Directors" see "Director." It means a person appointed or elected to sit on a board that manages the affairs of a corporation or other organisation by electing and exercising control over its officers. **See Garner B. (ed.) Black's Law Dictionary 8th ed.**

   "Director" includes any person occupying the position of director by whatever name called; and includes any person in accordance with whose directions or instructions the directors of the company are accustomed to act. See **Section 567 CAMA Cap. C20 LFN, 2004**

2. "Company" means a corporation or, less commonly, an association, partnership, or union that carries on a commercial or industrial enterprise
"Company" means a company formed and registered under this Act or, as the case may be, formed and registered in Nigeria before and in existence on the commencement of this Act. See **section 567 CAMA Cap. C20 LFN, 2004**
3. "Member" includes the heir, executor, administrator or other personal representative, as the case maybe, of the member. **Section 567 CAMA Cap C20 LFN, 2004**

Cross Reference

On shadow directors, see **section 245 CAMA Cap. C20, LFN 2004**

---

**Cases**

A 'company' or 'existing' company means....a company formed and registered in Nigeria before and in existence on the commencement of this Act. ***Agro Allied Dev. Ent. Ltd. v. Reefer*** **(2009) vol.31 W.R.N 1-185 at pg 7.**

A director is simply person duly appointed by the company to direct and manage the business of the company, irrespective of the fact that he is appointed by the board of directors of the company. ***Bernard Ojeyo Longe v. FBN*** **(2010) SC. march, 2010** .

A person will only lose the protection of section 60 only if he has actual knowledge that the appointment or qualification of the director is defective. ***Onwuka v. Taymani (1965) LL.R. 62***

**For Further Reading**

On director, duties, powers, see, Osunbor, O.A., The Company Director: His Appointment, powers and Duties; **Essays on Company Law**, pg 130.

## 245. Shadow director

(1) Without prejudice to the provisions of sections 244 and 250, and for the purposes of sections 253, 275 and 281 of this Act, "director"[1] shall include any person on whose instructions and directions the directors[1] are accustomed to act.

(2) Subject to sections 275, 280 and 281 of this Act, nothing contained in section 250 of this Act shall be deemed to derogate from the duties or liabilities of the duly appointed directors.[1]

(3) For the avoidance of doubt, the fact that a person in his professional capacity[2] advice and a director [1] acts on it shall not be construed[3] to make such a person under this Act a person in accordance with whose directions or instructions the director [1] of a company[4] is accustomed to act.

---

**Notes**

**Section 245(1)**

1. "Director"- means (1) one who manages, guides, or orders; a chief administrator (2) a person appointed or elected to sit on a board that manages the affairs of a corporation or other organisation by electing and exercising control over its officers. **Garner B. (ed.) Black's Law Dictionary 8th ed. Section 244 Companies and Allied Matters Act Cap C20 LFN, 2004**
   "Director" includes any person occupying the position of director by whatever name called; and includes any person in accordance with whose directions or instructions the directors of the company are accustomed to act **Section 567 Companies and Allied Matters Act Cap C20 LFN, 2004.**

**Section 245(3)**

2. "Professional Capacity" see "Capacity" – the role in which one performs an act in their corporate capacity **Garner B. (ed.) Black's Law Dictionary 8th ed.**
3. "Construe" means to analyze and explain the meaning of a sentence or passage **Garner B. (ed.) Black's Law Dictionary 8 th ed.**
4. "Company" means a corporation or, less commonly, an association, partnership, or union that carries on a commercial or industrial enterprise
   "Company" or "existing company" means a company formed and registered under this Act or, as the case may be, formed and registered in Nigeria before and in existence on the commencement of this Act. **Section 567 Companies and Allied Matters Act Cap C20 LFN, 2004.**

Cross Reference

On insolvent persons acting as directors, see **section 253 CAMA Cap. C20, LFN 2004**

On the recreation of a register of directors' shareholding, see **section 275 Cap. C20 LFN 2004**

On multiple directorship, see **section 281 CAMA Cap. C20, LFN 2004**

---

**Cases**

Directors have sometimes been called trustees, or commercial trustees, and sometimes they have been called managing partners. It does not matter what you call them so long as you understand what their true position is, which is that they are really commercial when managing a

trading concern for the benefit of themselves and all other shareholders in it. ***Iwuchukwu vs. Nwizu*** **(1994) 7 N.W.L.R (part357) 379 at 396.**
A person will only lose the protection of section 60 only if he has actual knowledge that the appointment or qualification of the director is defective. ***Onwuka v. Taymani (1965) LL.R. 62***

*Appointment of Directors*

## 246. Number of directors

(1) Every company [1] registered on or after the commencement of this Act shall have at least two directors [2] and every company [1] registered before that date shall before the expiration of six months from the commencement of this Act have at least two directors. [3]

(2) Any company [1] whose number of directors [2] falls below two, shall within one month of its so falling appoint new directors [2] and shall not carry on business after the expiration of one month, unless such new directors [2] are appointed.

(3) A director [2] or member [3] of a company [1] who knows that a company [1] carries on business after the number of directors [3] has fallen below two for more than 60 days shall be liable for all liabilities and debts incurred by the company [1] during that period when the company [1] so carried on business.

---

**Notes**
**Section 246(1)**

1. "Company" means a corporation or, less commonly, an association, partnership, or union that carries on a commercial or industrial enterprise. See **Garner B. (ed.) Black's Law Dictionary 8 th ed.**
2. "Company" or "existing company" means a company formed and registered under this Act or, as the case may be, formed and registered in Nigeria before and in existence on the commencement of this Act. **See section 567 CAMA, Cap. C20 LFN 2004**
3. "Director" see "director". It means a person appointed or elected to sit on a board that manages the affairs of a corporation or other organisation by electing and exercising control over its officers See **Garner B. (ed.) Black's Law Dictionary 8th ed.**
"Director" includes any person occupying the position of director by whatever name called; and includes any person in accordance with whose directions or instructions the directors of the company are accustomed to act. See **section 567 CAMA, Cap. 2004**

**Section 246(3)**

4. "Member" includes the heir, executor, administrator or other personal representative, as the case maybe, of the member. See **Section 567 CAMA CAP C20 LFN, 2004**

Cross Reference

On meaning of director see **section 244 CAMA Cap. C20, LFN 2004**

---

## 247. Appointment of first directors[1]

Subject to section 246 of this Act, the number of directors [1] and the names of the first directors [1] shall be determined in writing by the subscribers[2] of the memorandum of association [3] or a majority of them or the directors [1] may be named in the articles. [4]

---

**Notes**

**Section 247**

1. "Directors" see "Director" means (1) one who manages, guides, or orders; a chief administrator (2) a person appointed or elected to sit on a board that manages the affairs of a corporation or other organisation by electing and exercising control over its officers **Garner B. (ed.) Black's Law Dictionary 8th ed. Section 244 Companies and Allied Matters Act Cap C20 LFN, 2004**

   "Director" includes any person occupying the position of director by whatever name called; and includes any person in accordance with whose directions or instructions the directors of the company are accustomed to act. **Section 567 Companies and Allied Matters Act Cap C20 LFN, 2004**
2. "Subscribers" see "Subscriber" to pay money, normally once a year, to receive regular copies of a newspaper, magazine, etc. **Oxford Advanced Learner's Dictionary 6th ed.**
3. "Memorandum of Association" means a legal document setting up a corporation – either with or without limited liability – and including the company's name, purpose, and duration. **Garner B. (ed.) Black's Law Dictionary 8th ed.**

   "Memorandum of Association" see "Memorandum" - means the memorandum of association of a company as originally framed or as altered in pursuance of any enactment **Section 567 of the Companies and Allied Matters Act Cap C20 LFN, 2004**
4. "Articles" means the articles of association of a company, as originally framed or as altered by special resolution, including so far as they apply to the regulations contained in Table A in the First Schedules of the Companies Act, 1922 or in that Table as altered by any subsequent enactment or reprint of the laws, or in Table A in the First Schedule to this Act. **Section 567 CAMA Cap C20 LFN, 2004**

Cross Reference

For contents of a memorandum of Association, see section 27 **CAMA Cap C20 LFN, 2004.**

For contents of Articles of Association, see section 34 **CAMA Cap C20 LFN, 2004.**

---

**Cases**

The Articles of Association is the contract governing the relationship between shareholders and any infraction of such articles may confer on the shareholder adversely affected a right of action. ***Attorney General of Lagos State v. Eko Hotel Ltd &Oha Ltd*** **(2001) FWLR page. 1996 at 2000.**

---

## 248. Subsequent appointments of directors

(1) The members [1] at the annual general meeting [2] shall have power to re-elect or reject directors [3] and appoint new ones.

(2) In the event of all the directors [3] and shareholders [4] dying, any of the personal representatives [5] shall be able to apply to the court[6] for an order to convene a meeting [7] of all the personal representatives[5] of the shareholders [4] entitled to attend and vote at a general meeting[2] to appoint new directors [3] to manage the company [8], and if they fail to convene a meeting [7]the creditors,[9] if any, shall be able to do so.

---

**Notes**

**Section 248(1)**

1. "Members" member includes the heir, executor, administrator or other personal representative, as the case maybe, of the member. **Section 567 CAMA Cap C20 LFN, 2004**
2. "General meeting" see "Annual meeting" – a yearly meeting to elect or install officers or directors and to conduct other routine organisational business **Garner B. (ed.) Black's Law Dictionary 8 th ed.**
3. "Directors" see "Director" means (1) one who manages, guides, or orders; a chief administrator (2) a person appointed or elected to sit on a board that manages the affairs of a corporation or other organisation by electing and exercising control over its officers. **Garner B. (ed.) Black's Law Dictionary 8th ed. Section 244 Companies and Allied Matters Act Cap C20 LFN, 2004**

   "Director" includes any person occupying the position of director by whatever name called; and includes any person in accordance with whose directions or instructions the directors of the company are accustomed to act **Section 567 Companies and Allied Matters Act Cap C20 LFN, 2004**

**Section 248(2)**

4. "Shareholder" means one who owns or holds a share or shares in a company especially a corporation. **Garner B. (ed.) Black's Law Dictionary 8th ed.**
5. "Personal representative" means a person entitled to deal with a deceased person's estate in accordance with his will or under the rules relating to intestacy. See **Martin E. (ed) Oxford Dictionary of Law, 4th ed.**
   "Personal representatives" where customary law is applicable, includes successors appointed in respect of deceased contributories **; See section 567 CAMA CAP C20 LFN 2004**
6. "Court" means the Federal High Court and to the extent to which application may be made to it as; court includes the Court of Appeal and the Supreme Court. **See section 567, CAMA Cap C20 LFN, 2004**
7. "Meeting" means the gathering of people to discuss or act on matters in which they have a common interest; esp. the convening of a deliberate assembly to transact business. **Garner B. (ed.) Black's Law Dictionary 8th ed.**
8. "Company" means a corporation or, less commonly, an association, partnership, or union that carries on a commercial or industrial enterprise
   "Company" or "existing company" means a company formed and registered under this Act or, as the case may be, formed and registered in Nigeria before and in existence on the commencement of this Act. **Section 567 Companies and Allied Matters Act Cap C20 LFN, 2004**
9. "Creditors" see "Creditors" means one to whom a debt is owed; one who gives credit for money and goods **Garner B. (ed.) Black's Law Dictionary 8th ed.**

Cross Reference

On appointment of first directors, see **section 247 CAMA Cap C20 LFN 2004**

On the jurisdiction of the Federal High Court, see **section 251 Constitution of the Federal Republic of Nigeria, 1999 (as amended)**

---

## 249. Casual vacancy

(1) The board of directors [1] shall have power to appoint new directors[2] to fill any casual vacancy arising out of death, resignation, retirement or removal.

(2) Where a casual vacancy is filled by the directors [2], the person may be approved by the general meeting [3]at the next annual general meeting[3], and if not so approved, he shall forthwith cease to be a director[2].

(3) The directors[2] may increase the number of directors[2] so long as it does not exceed the maximum allowed by the articles[4],

but the general meeting[3] shall have power to increase or reduce the number of directors[2] generally and may determine in what rotation the directors[2] shall retire:
provided that such reduction shall not invalidate any prior act of the removed director.[1]

---

**Notes**
**Section 249 (1)**

1. "Board of Directors" means the governing body of a corporation, elected by the shareholders to establish corporate policy, appoint executive officers, and make major business and financial decisions See **Garner B. (ed.) Black's Law Dictionary 8 th ed.**
2. "Directors" see "Director" It means a person appointed or elected to sit on a board that manages the affairs of a corporation or other organisation by electing and exercising control over its officers See **Garner B. (ed.) Black's Law Dictionary 8th ed.**
   "Director" includes any person occupying the position of director by whatever name called; and includes any person in accordance with whose directions or instructions the directors of the company are accustomed to act. See **Section 567 CAMA CAP C20 LFN, 2004**
3. "General meeting" see "Annual meeting" means a yearly meeting to elect or install officers or directors and to conduct other routine organisational business. **Garner B. (ed.) Black's Law Dictionary 8 th ed.**

**Section 249(3)**

4. "Articles" means the articles of association of a company, as originally framed or as altered by special resolution, including so far as they apply to the regulations contained in Table A in the First Schedules of the Companies Act, 1922 or in that Table as altered by any subsequent enactment or reprint of the laws, or in Table A in the First Schedule to this Act. See **Section 567 CAMA Cap C20 LFN, 2004**

**Cross Reference**

On the meaning of and number of directors a company can have, see Section 244, 246, **CAMA Cap C20 LFN, 2004.**

---

**Cases**

The Articles of Association is the contract governing the relationship between shareholders and any infraction of such articles may confer on the shareholder adversely affected a right of action. ***Attorney General of Lagos State v. Eko Hotel Ltd &Oha Ltd*** **(2001) FWLR page. 1996** at **2000**

**For Further Reading**

On directors, see, Bakibinga, D. J. "Directors' Duty to Act Bona Fide in the Interest of the Company" (1990) 39 (2) **The International and Comparative Law Quarterly 451.**

## 250. Liability of a person where not duly appointed

Where a person not duly appointed as a director [1]acts as such on behalf of the company[2], his act shall not bind the company [2] and he shall be personally liable for such action:
Provided that where it is the company [2]which holds him out as director,[1] the company[2] shall be bound by his acts.

---

**Notes**

**Section 250**

1."Director" means (1) one who manages, guides, or orders; a chief administrator (2) a person appointed or elected to sit on a board that manages the affairs of a corporation or other organisation by electing and exercising control over its officers. **Garner B. (ed.) Black's Law Dictionary 8th ed.**

"Director" includes any person occupying the position of director by whatever name called; and includes any person in accordance with whose directions or instructions the directors of the company are accustomed to act. **Section 567 CAMA, Cap. C20, LFN 2004**

2. "Company" means a corporation - or, less commonly, an association, partnership, or union that carries on a commercial or industrial enterprise. **Garner B. (ed.) Black's Law Dictionary 8 th ed.**

"Company" or "existing company" means a company formed and registered under this Act or, as the case may be, formed and registered in Nigeria before and in existence on the commencement of this Act. **Section 567 CAMA, Cap. C20, LFN 2004**

**Cross Reference**

On meaning of Directors and appointment of first directors, see **section 244 & 246 CAMA Cap. C20, LFN 2004**

---

**Cases**

A person will only lose the protection of section 60 only if he has actual knowledge that the appointment or qualification of the director is defective. ***Onwuka v. Taymani (1965) LL.R. 62***

## 251. Share qualification of directors

(1) The shareholding qualification for directors [1] may be fixed by the articles of association[2] of the company[3]and unless and until so fixed no shareholding qualification shall be required.

(2) It shall be the duty of every director [1] who is by the articles[2] of the company[3] required to hold a specified share qualification, and who is not already so qualified, to obtain qualification within two months after his appointment.

(3) The office of director [1] of a company[3] shall be vacated if the director[1] does not within two months from the date of his appointment, obtain his qualification or after the expiration of the said period, he ceases at any time to hold his shareholding qualification.

(4) A person vacating office under this section shall be incapable of being re-appointed director of the company [3] until he has obtained his shareholding qualification.

(5) If, after the expiration of the said period, any unqualified person acts as a director [1] of the company,[2] he shall be liable to a fine ofN50 for every day between the expiration of the said period or the day on which he ceased to be qualified, as the case may be, and the last day on which it is proved that he acted as a director.

---

**Notes**
**Section 251(1)**

1. "Director" means (1) one who manages, guides, or orders; a chief administrator (2) a person appointed or elected to sit on a board that manages the affairs of a corporation or other organisation by electing and exercising control over its officers. **Garner B. (ed.) Black's Law Dictionary 8th ed.**
   "Director" includes any person occupying the position of director by whatever name called; and includes any person in accordance with whose directions or instructions the directors of the company are accustomed to act. **Section 567 CAMA, Cap. C20 LFN 2004**
2. "Articles" see "articles of association" means a governing document that sets forth the basic terms of a corporation's existence, including the number and classes of shares and the purposes and duration of the corporation. **Garner B., (ed.) Black's Law Dictionary 8 th ed.**
   "Articles" means the articles of association of a company, as originally framed or as altered by special resolution, including so far as they apply to the regulations contained in Table A in the First Schedules of the Companies Act, 1922 or in that Table as altered by any subsequent enactment or reprint of the laws, or in Table A in the First Schedule to this Act; **Section 567 CAMA, Cap. C20, LFN 2004**
3. "Company" means a corporation or less commonly, an association, partnership, or union that carries on a commercial or industrial enterprise. **Garner B., (ed.) Black's Law Dictionary 8 th ed.**
   "Company" or "existing company" means a company formed and registered under this Act or, as the case may be, formed and registered

in Nigeria before and in existence on the commencement of this Act. **Section 567 CAMA, Cap. C20, LFN 2004** .

Cross Reference

On contents of the Articles of Association, see section 33 **CAMA Cap C20 LFN, 2004.**

**Cases**

The Articles of Association is the contract governing the relationship between shareholders and any infraction of such articles may confer on the shareholder adversely affected a right of action. ***Attorney General of Lagos State v. Eko Hotel Ltd &Oha Ltd*** **(2001) FWLR page. 1996** at **2000**

## 252. Duty of directors to disclose age to the company

(1) Any person who is appointed or to his knowledge proposed to be appointed director [1] of a public company [2] and who is 70 or more years old shall disclose this fact to the members [3] at the general meeting[4].

(2) Any person who fails to disclose his age as required under this section shall be guilty of an offence and liable to a fine of N500.

**Notes**

**Section 252**

1. "Director" means a person appointed or elected to sit on a board that manages the affairs of a corporation or other organisation by electing and exercising control over its officers See **Garner B., (ed.) Black's Law Dictionary 8th ed.**
   "Director" includes any person occupying the position of director by whatever name called; and includes any person in accordance with whose directions or instructions the directors of the company are accustomed to act. **Section 567 CAMA, Cap. C20, LFN 2004.**
2. "Public company" any company other company other than a private company shall be a public company and its memorandum shall state that it is a public company. **Section 24 CAMA, Cap. C20 LFN 2004.**
3. "Member" member includes the heir, executor, administrator or other personal representative, as the case maybe, of the member. **Section 567 CAMA, Cap. C20, LFN 2004.**
4. "General meeting" see "Annual meeting" a yearly meeting to elect or install officers or directors and to conduct other routine organisational business. **Garner B. (ed.) Black's Law Dictionary 8 th ed.**

Cross Reference

For characteristics of a public company, see **section 24, CAMA Cap. C20 LFN, 2004.**
On appointment of first directors, see **section 246 CAMA Cap. C20, LFN 2004**
On meaning of offence, see **section 2 Criminal Code Cap. C38 LFN 2004**

---

## 253.Provisions as to insolvent persons[1] acting as directors[2]

(1) If any person, being an insolvent person [1], acts as director [2] of or directly or indirectly takes part in or is concerned in the management of any company,[3] he shall be guilty of an offence and liable on conviction to a fine ofN500, or to imprisonment for a term not less than six months or more than two years, or both.

(2) In this section, "company" includes an unregistered company.[4]

---

**Notes**
**Section 253(1)**

1. "Insolvent person" means any person in Nigeria who, in respect of any judgment, Act or court order against him, is unable to satisfy execution or other process issued thereon in favour of a creditor, and the execution or other process remains unsatisfied for not less than six weeks. See **section 567 CAMA, Cap. C20, LFN 2004**
2. "Director" means a person appointed or elected to sit on a board that manages the affairs of a corporation or other organisation by electing and exercising control over its officers See **Garner B. (ed.) Black's Law Dictionary 8th ed.**
   "Director" includes any person occupying the position of director by whatever name called; and includes any person in accordance with whose directions or instructions the directors of the company are accustomed to act. **Section 567 CAMA, Cap. C20, LFN 2004.**
3. "Company" means a corporation - or, less commonly, an association, partnership, or union that carries on a commercial or industrial enterprise. See **Garner B, (ed) Black's Law Dictionary 8 th ed.**
   "Company" or "existing company" means a company formed and registered under this Act or, as the case may be, formed and registered in Nigeria before and in existence on the commencement of this Act. See **Section 567 CAMA, Cap. C20, LFN 2004**

**Section 253(2)**

4. "Unregistered company" includes any partnership, association or company with the following exceptions-

(a) a company and any existing company registered under this Act; and
(b) a partnership, association or company which consists of less than eight members and is not a foreign partnership, association or company.

**Section 567 of the Companies and Allied Matters Act Cap C20 LFN, 2004**

---

## 254. Restraint of fraudulent persons

(1) Where-

(a) a person is convicted by a High Court of any offence in connection with the promotion, formation or management of a company[1]; or

(b) in the course of winding up [2] a company[1] it appears that a person-

(i) has been guilty of any offence for which he is liable (whether he has been convicted or not) under section 506 of this Act; or

(ii) has otherwise been guilty, while an officer [3] of the company[2], of any fraud in relation to the company [1] or of any breach of his duty to the company [1], the court[4] shall make an order that that person shall not be a director[5] of or in any way, whether directly or indirectly, be concerned or take part in the management of a company for a specified period not exceeding 10 years.

(2) In the foregoing subsection, the High Court and the court,[4] where used in relation to the making of an order against any person by virtue of paragraph (a) of subsection (1) of this section, include the court[4] before which he is convicted, as well as any court[4] having jurisdiction to wind up [2] the company,[1] and in relation to the granting of leave means any court [4] having jurisdiction to wind up[3] the company[1] as respects which leave is sought.

(3) A person intending to apply for the making of an order under this section by the court [4] having jurisdiction to wind-up[2] a company[1] shall give not less than ten days' notice of his intention to the person against whom the order is sought, and on the hearing of the application, the last mentioned person may appear and himself give evidence or call witnesses.

(4) An application for the making of an order under this section by the court[4] having jurisdiction to wind up [2] a company,[1] may be made by the official receiver [6], or by the liquidator [7] of the company[1] or by any person who is or has been a member [8] or creditor[9] of the company[1]; and on the hearing of any application for

an order under this section by the official receiver [6] or the liquidator,[7] or of any application for leave under this section by a person against whom an order has been made on the application of the official receiver[6] or liquidator[7], the official receiver[6] or liquidator[7]shall appear and call the attention of the court [4] to any matters which seem to him to be relevant, and may himself give evidence or call witnesses.

(5) An order may be made by virtue of paragraph (b) (ii) of subsection (1) of this section, notwithstanding that the person concerned may be criminally liable in respect of the matters on the ground of which the order is to be made, and for the purposes of the said paragraph (b) (ii) "officer" includes any person in accordance with whose directions or instructions the directors of the company have been accustomed to act.

(6) If any person acts in contravention of an order made under this section, he shall be guilty of an offence and in respect of each offence, be liable on conviction to a fine of N500 or to imprisonment for a term of not less than six months or more than two years, or both.

---

**Notes**
**Section 254(1)**

1. "Company" means a corporation or, less commonly, an association, partnership, or union that carries on a commercial or industrial enterprise. **Garner B. (ed) Black's Law Dictionary 8 [th] ed.**
   "Company" or "existing company" means a company formed and registered under this Act or, as the case may be, formed and registered in Nigeria before and in existence on the commencement of this Act. **Section 567 CAMA, Cap. C20, LFN 2004**
2. "Winding up" means the process of settling accounts and liquidating assets in anticipation of a partnership's or a corporation's dissolution. See **Garner B. (ed) Black's Law Dictionary 8 [th] ed.**
3. "Officer" is used in relation to a body corporate, includes a director, manager or secretary. **See section 567 CAMA, Cap. C20, LFN 2004.**
4. "Court" means the Federal High Court and to the extent to which application may be made to it as; court includes the Court of Appeal and the Supreme Court. **Section 567 CAMA, Cap. C20, LFN 2004**
5. "Director" means (1) one who manages, guides, or orders; a chief administrator (2) a person appointed or elected to sit on a board that manages the affairs of a corporation or other organisation by electing and exercising control over its officers. **Garner B. (ed) Black's Law Dictionary 8[th] ed.**

"Director" includes any person occupying the position of director by whatever name called; and includes any person in accordance with whose directions or instructions the directors of the company are accustomed to act. **Section 567 CAMA, Cap. C20, LFN 2004.**

6. "Official receiver" "Official Receiver" see "receiver" – a disinterested person appointed by a court, or by a corporation or other person, for the protection or collection of property that is the subject of diverse claims. **Garner B. (ed) Black's Law Dictionary 8 th ed.**
7. "Liquidator" means the act of adjourning; to end or postpone a proceeding. **Garner B. (ed) Black's Law Dictionary 8 th ed.**
8. "Member" member includes the heir, executor, administrator or other personal representative, as the case maybe, of the member. **Section 567 CAMA, Cap. C20, LFN 2004.**
9. "Creditor" means one to whom a debt is owed whether contractual or otherwise. **Garner B. (ed.) Black's Law Dictionary 8 th ed.**

**Cross Reference**

For establishment and composition of high courts in F.C.T and state, see sections 255, 256, 270 and 271 respectively of the Constitution of FRN, 1999.

On how a liquidator is appointed, see section 473, **CAMA Cap C20 LFN, 2004.**

A Liquidator owes a duty to the whole body of creditors and shareholders and to the court to make himself thoroughly acquainted with the affairs of the company and suppress or conceal anything coming to his knowledge in the course of his investigation which is material; ***Re J.A. Balogun* (1977) FRCR 122**

---

## 255. Appointment of director for life

A person may be appointed a director[1] for life provided that he shall be removable under section 262 of this Act.

---

**Notes**

**Section 255**

1. "Director" means (1) one who manages, guides, or orders; a chief administrator (2) a person appointed or elected to sit on a board that manages the affairs of a corporation or other organisation by electing and exercising control over its officers. **See Garner B. (ed) Black's Law Dictionary 8th ed.**

   "Director" includes any person occupying the position of director by whatever name called; and includes any person in accordance with whose directions or instructions the directors of the company are accustomed to act. **See section 567 CAMA, Cap. C20, LFN 2004.**

---

**Cases**

Where a Director claims to be appointed for life or some indefinite period, the terms of the terms of the appointment must be clear and definite; ***Odulana v. Globe Fishing Ind. Ltd*** **Suit FHC/L/55/60 07 30/6/81 (unreported)**

## 256. Right to appoint a director at any age

Subject to the provisions of this Act, a person may be appointed a director [1] of a public company [2] notwithstanding that he is 70 years or more of age but special notice shall be required of any resolution[3] appointing or approving the appointment of such a director[1] for the purposes of this section, and the notice given to the company[2] and by the company [2] to its members [4] shall state the age of the person to whom it relates.

---

**Notes**
**Section 256**

1. "Director" means (1) one who manages, guides, or orders; a chief administrator (2) a person appointed or elected to sit on a board that manages the affairs of a corporation or other organisation by electing and exercising control over its **Garner B. (ed) Black's Law Dictionary 8th ed.**
   "Director" includes any person occupying the position of director by whatever name called; and includes any person in accordance with whose directions or instructions the directors of the company are accustomed to act. **Section 567 CAMA, Cap. C20, LFN 2004.**
2. "Public company" any company other company other than a private company shall be a public company and its memorandum shall state that it is a public company. **Section 24 CAMA, Cap. C20 LFN 2004.**
3. "Resolution" means a main motion that formally expresses the sense, will, or action of a deliberative assembly. **Garner B. (ed) Black's Law Dictionary 8th ed.**
4. "Members" member includes the heir, executor, administrator or other personal representative, as the case may be, of the member. **Section 567 CAMA, Cap. C20, LFN 2004.**

Cross Reference

On types of resolution, see section 233 CAMA Cap C20 LFN, 2004.

On duty of directors to disclose age, see **section 252 CAMA Cap. C20, LFN 2004**

---

## 257. Disqualification for directorship

The following persons shall be disqualified from being director[1]-

(a) an infant, that is, a person under the age of 18 years;

(b) a lunatic[2] or person of unsound mind;

(c) a person disqualified under sections 253, 254 and 258 of this Act;

(d) a corporation[3] other than its representative appointed to the board for a given term.

---

**Notes**

**Section 257(1)**

1. "Director" means (1) one who manages, guides, or orders; a chief administrator (2) a person appointed or elected to sit on a board that manages the affairs of a corporation or other organisation by electing and exercising control over its officers. **Garner B. (ed) Black's Law Dictionary 8th ed.**
"Director" includes any person occupying the position of director by whatever name called; and includes any person in accordance with whose directions or instructions the directors of the company are accustomed to act. **Section 567 CAMA, Cap. C20, LFN 2004.**
2. "Lunatic" see "insane" – mentally deranged; suffering from one or more delusions or false beliefs that (1) have no foundation in reason or reality, (2) are not credible to any reasonable person of sound mind, and (3) cannot be overcome in a sufferer's mind by any amount of evidence or argument. **Garner B. (ed) Black's Law Dictionary 8 th ed.**
3. "Corporation" means an entity usually business having authority under law to act as a single person distinct from the shareholders who own it and having rights to issue stock and exist indefinitely; a group or succession of persons established in accordance with legal rules into a legal or juristic person that has legal personality distinct from the natural persons who make it up, exists indefinitely apart from them, and has the legal powers that its constitution gives it. **Garner B. (ed) Black's Law Dictionary 8th ed.**

---

## 258. Vacation of office of director

(1) The office of director [1] shall be vacated if the director [1]-

(a) ceases to be a director [1] by virtue of section 251 of this Act; or

(b) becomes bankrupt[2] or makes any arrangement[3] or composition[4] with his creditors[5] generally; or

(c) becomes prohibited from being a director [1] by reason of any order made under section 254 of this Act; or

(d) becomes of unsound mind; or

(e) resigns his office by notice in writing to the company [6].

(2) Where a director [1] presents himself for re-election, a record of his attendance at the meetings of the board during the preceding one year shall be made available to members [7] at the general meeting[8] where he is to be re-elected.

---

**Notes**
**Section 258**

1. "Director" means (1) one who manages, guides, or orders; a chief administrator (2) a person appointed or elected to sit on a board that manages the affairs of a corporation or other organisation by electing and exercising control over its officers. **Garner B. (ed) Black's Law Dictionary 8th ed.**
   "Director" includes any person occupying the position of director by whatever name called; and includes any person in accordance with whose directions or instructions the directors of the company are accustomed to act. **Section 567 CAMA, Cap. C20 LFN 2004.**
2. "Bankrupt" means a person who cannot meet current financial obligations; an insolvent person. **Garner B. (ed) Black's Law Dictionary 8th ed.**
3. "Arrangement" means any change in the rights or liabilities of members, debenture holders or creditors of a company or any class of them in the regulation of a company, other than a change effected under any other provision of this Act or by the unanimous agreement of all parties affected thereby. **Section 537, CAMA Cap C20 LFN, 2004.**
4. "Composition" means an agreement between a debtor and two or more creditors for the adjustment or discharge of an obligation for some lesser amount; an agreement among the debtor and two or more creditors that the debtor will pay the creditors less than their full claims in full satisfaction of their claims. **Garner B. (ed) Black's Law Dictionary 8th ed.**
5. "Creditors" see "Creditors" - one to whom a debt is owed; one who gives credit for money and goods. **Garner B. (ed) Black's Law Dictionary 8th ed.**
6. "Company" means a corporation or, less commonly, an association, partnership, or union that carries on a commercial or industrial enterprise. **Garner B. (ed) Black's Law Dictionary 8 th ed.**
   "Company" or "existing company" means a company formed and registered under this Act or, as the case may be, formed and registered in Nigeria before and in existence on the commencement of this Act. **Section 567 CAMA, Cap. C20, LFN 2004**
7. "Members" see "member". It includes the heir, executor, administrator or other personal representative, as the case may be, of the member; **Section 567 CAMA, Cap. C20, LFN 2004.**

8. "General meeting" see "Annual meeting" – a yearly meeting to elect or install officers or directors and to conduct other routine organisational business. **Garner B. (ed) Black's Law Dictionary 8 [th] ed.**

Cross Reference

For types of meeting, see part VIII, **CAMA Cap C20 LFN, 2004.**

On the requirement or otherwise of shareholding qualifications for directors, see **section 251 CAMA Cap.C20, LFN 2004**

## 259. Rotation of directors

(1) Unless the articles [1] otherwise provide, at the first annual general meeting[2] of the company[3] all the directors [4] shall retire from office, and at the annual general meeting [2] in every subsequent year one third of the directors [4] for the time being, or if their number is not three or a multiple of three, then the number nearest one third shall retire from office.

(2) The directors [4] to retire in every year shall be those who have been longest in office since their last election, but as between persons who became directors [4] on the same day those to retire shall (unless they otherwise agree among themselves) be determined by lot.

(3) The company [3] at the meeting[2] at which a director [4] retires in the manner mentioned in subsections (1) and (2) of this section, may fill the vacated office by electing a person to that office and in default, the retiring director [4] shall, if offering himself for re-election, be deemed to have been re-elected, unless at such meeting[2] it is expressly resolved not to fill such vacated office or unless a resolution[6] for the re-election of such director [4] shall have been put to the meeting [2] and lost.

(4) No person other than a director [4] retiring at the meeting[2]shall, unless recommended by the directors [4], be eligible for election to the office of director [4] at any general meeting [2] unless not less than three nor more than 21 days before the date appointed for the meeting[2] there shall have been left at the registered office [6] or head office of the company [3] notice in writing, signed by a member [7] duly qualified to attend and vote at the meeting [2] for which such notice is given, of his intention to propose such person for election, and also notice in writing signed by that person of his willingness to be elected.

**Notes**

**Section 259(1)**

1. "Articles" see "articles of association" - means a governing document that sets forth the basic terms of a corporation's existence, including the number and classes of shares and the purposes and duration of the corporation. See **Garner B. (ed) Black's Law Dictionary 8 th ed.**
"Articles" means the articles of association of a company, as originally framed or as altered by special resolution, including so far as they apply to the regulations contained in Table A in the First Schedules of the Companies Act, 1922 or in that Table as altered by any subsequent enactment or reprint of the laws, or in Table A in the First Schedule to this Act. See **Section 567 CAMA, Cap. C20, LFN 2004.**
2. "Annual general meeting" see "annual meeting" – a yearly meeting to elect or install officers or directors and to conduct other routine organizational business. See **Garner B. (ed) Black's Law Dictionary 8th ed.**
3. "Company" means a corporation - or, less commonly, an association, partnership, or union that carries on a commercial or industrial enterprise. See **Garner B. (ed) Black's Law Dictionary 8 th ed.**
"Company" or "existing company" means a company formed and registered under this Act or, as the case may be, formed and registered in Nigeria before and in existence on the commencement of this Act. **See section 567 CAMA, Cap. C20, LFN 2004.**
4. "Director" means (1) one who manages, guides, or orders; a chief administrator (2) a person appointed or elected to sit on a board that manages the affairs of a corporation or other organisation by electing and exercising control over its officers. **Garner B. (ed) Black's Law Dictionary 8th ed.**
"Director" includes any person occupying the position of director by whatever name called; and includes any person in accordance with whose directions or instructions the directors of the company are accustomed to act. See **Section 567 CAMA, CAP C20 LFN 2004**

**Section 259(3)**

5. "Resolution" means a main motion that formally expresses the sense, will, or action of a deliberative assembly. **Garner B (ed) Black's Law Dictionary 8th ed.**

**Section 259(4)**

6. "Registered office" means the official address of a registered company. It must be notified to the Companies Registry before registration of the company and it must appear on company letter-head and order forms. Documents may be served to a company's registered office and various registers and records may be inspected there. **Martins E. (ed.) Oxford Dictionary of Law 4 th ed.**
7. "Members" see "member." It includes the heir, executor, administrator or other personal representative, as the case may be, of the member. See **section 567 CAMA, Cap. C20, LFN 2004.**

Cross Reference

On obligation to provide notice and length of notice for meeting, see **section 217, CAMA., Cap. C20 LFN 2004**

For types of meeting, see generally **Part VIII, CAMA Cap. C20 LFN, 2004.**

On appointment of first and subsequent directors, see **section 247 & 248 CAMA Cap. C20, LFN 2004**

**Cases**

The Articles of Association is the contract governing the relationship between shareholders and any infraction of such articles may confer on the shareholder adversely affected a right of action. ***Attorney General of Lagos State v. Eko Hotel Ltd &Oha Ltd*** **(2001) FWLR page 1996** at **2000**

## 260. Validity of acts of directors

The acts of a director,[1] manager,[2] or secretary[3] shall be valid notwithstanding any defect that may afterwards be discovered in his appointment or qualification.

**Notes**

**Section 260**

1. "Director" means (1) one who manages, guides, or orders; a chief administrator (2) a person appointed or elected to sit on a board that manages the affairs of a corporation or other organisation by electing and exercising control over its officers. **Garner B. (ed) Black's Law Dictionary 8th ed.**

   "Director" includes any person occupying the position of director by whatever name called; and includes any person in accordance with whose directions or instructions the directors of the company are accustomed to act . **See section 567 CAMA, Cap. C20, LFN 2004.**
2. "Manager" means a person who administers or supervises the affairs of a business, office, or other organization. **Garner B. (ed) Black's Law Dictionary 8th ed.**
3. "Secretary" means (1) an administrative assistant (2) a corporate officer in charge of official correspondence, minutes of board meetings, and records of stock ownership and transfer(3) an officer charged with recording a deliberative assembly's proceedings. **Garner B (ed) Black's Law Dictionary 8th ed.**

Cross Reference

On appointment of first and subsequent directors, see **section 247 & 248 CAMA Cap. C20, LFN 2004**

**Cases**

The Company is distinct from its promoters or directors and a director is an agent of the company. Consequently, where a director enters into a contract in the name of or purporting to bind the company, it is the company, as principal that is liable, not the director . ***Dansa Foods (Nig.) Ltd v. Isong*** **(2011) ALL F.W.L.R. part 596 404-600 at p.595**

**For Further Reading**

On directors, their discretions, powers, see, Bakibinga, D.J., "Directors' Duty to Act Bona Fide in the Interest of the Company" (1990) 39 (2) **The International and Comparative Law Quarterly 451.**

## 261. Mode of voting on appointment of directors

(1) At a general meeting [1] of a company [2] other than a private company,[3] a motion for the appointment of two or more persons as directors[4] of the company[2] by a single resolution [5] shall not be made, unless resolution[5] that it shall be so made has first been agreed to by the meeting[1] without any vote being given against it.

(2) A resolution[5] moved in contravention of this section shall be void, whether or not it being so moved was objected to at the time: Provided that-

(a) this subsection shall not be taken as excluding the operation of section 260 of this Act; and

(b) where a resolution [5] so moved is passed, no provision for automatic re-appointment of retiring directors [4] in default of another appointment shall apply.

(3) For the purposes of this section, a motion for approving a person's appointment or for nominating a person for appointment shall be treated as a motion for his appointment.

(4) Nothing in this section shall apply to a resolution [5] altering the company's articles .[6]

---

**Notes**

**Section 261**

1. "Meeting" means the gathering of people to discuss or act on matters in which they have a common interest; esp. the convening of a deliberate assembly to transact business. **Garner B. (ed) Black's Law Dictionary 8th ed.**

2. “Company” means a corporation or, less commonly, an association, partnership, or union that carries on a commercial or industrial enterprise. **Garner B. (ed) Black’s Law Dictionary 8 th ed.**
"Company" or "existing company" means a company formed and registered under this Act or, as the case may be, formed and registered in Nigeria before and in existence on the commencement of this Act. **Section 567 CAMA, Cap. C20, 2004.**
3. “Private company” means one which is stated in its memorandum to be a private company. **Section 22 CAMA, Cap. C20, LFN 2004.**
4. “Director” means (1) one who manages, guides, or orders; a chief administrator (2) a person appointed or elected to sit on a board that manages the affairs of a corporation or other organisation by electing and exercising control over its officers. **Garner B. (ed) Black’s Law Dictionary 8th ed.**
"Director" includes any person occupying the position of director by whatever name called; and includes any person in accordance with whose directions or instructions the directors of the company are accustomed to act. **Section 567 CAMA, Cap. C20, LFN 2004.**
5. “Resolution” means a main motion that formally expresses the sense, will, or action of a deliberative assembly. **Garner B. (ed) Black’s Law Dictionary 8th ed.**

**Section 261(4)**

6. “Articles of Association” means a governing document that sets forth the basic terms of a corporation’s existence, including the number and classes of shares and the purposes and duration of the corporation. **Garner B. (ed) Black’s Law Dictionary 8 th ed.**
"Articles" means the articles of association of a company, as originally framed or as altered by special resolution, including so far as they apply to the regulations contained in Table A in the First Schedules of the Companies Act, 1922 or in that Table as altered by any subsequent enactment or reprint of the laws, or in Table A in the First Schedule to this Act. **Section 567 CAMA, Cap. C20, LFN 2004.**

Cross Reference

On types of resolution; see section **233 CAMA Cap C20 LFN, 2004**
On validity of acts of directors with defective appointment, see **section 260 CAMA Cap C20 LFN, 2004.**

---

**Cases**

The Articles of Association is the contract governing the relationship between shareholders and any infraction of such articles may confer on the shareholder adversely affected a right of action. ***Attorney General of Lagos State v Eko Hotel Ltd &Oha Ltd*** **(2001) FWLR page. 1996** at **2000**

## 262. Removal of directors

(1) A company[1] may by ordinary resolution[2] remove a director[3] before the expiration of his period of office,

notwithstanding anything in its articles[4] or in any agreement between it and him.

(2) A special notice shall be required of any resolution [2] to remove a director[3] under this section, or to appoint some other person instead of a director [3] so removed, at the meeting [5] at which he is removed, and on receipt of notice of an intended resolution [2] to remove a director[3] under this section, the company [1] shall forthwith send a copy of it to the director [3] concerned, and the director [3] (whether or not he is a member [6] of the company [1]) shall be entitled to be heard on the resolution [2] at the meeting. [5]

(3) Where notice is given of an intended resolution [2] to remove a director[3] under this section and the director [3] concerned makes with respect to it representations in writing to the company [1] (not exceeding a reasonable length) and requests their notification to members[6] of the company,[1] the company[1] shall, unless the representations are received by it too late for it to do so-

(a) in any notice of the resolution [2] given to members[6] of the company[1] state the fact of the representations having been made; and

(b) send a copy of the representations to every member of the company[1] to whom notice of the meeting [5] is sent (whether before or after receipt of the representations by the company[1]),

and if a copy of the representations is not sent as required in this section because it is received too late or because of the company's[1] default, the director[3] may (without prejudice to his right to be heard orally) require that the representations shall be read out at the meeting: [5]

Provided that copies of the representations need not be sent out and the representations need not be read out at the meeting [5] if, on the application either of the company[1] or any other person who claims to be aggrieved, the court [7] is satisfied that the rights conferred by this section are being abused to secure needless publicity for defamatory matter and the court [7] may order the company's [1] costs on an application under this section to be paid in whole or in part by the director,[3] notwithstanding that he is not a party to the application.

(4) A vacancy created by the removal of a director [3] under this section, if not filled at the meeting [5] at which he is removed, may be filled as a casual vacancy.

(5) A person appointed director [3] in place of a person removed under this section shall be treated, for the purpose of determining the time at which he or any other director [3] is to retire, as if he had become director[3] on the day on which the person in whose place he is appointed was last appointed a director. [3]

(6) Nothing in this section shall be taken as depriving a person removed under it of compensation or damages payable to him in respect of the termination of his appointment as a director [3] or of any appointment terminating with that as director, [3] or as derogating from any power to remove a director [3] which may exist apart from this section.

---

**Notes**
**Section 262**

1. "Company" means a corporation - or, less commonly, an association, partnership, or union that carries on a commercial or industrial enterprise. **Garner B. (ed) Black's Law Dictionary 8 th ed.**
   "Company" or "existing company" means a company formed and registered under this Act or, as the case may be, formed and registered in Nigeria before and in existence on the commencement of this Act. **Section 567 CAMA, Cap. C20, LFN 2004.**
2. "Ordinary resolution" means a decision reached by a simple majority (i.e. of more than 50%) of company members voting in person or by proxy. It is appropriate where no other type of resolution is expressly required by the Companies Acts or the articles of association. **Martins E. (ed.) Oxford Dictionary of Law 4 th ed.**
3. "Director" means (1) one who manages, guides, or orders; a chief administrator (2) a person appointed or elected to sit on a board that manages the affairs of a corporation or other organisation by electing and exercising control over its officers. **Garner B. (ed) Black's Law Dictionary 8th ed.**
   "Director" includes any person occupying the position of director by whatever name called; and includes any person in accordance with whose directions or instructions the directors of the company are accustomed to act. **Section 567 CAMA, Cap. C20, LFN 2004.**
4. "Articles" see "articles of association" means a governing document that sets forth the basic terms of a corporation's existence, including the number and classes of shares and the purposes and duration of the corporation. **Garner B. (ed) Black's Law Dictionary 8 th ed.**
   "Articles" means the articles of association of a company, as originally framed or as altered by special resolution, including so far as they apply to the regulations contained in Table A in the First Schedules of the Companies Act, 1922 or in that Table as altered by any subsequent enactment or reprint of the laws, or in Table A in the First Schedule to this Act. **Section 567 CAMA, Cap. C20, LFN 2004.**

**Section 262(2)**

5. "Meeting" means the gathering of people to discuss or act on matters in which they have a common interest; esp. the convening of a deliberate assembly to transact business. **Garner B. (ed) Black's Law Dictionary 8th ed.**
6. "Members" member includes the heir, executor, administrator or other personal representative, as the case may be, of the member; **Section 567 CAMA, Cap. C20, LFN 2004.**
7. "Court" used in relation to a company means the Federal High court, and to the extent to which application may be made to it as; court includes the Court of Appeal and the Supreme Court of Nigeria. See **Section 567 CAMA, Cap. C20, LFN 2004.**

**Cross Reference**

On types of resolution, see section 233 **CAMA Cap C20 LFN, 2004.**

**On appointment of first and subsequent directors, see sections 247 & 248** CAMA CAP C20, LFN 2004

---

**Cases**

The power to remove a director under the Articles of Association is made subject to the provisions of CAMA. ***Bernard Ojeyo Longe v. FBN.***

The Articles of Association is the contract governing the relationship between shareholders and any infraction of such articles may confer on the shareholder adversely affected a right of action. ***Attorney General of Lagos State v Eko Hotel Ltd &Oha Ltd*** **[2001] FWLR page. 1996 at 2000.**

The combined requirement of section 266(1) and 262 is that a director to be removed must be given notice of the meeting. ***Longe v. F.B.N*** **(2010) SC. 116/2007, delivered on 5/03/2010.**

Generally companies speak or express their decisions through resolutions, which must be validly passed. No member of a company has a right to unilaterally commit the company on any matter without its consent and approval. Let me emphatically say that no member of a company is allowed to wake up one morning and sell off the company. ***New Resources Int'l Ltd. & Anor. v. Ejike Oranusi (2010) LPELR-CA/L/461/08.***

*Proceedings of directors*

## 263. Proceedings of directors

(1) The directors [1] may meet together for the dispatch of business,[2] adjourn and otherwise regulate their meetings [3] as they think fit:

Provided that the first meeting [3] of the directors [1] shall be held not later than six months after the incorporation of the company. [4]

(2) Any question arising at any meeting [3] shall be decided by a majority of votes, and in case of an equality of votes, the chairman shall have a second or casting vote.

(3) A director [1] may, and the secretary [5] on the requisition of a director shall, at any time summon a meeting [3] of the directors. [1]

(4) The directors [1] may elect a chairman of their meetings [3] and determine the period for which he is to hold office; but if no such chairman is elected or if at any meeting [3] the chairman is not present within five minutes after the time appointed for holding the same, the directors [1] present may choose one of their number to be chairman of the meeting. [3]

(5) The directors [1] may delegate any of their powers to a managing director[6] or to committees consisting of such member [7] or members[7] of their body as they think fit and the managing director[6] or any committee so formed shall, in the exercise of the powers so delegated, conform to any regulations that may be made by the directors. [1]

(6) A committee may elect a chairman of its meeting; [3] and if no such chairman is elected, or if at any meeting [3] the chairman is not present within five minutes after the time appointed for holding the same, the members [7] present may choose one of their number to be chairman of the meeting. [3]

(7) A committee may meet and adjourn as it thinks proper, and any questions arising shall be determined by a majority of votes of the members [7] present, and in the case of equality of votes the chairman shall have a second or casting vote.

(8) A resolution [8] in writing, signed by all the directors [1] for the time being entitled to receive notice of a meeting [3] of the directors,[1] shall be as valid and effectual as if it had been passed at a meeting[3] of the directors [1] duly convened and held.

(9) In all the directors' [1] meetings[3] each director[1] shall be entitled to one vote.

---

**Notes**

**Section 263(1)**

1. "Director" means (1) one who manages, guides, or orders; a chief administrator (2) a person appointed or elected to sit on a board that manages the affairs of a corporation or other organisation by electing

and exercising control over its officer. **Garner B. (ed) Black's Law Dictionary 8th ed.**

"Director" includes any person occupying the position of director by whatever name called; and includes any person in accordance with whose directions or instructions the directors of the company are accustomed to act. **Section 567 CAMA, Cap. C20, LFN 2004.**

2. "Business" includes any trade, industry and profession and any occupation carried on for profit; **Section 588 CAMA, Cap. C20, LFN 2004.**
3. "Meeting" means the gathering of people to discuss or act on matters in which they have a common interest; esp. the convening of a deliberate assembly to transact business. **Garner B. (ed) Black's Law Dictionary 8th ed.**

**Section 263(2)**

4. "Company" means a corporation - or, less commonly, an association, partnership, or union that carries on a commercial or industrial enterprise. **Garner B. (ed) Black's Law Dictionary 8 th ed.**

"Company" or "existing company" means a company formed and registered under this Act or, as the case may be, formed and registered in Nigeria before and in existence on the commencement of this Act. **Section 567 CAMA, Cap. C20, LFN 2004.**

**Section 263(3)**

5. "Secretary" means (1) an administrative assistant (2) a corporate officer in charge of official correspondence, minutes of board meetings, and records of stock ownership and transfer(3) an officer charged with recording a deliberative assembly's proceedings . **See Garner B. (ed) Black's Law Dictionary 8 th ed.**
6. "Managing director" means a director to whom management powers have been delegated, either absolutely or subject to supervision, by the other directors of the company under terms of the articles of association. Managing directors are the agents of the company and have wide authority to act on its behalf. See **Martins E. (ed.) Oxford Dictionary of Law 4th ed.**
7. "Members" member includes the heir, executor, administrator or other personal representative, as the case may be, of the member; See **Section 567 CAMA, Cap. C20, LFN 2004.**
8. "Resolution" means a main motion that formally expresses the sense, will, or action of a deliberative assembly. See **Garner B. (ed) Black's Law Dictionary 8th ed.**

**Cross Reference**

On meaning of directors, see section 244 CAMA CAP C20 LFN 2004

**On appointment of first and subsequent directors, see sections 247 & 248 CAMA CAP C20, LFN 2004**

---

**Cases**

It is only when the directors act on a board that the re organs of or agents for the company and entitled to exercise the powers vested in them by the

Act or articles. ***Carib Construction co. Ltd v. Lynch*** **CCHCJ 12/73/29 HC Lagos at p.32**

Although there is inherent distinction between the different directors as to their duties and liabilities, the chairman of the board and the managing director may, by the articles of Association, and must, by their special access to and connection with the detailed machinery of control, be expected to be better informed than the other directors or the affairs of the company; ***Shonowo v. Adebayo*** **(1969) 2 A.L.R Com 419**

The committee has no power to add to their number or supply a vacancy. ***Hiojos v. WAAC Ltd*** **(1976) NCLR, 304, 312**

The managing director is only a director with powers of management conferred on him by the board. ***Atewologun v. Metro Motors Ltd*** **(1978) NCLR 346.**

**For Further Reading**

On directors, theirs discretions, powers, see, Bakibinga, D.J., "Directors' Duty to Act Bona Fide in the Interest of the Company" (1990) 39 (2) **The International and Comparative Law Quarterly 451**

---

## 264. Quorum

(1) Unless the articles [1] otherwise provide, the quorum [2] necessary for the transaction of the business of directors [3] shall be two where there are not more than six directors, [3] but where there are more than six directors, [3] the quorum [2] shall be one third of the number of directors, [3] and where the number of directors [3] is not a multiple of three, then the quorum [2] shall be one third to the nearest number.

(2) Where a committee of directors is appointed by the board of directors, [4] the board [4] shall fix its quorum, [2] but where no quorum [2] is fixed, the whole committee shall meet and act by a majority.

---

**Notes**

**Section 264(1)**

1. "Articles" see "articles of association" means a governing document that sets forth the basic terms of a corporation's existence, including the number and classes of shares and the purposes and duration of the corporation. **See Garner B. (ed) Black's Law Dictionary 8 th ed.**
"Articles" means the articles of association of a company, as originally framed or as altered by special resolution, including so far as they apply to the regulations contained in Table A in the First Schedules of

the Companies Act, 1922 or in that Table as altered by any subsequent enactment or reprint of the laws, or in Table A in the First Schedule to this Act. **Section 567 CAMA, Cap. C20, LFN 2004.**

2. "Quorum" means the minimum number of members (usually a majority of all the members) who must be present for a deliberative assembly to legally transact business. **Garner B. (ed) Black's Law Dictionary 8th ed.**

3. "Director" means (1) one who manages, guides, or orders; a chief administrator (2) a person appointed or elected to sit on a board that manages the affairs of a corporation or other organisation by electing and exercising control over its officers. **Garner B, (ed) Black's Law Dictionary 8th ed.**

   "Director" includes any person occupying the position of director by whatever name called; and includes any person in accordance with whose directions or instructions the directors of the company are accustomed to act. **Section 567 CAMA, Cap. C20 LFN 2004.**

4. "Board of directors" means (1) the governing body of a corporation, elected by the shareholders to establish corporate policy, appoint executive officers, make major business and financial decisions. (2)the governing body of a corporation, partnership , association, or other organization, elected by the shareholders or members to establish policy, elect or appoint officers and committees, and make other governing decisions. **Garner B. (ed) Black's Law Dictionary 8 th ed.**

**Cross Reference**

On proceedings of directors, see **section 263 CAMA**.

On meaning of directors, see **section 244 CAMA Cap. C20 LFN 2004**

On first appointment and subsequent appointment of directors, see **section 246 & 247 CAMA Cap. C20, LFN 2004**

---

**Cases**

Although there is inherent distinction between the different directors as to their duties and liabilities, the chairman of the board and the managing director may, by the articles of Association, and must, by their special access to and connection with the detailed machinery of control, be expected to be better informed than the other directors or the affairs of the company. See ***Shonowo v. Adebayo*** **(1969) 2 A.L.R Com 419**

The committee has no power to add to their number or supply a vacancy. ***Hiojos v. WAAC Ltd*** **(1976) NCLR, 304, 312**

The managing director is only a director with powers of management conferred on him by the board. ***Atewologun v. Metro Motors Ltd*** **(1978) NCLR 346**

**For further reading**

On directors, theirs discretions, powers, see, Bakibinga, D. J., "Directors' Duty to Act Bona Fide in the Interest of the Company" (1990) 39 (2) **The International and Comparative Law Quarterly 451**

## 265. Failure to have a quorum

Where the board [1] is unable to act because a quorum [2] cannot be formed, the general meeting [3] may act in place of the board [1] and where a committee is unable to act because a quorum [2] cannot be formed, the board [1] may act in place of the committee.

---

**Notes**
**Section 265**

1. "Quorum" means 1. The minimum number of members who must be present for a deliberative assembly to legally transact business 2. Notwithstanding anything contained in any Act or any other enactment, the quorum of any tribunal, commission of inquiry (including any appeal tribunal established for the purpose of hearing any appeal arising there from) shall not be less than two (including the chairman): **Garner B. (ed) Black's Law Dictionary 8 th ed.**
   Provided that the chairman and the member shall be present at every sitting of the tribunal, commission or inquiry throughout the duration of the trial or hearing. **Section 28 Interpretation Act Cap 123 LFN, 2004.**
2. "Board" means a group of persons having managerial, supervisory, or advisory powers. **Garner B. (ed) Black's Law Dictionary 8 th ed.**
3. **"General meeting"** see "Annual meeting" – a yearly meeting to elect or install officers or directors and to conduct other routine organisational business. **Garner B. (ed) Black's Law Dictionary 8 th ed.**

Cross Reference

On the formation of a committee, see section **64 CAMA CAP C20, LFN 2004**

On the number required for the formation of a quorum of the board or the committee, see **section 264 CAMA CAP C20, LFN 2004**

---

## 266. Notice of meeting

(1) Every director [1] shall be entitled to receive notice of the directors' [1] meetings,[2] unless he is disqualified by any reason under the Act from continuing with the office of director. [1]

(2) There shall be given 14 days' notice in writing to all directors entitled to receive notice unless otherwise provided in the articles.[3]

(3) Failure to give notice in accordance with subsection (2) of this section shall invalidate the meeting. [2]

(4) Unless the articles [3] otherwise provide, it shall not be necessary to give notice of a meeting [2] of directors [1] to any director [1] for the time being absent from Nigeria, provided that if he has given an address in Nigeria, the notice shall be sent to such an address.

---

**Notes**
**Section 266 (1)**

1. "Director" means (1) one who manages, guides, or orders; a chief administrator (2) a person appointed or elected to sit on a board that manages the affairs of a corporation or other organisation by electing and exercising control over its officers. **Garner B. (ed) Black's Law Dictionary 8th ed.**
   "Director" includes any person occupying the position of director by whatever name called; and includes any person in accordance with whose directions or instructions the directors of the company are accustomed to act. **Section 567 CAMA, Cap. C20, LFN 2004.**
2. "Meeting" means the gathering of people to discuss or act on matters in which they have a common interest; esp. the convening of a deliberate assembly to transact business. **Garner B. (ed) Black's Law Dictionary 8th ed.**

**Section 266(3)**

3. "Articles" see "articles of association" means a governing document that sets forth the basic terms of a corporation's existence, including the number and classes of shares and the purposes and duration of the corporation. **Garner B. (ed) Black's Law Dictionary 8 th ed.**
   "Articles" means the articles of association of a company, as originally framed or as altered by special resolution, including so far as they apply to the regulations contained in Table A in the First Schedules of the Companies Act, 1922 or in that Table as altered by any subsequent enactment or reprint of the laws, or in Table A in the First Schedule to this Act; **Section 567 CAMA, Cap. C20, LFN 2004.**

**Cross Reference**

On entitlement of a director to be removed to receive notice, see section 262 , **CAMA Cap C20 LFN, 2004.**

---

**Cases**

The combined requirement of section 266(1) and 262 is that a director to be removed must be given notice of the meeting. ***Longe v. F.B.N* (2010) SC 116/2007, delivered on 5/03/2010.**

*Remuneration and other payments*

## 267. Remuneration of directors

(1) The remuneration of the directors [1] shall, from time to time, be determined by the company [2] in general meeting [3] and such remuneration shall be deemed to accrue from day to day.

(2) The directors [1] may also be paid all travelling, hotel and other expenses properly incurred by them in attending and returning from meetings[3] of the directors [1] or any committee of the directors [1] or general meetings [3] of the company [2] or in connection with the business[4] of the company. [2]

(3) Where remuneration has been fixed by the articles, [5] it shall be alterable only by a special resolution. [6]

(4) A company [2] shall not be bound to pay remuneration to directors,[1] but where the company [2] agrees to pay, the directors [1] shall be paid such remuneration out of the fund of the company. [2]

(5) The amount of remuneration shall be a debt from the company[2] so that if directors [1] take office on the basis of the articles,[5] they shall be able to sue the company [2] on account of the debt or prove it in the liquidation. [6]

(6) A director [1] who receives more money than he is entitled to, shall be guilty of misfeasance and shall be accountable to the company[2] for such money.

(7) The remunerations of directors [1] shall be apportionable.

---

**Notes**
**Section 267**

1. "Director" means (1) one who manages, guides, or orders; a chief administrator (2) a person appointed or elected to sit on a board that manages the affairs of a corporation or other organisation by electing and exercising control over its officers. **Garner B. (ed) Black's Law Dictionary 8th ed.**
   "Director" includes any person occupying the position of director by whatever name called; and includes any person in accordance with whose directions or instructions the directors of the company are accustomed to act. **Section 567 CAMA, Cap. C20, LFN 2004.**
2. "Company" means a corporation - or, less commonly, an association, partnership, or union that carries on a commercial or industrial enterprise. **Garner B. (ed) Black's Law Dictionary 8 th ed.**
   "Company" or "existing company" means a company formed and registered under this Act or, as the case may be, formed and registered in Nigeria before and in existence on the commencement of this Act. **Section 567 CAMA, Cap. C20, LFN 2004.**
3. "Meeting" means the gathering of people to discuss or act on matters in which they have a common interest; esp. the convening of a deliberate assembly to transact business. **Garner B. (ed) Black's Law Dictionary 8th ed.**

4. "Business" includes any trade, industry and profession and any occupation carried on for profit. **Section 588 CAMA, Cap. C20, LFN 2004.**
5. "Articles" see "articles of association" means a governing document that sets forth the basic terms of a corporation's existence, including the number and classes of shares and the purposes and duration of the corporation. **Garner B. (ed) Black's Law Dictionary 8 th ed.**
"Articles" means the articles of association of a company, as originally framed or as altered by special resolution, including so far as they apply to the regulations contained in Table A in the First Schedules of the Companies Act, 1922 or in that Table as altered by any subsequent enactment or reprint of the laws, or in Table A in the First Schedule to this Act; **Section 567 CAMA, Cap. C20, LFN 2004.**
6. "Liquidation" See winding up. Means a procedure by which a company can be dissolved. It may be instigated by members or creditors of the company or by order of the court. In both cases the process involves the appointment of a liquidator to assume control of the company from its directors. He collects the assets, pays debts, and distributes any surplus to company members in accordance with their rights. **Martins E. (ed.) Oxford Dictionary of Law 4 th ed.**

**Cross Reference**

On obligation of company to hold annual general meetings, see section 213, **CAMA Cap C20 LFN, 2004.**

On the formation of a committee, **see section 64 CAMA CAP C20, LFN 2004**

---

## 268. Remuneration of a managing director

(1) A managing director [1] shall receive such remuneration (whether by way of salary, commission or participation in profits, or partly in one way and partly in another) as the directors [2] may determine.

(2) Where a managing director [1] is removed for any reason whatsoever under section 262 of this Act, he shall have a claim for breach of contract if there is any or where a contract could be inferred from the terms of the articles. [3]

(3) Where he performs some services without a contract, he shall be entitled to payment on a quantum meruit. [4]

---

**Notes**

**Section 268(1)**

1. "Managing director" means a director to whom management powers have been delegated, either absolutely or subject to supervision, by the other directors of the company under terms of the articles of association. Managing directors are the agents of the company and

have wide authority to act on its behalf. **Martins E. (ed.) Oxford Dictionary of Law 4th ed.**

2. "Director" means (1) one who manages, guides, or orders; a chief administrator (2) a person appointed or elected to sit on a board that manages the affairs of a corporation or other organisation by electing and exercising control over its officers. **Garner B. (ed) Black's Law Dictionary 8th ed.**

   "Director" includes any person occupying the position of director by whatever name called; and includes any person in accordance with whose directions or instructions the directors of the company are accustomed to act. **Section 567 CAMA, Cap. C20, LFN 2004.**

3. "Articles" see "articles of association" means a governing document that sets forth the basic terms of a corporation's existence, including the number and classes of shares and the purposes and duration of the corporation. **Garner B. (ed) Black's Law Dictionary 8 th ed.**

   "Articles" means the articles of association of a company, as originally framed or as altered by special resolution, including so far as they apply to the regulations contained in Table A in the First Schedules of the Companies Act, 1922 or in that Table as altered by any subsequent enactment or reprint of the laws, or in Table A in the First Schedule to this Act. See **section 567 CAMA, Cap. C20, LFN 2004.**

4. "Quantum meruit" the term is a Latin term which means "as much as he has deserved. **Garner B. (ed) Black's Law Dictionary 8 th ed.**

**Cross Reference**

On power of the board to appoint a managing director see section 263, **CAMA Cap C20 LFN, 2004.**

---

## 269. Prohibition of tax-free payments to directors

(1) It shall not be lawful for a company [1] to pay a director [2] remuneration (whether as director or otherwise) free of income tax,[3] or otherwise calculated by reference to or varying with the amount of his income tax, [3]or at or with the rate or standard rate of income tax,[3] except under a contract which was in force at the commencement of this Act, and provides expressly, and not by reference to the articles, for payment or remuneration as aforesaid.

(2) Any provision contained in a company's [1] articles[4] or in any contract other than such a contract as mentioned in subsection (1) of this section, or in any resolution [4] of a company[1] or the resolution of a company's [1] directors[2] for payment to a director [2] of remuneration as mentioned in subsection (1) of this section, shall have effect as if it provided for payment, as a gross sum subject to income tax,[3] of the net sum for which it actually provides.

(3) This section shall not apply to remuneration due before this Act comes into force or in respect of a period before it comes into force.

---

**Notes**
**Section 269(1)**

1. "Company" means a corporation - or, less commonly, an association, partnership, or union that carries on a commercial or industrial enterprise. See **Garner B. (ed) Black's Law Dictionary 8 th ed.**
"Company" means a company formed and registered under this Act or, as the case may be, formed and registered in Nigeria before and in existence on the commencement of this Act. See **Section 567 CAMA, Cap. C20, LFN 2004.**
2. "Directors" see"ditector." A director is one appointed or elected to sit on a board that manages the affairs of a corporation or other organisation by electing and exercising control over its officers. See **Garner B. (ed) Black's Law Dictionary 8th ed.**
"Director" includes any person occupying the position of director by whatever name called; and includes any person in accordance with whose directions or instructions the directors of the company are accustomed to act. See **Section 567 CAMA, Cap. C20, LFN 2004.**
3. "Income tax" means a tax on an individual's or entity's net income. **See Garner B. (ed) Black's Law Dictionary 8 th ed.**
4. Resolution" means a decision reached by a majority of the m embers at a company meeting. **See Martins E. Oxford Dictionary of Law 4th ed.**

**Cross Reference**

On law governing income tax of individuals in Nigeria, see the **Personal Income Tax Act (PITA) CAP P8 LFN 2004**

---

## 270. Prohibition of loans to directors in certain circumstances

(1) It shall not be lawful for a company [1] to make a loan [2] to any person who is its director [3] or a director [3] of its holding company,[4] or to enter into any guarantee [5] or provide any security [6] in connection with a loan [2] made to such a person as earlier mentioned by any other person:

Provided that nothing in this section shall apply-

(a) subject to subsection (2) of this section, to anything done to provide any such person as mentioned in this subsection with funds to meet expenditure incurred or to be incurred by him for the purposes of the company [1] or for the purpose of enabling him properly to perform his duties as an officer[7] of the company;[1] or

(b) in the case of a company[1] whose ordinary business includes the lending of money or the giving of guarantees[5] in connection with loans made by other persons, to anything done by the company[1] in the ordinary course of that business.

(2) Proviso (a) to subsection (1) of this section shall not authorise the making of any loan,[2] or the entering into any guarantee,[6] or the provision of any security[6] except-

(a) with the prior approval of the company[1] given at a general meeting[8] at which the purposes of the expenditure and the amount of the loan[2] or the extent of the guarantee[5] or security,[6] as the case may be, are disclosed; or

(b) on condition that, if the approval of the company[1] is not given as in subsection (2) (a) of this section at or before the next following annual general meeting,[8] the loan[2] shall be repaid or the liability under the guarantee[5] or security[6] shall be discharged, as the case may be, within six months from the conclusion of that meeting.[8]

(3) Where the approval of the company[1] is not given as required by any such condition, the directors[3] authorizing the making of the loan,[2] or the entering into the guarantee,[5] or the provision of the security,[6] shall be jointly and severally liable to indemnify the company[1] against any loss arising there from.

---

**Notes**

**Section 270**

1. "Company" means a corporation - or, less commonly, an association, partnership, or union that carries on a commercial or industrial enterprise. **Garner B. (ed) Black's Law Dictionary 8 th ed.**
   "Company" or "existing company" means a company formed and registered under this Act or, as the case may be, formed and registered in Nigeria before and in existence on the commencement of this Act. **Section 567 CAMA, Cap. C20, LFN 2004.**
2. "Loan" means (1) an act of lending; a grant of something for temporary use. (2) a thing lent for the brrower's temporary use; esp., a sum of money lent at interest. **Garner B. (ed.) Black's Law Dictionary 8th ed.**
3. "Director" means (1) one who manages, guides, or orders; a chief administrator (2) a person appointed or elected to sit on a board that manages the affairs of a corporation or other organisation by electing

and exercising control over its officers. **Garner B (ed.) Black's Law Dictionary 8th ed.**
"Director" includes any person occupying the position of director by whatever name called; and includes any person in accordance with whose directions or instructions the directors of the company are accustomed to act. **Section 567 CAMA, Cap. C20, LFN 2004.**

4. "Holding company" means a holding company as defined by section 338. **Section 567 CAMA, Cap. C20, LFN 2004.**
5. "Guarantee" means a secondary agreement in which a person (the guarantor) is liable for the debt or default of another (the principal debtor), who is the party primarily liable for the debt. A guarantee requires an independent consideration and must be evidenced in writing. A guarantor who has paid out on his guarantee has a right to be indemnified by the principal debtor. **Martins E. (ed.) Oxford Dictionary of Law 4th ed.**
6. "Security" means an instrument that evidences the holder's ownership rights in a firm. **Garner B. (ed) Black's Law Dictionary 8th ed.** See Securities. It includes shares, debentures, debenture stock, bonds, notes(other than promissory notes) and units under a unit trust scheme. **Section 567 CAMA, Cap. C20, LFN 2004.**
7. "Officer" means in relation to a body corporate, includes a director, manager or secretary; **Section 567 CAMA, Cap. C20, LFN 2004.**
8. "General meeting" see "Annual meeting" – a yearly meeting to elect or install officers or directors and to conduct other routine organisational business. **Garner B. (ed) Black's Law Dictionary 8th ed.**

**Cross Reference**

On proceedings of directors, see **section 263 CAMA Cap. C20,LFN 2004**
On meaning of directors, see **section 244 CAMA Cap. C20 LFN 2004**
On first appointment and subsequent appointment of directors, see **section 246 & 247 CAMA Cap. C20, LFN 2004**

---

## 271. Payment by company for loss of office, etc., to be approved

It shall not be lawful for a company [1] to make to any director [2] of the company[1], any payment by way of compensation for loss of office, or as consideration for or in connection with his retirement from office, unless particulars with respect to the proposed payment and the amount have been disclosed to members [3] of the company[1] and the proposal is approved by the company.

---

**Notes**
**Section 271**

1. "Company" means a company formed and registered under this Act or, as the case may be, formed and registered in Nigeria before and in existence on the commencement of this Act. See **section 567 CAMA Cap C20 LFN, 2004**.
2. "Director" includes any person occupying the position of director by whatever name called; and includes any person in accordance with whose directions or instructions the directors of the company are accustomed to act. **Section 567 CAMA Cap C20 LFN, 2004**.
3. "Members" see "member." It means one of the individuals of whom a deliberative assembly consists and who enjoys the full rights of participating in the organization-including the rights of making, debating and voting on motions- except to the extent that the organization reserves those rights to certain classes of membership. **Garner B. (ed.) Black's Law Dictionary 8th ed.**

Cross Reference

On meaning of directors, see **section 244 CAMA Cap. C20 LFN 2004**

On first appointment and subsequent appointment of directors, see **section 246 & 247 CAMA Cap. C20, LFN 2004**

---

## 272. Payment to director for loss of office, etc., or transfer of property illegal

(1) If in connection with the transfer of the whole or any part of the undertaking or property of a company [1], it is proposed to make any payment to a director of the company [1] by way of compensation for loss of office, or as consideration for or in connection with his retirement from office, the payment shall be unlawful unless particulars with respect to the proposal and the amount have been disclosed to members [2] of the company and the proposal is approved by the company [1].

(2) Where a payment declared by this section to be illegal is made to a director [3] of a company [1], the amount received shall be deemed to have been received by him in trust for the company.

---

**Notes**

**Section 272**

1. "Company" means a company formed and registered under this Act or, as the case may be, formed and registered in Nigeria before and in existence on the commencement of this Act. See **section 567 CAMA Cap C20 LFN, 2004**.
2. "Members" see "member." It means one of the individuals of whom a deliberative assembly consists and who enjoys the full rights of participating in the organization-including the rights of making, debating and voting on motions- except to the extent that the

organization reserves those rights to certain classes of membership. **Garner B. (ed.) Black's Law Dictionary 8 th ed.**

3. "Director" "includes any person occupying the position of director by whatever name called; and includes any person in accordance with whose directions or instructions the directors of the company are accustomed to act **Section 567 CAMA Cap. C20 LFN, 2004**

**Cross Reference**

On payment by company on loss of office to be disclosed to members and approved by company, see **section 271 CAMA Cap. C20, LFN 2004**

---

## 273. Directors to disclose payment for loss of office, etc., in certain cases

(1) Where, in connection with the transfer to any persons of all or any of the shares [1] in a company[2], being a transfer resulting from-

(a) an offer made to the general body of shareholders [3];

(b) an offer made by or on behalf of some other body corporate with a view to the company [2] becoming its subsidiary[4] or a subsidiary [4] of its holding company [5];

(c) an offer made by or on behalf of an individual with a view to his obtaining the right to exercise or control the exercise of not less than one third of the voting power at any general meeting [6] of the company [2]; or

(d) any other offer which is conditional on acceptance to a given extent payment is to be made to a director [7] of the company[2] by way of compensation for loss of office, or as consideration for or in connection with his retirement from office, it shall be the duty of that director [7] to do all things reasonably necessary to secure that particulars with respect to the proposed payment and the amount, are included in or sent with any notice of the offer made for their shares which is given to any shareholders [3].

(2) If-

(a) any such director [7] fails to do all things reasonably necessary as mentioned in this section; or

(b) any person who has been properly required by any such director[7] to include the said particulars in or send them with any such notice as aforesaid fails so to do, he shall be guilty of an offence and liable to a fine of ₦20.

(3) If-

(a) the requirements of subsection (1) of this section are not complied with in relation to any such payments as are mentioned there; or

(b) the making of the proposed payment is not, before the transfer of any shares [1] in pursuance of the offer, approved by a meeting[8] summoned for the purpose of the holders of the shares to which the offer relates and of other holders of shares[1] of the same class as any of the said shares [1], any sum received by the director [7] on account of the payment shall be deemed to have been received by him in trust for any person who has sold his shares as a result of the offer made, and the expenses incurred by him in distributing that sum amongst those persons shall be borne by him and not retained out of that sum.

(4) Where the shareholders [3] referred to in subsection (3) (b) of this section are not all the members of the company [2] and no provision is made by the articles [9] for summoning or regulating such a meeting[8] as is mentioned in that paragraph, the provisions of this Act and of the company's articles relating to general meetings [6] of the company[2] shall, for that purpose, apply to the meeting [8] either without modification or with such modification as the Commission [10] on the application of any person concerned may direct for the purpose of adapting them to the circumstances of the meeting. [8]

(5) If at a meeting [8] summoned for the purpose of approving any payment as required by paragraph (b) of subsection (3) of this section, a quorum [11] is not present and, after the meeting [8] has been adjourned to a later date, a quorum [11] is again not present, the payment shall, for the purposes of that subsection be deemed to have been approved.

---

**Notes**
**Section 273**

1. "Shares" see "share." It means the interests in a company's share capital of a member who is entitled to share in the capital or income of such company; and except where a distinction between stock and shares is expressed or implied, includes stock. **Section 567, CAMA Cap C20 LFN, 2004**
2. "Company" means a company formed and registered under this Act or, as the case may be, formed and registered in Nigeria before and in existence on the commencement of this Act. See **section 567 CAMA, Cap. C20 LFN 2004**

3. "Shareholders" means one who owns or holds a share or shares in a company especially a corporation. **Garner B. (ed.) Black's Law Dictionary 8th ed.**
4. "Subsidiary" means subordinate; under another's control; a corporation in which a parent corporation has a controlling share **Garner B. (ed.) Black's Law Dictionary 8 th ed.**
5. "Holding Company" means, in relation to a body corporate, a subsidiary as defined by section 338 of this Act. See **section 567 CAMA, Cap. C20 LFN 2004**
6. "General meeting" see "Annual meeting" – a yearly meeting to elect or install officers or directors and to conduct other routine organizational business. **Garner B. (ed.) Black's Law Dictionary 8th ed.**
7. "Director" includes any person occupying the position of director by whatever name called; and includes any person in accordance with whose directions or instructions the directors of the company are accustomed to act **Section 567 CAMA Cap C20 LFN, 2004** .
8. "Meeting" means the gathering of people to discuss or act on matters in which they have a common interest; especially the convening of a deliberative assembly to transact business. **Garner B. (ed.) Black's Law Dictionary 8th ed.**
9. "Articles" see "articles of association". It means a governing document that sets forth the basic terms of a corporation's existence, including the number and classes of shares and the purposes and duration of the corporation. See **Garner B. (ed) Black's Law Dictionary 8th ed.**

   "Articles" means the articles of association of a company, as originally framed or as altered by special resolution, including so far as they apply to the regulations contained in Table A in the First Schedules of the Companies Act, 1922 or in that Table as altered by any subsequent enactment or reprint of the laws, or in Table A in the First Schedule to this Act. See **Section 567 CAMA, CAP C20, LFN 2004.**
10. "Commission" means the Corporate Affairs Commission established under section 1 of this Act; **Sec. 567 CAMA, Cap. C20 , LFN 2004**
11. "Quorum" means the minimum number of members who must be present for a deliberative assembly to legally transact business. See **Garner B., (ed.) Black's Law Dictionary 8 th ed.**

**Cross Reference**

On payment by company on loss of office to be disclosed to members and approved by company, see **section 271 CAMA Cap. C20, LFN 2004**

On required quorum at meeting of members, see **section 239 CAMA Cap. C2- LFN 2004**

On meaning of offence, see **section 2, Criminal Code Cap. C38 LFN 2004**

---

**Cases**

A director is a person appointed or elected according to Law, authorized to manage and direct the affairs of a corporation or company. ***Olufosoye***

***v. Fakorede*** **(1993) 1 N.W.L.R 947.** See also ***Longe v. First Bank Nigeria Plc*** **(2006) 3 N.W.L.R 228 at 270.**

**For Further Reading**
On companies, directors, see, Bakibinga, D.J., "Directors' Duty to Act Bona Fide in the Interest of the Company" (1990) 39 (2) **The International and Comparative Law Quarterly 451.**

## 274. Provisions supplementary to sections 271 to 273

(1) Where, in proceedings for the recovery of any payment which has been received by any person in trust by virtue of subsections (1) and (2) of section 272 or subsections (1) and (3) of section 273 of this Act, it is shown that-

(a) the payment was made in pursuance of any arrangement entered into as part of the agreement for the transfer in question, or within one year but before two years after that agreement or the offer leading thereto; and

(b) the company[1] or any person to whom the transfer was made was privy to that arrangement, the payment shall be deemed, except in so far as the contrary is shown, to be one to which the subsections apply.

(2) If in connection with any such transfer as is mentioned in sections 272 and 273 of this Act-

(a) the price to be paid to a director [2] of the company[1] whose office is to be abolished or who is to retire from office for any shares in the company held by him is in excess of the price obtainable at the time by other holders of the like shares[3]; or

(b) any valuable consideration is given to any such director [2], the excess or the money value of the consideration, as the case may be, shall, for the purposes of that section, be deemed to have been a payment made to him by way of compensation for loss of office, or as consideration for or in connection with his retirement from office.

(3) It is hereby declared that references in sections 271 to 273 of this Act to payments made to any director of a company by way of compensation for loss of office or as consideration for or in connection with his retirement from office shall not include any bona fide payment by way of damages for breach of contract or by way of pension in respect of past services and for the purposes of

this subsection, "pension" includes any superannuation allowance, superannuation gratuity or similar payment.

(4) Nothing in section 272 or 273 of this Act shall be taken to prejudice the operation of any rule of law requiring disclosure to be made with respect to any such payments as are mentioned there, or with respect to any other like payments made, or to be made, to the directors of a company.

---

**Notes**
**Section 274(3)**

1. "Company" means a company formed and registered under this Act or, as the case may be, formed and registered in Nigeria before and in existence on the commencement of this Act. See **Section 567, CAMA Cap C20 LFN, 2004.**
2. "Shares" means the interests in a company's share capital of a member who is entitled to share in the capital or income of such company; and except where a distinction between stock and shares is expressed of implied includes stock. **See section 567 CAMA, Cap. C20, LFN 2004**
3. "Director" includes any person occupying the position of director by whatever name called; and includes any person in accordance with whose directions or instructions the directors of the company are accustomed to act; **Section 567 CAMA, Cap. C20, LFN 2004**

---

**Cases**

The definition of a company in section 650 of Companies and Allied Matters Act puts the matter beyond doubt. It defines a 'company' or 'existing' to mean....a company formed and registered in Nigeria before and in existence on the commencement of this Act. ***Agro Allied Dev. Ent. Ltd. v. Reefer*** **(2009) vol.31 W.R.N 1-185 at pg 7** .

By the provisions of Companies and Allied Matters Act, Section 115, shares are in the nature of personal estate and freely transferable but subject to statutory restrictions and the articles of the company. Members in a company have a right to transfer shares belonging to them therein and this right is unfettered unless there is an express restriction to that effect in the articles or constitution of the company. ***N.R.I. Ltd v. Oranusi*** **(2011) ALL F.W.L.R part 577. 625-824 at p.765** .

---

**Cross Reference**

On payment for loss of office to be disclosed to members and approved by the Company, see **section 271 CAMA Cap. C20, LFN 2004**

On when of payment to directors for loss of office or transfer of property is illegal, see **section 272 CAMA Cap. C20, LFN 2004**
On duty of director to disclose payment for loss of office in certain cases, see **section 273 CAMA Cap. C20, LFN 2004**
On the establishment of acontributory scheme for employees in the public and private sector and the establishment of the Pension Commission, **see generally Pension Reform Act Cap. P4 LFN 2004**

---

**For Further Reading**
On shares, directors, and company, see Orojo, J. Ola **Company Law and Practice in Nigeria** 3rd Edition, Mbeyi & Associates (Lagos, Nigeria) 1992.

*Disclosure of directors' interests*

## 275. Register of directors' share holding etc.

(1) Every company [1] shall keep a register showing as respects each director[2] of the company[1] (not being its holding company) the number, description and amount of any shares [3] in or debentures [4] of the company[1] or any other body corporate, being the company's subsidiary[5] or holding company [6], or a subsidiary [5] of the company's holding company,[6] which are held by or in trust for him or of which he has any right to become the holder (whether on payment or not):
Provided that the register need not include shares [3] in any body corporate which is the wholly-owned subsidiary [5] of another body corporate, and for this purpose, a body corporate shall be deemed to be the wholly-owned subsidiary [5] of another if it has no members [7] but that other and that other's wholly-owned subsidiaries [5] and its or their nominees.

(2) Where any shares [3] or debentures [4] fall to be or cease to be recorded in the said register in relation to any director by reason of a transaction entered into after the commencement of this Act and while he is a director, [2] the register shall also show the date of, and price or other consideration for the transaction:
Provided that where there is an interval between the agreement for any such transaction and the completion thereof, the date shall be that of the agreement.

(3) The nature and extent of a director's [2] interest or right in or over any shares [3] or debentures [4] recorded in relation to him in the said register shall, if he so requires, be indicated in the register.

(4) The company [1] shall not by virtue of anything done for the purposes of this section, be affected with notice of, or put upon inquiry as to the rights of any person in relation to any shares [3] or debentures[4].

(5) The said register shall, subject to the provisions of this section, be kept at the company's [1] registered or head office and shall be open to inspection during business hours (subject to such reasonable restrictions as the company [1] may by its articles or in general meeting impose, so that not less than two hours in each day be allowed for inspection) as follows-

(a) during the period beginning 14 days before the date of the company's annual general meeting [8] and ending three days after the date of its conclusion, it shall be open to the inspection of any member [7] or holder of debentures [4] of the company[1] and

(b) during that or any other period, it shall be open to the inspection of any person acting on behalf of the Commission.[9]

(6) In computing the 14 days and the three days mentioned in subsection (5) of this section, any day which is a Saturday or Sunday or a public holiday [10] shall be disregarded.

(7) Without prejudice to the rights conferred by subsection (5) of this section, the Commission [9] may, at any time, request for the production to it of a copy of the register, or any part thereof.

(8) The register shall also be produced at the commencement of the company's [1] annual general meeting [8] and remain open and accessible during the continuance of the meeting to any person attending the meeting.[8]

(9) If default is made in complying with subsection (1) or (2) of this section, or if any inspection required under this section is refused, or any copy required there under is not sent within a reasonable time, the company [1] and every officer [11] of the company [1] who is in default shall be guilty of an offence and liable to a fine of ₦500, and if default is made in complying with subsection (8) of this section, the company [1] and every officer of the company [1] who is in default shall be liable to a fine of ₦50.

(10) If any inspection required under this section is refused, the court[12] may, by order, compel an immediate inspection of the register.

(11) For the purposes of this section-

(a) any person, in accordance with whose directions or instructions the directors[2] of a company[1] are accustomed to act, shall be deemed to be a director[6] of the company;[1] and

(b) a director[2] of a company[1] shall be deemed to hold or to have any interest or right in or over, any shares[3] or debentures[4], if a permanent representative of the body corporate other than the company[1] holds them or has that interest or right in or over them, and either-

(i) that permanent representative is accustomed to act in accordance with his directions or instructions; or

(ii) he is entitled to exercise or control the exercise of one third or more of the voting power at any general meeting[8] of that body corporate.

---

**Notes**

**Section 275(11)**

1 "Company" means a company formed and registered under this Actor as the case may be , formed and registered in Nigeria before and in existence on the commencement of this Act **.See Section 567 CAMA, Cap. C20, LFN 2004** "Company" means a corporation - or, less commonly, an association, partnership, or union that carries on a commercial or industrial enterprise. **Garner B. (ed) Black's Law Dictionary 8th ed.**

2. "Directors" includes any person occupying the position of director by whatever name called; and includes any person in accordance with whose directions or instructions the directors of the company are accustomed to act. See **Section 567 CAMA, Cap. C20, LFN 2004**

3. "Shares " means the interests in a company's share capital of a member who is entitled to share in the capital or income of such company; and except where a distinction between stock and shares is expressed of implied includes stock. See **Section 567 CAMA, Cap. C20, LFN 200**

3. "Debentures" means a debt secured only by the debtor's earning power, not by a lien on any specific asset. 2. An instrument acknowledging such a deb**t. See Garner B. (ed) Black's Law Dictionary 8th ed.**

5. " subsidiary" means, in relation to a body corporate, a subsidiary as defined **by section 338 of this Act. Section 567 CAMA, Cap. C20, LFN 2004.**

6. Holding Company" means a holding company as defined by section 338. **Section 567 CAMA, Cap. C20, LFN 2004.**
7. Member" means one of the individuals of whom a deliberative assembly consists and who enjoys the full rights of participating in the organization-including the rights of making, debating and voting on motions- except to the extent that the organization reserves those rights to certain classes of membership. See **Garner B. (ed.) Black's Law Dictionary 8th ed.**
8. "Meeting" means the gathering of people to discuss or act on matters in which they have a common interest; especially the convening of a deliberative assembly to transact business. See **Garner B. (ed.) Black's Law Dictionary 8th ed.**
9. "Commission" means the Corporate Affairs Commission established under section 1 **of this Act; Section 567 CAMA, Cap. C20, LFN 2004.**
10. "Public Holiday" public holiday" means a day which is a public holiday-(a) as respects Lagos, by virtue of the Public Holidays Act;(b) as respects any other part of Nigeria, by virtue of any corresponding enactment in force in that part. See **section 18, Interpretation Act, Cap. I 23, LFN 2004**
11. "Officer" means in relation to a body corporate, includes a director, manager or secretary. **See section 567 CAMA, Cap. C20, LFN 2004.**
12. "Court" means the Federal High Court , and to the extent to which application may be made to it as: court includes the court of Appeal, and the Supreme Court of Nigeria. **See section 567 CAMA, Cap. C20, LFN, 2004.**

---

**Cases**

Directors have sometimes been called trustees, or commercial trustees, and sometimes they have been called managing partners. It does not matter what you call them so long as you understand what their true position is, which is that they are really commercial when managing a trading concern for the benefit of themselves and all other shareholders in it. ***Iwuchukwu vs. Nwizu*** **(1994) 7 N.W.L.R (part357) 379 at 396.**

**For Further Reading**

On Directors, company, see, Osunbor. O.A. ' **The Company Director: His Appointment, Powers and duties; Essays on Company Law.** Page 130.

## 276. General duty to give notice, etc.

(1) It shall be the duty of any director [1] of a company[2] to give notice to the company[2] of such matters relating to himself as may be necessary for the purposes of sections 275 and 277 of this Act except so far as it relates to loans made by the company [2] or by any

other person under a guarantee from or on a security provided by the company[2], to an officer [3] thereof.

(2) Any such notice given for the purposes of section 275 of this Act, shall be in writing and if it is not given at a meeting [4] of the directors[1], the director [1] giving it shall do all things reasonably necessary to secure that it is brought up and read at the next meeting[4] of directors [1] after it is given.

(3) Subsection (1) of this section shall, to the extent to which it applies in relation to directors, [1] apply to the like extent for-

(a) the purposes of section 277 of this Act in relation to officers other than directors; [1]

(b) the purposes of sections 276 and 277 of this Act in relation to persons who are or have at any time during the preceding five years been officers [3] of the company. [2]

(4) Any person who makes default in complying with the foregoing provisions of this section shall be guilty of an offence and liable to a fine of ₦50.

---

**Notes**
**Section 276**

1. "Company" means a company formed and registered under this Actor as the case may be , formed and registered in Nigeria before and in existence on the commencement of this Act . **See section 567 CAMA, Cap. C20, LFN 2004** "Company" means a corporation - or, less commonly, an association, partnership, or union that carries on a commercial or industrial enterprise. **Garner B. (ed) Black's Law Dictionary 8th ed.**
2. "Directors" includes any person occupying the position of director by whatever name called; and includes any person in accordance with whose directions or instructions the directors of the company are accustomed to act; **Section 567 CAMA, Cap. C20, LFN 2004**
3. "Officer" in relation to a body corporate, includes a director, manager or secretary. See **section 567 CAMA, Cap. C20 , LFN 2004**
4. "Meeting" means the gathering of people to discuss or act on matters in which they have a common interest especially the convening of a deliberate assembly to transact business. See **Garner B. (ed) Black's Law Dictionary 8th ed.**

Cross Reference

On meaning of offence, see **section 2, Criminal Code, Cap. C38, LFN 2004**

---

## 277. Disclosure by directors of interests in contracts

(1) Subject to the provisions of this section, it shall be the duty of a director [1] of a company [2] who is in any way, whether directly or indirectly, interested in a contract or proposed contract with the company, [2] to declare the nature of his interest at a meeting of the directors of the company. [2]

(2) In the case of a proposed contract, the declaration required by this section to be made by a director [1] shall be made at the meeting of the directors [1] at which the question of entering into the contract is first taken into consideration, or, if the director [1] was not at the date of that meeting [3] interested in the proposed contract, at the next meeting [3] of the directors held after he became so interested, and in a case where the director [1] becomes interested in a contract after it is made, the said declaration shall be made at the first meeting of the directors [1] held after he becomes so interested.

(3) For the purpose of this section, a general notice given to the directors [1] of a company [2] by a director to the effect that he is a member of a specified company [2] or firm and is to be regarded as interested in any contract which may, after the date of the notice, be made with that company [2] or firm, shall be deemed to be a sufficient declaration of interest in relation to any contract so made: Provided that any such notice shall not have effect unless it is given at a meeting of the directors or the director does all things reasonably necessary to secure that it is brought up and read at the next meeting of the directors after it is given.

(4) Any director [1] who fails to comply with the provisions of this section shall be guilty of an offence and liable to a fine of ₦100.

(5) Nothing in this section shall be taken to prejudice the operation of any rule of law restricting directors [1] of a company [2] from having any interest in contracts with the company. [2]

---

**Notes**
**Section 277(4)**

1. "Director" includes any person occupying the position of director by whatever name called; and includes any person in accordance with whose directions or instructions the directors of the company are accustomed to act . **Section 567 CAMA, Cap. C20, LFN 2004**

2. "Company" means a company formed and registered under this Actor as the case may be , formed and registered in Nigeria before and in existence on the commencement of this Act. **Section 567 CAMA, Cap. C20, LFN 2004**

"Company" means a corporation - or, less commonly, an association, partnership, or union that carries on a commercial or industrial enterprise . **Garner B. (ed) Black's Law Dictionary 8th ed.**

3. "Meeting" means the gathering of people to discuss or act on matters in which they have a common interest especially the convening of a deliberate assembly to transact business. See **Garner B. (ed) Black's Law Dictionary 8th ed.**

---

**Cases**

A director is a person appointed or elected according to Law, authorized to manage and direct the affairs of a corporation or company. ***Olufosoye v. Fakorede* (1993) 1 N.W.L.R 947.** See also ***Longe v. First Bank Nigeria Plc* (2006) 3 N.W.L.R 228 at 270.**

The definition of a company in section 650 of Companies and Allied Matters Act puts the matter beyond doubt. It defines a 'company' or 'existing' to mean….a company formed and registered in Nigeria before and in existence on the commencement of this Act. ***Agro Allied Dev. Ent. Ltd. v. Reefer* (2009) vol.31 W.R.N 1-185 at pg 7** .

---

## 278. Particulars with respect to directors in trade catalogues, etc.

(1) Every company [1] to which this section applies shall, in all trade circulars, show cards and business letters on or in which the company's [1] name appears and which are issued or sent by the company[1] to any person in Nigeria, state in legible characters with respect to every director [2] the following particulars-

(a) his present forename, [2] or the initials thereof, and present surname;

(b) any former forenames [2] and surnames;

(c) his nationality, if not a Nigerian:

Provided that, if special circumstances exist which the Commission [3] is of the opinion render it expedient that such an exemption should be granted, the Commission [3] may, subject to such conditions as it may prescribe by notice published in the Gazette, [4] exempt a company[1] from the obligations imposed by this subsection.

(2) This section shall apply to every company incorporated under this Act, or any enactment repealed by it.

(3) If a company [1] makes default in complying with this section, every officer of the company [1] who is in default shall be

guilty of an offence and liable on conviction for each offence to a fine of ₦50:

Provided that no proceedings shall be instituted under this section except by, or with the consent of, the Attorney-General of the Federation.

(4) For the purposes of this section-

(a) "initials" includes a recognized abbreviation of a forename;[2]

(b) references to a former forename [2] or surname in the case of a married woman do not include the name or surname by which she was known previous to the marriage; and

(c) "show cards" means cards containing or exhibiting articles dealt with, or samples or representations thereof.

---

**Notes**

**Section 278(3)**

1. " Company" means a company formed and registered under this Actor as the case may be , formed and registered in Nigeria before and in existence on the commencement of this Act. **Section 567 CAMA, Cap. C20, LFN 2004**

   "Company" means a corporation - or, less commonly, an association, partnership, or union that carries on a commercial or industrial enterprise. **Garner B. (ed) Black's Law Dictionary 8th ed.**
2. "Forename" " includes a Christian name and a personal name, and "surname" includes a patronymic.See **Section 588 CAMA Cap. C20 LFN 2004**
3. "Commission" **m**eans the Corporate Affairs Commission established under section 1 of this Act. **See Section 567 CAMA, Cap. C20, LFN 2004.**
4. "Gazette " means the official gazette of the Federation. See **section 567 CAMA, Cap. C20, LFN, 2004.**

**Cross Reference**

On how to become a citizen of Nigeria, **see Section 26 Constitution Federal Republic of Nigeria 1999** as amended.

On the appointment of the Attorney General of the Federation and the States **section 150 and 195 Constitution Federal Republic of Nigeria 1999** as **amended.**

---

*Duties of directors*

## 279. Duties of directors

(1) A director[1] of a company[2] stands in a fiduciary relationship[3] towards the company[2] and shall observe the utmost good faith towards the company[2] in any transaction with it or on its behalf.

(2) A director[1] shall also owe fiduciary relationship[3] with the company[2] in the following circumstances-

(a) where a director[1] is acting as agent[4] of a particular shareholder;[5]

(b) where even though he is not an agent[4] of any shareholder,[5] such a shareholder[5] or other person is dealing with the company's[2] securities.[6]

(3) A director[1] shall act at all times in what he believes to be the best interests of the company[2] as a whole so as to preserve its assets, further its business, and promote the purposes for which it was formed, and in such manner as a faithful, diligent, careful and ordinarily skilful director[1] would act in the circumstances.

(4) The matters to which the director[1] of a company[2] is to have regard in the performance of his functions include the interests of the company's[2] employees in general, as well as the interests of its members.[7]

(5) A director[1] shall exercise his powers for the purpose for which he is specified and shall not do so for a collateral purpose, and the power, if exercised for the right purpose, does not constitute a breach of duty, if it, incidentally, affects a member[7] adversely.

(6) A director[1] shall not fetter his discretion to vote in a particular way.

(7) Where a director[1] is allowed to delegate his powers under any provision of this Act, such a director shall not delegate the power in such a way and manner as may amount to an abdication of duty.

(8) No provision, whether contained in the articles[8] or resolutions[9] of a company[2], or in any contract, shall relieve any director[1] from the duty to act in accordance with this section or relieve him from any liability incurred as a result of any breach of the duties conferred upon him under this section.

(9) Any duty imposed on a director[1] under this section shall be enforceable against the director[1] by the company.[2]

---

**Notes**
**Section 279(1)**

1. "Director" includes any person occupying the position of director by whatever name called; and includes any person in accordance with whose directions or instructions the directors of the company are accustomed to act; **Section 567 CAMA, Cap. C20, LFN 2004.**
2. "Company" means a company formed and registered under this Actor as the case may be , formed and registered in Nigeria before and in existence on the commencement of this Act; **Section 567 CAMA, Cap. C20, LFN 2004.**
   "Company" means a corporation - or, less commonly, an association, partnership, or union that carries on a commercial or industrial enterprise. **Garner B. (ed) Black's Law Dictionary 8th ed.**
3. "Fiduciary relationship' means a relationship in which one person is under a duty to act for the benefit of another on matters within the scope of the relationship **Garner B. (ed) Black's Law Dictionary 8th ed.**
4. "Agent" means a person whose job is to act for, or manage the affairs of, other people in business, politics, etc **Oxford Advanced Learner's Dictionary 6th edition**
5. "Shareholders" It means one who owns or holds a share or shares in a company. **See Garner B. ed. Black's Law Dictionary 8th Ed**
6. "Securities" means collateral given or pledged to guarantee the fulfillment of an obligation especially the assurance that a creditor will be repaid usually with interest any money or credit extended to a debtor ; **Garner B. (ed) Black's Law Dictionary 8th ed.**
   "Securities" includes shares, debentures, debenture stock, bonds, notes (other than promissory notes) and units under a unit trust scheme. See **section 567 CAMA Cap. C20, LFN 2004**
7. "Members" member includes the heir, executor, administrator or other personal representative, as the case may be, of the member; **Section 567 CAMA, Cap. C20, LFN 2004.**
8. "Articles" means the articles of association of a company, as originally framed or as altered by special resolution, including so far as they apply to the regulations contained in Table A in the First Schedules of the Companies Act, 1992 or in that Table as altered by any subsequent enactment or reprint of the Laws, or in Table A in Schedule **1 to this Act; Section 567 CAMA, Cap. C20, LFN 2004**
9. "Resolution" means a decision reached by a majority of the m embers at a company meeting. **Martins, E. Oxford Dictionary of Law 4th ed.**

Cross Reference;

On Resolution see **Section 233 CAMA Cap. C20 LFN 2004** .

---

**Cases**

The entire Law of Contract is founded on the "Consensus" or "will" theory of contract, which asserts that contractual obligations are by

definition self imposed and in terms of the function of the of the courts, finds expression in the idea that the exclusive task of a court in contract cases is to discover what the parties have agreed and give effect to it except in cases of mistake, duress and illegality. ***Coop. Dev. Bank Plc v. Ekanem***
**(2009) 16 N.W.L.R. part 1168 443-658 at pg.588.**

**For Further Reading**
On directors, their duties as agents of the company, see Bakibinga, D.J., "Directors' Duty to Act Bona Fide in the Interest of the Company" (1990) 39 (2) **The International and Comparative Law Quarterly 451** .

## 280. Conflicts of duties and interests

(1) The personal interest of a director [1] shall not conflict with any of his duties as a director [1] under this Act.

(2) A director [1]shall not-

(a) in the course of management of affairs of the company; [2] or

(b) in the utilization of the company's property, make any secret profit or achieve other unnecessary benefits.

(3) A director [1] shall be accountable to the company [2] for any secret profit made by him or any unnecessary benefit derived by him contrary to the provisions of subsection (2) of this section.

(4) The inability or unwillingness of the company [2] to perform any functions or duties under its articles and memorandum [3] shall not constitute a defence to any breach of duty of a director under this Act.

(5) The duty not to misuse corporate information shall not cease by a director or an officer having resigned from the company, and he shall still be accountable and can be restrained by an injunction from misusing the information received by virtue of his previous position.

(6) Where a director [4] discloses his interests before the transaction and before the secret profits are made before the general meeting,[5] which may or may not authorise any resulting profits, he may escape liability,[6] but he shall not escape liability if he discloses only after he has made the secret profits, and in this case, he shall account for the profits.

**Notes**
**Section 280**

1. "Director" includes any person occupying the position of director by whatever name called; and includes any person in accordance with whose directions or instructions the directors of the company are accustomed to act. **See Section 567 CAMA, Cap. C20, LFN 2004**
2. "Company" means a company formed and registered under this Actor as the case may be, formed and registered in Nigeria before and in existence on the commencement of this Act; **Section 567 CAMA, Cap. C20, LFN 2004**
   "Company" means a corporation - or, less commonly, an association, partnership, or union that carries on a commercial or industrial enterprise. **Garner B. (ed) Black's Law Dictionary 8th ed.**
3. "Article" means the articles of association of a company, as originally framed or as altered by special resolution, including so far as they apply to the regulations contained in Table A in the First Schedules of the Companies Act, 1992 or in that Table as altered by any subsequent enactment or reprint of the Laws, or in Table A in Schedule 1 to this Act; **Section 567 CAMA, Cap. C20, LFN 2004**
4. "Memorandum" means the memorandum of association of a company as originally framed or as altered in pursuance of any enactment **Section 567 CAMA, Cap. C20, LFN 2004**
5. "general meeting" "see "Annual meeting" – a yearly meeting to elect or install officers or directors and to conduct other routine organisational business. **Garner B. (ed) Black's Law Dictionary 8th ed.**

---

**For Further Reading**
On directors, company, see, Sofowora, M.O **Modern Nigerian Company Law** Soft Associates, 2[nd] Edition 2002

## 281. Multiple directorships

The fact that a person holds more than one directorship shall not derogate from his fiduciary duties [1] to each company, including a duty not to use the property, opportunity or information obtained in the course of the management of one company [2] for the benefit of the other company, [2] or to his own or other person's advantage.

---

**Notes**
**Section 281**

1. "Fiduciary relationship" means a relationship in which one person is under a duty to act for the benefit of another on matters within the scope of the relationship **Garner B. (ed) Black's Law Dictionary 8th ed.**

2. Company" means a company formed and registered under this Actor as the case may be , formed and registered in Nigeria before and in existence on the commencement of this Act. See **Section 567 CAMA, Cap. C20, LFN 2004** "Company" means a corporation - or, less commonly, an association, partnership, or union that carries on a commercial or industrial enterprise. See **Garner B. (ed) Black's Law Dictionary 8th ed.**

Cross Reference

On appointment of directors, see **section 246 CAMA Cap. C20 LFN 2004**

On appointment of directors for life, see **section 248 CAMA Cap. C20 LFN 2004**

---

**Cases**

Where a Director claims to be appointed for life or some indefinite period, the terms of the terms of the appointment must be clear and definite; ***Odulana v. Globe Fishing Ind. Ltd*** **Suit FHC/L/55/60 07 30/6/81 (unreported)**

It is only when the directors act on a board that the re organs of or agents for the company and entitled to exercise the powers vested in them by the Act or articles. ***Carib Construction co. Ltd v. Lynch*** **CCHCJ 12/73/29 HC Lagos at p.32**

## 282. Duty of care and skill

(1) Every director [1] of a company [2]shall exercise the powers and discharge the duties of his office honestly, in good faith and in the best interests of the company, [2] and shall exercise that degree of care, diligence and skill which a reasonably prudent director [1] would exercise in comparable circumstances.

(2) Failure to take reasonable care in accordance with the provisions of section 282 of this Act, shall ground an action for negligence and breach of duty.

(3) Each director [1] shall be individually responsible for the actions of the board in which he participated, and the absence from the board's [3] deliberations, unless justified, shall not relieve a director[1] of such responsibility.

(4) The same standard of care in relation to the director's [1] duties to the company[2] shall be required for both executive and non-executive directors[1]:

Provided that additional liability and benefit may arise under the master and servant law in the case of an executive director [1] if there is an express or implied contract to that effect.

---

**Notes**
**Section 282**

1. "Director" includes any person occupying the position of director by whatever name called; and includes any person in accordance with whose directions or instructions the directors of the company are accustomed to act; **Section 567 CAMA, Cap. C20, LFN 2004**
2. "Company" means a company formed and registered under this Actor as the case may be, formed and registered in Nigeria before and in existence on the commencement of this Act; **Section 567 CAMA, Cap. C20, LFN 2004.**
   " Company" means a corporation - or, less commonly, an association, partnership, or union that carries on a commercial or industrial enterprise. **Garner B. (ed) Black's Law Dictionary 8th ed.**
3. "Board" see "board of directors". It means the governing body of a corporation, partnership, association, or other organization, elected by the shareholders or members to establish policy, elect or appoint officers and committees, and make other governing decisions. See **Garner B. (ed) Black's Law Dictionary 8 th ed.**

Cross Reference

On definition of directors, see **section 244 (1) CAMA Cap C20 LFN 2004**
On appointment of directors, see **section 246 CAMA Cap C20 LFN 2004**
On appointment of directors for life, see **section 248 CAMA Cap C20 LFN 2004**
On removal of directors, see **section 266 CAMA Cap C20, LFN 2004**

---

**For Further Reading**

On directors, see, Bakibinga, D.J., "Directors' Duty to Act Bona Fide in the Interest of the Company" (1990) 39 (2) **The International and Comparative Law Quarterly** 451.

## 283. Legal position of directors

(1) Directors[1] are trustees[2] of the company's[3] moneys, properties and their powers and as such must account for all the moneys over which they exercise control and shall refund any moneys improperly paid away, and shall exercise their powers honestly in the interest of the company and all the shareholders,[4] and not in their own or sectional interests.

(2) A director[1] may, when acting within his authority and the powers of the company, be regarded as agents of the company[3] under Part III of this Act.

---

**Notes**
**Section 283(2)**

1. "Directors" includes any person occupying the position of director by whatever name called; and includes any person in accordance with whose directions or instructions the directors of the company are accustomed to act. See **Section 567 CAMA, Cap. C20, LFN 2004**
2. "Trustee" means one who, having legal title to property holds it in trust for the benefit of another and owes a fiduciary duty to that beneficiary**. See Garner B. Ed. Black's Law Dictionary**
3. "Company" means a company formed and registered under this Actor as the case may be, formed and registered in Nigeria before and in existence on the commencement of this Act. See **Section 567 CAMA, Cap. C20, LFN 2004 "** Company" means a corporation - or, less commonly, an association, partnership, or union that carries on a commercial or industrial enterprise. **Garner B. (ed) Black's Law Dictionary 8th ed.**
4. "Shareholders" see "shareholder." It means one who owns or holds a share or shares in a company. **See Garner B. ed. Black's Law Dictionary 8th Ed**

**Cross Reference**

On definition of directors, see **section 244 (1) CAMA Cap C20 LFN 2004**
On appointment of directors, see **section 246 CAMA Cap C20 LFN 2004**
On appointment of directors for life, see **section 248 CAMA Cap C20 LFN 2004**
On removal of directors, see **section 266 CAMA Cap C20, LFN 2004**

**For Further Reading**

On directors, shareholders, see, Osunbor O. A. The Company Director: His Appointment, Powers and Duties; **Essays on Company Law** Page 130.

*Property transactions by directors*

## 284. Substantial property transactions involving directors, etc.

(1) Subject to the exceptions provided by section 285 of this Act, a company [1] shall not enter into an arrangement-

(a) whereby a director [2] of the company [1] or its holding company,[3] or a person connected with such a director [2], acquires or is to acquire one or more non-cash assets of the requisite value from the company; [1] or

(b) whereby the company [1] acquires or is to acquire one or more non-cash assets of the requisite value from such a director[1] or a person so connected, unless the arrangement is first approved by a resolution [4] of the company[2] in general meeting[5] and if the director[2] or connected person is a director[2] of its holding company[3] or a person connected with such a director,[2] by a resolution[4] in general meeting[5] of the holding company.[3]

(2) For the purpose of subsection (1) of this section, a non-cash asset is of the requisite value if, at the time the arrangement in question is entered into, its value is not less than ₦2,000 but (subject to that) exceeds ₦100,000 or twenty per cent of the company's asset value, that is-

(a) except in a case falling within paragraph (b) of this subsection the value of the company's net asset determined by reference to the accounts prepared and laid under Part XI in respect of the last preceding year in respect of which such accounts were so laid; and

(b) where no accounts have been so prepared and laid before that time, the amount of the company's called-up share capital.

(3) For the purposes of this section and sections 285 and 286 of this Act, a shadow director[6] shall be treated as a director.[2]

---

**Notes**
**Section 284**

1. " Company" means a company formed and registered under this Actor as the case may be , formed and registered in Nigeria before and in existence on the commencement of this Act . See **section 567 CAMA, Cap C20, LFN 2004.**
2. "Director" means (1) one who manages, guides, or orders; a chief administrator (2) a person appointed or elected to sit on a board that manages the affairs of a corporation or other organisation by electing and exercising control over its officer. See **Garner B. (ed) Black's Law Dictionary 8th ed.** "Director" includes any person occupying the position of director by whatever name called; and includes any person in accordance with whose directions or instructions the directors of the company are accustomed to act. **See section 567 CAMA, Cap. C20, LFN 2004**
3. "Holding Company" "means a holding company as defined by section 338. **See section 567CAMA, Cap. C20, LFN 2004.**
4. "Resolution" means a decision reached by a majority of the m embers at a company meeting. See **Martins, E. Oxford Dictionary of Law 4th ed.**
5. "General meeting" see "Annual meeting" – a yearly meeting to elect or install officers or directors and to conduct other routine

organisational business. See **Garner B. (ed) Black's Law Dictionary 8th ed.**

6. "Shadow Director" " includes any person on whose instructions and directions the director of a company is accustomed to act. **Section 245 CAMA, Cap. C20, LFN 2004.**

Cross Reference

On exceptions to the prohibition of directors acquiring non-cash assets of requisite value of a company, see **section 285 CAMA CAP C20, LFN 2004**.

## 285. Exceptions from section 284

(1) No approval shall be required to be given under section 284 of this Act by any body corporate [1] unless it is a company [2] within the meaning of this Act, or if it is a wholly-owned subsidiary[3] of anybody corporate. [1]

(2) Section 283 of this Act shall not apply to an arrangement for the acquisition of a non-cash asset if-

(a) the asset is to be acquired by a holding company [4] from any of its wholly-owned subsidiaries [3] or from a holding company[4] by any of its wholly-owned subsidiary [3] of a holding company[4] from another wholly-owned subsidiary [3] of that same holding company; [4] or

(b) the arrangement is entered into by a company [2] which is being wound up,[5] unless the winding up [5] is a member's voluntary winding up. [6]

(3) Subsection (1) (a) of section 284 of this Act shall not apply to an arrangement whereby a person is to acquire an asset from a company[2] of which he is a member, [7] if the arrangement is made with that person in his character as a member [7]

**Notes**
**Section 28**

1. "Body corporate" means an entity (usu. A business) having authority under law to act as a single person distinct from the shareholders who own it and having rights to issue stock and exist indefinitely; a group or succession of persons established in accordance with legal rules into a legal or juristic person that has a legal personality distinct from the natural persons who make it up, exists indefinitely apart from them, and has the legal powers that its constitution gives it. **Garner B. (ed) Black's Law Dictionary 8th (ed)**

2. "Company" means a company formed and registered under this Actor as the case may be, formed and registered in Nigeria before and in

existence on the commencement of this Act . See **Section 567 CAMA, Cap. C20, LFN 2004.**

3. "subsidiary" means, in relation to a body corporate, a subsidiary as defined by section 338 of this Act. **Section 567 CAMA, CAP C20, LFN 2004.**
4. "Holding Company" means a holding company as defined by section 338**. See section 567CAMA, Cap. C20, LFN 2004.**
5. "Wound up" see "winding up. "It means the process of settling accounts and liquidating assets in anticipation of a partnership's or a corporation's dissolution. See **section 462(4) CAMA, Cap. C20 LFN 2004**
6. "Members voluntary winding up" has the same meaning as assigned by section 462(4) of this Act. **See section 567 CAMA Cap. C20 LFN 2004**
7. "Member" means the heirs, executor administrator or other personal representative as the case may be, of the member. See **section 537 CAMA, Cap. C20, LFN 2004.**

**Cross Reference**

On prohibition of directors acquiring non-cash assets of requisite value of a company, see **section 284 CAMA Cap. C20 LFN 2004**

---

## 286. Liabilities arising from contravention of section 284

(1) An arrangement entered into by a company [1] in contravention of section 284 of this Act and any transaction entered into in pursuance of the arrangement (whether by the company [1] or any other person), shall be voidable at the instance of the company,[1] unless one or more of the conditions specified in subsection (2) of this section is satisfied.

(2) The conditions are that-

(a) restitution of any money or other asset which is the subject-matter of the arrangement or transaction is no longer possible or the company [1] has been indemnified in pursuance of this section by any other person for the loss or damage suffered by it; or

(b) any rights acquired bona fide for value and without actual notice of the contravention by any person who is a party to the arrangement or transaction would be affected by its avoidance; or

(c) the arrangement is, within a reasonable period, affirmed by the company[1] in general meeting [2] and, if it is an arrangement for the transfer of an asset to or by a director[3] of its holding company [4] or a person who is connected with such a director, [3] is so affirmed with the approval of the holding company [1]given by a resolution[5] in general meeting.[2]

(3) If an arrangement is entered into with a company [1] by a director[3] of the company [1]or its holding company[4] or a person connected with him in contravention of section 284 of this Act, that director[3] and the person so connected, and any other director [3] of the company[1] who authorizes the arrangement or any transaction entered into in pursuance of such an arrangement, shall be guilty of an offence and liable-

(a) to account to the company [1] for any gain which he has made directly or indirectly by the arrangement or transaction; and

(b) (jointly and severally with any other person liable under this subsection) to indemnify the company [1] for any loss or damage resulting from the arrangement or transaction.

(4) Subsection (3) of this section shall be without prejudice to any liability imposed otherwise than by that subsection, and is subject to the following two subsections; and the liability under subsection (3) of the section arises whether or not the arrangement or transaction entered into has been avoided in pursuance of subsection (1) of this section.

(5) If an arrangement is entered into by a company [1] and a person connected with a director [3]of the company[1] or its holding company[4] in contravention of section 284 of this Act, that director [3] shall not be liable under subsection (3) of this section if he shows that he took all reasonable steps to secure the company's compliance with that section.

(6) In any case, a person so connected and any such other director[3] as is mentioned in subsection (3) of this section shall not be so liable if he shows that at the time the arrangement was entered into, he did not know the relevant circumstances constituting the contravention.

(7) This section shall have effect with respect to references in sections 284, 285 and 286 of this Act to a person being "connected" with a director[3] of a company,[1] and to a director [3]being "associated with" or "controlling" a body corporate.

(8) A person is connected with a director of a company if he (not being himself a director of it) 1S-

(a) that director's spouse, child or step-child, including illegitimate child;

(b) except where the context otherwise requires, a body corporate with which the director [3] is associated; or

(c) a person acting in his capacity as trustee [6] of any trust, the beneficiaries [7]of which include-

(i) the director,[3] his spouse, any children or step-children; or

(ii) a body corporate with which he is associated, or of a trust whose terms confer a power on the trustees [6] that may be exercised for the benefit of the director [3], his spouse or any children or step-children of his, or any such body corporate; or

(d) a person acting in his capacity as partner of that director [4] or of any person who, by virtue of paragraphs (a), (b) or (c) of this subsection, is connected with that director [4].

---

**Notes**
**Section 286**

1. **"Company"** means a corporation - or, less commonly, an association, partnership, or union that carries on a commercial or industrial enterprise. **Garner B. (ed) Black's Law Dictionary 8th ed.**
"Company" or "existing company" means a company formed and registered under this Act or, as the case may be, formed and registered in Nigeria before and in existence on the commencement of this Act. **Section 567 CAMA, Cap. C20, LFN 2004.**
2. "General meeting" see "Annual meeting" – a yearly meeting to elect or install officers or directors and to conduct other routine organisational business. See **Garner B. (ed) Black's Law Dictionary 8th ed**
3. **"Directior"** means a person appointed or elected to sit on a board that manages the affairs of a corporation or other organization by electing and exercising control over its officers. **See Graner B. Ed. Black's Law Dictionary**
"Director" includes any person occupying the position of director by whatever name called; and includes any person in accordance with whose directions or instructions the directors of the company are accustomed to act. See **Section 567 CAMA, Cap. C20, LFN 2004.**
4. "Holding company means a holding company as defined by section 338. **See Section 567CAMA, Cap. C20 LFN 2004.**
5. "Resolution" means a decision reached by a majority of the m embers at a company meeting. See **Martins, E. (ed.) Oxford Dictionary of Law 4th ed.**

6. "Trustee" means one who, having legal title to property holds it in trust for the benefit of another and owes a fiduciary duty to that beneficiary. **See Garner B. ed. Black's Law Dictionary 8 th ed.**
7. "Beneficiaries" see "Beneficiary" it means 1. A person for whose benefit property is held in trust; especially one designated to benefit from an appointment, disposition, or assignment (as in a will, insurance policy, etc.), or to receive something as a result of a legal arrangement or instrument. 2. A person to whom another is in a fiduciary relation, whether the relation is one of agency, guardianship, or trust. **See Garner B. Ed. Black's Law Dictionary 8 th ed.**

Cross Reference

On meaning of offence, see **section 2, Criminal Code Cap. C38 LFN 2004**
On prohibition of directors acquiring non-cash assets of requisite value of a company, see **section 284 CAMA Cap. C20 LFN 2004**

---

**Cases**

A director is a person appointed or elected according to Law, authorized to manage and direct the affairs of a corporation or company. ***Olufosoye v. Fakorede* (1993) 1 N.W.L.R 947.** See also ***Longe v. First Bank Nigeria Plc* (2006) 3 N.W.L.R 228 at 270.**

## 287. Prohibition of secret benefits

(1) A director [1] shall not accept a bribe, a gift, or commission either in cash or kind from any person or a share in the profit of that person in respect of any transaction involving his company [2] in order to introduce his company [2] to deal with such a person.

(2) If a director [1] contravenes the provisions of section 287 (1) of this Act, he commits a breach of duty and the company [2] shall recover from the director [1] the actual gift and then sue him and the other person jointly and severally for damages sustained without any deduction in respect of what the director [1] has returned.

(3) Where the gift is made after the transaction has been completed in a form of unsolicited gift as a sign of gratitude, the director[1] may be allowed to keep the gift, provided he declares it before the board [3]and that fact shall also appear in the minutes book of the directors. [1]

(4) In all cases concerning secret benefits, the plea that the company[2] benefited or that the gift was accepted in good faithshall be no defence.

---

**Notes**

**Section 287**

1. " Directors" includes any person occupying the position of director by whatever name called; and includes any person in accordance with whose directions or instructions the directors of the company are accustomed to act **Section 567CAMA, Cap. C20, LFN 2004.**
2. "Company" means a corporation - or, less commonly, an association, partnership, or union that carries on a commercial or industrial enterprise. **Garner B. (ed) Black's Law Dictionary 8th ed.**
   "Company" or "existing company" means a company formed and registered under this Act or, as the case may be, formed and registered in Nigeria before and in existence on the commencement of this Act. **Section 567 CAMA, Cap. C20, LFN 2004.**
3. "Board" see "board of directors". It means the governing body of a corporation, elected by the shareholders to establish corporate policy, appoint executive officers, and make major business and financial decisions. See **Garner B. (ed.) Black's Law Dictionary 8 th ed.**

**Cross Reference**

On prohibition of directors acquiring non-cash assets of requisite value of a company, see **section 284 CAMA Cap. C20 LFN 2004**

---

**Cases**

Directors have sometimes been called trustees, or commercial trustees, and sometimes they have been called managing partners. It does not matter what you call them so long as you understand what their true position is, which is that they are really commercial when managing a trading concern for the benefit of themselves and all other shareholders in it. ***Iwuchukwu vs. Nwizu* (1994) 7 N.W.L.R (part357) 379 at 396**

*Miscellaneous matters relating to directors*

## 288. Directors with unlimited liability in respect of a limited company

(1) In a limited company [1] the liability of the directors [2] or managers[3] or of the managing director, [4] may, if so provided by the memorandum,[5] be unlimited.

(2) In a limited company [1] in which the liability of a director [2] or manager[3] is unlimited, the directors [2] and any managers[3] of the company[1] and the member[6] who proposes a person for election or appointment to the office of director [2] or manager, [3] shall add to that proposal a statement that the liability of the person holding that office shall be unlimited, and before the person accepts the office or acts therein, notice in writing that his liability shall be unlimited

shall be given to him by the following or one of the following persons, namely, the promoters [7] of the company[2], the directors [2] of the company[1], any managers [3] of the company and the secretary [8] of the company.[1]

(3) If any director, [2] manager[3], or promoter [7] makes default in adding such a statement, or if any promoter, [7] director[2] manager[3] or secretary[8] makes default in giving such a notice, he shall be guilty of an offence and liable to a fine of ₦100 and shall also be liable for any damage which the person so elected or appointed may sustain from the default.

---

**Notes**
**Section 288**

1. "Limited company" means a company having the liability of its members limited by the memorandum to the amount, if any, unpaid on the shares respectively held by them. See **Section 21(1)(a)CAMA, CAP C20 , LFN 2004.**
2. "Directors" see "director." It includes any person occupying the position of director by whatever name called; and includes any person in accordance with whose directions or instructions the directors of the company are accustomed to act. See **Section 567CAMA, CAP C20, LFN 2004**
3. "Managers" see "manager". It means one who is in charge of a corporation and in control of its business, or establishments, division, or departments, and who is vested with a certain amount of discretion and independent judgement. See **Garner B. (ed.) Black's Law Dictionary 8th ed.**
4. "Managing director" means a director to whom management powers have been delegated, either absolutely or subject to supervision, by the other directors of the company under terms of the articles of association. Managing directors are the agents of the company and have wide authority to act on its behalf. See **Martins E. (ed.) Oxford Dictionary of Law 4th ed**
5. "Memorandum" see "memorandum of association" it means a legal document setting up a corporation- either with or without limited liability –and including the company's name, purpose, and duration . See **Garner B. (ed) Black's Law Dictionary 8th ed.**
   "Memorandum" means the memorandum of association of a company as originally framed or as altered in pursuance of any enactment. See **Section 567 CAMA, CAP C20, LFN 2004.**
6. "Members" **see** "member." It includes the heir, executor, administrator or other personal representative, as the case may be, of the member. See **Section 567 CAMA, CAP C20, LFN 2004.**
7. "Promoter" is any person who undertakes to take part in forming a company with reference to a given project and to set it going and who

takes the necessary steps to accomplish that purpose, or who, with regard to a proposed or newly formed company, undertakes a part in raising capital for it, shall, prima facie, be deemed a promoter of the company. See **section 61 CAMA CAP C20 LFN 2004**

8. "Secretary" means a corporate officer in charge of official correspondence, minutes of board meetings, and records of stock ownership and transfer **. See Garner B. (ed) Black's Law Dictionary 8th ed.**

**Cross Reference**

On meaning of offence, see section 2, Criminal Code Cap. C38 LFN 2004

On distinction between a limited and an unlimited company, see section 21 CAMA Cap. C20, LFN 2004

On appointment of first and subsequent directors, see sections 247 & 248 CAMA Cap. C20, LFN 2004

---

**Cases**

Directors have sometimes been called trustees, or commercial trustees, and sometimes they have been called managing partners. It does not matter what you call them so long as you understand what their true position is, which is that they are really commercial when managing a trading concern for the benefit of themselves and all other shareholders in it. Iwuchukwu vs. Nwizu (1994) 7 N.W.L.R (part357) 379 at 396

Section 61 defines a promoter as- any person who undertakes to take part in forming a company with reference to a given project and to set it going and who takes the necessary steps to accomplish that purpose, or who, with regard to a proposed or newly formed company, undertakes a part in raising capital for it, shall, prima facie, be deemed a promoter of the company: Provided that a person acting in a professional capacity for persons engaged in procuring the formation of the company shall not thereby be deemed to be a promoter. Adeniji v. Starcola (Nigeria) Ltd. Suit No. M.135/70 unreported, H.C. Lagos.

---

**For Further Reading**

On general provisions on directors, see, Deji Sasegbon, **Nigerian Companies and Allied Matters Law and Practice**, DSC Publications, Lagos, (1st Ed., 1992)

## 289.Special resolution of limited company making liability of directors unlimited

(1) A limited company.[1] if so authorized by its articles,[2] may, by special resolution,[3] alter its memorandum[4] so as to render unlimited the liability of its directors[5] or managers,[6] or of any managing director.[7]

(2) Upon the passing of any such special resolution, [3] the provisions of it shall be as valid as if they had been originally contained in the memorandum. [4]

---

**Notes**
**Section 289**

1. "Limited company" means a company having the liability of its members limited by the memorandum to the amount, if any, unpaid on the shares respectively held by them. See **Section 21(1)(a)CAMA, Cap. C20 , LFN 2004.**
2. "Articles" means the articles of association of a company, as originally framed or as altered by special resolution, including so far as they apply to the regulations contained in Table A in the First Schedules of the Companies Act, 1992 or in that Table as altered by any subsequent enactment or reprint of the Laws , or in Table A in Schedule 1 to this Act. See **Section 567 CAMA, Cap. C20, LFN 2004**
3. "Special Resolution" means resolution passed by not less than three-fourths of the votes by such members of the company as being entitled to do so, vote by person or in proxy at a general meeting of which 21days notice, specifying the intention to propose the resolution is a special resolution, has been duly given. **Section 233(2) CAMA, Cap. C20, LFN 2004.**
4. "Memorandum" see "memorandum of association" it means a legal document setting up a corporation- either with or without limited liability –and including the company's name, purpose, and duration . See **Garner B. (ed) Black's Law Dictionary 8th ed.**
   "Memorandum" means the memorandum of association of a company as originally framed or as altered in pursuance of any enactment. See **Section 567 CAMA, Cap. C20, LFN 2004.**
5. "Directors" see "director." It includes any person occupying the position of director by whatever name called; and includes any person in accordance with whose directions or instructions the directors of the company are accustomed to act. See **Section 567CAMA, Cap. C20, LFN 2004**
6. "Managers" see "manager." It means one who is in charge of a corporation and in control of its business, or establishments, division, or departments, and who is vested with a certain amount of discretion and independent judgement. See **Garner B. (ed.) Black's Law Dictionary 8th ed.**
7. "Managing director" means a director to whom management powers have been delegated, either absolutely or subject to supervision, by the other directors of the company under terms of the articles of association. Managing directors are the agents of the company and have wide authority to act on its behalf. See **Martins E. (ed.) Oxford Dictionary of Law 4th ed.**

**Cross Reference**

**On types of resolution, see section 233 CAMA CAP C20, LFN 2004.**

---

**Cases**

Generally companies speak or express their decisions through resolutions, which must be validly passed. No member of a company has a right to unilaterally commit the company on any matter without its consent and approval. Let me emphatically say that no member of a company is allowed to wake up one morning and sell off the company. ***New Resources Int'l Ltd. & Anor. v. Ejike Oranusi (2010) LPELR-CA/L/461/08.***

Where the provisions of the Act and the Articles regarding such matters as notice of meetings, quorum, proceedings at and conduct of meetings, are not strictly complied with, any resolution passed at such meetings will be a nullity. ***Obikoya v. Ezenwani (1964) 2 All NLR 133***

## 290. Personal liability of directors and officers

(1) Where a company [1]

(a) receives money by way of loan for specific purpose; or

(b) receives money or other property by way of advance payment for the execution of a contract or project; and

(c) with intent to defraud, fails to apply the money or other property for the purpose for which it was received, every director[2] or other officer [3] of the company [1] who is in default shall be personally liable to the party from whom the money or property was received for a refund of the money or property so received and not applied for the purpose for which it was received:

Provided that nothing in this section shall affect the liability of the company[1] itself.

---

**Notes**

**Section 290 (1)**

1. "Company" means a corporation - or, less commonly, an association, partnership, or union that carries on a commercial or industrial enterprise. See **Garner B. (ed) Black's Law Dictionary 8th ed.**
"Company" means a company formed and registered under this Act or, as the case may be, formed and registered in Nigeria before and in existence on the commencement of this Act. **Section 567 CAMA, Cap. C20 LFN 2004.**

2. "Director" includes any person occupying the position of director by whatever name called; and includes any person in accordance with whose directions or instructions the directors of the company are accustomed to act. See **Section 567CAMA, Cap. C20 LFN 2004**
3. "Officer" in relation to a body corporate, includes a director, manager or secretary **Section 567 CAMA, Cap. C20 LFN 2004**

Cross Reference

On appointment of first and subsequent directors, see **sections 247 & 248 CAMA Cap. C20, LFN 2004**

On prohibition of directors acquiring non-cash assets of requisite value of a company, see **section 284 CAMA Cap. C20 LFN 2004**

On removal of directors, see **section 266 CAMA Cap. C20, LFN 2004**

---

## 291. Director's contract of employment for more than five years

(1) The provisions of this section shall apply in respect of any term of an agreement whereby a director's [1] employment with the company[2] of which he is a director [1] or, where he is the director [1] of a holding company[3], his employment within the group, is to continue or may be continued, otherwise than at the instance of the company[2] (whether under the original agreement entered into in pursuance of it or not), for a period of more than five years during which the employment-

(a) cannot be terminated by the company [2] by notice; or

(b) can be so terminated only in specified circumstances.

(2) In any such case where-

(a) a person is or is to be employed with a company [2] under an agreement which cannot be terminated by the company[2] by notice or can be so terminated only in specified circumstances; and

(b) more than six months before the expiration of the period for which he is or to be so employed, the company [2] enters into a further agreement otherwise than in pursuance of a right conferred by or under the original agreement on the other party to it under which he is to be employed with the company[2] or, where he is a director [1] of a holding company[3], within the group, this section shall apply as if to the period for which he is to be employed under that further agreement there were added a further period equal to the unexpired period of the original agreement.

(3) A company[2] shall not incorporate in an agreement such a term as is mentioned in subsection (1) of this section unless the term is first approved by a resolution [4] of the company[2] in general meeting[5] and in the case of a director [1] of a holding company[3], by a resolution[4] of that company[2] in general meeting.[5]

(4) No approval shall be required to be given under this section by any body corporate unless it is a company within the meaning of this Act, or if it is a wholly-owned subsidiary [6] of any body corporate.

(5) A resolution[4] of a company[2] approving such a term as is mentioned in subsection (1) of this section, shall not be passed at a general meeting[5] of the company[2] unless a written memorandum setting out the proposed agreement incorporating the term is available for inspection by members[7] of the company[2] both-

(a) at the company's [2] registered office[8] for not less than 15 days ending with the date of the meeting; [5] and

(b) at the meeting[5] itself.

(6) A term incorporated in an agreement in contravention of this section shall to the extent that it contravenes the section, be void; and that agreement and in a case where subsection (2) of this section applies, the original agreements shall be deemed each to contain a term entitling the company [2] to terminate it at any time by the giving of reasonable notice.

(7) In this section-

(a) "employment" includes employment under a contract for services; and

(b) "group" in relation to a director of a holding company, [3] means the group which consists of that company and its subsidiaries[6] and for purposes of this section, a shadow director[9] shall be treated as a director [1]

---

**Notes**
**Section 291**

1. "Directors" see "director." It means a person appointed or elected to sit on a board that manages the affairs of a corporation or other organisation by electing and exercising control over its officers. **See Garner B. (ed) Black's Law Dictionary 8th ed.**
"Director" includes any person occupying the position of director by whatever name called; and includes any person in accordance with whose directions or instructions the directors of the company are accustomed to act . See section **567 CAMA, Cap. C20 LFN 2004.**

2. "Company" means a corporation - or, less commonly, an association, partnership, or union that carries on a commercial or industrial enterprise. See **Garner B. (ed) Black's Law Dictionary 8th ed.** "Company" means a company formed and registered under this Act or, as the case may be, formed and registered in Nigeria before and in existence on the commencement of this Act. **See Section 567 CAMA, Cap. C20 LFN 2004.**
3. "Holding Company" means a holding company as defined by section 338 of this Act. **See Section 567 CAMA, Cap. C20 LFN 2004.**
4. "Resolution" **is** a formal expression of the opinion or will of an official body or public assembly adopted by a vote. See **Garner B. (ed) Black's Law Dictionary 8th ed.**
5. "General meeting" "Annual meeting" – a yearly meeting to elect or install officers or directors and to conduct other routine organisational business. **See Garner B. (ed) Black's Law Dictionary 8th ed.**
6. "Subsidiary" in relation to a body corporate, a subsidiary as defined by section 338 of this Act. **See Section 567 CAMA, Cap C20 LFN 2004.**
7. Members" see "member". It includes the heir, executor, administrator or other personal representative, as the case may be, of the member. See **Section 567 CAMA, Cap. C20 LFN 2004.**
8. "Registered office" means the official address of a registered company; It must be notified to the Companies Registry before registration of the company and it must appear on company letter-head and order forms. Documents may be served to a company's registered office and various registers and records may be inspected there. See **Martins E. (ed.) Oxford Dictionary of Law 4th ed.**
9. "Shadow director" " includes any person on whose instructions and directions the director of a company is accustomed to act. **See Section 245 CAMA, Cap. C20 LFN 2004.**

Cross Reference

On the registered offices of company and change therein, see **sections 35 & 547 CAMA Cap C20 LFN 2004**

On types of resolutions, see **section 233 CAMA Cap. C20, LFN 2004**

---

**Cases**

Generally employments fall into three categories, viz (a) master and servant; (b) where the servant holds an office at pleasure;(c) employment that is governed by statute. **See *Olaniyan v. University of Lagos (1985) 2 NWLR (Pt. 9) 599***

**For Further Reading**

On Directors, Officers and their liabilities see Okoli, C., "Criminal Liability of Corporations in Nigeria: A Current Perspective " **(1994) 38 Journal of African Law 35.**

**292. Register of directors and secretaries**

(1) Every company [1] shall keep at its registered office, [2] a register of its directors [3] and secretaries. [4]

(2) The register shall contain the following particulars with respect to each director [3], that is to say his present forename and surname, any former forename and surname, his usual residential address, his nationality, his business occupation, if any, particulars of any other directorships [3] held by him and the date of his birth: Provided that it shall not be necessary for the register to contain particulars of directorships held by a director [4] in companies [1] of which the whole company [1] is the wholly-owned subsidiary [5], or which are the wholly-owned subsidiaries [5] either of the company [1] or of another company [1] of which the company [1] is the wholly-owned subsidiary, [5] and for the purpose of this proviso-

(i) "company [1]" includes any body corporate [6] incorporated in Nigeria; and

(ii) a body corporate [6] shall be deemed to be the wholly-owned subsidiary [5] of another if it has no members [7] except that other and that other's wholly-owned subsidiaries [5] and its or their nominees.

(3) The register shall contain the following particulars with respect to the secretary [5], in the case of an individual, his present forename and surname, any former forenames and surname and his usual residential address; and in the case of a corporation its registered name and registered or head office.

(4) The company [1] shall within the periods respectively mentioned in subsection (5) of this section, send to the Commission [8] a return in the prescribed form containing the particulars specified in the register and notification in the prescribed form of any change among its directors or in its secretary or in any of the particulars contained in the register, specifying the date of the change.

(5) The periods referred to in subsection (4) of this section shall be the period within which-

(a) the return is to be sent which shall be a period of 14 days from the date of incorporation of the company; and

(b) the notification of a change is to be sent which shall be 14 days from the happening thereof:

Provided that, in the case of a return containing particulars with respect to any person who is the company's [3] secretary [4] at the commencement of this Act, the period shall be 14 days from the commencement of this Act.

(6) The register to be kept under this section shall during business hours (subject to such reasonable restrictions as the company may by its articles or in general meeting [9] impose, so that no less than two hours in each day be allowed for inspection) be open to inspection by any member of the company [3] without charge and by any other person on payment of 50k or such less sum as the company [3]may prescribe, for each inspection.

(7) If any inspection required under this section is refused, or if default is made in complying with the provisions of subsections (1), (2), (3) and (4) of this section, the company [3] and every officer[10] of the company[3] who is in default shall be guilty of an offence and liable to a fine of ₦50.

(8) In case of any such refusal or default as mentioned in subsection (7) of this section, the court may by order compel an inspection of the register or that the copies required be sent as provided in this section.

(9) For the purpose of this section-

(a) a person in accordance with whose directions or instruction the directors[3] of a company are accustomed to act shall be deemed to be a director [3] and officer of the company[1];

(b) references to a former forename or surname in the case of a married woman shall not include the name or surname by which she was known previous to the marriage.

---

**Notes**
**Section 292**

1. "Company" means a corporation - or, less commonly, an association, partnership, or union that carries on a commercial or industrial enterprise. **Garner B. (ed) Black's Law Dictionary 8th ed.**
"Company" or "existing company" means a company formed and registered under this Act or, as the case may be, formed and registered in Nigeria before and in existence on the commencement of this Act . **Section 567 CAMA, Cap. C20, LFN 2004.**
2. "Registered office" "the official way of referring to a Registry . **Oxford Advanced Learners Dictionary, New 7th Edition.** 3" Director" "means (1) one who manages, guides, or orders; a chief administrator (2) a person appointed or elected to sit on a board that manages the affairs of a corporation or other organisation by electing

and exercising control over its officers. **Garner B. (ed) Black's Law Dictionary 8th ed.**

3. "Director" includes any person occupying the position of director by whatever name called; and includes any person in accordance with whose directions or instructions the directors of the company are accustomed to act. **Section 567 CAMA, Cap. C20, LFN 2004.**
4. "Secretary" An administrative assistant. 2. A corporate officer in charge of official correspondence, minutes of board meetings, and records of stock ownership and transfer **Garner B. (ed) Black's Law Dictionary 8th (ed)**
5. "Subsidiaries" means, in relation to a body corporate, a subsidiary as defined by section 338 of this Act. **Section 567 CAMA, Cap. C20, LFN 2004.**
6. "Body corporate" see corporation. An entity (usu. A business) having authority under law to act as a single person distinct from the shareholders who own it and having rights to issue stock and exist indefinitely; a group or succession of persons established in accordance with legal rules into a legal or juristic person that has a legal personality distinct from the natural persons who make it up, exists indefinitely apart from them, and has the legal powers that its constitution gives it. **Garner B. (ed) Black's Law Dictionary 8 th (ed)**
7 "Members" "includes the heir, executor, administrator or other personal representative, as the case may be, of the member. **Section 567 CAMA, Cap. C20, LFN 2004.**
8. "Commission" means the Corporate Affairs Commission established under section 1 of this Act; Sect
9. "General meeting" see "Annual meeting" – a yearly meeting to elect or install officers or directors and to conduct other routine organisational business. **Garner B. (ed) Black's Law Dictionary 8th ed.**
10. "Officer "means in relation to a body corporate includes a director, manager or secretary; Section 567 **CAMA Cap. C20, LFN 2004.**

**Cross Reference**

On the registered offices of company and change therein, see **sections 35 & 547 CAMA Cap. C20 LFN 2004**

On meaning of offence, see **section 2, Criminal Code Act, Cap. C38, LFN 2004**

---

*CHAPTER 2*

*Secretaries*

## 293. Secretaries

(1) Every company[1] shall have a secretary.[2]

(2) Anything required or authorized to be done by or of the secretary[2] may, if the office is vacant or there is for any other

reason no secretary[2] capable of acting, be done by or of any assistant or deputy secretary[2] or, if there is no assistant or deputy secretary[2] capable of acting, by or of any officer [3] of the company[1] authorized generally or specially in that behalf by the directors. [4]

---

**Notes**
**Section 293**

1. "Company" means a corporation - or, less commonly, an association, partnership, or union that carries on a commercial or industrial enterprise. **See Garner B. (ed) Black's Law Dictionary 8th ed.**
   "Company" or "existing company" means a company formed and registered under this Act or, as the case may be, formed and registered in Nigeria before and in existence on the commencement of this Act. **See section 567 CAMA, Cap. C20, LFN 2004.**
2. "Secretary" means 1. An administrative assistant. 2. A corporate officer in charge of official correspondence, minutes of board meetings, and records of stock ownership and **transfer. See Garner B, (ed) Black's Law Dictionary 8th ed.**
3. "Officer" means in relation to a body corporate includes a director, manager or secretary; **Section 567 CAMA Cap. C20, LFN 2004.**
4. "Directors" see "director". It means a person appointed or elected to sit on a board that manages the affairs of a corporation or other organisation by electing and exercising control over its officers. See **Garner B. (ed) Black's Law Dictionary 8th ed.**
   "Director" includes any person occupying the position of director by whatever name called; and includes any person in accordance with whose directions or instructions the directors of the company are accustomed to act. See **Section 567 CAMA, Cap. C20 LFN 2004.**

**Cross Reference**

On duties of a company secretary, see **section 298 CAMA Cap. C20, LFN 2004**

On qualification of a company secretary, see **section 295 CAMA Cap. C20, LFN 2004**

---

**Cases**

A company secretary is a principal officer of the company. ***Okeowo v. Maglore*** (1979)11 SC 138. A company secretary is indeed a high ranking officer in the company set up and indeed part of the management of the company. ***Wimpey v. Balogun*** .**(1987) 2 NWLR 322** On members admitted to the Institute of Chartered Secretaries and Administration of Nigeria Act, 1991. Legal Practitioner is under LPA.

**For Further Reading**

On secretaries, their appointment, powers, duties see Orojo, J. Ola **Company Law and Practice in Nigeria** 3rd Edition, Mbeyi & Associates (Lagos, Nigeria) 1992 pages 336 – 346.

## 294. Avoidance of acts done by a person as director and secretary

A provision requiring or authorizing a thing to be done by or of a director [1] and the secretary [2] shall not be satisfied by its being done by or of the same person acting both as director [1] and as, or in place of the secretary. [2]

---

**Notes**

**Section 294.**

1. "Director" "means (1) one who manages, guides, or orders; a chief administrator (2) a person appointed or elected to sit on a board that manages the affairs of a corporation or other organisation by electing and exercising control over its officers. **Garner B. (ed) Black's Law Dictionary 8th ed.**

   "Director" includes any person occupying the position of director by whatever name called; and includes any person in accordance with whose directions or instructions the directors of the company are accustomed to act. **Section 567 CAMA, Cap. C20, LFN 2004.**
2. "Secretary" means 1. An administrative assistant. 2. A corporate officer in charge of official correspondence, minutes of board meetings, and records of stock ownership and transfer . **Garner B. (ed) Black's Law Dictionary 8th ed.**

Cross Reference

On duties of a company secretary, see **section 298 CAMA Cap. C20, LFN 2004**

On obligation of every company to have a company secretary, see **section 293 CAMA Cap. C20, LFN 2004**

---

**Cases**

A company secretary is a principal officer of the company. ***Okeowo v. Maglore*** (1979)11 SC 138.

A company secretary is indeed a high ranking officer in the company set up and indeed part of the management of the company . ***Wimpey v. Balogun***.**(1987) 2 NWLR 322**

**For Rurther Reading**

On secretaries, their appointment, powers, duties see Orojo, J. Ola **Company Law and Practice in Nigeria** 3rd Edition, Mbeyi & Associates (Lagos, Nigeria) 1992 pages 336 – 346.

## 295. Qualification of a secretary

It shall be the duty of a director [1] of a company[2] to take all reasonable steps to ensure that the secretary [3] of the company[2] is a person who appears to have the requisite knowledge and experience to discharge the functions of a secretary [3] of a company,[2] and in the case of a public company,[4] he shall be-

(a) a member of the Institute of Chartered Secretaries and Administrators; or

(b) a legal practitioner [5] within the meaning of the Legal Practitioners Act; or

[Cap. Lll.]

(c) a member of the Institute of the Chartered Accountants of Nigeria or such other bodies of accountants as are established from time to time by an Act; or

(d) any person who has held the office of the secretary [3] of a public company[4] for at least three years of the five years immediately preceding his appointment in a public company[4]; or

(e) a body corporate [6] or firm consisting of members each of whom is qualified under paragraphs (a), (b), (c), or (d) of this section.

---

**Notes**
**Section 295**

1. "Director" means (1) one who manages, guides, or orders; a chief administrator (2) a person appointed or elected to sit on a board that manages the affairs of a corporation or other organisation by electing and exercising control over its officers. **Garner B. (ed) Black's Law Dictionary 8th ed.**
"Director" includes any person occupying the position of director by whatever name called; and includes any person in accordance with whose directions or instructions the directors of the company are accustomed to act. **See Section 567 CAMA, Cap. C20, LFN 2004.**
2. "Company" means a corporation - or, less commonly, an association, partnership, or union that carries on a commercial or industrial enterprise. **Garner B. (ed) Black's Law Dictionary 8th ed.**
"Company" or "existing company" means a company formed and registered under this Act or, as the case may be, formed and registered in Nigeria before and in existence on the commencement of this Act. See **Section 567 CAMA, Cap. C20, LFN 2004.**
3"**Secretary**" means 1. An administrative assistant. 2. A corporate officer in charge of official correspondence, minutes of board

meetings, and records of stock ownership .See **Garner B. (ed) Black's Law Dictionary 8th ed.**

4"public company" any company other company other than a private company shall be a public company and its memorandum shall state that it is a public company. See **Section 24 CAMA, Cap. C20, LFN 2004.**

5. "Legal Practitioner" has the meaning assigned to it by the Legal Practitioners Act**. See Section 567 CAMA, Cap. C20 , LFN 2004**

6. "Body corporate" see corporation. An entity (usu. A business) having authority under law to act as a single person distinct from the shareholders who own it and having rights to issue stock and exist indefinitely ;a group or succession of persons established in accordance with legal rules into a legal or juristic person that has a legal personality distinct from the natural persons who make it up, exists indefinitely apart from them, and has the legal powers that its constitution gives it. **Garner B. (ed) Black's Law Dictionary 8th (ed)**

**Cross Reference**

On members admitted as chartered secretaries, see **the Institute of Chartered Secretaries and Administration of Nigeria Act, 1991.**

On the requirements for practice as a legal practitioner, see generally, **Legal Practitioners Act Cap. L11, LFN 2004**

On the establishment of the Institute of Chartered Accounts of Nigeria, See **Section 1 of the Institute of Chartered Accountants of Nigeria Act, Cap. I11, LFN, 2004.**

**Cases**

A company secretary is a principal officer of the company. ***Okeowo v Maglore*** (1979)11 SC 138.

A company secretary is indeed a high ranking officer in the company set up and indeed part of the management of the company . ***Wimpey v Balogun***.(**1987) 2 NWLR 322**

**For Further Reading**

On secretaries, their appointment, powers, duties see Orojo, J. Ola **Company Law and Practice in Nigeria** 3rd Edition, Mbeyi & Associates (Lagos, Nigeria) 1992 pages 336 – 346.

## 296. Appointment and removal of a secretary

(1) A secretary [1] shall be appointed by the directors [2] and, subject to the provisions of this section, may be removed by them.

(2) Where it is intended to remove the secretary [1] of a public company,[3] the board of directors [4] shall give him notice-

(a) stating that it is intended to remove him;

(b) setting out the grounds on which it is intended to remove him;

(c) giving him a period not less than seven working days within which to make his defence; and

(d) giving him an option to resign his office within a period of seven working days.

(3) Where, following the notice prescribed in subsection (2) of this section, the secretary [1] does not within the given period resign his office or make a defence, the board [4] may remove him from office and shall make a report to the next general meeting [5]; but where the secretary, without resigning his office, makes a defence and the board [4] does not consider it sufficient, if the ground-

(a) on which it is intended to remove him is that of fraud or serious misconduct, the board may remove him from office and shall report to the next general meeting [5]; and

(b) is other than of fraud or serious misconduct, the board [4] shall not remove him without the approval of the general meeting[5], but may suspend him and shall report to the next general meeting[5].

(4) Notwithstanding any rule of law, where a secretary [1] suspended under paragraph (b) of subsection (3) of this section is removed with the approval of the general meeting [5], the removal may take effect from such time as the general meeting [5] may determine.

---

**Notes**

**Section 296**

1. "Secretary" means 1. An administrative assistant. 2. A corporate officer in charge of official correspondence, minutes of board meetings, and records of stock ownership and transfer. **Garner B. (ed) Black's Law Dictionary 8th ed.**
2. " Director" " means (1) one who manages, guides, or orders; a chief administrator (2) a person appointed or elected to sit on a board that manages the affairs of a corporation or other organisation by electing and exercising control over its officers **. Garner B. (ed) Black's Law Dictionary 8th ed. "** Director" includes any person occupying the position of director by whatever name called; and includes any person in accordance with whose directions or instructions the directors of the company are accustomed to act **Section 567 CAMA, Cap. C20, LFN 2004.**

3. "Public company." any company other company other than a private company shall be a public company and its memorandum shall state that it is a public company **. Section 24 CAMA, Cap. C20, LFN 2004.**
4. "Board" is a group of people who have power to make a decision and control a company or other organization e.g. academic board (Oxford Advanced Learners Dictionary ,New 7th Edition.)
5. "General meeting" means the gathering of people to discuss or act on matters in which they have a common interest. **Garner. B. (ed) Black's Law Dictionary 8th ed.**

**Cross Reference**

On duties of a company secretary, see **section 298 CAMA Cap. C20, LFN 2004**

On obligation of every company to have a company secretary, see **section 293 CAMA Cap. C20, LFN 2004**

## Cases

"A company secretary is an officer of the company with extensive duties and responsibilities... He is no longer a mere clerk... he is certainly entitled to sign contracts connected with administrative side of a company's affair, such as employing staff, and ordering cars and so on and so forth ***Panorama Developments v. Fidelis Furnishing Fabrics (1971)***

**For Further Reading**

On Secretaries see Orojo, J. Ola **Company Law and Practice in Nigeria** 3rd Edition, Mbeyi & Associates (Lagos, Nigeria) 1992, Asomugha, E. Maduelosi **Company law in Nigeria under the Companies and Allied Matters Act** E .M. Asomugha (Lagos) 1994

## 297. Fiduciary interests of a secretary

A secretary[1] shall not owe fiduciary duties to the company, [2] but where he is acting as its agent he shall owe fiduciary duties to it, and as such shall be liable to the company [2] where he makes secret profits or lets his duties conflict with his personal interests, or uses confidential information he obtained from the company for his own benefit.

**Notes**

**Section 297**

1."Secretary" means 1. An administrative assistant. 2. A corporate officer in charge of official correspondence, minutes of board meetings, and records of stock ownership and transfer. **Garner B. (ed) Black's Law Dictionary 8th ed.**

2. "Company" means a corporation - or, less commonly, an association, partnership, or union that carries on a commercial or industrial enterprise. **Garner B. (ed) Black's Law Dictionary 8th ed.** "Company" or "existing company" means a company formed and registered under this Act or, as the case may be, formed and registered in Nigeria before and in existence on the commencement of this **Act. Section 567 CAMA, Cap. C20, LFN 2004.**

---

**Cases**

A company secretary is indeed a high ranking officer in the company set up and indeed part of the management of the company . ***Wimpey v. Balogun.*****(1987) 2 NWLR 322**

**For Further Reading**

On Secretaries see Orojo, J. Ola **Company Law and Practice in Nigeria** 3rd Edition, Mbeyi & Associates (Lagos, Nigeria) 1992, Asomugha, E. Maduelosi **Company law in Nigeria under the Companies and Allied Matters Act** E.M. Asomugha (Lagos) 1994

## 298. Duties of a secretary

(1) The duties of a secretary [1] shall include the following-

(a) attending the meeting[2] of the company,[3] the board[4] of directors[5] and its committees, rendering all necessary secretarial services in respect of the meeting [2] and advising on compliance by the meetings[2] with the applicable rules and regulations;

(b) maintaining the registers and other records required to be maintained by the company[3] under this Act;

(c) rendering proper returns and giving notification to the Commission[6] required under this Act;
and

(d) carrying out such administrative and other secretarial duties as directed by the director, [5] or the Company. [3]

(2) The secretary [1] shall not without the authority of the board [4] exercise any powers vested in the directors. [5]

---

**Notes**

**Section 298**

1. "Secretary" means 1. An administrative assistant. 2. A corporate officer in charge of official correspondence, minutes of board

meetings, and records of stock ownership and transfer. **Garner B. (ed) Black's Law Dictionary 8th ed.**

2. "Meeting" means the gathering of people to discuss or act on matters in which they have a common interest. **Garner B. (ed) Black's Law Dictionary 8th ed.**
3. "Company" means a corporation - or, less commonly, an association, partnership, or union that carries on a commercial or industrial enterprise. **Garner B. (ed) Black's Law Dictionary 8th ed.**
   "Company" or "existing company" means a company formed and registered under this Act or, as the case may be, formed and registered in Nigeria before and in existence on the commencement of this Act. **Section 567 CAMA, Cap. C20, LFN 2004.**
4. "Board" is a group of people who have power to make a decision and control a company or other organization e.g. academic board **Oxford Advanced Learners Dictionary ,New 7 th Edition.**
5. "Director" means (1) one who manages, guides, or orders; a chief administrator (2) a person appointed or elected to sit on a board that manages the affairs of a corporation or other organisation by electing and exercising control over its officers . **Garner B. (ed) Black's Law Dictionary 8th ed.**
   "Director" includes any person occupying the position of director by whatever name called; and includes any person in accordance with whose directions or instructions the directors of the company are accustomed to act **Section 567 CAMA, Cap. C20, LFN 2004.**
6. "Commission" means the Corporate Affairs Commission established under section 1 of this Act. See **Section 567 CAMA, Cap. C20, LFN 2004.**

**Cross Reference**

On obligation of every company to have a company secretary, see **section 293 CAMA Cap. C20, LFN 2004**

---

**Cases**

whether it is the director who himself calling or he is requesting the secretary to call a meeting of the board, it amount to same thing for it is the secretary who will gather the facilities for holding the meeting and take records of the minutes of the meeting . ***Okeowo v Miglore (1979) 11 SC.***

"A company secretary is an officer of the company with extensive duties and responsibilities... He is no longer a mere clerk... he is certainly entitled to sign contracts connected with administrative side of a company's affair, such as employing staff, and ordering cars and so on and so forth ***Panorama Developments v. Fidelis Furnishing Fabrics (1971)***

**For Further Reading**

On Secretaries see Orojo, J. Ola **Company Law and Practice in Nigeria** 3rd Edition, Mbeyi & Associates (Lagos, Nigeria) 1992, Asomugha, E. Maduelosi **Company law in Nigeria under the Companies and Allied Matters Act** E.M. Asomugha (Lagos) 1994

## *PART X*

### *Protection of minority against illegal and oppressive conduct*

### *Action by or against the company*

**299.** Only company may sue for wrong or ratify irregular conduct
Subject to the provisions of this Act, where an irregularity has been committed in the course of a company's [1] affairs or any wrong has been done to the company, [1] only the company [1] can sue to remedy that wrong and only the company [1] can ratify the irregular conduct.

---

**Notes**
**Section 299.**

1. "Company" means a corporation - or, less commonly, an association, partnership, or union that carries on a commercial or industrial enterprise. **Garner B. (ed) Black's Law Dictionary 8th ed.**
"Company" or "existing company" means a company formed and registered under this Act or, as the case may be, formed and registered in Nigeria before and in existence on the commencement of this Act. **Section 567 CAMA, Cap. C20, LFN 2004**

---

### 300. Protection of minority: injunction and declaration in certain cases

Without prejudice to the rights of members [1] under sections 303 to 308 and sections 310 to 312 of this Act or any other provisions of this Act, the court, [2] on the application of any member, [1] may by injunction or declaration restrain the company [3] from the following-

(a) entering into any transaction which is illegal or ultra vires;
(b) purporting to do by ordinary resolution [4] any act which by its constitution or the Act requires to be done by special resolution;[5]
(c) any act or omission affecting the applicant's individual rights as a member;

(d) committing fraud on either the company [3] or the minority shareholders[6] where the directors [7] fail to take appropriate action to redress the wrong done;

(e) where a company [3] meeting cannot be called in time to be of practical use in redressing a wrong done to the company or to minority shareholders [6]; and

(f) where the directors [7] are likely to derive a profit or benefit, or have profited or benefited from their negligence or from their breach of duty.

---

**Notes**
**Section 300**

1. "Members" includes the heir, executors, administrator or other personal representative, as the case may be, of the members" See **Section 567 CAMA, Cap. C20 LFN 2004 .**
   "Member" for the purpose of sections 300 & 301 (a) the personal representative of a deceased member; and (b) any person to whom shares have been transferred or transmitted by operation of law. See **section 302 CAMA Cap. C20, LFN 2004**
2. "Court" means the Federal High Court , and to the extent to which application may be made to it as: court includes the court of Appeal, and the Supreme Court of Nigeria. **See section 567 CAMA, Cap. C20 LFN 2004.**
3. "Company" means a corporation - or, less commonly, an association, partnership, or union that carries on a commercial or industrial enterprise. See **Garner B. (ed) Black's Law Dictionary 8th ed.**
   "Company" means a company formed and registered under this Act or, as the case may be, formed and registered in Nigeria before and in existence on the commencement of this Act. See **section 567 CAMA, Cap. C20 LFN 2004.**
4. "Ordinary resolution" is a resolution passed by a simple majority of votes cast by such members of the company as, being entitled to do so, vote in person or by proxy at a general meeting. See **section 233(1), CAMA Cap. C20 LFN 2004**
   "Ordinary resolution" means a decision reached by a simple majority (i.e. of more than 50%) of company members voting in person or by proxy. It is appropriate where no other type of resolution is expressly required by the Companies Acts or the articles of association. **See Martins E. (ed.) Oxford Dictionary of Law 4 th ed.**
5. "Special Resolution" means resolution passed by not less than three-fourths of the votes by such members of the company as being entitled to do so, vote by person or in proxy at a general meeting of which 21days notice, specifying the intention to propose the resolution is a special resolution, has been duly given. **See section 233(2) CAMA, Cap. C20 LFN 2004.**

6. "Shareholders" means one who owns or holds a share or shares in a company. See **Garner B. (ed) Black's Law Dictionary 8th ed.**

7. "Directors" see "director." A director is a person appointed or elected to sit on a board that manages the affairs of a corporation or other organisation by electing and exercising control over its officers. See **Garner B. (ed) Black's Law Dictionary 8th ed.**
"Director" includes any person occupying the position of director by whatever name called; and includes any person in accordance with whose directions or instructions the directors of the company are accustomed to act. **See Section 567 CAMA, Cap. C20 LFN 2004.**

**Cross Reference**

On members of a company,see **sections 79& 80 CAMA Cap. C20, LFN 2004**

On establishment and jurisdiction of the Federal High Court, see **section 249& 251 Constitution of the Federal Republic of Nigeria, 1999 (as amended)**

---

**Cases**

On meaning of fraud

"...any act which may amount to an infraction of fair dealing, or abuse of confidence, or unconscionable conduct, or abuse of power as between a trustee and his shareholders in the management of a company, is fraud. See ***Yalaju Amaye v. A.R.E.C ltd***

## 301. Personal and representative action

(1) Where a member [1] institutes a personal action to enforce a right due to him personally, he shall not be entitled to any damages but a declaration or injunction to restrain the company [2] and/or the directors[3] from doing a particular act.

(2) Where a member [1] institutes a representative action [4] on behalf of himself and other affected members [1] to enforce any rights due to them, he shall not be entitled to any damages but to a declaration or injunction to restrain the company [2] and/or directors [3] from doing a particular act.

(3) Where any member [1] institutes an action under this section, the court [5] may award costs to him personally whether or not his action succeeds.

(4) In any proceedings by a member [1] under section 300 of this Act, the court [5] may, if it thinks fit, order that the member [1] shall give security for costs.

---

**Notes**

**Section 301 (1)**

1. "Member" "includes the heir, executor, administrator or other personal representative, as the case may be, of the member. **Section 567 CAMA, Cap. C20,LFN 2004**
2. "Company" means a corporation - or, less commonly, an association, partnership, or union that carries on a commercial or industrial enterprise. **Garner B. (ed) Black's Law Dictionary 8th ed.**
   "Company" or "existing company" means a company formed and registered under this Act or, as the case may be, formed and registered in Nigeria before and in existence on the commencement of this Act . **Section 567 CAMA, Cap. C20, LFN 2004.**
3. "Director" means (1) one who manages, guides, or orders; a chief administrator (2) a person appointed or elected to sit on a board that manages the affairs of a corporation or other organisation by electing and exercising control over its officers. **Garner B. (ed) Black's Law Dictionary 8th ed.**
   "Director" includes any person occupying the position of director by whatever name called; and includes any person in accordance with whose directions or instructions the directors of the company are accustomed to act. **Section 567 CAMA, Cap. C20, LFN 2004.**
4. "Representative action" to act speak or speak officially for somebody and defend their interest, a person who brings on a legal action on behalf of a group. **Garner B. Blacks Law Dictionary, 8th ed.**
5. "Court" means the Federal High Court , and to the extent to which application may be made to it as: court includes the court of Appeal, and the Supreme Court of Nigeria. **See section 567 CAMA, CAP C20, LFN, 2004.**

Cross Reference

On establishment and jurisdiction of the Federal High Court, see **section 249& 251 Constitution of the Federal Republic of Nigeria, 1999** (as amended)

**Cases**

The effect of the provision of section 301 is to deprive the directors of the Company the power as duly authorized organ of the Company to authorize bringing an action in the name of the Company. The action is brought by the minority shareholder in the name of the company. See ***Agip(Nigeria ) Limited v. Agip Petroli International & Ors (2010) 5 NWLR part 1187***

## 302. Definition of member

For the purpose of sections 300 and 301 of this Act, "member" includes-

(a) the personal representative of a deceased member; and

(b) any person to whom shares have been transferred or transmitted by operation of law

### 303. Commencing derivative action

(1) Subject to the provisions of subsection (2) of this section, an applicant[1] may apply to the court [2] for leave to bring an action in the name or on behalf of a company, [3] or to intervene in an action to which the company[3] is a party, for the purpose of prosecuting, defending or discontinuing the action on behalf of the company [3].

(2) No action may be brought and no intervention may be made under subsection (1) of this section, unless the court [2] is satisfied that-

(a) the wrongdoers are the directors [4] who are in control, and will not take necessary action;

(b) the applicant has given reasonable notice to the directors [4] of the company[3] of his intention to apply to the court [2] under subsection (1) of this section if the directors [4] of the company do not bring, diligently prosecute or defend or discontinue the action;

(c) the applicant [1] is acting in good faith; and

(d) it appears to be in the best interest of the company [3] that the action be brought, prosecuted, defended or discontinued.

---

**Notes**

**Section 302(1)**

1. "Applicant"(a)a registered holder or beneficial owner and a former registered holder or beneficial owner, of a security of a company.(b)a director or a former officer of a company;(c)the commission or(d) any other person who in the discretion of the court is a proper person to make an application under section 303 of CAMA C 20 LFN 2004. **See section 309 CAMA, Cap. C20, LFN 2004**
2. "Court" means the Federal High Court , and to the extent to which application may be made to it as: court includes the court of Appeal, and the Supreme Court of Nigeria. **See section 567 CAMA, CAP C20, LFN, 2004.**
3. Company" means a corporation - or, less commonly, an association, partnership, or union that carries on a commercial or industrial enterprise. **Garner B. (ed) Black's Law Dictionary 8th ed.**
   "Company" or "existing company" means a company formed and registered under this Act or, as the case may be, formed and registered

in Nigeria before and in existence on the commencement of this Act . **See Section 567 CAMA, Cap. C20, LFN 2004.**

4. "Director" means (1) one who manages, guides, or orders; a chief administrator (2) a person appointed or elected to sit on a board that manages the affairs of a corporation or other organisation by electing and exercising control over its officers. **Garner B. (ed) Black's Law Dictionary 8th ed.**

   "Director" includes any person occupying the position of director by whatever name called; and includes any person in accordance with whose directions or instructions the directors of the company are accustomed to act **Section 567 CAMA, Cap. C20, LFN 2004.**

**Cross Reference**

On establishment and jurisdiction of the Federal High Court, see **section 249& 251 Constitution of the Federal Republic of Nigeria, 1999** (as amended)

**Cases**

It is consequently imperative that a minority shareholder whi intends to bring a derivative action in the name of the company must first and foremost apply for leave of court by way of originating summon on notice to the Company. See ***Agip(Nigeria ) Limited v. Agip Petroli International & Ors (2010) 5 NWLR part 1187 at 348***

## 304. Powers of the court

(1) In connection with an action brought or intervened under section 303 of this Act, the court [1] may, at any time, make any such order or orders as it thinks fit.

(2) Without prejudice to the generality of subsection (1) of this section, the court [1] may make one or more of the following orders, that is an order-

(a) authorizing the applicant [2] or any other person to control the conduct of the sanction;

(b) giving directions for the conduct of the action;

(c) directing that any amount adjudged payable by a defendant in the action shall be paid, in whole or in part, directly to former and present security holders of the company[3] instead of the company [3];

(d) requiring the company [3] to pay reasonable legal fees incurred by the applicant in connection with the proceedings.

**Notes**

**Section 304 (1)**

1. "Court" means the Federal High Court , and to the extent to which application may be made to it as: court includes the court of Appeal, and the Supreme Court of Nigeria. **See section 567 CAMA, CAP C20, LFN, 2004.**
2. "Applicant"(a)a registered holder or beneficial owner and a former registered holder or beneficial owner, of a security of a company.(b)a director or a former officer of a company;(c)the commission or(d) any other person who in the discretion of the court is a proper person to make an application under section 303 of this Act . **See Section 309 CAMA, Cap. C20, LFN 2004** .
3. "Company" means a corporation - or, less commonly, an association, partnership, or union that carries on a commercial or industrial enterprise. **Garner B. (ed) Black's Law Dictionary 8th ed.**
   "Company" or "existing company" means a company formed and registered under this Act or, as the case may be, formed and registered in Nigeria before and in existence on the commencement of this Act. **Section 567 CAMA, Cap. C20, LFN 2004** .

Cross Reference

On manner of commencing derivative action, see **section 303 CAMA Cap. C20, LFN 2004**

On establishment and jurisdiction of the Federal High Court, see **section 249& 251 Constitution of the Federal Republic of Nigeria, 1999 (as amended)**

## 305. Evidence of shareholders' approval not decisive

An application made or an action brought or intervened in under section 303 of this Act shall not be stayed or dismissed by reason only that it is shown that an alleged breach of a right or a duty owed to the company[1] has been or may be approved by the shareholders[2] of such company,[1] but evidence of approval by the shareholders[2] may be taken into account by the court [3] in making an order under section 304 of this Act.

**Notes**

**Section 305**

1. "Company "means a corporation - or, less commonly, an association, partnership, or union that carries on a commercial or industrial enterprise. **Garner B. (ed) Black's Law Dictionary 8th ed.**
   "Company" or "existing company" means a company formed and registered under this Act or, as the case may be, formed and registered in Nigeria before and in existence on the commencement of this Act . **Section 567 CAMA, Cap. C20, LFN 2004.**
2. " shareholders." It means one who owns or holds a share or shares in a company. **See Garner B. ed. Black's Law Dictionary 8th Ed**

3. "Court" means the Federal High Court, and to the extent to which application may be made to it as: court includes the court of Appeal, and the Supreme Court of Nigeria. **See section 567 CAMA, Cap. C20, LFN, 2004.**

Cross Reference

On manner of commencing derivative action, see **section 303 CAMA Cap. C20, LFN 2004**

On establishment and jurisdiction of the Federal High Court, see **section 249& 251 Constitution of the Federal Republic of Nigeria, 1999** (as amended)

---

## 306. Court's approval to discontinue

An application made or an action brought or intervened in under section 303 of this Act shall not be stayed, discontinued, settled or dismissed for want of prosecution without the approval of the court[1] given upon such terms as the court [1] thinks fit and, if the court[1] determines that the rights of any applicant [2] may be substantially affected by such stay, discontinuance, settlement or dismissal, the court [1] may order any party to the application or action to give notice to the applicant.

---

**Notes**

**Section 306**

1. "Court" means the Federal High Court , and to the extent to which application may be made to it as: court includes the court of Appeal, and the Supreme Court of Nigeria. **See section 567 CAMA, Cap. C20, LFN, 2004.**
2. "Applicant "(a) a registered holder or beneficial owner and a former registered holder or beneficial owner, of a security of a company.(b)a director or a former officer of a company;(c) the commission or(d) any other person who in the discretion of the court is a proper person to make an application under section 303 of this Act. **See Section 309 CAMA, Cap. C20, LFN 2004** .

Cross Reference

On manner of commencing derivative action, see **section 303 CAMA Cap. C20, LFN 2004**

On establishment and jurisdiction of the Federal High Court, see **section 249& 251 Constitution of the Federal Republic of Nigeria, 1999** (as amended)

---

## 307. No security for costs

An applicant[1] shall not be required to give security for costs in any application made or action brought or intervened in under section 303 of this Act.

---

**Notes**
**Section 307**

1. "Applicant" (a) a registered holder or beneficial owner and a former registered holder or beneficial owner, of a security of a company.(b)a director or a former officer of a company;(c) the commission or(d) any other person who in the discretion of the court is a proper person to make an application under section 303 of this Act.
   **See Section 309 CAMA, Cap. C20, LFN 2004** .

Cross Reference

On manner of commencing derivative action, see **section 303 CAMA Cap. C20, LFN 2004**

On establishment and jurisdiction of the Federal High Court, see **section 249& 251 Constitution of the Federal Republic of Nigeria, 1999 (as amended)**

---

## 308. Interim costs

In an application made or an action brought or intervened in under section 303 of this Act, the court [1] may at any time order the company[2] to pay to the applicant[3] interim costs before the final disposition of the application or action.

---

**Notes**
**Section 308**

1. "Court " means the Federal High Court , and to the extent to which application may be made to it as: court includes the court of Appeal, and the Supreme Court of Nigeria. **See section 567 CAMA, Cap. C20, LFN, 2004.**
2. " Company" "means a corporation - or, less commonly, an association, partnership, or union that carries on a commercial or industrial enterprise. **Garner B. (ed) Black's Law Dictionary 8th ed.**
   "Company" or "existing company" means a company formed and registered under this Act or, as the case may be, formed and registered in Nigeria before and in existence on the commencement of this Act. **Section 567 CAMA, Cap. C20, LFN 20004.**
3. "Applicant" means (a)a registered holder or beneficial owner and a former registered holder or beneficial owner, of a security of a company.(b)a director or a former officer of a company;(c)the commission or(d) any other person who in the discretion of the court is

a proper person to make an application under section 303 of this Act. **See Section 567 CAMA, Cap. C20, LFN 2004.**

## 309. Definition

In sections 303 to 308 of this Act, "applicant" means-

(a) a registered holder or a beneficial owner and a former registered holder or beneficial owner, of a security of a company;

(b) a director or an officer or a former director or officer of a company;

(c) the Commission; or

(d) any other person who in the discretion of the court, IS a proper person to make an application under section 303 of this Act.

Relief on the grounds of unfairly prejudicial and oppressive conduct

**Notes**

**Section 309**

1. "Security" means an instrument that evidences the holder's ownership rights in a firm. See **Garner B. (ed) Black's Law Dictionary 8 th ed.**
2. "Company" means a corporation - or, less commonly, an association, partnership, or union that carries on a commercial or industrial enterprise. See **Garner B. (ed) Black's Law Dictionary 8th ed.**
   "Company" means a company formed and registered under this Act or, as the case may be, formed and registered in Nigeria before and in existence on the commencement of this Act. See **section 567 CAMA, Cap. C20, LFN 2004.**
3. "Director" is a person appointed or elected to sit on a board that manages the affairs of a corporation or other organisation by electing and exercising control over its officers. See **Garner B. (ed) Black's Law Dictionary 8th ed.**
   "Director" includes any person occupying the position of director by whatever name called; and includes any person in accordance with whose directions or instructions the directors of the company are accustomed to act. **See Section 567 CAMA, Cap. C20, LFN 2004.**
4. "Officer" in relation to a body corporate includes a director, manager or secretary. See **section 567 CAMA Cap. C20, LFN 2004.**
5. "Commission" means the Corporate Affairs Commission established under section 1 of this Act. See **Section 567 CAMA, Cap. C20, LFN 2004.**

## 310. Application

(1) An application to the court [1] by petition for an order under section 311 of this Act in relation to a company [2] may be made by any of the following persons-

(a) a member [3] of the company; [2]

(b) a director [4] or officer [5] or former director [4] or officer of the company; [2]

(c) a creditor; [6]

(d) the Commission; [7] or

(e) any other person who, in the discretion of the court [1], is the proper person to make an application under section 311 of this Act.

(2) In sections 311 to 313 of this Act, "member" includes-

(a) the personal representative of a deceased member; and

(b) any person to whom shares have been transferred or transmitted by operation of law.

---

**Notes**
**Section 310**

1. "Court" means the Federal High Court , and to the extent to which application may be made to it as: court includes the court of Appeal, and the Supreme Court of Nigeria. **See section 567 CAMA, Cap. C20, LFN, 2004.**
2. "Company" means a corporation - or, less commonly, an association, partnership, or union that carries on a commercial or industrial enterprise. **Garner B. (ed) Black's Law Dictionary 8th ed.**
   "Company" or "existing company" means a company formed and registered under this Act or, as the case may be, formed and registered in Nigeria before and in existence on the commencement of this **Act. Section 567 CAMA, Cap. C20, LFN 2004.**
3. "Member" includes the heir, executors, administrator or other personal representative, as the case may be, of the members **Section 567 CAMA Cap. C 20 LFN 2004**
4. "Director" means (1) one who manages, guides, or orders; a chief administrator (2) a person appointed or elected to sit on a board that manages the affairs of a corporation or other organisation by electing and exercising control over its officers. **Garner B. (ed) Black's Law Dictionary 8th ed.**
   "Director" includes any person occupying the position of director by whatever name called; and includes any person in accordance with whose directions or instructions the directors of the company are accustomed to act. **Section 567 CAMA, Cap. C20, LFN 2004**
5. "Officer" " means in relation to a body corporate, includes a director, manager or secretary; **Section 567 CAMA, Cap. C20, LFN 2004** .

6. Creditor": - one to whom a debt is owed; one who gives credit for money and goods. **Garner B. (ed) Black's Law Dictionary 8th ed.**
7. "Commission" means the Corpora- one to whom a debt is owed; one who gives credit for money and goods. Garner B. (ed) Black's Law Dictionary 8th ed. te Affairs Commission established under section 1 of this Act; **Section 567 CAMA, Cap. C20, LFN 2004.**

**Cross Reference**

On transfer and transmission of shares, see **section 151-157 CAMA LFN 2004**.

On application for relief on the grounds of illegal or oppressive conduct of company affairs to be by petition, see **section 311 CAMA Cap. C20, LFN 2004**

On the establishment and jurisdiction of the Federal High Court, see **sections 249& 251 Constitution of the Federal Republic of Nigeria, 1999** (as amended)

---

## 311. Grounds upon which an application may be made

(1) An application for relief on the ground that the affairs of a company[1] are being conducted in an illegal or oppressive manner may be made to the court [2] by petition.

(2) An application to the court [2] by petition for an order under this section in relation to a company [1] maybe made-

(a) by a member [3] of the company [1] who alleges-

(i) that the affairs of the company [1] are being conducted in a manner that is oppressive or unfairly prejudicial to, or unfairly discriminatory against, a member [3] or members[3], or in a manner that is in disregard of the interests of a member or the members [3] as a whole; or

(ii) that an act or omission or a proposed act or omission, by or on behalf of the company [1] or a resolution[4], or a proposed resolution [4], of a class of members[3], was or would be oppressive or unfairly prejudicial to, or unfairly discriminatory against, a member[3] or members [3] or was or would be in a manner which is in disregard of the interest of a member[3] or the members [3] as a whole; or

(b) by any person mentioned in under para (b),(C) and (e) of subsection(1) of section 310 of this Act who alleges-

(i) that the affairs of the company [1] are being conducted In a manner oppressive or unfairly prejudicial to or discriminatory against or in a manner in disregard of the interest of that person ;

(ii) that ann act or omission, or proposed act or omission was or would be oppressive or unfairly prejudicial to, or unfairly discriminatory against or which is in manner disregard of the interest of that person; or

(c) by the commission[5] in a case where it appear to it in the exercise of its power s under the provision of this act or any other enactment that

(i) the affairs of the company[1] are being conducted in a manner that is oppressive or unfairly prejudicial to ,or in fairly discriminatory against a member or members[3] or in a manner which in is disregard or the public interest; or

(ii) any actual or proposed act of omission of the company[1] (including an act or omission on its behalf) which was or would be oppressive , or unfairly prejudicial to or unfairly discriminatory against a member[3] or members[3] in a manner which is in disregard of the public interest.

---

**Notes**
**Section 311(1)**

1. "Company" means a corporation - or, less commonly, an association, partnership, or union that carries on a commercial or industrial enterprise. **Garner B. (ed) Black's Law Dictionary 8th ed.**
   "Company" or "existing company" means a company formed and registered under this Act or, as the case may be, formed and registered in Nigeria before and in existence on the commencement of this Act. **Section 567 CAMA, Cap. C20, LFN 2004.**
2. "Court" means the Federal High Court , and to the extent to which application may be made to it as: court includes the court of Appeal, and the Supreme Court of Nigeria. **See section 567 CAMA, Cap. C20, LFN, 2004.**
3. "Member" includes the heir, executors, administrator or other personal representative, as the case may be, of the members. **section 567 CAMA Cap. C20 LFN 2004**
4. "resolution": formal statement of an opinion agreed on by committee or a council, especially by means of vote: to pass/ to adapt/ carry a resolution. **Oxford Advanced Learners Dictionary ,New 7 th Edition**
5. "Commission" means the Corporate Affairs Commission established under section 1 of this Act. See **Section 567 CAMA, Cap. C20, LFN 2004.**

Cross Reference

On application for relief on the grounds of illegal or oppressive conduct of company affairs to be by petition, see **section 311 CAMA Cap. C20, LFN 2004**

On the establishment and jurisdiction of the Federal High Court, see **sections 249& 251 Constitution of the Federal Republic of Nigeria, 1999(as amended)**

## 312. Powers of the court

(1) If the court [1] is satisfied that a petition under sections 310 and 311 of this Act is well founded, it may make such order or orders as it thinks fit for giving relief in respect of the matter complained of.

(2) Without prejudice to the generality of subsection (1) of this section, the court [1] may make one or more of the following orders that is, an order—

(a) that the company [2] be wound up; [3]

(b) for regulating the conduct of the affairs of the company [2] in future;

(c) for the purchase of the shares [4] of any member [5] by other members[5] of the company; [2]

(d) for the purchase of the shares [4] of any member [5] by the company[2] and for the reduction accordingly of the company's[2] capital; [6]

(e) directing the company [2] to institute, prosecute, defend or discontinue specific proceedings, or authorizing a member[5] or the company [2] to institute, prosecute, defend or discontinue specific proceedings in the name or on behalf of the company; [2]

(f) varying or setting aside a transaction or contract to which the company[2] is a party and compensating the company [2] or any other party to the transaction or contract;

(g) directing an investigation to be made by the Commission [7];

(h) appointing a receiver [8] or a receiver [8] and manager[9] of property of the company [2];

(i) restraining a person from engaging in specific conduct or from doing a specific act or thing;

(j) requiring a person to do a specific act or thing.

(3) Where an order that a company [2] be wound up[3] is made under this section, the provisions of this Act relating to winding up [3] of companies[2] shall apply, with such adaptations as are necessary,

as if the order had been made upon an application duly filed in the court[1] by the company[2].

(4) Where an order under this section makes any alteration or addition to the memorandum[10] or articles[11] of a company[2], then, notwithstanding anything in any other provision of this Act but subject to the provisions of the order, the company[2] shall not have power, without the leave of the court[1], to make any further alteration or addition to the memorandum[10] and articles[11] inconsistent with the provisions of the order but, subject to the foregoing provisions of this subsection, the alteration or addition shall have effect as if it had been duly made by a resolution[12] of the company[2].

(5) A certified true copy of an order made under this section altering or giving leave to alter a company[2]'s memorandum[10] or articles[11] shall, within 14 days from the making of the order or such longer period as the court[1] may allow, be delivered by the company[2] to the Commission[7] for registration; and if the company[2] makes default in complying with the provisions of this subsection, the company[2] and every officer[13] of it who is in default shall be guilty of an offence and liable to a fine of N50 and, for continued contravention, to a daily default fine of N25.

---

**Notes**
**Section 312**

1. "Court" means the Federal High Court , and to the extent to which application may be made to it as: court includes the court of Appeal, and the Supreme Court of Nigeria. **See section 567 CAMA, Cap. C20, LFN, 2004.**
2. "Company" means a corporation - or, less commonly, an association, partnership, or union that carries on a commercial or industrial enterprise. See **Garner B. (ed) Black's Law Dictionary 8th ed.**
   "Company" means a company formed and registered under this Act or, as the case may be, formed and registered in Nigeria before and in existence on the commencement of this Act. See **section 567 CAMA, Cap. C20, LFN 2004.**
3. "Wound up" see "winding up." It means the process of settling accounts and liquidating assets in anticipation of a partnership's or a corporation's dissolution. See **Garner B. (ed) Black's Law Dictionary 8th (ed).**
4. "Shares" see "share". It means the interest in a company share capital of a member who is entitled to share in the capital or income of such company. See **section 567 CAMA, Cap. C20, LFN, 2004**

5. "Member" includes the heir, executors, administrator or other personal representative, as the case may be of the members. See **section 567 CAMA, Cap. C20 LFN, 2004**
6. "Capital" means a fund representing the nominal value of shares issued by a registered company. See **Martins, E. (ed) Oxford Dictionary of Law 4th ed.**
7. "Commission" means the Corporate Affairs Commission established under section 1 of this Act. See **Section 567 CAMA, Cap. C20, LFN 2004.**
8. "Receiver" means a disinterested person appointed by a court, or by a corporation or other person, for the protection or collection of property that is the subject of diverse claims. See **Garner B. (ed) Black's Law Dictionary 8th ed.**

   "Receiver" includes a manager. See **section 567 CAMA, Cap. C20, LFN 2004**
9. "Manager" means one who is in charge of a corporation and in control of its business, or establishments, division, or departments, and who is vested with a certain amount of discretion and independent judgement. See **Garner B. (ed.) Black's Law Dictionary 8 th ed.**
10. "Memorandum see "memorandum of association" it means a legal document setting up a corporation- either with or without limited liability –and including the company's name, purpose, and duration . See **Garner B. (ed) Black's Law Dictionary 8th ed.**

    "Memorandum" means the memorandum of association of a company as originally framed or as altered in pursuance of any enactment. See **Section 567 CAMA, Cap. C20, LFN 2004.**
11. Articles" means the articles of association of a company, as originally framed or as altered by special resolution, including so far as they apply to the regulations contained in Table A in the First Schedules of the Companies Act, 1992 or in that Table as altered by any subsequent enactment or reprint of the Laws , or in Table A in Schedule 1 to this Act. See **Section 567 CAMA, Cap. C20, LFN 2004**
12. "Resolution**" is** a formal expression of the opinion or will of an official body or public assembly adopted by a vote. See **Garner B. (ed) Black's Law Dictionary 8th ed.**
13. **"**Officer" in relation to a body corporate, includes a director, manager or secretary; **Section 567 CAMA, Cap. C20, LFN 2004** .

Cross Reference

On the establishment and jurisdiction of the Federal High Court, see **sections 249& 251, Constitution of the Federal Republic of Nigeria, 1999( as amended)**

On types of resolution, see **section 233, CAMA CAP C20, LFN 2004**

---

**Cases**

It is settled Law that the duty of the Courts is simply to interpret the Law or Constitution as made by the Legislature or the framers of the constitution. It must therefore, be borne in mind always that the courts

cannot amend the constitution or statute neither can they change the words used in drafting same. ***Agro Allied Dev. Ent. Ltd. v. Reefer (* Supra).**
A receiver has duty to stop business, collect the debts and release the assets. But a manager has power to continue a business or a going concern: See ***Ponson Enterprise Nig. Ltd v. Njigha (2001) FWLR pt. 61 p. 3***

**For Further Reading**
on company, shares, winding up, see, Orojo, J. Ola **Company Law and Practice in Nigeria** 3[rd] Edition, Mbeyi & Associates (Lagos, Nigeria) 1992

## 313. Penalty for failure to comply with order of the court

Any person who contravenes or fails to comply with an order made under section 312 of this Act that is applicable to him, shall be guilty of an offence and be liable to a fine of N500 or imprisonment for a term of one year [1] or to both such fine and imprisonment.

---

**Notes**
**Section 313**
1. "Year" means a period of twelve months. See **section 18 Interpretation Act Cap. 132 LFN, 2004**

Cross Reference
On meaning of offence, see **section 2, Criminal Code Act, CAP C38, LFN, 2004**

---

*Investigation of companies and their affairs*

## 314. Investigation of a company on its own application or that of its members

(1) The Commission [1] may appoint one or more competent inspectors to investigate the affairs of a company [2] and to report on them in such manner as it may direct.

(2) The appointment may be made-

(a) in the case of a company [2] having a share capital [3], on the application of members [4] holding not less than one quarter of the class of shares [5] issued;

(b) in the case of a company [2] not having a share capital [3], on the application of not less than one quarter in number of the persons on the company's register of members; and

(c) in any other case, on application of the company [2].

(3) The application shall be supported by such evidence as the Commission[1] may require for the purpose of showing that the applicant or applicants have good reason for requiring the investigation.

---

**Notes**

**Section 314**

1. "Commission" means the Corporate Affairs Commission established under section 1 of this Act. See **section 567 CAMA, Cap. C20 LFN 2004**
2. "Company" means a corporation - or, less commonly, an association, partnership, or union that carries on a commercial or industrial enterprise. See **Garner B, (ed) Black's Law Dictionary 8th ed.**
   "Company" means a company formed and registered under this Act or, as the case may be, formed and registered in Nigeria before and in existence on the commencement of this Act. See **section 567 CAMA, Cap. C20, LFN 2004.**
3. "Share capital see "capital". "Capital" means a fund representing the nominal value of shares issued by a registered company. See **Martins, E. (ed) Oxford Dictionary of Law 4th ed.**
   "Members" see "member." It includes the heir, executor, administrator, or other personal representatives , as the case may be, of the member. See **section 567 CAMA, Cap. C20, LFN 2004.**
   **4.** "Shares" see "share". It means the interest in a company share capital of a member who is entitled to share in the capital or income of such company. See **section 567 CAMA Cap. C20 LFN, 2004.**

**Cross Reference**

On investigation of a Company by the Commission where the court declares that the Company's affairs ought to be investigated, see **section 315(1) CAMA Cap. C20, LFN 2004**

---

**Cases**

The Corporate Affairs Commission is conferred with the responsibility of registering companies operating in Nigeria by Statute, and under the said statute it can prohibit and restrict certain names to be registered. ***Mustapha v. CAC* (2009) Vol. 43 W.R.N. 1-171 pg 156.**

## 315. Other investigations of company

(1) The Commission [1] shall appoint one or more competent inspectors to investigate the affairs of a company [2] and report on them in such manner as it directs, if the court [3] by order declares that its affairs ought be so investigated.

(2) The Commission [1] may make such an appointment if it appears to it that there are circumstances suggesting that-

(a) the company's [2] affairs are being or have been conducted with intent to defraud its creditors [4] or the creditors of any other person, or in a manner which is unfairly prejudicial to some part of its members [5]; or

(b) any actual or proposed act or omission of the company [2] (including an act or omission on its behalf) is or would be so prejudicial, or that the company [2] was formed for any fraudulent or unlawful purpose; or

(c) persons concerned with the company's [2] formation or the management of its affairs have in connection therewith been guilty of fraud, misfeasance or other misconduct towards it or towards its members; [5] or

(d) the company's [2] members [5] have not been given all the information with respect to its affairs which they might reasonably expect.

(3) Subsections (1) and (2) of this section shall be without prejudice to the powers of the Commission [1] under section 322 of this Act, and the power conferred by subsection (2) of this section shall be exercisable with respect to a body corporate, notwithstanding that it is in a course of being voluntarily wound up.[6]

(4) Reference in subsection (2) of this section to a company's [2] members,[5] includes any of the following persons-

(a) the personal representatives [7] of a deceased member; and

(b) any person to whom shares have been transferred or transmitted by operation of law.

---

**Notes**

**Section 315 (1)**

1. "Commission" means the Corporate Affairs Commission established under section 1 of this Act. See **section 567 CAMA, Cap. C20 LFN 2004**

2. "Company" means a corporation - or, less commonly, an association, partnership, or union that carries on a commercial or industrial enterprise. See **Garner B. (ed) Black's Law Dictionary 8th ed.** "Company" means a company formed and registered under this Act or, as the case may be, formed and registered in Nigeria before and in existence on the commencement of this Act. See **section 567 CAMA, Cap. C20 LFN 2004.**
3. "Court" means the Federal High Court , and to the extent to which application may be made to it as: court includes the court of Appeal, and the Supreme Court of Nigeria. **See section 567 CAMA, Cap. C20, LFN, 2004.**
4. "Creditors" see "creditor". It means one to whom a debt is owed; one who gives credit for money and goods. See **Garner B. (ed) Black's Law Dictionary 8th ed.**
5. "Members" see "member". It includes the heir, executor, administrator, or other personal representatives, as the case may be, of the member. See **section 567 CAMA, Cap. C20, LFN, 2004.**
6. "Voluntary wound up" see "voluntary winding up." It means the dissolution of a company when the period, if any fixed for its duration by the articles expires or on the occurrence of an event of which its articles provide that the company is to be dissolved and the company in a general meeting pass a resolution requiring the company to be wound up. See **section 457 CAMA, Cap. C20, LFN 2004**
7. "Personal representative" where customary law is applicable, includes successors appointed in respect of deceased contributories. **See section 567 CAMA, Cap. C20 LFN 2004**

**Cross Reference**

On transfer and transmission of shares, see sections 151-157 CAMA, Cap. C20 LFN 2004.

On procedure for voluntary windingup see srctions 457-459, CAMA, Cap. C20 LFN 2004.

On criminal proceedingsby the Attorney General based on an investigation report by an inspector, see section 322 CAMA, Cap. C20 LFN 2004.

On the establishment and jurisdiction of the Federal High Court, see sections 249 &251 CAMA, Cap. C20, LFN 2004

---

**For Further Reading**

On shares, members, company, commission see, Kiser Barnes **Cases and Materials on Nigeria Company Law** (1992) Obafemi Awolowo University press Ltd, Ile-Ife, Nigeria

## 316. Inspectors powers during investigation

(1) If an inspector appointed under section 314 or 315 of this Act to investigate the affairs of a company [1] thinks it necessary for the purposes of his investigation to investigate also the affairs of

another body corporate [2] which is or at any relevant time has been the company's [1] subsidiary [3] or holding company, [4] or a subsidiary [3] of its holding company [4] or a holding company [4] of its subsidiary, [3] he shall report on the affairs of the other body corporate [2] so far as he thinks that the results of his investigation of its affairs are relevant to the investigation of the affairs of the company [1] first mentioned above.

(2) An inspector appointed under either section 314 or 315 of this Act may at any time in the course of his investigation, without the necessity of making an interim report, inform the Commission [5] of matters coming to his knowledge as a result of the investigation tending to show that an offence has been committed.

---

**Notes**
**Section 316 (1)**

1. "Company" means a corporation - or, less commonly, an association, partnership, or union that carries on a commercial or industrial enterprise. See **Garner B, (ed) Black's Law Dictionary 8th ed.**
   "Company" means a company formed and registered under this Act or, as the case may be, formed and registered in Nigeria before and in existence on the commencement of this Act. See **section 567 CAMA, Cap. C20 LFN 2004.**
2. "Body corporate" means an entity under law to act as a single person distinct from the shareholders who own it and have right to issue stock and exist indefinitely. See **Garner B, (ed) Black's Law Dictionary 8th ed.**
3. "Subsidiary" in relation to a body corporate, a subsidiary as defined by section 338 of this Act **. See Section 567 CAMA, Cap. C20 LFN 2004.**
4. "Holding Company" means a holding company as defined by section 338 of this Act **. See Section 567 CAMA, Cap. C20 LFN 2004.**

---

**For Further Reading**

On subsidiary and holding companies, see, Oserheimen A. Osunbor "The Agent-Only Subsidiary Company and The Control of Multinational Groups", **The International and Comparative Law Quaterly,** Vol. 38, No. 2 (Apr; 1989), pp 377 -387 published by Cambridge university press.
Akanki, J.O., **Essays on Company Law**, University of Lagos Press, 1992.

## 317. Production of documents and evidence to inspectors

(1) When an inspector is appointed under section 314 or 315 of this Act, it shall be the duty of all officers [1] and agents [2] of the

company[3], and of all officers [1] and agents[2] of any other body corporate[4] whose affairs are investigated under section 316 of this Act-

(a) to produce to the inspector all books [5] and documents[6] of or relating to the company [3] or, as the case may be, the other body corporate [4] which are in their custody or power;

(b) to attend before the inspector when required to do so; and

(c) otherwise to give the inspector all assistance in connection with the investigation which he is reasonably able to give.

(2) If the inspector considers that a person other than an officer[1] or agent of the company [3] or other body corporate [4] is or may be in possession of information concerning its affairs, he may require that person to produce to him any books [5] or documents [6] in his custody or power relating to the company [2] or other body corporate,[4] to attend before him and otherwise to give him all assistance in connection with the investigation which he is reasonably able to give; and it is that person's duty to comply with the requirement.

(3) An inspector may examine on oath [7] the officers[1] and agents[2] of the company[3] or other body corporate, [4] and any such person as is mentioned in subsection (2) of this section in relation to the affairs of the company [3] or other body, and administer an oath [7] accordingly.

(4) In this section, a reference to officers [1] or to agents includes past, as well as present, officers [1] or agents (as the case may be); and "agent" in relation to a company [3] or other body corporate,[4] includes its bankers and solicitors and persons employed by it as auditors, whether these persons are or are not officers [1] of the company[3] or other body corporate. [4]

(5) An answer given by a person to a question put to him in exercise of powers conferred by this section (whether as it has effect in relation to an investigation under any of sections 314 to 316 of this Act as applied by any other section in this Act) may be used in evidence against him.

---

**Notes**
**Section 317**

1. "Officer" in relation to a body corporate, includes a director, manager or secretary. See **section 567 CAMA, Cap. C20 LFN 2004** .

2. "Agent" does not include a legal practitioner acting as counsel for any person. See **section 567 CAMA, CAP C20 LFN 2004** .
3. "Company" means a corporation - or, less commonly, an association, partnership, or union that carries on a commercial or industrial enterprise. See **Garner B. (ed) Black's Law Dictionary 8th ed.**
   "Company" means a company formed and registered under this Act or, as the case may be, formed and registered in Nigeria before and in existence on the commencement of this Act. See **section 567 CAMA, Cap. C20 LFN 2004.**
4. "Body corporate" means an entity under law to act as a single person distinct from the shareholders who own it and have right to issue stock and exist indefinitely. See **Garner B. (ed) Black's Law Dictionary 8th ed.**
5. "Books" see "books and paper". It include accounts, deeds, writings, and documents. See **section 567 CAMA, Cap. C20 LFN 2004.**
6. "Documents" see "document." It includes summons, notice, order and other legal process, and register. See **section 567 CAMA, Cap. C20 LFN 2004.**
7. "Oath" means an affirmation or declaration made in accordance with the relevant law. See **18(1) Interpretation Act Cap. I 23 LFN 2004**

Cross Reference

On the appointment of auditors, see **section 357 CAMA Cap. C20, LFN 2004**

---

## 318.Power of inspector to call for directors' bank accounts

(1) If an inspector has reasonable grounds for believing that a director,[1] or past director,[1] of the company[2] or other body corporate[3] whose affairs he is investigating maintains or has maintained a bank account of any description (whether alone or jointly with another person and whether in Nigeria or elsewhere), into or out of which there has been paid-

(a) the emoluments or part of the emoluments of his office as such director,[1] particulars of which have not been disclosed in the financial statements[4] of the company[2] or other body corporate[3] for any financial year,[5] contrary to the provisions of Part V of the Fourth Schedule to this Act (in relation to particular in accounts of directors);

---

**Notes**
**Section 318**

1. "Director" means (1) one who manages, guides, or orders; a chief administrator (2) a person appointed or elected to sit on a board that

manages the affairs of a corporation or other organisation by electing and exercising control over its officers. **Garner B. (ed) Black's Law Dictionary 8th ed.**

"Director" includes any person occupying the position of director by whatever name called; and includes any person in accordance with whose directions or instructions the directors of the company are accustomed to act. See **section 567 CAMA, Cap. C20, LFN 2004.**

2. "Company" means a corporation - or, less commonly, an association, partnership, or union that carries on a commercial or industrial enterprise. **Garner B. (ed) Black's Law** Dictionary 8th ed.
3. "Company" or "existing company" means a company formed and registered under this Act or, as the case may be, formed and registered in Nigeria before and in existence on the commencement of this Act. See **section 567 CAMA, Cap. C20, LFN 2004.** Body corporate" see corporation. An entity (usu. A business) having authority under law to act as a single person distinct from the shareholders who own it and having rights to issue stock and exist indefinitely. See **Garner B. (ed) Black's Law Dictionary 8th ed.**
4. "Financial statements" see "financial statement". It means balance sheet, income statement or annual report that summarizes an individual or organization's financial condition on a specified date. **See Garner B. (ed) Black's Law Dictionary 8th ed.**
5. "Financial year" means the period of twelve months beginning from the first day of January in the year or such other date as the National Assembly may prescribe. See **section 318, Constitution of the Federal Republic of Nigeria, 1999(as amended)**

Cross Reference

On the regulation of banking business generally, see **Banks and other Financial Institutions Act (BOFIA) Cap. B3, LFN 2004**

---

**For Further Reading**

On directors, company, accounts, see, Iruchukwu, J.O. **The Company, The Sharehlder, The Director and the Law** , (Fourth Dimension Publishing Co. Ltd. 1994).

Anifalaja, J.O.,"Current Principles & Policies on Company Accounts," Essays on Company Law.

## 319.Obstruction of inspectors to be treated as contempt of court

(1) When an inspector is appointed under section 314 or 315 of this Act to investigate the affairs of a company, [1] the following applies in the case of-

(a) any officer[2] or agent[3] of the company; [1]

(b) any officer[2] or agent[3] of another body corporate [4] whose affairs are investigated under section 316 of this Act; and

(c) any such person as is mentioned in section 317 (2) of this Act.

(2) Subsection (4) of section 317 of this Act shall apply with regards to references in subsection (1) of this section to an officer [2] or agent. [3]

(3) If that person-

(a) refuses to produce any book [5] or document[6] which it is his duty under section 317 or 318 of this Act to produce; or

(b) refuses to attend before the inspector when required to do so; or

(c) refuses to answer any question put to him by the inspector with respect to the affairs of the company [1] or other body corporate[4] (as the case may be),

the inspector may certify the refusal in writing to the court.

(4) The court [7] may thereupon enquire into the case; and after hearing any witnesses who may be produced against or on behalf of the alleged offender and after hearing any statement which may be offered in defence, the court may punish the offender in like manner as if he had been guilty of contempt of the court.

---

**Notes**
**Section 319**

1. "Company" means a corporation - or, less commonly, an association, partnership, or union that carries on a commercial or industrial enterprise. See **Garner B. (ed) Black's Law Dictionary 8th ed.** "Company" or "existing company" means a company formed and registered under this Act or, as the case may be, formed and registered in Nigeria before and in existence on the commencement of this Act. See **Section 567 CAMA, Cap. C20, LFN 20004.**
2. "Officer" means in relation to a body corporate includes a director, manager or secretary; **Section 567 CAMA Cap. C20, LFN 2004.**
3. "Agent" does not include a legal practitioner acting as counsel for any person. **Garner. B. (ed) Black's Law Dictionary 8th ed.**
4. "Body corporate" see corporation. An entity (usu. A business) having authority under law to act as a single person distinct from the shareholders who own it and having rights to issue stock and exist indefinitely. See **Garner B. (ed) Black's Law Dictionary 8th ed.**
5. "Books" see "books and paper". It include accounts, deeds, writings, and documents. See **section 567 CAMA, CAP C20, LFN 2004.**
6. "Document" includes summons, notice, order and other legal process, and registers; **Section 567 CAMA, Cap. C20, LFN 2004**

"Court" means the Federal High Court, and to the extent to which application may be made to it as: court includes the court of Appeal, and the Supreme Court of Nigeria. **See section 567 CAMA, CAP C20, LFN, 2004.**

Cross Reference

On the establishment and jurisdiction of the Federal High Court, see **sections 249 & 251 CAMA Cap. C20, LFN 2004**

---

**Cases**

The rationale for contempt is to vindicate the dignity of the court as an institution and thereby, protect it from denigration and ensure the administration of justice. See ***FRN v. Joe Brown Akubueze SC 206/ 2004 delivered on 4/06/2010***

## 320. Inspector's report

(1) The inspector may, and if so directed by the Commission [1] shall, make interim reports to the Commission, [1] and on the conclusion of his investigation shall make a final report to it and any such report shall be written or printed, as the Commission [1] may direct.

(2) The Commission[1] may direct that a copy of the inspector's report be forwarded to the company [2]at its registered[3] or head office.

(3) Where an inspector is appointed under section 314 of this Act in pursuance of an order of the court [4], the Commission[1] shall furnish a copy of any of its reports to the court. [4]

(4) In any other case, the Commission [1]may, if it thinks fit-

(a) furnish a copy on request and on payment of the prescribed fee to-

(i) any member[5] of the company [2]or other body corporate[6] which is the subject of the report;

(ii) any person whose conduct is referred to in the report;

(iii) the auditors of that company [2] or body corporate; [6]

(iv) the applicants for the investigation;

(v) any other person whose financial interests appear to the Commission[1] to be affected by the matters dealt with in the report, whether as creditors [7] of the company[2] or body corporate, [6] or otherwise; and

(b) cause any such report to be printed and published.

---

**Notes**

**Section 320 (1)**

1. "Commission" means the Corporate Affairs Commission established under section 1 of this Act .See section 567 **CAMA, Cap. C20 LFN 2004**
2. " Company" means a corporation - or, less commonly, an association, partnership, or union that carries on a commercial or industrial enterprise. **Garner B. (ed) Black's Law Dictionary 8th ed.** " Company" or "existing company" means a company formed and registered under this Act or, as the case may be, formed and registered in Nigeria before and in existence on the commencement of this Act. **See section 567 CAMA, Cap. C20, LFN 20004.**
3. "Registered office" means the official address of a registered company; It must be notified to the Companies Registry before registration of the company and it must appear on company letter-head and order forms. Documents may be served to a company's registered office and various registers and records may be inspected there. See **Martins E. (ed.) Oxford Dictionary of Law 4 th ed.**
4. "Court" means the Federal High Court , and to the extent to which application may be made to it as: court includes the court of Appeal, and the Supreme Court of Nigeria. **See section 567 CAMA, Cap. C20, LFN, 2004.**
5. "Members" see "member". It includes the heir, executor, administrator, or other personal representatives , as the case may be, of the member. See **section 567 CAMA, Cap. C20, LFN, 2004.**
6. "Body corporate" see corporation. An entity (usu. A business) having authority under law to act as a single person distinct from the shareholders who own it and having rights to issue stock and exist indefinitely; a group or succession of persons established in accordance with legal rules into a legal or juristic person that has a legal personality distinct from the natural persons **Garner B. (ed) Black's Law Dictionary 8th ed.**
7. "Creditors" see "creditor." It means one to whom a debt is owed; one who gives credit for money and goods. See **Garner B. (ed) Black's Law Dictionary 8th ed.**

**Cross Reference**

On the registered offices of company and change therein, see **sections 35 & 547 CAMA Cap. C20 LFN 2004**

On the establishment and jurisdiction of the Federal High Court, see **sections 249 &251 CAMA Cap. C20, LFN 2004**

---

## 321.Power to bring civil proceedings on company's behalf

(1) If, from any report made under section 320 of this Act it appears to the Commission[1] that any civil proceedings ought in the public interest to be brought by the company[2] or any body

corporate,[3] the Commission[1] may itself bring such proceedings in the name and on behalf of the company [2] or the body corporate. [3]

(2) The Commission [1]shall indemnify the body corporate [3] against any costs or expenses incurred by it in or in connection with proceedings brought under this section; and any costs or expenses so incurred shall, if not otherwise recoverable, be defrayed out of the Consolidated Revenue Fund.

**Notes**

**Section 321 (1)**

1. "Commission" means the Corporate Affairs Commission established under section 1 of this Act. See section 567 **CAMA Cap. C 20 LFN 2004**
2. "Company" means a corporation - or, less commonly, an association, partnership, or union that carries on a commercial or industrial enterprise. See **Garner B. (ed) Black's Law Dictionary 8th ed.** "Company" or "existing company" means a company formed and registered under this Act or, as the case may be, formed and registered in Nigeria before and in existence on the commencement of this Act. **Section 567 CAMA, Cap. C20, LFN 2004.**
3. "Body corporate" means: An entity under law to act as a single person distinct from the shareholders who own it and have right to issue stock and exist indefinitely. See **Garner B. (ed) Black's Law Dictionary 8th ed.**

Cross Reference

On meaning of Consolidated Revenue Fund see **section 80 Constitution of the Federal Republic of Nigeria, 1999 ( as amended.)**

**Cases**

As a general principle, only natural persons, that is, human beings and juristic or artificial persons such as body corporate are competent to sue or be sued. Consequently, where either of the parties is not a legal person, the action is liable to be struck out as being incompetent. ***Ataguba & Company v. Gura Nigeria Ltd*** **S.C. 295/2000.**

## 322. Criminal proceedings and other proceedings by the Attorney-General of the Federation

(1) If, from any report made under section 320 of this Act, it appears that any person has, in relation to the company [1] or any body corporate[2] whose affairs have been investigated by virtue of section 316 of this Act, been guilty of any offence for which he is criminally liable, the report shall be referred to the Attorney-General of the Federation.

(2) If the Attorney-General of the Federation considers that the case referred to him is one in which a prosecution ought to be instituted, he shall direct action accordingly, and it shall be the duty of all officers [3]and agents[4] of the company [1]or other body corporate,[2] as the case may be (other than the defendant in the proceedings), to give all assistance in connection with the prosecution which they are reasonably able to give.

(3) If, from any report made under section 320 of this Act, it appears to the Commission[5] that proceedings ought in the public interest to be brought by anybody corporate [2] dealt with by the report for the recovery of damages in respect of any fraud, misfeasance or other misconduct in connection with the promotion or formation of that body corporate [2] or the management of its affairs, or for the recovery of any property of the body corporate [2] which has been misapplied or wrongfully retained, it may refer the case to the Attorney-General of the Federation for his opinion as to the bringing of proceedings for that purpose in the name of the body corporate and if proceedings are brought, it shall be the duty of all officers[3] and agents [4]of the company [1]or other body corporate [2] as the case may be (other than the defendants in proceedings), to give him all assistance in connection with the proceedings which they are reasonably able to give.

(4) Costs and expenses incurred by a body corporate [2] in or in connection with any proceedings brought by it under subsection (3) of this section shall, if not otherwise recoverable, be defrayed out of the Consolidated Revenue Fund

---

**Notes**
**Section 322 (3)**

1. "Company" means a corporation - or, less commonly, an association, partnership, or union that carries on a commercial or industrial enterprise. See **Garner B. (ed) Black's Law Dictionary 8th ed.** "Company" or "existing company" means a company formed and registered under this Act or, as the case may be, formed and registered in Nigeria before and in existence on the commencement of this Act. **See section 567 CAMA, Cap. C20, LFN 2004.**
2. "Body corporate" see corporation. An entity (usu. A business) having authority under law to act as a single person distinct from the shareholders who own it and having rights to issue stock and exist indefinitely; a group or succession of persons established in accordance with legal rules into a legal or juristic person that has a legal personality distinct from the natural persons . who make it up, exists

indefinitely apart from them, and has the legal powers that its constitution gives it. See **Garner B. (ed) Black's Law Dictionary 8th ed.**

3. "Officers" see "officer." In relation to a body corporate, includes a director, manager or secretary. **See section 567 CAMA, Cap. C20, LFN 2004.**
4. "Agents" "does not include a legal practitioner acting as counsel for any person. **See section 567 CAMA, Cap. C20, LFN 2004.**
5. "Commission" means the Corporate Affairs Commission established under section 1 of this Act. See **section 567 CAMA Cap. C 20 LFN 2004.**

Cross Reference

On meaning of Consolidated Revenue Fund see **section 80 Constitution of the Federal Republic of Nigeria, 1999 ( as amended.)**

On report by the inspector after investigation, see **section 320 CAMA Cap. C20, LFN 2004**

On the powers of the Attorney General of the Federation, **see section 174 Constitution of the Federal Republic of Nigeria, 1999(as amended)**

**For Further Reading**

On criminal proceedings on companies, see, Okoli, C. "Criminal Liability of Corporations in Nigeria: A Current Perspective" **(1994) 38 Journal of African Law 35.**

## 323. Power of the Commission to present winding-up petition

If, in the case of any body corporate [1] liable to be wound up [2] under this Act, it appears to the Commission [3] from a report made by an inspector under section 320 of this Act that it is expedient in the public interest that the body corporate [1] should be wound up, [2] the Commission[3] may (unless the body corporate is already wound up by the court) present a petition for it to be so wound up [2] if the court[4] thinks it just and equitable to do so.

**Notes**

**Section 323**

1. "Body Corporate" see corporation. An entity (usu. A business) having authority under law to act as a single person distinct from the shareholders who own it and having rights to issue stock and exist indefinitely; a group or succession of persons established in accordance with legal rules into a legal or juristic person that has a legal personality distinct from the natural persons . who make it up, exists indefinitely apart from them, and has the legal powers that its constitution gives it. See **Garner B. (ed) Black's Law Dictionary 8th ed.**

2. "Wound up" see "winding up". It is the process of settling accounts and liquidating assets in anticipation of a partnership's or a corporation's dissolution. See **Garner B. (ed) Black's Law Dictionary 8th ed.**
3. "Commission" means the Corporate Affairs Commission established under section 1 of this Act. See **section 567 CAMA, Cap. C 20 LFN 2004.**
4. "Court" when used in relation to a company, means the federal High court, and to the extent to which application maybe made to it as; court includes the court of appeal and the supreme court of Nigeria . **See Section 567 CAMA, Cap. C20, LFN 2004.**

Cross Reference

On modes of winding up companies, see **section 400, CAMA Cap. C20, LFN 2004**

On application for winding up to be by petition, **see section 410 CAMA Cap. C20 LFN 2004**

---

**Cases**

Care and utmost caution must be exercised by the court in its dealing with cases involving the termination of the life of a company. ***Air Via Ltd v. Oriental Airlines Ltd.* (2004) 9 N.W.L.R (PT.878) 298.**

## 324. Expenses of investigation

(1) The expenses of, an incidental to, an investigation by an inspector appointed by the Commission[1] under the foregoing provisions of this Act, shall be defrayed in the first instance out of the Consolidated Revenue Fund, but the following persons shall, to the extent mentioned, be liable to make repayment, that is to say-

(a) any person who is convicted on a prosecution instituted, as a result of the investigation by the Attorney-General of the Federation, or who is ordered to pay damages or restore any property in proceedings brought by virtue of subsection (3) of section 322 of this Act, may in the same proceedings be ordered to pay the said expenses to such extent as are specified in the order;

(b) any body corporate[2] in whose name proceedings are brought as aforesaid shall be liable to the extent of the amount or value of any sums or property recovered by it as a result of those proceedings;

(c) unless as the result of the investigation a prosecution is instituted by the Attorney-General of the Federation, the applicants for the investigation, where the inspector was appointed under section 314 of this Act, shall be liable to such extent (if any) as the Commission [1] may direct, and any amount for which a body corporate [2] is liable by virtue of paragraph (b) of this subsection, shall be a first charge on the sums or property mentioned in that paragraph.

(2) For the purposes of this section, any costs or expenses incurred by the Commission [1] in or in connection with proceedings brought by virtue of subsection (2) of section 321 of this Act, shall be treated as expenses of the investigation giving rise to the proceedings.

(3) Expenses to be defrayed by the Commission [1] under this section shall, so far as not recovered there under, be paid out of the appropriate Consolidated Revenue Fund.

---

**Notes**

**Section 324(1)**

1. "Commission" means the Corporate Affairs Commission established under section 1 of this **Act. See section 567 CAMA, Cap. C 20 LFN 2004**
2. "Body Corporate" see corporation. An entity (usu. A business) having authority under law to act as a single person distinct from the shareholders who own it and having rights to issue stock and exist indefinitely; a group or succession of persons established in accordance with legal rules into a legal or juristic person that has a legal personality distinct from the natural persons. who make it up, exists indefinitely apart from them, and has the legal powers that its constitution gives it. **See Garner B. (ed) Black's Law Dictionary 8th ed.**

**Cross Reference**

On meaning of Consolidated Revenue Fund see **section 80 Constitution of the Federal Republic of Nigeria, 1999 ( as amended.)**

On report by the inspector after investigation, see **section 320 CAMA Cap. C20, LFN 2004**

---

## 325.Inspectors' report to be used as evidence in legal proceedings

(1) A copy of any report of an inspector appointed under sections 314 and 315 of this Act, certified by the Commission [1]to be a true copy, shall be admissible in any legal proceedings [2] as evidence of the opinion of the inspector in relation to any matter contained in the report.

(2) A document[3] purporting to be such a certificate as is mentioned above shall be received in evidence and be deemed to be such a certificate, unless the contrary is proved.

---

**Notes**
**Section 325**

1. "Commission" means the Corporate Affairs Commission established under section 1 of this Act . **See Section 567 CAMA, Cap. C20, LFN 2004.**
2. "Legal proceeding" means any proceeding authorized by law and instituted in a court or tribunal to acquire a right or to enforce a remedy. See **Garner B. (ed.) Black's Law dictionary 8 th ed.**
3. "Document" "includes summons, notice, order and other legal process, and registers. See **Section 567 CAMA, Cap. C20, LFN 2004.**

**Cross Reference**

On documentary evidence in legal proceedings generally, see **section 83-120 Evidence Act 2011.**

On report by the inspector after investigation, see **section 320 CAMA Cap. C20, LFN 2004**

---

## 326. Appointment, etc., of inspectors to investigate ownership of a company

(1) Where it appears to the Commission[1] that there is good reason so to do, it may appoint one or more competent inspectors to investigate and report on the membership[2] of any company,[3] and otherwise with respect to the company,[3] for the purpose of determining the true persons who are or have been financially interested in the success or failure (real or apparent) of the company[3] or able to control or materially to influence the policy of the company.[3]

(2) The appointment of an inspector under this section may define the scope of his investigation, whether as respects the matter or the period to which it is to extend or otherwise and in particular may limit investigation to matters connected with particular shares[4] or debentures.[5]

(3) Where an application for an investigation under this section with respect to particular shares[4] or debentures[5] of a company[3] is made to the Commission[1] by members[2] of the company,[3] and the number of applicants or the amount of the shares[4] held by them is not less than that required for an application

for the appointment of an inspector under paragraphs (a) and (b) of subsection (2) of section 314 of this Act-

(a) the Commission[1] shall appoint an inspector to conduct that investigation, unless it is satisfied that the application is vexatious; and

(b) the inspector's appointment shall not exclude from the scope of his investigation any matter which the application seeks to include, except in so far as the Commission [1] is satisfied that it is reasonable for the matter to be investigated.

(4) Subject to the terms of an inspector's appointment, his powers shall extend to the investigation of any circumstances suggesting the existence of an arrangement or understanding which, though not legally binding, is or was observed or likely to be observed in practice and which is relevant to the purposes of his investigation.

---

**Notes**
**Section 326**

1. "Commission" means the Corporate Affairs Commission established under section 1 of this Act . **See Section 567 CAMA, Cap. C20, LFN 2004.**
2. "Company" means a corporation - or, less commonly, an association, partnership, or union that carries on a commercial or industrial enterprise. See **Garner B. (ed) Black's Law Dictionary 8th ed.** "Company" or "existing company" means a company formed and registered under this Act or, as the case may be, formed and registered in Nigeria before and in existence on the commencement of this Act. **Section 567 CAMA, Cap. C20, LFN 2004.**
3. "Shares" see "share." It means the interest in a company share capital of a member who is entitled to share in the capital or income of such company. **See section 567 CAMA, Cap C20 LFN, 2004.**
4. "Debentures" see "debenture." It means a written acknowledgement of indebtedness by the company, setting out the terms and conditions of the indebtedness, and includes debenture stock, bonds and any other securities of a company whether constituting a charge on the assets of the company or not. See **Section 567 CAMA, Cap. C20, LFN 2004.**
5. "Members" see "member." It includes the heir, executor, administrator, or other personal representatives, as the case may be, of the member. See **Garner B. (ed) Black's Law Dictionary 8th ed.**

**Cross Reference**

On report by the inspector after investigation, see **section 320 CAMA Cap. C20, LFN 2004**

**Cases**

The definition of a company in section 650 of Companies and Allied Matters Act puts the matter beyond doubt. It defines a 'company' or 'existing' to mean....a company formed and registered in Nigeria before and in existence on the commencement of this Act. ***Agro Allied Dev. Ent. Ltd. v. Reefer*** **(2009) vol.31 W.R.N 1-185 at pg 7** .

## 327. Provisions applicable to investigation

(1) For the purposes of any investigation under section 326 of this Act, the provisions of sections 316 to 320 of this Act shall apply with the necessary modifications to references to the affairs of the company[1] or those of any body corporate, [2] so however, that-

(a) the said sections shall apply in relation to all persons who are or have been, or whom the inspector has reasonable cause to believe to be or have been, financially interested in the success or failure or the apparent success or failure of the company [1]or any other body corporate [2] whose membership is investigated with that of the company; [1] or able to control or materially to influence the policy thereof, including persons concerned only on behalf of others, as they apply in relation to officers [3] and agents[4] of the company[1] or of the other body corporate, [2] as the case may be; and

(b) the Commission[5] shall not be bound to furnish the company[1] or any other person with a copy of any report by an inspector appointed under this section or with a complete copy thereof if he is of opinion that there is good reason for not divulging the contents of the reports or of part thereof, but shall keep a copy of any such report, or, as the case may be, the parts of any report, as regards which he is not of that opinion.

(2) The expenses of any investigation under section 326 of this Act shall be defrayed out of the Consolidated Revenue Fund

---

**Notes**
**Section 327**

1. "Company" " means a corporation - or, less commonly, an association, partnership, or union that carries on a commercial or industrial enterprise. See **Garner B. (ed) Black's Law Dictionary 8th ed.**

"Company" or "existing company" means a company formed and registered under this Act or, as the case may be, formed and registered in Nigeria before and in existence on the commencement of this Act. **Section 567 CAMA, Cap. C20, LFN 2004.**

2. "Body corporate" see corporation. An entity (usu. A business) having authority under law to act as a single person distinct from the shareholders who own it and having rights to issue stock and exist indefinitely; a group or succession of persons established in accordance with legal rules into a legal or juristic person that has a legal personality distinct from the natural persons . who make it up, exists indefinitely apart from them, and has the legal powers that its constitution gives it. **See Garner B. (ed) Black's Law Dictionary 8th ed.**
3. "Officers" see "officer." In relation to a body corporate includes a director, manager or secretary **. See Section 567 CAMA Cap. C20, LFN 2004.**
4. "Agents" see "agent." It does not include a legal practitioner acting as counsel for any person. **See Section 567 CAMA Cap. C20, LFN 2004.**
5. "Commission" means the Corporate Affairs Commission established under section 1 of this Act. **See Section 567 CAMA Cap. C20, LFN 2004.**

**Cross Reference**

On meaning of Consolidated Revenue Fund see **section 80 Constitution of the Federal Republic of Nigeria, 1999 ( as amended.)**

On powers of the inspector in an investigation, see **section 316 CAMA Cap. C20, LFN 2004**

On report by the inspector after investigation, see **section 320 CAMA Cap. C20, LFN 2004**

On obligation on officers and agents of a company under investigation to produce documents requested by the inspectior, see **section 317 CAMA Cap. C20, LFN 2004**

On obligation to produce director's bank account if requested by inspector, see **section 318 CAMA Cap. C20, LFN 2004**

---

## 328. Power to require information as to persons interested in shares, etc.

(1) Where it is made to appear to the Commission [1] that there is good reason to investigate the ownership of any shares [2] in or debentures[3] of a company[4] and that it is unnecessary to appoint an inspector for the purpose, the Commission [1] may require any person who it has reasonable cause to believe-

(a) to be or to have been interested in those shares [2]or debentures;[3] or

(b) to act or to have acted in relation to those shares [2]or debentures[3] as a legal practitioner [4]or an agent[5] of someone interested therein, to give to the Commission [1] any information which the person has or might reasonably be expected to obtain as to the present and past interest in those shares[2] or debentures[3] and the names and addresses of the persons interested, and of any persons who act or have acted on their behalf in relation to the shares [2] or debentures.[3]

(2) For the purposes of this section, a person shall be deemed to have an interest in a share [2]or debenture[3] if he has any right to acquire or dispose of the share [2] or debenture[3] or any interest therein or to vote in respect thereof, or if his consent is necessary for the exercise of any of the rights of other persons interested therein, or if other persons interested therein can be required or are accustomed to exercise their rights in accordance with his instructions.

(3) Any person who fails to give any information required of him under this section, or who, in giving any such information, makes any statement which he knows to be false in a material particular, or recklessly makes any statement which is false in a material particular shall be guilty of an offence and liable to a fine of N500 or to imprisonment for a term of six months or to both.

---

**Notes**
**Section 328**

1. "Commission" means the Corporate Affairs Commission established under section 1 of this Ac**t. See section 567 CAMA , Cap. C20 LFN, 2004.**
2. "Shares" see "share." It means the interests in a company's share capital of a member who is entitled to share in the capital or income of such company; and except where a distinction between stock and shares is expressed or implied, includes stock. See S **ection 567 CAMA, Cap. C20 LFN 2004.**
3. "Debenture" means a written acknowledgement of indebtedness by the company, setting out the terms and conditions of the indebtedness, and includes debenture stock, bonds and any other securities of a company whether constituting a charge on the assets of the company or not. See **Section 567 CAMA Cap. C20 LFN 2004.**
4. "Legal Practitioner" has the meaning assigned to it by the Legal Practitioners Act**. See section 567 CAMA, Cap. C20 LFN 2004**
5. "Company" means a corporation - or, less commonly, an association, partnership, or union that carries on a commercial or industrial enterprise**. See Garner B. (ed) Black's Law Dictionary 8th ed.**
"Company" means a company formed and registered under this Act or, as the case may be, formed and registered in Nigeria before and in

existence on the commencement of this Act. **Section 567 CAMA, Cap. C20 LFN 2004.**

Cross Reference

On transfer and transmission of shares, see **section 151 & 153 CAMA Cap. C20, LFN 2004**

On meaning of offence, see **section 2 Criminal Code Act, Cap. C38, LFN 2004**

On power of the Commission to impose restriction on shares during an investigation, see **section 329 CAMA Cap. C20, LFN 2004**

On the requirements for practice as a legal practitioner, see generally, **Legal Practitioners Act Cap. L11, LFN 2004**

---

**For Further Reading**

On company, shares, debenture, commission, see, Ola, C. S. **Company Law in Nigeria**, Heinemann Educational Books (Nig). 1999.

## 329. Power to impose restrictions on shares, etc.

(1) Where, in connection with an investigation under section 326 or 328 of this Act, it appears to the Commission [1] that there is difficulty in finding out the relevant facts about any share [2] (whether issued or to be issued), and that the difficulty is due wholly or mainly to the unwillingness of the persons concerned, or any of them, to assist the investigation as required by this Act, the Commission[1] may in writing direct that the shares [2]shall until further notice be subject to the restrictions imposed by this section.

(2) So long as any shares [2] are directed to be subject to the restrictions imposed by this section-

(a) any transfer of those shares, [2] or in case of unissued shares[2], any transfer of the right to be issued therewith and any issue thereof, shall be void;

(b) no voting rights shall be exercisable in respect of those shares; [2]

(c) no further shares [2] shall be issued in right of those shares [2] or in pursuance of any offer made to the holder thereof;

(d) except in a liquidation, no payment shall be made of any sums due from the company [3]on those shares, [2] whether in respect of capital [4] or otherwise.

(3) Where the Commission [1] directs shares to be subject to restrictions under this section, or refuses to direct that shares [2] shall cease to be subject thereto, any person aggrieved thereby may

appeal to the court[5], and the court may, if it sees fit, direct that the shares[2] shall cease to be subject to the said restrictions.

(4) Any direction or order of the court [5] that shares[2] shall cease to be subject to restrictions under this section, expressed to be made with a view to permitting a transfer of those shares, [2] may continue the restrictions mentioned in paragraphs (c) and (d) of subsection (2) of this section, either in whole or in part, so far as they relate to any right acquired or offer made before the transfer.

(5) Any person who-

(a) exercises or purports to exercise any right to dispose of any shares[2] which, to his knowledge, are for the time being subject to restrictions under this section; or

(b) votes in respect of any such shares, [2] whether as holder or proxy[6], or appoints a proxy [6] to vote in respect thereof; or

(c) being the holder of any such shares, [2] fails to notify that they are subject to the said restrictions, shall be guilty of an offence and liable to a fine of N500 or imprisonment for a term of six months, or to both.

(6) Where shares [2] in any company[3] are issued in contravention of the said restrictions, the company [5]and every officer[7] of the company[3] who is in default shall be guilty of an offence and liable to a fine of N500.

(7) A prosecution shall not be instituted under this section except by or with the consent of the Attorney-General of the Federation.

(8) This section shall apply in relation to debentures [8] as it applies in relation to shares. [2]

---

**Notes**

**Section 329**

1. "Commission" means the Corporate Affairs Commission established under section 1 of this Act ; **Section 567 CAMA, Cap. C20, LFN 2004.**
2. "Shares" see "share". It means the interests in a company's share capital of a member who is entitled to share in the capital or income of such company; and except where a distinction between stock and shares is expressed or implied, includes stock. See **Section 567 CAMA, Cap. C20, LFN 2004.**
3. "Company" " means a corporation –or, less commonly, an association, partnership, or union – that carries on a commercial or industrial enterprise. See **Garner B. (ed.) Black's Law Dictionary 8th ed.**

"Company" or "existing company" means a company formed and registered under the Act, or as the case may be, formed and registered in Nigeria before and in existence on the commencement of this Act . **See Section 567 CAMA, Cap. C20 LFN 2004**

4. "Capital" means a fund representing the nominal value of shares issued by a registered company. See **Martins E. (ed.) Oxford Dictionary of Law 4th ed.**
5. "Court" when used in relation to a company, means the federal High court, and to the extent to which application maybe made to it as; court includes the court of appeal and the supreme court of Nigeria . **See Section 567 CAMA, Cap. C20, LFN 2004.**
6. "Proxy" means one who is authorized to act as a substitute for another; a person who is authorized to vote another's stock shares . **See Garner B. ed. Black's Law Dictionary 8th ed.**
7. "Officer" "means in relation to a body corporate, includes a director, manager or secretary . **See section 567 CAMA, Cap. C20, LFN 2004.**
8. "Debentures" see "debenture". It means a written acknowledgement of indebtedness by the company, setting out the terms and conditions of the indebtedness and includes debenture stock, bonds and any other securities of any company whether constituting a charge on the assets of the company or not. "holder" is one who has legal possession of a negotiable instrument and is entitled to receive payment on it. **See section 567 CAMA, Cap. C20, LFN 2004.**

**Cross Reference**

On the establishment of the Office of the Attorney General of the Federation, see **section 150, Constitution of the Federal Republic of Nigeria, 1999 (as amended)**

On meaning of offence, see section **2, Criminal Code Cap. C38, LFN 2004**

---

**Cases**

It does not matter if the company's shares are owned substantially by one of the shareholders with only a very small fraction held by one or Few of others. ***Dunlop Nigerian Industries Ltd vs. Forward Nigerian Enterprises Ltd & Fafore*** **(1976) (1) A.L.R.**

## 330. Savings for legal practitioners and bankers

Nothing in the foregoing provisions of this Part of this Act shall require disclosure to the Commission [1] or to an inspector appointed by it by-

(a) a legal practitioner [2] of any privileged communication [3] made to him in that capacity, except as regards the name and address of his client; or

(b) a company's bankers as such, of any information as to the affairs of any of their customers other than the company. [4]

---

**Notes**

## Section 330

1. "Commission" means the Corporate Affairs Commission established under section 1 of this Act . **See Section 567 CAMA, Cap. C20, LFN 2004.**
2. "Legal Practitioner" has the meaning assigned to it by the Legal Practitioners Act. **See section 567 CAMA, Cap. C20 , LFN 2004**
3. "Privileged communication" means a communication that is protected by law from compelled disclosure in a legal proceeding or that cannot be used against the person who made it . **See Garner B. (ed.) Black's Law Dictionary, 8th ed.**
4. "Company" means a company formed and registered under the Act, or as the case may be, formed and registered in Nigeria before and in existence on the commencement of this Act. **See section 567 CAMA, Cap. C20 LFN 2004.**

**Cross Reference**

On the requirements for practice as a legal practitioner, see generally, **Legal Practitioners Act CAP L11, LFN 2004**

---

**Case Law**

A Legal Practitioner who is a gratuitous director of a company can appear as counsel for the company and is entitled to legal fees. ***I.B.W.A v. Imano* (1988) 3 N.W.L.R Pt.85, p. 633.**

*PART XI*

*Financial statements and audit*

*CHAPTER 1 - Financial statements*

*Accounting records*

### 331. Companies to keep accounting records

(1) Every company [1] shall cause accounting records to be kept in accordance with this section.

(2) The accounting records shall be sufficient to show and explain the transactions of the company and shall be such as to-

(a) disclose with reasonable accuracy, at any time, the financial position of the company; [1]and

(b) enable the directors [2] to ensure that any financial statements[3] prepared under this Part comply with the requirements of this Act as to the form and content of the company's financial statements. [3]

(3) The accounting records shall, in particular, contain-

(a) entries from day to day of all sums of money received and expended by the company, [1] and the matters in respect of which the receipt and expenditure took place; and

(b) a record of the assets and liabilities of the company. [1]

(4) If the business of the company [1]involves dealing in goods, the accounting records shall contain-

(a) statements of stocks[4] held by the company[1] at the end of each year of the company; [1]

(b) all statements of stock takings from which any such statement of stock[4] as is mentioned in paragraph (a) of this subsection has been or is to be prepared; and

(c) except in the case of goods sold by way of ordinary retail trade, statements of all goods sold and purchased, showing the goods and the buyers and sellers in sufficient detail to enable all these to be identified.

---

**Notes**
**Section 331**

1. "Company" means a corporation - or, less commonly, an association, partnership, or union that carries on a commercial or industrial enterprise. **See Garner B. (ed) Black's Law Dictionary 8th ed.**
   "Company" means a company formed and registered under this Act or, as the case may be, formed and registered in Nigeria before and in existence on the commencement of this Act. See Section **567 CAMA, Cap. C20, LFN 2004.**
2. "Directors" means (1) one who manages, guides, or orders; a chief administrator (2) a person appointed or elected to sit on a board that manages the affairs of a corporation or other organisation by electing and exercising control over its officers **. See Garner B. (ed) Black's Law Dictionary 8th ed.**
   "Director" includes any person occupying the position of director by whatever name called; and includes any person in accordance with whose directions or instructions the directors of the company are accustomed to act**. See Section 567 CAMA, Cap. C20, LFN 2004.**
3. "Financial statements" means balance sheet, income statement or annual report that summarizes an individual or organization's financial condition on a specified date. See **Garner B. (ed) Black's Law Dictionary 8th ed.**
4. "Stock" means the value of the shares in a company that has been sold. **See Oxford Advanced Learner's Dictionary 6[th] edition**

---

**For further Reading**

On company accounts, see, Anifalaja, J. O. "Current Principles & Policies on Company Accounts," **Essays on Company Law.**

---

## 332. Place and duration of records

(1) The accounting records of a company [1] shall be kept at its registered office[2] or such other place in Nigeria as the directors [3] think fit, and shall at all times be open to inspection by the officers [4]of the company. [1]

(2) Subject to any direction with respect to the disposal of records given under winding up [5] rules made under section 552 of this Act, accounting records which a company [1] is required by section 331 of this Act to keep shall be preserved by it for a period of six years from the date on which they were made.

---

**Notes**
**Section 332**

1. "Company" means a corporation - or, less commonly, an association, partnership, or union that carries on a commercial or industrial enterprise. See **Garner B. (ed) Black's Law Dictionary 8th ed.**
   "Company" means a company formed and registered under this Act or, as the case may be, formed and registered in Nigeria before and in existence on the commencement of this Act. **See Section 567 CAMA, Cap. C20, LFN 2004.**
2. "Registered office" means the official address of a registered company. It must be notified to the Companies Registry before registration of the company and it must appear on company letter-head and order forms. Documents may be served to a company's registered office and various registers and records may be inspected there.See **Martins E. (ed.) Oxford Dictionary of Law 4th ed.**
3. "Directors" see "director". It means (1) one who manages, guides, or orders; a chief administrator (2) a person appointed or elected to sit on a board that manages the affairs of a corporation or other organisation by electing and exercising control over its officers. **See Garner B, (ed) Black's Law Dictionary 8th ed.**
   "Director" includes any person occupying the position of director by whatever name called; and includes any person in accordance with whose directions or instructions the directors of the company are accustomed to act**. See Section 567 CAMA, Cap. C20, LFN 2004.**
4. "Officers" see "officer". In relation to a body corporate, officer includes a director, manager or secretary **. See Section 567 CAMA, Cap. C20, LFN 2004**
5. "Winding up" means the process of settling accounts and liquidating assets in anticipation of a partnership's or a corporation's dissolution. See **Garner B. (ed) Black's Law Dictionary 8th ed.**

**Cross Reference**

On penalty for non compliance of the requirement to keep accounting records, see **section 333 CAMA Cap. C20, LFN 2004**

---

**Cases**

The definition of a company in section 650 of Companies and Allied Matters Act puts the matter beyond doubt. It defines a 'company' or 'existing' to mean....a company formed and registered in Nigeria before and in existence on the commencement of this Act. ***Agro Allied Dev. Ent. Ltd. v. Reefer*** **(2009) vol.31 W.R.N 1-185 at pg 7** .

## 333. Penalties for non-compliance with sections 331 and 332

(1) If a company[1] fails to comply with any provision of section 331 or 332 (1) of this Act, every officer [2] of the company [1]who is in default shall be guilty of an offence unless he shows that he acted honestly and that in the circumstances in which the business of the company[1] was carried on, the default was excusable.

(2) An officer[2] of a company[1] shall be guilty of an offence if he fails to take all reasonable steps for securing compliance by the company[1] with section 332 of this Act, or has intentionally caused any default by the company [1] under it.

(3) A person guilty of an offence under this section, shall be liable to imprisonment for a term not exceeding six months or to a fine of N500.

---

**Notes**

**Section 333**

1. "Company" means a corporation - or, less commonly, an association, partnership, or union that carries on a commercial or industrial enterprise. **See Garner B. (ed) Black's Law Dictionary 8th ed.**
   "Company" means a company formed and registered under this Act or, as the case may be, formed and registered in Nigeria before and in existence on the commencement of this Act. **See Section 567 CAMA, Cap. C20, LFN 2004.**
2. "Officer" in relation to a body corporate, includes a director, manager or secretary. **See Section 567 CAMA, Cap. C20, LFN 2004**

**Cross Reference**

On meaning of offence, see **section 2, Criminal Code Cap. C38, LFN 2004**

On obligation of a company to maintain accounting records, see **section 331 CAMA Cap. C20 LFN 2004**

On duration of retention of accounting records by a company, see **section 332 CAMA Cap. C20 LFN 2004**

---

### 334. Directors' duty to prepare annual accounts

(1) In the case of every company, [1] the directors [2] shall in respect of each year of the company, [1] prepare financial statements [3] for the year[4].

(2) Subject to subsection (3) of this section, the financial statements[3] required under subsection (1) of this section shall include-

(a) statement of the accounting policies;

(b) the balance sheet as at the last day of the year; [4]

(c) a profit and loss account or, in the case of a company [1] not trading for profit, an income and expenditure account for the year;

(d) notes on the accounts; [5]

(e) the auditors' [6] reports;

(f) the directors' [2]report;

(g) a statement of the source and application of fund;

(h) a value-added statement for the year;

(i) a five-year financial summary; and

(j) in the case of a holding company, [7] the group financial statements.[8]

(3) The financial statements [3] of a private company [9] need not include the matters stated in paragraphs (a), (g), (h) and (i) of subsection (2) of this section.

(4) The directors [2] shall at their first meeting [10] after the incorporation of the company, [1] determine to what date in each year [4] financial statements[3] shall be made up, and they shall give notice of the date to the Commission [11] within 14 days of the determination.

(5) In the case of a holding company, [7] the directors [2] shall ensure that, except where in their opinion there are good reasons against it, the year [4] of each of its subsidiaries [12] shall coincide with the year[4] of the company. [1]

---

**Notes**
**Section 334**

1. "Company" means a corporation - or, less commonly, an association, partnership, or union that carries on a commercial or industrial enterprise. **See Garner B. (ed) Black's Law Dictionary 8 th ed.**
   "Company" means a company formed and registered under this Act or, as the case may be, formed and registered in Nigeria before and in existence on the commencement of this Act. See **Section 567 CAMA, Cap. C20, LFN 2004.**
2. "Directors" see "director." It means (1) one who manages, guides, or orders; a chief administrator (2) a person appointed or elected to sit on a board that manages the affairs of a corporation or other organisation by electing and exercising control over its officers. **See Garner B. (ed) Black's Law Dictionary 8th ed.**
   "Director" includes any person occupying the position of director by whatever name called; and includes any person in accordance with whose directions or instructions the directors of the company are accustomed to act. **Section 567 CAMA, Cap. C20, LFN 2004.**
3. "Financial statements" means: balance sheet, income statement or annual report that summarizes an individual or organization's financial condition on a specified date. **See Garner B. (ed) Black's Law Dictionary 8th ed.**
4. "Year" means a period of twelve months. See **section 18, Interpretation Act CAP 123 LFN, 2004.**
5. "Accounts" includes a company's group accounts, whether prepared in the form of accounts or not. **Section 567 CAMA, Cap. C20, LFN 2004.**
6. "Auditors" see "auditor". It means a person or firm, usually an accountant that formally examines an individual or an entity's financial records or status. **See Garner B. (ed) Black's Law Dictionary 8 th ed.**
7. "Holding Company" means a holding company as defined by section 338 of this Act. **See Section 567CAMA, Cap. C20, LFN 2004.**
8. "Group financial statements" means financial statements being accounts or statements which deal with the state of affairs and profit or loss of the company and the subsidiaries. **See section 336(1) CAMA, Cap. C20, LFN 2004.**
9. "Private company" means one which is stated in its memorandum to be a private company. **See section 22(1) CAMA, Cap. C20, LFN 2004.**
10. "Meeting" means the gathering of people to discuss or act on matters in which they have a common interest; esp. the convening of a deliberate assembly to transact business. See **Garner B. (ed) Black's Law Dictionary 8th ed.**
11. "Commission" means the Corporate Affairs Commission established under section 1 of this Act. See **Section 567,CAMA, Cap. C20, LFN 2004.**
12. "Subsidiaries" means, in relation to a body corporate, a subsidiary as defined by section 338 of this Act. See **Section 567 CAMA, Cap. C20, LFN 2004.**

**For Further Reading** Oon company accounts, Directors' duties, see, Anifalaje, J. O. "Current Principles & Policies on Company Accounts," **Essays on Company,** pg.205.
Bakibinga, D. J. "Directors' Duty to Act Bona Fide in the Interest of the Company" (1990) 39 (2) **The International and Comparative Law Quarterly 451.**

## 335.Form and content of individual financial statements

(1) The financial statements [1] of a company [2] prepared under section 334 of this Act, shall comply with the requirements of the Second Schedule to this Act (so far as applicable) with respect to their form and content, and with the accounting standards laid down in the Statements of Accounting Standards issued from time to time by the Nigerian Accounting Standards Board to be constituted by the Minister[3] after due consultation with such accounting bodies as he may deem fit in circumstances for this purposes:
Provided that such accounting standards do not conflict with the provisions of this Act or the Second Schedule to this Act.

(2) The balance sheet [4] shall give a true and fair view of the state of affairs of the company [2] as at the end of the year; [5] and the profit and loss account shall give a true and fair view of the profit or loss of the company [2] for the year. [5]

(3) The statement of the source and application of funds shall provide information on the generation and utilization of funds by the company[2] during the year. [5]

(4) The value added statement shall report the wealth created by the company[2] during the year [5] and its distribution among various interest groups such as the employees, the government [6], creditors [7], proprietors and the company. [2]

(5) The five-year financial summary shall provide a report for a comparison over a period of five years or more of vital financial information.

(6) Subsection (2) of this section shall override-

(a) the requirements of the Second Schedule to this Act; and

(b) all other requirements of this Act as to the matters to be included in the accounts [8] of a company [2] or in notes to those accounts;[8] and accordingly the provisions of subsections (7) and (8) of this section shall have effect.

(7) If the balance sheet[4] or profit and loss account drawn up in accordance with those requirements would not provide sufficient information to comply with subsection (2) of this section, any necessary additional information shall be provided in that balance sheet or profit and loss account, or in a note to the accounts.[8]

(8) If, owing to special circumstances in the case of any company,[2] compliance with any such requirement in relation to the balance sheet or profit and loss account would prevent compliance with subsection (2) of this section, (even if additional information were provided in accordance with subsection (4) of this section), the directors[9] shall depart from that requirement in preparing the balance sheet[4] or profit and loss account (so far as necessary) in order to comply with subsection (2) of this section.

(9) If the directors[9] depart from any such requirement, particulars of the departure, the reasons for it and its effects shall be given in a note to the accounts.[8]

(10) Subsections (1) to (9) of this section shall not apply to group accounts prepared under section 336 of this Act and subsections (1) and (2) of this section shall apply to a company's[2] profit and loss account (or require the notes otherwise required in relation to that account) if-

(a) the company[2] has subsidiaries;[10] and

(b) the profit and loss account is framed as a consolidated account dealing with all or any of the subsidiaries[10] of the company[2] as well as the company-[2]

- (i) complies with the requirements of this Act relating to consolidated profit and loss account; and
- (ii) shows how much of the consolidated profit and loss for the year[5] is dealt with in the individual financial statements[1] of the company.[2]

(11) If group financial statements[11] are prepared and advantage is taken of subsection (7) of this section, that fact shall be disclosed in a note to the group financial statements.[12]

---

**Notes**
**Section 335**

1. "Financial statements" means balance sheet, income statement or annual report that summarizes an individual or organization's financial condition on a specified date. **See Garner B. (ed) Black's Law Dictionary 8[th] ed.**

2. "Company" means a corporation - or, less commonly, an association, partnership, or union that carries on a commercial or industrial enterprise. **See Garner B. (ed) Black's Law Dictionary 8 th ed.**
"Company" means a company formed and registered under this Act or, as the case may be, formed and registered in Nigeria before and in existence on the commencement of this Act. See **Section 567 CAMA, Cap. C20, LFN 2004** .
3. "Minister" means the minister charged with responsibility for trade; and "ministry" shall be constituted accordingly. See **Section 567 CAMA, Cap. C20, LFN 2004.**
4. "Balance sheet" means A statement of an entity's current financial position, disclosing the value of the entity's asset, liabilities and owner's equity. See **Garner B. (ed) Black's Law Dictionary 8 th ed.**
5. "Year" means a period of twelve months. See **section 18, Interpretation Act CAP 123 LFN, 2004.**
6. "Government" includes government of the federation, or of any state, or local government council or any person who exercises power or authority on its behalf. See **section 318 Constitution of the Federal Republic of Nigeria, 1999 (as amended)**
7. "Creditors" see "creditor". It means one to whom a debt is owed; one who gives credit for money and goods. See **Garner B. (ed) Black's Law Dictionary 8th ed.**
8. "Accounts" includes a company's group accounts, whether prepared in the form of accounts or not. **See Section 567 CAMA, Cap. C20, LFN 2004.**
9. "Directors" see "director". It means (1) one who manages, guides, or orders; a chief administrator (2) a person appointed or elected to sit on a board that manages the affairs of a corporation or other organisation by electing and exercising control over its officers. **See Garner B. (ed) Black's Law Dictionary 8th ed.**
"Director" includes any person occupying the position of director by whatever name called; and includes any person in accordance with whose directions or instructions the directors of the company are accustomed to act. See **Section 567 CAMA, Cap. C20, LFN 2004.**
10. "Subsidiaries" means, in relation to a body corporate, a subsidiary as defined by section 338 of this Act. See **Section 567 CAMA, Cap. C20, LFN 2004.**
11. "Group financial statements" means financial statements being accounts or statements which deal with the state of affairs and profit or loss of the company and the subsidiaries. **See section 336(1) CAMA, Cap. C20, LFN 2004.**

**Cross Reference**

On power of Nigerian Accounting Standard Board to alter accounting requirements, see section **356 CAMA, LFN, Section 6, Nigerian Accounting Standard Board Act, 2003.**

On the appointment of Ministers, See **section 147 of the Constitution of the Federal Republic of Nigeria 1999 as amended.**

**336. Group financial statements of holding company**

(1) If, at the end of a year [1] a company[2] has subsidiaries,[3] the directors[4] shall, as well as preparing individual accounts [5] for that year,[1] also prepare group financial statements [6] being accounts[7] or statements which deal with the state of affairs and profit or loss of the company[2] and the subsidiaries.[3]

(2) The provisions of subsection (1) of this section shall not apply if the company[2] is a wholly owned subsidiary [3] of another body corporate incorporated in Nigeria.

(3) A group financial statement [6] may not deal with a subsidiary,[3] if the directors [4] of the company[2] are of the opinion that-

(a) it is impracticable, or would be of no real value to the members,[8] in view of the insignificant amounts involved; or

(b) it would involve expense or delay out of proportion to its value to members[8] of the company;[2] or

(c) the result would be misleading, or harmful to the business of the company[2] or any of its subsidiaries;[3] or

(d) the business of the holding company [9] and that of the subsidiary[3] are so different that they cannot reasonably be treated as a single undertaking.

(4) The group financial statements of a company [2] shall consist of a consolidated-

(a) balance sheet[10] dealing with the state of affairs of the company[2] and all the subsidiaries [3] of the company;[2] and

(b) profit and loss account of the company [2] and its subsidiaries.[3]

(5) If the directors [4] are of the opinion that it is better for the purpose of presenting the same or equivalent information about the state of affairs and profit or loss of the company [2] and its subsidiaries,[3] and that to so present it may be readily appreciated by the members[8] of the company,[2] the group financial statements [6] may be prepared in a form not consistent with subsection (1) of this section and in particular the group financial statement [6] may consist of-

(a) more than one set of consolidated financial statements [6] dealing respectively with the company [2] and one group of subsidiaries[3] and with other groups of subsidiaries; [3] or

(b) separate financial statements[6] dealing with each of the subsidiaries;[3] or

(c) statements expanding the information about the subsidiaries[3] in individual financial statements[6] of the company,[2] or in any other form.

(6) The group financial statements[6] may be wholly or partly incorporated in the individual balance sheet[10] and profit and loss account of the holding company.[9]

---

**Notes**
**Section 336**

1. "Year" means a period of twelve months. See **section 18, Interpretation Act CAP I 23 LFN 2004.**
2. "Company" means a corporation - or, less commonly, an association, partnership, or union that carries on a commercial or industrial enterprise. **See Garner B. (ed) Black's Law Dictionary 8[th] ed.**
"Company" means a company formed and registered under this Act or, as the case may be, formed and registered in Nigeria before and in existence on the commencement of this Act**. See Section 567 CAMA, Cap. C20, LFN 2004.**
3. "Subsidiaries" means, in relation to a body corporate, a subsidiary as defined by section 338 of this Act. **See Section 567 CAMA, Cap. C20, LFN 2004.**
4. "Directors" see "director." It means (1) one who manages, guides, or orders; a chief administrator (2) a person appointed or elected to sit on a board that manages the affairs of a corporation or other organisation by electing and exercising control over its officers. **See Garner B. (ed) Black's Law Dictionary 8[th] ed.**
"Director" includes any person occupying the position of director by whatever name called; and includes any person in accordance with whose directions or instructions the directors of the company are accustomed to act. See **Section 567 CAMA, Cap. C20, LFN 2004.**
5. "Accounts" includes a company's group accounts, whether prepared in the form of accounts or not. See **Section 567 CAMA, Cap. C20, LFN 2004.**
6. "Group Financial statement" means financial statements being accounts or statements which deal with the state of affairs and profit or loss of the company and the subsidiaries. **See section 336(1) CAMA, Cap. C20, LFN 2004**.
7. "Body corporate" see corporation. An entity (usu. A business) having authority under law to act as a single person distinct from the shareholders who own it and having rights to issue stock and exist indefinitely; a group or succession of persons established in accordance with legal rules into a legal or juristic person that has a legal personality distinct from the natural persons who make it up, exists indefinitely apart from them, and has the legal powers that its

constitution gives it. See **Garner B. (ed) Black's Law Dictionary 8 th ed.**

8. "Members" see "member". It includes the heir, executor, administrator or other personal representative, as the case may be, of the member. See **Section 567 CAMA, Cap. C20,LFN 2004.**
9. "Holding Company" means a holding company as defined by section 338 of this Act. See **Section 567 CAMA, Cap. C20, LFN 2004.**
10. "Balance sheet" means A statement of an entity's current financial position, disclosing the value of the entity's asset, liabilities and owner's equity. See **Garner B. (ed) Black's Law Dictionary 8th ed** .

**Cross Reference**

On contents of a financial statement, see **section 334 CAMA Cap. C20, LFN 2004.**

---

**For Further Reading**

**On accounting records of company, see, Deji Sasegbon, Nigerian Companies and Allied Matters Law & Practice, DSC Publications, Lagos (1st Ed., 1992)**

## 337. Form and content of group financial statements

(1) The group financial statements [1] of a holding company [2] shall comply with the requirements of the Second Schedule to this Act, so far as applicable to group financial statements [1] in the form in which those accounts [3] are prepared with respect to the form and content of those statements and any additional information to be provided by way of notes to those accounts. [3]

(2) Group financial statements [1] together with any notes thereon shall give a true and fair view of the state of affairs and profit or loss of the company [4] and the subsidiaries [5] dealt with by those statements as a whole.

(3) Subsection (2) of this section shall override-

(a) the requirements of the Second Schedule to this Act; and

(b) all the requirements of this Act as to the matters to be included in group financial statements [1] or in notes to those statements and accordingly subsections (4) and (5) of this section shall have effect.

(4) If group financial statements [1] are not in accordance with the requirements of this Act by not providing sufficient information in compliance with subsection (2) of this section, any necessary additional information shall be provided in, or in a note to, the group financial statements. [1]

(5) If, owing to special circumstances in the case of any company, [4] compliance with any such requirements in relation to its

group financial statements[1] would prevent the statements from complying with subsection (2) of this section, (even if additional information were provided in accordance with subsection (4) of this section, the directors[6] may depart from that requirement in preparing the group financial statements [1]).

---

**Notes**
**Section 337**

1. "Group financial statements" means financial statements being accounts or statements which deal with the state of affairs and profit or loss of the company and the subsidiaries. **See section 336(1) CAMA, Cap. C20, LFN 2004** .
2. "Holding company" means a holding company as defined by section 338 of this Act**. See Section 567 CAMA, Cap. C20, LFN 2004.**
3. "Accounts" includes a company's group accounts, whether prepared in the form of accounts or no**t. See Section 567 CAMA, Cap. C20, LFN 2004.**
4. "Company" means a corporation - or, less commonly, an association, partnership, or union that carries on a commercial or industrial enterprise. See **Garner B. (ed) Black's Law Dictionary 8 th ed.**
   "Company" means a company formed and registered under this Act or, as the case may be, formed and registered in Nigeria before and in existence on the commencement of this Act. See **Section 567 CAMA Cap. C20, LFN 2004** .
5. "Subsidiaries" means, in relation to a body corporate, a subsidiary as defined by section 338 of this Act . **Section 567 CAMA, Cap. C20, LFN 2004.**
6. "Directors" see "director". It means (1) one who manages, guides, or orders; a chief administrator (2) a person appointed or elected to sit on a board that manages the affairs of a corporation or other organisation by electing and exercising control over its officers. **See Garner B. (ed) Black's Law Dictionary 8 th ed.**
   "Director" includes any person occupying the position of director by whatever name called; and includes any person in accordance with whose directions or instructions the directors of the company are accustomed to act. **See Section 567 CAMA, Cap. C20, LFN 2004.**

---

## 338. Meaning of "holding company", "subsidiary" and "wholly-owned subsidiary"

(1) Subject to subsection (4) of this section, a company [1] shall for the purposes of this Act be deemed to be a subsidiary [2] of another company[1] if-

(a) the company-[1]

(i) is a member[3] of it and controls the composition of its board of directors; [4] or

(ii) holds more than half in nominal value of its equity share capital;[5] or

(b) the first-mentioned company is subsidiary[2] of any company[1] which is that other's subsidiary. [2]

(2) For the purposes of subsection (1) of this section, the composition of the board of directors[4] of a company[1] shall be deemed to be controlled by another company[1] if that other company[1] by the exercise of some power, without the consent or concurrence of any other person, can appoint or remove the holders of all or majority of the directors. [6]

(3) For purposes of subsection (2) of this section, the other company[1] shall be deemed to have power to appoint a director [4] with respect to which any of the following conditions is satisfied that-

(a) a person cannot be appointed to it without the exercise in his favour by the other company [1] of such power as is mentioned in this section; or

(b) the appointment of a person to the directorship follows necessarily from his appointment as director[6] of the other company;[1] or

(c) the directorship is held by the other company [1] itself or by a subsidiary[2] of it.

(4) In determining whether one company [1] is a subsidiary[2] of another-

(a) any shares[7] held or power exercisable by the other in a fiduciary capacity shall be treated as not held or exercisable by it;

(b) subject to paragraphs (c) and (d) of this subsection, any shares[6] held or power exercisable-

(i) by any person as nominee for the other (except where the other is concerned only in a fiduciary capacity); or

(ii) by, or by a nominee for, a subsidiary [2] or the other (not being a subsidiary[2] which is concerned only in a fiduciary capacity), shall be treated as held or exercisable by the other;

(c) any shares[7] held or power exercisable by any person by virtue of the provisions of any debentures [8] of the first-mentioned company[1] or of a trust deed [9] for securing any issue of such debentures[8] shall be disregarded;

(d) any shares[7] held or power exercisable by, or by a nominee for, the other or its subsidiary [2] (not being held or exercisable as mentioned in paragraph (c) of this subsection), shall be treated as not held or exercisable by the other, if the ordinary business of the other or its subsidiary [2] (as the case may be) includes the lending of money and the shares[7] are held or the power is exercisable as above mentioned by way of security only for the purposes of a transaction entered into in the ordinary course of that business.

(5) For the purposes of this Act-

(a) a company[1] shall be deemed to be the holding company [10] of another, if the other is its subsidiary; [2] and

(b) a body corporate [11] shall be deemed to be the wholly-owned subsidiary[2] of another, if it has no member [3] except that other and that other's wholly owned subsidiaries [2] are its or their nominees.

(6) In this section, "company" [1] includes anybody corporate.

---

**Notes**
**Section 338**

1. '"Company" means a corporation - or, less commonly, an association, partnership, or union that carries on a commercial or industrial enterprise. **See Garner B. (ed) Black's Law Dictionary 8 th ed.** "Company" means a company formed and registered under this Act or, as the case may be, formed and registered in Nigeria before and in existence on the commencement of this Act. See **Section 567 CAMA, Cap. C20, LFN 20004.**
2. "Subsidiary" see "subsidiaries." In relation to a body corporate, a subsidiary as defined by section 338 of this Act. **See Section 567 CAMA, Cap. C20, LFN 2004.**
3. "Member" includes the heir, executor, administrator or other personal representative, as the case may be, of the member. See **Section 567 CAMA, Cap. C20, LFN 2004.**
4. "Board of directors" means the governing body of a corporation, elected by the shareholders to establish corporate policy, appoint executive officers, and make major business and financial decisions. See **Garner B. (ed.) Black's Law Dictionary 8 th ed.**
5. "Equity share capital" means a share capital other than a preference share capital. See **Section 567 CAMA, Cap. C20, LFN 2004.**
6. "Director" means (1) one who manages, guides, or orders; a chief administrator (2) a person appointed or elected to sit on a board that manages the affairs of a corporation or other organisation by electing

and exercising control over its officers. **See Garner B. (ed) Black's Law Dictionary 8th ed.**

"Director" includes any person occupying the position of director by whatever name called; and includes any person in accordance with whose directions or instructions the directors of the company are accustomed to act. See **Section 567 CAMA, Cap. C20, LFN 2004.**

7. "Shares" see "share." It means the interests in a company's share capital of a member who is entitled to share in the capital or income of such company; and except where a distinction between stock and shares is expressed or implied, includes stock; **Section 567 CAMA, Cap. C20, LFN 2004.**
8. "Debentures" means a written acknowledgement of indebtedness by the company, setting out the terms and conditions of the indebtedness, and includes debenture stock, bonds and any other securities of a company whether constituting a charge on the assets of the company or not. See **Section 567 CAMA, Cap. C20, LFN 2004.**
9. "Trust Deed" means the instrument that creates a trust. See **Garner B. (ed) Black's Law Dictionary 8th ed.**
10. "Holding Company" means a holding company as defined by section 338 of this Act. See **Section 567 CAMA Cap. C20, LFN 2004** .
11. "Body Corporate" see corporation. An entity (usu. A business) having authority under law to act as a single person distinct from the shareholders who own it and having rights to issue stock and exist indefinitely; a group or succession of persons established in accordance with legal rules into a legal or juristic person that has a legal personality distinct from the natural person. See **Garner B. (ed) Black's Law Dictionary 8th ed.**

---

**Cases**

It is clearly a necessary incident of company law that the concurrence of a holding company is *sine qua non* to the acquisition of shares in its subsidiary. ***Seaways Ltd v. Nig. Dredging R & G Ltd* (1977) 5 SC at 35.** a

**For Further Reading** On holding companies and their subsidiaries, see, Oserheimen A. Osunbor "The Agent-Only Subsidiary Company and The Control of Multinational Groups", **The International and Comparative law Quarterly,** Vol. 38, No. 2 (Apr; 1989), pp 377 -387 published by Cambridge university press.

---

## 339.Additional disclosure required in notes to financial statements

(1) The additional matters contained in the Third Schedule to this Act shall be disclosed in the company's [1] financial statements[2] for the year; [3] and in that Schedule, where a thing is required to be stated or shown or information is required to be given, it shall be

construed to mean that the thing shall be stated or shown, or the information is to be given in a note to those statements.

(2) In the Third Schedule to this Act-

(a) Parts I and II deal respectively with the disclosure of particulars of the subsidiaries[4] of the company[1] and its shareholders;[5]

(b) Part III deals with the disclosure of financial information relating to subsidiaries;[4]

(c) Part IV requires a subsidiary[4] company to disclose its ultimate holding company;[6]

(d) Part V deals with the emoluments of directors,[7] including emoluments waived, pensions of directors[7] and compensation for loss of office to directors[7] and past directors;[7] and

(e) Part VI deals with disclosure of the number of the employees of the company[1] who are remunerated at higher rates.

(3) Whenever it is stated in the Third Schedule to this Act that this subsection shall apply to certain particulars or information, the particulars or information shall be annexed to the annual return[8] first made by the company[1] after copies of its financial statements[2] have been laid before its shareholders[5] in a general meeting[9] and if a company[1] fails to satisfy an obligation thus imposed, the company[1] and every officer[10] of it who is in default shall be guilty of an offence and liable to a fine of N50 and for continued contravention, to a daily default fine of N10.

(4) It shall be the duty of any director[7] of a company[1] to give notice to the company[1] of such matters relating to himself as may be necessary for the purposes of Part V of the Third Schedule to this Act and this applies to persons who are or have at any time in the preceding three years been officers as it applies to directors.[7]

(5) A person who makes default in complying with the provisions of subsection (4) of this section, shall be guilty of an offence and liable to a fine of N10 for every day during which the default continues.

---

**Notes**
**Section 339**

1. "Company" means a corporation - or, less commonly, an association, partnership, or union that carries on a commercial or industrial enterprise. **See Garner B. (ed) Black's Law Dictionary 8 th ed.** "Company" means a company formed and registered under this Act or, as the case may be, formed and registered in Nigeria before and in existence on the commencement of this Act. See **Section 567 CAMA, Cap. C20, LFN 2004.**
2. "Financial statements" means balance sheet, income statement or annual report that summarizes an individual or organization's financial condition on a specified date. **See Garner B. (ed) Black's Law Dictionary 8th ed.**
3. "Year" means a period of twelve months. See **section 18 Interpretation Act CAP 123 LFN, 2004.**
4. "Subsidiaries" means, in relation to a body corporate, a subsidiary as defined by section 338 of this Act. **See Section 567 CAMA, Cap. C20, LFN 2004.**
5. "Share holders'' means one who owns or holds a share or shares in a company. **See Garner B. (ed) Black's Law Dictionary 8 th ed.**
6. "Holding Company" means a holding company as defined by section 338 of this Act. See **Section 567 CAMA, Cap. C20, LFN 2004.**
7. "Directors" see "director". A director is (1) one who manages, guides, or orders; a chief administrator (2) a person appointed or elected to sit on a board that manages the affairs of a corporation or other organisation by electing and exercising control over its officers. **See Garner B. (ed) Black's Law Dictionary 8 th ed.** "Director" includes any person occupying the position of director by whatever name called; and includes any person in accordance with whose directions or instructions the directors of the company are accustomed to act. **Section 567 CAMA, Cap. C20, LFN 2004.**
8. "Annual Return" means the return required to be made, in the case of a company limited by shares under sections 371 and 372 and, in the case of a company limited by guarantee, under section 373 of this Act. See **Section 567 CAMA, Cap. C20, LFN 2004.**
9. "General Meeting" see "Annual meeting" – a yearly meeting to elect or install officers or directors and to conduct other routine organisational business. See **Garner B. (ed) Black's Law Dictionary 8th ed.**

**Cross Reference**

On remuneration and other payments of directors see **section 267-274, CAMA Cap. C20 LFN 2004**

On meaning of offence, see **section 2 Criminal Code Cap. C38, LFN 2004**

---

## 340. Disclosure of loans in favor of directors and connected persons

(1) The group financial statements [1] of a holding company [2] for a year [3] shall comply with Part I of the Fourth Schedule to this Act

(so far as applicable) as regards the disclosure of transactions, arrangements and agreements mentioned therein, including loans, quasi loans and other dealings in favour of directors. [4]

(2) In the case of a company [5] other than a holding company, [2] its individual accounts shall comply with Part I of the Fourth Schedule to this Act (so far as applicable) as regards disclosure matters contained therein.

(3) Particulars which are required to be contained in Part I of the Fourth Schedule to this Act in any financial statements [6] shall be required in respect of shadow directors [7] as well as a director [4] given by way of notes.

(4) Where by virtue of subsection (2) or (3) of section 336 of this Act, a company [5] does not prepare group financial statements [1] for a year, [3] it shall disclose such matters in its individual statements as would have been disclosed in group financial statements. [1]

(5) The requirements of this section shall apply with such modifications as are necessary to bring them in line with Part I of the Fourth Schedule to this Act (including with particulars of exceptions in respect of recognised banks) it shall disclose.

---

**Notes**
**Section 340**

1. "Group financial statements" means financial statements being accounts or statements which deal with the state of affairs and profit or loss of the company and the subsidiaries. **See section 336(1) CAMA, Cap. C20, LFN 2004** .
2. "Holding Company" means a holding company as defined by section 338 of this Act. See **Section 567 CAMA, Cap. C20, LFN 2004.**
3. "Year" means a period of twelve months. See **section 18, Interpretation Act Cap. 123 LFN, 2004.**
4. "Directors" see "director". A director is (1) one who manages, guides, or orders; a chief administrator (2) a person appointed or elected to sit on a board that manages the affairs of a corporation or other organisation by electing and exercising control over its officers. See **Garner B. (ed) Black's Law Dictionary 8 th ed.**
   "Director" includes any person occupying the position of director by whatever name called; and includes any person in accordance with whose directions or instructions the directors of the company are accustomed to act. See **Section 567 CAMA, Cap. C20, LFN 2004.**
5. "Company" means a corporation - or, less commonly, an association, partnership, or union that carries on a commercial or industrial enterprise. See **Garner B. (ed) Black's Law Dictionary 8th ed.**

"Company" means a company formed and registered under this Act or, as the case may be, formed and registered in Nigeria before and in existence on the commencement of this Act. See **Section 567 CAMA, Cap. C20, LFN 2004.**

6. "Shadow directors" are persons on whose instructions and directions the director of a company is accustomed to act. See **Section 245 CAMA, Cap. C20, LFN 2004.**

**Cross Reference**

On remuneration and other payments of directors see **section 267-274, CAMA Cap. C20 LFN 2004**

---

**Cases**

Directors have sometimes been called trustees, or commercial trustees, and sometimes they have been called managing partners. It does not matter what you call them so long as you understand what their true position is, which is that they are really commercial when managing a trading concern for the benefit of themselves and all other shareholders in it. ***Iwuchukwu vs. Nwizu*** **(1994) 7 N.W.L.R (pt357) 379 at 396.**

## 341. Disclosure of loans, etc., to officers of the company and statements of amounts outstanding

(1) The group financial statements [1] of a holding company [2] for a year [3] shall comply with Part II of the Fourth Schedule to this Act (so far as applicable) as regards transactions, arrangements and agreements made by the company [4] or a subsidiary [5] of it for persons who at any time during that year were officers [6] of the company but not directors. [7]

(2) In the case of a company other than a holding company, [2] its individual accounts shall comply with Part II of the Fourth Schedule to this Act (so far as applicable) as regards matters contained therein.

(3) Subsections (1) and (2) of this section shall not apply in relation to any transaction or agreement made by a recognised bank for any of its officers [6] or for any of the officers [6] of its holding company. [2]

(4) Particulars required by Part II of the Fourth Schedule to this Act to be in any accounts shall be given by way of notes to the accounts.

(5) Where by virtue of subsection (2) or (3) of section 336 of this Act, a company [4] does not prepare group financial statements [1]

for a year, [3] it shall disclose this fact in its individual financial statements[8] as required by subsection (1) of this section.

---

**Notes**
**Section 341**

1. "Group financial statements" means financial statements being accounts or statements which deal with the state of affairs and profit or loss of the company and the subsidiaries. **See section 336(1) CAMA, Cap. C20, LFN 2004** .
2. "Holding company" means a holding company as defined by section 338 of this Act. See **Section 567 CAMA, Cap. C20, LFN 2004.**
3. "Year" means a period of twelve months. **See section 18, Interpretation Act Cap. 123 LFN, 2004.**
4. "Company" " means a corporation - or, less commonly, an association, partnership, or union that carries on a commercial or industrial enterprise. **See Garner B. (ed) Black's Law Dictionary 8th ed.**
   "Company" means a company formed and registered under this Act or, as the case may be, formed and registered in Nigeria before and in existence on the commencement of this Act. See **Section 567 CAMA, Cap. C20, LFN 2004.**
5. "Subsidiary" see "subsidiaries." " Subsidiaries" means, in relation to a body corporate, a subsidiary as defined by section 338 of this Act. See **Section 567 CAMA, Cap. C20, LFN 2004.**
6. "Officers" see "officer". In relation to a body corporate, officer includes a director, manager or secretary. See **Section 567 CAMA Cap. C20, LFN 2004.**
7. "Directors" see "director". A director is (1) one who manages, guides, or orders; a chief administrator (2) a person appointed or elected to sit on a board that manages the affairs of a corporation or other organisation by electing and exercising control over its officers. See **Garner B. (ed) Black's Law Dictionary 8 th ed.**
   "Director" includes any person occupying the position of director by whatever name called; and includes any person in accordance with whose directions or instructions the directors of the company are accustomed to act. See **Section 567 CAMA, Cap. C20, LFN 2004.**
9. "Financial statement" means balance sheet, income statement or annual report that summarizes an individual or organization's financial condition on a specified date. **Garner B. (ed) Black's Law Dictionary 8th ed.**

**Cross Reference**

On prohibition of loans to directors in certain circumstances, see **section 270 CAMA Cap. C20, LFN 2004**

---

*Directors' reports*

**342. Directors' report**

(1) In the case of every company, [1] there shall be prepared in respect of each year, [2] a report by the directors- [3]

(a) containing a fair view of the development of the business of the company[1] and its subsidiaries[4] during the year[2] and of their position at the end of it; and

(b) stating the amount (if any) which they recommend should be paid as dividend[5] and the amount (if any) which they propose to carry to reserves.

(2) The directors' [3] report shall state the names of the persons who, at any time during the year, were directors [3] of the company,[1] and the financial activities of the company[1] and its subsidiaries[4] in the course of the year [2] and any significant change in those activities in the year. [2]

(3) The report shall also state the matters, and give the particulars, required by Part I of the Fifth Schedule to this Act.

(4) Part II of the Fifth Schedule to this Act shall apply as regards the matters to be stated in the report of the directors [3] in the circumstances specified therein.

(5) Part III of the Fifth Schedule to this Act shall apply as regards the matters to be stated in the directors' [3] report relative to the employment, training and advancement of disabled persons, the health, safety and welfare at work of the employees of the company[1] and the involvement of employees in the affairs, policy and performance of the company. [1]

(6) In respect of any failure to comply with the requirements of this Act as to the matters to be stated and the particulars to be given in the directors' [3] report, every person who was a director [3] of the company[1] immediately before the end of the period prescribed for laying and delivering financial statements [7] shall be guilty of an offence and liable on conviction to a term of imprisonment for not more than six months or to a fine of N500.

(7) In proceedings for an offence under subsection (6) of this section, it shall be a defence for the person to prove that he took all reasonable steps for securing compliance with the requirements in question.

**Notes**

**Section 342**

1. "Company" means a corporation - or, less commonly, an association, partnership, or union that carries on a commercial or industrial enterprise. **See Garner B. (ed) Black's Law Dictionary 8 th ed.**
   "Company" means a company formed and registered under this Act or, as the case may be, formed and registered in Nigeria before and in existence on the commencement of this Act. See **Section 567 CAMA, Cap. C20 LFN 2004.**
2. "Year" means a period of twelve months. See **section 18, Interpretation Act Cap. 123 LFN, 2004** .
3. "Directors" see "director." A director is one who manages, guides, or orders; a chief administrator (2) a person appointed or elected to sit on a board that manages the affairs of a corporation or other organisation by electing and exercising control over its officers. See **Garner B. (ed) Black's Law Dictionary 8th ed.**
   "Director" includes any person occupying the position of director by whatever name called; and includes any person in accordance with whose directions or instructions the directors of the company are accustomed to act. See **Section 567 CAMA, Cap. C20, LFN 2004.**
4. "Subsidiaries" means, in relation to a body corporate, a subsidiary as defined by section 338 of this Act. See **Section 567 CAMA, Cap. C20, LFN 2004.**
5. "Dividend" means a portion of a company's earnings or profits distributed prorate to its shareholders, usually in the form of cash or additional shares. See **Garner B. (ed) Black's Law Dictionary 8 th ed**.
   "Dividend" means a proportion of the distributed profits of the company which may be a fixed annual percentage, as in the case of preference shares, or it may be variable according to the prosperity or other circumstances of the company, as in the case of equity shares; See **section 567 CAMA, Cap. C20, LFN 2004.**
6. "Financial Statements" means balance sheet, income statement or annual report that summarizes an individual or organization's financial condition on a specified date. **See Garner B. (ed) Black's Law Dictionary 8 th ed.**

**Cross Reference**

On duties of director, see **section 279 CAMA Cap. C20, LFN 2004**

---

**Cases**

A director is a person appointed or elected according to Law, authorized to manage and direct the affairs of a corporation or company. ***Olufosoye v. Fakorede*** **(1993) 1 N.W.L.R 947.** See also ***Longe v. First Bank Nigeria Plc*** **(2006) 3 N.W.L.R 228 at 270.**

**For Further Reading**

On directors their duties, powers see, Osunbor, O. A. The Company Director: His Appointment, Powers and Duties; Essays on Company Law.

## 343.Signing of balance sheet and documents to be annexed thereto

(1) A company's [1] balance sheet[2] and every copy of it which is laid before the company [1] in general meeting [3] or delivered to the Commission[4] shall be signed on behalf of the board [5] by two of the directors[6] of the company. [1]

(2) If a copy of the balance sheet [2]

(a) is laid before the company [1] or delivered to the Commission[4] without being signed as required by this section; or

(b) not being a copy so laid or delivered, is issued, circulated or published in a case where the balance sheet [2] has not been signed as so required or where (the balance sheet [2] having been so signed) the copy does not include a copy of the signature as the case may be, the company [1] and every officer[7] of it who is in default shall be guilty of an offence and liable on conviction to a fine of ₦300.

(3) A company's [1] profit and loss account and, so far as not incorporated in its individual balance sheet [2] or profit and loss account, any group accounts of a holding company, [8] shall be annexed to the balance sheet, [2] and the auditors' [9] report and the directors' [6] report shall also be attached to the balance sheet. [2]

(4) The balance sheet [2] and the profit and loss account annexed to it shall be approved by the board of directors [5] and signed on their behalf by two directors [6] authorised to do so.

---

**Notes**

**Section 343**

1. "Company" means a corporation - or, less commonly, an association, partnership, or union that carries on a commercial or industrial enterprise. **See Garner B. (ed) Black's Law Dictionary 8 [th] ed.** "Company" or "existing company" means a company formed and registered under this Act or, as the case may be, formed and registered in Nigeria before and in existence on the commencement of this Act. **See Section 567 CAMA, Cap. C20, LFN 2004** .

2. "Balance Sheet" means A statement of an entity's current financial position, disclosing the value of the entity's asset, liabilities and owner's equity. **See Garner B. (ed) Black's Law Dictionary 8 th ed.**
3. "General Meeting" see "Annual meeting" – a yearly meeting to elect or install officers or directors and to conduct other routine organisational business. **See Garner B, (ed) Black's Law Dictionary 8 th ed.**
4. "Commission" means the Corporate Affairs Commission established under section 1 of this Act. See **Section 567 CAMA, Cap. C20, LFN 2004.**
5. "Board" see" Board of directors." It means the governing body of a corporation, elected by the shareholders to establish corporate policy, appoint executive officers, and make major business and financial decisions. See **Garner B., (ed.) Black's Law Dictionary 8 th ed.**
6. "Directors" see "director". A director is (1) one who manages, guides, or orders; a chief administrator (2) a person appointed or elected to sit on a board that manages the affairs of a corporation or other organisation by electing and exercising control over its officers. **See Garner B. (ed) Black's Law Dictionary 8th ed.**

   "Director" includes any person occupying the position of director by whatever name called; and includes any person in accordance with whose directions or instructions the directors of the company are accustomed to act. See **Section 567 CAMA, Cap. C20, LFN 2004.**
7. "Officer" means in relation to a body corporate, includes a director, manager or secretary. See **Section 567 CAMA, Cap. C20, LFN 2004.**
8. "Holding Company" means a holding company as defined by section 338 of this Act. **See Section 567 CAMA, Cap. C20, LFN 2004.**
9. "Auditors" see" auditor." It means a person or firm, usually an accountant that formally examines an individual or an entity's financial records or status. See **Garner B. (ed) Black's Law Dictionary 8 th ed.**

**Cross Reference**

On obligation to prepare directors report, see **section 342, CAMA Cap. C20, LFN 2004**

On obligation of auditor to prepare auditor's report, see **section 359,CAMA Cap. C20 LFN 2004.**

---

**Cases**

The Corporate Affairs Commission is conferred with the responsibility of registering companies operating in Nigeria by Statute, and under the said statute it can prohibit and restrict certain names to be registered. ***Mustapha v. CAC*** **(2009) Vol. 43 W.R.N. 1-171 pg 156.**

## 344. Persons entitled to receive financial statements as of right

(1) In the case of every company, [1] a copy of the company's [1] financial statements[2] for the year [3] shall, not less than 21 days before the date of the meeting [4] at which they are to be laid in accordance

with section 345 of this Act be sent to each of the following persons-

(a) every member[5] of the company[1] (whether or not entitled to receive notice of general meetings[4]);

(b) every holder of the company's[1] debentures,[6] (whether or not so entitled); and

(c) all persons other than members[5] and debenture holders,[7] being persons so entitled.

(2) In the case of a company[1] not having a share capital,[8] subsection (1) of this section shall not require a copy of the financial statements[2] to be sent to a member[5] of the company[1] who is not entitled to receive notices of general meetings[4] of the company,[1] or to a holder of the company's[1] debenture[6] who is not so entitled.

(3) Subsection (1) of this section shall not require copies of the financial statements[2] to be sent to-

(a) a member[5] of the company[1] or a debenture holder,[7] being in either case a person who is not entitled to receive notices of general meetings,[4] and of whose address the company[1] is unaware; or

(b) more than one of the joint holders of any shares[9] or debentures[6] none of whom are entitled to receive such notices; or

(c) those who are not so entitled in the case of joint holders of shares[9] or debentures,[6] some of whom are not entitled to receive such notices.

(4) If copies of the financial statements[2] are sent less than 21 days before the date of the meeting,[4] it shall, notwithstanding that fact, be deemed to have been duly sent if it is so agreed by all the members[5] entitled to attend and vote at the meeting.[4]

(5) If default is made in complying with subsection (1) of this section, the company[1] and every officer[10] of it who is in default shall be guilty of an offence and is liable to a fine of ₦250.

---

**Notes**
**Section 344**

1. "Company" means a corporation - or, less commonly, an association, partnership, or union that carries on a commercial or industrial enterprise. See **Garner B. (ed) Black's Law Dictionary 8th ed.**

"Company" means a company formed and registered under this Act or, as the case may be, formed and registered in Nigeria before and in existence on the commencement of this Act. See **Section 567 CAMA, Cap. C20, LFN 2004.**

2. "Financial statements" means balance sheet, income statement or annual report that summarizes an individual or organization's financial condition on a specified date. **See Garner B. (ed) Black's Law Dictionary 8 th ed.**
3. "Year" means a period of twelve months. See **section 18, Interpretation Act Cap. 123 LFN, 2004.**
4. "Meeting" means the gathering of people to discuss or act on matters in which they have a common interest; esp. the convening of a deliberate assembly to transact business. See **Garner B. (ed) Black's Law Dictionary 8th ed.**
5. "Member" includes the heir, executive, administrator or other personal representative, as the case maybe, of the member **. See Section 567 CAMA, Cap. C20, LFN 2004.**
6. "Debentures" means a written acknowledgement of indebtedness by the company, setting out the terms and conditions of the indebtedness, and includes debenture stock, bonds and any other securities of a company whether constituting a charge on the assets of the company or not. **See section 567 CAMA, Cap. C20, LFN 2004.**
7. "Debenture holder" see "debenture" and "holder". Debenture means a written acknowledgement of indebtedness by the company, setting out the terms and conditions of the indebtedness and includes debenture stock, bonds and any other securities of any company whether constituting a charge on the assets of the company or not. **See section 567 CAMA, Cap. C20, LFN 2004.** "Holder" is one who has legal possession of a negotiable instrument and is entitled to receive payment on it. See **Garner B. (ed) Black's Law Dictionary 8 th ed.**
8. "Share Capital" See capital. It means a fund representing the nominal value of shares issued by a registered company. See **Martins E. (ed.) Oxford Dictionary of Law 4 th ed.**
9. "Shares" see "share". It means the interests in a company's share capital of a member who is entitled to share in the capital or income of such company; and except where a distinction between stock and shares is expressed or implied, includes stock. See **Section 567 CAMA, Cap. C20, LFN 2004.**
10. "Officer" means in relation to a body corporate, includes a director, manager or secretary. See **Section 567 CAMA, Cap. C20, LFN 2004.**

**Cross Reference.**

On obligation to provide notice of meeting and length of notice: see section 217, **CAMA Cap. C20, LFN 2004**

On obligation of a company to hold general meeting see section 213, **CAMA Cap. C20, LFN 2004**

On meaning of offence, see **section 2, Criminal Code Act, Cap. C38 LFN 2004**

### 345. **Directors' duty to lay and deliver financial statements**

(1) In respect of each year, [1] the directors [2] shall at a date not later than 18 months after incorporation of the company [3] and subsequently once at least in every year, [1] lay before the company [3] in general meeting [4] copies of the financial statements [5] of the company [3] made up to a date not exceeding nine months previous to the date of the meeting. [4]

(2) The auditors' [6] report shall be read before the company [3] in general meeting, [4] and be open to the inspection of any member [7] of the company. [3]

(3) In respect of each year, [1] the directors [2] shall deliver with the annual return [8] to the Commission [9] a copy of the balance sheet, [10] the profit and loss account and the notes on the statements which were laid before the general meeting [4] as required by this section.

(4) In the case of an unlimited company, [11] the directors [2] shall not be required by subsection (3) of this section to deliver a copy of the accounts [12] if-

(a) at no time during the accounting reference period has the company [3] been, to its knowledge, the subsidiary [13] of a company [3] that was then limited and at no such time, to its knowledge, have there been held or been exercisable, by or on behalf of two or more companies that were then limited, shares [14] or powers which, if they had been held or been exercisable by one of them, would have made the company [3] its subsidiary; [13] and

(b) at no such time has the company [3] been the holding company [15] of a company [3] which was then limited.

(5) References in this section to a company [3] that was limited at a particular time are to a body corporate [16] (under whatever law incorporated) the liability of whose members [7] was at that time limited.

---

**Notes**
**Section 345**

1. "Year" means a period of twelve months. See **section 18, Interpretation Act Cap. 123 LFN, 2004.**
2. "Directors" see "director". A director is (1) one who manages, guides, or orders; a chief administrator (2) a person appointed or elected to sit on a board that manages the affairs of a corporation or other organisation by electing and exercising control over its officers. **See Garner B. (ed.) Black's Law Dictionary 8 th ed.**

Directors" includes any person occupying the position of director by whatever name called; and includes any person in accordance with whose directions or instructions the directors of the company are accustomed to act. See **Section 567 CAMA, Cap. C20, LFN 2004.**

3. "Company" means a corporation - or, less commonly, an association, partnership, or union that carries on a commercial or industrial enterprise. **See Garner B. (ed.) Black's Law Dictionary 8 th ed.**

   "Company" means a company formed and registered under this Act or, as the case may be, formed and registered in Nigeria before and in existence on the commencement of this Act. See **Section 567 CAMA, Cap. C20, LFN 2004.**

4. "General meeting" see "Annual meeting" – a yearly meeting to elect or install officers or directors and to conduct other routine organisational business. See **Garner B. (ed.) Black's Law Dictionary 8th ed.**

5. "Financial statements" means balance sheet, income statement or annual report that summarizes an individual or organization's financial condition on a specified date**. See Garner B. (ed.) Black's Law Dictionary 8th ed.**

6. "Auditors" see "auditor". It means a person or firm, usually an accountant that formally examines an individual or an entity's financial records or status. See **Garner B. (ed.) Black's Law Dictionary 8 th ed.**

7. "Member" includes the heir, executive, administrator or other personal representative, as the case maybe, of the member **. See Section 567 CAMA, Cap. C20, LFN 2004.**

8. "Annual return" means the return required to be made, in the case of a company limited by shares under sections 371 and 372 and, in the case of a company limited by guarantee, under section 373 of this Act. See **Section 567 CAMA, Cap. C20, LFN 2004.**

9. "Commission" means the Corporate Affairs Commission established under section 1 of this Act. See **Section 567 CAMA, Cap. C20, LFN 2004.**

10. "Balance sheet" means A statement of an entity's current financial position, disclosing the value of the entity's asset, liabilities and owner's equity. **See Garner B. (ed.) Black's Law Dictionary 8 th ed.**

11. "Unlimited company" has the meaning assigned to it by section 21(1) of this Act. See **Section 567 CAMA, Cap. C20, LFN 2004.**

12. "Accounts" includes a company's group accounts, whether prepared in the form of accounts or not;. See **Section 567 CAMA, Cap. C20, LFN 2004.**

13. "Subsidiary" see "subsidiaries". " Subsidiaries in relation to a body corporate, a subsidiary as defined by section 338 of this Act. **See Section 567 CAMA, Cap. C20, LFN 2004.**

14. "Shares" see "share". It means the interests in a company's share capital of a member who is entitled to share in the capital or income of such company; and except where a distinction between stock and

shares is expressed or implied, includes stock. See **Section 567 CAMA, Cap. C20, LFN 2004.**

15. "Holding Company" means a holding company as defined by section 338 of this Act. **See Section 567 CAMA, Cap. C20, LFN 2004.**
16. Body corporate" see corporation. An entity (usu. A business) having authority under law to act as a single person distinct from the shareholders who own it and having rights to issue stock and exist indefinitely; a group or succession of persons established in accordance with legal rules into a legal or juristic person that has a legal personality distinct from the natural persons who make it up, exists indefinitely apart from them, and has the legal powers that its constitution gives it. **See Garner B. (ed.) Black's Law Dictionary 8 th ed.**

**Cross Reference**

On obligation of Auditor to make report, see **section 359 CAMA Cap. C20, LFN 2004**

On persons entitled to receive the financial statement of a company as of right, see **section 343 CAMA Cap. C20, LFN 2004**

On penalty for failure of director to deliver financial report, see **section 346 CAMA Cap. C20, LFN 2004**

---

**For Further Reading**

On directors' duties, see, Bakibinga, D. J. "Directors' Duty to Act Bona Fide in the Interest of the Company" (1990) 39 (2) **The International and Comparative Law Quarterly 451.**

## 346. Penalty for non-compliance with section 345

(1) If in a year [1] any of the requirements of section 345 (1) or (3) of this Act is not complied with by any company, [2] every person who immediately before the end of that period was a director [3] of the company[2] shall in respect of each of those subsections which is not so complied with, be guilty of an offence and liable to a daily default fine of N50 in the case of a small company, [4] a company limited by guarantee[5] or an unlimited company, [6] and N500 in the case of any other company. [1]

(2) If a person is charged with an offence in respect of any of the requirements of subsection (1) or (3) of section 345 of this Act, it shall be a defence for him to prove that he took all reasonable steps for securing that those requirements be complied with before the end of the period allowed for laying and delivering accounts.

(3) In proceedings under this section with respect to a requirement to lay a copy of a document [7] before a company[2] in general meeting,[8] or to deliver a copy of a document [6] to the

Commission,[9] it shall not be a defence to prove that the document[6] in question was not in fact prepared as required by this Part of this Act.

---

**Notes**
**Section 346**

1. "Year" means a period of twelve months. See **section 18, Interpretation Act Cap. 123 LFN, 2004.**
2. "Company" means a corporation - or, less commonly, an association, partnership, or union that carries on a commercial or industrial enterprise. **See Garner B. (ed.) Black's Law Dictionary 8 th ed.**
"Company" means a company formed and registered under this Act or, as the case may be, formed and registered in Nigeria before and in existence on the commencement of this Act. See **Section 567 CAMA, Cap. C20, LFN 2004.**
3. "Director" means (1) one who manages, guides, or orders; a chief administrator (2) a person appointed or elected to sit on a board that manages the affairs of a corporation or other organisation by electing and exercising control over its officers. **See Garner B. (ed.) Black's Law Dictionary 8th ed.**
"Director" includes any person occupying the position of director by whatever name called; and includes any person in accordance with whose directions or instructions the directors of the company are accustomed to act. See **Section 567 CAMA, Cap. C20, LFN 2004.**
4. "Small Company" has the meaning assigned to it under section 351 of this Act. See **Section 567 CAMA, Cap. C20, LFN 2004.**
5. "Company Limited by Guarantee" has the meaning assigned to it by section 21 CAMA. **See Section 567 CAMA, Cap. C20, LFN 2004.**
6. "Unlimited Company" has the meaning assigned to it by section 21(1) of this Act. See **Section 567 CAMA, Cap. C20, LFN 2004.**
7. "Document" includes summons, notice, order and other legal process, and registers. **See Section 567 CAMA, Cap. C20, LFN 2004.**
8. "General Meeting" see "Annual meeting" – a yearly meeting to elect or install officers or directors and to conduct other routine organisational business. **See Garner B. (ed.) Black's Law Dictionary 8 th ed.**
9. "Commission" means the Corporate Affairs Commission established under section 1 of this Act. See **Section 567 CAMA, Cap. C20, LFN 2004.**

---

## 347. Default order in case of non-compliance

(1) If-

(a) in respect of a year,[1] any of the requirements of subsections (1) and (3) of section 345 of this Act has not been complied with by a company[2] before the end of the period allowed for laying and delivering financial statements;[3] and

(b) the directors[4] of the company[2] fail to make good the default within 14 days after the service of a notice on them requiring compliance, the court[5] may on application by any member[6] or creditor[7] of the company[2] or by the Commission[8] make an order directing the directors[4] (or any of them) to make good the default within such time as may be specified in the order.

(2) The court's[5] order may provide that all costs of and incidental to the application shall be borne by the directors.[4]

(3) Nothing in this section shall affect the provisions of section 346 of this Act.

---

**Notes**
**Section 347**

1. "Year" means a period of twelve months. See **section 18, Interpretation Act CAP 123 LFN, 2004.**
2. "Company" means a corporation - or, less commonly, an association, partnership, or union that carries on a commercial or industrial enterprise. **See Garner B. (ed.) Black's Law Dictionary 8[th] ed.**
   "Company" means a company formed and registered under this Act or, as the case may be, formed and registered in Nigeria before and in existence on the commencement of this Act. See **Section 567 CAMA, Cap. C20, LFN 2004.**
3. "Financial statements" means balance sheet, income statement or annual report that summarizes an individual or organization's financial condition on a specified date. **See Garner B. (ed.) Black's Law Dictionary 8[th] ed.**
4. "Director" means (1) one who manages, guides, or orders; a chief administrator (2) a person appointed or elected to sit on a board that manages the affairs of a corporation or other organisation by electing and exercising control over its officers. **See Garner B. (ed.) Black's Law Dictionary 8[th] ed.**
   "Director" includes any person occupying the position of director by whatever name called; and includes any person in accordance with whose directions or instructions the directors of the company are accustomed to act. See **Section 567 CAMA, Cap. C20, LFN 2004.**
5. "Court" when used in relation to a company, means the federal High court, and to the extent to which application maybe made to it as; court includes the court of appeal and the supreme court of Nigeria. See **Section 567 CAMA, Cap. C20, LFN 2004.**
6. "Member" includes the heir, executive, administrator or other personal representative, as the case maybe, of the member . **See Section 567 CAMA, Cap. C20, LFN 2004.**

7. "Creditor" means one to whom a debt is owed; one who gives credit for money and goods. **See Garner B. (ed.) Black's Law Dictionary 8th ed.**

8. "Commission" means the Corporate Affairs Commission established under section 1 of this Act. See **Section 567 CAMA, Cap. C20, LFN 2004.**

**Cross Reference**

On obligation of directors to prepare financial statement of a company, see **section 334, CAMA Cap. C20, LFN 2004.**

On establishment and jurisdiction of the Federal High Court, see **sections 249& 251 Constitution of the Federal Republic of Nigeria, 1999( as amended)**

---

## 348. Penalty for laying or delivering defective financial statements

(1) If any financial statements [1] of a company [2] (other than its group financial statement [3]) of which a copy is laid before the shareholders [4] in general meeting [5] or delivered to the Commission [6] do not comply with the requirement of this Act as to the matters to be included in, or in a note to, those financial statements, [1] every person who at the time when the copy is laid or delivered is a director [7] of the company [2] shall be guilty of an offence and in respect of each offence, liable to a fine of N100.

(2) If any group financial statements [3] of which a copy is laid before a company [2] in a general meeting [5] or delivered to the Commission [6] do not comply with section 345 (4) and (5) or section 346 of this Act and with the other requirements of this Act as to the matters to be included in or in a note to those financial statements, [1] every person who at the time when the copy was so laid or delivered was a director [7] of the company [2] shall be guilty of an offence and liable to a fine of N250.

(3) In proceedings against a person for an offence under this section, it shall be a defence for him to prove that he took all reasonable steps for securing compliance with the requirements in question.

---

**Notes**

**Section 348**

1. "Financial statements" means balance sheet, income statement or annual report that summarizes an individual or organization's financial condition

on a specified date. **See Garner B. (ed.) Black's Law Dictionary 8 th ed.**

2. "Company" means a corporation - or, less commonly, an association, partnership, or union that carries on a commercial or industrial enterprise. **See Garner B. (ed.) Black's Law Dictionary 8 th ed.**
   "Company" means a company formed and registered under this Act or, as the case may be, formed and registered in Nigeria before and in existence on the commencement of this Act. See **Section 567 CAMA, Cap. C20, LFN 2004.**
3. "Group financial statements" means financial statements being accounts or statements which deal with the state of affairs and profit or loss of the company and the subsidiaries. **See section 336(1) CAMA, Cap. C20, LFN 2004.**
4. "Shareholders" see "shareholder". It means one who owns or holds a share or shares in a company. **See Garner B. (ed.) Black's Law Dictionary 8th ed.**
5. "General Meeting" see "Annual meeting" – a yearly meeting to elect or install officers or directors and to conduct other routine organisational business. **See Garner B. (ed.) Black's Law Dictionary 8 th ed.**
6. "Commission" means the Corporate Affairs Commission established under section 1 of this Act. See **Section 567 CAMA, Cap. C20, LFN 2004.**
7. "Director" means (1) one who manages, guides, or orders; a chief administrator (2) a person appointed or elected to sit on a board that manages the affairs of a corporation or other organisation by electing and exercising control over its officers. **See Garner B. (ed.) Black's Law Dictionary 8th ed.**
   "Director" includes any person occupying the position of director by whatever name called; and includes any person in accordance with whose directions or instructions the directors of the company are accustomed to act. See **Section 567 CAMA, Cap. C20, LFN 2004.**

**Cross Reference**

On meaning of offence, see **section 2 Criminal Code Act Cap. C38, LFN 2004**

On obligation of directors to prepare financial statement of a company, see **section 334, CAMA Cap. C20, LFN 2004.**

---

## 349. Shareholders' right to obtain copies of financial statements

(1) Any member[1] of a company,[2] whether or not he is entitled to have sent to him copies of the company's[2] financial statements[3] and any holder of the company's[2] debentures[4] (whether or not so entitled) shall be entitled to be furnished (on demand and without charge) with a copy of the company's[2] last financial statements.[3]

(2) If, when a person makes a demand for a document [5] with which he is entitled by this section to be furnished, default is made in complying with the demand within seven days after its making, the company[2] and every officer[6] of it who is in default shall be guilty of an offence and liable to a daily default fine of N=100, unless it is proved that the person has already made a demand for, and been furnished with, a copy of the documents.

---

**Notes**
**Section 349**

1. "Member" includes the heir, executive, administrator or other personal representative, as the case maybe, of the member . See **Section 567 CAMA, Cap. C20, LFN 2004.**
2. "Company" means a corporation - or, less commonly, an association, partnership, or union that carries on a commercial or industrial enterprise. **See Garner B. (ed.) Black's Law Dictionary 8 th ed.**
   "Company" means a company formed and registered under this Act or, as the case may be, formed and registered in Nigeria before and in existence on the commencement of this Act. See **Section 567 CAMA, Cap. C20, LFN 2004.**
3. "Financial statements" means balance sheet, income statement or annual report that summarizes an individual or organization's financial condition on a specified date. **See Garner B. (ed.) Black's Law Dictionary 8th ed.**
4. "Debentures" see "debenture." It means a written acknowledgement of indebtedness by the company, setting out the terms and conditions of the indebtedness, and includes debenture stock, bonds and any other securities of a company whether constituting a charge on the assets of the company or not. See **Section 567 CAMA, Cap. C20, LFN 2004.**
5. "Document" includes summons, notice, order and other legal process, and registers. See **Section 567 CAMA, Cap. C20, LFN 2004.**
6. "Officer" means in relation to a body corporate, includes a director, manager or secretary. See **Section 567 CAMA, Cap. C20, LFN 2004.**

**Cross Reference**

On obligation of directors to prepare financial statement of a company, see **section 334, CAMA Cap. C20, LFN 2004.**

On meaning of offence, see **section 2, Criminal Code Act, Cap. C38 LFN** 2004

---

**Cases**

A registered holder of shares in a company becomes entitled to certain rights, benefits and privileges. Except as otherwise provided by the Law

and the provisions of the memorandum and Articles of Association of the company, he has the right to sell, mortgage or otherwise dispose of the shares. He is entitled to receive dividends on the shares registered in his name and to keep the dividends so received for his own use. In other words, the essence of being registered as an owner or a holder of shares in a company is that one is inter alia, entitled to enjoy in one's right the foregoing rights, benefits and privileges. ***Kotoye vs. Saraki* (1994) 7 N.W.L.R (part 357) 414** .
Entry in the register of the company is another method of proof of being a shareholder, but it is not the only method nor can the absence of that method of proof invalidate other methods. ***Ponmile v. Sparks Electrics (Nig) Ltd* (1986) 2 N.W.L.R pg 519.**

**For Further Reading**
On shareholders, see, Olufemi Amao and Kenneth Amaeshi "Galvanizing Shareholder Activism: A Prerequisite for Effective Corporate Governance and Accountability in Nigeria" **(2008) 82 Journal of Business Ethics 119-130.**

## 350. Entitlement to deliver financial statements in modified form

(1) In certain cases a company's [1] directors[2] may, in accordance with Part 1 of the Seventh Schedule to this Act, deliver modified financial statements[3] in respect of a year as a small company.[4]

(2) For the purposes of sections 351 to 353 and the Seventh Schedule to this Act, "deliver" means deliver to the Commission.[5]

---

**Notes**
**Section 350**

1. "Company" means a corporation - or, less commonly, an association, partnership, or union that carries on a commercial or industrial enterprise. **See Garner B. (ed.) Black's Law Dictionary 8 th ed.**
"Company" means a company formed and registered under this Act or, as the case may be, formed and registered in Nigeria before and in existence on the commencement of this Act. See **Section 567 CAMA, Cap. C20, LFN 2004.**
2. "Directors" see "Director." "Director means (1) one who manages, guides, or orders; a chief administrator (2) a person appointed or elected to sit on a board that manages the affairs of a corporation or other organisation by electing and exercising control over its officers. **See Garner B. (ed.) Black's Law Dictionary 8 th ed.**
"Director" includes any person occupying the position of director by whatever name called; and includes any person in accordance with whose

directions or instructions the directors of the company are accustomed to act. See **Section 567 CAMA, Cap. C20, LFN 2004.**

3. "Financial statements" means balance sheet, income statement or annual report that summarizes an individual or organization's financial condition on a specified date. **See Garner B. (ed.) Black's Law Dictionary 8 th ed.**
4. "Small Company" has the meaning assigned to it under section 351 of this Act. See **Section 567 CAMA, Cap. C20, LFN 2004.**
5. "Commission" means the Corporate Affairs Commission established under section 1 of this Act. See **Section 567 CAMA, Cap. C20, LFN 2004.**

---

## 351. Qualification of a small company

(1) A company [1] qualifies as a small company [2] in a year [3] if for that year [3] the following conditions are satisfied-

(a) it is a private company [4] having a share capital; [5]

(b) the amount of its turnover for that year [3] is not more than N2 million or such amount as may be fixed by the Commission; [6]

(c) its net assets value is not more than N 1 million or such amount as may be fixed by the Commission; [6]

(d) none of its members [7] is an alien;

(e) none of its members [7] is a Government or a Government corporation or agency or its nominee; and

(f) the directors [8] between them hold not less than 51 per cent of its equity share capital. [9]

(2) In applying subsection (1) of this section, to a period which is a company's [2] year [3] but not in fact a year, [3] the maximum figures for turnover in paragraph (b) of that subsection shall be proportionately adjusted.

---

**Notes**
**Section 351**

1. "Company" means a corporation - or, less commonly, an association, partnership, or union that carries on a commercial or industrial enterprise. **Garner B. (ed.) Black's Law Dictionary 8 th ed.**
   "Company" or "existing company" means a company formed and registered under this Act or, as the case may be, formed and registered in Nigeria before and in existence on the commencement of this Act. See **Section 567 CAMA, Cap. C20, LFN 2004.**
2. "Small company" has the meaning assigned to it under section 351 of this Act. **See section 567 CAMA, Cap. C20, LFN 2004.**

3. "Year" means a period of twelve months. See **section 18 Interpretation Act Cap. 192 LFN, 1990.**
4. "Private company" means one which is stated in its memorandum to be a private company. **See section 567 CAMA, Cap. C20, LFN 2004.**
5. "Share Capital" See capital. means a fund representing the nominal value of shares issued by a registered company. See **Martins E. (ed.) Oxford Dictionary of Law 4th ed.**
6. "Commission" means the Corporate Affairs Commission established under section 1 of this Act. **See section 567 CAMA, Cap. C20, LFN 2004.**
7. "Members" includes the heir, executive, administrator or other personal representative, as the case maybe, of the member . **See section 567 CAMA, Cap. C20, LFN 2004.**
8. "Directors" means (1) one who manages, guides, or orders; a chief administrator (2) a person appointed or elected to sit on a board that manages the affairs of a corporation or other organisation by electing and exercising control over its officers. **See Garner B. (ed.) Black's Law Dictionary 8th ed.**
   "Directors" includes any person occupying the position of director by whatever name called; and includes any person in accordance with whose directions or instructions the directors of the company are accustomed to act. **See section 567 CAMA, Cap. C20, LFN 2004.**
9. "Equity share capital" means a share capital other than a preference share capital. **See section 567 CAMA C20, LFN 2004.**

**Cross Reference**

On obligation of directors to prepare financial statement of a company, see **section 334, CAMA Cap. C20, LFN 2004.**

On entitlement of a small company to deliver modified financial statements, see **section 350 CAMA Cap. C20 LFN 2004**

---

## 352.Modified individual financial statements

(1) The directors [1] of a company[2] may (subject to section 353 of this Act where the company [2]has subsidiaries[3]) deliver individual financial statements [4]modified as for a small company [5] in the cases specified in subsections (2) and (3) of this section; and Part 1 of the Seventh Schedule shall apply with respect to the delivery of financial statements[4] so modified.

(2) In respect of the company's [2] first year the directors [1] may deliver financial statements[4] modified as for a small company, [5] if in that year it qualifies as small.

(3) The directors [1] may in respect of a company's [2] year subsequent to the first-

(a) Deliver financial statements[4] modified as for a small company[5] if the company[2] qualifies as small and it also so qualified in the preceding year;

(b) deliver financial statements[4] modified as for a small company [5](although not qualifying in that year as small), if in the preceding year it so qualified and the directors[1] were entitled to deliver financial statements [4]so modified in respect of that year;

(c) deliver financial statements [4]modified as for a small company [5]if, in that year the company[2] qualifies as small and the directors[1] were entitled under paragraph (b) of this subsection to deliver financial statements[4] so modified for the preceding year (although the company [2]did not in that year qualify as small).

---

**Notes**
**Section 352(1)**

1. "Directors" see "Director". "Director means (1) one who manages, guides, or orders; a chief administrator (2) a person appointed or elected to sit on a board that manages the affairs of a corporation or other organisation by electing and exercising control over its officers. **See Garner B. (ed.) Black's Law Dictionary 8 th ed.**
   "Director" includes any person occupying the position of director by whatever name called; and includes any person in accordance with whose directions or instructions the directors of the company are accustomed to act. See **Section 567 CAMA, Cap. C20, LFN 2004.**
2. "Company" means a corporation - or, less commonly, an association, partnership, or union that carries on a commercial or industrial enterprise. **See Garner B. (ed.) Black's Law Dictionary 8 th ed.**
   "Company" means a company formed and registered under this Act or, as the case may be, formed and registered in Nigeria before and in existence on the commencement of this Act. See **Section 567 CAMA, Cap. C20, LFN 2004.**
3. "Subsidiaries" means, in relation to a body corporate, a subsidiary as defined by section 338 of this Act. See **Section 567 CAMA, Cap. C20, LFN 2004.**
4. "Financial statements" means balance sheet, income statement or annual report that summarizes an individual or organization's financial condition on a specified date. **See Garner B. (ed.) Black's Law Dictionary 8th ed.**
5. "Small Company" has the meaning assigned to it under section 351 of this Act. See **Section 567 CAMA, Cap. C20, LFN 2004.**

Cross Reference

On entitlement of a small company to deliver modified financial statements, see **section 350 CAMA Cap. C20 LFN 2004**

---

## 53. Modified financial statements of holding company

(1) This section shall apply to a holding company [1] where in respect of a year section 336 of this Act requires the preparation of group financial statements [2] for the company [3] and its subsidiaries. [4]

(2) The directors [5] of the holding company [1] may not under section 352 of this Act deliver financial statements [6] modified as for a small company,[7] unless the group (that is to say, the holding company[1] and its subsidiaries [5] together) is in that year a small group and the group is small if it would so qualify under section 351 of this Act (applying that section as directed by subsections (3) and (4) of this section, if it were all one company. [4]

(3) The figures to be taken into account in determining whether the group is small shall be the group account figures, that is-

(a) where the group financial statements [2] are prepared as consolidated financial statements,[3] the figures for turnover and balance sheet[8] total; and

(b) where the group financial statements [3] are not prepared as consolidated financial statements,[3] the corresponding figures given in the group financial statements, [3] with such adjustment as would have been made if the statements had been prepared in consolidated form; aggregated in either case with the relevant figures for the subsidiaries [5] (if any) omitted from the group accounts (excepting those for any subsidiary[5] omitted under section 336 (3) (a) of this Act on the ground of impracticability).

(4) In the case of each subsidiary [5] omitted from the group financial statements,[3] the figures relevant as regards turnover, and balance sheet[8] total shall be those which are included in the financial statements[3] of that subsidiary [5] prepared in respect of its relevant year (with such adjustment as would have been made if those figures had been included in group financial statements [3] prepared in consolidated form).

(5) For the purposes of subsection (4) of this section, the relevant year[2] of the subsidiary [5] shall be-

(a) if its year[2] ends with that of the holding company[1] to which the group financial statements[3] relate, that year;[2] and

(b) if not, the subsidiary's[5] year[2] ending last before the end of the year[2] of the holding company.[1]

(6) If the directors[5] are entitled to deliver modified financial statements[6] they may also deliver modified group financial statements,[3] and such group financial statements-[3]

(a) if consolidated, may be in accordance with Part II of the Seventh Schedule (while otherwise comprising or corresponding with group financial statements[3] prepared under section 336 of this Act); and

(b) if not consolidated, may be such as (together with any notes) give the same or equivalent information as required by paragraph (a) of this subsection,

and Part III to the Seventh Schedule to this Act shall apply to modified group financial statements[3] whether consolidated or not.

---

**Notes**
**Section 353**

1. "Holding company" means a holding company as defined by section 338 of this Act. **Section 567 CAMA, Cap. C20, LFN 2004.**
2. "Year" means a period of twelve months. See **section 18, Interpretation Act CAP 192 LFN, 1990.**
3. "Group Financial statements" means financial statements being accounts or statements which deal with the state of affairs and profit or loss of the company and the subsidiaries. **See section 336(1) CAMA, Cap. C20, LFN 2004** .
4. "Companies" "means a corporation - or, less commonly, an association, partnership, or union that carries on a commercial or industrial enterprise. **Garner B. (ed.) Black's Law Dictionary 8th ed.**

   "Company" or "existing company" means a company formed and registered under this Act or, as the case may be, formed and registered in Nigeria before and in existence on the commencement of this Act . **Section 567 CAMA, Cap. C20, LFN 2004.**
5. "Subsidiaries" subsidiary means, in relation to a body corporate, a subsidiary as defined by section 338 of this Act. **Section 567 CAMA, Cap. C20, LFN 2004.**
6. "Financial statement" means balance sheet, income statement or annual report that summarizes an individual or organization's financial

condition on a specified date. **See Garner B. (ed.) Black's Law Dictionary 8th ed.**

Directors" means (1) one who manages, guides, or orders; a chief administrator (2) a person appointed or elected to sit on a board that manages the affairs of a corporation or other organisation by electing and exercising control over its officers. **Garner B. (ed.) Black's Law Dictionary 8th ed.**

"Director" includes any person occupying the position of director by whatever name called; and includes any person in accordance with whose directions or instructions the directors of the company are accustomed to act; **Section 567 CAMA, Cap. C20, LFN 2004.**

7. "Small company" has the meaning assigned to it under section 351 of this Act. **Section 567 CAMA, Cap. C20, LFN 2004.**
8. "Balance sheet" means A statement of an entity's current financial position, disclosing the value of the entity's asset, liabilities and owner's equity. **Garner B. (ed.) Black's Law Dictionary 8 th ed.**

---

## 354. Publication by a company of full individual or group financial statements

(1) This section shall apply to the publication by a company [1] of full individual or group financial statements, [2] that is to say, the statements required by section 345 of this Act to be laid before the company[1] in general meeting[3] and delivered to the Commission, [4] including the directors' [5] report, unless dispensed with under paragraph 3 of the Sixth Schedule to this Act, but does not apply to interim financial statements.[2]

(2) If a company[1] publishes individual financial statements[6] (modified or other) for a year, it shall publish with them the relevant auditors'[7] report.

(3) If a company[1] required by section 336 of this Act to prepare group financial statements[2] for a year, publishes individual financial statements[6] for that year, it shall also publish with them its group financial statements[2] (which may be modified financial statements[2] but only if the individual financial statements[6] are modified).

(4) If a company[1] publishes group financial statements[2] (modified or not) otherwise than together with its individual financial statements,[6] it shall publish with them the relevant auditors'[7] report.

(5) References in this section to the relevant auditor's [7] report are to the auditors'[7] report under section 359 of this Act or, in the case of modified financial statements[2] (individual or group), the

auditors'[7] special report under paragraph 10 of the Sixth Schedule to this Act.

(6) A company[1] which contravenes any provision of this section and any officer[8] of it who is in default, shall be guilty of an offence and liable to a daily default fine of N100.

---

**Notes**
**Section 354(1)**

1. "Company" means a corporation - or, less commonly, an association, partnership, or union that carries on a commercial or industrial enterprise. **See Garner B. (ed.) Black's Law Dictionary 8 th ed.**
"Company" means a company formed and registered under this Act or, as the case may be, formed and registered in Nigeria before and in existence on the commencement of this Act. See **Section 567 CAMA, Cap. C20, LFN 2004.**
2. "Group Financial Statements" means financial statements being accounts or statements which deal with the state of affairs and profit or loss of the company and the subsidiaries. **See section 336(1) CAMA, Cap. C20, LFN 2004** .
3. "General meeting" see "Annual meeting" – a yearly meeting to elect or install officers or directors and to conduct other routine organisational business. **See Garner B. (ed.) Black's Law Dictionary 8th ed.**
4. "Commission" means the Corporate Affairs Commission established under section 1 of this Act. See **Section 567 CAMA, Cap. C20, LFN 2004.**
5. "Directors" see "Director." "Director means (1) one who manages, guides, or orders; a chief administrator (2) a person appointed or elected to sit on a board that manages the affairs of a corporation or other organisation by electing and exercising control over its officers. **See Garner B. (ed.) Black's Law Dictionary 8 th ed.**
"Director" includes any person occupying the position of director by whatever name called; and includes any person in accordance with whose directions or instructions the directors of the company are accustomed to act. See **Section 567 CAMA, Cap. C20, LFN 2004.**
6. "Financial statement" means balance sheet, income statement or annual report that summarizes an individual or organization's financial condition on a specified date**. See Garner B. (ed.) Black's Law Dictionary 8th ed.**
7. "Auditor" means a person or firm, usually an accountant that formally examines an individual or an entity's financial records or status. **See Garner B. (ed.) Black's Law Dictionary 8 th ed.**
8. "Officer" means in relation to a body corporate, includes a director, manager or secretary; **Section 567 CAMA, Cap. C20, LFN 2004.**

Cross Reference

On meaning of offence, see **section 2 Criminal Code Act Cap. C20, LFN 2004**

On entitlement of a small company to deliver modified financial statements, see **section 350 CAMA Cap. C20 LFN 2004**

On obligation of directors to prepare financial statement of a company, see **section 334, CAMA Cap. C20, LFN 2004.**

---

**For Further Reading**

On a company's financial statement, see, Anifalaja, J. O. "Current Principles & Policies on Company Accounts," **Essays on Company Law**.

## 355. Publication of abridged financial statements

(1) This section shall apply to the publication by a company [1] of abridged financial statements,[2] that is to say, any balance sheet [3] or profit and loss account relating to a year of the company [1] or purporting to deal with any such year, otherwise than as part of full financial statements[2] (individual or group) to which section 354 of this Act applies.

(2) The reference in subsection (1) of this section to a balance sheet[3] or profit and loss account, in relation to financial statements [2] published by a holding company,[4] includes an account in any form purporting to be a balance sheet [3] or profit and loss account for the group consisting of the holding company [4] and its subsidiaries.[5]

(3) If the company[1] publishes abridged financial statements,[2] it shall publish with those statements, a statement indicating-

(a) that the statements are not full financial statements; [2]

(b) whether full individual or full group financial statements [2] according as the abridged statements deal solely with the company's[1] own affairs or with the affairs of the company and any subsidiaries[5] have been delivered to the Commission[6] or, in the case of an unlimited company [7] exempted under subsection (4) of section 345 of this Act, from the requirement to deliver financial statements, [2] that the company[1] is so exempted;

(c) whether the company's [1] auditors[8] have made a report under section 359 of this Act on the company's [1] financial statements[2] for any year with which the abridged financial statements[2] purport to deal; and

(d) whether any report so made was unqualified (meaning that it was a report, without qualification, to the effect that in the opinion of the person making it, the company's [1] financial statements[2] had been properly prepared).

(4) Where a company [1] publishes abridged financial statements,[2] it shall not publish with those statements any such report of the auditors [8] as is mentioned in subsection (3) (c) of this section.

(5) A company[1] which contravenes any provision of this section and any officers[9] of it who is in default, shall be guilty of an offence and liable to a daily default fine of N100.

---

**Notes**

**Section 355**

1. "Company" means a corporation - or, less commonly, an association, partnership, or union that carries on a commercial or industrial enterprise. See **Garner B. (ed.) Black's Law Dictionary 8 th ed.** "Company" means a company formed and registered under this Act or, as the case may be, formed and registered in Nigeria before and in existence on the commencement of this Act. See **Section 567 CAMA, Cap. C20, LFN 2004.**
2. "Group financial statements" means financial statements being accounts or statements which deal with the state of affairs and profit or loss of the company and the subsidiaries. **See section 336(1) CAMA, Cap. C20, LFN 2004** .
3. "Balance sheet" means a statement of an entity's current financial position, disclosing the value of the entities assets, liabilities and owner equity. **Garner B. (ed.) Black's Law Dictionary 8 th ed.**
4. "Holding company" means a holding company as defined by section 338 of this Act. See **Section 567 CAMA, Cap. C20, LFN 2004.**
5. "Subsidiaries" **see** "subsidiary." In relation to a body corporate, means asubsidiary as defined by section 338 of this Act. **Section 567 CAMA, Cap. C20, LFN 2004.**
6. "Commission" means the Corporate Affairs Commission established under section 1 of this Act. See **Section 567 CAMA, Cap. C20, LFN 2004.**
7. "Unlimited company" has the meaning assigned to it by section 21(1) of this Act. See **Section 567 CAMA, Cap. C20, LFN 2004.**
8. "Auditors" see "auditor." It means a person or firm, usually an accountant that formally examines an individual or an entity's financial records or status. See **Garner B. (ed.) Black's Law Dictionary 8 th ed.**
9. "Officers" see "officer". In relation to a body corporate, officer includes a director, manager or secretary. See **Section 567 CAMA, Cap. C20, LFN 2004.**

**Cross Reference**

On meaning of offence, see **section 2, Criminal Code, Cap. C38 LFN 2004**

## 356. Power to alter accounting requirements

(1) The Minister[1] may after consultation with the Nigerian Accounting Standards Board by regulations in a statutory instrument-

(a) add to the classes of documents-

(i) to be comprised in a company's [2] financial statements[3] for a year to be laid before the company [2] in general meeting[4] as required by section 345, of this Act; or

(ii) to be delivered to the Commission[5] under that section, and make provision as to the matters to be included in any document to be added to either class; or

(b) modify the requirements of this Act as to the matters to be stated in a document of any such class; or

(c) reduce the classes of documents to be delivered to the Commission[5] under section 343 of this Act.

**Notes**

**Section 356**

1. "Minister" means the minister charged with responsibility for trade; and "ministry" shall be constituted accordingly. See **Section 567 CAMA, Cap. C20, LFN 2004.**
2. "Company" means a corporation - or, less commonly, an association, partnership, or union that carries on a commercial or industrial enterprise. **See Garner B. (ed.) Black's Law Dictionary 8 th ed.** "Company" means a company formed and registered under this Act or, as the case may be, formed and registered in Nigeria before and in existence on the commencement of this Act. See **Section 567 CAMA Cap. C20, LFN 2004.**
3. "Financial statement means balance sheet, income statement or annual report that summarizes an individual or organization's financial condition on a specified date. **See Garner B. (ed.) Black's Law Dictionary 8th ed.**
4. "General meeting" see "Annual meeting" – a yearly meeting to elect or install officers or directors and to conduct other routine organisational business. **See Garner B. (ed.) Black's Law Dictionary 8th ed.**
5. "Commission" means the Corporate Affairs Commission established under section 1 of this Act. See **Section 567 CAMA, Cap. C20, LFN 2004.**

Cross Reference

On preparation of group financial statements, see **section 336 CAMA Cap. C20, LFN 2004**
On statutory mandate of the Accounting Standard Board, see generally **Nigerian Accounting Standard Board Act, 2003.**
On the appointment of Ministers, See **section 147 of the Constitution of the Federal Republic of Nigeria 1999 as amended.**

---

## 357. Appointment of auditors

(1) Every company [1] shall at each annual general meeting [2] appoint an auditor[3] or auditors to audit the financial statements [4] of the company,[1] and to hold office from the conclusion of that, until the conclusion of the next, annual general meeting. [2]

(2)At any annual general meeting [2] a retiring auditor, [3] however appointed, shall be re-appointed without any resolution [5] being passed unless-

(a) he is not qualified for re-appointment; or

(b) a resolution [5] has been passed at that meeting appointing some other person instead of him or providing expressly that he shall not be re-appointed; or

(c) he has given the company [1] notice in writing of his unwillingness to be re-appointed:

Provided that where notice is given of an intended resolution[5] to appoint some person or persons in place of a retiring auditor, [3] and by reason of the death, incapacity or disqualification of that person or of all those persons, as the case may be, the resolution [5] cannot be proceeded with, the retiring auditor shall not be automatically re-appointed by virtue of this subsection.

(3) Where at an annual general meeting, [2] no auditors[3] are appointed or re-appointed, the directors [6] may appoint a person to fill the vacancy.

(4) The company [1] shall, within one week of the power of the directors[6] under subsection (3) of this section becoming exercisable, give notice of that fact to the Commission [7] and if a company [1] fails to give notice as required by this subsection, the company [1] and every officer[8]of the company[1] who is in default shall be guilty of an offence and liable to a fine of Nl00 for every day during which the default continues.

(5) Subject as hereinafter provided, the first auditors [3] of a company[1] may be appointed by the directors [6] at any time before the

company[1] is entitled to commence business and auditors [3] so appointed shall hold office until the conclusion of the next annual general meeting:[2]

Provided that-

(a) the company [1] may at a general meeting [2] remove any such auditors[3] and appoint in their place any other person who has been nominated for appointment by any member [9] of the company[1] and of whose nomination notice has been given to the members[9] of the company[1] not less than 14 days before the date of the meeting; [2] and

(b) if the directors [6] fail to exercise their powers under this subsection; the company[1] may, in a general meeting [2] convened for that purpose, appoint the first auditors [3] and thereupon the said powers of the directors [6] shall cease.

(6) The directors [6] may fill any casual vacancy in the office of auditor[3] but while any such vacancy continues, the surviving or continuing auditor[3] or auditors, if any, may act.

---

**Notes**

**Section 357 (1)**

1. "Company" means a corporation - or, less commonly, an association, partnership, or union that carries on a commercial or industrial enterprise. **See Garner B. (ed.) Black's Law Dictionary 8 th ed.**
   "Company" means a company formed and registered under this Act or, as the case may be, formed and registered in Nigeria before and in existence on the commencement of this Act. See **Section 567 CAMA, Cap C20, LFN 2004.**
2. "General Meeting" see "Annual meeting" – a yearly meeting to elect or install officers or directors and to conduct other routine organisational business. **See Garner B. (ed.) Black's Law Dictionary 8th ed.**
3. "Auditor" means a person or firm, usually an accountant that formally examines an individual or an entity's financial records or status. **Garner B. (ed.) Black's Law Dictionary 8 th ed.**
4. "Financial Statements" means balance sheet, income statement or annual report that summarizes an individual or organization's financial condition on a specified date. **Garner B. (ed.) Black's Law Dictionary 8th ed.**
5. "Resolution" means formal action by a corporate board of directors or other corporate body authorizing a particular act transaction or appointment. See **Garner B. (ed.) Black's Law Dictionary 8 th ed.**
6. "Director" includes any person occupying the position of director by whatever name called; and includes any person in accordance with

whose directions or instructions the directors of the company are accustomed to act. See **Section 567 CAMA, Cap. C20, LFN 2004.**

7. "Commission" means the Corporate Affairs Commission established under section 1 of this Act. See **Section 567 CAMA, Cap. C20, LFN 2004.**

8. "Officers" see "officer". In relation to a body corporate, includes a director, manager or secretary. See **Section 567 CAMA, Cap. C20, LFN 2004.**

9. "Member" includes the heir, executive, administrator or other personal representative, as the case maybe, of the member . **See Section 567 CAMA, Cap. C20, LFN 2004.**

**Cross References**

On preparation of group financial statements, see **section 336 CAMA Cap. C20, LFN 2004**

On statutory mandate of the Accounting Standard Board, see generally **Nigerian Accounting Standard Board Act, 2003.**

On the appointment of Ministers, See **section 147 of the Constitution of the Federal Republic of Nigeria 1999 as amended.**

---

**Cases**

Generally companies speak or express their decisions through resolutions, which must be validly passed. No member of a company has a right to unilaterally commit the company on any matter without its consent and approval. Let me emphatically say that no member of a company is allowed to wake up one morning and sell off the company. ***New Resources Int'l Ltd. & Anor. v. Ejike Oranusi (2010) LPELR-CA/L/461/08.***

## 358. Qualification of auditors

(1) The provisions of the Institute of Chartered Accountants of Nigeria Act shall have effect in relation to any investigation or audit for the purpose of this Act so however that none of the following persons shall be qualified for appointment as auditor [1] of a company,[2] that is-

[Cap. 111.]

(a) an officer[3] or servant of the company; [2]

(b) a person who is a partner of or in the employment of an officer[3] or servant of the company; [2] or

(c) a body corporate, [4]

[1990 No. 32.]

and references in the subsection to an officer [3] or servant shall be construed as not including references to an auditor. [1]

(2) In the application of subsection (1) of this section, the disqualification shall extend and apply to persons who in respect of any period of an audit were in the employment of the company or were otherwise connected therewith in any manner.

(3) A person shall also not qualify for appointment as an auditor[1] of a company[2] if he is, under subsection (6) of this section, disqualified for appointment as auditor[2] of any other body corporate[4] which is that company's[2] subsidiary[5] or holding company[6] or a subsidiary[5] of that company's[2] holding company,[6] or would be so disqualified if the body corporate[4] were a company.[2]

(4) Notwithstanding subsections (1), (2) and (3), of this section, a firm is qualified for appointment as auditor[1] of a company[2] if, but only if, all the partners are qualified for appointment as auditors[1] of it.

(5) No person shall act as auditor[1] of a company[2] at a time when he knows that he is disqualified for appointment to that office and if an auditor[1] of a company[2] to his knowledge becomes so disqualified during his term of office, he shall thereupon vacate his office and give notice in writing to the company that he has vacated it by reason of that disqualification.

(6) A person who acts as auditor[1] in contravention of subsection (5), of this section or fails without reasonable excuse to give notice of vacating his office as required by that subsection, shall be guilty of an offence and liable to a fine of N500 and, for continued contravention, to a daily default fine of N50.

---

**Notes**
**Section 358**

"Auditor" means a person or firm usually an accountant or an accounting firm that formally examines an individuals or entity's financial record or status. **See Garner B. (ed.) Black's Law Dictionary 8th ed.**

1. "Company" means a company formed and registered under this Act or, as the case may be, formed and registered in Nigeria before and in existence on the commencement of this Act. **See Section 567 CAMA, Cap. C20, LFN 2004.**
2. "Officer" in relation to a body corporate, includes a director, manager or secretary. See **Section 567 CAMA, Cap. C20, LFN 2004.**
3. "Body corporate" see corporation. An entity (usu. A business) having authority under law to act as a single person distinct from the shareholders who own it and having rights to issue stock and exist indefinitely; a group or succession of persons established in accordance

with legal rules into a legal or juristic person that has a legal personality distinct from the natural persons who make it up, exists indefinitely apart from them, and has the legal powers that its constitution gives it. **See Garner B. (ed.) Black's Law Dictionary 8 th ed.**

4. "Subsidiary" in relation to a body corporate, is as defined by section 338 of this Act. See **Section 567 CAMA, Cap. C20, LFN 2004.**
5. "Holding company" means a holding company as defined by section 338 of this Act. **See section 567 CAMA, Cap. C20, LFN 2004.**

**Cross Reference**

As to when persons are deemed to practice as accountants generally, see **section 14, Institute of Chartered Accountants of Nigeria (ICAN) Act Cap. I11, LFN, 2004.**

---

**Cases**

On relationship between a subsidiary and holding company

It is trite that the relationship between a parent and subsidiary company is apposite to agency. See ***Opuo v NNPC(2001)14 NWLR***

**or Further Reading**

On holding company and its subsidiaries, see, Oserheimen A. Osunbor "The Agent-Only Subsidiary Company and The Control of Multinational Groups", **The International and Comparative law Quaterly,** Vol. 38, No. 2 (Apr; 1989), pp 377 -387 published by Cambridge university press.

## 359. Auditors' report

(1) The auditors [1] of a company[2] shall make a report to its members[3] on the accounts[4] examined by them, and on every balance sheet[5] and profit and loss account, and on all group financial statements,[6] copies of which are to be laid before the company[2] in a general meeting[7] during the auditors' [1] tenure of office.

(2) The auditors' [1] report shall state the matters set out in the Sixth Schedule to this Act.

(3) In addition to the report made under subsection (1) of this section, the auditor[1] shall in the case of a public company [8] also make a report to an audit committee [9] which shall be established by the public company.[8]

(4) The audit committee[9] referred to in subsection (3) of this section, shall consist of an equal number of directors [10] and representatives of the shareholders [11] of the company[2] (subject to a maximum number of six members [3]) and shall examine the

auditors'[1] report and make recommendations thereon to the annual general meeting[7] as it may think fit:

Provided, however, that such member of the audit committee [9] shall not be entitled to remuneration and shall be subject to re-election annually.

(5) Any member may nominate a shareholder [11] as a member[3] of the audit committee[9] by giving notice in writing of such nomination to the secretary [12] of the company[2] at least 21 days before the annual general meeting. [7]

(6) Subject to such other additional functions and powers that the company's [2] articles of association [13] may stipulate, the objectives and functions of the audit committee [9] shall be to-

(a) ascertain whether the accounting and reporting policies of the company[2] are in accordance with legal requirements and agreed ethical practices;

(b) review the scope and planning of audit requirements;

(c) review the findings on management matters in conjunction with the external auditor [1] and departmental responses thereon;

(d) keep under review the effectiveness of the company's [2] system of accounting and internal control;

(e) make recommendations to the Board [14] in regard to the appointment, removal and remuneration of the external auditors[1] of the company; [2] and

(f) authorise the internal auditor [1] to carry out investigations into any activities of the company [2] which may be of interest or concern to the committee. [9]

---

**Notes**
**Section 359**

1. "Auditors" see "auditor." It means a person or firm usually an accountant or an accounting firm that formally examines an individuals or entity's financial record or status. See **Garner B. (ed) Black's Law Dictionary 8th ed.**
2. "Company" means a corporation - or, less commonly, an association, partnership, or union that carries on a commercial or industrial enterprise.See **Garner B. (ed) Black's Law Dictionary 8 th ed.**
   " Company" means a company formed and registered under this Act or, as the case may be, formed and registered in Nigeria before and in existence on the commencement of this Act **. See Section 567 CAMA, Cap. C20, LFN 2004.**

3. "Members" see "member". It includes the heir, executive, administrator or other personal representative, as the case maybe, of the member.See **Section 567 CAMA, Cap. C20, LFN 2004** .
4. "Accounts" includes a company's group accounts, whether prepared in the form of accounts or not. See **section 567 CAMA, Cap. C20, LFN 2004**.
5. "Balance sheet" means a statement of an entity's current financial position, disclosing the value of the entity's asset, liabilities and owner's equity. See **Garner B. (ed) Black's Law Dictionary 8 th ed.**
6. "Group financial statements" means financial statements being accounts or statements which deal with the state of affairs and profit or loss of the company and the subsidiaries. **See section 336(1) CAMA, Cap/ C20, LFN 2004** .
7. "General meeting" see "Annual meeting" – a yearly meeting to elect or install officers or directors and to conduct other routine organizational business. See **Garner B. (ed) Black's Law Dictionary 8th ed.**
8. "Public company" any company other company other than a private company shall be a public company and its memorandum shall state that it is a public company. **See section 24 CAMA, Cap. C20, LFN 2004.**
9. "Audit committee" means a committee appointed by the board of an organization especially a corporation to oversee the financial reporting process, select an independent auditor and receive the audit . **See Garner B. (ed) Black's Law Dictionary 8 th ed.**
10. "Directors" see "director". It includes any person occupying the position of director by whatever name called; and includes any person in accordance with whose directions or instructions the directors of the company are accustomed to act; **Section 567 CAMA, Cap. C20, LFN 2004.**
11. "Shareholder" one who owns or holds a share or shares in a company especially a corporation **Garner B. (ed) Black's Law Dictionary 8 th ed.**
12. "Secretary" means a corporate officer in charge of official correspondence, minutes of board meetings, and records of stock ownership and transfer(3) an officer charged with recording a deliberative assembly's proceedings. See **Garner B. (ed) Black's Law Dictionary 8th ed.**
13. "Articles of Association" means the articles of association of a company, as originally framed or as altered by special resolution including so far as they apply to the regulations contained in Table A in the first schedules of the Companies Act, 1922 or in that Table as altered by any subsequent enactment or reprint of the Laws, or in Table A in schedule 1 to this Act' **see section 567 CAMA, Cap. C20, LFN 2004.**
14. "Board" see "board of directors." It means the governing body of a corporation, elected by the shareholders to establish corporate policy, appoint executive officers, and make major business and financial decisions. See **Garner B. (ed.) Black's Law Dictionary 8 th ed.**

**Cross Reference**

On statutory power of Nigerian Accounting Standard Board to alter accounting requirements, see **section 356 CAMA** and section 6, **Nigerian Accounting Standard Board Act, 2003.**

**For Further Reading**

On the functions of an auditor, see Anifalaje, J. O. "Current Principles & Policies on Company Accounts," **Essays on Company Law**

## 360. Auditors' duties and powers

(1) It shall be the duty of the company's [1] auditors,[2] in preparing their report to carry out such investigations as may enable them to form an opinion as to the following matters whether-

(a) proper accounting records have been kept by the company[1] and proper returns adequate for their audit have been received from branches not visited by them;

(b) the company's [1] balance sheet[3] and (if not consolidated) its profit and loss account are in agreement with the accounting records and returns.

(2) If the auditors [2] are of opinion that proper accounting records have not been received from branches not visited by them, or if the balance sheet [3] and (if not consolidated) the profit and loss account are not in agreement with the accounting records and returns, the auditors [2] shall state that fact in their report.

(3) Every auditor [2] of a company [1] shall have a right of access at all times to the company's [1] books, accounts [4] and vouchers, and be entitled to require from the company's [1] office such information and explanations as he thinks necessary for the performance of the auditor's [2] duties.

(4) If the requirements of Part V and VI of the Third Schedule and Parts I to III of the Fourth Schedule to this Act are not complied with in the accounts, [4] it shall be the auditors' [2] duty to include in their report, so far as they are reasonably able to do so, a statement giving the required particulars.

[Third Schedule. Fourth Schedule.]

(5) It shall be the auditors' [2] duty to consider whether the information given in the directors' [5] report for the year for which the accounts[4] are prepared is consistent with those accounts; [4] and if they are of opinion that it is not, they shall state that fact in their report.

---

**Notes**
**Section 360**

1. "Company" means a corporation - or, less commonly, an association, partnership, or union that carries on a commercial or industrial enterprise. See **Garner B. (ed) Black's Law Dictionary 8 th ed**.
   "Company" means a company formed and registered under this Act or, as the case may be, formed and registered in Nigeria before and in existence on the commencement of this Act. See section **567 CAMA, Cap. C20, LFN 2004.**
2. "Auditors" see "auditor." It means a person or firm usually an accountant or an accounting firm that formally examines an individuals or entity's financial record or status. See **Garner B. (ed) Black's Law Dictionary 8th ed.**
3. "Balance sheet" means a statement of an entity's current financial position, disclosing the value of the entity's asset, liabilities and owner's equity. See **Garner B. (ed) Black's Law Dictionary 8 th ed.**
4. "Accounts" includes a company's group accounts, whether prepared in the form of accounts or not. See **section 567 CAMA, Cap. C20, LFN 2004.**
5. "Directors" means (1) one who manages, guides, or orders; a chief administrator (2) a person appointed or elected to sit on a board that manages the affairs of a corporation or other organisation by electing and exercising control over its officers.See **Garner B. (ed) Black's Law Dictionary 8th ed.**
6. "Director" includes any person occupying the position of director by whatever name called; and includes any person in accordance with whose directions or instructions the directors of the company are accustomed to act. See **section 567 CAMA, Cap. C20, LFN 2004.**

**Cross Reference**

On duty of company to ensure preparation of auditor's report, see **section 359, CAMA, Cap. C20 LFN 2004**

On obligation of director to prepare director's report see **section 342, CAMA, Cap C20, LFN 2004.**

---

## 361. Remuneration of auditors

(1) The remuneration of the auditors of a company-

(a) in the case of an auditor [1] appointed by the directors, [2] may be fixed by the directors; [2] or

(b) shall, subject to the foregoing paragraph, be fixed by the company[3] in general meeting[4] or in such manner as the company[3] in general meeting[4] may determine.

(2) For the purposes of subsection (7) of this section, "remuneration" includes sums paid by the company [3] in respect of the auditors' [1] expenses.

---

**Notes**
**Section 361**

1. "Auditor" A person or firm usually an accountant or an accounting firm that formally examines an individuals or entity's financial record or status. See **Garner B. (ed) Black's Law Dictionary 8 th ed.**
2. "Directors" means (1) one who manages, guides, or orders; a chief administrator (2) a person appointed or elected to sit on a board that manages the affairs of a corporation or other organisation by electing and exercising control over its officer. See **Garner B. (ed) Black's Law Dictionary 8th ed.**
   "Director" includes any person occupying the position of director by whatever name called; and includes any person in accordance with whose directions or instructions the directors of the company are accustomed to act. See **Section 567 CAMA, Cap. C20, LFN 2004.**
3. "Company" mean a corporation - or, less commonly, an association, partnership, or union that carries on a commercial or industrial enterprise. See **Garner B. (ed) Black's Law Dictionary 8 th ed.**
   "Company" or "existing company" means a company formed and registered under this Act or, as the case may be, formed and registered in Nigeria before and in existence on the commencement of this Act. See **Section 567 CAMA, Cap. C20, LFN 2004.**
4. "General meeting" see "Annual meeting" – a yearly meeting to elect or install officers or directors and to conduct other routine organisational businesss. See **Garner B. (ed) Black's Law Dictionary 8th ed.**

---

## 362. Removal of auditors

(1) A company [1] may by ordinary resolution [2] remove an auditor[3] before the expiration of his term of office, notwithstanding anything in any agreement between it and him.

(2) Where a resolution [2] removing an auditor [3] is passed at a general meeting[4] of a company, [1] the company[1] shall within 14 days give notice of that fact in the prescribed form to the Commission [5] and if a company[1] fails to give the notice required by this subsection, the company [1] and every officer [6] of it who is in default shall be guilty of an offence and liable to a daily default fine of N100.

(3) Nothing in this section shall be taken as depriving a person removed under it of compensation or damages payable to him in respect of the termination of his appointment as auditor [3] or of any appointment terminating with that as auditor. [3]

---

**Notes**
**Section 362**

1. "Company" means a corporation - or, less commonly, an association, partnership, or union that carries on a commercial or industrial enterprise. See **Garner B. (ed) Black's Law Dictionary 8th ed.**
   "Company" means a company formed and registered under this Act or, as the case may be, formed and registered in Nigeria before and in existence on the commencement of this Act. **See Section 567 CAMA, Cap. C20, LFN 2004.**
2. "Ordinary Resolution" means formal action by a corporate board of directors or other corporate body authorizing a particular act transaction or appointment. See **Garner B. (ed) Black's Law Dictionary 8th ed.**
3. "Auditor" means a person or firm usually an accountant or an accounting firm that formally examines an individuals or entity's financial record or status.See **Garner B. (ed) Black's Law Dictionary 8th ed.**
4. "General meeting" see "Annual meeting" – a yearly meeting to elect or install officers or directors and to conduct other routine organisational business. See **Garner B. (ed) Black's Law Dictionary 8th ed.**
5. "Commission" means the Corporate Affairs Commission established under section 1 of this Act. **See Section 567 CAMA, Cap. C20, LFN 2004.**
6. "Officer" in relation to a body corporate, includes a director, manager or secretary. **See section 567 CAMA, Cap. C20, LFN 2004.**

**Cross Reference**

On meaning of offence, see **section 2, Criminal Code, Cap. C38, LFN 2004**
On appointment of auditors, see **section 357 CAMA Cap. C20, LFN 2004**
On types of resolutions, see **section 233 CAMA Cap. C20 LFN 2004**

---

For further reading on auditors and auditors liability , see Chua, S. **"The Auditors' Liability in Negligence in respect of Auditors' report"** Business Law Journal 1995, pg. 1

## 363. Auditors' right to attend company's meetings

(1) A company's [1] auditors[2] shall be entitled to attend any general meeting[3] of the company[1] and to receive all notices of and other communications relating to any general meeting [3] which a

member[4] of the company[1] is entitled to receive and to be heard at any general meeting[3] which they attend on any part of the business of the meeting[3] which concerns them as auditor.[2]

(2) An auditor[2] of a company[2] who has been removed shall be entitled to attend-

(a) the general meeting[3] at which his term of office would otherwise have expired; and

(b) any general meeting[3] at which it is proposed to fill the vacancy caused by his removal, and to receive all notices of, and other communications relating to, any such meeting[3] which any member[4] of the company[1] is entitled to receive, and to be heard at any such meeting[3] which he attends on any part of the business of the meeting[3] which concerns him as former auditor[2] of the company.[1]

---

**Notes**
**Section 363(1)**

1. "Company" mean a corporation - or, less commonly, an association, partnership, or union that carries on a commercial or industrial enterprise. See **Garner B. (ed) Black's Law Dictionary 8 th ed.** "Company" or "existing company" means a company formed and registered under this Act or, as the case may be, formed and registered in Nigeria before and in existence on the commencement of this Act. See **section 567 CAMA, Cap. C20, LFN 2004.**
2. "Auditors" A person or firm usually an accountant or an accounting firm that formally examines an individuals or entity's financial record or status. See **Garner B, (ed) Black's Law Dictionary 8 th ed.**
3. "General meeting" see "Annual meeting" – a yearly meeting to elect or install officers or directors and to conduct other routine organisational business. See **Garner B. (ed) Black's Law Dictionary 8th ed.**
4. "Member" includes the heir, executive, administrator or other personal representative,as the case maybe, of the member. See **section 567 CAMA, Cap. C20, LFN 2004.**

**Cross Reference**

On obligation to provide notice and length of notice for meeting, see **section 217, CAMA, Cap. C20, LFN 2004.**

On appointment of auditors, see **section 357 CAMA Cap. C20, LFN 2004**

---

## 364. Supplementary provisions relating to auditors

(1) A special notice shall be required for a resolution[1] at a general meeting[2] of a company-[3]

(a) appointing as auditor[4] a person other than a retiring auditor;[4] or

(b) filling a casual vacancy in the office of auditor; [4] or

(c) re-appointing as auditor[4] a retiring auditor[4] who was appointed by the directors to fill a casual vacancy; or

(d) removing an auditor[4] before the expiration of his term of office.

(2) On receipt of notice of such an intended resolution [1] as is mentioned in subsection (1), the company[3] shall forthwith send a copy of it-

(a) to the person proposed to be appointed or removed, as the case may be;

(b) in a case within subsection (1) (a) of this section, to the retiring auditors;[3] and

(c) where, in a case within subsection (1) (b) or (c) of this section, the casual vacancy was caused by the resignation of an auditor,[3] to the auditor[3] who resigned.

(3) Where notice is given of such a resolution [1] as is mentioned in subsection (1) (a) or (d) of this section and the retiring auditor[4] (or, as the case may be, the auditor [4] proposed to be removed) makes with respect to the intended resolution [1] representations in writing to the company[3] not exceeding a reasonable length, and requests their notification to members [5] of the company,[3] the company[3] shall (unless the representations are received by it too late for it to do so)-

(a) in any notice of the resolution [1] given to members[5] of the company,[3] state the fact of the representations having been made; and

(b) send a copy of the representations to every member [5] of the company[3] to whom notice of the meeting is or has been sent.

(4) If a copy of any such representations is not sent out as required by subsection (3) of this section because they were received too late or because of the company's [3] default, the auditor[4] may (without prejudice to his right to be heard orally) require that the representations shall be read out at the meeting. [2]

(5) Copies of the representations need not be sent out and the representations need not be read out at the meeting [2] if, on the application either of the company[3] or of any other person claiming to be aggrieved, the court [6] is satisfied that the rights conferred by

this section are being abused to secure needless publicity for defamatory matter; and the court [6] may order the company's [3] costs on the application to be paid in whole or in part by the auditor, [4] notwithstanding that he is not a party to the application.

---

**Notes**
**Section 364**

1. "Resolution" means formal action by a corporate board of directors or other corporate body authorizing a particular act transaction or appointment. See **Garner B. (ed) Black's Law Dictionary 8 th ed.**
2. "General meeting" see "Annual meeting" – a yearly meeting to elect or install officers or directors and to conduct other routine organisational business. See **Garner B. (ed) Black's Law Dictionary 8th ed.**
3. "Company" means a corporation - or, less commonly, an association, partnership, or union that carries on a commercial or industrial enterprise. See **Garner B. (ed) Black's Law Dictionary 8 th ed.** "Company" means a company formed and registered under this Act or, as the case may be, formed and registered in Nigeria before and in existence on the commencement of this Act. **See section 567 CAMA, Cap. C20, LFN 2004.**
4. "Auditor" means person or firm usually an accountant or an accounting firm that formally examines an individuals or entity's financial record or status. See **Garner B. (ed) Black's Law Dictionary 8th ed.**
5. "Members" see "member." It includes the heir, executive, administrator or other personal representative, as the case maybe, of the member. **See section 567 CAMA, Cap. C20, LFN 2004** .
6. "Court" used in relation to a company, means the Federal High Court, and to the extent to which application may be made to it as; court includes the Court of Appeal and the Supreme Court of Nigeria **. See section 567 CAMA, Cap. C20, LFN 2004.**

Cross Reference

On establishment and jurisdiction of the Federal High Court, see **section 249 & 251 Constitution of the Federal Republic of Nigeria, 1999** (as amended)

---

**For Further Reading**

On auditors and auditors liability **, see Chua, S. "The Auditors' Liability in Negligence in respect of Auditors' report" Business Law Journal 1995, pg. 1**

## 365. Resignation of auditors

(1) An auditor[1] of a company[2] may resign his office by depositing a notice in writing to that effect at the company's [2] registered office;[3] and any such notice shall operate to bring his term of office to an end on the date of which the notice is deposited, or on such later date as may be specified in it.

(2) An auditor's [1] notice of resignation shall not be effective unless it contains either-

(a) a statement to the effect that there are no circumstances connected with his resignation which he considers should be brought to the notice of the members [4] or creditors[5] of the company;[2] or

(b) a statement of any such circumstances as are mentioned above.

(3) Where a notice under this section is deposited at a company's[2] registered office,[3] the company shall within 14 days send a copy of the notice-

(a) to the Commission;[5] and

(b) if the notice contained a statement under subsection (2) (b) of this section, to every person who under section 344 of this Act is entitled to be sent copies of the financial statements.[6]

(4) The company[2] or any person claiming to be aggrieved may, within 14 days of the receipt by the company of a notice containing a statement under subsection (2) (b) of this section, apply to the court[7] for an order under subsection (5) of this section.

(5) If on such an application the court [7] is satisfied that the auditor[1] is using the notice to secure needless publicity for defamatory matter, it may, by order, direct that copies of the notice need not be sent out; and the court [7] may further order the company's[2] costs on the application to be paid in whole or in part by the auditor,[1] notwithstanding that he is not a party to the application.

(6) The company[2] shall, within 14 days of the court's [7] decision, send to the persons mentioned in subsection (3) of this section-

(a) if the court[7] makes an order under subsection (5) of this section, a statement setting out the effect of the order;

(b) if not, a copy of the notice containing the statement under subsection (2) (b) of this section.

(7) If default is made in complying with the provisions of subsection (3) or (6) of this section, the company and every officer

of it who is in default shall be guilty of an offence and liable to a daily default fine ofN100.

---

**Notes**

**Section 365**

1. "Auditor" means a person or firm usually an accountant or an accounting firm that formally examines an individuals or entity's financial record or status. See **Garner B. (ed) Black's Law Dictionary 8th ed.**
2. "Company" means a corporation - or, less commonly, an association, partnership, or union that carries on a commercial or industrial enterprise. See **Garner B. (ed) Black's Law Dictionary 8 th ed.**
   "Company" or "existing company" means a company formed and registered under this Act or, as the case may be, formed and registered in Nigeria before and in existence on the commencement of this Act . **Section 567 Cap. C20, LFN 2004.**
3. "Registered office" means the official address of a registered company. It must be notified to the Companies Registry before registration of the company and it must appear on company letter-head and order forms. Documents may be served to a company's registered office and various registers and records may be inspected there.See **Martins E. (ed.) Oxford Dictionary of Law 4 th ed.**
4. "Member" includes the heir, executive, administrator or other personal representative,as the case maybe, of the member. See **Section 567 CAMA, Cap. C20, LFN 2004.**
5. "Commission" means the Corporate Affairs Commission established under section 1 of this Act . **See section 567 CAMA, Cap. C20, LFN 2004.**
6. "Financial statements" means balance sheet, income statement or annual report that summarizes an individual or organization's financial condition on a specified date. **Garner B. (ed) Black's Law Dictionary 8 th ed.**
7. "Court" used in relation to a company, means the Federal High Court, and to the extent to which application may be made to it as; court includes the Court of Appeal and the Supreme Court of Nigeria. See **Section 567 CAMA, Cap. C20, LFN 2004.**

**Cross Reference**

On the establishment and jurisdiction of the Federal High Court, see **sections 249 & 251, Constitution of the Federal republic of Nigeria, 1999( as amended)**

On meaning of offence, see **section 2, Criminal Code, Cap. C38, LFN 2004**

On preparation of group financial statmeents, see **section 336 CAMA Cap. C20, LFN 2004**

---

**For Further Reading**

On auditors and auditors liability, **see Chua, S., "The Auditors' Liability in Negligence in respect of Auditors' report" Business Law Journal 1995, pg. 1**

**366. Right of resigning auditor to requisition company meeting**

(1) Where an auditor's [1] notice of resignation contains a statement under section 365 (2) (b) of this Act, there may be deposited with the notice a requisition signed by the auditor [1] calling on the directors [2] of the company [3] forthwith duly to convene an extraordinary general meeting [4] of the company [3] for the purpose of receiving and considering such explanation of the circumstances connected with his resignation as he may wish to place before the meeting.[4]

(2) Where an auditor's [1] notice of resignation contains such a statement, the auditor may request the company [3] to circulate to its members [5] before-

(a) the general meeting [6] at which his term of office would otherwise have expired; or

(b) any general meeting [6] at which it is proposed to fill the vacancy caused by his resignation or convened on his requisition, a statement in writing (not exceeding a reasonable length) of the circumstances connected with his resignation.

(3) If a resigning auditor [1] requests the circulation of a statement by virtue of subsection (2) of this section, the company shall (unless the statement is received by it too late for it to comply)-

(a) in any notice of the meeting [4] given to members [5] of the company,[3] state the fact of the statement having been made; and

(b) send a copy of the statement to every member [5] of the company [3] to whom notice of the meeting [4] is or has been sent.

(4) If the directors [2] do not within 21 days from the date of the deposit of a requisition under this section proceed duly to convene a meeting [4] for a day not more than 28 days after the date on which the notice convening the meeting [4] is given, every director [2] who fails to take all reasonable steps to secure that a meeting [4] is convened as mentioned above shall be guilty of an offence and liable to a fine of N500.

(5) If a copy of the statement mentioned in subsection (2) of this section is not sent out as required by subsection (3) of this

section because it was received too late or because of the company's[3] default, the auditor[1] may (without prejudice to his right to be heard orally) require that the statement shall be read out at the meeting.[4]

(6) Copies of a statement need not be sent out and the statement need not be read out at the meeting[4] if, on the application either of the company[3] or of any other person who claims to be aggrieved, the court[6] is satisfied that the rights conferred by this section are being abused to secure needless publicity for defamatory matter; and the court[6] may order the company's[3] costs on such an application to be paid in whole or in part by the auditor,[1] notwithstanding that he is not a party to the application.

(7) An auditor[1] who has resigned his office shall be entitled to attend any such meeting[4] as is mentioned in subsection (2) (a) or (b) of this section and to receive all notices of and other communications relating to any such meeting[4] which any member[5] of the company[3] is entitled to receive, and to be heard at any such meeting[4] which concerns him as former auditor[1] of the company.[3]

---

**Notes**
**Section 366**

1. "Auditor" means a person or firm usually an accountant or an accounting firm that formally examines an individuals or entity's financial record or status. See **Garner B. (ed) Black's Law Dictionary 8th ed.**
2. "Directors" means (1) one who manages, guides, or orders; a chief administrator (2) a person appointed or elected to sit on a board that manages the affairs of a corporation or other organisation by electing and exercising control over its officers. See **Garner B. (ed) Black's Law Dictionary 8th ed.**
   "Director" includes any person occupying the position of director by whatever name called; and includes any person in accordance with whose directions or instructions the directors of the company are accustomed to act.See **Section 567 CAMA, Cap. C20, LFN 2004.**
3. "Company" means a corporation - or, less commonly, an association, partnership, or union that carries on a commercial or industrial enterprise. **Garner B. (ed) Black's Law Dictionary 8th ed.**
   "Company" or "existing company" means a company formed and registered under this Act or, as the case may be, formed and registered in Nigeria before and in existence on the commencement of this Act. **Section 567 CAMA, Cap. C20, LFN 2004.**

4. Extraordinary general meeting: A meeting that is not a regular meeting. A meeting called for a special purpose.See **Garner B. (ed) Black's Law Dictionary 8th ed.**
5. "Members" includes the heir, executive, administrator or other personal representative, as the case maybe, of the member. See **Section 567 CAMA, Cap. C20, LFN 2004** .
6. "General meeting" see "Annual meeting" – a yearly meeting to elect or install officers or directors and to conduct other routine organisational business. **Garner B. (ed) Black's Law Dictionary 8 th ed.**
7. "Court" used in relation to a company , means the Federal High Court, and to the extent to which application may be made to it as; court includes the Court of Appeal and the Supreme Court of Nigeria. See **Section 567 CAMA, Cap. C20, LFN 2004.**

Cross Reference

On types of meetings, see **section 215 -217 CAMA Cap. C20, LFN 2004**
On meaning of offence, see **section 2, Criminal Code, Cap. C38, LFN 2004**

---

**For Further Reading**
On auditors and auditors liability, **see Chua, S., "The Auditors' Liability in Negligence in respect of Auditors' report" Business Law Journal 1995, pg. 1**

## 367. Powers of auditors in relation to subsidiaries

(1) Where a company has a subsidiary, then-

(a) if the subsidiary [1] is a body corporate [2] incorporated[3] in Nigeria it shall be the duty of the subsidiaries [1] and its auditors[4] to give the auditors [4] of the holding company[5] such information and explanation as those auditors [4] may reasonably require for the purposes of their duties as auditors[4] of the holding company; [5]

(b) in any other case, it shall be the duty of the holding company,[5] if required by its auditors [4] to do so, to take all such steps as are reasonably open to it to obtain from the subsidiary[1] such information and explanation as are mentioned above.

(2) If a subsidiary [1] or holding company [5] fails to comply with the provisions of subsection (1) of this section, the subsidiary [1] or holding company,[5] and every officer [6] of it who is in default, shall be guilty of an offence and liable to a fine; and if an auditor [4] fails without reasonable excuse to comply with paragraph (a) of the subsection, he shall be guilty of an offence and so liable.

---

**Notes**
**Section 367**

1. "Company" Company" means a corporation - or, less commonly, an association, partnership, or union that carries on a commercial or industrial enterprise. See **Garner B. (ed) Black's Law Dictionary 8 th ed.**
   "Company" means a company formed and registered under this Act or, as the case may be, formed and registered in Nigeria before and in existence on the commencement of this Act. **See section 567 CAMA, Cap. C20, LFN 2004.**
2. "Subsidiary" subsidiary means, in relation to a body corporate, a subsidiary as defined by section 338 of this Act. **See Section 567 CAMA, Cap. C20, LFN 2004.**
3. "Body Corporate" means an entity usually a business having authority under law to act as a single person distinct from the shareholders who own it and having rights to issue stocks and exit indefinitely. See **Garner B. (ed) Black's Law Dictionary 8 th ed.**
4. "Auditors" A person or firm usually an accountant or an accounting firm that formally examines an individuals or entity's financial record or status. See **Garner B. (ed) Black's Law Dictionary 8 th ed.**
5. "Holding company" means a holding company as defined by section 338 of this Act. See **Section 567 CAMA, Cap. C20, LFN 2004.**
6. "Officer" in relation to a body corporate, includes a director, manager or secretary. **See Section 567 CAMA, Cap. C20, LFN 2004.**

---

**For Further Reading**

On holding companies and subsidiaries, see, Oserheimen A. Osunbor 'The Agent-Only Subsidiary Company and The Control of Multinational Groups', **The International and Comparative law Quaterly, Vol. 38, No. 2 (Apr; 1989),** pp 377 - 387 published by Cambridge university press.

on auditors and auditors liability, **see Chua, S. "The Auditors' Liability in Negligence in respect of Auditors' report" Business Law Journal 1995, pg. 1**

## 368. Liability of auditors for negligence

(1) A company's [1] auditor[2] shall in the performance of his duties, exercise all such care, diligence and skill as is reasonably necessary in each particular circumstance.

(2) Where a company [1] suffers loss or damage as a result of the failure of its auditor [2] to discharge the fiduciary duty imposed on him by subsection (1) of this section, the auditor [2] shall be liable for

negligence and the directors [3] may institute an action for negligence against him in the court. [4]

(3) If the directors [3] fail to institute an action against the auditor[2] under subsection (2) of this section, any member [5] may do so after the expiration of 30 days' notice to the company [1] of his intention to institute such action.

---

**Notes**
**Section 368**

1. "Company" means a corporation - or, less commonly, an association, partnership, or union that carries on a commercial or industrial enterprise. See **Garner B. (ed) Black's Law Dictionary 8 th ed.**
   "Company" means a company formed and registered under this Act or, as the case may be, formed and registered in Nigeria before and in existence on the commencement of this Act**. See section 567 CAMA, Cap. C20, LFN 2004.**
2. "Auditor" means a person or firm usually an accountant or an accounting firm that formally examines an individuals or entity's financial record or status. See **Garner B. (ed) Black's Law Dictionary 8th ed.**
3. "Directors" means a person appointed or elected to sit on a board that manages the affairs of a corporation or other organisation by electing and exercising control over its officers. See **Garner B. (ed) Black's Law Dictionary 8th ed**.
   "Director" includes any person occupying the position of director by whatever name called; and includes any person in accordance with whose directions or instructions the directors of the company are accustomed to act**. See Section 567 CAMA, Cap. C20, LFN 2004.**
4. "Court" used in relation to a company , means the Federal High Court, and to the extent to which application may be made to it as; court includes the Court of Appeal and the Supreme Court of Nigeria. See **Section 567 CAMA, Cap. C20, LFN, 2004.**
5. "Member" includes the heir, executive, administrator or other personal representative, as the case maybe, of the member. See **Section 567 CAMA, Cap. C20, LFN 2004.**

**Cross Reference**

On establishment at jurisdiction of the Federal High Court, see **sections 249 & 251 Constitution of the Federal Republic of Nigeria, 1999( as amended)**

On meaning of offence, see **section 2, Criminal Code, Cap. C38, LFN 2004**

---

**For Further Reading**

On auditors and auditors liability **, see Chua, S. "The Auditors' Liability in Negligence in respect of Auditors' report" Business Law Journal 1995, pg. 1**

## 369. False statements to auditors

(1) An officer[1] of a company[2] commits an offence if he knowingly or recklessly makes to a company's [2] auditors[3] a statement (whether written or oral) which-

(a) conveys or purports to convey any information or explanation which the auditors[3] require, or are entitled to require, as auditors [3] of the company; [2] and

(b) is misleading, false or deceptive in a material particular.

(2) A person guilty of an offence under this section shall be liable to imprisonment for one year or to a fine of N500 or both.

---

**Notes**

**Section 369**

1. "Officer" in relation to a body corporate, includes a director, manager or secretary. see **Section 567 CAMA, Cap. C20, LFN 2004.**
2. "Company" means a corporation - or, less commonly, an association, partnership, or union that carries on a commercial or industrial enterprise. See **Garner B. (ed) Black's Law Dictionary 8th ed.**

   "Company" or "existing company" means a company formed and registered under this Act or, as the case may be, formed and registered in Nigeria before and in existence on the commencement of this Act. **Section 567 CAMA, Cap. C20, LFN 2004.**
3. "Auditors" see "auditor." It means a person or firm usually an accountant or an accounting firm that formally examines an individuals or entity's financial record or status.Se **Garner B. (ed) Black's Law Dictionary 8th ed.**

Cross Reference

On meaning of offence, see **section 2, Criminal Code, Cap. C38, LFN 2004**

---

**For Further Reading**

On auditors and auditors liability **, see Chua, S. "The Auditors' Liability in Negligence in respect of Auditors' report" Business Law Journal 1995, pg. 1**

*PART XII*

*Annual returns*

## 370. Annual return by company limited by shares or guarantee

Every company[1] shall, once at least in every year[2] make and deliver to the Commission[3] an annual return[4] in the form, and containing the matters specified in sections 371, 372 or 373 of this Act as may be applicable:

Provided that a company[1] need not make a return[4] under this section either in the year[2] of its incorporation[5] or, if it is not required by section 213 of this Act to hold an annual general meeting[6] during the following year,[2] in that year.[2]

---

**Notes**

**Section 370**

1. "Company" means a corporation - or, less commonly, an association, partnership, or union that carries on a commercial or industrial enterprise. See **Garner B. (ed) Black's Law Dictionary 8th ed.** "Company" or "existing company" means a company formed and registered under this Act or, as the case may be, formed and registered in Nigeria before and in existence on the commencement of this Act. See **Section 567 CAMA, Cap. C20, LFN 2004.**
2. "Year" means a period of twelve months.See **section 18, Interpretation Act Cap. 123 LFN, 1990** .
3. "Commission" means the Corporate Affairs Commission established under section 1 of this Act. See **Section 567 CAMA, Cap. C20, LFN 2004.**
4. "Annual return" means the return required to be made, in the case of a company limited by shares under sections 371 and 372 and, in the case of a company limited by guarantee, under section 373 of the Companies and Allied matters Act.See **Section 567 CAMA, Cap. C20, LFN 2004.**
6. "Annual general meeting" means a yearly meeting to elect or install officers or directors and to conduct other routine organizational business. An organizational governing document usually specify the time and place of such a meeting. See **Garner B. (ed) Black's Law Dictionary 8th ed.**

Cross Reference

On annual return by a company having shares other than a small company, see **section 371 CAMA Cap. C20 LFN 2004**
On returns by a small company, see **section 372 CAMA Cap. C20 LFN 2004**
On returns by companies limited by guarantee, see **section 373 CAMA Cap. C20 LFN 2004**

**For Further Reading**
On annual returns, see Anifalaje, J.O., "Current Principles & Policies on Company Accounts," **Essays on Company Law,** p. 208

## 371. Annual return by company having shares other than small company

(1) The annual return [1] by a company[2] having shares[3] other than a small company[4] shall contain with respect to the registered office[5] of the company,[2] registers of members[6] and debenture holders,[7] shares[3] and debentures,[8] indebtedness, past and present members[6] and directors[9] and secretary,[10] the matters specified in Part I of the Eighth Schedule to this Act, and the said return [1] shall be in the form set out in Part II of that Schedule or as near to it as circumstances admit.
[Eighth Schedule.]

(2) Where the company[2] has converted any of its shares [3] into stock and given notice of the conversion to the Commission, [11] the list referred to in paragraph 5 of Part I of the Eighth Schedule to this Act shall state the amount of stock held by each of the existing members[6] instead of the amount of shares [3] and the particulars relating to shares[3] required by that paragraph.
[Eighth Schedule.]

(3) The return [1] may, in any year, if the return [1] for either of the two immediately preceding years has given, as at the date of that return,[1] the full particulars required by the said paragraph 5 of the Eighth Schedule to this Act, give only such particulars required by that paragraph as relate to persons ceasing to be or becoming members[6] since the date of the last return and to shares [3] transferred since that date in the amount of stock held by a member. [6]
[Eighth Schedule.]

**Notes**
**Section 371**

1. "Annual return" means the return required to be made, in the case of a company limited by shares under sections 371 and 372 and, in the case of a company limited by guarantee, under section 373 of this Act; **Section 567 CAMA, Cap. C20, LFN 2004.**
2. "Company" means a corporation - or, less commonly, an association, partnership, or union that carries on a commercial or industrial enterprise. **Garner B. (ed) Black's Law Dictionary 8 th ed.**
   "Company" or "existing company" means a company formed and registered under this Act or, as the case may be, formed and registered in Nigeria before and in existence on the commencement of this Act. **Section 567 CAMA, Cap. C20, LFN 2004.**
3. "Shares" see" share." It means the interests in a company's share capital of a member who is entitled to share in the capital or income of such company; and except where a distinction between stock and shares is expressed or implied, includes stock; **Section 567 CAMA, CAP C20, LFN 2004**.
4. "Small company" has the meaning assigned to it by section 351 of this Act. **Section 567 CAMA, Cap. C20, LFN 2004.**
5. "Registered office" means the official address of a registered company. It must be notified to the Companies Registry before registration of the company and it must appear on company letter-head and order forms. Documents may be served to a company's registered office and various registers and records may be inspected there. See **Martins E. (ed.) Oxford Dictionary of Law 4 th ed.**
6. "Members" see "member." It includes the heir, executive, administrator or other personal representative, as the case maybe, of the member. **Section 567 CAMA, Cap. C20, LFN 2004** .
7. "Debenture holders" see "debenture" and "holder". Debenture means a written acknowledgement of indebtedness by the company, setting out the terms and conditions of the indebtedness and includes debenture stock, bonds and any other securities of any company whether constituting a charge on the assets of the company or not. See **Section 567 CAMA, Cap. C20, LFN 2004.** "Holder" is one who has legal possession of a negotiable instrument and is entitled to receive payment on it. See **Garner B. (ed) Black's Law Dictionary 8 th ed.**
8. "Debenture" means a written acknowledgement of indebtedness by the company, setting out the terms and conditions of the indebtedness, and includes debenture stock, bonds and any other securities of a company whether constituting a charge on the assets of the company or not. See **Section 567 CAMA, Cap. C20, LFN 2004.**
9. "Director" includes any person occupying the position of director by whatever name called; and includes any person in accordance with whose directions or instructions the directors of the company are accustomed to act. See **Section 567 CAMA, Cap. C20, LFN 2004.**
10. "Secretary" means a corporate officer in charge of official correspondence, minutes of board meetings, and records of stock ownership and transfer(3) an officer charged with recording a deliberative assembly's proceedings . See **Garner B. (ed) Black's Law Dictionary 8th ed.**

11. "Commission" means the Corporate Affairs Commission established under section 1 of this Act. See **Section 567 CAMA, Cap. C20, LFN 2004.**

Cross Reference

On obligation to keep register of members, see **section 83, CAMA Cap. C20 LFN 2004**

On obligation to keep register of debenture holders, see **section 193, CAMA Cap. C20 LFN 2004**

On procedure for conversion of shares to stock, see **section 101, CAMA Cap. C20 LFN**

---

## 372. Annual return by small company

The annual return[1] by a small company[2] shall contain the matters specified in Part I of the Ninth Schedule to this Act and the return shall be in the form set out in Part II of that Schedule or as near to it as circumstances admit.

---

**Notes**
**Section 372**

1. "Annual return" means the return required to be made, in the case of a company limited by shares under sections 371 and 372 and, in the case of a company limited by guarantee, under section 373 of this Act. See **Section 567 CAMA C20, LFN 2004**
2. " Small Company" " has the meaning assigned to it by section 351 of this Act. **See section 567 CAMA, Cap. C20, LFN 2004**

---

## 373. Annual return by company limited by guarantee

(1) The annual return[1] by a company limited by guarantee[2] shall be in the form prescribed in the Tenth Schedule to this Act or as near to it as circumstances admit.

[Tenth Schedule.]

(2) There shall be annexed to the return[1] a statement containing particulars of the total amount of the indebtedness of the company[3] in respect of all mortgages[4] and charges[5] which are required to be registered with the Commission[6] under this Act.

(2) There shall be annexed to the return[1] a statement containing particulars of the total amount of the indebtedness of the company[3] in respect of all mortgages[4] and charges[5] which are required to be registered with the Commission[6] under this Act.

---

**Notes**
**Section 373(1)**

1. "Annual return" means the return required to be made, in the case of a company limited by shares under sections 371 and 372 and, in the case of a company limited by guarantee, under section 373 of this Act. See **Section 567 CAMA, Cap. C20, LFN 2004**
2. "Company limited by guarantee" has the meaning assigned to it by section 21 CAMA. **See section 567 CAMA, Cap C20, LFN 2004.**
3. "Company" means a corporation - or, less commonly, an association, partnership, or union that carries on a commercial or industrial enterprise. See **Garner B. (ed) Black's Law Dictionary 8th ed.** "Company" or "existing company" means a company formed and registered under this Act or, as the case may be, formed and registered in Nigeria before and in existence on the commencement of this Act. See **Section 567 CAMA, Cap. C20, LFN 2004.**
4. "Mortgages": A conveyance of title to property that is given as security for the payment of a debt or the performance of a duty and that will become void upon payment or performance according to the stipulated terms. See **Garner B. (ed) Black's Law Dictionary 8 th edition**
5. "Charge" means an encumbrance, lien or claim. See **Garner B. ed. Black's Law Dictionary 8th ed.**
6. "Commision" means the Corporate Affairs Commission established under section 1 of this Act **. See section 567 CAMA Cap. C20, LFN 2004.**

Cross Reference

On registration of a company, see generally **sections 35-37 CAMA Cap. C20 LFN 2004**

---

**For Further Reading**

On annual returns, see Anifalaje, J. O. "Current Principles & Policies on Company Accounts," Essays on Company Law, p. 208

## 374. Time for completion of annual return

The annual return [1] shall be completed within 42 days after the annual general meeting[2] for the year, [3] whether or not that meeting [2] is the first or only ordinary general meeting [2] of the company[4] in that year,[3] and the company[4] shall forthwith forward to the Commission[5] a copy signed both by a director [6] and by the secretary[7] of the company[4].

**Notes**
**Section 374**

1. "Annual Return" means the return required to be made, in the case of a company limited by shares under sections 371 and 372 and, in the case of a company limited by guarantee, under section 373 of this Act. See **section 567 CAMA Cap. C20, LFN 2004**
2. "Annual general meeting" see "Annual meeting" – a yearly meeting to elect or install officers or directors and to conduct other routine organisational business. **See Garner B. (ed) Black's Law Dictionary 8th ed.**
3. "Year" means a period of twelve months. See section 18, **Interpretation Act Cap. 123 LFN, 2004.**
4. "Company" means a company formed and registered under this Act or, as the case may be, formed and registered in Nigeria before and in existence on the commencement of this Act. **See section 567, CAMA Cap. C20, LFN 2004**
5. "Commission" means the Corporate Affairs Commission established under section 1 of this Act **. See section 567 CAMA Cap. C20, LFN 2004.**
6. "Director" means any person occupying the position of director by whatever name called; and includes any person in accordance with whose directions or instructions the directors of the company are accustomed to act; **See section 567 CAMA Cap. C20, LFN 2004**
7. "Secretary" means corporate officer in charge of official correspondence, minutes of board meetings and records of stock ownership and transfer. See **Garner B. (ed) Black's Law Dictionary, 8th Ed.**

Cross Reference

On annual return by a company having shares other than a small company, see **section 371 CAMA Cap. C20 LFN 2004**

On returns by a small company, see **section 372 CAMA Cap. C20 LFN 2004**

On returns by companies limited by guarantee, see **section 373 CAMA Cap. C20 LFN 2004**

---

**For Further Reading**

On annual returns, see Anifalaje, J. O. "Current Principles & Policies on Company Accounts", Essays on Company Law, p. 208

## 375. Documents to be annexed to annual return

(1) Subject to the provisions of section 377 of this Act, there shall be annexed to the annual return [1]-

(a) a written copy, certified both by a director [2] and by the secretary[3] of the company[4] to be a true copy, of every balance sheet[5] and profit and loss account laid before the company[4] in general meeting[6] held in the year[7] to which the return relates (including every document[8] required by law to be annexed to the balance sheet[5]); and

(b) a copy, certified as aforesaid, of the report of the auditors[9] on, and of the report of the directors[2] accompanying, each such balance sheet[5].

(2) If any such balance sheet[5] as is mentioned in subsection (1) of the section or document[8] required by law to be annexed does not comply with the requirement of the law as in force at the date of the audit[10] with respect to the form of balance sheets[5] or documents[8] aforesaid, as the case may be, there shall be made such additions to and corrections in the copy as would have been required to be made in the balance sheet[5] or document in order to comply with the requirements, and the fact that the copy has been so amended shall be stated on it.

---

**Notes**
**Section 375**

1. "Annual Return" means the return required to be made, in the case of a company limited by shares under sections 371 and 372 and, in the case of a company limited by guarantee, under section 373 of this Act. See **section 567 CAMA Cap. C20 LFN 2004.**
2. "Director" means any person occupying the position of director by whatever name called; and includes any person in accordance with whose directions or instructions the directors of the company are accustomed to act. See **section 567 CAMA Cap. C20 LFN 2004**
3. "Secretary" means a corporate officer in charge of official correspondence, minutes of board meetings and records of stock ownership and transfer. See **Garner B. (ed) Black's Law Dictionary, 8th ed**.
4. "Company" means a company formed and registered under this Act or, as the case may be, formed and registered in Nigeria before and in existence on the commencement of this Act. See **section 567 CAMA Cap. C20 LFN 2004**
5. "Balance sheet" means a statement of an entity's financial position, disclosing the value of the entity's assets, liabilities and owner equity. See **Garner B. (ed) Black's law dictionary 8 th ed**
6. "General Meeting" see "Annual meeting" – a yearly meeting to elect or install officers or directors and to conduct other routine organisational business. **See Garner B. (ed) Black's Law Dictionary 8th ed.**

7. "Year" means a period of twelve months. See **section 18 Interpretation Act Cap. 192 LFN, 2004**
8. "Document" includes summons, notice, order and other legal process, and register. See **section 567 CAMA Cap. C20 LFN 2004.**
9. "Auditors" means a person or firm usually an accountant or an accounting firm that formally examines an individuals or entity's financial record or status. See **Garner B. (ed) Black's law dictionary 8th ed.**
10. "Audit"means a formal examination of an individuals or organizations accounting records, financial situation, or compliance with some other set of standards.See **Garner B. (ed) Black's law dictionary 8th ed.**

Cross Reference

On the appointment of auditors, see **section 357 CAMA Cap. C20 LFN 2004**

On time for completion of annual return, see **section 375 CAMA Cap. C20 LFN 2004**

---

**For Further Reading**

On annual returns, see Anifalaje, J. O. "Current Principles & Policies on Company Accounts", **Essays on Company Law,** p. 208

### 376. Certificates by private company and small company in annual return

(1) A private company [1] shall send with the annual return [2] required by sections 371, 372 or 373 of this Act a certificate signed both by a director [3] and by the secretary [4] of the company [5] that the company[5] has not, since the date of the last return, or, in the case of a first return, since the date of the incorporation of the company,[5] issued any invitation to the public to subscribe for any shares[6] or debentures [7] of the company, [5] and, where the annual return[2] discloses the fact that the number of members [8] of the company[5] exceeds fifty, also a certificate so signed that the excess consists wholly of persons who under subsection (3) of section 22 of this Act are not included in reckoning the number of fifty.

(2) A small company [9] shall in addition to the certificate required under subsection (1) of this section, send with the annual return[2] a certificate signed by a director [3] and the secretary [4] that-

(a) it is a private company [1] limited by shares [6];

(b) the amount of its turn-over for that year is not more than ₦ 2 million or such amount as may be fixed by the Commission[10];

(c) its net assets value is not more than N 1 million or such amount as may be fixed by the Commission [10];

(d) none of its members [8] is an alien [11];

(e) none of its members is a Government, [12] a Government [12] agent or nominee; and

(f) the directors [3] among them hold not less than 51 per cent of the equity share [13] capital of the company. [5]

---

**Notes**
**Section 376**

1. "Private company" means one which is stated in its memorandum to be a private company. **See section 567 CAMA, Cap. C20, LFN 2004.**
2. "Annual Return" means the return required to be made, in the case of a company limited by shares under sections 371 and 372 and, in the case of a company limited by guarantee, under section 373 of this Act. **See section 567 CAMA, Cap. C20, LFN 2004.**
3. "Director": means any person occupying the position of director by whatever name called; and includes any person in accordance with whose directions or instructions the directors of the company are accustomed to act. **See section 567 CAMA, Cap. C20, LFN 2004.**
4. "Secretary" means a corporate officer in charge of official correspondence, minutes of board meetings and records of stock ownership and transfer. See. **Garner; Black's Law Dictionary, 8th Edition.**
5. **"Company"** means a company formed and registered under this Act or, as the case may be, formed and registered in Nigeria before and in existence on the commencement of this Act. See **section 567, CAMA Cap. C20, LFN 2004.**
6. "Shares" see "share." It means the interests in a company's share capital of a member who is entitled to share in the capital or income of such company; and except where a distinction between stock and shares is expressed or implied, includes stock. **See section 567 CAMA, Cap. C20, LFN 2004.**
7. "Debenture" means a written acknowledgement of indebtedness by the company, setting out the terms and conditions of the indebtedness, and includes debenture stock, bonds and any other securities of a company whether constituting a charge on the assets of the company or not. **See section 567 CAMA, Cap. C20, LFN 2004.**
8. "Members" see "member". It includes the heir, executor, administrator or other personal representative, as the case may be, of the member. **See section 567 CAMA, Cap. C20, LFN 2004.**
9. "Small Company" "has the meaning assigned to it by section 351 of this Act. See **section 567 CAMA, Cap. C20, LFN 2004.**

10. "Commission" means the Corporate Affairs Commission established under section 1 of this Act . **See section 567 CAMA Cap. C20, LFN 2004.**
11. "Alien" means a person or association, whether corporate or unincorporated, other than a Nigeria citizen or association. See s **ection 567 CAMA Cap. C20, LFN 2004**
12. "Government" includes government of the federation, or of any state, or local government council or any person who exercises power or authority on its behalf. See **section 318 Constitution of the Federal Republic of Nigeria, 1999 (as amended)**
13. "Equity Share" means a share other than a preference share; and "equity capital" shall be construed accordingly. See **section 567 CAMA, Cap. C20 LFN 2004**

**Cross Reference**

On characteristics of a private company, **see S. 376(1) CAMA, Cap. C20 LFN 2004**

On annual return by a company having shares other than a small company, see **section 371 CAMA Cap. C20 LFN 2004**

On returns by a small company, see **section 372 CAMA Cap. C20 LFN 2004**

On returns by companies limited by guarantee, see **section 373 CAMA Cap. C20 LFN 2004**

---

**For Further Reading**

On annual returns, see Anifalaje, J. O. "Current Principles & Policies on Company Accounts", **Essays on Company Law,** p. 208

## 377. Exception in certain cases of unlimited companies and small companies from requirements of section 375

(1) An unlimited company[1] shall be exempted from the requirements imposed by section 375 of this Act as to documents[2] to be annexed to the annual return[3] if, but only if-

(a) at no time during the period to which the return relates has it been, to its knowledge, the subsidiary[4] of a company[5] that was then limited and at no such time, to its knowledge, have there been held or exercisable by or on behalf of two or more companies[5] that were limited, shares[6] or powers which, had they been held or exercisable by one of them, would have made the company its subsidiary[4];

(b) at no such time has it been the holding company[7] of a company[5] that was then limited.

(2) A small company[8] shall also be exempted from the requirements imposed by section 375 of this Act provided that it complies with the provision of section 351 of this Act.

---

**Notes**
**Section 377**

1. "Unlimited company" has the meaning assigned to it by section 21(1) of this Act. **See section 567 CAMA, Cap. C20, LFN 2004.**
2. "Document" includes summons, notice, order and other legal process, and register. See **section 567 CAMA Cap. C20 LFN 2004.**
3. "Annual Returns" means the return required to be made, in the case of a company limited by shares under sections 371 and 372 and, in the case of a company limited by guarantee, under section 373 of this Act. See **section 567 CAMA CAP C20 LFN 2004.**
4. "Subsidiary" means, in relation to a body corporate, a subsidiary as defined by section 338 of this Act. See **Section 567 CAMA, CAP C20, LFN 2004.**
5. "Company" means a company formed and registered under this Act or, as the case may be, formed and registered in Nigeria before and in existence on the commencement of this Act. See **section 567, CAMA Cap. C20, LFN 2004.**
6. "Shares" see 'share." It means the interests in a company's share capital of a member who is entitled to share in the capital or income of such company; and except where a distinction between stock and shares is expressed or implied, includes stock. See **Section 567 CAMA, Cap. C20, LFN 2004.**
7. "Holding company" means a holding company as defined by section 338 of this Act.See **Section 567 CAMA, Cap. C20, LFN 2004.**
8. "Small Company" has the meaning assigned to it by section 351 of this Act. See **Section 567 CAMA, Cap. C20, LFN 2004.**

**Cross Reference**

On Characteristics of a small company, see **section 351, CAMA CAP C20, LFN 2004**

On onligation of companies to send certificate of compliance with the requirements of Annual returns to the COmmisssion, **see section 375 CAMA CAP C20, LFN 2004**

---

**For Further Reading**

On holding companies and their subsidiaries, see, Oserheimen A. Osunbor "The Agent-Only Subsidiary Company and The Control of Multinational Groups", **The International and Comparative Law Quaterly, Vol. 38, No. 2 (Apr 1989), pp 377 -387** published by Cambridge university press.

**378. Penalty for non-compliance with sections 370 to 376**

(1) If a company [1] required to comply with any of the provisions of sections 370 to 376 of this Act fails to do so, the company and every director [2] or officer [3] of the company [1] who is in default shall be guilty of an offence and liable to a fine of N 1,000 in the case of a public company [4] and N 100 in the case of a private company.[5]

(2) For the purposes of subsection (1) of this section, "officer" includes any person in accordance with those directions or instructions the directors of the company are accustomed to act.

---

Notes

Section 378

1. "Company" means a company formed and registered under this Act or, as the case may be, formed and registered in Nigeria before and in existence on the commencement of this Act. See section 567, CAMA Cap. C20, LFN 2004.
2. "Directors" : means any person occupying the position of director by whatever name called; and includes any person in accordance with whose directions or instructions the directors of the company are accustomed to act. See section 567, CAMA Cap. C20, LFN 2004.
3. "Officer" in relation to a body corporate, includes a director, manager or secretary; Section 567 CAMA, Cap. C20, LFN 2004.
   For the purpose of section 378, "officer" includes any person in accordance with those directions or instructions the directors of the company are accustomed to act. See section 378 CAMA Cap. C20, LFN 2004
4. "Public company" is any company other company other than a private company shall be a public company and its memorandum shall state that it is a public company. See section 24 CAMA, Cap. C20, LFN 2004.
5. "Private company" is one which is stated in its memorandum to be a private company. See Section 22 CAMA Cap. C20 LFN 2004

Cross Reference

On meaning of offence, see section 2, Criminal Code, Cap. C38, LFN 2004

On obligation of companies to send certificate of compliance with the requirements of Annual returns to the COmmisssion, see section 375 CAMA Cap. C20, LFN 2004

On characteristics of a private company, see section 37(1) CAMA Cap. C20, LFN 2004

On annual return by a company having shares other than a small company, see section 371 CAMA Cap. C20 LFN 2004
On returns by a small company, see section 372 CAMA Cap. C20 LFN 2004
On returns by companies limited by guarantee, see section 373 CAMA Cap. C20 LFN 2004

---

**For Further Reading**
On annual returns, see Anifalaje, J. O. "Current Principles & Policies on Company Accounts," **Essays on Company Law**, p. 208

## *PART XIII*

### *Dividends and profits*

### 379. Declaration of dividends and payment of interim dividend

(1) A company [1] may, in general meeting, [2] declare dividends [3] in respect of any year [4] or other period only on the recommendation of the directors [5].

(2) The company [1] may from time to time pay to the members [6] such interim dividends [3] as appear to the directors [5] to be justified by the profits of the company [1].

(3) The general meeting [2] shall have power to decrease the amount of dividend [3] recommended by the directors, [5] but shall have no power to increase the recommended amount.

(4) Where the recommendation of the directors [5] of a company [1] with respect to the declaration of a dividend [3] is varied in accordance with subsection (3) of this section by the company in general meeting, [2] a statement to that effect shall be included in the relevant annual return. [7]

(5) Subject to the provisions of this Act, dividends [3] shall be payable to the shareholders [8] only out of the distributable profits of the company. [1]

---

**Notes**
**Section 379**

1. "Company" means a company formed and registered under this Act or, as the case may be, formed and

registered in Nigeria before and in existence on the commencement of this Act. **See section 567, CAMA Cap. C20, LFN 2004.**

2. "General meeting"see "Annual meeting" – a yearly meeting to elect or install officers or directors and to conduct other routine organisational business. **See Garner B (ed) Black's Law Dictionary 8th ed.**
3. "Dividends" see "dividend." It means a proportion of the distributed profits of the company which may be a fixed annual percentage, as in the case of preference shares, or it may be variable according to the prosperity or other circumstances of the company, as in the case of equity shares; See **section 567, CAMA Cap. C20, LFN 2004.**
4. Year" means a period of twelve months. See **section 18 Interpretation Act Cap. 1 23 LFN, 2004**
5. "Directors": means any person occupying the position of director by whatever name called; and includes
   any person in accordance with whose directions or instructions the directors of the company are accustomed to act; **See section 567 CAMA, Cap. C20 LFN 2004**
6. "Members" includes the heir, executor, administrator or other personal representative, as the case may be, of the member. **See section 567 CAMA, Cap. C20, LFN 2004.**
7. "Annual return"means the return required to be made, in the case of a company limited by shares under sections 371 and 372 and, in the case of a company limited by guarantee, under section 373 of this Act. See **section 567 CAMA Cap, C20, LFN 2004**
8. "Shareholder" means one who owns or holds a share or shares in a company. **See Garner B. (ed) Black's Law Dictionary 8 th ed.**

**Cross Reference**

On distributable Profits of a company, see **section 380, CAMA CAP C20, LFN 2004**

**Cases**

Dividends are the payment made out of profits to shareholders of a company from time to time. ***Kotoye v. Saraki (1994) 7 NWLR. 357, 414***

**For Further Reading**

On dividends, profits of companies, see, Deji Sasegbon, Nigerian Companies And Allied Matters Law & Practice, Dsc Publications, Lagos (1st Ed.,1992)

## 380. Distributable profits

Subject to the company[1] being able to pay its debts as they fall due, the company[1] may pay dividends[2] out of the following profits-

(a) profits arising from the use of the company's property although it is a wasting asset;
(b) revenue reserves;
(c) realised profit on a fixed asset sold, but where more than one asset is sold, the net realised profit on the assets sold.

**Notes**
**Section 380**

1. "Company:" means a company formed and registered under this Act or, as the case may be, formed and registered in Nigeria before and in existence on the commencement of this Act. **See section 567, CAMA Cap. C20 LFN 2004**
2. "Dividends" A portion of a company's earnings or profits distributed pro rata to its shareholders usually in the form of cash or additional shares.means a proportion of the distributed profits of the company which may be a fixed annual percentage, as in the case of preference shares, or it may be variable according to the prosperity or other circumstances of the company, as in the case of equity shares; **See Section 567 CAMA Cap. C20 LFN 2004**

**Cross Reference**

On declaration of dividends and payment of interim dividend, **see section 379, CAMA Cap. C20, LFN 2004**

**Cases**

Dividends are the payment made out of profits to shareholders of a company from time to time. ***Kotoye v. Saraki (1994) 7 NWLR. 357, 414***

**For Further Reading**

On dividends, profits of companies, see, Deji Sasegbon, Nigerian Companies And Allied Matters Law & Practice, Dsc Publications, Lagos (1st Ed.,1992)

## 381. Restriction on declaration and payment of dividends

A company[1] shall not declare or pay dividend [2] if there are reasonable grounds for believing that the company [1] is or would be, after the payment, unable to pay its liabilities as they become due.

**Notes**
**Section 381**

1. "Company" means a company formed and registered under this Act or, as the case may be, formed and registered in Nigeria before and in

existence on the commencement of this Act. **See section 567, CAMA Cap. C20 LFN 2004**

2. "Dividend"means portion of a company's earnings or profits distributed pro rata to its shareholders usually in the form of cash or additional shares.

means a proportion of the distributed profits of the company which may be a fixed annual percentage, as in the case of preference shares, or it may be variable according to the prosperity or other circumstances of the company, as in the case of equity shares; **See S. 567 CAMA Cap. C20 LFN 2004**

**Cross Reference**

On declaration of dividends and payment of interim dividend, see **section 379, CAMA Cap. C20, LFN 2004**

On distributable Profits of a company, see **section 380, CAMA Cap. C20, LFN 2004**

---

**Cases**

Dividend is the payment made out of profits to the shareholder of a company from time to time: ***See Kotoye v Saraki (1994) 7 NWLR pt. 357, 414.***

## 382. Unclaimed dividends

(1) Where dividends[1] are returned to the company[2] unclaimed, the company[2] shall send a list of the names of the persons entitled with the notice of the next annual general meeting[3] to the members[4].

(2) After the expiration of three months of the notice mentioned in subsection (1) of this section, the company[2] may invest the unclaimed dividend[1] for its own benefit in an investment outside the company and no interest shall accrue on the dividends[1] against the company[2].

(3) Where dividends[1] have been sent to members[4] and there is an omission to send to some members[4] due to the fault of the company,[2] the dividends[1] shall earn interest at the current bank rate from three months after the date on which they ought to have been posted.

(4) For the purpose of liability, the date of posting the dividend[1] warrant shall be deemed to be the date of payment and proof of whether it has been sent is a question of fact.

---

**Notes**

**Section 382(1)**

1. "Dividends" see"dividend". It means a proportion of the distributed profits of the company which may be a fixed annual percentage, as in the case of preference shares, or it may be variable according to the prosperity or other circumstances of the company, as in the case of equity shares. **See section 567, CAMA Cap. C20 LFN 2004.**
2. "Company:" means a company formed and registered under this Act or, as the case may be, formed and registered in Nigeria before and in existence on the commencement of this Act. **See section 567, CAMA Cap. C20 LFN 2004.**
3. "Annual general meeting" see "annual meeting." It means a yearly meeting to elect or install officers or directors and to conduct other routine organisational business. **See Garner B, (ed) Black's Law Dictionary 8th ed.**
4. "Members" see "member." It includes the heir, executor, administrator or other personal representative, as the case may be, of the member. **See section 567 CAMA Cap. C20 LFN 2004**

**Cross Reference**

On declaration of dividends and payment of interim dividend, see **section 379, CAMA CAP C20, LFN 2004**

On distributable Profits of a company, see **section 380, CAMA Cap. C20, LFN 2004**

On restriction on declaratrion and payment of dividend, see **section 381 CAMA Cap. C20 LFN 2004**

---

**Cases**

Dividend is the payment made out of profits to the shareholder of a company from time to time: ***See Kotoye v Saraki (1994) 7 NWLR pt. 357,414.***

## 383. Reserve and capitalisation

(1) The directors [1] may, before recommending any dividend [2], set aside out of the profits of the company [3] such sums as they think proper as a reserve or reserves which shall, at the discretion of the directors,[1] be applicable for any purpose to which the profits of the company[3] may be properly applied, and pending such application may, at the like discretion, either be employed in the business of the company[3] or be invested in such investments (other than shares [4] of the company[3]) as the directors [1] may from time to time think fit; and the directors[1] may also without placing the same to reserve, carry forward any profits which they may think prudent not to distribute.

(2) The company [3] in general meeting [5] may upon the recommendation of the directors [1] resolve that it is desirable to capitalise any part of the amount for the time being standing to the credit of any of the company's [3] reserve accounts or to the credit of the profit and loss account or otherwise available for distribution.

(3) Such sum may be set free for distribution among the members[6] who would have been entitled to dividends [2] in the same proportions on condition that the same be not paid in cash but be applied either on or towards paying up any amounts for the time being unpaid on any shares [4] held by such members [6] respectively or paying up in full unissued shares [7] or debentures [8] of the company [3] to be allotted and distributed to creditors [9] as fully paid up.

(4) The company [3] may decide by a resolution [10] what part is to be distributed in cash or in shares [4] and the directors [1] shall give effect to such resolution. [10]

(5) Share premium account [11] and a capital redemption reserve fund may, for the purposes of this subsection, only be applied in the paying up of unissued shares [8] to be issued to members [6] of the company as fully paid bonus shares [12].

(6) Where a resolution [10] is under subsections (2) to (5) of this section passed, the directors [1] shall make all appropriations and applications of the undivided profits resolved to be capitalised thereby, and all allotments and issues of fully-paid shares [12] or debentures[8], if any, and generally do all acts and things required to give effect to it.

(7) The directors [1] shall have power to make such provision by the issue of fractional certificates or by payment in cash or otherwise as they think fit in the case of shares [4] or debentures [8] becoming distributable in fractions.

(8) Any person may be authorised by the directors [1] to enter on behalf of all the members [6] entitled under this section into an agreement with the company [3] to provide for the allotment to them respectively, credited as fully paid up, of any further shares [4] or debentures[8] to which they may be entitled upon such capitalisation, or (as the case may require) for the payment up by the company [3] on their behalf, of the amounts or any part of the amounts remaining unpaid on their existing shares [4], and any agreement made under such authority shall be effective and binding on all such members [6]

**Notes**
**Section 383**

1. "Director" includes any person occupying the position of director by whatever name called; and includes
any person in accordance with whose directions or instructions the directors of the company are accustomed to act; See section 567 CAMA Cap. C20 LFN 2004.
2. "Dividend" means a proportion of the distributed profits of the company which may be a fixed annual percentage, as in the case of preference shares, or it may be variable according to the prosperity or other circumstances of the company, as in the case of equity shares. See section 567 CAMA Cap. C20 LFN 2004
3. "Company" means a company formed and registered under this Act or, as the case may be, formed and
registered in Nigeria before and in existence on the commencement of this Act. See section 567, CAMA Cap. C20 LFN 2004.
4. "Shares" see "share." It means the interests in a company's share capital of a member who is entitled to share in the capital or income of such company; and except where a distinction between stock and shares is expressed or implied, includes stock. See S. 567 CAMA Cap. C20 LFN 2004
5. "General meeting" see "annual meeting." It means a yearly meeting to elect or install officers or directors and to conduct other routine organisational business. See Garner B. (ed) Black's Law Dictionary 8th ed.
6. "Members" see "member." It includes the heir, executor, administrator or other personal representative, as the case may be, of the member; See section **567 CAMA Cap. C20 LFN 2004**
7. "Unissued Shares" see shares. "Shares" means the interests in a company's share capital of a member who is entitled to share in the capital or income of such company; and except where a distinction between stock and shares is expressed or implied, includes stock; **See S. 567 CAMA Cap. C20 LFN 2004**
8. "Debentures" see"debenture". It means a written acknowledgement of indebtedness by the company, setting out the terms and conditions of the indebtedness, and includes debenture stock, bonds and any other securities of a company whether constituting a charge on the assets of the company or not. See **section 567 CAMA Cap. C20, LFN 2004**
9. "Creditors" see "creditor." It means one to whom a debt is owned; one who gives credit for money or goods. See **Garner B. (ed) Black's Law Dictionary, 8$^{th}$ ed.**
10. "Resolution" means a formal action by a corporate board of directors or other corporate body authorizing a particular act, transaction or appointment. See **Garner B. (ed) Black's Law Dictionary, 8 $^{th}$ ed.**
11. "Share premium account" means the amount paid by shareholders to a company on the purchase of the company's shares which is in excess of the nominal value of the shares, reflecting the market values of the

shares. It is paid into the company's share premium account. See **Sheila B. Osborne Concise Law Dictionary 9 th ed**
"Share premium account" means the account where a sum equal to the aggregate amount or value of the premium from shares issued at a premium by a company is transferred. See **section 120 (2) CAMA, Cap. C20, LFN 2004.**

12. "Fully-paid Shares" see shares, which means the interests in a company's share capital of a member who is entitled to share in the capital or income of such company; and except where a distinction between stock and shares is expressed or implied, includes stock **. See section 567 CAMA Cap. C20 LFN 2004**

---

**For Further Reading**
On directors, theirs discretions, powers, see, Bakibinga, D. J. "Directors' Duty to Act Bona Fide in the Interest of the Company" **(1990) 39 (2) The International and Comparative Law Quarterly 451.**

## 384. Employees' shares and profit sharing

If under his contract of service, an employee is entitled to share in the profits of the company [1] as an incentive, he shall be entitled to share in the profits of the company [1], whether or not dividends[2] have been declared.

---

**Notes**
**Section 384**

1. "Company:" means a company formed and registered under this Act or, as the case may be, formed and registered in Nigeria before and in existence on the commencement of this Act. **See section 567, CAMA Cap. C20 LFN 2004**
2. "Dividend:" A portion of a company's earnings or profits distributed pro rata to its shareholders usually in the form of cash or additional shares. means a proportion of the distributed profits of the company which may be a fixed annual percentage, as in the case of preference shares, or it may be variable according to the prosperity or other circumstances of the company, as in the case of equity shares; **See S. 567 CAMA Cap. C20 LFN 2004**

---

## 385.Right of the shareholders to sue for dividends

Dividends[1] shall be special debts due to, and recoverable by, shareholders[2] within 12 years, and actionable only when declared.

---

**Notes**
**Section 385**

1. "Dividends"see "dividened." It means a proportion of the distributed profits of the company which may be a fixed annual percentage, as in the case of preference shares, or it may be variable according to the prosperity or other circumstances of the company, as in the case of equity shares. **See section 567 CAMA Cap. C20 LFN 2004**
2. "Shareholder" means one who owns or holds a share or shares in a company. **See Garner B, (ed) Black's Law Dictionary 8 th ed.**

**Cross Reference**

On declaration of dividends and payment of interim dividend, see **section 379, CAMA Cap. C20, LFN 2004**

On distributable Profits of a company, see **section 380, CAMA Cap. C20, LFN 2004**

On restriction on declaratrion and payment of dividend, see **section 381 CAMA Cap. C20 LFN 2004**

---

**Cases**

Once dividend is declared, shareholders are entitled to be paid dividends in proportion to the nominal amount held and they can sue for the dividend within twelve years after being declared: ***AG Federation v. Ijewere (1980) 4 NWLR pt. 37, p. 659.***

**For Further Reading**

On shares, shareholders, see, Olufemi Amao and Kenneth Amaeshi "Galvanizing Shareholder Activism: A Prerequisite for Effective Corporate Governance and Accountability in Nigeria" **(2008) 82 Journal of Business Ethics 119-130**.

---

## 386. Liability for paying dividend out of capital

(1) All directors[1] who knowingly pay, or are party to the payment of dividend[2] out of capital[3] or otherwise in contravention of this Part of this Act, shall be personally liable jointly and severally to refund to the company[4] any amount so paid.

(2) Such directors[1] shall have the right to recover the dividend[2] from shareholders[5] who receive it with knowledge that the company[4] had no power to pay it.

---

**Notes**

**Section 386**

1. "Directors" see "director." It includes any person occupying the position of director by whatever name called; and includes any person in accordance with whose directions or instructions the directors of the company are accustomed to act. **See section 567 CAMA Cap. C20 LFN 2004**
2. "Dividend" means a proportion of the distributed profits of the company which may be a fixed annual percentage, as in the case of preference shares, or it may be variable according to the prosperity or other circumstances of the company, as in the case of equity shares; **See section 567 CAMA Cap. C20 LFN 2004**
3. "Capital" means a fund representing the nominal value of shares issued by a registered company. See **Martins E. (ed.) Oxford Dictionary of Law 4th ed**
4. "Company" means a company formed and registered under this Act or, as the case may be, formed and registered in Nigeria before and in existence on the commencement of this Act. **See section 567, CAMA Cap. C20 LFN 2004**
5. "Shareholders" see "shareholder." It means one who owns or holds a share or shares in a company. **See Garner B. (ed) Black's Law Dictionary 8th ed.**

Cross Reference

On declaration of dividends and payment of interim dividend, see **section 379, CAMA Cap. C20, LFN 2004**

On distributable Profits of a company, see **section 380, CAMA Cap. C20, LFN 2004**

On restriction on declaratrion and payment of dividend, see **section 381 CAMA Cap. C20 LFN 2004**

On right of shaewholders to sue for dividends, see **section 385 CAMA Cap. C20, LFN 2004**

---

**Cases**

Once dividend is declared, shareholders are entitled to be paid dividends in proportion to the nominal amount held and they can sue for the dividend within twelve years after being declared.See ***AG Federation v. Ijewere*** **(1980) 4 NWLR pt. 37, p. 659.**

*PART XIV*

*Receivers and managers*

*Appointment of receivers and managers*

## 387. Disqualification for appointment as a receiver or manager

(1) The following persons shall not be appointed or act as receivers[1] or managers[2] of any property ndertaking of any company[3]-

(a) an infant;

(b) any person found by a competent court [4] to be of unsound mind;

(c) a body corporate [5];

(d) an undischarged bankrupt [6], unless he shall have been given leave to act as a receiver [1] or manager[2] of the property or undertaking of the company [3] by the court[4] by which he was adjudged bankrupt; [6]

(e) a director [6]7or auditor[8] of the company[3];

(f) any person convicted of any offence involving fraud, dishonesty, official corruption or moral turpitude and who is disqualified under section 254 of this Act.

(2) Any appointment made in contravention of the provisions of subsection (1) of this section shall be void and if any of the persons named in paragraphs (c), (d), ( e) and (f) of that subsection shall act as a receiver [1] or manager, [2] he shall be guilty of an offence and liable to a fine not exceeding N2,000 in the case of a body corporate[5] or, in the case of an individual, to imprisonment for a term not exceeding six months or to a fine not exceeding N500.

(3) Where any of the persons mentioned in subsection (1) of this section is at the commencement of this Act acting as a receiver [1] or manager, [2] he may be removed by the court [4] on an application by a person interested.

---

**Notes**
**Section 387**

1. "Receiver" means a disinterested person appointed by a court, or by a corporation or other person, for the protection or collection of property that is the subject of diverse claims. See **Garner B. (ed) Black's Law Dictionary 8th ed.**
   "Receiver" includes a manager. See **section 567 CAMA, Cap. C20, LFN 2004**
2. "Manager" means one who is in charge of a corporation and in control of its business, or establishments, division, or departments, and who is vested with a certain amount of discretion and independent jugement. See **Garner B. (ed.) Black's Law Dictionary 8 th ed.**
3. "Company" means a company formed and registered under this Act or, as the case may be, formed and registered in Nigeria before and in

existence on the commencement of this Act. **See section 567, CAMA Cap. C20 LFN 2004**

4. "Court" used in relation to a company, means the Federal High Court, and to the extent to which application may be made to it as; court includes the Court of Appeal and the Supreme Court of Nigeria. See **Section 567 CAMA, Cap. C20, LFN, 2004.**
5. "Body Corporate" means entity usually a business having authority under law to act as a single person distinct from the shareholders who own it and having rights to issue stocks and exit indefinitely. See **Garner B. (ed) Black's law dictionary 8 th ed**
6. "Bankrupt" means a person who cannot meet current financial obligations; an insolvent person. See **Garner B. (ed) Black's Law Dictionary 8th ed.**
7. "Director"includes any person occupying the position of director by whatever name called; and includes any person in accordance with whose directions or instructions the directors of the company are accustomed to act. **See section 567 CAMA Cap. C20 LFN 2004.**
8. "Auditors" means a person or firm usually an accountant or an accounting firm that formally examines an individuals or entity's financial record or status. See **Garner B. (ed) Black's law dictionary 8th ed.**

**Cross Reference**

On duties of a receiver, see **section 393, CAMA Cap. C20, LFN 2004**

On appointment and duties of a director see **sections 246 & 279 CAMA Cap. C20, LFN 2004**

On appointment and duties of an auditor see s **ections 357 & 360 CAMA Cap. C30 LFN 2004**

On establishment and jurisdiction of the Federal High Court, see **sections 249 & 251 Constitution of the Federal Republic of Nigeria, 1999** (as amended)

---

**Cases**

A receiver has duty to stop business, collect the debts and release the assets. But a manager has power to continue a business or a going concern: ***Ponson Enterprise Nig. Ltd v. Njigha (2001) FWLR pt. 61 p. 3***

**For Further Reading**

On receivers, their duties, powers, see, Ephraim Madeueulosi Asomugha **Company law in Nigeria under the companies and Allied Matters Act,** (1994) E.M. Asumughai Lagos.

## 388. Power of the court to appoint official receiver for debenture holders and others

Where an application is made to the court [1] to appoint a receiver[2] on behalf of the debenture holder [3] or other creditors [4] of a company[5] which is being wound up[6] by the court,[1] an official receiver[2] may be appointed.

---

**Notes**
**Section 388**

1. "Court" used in relation to a company, means the Federal High Court, and to the extent to which application may be made to it as; court includes the Court of Appeal and the Supreme Court of Nigeria. See **Section 567 CAMA, Cap. C20, LFN, 2004.**
2. "Official receiver" means the officer by whatever name called or known charged with control of affairs in bankruptcy and if the appointment is vacant for any reason whatsoever, means the sheriff. See **section 567, CAMA Cap. C20 LFN 2004**
   For the purpose of this Act and so far as it relates to the winding up of companies by the court, "official receiver" means the Deputy Chief Registrar of the Federal High Court or an officer designated for the purpose by the Chief Judge of the Court. See **section 419 CAMA Cap. C20, LFN 2004**
3. "Debenture Holder:" "see "debenture" and "holder." Debenture means a written acknowledgement of indebtedness by the company, setting out the terms and conditions of the indebtedness and includes debenture stock, bonds and any other securities of any company whether constituting a charge on the assets of the company or not. See **section 567 CAMA, Cap. C20, LFN 2004.** "Holder" is one who has legal possession of a negotiable instrument and is entitled to receive payment on it.. See **Garner B, (ed) Black's Law Dictionary 8th ed.**
4. "Creditors" see "creditor". It means one to whom a debt is owed; one who gives credit for money or goods. See **Garner B. (ed) Black's Law Dictionary, 8th ed.**
5. "Company" means a company formed and registered under this Act or, as the case may be, formed and
   registered in Nigeria before and in existence on the commencement of this Act. **See section 567, CAMA Cap. C20 LFN 2004**
6. "Wound up" see "winding up". It the process of settling accounts and liquidating assets in anticipation of a partnership's or a corporation's dissolution. See **Garner B. (ed) Black's Law Dictionary, 8th ed.**

**Cross Reference**

On duties of receiver see **Section 393, CAMA Cap. C20, LFN 2004.**

On winding up of companies generally, **see Part XV, CAMA Cap. C20 LFN 2004**

On the establishment and jurisdiction of the Federal High Court, see **sections 249& 251 Constitution of the Federal Republic of Nigeria, 1999(as amended)**

---

**Cases**

The appointment of a receiver does not prevent the director from exercising their power as long as their acts do not threaten the assets subject to the debenture holders' charge. The directors' powers are automatically restored when receivership ends. ***Newhart Developments v. Cooperative Commercial Bank Ltd* (1978) 2 WLR 636.**

## 389. Appointment of receivers and managers by the court

(1) Notwithstanding the provisions of paragraph (d) of subsection (1) of section 209 of this Act, the court [1] may, on the application of a person interested, appoint a receiver [2] or a receiver [2] and manager[3] of the property or undertaking of a company [4] if-

(a) the principal money borrowed by the company [4] or the interest is in arrears; or

(b) the security or property of the company is in jeopardy.

(2) A receiver [2] or manager [3] of any property or undertaking of a company[4] appointed by the court [1]; shall be deemed to be an officer of the court [1] and not of the company [4] and shall act in accordance with the directions and instructions of the court [1].

---

**Notes**
**Section 389**

1. "Court" used in relation to a company, means the Federal High Court, and to the extent to which application may be made to it as; court includes the Court of Appeal and the Supreme Court of Nigeria. See **Section 567 CAMA, Cap. C20, LFN, 2004.**
2. "Receiver" means a disinterested person appointed by a court, or by a corporation or other person, for the protection or collection of property that is the subject of diverse claims. See **Garner B. (ed) Black's Law Dictionary 8th ed.**
   "Receiver" includes a manager. See **section. 567 CAMA, Cap. C20, LFN 2004.**
3. "Manager" means one who is in charge of a corporation and in control of its business, or establishments, division, or departments, and who is vested with a certain amount of discretion and independent jugement. See **Garner, B. (ed.) Black's Law Dictionary 8 th ed.**
4. "Company" means a company formed and registered under this Act or, as the case may be, formed and
   registered in Nigeria before and in existence on the commencement of this Act. **See section 567, CAMA Cap. C20 LFN 2004**

**Cross Reference**

On duties of receiver see **section 393, CAMA Cap. C20 LFN 2004**

On winding up of companies generally, see **Part XV, CAMA Cap. C20 LFN 2004**

On the estavlishment and jurisdiction of the Federal High Court, see **sections 249& 251 Constitution of the Federal Republic of Nigeria, 1999(as amended)**
On duties and powers of the receiver or manager, see **section 393 CAMA Cap. C20. LFN 2004**

**Cases**
A receiver has duty to stop business, collect the debts and release the assets. But a manager has power to continue a business or a going concern: ***Ponson Enterprise Nig. Ltd v. Njigha (2001) FWLR pt. 61 p. 3***

**For Further Reading**
On receivers, their duties, powers, see, Ephraim Madeueulosi Asomugha **Company law in Nigeria under the companies and Allied Matters Act,** (1994) E.M. Asumughai Lagos.

## 390.Receivers and managers appointed out of court

(1) A receiver [1] or manager [2] of any property or undertaking of a company[3] appointed out of court [4] under a power contained in any instrument shall, subject to section 393 of this Act, be deemed to be an agent of the person or persons on whose behalf he is appointed and, if appointed manager of the whole or any part of the undertaking of a company, [3] he shall be deemed to stand in a fiduciary relationship to the company [3] and observe the utmost good faith towards it in any transaction with it or on its behalf.

(2) Such a manager [2]-

(a) shall act at all times in what he believes to be the best interests of the company [3] as a whole so as to preserve its assets, further its business, and promote the purposes for which it was formed, and in such manner as a faithful, diligent, careful and ordinarily skilful manager [2] would act in the circumstances;

(b) in considering whether a particular transaction or course of action is in the best interest of the company [3] as a whole, may have regard to the interests of the employees, as well as the members [5] of the company, [3] and, when appointed by, or as a representative of, a special class of members[5] or creditors [6] may give special, but not exclusive, consideration to the interests of that class.

(3) Nothing contained in the articles [7] of a company, [3] or in any contract, or in any resolution [8] of a company, [3] shall relieve any manager[2] from the duty to act in accordance with subsection (2) of this section or relieve him from any liability incurred as a result of any breach of such duty.

---

**Notes**
**Section 390**

1. "Receiver" means a disinterested person appointed by a court, or by a corporation or other person, for the protection or collection of property that is the subject of diverse claims. See **Garner B. (ed) Black's Law Dictionary 8th ed.**
   "Receiver" includes a manager. See **section. 567 CAMA, Cap. C20, LFN 2004.**
2. "Manager" means one who is in charge of a corporation and in control of its business, or establishments, division, or departments, and who is vested with a certain amount of discretion and independent jugement. See **Garner, B.(ed.) Black's Law Dictionary 8 th ed.**
3. "Company" means a company formed and registered under this Act or, as the case may be, formed and
   registered in Nigeria before and in existence on the commencement of this Act**. See section 567, CAMA Cap. C20 LFN 2004**
4. "Court" used in relation to a company , means the Federal High Court, and to the extent to which application may be made to it as; court includes the Court of Appeal and the Supreme Court of Nigeria. See **Section 567 CAMA, Cap. C20, LFN, 2004.**
5. "Members" see "member"It includes the heir, executor, administrator or other personal representative, as the case may be,of the member; **See section 567 CAMA Cap. C20 LFN 2004.**
6. "Creditors" see "creditor". It means one to whom a debt is owed; one who gives credit for money or goods. See **Garner B. (ed) Black's Law Dictionary, 8th ed.**
7. "Articles"means the articles of association of a company, as originally framed or as altered by special resolution including so far as they apply to the regulations contained in Table A in the first schedules of the Companies Act, 1922 or in that Table as altered by any subsequent enactment or reprint of the Laws, or in Table A in schedule 1 to this Act' **see section 567 CAMA Cap. C20 LFN 2004.**
8. "Resolution": means formal action by a corporate board of directors or other corporate body authorizing a particular act, transaction or appointment. See **Garner B. (ed.) Black's Law Dictionary 8 th ed.**

**Cross Reference**

On duties of receiver see **section 393, CAMA Cap C20 LFN 2004**

On winding up of companies generally, see **Part XV, CAMA Cap C20 LFN 2004**

On the estavlishment and jurisdiction of the Federal High Court, see **sections 249& 251 Constitution of the Federal Republic of Nigeria, 1999(as amended)**
On duties and powers of the receiver or manager, see **section 393 CAMA Cap. C20. LFN 2004**

**Cases**
By section 390(1) CAMA, a receiver/manager appointed out of court by a charge (in this case the bank) is the agent of the bank which appointed him ***:Unibiz Nig. Ltd. v Commercial Bank Credit Lyonnais (2001) 7 NWLR pt. 713***

**For Further Reading**
On the duty of courts to appoint receivers and managers, see, Orojo, J. Ola **Company Law and Practice in Nigeria** 3rd Edition, Mbeyi & Associates (Lagos, Nigeria) 1992.

## 391.Power of a receiver or manager appointed out of court to apply to the court for directions

A receiver[1] or manager[2] of the property of a company[3] appointed in accordance with the provisions of subsection (1) of section 390 of this Act may apply to the court[4] for direction in relation to any particular matter arising in connection with the performance of his functions, and on any such application, the court[4] may give such directions or make such order declaring the rights of persons before the court[4] or otherwise, as it thinks just.

**Notes**
**Section 391**

1. "Receiver" means a disinterested person appointed by a court, or by a corporation or other person, for the protection or collection of property that is the subject of diverse claims. See **Garner B. (ed) Black's Law Dictionary 8th ed.**
   "Receiver" includes a manager. See **section. 567 CAMA, Cap. C20, LFN 2004.**
2. "Manager" means one who is in charge of a corporation and in control of its business, or establishments, division, or departments, and who is vested with a certain amount of discretion and independent jugement. See **Garner B. (ed.) Black's Law Dictionary 8 th ed.**
3. "Company" means a company formed and registered under this Act or, as the case may be, formed and

registered in Nigeria before and in existence on the commencement of this Act. **See section 567, CAMA Cap. C20 LFN 2004**

4. "Court" used in relation to a company , means the Federal High Court, and to the extent to which application may be made to it as; court includes the Court of Appeal and the Supreme Court of Nigeria. See **Section 567 CAMA, Cap. C20, LFN, 2004.**

Cross Reference

On duties of receiver see **section 393, CAMA Cap. C20 LFN 2004**

On winding up of companies generally, see **Part XV, CAMA Cap. C20 LFN 2004**

On the estavlishment and jurisdiction of the Federal High Court, see **sections 249& 251 Constitution of the Federal Republic of Nigeria, 1999(as amended)**

On position of a receiver or manager appointed by the court in relation to the company, see **section 390 CAMA Cap. C20, LFN 2004**

On duties and powers of the receiver or manager, see **section 393 CAMA Cap. C20. LFN 2004**

---

**Cases**

A receiver has duty to stop business, collect the debts and release the assets. But a manager has power to continue a business or a going concern: ***Ponson Enterprise Nig. Ltd v. Njigha (2001) FWLR pt. 61 p. 3***

## 392.Notification that a receiver or manager has been appointed

(1) Where a receiver [1] or manager[2] of the property of a company[3] has been appointed, notice shall be given to the Commission[4] within 14 days, indicating the terms of and remuneration for the appointment, and every invoice, order for goods or business letter issued by or on behalf of the company, [3] or the receiver[1] or manager[2] or the liquidator[5] of the company,[3] being a document on or in which the company's name appears, shall contain a statement that a receiver [1] or manager[2] has been appointed.

(2) If default is made in complying with this section, the company[3] and any of the following persons, who knowingly and wilfully authorises or permits the default, namely, any officer of the company, any liquidator[5] of the company[3] and any receiver[1] or manager,[2] shall be guilty of an offence and liable to a fine not exceeding N25 for every day during which the default continues.

---

**Notes**
**Section 392**

1. "Receiver" means a disinterested person appointed by a court, or by a corporation or other person, for the protection or collection of property that is the subject of diverse claims. See **Garner B. (ed) Black's Law Dictionary 8th ed.**
"Receiver" includes a manager. See **section. 567 CAMA, Cap. C20, LFN 2004.**
2. "Manager" means one who is in charge of a corporation and in control of its business, or establishments, division, or departments, and who is vested with a certain amount of discretion and independent jugement. See **Garner B. (ed.) Black's Law Dictionary 8 th ed.**
3. "Company" means a company formed and registered under this Act or, as the case may be, formed and registered in Nigeria before and in existence on the commencement of this Act. **See section 567 CAMA Cap. C20 LFN 2004.**
4. "Commission": means the Corporate Affairs Commission established under section 1 of this Act **. See section 567 CAMA Cap. C20, LFN 2004.**
5. "Liquidator" means a person appointed to wind up a business's affairs, especially by selling off its assets. **See Garner B. (ed.) Black's Law Dictionary 8th ed.**

Cross Reference

On meaning of offence, see **section 2, Criminal Code Cap. C38, LFN 2004**

On duties and powers of the receiver or manager, see **section 393 CAMA Cap. 20. LFN 2004**

On how a liquidator is appointed, see **section 473, CAMA Cap C20 LFN, 2004.**

**Cases**

A Liquidator owes a duty to the whole body of creditors and shareholders and to the court to make himself thoroughly acquainted with the affairs of the company and suppress or conceal anything coming to his knowledge in the course of his investigation which is material; ***Re J.A. Balogun*** **(1977) FRCR 122**

## 393. Duties, powers, etc, of receivers and managers

(1) A person appointed a receiver [1] of any property of a company[2] shall, subject to the rights of prior encumbrances take possession of and protect the property, receive the rents and profits and discharge all out-goings in respect thereof and realise the security for the benefit of those on whose behalf he is appointed, but unless appointed manager, [3] he shall not have power to carry on any business or undertaking.

(2) A person appointed manager [3] of the whole or any part of the undertaking of a company [2] shall manage the same with a view to the beneficial realisation of the security of those on whose behalf he is appointed.

(3) Without prejudice to subsection (1) or (2) of this section, where a receiver [1] or manager [2] is appointed for the whole or substantially the whole of a company's [2] property, the powers conferred on him by the debentures [4] by virtue of which he was appointed shall be deemed to include (except in so far as they are inconsistent with any of the provisions of those debentures) the powers specified in the Eleventh Schedule to this Act.
[Eleventh Schedule.]

(4) As from the date of appointment of a receiver [1] or manager,[3] the powers of the directors [5] or liquidators [6] in a members' voluntary winding up[7] to deal with the property or undertaking over which he is appointed shall cease unless and until the receiver [1] or manager[3] is discharged.

(5) If, on the appointment of a receiver [1] or manager [3], the company[2] is being wound up [8] under the provision relating to creditors' voluntary winding up, [9] or the property concerned is in the hands of some other officer of the court, [10] the liquidator [6] or officer shall not be bound to relinquish control of such property to the receiver [1] or manager [3] except under the order of the court. [10]

---

**Notes**
**Section 393**

1. "Receiver" means a disinterested person appointed by a court, or by a corporation or other person, for the protection or collection of property that is the subject of diverse claims. See **Garner B. (ed) Black's Law Dictionary 8th ed.**
   "Receiver" includes a manager. See **section. 567 CAMA, Cap. C20, LFN 2004.**
2. "Company" means a company formed and registered under this Act or, as the case may be, formed and
   registered in Nigeria before and in existence on the commencement of this Act. **See section 567 CAMA Cap. C20 LFN 2004.**
3. "Manager" means one who is in charge of a corporation and in control of its business, or establishments, division, or departments, and who is vested with a certain amount of discretion and independent jugement. See **Garner B. (ed.) Black's Law Dictionary 8 th ed.**
4. "Debentures": means a written acknowledgement of indebtedness by the company, setting out the terms and conditions of the indebtedness,

and includes debenture stock, bonds and any other securities of a company whether constituting a charge on the assets of the company or not. See **section 567 CAMA Cap. C20 LFN 2004**

5. "Directors" see"director." It includes any person occupying the position of director by whatever name called; and includes any person in accordance with whose directions or instructions the directors of the company are accustomed to act. **See section567 CAMA Cap. C20 LFN 2004.**
6. "Liquidator:"means a person who is appointed to wind up a business's affairs esp. by selling off its assets. See **Garner B. (ed) Black's Law Dictionary, 8th ed.**
7. "Members' voluntary winding up"has the meaning assigned to it by **section 462(4) of this Act. See section 567 CAMA Cap. C20 LFN 2004**
8. "Wound up" see "winding up." It means the process of settling accounts and liquidating assets in anticipation of a partnership's or a corporation's dissolution.See **Garner B. (ed) Black's Law Dictionary, 8th ed.**
9. "Creditors' voluntary winding up"has the meaning assigned to it by section 462(4) of this Act. **See section 567 CAMA Cap. C20 LFN 2004**
10. "Court" used in relation to a company, means the Federal High Court, and to the extent to which application may be made to it as; court includes the Court of Appeal and the Supreme Court of Nigeria. See **Section 567 CAMA, Cap. C20, LFN, 2004.**

Cross Reference

On winding up of companies generally, see **Part XV, CAMA Cap. C20 LFN 2004**

On the estavlishment and jurisdiction of the Federal High Court, see **sections 249& 251 Constitution of the Federal Republic of Nigeria, 1999(as amended)**

On position of a receiver or manager appointed by the court in relation to the company, see **section 390 CAMA Cap. C20, LFN 2004**

---

**Cases**

On appointment of receiver, the powers of management of the company's business became vested in the receiver, but on quite a number of matters not related to management ,the directors can still act ***: UBA Trustees Ltd. v. Nigergrob Ceramic Ltd. (1987) 3 NWLR pt 62, p. 600.***

Where a receiver or manager is appointed for the whole o substantially the whole of a company's property, the powers conferred on him by the debentures by virtue of which he was appointed, shall be deemed to include, except in so far as they are with any of these debentures, the powers specified in the eleventh schedule to the Act ***: Onafowokan & 2 Ors v. Wema Bank & 2 Ors 88/2004 SC delivered 13/05/2010.***

Whilst receivership and manager open exclusively dominate the company affairs and dealings with the outside world, it does not affect the internal domestic structure of the company *: **Unibiz (Nig.) Ltd. v. Commercial Bank Credit Lyonnais Nig. Ltd.(for and on behalf of Babington Ashaye (2001) 7NWLR (pt 713) 534.***

## 394. Liabilities of receivers and managers on contracts

(1) A receiver [1] or manager [2] of any property or undertaking of a company[3] shall be personally liable on any contract entered into by him except in so far as the contract otherwise expressly provides.

(2) As regards contracts entered into by a receiver [1] or manager[2] in the proper performance of his functions, such receiver [1] or manager[2] shall, subject to the rights of any prior incumbrancers, be entitled to an indemnity in respect of liability thereon out of the property over which he has been appointed to act as receiver or manager[2].

(3) A receiver [1] or manager [2] appointed out of court [4] under a power contained in any instrument shall also be entitled, as regards contracts entered into by him with the express or implied authority of those appointing him, to an indemnity in respect of liability thereon from those appointing him to the extent to which he is unable to recover in accordance with subsection (2) of this section.

---

**Notes**
**Section 394**

1. "Receiver" means a disinterested person appointed by a court, or by a corporation or other person, for the protection or collection of property that is the subject of diverse claims. See **Garner B. (ed) Black's Law Dictionary 8th ed.**
   "Receiver" includes a manager. See **section. 567 CAMA, Cap. C20, LFN 2004.**
2. "Manager" means one who is in charge of a corporation and in control of its business, or establishments, division, or departments, and who is vested with a certain amount of discretion and independent jugement. See **Garner, B. (ed.) Black's Law Dictionary 8 th ed.**
3. "Company" means a company formed and registered under this Act or, as the case may be, formed and
   registered in Nigeria before and in existence on the commencement of this Act. **See section 567, CAMA Cap. C20 LFN 2004**
4. "Court" used in relation to a company, means the Federal High Court, and to the extent to which application may be made to it as; court

includes the Court of Appeal and the Supreme Court of Nigeria. See **Section 567 CAMA, Cap. C20, LFN, 2004.**

**Cross Reference**

On duties of receiver and manager,see **section 393, CAMA Cap. C20 LFN 2004**

On winding up of companies generally, see **Part XV, CAMA Cap. C20 LFN 2004**

On the estavlishment and jurisdiction of the Federal High Court, see **sections 249& 251 Constitution of the Federal Republic of Nigeria, 1999(as amended)**

On position of a receiver or manager appointed by the court in relation to the company, see **section 390 CAMA Cap. C20, LFN 2004**

On duties and powers of the receiver or manager, see **section 393 CAMA Cap. C20. LFN 2004**

---

**Cases**

A receiver has duty to stop business, collect the debts and release the assets. But a manager has power to continue a business or a going concern: ***Ponson Enterprise Nig. Ltd v. Njigha (2001) FWLR pt. 61 p. 3***

On appointment of receiver, the powers of management of the company's business became vested in the receiver, but on quite a number of matters not related to management ,the directors can still act ***: UBA Trustees Ltd. v. Nigergrob Ceramic Ltd. (1987) 3 NWLR pt 62, p. 600.***

Where a receiver or manager is appointed for the whole or substantially the whole of a company's property, the powers conferred on him by the debentures by virtue of which he was appointed, shall be deemed to include, except in so far as they are with any of these debentures, the powers specified in the eleventh schedule to the Act ***: Onafowokan & 2 Ors v. Wema Bank & 2 Ors 88/2004 SC delivered 13/05/2010.***

Whilst receivership and manager open exclusively dominate the company affairs and dealings with the outside world, it does not affect the internal domestic structure of the company ***: Unibiz (Nig.) Ltd. v. Commercial Bank Credit Lyonnais Nig. Ltd.(for and on behalf of Babington Ashaye (2001) 7NWLR (pt 713) 534.***

## 395.Power of court to fix remuneration on application of liquidator

(1) The court[1] may, on the application of the company [2] or the liquidator[3] of a company,[2] by order fix the amount to be paid by way of remuneration to any person who, under the powers contained in any instrument, has been appointed as receiver [4] or manager[5] of the property of the company. [5]

(2) The powers of the court [1] under subsection (1) of this section shall, where no previous order has been made with respect thereto under that subsection-

(a) extend to fixing the remuneration for any period before the making of the order or the application therefor; and

(b) be exercisable notwithstanding that the receiver [4] or manager[5] has died or ceased to act before the making of the order or the application therefor; and

(c) extend, where the receiver [4] or manager [5] has been paid or has retained for his remuneration for any period before the making of the order any amount in excess of that so fixed for that period, to requiring him or his personal representatives [6] to account for the excess or such part thereof as may be specified in the order:

Provided that the power conferred by paragraph (c) of this subsection shall not be exercised as respects any period before the making of the application for the order unless in the opinion of the court there are special circumstances making it proper for the power to be so exercised.

(3) The court [1] may, from time to time, on an application made either by the company [2] or the liquidator [3] or by the receiver [4] or manager, [5] vary or amend an order made under subsection (1) of this section.

(4) This section shall apply whether the receiver [4] or manager [5] has been appointed before or after the commencement of this Act, and to periods before, as well as to periods after, the commencement of this Act.

---

**Notes**
**Section 395**

1. "Court" used in relation to a company, means the Federal High Court, and to the extent to which application may be made to it as; court includes the Court of Appeal and the Supreme Court of Nigeria. See **Section 567 CAMA, Cap. C20, LFN, 2004.**
2. "Company" means a company formed and registered under this Act or, as the case may be, formed and registered in Nigeria before and in existence on the commencement of this Act. **See section 567 CAMA Cap. C20 LFN 2004**
3. "Liquidator" means a person who is appointed to wind up a business's affairs esp. by selling off its assets. See **Garner B. (ed) Black's Law Dictionary, 8th ed.**

4. "Receiver" means a disinterested person appointed by a court, or by a corporation or other person, for the protection or collection of property that is the subject of diverse claims. See **Garner B. (ed) Black's Law Dictionary 8th ed.**

"Receiver" includes a manager. See **section. 567 CAMA, Cap. C20, LFN 2004.**

5. "Manager" means one who is in charge of a corporation and in control of its business, or establishments, division, or departments, and who is vested with a certain amount of discretion and independent jugement. See **Garner B. (ed.) Black's Law Dictionary 8 th ed.**

6. "Personal Representatives" where customary law is applicable, includes successors appointed in respect of deceased contributories ; **See section 567 CAMA Cap. C20 LFN 2004**

**Cross Reference**

On duties of receiver and manager,see **section 393, CAMA Cap. C20 LFN 2004**

On winding up of companies generally, see **Part XV, CAMA Cap. C20 LFN 2004**

On the establishment and jurisdiction of the Federal High Court, see **sections 249& 251 Constitution of the Federal Republic of Nigeria, 1999(as amended)**

On position of a receiver or manager appointed by the court in relation to the company, see **section 390 CAMA Cap. C20, LFN 2004**

On duties and powers of the receiver or manager, see **section 393 CAMA Cap. C20. LFN 2004**

---

**Cases**

A Liquidator owes a duty to the whole body of creditors and shareholders and to the court to make himself thoroughly acquainted with the affairs of the company and not suppress or conceal anything coming to his knowledge in the course of his investigation which is material; ***Re J.A. Balogun* (1977) FRCR 122**

## 396. Provisions as to information where receiver or manager appointed

(1) Where a receiver [1] or manager [2] of the whole or substantially the whole of the property of a company [3] (in this section and in section 397 of this Act referred to as "the receiver" [1]) has been appointed on behalf of the holders of any debentures [4] of the company[3] secured by a floating charge [5], then, subject to the provisions of this section and of section 397 of this Act-

(a) the receiver [1] shall forthwith send notice to the company [3] of his appointment and the terms; and

(b) there shall, within 14 days after receipt of the notice, or such longer period as may be allowed by the court [6] or by the receiver, [1] be made out and submitted to the receiver [1] in accordance with section 397 of this Act, a statement in the prescribed form as to the affairs of the company [3]; and

(c) The receiver [1] shall within two months after receipt of the said statement send-

(i) To the Commission [7] or to the court [6] a copy of the statement and of any comments he sees fit to make thereon and in the case of the Commission [7] also a summary of the statement and of his comments, if any, thereon;

(ii) to the company [3] a copy of any such comments as aforesaid or if he does not see fit to make any comment, a notice to that effect; and

(iii) to any trustees [8] for the debenture holders [9] on whose behalf he has been appointed and, so far as he is aware of their addresses, to all such debenture holders, [9] a copy of the said summary.

(2) The receiver [1] shall within two months, or such longer period as the court [6] may allow after the expiration of the period of 12 months from the date of his appointment and of every subsequent period of 12 months, and within two months, or such longer period as the court [6] may allow after he ceases to act as receiver [1] or manager [2] of the property of the company [3], send to the Commission [7], to any trustees [8] for the debenture holders [9] of the company [3] on whose behalf he was appointed, to the company [3] and (so far as he is aware of their addresses) to all such debenture holders, [9] an abstract in the prescribed form showing his receipts and payments during that period of 12 months, or, where he ceases to act as aforesaid, during the period from the end of the period to which the last preceding abstract relates up to the date of his so ceasing, and the aggregate amounts of his receipts and of his payments during all preceding periods since his appointment.

(3) Where the receiver [1] is appointed under the powers contained in any instrument, this section shall have effect-

(a) with the omission of the references to the court in subsection (1) of this section; and

(b) with the substitution for the references to the court [6] in subsection (2) of this section, of references to the Commission [7];

and in any other case references to the court [6] shall be taken as referring to the court [6] by which the receiver was appointed.

(4) Subsection (1) of this section shall not apply in relation to the appointment of a receiver [1] or manager [2] to act with an existing receiver [1] or manager [2] or in place of a receiver [1] or manager [2] dying or ceasing to act, except that, where that subsection applies to a receiver [1] or manager [2] who dies or ceases to act before it has been fully complied with, the references in paragraphs (b) and (c) thereof to the receiver [1] shall, subject to subsection (5) of this section, include references to his successor and to expression "the receiver" [1] where used in, or in relation to, subsection (2) of this section.

(5) This section and section 397 of this Act, where the company [3] is being wound up [10], shall apply notwithstanding that the receiver [1] or manager [2] and the liquidator [11] are the same person.

(6) Nothing in subsection (2) of this section shall be taken to prejudice the duty of the receiver [1] to render proper accounts of his receipts and payments to the persons to whom, and at the times at which, he may be required to do so apart from that subsection.

(7) If the receiver [1] makes default in complying with the requirements of this section, he shall be guilty of an offence and liable to a fine of N=25 for every day during which the default continues.

---

**Notes**

**Section 396(1)**

1. "Receiver" means a disinterested person appointed by a court, or by a corporation or other person, for the protection or collection of property that is the subject of diverse claims. See **Garner B. (ed) Black's Law Dictionary 8th ed.**
   "Receiver" includes a manager. See **section. 567 CAMA, Cap. C20, LFN 2004.**
2. "Manager" means one who is in charge of a corporation and in control of its business, or establishments, division, or departments, and who is vested with a certain amount of discretion and independent jugement. See **Garner, B. (ed.) Black's Law Dictionary 8 th ed.**
3. "Company" means a company formed and registered under this Act or, as the case may be, formed and registered in Nigeria before and in existence on the commencement of this Act. **See section 567, CAMA Cap. C20 LFN 2004.**
4. "Debentures" see"debenture. "It means a written acknowledgement of indebtedness by the company, setting out the terms and conditions of the indebtedness, and includes debenture stock, bonds and any other

securities of a company whether constituting a charge on the assets of the company or not. See **section 567, CAMA Cap. C20 LFN 2004.**

5. "Floating charge" see floating lien. It means a charge that continues to exist even when the collateral changes in character, classification or location. See **Garner B. (ed.) Black's Law Dictionary 8th ed.**
A "floating charge" means an equitable charge over the whole or a specified part of the company's undertakings and assets, including cash and uncalled capital of the company both present and future, but so that the charge shall not preclude the company from dealing with such assets until- (a) the security becomes enforceable and the holder thereof, pursuant to a power in that behalf in the debenture or the deed securing the same, appoints a receiver or manager or enters into possession of such assets; or (b) the court appoints a receiver or manager of such assets on the application of the holder; or (c) the company goes into liquidation. See section 178 **CAMA Cap. C20 LFN, 2004**
6. "Court" used in relation to a company , means the Federal High Court, and to the extent to which application may be made to it as; court includes the Court of Appeal and the Supreme Court of Nigeria. See **Section 567 CAMA, Cap. C20, LFN, 2004.**
7. "Commission" means the Corporate Affairs Commission established under section 1 of this Act **. See section 567 CAMA Cap. C20, LFN 2004.**
8. "Trustee" means one who, having legal title to property holds it in trust for the benefit of another and owes a fiduciary duty to that beneficiary**. See Garner B. ed. Black's Law Dictionary 8 th ed.**
9. "Debenture Holder" "see "debenture" and "holder." Debenture means a written acknowledgement of indebtedness by the company, setting out the terms and conditions of the indebtedness and includes debenture stock, bonds and any other securities of any company whether constituting a charge on the assets of the company or not. **See section 567 CAMA, Cap. C20, LFN 2004.**
"Holder" is one who has legal possession of a negotiable instrument and is entitled to receive payment on it. **See Garner B. ed. Black's Law Dictionary 8th ed.**
10. "Wound up" see "winding up." It means the process of settling accounts and liquidating assets in anticipation of a partnership's or a corporation's dissolution. **See Garner B. ed. Black's Law Dictionary 8th ed.**

**Cross Reference**

On duties of receiver and manager,see **section 393, CAMA Cap. C20 LFN 2004**

On winding up of companies generally, see **Part XV, CAMA Cap. C20 LFN 2004**

On the estavlishment and jurisdiction of the Federal High Court, see **sections 249& 251 Constitution of the Federal Republic of Nigeria, 1999(as amended)**

On position of a receiver or manager appointed by the court in relation to the company, see **section 390 CAMA Cap. C20, LFN 2004**

On duties and powers of the receiver or manager, see **section 393 CAMA Cap. C20. LFN 2004**
On obligation of appointed receiver to inform the company of the terms of appointment, **see section 396 CAMA Cap. C20, LFN 2004**
On meaning of offence, see **section 2, Criminal Code Cap. C38, LFN 2004**

---

## 397. Special provisions as to statement submitted to receiver

(1) The statements as to the affairs of a company [1] required by section 396 of this Act, to be submitted to the receiver [2] (or his successor) shall show as at the date of the receiver's [2] appointment, the particulars or the company's [1] assets, debts and liabilities, the names, residences and occupations of its creditors [3], the securities [4] held by them respectively, the dates when the securities [4] were respectively given and such further or other information as may be prescribed.

(2) The statement shall be submitted by, and be verified by, affidavit of one or more of the persons who are at the date of the receiver's [2] appointment the directors [5], and by the person who is at that date the secretary [6] of the company [1], or by such of the persons hereafter in this subsection mentioned as the receiver [2] (or his successor), subject to the direction of the court [7], may require to submit and verify the statement, that is to say, persons-

(a) who are or have been officers [8] of the company [1];

(b) who have taken part in the formation of the company [1] at any time within one year before the date of the receiver's [2] appointment;

(c) who are in the employment of the company [1], or have been in the employment of the company [1] within the year, and are in the opinion of the receiver [2] capable of giving the information required;

(d) who are or have been within the said year officers [8] of or in the employment of a company [1] which is, or within the said year was, an officer [8] of the company [1] to which the statement relates.

(3) Any person making the statement and affidavit shall be allowed, and shall be paid by the receiver [2] (or his successor) out of his receipts, such costs and expenses incurred in and about the preparation and making of the statement and affidavit as the

receiver[2] (or his successor) may consider reasonable, subject to an appeal to the court[7].

(4) Where the receiver[2] is appointed under the powers contained in any instrument, this section shall have effect with the substitution for references to the court[7] of references to the Commission[9] and references to an affidavit, of references to a statutory declaration[10]; and in any other case references to the court[7] shall be taken as referring to the court by which the receiver[2] was appointed.

(5) If any person without reasonable excuse makes default in complying with the requirements of this section, he shall be guilty of an offence and liable to a fine of ₦50 for every day during which the default continues.

(6) References in this section to the receiver's[1] successor shall include a continuing receiver[2] or manager[11].

---

**Notes**

**Section 397**

1. "Company" means a company formed and registered under this Act or, as the case may be, formed and registered in Nigeria before and in existence on the commencement of this Act. **See section 567 CAMA Cap. C20 LFN 2004.**
2. "Receiver" means a disinterested person appointed by a court, or by a corporation or other person, for the protection or collection of property that is the subject of diverse claims. See **Garner B. (ed) Black's Law Dictionary 8th ed.**
   "Receiver" includes a manager. See **section. 567 CAMA, Cap. C20, LFN 2004.**
3. "Creditors" see "creditor". It means one to whom a debt is owed; one who gives credit for money or goods. **See Garner B. (ed) Black's Law Dictionary, 8th ed.**
4. "Securities"includes shares, debentures, debenture stock, bonds, notes (other than promissory notes) and units under a unit trust scheme; **See section 567 CAMA Cap. C20 LFN 2004**
5. "Directors" see "director." It includes any person occupying the position of director by whatever name called; and includes any person in accordance with whose directions or instructions the directors of the company are accustomed to act. **See section 567 CAMA Cap. C20 LFN 2004**
6. "Secretary" means corporate officer in charge of official correspondence, minutes of board meetings and records of stock ownership and transfer. See. **Garner B. (ed.) Black's Law Dictionary, 8th ed.**

7. "Court" used in relation to a company , means the Federal High Court, and to the extent to which application may be made to it as; court includes the Court of Appeal and the Supreme Court of Nigeria. See **Section 567 CAMA, Cap. C20, LFN, 2004.**
8. "Officer"in relation to a body corporate, includes a director, manager or secretary; **Section 567 CAMA, Cap. C20, LFN 2004.** For the purpose of section 378, "officer" includes any person in accordance with those directions or instructions the directors of the company are accustomed to act. See **section 378 CAMA Cap. C20, LFN 2004**
9. "Commission" means the Corporate Affairs Commission established under section 1 of this Act **. See section 567 CAMA Cap. C20, LFN 2004.**
10. "Statutory Declaration" means a declaration voluntarily made under the Oaths Act and in Nigeria includes one so made under any other enactment or law providing for the taking of a voluntary declaration. See **section 567 CAMA Cap. C20 LFN 2004**
11. "Manager" means one who is in charge of a corporation and in control of its business, or establishments, division, or departments, and who is vested with a certain amount of discretion and independent jugement. See **Garner B. (ed.) Black's Law Dictionary 8 [th] ed**

**Cross Reference**

On duties of receiver and manager,see **section 393, CAMA Cap. C20 LFN 2004**

On winding up of companies generally, see **Part XV, CAMA Cap. C20 LFN 2004**

On the estavlishment and jurisdiction of the Federal High Court, see **sections 249& 251 Constitution of the Federal Republic of Nigeria, 1999(as amended)**

On position of a receiver or manager appointed by the court in relation to the company, see **section 390 CAMA Cap. C20, LFN 2004**

On duties and powers of the receiver or manager, see **section 393 CAMA Cap. C20. LFN 2004**

On obligation of appointed receiver to inform the company of the terms of appointment, **see section 396 CAMA Cap. C20, LFN 2004**

On meaning of offence, see **section 2, Criminal Code Cap. C38, LFN 2004**

For provisions in taking an affidavit generally, see **section 117 Evidence Act, 2011**

---

*Accounts by receiver or manager*

## 398.Delivery to Commission of accounts of receivers and managers

(1) Except where section 396 (2) of this Act applies, every receiver[1] or manager[2] of the property of a company [3] who has been appointed under the powers contained in any instrument shall, within one month or such longer periods as the Commission [4] may

allow, after the expiration of the period of six months from the date of his appointment, and of every subsequent period of six months, and within one month after he ceases to act as receiver [1] or manager[2], deliver to the Commission [4] for registration an abstract in the prescribed form showing his receipts and his payments during that period of six months, or where he ceases to act as aforesaid, during the period from the end of the period to which the last preceding abstract relates, up to the date of his ceasing, and the aggregate amount of his receipts and of his payments during all preceding periods since his appointment.

(2) Every receiver [1] or manager [2] who makes default in complying with the provisions of this section shall be guilty of an offence and liable to a fine of ₦25 for every day during which the default continues.

---

**Notes**
**Section 398**

1. "Receiver" means a disinterested person appointed by a court, or by a corporation or other person, for the protection or collection of property that is the subject of diverse claims. See **Garner B. (ed) Black's Law Dictionary 8th ed.**
   "Receiver" includes a manager. See **section. 567 CAMA, Cap. C20, LFN 2004.**
2. "Manager" means one who is in charge of a corporation and in control of its business, or establishments, division, or departments, and who is vested with a certain amount of discretion and independent jugement. See **Garner B. (ed.) Black's Law Dictionary 8 th ed.**
3. "Company" means a company formed and registered under this Act or, as the case may be, formed and registered in Nigeria before and in existence on the commencement of this Act. **See section 567, CAMA Cap. C20 LFN 2004.**
4. "Commission" means the Corporate Affairs Commission established under section 1 of this Act . **See section 567 CAMA Cap. C20, LFN 2004.**

**Cross Reference**

On duties of receiver and manager,see **section 393, CAMA Cap. C20 LFN 2004**

On winding up of companies generally, see **Part XV, CAMA Cap. C20 LFN 2004**

On the estavlishment and jurisdiction of the Federal High Court, see **sections 249& 251 Constitution of the Federal Republic of Nigeria, 1999(as amended)**

On position of a receiver or manager appointed by the court in relation to the company, see **section 390 CAMA Cap. C20, LFN 2004**

On duties and powers of the receiver or manager, see **section 393 CAMA Cap. C20. LFN 2004**
On obligation of appointed receiver to inform the company of the terms of appointment, **see section 396 CAMA Cap. C20, LFN 2004**
On meaning of offence, see **section 2, Criminal Code Cap. C38, LFN 2004**

**Cases**
A receiver has duty to stop business, collect the debts and release the assets. But a manager has power to continue a business or a going concern: ***Ponson Enterprise Nig. Ltd v. Njigha (2001) FWLR pt. 61 p. 3***

*Duty as to returns*

## 399. Enforcement of duty of receivers and managers to make returns, etc.

(1) If any receiver[1] or manager[2] of the property of a company[3] having-

(a) made default in filing, delivering or making any returns, account or other document, or in giving any notice which a receiver[1] or manager[2] is by law required to file, delivers, makes or gives or fails to make good the default within 14 days after the service on him of a notice requiring him to do so; or

(b) been appointed under the powers contained in any instrument has, after being required at any time by the liquidator[4] of the company[3] so to do, fails to render proper accounts of his receipts and payment and to vouch the same and to pay over to the liquidator[4] the amount properly payable to him, the court[5] may, on an application made for the purpose, make an order directing the receiver[1] or manager[2], as the case may be; to make good the default within such time as may be specified in the order.

(2) In the case of any such default as is mentioned in paragraph (a) of subsection (1) of this section, an application for the purposes of this section may be made by any member[5] or by the Commission[6], and in the case of any such default as is mentioned in paragraph (b) of that subsection, the application shall be made by the liquidator[4], and in either case the order may provide that all costs shall be borne by the receiver[1] or manager[2], as the case may be.

(3) Nothing in this section shall be taken to prejudice the operation of any enactment imposing penalties on receivers [1] in respect of any such default as is mentioned in subsection (1) of this section.

---

**Notes**
**Section 399**

1. "Receiver" means a disinterested person appointed by a court, or by a corporation or other person, for the protection or collection of property that is the subject of diverse claims. See **Garner B. (ed) Black's Law Dictionary 8th ed.**
   "Receiver" includes a manager. See **section. 567 CAMA, Cap. C20, LFN 2004.**
2. "Manager" means one who is in charge of a corporation and in control of its business, or establishments, division, or departments, and who is vested with a certain amount of discretion and independent jugement. See **Garner B. (ed.) Black's Law Dictionary 8 th ed.**
3. "Company" means a company formed and registered under this Act or, as the case may be, formed and registered in Nigeria before and in existence on the commencement of this Act. **See section 567, CAMA Cap. C20 LFN 2004.**
4. "Liquidator" means a person who is appointed to wind up a business's affairs esp. by selling off its assets. See **Garner B. (ed) Black's Law Dictionary, 8th ed.**
5. "Court" used in relation to a company , means the Federal High Court, and to the extent to which application may be made to it as; court includes the Court of Appeal and the Supreme Court of Nigeria. See **Section 567 CAMA, Cap. C20, LFN, 2004.**
   "Commission" means the Corporate Affairs Commission established under section 1 of this Act **. See section 567 CAMA Cap. C20, LFN 2004.**

**Cross Reference**

On duties of receiver and manager,see **section 393, CAMA Cap. C20 LFN 2004**

On winding up of companies generally, see **Part XV, CAMA Cap. C20 LFN 2004**

On the establishment and jurisdiction of the Federal High Court, see **sections 249& 251 Constitution of the Federal Republic of Nigeria, 1999(as amended)**

On position of a receiver or manager appointed by the court in relation to the company, see **section 390 CAMA Cap. C20, LFN 2004**

On duties and powers of the receiver or manager, see **section 393 CAMA Cap. C20. LFN 2004**

On obligation of appointed receiver to inform the company of the terms of appointment, **see section 396 CAMA Cap. C20, LFN 2004**

On meaning of offence, see **section 2, Criminal Code Cap. C38, LFN 2004**

**Cases**

A Liquidator owes a duty to the whole body of creditors and shareholders and to the court to make himself thoroughly acquainted with the affairs of the company and not suppress or conceal anything coming to his knowledge in the course of his investigation which is material; ***Re J.A. Balogun*** **(1977) FRCR 122**

*Construction of references*

## 400.Construction of references to receivers and managers

It is hereby declared that, except where the context otherwise requires-

(a) any reference in this Act to a receiver [1] or manager[2] of the property of a company [3], or to a receiver [1] thereof, includes a reference to a receiver [1] or manager[2], or as the case may be to a receiver[1] of part only of that property and to a receiver[1] only of the income arising from that property or from part thereof; and

(b) any reference in this Act to the appointment of a receiver [1] or manager[2] under powers contained in any instrument, includes a reference to an appointment made under powers which, by virtue of any enactment, are implied in and have effect as if contained in an instrument.

---

**Notes**
**Section 400**

1. "Receiver" means a disinterested person appointed by a court, or by a corporation or other person, for the protection or collection of property that is the subject of diverse claims. See **Garner B, (ed) Black's Law Dictionary 8th ed.**
   "Receiver" includes a manager. See **section. 567 CAMA, Cap. C20, LFN 2004.**
2. "Manager" means one who is in charge of a corporation and in control of its business, or establishments, division, or departments, and who is vested with a certain amount of discretion and independent jugement. See **Garner, B.(ed.) Black's Law Dictionary 8 th ed.**
3. "Company" means a company formed and registered under this Act or, as the case may be, formed and
   registered in Nigeria before and in existence on the commencement of this Act. **See section 567, CAMA Cap. C20 LFN 2004.**

Cross Reference

On duties of receiver and manager,see **section 393, CAMA Cap. C20 LFN 2004**

---

**Cases**

On appointment of receiver, the powers of management of the company's business became vested in the receiver, but on quite a number of matters not related to management ,the directors can still act ***: UBA Trustees Ltd. v. Nigergrob Ceramic Ltd. (1987) 3 NWLR pt 62, p. 600.***

Where a receiver or manager is appointed for the whole or substantially the whole of a company's property, the powers conferred on him by the debentures by virtue of which he was appointed, shall be deemed to include, except in so far as they are with any of these debentures, the powers specified in the eleventh schedule to the Act ***: Onafowokan & 2 Ors v. Wema Bank & 2 Ors 88/2004 SC delivered 13/05/2010.***

*PART XV*

*Winding up of companies*

*Chapter 1 - Preliminary*

*Modes of winding up*

## 401. Modes of winding up

(1) The winding up [1] of a company [2] may be effected-

(a) by the court [3]; or

(b) voluntarily; or

(c) subject to the supervision of the court [3].

(2) The provisions of this Act with respect to winding up [1] shall apply, unless the contrary appears, to the winding up [1] of a company[2] in any of those modes.

---

**Notes**

**Section 401**

1. "Winding up" means the process of settling accounts and liquidating assets in anticipation of a partnership's or a corporations dissolution. See **Garner B. (ed.) Black's Law Dictionary 8 [th] ed.**
2. "Company" means a company formed and registered under this Act or, as the case may be, formed and registered in Nigeria before and in existence on the commencement of this Act. **See section 567 CAMA Cap. C20 LFN 2004**

3. "Court" used in relation to a company, means the Federal High Court, and to the extent to which application may be made to it as; court includes the Court of Appeal and the Supreme Court of Nigeria. See **Section 567 CAMA, Cap. C20, LFN, 2004.**

Cross Reference

On the establishment and jurisdiction of the Federal High Court, see **sections 249& 251 Constitution of the Federal Republic of Nigeria, 1999(as amended)**

---

**Cases**

Care and utmost caution must be exercised by the court in its dealing with cases involving the termination of the life of a company. ***Air Via Ltd v. Oriental Airlines Ltd.*** **(2004) 9 N.W.L.R (PT.878) 298.**

*Contributories*

## 402. Liability as contributories of present and past members

In the event of a company [1] being wound up, [2] every present and past member[3] shall be liable to contribute to the assets of the company[1] as provided in section 92 of this Act.

---

**Notes**

**Section 402**

1. "Company" means a company formed and registered under this Act or, as the case may be, formed and registered in Nigeria before and in existence on the commencement of this Act. **See section 567 CAMA Cap. C20 LFN 2004.**
2. "Wound up" see "winding up" means the process of settling accounts and liquidating assets in anticipation of a partnership's or a corporations dissolution. See **Garner B. (ed.) Black's Law Dictionary 8th ed.**
3. "Member" includes the heir, executor, administrator or other personal representative, as the case maybe, of the member; See **section 567 CAMA Cap. C20 LFN 2004**

Cross Reference

On liability of members of a company prior to and during winding up, see **section 92 CAMA Cap. C20, LFN 2004**

On modes of winding up a company, see **section 401 CAMA Cap. C20 LFN 2004**

---

**Cases**

A just and equitable ground is one of the grounds upon which a court having jurisdiction can rely to make an order for winding up a company. See Section 408(e) of the Companies and Allied Matters Act, cap 59, Laws of the Federation of Nigeria 1990. Section 408(e) of same law contained in cap c20 of Laws of the Federation of Nigeria 2004. A just and equitable ground for winding up a company is a remedy most suitable for contributories. Where a contributory brings a petition under this head as was found by the trial court and where the trial court is of the opinion that the petitioner is entitled to the order of winding up, it must make the order unless it appears to the court that some other remedy is available to the petitioner and that he is acting unreasonably in seeking a winding up order instead of pursuing that other remedy. ***Ado Ibrahim & Company Ltd v. Bendel Cement Company Ltd*** **(2007) S.C. 284/2001.**

Care and utmost caution must be exercised by the court in its dealing with cases involving the termination of the life of a company. ***Air Via Ltd v. Oriental Airlines Ltd.*** **(2004) 9 N.W.L.R (PT.878) 298.**

**For Further Reading**

On winding up of company, see Sofowora, M. O. **Modern Nigerian Company Law** Soft Associates, 2[nd] Edition 2002.

## 403. Definition of contributory

The term "contributory" [1] means every person liable to contribute to the assets of a company [2] in the event of its being wound up[3] and for the purposes of all proceedings for determining and all proceedings prior to the final determination of the persons who are to be deemed contributories, [1] the expression shall include any person alleged to be a contributory. [1]

---

**Notes**
**Section 403**

1. "Contributories" see ''contributory" which means every person liable to contribute to the assets of a company in the event of its being wound up and for the purposes of all proceedings for determining, and all proceedings prior to the final determination of, the persons who are to be deemed contributories, the expression includes any person alleged to be contributory. See **section 567 CAMA Cap. C20, LFN 2004**
2. "Company" means a company formed and registered under this Act or, as the case may be, formed and registered in Nigeria before and in existence on the commencement of this Act. See **section 567, CAMA Cap. C20 LFN 2004.**
3. "Wound up" see "winding up" which means the process of settling accounts and liquidating assets in anticipation of a partnership's or a

corporation's dissolution. See **Garner B. (ed.) Black's Law Dictionary 8th ed.**

Cross Reference

On modes of winding up a company, see **section 401 CAMA Cap. C20 LFN 2004**

## 404. Nature of liability of contributory

The liability of a contributory [1] shall create a debt of the nature of a specialty accruing and due from him at the time when his liability commenced, but payable at the times when calls are made for enforcing the liability.

**Notes**

**Section 404**

1. "Contributory" means every person liable to contribute to the assets of a company in the event of its being wound up and for the purposes of all proceedings for determining, and all proceedings prior to the final determination of, the persons who are to be deemed contributories, the expression includes any person alleged to be contributory. See **section 567 CAMA Cap. C20, LFN 2004**

Cross Reference

On definition of contributory, **see section 403 CAMA Cap. C20, LFN 2004**

## 405. Contributories in case of death of member

(1) If a contributory [1] dies either before or after he has been placed on the list of contributories [1], his personal representatives [2] and his heirs and devisees, shall be liable in due course of administration to contribute to the assets of the company [3] in discharge of his liability and they shall be contributories [1] accordingly.

(2) Where the personal representatives [2] are placed on the list of contributories [1], the heirs or devisees need not be added; but they may be added as and when the court [4] thinks fit.

(3) If the personal representatives [2] make default in paying any money ordered to be paid by them, proceedings may be taken for administering the whole or any part of the estate of the deceased contributory,[1] and for compelling payment out of it of the money due.

**Notes**

**Section 405**

1. "Contributory" means every person liable to contribute to the assets of a company in the event of its being wound up and for the purposes of all proceedings for determining, and all proceedings prior to the final determination of, the persons who are to be deemed contributories, the expression includes any person alleged to be contributory. See **section 567 CAMA Cap. C20, LFN 2004**
2. "Personal Representative" where customary law is applicable, includes successors appointed in respect of deceased contributories **; See section 567 CAMA Cap. C20 LFN 2004.**
3. "Company" means a company formed and registered under this Act or, as the case may be, formed and registered in Nigeria before and in existence on the commencement of this Act. **See section 567, CAMA Cap. C20 LFN 2004**
4. "Court" used in relation to a company, means the Federal High Court, and to the extent to which application may be made to it as; court includes the Court of Appeal and the Supreme Court of Nigeria. See **Section 567 CAMA, Cap. C20, LFN, 2004.**

**Cross Reference**

On the establishment and jurisdiction of the Federal High Court, see **sections 249 & 251 Constitution of the Federal Republic of Nigeria, 1999(as amended)**

---

## 406. Contributories in case of bankruptcy of member

(1) If a contributory [1] becomes bankrupt[2], either before or after he has been placed on the list of contributories [1], then-

(a) his trustee in bankruptcy [3] shall represent him for all the purposes of the winding-up[4], and shall be a contributory [1] accordingly, and may be called on to admit to proof against the estate of the bankrupt [2], or otherwise to allow to be paid out of his assets in due course of law, any money due from the bankrupt [2] in respect of his liability to contribute to the assets of the company [5]; and

(b) there may be proved against the estate of the bankrupt [2] the estimated value of his liability to future calls as well as calls already made.

(2) The provisions of this section shall extend and apply with all necessary changes to the case of an insolvent person [5].

---

**Notes**

**Section 406**

1. "Contributory" means every person liable to contribute to the assets of a company in the event of its being wound up and for the purposes of all proceedings for determining, and all proceedings prior to the final determination of, the persons who are to be deemed contributories, the expression includes any person alleged to be contributory. See **section 567 CAMA Cap. C20, LFN 2004**
2. "Bankrupt" means person who cannot meet current financial obligations; an insolvent person. See **Garner B. (ed) Black's law dictionary 8th ed.**
3. "Trustee in bankruptcy" means a person in whom the property of a bankrupt is vested for the benefit of the bankrupt's creditors. See Martine E. (ed.), Oxford Dictionaly of Law, 4 th ed.
4. "Winding up:" the process of settling accounts and liquidating assets in anticipation of a partnership's or a corporations dissolution. See **Garner B. (ed) Black's law dictionary 8th ed.**
5. "Insolvent person" means any person in Nigeria who, in respect of any judgment, Act or court order against him, is unable to satisfy execution or other process issued thereon in favour of a creditor, and the execution or other process remains unsatisfied for not less than six weeks. See **section 567 CAMA Cap. C20, LFN 2004**

**Cross Reference**

On the appointment of a trustee in bankruptcy, see **section 21, Bankruptcy Act Cap. B2 LFN 2004**

*CHAPTER 2*

*Winding up by the court*

*Jurisdiction*

## 407. Jurisdiction as to winding up

(1) The court [1] having jurisdiction to wind up [2] a company [3] shall be the Federal High Court within whose area of jurisdiction the registered office or head office of the company [3] is situate.

(2) For the purpose of this section, "registered office" or "head office" means the place which has longest been the registered office or head office of the company during the six months immediately preceding the presentation of the petition for winding up [2].

**Notes**

**Section 407(1)**

1. "Court" used in relation to a company , means the Federal High Court, and to the extent to which application may be made to it as; court

includes the Court of Appeal and the Supreme Court of Nigeria. See **Section 567 CAMA, Cap. C20, LFN, 2004.**

2. "Wind up" see "winding up." It is the process of settling accounts and liquidating assets in anticipation of a partnership's or a corporation's dissolution. See **Garner B. (ed) Black's law dictionary 8th ed.**
3. "Company" means a company formed and registered under this Act or, as the case may be, formed and registered in Nigeria before and in existence on the commencement of this Act. **See section 567, CAMA Cap. C20 LFN 2004**

Cross Reference

On the establishment of Federal High Court and its respective jurisdiction: see Sections 249 and 251 of the Constitution of the Federal Republic of Nigeria,1999 (as amended)

On obligation to provide a registered address see section 251 of the Constitution of the Federal Republic of Nigeria,1999 (as amended)

On the appointment of a trustee in bankruptcy, see **section 21, Bankruptcy Act Cap. B2 LFN 2004**

On application for winding up to be by petition, **see section 410 CAMA Cap. C20 LFN 2004**

**Cases**

Care and utmost caution must be exercised by the court in its dealing with cases involving the termination of the life of a company. ***Air Via Ltd v. Oriental Airlines Ltd.*** **(2004) 9 N.W.L.R (PT.878) 298.**

## 408. Circumstances in which companies may be wound up by court

A company[1] may be wound up[2] by the court[3] if-

(a) the company[1] has by special resolution[4] resolved that the company[1] be wound up[2] by the court[3];
(b) default is made in delivering the statutory report[5] to the Commission[6] or in holding the statutory meeting[7];
(c) the number of members[8] is reduced below two;
(d) the company[1] is unable to pay its debts;
(e) the court[3] is of opinion that it is just and equitable that the company[1] should be wound up[2]

**Notes**

**Section 408**

1. "Company" means a company formed and registered under this Act or, as the case may be, formed and

registered in Nigeria before and in existence on the commencement of this Act. **See section 567, CAMA Cap. C20 LFN 2004**

2. "Wound up" see "winding up". It is the process of settling accounts and liquidating assets in anticipation of a partnership's or a corporation's dissolution. See **Garner B. (ed) Black's law dictionary 8th ed.**
3. "Court" used in relation to a company , means the Federal High Court, and to the extent to which application may be made to it as; court includes the Court of Appeal and the Supreme Court of Nigeria. See **Section 567 CAMA, Cap. C20, LFN, 2004.**
4. "Special Resolution" means resolution passed by not less than three-fourths of the votes by such members of the company as being entitled to do so, vote by person or in proxy at a general meeting of which 21days notice, specifying the intention to propose the resolution is a special resolution, has been duly given. **See section 233(2) CAMA, Cap. C20 , LFN 2004.**
5. "Statutory report" has the meaning assigned to it by section 211 (2) of this Act. See **Section 567 CAMA, Cap. C20, LFN, 2004.**
6. "Commission" means the Corporate Affairs Commission established under section 1 of this Act **. See section 567 CAMA Cap. C20, LFN 2004.**
7. "Statutory Meeting" means the meeting required to be held by section 211 (1) of this Act. **See section 567 CAMA Cap. C20, LFN 2004.**
8. "Members" see "member" It means one of the individuals of whom a deliberative assembly consists and who enjoys the full rights of participating in the organization-including the rights of making, debating and voting on motions- except to the extent that the organization reserves those rights to certain classes of membership. **Garner B. ed. Black's Law Dictionary 8th ed.**

   "Member"includes the heir, executor, administrator or other personal representative, as the case maybe, of the member; **See section 567 CAMA Cap. C20 LFN 2004**

Cross Reference

On the establishment of Federal High Court and its respective jurisdiction, see **sections 249 & 251 Constitution of the Federal Republic of Nigeria, 1999 (as amended)**

Cases

A just and equitable ground is one of the grounds upon which a court having jurisdiction can rely to make an order for winding up a company. See **Section 408(e) of the Companies and Allied Matters Act,Cap. 59, Laws of the Federation of Nigeria 1990** . Section 408(e) of same law contained in **Cap. C.20 of Laws of the Federation of Nigeria 2004.** ***Ado Ibrahim & Company Ltd v. Bendel Cement Company Ltd*** **[2007] S.C. 284/2001.**

## 409. Definition of inability to pay debts

A company[1] shall be deemed to be unable to pay its debts if-

(a) a creditor[2], by assignment or otherwise, to whom the company[1] is indebted in a sum exceeding N2,000, then due, has served on the company[1], by leaving it at its registered office or head office, a demand under his hand requiring the company[1] to pay the sum so due, and the company[1] has for three weeks thereafter neglected to pay the sum or to secure or compound for it to the reasonable satisfaction of the creditor[2]; or

(b) execution or other process issued on a judgment, Act or order of any court[3] in favour of a creditor[2] of the company[1] is returned unsatisfied in whole or in part; or

(c) the court[3], after taking into account any contingent or prospective liability of the company[1], is satisfied that the company[1] is unable to pay its debts.

---

**Notes**
**Section 409**

1. "Company" means a company formed and registered under this Act or, as the case may be, formed and
registered in Nigeria before and in existence on the commencement of this Act. **See section 567, CAMA Cap. C20 LFN 2004**
2. "Creditor" means one to whom a debt is owed; one who gives credit for money or goods. **See Garner B. (ed) Black's Law Dictionary, 8 th ed.**
3. "Court" used in relation to a company, means the Federal High Court, and to the extent to which application may be made to it as; court includes the Court of Appeal and the Supreme Court of Nigeria. See **Section 567 CAMA, Cap. C20, LFN, 2004.**

Cross Reference

On the establishment of Federal High Court and its respective jurisdiction, see **sections 249 & 251 Constitution of the Federal Republic of Nigeria, 1999 (as amended)**

On obligation on a company to provide a registered address and notify of any change there in, see **sections 35 & 574 CAMA Cap. C20, LFN 2004**

---

*Petitions for winding up and effects thereof*

## 410. Provisions as to application for winding up

(1) An application to the court [1] for the winding up [2] of a company[3] shall be by petition presented subject to the provisions of this section, either by-

(a) the company [3];

(b) a creditor [4], including a contingent or prospective creditor [4] of the company [3];

(c) the official receiver [5];

(d) a contributory [6];

(e) a trustee in bankruptcy [7] to, or a personal representative [8] of, a creditor [4] or contributory [6];

(f) the Commission [9] under section 323 of this Act;

(g) a receiver, [10] if authorised by the instrument under which he was appointed; or

(h) by all or any of those parties, together or separately.

(2) Notwithstanding anything in subsection (1) of this section-

(a) a contributory [6] shall not be entitled to present a petition for winding up [2] a company [3] unless-

(i) the number of members [11] is reduced below two; or

(ii) the shares in respect of which he is contributory [6] or some of them, were originally allotted to him or have been held by him, and registered in his name, for at least six months during the 18 months before the commencement of the winding up [2], or have devolved on him through the death of a former holder;

(b) a winding-up [2] petition shall not, if the ground of the petition is default in delivering the statutory report [12] to the Commission[9] or in holding the statutory meeting, [13] be presented by any person except a shareholder, [14] or before the expiration of 14 days after the last day on which the meeting[13] should have been held;

(c) the court [1] shall not hear a winding-up [2] petition presented by a contingent or prospective creditor [4] until sufficient security for costs has been given, and a prima facie case for winding up [2] has been established to its satisfaction;

(d) in any case falling within section 320 or 321 of this Act (proceedings on inspector's reports) or paragraph (e) of section 408 of this Act, a winding-up [2] petition may be presented by the Commission [9] with the approval of the Attorney-General of the Federation.

(3) Where a company [3] is being wound up voluntarily [15] or subject to supervision, a winding-up [2] petition may be presented by the official receiver [5] attached to the court, [1] as well as by any other person authorised in that behalf under the other provisions of this section; but the court [1] shall not make a winding-up [2] order on any such petition unless it is satisfied that the voluntary winding up [15] or winding up [2] subject to supervision cannot be continued with due regard to the interests of the creditors [4] or contributories [6].

(4) A contributory [6] shall be entitled to present a winding-up [2] petition notwithstanding that there may not be assets available on the winding up [2] for distribution to contributories [6].

---

**Notes**
**Section 410**

1. "Court" used in relation to a company , means the Federal High Court, and to the extent to which application may be made to it as; court includes the Court of Appeal and the Supreme Court of Nigeria. See **Section 567 CAMA, Cap. C20, LFN, 2004.**
2. "Winding up" is the process of settling accounts and liquidating assets in anticipation of a partnership's or a corporation's dissolution. See **Garner B. (ed) Black's law dictionary 8th ed.**
3. "Company" means a company formed and registered under this Act or, as the case may be, formed and registered in Nigeria before and in existence on the commencement of this Act. **See section 567, CAMA Cap. C20 LFN 2004**
4. "Creditor" means one to whom a debt is owed; one who gives credit for money or goods. **See Garner B. (ed) Black's Law Dictionary, 8 th ed.**
5. "Official receiver" means the officer by whatever name called or known charged with control of affairs in bankruptcy and if the appointment is vacant for any reason whatsoever, means the sheriff. See **section 567, CAMA Cap. C20 LFN 2004**
   For the purpose of this Act and so far as it relates to the winding up of companies by the court, "official receiver" means the Deputy Chief Registrar of the Federal High Court or an officer designated for the purpose by the Chief Judge of the Court. See **section 419 CAMA Cap. C20, LFN 2004**
6. "Contributory" means every person liable to contribute to the assets of a company in the event of its being wound up and for the purposes of all proceedings for determining, and all proceedings prior to the final determination of, the persons who are to be deemed contributories, the expression includes any person alleged to be contributory. See **section 567 CAMA Cap. C20, LFN 2004**
7. "Trustee in bankruptcy"

8. "Personal Representative" where customary law is applicable, includes successors appointed in respect of deceased contributories. See **section 567 CAMA Cap. C20, LFN 2004**
9. "Commission" means the Corporate Affairs Commission established under section 1 of this Act **. See section 567 CAMA Cap. C20, LFN 2004.**
10. "Receiver" means a disinterested person appointed by a court, or by a corporation or other person, for the protection or collection of property that is the subject of diverse claims. See **Garner B, (ed) Black's Law Dictionary 8th ed.**
    "Receiver" includes a manager. See **section. 567 CAMA, Cap. C20, LFN 2004.**
11. "Members" see "member" It means one of the individuals of whom a deliberative assembly consists and who enjoys the full rights of participating in the organization-including the rights of making, debating and voting on motions- except to the extent that the organization reserves those rights to certain classes of membership. **Garner B. ed. Black's Law Dictionary 8th ed.**
    "Member"includes the heir, executor, administrator or other personal representative, as the case maybe, of the member; **See section 567 CAMA Cap. C20 LFN 2004**
12. "Statutory report" has the meaning assigned to it by section 211 (2) of this Act. See **Section 567 CAMA, Cap. C20, LFN, 2004.**
13. "Statutory Meeting" means the meeting required to be held by section 211 (1) of this Act. **See section 567 CAMA Cap. C20, LFN 2004.**
14. "Shareholder" means one who owns or holds a share or shares in a company. **See Garner B, (ed) Black's Law Dictionary 8 th ed.**
15. "Wound up voluntarily" see"voluntary winding up". It means the dissolution of a company when the period, if any fixed for its duration by the articles expires or on the occurrence of an event of which its articles provide that the company is to be dissolved and the company in a general meeting pass a resolution requiring the company to be wound up . See **section 457 CAMA Cap. C20, LFN 2004**

**Cross Reference**

On the establishment of the Office of the Attorney General of the Federation, see **section 150, Constitution of the Federal Republic of Nigeria, 1999 (as amended)**

On winding up proceedings, see generally the Companies Winding up rules 2001

---

**For Further Reading**

On winding up of company, see Sofowora, M.O **Modern Nigerian Company Law** Soft Associates, 2 nd Edition 2002.

## 411. Powers of court on hearing petition

(1) On hearing a winding-up [1] petition the court[2] may dismiss it, or adjourn the hearing conditionally or unconditionally, or make any interim order, or any other order that it thinks fit; but the court[2] shall not refuse to make a winding-up [1] order on the ground only that the assets of the company [3] have been mortgaged to an amount equal to or in excess of those assets, or that the company [3] has no assets.

(2) Unless it appears to the court [2] that some other remedy is available and that the petitioners are acting unreasonably in seeking a winding-up[1] order instead of pursuing that remedy, the court [2], on hearing a petition by contributory [4] members[5] of a company[3] for relief by winding up [1] on the ground that it would be just and equitable so to do, shall make the order as prayed if of opinion that the petitioners are entitled to the relief sought.

(3) Where a petition is presented on the ground of default in delivering the statutory report [6] to the Commission[7] or in holding the statutory meeting[8], the court[2], instead of making a winding-up [1] order, may direct the delivery of the statutory report [6] or the holding of a meeting[8], as the case may require, and order the costs to be paid by the persons who, in the opinion of the court [2], are responsible for the default.

---

**Notes**
**Section 411**

1. "Winding up" is the process of settling accounts and liquidating assets in anticipation of a partnership's or a corporation's dissolution. See **Garner B. (ed) Black's law dictionary 8th ed.**
2. "Court" used in relation to a company, means the Federal High Court, and to the extent to which application may be made to it as; court includes the Court of Appeal and the Supreme Court of Nigeria. See **Section 567 CAMA, Cap. C20, LFN, 2004.**
3. "Company" means a company formed and registered under this Act or, as the case may be, formed and registered in Nigeria before and in existence on the commencement of this Act. **See section 567, CAMA Cap. C20 LFN 2004**
4. "Contributory" means every person liable to contribute to the assets of a company in the event of its being wound up and for the purposes of all proceedings for determining, and all proceedings prior to the final determination of, the persons who are to be deemed contributories, the expression includes any person alleged to be contributory. See **section 567 CAMA Cap. C20, LFN 2004**
5. "Members" see "member" It means one of the individuals of whom a deliberative assembly consists and who enjoys the full rights of

participating in the organization-including the rights of making, debating and voting on motions- except to the extent that the organization reserves those rights to certain classes of membership. **Garner B. ed. Black's Law Dictionary 8th ed.**
"Member"includes the heir, executor, administrator or other personal representative, as the case maybe, of the member; **See section 567 CAMA Cap. C20 LFN 2004**

6. "Statutory report" has the meaning assigned to it by section 211 (2) of this Act. See **Section 567 CAMA, Cap. C20, LFN, 2004.**
7. "Commission" means the Corporate Affairs Commission established under section 1 of this Act . **See section 567 CAMA Cap. C20, LFN 2004.**
8. "Statutory Meeting" means the meeting required to be held by section 211 (1) of this Act. **See section 567 CAMA Cap. C20, LFN 2004.**

**Cross Reference**

On the establishment of Federal High Court and its respective jurisdiction, see **sections 249 & 251 Constitution of the Federal Republic of Nigeria, 1999** (as amended)

On winding up proceedings, see generally the Companies Winding up rules 2001

---

**Cases**

Care and utmost caution must be exercised by the court in its dealing with cases involving the termination of the life of a company. ***Air Via Ltd v. Oriental Airlines Ltd.*** **(2004) 9 N.W.L.R (Pt.878) 298.**

For Further Reading on winding up of company, see Sofowora, M.O Modern Nigerian Company Law Soft Associates, 2 nd Edition 2002.

## 412.Power to stay or restrain proceedings against company

Where a winding-up[1] petition has been presented and an action or other proceeding against a company [2] is instituted or pending in any court[3] (in this section referred to as "the court concerned"), the company[2] or any creditor [4] or contributory [5] may, before the making of the winding-up[1] order, apply to the court [3] concerned for an order staying proceedings; and the court [3] concerned may, with or without imposing terms, stay or restrain proceedings, or if it thinks fit, refer the case to the court [3] hearing the winding-up[1] petition.

---

**Notes**
**Section 412**

1. "Winding up" is the process of settling accounts and liquidating assets in anticipation of a partnership's or a corporation's dissolution. See **Garner B. (ed) Black's law dictionary 8th ed.**
2. "Company" means a company formed and registered under this Act or, as the case may be, formed and
registered in Nigeria before and in existence on the commencement of this Act. **See section 567, CAMA Cap. C20 LFN 2004**
3. "Court" used in relation to a company , means the Federal High Court, and to the extent to which application may be made to it as; court includes the Court of Appeal and the Supreme Court of Nigeria. See **Section 567 CAMA, Cap. C20, LFN, 2004.**
4. "Creditor" means one to whom a debt is owed; one who gives credit for money or goods. **See Garner B. (ed) Black's Law Dictionary, 8 th ed.**
5. "Contributory" means every person liable to contribute to the assets of a company in the event of its being wound up and for the purposes of all proceedings for determining, and all proceedings prior to the final determination of, the persons who are to be deemed contributories, the expression includes any person alleged to be contributory. See **section 567 CAMA Cap. C20, LFN 2004**

Cross Reference

On the establishment of Federal High Court and its respective jurisdiction, see **sections 249 & 251 Constitution of the Federal Republic of Nigeria, 1999** (as amended)

On winding up proceedings, see generally the Companies Winding up rules 2001

---

**Cases**

The application for stay of proceedings may be brought where there is an interlocutory appeal or final appeal in an action between parties. It may also be brought where there is a concurrent action between parties in respect of thr same or substiantially the same subject matter... In all these cases, the rationale is that the action ought, in the interest of justice to be stayed to enable the preservation od the subject matter in dispute. This discretion exists and may be exercised whether the res is tangible or intangible See ***Akilu v. GAni Fawehinmi (No.2)***

All Courts have an impeded discretion to grant or refuse a stay of proceedins or execution of proceedings before them but the discretion ought to be exercised both judicially as well as judiciously. See ***Okafor v. Nnaife (1987) 4 N.W.L.R (Pt. 64) 129***

**For Further Reading**

On winding up of company, see Sofowora, M.O **Modern Nigerian Company Law** Soft Associates, 2nd Edition 2002.

## 413. Avoidance of dispositions of property, etc., after commencement of winding up

In a winding up[1] by the court,[2] any disposition of the property of the company,[3] including things in action and any transfer of shares,[4] or alteration in the status of the members[5] of the company[3], made after the commencement of the winding up[1] shall, unless the court[2] otherwise orders, be void.

---

**Notes**
**Section 413**

1. "Winding up" is the process of settling accounts and liquidating assets in anticipation of a partnership's or a corporation's dissolution. See **Garner B. (ed) Black's law dictionary 8th ed.**
2. "Court" used in relation to a company, means the Federal High Court, and to the extent to which application may be made to it as; court includes the Court of Appeal and the Supreme Court of Nigeria. See **Section 567 CAMA, Cap. C20, LFN, 2004.**
3. "Company" means a company formed and registered under this Act or, as the case may be, formed and
registered in Nigeria before and in existence on the commencement of this Act. **See section 567, CAMA Cap. C20 LFN 2004**
4. "Shares" see "share." It means the interest in a company's share capital of a member who is entitled to share in the capital or income of such company: and except where a distinction between stock and shares is expressed or implied, includes stock. **See section 567CAMA Cap. C20 LFN 2004**
5. "Members" see "member" It means one of the individuals of whom a deliberative assembly consists and who enjoys the full rights of participating in the organization-including the rights of making, debating and voting on motions- except to the extent that the organization reserves those rights to certain classes of membership. See **Garner B. ed. Black's Law Dictionary 8th ed.**
"Member"includes the heir, executor, administrator or other personal representative, as the case maybe, of the member; **See section 567 CAMA Cap. C20 LFN 2004**

**Cross Reference**

On the establishment of Federal High Court and its respective jurisdiction, see **sections 249 & 251 Constitution of the Federal Republic of Nigeria, 1999 (as amended)**

On transfer of shares of a company, see **section 151 CAMA, Cap. C 20, LFN 2004**

On winding up proceedings, see generally the Companies Winding up rules 2001

---

**For Further Reading**
On winding up of company, see Sofowora, M.O **Modern Nigerian Company Law** Soft Associates, 2[nd] Edition 2002.

## 414. Avoidance of attachments, etc.

Where a company[1] is being wound up[2] by the court[3], any attachment[4], sequestration[5], distress or execution put in force against the estate or effects of the company[1] after the commencement of the winding up[2] shall be void.

---

**Notes**
**Section 414**

1. "Company" means a company formed and registered under this Act or, as the case may be, formed and registered in Nigeria before and in existence on the commencement of this Act. **See section 567, CAMA Cap. C20 LFN 2004**
2. "Wound up" see "winding up" which means the process of settling accounts and liquidating assets in anticipation of a partnership's or a corporation's dissolution. See **Garner B. ed. Black's Law Dictionary 8th ed.**
3. "Court" used in relation to a company, means the Federal High Court, and to the extent to which application may be made to it as; court includes the Court of Appeal and the Supreme Court of Nigeria. See **Section 567 CAMA, Cap. C20, LFN, 2004.**
4. "Attachment" means the seizing of a person's property to secure a judgment or to be sold in satisfaction of udgment. See **Garner B.(ed) Black's Law Dictionary 8[th] ed**
5. "Sequestration" means the process by which property is removed from the possessor pending the outcome f a dispute in which two or more parties contend for it. See **Garner B. ed) Black's Law Dictionary 8[th] ed**

Cross Reference

On the establishment of Federal High Court and its respective jurisdiction, see **sections 249 & 251 Constitution of the Federal Republic of Nigeria, 1999 (as amended)**

On power of court to order a writ of sequestration against property,see **section 82 Sheriffs and Civil Process Act Cap. s 6, LFN 2004**

On winding up proceedings, see generally the Companies Winding up rules 2001

---

*Commencement of winding up*

## 415. Commencement of a winding up by the court

(1) Where, before the presentation of a petition for the winding up[1] of a company[2] by the court[3], a resolution[4] has been passed by the company[2] for voluntary winding up[5], the winding up[1] of the company[2] shall be deemed to have commenced at the time of the passing of the resolution[4], and unless the court[3], on proof of fraud or mistake, thinks fit otherwise to direct, all proceedings taken in the voluntary winding up[5] shall be deemed to have been validly taken.

(2) In any other case, the winding up[1] of a company[2] by the court[3] shall be deemed to commence at the time of the presentation of the petition for the winding up.[1]

---

**Notes**

**Section 415**

1. "Winding up" means the process of settling accounts and liquidating assets in anticipation of a partnership's or a corporation's dissolution. See **Garner B. ed. Black's Law Dictionary 8th ed.**
2. "Company" means a company formed and registered under this Act or, as the case may be, formed and registered in Nigeria before and in existence on the commencement of this Act. **See section 567, CAMA Cap. C20 LFN 2004**
3. "Court" used in relation to a company, means the Federal High Court, and to the extent to which application may be made to it as; court includes the Court of Appeal and the Supreme Court of Nigeria. See **Section 567 CAMA, Cap. C20, LFN, 2004.**
4. "Resolution" means a main motion that formally expresses the sense, will, or action of a deliberative assembly. See **Garner B. (ed) Black's Law Dictionary, 8th ed**
5. "Voluntary winding up" means the dissolution of a company when the period, if any fixed for its duration by the articles expires or on the occurrence of an event of which its articles provide that the company is to be dissolved and the company in a general meeting pass a resolution requiring the company to be wound up . See **section 457 CAMA Cap. C20, LFN 2004**

Cross Reference

On the passing of a resolution to wind up a company voluntarily, see **section 458 CAMA Cap. C20, LFN 2004**

On winding up proceedings, see generally the Companies Winding up rules 2001

On the establishment of Federal High Court and its respective jurisdiction, see **sections 249 & 251 Constitution of the Federal Republic of Nigeria, 1999 (as amended)**

---

**For Further Reading**

On commencement of winding up proceedings, see, Asomugha, E. Maduelosi **Company law in Nigeria under the Companies and Allied Matters Act** E.M. Asomugha (Lagos) 1994

*Consequences of winding-up order*

## 416. Copy of order to be forwarded to Commission

On the making of a winding-up[1] order, a copy of the order shall forthwith be forwarded by the company, [2] or otherwise as may be prescribed, to the Commission, [3] which shall make a minute thereof in its books relating to the company [2].

**Notes**
**Section 416**

1. "Winding up" means the process of settling accounts and liquidating assets in anticipation of a partnership's or a corporation's dissolution . **See Garner B. (ed) Black's Law Dictionary, 8th ed.**
2. "Company" means a company formed and registered under this Act or, as the case may be, formed and registered in Nigeria before and in existence on the commencement of this Act. **See section 567, CAMA Cap. C20 LFN 2004**
3. "Commission" means the Corporate Affairs Commission established under section 1 of this Act . **See section 567 CAMA Cap. C20, LFN 2004.**

**Cross Reference**

On commencement of winding up by the Court, see **section 415 CAMA Cap.C20, LFN 2004**

**Cases**

A just and equitable ground is one of the grounds upon which a court having jurisdiction can rely to make an order for winding up a company. **See Section 408(e) of the Companies and Allied Matters Act, Cap 59, Laws of the Federation of Nigeria 1990.** Section 408(e) of same law contained in Cap. C20 of Laws of the Federation of Nigeria 2004. A just and equitable ground for winding up a company is a remedy most suitable for contributories. Where a contributory brings a petition under this head as was found by the trial court and where the trial court is of the opinion that the petitioner is entitled to the order of winding up, it must make the order unless it appears to the court that some other remedy is available to the petitioner and that he is acting unreasonably in seeking a winding up order instead of pursuing that other remedy. ***Ado Ibrahim & Company Ltd v. Bendel Cement Company Ltd*** **(2007) S. C. 284/2001.**

## 417. Actions stayed on winding-up order

If a winding-up[1] order is made or a provisional liquidator [2] is appointed, no action or proceeding shall be proceeded with or commenced against the company[3] except by leave of the court [4] given on such terms as the court [4] may impose.

---

**Notes**
**Section 417**

1. "Winding up" means the process of settling accounts and liquidating assets in anticipation of a partnership's or a corporation's dissolution.See **Garner B. (ed) Black's Law Dictionary, 8th ed.**
2. "Provisional Liquidator" means a person who is temporarily appointed to wind up a business's affairs esp. by selling off its assets. **See Garner B. Black's Law Dictionary, 8 th ed.**
3. "Company" means a company formed and registered under this Act or, as the case may be, formed and registered in Nigeria before and in existence on the commencement of this Act. **See section 567, CAMA Cap. C20 LFN 2004.**
4. "Court" used in relation to a company, means the Federal High Court, and to the extent to which application may be made to it as; court includes the Court of Appeal and the Supreme Court of Nigeria. See **Section 567 CAMA, Cap. C20, LFN, 2004.**

**Cross Reference**

On the establishment of Federal High Court and its respective jurisdiction, see **sections 249 & 251 Constitution of the Federal Republic of Nigeria, 1999 (as amended)**

On winding up proceedings, see generally the Companies Winding up rules 2001

---

## 418. Effect of winding-up order

An order for winding up [1] a company[2] shall operate in favour of all the creditors [3] and of all the contributories [4] of the company[2] as if made on the joint petition of a creditor [3] and of a contributory [4].

---

**Notes**
**Section 418**

1. "Winding up" means the process of settling accounts and liquidating assets in anticipation of a partnership's or a corporation's dissolution . **See Garner B. (ed) Black's Law Dictionary, 8th ed.**
2. "Company" means a company formed and registered under this Act or, as the case may be, formed and registered in Nigeria before and in

existence on the commencement of this Act. **See section 567, CAMA Cap. C20 LFN 2004**

3. "Creditors" means one to whom a debt is owed; one who gives credit for money or goods. **See Garner B. (ed) Black's Law Dictionary, 8 th ed.**
4. "Contributory" means every person liable to contribute to the assets of a company in the event of its being wound up and for the purposes of all proceedings for determining and all proceedings prior to the final determination of the persons who are to be deemed contributories, the expression shall include any person alleged to be a contributory. See section **567 CAMA Cap. C20 LFN 2004**

Cross Reference

On winding up proceedings, see generally the Companies Winding up rules 2001

On commencement of winding up by the Court, see **section 415 CAMA Cap.C20, LFN 2004**

**For Further Reading**

On commencement of winding up proceedings, see, Asomugha, E. Maduelosi **Company law in Nigeria under the Companies and Allied Matters Act** E.M. Asomugha (Lagos) 1994

*Official receiver*

## 419. Definition of official receiver

(1) For the purpose of this Act and so far as it relates to the winding up[1] of companies[2] by the court, "official receiver" means the Deputy Chief Registrar of the Federal High Court or an officer designated for the purpose by the Chief Judge of the Court.

(2) Any such officer shall, for the purpose of his duties under this Act, be styled "the official receiver".

**Notes**

**Section 419**

1. "Winding up" means the process of settling accounts and liquidating assets in anticipation of a partnership's or a corporation's dissolution.See **Garner B. (ed) Blacks' Law Dictionary, 8th ed.**
2. "Companies" see"company." It means a company formed and registered under this Act or, as the case may be, formed and registered in Nigeria before and in existence on the commencement of this Act. **See section 567, CAMA Cap. C20 LFN 2004**

Cross Reference

On the establishment of the Federal High Court, see section 249, **Constitution of the Federal Republic of Nigeria, 1999 (as amended)**
On the appointment of the Chief Judge of the Federal High Court, see section 250 **Constitution of the Federal Republic of Nigeria, 1999(as amended)**

---

## 420. Statement of company's affairs to be submitted to official receiver

(1) Where the court [1] has made a winding-up [2] order or appointed a provisional liquidator [3] there shall, unless the court [1] thinks fit to order otherwise and so orders, be made out and submitted to the official receiver [4] a statement as to the affairs of the company[5] in the prescribed form, verified by affidavit, and showing the particulars of its assets, debts and liabilities, the names, residences and occupations of its creditors [6], the securities [7] held by them respectively, the dates when the securities [7] were respectively given, the list of members [8] and the list of charges [9] and such further or other information as may be prescribed or as the official receiver[4] may require.

(2) The statement shall be submitted and verified by one or more of the persons who are at the relevant date the directors [10] and the person who is at that date the secretary [11] of the company,[5] or by such of the persons mentioned in this subsection as the official receiver,[4] subject to the direction of the court, [1] may require to submit and verify the statement, that is to say persons who-

(a) are or have been officers [12] of the company[5];

(b) have taken part in the formation of the company [5] at any time within one year before the relevant date;

(c) have been or are in the employment of the company [5] within the said year, and are in the opinion of the official receiver[4] capable of giving the information required;

(d) are or have been within the said year officers [12] of or in the employment of a company[5] which is, or within the said year was, an officer [12] of the company[5] to which the statement relates.

(3) The statement shall be submitted within 14 days from the relevant date or within such extended time as the official receiver [4] or the court [1] may for special reasons appoint.

(4) Any person making or concurring in making the statement and affidavit required by this section shall be allowed, and shall be

paid by the official receiver [4] or provisional liquidator, [3] as the case may be, out of the assets of the company [5] such costs and expenses incurred in and about the preparation and making of the statement and affidavit as the official receiver [4] may consider reasonable, subject to an appeal to the court [1].

(5) If any person, without reasonable excuse, makes default in complying with the requirements of this section, he shall be guilty of an offence and liable to a fine of N25 for every day during which the default continues.

(6) Any person stating himself in writing to be a creditor [6] or contributory[13] of the company[5] shall be entitled by himself or by his agent at all reasonable times, on a payment of the prescribed fee to inspect the statement submitted in pursuance of this section, and to a copy of or extract from it.

(7) Any person untruthfully so stating himself to be a creditor[6] or contributory [13] shall be guilty of contempt of court [1] and shall, on the application of the liquidator [3] or of the official receiver,[4] be punishable accordingly.

(8) In this section, the expression "the relevant date" means, in a case where a provisional liquidator [3] is appointed, the date of his appointment and in a case where no such appointment is made, the date of the winding-up[2] order.

---

**Notes**
**Section 420**

1. "Court" used in relation to a company , means the Federal High Court, and to the extent to which application may be made to it as; court includes the Court of Appeal and the Supreme Court of Nigeria. See **Section 567 CAMA, Cap. C20, LFN, 2004.**
2. "Winding-up means the process of settling accounts and liquidating assets in anticipation of a partnership's or a corporation's dissolution. See **Garner B. (ed) Blacks' Law Dictionary, 8th ed.**
3. "Provisional Liquidator" means a person who is temporarily appointed to wind up a business's affairs esp. by selling off its assets. **See Garner B. Black's Law Dictionary, 8 th ed.**
4. "Official receiver" means the officer by whatever name called or known charged with control of affairs in bankruptcy and if the appointment is vacant for any reason whatsoever, means the sheriff. See **section 567, CAMA Cap. C20 LFN 2004**
   For the purpose of this Act and so far as it relates to the winding up of companies by the court, "official receiver" means the Deputy Chief Registrar of the Federal High Court or an officer designated for the

purpose by the Chief Judge of the Court. See **section 419 CAMA CAap.C20, LFN 2004**

5. "Company" means a company formed and registered under this Act or, as the case may be, formed and registered in Nigeria before and in existence on the commencement of this Act. See **section 567, CAMA Cap. C20 LFN 2004.**
6. "Creditors" see "creditor." It means one to whom a debt is owed; one who gives credit for money or goods. **See Garner B. (ed) Black's Law Dictionary, 8th ed.**
7. "Securities" includes shares, debentures, debenture stock, bonds, notes (other than promissory notes)
   and units under a unit trust scheme; **See S.567 CAMA Cap. C20 LFN 2004**
8. "Members" see"member." It includes the heir, executor, administrator or other personal representative, as the case may be, of the member; **See section 567 CAMA Cap. C20 LFN 2004**
9. "Charges" see "charge." It means an incumbrance, lien or claim, a burden or load, an obligation or duty or liability. See **Garner B. (ed) Black's law dictionary 8th ed.**
10. "Directors" see "director." It includes any person occupying the position of director by whatever name called; and includes any person in accordance with whose directions or instructions the directors of the company are accustomed to act. See **section 567 CAMA Cap. C20 LFN 2004**
11. "Secretary" means a corporate officer in charge of official correspondence, minutes of board meetings and records of stock ownership and transfer. See **Garner B. (ed) Black's law dictionary 8th ed.**
12. "Officers" see "officer". In relation to a body corporate, officer includes a director, manager or secretary. See **section 567 CAMA, Cap. C20, LFN 2004.**
13. "Contributory" means every person liable to contribute to the assets of a company in the event of its being wound up and for the purposes of all proceedings for determining and all proceedings prior to the final determination of the persons who are to be deemed contributories, the expression shall include any person alleged to be a contributory. See **section 567 CAMA Cap. C20 LFN 2004**

**Cross Reference**

On winding up proceedings, see generally the Companies Winding up rules 2001

On commencement of winding up by the Court, see **section 415 CAMA Cap. C20, LFN 2004**

---

**Cases**

On appointment of receiver, the powers of management of the company's business became vested in the receiver, but on quite a number of matters not related to management ,the directors can still act: ***UBA Trustees Ltd. v. Nigergrob Ceramic Ltd. (1987) 3 NWLR pt 62, p. 600.***

Where a receiver or manager is appointed for the whole o substantially the whole of a company's property, the powers conferred on him by the debentures by virtue of which he was appointed, shall be deemed to include, except in so far as they are with any of these debentures, the powers specified in the eleventh schedule to the Act: ***Onafowokan & 2 Ors v. Wema Bank & 2 Ors 88/2004 SC delivered 13/05/2010.***

Whilst receivership and manager open exclusively dominate the company affairs and dealings with the outside world, it does not affect the internal domestic structure of the company: ***Unibiz (Nig.) Ltd. v. Commercial Bank Credit Lyonnais Nig. Ltd.(for and on behalf of Babington Ashaye (2001) 7NWLR (pt 713) 534.***

Whilst receivership and manager open exclusively dominate the company affairs and dealings with the outside world, it does not affect the internal domestic structure of the company: ***Unibiz (Nig.) Ltd. v. Commercial Bank Credit Lyonnais Nig. Ltd.(for and on behalf of Babington Ashaye (2001) 7NWLR (pt 713) 534.***

The rationale for contempt is to vindicate the dignity of the court as an institution and thereby, protect it from denigration and ensure the administration of justice. See ***FRN v. Joe Brown Akubueze SC 206/ 2004 delivered on 4/06/2010***

## 421. Report by official receiver

(1) If a winding-up[1] order is made, the official receiver [2] shall as soon as practicable after receipt of the statement to be submitted under section 420 of this Act or where the court [3] orders that no statement shall be submitted, as soon as practicable after the date of the order, submit a preliminary report to the court [3]-

(a) as to the amount of capital [4] issued, subscribed and paid up, and the estimated amount of assets and liabilities; and

(b) if the company[5] has failed, as to the causes of the failure; and

(c) whether, in his opinion, further inquiry is desirable as to any matter relating to the promotion, formation or failure of the company.[5]

(2) The official receiver[2] may if he thinks fit, make further reports, stating the manner in which the company [5] was formed and whether in his opinion fraud has been committed by any person in its promotion or formation, or by any officer [6] of the company[5] in relation to the company[5] since its formation and the reports may include any other matters which, in his opinion, it is desirable to bring to the notice of the court. [3]

(3) If any further report under this section indicates the commission of fraud, the court [3] shall have the further powers

provided in section 450 of this Act (which confers authority to order public examination of certain officials).

---

**Notes**
**Section 421**

1. "Winding up" means the process of settling accounts and liquidating assets in anticipation of a partnership's or a corporation's dissolution. See **Garner B. (ed) Black's law dictionary 8th ed** .
2. "Official receiver" means the officer by whatever name called or known charged with control of affairs in bankruptcy and if the appointment is vacant for any reason whatsoever, means the sheriff. See **section 567, CAMA Cap. C20 LFN 2004**
   For the purpose of this Act and so far as it relates to the winding up of companies by the court, "official receiver" means the Deputy Chief Registrar of the Federal High Court or an officer designated for the purpose by the Chief Judge of the Court. See **section 419 CAMA Cap. C20, LFN 2004**
3. "Court" used in relation to a company , means the Federal High Court, and to the extent to which application may be made to it as; court includes the Court of Appeal and the Supreme Court of Nigeria. See **Section 567 CAMA, Cap. C20, LFN, 2004.**
4. "Capital" means a fund representing the nominal value of shares issued by a registered company. See **Martins E. (ed.) Oxford Dictionary of Law 4th ed**
5. "Company" means a company formed and registered under this Act or, as the case may be, formed and registered in Nigeria before and in existence on the commencement of this Act. See **Section 567 CAMA, Cap. C20, LFN, 2004.**
6. "officer" in relation to a body corporate, includes a director, manager or secretary. See **section 567 CAMA Cap. C20 LFN 2004.**

**Cross Reference**

On winding up proceedings, see generally the Companies Winding up rules 2001

On commencement of winding up by the Court, see **section 415 CAMA Cap. C20, LFN 2004**

On meaning of official receiver, see **section 419 CAMA Cap. C20 LFN 2004**

---

**For Further Reading**

On commencement of winding up proceedings, see, Asomugha, E. Maduelosi **Company law in Nigeria under the Companies and Allied Matters Act** E.M. Asomugha (Lagos) 1994

*Liquidators*

## 422. Appointment, remuneration and title of liquidators

(1) The court [1] may appoint a liquidator [2] or liquidators [2] for the purpose of conducting the proceedings in winding up [3] a company [4] and performing such duties in reference thereto as the court [1] may impose and where there is a vacancy, the official receiver [5] shall by virtue of his office, act as liquidator [2] until such time as the vacancy is filled.

(2) At any time after the presentation of a petition and before the making of a winding-up [3] order, the appointment shall be provisional and the court [1] making the appointment may limit and restrict the powers of the liquidator [2] by the order appointing him.

(3) In the application of the foregoing provisions of this section-

(a) if a provisional liquidator [6] is to be appointed before the making of a winding-up [3] order, the official receiver, [5] or any other fit person, may be so appointed;

(b) on the making of a winding-up [3] order, if no liquidator [2] is appointed, the official receiver [5] shall by virtue of his office become the liquidator [2];

(c) the official receiver [5] in his capacity as provisional liquidator [6] shall, and in any other case may, summon meetings of creditors [7] and contributories [8] of the company [4] to be held separately for the purpose of determining whether or not an application is to be made to the court for appointing a liquidator [2] in place of the official receiver [5];

(d) if a person other than the official receiver [5] is appointed liquidator, [2] he shall not be capable of acting in that capacity until he has notified his appointment to the Commission [9] and given security in the prescribed manner to the satisfaction of the court [1].

(4) If more than one liquidator [2] of a company [4] is appointed by the court, [1] the court [1] shall declare whether anything by this Act required or authorised to be done by a liquidator [2] is to be done by all or anyone or more of them.

(5) A liquidator [2] appointed by the court [1] may resign, or, on cause shown, be removed by the court [1]; and any vacancy in the office of a liquidator [2] so appointed shall be filled by the court. [1]

(6) Where a person other than the official receiver [5] is appointed a liquidator, [2] he shall receive salary in an amount, or

remuneration by way of percentage or otherwise, as the court [1] may direct; and, if more such persons than one are appointed liquidators,[2] their remuneration shall be distributed among them in such proportions as the court [1] directs.

(7) Where a liquidator [2] of a company [4] is appointed, he shall, after his individual name-

(a) if he is the official receiver, [5] be described as "official receiver[5] and liquidator[2] of (add here name of the company[4])"; and

(b) in any other case be described as "liquidator [2] of (add here name of the company [4])."

(8) The acts of a liquidator [2] shall be valid notwithstanding any defects that may afterwards be discovered in his appointment or qualification.

(9) If a liquidator [2] is appointed under this section, all the powers of the directors [10] shall cease, except so far as the court [1] may by order sanction the continuance thereof.

---

**Notes**
**Section 422**

1. "Court" used in relation to a company, means the Federal High Court, and to the extent to which application may be made to it as; court includes the Court of Appeal and the Supreme Court of Nigeria. See **Section 567 CAMA, Cap. C20, LFN, 2004.**
2. "Liquidator" means a person who is appointed to wind up a business's affairs esp. by selling off its assets. See **Garner B. (ed) Black's Law Dictionary, 8th ed**
3. "Winding-up" means the process of settling accounts and liquidating assets in anticipation of a partnership's or a corporation's dissolution. See **Garner B. (ed) Black's law dictionary 8th ed.**
4. "Company" means a company formed and registered under this Act or, as the case may be, formed and registered in Nigeria before and in existence on the commencement of this Act. See **section 567, CAMA Cap. C20 LFN 2004.**
5. "Official receiver" means the officer by whatever name called or known charged with control of affairs in bankruptcy and if the appointment is vacant for any reason whatsoever, means the sheriff. See **section 567, CAMA Cap. C20 LFN 2004**

   For the purpose of this Act and so far as it relates to the winding up of companies by the court, "official receiver" means the Deputy Chief Registrar of the Federal High Court or an officer designated for the purpose by the Chief Judge of the Court. See **section 419 CAMA Cap. C20, LFN 2004**

6. "Provisional liquidator" means a person who is temporarily appointed to wind up a business's affairs esp. by selling off its assets. **See Garner B. Black's Law Dictionary, 8 th ed.**
7. "Creditors" means one to whom a debt is owed; one who gives credit for money or goods. See **Garner B. (ed) Black's Law Dictionary, 8 th ed.**
8. "Contributories" see "contributory."It means every person liable to contribute to the assets of a company in the event of its being wound up and for the purposes of all proceedings for determining and all proceedings prior to the final determination of the persons who are to be deemed contributories, the expression shall include any person alleged to be a contributory. See **section 567, CAMA Cap. C20 LFN 2004**
9. "Commission" means the Corporate Affairs Commission established under section 1 of this Act . **See section 567 CAMA Cap. C20, LFN 2004.**
10. "Director" includes any person occupying the position of director by whatever name called; and includes any person in accordance with whose directions or instructions the directors of the company are accustomed to act; **See S. 567 CAMA Cap. C20 LFN 2004**

**Cross Reference**

On winding up proceedings, see generally the Companies Winding up rules 2001

On commencement of winding up by the Court, see **section 415 CAMA Cap. C20, LFN 2004**

On meaning of official receiver, see **section 419 CAMA Cap. C20 LFN 2004**

On the establishment of Federal High Court and its respective jurisdiction, see **sections 249 & 251 Constitution of the Federal Republic of Nigeria, 1999 (as amended)**

---

**For Further Reading**

On commencement of winding up proceedings, see, Asomugha, E. Maduelosi *Company law in Nigeria under the Companies and Allied Matters Act* E.M. Asomugha (Lagos) 1994

## 423. Custody of company's property

In a winding up [1] by the court [2] the liquidator [3] shall take into his custody, or under his control, all the property and choses in action to which the company [4] is or appears to be entitled.

---

**Notes**
**Section 423**

1. "Winding up" means the process of settling accounts and liquidating assets in anticipation of a partnership's or a corporation's dissolution. **Garner B. (ed) Black's law dictionary 8th ed** .
2. "Court" used in relation to a company, means the Federal High Court, and to the extent to which application may be made to it as; court includes the Court of Appeal and the Supreme Court of Nigeria. See **Section 567 CAMA, Cap. C20, LFN, 2004.**
3. "Liquidator": means a person who is appointed to wind up a business's affairs esp. by selling off its assets **Garner B. (ed) Black's Law Dictionary, 8th ed.**
4. "Company" means a company formed and registered under this Act or, as the case may be, formed and registered in Nigeria before and in existence on the commencement of this Act. **See section 567, CAMA Cap. C20 LFN 2004**

Cross Reference

On the establishment of Federal High Court and its respective jurisdiction, see **sections 249 & 251 Constitution of the Federal Republic of Nigeria, 1999 (as amended)**

On winding up proceedings, see generally the Companies Winding up rules 2001

---

**Cases**

A Liquidator owes a duty to the whole body of creditors and shareholders and to the court to make himself thoroughly acquainted with the affairs of the company and not suppress or conceal anything coming to his knowledge in the course of his investigation which is material; ***Re J. A. Balogun* (1977) FRCR 122**

**For Further Reading**

On commencement of winding up proceedings, see, Asomugha, E. Maduelosi **Company law in Nigeria under the Companies and Allied Matters Act** E.M. Asomugha (Lagos) 1994

## 424. Vesting of property of company in liquidator

Where a company [1] is being wound up [2] by the court [3], the court [3] may on the application of the liquidator [4] by order direct that all or any part of the property of whatsoever description belonging to the company[1] or held by trustees [5] on its behalf shall vest in the liquidator[4] by his official name, and thereupon, but subject to the requirements of registration under any particular enactment, the property to which the order relates shall vest accordingly; and the liquidator[4] may, after giving such indemnity, if any, as the court [3] may direct, bring or defend in his official name any action or other legal proceeding which relates to that property or which it is necessary to bring or defend for the purpose of effectually winding up[2] the company[1] and recovering its property.

---

**Notes**
**Section 424**

1. "Company" means a company formed and registered under this Act or, as the case may be, formed and registered in Nigeria before and in existence on the commencement of this Act. See **section 567, CAMA Cap. C20 LFN 2004**
2. "Wound up" see "winding up." It means the process of settling accounts and liquidating assets in anticipation of a partnership's or a corporation's dissolution. **Garner B. (ed) Black's law dictionary 8th ed.**
3. "Court" used in relation to a company , means the Federal High Court, and to the extent to which application may be made to it as; court includes the Court of Appeal and the Supreme Court of Nigeria. See **Section 567 CAMA, Cap. C20, LFN, 2004.**
4. "Liquidator" means a person who is appointed to wind up a business's affairs esp. by selling off its assets. See **Garner B. (ed) Black's Law Dictionary, 8th ed**

Cross Reference

On the establishment of Federal High Court and its respective jurisdiction, see **sections 249 & 251 Constitution of the Federal Republic of Nigeria, 1999** (as amended)

On winding up proceedings, see generally the Companies Winding up rules 2001

---

**Cases**

A Liquidator owes a duty to the whole body of creditors and shareholders and to the court to make himself thoroughly acquainted with the affairs of the company and not suppress or conceal anything coming to his knowledge in the course of his investigation which is material; ***Re J.A. Balogun* (1977) FRCR 122**

**For Further Reading**

On commencement of winding up proceedings, see, Asomugha, E. Maduelosi **Company law in Nigeria under the Companies and Allied Matters Act** E.M. Asomugha (Lagos) 1994

## 425. Powers of liquidator

(1) The liquidator [1] in a winding up [2] by the court [3] shall have power, with the sanction either of the court [3] or of the committee of inspection, to-

(a) bring or defend any action or other legal proceeding in the name and on behalf of the company [4];

(b) carry on the business of the company [4] so far as may be necessary for its beneficial winding up [2];

(c) appoint a legal practitioner [5] or any other relevant professional to assist him in the performance of his duties;

(d) pay any classes of creditors [6] in full;

(e) make any compromise or arrangement with creditors [6] or persons claiming to be creditors [6], or having or alleging themselves to have any claim, present or future, certain or contingent, ascertained or sounding only in damages against the company [4], or whereby the company [4] may be rendered liable;

(f) compromise all calls and liabilities to calls, debts and liabilities capable of resulting in debts, and all claims, present or future, certain or contingent, ascertained or sounding only in damages, subsisting or supposed to subsist between the company [4] and a contributory [7] or alleged contributory [7] or other debtor or person apprehending liability to the company [4], and all questions in any way relating to or affecting the assets or the winding up [2] of the company [4], on such terms as may be agreed, and take any security for the discharge of any such call, debt, liability or claim and give a complete discharge in respect thereof;

(2) The liquidator [1] in winding up [2] by the court [3] shall have power to-

(a) sell the property of the company [4] of whatever nature by public auction or private contract, with power to transfer the whole thereof to any person or company [4] or to sell the same in parcels;

(b) do all acts and to execute, in the name and on behalf of the company, [4] all deeds, receipts and other documents, and for that purpose to use, when necessary, the company's seal [8];

(c) prove, rank and claim in the bankruptcy [9], insolvency [10] or sequestration[11] of any contributory [7] for any balance against his estate, and to receive dividends [12] in the bankruptcy,[9] insolvency[10] or sequestration [11] in respect of that balance as a separate debt due from the bankrupt [9] or insolvent[10], and rateably with the other separate creditors [6];

(d) draw, accept, make and indorse any bill of exchange or promissory note in the name and on behalf of the company[4] with the same effect with respect to the liability of the company[4] as if the bill or note had been drawn, accepted, made or indorsed by or on behalf of the company[4] in the course of its business;

(e) raise on the security of the assets of the company [4] any money requisite;

(f) take out in his official name letters of administration to any deceased contributory [7], and to do in his official name any other act necessary for obtaining payment of any money due from a contributory [7] or his estate which cannot be conveniently done in the name of the company [4], and in all such cases the money due shall, for the purpose of enabling the liquidator [1] to take out the letters of administration or recover the money, be deemed to be due to the liquidator [1] himself;

(g) appoint an agent to do any business which the liquidator [1] is unable to do himself;

(h) do all such other things as may be necessary for winding up the affairs of the company [4] and distributing its assets.

(3) The exercise by the liquidator [1] in a winding up [2] by the court[3] of the powers conferred by this section shall be subject to the control of the court [3], and any creditor [6] or contributory [7] may apply to the court[3] with respect to any exercise or proposed exercise of any of those powers.

---

**Notes**
**Section 425**

1. "Liquidator" means a person who is appointed to wind up a business's affairs esp. by selling off its assets. **See Garner B. (ed) Black's Law Dictionary, 8th ed.**

2. "Winding up" means the process of settling accounts and liquidating assets in anticipation of a partnership's or a corporation's dissolution. **See Garner B. (ed) Black's Law Dictionary, 8 th ed.**
3. "Court" used in relation to a company , means the Federal High Court, and to the extent to which application may be made to it as; court includes the Court of Appeal and the Supreme Court of Nigeria. See **Section 567 CAMA, Cap. C20, LFN, 2004.**
4. "Company" means a company formed and registered under this Act or, as the case may be, formed and registered in Nigeria before and in existence on the commencement of this Act. See **Section 567, CAMA Cap. C20 LFN 2004**
5. Legal Practitioner" has the meaning assigned to it by the Legal Practitioners Act. **See section 567 CAMA, Cap. C20 , LFN 2004**
6. "Creditor" means one to whom a debt is owed; one who gives credit for money or goods. See **Garner B. (ed) Black's Law Dictionary, 8 th ed.**
7. "Contributory" means every person liable to contribute to the assets of a company in the event of its being wound up and for the purposes of all proceedings for determining and all proceedings prior to the final determination of the persons who are to be deemed contributories, the expression shall include any person alleged to be a contributory. See **Section 567, CAMA Cap. C20 LFN 2004**
8. "Common seal" means a design embossed or stamped on paper to authenticate, confirm, or attest; an impression or sign that has legal consequence when applied to an instrument. The purpose of a seal is to secure or prove authenticity. See **Garner, B. (ed.) Black's Law Dictionary, 8th ed**
9. "Bankruptcy" means statutory procedure by which a debtor obtains financial relief and undergoes a judicially supervised reorganization or liquidation of the debtors assets for the benefit of creditors. See **Garner B. (ed) Black's law dictionary 8th ed.**
10. "Insolvency " see insolvent person". It means any person in Nigeria who, in respect of any judgment, Act or court order against him, is unable to satisfy execution or other process issued thereon in favour of a creditor, and the execution or other process remains unsatisfied for not less than six weeks. See **section 567 CAMA Cap. C20, LFN 2004.**
11. "Sequestration": The process by which property is removed from the possessor pending the outcome of a dispute in which two or more parties contend for it. **Garner B. (ed) Black's Law Dictionary 9th ed.**
12. "Dividends" means a proportion of the distributed profits of the company which may be a fixed annual percentage, as in the case of preference shares, or it may be variable according to the prosperity or other circumstances of the company, as in the case of equity shares. See **section 567 CAMA Cap. C20, LFN 2004.**

Cross Reference

On the establishment of Federal High Court and its respective jurisdiction, see **sections 249 & 251 Constitution of the Federal Republic of Nigeria, 1999 (as amended)**
On power of court to order a writ of sequestration against property,see **section 82 Sheriffs and Civil Process Act Cap. s 6, LFN 2004**
On the requirements for practice as a legal practitioner, see generally, **Legal Practitioners Act Cap. L11, LFN 2004**
On winding up proceedings, see generally the Companies Winding up rules 2001
On obligation of the company to have and use common seal, see **section 74 CAMA, Cap. C20, LFN 2004**
On declaration of dividends and payment of interim dividend, see **section 379, CAMA Cap. C20, LFN 2004**
On restriction on declaratrion and payment of dividend, see **section 381 CAMA Cap. C20 LFN 2004**
On appointment of committee of inspection in voluntary winding up, **see sec. 474, CAMA,**
On appointment of committee of inspection, where winding up is by court, see **sec. 433 CAMA**

## 426.Liquidator to give information, etc. to official receiver

If during the winding up [1] of a company [2] by the court [3] a person other than the official receiver [4] is appointed liquidator, [5] he shall give the official receiver [4] such information and access to and facilities for inspecting the books and documents [6] of the company, [2] and generally any aid requisite or necessary for enabling that officer[7] to perform his duties under this Act.

**Notes**
**Section 426**

1. "Winding up" means the process of settling accounts and liquidating assets in anticipation of a partnership's or a corporation's dissolution. See **Garner B. (ed) Black's law dictionary 8th ed.**
2. "Company" means a company formed and registered under this Act or, as the case may be, formed and registered in Nigeria before and in existence on the commencement of this Act. See **section 567, CAMA Cap. C20 LFN 2004**
3. "Court" used in relation to a company, means the Federal High Court, and to the extent to which application may be made to it as; court includes the Court of Appeal and the Supreme Court of Nigeria. See **Section 567 CAMA, Cap. C20, LFN, 2004.**
4. "Official receiver" means the officer by whatever name called or known charged with control of affairs in bankruptcy and if the appointment is vacant for any reason whatsoever, means the sheriff. See **section 567, CAMA Cap. C20 LFN 2004**

For the purpose of this Act and so far as it relates to the winding up of companies by the court, "official receiver" means the Deputy Chief Registrar of the Federal High Court or an officer designated for the purpose by the Chief Judge of the Court. See **section 419 CAMA Cap. C20, LFN 2004**

5. "Liquidator" means a person who is appointed to wind up a business's affairs esp. by selling off its assets. See **Garner B. (ed) Black's Law Dictionary, 8th ed.**
6. "Documents" see "document." It includes summons, notice, order and other legal process, and register. See **section 567 CAMA Cap. C20 LFN 2004.**
7. "officer" in relation to a body corporate, includes a director, manager or secretary. See **section 567 CAMA Cap. C20 LFN 2004.**

**Cross Reference**

On appointment of liquidator by the court, see **section 422 CAMA Cap. C20, LFN 2004**

On the establishment and jurisdiction of the Federal High Court, see **sections 249 &251 Constitution of the Federal Republic of Nigeria, 1999 (as amended)**

On winding up proceedings, see generally the Companies Winding up rules 2001

On commencement of winding up by the Court, see **section 415 CAMA Cap.C20, LFN 2004**

---

**For Further Reading**

On commencement of winding up proceedings, see, Asomugha, E. Maduelosi **Company law in Nigeria under the Companies and Allied Matters Act** E.M. Asomugha (Lagos) 1994

## 427. Exercise and control of liquidator's powers

(1) Subject to the provisions of this Act, the liquidator [1] of a company[2] being wound up[3] by the court[4] shall, in the administration and distribution of the assets of the company [2] among its creditors [5], have regard to directions given by resolution [6] of the creditors [5] or contributories[7] at any general meeting, [8] or by the committee of inspection; so however that directions given by the creditors [5] or contributories[7] at any general meeting [8] shall, in case of conflict, override directions given by the committee of inspection.

(2) The liquidator [1] may summon general meetings [8] of the creditors[5] or contributories [7] for the purpose of ascertaining their wishes, and it shall be his duty to summon meetings [8] at such times as the creditors [5] or contributories [7] by resolution[6] either at the meeting[8] appointing the liquidator [1] or otherwise, may direct, or

whenever requested in writing to do so by one tenth in value of the creditors[5] or contributories[7], as the case may be.

(3) The liquidator[1] may apply to the court[4] in the manner prescribed for directions in relation to any particular matter arising under the winding up[3].

(4) Subject to the provisions of this Act, the liquidator[1] shall use his own discretion in the management of the estate and its distribution among the creditors[5].

(5) Any persons aggrieved by an act or decision of the liquidator,[1] may apply to the court[4] for such order in the premises as it thinks just; and the court[4] may confirm, reverse, or modify the act or decision.

---

**Notes**
**Section 427**

1. "Liquidator:" means a person who is appointed to wind up a business's affairs esp. by selling off its assets. See **Garner B. (ed) Black's Law Dictionary, 8th ed**
2. "Company" means a company formed and registered under this Act or, as the case may be, formed and registered in Nigeria before and in existence on the commencement of this Act. See **section 567, CAMA Cap. C20 LFN 2004**
3. "Wound up" see "winding up". It means the process of settling accounts and liquidating assets in anticipation of a partnership's or a corporation's dissolution. **Garner B. (ed) Black's law dictionary 8th ed.**
4. "Court" used in relation to a company , means the Federal High Court, and to the extent to which application may be made to it as; court includes the Court of Appeal and the Supreme Court of Nigeria. See **Section 567 CAMA, Cap. C20, LFN, 2004.**
5. "Creditors" means one to whom a debt is owed; one who gives credit for money or goods. **See Garner B. (ed) Black's Law Dictionary, 8 th ed.**
6. "Resolutions" see "resolution." It is the main motion that formally expresses the sense, will, or action of a deliberative assembly . **See Garner B. (ed) Black's Law Dictionary, 8th ed.**
7. "Contributories" see" contributory". It means every person liable to contribute to the assets of a company in the event of its being wound up and for the purposes of all proceedings for determining and all proceedings prior to the final determination of the persons who are to be deemed contributories, the expression shall include any person alleged to be a contributory . See **section 567, CAMA Cap. C20 LFN 2004**
8. "General meeting" see "annual meeting". It means a yearly meeting to elect or install officers or directors and to conduct other routine

organisational business. **See Garner B. (ed) Black's Law Dictionary 8th ed.**

Cross Reference

On appointment of liquidator by the court, see **section 422 CAMA Cap. C20, LFN 2004**

On the establishment and jurisdiction of the Federal High Court, see **sections 249 &251 Constitution of the Federal Republic of Nigeria, 1999 (as amended)**

On types of resolution that can be passed, see **section 233 CAMA Cap. C20 LFN 2004**

On types of meetings, see generally **sections 211, 213 & 215 CAMA Cap. C20, LFN 2004**

On appointment of committee of inspection in voluntary winding up, see section **474, CAMA, Cap. C20, LFN 2004**

On appointment of committee of inspection, where winding up is by court, see **section 433 CAMA, Cap. C20 LFN 2004**

**Cases**

A Liquidator owes a duty to the whole body of creditors and shareholders and to the court to make himself thoroughly acquainted with the affairs of the company and suppress or conceal anything coming to his knowledge in the course of his investigation which is material; ***Re J.A. Balogun*** **(1977) FRCR 122.**

## 428.Payments by liquidator into companies' liquidation account

(1) Every liquidator[1] of a company[2] being wound up[3] by the court[4] shall, in such manner and at such times as the Commission[5] directs, pay moneys received by him into the public fund of the Federation kept by the Commission[5] under and for the purposes of this Act and known as "the Companies Liquidation Account", and the Accountant-General of the Federation shall furnish him with a certificate of receipt for the money so paid:

Provided that, if the committee of inspection satisfies the Commission[5] that for the purpose of carrying on the business of the company[2] or of obtaining advances, or for any other reason, it is for the advantage of the creditors[6] or contributories[7] that the liquidator[1] should have an account with any bank, the Commission[5] shall, on the application of the committee of inspection, authorise the liquidator[1] to make his payments into and out of such bank in Nigeria as the committee may select, and thereupon those payments shall be made in the prescribed manner.

(2) If the liquidator[1] of a company[2] being wound up[3] as aforesaid, at any time retains for more than ten days an amount in excess of either N500 or, in any particular case, such other amount as the Commission[5] may approve, and fails to satisfy the Commission[5] as to the need for the retention beyond that time, the liquidator[1] shall pay interest on the amount so retained in excess, at the rate of twenty per cent per annum, and shall be liable to-

(a) disallowance of the whole or such part of his remuneration as the Commission[5] thinks fit; and

(b) removal from office, and in addition, he shall be liable to pay any expenses occasioned by the retention.

(3) A liquidator[1] of a company[2] which is being wound up[3] by the court[4] shall not pay any sums received by him as liquidator [1] into his private banking account.

---

**Notes**
**Section 428**

1. "Liquidator" means a person who is appointed to wind up a business's affairs esp. by selling off its assets. See **Garner B. (ed) Black's law dictionary 8th ed.**
2. "Company" means a company formed and registered under this Act or, as the case may be, formed and registered in Nigeria before and in existence on the commencement of this Act. See **section 567, CAMA Cap. C20 LFN 2004.**
3. "Wound up" see "winding up." It means the process of settling accounts and liquidating assets in anticipation of a partnership's or a corporation's dissolution. **Garner B. (ed) Black's law dictionary 8th ed.**
4. "Court" used in relation to a company , means the Federal High Court, and to the extent to which application may be made to it as; court includes the Court of Appeal and the Supreme Court of Nigeria. See **Section 567 CAMA, Cap. C20, LFN, 2004.**
5. "Commission" means the Corporate Affairs Commission established under section 1 of this Act **. See section 567 CAMA Cap. C20, LFN 2004.**
6. "Creditors" means one to whom a debt is owed; one who gives credit for money or goods. See **Garner B. (ed) Black's Law Dictionary, 8 th ed.**
7. "Contributories" see "contributory". It means every person liable to contribute to the assets of a company in the event of its being wound up and for the purposes of all proceedings for determining and all proceedings prior to the final determination of the persons who are to be deemed contributories, the expression shall include any person

alleged to be a contributory . **See section 567 CAMA Cap. C20, LFN 2004.**

Cross Reference

On appointment of liquidator by the court, see **section 422 CAMA Cap. C20, LFN 2004**

On the establishment and jurisdiction of the Federal High Court, see **sections 249 &251 Constitution of the Federal Republic of Nigeria, 1999 (as amended)**

On the establishment of the office of the Accountant General see **Civil Service re-Organization Decree No. 43, 1988.**

On appointment of committee of inspection in voluntary winding up, see **section 474, CAMA, Cap. C20, LFN 2004**

On appointment of committee of inspection, where winding up is by court, see **section 433 CAMA Cap. C20, LFN 2004**

On power of court to order payment into companies liquidation account, see **section 443 CAMA Cap. C20, LFN 2004**

On definition of companies liquidation account, see **section 527 CAMA Cap. C20, LFN 2004**

---

**Cases**

A Liquidator owes a duty to the whole body of creditors and shareholders and to the court to make himself thoroughly acquainted with the affairs of the company and suppress or conceal anything coming to his knowledge in the course of his investigation which is material; ***Re J.A. Balogun* (1977) FRCR 122**

## 429. Audit, etc., of liquidator's account

(1) Every liquidator [1] of a company [2] being wound up [3] by the court[4] shall, at such times as may be prescribed, but not less than twice in each year during his tenure of office, send to the Commission[5] an account of his receipts and payments as liquidator [1].

(2) The account shall be in duplicate in the prescribed form, and shall be verified by a statutory declaration [6] in the prescribed form.

(3) The Commission [5] shall cause the account to be audited [7], and for the purpose of the audit [7] the liquidator[1] shall furnish the Commission[5] with such vouchers and information as the Commission[5] may require, and the Commission [5] may at any time require the production of, and may inspect, any books [8] or accounts[9] kept by the liquidator [1].

(4) When the account has been audited [7], one copy shall be filed and kept by the Commission [5], and the other copy shall be with

the court[4] and each shall be open to inspection by any creditor [10] or other person interested, on payment of the prescribed fee.

(5) The Commission[5] shall cause the account when audited[7], or a summary thereof, to be printed, and shall send a printed copy of the account or summary by post to every creditor [10] and contributory.[11]

---

**Notes**
**Section 429**

1. "Liquidator" means a person who is appointed to wind up a business's affairs esp. by selling off its assets. See **Garner B. (ed) Black's Law Dictionary, 8th ed.**
2. "Company" means a company formed and registered under this Act or, as the case may be, formed and registered in Nigeria before and in existence on the commencement of this Act. See section **567, CAMA Cap. C20 LFN 2004**
3. "Wound up" see "winding up." It means the process of settling accounts and liquidating assets in anticipation of a partnership's or a corporation's dissolution.See **Garner B. (ed) Black's law dictionary 98h ed.**
4. "Court" used in relation to a company, means the Federal High Court, and to the extent to which application may be made to it as; court includes the Court of Appeal and the Supreme Court of Nigeria. See **Section 567 CAMA, Cap. C20, LFN, 2004.**
5. "Commission" means the Corporate Affairs Commission established under section 1 of this Act **. See section 567 CAMA Cap. C20, LFN 2004.**
6. "Statutory declaration" means a declaration voluntarily made under the Oaths Act and in Nigeria includes one so made under any other enactment or law providing for the taking of a voluntary declaration. See **section 567 CAMA Cap. C20, LFN 2004**
7. "Audited" see" audit". It is a formal examination of an individual's or organisation accounting records, financial situation, or compliance with some other set of standards **. See Garner B. (ed) Black's Law Dictionary, 8th ed.**
8. "Books" see "book or paper". It include accounts, deeds, writings, and documents; **See section 567 CAMA Cap. C20 LFN 2004.**
9. "Accounts" includes a company's group accounts, whether prepared in the form of accounts or not. **See section 567 CAMA Cap. C20 LFN 2004.**
10. "Creditor" means one to whom a debt is owed; one who gives credit for money or goods **. See Garner B. (ed) Black's Law Dictionary, 8th ed.**
11. "Contributory" means every person liable to contribute to the assets of a company in the event of its being wound up and for the purposes of all proceedings for determining and all proceedings prior to the final

determination of the persons who are to be deemed contributories; the expression shall include any person alleged to be a contributory. **See section 567 CAMA Cap. C20 LFN 2004**

Cross Reference

On appointment of liquidator by the court, see **section 422 CAMA Cap. C20, LFN 2004**

On books to be kept by a liquidator appointed by court, see **section 430 CAMA Cap. C20 LFN 2004**

On the establishment and jurisdiction of the Federal High Court, see **sections 249 &251 Constitution of the Federal Republic of Nigeria, 1999 (as amended)**

**Cases**

A Liquidator owes a duty to the whole body of creditors and shareholders and to the court to make himself thoroughly acquainted with the affairs of the company and suppress or conceal anything coming to his knowledge in the course of his investigation which is material; ***Re J.A. Balogun* (1977) FRCR 122**

## 430. Books to be kept by liquidator

Every liquidator [1] of a company [2] which is being wound up [3] by the court[4] shall, in the manner prescribed, keep proper books [5] in which he shall cause to be made entries or minutes of proceedings at meetings,[6] and of such other matters as may be prescribed, and any creditor[7] or contributory [8] may, subject to the control of the court,[4] personally or by his agent inspect any such books [5].

**Notes**

**Section 430**

1. "Liquidator" means a person who is appointed to wind up a business's affairs esp. by selling off its assets. **See Garner B. (ed) Black's Law Dictionary, 8th ed.**
2. "Company" means a company formed and registered under this Act or, as the case may be, formed and registered in Nigeria before and in existence on the commencement of this Act. **See section 567, CAMA Cap. C20 LFN 2004**
3. "Wound up" see "winding up." It means the process of settling accounts and liquidating assets in anticipation of a partnership's or a corporation's dissolution.See **Garner B. (ed) Black's law dictionary 8th ed.**
4. "Court" used in relation to a company , means the Federal High Court, and to the extent to which application may be made to it as; court includes the Court of Appeal and the Supreme Court of Nigeria. See **Section 567 CAMA, Cap. C20, LFN, 2004.**
5. "Books" see "book or paper." It include accounts, deeds, writings, and documents; See **section 567 CAMA Cap. C20 LFN 2004**

6. "Meetings" see "meeting." It means the gathering of people to discuss or act on matters in which they have a common interest; especially the convening of a deliberative assembly to transact business. **See Graner B. Ed. Black's Law Dictionary 8 th ed.**
7. "Creditor" means one to whom a debt is owed; one who gives credit for money or goods. See **Garner B. (ed) Black's Law Dictionary, 8 th ed.**
8. "Contributory" means every person liable to contribute to the assets of a company in the event of its being wound up and for the purposes of all proceedings for determining and all proceedings prior to the final determination of the persons who are to be deemed contributories, the expression shall include any person alleged to be a contributory. **See section 567 CAMA Cap. C20, LFN 2004**

**Cross Reference**

On appointment of liquidator by the court, see **section 422 CAMA Cap. C20, LFN 2004**

---

**Cases**

A Liquidator owes a duty to the whole body of creditors and shareholders and to the court to make himself thoroughly acquainted with the affairs of the company and suppress or conceal anything coming to his knowledge in the course of his investigation which is material; ***Re J.A. Balogun*** **(1977) FRCR 122**

**For Further Reading**

On commencement of winding up proceedings, see, Asomugha, E. Maduelosi **Company law in Nigeria under the Companies and Allied Matters Act** E.M. Asomugha (Lagos) 1994

## 431. Release of liquidator

(1) Where the liquidator [1] of a company [2] being wound up [3] by the court [4] has realised all the property of the company, [2] or so much of it as may, in his opinion, be realised without needlessly protracting the liquidation, and has distributed a final dividend [5], if any, to the creditors, [6] and adjusted the rights of the contributories [7] among themselves, and made a final return, if any, to the contributories, [7] or has resigned, or has been removed from his office, the Commission [8] shall, on the application of the liquidator, [1] cause a report on the accounts [9] of the liquidator [1] to be prepared.

(2) The Commission [8] shall consider the report referred to in subsection (1) of this section together with any objection that may be raised by any creditor, [6] or contributory, [7] or person interested against the release of the liquidator, [1] and may grant or withhold the

release as it deems fit subject nevertheless to an appeal to the court.[4]

(3) If the release of a liquidator [1] is withheld, the court [4] may, on the application of any creditor, [6] or contributory, [7] or person interested, make such order as it thinks just, charging the liquidator[1] with the consequences of any act or default which he may have done or made contrary to his duty.

(4) An order of the Commission [8] releasing the liquidator [1] shall discharge him from all liability in respect of any act done or default made by him in the administration of the affairs of the company,[2] or otherwise in relation to his conduct as liquidator [1]; but any such order may be revoked on proof that it was obtained by fraud or by suppression or concealment of any material fact.

(5) Where the liquidator [1] has not previously resigned or been removed, his release shall operate as a removal of him from his offce.

---

**Notes**
**Section 431**

1. "Liquidator" means a person who is appointed to wind up a business's affairs esp. by selling off its assets. **See Garner B. (ed) Black's Law Dictionary, 8th ed.**
2. "Company" means a company formed and registered under this Act or, as the case may be, formed and registered in Nigeria before and in existence on the commencement of this Act. **See section 567, CAMA Cap. C20 LFN 2004**
3. "Wound up" see "winding up". It means the process of settling accounts and liquidating assets in anticipation of a partnership's or a corporation's dissolution.See **Garner B. (ed) Black's law dictionary 8th ed.**
4. "Court" used in relation to a company , means the Federal High Court, and to the extent to which application may be made to it as; court includes the Court of Appeal and the Supreme Court of Nigeria. See **Section 567 CAMA, Cap. C20, LFN, 2004.**
5. "Dividend" means a proportion of the distributed profits of the company which may be a fixed annual percentage, as in the case of preference shares, or it may be variable according to the prosperity or other circumstances of the company, as in the case of equity shares. See **section 567 CAMA Cap. C20, LFN 2004.**
6. "Creditors" see "creditor". It means one to whom a debt is owed; one who gives credit for money or goods. See **Garner B. (ed) Black's Law Dictionary, 8th ed.**
7. "Contributories" see "contributory." It means every person liable to contribute to the assets of a company in the event of its being wound

up and for the purposes of all proceedings for determining and all proceedings prior to the final determination of the persons who are to be deemed contributories, the expression shall include any person alleged to be a contributory . **See section 567 CAMA Cap. C20, LFN 2004.**

8. "Commission" means the Corporate Affairs Commission established under section 1 of this Act . **See section 567 CAMA Cap. C20, LFN 2004.**
9. "Accounts:" includes a company's group accounts, whether prepared in the form of accounts or not. **See Ssection 567 CAMA Cap. C20 LFN 2004**

**Cross Reference**

On declaration of dividends and payment of interim dividend, see **section 379, CAMA Cap. C20, LFN 2004**

On restriction on declaratrion and payment of dividend, see **section 381 CAMA Cap. C20 LFN 2004**

On appointment of liquidator by the court, see **section 422 CAMA Cap. C20, LFN 2004**

On audit on liquidator's account, see **section 429 CAMA Cap. C20 LFN 2004**

---

**Cases**

A Liquidator owes a duty to the whole body of creditors and shareholders and to the court to make himself thoroughly acquainted with the affairs of the company and suppress or conceal anything coming to his knowledge in the course of his investigation which is material; ***Re J.A. Balogun*** **(1977) FRCR 122**

**For Further Reading**

On commencement of winding up proceedings, see, Asomugha, E. Maduelosi **Company law in Nigeria under the Companies and Allied Matters Act** E.M. Asomugha (Lagos) 1994

## 432. Control over liquidators

(1) The Commission[1] shall take cognisance of the conduct of liquidators[2] of companies[3] which are being wound up[4] by the court[5] and if a liquidator[2] does not faithfully perform his duties and duly observe all the requirements imposed on him by any enactment, or other-wise with respect to the performance of his duties, or if any complaint is made to the Commission[1] by any creditor[6] or contributory[7] in regard thereto, the Commission[1] shall inquire into the matter, and may take such action thereon as it thinks fit, including the direction of a local investigation of the books[8] and vouchers of the liquidator.[1]

(2) The Commission [1] may at any time require the liquidator [2] of a company [3] being wound up [4] by the court [5] to answer any inquiry in relation to any winding up [4] in which he is engaged and if the Commission [1] thinks fit, it may apply to the court [5] to examine the liquidator [2] or any other person on oath [9] concerning the winding up [4].

---

**Notes**
**Section 432**

1. "Commission" means the Corporate Affairs Commission established under section 1 of this Act . **See section 567 CAMA Cap. C20, LFN 2004.**
2. "Liquidators": means a person who is appointed to wind up a business's affairs esp. by selling off its assets. See **Garner B. (ed) Black's Law Dictionary, 8 th ed.**
3. "Companies" see "company." It means a company formed and registered under this Act or, as the case may be, formed and registered in Nigeria before and in existence on the commencement of this Act. See **section 567, CAMA Cap. C20 LFN 2004**
4. "Wound up" see "winding up." It means the process of settling accounts and liquidating assets in anticipation of a partnership's or a corporation's dissolution. See **Garner B. (ed) Black's law dictionary 8th ed.**
5. "Court" used in relation to a company , means the Federal High Court, and to the extent to which application may be made to it as; court includes the Court of Appeal and the Supreme Court of Nigeria. See **Section 567 CAMA, Cap. C20, LFN, 2004.**
6. "Creditor" means one to whom a debt is owed; one who gives credit for money or goods. **See Garner B. (ed) Black's Law Dictionary, 8 th ed.**
7. "Contributory" means every person liable to contribute to the assets of a company in the event of its being wound up and for the purposes of all proceedings for determining and all proceedings prior to the final determination of the persons who are to be deemed contributories; the expression shall include any person alleged to be a contributory **. See section 567 CAMA Cap. C20 LFN 2004**
8. "Books" see "book or paper." It includes accounts, deeds, writings, and documents; **See section 567 CAMA Cap. C20 LFN 2004**
9. "Oath" means an affirmation or declaration made in accordance with the relevant law. See **18(1) Interpretation Act Cap. I 23 LFN 2004**

**Cross Reference**

On appointment of liquidator by the court, see **section 422 CAMA Cap. C20, LFN 2004**

On audit of liquidator's account, see **section 429 CAMA Cap. C. 20 LFN 2004**

On the requirement of Oral evidence to be on oath or affirmation. See **section 205 Evidence Act, 2011**

*Committee of inspection, special manager, etc.*

## 433. Power to appoint committee of inspection after meeting of creditors and others

(1) Where a winding-up [1] order is made by the court [2], it shall be the business of the separate meetings of creditors [3] and contributories[4] summoned for the purpose of determining whether or not to apply to the court [2] for an order appointing a liquidator [5] in place of the official receiver, [6] to determine whether or not application should be made to the court [2] for the appointment of a committee of inspection to act with the liquidator [5], and who are to be members of the committee, if the appointment is made.

(2) The court [2] may make any appointment and order required to give effect to any determination under this section and if there is a difference between the determinations of the meetings of the creditors [3] and contributories [4] in respect of the matters aforesaid, the court[2] shall decide the difference and make any order it thinks necessary.

**Notes**
**Section 433**

1. "Winding up" means the process of settling accounts and liquidating assets in anticipation of a partnership's or a corporation's dissolution. See **Garner B. (ed) Black's law dictionary 9th ed.**
2. "Court" used in relation to a company , means the Federal High Court, and to the extent to which application may be made to it as; court includes the Court of Appeal and the Supreme Court of Nigeria. See **Section 567 CAMA, Cap. C20, LFN, 2004.**
3. "Creditors" see "creditor" means one to whom a debt is owed; one who gives credit for money or goods. **See Garner B. (ed) Black's Law Dictionary, 8th ed.**
4. "Contributory" means every person liable to contribute to the assets of a company in the event of its being wound up and for the purposes of all proceedings for determining and all proceedings prior to the final determination of the persons who are to be deemed contributories; the expression shall include any person alleged to be a contributory . **See section 567 CAMA Cap. C20 LFN 2004**
5. "Liquidator" means a person who is appointed to wind up a business's affairs esp. by selling off its assets. **See Garner B. (ed) Black's Law Dictionary, 8th ed**

6. “Official receiver" means the officer by whatever name called or known charged with control of affairs in bankruptcy and if the appointment is vacant for any reason whatsoever, means the sheriff. See **section 567, CAMA Cap. C20 LFN 2004**
For the purpose of this Act and so far as it relates to the winding up of companies by the court, "official receiver" means the Deputy Chief Registrar of the Federal High Court or an officer designated for the purpose by the Chief Judge of the Court. See **section 419 CAMA Cap. C20, LFN 2004**

**Cross Reference**

On the establishment and jurisdiction of the Federal High Court, see **sections 249& 251 Constitution of the Federal Republic of Nigeria 1999 as (amended)**

On the nature and liability of a contributory, see **section 404 CAMA Cap. C20, LFN 2004**

---

## 434. Powers, etc., of committee of inspection

(1) A committee of inspection appointed under this Act shall consist of creditors [1] and contributories [2] of the company [3] or persons holding general powers of attorney from creditors [1] or contributories[2] in such proportions as may be agreed on by the meetings of creditors [1] and contributories [2] or as, in case of difference may be determined by the court [4].

(2) A committee of inspection shall meet at the time or times appointed, so however that there shall be a meeting at least once in every month during its existence; but the liquidator [5] or any member of the committee may convene a meeting as and when necessary.

(3) A meeting of a committee of inspection shall be deemed convened if a majority of members are present; but at any such meeting the committee may act by a majority of the members present.

(4) A member of the committee may resign by notice in writing signed by him and delivered to the liquidator [5].

(5) If a member of the committee becomes bankrupt [6] or compounds or arranges with his creditors [1] or is absent from five consecutive meetings of the committee without leave of those members who together with himself represent the creditors [1] or contributories[2], as the case may be, his office shall thereupon become vacant.

(6) A member of the committee may be removed by an ordinary resolution [7] at a meeting of creditors, [1] if he represents creditors, [1] or of contributories [2], if he represents contributories, [2] of

which seven days' notice has been given, stating the object of the meeting.

(7) On a vacancy occurring in the committee, the liquidator [5] shall forthwith summon a meeting of creditors [1] or of contributories,[2] as the case may require, to fill the vacancy, and the meeting may, by resolution, [8] reappoint the same or appoint another creditor[1] or contributory [2] to fill the vacancy:

Provided that if the liquidator [5], having regard to the position in the winding up,[9] is of the opinion that it is unnecessary for the vacancy to be filled he may apply to the court [3] and the court[3] may make an order that the vacancy shall not be filled, or shall not be filled except in such circumstances as may be specified in the order.

(8) The continuing members of the committee, if not less than two, may act notwithstanding any vacancy in the committee.

---

**Notes**
**Section 434**

1. "Creditor" means one to whom a debt is owed; one who gives credit for money or goods.See **Garner B. (ed) Black's Law Dictionary, 8 th ed.**
2. "Contributory" means every person liable to contribute to the assets of a company in the event of its being wound up and for the purposes of all proceedings for determining and all proceedings prior to the final determination of the persons who are to be deemed contributories; the expression shall include any person alleged to be a contributory **. See section 567 CAMA Cap. C20 LFN 2004**
3. "Company" means a company formed and registered under this Act or, as the case may be, formed and registered in Nigeria before and in existence on the commencement of this Act. See Section **567, CAMA Cap. C20 LFN 2004**
4. "Court" used in relation to a company , means the Federal High Court, and to the extent to which application may be made to it as; court includes the Court of Appeal and the Supreme Court of Nigeria. See **Section 567 CAMA, Cap. C20, LFN, 2004.**
5. "Liquidator" means a person who is appointed to wind up a business's affairs esp. by selling off its assets. See **Garner B. (ed) Black's Law Dictionary, 8th ed**.
6. "Bankrupt" means a person who cannot meet current financial obligations; an insolvent person. See **Garner B. (ed) Black's Law Dictionary, 8th ed**
7. "Ordinary resolution" is a resolution passed by a simple majority of votes cast by such members of the company as, being entitled to do so,

vote in person or by proxy at a general meeting. See **section 233(1), CAMA Cap. C20, LFN, 2004**

8. "Resolution" means the main motion that formally expresses the sense, will, or action of a deliberative assembly. See **Garner B. (ed) Black's Law Dictionary, 8th ed**
9. "Winding up" which means the process of settling accounts and liquidating assets in anticipation of a partnership's or a corporation's dissolution. See **Garner B. (ed) Black's Law Dictionary, 8th ed**

Cross Reference

On appointment of committee of inspectors after meetings of the creditor, see **section 433 CAMA Cap. C20,LFN 2004**

On the establishment and jurisdiction of the Federal High Court, see **sections 249& 251 Constitution of the Federal Republic of Nigeria 1999 as (amended)**

On the nature of liability of a contributory, see **section 404 CAMA Cap. C20, LFN 2004**

---

## 435.Powers where no committee of inspection is appointed

Where, in the case of winding up, [1] there is no committee of inspection, the Commission[2] may, on the application of the liquidator[3], if he thinks fit, do any act or thing or give any direction or permission which is by this Act authorised or required to be done or given by the committee

---

**Notes**

**Section 435**

1. "Winding up" means the process of settling accounts and liquidating assets in anticipation of a partnership's or a corporation's dissolution. See **Garner B. (ed) Black's law dictionary 8th ed** .
2. "Commission" means the Corporate Affairs Commission established under section 1 of this Act **. See section 567 CAMA Cap. C20, LFN 2004.**
3. "Liquidatior" means a person who is appointed to wind up a business's affairs esp. by selling off its assets. **See Garner B. (ed) Black's Law Dictionary, 8th ed**.

Cross Reference

On appointment of committee of inspectors after meetings of the creditor, see **section 433 CAMA Cap. C20,LFN 2004**

On appointment of liquidator by the court, see **section 422 CAMA Cap. C20, LFN 2004**

On audit on liquidator's account, see **section 429 CAMA Cap. CO20 LFN 2004**

---

**Cases**

A Liquidator owes a duty to the whole body of creditors and shareholders and to the court to make himself thoroughly acquainted with the affairs of the company and suppress or conceal anything coming to his knowledge in the course of his investigation which is material; ***Re J.A. Balogun*** **(1977) FRCR 122**

**For Further Reading**

On commencement of winding up proceedings, see, Asomugha, E. Maduelosi *Company law in Nigeria under the Companies and Allied Matters Act* E.M. Asomugha (Lagos) 1994

## 436. Power to appoint special manager

(1) Where the official receiver [1] becomes the liquidator [2] of a company,[3] whether provisionally or otherwise, he may, if satisfied that the nature of the estate or business of the company, [3] or the interests of the creditors [4] or contributories [5] generally, require the appointment of a special manager of the estate or business of the company[3] other than himself, apply to the court [6] for an order appointing a special manager[7] to act during such time as the court [6] may direct, with such powers, including those of a receiver [1] or manager,[7] as may be entrusted to him by the court, [6] and the court [6] may make any order necessary.

(2) A special manager [7] appointed under this section shall receive remuneration as fixed by the court, [6] and shall give security [8] and account in such manner as the Commission [9] directs.

---

**Notes**

**Section 436**

1. "Official receiver" means the officer by whatever name called or known charged with control of affairs in bankruptcy and if the appointment is vacant for any reason whatsoever, means the sheriff. See **section 567, CAMA Cap. C20 LFN 2004**

   For the purpose of this Act and so far as it relates to the winding up of companies by the court, "official receiver" means the Deputy Chief Registrar of the Federal High Court or an officer designated for the purpose by the Chief Judge of the Court. See **section 419 CAMA Cap. C20, LFN 2004**
2. "Liquidator" means a person who is appointed to wind up a business's affairs esp. by selling off its assets. **See Garner B. (ed) Black's Law Dictionary, 8th ed.**:

3. "Company" means a company formed and registered under this Act or, as the case may be, formed and registered in Nigeria before and in existence on the commencement of this Act. See section **567, CAMA Cap. C20 LFN 2004**
4. "Creditors" see "creditor." It means one to whom a debt is owed; one who gives credit for money or goods. **See Garner B. (ed) Black's Law Dictionary, 8th ed.**
5. "Contributory" means every person liable to contribute to the assets of a company in the event of its being wound up and for the purposes of all proceedings for determining and all proceedings prior to the final determination of the persons who are to be deemed contributories; the expression shall include any person alleged to be a contributory **. See section 567 CAMA Cap. C20 LFN 2004**
6. "Court" used in relation to a company, means the Federal High Court, and to the extent to which application may be made to it as; court includes the Court of Appeal and the Supreme Court of Nigeria. See **Section 567 CAMA, Cap. C20, LFN, 2004.**
7. "Manager" means a person who administers or supervises the affairs of a business, office, or other organization. See **Garner B. (ed) Black's Law Dictionary, 8th ed.**
8. "Security" includes shares, debentures, debenture stock, bonds, notes (other than promissory notes)
   and units under a unit trust scheme; **See section 567 CAMA Cap. C20 LFN 2004**
9. "Commission" means the Corporate Affairs Commission established under section 1 of this Act **. See section 567 CAMA Cap. C20, LFN 2004.**

Cross Reference

On appointment of committee of inspectors after meetings of the creditor, see **section 433 CAMA Cap. C20, LFN 2004**

On appointment of liquidator by the court, see **section 422 CAMA Cap. C20, LFN 2004**

On meaning of official receiver, see **section 419 CAMA Cap. C20 LFN 2004**

On winding up proceedings, see generally the Companies Winding up rules 2001

On commencement of winding up by the Court, see **section 415 CAMA Cap. C20, LFN 2004**

---

**For Further Reading**

On commencement of winding up proceedings, see, Asomugha, E. Maduelosi **Company law in Nigeria under the Companies and Allied Matters Act** E.M. Asomugha (Lagos) 1994

## 437. Official receiver as receiver for debenture holders, etc.

It is hereby declared that where application is made to the court[1] to appoint a receiver[2] on behalf of the debenture holders[3] or other creditors[4] of a company[5] being wound up[6] by the court[1], the official receiver[3] may be so appointed.

---

**Notes**
**Section 437**

1. "Court" used in relation to a company, means the Federal High Court, and to the extent to which application may be made to it as; court includes the Court of Appeal and the Supreme Court of Nigeria. See **Section 567 CAMA, Cap. C20, LFN, 2004.**
2. "Receiver" means a disinterested person appointed by a court, or by a corporation or other person, for the protection or collection of property that is the subject of diverse claims. See **Garner B. (ed) Black's Law Dictionary 8th ed.**
   "Receiver" includes a manager. See **section. 567 CAMA, Cap. C20, LFN 2004.**
3. "Official receiver" means the officer by whatever name called or known charged with control of affairs in bankruptcy and if the appointment is vacant for any reason whatsoever, means the sheriff. See **section 567, CAMA Cap. C20 LFN 2004**
   For the purpose of this Act and so far as it relates to the winding up of companies by the court, "official receiver" means the Deputy Chief Registrar of the Federal High Court or an officer designated for the purpose by the Chief Judge of the Court. See **section 419 CAMA Cap. C20, LFN 2004**
3. "Debenture Holder" "see "debenture" and "holder." Debenture means a written acknowledgement of indebtedness by the company, setting out the terms and conditions of the indebtedness and includes debenture stock, bonds and any other securities of any company whether constituting a charge on the assets of the company or not. **See 567 CAMA Cap. C20, LFN 2004** . "Holder" is one who has legal possession of a negotiable instrument and is entitled to receive payment on it. See **Garner B. (ed) Black's Law Dictionary, 8 th ed.**
4. "Creditors" see "creditor". It means one to whom a debt is owed; one who gives credit for money or goods. See **Garner B. (ed) Black's Law Dictionary, 8th ed.**
5. "Company" means a company formed and registered under this Act or, as the case may be, formed and registered in Nigeria before and in existence on the commencement of this Act.See **section 567, CAMA Cap. C20 LFN 2004**
6. "Wound up" see "winding up." It means the process of settling accounts and liquidating assets in anticipation of a partnership's or a

corporation's dissolution. See **Garner B. (ed) Black's law dictionary 8th ed.**

Cross Reference

On meaning of official receiver, see **section 419 CAMA Cap. C20 LFN 2004**

On winding up proceedings, see generally the Companies Winding up rules 2001

On commencement of winding up by the Court, see **section 415 CAMA Cap. C20, LFN 2004**

---

**For Further Reading**

On commencement of winding up proceedings, see, Asomugha, E. Maduelosi **Company law in Nigeria under the Companies and Allied Matters Act** E.M. Asomugha (Lagos) 1994

*General Powers of court in case of winding up by court*

## 438. Power to stay winding up

(1) The court [1] may at any time after an order for winding up,[2] on the application either of a liquidator [3] or the official receiver[4] or any creditor [5] or contributory,[6] and on proof to the satisfaction of the court[1] that all proceedings in relation to the winding up[2] ought to be stayed, make an order staying the proceedings either altogether or for a limited time, on such terms and conditions as the court[1] thinks fit.

(2) The court [1] may, at any time after an order for winding up,[2] on the application either of the liquidator [3] or a creditor,[5] and after having regard to the wishes of the creditors [5] and contributories,[6] make an order directing that the winding up [2], ordered by the court, [1] shall be conducted as a creditors' [5] voluntary winding up,[2] and if the court [1] does so, the winding up [2] shall be so conducted.

(3) On any application under this section, the court [1] may, before making an order, require the official receiver [4] to furnish to the court[1] a report with respect to any facts or matters which are in his opinion relevant to the application.

(4) A copy of every order made under this section shall forthwith be forwarded by the company [7], or otherwise as may be prescribed, to the Commission [8], which shall make a minute of the order in its books [9] relating to the company. [7]

(5) If default is made in lodging a copy of an order made under this section with the Commission [8] as required by subsection (4) of this section, every officer [10] of the company [8] or other person who knowingly authorises or permits the default shall be guilty of an offence punishable by a daily default fine of N25.

---

**Notes**
**Section 438**

1. "Court" used in relation to a company, means the Federal High Court, and to the extent to which application may be made to it as; court includes the Court of Appeal and the Supreme Court of Nigeria. See **Section 567 CAMA, Cap. C20, LFN, 2004.**
2. "Winding up" means the process of settling accounts and liquidating assets in anticipation of a partnership's or a corporation's dissolution. See **Garner B. (ed) Black's law dictionary 9th ed.**
3. "Liquidator" means a person who is appointed to wind up a business's affairs esp. by selling off its assets. **See Garner B, (ed) Black's Law Dictionary, 8th ed**
   A person responsible for closing down a business and using any profits from the sale to pay its debts **Oxford Advanced leaner's Dictionary. 6th ed**
4. "Official receiver" means the officer by whatever name called or known charged with control of affairs in bankruptcy and if the appointment is vacant for any reason whatsoever, means the sheriff. See **section 567, CAMA Cap. C20 LFN 2004**
   For the purpose of this Act and so far as it relates to the winding up of companies by the court, "official receiver" means the Deputy Chief Registrar of the Federal High Court or an officer designated for the purpose by the Chief Judge of the Court. See **section 419 CAMA Cap. C20, LFN 2004**
5. "Creditor" means one to whom a debt is owed; one who gives credit for money or goods. **See Garner B. (ed) Black's Law Dictionary, 8th ed.**
6. "Contributories" see "contributory". It means every person liable to contribute to the assets of a company in the event of its being wound up and for the purposes of all proceedings for determining and all proceedings prior to the final determination of the persons who are to be deemed contributories, the expression shall include any person alleged to be a contributory**. See section 567 CAMA Cap. C20 LFN 2004**
7. "Company" means a company formed and registered under this Act or, as the case may be, formed and registered in Nigeria before and in existence on the commencement of this Act. See **section 567, CAMA Cap. C20 LFN 2004**
8. "Commission" means the Corporate Affairs Commission established under section 1 of this Act **. See section 567 CAMA Cap. C20, LFN 2004.**

9. "Books" "book or paper" include accounts, deeds, writings, and documents; **See section 567 CAMA Cap. C20 LFN 2004**
10. "Officer" in relation to a body corporate, includes a director, manager or secretary. See **section 567 CAMA Cap. C20 LFN 2004**

**Cross Reference**

On winding up proceedings, see generally the Companies Winding up rules 2001

On commencement of winding up by the Court, see **section 415 CAMA Cap. C20, LFN 2004**

On establishment and jurisdiction of the Federal High Court, see **sections 249&251 Constitution of the Federal Republic of Nigeria 1999( as amended)**

---

**For Further Reading**

On commencement of winding up proceedings, see, Asomugha, E. Maduelosi **Company law in Nigeria under the Companies and Allied Matters Act** E.M. Asomugha (Lagos) 1994

## 439.Settlement of list of contributories and application of assets

(1) As soon as may be after making a winding-up [1] order, the court[2] shall settle a list of contributories, [3] and may rectify the register of members[4] in all cases where rectification is required in pursuance of this Act, and the court [2] shall cause the assets of the company[5] to be collected, and applied in discharge of its liabilities: Provided that where it appears to the court [2] that it will not be necessary to make calls on or adjust the rights of contributories, [3] the court[2] may dispense with the settlement of a list of contributories.[3]

(2) In settling the list of contributories, [3] the court[2] shall distinguish between persons who are contributories [3] in their own right and persons who are contributories [3] as being representatives of or liable for the debts of others.

---

**Notes**

**Section 439**

1. "Winding-up order" means the process of settling accounts and liquidating assets in anticipation of aPartnership's or a corporation's dissolution **See Garner B. (ed) Black's Law Dictionary, 8 th ed.**

2. "Court" A court that has the power and authority to do a particular act; one recognised by law as Possessing the right to adjudicate a controversy.
3. "Contributory" means every person liable to contribute to the assets of a company in theevent of its being wound up and for the purposes of all proceedings for determining and all proceedings prior to the final determination of the persons who are to be deemed contributories, the expression shall include any person alleged to be a contributory. See Company Allied Matters Act s.403

   One who contributes or who has a duty to contribute. A person who, as a result of being or representing a past or present member of a corporation, is liable to contribute to the corporation's debts upon its winding up. **Garner B. (ed) Blacks' Law Dictionary, 8 th ed.**
4. "Members" includes the heir, executor, administrator or other personal representative, as the case may be, of the member; **See section 567 CAMA Cap. C20 LFN 2004**
5. "Company" means a company formed and registered under this Act or, as the case may be,formed and registered in Nigeria before and in existence on the commencement of this Act. **See section 567, CAMA Cap. C20 LFN 2004**

**Cross Reference**

On obligation to keep register of members see **section 83 CAMA Cap. C20, LFN 2004**

On establishment and jurisdiction of the Federal High Court, see **sections 249 &251 Constitution of the Federal Republic of Nigeria 1999(as amended)**

On winding up proceedings, see generally the Companies Winding up rules 2001

**For Further Reading**

On commencement of winding up proceedings, see, Asomugha, E. Maduelosi **Company law in Nigeria under the Companies and Allied Matters** *Act* E.M. Asomugha (Lagos) 1994

## 440. Delivery of property to liquidator

The court[1] may, at any time after making a winding-up [2] order require any contributory [3] for the time being on the list of contributories[3] and any trustee,[4] receiver,[5] banker, agent, or officer [6] of the company[7] to pay, deliver, convey, surrender or transfer forthwith, or within such time as the court [1] directs, to the liquidator[8] any money, property, or books and papers [9] in his hands, to which the company[7] is prima facie entitled.

---

**Notes**

**Section 440**

1. "Court" used in relation to a company, means the Federal High Court, and to the extent to which application may be made to it as; court includes the Court of Appeal and the Supreme Court of Nigeria. See **Section 567 CAMA, Cap. C20, LFN, 2004.**
2. "Winding-up order" the process of settling accounts and liquidating assets in anticipation of a partnership's or a corporation's dissolution. See **Garner B. (ed) Black's Law Dictionary, 8 th ed**
3. "Contributory"means every person liable to contribute to the assets of a company in the event of its being wound up and for the purposes of all proceedings for determining and all proceedings prior to the final determination of the persons who are to be deemed contributories, the expression shall include any person alleged to be a contributory **. See section 567 CAMA Cap. C20 LFN 2004**
4. "Trustee" means one who, having legal title to property holds it in trust for the benefit of another and owes a fiduciary duty to that beneficiary**. See Garner B. ed. Black's Law Dictionary 8 th ed.**
5. "Receiver" means a disinterested person appointed by a court, or by a corporation or other person, for the protection or collection of property that is the subject of diverse claims. See **Garner B. (ed) Black's Law Dictionary 8th ed.**

   "Receiver" includes a manager. See **section. 567 CAMA, Cap. C20, LFN 2004.**
6. "Officer" in relation to a body corporate, includes a director, manager or secretary. See **section 567 CAMA Cap. C20 LFN 2004**
7. "Company" means a company formed and registered under this Act or, as the case may be, formed and registered in Nigeria before and in existence on the commencement of this Act. See section **567, CAMA Cap. C20 LFN 2004.**
8. "Liquidator" means a person who is appointed to wind up a business's affairs esp. by selling off its assets. See **Garner B, (ed) Black's Law Dictionary 8th ed.**
9. "Books and Papers" see "book or paper." It include accounts, deeds, writings, and documents; **See section 567 CAMA Cap. C 20 LFN 2004**

**Cross Reference**

On establishment and jurisdiction of the Federal High Court, see **sections 249 &251 Constitution of the Federal Republic of Nigeria 1999(as amended)**

On winding up proceedings, see generally the Companies Winding up rules 2001

On the nature of liability of a contributory, see **section 404 CAMA Cap. C20, LFN 2004**

---

**Cases**

On appointment of receiver, the powers of management of the company's business became vested in the receiver, but on quite a number of matters

not related to management ,the directors can still act ***: UBA Trustees Ltd. v. Nigergrob Ceramic Ltd. (1987) 3 NWLR pt 62, p. 600.***
Where a receiver or manager is appointed for the whole or substantially the whole of a company's property, the powers conferred on him by the debentures by virtue of which he was appointed, shall be deemed to include, except in so far as they are with any of these debentures, the powers specified in the eleventh schedule to the Act ***: Onafowokan & 2 Ors v. Wema Bank & 2 Ors 88/2004 SC delivered 13/05/2010.***

## 441. Payments by contributory to company and set-off allowance

(1) The court [1] may, at any time after making a winding-up [2] order, make an order on any contributory [3] for the time being on the list of contributories [3] to pay, in the manner directed by the order; any money due from him or from the estate of the person whom he represents to the company, [4] exclusive of any money payable by him or the estate by virtue of any call in pursuance of this Act.

(2) The court [1] making an order under this section-

(a) in the case of an unlimited company [5], may allow to the contributory[3] by way of set-off any money due to him or to the estate which he represents from the company [4] of any independent dealing or contract with the company, [4] but not any money due to him as a member [6] of the company[4] in respect of any dividend [7] or profit;

(b) in the case of a limited company, [4] may make to any director[8] or manager[9] whose liability is unlimited or to his estate, the like allowance as in paragraph (a) of this subsection.

(3) In the case of any company, [4] limited or unlimited, when all the creditors [10] are paid in full, the money due on any account whatever to a contributory [3] from the company [4] may be allowed to him by way of set-off against any subsequent call.

---

**Notes**
**Section 441**

1. "Court" used in relation to a company, means the Federal High Court, and to the extent to which application may be made to it as; court includes the Court of Appeal and the Supreme Court of Nigeria. See **Section 567 CAMA, Cap. C20, LFN, 2004.**

2. "Winding-up" means the process of settling accounts and liquidating assets in anticipation of a partnership's or a corporation's dissolution. See **Garner B. (ed) Black's Law Dictionary, 8 th ed.**
3. "Contributory"means every person liable to contribute to the assets of a company in the event of its being wound up and for the purposes of all proceedings for determining and all proceedings prior to the final determination of the persons who are to be deemed contributories, the expression shall include any person alleged to be a contributory . See **section 567 CAMA Cap. C20 LFN 2004**
4. "Company" means a company formed and registered under this Act or, as the case may be, formed and registered in Nigeria before and in existence on the commencement of this Act. See **section 567, CAMA Cap. C20 LFN 2004.**
5. "Unlimited Company" is a company not having any limit on the liability of its members (in this Act termed "an unlimited company"). See **Section 21(1)(c) CAMA Cap. C20 LFN 2004** .
6. "Member" includes the heir, executor, administrator or other personal representative, as the case may be, of the member; See **section 567, CAMA Cap. C20 LFN 2004.**
7. "Dividend" means a proportion of the distributed profits of the company which may be a fixed annual percentage, as in the case of preference shares, or it may be variable according to the prosperity or other circumstances of the company, as in the case of equity shares. See **section 567 CAMA Cap. C20, LFN 2004.**
8. "Director" means a person appointed or elected to sit on a board that manages the affairs of a corporation or other organization by electing and exercising control over its officers See **Garner B. (ed) Black's Law Dictionary, 8 th ed.**
9. "Manager" means a person who administers or supervises the affairs of a business, office, or other organization. **See Garner B. (ed) Black's Law Dictionary, 8 th ed.**
10. "Creditors" see "creditor." It means one to whom a debt is owed; one who gives credit for money or goods. **See Garner B. (ed) Black's Law Dictionary, 8 th ed.**

**Cross Reference**

On declaration of dividends and payment of interim dividend, see **section 379, CAMA Cap. C20, LFN 2004**

On restriction on declaratrion and payment of dividend, see **section 381 CAMA Cap. C20 LFN 2004**

On appointment of liquidator by the court, see **section 422 CAMA Cap. C20, LFN 2004**

On audit on liquidator's account, see **section 429 CAMA Cap. C20 LFN 2004**

On the establishment and jurisdiction of the Federal High Court, see **sections 249& 251 Constitution of the Federal Republic of Nigeria, 1999 (as amended)**

---

## 442. Power of Court to make calls

(1) The court [1] may, at any time after making a winding –up [2] order, and either before or after it has ascertained the sufficiency of the assets of the company[3], make calls on all or any of the contributories[4] for the time being settled on the list of the contributories[4] to the extent of their liability, for payment of any money which the court[1] considers necessary to satisfy the debts and liabilities of the company,[3] and the costs, charges and expenses of winding-up,[1] and or the adjustment of the rights of the contributories[4] among themselves, and make an order for payment of any calls so made.

(2) In making a call under this section, the court [1] shall take into consideration the probability that some of the contributories [4] may fail, wholly or partially to pay the call.

---

**Notes**
**Section 442**

1. "Court" used in relation to a company, means the Federal High Court, and to the extent to which application may be made to it as; court includes the Court of Appeal and the Supreme Court of Nigeria. See **Section 567 CAMA, Cap. C20, LFN, 2004.**
2. "Winding-up" means the process of settling accounts and liquidating assets in anticipation of a partnership or dissolution. **See Garner B. (ed) Black's Law Dictionary 8th ed**
3. "Company" means a company formed and registered under this Act or, as the case may be, formed and registered in Nigeria before and in existence on the commencement of this Act. See section **567, CAMA Cap. C20 LFN 2004**
4. "Contributories" see"Contributory." It means every person liable to contribute to the assets of a company in the event of its being wound up and for the purposes of all proceedings for determining and all proceedings prior to the final determination of the persons who are to be deemed contributories, the expression shall include any person alleged to be a contributory. See **section 567 CAMA Cap. C20 LFN 2004**

**Cross Reference**

On appointment of liquidator by the court, see **section 422 CAMA Cap. C20, LFN 2004**

On audit on liquidator's account, see **section 429 CAMA Cap. C20 LFN 2004**

On the establishment and jurisdiction of the Federal High Court, see **sections 249& 251 Constitution of the Federal Republic of NIgeria, 1999 (as amended)**

---

**For Further Reading**

On commencement of winding up proceedings, see, Asomugha, E. Maduelosi **Company law in Nigeria under the Companies and Allied Matters Act** E.M. Asomugha (Lagos) 1994

## 443.Power to order payment into companies liquidation account

(1) The court [1] may order any contributory [2], purchaser or other person from whom money is due to the company [3] to pay it into the company's [3] liquidation account[4] referred to in section 428 of this Act to the account of the liquidator [5] instead of direct to the liquidator[5] and any such order may be enforced in the same manner as if it had directed payment to the liquidator. [5]

(2) Moneys and securities [5] paid or delivered into the company's [3] liquidation account[4] in the event of a winding up [6] by the court[1] shall be subject in all respects to any relevant order of the court[1]

---

**Notes**

**Section 443**

1. "Court" used in relation to a company, means the Federal High Court, and to the extent to which application may be made to it as; court includes the Court of Appeal and the Supreme Court of Nigeria. See **Section 567 CAMA, Cap. C20, LFN, 2004.**
2. "Contributories" see"Contributory". It means every person liable to contribute to the assets of a company in the event of its being wound up and for the purposes of all proceedings for determining and all proceedings prior to the final determination of the persons who are to be deemed contributories, the expression shall include any person alleged to be a contributory . See **section 567 CAMA Cap. C20 LFN 2004**
3. "Company" means a company formed and registered under this Act or, as the case may be, formed and registered in Nigeria before and in existence on the commencement of this Act. See section **567, CAMA Cap. C20 LFN 2004**
4. "Companies liquidation account" means kept on behalf of the commission by the Accountant-General of the Federation, into which shall be paid all moneys received by the Commission1 in respect of proceedings under this act in connection with the winding up of companies. **See section 527 CAMA Cap. C20, LFN 2004**
5. "Liquidator" means a person who is appointed to wind up a business's affairs esp. by selling off its assets. See **Garner B. (ed) Black's Law Dictionary 8th ed.**

6. "Securities" includes shares, debentures, debenture stock, bonds, notes (other than promissory notes) and units under a unit trust scheme. See **section 567 CAMA Cap. C20, LFN 2004**

Cross Reference

On company's liquidation account, see **section 428 CAMA Cap. C20 LFN 2004**

On appointment of liquidator by the court, see **section 422 CAMA Cap. C20, LFN 2004**

On the establishment and jurisdiction of the Federal High Court, see **sections 249& 251 Constitution of the Federal Republic of NIgeria, 1999 (as amended)**

On payment of a liquidator into companies liquidation account, see **section 428 CAMA Cap. C20 LFN 2004**

---

**For Further Reading**

On commencement of winding up proceedings, see, Asomugha, E. Maduelosi **Company law in Nigeria under the Companies and Allied Matters Act** E.M. Asomugha (Lagos) 1994

## 444. Order on contributory to be conclusive evidence

(1) An order made by the Court [1] on a Contributory [2] shall, subject to any right of Appeal [3], be conclusive evidence that money, if any thereby appearing to be due or ordered to be paid, is due.

(2) All other pertinent matters stated in the order shall be taken to be truly stated as against all persons and in all proceedings, except proceedings against the land of a deceased Contributory, [2] when the order shall be only prima facie evidence for the purpose of charging his land, unless his heirs or devisees were on the list of Contributories [2] at the time the order was made.

---

**Notes**

**Section 444 (1)**

1. "Court" used in relation to a company, means the Federal High Court, and to the extent to which application may be made to it as; court includes the Court of Appeal and the Supreme Court of Nigeria. See **Section 567 CAMA, Cap. C20, LFN, 2004.**
2. "Contributory"means every person liable to contribute to the assets of a company in the event of its being wound up and for the purposes of all proceedings for determining and all proceedings prior to the final determination of the persons who are to be deemed contributories, the expression shall include any person alleged to be a contributory . See **section 567 CAMA Cap. C20 LFN 2004.**

Cross Reference

On the establishment and jurisdiction of the Federal High Court, see **sections 249& 251 Constitution of the Federal Republic of NIgeria, 1999 (as amended)**
As to the manner of appeals in the Federal High Court, see **section 241 and section 242 of the 1999 Constitution (as amended)**

---

**Cases**
A Court is duty bound to confine its decisions to issues raised by the parties. The Court has no power to formulate cases for the parties or to speculate on the evidence parties ought to proffer otherwise it might find itself covered by the dust of conflict. ***Anambra State Envi. Sani. Auth. v. Ekwenem* (2009) Vol. 45 W.R.N. 1-175 at p.12**
A just and equitable ground is one of the grounds upon which a court having jurisdiction can rely to make an order for winding up a company. See Section 408(e) of the **Companies and Allied Matters Act, Cap 59, Laws of the Federation of Nigeria 1990.** Section 408(e) of same law contained in Cap c20 of Laws of the Federation of Nigeria 2004. A just and equitable ground for winding up a company is a remedy most suitable for contributories. Where a contributory brings a petition under this head as was found by the trial court and where the trial court is of the opinion that the petitioner is entitled to the order of winding up, it must make the order unless it appears to the court that some other remedy is available to the petitioner and that he is acting unreasonably in seeking a winding up order instead of pursuing that other remedy. ***Ado Ibrahim & Company Ltd v. Bendel Cement Company Ltd* (2007) S.C. 284/2001.**

**For Further Reading**
On company's winding up, see, Ayua, I.A **Nigerian Company Law** G. Burn (Leighton Buzzard, Bedfordshire, United Kingdom) 1984.

## 445. Power to exclude creditors not proving in time

The Court [1]may fix a time or times within which Creditors [2] are to prove their debts or claims, or be excluded from the benefit of any distribution made before those debts are proved.

---

**Notes**
**Section 445**

1. "Court" used in relation to a company, means the Federal High Court, and to the extent to which application may be made to it as; court includes the Court of Appeal and the Supreme Court of Nigeria. See **Section 567 CAMA, Cap. C20, LFN, 2004.**

2. "Creditors" see "creditor." It means one to whom a debt is owed; one who gives credit for money or goods. See **Garner B. (ed) Black's Law Dictionary, 8th ed.**

Cross Reference

On the establishment and jurisdiction of the Federal High Court, see **sections 249& 251 Constitution of the Federal Republic of NIgeria, 1999** (as amended)

**Cases**

A secured creditor is a entitled to realise his security and to give credit for the realised or estimated value of the security unless he surrenders it and he cannot be restrained by an action from doing so. ***Alitalia Airlines Ltd. v.N.I.D.B. Ltd.*** **(1967) F.N.L.R.134.**

**For Further Reading**

On winding up, creditors, contributories, see, Orojo, J. Ola **Company Law and Practice in Nigeria** 3rd Edition, Mbeyi & Associates (Lagos, Nigeria) 1992.p.p 455-503.

## 446. Adjustment of rights of contributories

The Court[1] shall adjust the rights of the Contributories [2] among themselves, and distribute any surplus among the persons entitled thereto.

**Notes**

**Section 446**

1. "Court" used in relation to a company , means the Federal High Court, and to the extent to which application may be made to it as; court includes the Court of Appeal and the Supreme Court of Nigeria. See **Section 567 CAMA, Cap. C20, LFN, 2004.**
2. "Contributories" see "contributory." It means every person liable to contribute to the assets of a company in the event of its being wound up and for the purposes of all proceedings for determining and all proceedings prior to the final determination of the persons who are to be deemed contributories, the expression shall include any person alleged to be a contributory . See **section 567 CAMA Cap. C20 LFN 2004**

Cross Reference

On the establishment and jurisdiction of the Federal High Court, see **sections 249& 251 Constitution of the Federal Republic of Nigeria, 1999** (as **amended**)

On winding up proceedings, see generally the Companies Winding up rules 2001

On the nature of liability of a contributory, see **section 404 CAMA Cap. C20, LFN 2004**

---

**Cases**

An application may be made by summons to determine whether or not a person is a contributory, but such application should not be made unless the liquidator has failed to appoint a time and place for the purpose or has made a decision which is not acceptable to the alleged contributory. ***Sulaiman v. Muslim Bank (W.A.) Ltd.*** **(1970) 1 A.L.R. Comm 388.**

## 447. Inspection of books by creditors and contributories

(1) The Court [1] may, at any time after making a Winding-up [2] order, make such order for inspection of the Books and Papers [3] of the Company[4] by Creditors [5] and Contributories [6] as the court [1] thinks just, and any Books and Papers [3] in the possession of the Company [4] may be inspected by Creditors [5] or Contributories [6] accordingly, but not further or otherwise.

(2) Nothing in this section shall be taken as excluding or restricting any statutory rights of government department or person acting under the authority of a government department.

---

**Notes**

**Section 447**

1. "Court" used in relation to a company, means the Federal High Court, and to the extent to which application may be made to it as; court includes the Court of Appeal and the Supreme Court of Nigeria. See **Section 567 CAMA, Cap. C20, LFN, 2004.**
2. "Winding-up" means the process of settling accounts and liquidating assets in anticipation of
a partnership or dissolution. See **Garner B. (ed) Black's Law Dictionary, 8th ed.**
3. "Books and Papers" see "book or paper." It include accounts, deeds, writings, and documents. See **Section 567 CAMA, Cap. C20, LFN, 2004.**
4. "Company" means a company formed and registered under this Act or, as the case may be, formed and
registered in Nigeria before and in existence on the commencement of this Act. **Section 567, CAMA Cap. C20, LFN 2004.**
5. "Creditors" means one to whom a debt is owed; one who gives credit for money or goods. See **Garner B. (ed) Black's Law Dictionary, 8 th ed.**
6. "Contributories" see "Contributory." It means every person liable to contribute to the assets of a company in the event of its being wound

up and for the purposes of all proceedings for determining and all proceedings prior to the final determination of the persons who are to be deemed contributories, the expression shall include any person alleged to be a contributory. See **section 567 CAMA Cap. C20 LFN 2004**

Cross Reference

On the establishment and jurisdiction of the Federal High Court, see **sections 249& 251 Constitution of the Federal Republic of Nigeria, 1999 (as amended)**

On winding up proceedings, see generally the Companies Winding up rules 2001

On the nature of liability of a contributory, see **section 404 CAMA Cap. C20, LFN 2004**

---

**Cases**

An application may be made by summons to determine whether or not a person is a contributory, but such application should not be made unless the liquidator has failed to appoint a time and place for the purpose or has made a decision which is not acceptable to the alleged contributory. See ***Sulaiman v. Muslim Bank (W.A.) Ltd.*** **(1970) 1 A.L.R. Comm 388.**

## 448.Power to order costs of winding up to be paid out of assets

The Court[1] may, in the event of the Assets being insufficient to satisfy the liabilities, make an order as to the payment out of the Assets of the costs, charges and expenses incurred in the Winding up[2] in such order of priority as the Court [1] thinks just.

---

**Notes**

**Section 448**

1. "Court" used in relation to a company, means the Federal High Court, and to the extent to which application may be made to it as; court includes the Court of Appeal and the Supreme Court of Nigeria. See **Section 567 CAMA, Cap. C20, LFN, 2004.**
2. "Winding-up" means the process of settling accounts and liquidating assets in anticipation of a partnership or dissolution. See **Garner B. (ed) Black's Law Dictionary, 8 th ed.**

Cross Reference

On the establishment and jurisdiction of the Federal High Court, see **sections 249& 251 Constitution of the Federal Republic of Nigeria, 1999 (as amended)**

On winding up proceedings, see generally the Companies Winding up rules 2001

On the nature of liability of a contributory, see **section 404 CAMA Cap. C20, LFN 2004**

---

**Cases**

Care and utmost caution must be exercised by the court in its dealing with cases involving the termination of the life of a company. ***Air Via Ltd v. Oriental Airlines Ltd.*** **(2004) 9 N.W.L.R (PT.878) 298.**

## 449. Power to summon persons suspected of having property of company, etc.

(1) The Court [1] may, at any time after the appointment of a provisional Liquidator [2] or the making of a Winding-up [3] order, summon before it any Officer [4] of the Company [5] or person known or suspected to have in his possession any property of the Company [5] or supposed to be indebted to the Company [5], or any person who the Court [1] deems capable of giving information concerning the promotion, formation, trade, dealings, affairs or property of the Company [5].

(2) The Court [1] may examine on Oath [6] any person so summoned concerning the matters aforesaid either by word of mouth or on written interrogatories, and may reduce his answers to writing and require him to sign them.

(3) The Court [1] may require any person summoned under subsection (1) of this section, to produce Books and Papers [7] in his custody or power relating to the company [5] but, where any such person claims a lien on Books or Papers [7] produced by him, the production shall be without prejudice to the lien, and the Court [1] shall have jurisdiction in the Winding up [3] to determine all questions relating to that lien.

(4) If any person so summoned as aforesaid, after being tendered a reasonable sum for his expenses, refuses to come before the Court [1] at the time appointed, not having lawful impediment (made known to the court at the time of its sitting and allowed by it), the Court [1] may cause him to be apprehended and brought before the Court [1] for examination.

---

**Notes**

**Section 449**

1. "Court" used in relation to a company, means the Federal High Court, and to the extent to which application may be made to it as; court

includes the Court of Appeal and the Supreme Court of Nigeria. See **Section 567 CAMA, Cap. C20, LFN, 2004.**

2. "Provisional Liquidator" means a person who is temporarily appointed to wind up a business's affairs esp. by selling off its assets. **See Garner B. Black's Law Dictionary, 8 th ed.**
3. "Winding-up" means the process of settling accounts and liquidating assets in anticipation of a partnership or dissolution. **See Garner B. Black's Law Dictionary, 8th ed.**
4. "Officer" in relation to a body corporate, includes a director, manager or secretary. See **section 567 CAMA Cap. C20 LFN 2004**
5. "Company" means a company formed and registered under this Act or, as the case may be, formed and registered in Nigeria before and in existence on the commencement of this Act.See **Section 567, CAMA Cap. C20, LFN 2004**
6. "Oath" means an affirmation or declaration made in accordance with the relevant law. See section **18(1) Interpretation Act Cap. I 23 LFN 2004** .
7. Books and Papers" see "book or paper." It include accounts, deeds, writings, and documents. See **Section 567 CAMA, Cap. C20, LFN 2004.**

Cross Reference

On the establishment and jurisdiction of the Federal High Court, see **sections 249& 251 Constitution of the Federal Republic of Nigeria, 1999 (as amended)**

On winding up proceedings, see generally the Companies Winding up rules 2001

On the requirement of Oral evidence to be on oath or affirmation. See **section 205 Evidence Act, 2011**

**Cases**

Care and utmost caution must be exercised by the court in its dealing with cases involving the termination of the life of a company.See ***Air Via Ltd v. Oriental Airlines Ltd.*** **(2004) 9 N.W.L.R (Pt.878) 298.**

## 450. Power to order public examination of promoters, etc.

(1) Where an order is made for winding up [1] a company[2] by the court[3] and the official receiver [4] makes a further report under this act stating that in his opinion a fraud has been committed by any person in the promotion or formation of the company, [2] or by any director[5] or other officer [6] of the company[2] in relation to the company[2] since its formation, the court [3] may, after consideration of the report, direct that any person who has taken any part in the promotion or formation of the company, [2] or has been a director [5] or

officer[6] of the company,[2] shall attend before the court[3] on a day appointed by the court[3] for that purpose, and be publicly examined as to the promotion or formation or the conduct of the business of the company[2], or as to his conduct and dealing as director[5] or officer[6] thereof.

(2) The official receiver[4] shall take part in the examination, and for that purpose may, if specially authorised by the commission[7] in that behalf, employ a legal practitioner.[8]

(3) The liquidator,[9] where the official receiver[4] is not the liquidator,[9] and any creditor[10] or contributory,[11] may also take part in the examination, either personally or by a legal practitioner.[8]

(4) The Court[3] may put such questions to the person examined as the court[3] thinks fit.

(5) The person examined shall be examined on oath[12], and shall answer all such questions as the court[3] may put or allow to be put to him.

(6) A person ordered to be examined under this section shall at his own cost, before his examination, be furnished with a copy of the official receiver's[4] report, and may at his own cost employ a legal practitioner[8] who shall be at liberty to put to him such questions as the court[3] may deem just for the purpose of enabling him to explain or qualify any answers given by him:
Provided that if any such person applies to the court[3] to be exculpated from any charges made or suggested against him, it shall be the duty of the official receiver[4] to appear on the hearing of the application and call the attention of the court[3] to any matters which appear to the official receiver[4] to be relevant, and if the court[3] after hearing any evidence given or witnesses called by the official receiver[4], grants the application, the court[3] may allow the applicant such costs as in its discretion it may think fit.

(7) Notes of the examination shall be taken down in writing, and shall be read over to or by, and signed by, the person examined, and may thereafter be used in evidence against him, and shall be open to the inspection of any creditor[10] or contributory[11] at all reasonable times.

(8) The Court[3] may, if it thinks fit, adjourn the examination from time to time.

(9) An examination under this section may, if the court[3] so directs, and subject to general rules made under section 453 of this act, be held before any magistrate, and the powers of the court[3]

under this section as to the conduct of the examination but not as to costs, may be exercised by the magistrate before whom the examination is held.

---

**Notes**
**Section 450**

1. "Winding-up" means the process of settling accounts and liquidating assets in anticipation of
a partnership or dissolution. **See Garner B. Black's Law Dictionary, 8th ed.**
2. "Company" means a company formed and registered under this Act or, as the case may be, formed and
registered in Nigeria before and in existence on the commencement of this Act.See **Section 567, CAMA Cap. C20, LFN 2004**
3. "Court" used in relation to a company , means the Federal High Court, and to the extent to which application may be made to it as; court includes the Court of Appeal and the Supreme Court of Nigeria. See **Section 567 CAMA, Cap. C20, LFN, 2004**
4. "Official receiver" means the officer by whatever name called or known charged with control of affairs in bankruptcy and if the appointment is vacant for any reason whatsoever, means the sheriff. See **section 567, CAMA Cap. C20 LFN 2004**
For the purpose of this Act and so far as it relates to the winding up of companies by the court, "official receiver" means the Deputy Chief Registrar of the Federal High Court or an officer designated for the purpose by the Chief Judge of the Court. See **section 419 CAMA Cap. C20, LFN 2004**
5. "Director" includes any person occupying the position of director by whatever name called; and includes any person in accordance with whose directions or instructions the directors of the company are accustomed to act .See **section 567, CAMA Cap. C20 LFN 2004**
6. "Officer" in relation to a body corporate, includes a director, manager or secretary. See **section 567 CAMA Cap. C20 LFN 2004**
7. "Commission" means the Corporate Affairs Commission established under section 1 of this Act **. See section 567 CAMA Cap. C20, LFN 2004.**
8. "Legal practitioner" has the meaning assigned to it by the Legal Practitioners Act. See **section 567 CAMA, Cap. C20, LFN 2004.**
9. "Liquidator" means a person who is appointed to wind up a business's affairs esp. by selling off its assets. . **See Garner B, Black's Law Dictionary, 8th ed.**
10. "Creditor" means one to whom a debt is owed; one who gives credit for money or goods. **Garner B. (ed) Black's Law Dictionary, 8 th ed.**
11. "Contributory".means every person liable to contribute to the assets of a company in the event of its being wound up and for the purposes of all proceedings for determining and all proceedings prior to the final determination of the persons who are to be deemed contributories, the

expression shall include any person alleged to be a contributory . See **section 567 CAMA Cap. C20 LFN 2004**

12. "Oath" means an affirmation or declaration made in accordance with the relevant law, See section **18(1) Interpretation Act Cap. I 23 LFN 2004**

Cross Reference

On the requirements for practice as a legal practitioner, see generally, **Legal Practitioners Act Cap. L11, LFN 2004**

On promoters, see **section 61 CAMA Cap. C20, LFN 2004**

On meaning of official receiver, see **section 419 Cap. C20, LFN 2004**

On powers to enforce orders of court, see **section 453 CAMA Cap. C20, LFN 2004**

On examination of witnesses see generally see **Part XII, Evidence Act 2011**

On the requirement of Oral evidence to be on oath or affirmation. See **section 205 Evidence Act, 2011**

On the establishment and jurisdiction of the Federal High Court, see **sections 249& 251 Constitution of the Federal Republic of Nigeria, 1999 (as amended)**

---

**Cases**

Section 61 defines a promoter as- any person who undertakes to take part in forming a company with reference to a given project and to set it going and who takes the necessary steps to accomplish that purpose, or who, with regard to a proposed or newly formed company, undertakes a part in raising capital for it, shall, prima facie, be deemed a promoter of the company: Provided that a person acting in a professional capacity for persons engaged in procuring the formation of the company shall not thereby be deemed to be a promoter. ***Adeniji v. Starcola (Nigeria) Ltd.*** **Suit No. M.135/70 unreported, H.C. Lagos.**

---

**For Further Reading**

On promoters, see, Orojo, J. Ola **Company Law and Practice in Nigeria** 3rd Edition, Mbeyi & Associates (Lagos, Nigeria) 1992. P.p 74-78.

## 451. Power to arrest absconding contributory

The court,[1] at any time either before or after making a winding-up[2] order, on proof of probable cause for believing that a contributory[3] is about to quit nigeria or otherwise to abscond, or to remove or conceal any of his property for the purpose of evading payment of calls, or of avoiding examination respecting the affairs of the company,[4] may cause the contributory[3] to be arrested, and his books and papers[5] and movable personal property, to be seized, and him and them to be safely kept until such time as the court [1] may order.

(2) Moneys and securities [6] paid or delivered into the company's liquidation account[7] in the event of a winding up [2] by the court[1] shall be subject in all respects to any relevant order of the court.[1]

---

**Notes**
**Section 451**

1. "Court" used in relation to a company, means the Federal High Court, and to the extent to which application may be made to it as; court includes the Court of Appeal and the Supreme Court of Nigeria. See **Section 567 CAMA, Cap. C20, LFN, 2004**
2. "Winding-up" means the process of settling accounts and liquidating assets in anticipation of
   a partnership or dissolution. **See Garner B. (ed.) Black's Law Dictionary, 8th ed.**
3. "Contributory." means every person liable to contribute to the assets of a company in the event of its being wound up and for the purposes of all proceedings for determining and all proceedings prior to the final determination of the persons who are to be deemed contributories, the expression shall include any person alleged to be a contributory . See **section 567 CAMA Cap. C20 LFN 2004**
4. "Company" means a company formed and registered under this Act or, as the case may be, formed and registered in Nigeria before and in existence on the commencement of this Act. **See section 567, CAMA Cap. C20, LFN 2004**
5. "Books and Papers" see "book or paper" include accounts, deeds, writings, and documents. See **Section. 567 CAMA Cap. C20, LFN 2004**
6. **"Securities"** includes shares, debentures, debenture stock, bonds, notes (other than promissory notes) and units under a unit trust scheme. See **section 567 CAMA Cap. C20, LFN 2004**
7. "Companies liquidation account" means kept on behalf of the commission by the Accountant-General of the Federation, into which shall be paid all moneys received by the Commission1 in respect of proceedings under this act in connection with the winding up of companies. **See section 527 CAMA Cap. C20, LFN 2004**

**Cross Reference**

On opening a company liquidation Account, see **section 428 CAMA Cap. C20, LFN 2004**

On the nature of liability of a contributory, see **section 404 CAMA Cap. C20, LFN 2004**

On the establishment and jurisdiction of the Federal High Court, see **sections 249& 251 Constitution of the Federal Republic of Nigeria, 1999** (as amended)

**Cases**

If a contributory petitions on the ground that the accounts and information about the company were not supplied, he need not prove that there will be assets to distribute. ***Attorney-General for Lagos State v. Nigerian Oxygen & Allied Gases Ltd.*** **Suit No. FRC/L/M3/77 of 13/3/80.**

## 452. Powers of court cumulative

Any powers by this act conferred on the court [1] shall be in addition to and not in restriction of any existing powers of instituting proceedings against any contributory [2] or debtor [3] of the company[4], or the estate of any contributory [2] or debtor [3], for the recovery of any call or other sums.

**Notes**

**Section 452**

1. "Court" means the Federal High Court and to the extent to which application may be made to it as; court includes the Court of Appeal and the Supreme Court. See **Section 567, CAMA, Cap. C20 LFN 2004**
2. "Contributory" means a person liable to contribute to the assets of a company in the event of it being wound up; and for the purpose of all proceedings for determining, and all proceedings prior to the final determination of, the persons who are to be deemed contributories, the expression includes any person alleged to be a contributory. See **Section 567, CAMA Cap. C20, LFN 2004**

   "Contributory" means a person who, as a result of representing a past or present member of a corporation, is liable to contribute to the corporations debts upon its winding up **See Garner B, (ed.) Black's Law Dictionary, 8th ed.**
3. "Debtor" means one who owes an obligation to another esp. an obligation to pay money. **See Garner B. (ed.) Black's Law Dictionary, 8th ed.**
4. "Company" means a corporation –or, less commonly, an association, partnership, or union – that carries on a commercial or industrial enterprise. **Black's Law Dictionary 8thed**

   "Company" means a company formed and registered under the Act, or as the case may be, formed and registered in Nigeria before and in existence on the commencement of this Act. **Section 567, CAMA,Cap. C20 LFN 2004**

Cross Reference

On the nature of liability of a contributory, see **section 404 CAMA Cap. C20, LFN 2004**

On the establishment and jurisdiction of the Federal High Court, see **sections 249& 251 Constitution of the Federal Republic of Nigeria, 1999 (as amended)**

---

**Cases**

Care and utmost caution must be exercised by the court in its dealing with cases involving the termination of the life of a company.See ***Air Via Ltd v. Oriental Airlines Ltd.*** **(2004) 9 N.W.L.R (PT.878) 298.**

## 453. Delegation to liquidator of certain powers of court

(1) Provision may be made by rules for enabling or requiring all or any of the powers and duties conferred and imposed on the court[1] by this act, in respect of the matters following, to be exercised or performed by the liquidator [2] as an officer of the court, [1] and subject to the control of the court, [1] that is to say, the powers and duties of the court [1] in respect of-

(a) the holding and conducting of meetings [3] to ascertain the wishes of creditors [4] and contributories [5];

(b) the settling of lists of contributories [5] and the rectifying of the register of members [6] where required, and the collecting and applying of the assets;

(c) requiring delivery of property or documents [7] to the liquidator[2];

(d) the making of calls;

(e) the fixing of a time within which debts and claims shall be proved.

(2) Nothing in this section shall authorise the liquidator, [2] without the special leave of the court, [1] to rectify the register of members,[6] or, without either the special leave of the court [1] or the sanction of the committee of inspection, to make any call.

---

**Notes**

**Section 453(1)**

1. "Court" means the Federal High Court and to the extent to which application may be made to it as; court includes the Court of Appeal and the Supreme Court. See **Section 567, CAMA, Cap. C20 LFN 2004**
2. "Liquidator" means a person appointed to wind up business affairs, especially by selling off its assets. See **Graner B. ed. Black's Law Dictionary, 8th ed.**

3. "Meeting" means the gathering of people to discuss or act on matters in which they have a common interest; especially the convening of a deliberative assembly to transact business. **See Graner B. Ed. Black's Law Dictionary, 8th ed.**
4. "Creditor" means a person or entity with a definite claim against another , especially a claim that is capable of adjustment and liquidation. See **Garner B. (ed.), Black's law Dictionary, 8 th ed.**
5. "Contributories" see "Contributory." It means a person liable to contribute to the assets of a company in the event of it being wound up; and for the purpose of all proceedings for determining, and all proceedings prior to the final determination of, the persons who are to be deemed contributories, the expression includes any person alleged to be a contributory. See **Section 567, CAMA, Cap. C20 LFN 2004**
   "Contributory" means a person who, as a result of representing a past or present member of a corporation, is liable to contribute to the corporations debts upon its winding up. **Garner B. (ed. )Black's Law Dictionary 8th ed.**
6. "Members" see "member." It means one of the individuals of whom a deliberative assembly consists and who enjoys the full rights of participating in the organization-including the rights of making, debating and voting on motions- except to the extent that the organization reserves those rights to certain classes of membership. **Garner B. (ed. )Black's Law Dictionary 8th ed.**
   It includes the heir, executor, administrator or other personal representative as the case may be, of the member. See **Section 567 CAMA, Cap. C20 LFN 2004**
7. "Document" includes summons, notice, order and other legal processes, and registers. See **Section 567 CAMA, Cap. C20 LFN 2004**

**Cross Reference**

On the various types of meeting a company should hold, see **sections 211,213 and 215, CAMA, Cap. C20 LFN 2004**

On obligation of a Company to maintain a Register of Members, see **section 83, CAMA, Cap. C20 LFN 2004**

---

**Cases**

The liquidator may be likened to an undertaker, by virtue of the Company's total in disposition goes into preparation for the "burial" of the company but the actual burial of the company takes place on its death at its dissolution. ***Co-Operative and Commerce Bank (NIG.)Ltd v. Alex O. Onwuchekwa*** **(2000)3 NWLR (Pt. 647) 67**

## 454. Dissolution of company

(1) If the affairs of a Company [1] have been fully Wound up [2] and the Liquidator[3] makes an application in that behalf, the Court [4]

shall order the dissolution of the Company [1] and the Company [1] shall be dissolved accordingly from the date of the order.

(2) A copy of the order shall, within 14 days from the date when made, be forwarded by the Liquidator [3] to the Commission [5] who shall make in its books a minute of the dissolution of the Company. [1]

(3) If the Liquidator [3] makes default in complying with the requirements of this section, he shall be guilty of an offence and liable to a fine of N25 for every day during which he is in default.

---

**Notes**

**Section 454(1)**

1. "Company" means a corporation –or, less commonly, an association, partnership, or union – that carries on a commercial or industrial enterprise. See **Garner B. (ed.), Black's Law Dictionary 8th ed.** "Company" means a company formed and registered under the Act, or as the case may be, formed and registered in Nigeria before and in existence on the commencement of this Act. See **Section 567, CAMA, Cap. C20, LFN 2004**
2. "Wound-up" see "winding-up." It means the process of settling accounts and liquidating assets in anticipation of dissolution. See **Garner B. (ed.), Black's Law Dictionary 8th ed.**
3. "Liquidator" means a person appointed to wind up business affairs, especially by selling off its assets. **See Garner B. (ed.), Black's Law Dictionary 8th ed.**
4. "Court" means the Federal High Court and to the extent to which application may be made to it as; court includes the Court of Appeal and the Supreme Court. See **Section 567, CAMA, Cap. C20 LFN 2004**

**Section 454(2)**

5. "Commission" means the Corporate Affairs Commission established under section 1 of this Act . **See section 567 CAMA Cap. C20, LFN 2004.**

**Cross Reference**

On Winding Up of Companies, see generally **Part XV of CAMA, Cap. C20 LFN 2004**

On meaning of offence, **see section 2, Criminal Code, Cap. C38, LFN 2004**

---

**Cases**

It is clear from the principle enunciated in ***Tesi Opebiyi v. Shittu Oshoboja & anor*. (1976) 9&10 SC 195** … and by virtue of section 454(1) and (2)…, a Company dies on its dissolution. The revocation of the licence of that Company where it is a bank, and the further order of court winding same up may indicate the acute disposition, and extreme position of ineffectiveness of the Company but not so the fact of its death. The liquidator may be likened to an undertaker, by virtue of the Company's total in disposition goes into preparation for the "burial" of the company but the actual burial of the company takes place on its death at its dissolution. ***Co-Operative and Commerce Bank (NIG.)Ltd v. Alex O. Onwuchekwa*** **(2000)3 NWLR (Pt. 647) 67**

*Enforcement of and appeals from orders*

## 455. Power to enforce orders

An order made by a Court [1] under this Act may be enforced in the same manner as orders made in any action pending therein.

---

**Notes**

**Section 455**

"Court" means the Federal High Court and to the extent to which application may be made to it as; court includes the Court of Appeal and the Supreme Court. **See section 567, CAMA, LFN 2004**

Cross Reference

On establishment and jurisdiction of the Federal High Court, see **section 249 & 251, Constitution of the Federal Republic of Nigeria, 1999 (as amended)**

---

## 456. Appeals from orders

Subject to rules of court [1], an appeal from any order or decision made or given in the winding up [2] of a company [3] by the court [1] under this act, shall lie in the same manner and subject to the same conditions as an appeal from any order or decision of the court [1] in cases within its ordinary jurisdiction [4].

---

**Notes**

**Section 456**

1. "Court" means the Federal High Court and to the extent to which application may be made to it as; court includes the Court of Appeal and the Supreme Court. See **Section 567 CAMA, CAP C20 LFN 2004**

2. "Winding up" means the process of settling accounts and liquidating assets in anticipation of a partnership or dissolution. See **Garner B. (ed.) Black's Law Dictionary 8 th ed.**
3. "Company" means a corporation –or, less commonly, an association, partnership, or union – that carries on a commercial or industrial enterprise. See **Garner B. (ed.) Black's Law Dictionary 8 th ed.** "Company" means a company formed and registered under the Act, or as the case may be, formed and registered in Nigeria before and in existence on the commencement of this Act. See **Section 567 CAMA, CAP C20 LFN 2004**
4. "Jurisdiction" means a courts powers to decide a case or decree. **Garner B. (ed.) Black's Law Dictionary 8 th ed.**

**Cross Reference**

As to the manner of appeals in the Federal High Court, see **section 241 and section 242 of the 1999 Constitution (as amended)**

---

**Cases**

On a court of competent jurisdiction:

In ***Madukolu v. Nkemdilim (1962)2 NSCC 374 at 379-380*** , this court stated that "a court is properly constituted as regards the number and qualification of its members on the bench , and no member is disqualified for one reason or the other and the subject matter of the case is within the jurisdiction and there is no feature in the case which prevents the court from exercising its jurisdiction and the case coming up before the court was initiated by due process of law and upon fufilment if any condition precedent to the exercise of jurisdiction." See ***SLB Consortium v. Nigerin National Peroleum Corporation (NNPC) SC 180/2008 delivered 15/04/11***

*Chapter 3 -Voluntary Winding Up*

*Resolutions for and commencement of voluntary winding up*

## 457. Any Company[1] may be wound up[2] Voluntarily

(a) when the period, if any, fixed for the duration of the company[1] by the articles[3] expires, or the event, if any, occurs, on occurrence of which the articles [3] provided that the company[1] is to be dissolved and the company [1] in general meeting[4] has passed a resolution[5] requiring the company[1] to be wound up[2] voluntarily;

(b) if the company[1] resolves by special Resolution[6] that the Company[1] be Wound up[2] voluntarily; and references in this Act to a "resolution for voluntary Winding up" means a resolution passed under any of the paragraphs of this section.

---

**Notes**
**Section 457**

1. "Company" means a corporation –or, less commonly, an association, partnership, or union – that carries on a commercial or industrial enterprise. See **Garner B. (ed.) Black's Law Dictionary 8 th ed.** "Company" means a company formed and registered under the Act, or as the case may be, formed and registered in Nigeria before and in existence on the commencement of this Act. See **Section 567, CAMA, Cap. C20 LFN 2004**
2. "Wound up" see "Winding up" means the process of settling accounts and liquidating assets in anticipation of a partnership or dissolution. See **Garner B. (ed.) Black's Law Dictionary 8 th ed.**
3. "Articles" means the articles of association of a company, as originally framed or as altered by special resolution including so far as they apply to the regulations contained in Table A I the First Schedules of the Companies Act 1922 or in that Table as altered by any subsequent enactment or reprint of the laws, or in Table A in Schedule 1. See **Section 567, CAMA, Cap. C20 LFN 2004.**
4. "General meeting" see "annual meeting." It means a yearly meeting to elect or install officers or directors and to conduct other routine organisational business**. See Garner B. (ed) Black's Law Dictionary 8th ed.**
5. "Resolution" means a main motion that formally expresses the sense, will, or action of a deliberative assembly. See **Garner B. (ed.) Black's Law Dictionary 8th ed.**

**Cross Reference**

On the Obligation to register the Articles of Association, the form and content of same, see **sections 33 & 34, CAMA, LFN 2004**

On procedure applicable in Winding up under the Act, see generally **Companies Winding-up Rules, 2001**

On consequences of Voluntary winding up, **see section 460 & 461, CAMA, Cap. 20 LFN 2004**

On types of resolutions, see **section 233, CAMA, Cap. C20 LFN 2004**

On dissolution of a Company, see **section 452, CAMA, Cap. C20 LFN 2004**

---

**For Further Reading**

On winding up proceedings, see, Asomugha, E. Maduelosi **Company law in Nigeria under the Companies and Allied Matters Act** E.M. Asomugha (Lagos) 1994

## 458. Notice of resolution to wind up voluntarily

(1) If a company [1] passes a resolution [2] for voluntary winding up[3] it shall, within 14 days after the passing of the resolution, [2] give notice of the resolution [2] by advertisement in the gazette [4] or two daily newspapers and to the Commission. [5]

(2) If default is made in complying with this section, the company[1] and every officer [6] of the company [1] who is in default shall be liable to a fine of n500 and for the purposes of this subsection the liquidator[7] of the company [1] shall be deemed to be an officer [6] of the company. [1]

---

**Notes**

**Section 458(1)**

1. Company" means a corporation –or, less commonly, an association, partnership, or union – that carries on a commercial or industrial enterprise. See **Garner B. (ed.) Black's Law Dictionary 8 th ed.** "Company" means a company formed and registered under the Act, or as the case may be, formed and registered in Nigeria before and in existence on the commencement of this Act. Seee **Section 567, CAMA, LFN 2004**
2. "Resolution" means a main motion that formally expresses the sense, will, or action of a deliberative assembly. See **Garner B. (ed.) Black's Law Dictionary 8th ed.**
3. "Voluntary winding up" Means the dissolution of a company when the period, if any fixed for its duration by the articles expires or on the occurrence of an event of which its articles provide that the company is to be dissolved and the company in a general meeting pass a resolution requiring the company to be wound up . See **section 457 CAMA Cap. C20, LFN 2004**
4. "Gazette" means the official Gazette of the Federation. See **Section 567, CAMA, Cap. C20 LFN 2004**

**Section 458(2)**

5. "Commission" means the Corporate Affairs Commission established under section 1 of this Act **. See section 567 CAMA Cap. C20, LFN 2004.**
6. "Officer" in relation to a body corporate, includes a director, manager or secretary. **See section 567, CAMA, Cap. C20 LFN 2004.**
7. "Liquidator" means a person appointed to wind up business affairs, especially by selling off its assets. **See Graner B. ed. Black's Law Dictionary, 8th ed.**

**Cross Reference**

On types of resolutions **, see section 233, CAMA, LFN 2004**

On consequences of Voluntary winding up, **see section 460 & 461, CAMA, LFN 2004**

---

**Cases**

The liquidator may be likened to an undertaker, by virtue of the Company's total in disposition goes into preparation for the "burial" of the company but the actual burial of the company takes place on its death at its dissolution. ***Co-Operative and Commerce Bank (NIG.)Ltd v. Alex O. Onwuchekwa* (2000) 3 NWLR (Pt. 647) 67**

## 459. Commencement of voluntary winding up

A voluntary winding up [1] shall be deemed to commence at the time of the passing of the resolution [2] for voluntary winding up. [1]

---

**Notes**
**Section 459**

1. "Voluntary winding up" Means the dissolution of a company when the period, if any fixed for its duration by the articles expires or on the occurrence of an event of which its articles provide that the company is to be dissolved and the company in a general meeting pass a resolution requiring the company to be wound up. See **section 457 CAMA Cap. C20, LFN 2004**
2. "Resolution" means a main motion that formally expresses the sense, will, or action of a deliberative assembly. See **Garner B. (ed.) Black's Law Dictionary 8th ed.**

Cross Reference

On consequences of Voluntary winding up, **see section 460 & 461, CAMA, LFN 2004**

On types of resolutions , **see section 233, CAMA, LFN 2004**

On procedure applicable in Winding up under the Act, see generally **Companies Winding-up Rules, 2001**

---

**For Further Reading**

On winding up proceedings, see, Asomugha, E. Maduelosi **Company law in Nigeria under the Companies and Allied Matters** *Act* E. M. Asomugha (Lagos) 1994.

*Consequences of voluntary winding up*

**460**. In case of voluntary winding up, [1] the company[2] shall, from the commencement of the winding up, [1] cease to carry on its business, except so far as may be required for the beneficial winding up[1] thereof:

Provided that the corporate state and corporate powers of the company[2] shall, notwithstanding anything to the contrary in its articles,[4] continue until it is dissolved.

**Notes**
**Section 460**

1. "Voluntary winding-up" Means the dissolution of a company when the period, if any fixed for its duration by the articles expires or on the occurrence of an event of which its articles provide that the company is to be dissolved and the company in a general meeting pass a resolution requiring the company to be wound up. See **section 457 CAMA Cap.C20, LFN 2004**
2. "Company" means a corporation –or, less commonly, an association, partnership, or union – that carries on a commercial or industrial enterprise. See **Garner B., (ed.) Black's Law Dictionary 8 th ed.** "Company" means a company formed and registered under the Act, or as the case may be, formed and registered in Nigeria before and in existence on the commencement of this Act. See **Section 567, CAMA, Cap. C20 LFN 2004**
3. "Articles" means the articles of association of a company, as originally framed or as altered by special resolution including so far as they apply to the regulations contained in Table A I the First Schedules of the Companies Act 1922 or in that Table as altered by any subsequent enactment or reprint of the laws, or in Table A in Schedule 1. **See section 567, CAMA, Cap. C20 LFN 2004.**

Cross Reference

On dissolution of a Company, see **section 454, CAMA, LFN 2004**

**For Further Reading**

On winding up proceedings, see, Asomugha, E. Maduelosi **Company law in Nigeria under the Companies and Allied Matters Act** E. M. Asomugha (Lagos) 1994

## 461.Avoidance of transfer, etc. after commencement of voluntary winding up

Any transfer of shares, [1] not being a transfer made to or with the sanction of the liquidator, [2] and any alteration in the status of the members[3] of the company, [4] made after the commencement of a voluntary winding up, [5] shall be void.

**Notes**
**Section 461**

1. "Shares" see "share." It means the interests in the company's shares capital of a member who is entitled to share in the capitalor income of such company, and except where a distinction between stock and

shares is expressed or implied, includes stock. See **section 567 CAMA Cap. C20, LFN 2004**

2. "Liquidator" means a person appointed to wind up business affairs, especially by selling off its assets. See **Graner B. Ed. Black's Law Dictionary, 8th ed.**
3. "Members" see "member." It means one of the individuals of whom a deliberative assembly consists and who enjoys the full rights of participating in the organization-including the rights of making, debating and voting on motions- except to the extent that the organization reserves those rights to certain classes of membership. See **Garner B. ed. Black's Law Dictionary 8th ed.**
"Member" includes the heir, executor, administrator or other personal representative as the case may be, of the member. **Section 567 CAMA, Cap. C20 LFN 2004**
4. "Company" means a corporation –or, less commonly, an association, partnership, or union – that carries on a commercial or industrial enterprise. See **Garner B. (ed.) Black's Law Dictionary 8th ed.**
"Company" means a company formed and registered under the Act, or as the case may be, formed and registered in Nigeria before and in existence on the commencement of this Act. **See section 567, CAMA, Cap. C20 LFN 2004**
5. "Voluntary winding-up" Means the dissolution of a company when the period, if any fixed for its duration by the articles expires or on the occurrence of an event of which its articles provide that the company is to be dissolved and the company in a general meeting pass a resolution requiring the company to be wound up . See **section 457 CAMA Cap. C20, LFN 2004**

**Cross Reference**

On how shares are transferred, see **section 151, CAMA, LFN 2004**

---

**Cases**

The liquidator may be likened to an undertaker, by virtue of the Company's total in disposition goes into preparation for the "burial" of the company but the actual burial of the company takes place on its death at its dissolution. ***Co-Operative and Commerce Bank (Nig.)Ltd v. Alex O. Onwuchekwa (2000) 3 NWLR (Pt. 647) 67.***

*Declaration of solvency*

## 462.Statutory declaration of solvency where proposal to wind up voluntarily

(1) Where on or after the commencement of this act, it is proposed to wind up[1] a company[2] voluntarily, the directors[3] of the company[2] or, in the case of a company[2] having more than two directors,[3] the majority of the directors,[3] may at a meeting[4] of the directors[3] make a statutory declaration[5] to the effect that they have

made a full inquiry into the affairs of the company [2] and that, having so done, they have formed the opinion that the company [2] will be able to pay its debts in full within such period, not exceeding 12 months from the commencement of the winding up, [1] as is specified in the declaration. [5]

(2) A declaration [5] made as aforesaid shall have no effect for the purposes of this Act unless-

(a) it is made within the five weeks immediately preceding the date of the passing of the resolution [6] for winding up [1] the company[2] and is delivered to the commission [7] for registration before that date; and

(b) it embodies a statement of the company's [2] assets and liabilities as at the latest practicable date before the making of the declaration. [5]

(3) Any director [3] of a company [2] making a declaration [5] under this section without having reasonable grounds for the opinion that the company[2] will be able to pay its debts in full within the period specified in the declaration, [5] shall be guilty of an offence and liable on conviction to a fine of N1,500 or to imprisonment for a term of three months, or to both; and if the company [2] is wound up [1] in pursuance of a resolution [6] passed within the period of five weeks after the making of the declaration, [5] but its debts are not paid or provided for in full within the period stated in the declaration, [5] it shall be presumed, until the contrary is shown, that the director [3] did not have reasonable grounds for his opinion.

(4) A winding up [1] in any case where a declaration [5] has been made and delivered in accordance with this section, shall in this act be referred to as "a members' voluntary winding up" and a winding up[1] in any case where a declaration has not been made and delivered as aforesaid shall in this act be referred to as "a creditors' voluntary winding up."

(5) Subsections (1) to (3) of this section shall not apply to a winding up[1] commenced before the commencement of this act.

---

**Notes**

**Section 462(1)**

1. "Wind-up" see "Winding-up." It means the process of settling accounts and liquidating assets in anticipation of a partnership or dissolution. See **Garner B. (ed.) Black's Law Dictionary 8 [th]ed.**

2. "Company" means a corporation –or, less commonly, an association, partnership, or union – that carries on a commercial or industrial enterprise. See **Garner B. (ed.) Black's Law Dictionary 8 th ed.** "Company" means a company formed and registered under the Act, or as the case may be, formed and registered in Nigeria before and in existence on the commencement of this Act. See **Section 567, CAMA, Cap. C20 LFN 2004.**
3. "Directors" see "Director". A director includes any person occupying the position of director by whatever name called, and includes any person in accordance with whose directions or instructions the directors of the company are accustomed to act. See **Section 567, CAMA, Cap. C20 LFN 2004.**
4. "Meeting" means the gathering of people to discuss or act on matters in which they have a common interest; especially the convening of a deliberative assembly to transact business. See **Garner B. ed. Black's Law Dictionary, 8 th ed.**
5. "Statutory declaration" means a declaration voluntarily made under the Oaths Act 1963 and in Nigeria, includes one so made under any other enactment or law providing for the taking of voluntary declaration. **See section 567, CAMA, Cap. C20 LFN 2004.**

**Section 462(2)**

6. "Resolution" means a main motion that formally expresses the sense, will, or action of a deliberative assembly. See **Garner B. (ed.) Black's Law Dictionary 8th ed.**
7. "Commission" means the Corporate Affairs Commission established under section 1 of this Act **. See section 567 CAMA Cap. C20, LFN 2004.**

**Cross Reference**

On consequences of Voluntary winding up, **see section 460 & 461, CAMA, Cap. C20 LFN 2004**

On types of resolutions **, see section 233, CAMA, Cap. C20 LFN 2004**

On procedure applicable in Winding up under the Act, see generally **Companies Winding-up Rules, 2001**

---

**For Further Reading**

On winding up proceedings, see, Asomugha, E. Maduelosi **Company law in Nigeria under the Companies and Allied Matters Act** E. M. Asomugha (Lagos) 1994.

*Provisions applicable to a members' voluntary winding-up*

## 463. Provisions applicable to a members' voluntary winding-up

The provisions following, that is to say, sections 464 to 470 of this Act, shall, subject to the alternative provision in section 469 of this Act, apply in relation to a members' voluntary Winding up. [1]

---

**Notes**
**Section 463**

1. "Members voluntary winding-up" has the meaning assigned to it by section 462 (4) of this Act. See **section 567 CAMA Cap. C20 LFN 2004**

**Cross Reference**

On distinction between members voluntary winding-up and creditors voluntary winding-up, see **section 462(4), CAMA, LFN 2004**

On power of the company to appoint a liquidator, see **section 464 CAMA Cap. C20 LFN 2004**

---

**For Further Reading**

On winding up proceedings, see, Asomugha, E. Maduelosi *Company law in Nigeria under the Companies and Allied Matters Act* E.M. Asomugha (Lagos) 1994

## 464. Power to appoint, etc., liquidators

(1) The company [1] in general meeting [2] shall appoint one or more liquidators [3] for the purpose of winding up [4] the affairs and distributing the assets of the company, [1] and may fix the remuneration to be paid to him or them.

(2) If a liquidator [3] is appointed under this section, all the powers of the directors [6] shall cease, except so far as the company [1] in general meeting [2] or the liquidator [3] sanctions the continuance thereof.

---

**Notes**
**Section 464(1)**

1. "Company" means a corporation –or, less commonly, an association, partnership, or union – that carries on a commercial or industrial enterprise. See **Garner B. (ed.) Black's Law Dictionary 8th ed** .
   "Company" means a company formed and registered under the Act, or as the case may be, formed and registered in Nigeria before and in existence on the commencement of this Act. See **section 567, CAMA, Cap C20 LFN 2004.**
2. "Meeting" means the gathering of people to discuss or act on matters in which they have a common interest; especially the convening of a

deliberative assembly to transact business. See **Garner B. (ed.) Black's Law Dictionary, 8th ed.**

3. "Liquidator" means a person appointed to wind up business affairs, especially by selling off its assets. See **Garner B. (ed.) Black's Law Dictionary, 8th ed.**
4. "Winding-up" means the process of settling accounts and liquidating assets in anticipation of a partnership or dissolution. See **Garner B. (ed.)Black's Law Dictionary 8th ed.**
5. "Directors" see "Director." A director includes any person occupying the position of director by whatever name called, and includes any person in accordance with whose directions or instructions the directors of the company are accustomed to act. See **Section 567, CAMA, Cap. C20 LFN 2004.**

**Cross Reference**

For types of general meeting see **section 213 & section 215, CAMA, LFN 2004**

---

**Cases**

The liquidator may be likened to an undertaker, by virtue of the Company's total in disposition goes into preparation for the "burial" of the company but the actual burial of the company takes place on its death at its dissolution. ***Co-Operative and Commerce Bank (NIG.)Ltd v. Alex O. Onwuchekwa* (2000) 3 NWLR (Pt. 647) 67.**

**For Further Reading**

On winding up proceedings, see, Asomugha, E. Maduelosi **Company law in Nigeria under the Companies and Allied Matters Act** E.M. Asomugha (Lagos) 1994

## 465. Power to fill vacancy in office of liquidators

(1) If a vacancy occurs by death, resignation or otherwise in the office of a liquidator [1] appointed by the company, [2] the company [2] in general meeting [3] may, subject to any arrangement with its creditors, [4] fill the vacancy; and for that purpose a general meeting [3] may be convened by any contributory [5] or, if there were more liquidators [1] than one, by the continuing liquidators. [1]

(2) The general meeting [3] shall be held in the manner provided by this act or by the articles, [6] or in such manner as may, on application by any contributory [5] or by the continuing liquidators, [1] be determined by the court. [7]

---

**Notes**
**Section 465(1)**

1. "Liquidator" means a person appointed to wind up business affairs, especially by selling off its assets.See **Graner B. (ed.) Black's Law Dictionary, 8 th ed.**
2. "Company" means a corporation –or, less commonly, an association, partnership, or union – that carries on a commercial or industrial enterprise. See **Garner B. (ed.) Black's Law Dictionary 8 th ed.**
   "Company" means a company formed and registered under the Act, or as the case may be, formed and registered in Nigeria before and in existence on the commencement of this Act. See **Section 567, CAMA, Cap. C20 LFN 2004.**
3. "Meeting" means the gathering of people to discuss or act on matters in which they have a common interest; especially the convening of a deliberative assembly to transact business. See **Garner B. (ed.) Black's Law Dictionary, 8 th ed.**
4. "Creditor" means a person or entity with a definite claim against another, especially a claim that is capable of adjustment and liquidation. See **Garner B. (ed.), Black's law Dictionary, 8 th ed.**
5. "Contributory" means a person liable to contribute to the assets of a company in the event of it being wound up; and for the purpose of all proceedings for determining, and all proceedings prior to the final determination of, the persons who are to be deemed contributories, the expression includes any person alleged to be a contributory. See **Section 567, CAMA, Cap. C20 LFN 2004**
6. "Articles" means the articles of association of a company, as originally framed or as altered by special resolution including so far as they apply to the regulations contained in Table AI the First Schedules of the Companies Act 1922 or in that Table as altered by any subsequent enactment or reprint of the laws, or in Table A in Schedule 1. See **Section 567, CAMA, Cap. C20 LFN 2004.**

**Cross Reference**

For types of general meeting see **section 213 & section 215, CAMA, LFN Cap. C20 2004**

On power of company to appoint liquidators, see **section 464 CAMA Cap. C20 LFN 2004**

**Cases**

The liquidator may be likened to an undertaker, by virtue of the Company's total in disposition goes into preparation for the "burial" of the company but the actual burial of the company takes place on its death at its dissolution. ***Co-Operative and Commerce Bank (NIG. )Ltd v. Alex O. Onwuchekwa*** **(2000)3 NWLR (Pt. 647) 67.**

**For Further Reading**

On winding up proceedings, see, Asomugha, E. Maduelosi **Company law in Nigeria under the Companies and Allied Matters Act** E. M. Asomugha (Lagos) 1994.

---

## 466. Liquidator to call creditors' meeting on insolvency

(1) If, in the case of a winding up [1] commenced after the commencement of this act, the liquidator [2] is at any time of opinion that the company[3] will not be able to pay its debts in full within the period stated in the declaration [4] under section 462 of this act, he shall forthwith summon a meeting of the creditors, [5] and lay before the meeting[6] a statement of the assets and liabilities of the company.[3]

(2) If the liquidator [2] fails to comply with this section, he shall be guilty of an offence and liable to a fine of N500.

---

**Notes**

**Section 466(1)**

1. "Winding-up" means the process of settling accounts and liquidating assets in anticipation of a partnership or dissolution. See **Garner B. (ed.) Black's Law Dictionary 8 th ed.**
2. "Liquidator" means a person appointed to wind up business affairs, especially by selling off its assets. See **Garner B. Ed. Black's Law Dictionary, 8th ed.**
3. "Company" means a corporation –or, less commonly, an association, partnership, or union – that carries on a commercial or industrial enterprise. See **Garner B. (ed.) Black's Law Dictionary 8 th ed.**
   "Company" or "existing company" means a company formed and registered under the Act, or as the case may be, formed and registered in Nigeria before and in existence on the commencement of this Act. **See section 567, Cap. C20 CAMA, LFN 2004.**
4. "Declaration" see "Statutory Declaration . It means a declaration voluntarily made under the Oaths Act 1963 and in Nigeria, includes one so made under any other enactment or law providing for the taking of voluntary declaration. **See section 567, CAMA, Cap. C20LFN 2004.**
5. "Creditors" see "Creditor". It means a person or entity with a definite claim against another , especially a claim that is capable of adjustment and liquidation. See **Garner B. (ed.), Black's law Dictionary, 8 th ed.**
   A creditor is person or company that somebody owes money to. See **Oxford advanced Learners Dictionary 6th ed.**
6. "Meeting" means the gathering of people to discuss or act on matters in which they have a common interest; especially the convening of a

deliberative assembly to transact business. See **Garner B. Ed. Black's Law Dictionary, 8[th] ed.**

Cross Reference

For types of general meeting see **section 213 & section 215, CAMA, LFN Cap. C20 2004**

On power of company to appoint liquidators, see **section 464 CAMA Cap. C20 LFN 2004**

On Statutory declaration of solvency by directors of the Company, where proposal to wind up voluntarily, see **section 462 CAMA Cap. C20 LFN 2004**

On meaning of offence, see **section 2, Criminal Code Act, Cap. C38 LFN 2004**

---

**Cases**

The liquidator may be likened to an undertaker, by virtue of the Company's total in disposition goes into preparation for the "burial" of the company but the actual burial of the company takes place on its death at its dissolution. ***Co-Operative and Commerce Bank (NIG.)Ltd v. Alex O. Onwuchekwa*** **(2000) 3 NWLR (Pt. 647) 67.**

**For Further Reading**

On winding up proceedings, see, Asomugha, E. Maduelosi *Company law in Nigeria under the Companies and Allied Matters* **Act E. M. Asomugha** (Lagos) 1994.

---

## 467. Liquidator to call general meeting at end of each year

(1) Subject to the provisions of section 469 of this act, in the event of the winding up[1] continuing for more than one year, the liquidator[2] shall summon a general meeting[3] of the company[4] at the end of the first year[5] from the commencement of the winding up,[1] and of each succeeding year[5], or at the first convenient date within three months from the end of the year[5] or such longer period as the commission[6] may allow, and shall lay before the meeting an account of his acts and dealings and of the conduct of the winding up[1] during the preceding year.[5]

(2) If the liquidator[2] fails to comply with this section, he shall be guilty of an offence and liable to a fine of N50.

---

**Notes**

**Section 467(1)**

1. "Winding-up" means the process of settling accounts and liquidating assets in anticipation of a partnership or dissolution. See **Garner B. (ed.) Black's Law Dictionary 8 th ed.**
2. "Liquidator" means a person appointed to wind up business affairs, especially by selling off its assets. See **Garner B. Ed. Black's Law Dictionary, 8 th ed.**
3. "Meeting" means the gathering of people to discuss or act on matters in which they have a common interest; especially the convening of a deliberative assembly to transact business. See **Garner B. Ed. Black's Law Dictionary, 8 th ed.**
4. "Company" means a corporation –or, less commonly, an association, partnership, or union – that carries on a commercial or industrial enterprise. See **Garner B. (ed.) Black's Law Dictionary 8 th ed.**
   "Company" or "existing company" means a company formed and registered under the Act, or as the case may be, formed and registered in Nigeria before and in existence on the commencement of this Act. **See section 567, CAMA, Cap. C20 LFN 2004.**
5. "Year" means a period of twelve months. **Section 18, Interpretation Act, Cap. I23 LFN 2004**
6. "Commission" except where referred to in Part XVII means the Corporate Affairs Commission established under section 1 of this Act. **See section 567, CAMA, Cap. 20 LFN 2004.**

Cross Reference

For types of general meeting see **section 213 & section 215, CAMA, LFN Cap. C20 2004**

On power of company to appoint liquidators, see **section 464 CAMA Cap. C20 LFN 2004**

On meaning of offence, see **section 2, Criminal Code Act, Cap. C38 LFN 2004**

On the alternative provisions as to annual and final meetings in insolvency cases, see **section 469 CAMA Cap. C20, LFN 2004**

---

**Cases**

The liquidator may be likened to an undertaker, by virtue of the Company's total in disposition goes into preparation for the "burial" of the company but the actual burial of the company takes place on its death at its dissolution. ***Co-Operative and Commerce Bank (NIG.)Ltd v. Alex O. Onwuchekwa* (2000) 3 NWLR (Pt. 647) 67.**

**For Further Reading**

On winding up proceedings, see, Asomugha, E. Maduelosi **Company law in Nigeria under the Companies and Allied Matters** *Act* E. M. Asomugha (Lagos) 1994

## 468. Final meeting and dissolution

(1) Subject to the provisions of section 469 of this act, as soon as the affairs of the company [1] are fully wound up,[2] the liquidator[3] shall prepare an account of the winding up, [2] showing how the winding up[2] has been conducted and the property of the company[1] has been disposed of; and when the account is prepared, he shall call a general meeting [4] of the company [1] for the purpose of laying before it the account, and giving any explanation thereof.

(2) The Meeting [4] shall be called by notice published in the Gazette[5] and in some newspaper printed in Nigeria and circulating in the locality where the meeting is being called, specifying the time, place and object thereof, and published one month at least before the Meeting. [4]

(3) Within seven days after the meeting, [4] the liquidator [3] shall send to the commission [6] a copy of the account, and shall make a return to it of the holding of the meeting [4] and of its date and if the copy is not sent or the return is not made in accordance with this subsection, the liquidator [3] shall be guilty of an offence and liable to fine of N15 for every day during which the default continues:
Provided that, if a quorum [7] is not present at the meeting, [4] the liquidator[3] shall in lieu of the return hereinbefore mentioned, make a return that the meeting [4] was duly summoned and that no quorum [7] was present thereat, and upon such a return being made, the provisions of this subsection as to the making of the return shall be deemed to have been complied with.

(4) The Commission, [6] on receiving the account and the appropriate return, shall forth-with register them, and on the expiration of three months from the registration of the return, the company shall be deemed to be dissolved:
Provided that the court [8] may, on the application of the liquidator [3] or of any other person who appears to the court [8] to be interested, make an order deferring the date at which the dissolution of the company is to take effect for such time as the court [8] thinks fit.

(5) It shall be the duty of the person on whose application an order of the court [8] under this section is made, within seven days after the making of the order, to deliver to the Commission [6] an office copy of the order for registration, and if that person fails so to do he shall be liable to a fine of N20 for every day during which the default continues.

(6) If the liquidator[3] fails to call a general meeting of the company[1] as required by this section, he shall be guilty of an offence and liable to a fine of N50.

---

**Notes**

**Section 468(1)**

1. "Company" means a corporation –or, less commonly, an association, partnership, or union – that carries on a commercial or industrial enterprise. See **Garner B. (ed.) Black's Law Dictionary 8 th ed.** "Company" means a company formed and registered under the Act, or as the case may be, formed and registered in Nigeria before and in existence on the commencement of this Act. See **Section 567, CAMA, Cap. C20 LFN 2004.**
2. "Winding-up" means the process of settling accounts and liquidating assets in anticipation of a partnership or dissolution. See **Garner B. (ed.) Black's Law Dictionary 8 thed.**
3. "Liquidator" means a person appointed to wind up business affairs, especially by selling off its assets. See **Graner B. Ed. Black's Law Dictionary, 8th ed.**
4. "Meeting" means the gathering of people to discuss or act on matters in which they have a common interest; especially the convening of a deliberative assembly to transact business. **See Garner B. Ed. Black's Law Dictionary, 8th ed**

**Section 468(2)**

5. "Gazette" means the official Gazette of the Federation. **See section 567, CAMA, Cap. C20 LFN 2004**
6. "Commission" means the Corporate Affairs Commission established under section 1 of this Act . **See section 567 CAMA Cap. C20, LFN 2004.**

**Section 468(4)**

7. "Quorum" means the minimum number of members who must be present for a deliberative assembly. See **Garner B. (ed.), Blacks' Law Dictionary 8th ed.**
8. "Court" means the Federal High Court and to the extent to which application may be made to it as; court includes the Court of Appeal and the Supreme Court. See **Section 567, CAMA, Cap. C20 LFN 2004**

**Cross Reference**

On power of company to appoint liquidators, see **section 464 CAMA Cap. C20 LFN 2004**

On meaning of offence, see **section 2, Criminal Code Act, Cap. C38 LFN 2004.**

---

**Cases**

The liquidator may be likened to an undertaker, by virtue of the Company's total in disposition goes into preparation for the "burial" of the company but the actual burial of the company takes place on its death at its dissolution. ***Co-Operative and Commerce Bank (NIG.)Ltd v. Alex O. Onwuchekwa*** **(2000)3 NWLR (Pt. 647) 67.**

For further reading on winding up proceedings, see, Asomugha, E. Maduelosi *Company law in Nigeria under the Companies and Allied Matters Act* E.M. Asomugha (Lagos) 1994

## 469. Alternative provisions as to annual and final meetings in insolvency cases

Where section 466 of this Act has effect, sections 477 and 478 thereof shall apply to the winding up [1] to the exclusion of the two last foregoing sections, as if the winding up [1] were a creditors' voluntary winding up [2] and not a members' voluntary winding up; [3] Provided that the liquidator [4] shall not be required to summon a meeting[5] of creditors [6] under section 477 of this Act at the end of the first year from the commencement of the winding up, [1] unless the meeting[5] held under section 466 of this Act is held more than three months before the end of that year.

**Notes**

**Section 469**

1. "Winding-up" means the process of settling accounts and liquidating assets in anticipation of a partnership or dissolution. See **Garner B. (ed.) Black's Law Dictionary 8 th ed.**
2. "Creditors' voluntary winding up" has the meaning assigned to it by section 462(4) of this Act. See section **567 CAMA, Cap. C20 , LFN 2004**
3. "Members voluntary winding up" has the meaning assigned to it by section 462 (4) of this Act. See **section 567 CAMA Cap. C20 LFN 2004**
4. "Liquidator" means a person appointed to wind up business affairs, especially by selling off its assets. **See Graner B. Ed. Black's Law Dictionary, 8 th ed.**
5. "Meeting" means the gathering of people to discuss or act on matters in which they have a common interest; especially the convening of a deliberative assembly to transact business. See **Garner B. Ed. Black's Law Dictionary, 8 th ed.**
6. "Creditors" see "creditor." It means a person or entity with a definite claim against another, especially a claim that is capable of adjustment and liquidation. See **Garner B. (ed.), Black's law Dictionary, 8 th ed.**

**Cross Reference**

On distinction between members voluntary winding-up and creditors voluntary winding-up, see **section 462(4), CAMA, LFN 2004.**

On when a Liquidator calls for creditors' meeting on insolvency, see **section 466 CAMA Cap. C20 LFN 2004**

On obligation of the liquidator to call on a meeting of the company and creditor yearly, under a voluntary winding up see **section 477 CAMA Cap. C20, LFN 2004**

On final dissolution of a company under a voluntary winding up see **section 478 CAMA Cap. C20, LFN 2004**

**Cases**

The liquidator may be likened to an undertaker, by virtue of the Company's total in disposition goes into preparation for the "burial" of the company but the actual burial of the company takes place on its death at its dissolution. ***Co-Operative and Commerce Bank (NIG.)Ltd v. Alex O. Onwuchekwa*** **(2000)3 NWLR (Pt. 647) 67.**

---

**For Further Reading**

On winding up proceedings, see, Asomugha, E. Maduelosi **Company law in Nigeria under the Companies and Allied Matters Act** E.M. Asomugha (Lagos) 1994.

## 470.Books and accounts during members' voluntary winding up

(1) The liquidator [1] in a members' voluntary winding up [2] shall keep proper records and books of account with respect to his acts and dealings and of the conduct of the winding up [2] and of all receipts and payments by him and so long as he carries on the business of the company,[3] shall keep a distinct account of the trading.

(2) In the event of the winding up [2] continuing for more than a year, the liquidator [1] shall summon a general meeting [4] of the company[3] at the end of the first year from the commencement of the winding up[2] and of each succeeding year, or at the first convenient date within three months of the end of the year or such longer period as the Commission [5] may allow, and shall lay before the meeting an account of his acts and dealings and of the conduct of the winding up[2] during the preceding year and of the trading during such time as the business of the company [3] has been carried on, and within 28 days thereafter shall send a copy of such accounts to the commission[5] for registration.

(3) So soon as the affairs of the company [3] are fully wound up,[2] the liquidator[1] shall prepare and send to every member [6] of the company[3] final accounts of the winding up [2] showing how the winding up[2] has been conducted, the result of the trading during

such time as the business of the company [3] has been carried on, and how the property of the company [3] has been disposed of, and thereupon shall convene a general meeting [4] of the company [3] for the purpose of laying before it such accounts and of giving an explanation thereof.

(4) Within 28 days after the meeting [4] referred to in the immediately preceding subsection, the liquidator [1] shall send to the commission[5] for registration copies of the accounts laid before the meeting[4] and a statement of the holding of the meeting [4] and of its date:

Provided that if a quorum [7] was not present at the meeting [4] the liquidator,[1] in lieu of the statement hereinbefore mentioned, shall send a statement that the meeting [4] was duly convened and that no quorum[7] was present thereat.

(5) The records, books and accounts referred to in this section shall be in such form, if any, as the Commission [5] may from time to time prescribe and shall give a true and fair view of the matters therein recorded and of the administration of the company's [3] affairs and of the winding up. [2]

(6) The accounts referred to in subsections (2) and (3) of this section, shall be audited by the auditor [8] of the company [3] prior to being laid before the company [3] in general meeting [4] in accordance with such subsections and the auditors [8] shall state in a report annexed thereto whether, in their opinion and to the best of their information-

(a) they have obtained all the information and explanations necessary for the purpose of their audit;

(b) proper books and records have been maintained by the liquidator[1] in accordance with this act, and such accounts are in accordance with the books and records and give all the information required by this act in the manner therein required and give a true and fair view of the matters stated in such accounts:

Provided that such audit and auditors [8]' report shall not be required if-

(i) the liquidator, [1] or one of the liquidators [1] if more than one, is duly qualified under the provisions of this act for appointment as auditor [8] of a public company [9]; and

(ii) on or after his appointment as liquidator, [1] the company[3] resolved by special resolution [10] that the accounts shall not be audited in accordance with this subsection.

(7) meetings[4] required to be convened under this section or the immediately foregoing section, shall be convened and held, so far as may be, in accordance with the provisions of this act and the regulations of the company [3] relating to general meetings [4]

(8) The liquidator [1] shall preserve the books and papers [11] of the company[3] and of the liquidator [1] for a period of five years from the dissolution of the company[3] but thereafter may destroy such books and papers [11] unless the Commission [5] shall otherwise direct, in which event he shall not destroy the same until the Commission [5] consents in writing.

(9) If a liquidator [1] should fail to comply with any of the provisions of this section, he shall be guilty of an offence and liable to a fine not exceeding N230 for each default.

---

**Notes**

**Section 470(1)**

1. "Liquidator" means a person appointed to wind up business affairs, especially by selling off its assets. See **Graner B. Ed. Black's Law Dictionary, 8 th ed.**
2. "Members voluntary winding up" has the meaning assigned to it by section 462 (4) of this Act. See **section 567 CAMA Cap. C20 LFN 2004**
3. "Company" means a corporation –or, less commonly, an association, partnership, or union – that carries on a commercial or industrial enterprise. See **Garner B. (ed.) Black's Law Dictionary 8th ed.**

   "Company" means a company formed and registered under the Act, or as the case may be, formed and registered in Nigeria before and in existence on the commencement of this Act.See **section 567, CAMA, Cap. C20 LFN 2004.**

**Section 470(2)**

4. "Meeting" means the gathering of people to discuss or act on matters in which they have a common interest; especially the convening of a deliberative assembly to transact business. See **Garner B. Ed. Black's Law Dictionary, 8 th ed.**

**Section 470(3)**

5. "Commission" means the Corporate Affairs Commission established under section 1 of this Act . **See section 567 CAMA Cap. C20, LFN 2004.**
6. "Members" see "member."It means one of the individuals of whom a deliberative assembly consists and who enjoys the full rights of participating in the organization-including the rights of making, debating and voting on motions- except to the extent that the organization reserves those rights to certain classes of membership. See **Garner B. ed. Black's Law Dictionary 8th ed.**

   It includes the heir, executor, administrator or other personal representative as the case may be, of the member. **section 567 of CAMA, Cap. C20 LFN 2004.**

**Section 470(4)**

7. "Quorum" means the minimum number of members who must be present for a deliberative assembly. See **Garner B. (ed.), Blacks' Law Dictionary 8th ed.**

**Section 470(6)**

8. "Auditor" means a person appointed to examine the books of account and the accounts of a registered company and to report upon them to members of the Company. See **Martin E, ( ed.) A Dictionary of Law, 4 th ed.**
9. "Public company" means any company other than a private company and is stated in its memorandum of Association that it is a public company. See **section 24 CAMA Cap. C20, LFN 2004**
10. "Resolution" means a main motion that formally expresses the sense, will, or action of a deliberative assembly.See **Garner B. (ed.) Black's Law Dictionary 8 th ed.**

**Section 470(8)**

11. "Books and paper" includes account deeds, writings and documents.See s**ection 567 CAMA, Cap. C20, LFN 2004**

**Cross Reference**

On distinction between a public and a private company, see **section 22 & 24 CAMA, Cap. C20 LFN 2004**

For types of general meeting see **section 213 & section 215, CAMA, LFN 2004**

On the qualification of auditors, auditor's duties and powers, see **section 358 & 360 CAMA, Cap. C20 LFN 2004.**

On distinction between members voluntary winding-up and creditors voluntary winding-up, see **section 462(4), CAMA, LFN 2004**

---

**Cases**

The liquidator may be likened to an undertaker, by virtue of the Company's total in disposition goes into preparation for the "burial" of the company but the actual burial of the company takes place on its death at its dissolution. ***Co-Operative and Commerce Bank (NIG.)Ltd v. Alex O. Onwuchekwa*** **(2000)3 NWLR (Pt. 647) 67.**

**For Further Reading**

On winding up proceedings, see, Asomugha, E. Maduelosi **Company law in Nigeria under the Companies and Allied Matters Act** E.M. Asomugha (Lagos) 1994

*Provisions applicable to a creditors' voluntary winding up*

## 471. Provisions applicable to Creditors' Winding up voluntarily

The provisions following, that is to say sections 472 to 478 of this Act, shall apply in relation to a creditors' voluntary winding up.[1]

---

**Notes**

**Section 471**

1. "Creditors' voluntary winding up "has the meaning assigned to it by section 462(4) of this Act. See section **567 CAMA, Cap. C20 , LFN 2004**

**Cross Reference**

On distinction between members voluntary winding-up and creditors voluntary winding-up, see **section 462(4), CAMA, LFN 2004.**

---

**Cases**

The liquidator may be likened to an undertaker, by virtue of the Company's total in disposition goes into preparation for the "burial" of the company but the actual burial of the company takes place on its death at its dissolution. ***Co-Operative and Commerce Bank (NIG.)Ltd v. Alex O. Onwuchekwa*** **(2000)3 NWLR (Pt. 647) 67.**

**For Further Reading**

On winding up proceedings, see, Asomugha, E. Maduelosi **Company law in Nigeria under the Companies and Allied Matters Act** E.M. Asomugha (Lagos) 1994.

## 472. Meeting of creditors

(1) The Company [1] shall cause a meeting of the Creditors [2] of the company[1] to be summoned for the day, or the day next following the day, on which there is to be held the meeting [3] at which the Resolution[4] for voluntary Winding up [5] is to be proposed, and shall cause the notices of the meeting [3] of creditors [2] to be sent by post to the creditors [2] simultaneously with the sending of the notices of the meetings [3] of the company [1].

(2) The Company [1] shall cause notice of the meeting [3] of the Creditors [2] to be published once in the Gazette [6] and once at least in two newspapers printed in Nigeria and circulating in the district where the registered office or principal place of business of the company[1] is situate.

(3) The directors [7] of the company [1] shall-

(a) cause a full statement of the position of the company's [1] affairs together with a list of the creditors [2] of the company[1] and the estimated amount of their claims to be laid before the meeting [3] of the creditors [2] to be held as aforesaid; and

(b) appoint one of their number to preside at the said meeting[3].

(4) It shall be the duty of the director [7] so appointed to attend the meeting[3] and preside thereat.

(5) If the meeting [3] of the company at which the resolution [4] for voluntary winding up [5] is to be proposed, is adjourned and the resolution[4] is passed at an adjourned meeting, any resolution [4] passed at the meeting [3] of the creditors [2] held in pursuance of subsection (1) of this section shall have effect as if it had been passed immediately after the passing of the resolution [4] for winding up[2] the company. [1]

(6) If default is made by-

(a) the company [1] in complying with subsection (1) or (2) of this section;

(b) the directors [7] of the company [1] in complying with subsection (3) of this section;

(c) any director [7] of the company [1] appointed to preside, in complying with subsection (4) of this section,

the company, [1] directors [7] or director, [7] as the case may be, shall be guilty of an offence and liable to a fine of N250 and in the case of default by the company, [1] every officer [8] of the company[1] who is in default shall be liable to the like penalty.

---

**Notes**

**Section 472(1)**

1. "Company" means a company formed and registered under the Act, or as the case may be, formed and registered in Nigeria before and in existence on the commencement of this Act.See s **ection 567, CAMA, Cap. C20 LFN 2004.**
2. "Creditor" means a person or entity with a definite claim against another, esp. a claim that is capable of adjustment and liquidation. See **Garner B. ed. Black's Law Dictionary 8th ed.**
3. "Meeting" means a coming together of persons; an assembly of a number of persons for the purpose of discussing and acting upon some matters. See **Garner B.(ed.) Black's Law Dictionary 8th ed.**
4. "Resolution" means a main motion that formally expresses the sense, will, or action of a deliberative assembly. See **Garner B. (ed.) Black's Law Dictionary 8th ed.**
5. "Winding up" means the process of settling accounts and liquidating assets in anticipation of a partnership or dissolution . See **Garner B. (ed.) Black's Law Dictionary 8th ed.**

**Section 472(2)**

6. "Gazette" means the official Gazette of the Federation. **See section 567, CAMA, Cap. C20 LFN 2004**

**Section 472(3)**

7. "Directors" see "Director." It includes any person occupying the position of director by whatever name called: and includes any person in accordance with whose directions or instructions the directors of the company are accustomed to act. See **section 567 CAMA Cap. C20, LFN 2004**

**Section 472(6)**

8. "Officer" in relation to a body corporate, includes a director, manager or secretary. **See Garner B. (ed) Black's Law Dictionary, 8th ed.**

**Cross Reference**

On appointment of committee of inspection in voluntary winding up, see **section 474 CAMA Cap. C20, LFN 2004**

On meaning of offence, see **section 2, Criminal Code, Cap. C38, LFN 2004**

---

**Cases**

The Company is distinct from its promoters or directors and a director is an agent of the company. Consequently, where a director enters into a contract in the name of or purporting to bind the company, it is the company, as principal that is liable, not the director . ***Dansa Foods (Nig.) Ltd v. Isong*** **(2011) ALL F.W.L.R. part 596 404-600 at p.595**

**For Further Reading**
On memorandum, directors, company, see Kiser Barnes, **Cases and Materials on Nigeria Company Law** (1992) Obafemi Awolowo University press Ltd, Ile-Ife, Nigeria

## 473.Appointment of liquidator and cesser of directors' powers

(1) The creditors [1] and the company[2] at their respective meetings[3] mentioned in section 472 of this act may nominate a person to be liquidator[4] for the purpose of winding up [5] the affairs and distributing the assets of the company [2], and if the creditors [1] and the company[2] nominate different persons, the person nominated by the creditors[1] shall be liquidator,[4] and if no person is nominated by the creditors[1] the person if any, nominated by the company, [2] shall be liquidator:[4]
Provided that in the case of different persons being nominated, any director,[6] member[7] or creditor[1] of the company[2] may, within seven days after the date on which the nomination was made by the creditors,[1] apply to the court for an order directing that the persons nominated as liquidator[4] by the company[2] shall be liquidator[4] instead of or jointly with the person nominated by the creditors, [1] or appointing some other person to be liquidator [4] instead of the person appointed by the creditors. [1]
(2) On the appointment of a liquidator, [4] all the powers of the directors[6] shall cease, except so far as the committee of inspection, or if there is no such committee, the creditors, [1] sanction the continuance thereof.

---

**Notes**
**Section 473(1)**

1. "Creditor" means a person or entity with a definite claim against another, esp. a claim that is capable of adjustment and liquidation. See **Garner B. (ed.) Black's Law Dictionary 8th ed.**
2. "Company" means a company formed and registered under the Act, or as the case may be, formed and registered in Nigeria before and in existence on the commencement of this Act. See **section 567, CAMA, LFN 2004.**
3. "Meeting" means the gathering of people to discuss or act on matters in which they have a common interest. See **Garner B. (ed.) Black's Law Dictionary 8[th] ed.**

4. "Liquidator" means a person appointed to wind up business affairs, esp. by selling off its assets. See **Garner B. (ed.) Black's Law Dictionary 8th ed.**
5. "Winding up" means the process of settling accounts and liquidating assets in anticipation of a partnership or dissolution. **Black's Law Dictionary 8th ed**
6. "Director" includes any person occupying the position of director by whatever name called: and includes any person in accordance with whose directions or instructions the directors of the company are accustomed to act. See **section 567 CAMA Cap. C20, LFN 2004**
7. "Member" means one of the individuals of whom a deliberative assembly consists and who enjoys the full rights of participating in the organization-including the rights of making, debating and voting on motions- except to the extent that the organization reserves those rights to certain classes of membership. **See Garner B. ed. Black's Law Dictionary 8th ed.**

   It includes the heir, executor, administrator or other personal representative as the case may be, of the member. **See section 567 CAMA Cap. C20 LFN 2004**

**Cross Reference**

On the appointment of committee of inspection see **section 474 CAMA Cap. C20, LFN 2004**

---

**Cases**

The liquidator may be likened to an undertaker, by virtue of the Company's total in disposition goes into preparation for the "burial" of the company but the actual burial of the company takes place on its death at its dissolution. ***Co-Operative and Commerce Bank (NIG.)Ltd v. Alex O. Onwuchekwa*** **(2000)3 NWLR (Pt. 647) 67.**

**For Further Reading**

On winding up proceedings, see, Asomugha, E. Maduelosi **Company law in Nigeria under the Companies and Allied Matters Act** E.M. Asomugha (Lagos) 1994

## 474. Appointment of committee of inspection

(1) The creditors [1]at the meeting[2] to be held in pursuance of section 472 of this act or at any subsequent meeting [2] may, if they think fit, appoint a committee of inspection consisting of not more than five persons, and if such a committee is appointed, the company[3] may, either at the meeting [2] at which the resolution for voluntary winding up[4] is passed or at any time subsequently in general meeting,[2] appoint such number of persons as they think fit to act as members of the committee not exceeding five in number:

Provided that the creditors [1] may, if they think fit, resolve that all or any of the persons so appointed by the company [3] shall not be members of the committee of inspection, and if the creditors [1] so resolve, the persons mentioned in the resolution [5] shall not, unless the court[6] otherwise directs, be qualified to act as members of the committee, and on any application to the court [6] under this provision the court[6] may, if it thinks fit, appoint other persons to act as such members in place of the persons mentioned in the resolution [5].

(2) Subject to the provisions of this section and to general rules made under this Act, the provisions of section 434 of this Act (except subsection (1) of this section), shall apply with respect to a committee of inspection appointed under this section as they apply with respect to a committee of inspection appointed in a winding up[7] by the court [6].

---

**Notes**

**Section 474(1)**

1. "Creditor" means a person or entity with a definite claim against another, esp. a claim that is capable of adjustment and liquidation. See **Garner B. (ed.) Black's Law Dictionary 8th ed.**
2. "Meeting" means the gathering of people to discuss or act on matters in which they have a common interest. See **Garner B. (ed.) Black's Law Dictionary 8th ed.**
3. "Company" means a company formed and registered under the Act, or as the case may be, formed and registered in Nigeria before and in existence on the commencement of this Act.See s **ection 567, CAMA, Cap. C20 LFN 2004.**
4. "Resolution for voluntary winding up" has the meaning assigned to it by section 457 of this Act. See **section 567 CAMA Cap. C20 LFN 2004**
5. "Resolution" means a main motion that formally expresses the sense, will, or action of a deliberative assembly. See **Garner B. (ed.) Black's Law Dictionary 8th ed.**
6. "Court" means the Federal High Court and to the extent to which application may be made to it as; court includes the Court of Appeal and the Supreme Court. See **section 567, CAMA Cap. C20 LFN 2004.**
7. "Winding up" means the process of settling accounts and liquidating assets in anticipation of a partnership or dissolution. See **Garner B.(ed.) Black's Law Dictionary 8th ed.**

**Cross Reference**

On distinction between members voluntary winding-up and creditors voluntary winding-up, see **section 462(4), CAMA, LFN 2004**

On the appointment of committee of inspection see **section 474 CAMA Cap. C20, LFN 2004**

On the establishment and jurisdiction of the Federal High Court, see **section 249 & 251 of the Constitution of the Federal Republic of Nigeria, 1999 (as amended)**

**Cases**

The liquidator may be likened to an undertaker, by virtue of the Company's total in disposition goes into preparation for the "burial" of the company but the actual burial of the company takes place on its death at its dissolution. ***Co-Operative and Commerce Bank (NIG.)Ltd v. Alex O. Onwuchekwa* (2000)3 NWLR (Pt. 647) 67.**

**For Further Reading**

On winding up proceedings, see, Asomugha E. Maduelosi **Company law in Nigeria under the Companies and Allied Matters Act** E.M. Asomugha (Lagos) 1994.

## 475. Fixing of liquidators' remuneration

The committee of inspection, or if there is no such committee, the creditors [1], may fix the remuneration to be paid to the liquidator [2] or liquidators. [2]

**Notes**

**Section 475**

1. "Creditors" see "creditor." It means a person or entity with a definite claim against another, esp. a claim that is capable of adjustment and liquidation. See **Garner B. (ed.) Black's Law Dictionary 8th ed.**
2. "Liquidator" means a person appointed to wind up business affairs, esp. by selling off its assets. See **Garner B. (ed.) Black's Law Dictionary 8th ed.**

**Cross Reference**

On the appointment of committee of inspection see **section 474 CAMA Cap. C20, LFN 2004**

**Cases**

The liquidator may be likened to an undertaker, by virtue of the Company's total in disposition goes into preparation for the "burial" of the company but the actual burial of the company takes place on its death at its dissolution. ***Co-Operative and Commerce Bank (NIG.)Ltd v. Alex O. Onwuchekwa* (2000)3 NWLR (Pt. 647) 67**

## 476. Power to fill vacancy in the office of liquidator

If a vacancy occurs, by death, resignation or otherwise, in the office of a Liquidator [1], other than a liquidator [1] appointed by, or by the direction of the court [2], the Creditors [3] may fill the Vacancy.

---

**Notes**
**Section 476**

1. "Liquidator" means a person appointed to wind up business affairs, esp. by selling off its assets. See **Garner B. (ed.) Black's Law Dictionary 8th ed.**
2. "Court" means the Federal High Court and to the extent to which application may be made to it as; court includes the Court of Appeal and the Supreme Court. See **section 567, CAMA Cap. C20 LFN 2004.**
3. "Creditor" means a person or entity with a definite claim against another, esp. a claim that is capable of adjustment and liquidation. See **Garner B. (ed.) Black's Law Dictionary 8th ed.**

**Cross Reference**

On the establishment and jurisdiction of the Federal High Court, see **section 249 & 251 of the Constitution of the Federal Republic of Nigeria, 1999( as amended)**

On the Appointment, remuneration and title of liquidators, see **section 422 CAMA Cap. C20 LFN 2004**

---

**Cases**

The liquidator may be likened to an undertaker, by virtue of the Company's total in disposition goes into preparation for the "burial" of the company but the actual burial of the company takes place on its death at its dissolution. ***Co-Operative and Commerce Bank (NIG.)Ltd v. Alex O. Onwuchekwa* (2000)3 NWLR (Pt. 647) 67.**

**For Further Reading**

On winding up proceedings, see, Asomugha, E. Maduelosi **Company law in Nigeria under the Companies and Allied Matters Act** E. M. Asomugha (Lagos) 1994

## 477.Liquidator to call meetings of company and others at the end of each year

(1) In the event of the winding up [1] continuing for more than one year, the liquidator [2] shall summon a general meeting [3] of the company[4] and a meeting [3] of the creditors [5] at the end of the first year from the commencement of the winding up, [1] and of each succeeding year, or at the first convenient date within three months

from the end of year, or such longer period as the commission [6] may allow, and shall lay before the meetings [3] an account of his acts and dealings and of the conduct of the winding up [1] during the preceding year.

(2) If the liquidator [2] fails to comply with the provisions of this section, he shall be guilty of an offence and liable to a fine of N50.

---

**Notes**
**Section 477(1)**

1. "Winding up" means the process of settling accounts and liquidating assets in anticipation of a partnership or dissolution. **Black's Law Dictionary 8thed**
2. "Liquidator" means a person appointed to wind up business affairs, esp. by selling off its assets. **Black's Law Dictionary 8thed**
3. "Meeting" means the gathering of people to discuss or act on matters in which they have a common interest; especially the convening of a deliberative assembly to transact business. See **Garner B. (ed.) Black's Law Dictionary, 8 th ed.**
4. "Company" means a company formed and registered under the Act, or as the case may be, formed and registered in Nigeria before and in existence on the commencement of this Act. See s **ection 567, CAMA, Cap. C20 LFN 2004.**
5. "Creditor" means a person or entity with a definite claim against another , esp. a claim that is capable of adjustment and liquidation. See **Garner B. (ed.) Black's Law Dictionary, 8 th ed.**
6. "Commission" means the Corporate Affairs Commission established under section 1 of this Act, See s **ection 567, CAMA, Cap. C20 LFN 2004.**

**Cross Reference**

For types of general meeting, see s **ection 213 & section 215, CAMA, LFN 2004**

On the Appointment, remuneration and title of liquidators, see **section 422 CAMA Cap. C20 LFN 2004**

On the meaning of offence, see **section 2, Criminal Code Cap. C38, LFN 2004**

---

**Cases**

The liquidator may be likened to an undertaker, by virtue of the Company's total in disposition goes into preparation for the "burial" of the company but the actual burial of the company takes place on its death at its dissolution. ***Co-operative and Commerce Bank (Nig.)Ltd v. Alex O. Onwuchekwa*** **(2000)3 NWLR (Pt. 647) 67.**

**For Further Reading**

On winding up proceedings, see, Asomugha, E. Maduelosi **Company law in Nigeria under the Companies and Allied Matters Act** E. M. Asomugha (Lagos) 1994

## 478. Final meeting and dissolution

(1) As soon as the affairs of the company [1] are fully wound up,[2] the liquidator[3] shall prepare an account of the Winding up, [1] showing how the winding up[1] has been conducted and the property of the Company[1] has been disposed of, and thereupon he shall call a general meeting[3] of the company[1] and a meeting[4] of the Creditors [5] for the purpose of laying the account before the meetings [4] and giving any explanation thereof.

(2) Each such meeting[4] shall be called by notice published in the Gazette[6] and in some newspapers printed in Nigeria and circulating in the locality where the meeting[4] is being called, specifying the time, place and object thereof, and published one month at least before the meeting. [4]

(3) Within seven days after the date of the meeting, [4] or if the meetings[4] are not held on the same date, after the date of the later meeting,[4] the Liquidator[3] shall send to the Commission[7] a copy of the account, and shall make a return to it of the holding of the meetings[4] and of their dates, and if the copy is not sent or the return is not made in accordance with this subsection, the liquidator [3] shall be guilty of an offence and liable to a fine of N25 for every day during which the default continues:

Provided that, if a quorum [8] is not present at either such meetings [3] the liquidator[3] shall, in lieu of the return hereinbefore mentioned, make a return that the meeting [4] was duly summoned and that no quorum[8] was present; and upon such a return being made the provisions of this subsection as to the making of the return shall, in respect of that meeting[4], be deemed to have been complied with.

(4) The Commission,[7] on receiving the account, and, in respect of each such meeting,[4] either of the returns mentioned above, shall forthwith register them, and on the expiration of three months from the registration thereof, the company [1] shall be deemed to be dissolved:

Provided that the court[9] may, on the application of the liquidator [3] or of any other person who appears to the court [9] to be interested, make an order deferring the date at which the Dissolution of the company[1] is to take effect for such time as the court [9] thinks fit.

(5) It shall be the duty of the person on whose application an order of the court [9] under this section is made, within seven days after the making of the order, to deliver to the Commission [7] an office copy of the order for registration, and if that persons fails so to do he shall be guilty of an offence and liable to a fine of N25 for every day during which the default continues.

(6) If the liquidator [3] fails to call a general meeting [4] of the company[1] or a meeting [4] of the creditors [5] as required by this section, he shall be guilty of an offence and liable to a fine of N250.

---

**Notes**
**Section 478(1)**

1. "Company" means a company formed and registered under the Act, or as the case may be, formed and registered in Nigeria before and in existence on the commencement of this Act. See s **ection 567, CAMA Cap. C20 LFN 2004.**
2. "Wound up" see "winding up," It means the process of settling accounts and liquidating assets in anticipation of a partnership or dissolution. See **Garner B. (ed.) Black's Law Dictionary, 8 th ed.**
3. "Liquidator" means a person appointed to wind up business affairs, esp. by selling off its assets. See **Garner B. (ed.) Black's Law Dictionary, 8th ed.**
4. "Meeting" means the gathering of people to discuss or act on matters in which they have a common interest; especially the convening of a deliberative assembly to transact business. See **Garner B. (ed.) Black's Law Dictionary, 8 th ed.**
5. "Creditor" means a person or entity with a definite claim against another , esp. a claim that is capable of adjustment and liquidation. See **Garner B. (ed.) Black's Law Dictionary, 8 th ed.**

**Section 478(2)**

6. "Gazette" means the official Gazette of the Federation. See **section 567, CAMA Cap. C20 LFN 2004.**

**Section 478(3)**

7. "Commission" means the Corporate Affairs Commission established under section 1 of this Act, See s **ection 567, CAMA, Cap. C20 LFN 2004.**

**Section 478(4)**

8. "Quorum" means the minimum number of members who must be present for a deliberative assembly. See **Garner B. (ed) Black's Law Dictionary 8th ed.**
9. "Court" means the Federal High Court and to the extent to which application may be made to it as; court includes the Court of Appeal and the Supreme Court. **See section 567 CAMA Cap. C20 LFN, 2004**

Cross Reference

On appointment, remuneration and title of liquidators, see **section 422 CAMA Cap. C20 LFN 2004**

On quorum for directors see **section 264 CAMA Cap. C20 LFN 2004**

On quorum and adjournment of meeting, see **section 239 CAMA Cap. C20, LFN 2004**

On establishment and jurisdiction of the Federal High Court, see **section 249 & 251, Constitution of the Federal Republic of Nigeria, 1999 (as amended)**

---

**Cases**

Where the provisions of the Act and the articles regarding such matters as notice of meetings, quorum, proceedings at and conduct of meetings, are not strictly complied with, any resolution passed at such meetings will be a nullity. ***Obikoya v. Ezenwani (1964) 2 All NLR 133.***

*Provisions applicable to every voluntary winding up*

## 479. Provisions applicable to every voluntary winding up

The provisions following, that is to say, sections 480 to 485 of this act, shall apply to every voluntary winding up, [1] whether a members' [2] or a creditors' [3] winding up.

---

**Notes**
**Section 479**

1. "Winding up" means the process of settling accounts and liquidating assets in anticipation of a partnership or dissolution. See **Garner B. (ed.) Black's Law Dictionary, 8 th ed.**
2. "Members voluntary winding up" has the meaning assigned to it by section 462 (4) of this Act. See **section 567, CAMA Cap. C20 LFN 2004.**
3. "Creditors voluntary winding up" has the meaning assigned to it by section 462 (4) of this Act. See **section 567, CAMA Cap. C20 LFN 2004.**

Cross Reference

on procedure for voluntary winding up see **section 457-459 CAMA Cap. C20 LFN 2004**.

---

## 480. Distribution of property of company

Subject to the provisions of this act as to preferential payments, the property of a company [1] shall, on its winding up, [2] be applied in satisfaction of its liabilities pari passu and, subject to such application shall, unless the articles [3] otherwise provide, be distributed among the members [4] according to their rights and interests in the company. [1]

---

**Notes**
**Section 480**

1. "Company" means a company formed and registered under the Act, or as the case may be, formed and registered in Nigeria before and in existence on the commencement of this Act. See s **ection 567, CAMA Cap. C20 LFN 2004**
2. "Winding up" means the process of settling accounts and liquidating assets in anticipation of a partnership or dissolution. See **Garner B. (ed.) Black's Law Dictionary, 8 th ed.**
3. "Articles" means the articles of association of a company, as originally framed or as altered by special resolution including so far as they apply to the regulations contained in table A in the first schedules of the companies Act, 1922 or in that table as altered by any subsequent enactment or reprint of the laws, or in table A in schedule 1 to this Act. See **section 567 CAMA Cap. C20 LFN, 2004**

**Cross Reference**

On form and content of the Articles of Association, see **section 34 CAMA Cap. C20 LFN 2004**

On preferential payments, see **section 494 CAMA Cap. C20, LFN 2004**

---

**Cases**

By the provisions of Companies and Allied Matters Act, Section 115, shares are in the nature of personal estate and freely transferable but subject to statutory restrictions and the articles of the company. Members in a company have a right to transfer shares belonging to them therein and this right is unfettered unless there is an express restriction to that effect in the articles or constitution of the company. ***N.R.I. Ltd v. Oranusi* [2011] ALL F.W.L.R part 577. 625-824 at p.765** .

The Articles of Association is the contract governing the relationship between shareholders and any infraction of such articles may confer on the shareholder adversely affected a right of action See ***Attorney General of Lagos State v Eko Hotel Ltd &Oha Ltd (2001) FWLR page 1996*** *at 2000*

**For Further Reading** On memorandum, articles of Association, see Ephraim Madeueulosi Asomugha, **Company law in Nigeria under the companies and Allied Matters Act,** (1994) E.M. Asumughai Lagos

## 481.Powers, etc., of liquidator in every voluntary winding up

(1) The Liquidator [1] may-

(a) in the case of a members' voluntary winding up, [2] with the sanction of special resolution[3] of the company,[4] and, in the case of a creditors' voluntary winding up, [5] with the sanction of the court[6] or, the committee of inspection or if there is no such committee, a meeting [7] of the creditors, [8] exercise any of the powers given by paragraphs (d), (e) and (f) of section 425 (1) of this act to a liquidator [1] in a winding up[9] by the court [6];

(b) without sanction, exercise any of the other powers given by this act to the liquidator [1] in a winding up [8] by the court[6];

(c) exercise the power of the court [6] under this act of settling a list of contributories, [10] and the list of contributories [10] shall be prima facie evidence of the liability of the persons named therein to be contributories [10];

(d) exercise the court's [6] power of making calls;

(e) summon general meetings[7] of the company[4] for the purpose of obtaining the sanction of the company [4] by special resolution[3] or for any other purpose he may think fit.

(2) The liquidator [1] shall pay the debts of the company [4] and shall adjust the rights of the contributories [10] among themselves.

(3) Where several liquidators [1] are appointed, any power given by this Act may be exercised by such one or more of them as may be determined by any number not less than two.

---

**Notes**

**Section 481(1)**

1. "Liquidator" means a person appointed to wind up business affairs, esp. by selling off its assets. See **Garner B. (ed.) Black's Law Dictionary, 8th ed.**
2. "Members voluntary winding up" has the meaning assigned to it by section 462 (4) of this Act. See **section 567, CAMA Cap. C20 LFN 2004.**
3. "Special Resolution" means a resolution passed by not less than three fourths of the votes cast by such members of the company as, being entitled to do so, vote in person or by proxy at a general meeting of which 21 days' notice, specifying the intention to propose the resolution as a special resolution, has been duly given. See **Section 233(2)CAMA Cap. C20, LFN,2004** .

4. "Company" means a company formed and registered under the Act, or as the case may be, formed and registered in Nigeria before and in existence on the commencement of this Act. See s **ection 567, CAMA Cap. C20 LFN 2004**
5. "Creditors voluntary winding up" has the meaning assigned to it by section 462 (4) of this Act. See **section 567, CAMA Cap. C20 LFN 2004.**
6. "Court" means the Federal High Court and to the extent to which application may be made to it as; court includes the Court of Appeal and the Supreme Court. **See section 567 CAMA Cap. C20 LFN, 2004**
7. "Meeting" means the gathering of people to discuss or act on matters in which they have a common interest. See **Garner B. (ed.) Black's Law Dictionary 8th ed.**
8. "Creditors" means a person or entity with a definite claim against another, esp. a claim that is capable of adjustment and liquidation. See **Garner B. (ed.) Black's Law Dictionary, 8 th ed.**
9. "Winding up" means the process of settling accounts and liquidating assets in anticipation of a partnership or dissolution. See **Garner B. (ed.) Black's Law Dictionary, 8 th ed.**
10. "Contributories" see "contributory." It means every person liable to contribute to the assets of a company in the event of its being wound up and for the purposes of all proceedings for determining, and all proceedings prior to the final determination of, the persons who are to be deemed contributories. See **section 567, CAMA Cap. C20 LFN 2004.**

**Cross Reference**

On procedure for voluntary windingup see **section 457-459 CAMA Cap. C20 LFN 2004**.

On appointment, remuneration and title of liquidators, see **section 422 CAMA Cap. C20 LFN 2004**

On nature and liability of contributories, see **section 404 CAMA Cap. C20 LFN 2004**.

**Cases**

An application may be made by summons to determine whether or not a person is a contributory, but such application should not be made unless the liquidator has failed to appoint a time and place for the purpose or has made a decision which is not acceptable to the alleged contributory. ***Sulaiman v. Muslim Bank (W.A.) Ltd.*** **(1970) 1 A.L.R. Comm 388.**

**For Further Reading**

On winding up proceedings, see, Asomugha, E. Maduelosi **Company law in Nigeria under the Companies and Allied Matters Act** E.M. Asomugha (Lagos) 1994

## 482. Power of court to appoint, etc., liquidator

If, in any voluntary winding up, [1] there is no liquidator [2] acting, the court[3] may appoint a liquidator [2] and in any case the court [3] may, on cause shown, remove a liquidator [2] and appoint another liquidator,[2]

---

**Notes**
**Section 482**

1. "Winding up" means the process of settling accounts and liquidating assets in anticipation of a partnership or dissolution. See **Garner B. (ed.) Black's Law Dictionary, 8 th ed.**
2. "Liquidator" means a person appointed to wind up business affairs, esp. by selling off its assets. See **Garner B. (ed.) Black's Law Dictionary, 8th ed.**
3. "Court" means the Federal High Court and to the extent to which application may be made to it as; court includes the Court of Appeal and the Supreme Court.See **section 567 CAMA Cap. C20 LFN, 2004**

Cross Reference

On procedure for voluntary windingup see **section 457-459 CAMA Cap. C20 LFN 2004**.

On appointment, remuneration and title of liquidators, see **section 422 CAMA Cap. C20 LFN 2004**

On establishment and jurisdiction of the Federal High Court, see **section 249 & 251, Constitution of the Federal Republic of Nigeria, 1999** (as amended).

---

**For Further Reading**

On winding up proceedings, see, Asomugha, E. Maduelosi Company law in Nigeria under the Companies and Allied Matters Act E. M. Asomugha (Lagos) 1994.

## 483.Power to apply to court to determine questions or exercise powers

(1) The Liquidator [1] or any Contributory [2] or Creditor [3] may apply to the court [4] to determine any question arising in the Winding up[5] of a Company, [6] to exercise, as respects the enforcing of calls or any other matter, all or any of the powers which the court [4] might exercise if the company [6] were being wound up [5] by the court. [4]

(2) If the court [4] is satisfied that the determination of the question or the required exercise of power will be just and beneficial, it may give effect wholly or partially to the application on such terms and conditions as it thinks fit, or make such other order as the case may require.

(3) A copy of an order made under this section staying the proceedings in the winding up, [2] shall forthwith be forwarded by the company,[6] or otherwise as may be prescribed, to the Commission, [7] which shall make a minute of the order in its books relating to the company.[6]

---

**Notes**
**Section 483**

1. "Liquidator" means a person appointed to wind up business affairs, esp. by selling off its assets. See **Garner B. (ed.) Black's Law Dictionary, 8th ed.**
2. Contributory" means every person liable to contribute to the assets of a company in the event of its being wound up and for the purposes of all proceedings for determining, and all proceedings prior to the final determination of, the persons who are to be deemed contributories. See **section 567, CAMA Cap. C20 LFN 2004.**
3. "Creditor" means a person or entity with a definite claim against another, esp. a claim that is capable of adjustment and liquidation. See **Garner B. (ed.) Black's Law Dictionary, 8 th ed.**
4. "Court" means the Federal High Court and to the extent to which application may be made to it as; court includes the Court of Appeal and the Supreme Court.See **section 567 CAMA Cap. C20 LFN, 2004**
5. "Winding up" means the process of settling accounts and liquidating assets in anticipation of a partnership or dissolution. See **Garner B. (ed.) Black's Law Dictionary, 8 th ed.**
6. "Company" means a company formed and registered under the Act, or as the case may be, formed and registered in Nigeria before and in existence on the commencement of this Act. See s **ection 567, CAMA Cap. C20 LFN 2004**

**Section 483 (3)**

7. "Commission" means the Corporate Affairs Commission. **See section 567 CAMA, Cap. C20 , LFN 2004**

**Cross Reference**

On procedure for voluntary windingup see **section 457-459 CAMA Cap. C20 LFN 2004**.

On appointment, remuneration and title of liquidators, see **section 422 CAMA Cap. C20 LFN 2004**

On power of court to remove and appoint another liquidator in a voluntary winding up, see **section 482 CAMA Cap. C20, LFN 2004**

On establishment and jurisdiction of the Federal High Court, see **section 249 & 251, Constitution of the Federal Republic of Nigeria, 1999 (as amended).**

---

**For Further Reading**

On winding up proceedings, see, Asomugha E. Maduelosi **Company law in Nigeria under the Companies and Allied Matters Act** E.M. Asomugha (Lagos) 1994.

### 484. Costs of voluntary winding up

All costs, charges and expenses properly incurred in the Winding up,[1] including the Remuneration of the Liquidator, [2] shall be payable out of the Assets of the Company [3] in priority to all other claims.

---

**Notes**
**Section 484**

1. "Winding up" means the process of settling accounts and liquidating assets in anticipation of a partnership or dissolution. See **Garner B. (ed.) Black's Law Dictionary, 8 th ed.**
2. "Liquidator" means a person appointed to wind up business affairs, esp. by selling off its assets. See **Garner B. (ed.) Black's Law Dictionary, 8th ed.**
3. "Company" means a company formed and registered under the Act, or as the case may be, formed and registered in Nigeria before and in existence on the commencement of this Act. See s **ection 567, CAMA Cap. C20 LFN 2004**

**Cross Reference**

On procedure for voluntary windingup see **section 457-459 CAMA Cap. C20 LFN 2004**

On appointment, remuneration and title of liquidators, see **section 422 CAMA Cap. C20 LFN 2004**

---

**For Further Reading**

On winding up proceedings, see, Asomugha E. Maduelosi **Company law in Nigeria under the Companies and Allied Matters Act** E.M. Asomugha (Lagos) 1994.

### 485. Saving of rights of creditors and contributories

The Winding up[1] of a Company[2] shall not bar the right of any Creditor[3] or Contributory [4] to have it wound up [1] by the court[5]; but where the applicant for winding up [1] is a contributory, [4] an order shall not be made unless the court [5] is satisfied that the rights of contributories[4] shall be prejudiced by the members' [6] or creditors' voluntary winding up, [7] as the case may be.

---

**Notes**

**Section 485**

1. "Winding up" means the process of settling accounts and liquidating assets in anticipation of a partnership or dissolution . See **Garner B. (ed.) Black's Law Dictionary, 8 th ed.**
2. "Company" means a company formed and registered under the Act, or as the case may be, formed and registered in Nigeria before and in existence on the commencement of this Act. See s **ection 567, CAMA Cap. C20 LFN 2004**
3. "Creditor" means a person or entity with a definite claim against another, esp. a claim that is capable of adjustment and liquidation. See **Garner B. (ed.) Black's Law Dictionary, 8 th ed.**
4. "Contributory" means every person liable to contribute to the assets of a company in the event of its being wound up and for the purposes of all proceedings for determining, and all proceedings prior to the final determination of, the persons who are to be deemed contributories. See **section 567, CAMA Cap. C20 LFN 2004.**
5. "Court" means the Federal High Court and to the extent to which application may be made to it as; court includes the Court of Appeal and the Supreme Court.See **section 567 CAMA Cap. C20 LFN, 2004**
6. "Members voluntary winding up"has the meaning assigned to it by section 462 (4) of this Act. See **section 567, CAMA Cap. C20 LFN 2004.**
7. "Creditors voluntary winding up" has the meaning assigned to it by section 462 (4) of this Act. See **section 567, CAMA Cap. C20 LFN 2004.**

**Cross Reference**

On nature and liability of contributories, see **section 404 CAMA Cap. C20 LFN 2004**.

---

**Cases**

An application may be made by summons to determine whether or not a person is a contributory, but such application should not be made unless the liquidator has failed to appoint a time and place for the purpose or has made a decision which is not acceptable to the alleged contributory. ***Sulaiman v. Muslim Bank (W.A.) Ltd.*** **(1970) 1 A.L.R. Comm 388.**

*CHAPTER 4 - Winding up subject to supervision of court*

## 486. Power to order winding up subject to supervision

If a company[1] passes a resolution[2] for voluntary winding up,[3] the court[4] may on petition order that the voluntary winding up[3] shall continue but subject to such supervision of the court,[4] and with such liberty for creditors,[5] contributories,[6] or others to apply to the court,[4] and generally on such terms and conditions, as the court [4] thinks just.

---

**Notes**
**Section 486**

1. "Company" means a company formed and registered under the Act, or as the case may be, formed and registered in Nigeria before and in existence on the commencement of this Act. See s **ection 567, CAMA Cap. C20 LFN 2004.**
2. "Resolution for voluntary winding up" has the meaning assigned to it by section 457 of this Act. See s **ection 567, CAMA Cap. C20 LFN 2004.**
3. "Winding up" means the process of settling accounts and liquidating assets in anticipation of a partnership or dissolution . See **Garner B. (ed.) Black's Law Dictionary, 8 th ed.**
4. "Court" means the Federal High Court and to the extent to which application may be made to it as; court includes the Court of Appeal and the Supreme Court.See **section 567 CAMA Cap. C20 LFN, 2004**
5. "Creditors" see "creditor." It means a person or entity with a definite claim against another, esp. a claim that is capable of adjustment and liquidation. See **Garner B. (ed.) Black's Law Dictionary, 8 th ed.**
6. "Contributories" see "contributory." It means every person liable to contribute to the assets of a company in the event of its being wound up and for the purposes of all proceedings for determining, and all proceedings prior to the final determination of, the persons who are to be deemed contributories. See **section 567, CAMA Cap. C20 LFN 2004**

**Cross Reference**

On nature and liability of contributories, see **section 404 CAMA Cap. C20 LFN 2004**.

On types of resolution, see **section 233 CAMA Cap. C20 LFN 2004**

On procedure for voluntary windingup see **section 457-459 CAMA Cap. C20 LFN 2004**.

On requirement for winding up application to be be by petition, see **section 410 CAMA Cap. C20, LFN 2004**

---

**Cases**

An application may be made by summons to determine whether or not a person is a contributory, but such application should not be made unless the liquidator has failed to appoint a time and place for the purpose or has made a decision which is not acceptable to the alleged contributory. ***Sulaiman v. Muslim Bank (W.A.) Ltd.*** **(1970) 1 A.L.R. Comm 388.**

**For Further Reading**

On winding up proceedings, see, Asomugha E. Maduelosi **Company law in Nigeria under the Companies and Allied Matters Act** E. M. Asomugha (Lagos) 1994

## 487.Effect of petition for winding up subject to supervision

A petition for the continuance of a voluntary winding up [1] subject to the supervision of the court [2] shall, for the purpose of giving jurisdiction to the court [2] over actions, be deemed to be a petition for winding up [3] by the court. [2]

---

**Note**
**Section 487**

1. "Voluntary winding up" means the dissolution of a company when the period, if any fixed for its duration by the articles expires or on the occurrence of an event of which its articles provide that the company is to be dissolved and the company in a general meeting pass a resolution requiring the company to be wound up. See **section 457 CAMA Cap. C20, LFN 2004**
2. "Court" means the Federal High Court and to the extent to which application may be made to it as; court includes the Court of Appeal and the Supreme Court.See **section 567 CAMA Cap. C20 LFN, 2004**
3. "Winding up" means the process of settling accounts and liquidating assets in anticipation of a partnership or dissolution . See **Garner B. (ed.) Black's Law Dictionary, 8 th ed.**

Cross Reference

On establishment and jurisdiction of the Federal High Court, see **section 249 & 251, Constitution of the Federal Republic of Nigeria, 1999 (as amended)**

On requirement for winding up application to be be by petition, see **section 410 CAMA Cap. C20, LFN 2004**

---

**Cases**

On a court of competent jurisdiction:

In ***Madukolu v. Nkemdilim (1962)2 NSCC 374 at 379-380*** , this court stated that "a court is properly constituted as regards the number and qualification of its members on the bench, and no member is disqualified for one reason or the other and the subject matter of the case is within the jurisdiction and there is no feature in the case which prevents the court from exercising its jurisdiction and the case coming up before the court was initiated by due process of law and upon fufilment if any condition precedent to the exercise of jurisdiction." See ***SLB Consortium v. Nigerin National Peroleum Corporation (NNPC) SC 180/2008 delivered 15/04/11***

**For Further Reading**

On winding up proceedings, see, Asomugha, E. Maduelosi **Company law in Nigeria under the Companies and Allied Matters Act** E. M. Asomugha (Lagos) 1994.

## 488. Application of sections 413 and 414

A Winding up[1] subject to the supervision of the court [2] shall, for the purposes of sections 413 and 414 of this Act, be deemed to be a winding up[1] by the court. [2]

---

**Notes**
**Section 488**

1. "Winding up" means the process of settling accounts and liquidating assets in anticipation of a partnership or dissolution . See **Garner B. (ed.) Black's Law Dictionary, 8 th ed.**
2. "Court" means the Federal High Court and to the extent to which application may be made to it as; court includes the Court of Appeal and the Supreme Court.See **section 567 CAMA Cap. C20 LFN, 2004**

Cross Reference

On establishment and jurisdiction of the Federal High Court, see **section 249 & 251, Constitution of the Federal Republic of Nigeria, 1999** (as amended)

---

**Cases**

On a court of competent jurisdiction:

In ***Madukolu v. Nkemdilim (1962)2 NSCC 374 at 379-380*** , this court stated that "a court is properly constituted as regards the number and qualification of its members on the bench , and no member is disqualified for one reason or the other and the subject matter of the case is within the jurisdiction and there is no feature in the case which prevents the court from exercising its jurisdiction and the case coming up before the court was initiated by due process of law and upon fufilment if any condition precedent to the exercise of jurisdiction." See ***SLB Consortium v. Nigerin National Peroleum Corporation (NNPC) SC 180/2008 delivered 15/04/11***

**For Further Reading**

On winding up proceedings, see, Asomugha, E. Maduelosi **Company law in Nigeria under the Companies and Allied Matters Act** E. M. Asomugha (Lagos) 1994.

## 489. Power of court to appoint, etc. liquidators

(1) Where an order is made for a winding up [1] subject to supervision, the court [2] may by the same or any subsequent order appoint an additional liquidator. [3]

(2) A liquidator [3] appointed by the court [2] under this section shall have the same powers, be subject to the same obligations, and in all respects stand in the same position, as if he had been duly appointed in accordance with the provisions of this act with respect to the appointment of liquidators [3] in a voluntary winding up. [4]

(3) The court [2] may remove any liquidator [3] so appointed by the court [2] or any liquidator [3] continued under the supervision order, and may fill any vacancy occasioned by the removal, or by death or resignation.

---

**Notes**
**Section 489**

1. "Winding up" means the process of settling accounts and liquidating assets in anticipation of a partnership or dissolution . See **Garner B. (ed.) Black's Law Dictionary, 8 th ed.**
2. "Court" means the Federal High Court and to the extent to which application may be made to it as; court includes the Court of Appeal and the Supreme Court.See **section 567 CAMA Cap. C20 LFN, 2004**
3. "Liquidator" means a person appointed to wind up business affairs, esp. by selling off its assets. See **Garner B. (ed.) Black's Law Dictionary, 8th ed.**
4. "Voluntary winding up" means the dissolution of a company when the period, if any fixed for its duration by the articles expires or on the occurrence of an event of which its articles provide that the company is to be dissolved and the company in a general meeting pass a resolution requiring the company to be wound up. See **section 457 CAMA Cap. C20, LFN 2004**

**Cross Reference**

On establishment and jurisdiction of the Federal High Court, see **section 249 & 251, Constitution of the Federal Republic of Nigeria, 1999 (as amended)**

On disposition of company property and shares after commencement of winding up proceedings under supervision of court being void, see **sections 413 & 414 CAMA Cap. C20 LFN 2004**

On requirement for winding up application to be be by petition, see **section 410 CAMA Cap. C20, LFN 2004**

On power of court to order winding up subject to supervision, **see section 486 CAMA Cap. C20 LFN 2004**

---

**For Further Reading**

On winding up proceedings, see, Asomugha, E. Maduelosi **Company law in Nigeria under the Companies and Allied Matters Act** E. M. Asomugha (Lagos) 1994.

## 490. Effect of supervision order

(1) Where an order is made for a Winding up [1] subject to supervision, the Liquidator [2] may, subject to any restrictions imposed by the court, [3] exercise all his powers, without the sanction or intervention of the court, [3] in the same manner as if the Company[4] were being wound up [1] voluntarily:
Provided that the powers specified in paragraphs ( d), (e) and (f) of section 425 (1) of this Act shall not be exercised by the liquidator [2] except with the sanction of the court [3] or, in a case where before the order the winding up [1] was a creditors' voluntary winding up, [5] with the sanction of the court [3] or the committee of inspection, or (if there is no such committee) a meeting [6] of the Creditors. [7]

(2) A winding up [1] subject to the supervision of the court [3] shall not amount to a winding-up [1] by the court [3] for the purpose of the provisions of this Act as specified in the Twelfth Schedule to this Act (dealing with provisions which do not apply in the case of winding up subject to the supervision of the court) but, subject to this, an order for a winding up [1] subject to supervision shall for all purposes be an order for winding up by the court:
[Twelfth Schedule.]
Provided that where the order for winding up [1] subject to supervision of the committee was made in relation to a creditors' voluntary winding[5] up in which a committee of inspection had been appointed, the order shall be deemed to be an order for winding up [1] by the court [3] for the purposes of section 434 of this Act, (except subsection (1) thereof) save insofar as the operation of that section is excluded in a voluntary winding up [1] by general rules made under this Act.

---

**Notes**
**Section 490(1)**

1. "Winding up" means the process of settling accounts and liquidating assets in anticipation of a partnership or dissolution. **See Garner B. (ed.) Black's Law Dictionary, 8th ed.**
2. "Liquidator" means a person appointed to wind up business affairs, esp. by selling off its assets. See **Garner B. (ed.) Black's Law Dictionary, 8th ed.**

"Liquidator" means a person responsible for closing down a business and using any profits from the sale to pay its debts. See **Oxford Advanced Learners Dictionary, 6 th ed**

3. "Court" means the Federal High Court and to the extent to which application may be made to it as; court includes the Court of Appeal and the Supreme Court.See **section 567 CAMA Cap. C20 LFN, 2004**
4. "Company" means a company formed and registered under the Act, or as the case may be, formed and registered in Nigeria before and in existence on the commencement of this Act. See s **ection 567, CAMA Cap. C20 LFN 2004**
5. "Creditors' voluntary winding up" has the meaning assigned to it by section 462(4) of this Act. See section **567 CAMA, Cap. C20, LFN 2004**
6. "Meeting" means the gathering of people to discuss or act on matters in which they have a common interest. See **Garner B. (ed.) Black's Law Dictionary 8 th ed.**
7. "Creditors" see "creditor." It means a person or entity with a definite claim against another, esp. a claim that is capable of adjustment and liquidation. See **Garner B. (ed.) Black's Law Dictionary, 8 th ed.**

Cross Reference

On distinction between members voluntary winding-up and creditors voluntary winding-up, see **section 462(4), CAMA, LFN 2004.**

On the appointment of committee of inspection by creditors see **section 474 CAMA Cap. C20, LFN 2004**

On powers of the Committee of inspection, see **section 434 CAMA Cap. C20, LFN 2004**

On power of court to order winding up subject to supervision, see **section 486 CAMA Cap. C20 LFN 2004**

---

**Cases**

The liquidator may be likened to an undertaker, by virtue of the Company's total in disposition goes into preparation for the "burial" of the company but the actual burial of the company takes place on its death at its dissolution. ***Co-Operative and Commerce Bank (NIG.)Ltd v. Alex O. Onwuchekwa*** **(2000) 3 NWLR (Pt. 647) 67**

**For Further Reading**

On winding up proceedings, see, Asomugha E. Maduelosi **Company law in Nigeria under the Companies and Allied Matters Act** E. M. Asomugha (Lagos) 1994.

*Chapter 5 - Provisions Applicable To Every Mode Of Winding Up*

## 491. Liquidator to give notice of appointment

(1) The liquidator[1] shall, within 14 days after his appointment, publish in the gazette[2] and in two daily newspapers and deliver to the commission[3] for registration a notice of his appointment in such form as the commission[3] may from time to time approve.

(2) If the liquidator[1] fails to comply with the requirements of this section, he shall be guilty of an offence and liable to a fine of N25 for every day during which the default continues.

---

**Notes**
**Section 491**

1. "Liquidator" means a person appointed to wind up business affairs, esp. by selling off its assets. See **Garner B. (ed.) Black's Law Dictionary, 8[th] ed.**
   "Liquidator" means a person responsible for closing down a business and using any profits from the sale to pay its debts. See **Oxford Advanced Learners Dictionary, 6[th]ed**
2. "Gazette" means the official Gazette of the Federation. See section **567 CAMA, Cap. C20 , LFN 2004**
3. "Commission" means the Corporate Affairs Commission established under section 1 of this Act. See section **567 CAMA, Cap. C20 , LFN 2004**

Cross Reference

On meaning of offence, see **section 2, Criminal Code, Cap. C38 LFN 2004**
On appointment, remuneration and title of liquidators, see **section 422 CAMA Cap. C20 LFN 2004**

---

**For Further Reading**
On winding up proceedings, see, Asomugha E. Maduelosi **Company law in Nigeria under the Companies and Allied Matters Act** E. M. Asomugha (Lagos) 1994.

*Proof and ranking of claims*

## 492. Debts of all descriptions may be proved

In every winding up[1] (subject, in the case of insolvent companies,[2] to the application in accordance with the provisions of this act of the law of bankruptcy), all debts payable on a contingency, and all claims against the company,[3] present or future, certain or contingent, ascertained or sounding only in damages, shall be admissible to proof against the company,[3] a just estimate being made, so far as possible, of the value of such debts or claims as may be subject to any contingency or sound only in damages, or for some other reasons do not bear a certain value.

**Notes**

Section 492

1. "Winding up" means the process of settling accounts and liquidating assets in anticipation of a partnership or dissolution. See **Garner B. (ed.) Black's Law Dictionary, 8th ed.**
2. "Insolvent companies" see insolvent person. "where used in this Act means any person in Nigeria who, in respect of any judgment, Act or court order against him, is unable to satisfy execution or other process issued thereon in favour of a creditor, and the execution or other process remains unsatisfied for not less than six weeks. See **section 567 CAMA Cap. C20, LFN 2004**
3. "Company" means a company formed and registered under the Act, or as the case may be, formed and registered in Nigeria before and in existence on the commencement of this Act. See s **ection 567, CAMA Cap. C20 LFN 2004**

Cross Reference

On modes of winding up of a company, see **section 401 CAMA Cap. C20 LFN 2004**

**For Further Reading**

On winding up proceedings, see, Asomugha, E. Maduelosi **Company law in Nigeria under the Companies and Allied Matters Act** E. M. Asomugha (Lagos) 1994.

## 493. Application of bankruptcy rules in certain cases

In the winding up[1] of an insolvent company[2] registered in Nigeria the same rules shall prevail and be observed with regard to the respective rights of secured[3] and unsecured creditors[4] and to debts provable and to the valuation of annuities and future and contingent liabilities as are in force for the time being under the law of bankruptcy[5] in Nigeria with respect to the estates of persons adjudged bankrupt, and all persons who in any such case would be entitled to prove for and receive dividends[6] out of the assets of the company[7] may come in under the winding up[1] and make such claims against the company[7] as they respectively are entitled to by virtue of this section.

**Notes**

Section 493

1. "Winding up" means the process of settling accounts and liquidating assets in anticipation of a partnership or dissolution. See **Garner B. (ed.) Black's Law Dictionary, 8th ed.**
2. "Insolvent company" see insolvent person. "Where used in this Act means any person in Nigeria who, in respect of any judgment, Act or court order against him, is unable to satisfy execution or other process issued thereon in favour of a creditor, and the execution or other process remains unsatisfied for not less than six weeks. See **section 567 CAMA Cap. C20, LFN 2004** means a company formed and registered under the Act, or as the case may be, formed and registered in Nigeria before and in existence on the commencement of this Act. See s**ection 567, CAMA Cap. C20 LFN 2004**
3. "Secured creditors" means a person who holds some security, such as a mortgage, for money he lent. If the debtor becomes bankrupt, the creditor has a choice. See **Martin E. (ed.) Oxford Dictionary of Law 4th ed.**
4. "Unsecured creditors" means a a person who has lent money without obtaining any security. See **Martin E. (ed.) Oxford Dictionary of Law 4th ed.**
5. "Bankruptcy" means the state of a person who has been adjudged by a court to be insolvent. See **Martin E. (ed.) Oxford Dictionary of Law 4th ed.**
6. "Dividends"see "dividend." It means a proportion of the distributed profits of the company which may be a fixed annual percentage, as in the case of preference shares, or it may be variable according to the prosperity or other circumstances of the company, as in the case of equity shares. See **Section 567 CAMA, Cap. C20, LFN 2004.**
7. "Company" means a company formed and registered under the Act, or as the case may be, formed and registered in Nigeria before and in existence on the commencement of this Act.. See s **ection 567, CAMA Cap. C20 LFN 2004.**

**Cross Reference**

On the laws governing bankruptcy in Nigeria, see generally, **Bankruptcy Act Cap. B2 LFN 2004.**

On declaration of dividends and payment of interim dividend, see **section 379, CAMA Cap. C20, LFN 2004.**

---

**For Further Reading**

On winding up proceedings, see, Asomugha, E. Maduelosi **Company law in Nigeria under the Companies and Allied Matters Act** E. M. Asomugha (Lagos) 1994

**Cases.**

Once dividend is declared, shareholders are entitled to be paid dividends in proportion to the nominal amount held and they can sue for the dividend within twelve years after being declared: ***AG Federation v. Ijewere*** **(1980) 4 NWLR pt. 37, p. 659.**

### 494. Preferential payments

(1) In a Winding up [1] there shall be paid in priority to all other debts-

(a) all local rates and charges due from the Company [2] at the relevant date, and having become due and payable within 12 months next before that date, and all pay-as-you-earn tax deductions, assessed taxes, land tax, property or income tax assessed on or due from the company [2] up to the annual day of assessment next before the relevant date, and in the case of pay-as-you-earn tax deductions not exceeding deductions made in respect of one year of assessment and, in any other case, not exceeding in the whole one year's assessment;

(b) deductions under the Nigeria Social Insurance Trust Fund Act;

[Cap. N88.]

(c) all wages or salary of any clerk or servant in respect of services rendered to the company [2];

(d) all wages of any workman or labourer, whether payable for time or for piece work, in respect of services rendered to the company[2];

(e) all accrued holiday remuneration becoming payable to any clerk, servant, workman or labourer (or in the case of his death to any other person in his rights) on the termination of his employment before or by the effect of the winding up[1] order or resolution [3];

(f) unless the company[1] is being wound up[1] voluntarily merely for the purpose of reconstruction or of amalgamation with another company or unless the company[2] has at the commencement of the winding up [1] under such a contract with insurers as is mentioned in section 26 of the Workmen's Compensation Act,* rights capable of being transferred to and vested in the workman, all amounts due in respect of any compensation or liability for compensation under the Act aforesaid, accrued before the relevant date.

[Cap. W6.]

(2) Where any compensation under the Workmen's Compensation Act* is a weekly payment, the amount due in respect thereof shall, for the purpose of paragraph (e) of subsection (1) of this section, be taken to be the amount of the lump sum for which the weekly payment could, if redeemable, be redeemed if the employer made an application for that purpose under the aforesaid Act.

(3) Where any payment on account of wages or salary has been made to any clerk, servant, workman or labourer in the employment of a company out of the money advanced by some persons for that purpose, that person shall in a winding up [1] have a right of priority in respect of the money so advanced and paid up to the amount by which the sum in respect of which that clerk, servant, workman or labourer would have been entitled to priority in the winding up[1] has been diminished by reason of the payment having been made.

(4) The foregoing debts shall-

(a) rank equally among themselves and be paid in full, unless the Assets are insufficient to meet them, in which case they shall abate in equal proportions; and

(b) so far as the assets of the company [2] available for payment of general Creditors [4] are insufficient to meet them, have priority over the claims of holders of debentures [5] under any floating charge[6] created by the company [2] and be paid accordingly out of any property comprised in or subject to that charge.[7]

(5) Subject to the retention of such sums as may be necessary for the costs and expenses of the winding up, [1] the foregoing debts shall be discharged forthwith so far as the assets are sufficient to meet them.

(6) In this section "the relevant date" means-

(a) in the case of a company [2] ordered to be wound up [1] compulsorily which had not previously commenced to be wound up[1] voluntarily, the date of the winding-up [1] order; and

(b) in any other case, the date of the commencement of the winding up.[1]

**Notes**
**Section 494(1)**

1. "Winding up" means the process of settling accounts and liquidating assets in anticipation of a partnership or dissolution. See **Garner B. (ed.) Black's Law Dictionary, 8th ed.**
2. "Company" means a company formed and registered under the Act, or as the case may be, formed and registered in Nigeria before and in existence on the commencement of this Act. See s **ection 567, CAMA Cap. C20 LFN 2004**
3. "Resolution" means a main motion that formally expresses the sense, will, or action of a deliberative assembly. See **Garner B. (ed.) Black's Law Dictionary 8th ed.**
4. "Creditors" see "creditor." It means a person or entity with a definite claim against another , esp. a claim that is capable of adjustment and liquidation. See **Garner B. (ed.) Black's Law Dictionary, 8 th ed.**
5. "Debenture holders" see "debenture" and "holder." Debenture means a written acknowledgement of indebtedness by the company, setting out the terms and conditions of the indebtedness and includes debenture stock, bonds and any other securities of any company whether constituting a charge on the assets of the company or not. **See 567 CAMA Cap. C20, LFN 2004** . "Holder" is one who has legal possession of a negotiable instrument and is entitled to receive payment on it. See **Garner B. (ed) Black's Law Dictionary, 8 th ed.**
6. "Floating Charge" see floating lien. It means a charge that continues to exist even when the collateral changes in character, classification or location**. See Garner B. (ed.) Black's Law Dictionary 8th ed.**
   A "floating charge" means an equitable charge over the whole or a specified part of the company's undertakings and assets, including cash and uncalled capital of the company both present and future, but so that the charge shall not preclude the company from dealing with such assets until- (a) the security becomes enforceable and the holder thereof, pursuant to a power in that behalf in the debenture or the deed securing the same, appoints a receiver or manager or enters into possession of such assets; or (b) the court appoints a receiver or manager of such assets on the application of the holder; or (c) the company goes into liquidation. See **section 178 CAMA Cap. C20 LFN, 2004**
7. **"charge"** means an incumbrance, lien or claim, a burden or load, an obligation or duty or liability. See **Garner B. (ed) Black's law dictionary 8th ed.**

**Cross Reference**

On the regulation of pay as you earn tax deductions in Nigeria, see generally **Personal Income Tax Act (PITA) Cap. P8 LFN 2004**

On taxes on income of companies, see generally, **Companies Income Tax Act, Cap. C21, LFN 2004**

On the categories of contributions to be made under the Nigeria Social Insurance Trust Fund Act, see **section 12, Nigeria Socila Insurance Trust Fund (NSITF) Act, Cap. N88, LFN 2004**

On national minimum wages of workers and categories of workers that it applies to, see generally **National Minimum Wage Act (as amended), Cap. N61, LFN 2004**

* The Workmens Compensation Act, Cap. W6 LFN 2004, has been repealed by section 72, Employees' Compensation Act 2010.

---

*Effect of winding up on antecedent and other transactions*

## 495. Fraudulent preference

(1) Any conveyance, mortgage, [1] delivery of goods, payment, execution or other act relating to property which would, if made or done by or against an individual, be deemed in his bankruptcy [2] a fraudulent preference, shall, if made or done by or against a company[3], be deemed, in the event of its being wound up, [4] a fraudulent preference of its creditors, [5] and be invalid accordingly.
(2) Any conveyance or assignment by a Company [3] of all its property to trustees for the benefit of all its creditors [5] shall be void.

(3) For the purposes of this section, the presentation of a petition for Winding up [4] in the case of a winding up [4] by or subject to the supervision of the court, [6] and a resolution [7] for winding up [4] in the case of a voluntary winding up, [8] shall be deemed to correspond with the act of bankruptcy in the case of an individual.

---

**Notes**
**Section 495**

1. "Mortgage" means a conveyance of title to property that is given as security for the payment of a debt or the performance of a duty and that will become void upon payment or performance according to the stipulated terms. See **Garner B. (ed.) Black's Law Dictionary, 8th ed.**
2. "Bankruptcy" means the state of a person who has been adjudged by a court to be insolvent. See **Martin E. (ed.) Oxford Dictionary of Law 4th ed.**
3. "Company" means a company formed and registered under the Act, or as the case may be, formed and registered in Nigeria before and in existence on the commencement of this Act.. See s **ection 567, CAMA CAP C20 LFN 2004**

4. "Wound up" see"winding up." It means the process of settling accounts and liquidating assets in anticipation of a partnership or dissolution. See **Garner B. (ed.) Black's Law Dictionary, 8th ed.**
5. "Creditor" means a person or entity with a definite claim against another, esp. a claim that is capable of adjustment and liquidation. See **Garner B. (ed.) Black's Law Dictionary, 8 th ed.**
6. "Court" means the Federal High Court and to the extent to which application may be made to it as; court includes the Court of Appeal and the Supreme Court.See **section 567 CAMA CAP C20 LFN, 2004**
7. "Resolution" means a main motion that formally expresses the sense, will, or action of a deliberative assembly. See **Garner B. (ed.) Black's Law Dictionary 8th ed.**
8. "Voluntary winding up" means the dissolution of a company when the period, if any fixed for its duration by the articles expires or on the occurrence of an event of which its articles provide that the company is to be dissolved and the company in a general meeting pass a resolution requiring the company to be wound up. See **section 457 CAMA CAP C20, LFN 2004**

**Cross Reference**

On the laws governing bankruptcy in Nigeria, see generally, **Bankruptcy Act Cap. B2 LFN 2004**

On requirement for winding up application to be be by petition, see **section 410 CAMA Cap. C20, LFN 2004**

On power of court to order winding up subject to supervision, see **section 486 CAMA Cap. C20 LFN 2004**

---

## 496.Liabilities and rights of certain fraudulently preferred persons

(1) Where anything made or done after the commencement of this Act is void under section 495 of this Act as a fraudulent preference of a person interested in property mortgaged or charged to secure the company's [1] debt, the person preferred shall, without prejudice to any liabilities or rights arising apart from this provision, be subject to the same liabilities, and have the same rights, as if he had undertaken to be personally Liable as surety for the debt, to the extent of the charge on the property or have value of his interest, whichever is the less, and the value of the said person's interest shall be determined as at the date of the transaction constituting the fraudulent preference, and shall be determined as if the interest were free of all incumbrances other than those to which the charge for the company's [1] debt was the subject.

(2) Where for the purposes of this section, application is made to the court[2] with respect to any payment on the ground that the payment was fraudulent preference of a surety or Guarantor, [3] the court shall have jurisdiction to determine any questions with respect to the payment arising between the person to whom the payment was made and the surety or Guarantor, [3] and to grant relief in respect thereof, notwithstanding that it is not necessary so to do for the purposes of the winding up, [4] and for that purpose may give leave to bring in the surety or Guarantor [3] as a third party as in the case of an action for the recovery of the sum paid.

(3) Subsection (2) of this section shall apply, with the necessary modifications, in relation to transactions other than the payment of money, as it applies in relation to payments.

---

**Notes**
**Section 496(1)**

1. "Company" means a company formed and registered under the Act, or as the case may be, formed and registered in Nigeria before and in existence on the commencement of this Act.. See s **ection 567, CAMA Cap. C20 LFN 2004**
2. "Court" means the Federal High Court and to the extent to which application may be made to it as; court includes the Court of Appeal and the Supreme Court.See **section 567 CAMA Cap. C20 LFN, 2004**
3. "Guarantor" means one who makes a guaranty or gives security for a debt. **See Garner B. (ed.) Black's Law Dictionary 8th ed.**
4. "Winding up" means the process of settling accounts and liquidating assets in anticipation of a partnership or dissolution. See **Garner B. (ed.) Black's Law Dictionary, 8th ed.**

Cross Reference

On establishment and jurisdiction of the Federal High Court, see **section 249 & 251, Constitution of the Federal Republic of Nigeria, 1999** (as amended)

---

## 497. Avoidance of attachments, etc., on winding up subject to supervision of the court

Where a Company[1] is being wound up[2] subject to the supervision of the court, any Attachment, sequestration or execution put in force against the estate or effects of the company[1] after the commencement of the Winding up[2], shall be void.

---

**Notes**
**Section 497**

1. "Company" means a company formed and registered under the Act, or as the case may be, formed and registered in Nigeria before and in existence on the commencement of this Act. See s **ection 567, CAMA Cap. C20 LFN 2004.**
2. "Wound up" see "winding up." It means the process of settling accounts and liquidating assets in anticipation of a partnership or dissolution. See **Garner B. (ed.) Black's Law Dictionary, 8th ed.**

**Cross Reference**

On disposition of company property and shares after commencement of winding up proceedings under supervision of court being void, see **sections 413 & 414 CAMA CAP C20 LFN 2004**

On requirement for winding up application to be be by petition, see **section 410 CAMA CAP C20, LFN 2004**

On power of court to order winding up subject to supervision, **see section 486 CAMA CAP C20 LFN 2004**

## 498. Effect of floating charge

Where a company [1] is being wound up, [2] a floating charge [3] on the undertaking or property of the company [1] created within three months of the commencement of the winding up [2] shall, unless it is proved that the company [1] immediately after the creation of the charge was solvent, be invalid, except to the amount of any cash paid to the company [1] at the time of or subsequently to the creation of, and in consideration for, the charge, together with interest on that amount at the current bank rate.

**Notes**
**Section 498**

1. "Company" means a company formed and registered under the Act, or as the case may be, formed and registered in Nigeria before and in existence on the commencement of this Act.See **section 567, CAMA CAP C20 LFN 2004.**
2. "Wound up" see"winding up." It means the process of settling accounts and liquidating assets in anticipation of a partnership or dissolution. See **Garner B. (ed.) Black's Law Dictionary, 8th ed.**
3. "Floating charge" see floating lien. It means a charge that continues to exist even when the collateral changes in character, classification or location. See **Garner B. (ed.) Black's Law Dictionary 8th ed.**
   A "floating charge" means an equitable charge over the whole or a specified part of the company's undertakings and assets, including cash and uncalled capital of the company both present and future, but so

that the charge shall not preclude the company from dealing with such assets until- (a) the security becomes enforceable and the holder thereof, pursuant to a power in that behalf in the debenture or the deed securing the same, appoints a receiver or manager or enters into possession of such assets; or (b) the court appoints a receiver or manager of such assets on the application of the holder; or (c) the company goes into liquidation. See **section 178 CAMA CAP C20 LFN, 2004**

4. "Charge" means an incumbrance, lien or claim, a burden or load, an obligation or duty or liability. See **Garner B. (ed) Black's law dictionary 8th ed.**

Cross Reference

On priority of fixed charge over floating charge, see section 179 CAMA CAP C20, LFN 2004

## 499. Disclaimer of onerous property

(1) Where any part of the property of a company [1] which is being wound up[2] consists of land of any tenure burdened with onerous covenants,[3] of shares[4] or stock in companies,[1] of unprofitable contracts, or of any other property that is unsaleable, or not readily saleable, by reason of its binding the possessor thereof to the performance of any onerous act or to the payment of any sum of money, the liquidator [5] of the company,[1] notwithstanding that he has endeavoured to sell or has taken possession of the property or exercised any act of ownership in relation thereto, may, with the leave of the court [6], and subject to the provisions of this section, by writing signed by him, at any time within 12 months after the commencement of the winding up [2] or such extended period as may be allowed by the court [6], disclaim the property:
Provided that, where any such property has not come to the knowledge of the liquidator[5] within one month after the commencement of the winding up,[2] the power under this section of disclaiming the property may be exercised at any time within 12 months after he has become aware thereof or such extended period as may be allowed by the court. [6]

(2) A Disclaimer under this section shall operate to determine, as from the date of the disclaimer, the rights, interest and liabilities of the company,[1] and the property of the company,[1] in or in respect of the property disclaimed, but shall not, except so far as is necessary for the purpose of releasing the company [1] and

the property of the company [1] from liability, affect the rights or liabilities of any other person.

(3) The court, [6] before or on granting leave to disclaim, may require such notices to be given to persons interested, and impose such terms as a condition of granting leave, and make such other order in the matter as the court [6] thinks just.

(4) The liquidator [5] shall not be entitled to disclaim any property under this section in any case where an application in writing has been made to him by any persons interested in the property requiring him to decide whether or not he will disclaim, and the liquidator [5] has not, within a period of 28 days after the receipt of the application or such further period as may be allowed by the court [6], given notice to the applicant that he intends to apply to the court [6] for leave to disclaim, and, in the case of a Contract, if the liquidator, [5] after such an application, does not within that period or further period disclaim the contract, the company [1] shall be deemed to have adopted it.

(5) The court [6] may, on the application of any person who is, as against the liquidator, [5] entitled to the benefit or subject to the burden of a contract on such terms as to payment by or to either party, of damages for the non-performance of the contract, or otherwise as the court [6] thinks just and any damages payable under the order to any such person may be proved by him as a debt in the winding up. [2]

(6) The court [6] may, on an application by any person who claims any interest in any property disclaimed under this section, or is under any liability not discharged by this Act in respect of any disclaimed property, and on hearing any such persons as it thinks fit, make an order for the vesting of the property in or the delivery of the property to any persons entitled thereto, or to whom it may seem just that the property should be delivered by way of compensation for such liability as aforesaid, or a trustee [7] for him, and on such terms as the court [6] thinks just and on any such vesting order being made, the property comprised therein shall vest accordingly in the person therein named in that behalf without any conveyance or assignment for the purpose.

(7) Where the property disclaimed is of a Leasehold [8] nature the court [6] shall not make a vesting order in favour of any person claiming under the company [1], whether as an under-lessee or as a mortgagee by demise, a Mortgage [9] by way of legal charge or

Mortgage,[9] as the case may be, except upon the terms of making that person-

(a) subject to the same liabilities and obligations as those to which the company[1] was subject under the lease in respect of the property at the commencement of the winding up [2]; or

(b) if the court[6] thinks fit, subject only to the same liabilities and obligations as if the lease had been assigned to that person at that date, and in either event if the case so requires, as if the lease had comprised only the property comprised in the vesting order, and any mortgagee or under-lessee declining to accept a vesting order upon such terms shall be excluded from all interest in and security upon the property, and if there is no person claiming under the company[1] who is willing to accept an order upon such terms, the court [6] shall have power to vest the estate and interest of the company [1] in the property in any person liable, either personally or in a representative character, and either alone or jointly with the company, to perform the lessee's covenants in the lease, freed and discharged from all estates, incumbrances and interests created therein by the company. [1]

(8) Any person injured by the operation of a disclaimer under this section shall be deemed to be a creditor of the company [1] to the amount of the injury, and may accordingly prove the amount as a debt in the winding up. [2]

---

**Notes**
**Section 499(1)**

1. "Company" means a company formed and registered under the Act, or as the case may be, formed and registered in Nigeria before and in existence on the commencement of this Act.See **section 567, CAMA Cap. C20 LFN 2004.**
2. "Wound up" see"winding up." It means the process of settling accounts and liquidating assets in anticipation of a partnership or dissolution. See **Garner B. (ed.) Black's Law Dictionary, 8th ed.**
3. "Covenants" means promise contained in a deed which is binding even if not supported by consideration. See **Martin E. (ed.) Oxford Dictionary of Law 4th ed.**
4. "Shares" see "share." It means the interests in the company's shares capital of a member who is entitled to share in the capitalor income of such company, and except where a distinction between stock and

shares is expressed or implied, includes stock. See **section 567, CAMA Cap. C20 LFN 2004.**

5. "Liquidator" means a person appointed to wind up business affairs, esp. by selling off its assets. See **Garner B. (ed.) Black's Law Dictionary, 8th ed.**
6. "Court" means the Federal High Court and to the extent to which application may be made to it as; court includes the Court of Appeal and the Supreme Court.See **section 567 CAMA Cap. C20 LFN, 2004**

**Section 499(6)**

7. "Trustee" One who having legal title to property holds it in trust for the benefit of another and owes a fiduciary duty to that beneficiary. See **Garner B(ed) Black's law dictionary 8th ed.**

**Section 499(7)**

8. "Leasehold" means a tenants possessory estate in land or premises, the four types being the tenancy for years, the periodic tenancy, the tenancy at will, and the tenancy at sufferance. See **Garner B. (ed.) Black's Law Dictionary, 8th ed.**
9. "Mortgage" means a conveyance of title to property that is given as security for the payment of a debt or the performance of a duty and that will become void upon payment or performance according to the stipulated terms. See **Garner B. (ed.) Black's Law Dictionary, 8th ed.**

**Cross Reference**

On establishment and jurisdiction of the Federal High Court, see **section 249 & 251, Constitution of the Federal Republic of Nigeria, 1999 (as amended)**

On appointment, remuneration and title of liquidators, see **section 422 CAMA Cap. C20 LFN 2004**

---

**Cases**

By the provisions of Companies and Allied Matters Act, Section 115, shares are in the nature of personal estate and freely transferable but subject to statutory restrictions and the articles of the company. Members in a company have a right to transfer shares belonging to them therein and this right is unfettered unless there is an express restriction to that effect in the articles or constitution of the company. ***N.R.I. Ltd v. Oranusi*** **[2011] ALL F.W.L.R part 577. 625-824 at p.765** .

## 500. Restriction of rights of creditor as to execution, etc., on winding up of company

(1) Where a Creditor [1] issues execution against any goods or land of a Company, [2] or attaches any debt due to the Company, [2] and the company[2] is subsequently wound up, [3] the Creditor [1] shall not be entitled to retain the benefit of the execution or attachment against the liquidator[4] in the winding up [3] of the company, [2] unless he has

completed the execution or attachment before the commencement of the Winding up;[3]

Provided that-

(a) where any creditor[1] has had notice of a meeting[5] having been called at which a Resolution[6] for voluntary winding up[7] is to be proposed, the date on which the creditor[1] so had notice shall, for the purposes of the foregoing provision, be substituted for the date of the commencement of the winding up[3];

(b) if a person purchases in good faith under a sale by the sheriff any goods of a company[2] on which an execution has been levied, he shall acquire a good title to them against the liquidator[4];

(c) the rights conferred by this subsection on the liquidator[4] may be set aside by the court[8] in favour of the creditor[1] to such extent and subject to such terms as the court[8] thinks fit.

(2) For the purposes of this section, an execution against goods shall be taken to be completed by seizure and sale, and an attachment of a debt shall be deemed to be completed by receipt of the debt, and an execution against land shall be deemed to be completed by seizure and, in the case of an equitable interest, by the appointment of a receiver.[9]

---

**Notes**

**Section 500**

1. "Creditor" means one to whom a debt is owed; one who gives credit for money or goods. See **Garner B. (ed) Black's Law Dictionary, 8th ed.**
2. "Company" means a company formed and registered under this Act or, as the case may be, formed and registered in Nigeria before and in existence on the commencement of this Act. **See section 567, CAMA Cap. C20 LFN 2004**
3. "Wound up" see "winding up." It means the process of settling accounts and liquidating assets in anticipation of a partnership's or a corporation's dissolution. See **Garner B. (ed) Black's law dictionary 8th ed.**
4. "Liquidators" means a person who is appointed to wind up a business's affairs esp. by selling off its assets. See **Garner B. (ed) Black's Law Dictionary, 8[th] ed.**
5. "Meeting" means the gathering of people to discuss or act on matters in which they have a common interest; especially the convening of a

deliberative assembly to transact business. See **Garner B. Ed. Black's Law Dictionary, 8th ed.**

6. "Resoultion" means a main motion that formally expresses the sense, will, or action of a deliberative assembly.See **Garner B. (ed.) Black's Law Dictionary 8th ed.**
7. "Voluntary Winding up" has the meaning assigned to it by **section 462(4) CAMA Cap. C20 LFN 2004.**
8. "Court" means the Federal High Court and to the extent to which application may be made to it as; court includes the Court of Appeal and the Supreme Court. See **section567 CAMA Cap. C20, LFN 2004**
9. "Receiver" means a disinterested person appointed by a court, or by a corporation or other person, for the protection or collection of property that is the subject of diverse claims. See **Garner B. (ed) Black's Law Dictionary 8th ed.**

   "Receiver" includes manager. **Section 567 CAMA, Cap. C20 , LFN 2004**

Cross Reference

On distinction between members voluntary winding-up and creditors voluntary winding-up, see **section 462(4), CAMA, Cap. C20 LFN 2004**

On how a liquidator is appointed, see **section 473, CAMA Cap. C20 LFN, 2004.**

On sale of goods by Sherrif, see generally **section 29-31, Sherrif and Civil Processes Act, Cap. LFN 2004**

---

**Cases**

A Liquidator owes a duty to the whole body of creditors and shareholders and to the court to make himself thoroughly acquainted with the affairs of the company and suppress or conceal anything coming to his knowledge in the course of his investigation which is material; ***Re J. A. Balogun*** **(1977) FRCR 122**

On appointment of receiver, the powers of management of the company's business became vested in the receiver, but on quite a number of matters not related to management ,the directors can still act: ***UBA Trustees Ltd. v. Nigergrob Ceramic Ltd. (1987) 3 NWLR pt 62, p. 600.***

## 501. Duty of sheriff as to goods taken in execution

(1) Subject to the provisions of subsection (3) of this section, where any goods of a Company [1] are taken in execution and before the sale thereof or the completion of the execution by the receipt or recovery of the full amount of the levy, notice is served on the Sheriff that a provisional Liquidator [2] has been appointed or that a Winding-up[3] order has been made or that a Resolution [4] for voluntary winding up[5] has been passed, the sheriff shall, on being so required, deliver the goods and any money seized or received in

part satisfaction of the execution to the liquidator [2], but the costs of the execution shall be a first charge on the goods or money so delivered, and the Liquidator [2] may sell the goods, or a sufficient part thereof, for the purpose of satisfying that charge.

(2) Subject to the provisions of subsection (3) of this section, where under an execution in respect of a judgment for a sum exceeding N100 the goods of a Company [1] are sold or money is paid in order to avoid the sale, the Sheriff shall deduct the costs of the execution from the proceeds of the sale or the money paid, and retain the balance for 14 days and if within that time notice is served on him of a petition for the winding up of the Company [1] having been presented or of a meeting having been called at which there is to be proposed a resolution for the voluntary winding up [5] of the company[1] and an order is made or a resolution [4] is passed, as the case may be, for the winding up [3] of the Company, [1] the sheriff shall pay the balance to the liquidator, [2] who shall be entitled to retain it as against the execution creditor. [6]

(3) The rights conferred by this section on the Liquidator [2] may be set aside by the court [7] in favour of the Creditor [6] to such extent and subject to such terms as the court thinks fit.

(4) In this section and section 500 of this Act-

(a) "goods" includes chattels personal; and

(b) "sheriff' includes any officer charged with the execution of a writ or other process.

---

**Notes**
**Section 501**

1. "Company" means a company formed and registered under this Act or, as the case may be, formed and registered in Nigeria before and in existence on the commencement of this Act. **See section 567, CAMA C20 LFN 2004**
2. "Liquidator" means a person who is appointed to wind up a business's affairs esp. by selling off its assets. See **Garner B. (ed) Black's Law Dictionary, 8th ed.**
3. "Winding up" means the process of settling accounts and liquidating assets in anticipation of a partnership's or a corporation's dissolution. See **Garner B. (ed) Black's law dictionary 8th ed.**
4. "Resolution" means a main motion that formally expresses the sense, will, or action of a deliberative assembly.See **Garner B. (ed.) Black's Law Dictionary 8th ed.**
5. "Voluntary winding up" has the meaning assigned to it by **section 462(4) CAMA Cap. C20 LFN 2004.**

6. "Creditor" means one to whom a debt is owed; one who gives credit for money or goods. See **Garner B. (ed) Black's Law Dictionary, 8th ed.**
7. "Court" means the Federal High Court and to the extent to which application may be made to it as; court includes the Court of Appeal and the Supreme Court. See **section567 CAMA Cap. C20, LFN 2004**

**Cross Reference**

On distinction between members voluntary winding-up and creditors voluntary winding-up, see **section 462(4), CAMA, Cap. C20 LFN 2004**

On how a liquidator is appointed, see **section 473, CAMA Cap. C20 LFN, 2004.**

On sale of goods by Sherrif, see generally **section 29-31, Sherrif and Civil Processes Act, Cap. LFN 2004**

*Offences antecedent to or in course of winding up*

## 502. Offences by officers of company in liquidation

(1) If any person, being a past or present officer [1] of a Company[2] which at the time of the commission of the alleged offence is being wound up,[3] whether by or under the supervision of the court[4] or voluntarily, or is subsequently ordered to be wound up[3] by the court[4] or subsequently passes a resolution [5] for voluntary winding up[6]-

(a) does not to the best of his knowledge and belief fully and truly discover or deliver to the Liquidator [7] all the property, landed and personal, of the Company, [2] and how and to whom, for what consideration and when, the Company[2] disposed of any part thereof, except such part as has been disposed of in the ordinary way of the business of the company[2]; or

(b) does not deliver up to the Liquidator, [7] or as he directs, all such part of the real and personal property of the company[2] as is in his custody or under his control, and which he is required by law to deliver up; or

(c) does not deliver up to the Liquidator [7]; or as he directs, all books and papers in his custody or under his control belonging to the company[2] and which he is required by law to deliver up; or

(d) within 12 months next before the commencement of the Winding up[3] or at any time thereafter, conceals any part of the property of the company [2] to the value of N100 or upwards, or conceals any debt due to or from the company[2]; or

(e) within 12 months next before the commencement of the winding up[3] or at any time thereafter, fraudulently removes any part of the property of the company [2] to the value of N100 or upwards; or

(f) makes any material omission in any statement relating to the affairs of the company [2]; or

(g) knowing or believing that a false debt has been proved by any person under the winding up, [3] fails for the period of one month to inform the liquidator [7] thereof; or

(h) after the commencement of the winding up [3], prevents the production of any book or paper affecting or relating to the property or affairs of the company [2]; or

(i) within 12 months next before the commencement of the winding up[3] or at any time thereafter -

(i) conceals, destroys, mutilates or falsifies, or is privy to the concealment, destruction, mutilation or falsification of the book or paper affecting or relating to the property or affairs of the company [2]; or

(ii) makes or is privy to the making of any false entry in any book or paper affecting or relating to the property or affairs of the company [2]; or

(iii) fraudulently parts with, alters or makes any omission in, or is privy to the fraudulently parting with, altering or making any omission in any document [8] affecting or relating to the property or affairs of the company[2]; or

(iv) at any meeting[9] of the creditors [10] of the company,[2] attempts to account for any part of the property of the company[2] by fictitious losses or expenses; or

(v) made false representation or other fraud, obtained any property for or on behalf of the company [2] on credit which the company[2] does not subsequently pay for; or

(vi) under the false pretence that the company [2] is carrying on its business, obtains on credit, for or on behalf of the company[2] any property which the company [2] does not subsequently pay for; or

(vii) pawns, pledges or disposes of any property of the company[2] which has been obtained on credit and has not been paid for, unless such pawning, pledging, or disposing is in the ordinary way of the business of the company[2]; or

(j) is guilty of any false representation or other fraud for the purpose of obtaining the consent of the creditors [10] of the company[2] or any of them to an agreement with reference to the affairs of the company [2] or to the winding up,[3] he shall be guilty of an offence and shall, in the case of the offences mentioned respectively in sub-paragraphs (iv), (v) and (vi) of this subsection, be liable on conviction to imprisonment for a term of 12 months, and in the case of any other offence under this subsection, shall be liable on conviction to imprisonment for a term of two years:

Provided that it shall be a good defence to a charge under any of paragraphs (a), (b), (c), (d), (f), (v) and (vi) of this subsection, if the accused proves that he had no intent to defraud, and to a charge under any of paragraphs (h), (i) and (j), if he proves he had no intention to conceal the state of affairs of the company or to defeat the law.

(2) Where any person pawns, pledges or disposes of any property in circumstances which amount to an offence under sub-paragraph (vii) of paragraph (i) of subsection (1) of this section, every person who takes in pawn or pledge, or otherwise receives the property knowing it to be pawned, pledged or disposed of in such circumstances as aforesaid, shall be guilty of an offence, and on conviction thereof liable to be punished in the same way as if he had received the property knowing it to have been obtained in circumstances amounting to an offence.

(3) For the purposes of this section, "officer" [1] includes any person in accordance with whose directions or instructions the directors of a company have been accustomed to act.

---

**Notes**
**Section 502(1)**

1. "Officer" in relation to a body corporate, includes a director, manager or secretary. See **section 567 CAMA Cap. C20, LFN 2004**
2. "Company" means a company formed and registered under this Act or, as the case may be, formed and registered in Nigeria before and in existence on the commencement of this Act. **See section 567, CAMA C20 LFN 2004**
3. "Wound up" see "winding up." It means the process of settling accounts and liquidating assets in anticipation of a partnership's or a corporation's dissolution. See **Garner B. (ed) Blacks' Law Dictionary, 8th ed.**
4. "Court" means the Federal High Court and to the extent to which application may be made to it as; court includes the Court of Appeal and the Supreme Court. See **section567 CAMA Cap. C20, LFN 2004**
5. "Resolution" means a main motion that formally expresses the sense, will, or action of a deliberative assembly.See **Garner B. (ed.) Black's Law Dictionary 8th ed.**
6. "Voluntary wound up" has the meaning assigned to it by **section 462(4) CAMA Cap. C20 LFN 2004.**
7. "Liquidator" means a person who is appointed to wind up a business's affairs esp. by selling off its assets. See **Garner B(ed) Black's Law Dictionary, 8th ed.**
8. "Document" includes summons, notice, order and other legal process, and register. See **section 567 CAMA Cap. C20, LFN 2004**
9. "Meeting" means an assembling of a number of persons for the purpose of discussing and acting upon some matter or matters in which they have a common interest. See **Garner B.(ed) Black's Law Dictionary, 8th ed.**
10. "Creditor" means one to whom a debt is owed whether contractual or otherwise. See **Garner B. (ed.) Black's Law Dictionary 8th ed.**

---

## 503. Falsification of books

If any officer [1] or Contributory [2] of any Company [3] being wound up[4] destroys, mutilates, alters or falsifies any books, papers or securities, or makes or is privy to the making of any false or fraudulent entry in any register, book of account or document [5] belonging to the company[3] with intent to defraud or deceive any person, he shall be guilty of an offence and liable on conviction to imprisonment for a term of two years or a fine of N2,500.

---

**Notes**
**Section 503**

1. "Officer" in relation to a body corporate, includes a director, manager or secretary. See **section 567 CAMA Cap. C20, LFN 2004.**
2. "Contributory" means every person liable to contribute to the assets of a company in the event of its being wound up and for the purposes of all proceedings for determining and all proceedings prior to the final determination of the persons who are to be deemed contributories, the expression shall include any person alleged to be a contributory. **See section403 CAMA Cap. C20 LFN 2004.**
   "Contributory" means one who contributes or who has a duty to contribute. A person who, as a result of being or representing a past or present member of a corporation, is liable to contribute to the corporation's debts upon its winding up. **See Garner B. (ed) Black's Law Dictionary, 8th ed.**
3. "Company" means a company formed and registered under this Act or, as the case may be, formed and registered in Nigeria before and in existence on the commencement of this Act. **See section 567, CAMA C20 LFN 2004.**
4. "Wound up" see "winding up." It means the process of settling accounts and liquidating assets in anticipation of a partnership's or a corporation's dissolution. See **Garner B. (ed) Blacks' Law Dictionary, 8th ed.**
5. "Document" includes summons, notice, order and other legal process, and register. See **section 567 CAMA Cap. C20, LFN 2004**

Cross Reference

On the meaning of offence, see **section 2, Criminal Code Cap. C38 LFN 2004**

---

## 504. Frauds by officers of companies in liquidation

If any person, being at the time of the commission of the alleged offence an officer[1] of a Company[2] which is subsequently ordered to be wound up[3] by the court,[4] or subsequently passes a resolution[5] for voluntary winding up[6]-

(a) has by false pretences or by means of any other fraud induced any person to give credit to the Company[2]; or

(b) with intent to defraud creditors[7] of the company,[2] has made or caused to be made any gift or transfer of or charge on, or has caused or connived at the levying of any execution against, the property of the company[2]; or

(c) with intent to defraud creditors[7] of the company,[2] has concealed or removed any part of the property of the company[2] since, or within two months before, the date of any unsatisfied judgment or order for payment of money obtained against the company[3], he shall be guilty of an offence and liable on conviction to imprisonment for a term of two years.

---

**Notes**

**Section 504**

1. "Officer" in relation to a body corporate, includes a director, manager or secretary. See **section 567 CAMA Cap. C20, LFN 2004**
2. "Company" means a company formed and registered under this Act or, as the case may be, formed and registered in Nigeria before and in existence on the commencement of this Act. **See section 567, CAMA C20 LFN 2004**
3. "Wound up" see "winding up." It means the process of settling accounts and liquidating assets in anticipation of a partnership's or a corporation's dissolution. See **Garner B. (ed) Blacks' Law Dictionary, 8th ed.**
4. "Court" means the Federal High Court and to the extent to which application may be made to it as; court includes the Court of Appeal and the Supreme Court. See **section567 CAMA Cap. C20, LFN 2004**
5. "Resolution" means a main motion that formally expresses the sense, will, or action of a deliberative assembly. See **Garner B. (ed.) Black's Law Dictionary 8th ed.**
6. "Voluntary wound up" has the meaning assigned to it by **section 462(4) CAMA Cap. C20 LFN 2004**
7. "Creditor" means one to whom a debt is owed; one who gives credit for money or goods. See **Garner B. (ed) Black's Law Dictionary, 8 th ed.**

Cross Reference

On meaning of offence, see **section 2, Criminal Code Cap. C38, LFN 2004**

---

## 505. Liability where proper accounts not kept

(1) If, where a company [1] is wound up, [2] it is shown that proper books of account were not kept by the company [1] throughout the period of two years immediately preceding the commencement of the Winding up [2] or the period between the incorporation [3] of this company [1] and the commencement of the winding up, [2] whichever is the shorter, every officer [4] of the Company [1] who is in default shall, unless he shows that he acted honestly and that in the circumstances in which the business of the company [1] was carried on the default was excusable, be guilty of an offence and be liable on conviction in the court to a fine of N250.

(2) For the purposes of this section, proper books of account shall be deemed not to have been kept in the case of any Company [1]

if there have not been kept such books of accounts as are necessary to exhibit and explain the transactions and financial position of the trade or business of the company, including books containing entries from day to day in sufficient detail of all cash received and cash paid; and, where the trade or business has involved dealing in goods, statements of the annual stocktakings and (except in case of goods sold by way of ordinary retail trade) of all goods sold and purchased, showing the goods and the buyers and sellers thereof in sufficient details to enable those goods and those buyers and sellers to be identified.

---

**Notes**
**Section 505(1)**

1. "Company" means a company formed and registered under this Act or, as the case may be, formed and registered in Nigeria before and in existence on the commencement of this Act. **See section 567, CAMA C20 LFN 2004**
2. "Wound up" see "winding up." It means the process of settling accounts and liquidating assets in anticipation of a partnership or dissolution. See **Garner B. (ed.) Black's Law Dictionary 8 th ed.**
3. "Incorporation" means the formation of an association that has corporate personality, i.e a personality distinct from its members. **Martins, E. (ed.) Oxford Dictionary of Law 4th ed.**
4. "Officer" in relation to a body corporate, includes a director, manager or secretary. See **section 567 CAMA Cap. C20, LFN 2004**

Cross Reference

On meaning of offence, see **section 2, Criminal Code Cap. C38, LFN 2004**

---

## 506. Responsibility for fraudulent trading

(1) If, in the course of the winding up [1] of a company,[2] it appears that any business of the company [2] has been carried on in a reckless manner or with intent to defraud creditors [3] of the company[2] or creditors [3] of any other person for any fraudulent purpose, the court, [4] on the application of the official receiver, [5] or the Liquidator[6] or any Creditor [3] or Contributory [7] of the company,[2] may, if it thinks proper so to do, declare that any persons who were knowingly parties to the carrying on of the business in manner aforesaid shall be personally responsible, without any limitation of Liability for all or any of the debts or other liabilities of the Company[2] as the court [4] may direct.

(2) Where the court [4] makes a declaration as to responsibility for debts or liabilities under subsection (1) of this section, it may give any direction it thinks proper for the purpose of giving effect to that declaration, and in particular the court [4] may make provision for making the Liability of any such person under the declaration a charge on any debt or obligation due from the Company [2] to him, or on any mortgage[8] or charge[9] or any interest in any mortgage [8] or charge[9] or any assets of the Company [2] held by or vested in him, or any Company[2] or person on his behalf, or any person claiming as assignee from or through the person liable or any Company [2] or person acting on his behalf, and may from time to time make any further order necessary for enforcing any charge imposed under this subsection.

(3) Where any business of a Company [2] is carried on with such intent or for such purpose as is mentioned in subsection (1) of this section (other than recklessly), every person who was knowingly a party to the carrying on of the business in manner aforesaid, shall be guilty of an offence, and liable on conviction to a fine of N2,500 or to imprisonment for a term of two years, or to both.

(4) In its operation, this section shall have effect, so however that-

(a) a declaration may be made notwithstanding that the person concerned may be criminally liable in respect of matters which are grounds for the declaration and a declaration, if made, shall be deemed to be a final judgment of the court;

(b) the official receiver [5] or the Liquidator, [6] as the case may be, on the hearing of an application to the court, [4] may himself give evidence or call witnesses;

(c) there shall be included in the expression "assignee" any person to whom or in whose favour by the direction of the person liable the debt, obligation, mortgage, [8] or charge [9] was created, issued or transferred, or the interest created, other than any person being an assignee for valuable consideration given in good faith and without notice of any of the matters on the ground of which the declaration is made;

(d) "valuable consideration" shall not include consideration by way of marriage.

---

**Notes**

**Section 506(1)**

1. "Winding up" means the process of settling accounts and liquidating assets in anticipation of a partnership or dissolution. See **Garner B. (ed.) Black's Law Dictionary 8 th ed.**
2. "Company" means a company formed and registered under this Act or, as the case may be, formed and registered in Nigeria before and in existence on the commencement of this Act. **See section 567, CAMA C20 LFN 2004**
3. "Creditor" means one to whom a debt is owed; one who gives credit for money or goods. See **Garner B. (ed) Black's Law Dictionary, 8 th ed.**
4. "Court" means the Federal High Court and to the extent to which application may be made to it as; court includes the Court of Appeal and the Supreme Court. See **section567 CAMA Cap. C20, LFN 2004**
5. "Official Receiver" means the officer by whatever name called or known charged with control of affairs in bankruptcy and if the appointment is vacant for any reason whatsoever, means the sheriff. See **section 567 CAMA Cap. C20, LFN 2004**
6. "Liquidator" means a person who is appointed to wind up a business's affairs esp. by selling off its assets. See **Garner B. (ed) Black's Law Dictionary, 8th ed.**
7. "Contributory" means every person liable to contribute to the assets of a company in the event of its being wound up and for the purposes of all proceedings for determining and all proceedings prior to the final determination of the persons who are to be deemed contributories, the expression shall include any person alleged to be a contributory. **See section 403 CAMA Cap. C20 LFN 2004**

   "Contributory" means one who contributes or who has a duty to contribute. A person who, as a result of being or representing a past or present member of a corporation, is liable to contribute to the corporation's debts upon its winding up. **See Garner B. (ed) Black's Law Dictionary, 8th ed.**
8. "Mortgage" means a conveyance of title to property that is given as security for the payment of a debt or the performance of a duty and that will become void upon payment or performance according to the stipulated terms. See **Garner B. (ed) Black's Law Dictionary, 8th ed.**
9. "Charge" means an encumbrance, lien or claim. **Garner B. (ed.) Black's Law Dictionary 8th ed.**

**Cross Reference**

On how a liquidator is appointed, see **section 473, CAMA Cap. C20 LFN, 2004.**

On modes of winding up a company, see **section 401, CAMA Cap. C20, LFN 2004**

On the establishment of the Federal High Court and its jurisdiction, see **section 249 &251, Constiution of the Federal Republic of Nigeria, 1999(as amended).**

**Cases**

A Liquidator owes a duty to the whole body of creditors and shareholders and to the court to make himself thoroughly acquainted with the affairs of the company and suppress or conceal anything coming to his knowledge in the course of his investigation which is material; ***Re J.A. Balogun* (1977) FRCR 122**

## 507.Power of court to assess damages against delinquent directors, etc.

(1) If, in the course of Winding up [1] a Company,[2] it appears that any person who has taken part in the formation or promotion of the Company,[2] or any past or present director, [3] manager[4] or Liquidator,[5] or any officer[6] of the Company,[2] has misapplied or retained or become liable or accountable for any money or Property of the Company[2], or been guilty of any misfeasance or breach of duty in relation to the company [2] which would involve civil liability at the suit of the company, [2] the court[7] may, on the application of the official receiver,[8] or of the liquidator, [5] or of any creditor [9] or contributory[10] examine into the conduct of the promoter, [11] director,[3] liquidator[5] or officer,[6] and compel him to repay or restore the money or property or any part thereof respectively with interest at such rates as the court thinks just, or to contribute such sum to the assets of the company[2] by way of compensation in respect of the misapplication, retainer, misfeasance or breach of trust as the court thinks just.

(2) The provisions of this section shall extend to any receiver of the property of a Company, [2] and shall in any case have effect notwithstanding that the offence is one for which the offender may be criminally liable.

(3) Where an order for payment of money is made under this section, the order shall be deemed to be a final judgment of the court.[7]

**Note**

**Section 507(1)**

1. "Winding up" means the process of settling accounts and liquidating assets in anticipation of a partnership or dissolution. See **Garner B. (ed.) Black's Law Dictionary 8 th ed.**
2. "Company" means a company formed and registered under this Act or, as the case may be, formed and registered in Nigeria before and in existence on the commencement of this Act. **See section 567, CAMA C20 LFN 2004**
3. "Director" includes any person occupying the position of director by whatever name called; and includes any person in accordance with whose directions or instructions the directors of the company are accustomed to act. See **section 567 CAMA Cap. C20, LFN 2004**
4. "Manager" means a person who administers or supervises the affairs of a business, office, or other organization. See **Garner B. (ed) Black's Law Dictionary, 8th ed.**
5. "Liquidator" means a person who is appointed to wind up a business's affairs esp. by selling off its assets. See **Garner B. (ed) Black's Law Dictionary, 8 th ed.**
6. "Officer" in relation to a body corporate, includes a director, manager or secretary. See **section 567 CAMA Cap. C20, LFN 2004**
7. "Court" means the Federal High Court and to the extent to which application may be made to it as; court includes the Court of Appeal and the Supreme Court. See **section567 CAMA Cap. C20, LFN 2004**
8. "official Reciever" means the officer by whatever name called or known charged with control of affairs in bankruptcy and if the appointment is vacant for any reason whatsoever, means the sheriff. See **section 567 CAMA Cap. C20, LFN 2004**
9. "Creditor" means one to whom a debt is owed; one who gives credit for money or goods. See **Garner B. (ed) Black's Law Dictionary, 8 th ed.**
10. "Contributory" means every person liable to contribute to the assets of a company in the event of its being wound up and for the purposes of all proceedings for determining and all proceedings prior to the final determination of the persons who are to be deemed contributories, the expression shall include any person alleged to be a contributory. See **section 403 CAMA Cap. C20 LFN 2004**

    "Contributory" means one who contributes or who has a duty to contribute. A person who, as a result of being or representing a past or present member of a corporation, is liable to contribute to the corporation's debts upon its winding up. See **Garner B. (ed) Black's Law Dictionary, 8th ed.**
11. "Promoter" means Any person who undertakes to take part in forming a company1 with reference to a given project and to set it going and who takes the necessary steps to accomplish that purpose, or who, with regard to a proposed or newly formed company1, undertakes a part in raising capital for it. See **section 61 CAMA Cap. C20, LFN 2004**

**Cross Reference**

On meaning of offence, see **section 2, Criminal Code, Cap. C38, LFN 2004**

**Cases**

Section 61 defines a promoter as- any person who undertakes to take part in forming a company with reference to a given project and to set it going and who takes the necessary steps to accomplish that purpose, or who, with regard to a proposed or newly formed company, undertakes a part in raising capital for it, shall, prima facie, be deemed a promoter of the company: Provided that a person acting in a professional capacity for persons engaged in procuring the formation of the company shall not thereby be deemed to be a promoter. ***Adeniji v. Starcola (Nigeria) Ltd.*** **Suit No. M.135/70 unreported, H.C. Lagos.**

Whilst receivership and manager open exclusively dominate the company affairs and dealings with the outside world, it does not affect the internal domestic structure of the company ***: Unibiz (Nig.) Ltd. v. Commercial Bank Credit Lyonnais Nig. Ltd.(for and on behalf of Babington Ashaye (2001) 7NWLR (pt 713) 534.***

**For Further Reading**

On promoters, see, Orojo, J. Ola **Company Law and Practice in Nigeria** 3rd Edition, Mbeyi & Associates (Lagos, Nigeria) 1992. P.p 74-78.

## 508. Prosecution of delinquent officers and members of a company

(1) If it appears to the court, [1] in the course of Winding up [2] by, or subject to the supervision of the court, [1] that any past or present officer, [3] or any member [4] of the company [5] has been guilty of any offence in relation to the Company [5] for which he is criminally liable, the court [1] may, either on the application of any person interested in the Winding up [2] or of its own motion direct the Liquidator[6] to refer the matter to the Attorney-General of the Federation.

(2) If it appears to the Liquidator [6] in the course of a voluntary winding up[7] that any past or present officer, [3] or any member [4] of the Company[5] has been guilty of any offence in relation to the Company[5] for which he is criminally liable, he shall forthwith report the matter to the Attorney-General of the Federation and shall furnish him such information and give to him such access to and facilities for inspecting and taking copies of any documents [8] being information or documents [8] in the possession or under the control of the Liquidator [6] and relating to the matter in question, as he may require.

(3) Where any report is made under subsection (2) of this section to the Attorney-General of the Federation he may, if he thinks fit, apply to the court [1] for an order conferring on him or any person designated by him for the purpose with respect to the company[5] concerned, all such powers of investigating the affairs of the company[2] as are provided by this Act in the case of a Winding up[2] by the court. [1]

(4) If it appears to the court [1] in the course of a voluntary Winding up[7] that any past or present officer, [3] or any member [4] of the Company[5] has been guilty as aforesaid, and that no report with respect to the matter has been made by the Liquidator [6] to the Attorney-General of the Federation under subsection (2) of this section, the court [1] may on the application of any person interested in the Winding up [2] or of its own motion, direct the Liquidator [6] to make such a report, and on a report being made accordingly, the provisions of this section shall have effect as though the report had been made in pursuance of the provisions of subsection (2) of this section.

(5) If, where any matter is reported or referred to the Attorney-General of the Federation under this section, he considers that the case is one in which a prosecution ought to be instituted, he shall institute proceedings accordingly, and it shall be the duty of the Liquidator[6] and of every other officer [3] and agent of the Company[5] past and present (other than the defendant in the proceedings) to give him all assistance in connection with the prosecution which he is reasonably able to give and it is hereby declared for the purposes of this subsection, that the expression "agent" in relation to a Company [5] includes any banker or solicitor of the Company[5] and any person employed by the Company [5] as auditor, whether that person is or is not an officer [3] of the Company[5].

(6) If any person fails or neglects to give assistance in the manner required by subsection (3) of this section, the court may, on the application of the Attorney-General of the Federation, direct that person to comply with the requirements of the said subsection, and where any such application is made with respect to a Liquidator[6] the court, [1] may, unless it appears that the failure or neglect to comply was due to the Liquidator [6] not having in his hands sufficient assets of the Company [5] to enable him so to do,

direct that the costs of the application shall be borne by the Liquidator[6] personally.

---

**Notes**

**Section 508(1)**

1. "Court" means the Federal High Court and to the extent to which application may be made to it as; court includes the Court of Appeal and the Supreme Court. See **section567 CAMA Cap. C20, LFN 2004**
2. "Winding up" means the process of settling accounts and liquidating assets in anticipation of a partnership or dissolution. See **Garner B. (ed.) Black's Law Dictionary 8 th ed.**
3. "Officer" in relation to a body corporate, includes a director, manager or secretary. See **section 567 CAMA Cap. C20, LFN 2004**
4. "Member" includes the heir, executor, administrator, or other personal representatives, as the case may be, of the member. See **section 567 CAMA Cap. C20 LFN 2004**
5. "Company" means a company formed and registered under this Act or, as the case may be, formed and registered in Nigeria before and in existence on the commencement of this Act. **See section 567, CAMA C20 LFN 2004**
6. "Liquidator" means a person who is appointed to wind up a business's affairs esp. by selling off its assets. See **Garner B(ed) Black's Law Dictionary, 8th ed.**

**Section 508(2)**

7. "Voluntary winding up" has the meaning assigned to it by **section 462(4) CAMA Cap. C20 LFN 2004**
8. "Documents" includes summons, notice, order and other legal process, and register. See **section 567 CAMA Cap. C20, LFN 2004**

**Cross Reference**

On the establishment of the Office of the Attorney General of the Federation, see **section 150, Constitution of the Federal Republic of Nigeria, 1999 (as amended)**

On the establishment of the Federal High Court and its jurisdiction, see **section 249 &251, Constitution of the Federal Republic of Nigeria, 1999(as amended)**

---

*Supplementary provisions as to winding up*

## 509. Disqualifications for appointment as liquidator

(1) The following persons shall not be competent to be appointed or to act as Liquidator [1] of a Company, [2] whether in a Winding up[3] by, or under the supervision of the court, [4] or in a voluntary winding up[5]-

(a) an infant;

(b) anyone found by the court to be of unsound mind;
(c) a body corporate;
(d) an undischarged bankrupt [6];
(e) any director [7] of the company [2] under Liquidation;
(f) any person convicted of any offence involving fraud, dishonesty, official corruption or moral turpitude and in respect of whom there is a subsisting order under section 254 of this Act.

(2) Any appointment made in contravention of the provisions of subsection (1) of this section shall be void and if any of the persons named in paragraphs (c), (d) (e), and (f) of that subsection shall act as a Liquidator [1] of the Company, [2] he shall be guilty of an offence and liable to a fine not exceeding N2,500 in the case of a body corporate or, in the case of an individual, to imprisonment for a term not exceeding six months or to a fine not exceeding N500 or to both such imprisonment and fine.

---

**Notes**
**Section 509 (1)**

1. "Liquidator" means a person appointed to wind up business affairs, esp. by selling off its assets. See **Garner B. (ed) Black's Law Dictionary, 8th ed.**
2. "Company" means a company formed and registered under this Act or, as the case may be, formed and registered in Nigeria before and in existence on the commencement of this Act. **See section 567, CAMA C20 LFN 2004**
3. "Winding up" means the process of settling accounts and liquidating assets in anticipation of a partnership or dissolution. See **Garner B. (ed.) Black's Law Dictionary 8 th ed.**
4. "Court" means the Federal High Court and to the extent to which application may be made to it as; court includes the Court of Appeal and the Supreme Court. See **section567 CAMA Cap. C20, LFN 2004**
5. "Voluntary winding up" has the meaning assigned to it by **section 462(4) CAMA Cap. C20 LFN 2004**
6. "Bankrupt" means a person who cannot meet current financial obligations; an insolvent person. **Garner B. (ed) Black's Law Dictionary 8th ed.**
7. "Director" includes any person occupying the position of director by whatever name called; and includes any person in accordance with whose directions or instructions the directors of the company are accustomed to act. See **section 567 CAMA Cap. C20, LFN 2004**

**Cross Reference**

On meaning of offence, see **section 2, Criminal Code, Cap. C38, LFN 2004**

On the establishment of the Federal High Court and its jurisdiction, see **section 249 &251, Constitution of the Federal Republic of Nigeria, 1999(as amended)**

As to when a debtor commits an act of bankruptcy, see **section 1, Bankruptcy Act, Cap. B2, LFN 2004.**

---

## 510.Corrupt inducement affecting appointment as liquidator

Any person who gives or agrees or offers to give to any member[1] or creditor [2] of a company[3] any valuable consideration with a view to securing his own appointment or nomination, or to securing or preventing the appointment or nomination of some person other than himself as the company's [3] liquidator,[4] shall be guilty of an offence and liable to a fine of n250.

---

**Notes**

**Section 510**

1. "Member" includes the heir, executor, administrator, or other personal representatives, as the case may be, of the member. See **section 567 CAMA Cap. C20 LFN 2004**
2. "Creditor" means one to whom a debt is owed; one who gives credit for money or goods. See **Garner B. (ed) Black's Law Dictionary, 8 th ed.**
3. "Company" means a company formed and registered under this Act or, as the case may be, formed and registered in Nigeria before and in existence on the commencement of this Act. **See section 567, CAMA C20 LFN 2004**
4. "Liquidator" means a person appointed to wind up business affairs, esp. by selling off its assets. See **Garner B. (ed) Black's Law Dictionary, 8th ed.**

Cross Reference

On meaning of offence, see **section 2, Criminal Code, Cap. C38, LFN 2004**

---

## 511.Enforcement of duty of liquidator to make returns, etc.

(1) If a liquidator [1] makes default in filing, delivering or making any return, account or other document, [2] or in giving any notice which he is by law required to file, deliver, make or give, and fails to make good the default within 14 days after the service on him of a notice requiring him to do so, the court [3] may, on an application made to the court [3] by any contributory [4] or Creditor [5] of

the Company[6] or by the commission, make an order directing the liquidator[1] to make good the default within such time as is specified in the order.

(2) Any order under this section may provide that the costs of any expenses incidental to the application shall be borne by the liquidator[1] and nothing in this section shall be taken to prejudice the operation of any enactment imposing penalties on a liquidator [1] in respect of any such default.

---

**Notes**
**Section 511(1)**

1. "Liquidator" means a person appointed to wind up business affairs, esp. by selling off its assets. See **Garner B. (ed) Black's Law Dictionary, 8th ed.**
2. "Document" includes summons, notice, order and other legal process, and register. See **section 567 CAMA Cap. C20, LFN 2004.**
3. "Court" means the Federal High Court and to the extent to which application may be made to it as; court includes the Court of Appeal and the Supreme Court. See **section567 CAMA Cap. C20, LFN 2004**
4. "Contributory" means every person liable to contribute to the assets of a company in the event of its being wound up and for the purposes of all proceedings for determining and all proceedings prior to the final determination of the persons who are to be deemed contributories, the expression shall include any person alleged to be a contributory. See **section 403 CAMA Cap. C20 LFN 2004.**
   "Contributory" means one who contributes or who has a duty to contribute. A person who, as a result of being or representing a past or present member of a corporation, is liable to contribute to the corporation's debts upon its winding up. See **Garner B. (ed) Black's Law Dictionary, 8th ed.**
5. "Creditor" means one to whom a debt is owed; one who gives credit for money or goods. See **Garner B. (ed) Black's Law Dictionary, 8 th ed.**
6. "Company" means a company formed and registered under this Act or, as the case may be, formed and registered in Nigeria before and in existence on the commencement of this Act. **See section 567, CAMA C20 LFN 2004**

**Cross Reference**

On meaning of offence, see **section 2, Criminal Code, Cap. C38, LFN 2004**

On the establishment of the Federal High Court and its jurisdiction, see **section 249 &251, Constitution of the Federal Republic of Nigeria, 1999(as amended).**

## 512. Notification that a company is in liquidation

(1) Where a company[1] is being wound up,[2] whether by or under the supervision of the court[3] or voluntarily, every invoice, order for goods or business letter issued by or on behalf of the company[1] or a liquidator[4] of the company,[1] or a receiver[5] or manager[6] of the property of the company,[1] being a document[7] on or in which the name of the company[1] appears, shall contain a statement that the company[1] is being wound up.[2]

(2) If default is made in complying with the provisions of this section, the company[1] and any of the following persons who knowingly and wilfullyauthorises or permits the default, namely, any officer[8] of the company,[1] any liquidator[2] of the company[1] and any receiver[5] or manager,[6] shall be guilty of an offence and liable to a fine of N100.

---

**Notes**

**Section 512(1)**

1. "Company" means a company formed and registered under this Act or, as the case may be, formed and registered in Nigeria before and in existence on the commencement of this Act. **See section 567, CAMA C20 LFN 2004.**
2. "Wound up" see "winding up." It means the process of settling accounts and liquidating assets in anticipation of a partnership or dissolution. See **Garner B. (ed.) Black's Law Dictionary 8 th ed.**
3. "Court" means the Federal High Court and to the extent to which application may be made to it as; court includes the Court of Appeal and the Supreme Court. See **section567 CAMA Cap. C20, LFN 2004.**
4. "Liquidator" means a person appointed to wind up business affairs, esp. by selling off its assets. See **Garner B. (ed) Black's Law Dictionary, 8th ed.**
5. "Receiver" means a disinterested person appointed by a court, or by a corporation or other person, for the protection or collection of property that is subject of diverse claims. See **Garner B. (ed.) Black's Law Dictionary 8th ed.**

   "Receiver includes manager. See **section 567 CAMA Cap. C20, LFN 2004.**
6. "Manager" means a person who administers or supervises the affairs of a business, office, or other organization. See **Garner B. (ed) Black's Law Dictionary, 8th ed.**
7. "Document" includes summons, notice, order and other legal process, and register. See **section 567 CAMA Cap. C20, LFN 2004.**

**Cross Reference**

On meaning of offence, see **section 2, Criminal Code, Cap. C38, LFN 2004**

On the establishment of the Federal High Court and its jurisdiction, see **section 249 &251, Constitution of the Federal Republic of Nigeria, 1999(as amended).**

---

## 513. Exemption from Stamp duty

(1) In the case of a winding up [1] by the court, [2] or a creditors' voluntary winding up[3]-

(a) every assurance relating to any property of the company [4], or to any mortgage, [5] charge[6] or other encumbrance thereon or any right or interest in any property, in any event forming part of the assets of the company [4] and which, after the execution of the assurance, either at law or in equity is, or remains part of the assets of the company[4]; and

(b) every power of Attorney [7], proxy paper, writ, order, certificate, affidavit, [8] bond or other instrument or writing relating solely to the property of any company [4] which is being so wound up, [1] or to any proceeding under any such winding up,[1] shall be exempted from duties chargeable under any law, enactment relating to stamp duties.

(2) In this section, "assurance" includes any deed, Conveyance, instrument, discharge, assignment or surrender.

---

**Notes**

**Section 513 (1)**

1. "Winding up" means the process of settling accounts and liquidating assets in anticipation of a partnership or dissolution. See **Garner B. (ed) Black's Law Dictionary, 8th ed.**
2. "Court" means the Federal High Court and to the extent to which application may be made to it as; court includes the Court of Appeal and the Supreme Court. See **section567 CAMA Cap. C20, LFN 2004**
3. "Voluntary winding up" has the meaning assigned to it by **section 462(4) CAMA Cap. C20 LFN 2004**
4. "Company" means a company formed and registered under this Act or, as the case may be, formed and registered in Nigeria before and in existence on the commencement of this Act. **See section 567, CAMA C20 LFN 2004**
5. "Mortgage" means a conveyance of title to property that is given as security for the payment of a debt or the performance of a duty and that will become void upon payment or performance according to the stipulated terms. See **Garner B. (ed) Black's Law Dictionary, 8th ed.**

6. "Charge" means an encumbrance, lien or claim. See **Garner B. (ed.) Black's Law Dictionary 8th ed.**
7. "Power of attorney" means an instrument granting someone authority to act as agent. See **Garner B. (ed) Black's Law Dictionary, 8th ed.**
8. "Affidavit" means a voluntary declaration of facts written down and sworn to by the declarant before an officer authorized to administer oaths, such as a notary public. See **Garner B. (ed) Black's Law Dictionary, 8th ed.**

**Cross Reference**

On instruments on which stamp duties are paid, see generally, **Stamp Duties Act Cap. 58 LFN 2004**

On creditors voluntary winding up see **sections 471-478CAMA Cap. C20, LFN 2004.**

---

## 514. Books of company to be evidence

Where a company [1] is being wound up, [2] all books and papers of the company[1] and of the liquidators [3] shall, as between the contributories[4] of the company, [1] be prima facie evidence of the truth of all matters purporting to be therein recorded.

---

**Notes**

**Section 514**

1. "Company" means a company formed and registered under this Act or, as the case may be, formed and registered in Nigeria before and in existence on the commencement of this Act. **See section 567, CAMA C20 LFN 2004**
2. "Wound up" see "winding up". It means the process of settling accounts and liquidating assets in anticipation of a partnership or dissolution. **See Garner B. (ed) Black's Law Dictionary, 8th ed.**
3. "Liquidators" see "liquidator". It means a person appointed to wind up business affairs, esp. by selling off its assets. See **Garner B. (ed) Black's Law Dictionary, 8 th ed.**

   A business organization that makes money by producing or selling goods and services. **Oxford Advanced Learners Dictionary. 6 th ed.**
4. " Contributories" see "Contributory." It means means every person liable to contribute to the assets of a company in the event of its being wound up and for the purposes of all proceedings for determining and all proceedings prior to the final determination of the persons who are to be deemed contributories, the expression shall include any person alleged to be a contributory. See **section 403 CAMA Cap. C20 LFN 2004**

   "Contributory" means one who contributes or who has a duty to contribute. A person who, as a result of being or representing a past or present member of a corporation, is liable to contribute to the corporation's debts upon its winding up. See **Garner B. (ed) Black's Law Dictionary, 8th ed.**

Cross Reference

On production of the books of account as primary evidence to prove its content, see **section 86 Evidence Act, 2011**

---

## 515. Disposal of books, etc., of company

(1) where a company [1] is being wound up [2] and is about to be dissolved, the books and papers [3] of the company [1] and of the liquidators [4] may be disposed of as follows, that is to say-

(a) in the case of a winding up [2] by or subject to the supervision of the court, [5] in such way as the court [5] directs;

(b) in the case of a members' voluntary winding up, [6] in such way as the company [1] by special resolution [7] directs and, in the case of a creditors voluntary winding up, [8] in such way as the committee of inspection or, if there is no such committee, as the creditors [9] of the company [1], may direct.

(2) After five years from the dissolution of the com pany [1] no responsibility shall rest on the company, [1] the liquidators, [4] or any person to whom the custody of the books and papers [3] has been committed, by reason of any book or paper [3] not being forthcoming to any person claiming to be interested therein.

(3) Provisions may be made by general rules for enabling the Commission [9] to prevent, for such period (not exceeding five years from the dissolution of the company [1]) as it may think proper, the destruction of the books and papers [3] of a company [1] which has been wound up, [2] and for enabling any creditor [10] or contributory [11] of the company [1] to make representations to it and to appeal to the court [5] from any direction which may be given by it in the matter.

(4) If any person acts in contravention of any general rules made for the purposes of this section or of any direction of the Commission [9] there under, he shall be guilty of an offence and liable to a fine of N 1,000.

---

**Notes**

**Section 515(1)**

1. "Company" means a company formed and registered under this Act or, as the case may be, formed and registered in Nigeria before and in

existence on the commencement of this Act. **See section 567, CAMA C20 LFN 2004**

2. "Wound up" see "winding up." It means the process of settling accounts and liquidating assets in anticipation of a partnership or dissolution. See **Garner B. (ed) Black's Law Dictionary, 8th ed.**
3. "Books and Papers" include accounts, deeds, writings, and documents. See **section 567 CAMA, Cap. C20, LFN 2004.**
4. "Liquidators" see "liquidator". It means a person appointed to wind up business affairs, esp. by selling off its assets. See **Garner B. (ed) Black's Law Dictionary, 8 th ed**
5. "Court" used in relation to a company , means the Fedeal High Court, and to the extent to which application may be made to it as; court includes the Court of Appeal and the Supreme Court of Nigeria. See **Section 567 CAMA, Cap. C20 , LFN 2004.**
6. "Members Voluntary winding up" has the meaning assigned to it by **section 462(4) CAMA Cap. C20 LFN 2004. See section 567 CAMA Cap. C20, LFN 2004**
7. "Special Resoluion" means resolution passed by not less than three-fourths of the votes by such members of the company as being entitled to do so, vote by person or in proxy at a general meeting of which 21days notice, specifying the intention to propose the resolution is a special resolution, has been duly given. See **Section 233(2) CAMA, Cap. C20, LFN 2004**
8. "Creditor's voluntary Winding up" has the meaning assigned to it by section 462(4) of this Act. See **section 567 CAMA, Cap. C20, LFN 2004**
9. "Commission" means the Corporate Affairs Commission,established under Section 1 of this Act. **See section 567 CAMA, Cap. C20, LFN 2004**
10. "Creditors" means one to whom a debt is owed; one who gives credit for money or goods. See **Garner B. (ed) Black's Law Dictionary, 8 th ed.**
11. "Contributory" means means every person liable to contribute to the assets of a company in the event of its being wound up and for the purposes of all proceedings for determining and all proceedings prior to the final determination of the persons who are to be deemed contributories, the expression shall include any person alleged to be a contributory. See **section 403 CAMA Cap. C20 LFN 2004**

    "Contributory" means one who contributes or who has a duty to contribute. A person who, as a result of being or representing a past or present member of a corporation, is liable to contribute to the corporation's debts upon its winding up. See **Garner B. (ed) Black's Law Dictionary, 8th ed.**

**Cross Reference**

On members voluntary Winding up, **see sections 463-470 CAMA Cap. C20, LFN 2004**

On creditors voluntary winding up see **sections 471-478 CAMA Cap. C20, LFN 2004**

**516. Information as to pending liquidations and disposal of unclaimed assets**

(1) If where a Company [1] is being Wound up,[2] the Winding up[2] is not concluded within one year after its commencement, the Liquidator[3] shall, at such intervals as may be prescribed, until the Winding up[2] is concluded, send to the Commission [4] a statement in the prescribed form and containing the prescribed particulars with respect to the proceedings in and position of the Liquidation.

(2) Any person stating himself in writing to be a Creditor [5] or Contributory[6] of the Company[1] shall be entitled, by himself or by his agent at all reasonable times, on payment of the prescribed fee, to inspect the statement, and to receive a copy thereof or extract therefrom; but any person untruthfully so stating himself to be Creditor[5] or Contributory [6] shall be guilty of contempt of court, [7] and shall be punishable accordingly on the application of the Liquidator [3] or of the Official Receiver. [8]

(3) If a Liquidator [3] fails to comply with the requirements of this section, he shall be guilty of an offence and liable to a fine of N50 for each day during which the default continues.

(4) If it appears from any such statement or otherwise that a Liquidator[3] has in his custody or under his control any money representing unclaimed or undistributed assets of the company [1] which have remained unclaimed or undistributed for six months after the date of their receipt, the Liquidator [3] shall forthwith pay the same to the companies Liquidation account[9] mentioned in section 257 of this Act and shall be entitled to a certificate of receipt in the prescribed form for the money so paid, which shall be an effectual discharge to him.

(5) For the purposes of ascertaining and getting in any money payable into the companies Liquidation account[9] in pursuance of this section, the following powers may be exercised by the authorities named, that is to say-

(a) the Commission[4] may at any time order any such Liquidator[3] to submit to it an account verified by affidavit of the sums received and paid by him under or in pursuance of the Liquidation, and may direct and enforce an audit of the account and if the Liquidator [3] fails to submit the account within such reasonable time as the

Commission[4] directs, he shall be guilty of contempt of Court[7] and may, on the application of the Commission [4] to the Court[7] made for the purpose, be punished accordingly; and

(b) the Court[7] may, if default is made in submitting the account referred to in paragraph (a) of this section-

(i) by warrant addressed to any police officer, cause the Liquidator[3] to be arrested, and all books, papers and money or goods, relating to the liquidation in his possession to be seized and him and them to be safely kept until such time as the Court [7] may order;

(ii) at any time by order addressed to the Postmaster-General of the Nigerian Postal Service require that, for a period of not more than three months, letters addressed to the Liquidator [3] and sent through the post, be in course of post, redirected, sent or delivered to or at any place or places mentioned in the order;

(iii) summon the Liquidator [3] or his wife, or any person known or suspected to have in his possession any books, or papers relating to the liquidation and any money or goods belonging to the Liquidator [3] or representing any unclaimed or undistributed assets of the Company[1] as aforesaid, or summon any person whom the court[7] deems capable of giving information respecting any such books, papers, money, goods or other assets, and require any person summoned under this paragraph to produce documents [10] in his custody or under his control relating to the Liquidator's [3] dealings with the property of the company[1];

(iv) where any person on examination before it admits that he is indebted to the company, by order made on the application of the Official Receiver [8] or Liquidator,[3] direct payment to the Official Receiver [8] or Liquidator,[3] as the case may be, of the amount admitted, or any part thereof, either in full discharge of the whole amount in question or not at such time and in such manner as the court [7] thinks fit, with or without costs of the examination;

(v) Examine on Oath[11], either by word of mouth or written interrogatories, any person so brought before it concerning the Liquidator[3] and his dealings with the property of the company[1];

(vi) if any person on examination before the Court[7] admits that he has in his possession any money properly payable into the company's liquidation account[9] in pursuance of this section, order him to pay any such money forthwith into that account.

(6) Any person claiming to be entitled to money paid into the company's liquidation account[10] in pursuance of this section may apply to the Commission[4] for payment, and the Commission,[4] if the Liquidator[3] certifies the claim, may make an order for payment accordingly.

(7) An appeal shall lie to the Court[7] by any person claiming to be dissatisfied with the decision of the Commission[4] in respect of any claim made under this section.

---

**Notes**
**Section 516**

1. "Company" means a company formed and registered under this Act or, as the case may be, formed and registered in Nigeria before and in existence on the commencement of this Act. **See section 567, CAMA C20 LFN 2004**
2. "Wound up" see "winding up." It means the process of settling accounts and liquidating assets in anticipation of a partnership or dissolution. See **Garner B. (ed) Black's Law Dictionary, 8th ed.**
3. "Liquidator" means a person appointed to wind up business affairs, esp. by selling off its assets. See **Garner B. (ed) Black's Law Dictionary, 8th ed.**
4. "Commission" means the Corporate Affairs Commission,established under Section 1 of this Act. **See section 567 CAMA, Cap. C20 , LFN 2004**

**Section 516(2)**

5. "Creditor" means one to whom a debt is owed; one who gives credit for money or goods. See **Garner B. (ed) Black's Law Dictionary, 8 th ed.**
6. "Contributory" means means every person liable to contribute to the assets of a company in the event of its being wound up and for the purposes of all proceedings for determining and all proceedings prior to the final determination of the persons who are to be deemed contributories, the expression shall include any person alleged to be a contributory. See **section 403 CAMA Cap. C20 LFN 2004**

"Contributory" means one who contributes or who has a duty to contribute. A person who, as a result of being or representing a past or present member of a corporation, is liable to contribute to the corporation's debts upon its winding up. See **Garner B. (ed) Black's Law Dictionary, 8th ed.**

7. "Court" used in relation to a company , means the Fedeal High Court, and to the extent to which application may be made to it as; court includes the Court of Appeal and the Supreme Court of Nigeria. See **Section 567 CAMA, Cap. C20 , LFN 2004**
8. "Official Receiver" **Section 567 CAMA, Cap. C20 , LFN 2004**
9. "Companies Liquidation Account" means the account kept on behalf of the Commission pursuant to section 428 of this Act. See **section 567 CAMA Cap. C20, LFN 2004**
10. "Documents" includes summons, notice, order and other legal process, and register. See **section 567 CAMA Cap. C20, LFN 2004.**
11. "Oath" means an affirmation or declaration made in accordance with the relevant law. See **section 18(1) Interpretation Act LFN 2004**

Cross Reference

On opening a company liquidation Account, see **section 428 CAMA Cap. C20, LFN 2004**

---

## 517. Resolutions passed at adjourned meetings of creditors, etc.

Where a resolution[1] is passed at an adjourned meeting[2] of any creditors[3] or contributories[4] of a company[5], the resolution[1] shall, for all purposes, be treated as having been passed on the date on which it was in fact passed, and shall not be deemed to have been passed on any earlier date.

---

**Notes**

**Section 517**

1. "Resolution" means formal statement of an opinion agreed on by a committee or a council, especially by means of a vote. **Oxford Advanced Learners Dictionary, 7th ed.**
2. "Meeting" means a coming together of persons; an assembly of a number of persons for the purpose of discussing and acting upon some matters, **Black's Law Dictionary 6th ed**
3. "Creditor" means one to whom a debt is owed; one who gives credit for money or goods. See **Garner B. (ed) Black's Law Dictionary, 8th ed.**
4. "Contributory" means means every person liable to contribute to the assets of a company in the event of its being wound up and for the purposes of all proceedings for determining and all proceedings prior to the final determination of the persons who are to be deemed contributories, the expression shall include any person alleged to be a contributory. See **section 403 CAMA Cap. C20 LFN 2004.**

"Contributory" means one who contributes or who has a duty to contribute. A person who, as a result of being or representing a past or present member of a corporation, is liable to contribute to the corporation's debts upon its winding up. See **Garner B. (ed) Black's Law Dictionary, 8th ed.**

5. "Company" means a company formed and registered under this Act or, as the case may be, formed and registered in Nigeria before and in existence on the commencement of this Act. **See section 567, CAMA C20 LFN 2004**

Cross Reference

On types of resolution see **section 233 CAMA Cap. C20,LFN 2004**

---

## 518. Power to make over assets to employees

(1) On the winding up[1] of a company[2] (whether by the court[3] or voluntarily), the liquidator[4] may, subject to the following provisions of this section, make any payment which the company[2] has, before the commencement of the winding up,[1] decided to make under section 566 of this Act.

(2) The power which a company[2] may exercise by virtue only of section 566 of this act may be exercised by the liquidator[4] after the winding up[1] has commenced if, after the company's[2] liabilities have been fully satisfied and provision has been made for the costs of the winding up,[1] the exercise of that power has been sanctioned by such resolution[5] of the company[2] as would be required of the company[2] itself by subsection (3) of section 566 of this act before that commencement, as if paragraph (b) of that subsection were omitted and any other requirement applicable to its exercise by the company[2] had been met.

(3) Any payment which may be made by a company[2] under this section may be made out of the company's[2] assets which are available to the members[6] on the winding up.[1]

(4) On a winding up[1] by the court,[3] the exercise by the liquidator[4] of his powers under this section shall be subject to the court's[3] control and any creditor[7] or contributory[8] may apply to the court[3] with respect to any exercise or proposed exercise of the power.

---

**Notes**

**Section 518(1)**

1. "Winding up" means the process of settling accounts and liquidating assets in anticipation of a partnership or dissolution. **Black's Law Dictionary 8th ed.**
2. "Company" means a corporation –or, less commonly, an association, partnership, or union – that carries on a commercial or industrial enterprise. **Black's Law Dictionary, 8 th ed.** A business organization that makes money by producing or selling goods and services. **Oxford Advanced Learners Dictionary. 6 th ed.**
3. "Court" means the Fedeal High Court, and to the extent to which application may be made to it as; court includes the Court of Appeal and the Supreme Court of Nigeria; **Section 567 CAMA, Cap. C20 , LFN 2004**
4. "Liquidator" means a person appointed to wind up business affairs, esp. by selling off its assets. **Black's Law Dictionary 8th ed.** A person responsible for closing down a business and using any profits from the sale to pay its debts. **Oxford Advanced Learners Dictionary, 6 th ed**
5. "Resolution" means formal statement of an opinion agreed on by a committee or a council, especially by means of a vote. **Oxford Advanced Learners Dictionary, 7 th ed**
6. "Members" means the heir, executors, administrator or other personal representative, as the case may be of the member. **Section 567 CAMA, Cap. C20 , LFN 2004**
7. "Creditors" means a person or entity with a definite claim against another, esp. a claim that is capable of adjustment and liquidation. **Black's Law Dictionary 8thed.** A person, company somebody owes money to. **Oxford Advanced Learners Dictionary 6 th ed.**
8. "Contributory" means a person who, as a result of representing a past or present member of a corporation, is liable to contribute to the corporations debts upon its winding up. **Black's Law Dictionary 8th ed.**

Cross Reference

On modes of winding up a company, **see section 400 CAMA Cap. C20, LFN 2004**

On distribution of company property upon winding up, see **section 480 CAMA Cap. C20 LFN 2004**

On the power of a company to provide for employees on cessation or transfer of business, see section **566 CAMA Cap. C20 LFN 2004**

On the establishment and jurisdiction of the Federal High Court, see **section 249&251 Constitution od the Federal Republic of Nigeria, 1999(as amended)**

---

**Cases**

A Liquidator owes a duty to the whole body of creditors and shareholders and to the court to make himself thoroughly acquainted with the affairs of the company and suppress or conceal anything coming to his knowledge in the course of his investigation which is material; ***Re J.A. Balogun*** **(1977) FRCR 122**

*Supplementary powers of court*

## 519. Meetings to ascertain wishes of creditors and others

(1) The court [1] may, as to all matters relating to the winding up[2] of a company[3], have regard to the wishes of the creditors [4] or contributories[5] of the company[3], as proved to it by any sufficient evidence, and may, if it thinks fit, for the purposes of ascertaining those wishes, direct meetings [6] of the creditors [4] or contributories [5] to be called, held and conducted in such manner as the court [1] directs and may appoint a person to act as chairman of any such meeting [4] and to report the result thereof to the court [1].

(2) In the case of creditors, [4] regard shall be had to the value of each creditor's [4] debt.

(3) In the case of contributories, [5] regard shall be had to the number of votes conferred on each contributory [5] by this act or the articles.[7]

---

**Notes**
**Section 519 (1)**

1. "Courts" means the Fedeal High Court, and to the extent to which application may be made to itas; court includes the Court of Appeal and the Supreme Court of Nigeria; **Section 567 CAMA, Cap. C20,LFN 2004**
2. "Winding up" means the process of settling accounts and liquidating assets in anticipation of a partnership or dissolution. **Black's Law Dictionary 8th ed.**
3. "Company" means a corporation –or, less commonly, an association, partnership, or union – that carries on a commercial or industrial enterprise. **Black's Law Dictionary, 8 th ed.** A business organization that makes money by producing or selling goods and services. **Oxford Advanced Learners Dictionary. 6 th ed.**
4. "Creditors" means a person or entity with a definite claim against another, esp. a claim that is capable of adjustment and liquidation. **Black's Law Dictionary 8thed.** A person, company somebody owes money to. **Oxford Advanced Learners Dictionary 6th ed.**
5. "Contributories" means persons who, as a result of representing a past or present member of a corporation, is liable to contribute to the corporations debts upon its winding up. **Black's LawDictionary 8th ed.**
6. "Meetings" coming together of persons; an assembly of a number of persons for the purpose of discussing and acting upon some matters, **Black's Law Dictionary 6thed**

7. "Articles" means the articles of association of a company, as originally framed or as altered by special resolution. **Section 567 CAMA, Cap. C20 , LFN 2004** .

Cross Reference

On form and content of the Articles of Association, see **section 34 CAMA Cap. C20 LFN 2004**

---

## 520. Judicial notice of signatures of officers of court, etc

In all proceedings under this part of this act, all courts [1], judges, and persons judicially acting, and all officers, judicial or ministerial, of any court [1] or employed in enforcing the process of any court[1], shall take judicial notice of the signature of any officer of court and also of the official seal or stamp of a court [1] appended to or impressed on any document [2] made, issued or signed under the provisions of this part of this act, or on any official copy of any such document.[2]

---

**Notes**

**Section 520**

1. "Courts" the Fedeal High Court, and to the extent to which application may be made to it as; court includes the Court of Appeal and the Supreme Court of Nigeria; **Section 567 CAMA, Cap. C20, LFN 2004**
2. "Document" means summons, notice, order and other legal process, and registers. **Section 567 CAMA, Cap. C20, LFN 2004.**

Cross Reference

On the non-reqirement to prove facts judicially taken notice of, see **section 122(1) Evidence Act 2011**

On the obligation of the court to take judicial notice of signatures of judicial officers, see **section 122 (2) (j) Evidence Act, 2011**

On the obligation of the court to take judicial notice of the seal of all courts in Nigeria, see **section 122(2) ( e) Evidence Act, 2011**

---

## 521.Judicial notice of signatures of certain government officials

(1) Documents[1] purporting to be orders or certificates made or issued by the Attorney-General of the Federation or the Commission[2] for the purposes of this Act and to be signed by the Attorney-General of the Federation or the Accountant-General of the Federation, or under the seal of the Commission [2] or signed by any person authorized in that behalf by them or, it, and in proper case to be sealed where necessary, shall be received in evidence and

deemed to be such orders, or certificates without further proof, unless the contrary is shown.

(2) A certificate signed by the Attorney-General of the Federation or the Accountant-General of the Federation or under the seal of the Commission[2] that any order made, certificate issued, or act done, is the order, certificate or act of the Attorney-General of the Federation, Accountant-General of the Federation or the Commission,[2] as the case may be, shall be conclusive of the fact so certified.

---

**Notes**
**Section 521**

1. "Document" means summons, notice, order and other legal process, and registers. **Section 567 CAMA, Cap. C20 , LFN 2004**
2. "Commission" means the Corporate Affairs Commission. **Section 567 CAMA, Cap. C20 , LFN 2004**

**Cross Reference**

On effect of judicial notice on court, see **section 122 (1) , Evidence Act 2011**

On establishment of the position of Attorney-.General of the Federation, see **section150 Constitution of the Federal Republic of Nigeria, 1999 (as amended)**

On powers of the Attorney-General of the Federation, see section 174, **Constitution of the Federal Republic of Nigeria, 1999 (as amended)**

On the establishment of the office of the Accountant General see **Civil Service re-Organization Decree No. 43, 1988**

---

## 522. Special commissioners for receiving evidence

(1) Where a Company[1] is in course of being Wound up,[2] all magistrates shall be commissioners for the purpose of taking evidence under this Act and the court[3] may refer the whole or any part of the examination of any witnesses under this Act to any person hereby appointed commissioner.

(2) Every commissioner shall, in addition to any powers which he might lawfully exercise as a magistrate, have in the matter so referred to him all the same powers as the Court[3] of summoning and examining witnesses, of requiring the production or delivery of documents, of punishing defaults by witnesses and of allowing costs and expenses to witnesses.

(3) The examination so taken shall be returned or reported to the Court[3] in such manner as that Court[3] directs.

**Notes**
**Section 522(1)**

1. "Company" means a corporation –or, less commonly, an association, partnership, or union – that carries on a commercial or industrial enterprise. **Black's Law Dictionary, 8 th ed.** A business organization that makes money by producing or selling goods and services. **Oxford Advanced Learners Dictionary.6 th ed.**
2. "Wound up" means the process of settling accounts and liquidating assets in anticipation of a partnership or dissolution. **Black's Law Dictionary 8th ed.**
3. "Courts" means the Fedeal High Court, and to the extent to which application may be made to it as; court includes the Court of Appeal and the Supreme Court of Nigeria; **Section 567 CAMA, Cap. C20, LFN 2004.**

Cross Reference;

On examination of witnesses, see section of Evidence Act

## 523. Affidavits in Nigeria and elsewhere

An Affidavit[1] required to be sworn under the provisions or for the purposes of this Part of this Act may be sworn in Nigeria or elsewhere in accordance with the provisions of the Oaths Act or under any other enactment or law providing for the administration of Oaths[2] and all courts, Judges, commissioners, and persons acting judicially shall take judicial notice of the seal or stamp or signatures (as the case may be) of any court, Judge, person, consul, or vice-consul, attached, appended, or subscribed to any such affidavit, or to any other Document to be used for the purposes of this Part of this Act.
[Cap. O1.]

**Notes**
**Section 523**

1. "Affidavit" means a voluntary declaration of facts written down and sworn to by the declarant before an officer authorized to administer oaths, such as a notary public. **Black's Law Dictionary 8th ed.**
   A written statement that you swear is true and can be used as evidence in court. **Oxford Advanced Learners Dictionary. 6 th ed.**
2. "Oath" means an affirmation or declaration made in accordance with the relevant law, **18(1) Interpretation Act LFN 2004**
3. "Document" means summons, notice, order and other legal process, and registers. **Section 567 CAMA, Cap. C20, LFN 2004.**

**Cross Reference**

On the form of an affidavit, see **section 117 Evidence Act, 2011**

On effect of Judicial notice, **see 122 Evidence Act, 2011**

---

*Provisions as to dissolution*

## 524. Power of court to avoid dissolution of company

(1) Where a Company [1]has been dissolved, the Court [2] may at any time within two years of the date of the dissolution, on an application being made for the purpose by the Liquidator [3] of the Company[1] or by any other person who appears to the Court [2] to be interested, make an order, upon such terms as the Court [2] may think fit, declaring the dissolution to have been void, and thereupon such proceedings may be taken as might have been taken if the Company[1] had not been dissolved.

(2) It shall be the duty of the person on whose application the order was made, within seven days after the making of the order, or such further time as the Court [2] may allow, to deliver to the Commission[3] for registration an office copy of the order, and if that person fails so to do he shall be liable to a fine ofN25 for every day during which the default continues.

---

**Notes**

**Section 524(1)**

1. "Company" means a corporation –or, less commonly, an association, partnership, or union – that carries on a commercial or industrial enterprise. **Black's Law Dictionary, 8 th ed**

   A business organization that makes money by producing or selling goods and services. **Oxford Advanced Learners Dictionary. 6 th ed.**
2. "Courts" means the Federal High Court, and to the extent to which application may be made to it as; court includes the Court of Appeal and the Supreme Court of Nigeria; **Section 567 CAMA, Cap. C20 , LFN 2004 .**
3. "Commission" means a body of persons acting under lawful authority to perform certain public services. **Black's Law dictionary, 8th ed.**

   An official group of people who have been given the responsibility to control something, usually for the government. **Oxford advanced learners dictionary 6th ed.**

**Cross Reference**

On modes of winding up a company, see **section 401, CAMA Cap. C20, LFN 2004**

On dissolution of a company, see **sections 454 & 478 CAMA Cap. C20, LFN 2004**

On how a liquidator is appointed, see **section 473, CAMA Cap. C20 LFN, 2004.**

On the establishment of the Federal High Court and its jurisdiction, see **section 249 &251, Constiution of the Federal Republic of Nigeria, 1999(as amended)**

---

**Cases**

A Liquidator owes a duty to the whole body of creditors and shareholders and to the court to make himself thoroughly acquainted with the affairs of the company and suppress or conceal anything coming to his knowledge in the course of his investigation which is material; ***Re J.A. Balogun*** **(1977) FRCR 122**

## 525. Power of Commission to strike off defunct company

(1) Where the Commission [1] has reasonable cause to believe that a company[2] is not carrying on business or in operation, it may send to the company[2] by post a letter inquiring whether the company[2] is carrying on business or in operation.

(2) If the Commission [1] does not within one month of sending the letter receive any answer thereto, it shall within 14 days after the expiration of the month send to the company [2] by post a registered letter referring to the first letter, and stating that no answer thereto has been received, and that if an answer is not received to the second letter within one month from the date thereof, notice shall be published in the gazette [3] with a view to striking the name of the company [2] off the register.

(3) If the Commission [1] receives an answer to the effect that the company[2] is not carrying on business or in operation, or does not within one month after sending the second letter receive any answer, it may publish in the gazette [3], and send to the company [2] by post, a notice that at the expiration of three months from the date of that notice the name of the company [2] mentioned therein shall, unless cause is shown to the contrary, be struck off the register and the company[2] shall be dissolved.

(4) If, in any case where a company [2] is being wound up, [4] the Commission[1] has reasonable cause to believe either that no liquidator[5] is acting, or that the affairs of the company [2] are fully wound up,[4] and the returns required to be made by the liquidator [5] have not been made for a period of six consecutive months, the

Commission[1] shall publish in the gazette[3] and send to the company[2] or the liquidator,[5] if any, a like notice as is provided in subsection (3) of this section.

(5) At the expiration of the time mentioned in the notice the Commission[1] may, unless cause to the contrary is previously shown by the company,[2] strike its name off the register, and shall publish notice thereof in the gazette[4] and on the publication in the gazette[3] of notice as aforesaid, the company shall be dissolved:

Provided that-

(a) the liability, if any, of every director[6], managing officer[7] and member[8] of the company[2] shall continue and may be enforced as if the company[2] had not been dissolved; and

(b) nothing in this subsection shall affect the power of the court[9] to wind up[4] a company[2] the name of which has been struck off the register.

(6) Any company[2] or member[8] or creditor[10] aggrieved by the striking off the register of the company[2] under this section may apply to the court[9] at any time before the expiration of 20 years from the publication of the notice under subsection (5) of this section, for an order restoring the company[2] to the register; and if the court[9] is satisfied that, at the time of the striking off, the company[2] was carrying on business or in operation, or that otherwise it is just to restore it to the register, the court[9] may order the name of the company[2] to be restored to the register; and an order under this subsection may include any directions the court[9] thinks fit, and provision may be made therein for placing the company[2] and all other persons in the same position, as nearly as may be as, if the name of the company[2] had not been struck off the register; and upon delivery of an office copy to the Commission[1] for registration, the order shall have effect according to its tenor and may be registered accordingly.

(7) Any notice to a liquidator[5] to be sent under this section may be addressed to the liquidator[5] at his last known place of business, and any letter or notice to be sent under this section to a company[2] may be addressed to the company[2] at its registered or head office.

---

**Notes**
**Section 525(1)**

1. "Commission" means the Corporate Affairs Commission,established under Section 1 of this Act. **See section 567 CAMA, CAP C20, LFN 2004**
2. "Company" means a corporation –or, less commonly, an association, partnership, or union – that carries on a commercial or industrial enterprise See **Garner B(ed) Black's Law Dictionary, 8 th ed.**
   "Company" means a company formed and registered under this Act or, as the case may be, formed and registered in Nigeria before and in existence on the commencement of this Act. **See section 567, CAMA C20 LFN 2004**

**Section 525(2)**

3. "Gazette" means official gazette of the Federation. See **Section 567 CAMA CAP C20 LFN 2004**

**Section 525(4)**

4. "Wound up" see "winding up." It means the process of settling accounts and liquidating assets in anticipation of a partnership or dissolution. See **Garner B(ed) Black's Law Dictionary, 8 th ed.**
5. "Liquidator" means a person appointed to wind up business affairs, esp. by selling off its assets. See **Garner B. (ed) Black's Law Dictionary, 8th ed.**
6. "Director" means any person occupying the position of a director by whatever name called and includes any person in accordance with whose direction or instructions the directors of the company are accustomed to act. See **Section 567 CAMA, CAP C20 , LFN 2004.**
7. "Officer" in relation to a body corporate, includes a director, manager or secretary. See **Section 567 CAMA, CAP C20 , LFN 2004.**
8. "Member" includes the heir, executors, administrator or other personal representative, as the case may be of the member. **Section 567 CAMA, CAP C20 , LFN 2004**
9. "Court" means the Fedeal High Court, and to the extent to which application may be made to it as; court includes the Court of Appeal and the Supreme Court of Nigeria. See **Section 567 CAMA, CAP C20 , LFN 2004**
10. "Creditor" means one to whom a debt is owed; one who gives credit for money or goods. See **Garner B. (ed) Black's Law Dictionary, 8 th ed.**

**Cross Reference**

On registration of a company's memorandum and articles and effect thereof , see sec. 36 and 37 CAMA CAP C20, LFN 2004

On modes of winding up a company, see **section 401, CAMA CAP C20, LFN 2004**

On dissolution of a company, see **sections 454 & 478 CAMA CAP C20, LFN 2004**

On the establishment of the Federal High Court and its jurisdiction, see **section 249 &251, Constiution of the Federal Republic of Nigeria, 1999(as amended)**

## 526. Property of dissolved company to be declared as bona vacantia

Where a Company[1] is dissolved, all property and rights whatsoever vested in or held on trust for the Company [1] immediately before its dissolution, including leasehold Property (but not including property held by the Company [1] on trust for any other person) shall, subject and without prejudice to any order which may at any time be made by the Court [2] under section 524 or 525 of this Act, be deemed to be vested in the State without further assurance, as Bona vacantia.[3]

---

**Notes**
**Section 526**

1. "Company" means a corporation –or, less commonly, an association, partnership, or union – that carries on a commercial or industrial enterprise. See **Garner B(ed) Black's Law Dictionary, 8 th ed.**
   "Company" means a company formed and registered under this Act or, as the case may be, formed and registered in Nigeria before and in existence on the commencement of this Act. **See section 567, CAMA Cap. C20 LFN 2004**
2. "Property" means everything which is or may be the subject of ownership. See **Garner B. (ed) Black's Law Dictionary, 8 th ed.**
3. "Court" means the Fedeal High Court, and to the extent to which application may be made to it as; court includes the Court of Appeal and the Supreme Court of Nigeria. See **Section 567 CAMA, Cap. C20, LFN 2004**
4. "Bona Vacantia" means an ownerless property; goods without an owner. See **Garner,B.(ed) Black's Law Dictionary 8 th Ed.**

**Cross Reference:**

On procedure in dissolution of company by the Corporate Affairs Commission. See section **525 CAMA Cap. C20, LFN 2004**

---

## 527. Companies liquidation account defined

(1) There shall continue to be an account called the companies liquidation account, kept on behalf of the commission [1] by the accountant-general of the federation, into which shall be paid all moneys received by the commission [1] in respect of proceedings under this act in connection with the winding up [2] of companies.[3]

(2) All payments out of money standing to the credit of the commission[1] in the companies liquidation account shall be made by the accountant-general in the prescribed manner.

---

**Notes**
**Section 527**

1. "Commission" means the Corporate Affairs Commission,established under Section 1 of this Act. **See section 567 CAMA, CAP C20 , LFN 2004**
2. "Winding up" means the process of settling accounts and liquidating assets in anticipation of a partnership or dissolution. See **Garner B. (ed) Black's Law Dictionary, 8 th ed.**

Cross Reference:

On the establishment of the office of the Accountant General **see Civil Service re-Organization Decree No. 43, 1988**

On payment by a liquidator into companies' liquidation account, see **section 428 CAMA Cap. C20 LFN 2004**

On power of court to order payment into companies liquidation account, see **section 443 CAMA Cap. C20, LFN 2004**

---

## 528.Investment of surplus funds in government securities, etc.

(1) If the cash balance standing to the credit of the companies liquidation account[1] is in excess of the amount which in the opinion of the commission[2] is required for the time being to answer demands in respect of companies[3] estates, the commission[2] shall notify the excess to the accountant-general of the federation and the accountant-general of the federation may invest the excess or any part thereof, in government securities, [3] to be placed to the credit of such account as he may deem fit in the circumstances.

(2) If any part of the money so invested is, in the opinion of the commission[2], required to answer any demands in respect of companies'[3] estates, the commission[2] shall notify to the accountant-general of the federation the amount so required, and the accountant-general of the federation shall thereupon repay to the commission[2] such sum as may be required to the credit of the companies liquidation account,[1] and for that purpose may direct the sale of such part of the securities [3] as may be necessary.

(3) The dividends[4] on investments under this section shall be paid to such account as the accountant-general of the federation may direct, and regard shall be had to the amount thus derived in fixing the fees payable in respect of proceedings in the winding up [5] of companies.[3]

---

**Notes**
**Section 528(2)**

1. "Companies liquidation account" means kept on behalf of the commission by the Accountant-General of the Federation, into which shall be paid all moneys received by the Commission in respect of proceedings under this act in connection with the winding up of companies. See **section 527 CAMA Cap. C20, LFN 2004**
2. "Commission" means the Corporate Affairs Commission,established under Section 1 of this Act. **See section 567 CAMA, Cap. C20, LFN 2004**
3. "Companies" see "Company." It means a corporation –or, less commonly, an association, partnership, or union – that carries on a commercial or industrial enterprise. See **Garner B(ed) Black's Law Dictionary, 8th ed.**
   "Company" means a company formed and registered under this Act or, as the case may be, formed and registered in Nigeria before and in existence on the commencement of this Act. **See section 567, CAMA Cap. C20 LFN 2004**
4. "Securities" are collaterals given or pledged to guarantee the fulfillment of an obligation, especially, the assurance that a creditor will be repaid (usually, with interest.) **See Garner B. (ed) Black's Law Dictionary, 8th ed.**
   "Securities" includes shares, debentures, debenture stock, bonds, notes (other than promissory notes) and units under a unit trust scheme. See **section 567 CAMA Cap. C20, LFN 2004**
5. "Dividends" see "dividend." It means a proportion of the distributed profits of the company which may be a fixed annual percentage, as in the case of preference shares, or it may be variable according to the prosperity or other circumstances of the company, as in the case of equity shares. See **Section 567 CAMA, Cap. C20, LFN 2004**
6. "Winding up" means the process of settling accounts and liquidating assets in anticipation of a partnership or dissolution. See **Garner B. (ed) Black's Law Dictionary, 8th ed.**

Cross Reference

On the establishment of the office of the Accountant General, see **Civil Service Re- Organisation Decree no. 43, 1988.**

On payment by a liquidator into companies' liquidation account, see **section 428 CAMA Cap. C20 LFN 2004**

On power of court to order payment into companies liquidation account, see **section 443 CAMA Cap. C20, LFN 2004**

---

## 529. Separate accounts of particular estates

(1) An account shall be kept by the Commission [1] of the receipts and payments in the winding up [2] of each company, [3] and, when the cash balance standing to the credit of the account of any

company[3] is in excess of the amount which, in the opinion of the committee of inspection,[4] is required for the time being to answer demands in respect of that company's [3] estate, the Commission [1] shall, on the request of the committee, [4] invest the amount not so required in Government securities, [5] to be placed to the credit of the said account for the benefit of the company. [3]

(2) If any part of the money so invested is, in the opinion of the committee of inspection,[4] required to answer any demands in respect of the estate of the company, [3] the commissioner shall, on the request of that committee, [4] raise such sum as may be required by the sale of such part of the said securities [5] as may be necessary.

(3) The dividends[6] on investments under this section shall be paid to the credit of the company. [3]

(4) Where the balance at the credit of any company's account in the hands of the Commission [1] exceeds N10,000 and the liquidator[7] gives notice to the Commission [1] that the excess is not required for the purposes of the liquidation, the company shall be entitled to interest on the excess at the current bank rate.

---

**Notes**
**Section 529(1 )**

1. "Commission" means the Corporate Affairs Commission,established under Section 1 of this Act. **See section 567 CAMA, Cap. C20 , LFN 2004**
2. "Winding up" means the process of settling accounts and liquidating assets in anticipation of a partnership or dissolution . **See Garner, B.(ed.) Black's Law Dictionary 8 th ed.**
3. "Company" means a corporation –or, less commonly, an association, partnership, or union – that carries on a commercial or industrial enterprise. See **Garner B(ed) Black's Law Dictionary, 8 th ed.**
   "Company" means a company formed and registered under this Act or, as the case may be, formed and registered in Nigeria before and in existence on the commencement of this Act. **See section 567, CAMA C20 LFN 2004**
4. "Securities" are collaterals given or pledged to guarantee the fulfillment of an obligation, especially, the assurance that a creditor will be repaid (usually, with interest.) See **Garner B. (ed) Black's Law Dictionary, 8 th ed.**
   "Securities" includes shares, debentures, debenture stock, bonds, notes (other than promissory notes) and units under a unit trust scheme. See **section 567 CAMA Cap. C20, LFN 2004**

5. "Dividends" means a proportion of the distributed profits of the company which may be a fixed annual percentage, as in the case of preference shares, or it may be variable according to the prosperity or other circumstances of the company, as in the case of equity shares. See **567 CAMA, Cap. C20, LFN 2004**
6. "Liquidator" means a person appointed to wind up business affairs, esp. by selling off its assets See **Garner B(ed) Black's Law Dictionary, 8th ed.**

**Cross Reference**

On appointment of committee of inspection in voluntary winding up, see **section 474, CAMA,**

On appointment of committee of inspection, where winding up is by court, see **section 433 CAMA**

---

**Cases**

The Corporate Affairs Commission is conferred with the responsibility of registering companies operating in Nigeria by Statute, and under the said statute it can prohibit and restrict certain names to be registered. ***Mustapha v. CAC* (2009) Vol. 43 W.R.N. 1-171 pg 156.**

*Returns by officers of courts*

## 530. Returns by officers in winding up

The officers of the courts [1] acting in the winding up [2] of companies[3] shall make to the Commission [4] such returns of the business of their respective courts [1] and offices, at such times, and in such manner and form as may be prescribed, and from those returns the Commission [4] shall cause books to be prepared which shall be opened for public information and searches.

---

**Notes**

**Section 530**

1. "Courts" means the Federal High Court, and to the extent to which application may be made to it as; Court also includes the Court of Appeal and the Supreme Court of Nigeria. See **section 567 CAMA, Cap. C20, LFN 2004**
2. "Winding up" means the process of settling accounts and liquidating assets in anticipation of a partnership or dissolution. **Garner, B. ed.) Black's Law Dictionary 8th ed.**
3. "Companies" means a corporation –or, less commonly, an association, partnership, or union – that carries on a commercial or industrial enterprise. **Garner, B.(ed.) Black's Law Dictionary 8 th ed.**

4. "Commission" means the Corporate Affairs Commission, established under Section 1 of this Act. **See section 567 CAMA, Cap. C20, LFN 2004.**

Cross Reference

On modes of winding up a company, see **section 401, CAMA Cap. C20, LFN 2004**

On dissolution of a company, see **sections 454 & 478 CAMA Cap. C20, LFN 2004**

On the establishment of the Federal High Court and its jurisdiction, see **section 249 &251, Constiution of the Federal Republic of Nigeria, 1999(as amended)**

---

**Cases**

A just and equitable ground is one of the grounds upon which a court having jurisdiction can rely to make an order for winding up a company. See Section 408(c) of the Companies and Allied Matters Act, Cap. 59, Laws of the Federation of Nigeria 1990. Section 408(e) of same law contained in cap c20 of Laws of the Federation of Nigeria 2004. A just and equitable ground for winding up a company is a remedy most suitable for contributories. Where a contributory brings a petition under this head as was found by the trial court and where the trial court is of the opinion that the petitioner is entitled to the order of winding up, it must make the order unless it appears to the court that some other remedy is available to the petitioner and that he is acting unreasonably in seeking a winding up order instead of pursuing that other remedy. ***Ado Ibrahim & Company Ltd v. Bendel Cement Company Ltd* (2007) S. C. 284/2001.**

**For Further Reading**

On companies, winding up, commission, see, Asomugha, E. Maduelosi **Company law in Nigeria under the Companies and Allied Matters Act** E.M. Asomugha (Lagos) 1994.

*Accounts to be prepared annually*

## 531.Annual accounts of company winding up and disposal

(1) The Commission[1] and every officer by whom fees are taken under this Act in relation to the winding up [2] of companies[3], shall make returns and give information to the Accountant-General of the Federation in such form as he may require; and the accounts of the Commission[1] relating to the winding up [2] of companies[3] shall be audited as soon as may be after the end of each year in the

manner prescribed by the Constitution of the Federal Republic of Nigeria, 1999.

(2) The Accountant-General of the Federation shall, before the end of each year in which the audit is made, prepare for submission to the President an account of the winding up [2] of companies,[3] as audited by the Accountant-General for the Federation, showing in respect of such winding up, [2] the receipts and expenditure during the previous year, and any other matters which the President or the Minister [4], as the case may be, may require.

---

**Notes**
**Section 531**

1. "Commission" "means the Corporate Affairs Commission,established under Section 1 of this Act.See **section 567 CAMA, Cap. C20, LFN 2004**
2. **"Winding up"** means the process of settling accounts and liquidating assets in anticipation of a partnership or dissolution. See **Garner, B. (ed.) Black's Law Dictionary 8 th ed.**
3. "Companies" see "company." It means a corporation –or, less commonly, an association, partnership, or union – that carries on a commercial or industrial enterprise. See **Garner B. (ed) Black's Law Dictionary, 8th ed.**
   "Company" means a company formed and registered under this Act or, as the case may be, formed and registered in Nigeria before and in existence on the commencement of this Act. See **section 567, CAMA Cap. C20 LFN 2004**
4. "Minister" means the minister charged with responsibility for trade; and "ministry" shall be constituted accordingly. See **Section 567 CAMA, Cap. C20, LFN 2004.**

**Cross Reference**

On the establishment of the Office of the President of Nigeria, See **section 130 of the Constitution of the Federal Republic of Nigeria 1999 as amended.**

On the appointment of Ministers, See **section 147 of the Constitution of the Federal Republic of Nigeria 1999 as amended.**

On the establishment of the office of the Accountant General see **Civil Service re-Organization Decree No. 43, 1988.**

On audit of account of public offices of the Federation, see **section 85(2)&(3), Constitution of the Federation of Nigeria, 1999(as amended)**

---

**For Further Reading**

On company's accounts, see, Anifalaja, J. O."Current Principles & Policies on Company Accounts," E **ssays on Company Accounts.**

*Chapter 6 - Winding Up Of Unregistered Companies*

**532. Winding up of unregistered company**

Subject to the provisions of this Part of this Act, an unregistered company[1] may be wound up[2] under this Act and all the provisions of this Act, with respect to winding up [2] shall apply to an unregistered company,[1] with the following exceptions-

(a) the principal place of business of an unregistered company[1] shall for all the purposes of the winding up [2] be deemed to be the registered office of the company [1];

(b) an unregistered company [1] shall not be wound up[2] under this Act voluntarily or subject to supervision;

(c) an unregistered company [1] may be wound up[2] if-

(i) the company[1] is dissolved, or has ceased to carry on business or is carrying on business only for the purpose of winding up[2] its affairs;

(ii) the company[1] is unable to pay its debts;

(iii) the court[3] is of opinion that it is just and equitable that the company[1] should be wound up[2];

(d) an unregistered company [1] shall, for purposes of this Act, be deemed to be unable to pay its debts if-

(i) a creditor,[4] by assignment or otherwise, to whom the company[1] is indebted in a sum exceeding N100 then due, has served on the company,[1] by leaving it at its principal place of business, or by delivering to the secretary[5] or some director,[6] manager,[7] or principal officer[8] of the company,[1] or by otherwise serving in such manner as the court[3] may approve or direct, a demand under his hand requiring the company [1] to pay the sum so due, and the company [1] has for 21 days after the service of the demand neglected to pay the sum, or to secure or compound for it to the satisfaction of the creditor;[4]

(ii) any action or other proceedings has been instituted against any member[9] for any debt or demand due from the company,[1] or from him in his capacity as a member,[9] and notice in writing of the institution of the action or proceeding having been served on the company[1] by leaving it at its principal place of business, or by delivering it to the secretary, [5] or some director, [6] manager, [7] or principal officer [8] of the company, [1] or by otherwise serving the notice in such manner as the court [3] may approve or direct, the company[1] has not within 28 days after service of the notice secured, or compounded for the debt or demand or procured the action or proceeding to be stayed, or within that period has not indemnified the defendant to his reasonable satisfaction against the action or proceeding, and against all costs, damages and expenses to be incurred by him by reason of the same;

(iii) execution or other process issued on a judgment, act or order obtained in any court [3] in favour of a creditor[4] against the company, [1] or any member [9] thereof as such, or any person authorised to be sued as nominal defendant on behalf of the company [1], is returned unsatisfied;

(iv) it is otherwise proved to the satisfaction of the court [3] that the company [1] is unable to pay its debt

**Notes**
**Section 532**

1. Unregistered company" means and includes any partnership, association or company with the following exceptions- (a) a company and any existing company registered under this Act; and (b) a partnership, association or company which consists of less than eight members and is not a foreign partnership, association or company. See **section 567 CAMA, Cap. C20 , LFN 2004.**
2. "Wound up" see "winding up." It means the process of settling accounts and liquidating assets in anticipation of a partnership or dissolution. **Garner B. (ed.) Black's Law Dictionary 8 th ed.**
3. "Court" "means the Federal High Court, and to the extent to which application may be made to it as; Court also includes the Court of Appeal and the Supreme Court of Nigeria. See **section 567 CAMA, Cap. C20, LFN 2004**
4. "Creditor" "means a person or entity with a definite claim against another, esp. a claim that is capable of adjustment and liquidation. See **Garner B. (ed.) Black's Law Dictionary 8 th ed.**
5. "Secretary" means an officer charged with the direction and management of that part of the business of the company which is concerned with keeping records, the official correspondence, with

giving and receiving notices, countersigning documents. See **Garner B. (ed.) Black's Law Dictionary 8 th ed.**

6. "Director" means any person occupying the position of a director by whatever name called and includes any person in accordance with whose direction or instructions the directors of the company are accustomed to act. See **section 567 CAMA, Cap. C20 , LFN 2004**
7. "Manager" means one who is in charge or corporation and control of its business. **See Garner B. (ed.) Black's Law Dictionary 8 th ed.**
8. 'Officer" in relation to a body corporate, includes a director, manager or secretary. See **section 567 CAMA, Cap. C20, LFN 2004**
9. "Member" includes the heir, executors, administrator or other personal representative, as the case may be of the member **section 567 CAMA, Cap. C20, LFN 2004.**

---

## 533. Contributories in winding up unregistered company

(1) In the event of an unregistered company [1] being wound[2] up every person shall be deemed to be a contributory [3] who is liable to pay or contribute to the payment of any debt or liability of the company[1], or to pay or contribute to the payment of any sum for the adjustment of the rights of the members [4] among themselves, or to pay or contribute to the payment of the costs and expenses of winding up[2] the company, [1] and every contributory [3] shall be liable to contribute to the assets of the company [1] all sums due from him in respect of any such liability as aforesaid.

(2) In the event of the death, bankruptcy, [6] or insolvency of any contributory, [3] the provisions of this Act with respect to the personal representatives, [5] heirs, and devisees of deceased contributories, [3] and the trustees of bankrupt [6] or insolvent contributories, [3] as the case may be, shall apply.

---

**Notes**
**Section 533**

1. Unregistered company" means and includes any partnership, association or company with the following exceptions- (a) a company and any existing company registered under this Act; and (b) a partnership, association or company which consists of less than eight members and is not a foreign partnership, association or company. See **section 567 CAMA, Cap. C20, LFN 2004.**

2. "Wound up" see "winding up." It means the process of settling accounts and liquidating assets in anticipation of a partnership or dissolution. **Garner B. (ed.) Black's Law Dictionary 8 th ed.**
3. "Contributory" means every person liable to contribute to the assets of a company in the event of its being wound up and for the purposes of all proceedings for determining and all proceedings prior to the final determination of the persons who are to be deemed contributories, the expression shall include any person alleged to be a contributory. See **section 567 CAMA Cap. C20 LFN 2004**
4. "Members" see"member." It includes the heir, executors, administrator or other personal representative, as the case may be of the member **section 567 CAMA, Cap. C20 , LFN 2004.**
5. "Bankruptcy" means the state of a person who has been adjudged by a court to be insolvent. See **Martin E. (ed.) Oxford Dictionary of Law 4th ed.**
6. "Personal representatives" a person who manages the legal affairs of another because of incapacity or death, such as the executor of an estate. See **Garner B. (ed.) Black's Law Dictionary 8 th ed.7**
7. "Trustee of bankrupt" is a statutory procedure by which a debtor obtains financial relief and undergoes a judicially supervised reorganization or liquidation of the debtor's assets for the benefit of creditors. **See Garner B. (ed.) Black's Law Dictionary 8 th ed.**

Cross Reference

On the laws governing bankruptcy in Nigeria, see generally, **Bankruptcy Act Cap. B2 LFN 2004**

On winding up of unregistered companies, see **section 533 CAMA Cap. C20, LFN 2004**

---

**For Further Reading**

On unregistered companies, windng up, contributories, insolvency, see, Orojo, J. Ola Company Law and Practice in Nigeria 3rd Edition, Mbeyi & Associates (Lagos, Nigeria) 1992.

## 534. Power of court to stay or restrain proceedings

The provisions of this Act with respect to staying and restraining actions and proceedings against a company [1] at any time after the presentation of a petition for winding up [2] and before the making of a winding-up[2] order shall, in the case of an unregistered company,[3] where the application to stay or restrain is by a creditor,[4] extend to actions and proceedings against any contributory[5] of the company.[1]

---

**Notes**

**Section 534**

1. "Company" means a corporation – r, less commonly, an association, partnership, or union – that carries on a commercial or industrial enterprise. See **Garner B. (ed) Black's Law Dictionary, 8th ed.**
   "Company" means a company formed and registered under this Act or, as the case may be, formed and registered in Nigeria before and in existence on the commencement of this Act. See **section 567, CAMA Cap. C20 LFN 2004**
2. Winding up" means the process of settling accounts and liquidating assets in anticipation of a partnership or dissolution. See **Garner B. ed.) Black's Law Dictionary 8th ed.**
3. Unregistered company" means and includes any partnership, association or company with the following exceptions- (a) a company and any existing company registered under this Act; and (b) a partnership, association or company which consists of less than eight members and is not a foreign partnership, association or company. See **section 567 CAMA, Cap. C20, LFN 2004.**
4. "Creditor" means a person or entity with a definite claim against another, esp. a claim that is capable of adjustment and liquidation. See **Garner B. (ed.) Black's Law Dictionary 8 th ed.**
5. "Contributory" means every person liable to contribute to the assets of a company in the event of its being wound up and for the purposes of all proceedings for determining, and all proceedings prior to the final determination of, the persons who are to be deemed contributories, the expression includes any person alleged to be contributory **. See section 567 CAMA, Cap. C20 , LFN 2004.**

**Cross Reference**

On winding up of unregistered companies, see **section 533 CAMA Cap. C20, LFN 2004**

On requirement for winding up application to be be by petition, see **section 410 CAMA Cap. C20, LFN 2004**

---

**Cases**

A Court is duty bound to confine its decisions to issues raised by the parties. The Court has no power to formulate cases for the parties or to speculate on the evidence parties ought to proffer otherwise it might find itself covered by the dust of conflict. ***Anambra State Envi. Sani. Auth. v. Ekwenem*** **(2009) Vol. 45 W.R.N. 1-175 at p.12.**

## 535. Action, etc., stayed on winding-up order

Where an order has been made for winding up [1] an unregistered company,[2] no action or proceeding shall be proceeded with or commenced against any contributory [3] of the company [2] in respect of any debt of the company [2] except by leave of the court, [4] and subject to such terms as the court [4] may impose.

---

**Notes**
**Section 535**

1. "Winding up" means the process of settling accounts and liquidating assets in anticipation of a partnership or dissolution. See **Garner B. (ed.) Black's Law Dictionary 8 th ed.**
2. "Unregistered company" means and includes any partnership, association or company with the following exceptions- (a) a company and any existing company registered under this Act; and (b) a partnership, association or company which consists of less than eight members and is not a foreign partnership, association or company. See **section 567 CAMA, Cap. C20, LFN 2004.**
3. "Contributory" means one who contributes or who has a duty to contribute.
   See **Garner B. (ed.) Black's Law Dictionary 8 th ed.**
   "Contributory" means every person liable to contribute to the assets of a company in the event of its being wound up and for the purposes of all proceedings for determining, and all proceedings prior to the final determination of, the persons who are to be deemed contributories, the expression includes any person alleged to be contributory. See section **567 CAMA, Cap. C20 , LFN 2004.**
4. **"Court"** means the Federal High Court, and to the extent to which application may be made to it as; Court also includes the Court of Appeal and the Supreme Court of Nigeria. See section **567 CAMA, Cap. C20, LFN 2004.**

**Cross Reference**

On winding up of unregistered companies, see **section 533 CAMA Cap. C20, LFN 2004**

On power of court to restrain proceedings in winding up of unregistered company, **see section 534 CAMA Cap. C20, LFN 2004**

## 536. Provisions of this Part to be cumulative

The provisions of this Part of this Act with respect to unregistered companies[1] shall be in addition to and not in restriction of any provisions hereinbefore in this Act contained with respect to winding up[2] companies[3] by the court,[4] and the court[4] or liquidator[5] may exercise any powers to do any act in the case of unregistered companies[1] which might be exercised or done by it or him in winding up[2] companies[3] formed and registered under this Act; but an unregistered company[1] shall not, except in the event of its being wound up,[2] be deemed to be a company[3] under this Act, and then only to the extent provided by this Part of this Act.

**Notes**
**Section 536**

1. "Unregistered companies" see "unregistered company," It means and includes any partnership, association or company with the following exceptions- (a) a company and any existing company registered under this Act; and (b) a partnership, association or company which consists of less than eight members and is not a foreign partnership, association or company. See **section 567 CAMA, CAP C20, LFN 2004**
2. "Winding up" means the process of settling accounts and liquidating assets in anticipation of a partnership or dissolution. See **Garner B. (ed.) Black's Law Dictionary 8 th ed.**

   "Companies" see "company." It means a corporation –or, less commonly, an association, partnership, or union – that carries on a commercial or industrial enterprise. See **Garner B. (ed) Black's Law Dictionary, 8th ed.**
3. "Company" means a company formed and registered under this Act or, as the case may be, formed and registered in Nigeria before and in existence on the commencement of this Act. See **section 567, CAMA C20 LFN 2004**
4. "Court" means the Federal High Court, and to the extent to which application may be made to it as; Court also includes the Court of Appeal and the Supreme Court of Nigeria.See **section 567 CAMA, CAP C20, LFN 2004**
5. " Liquidator" means a person appointed to wind up business affairs, esp. by selling off its assets. See **Garner B. (ed) Black's Law Dictionary, 8th ed.**

**Cross Reference**

On winding up of unregistered companies, see **section 533 CAMA Cap. C20, LFN 2004.**

On power of court to restrain proceedings in winding up of unregistered company, **see section 534 CAMA Cap. C20, LFN 2004.**

---

**For Further Reading**

On companies, winding up, partnership, see, Akaki, J. O **Essays on Company Law,** University of Lagos Press, 1992.

*PART XVI*

*Arrangements and compromise*

## 537. Definition of "arrangement"

In this Part of this Act, the expression "arrangement" means any change in the rights or liabilities of members, [1] debenture holders[2] or creditors [3] of a company [4] or any class of them or in the regulation of a company, [4] other than a change effected under any other provision of this Act or by the unanimous agreement of all parties affected thereby.

---

**Notes**
**Section 537.**

1. "Members'' see "member." It includes the heir, executors, administrator or other personal representative, as the case may be of the member. See **section 567 CAMA, CAP C20, LFN 2004.**
2. "Debenture holders" see "denebture" and "holder." "Debenture" means a written acknowledgement of indebtedness by the company, setting out the terms and conditions of the indebtedness and includes debenture stock, bonds and any other securities of any company whether constituting a charge on the assets of the company or not. **See 567 CAMA CAP C20, LFN 2004**. "Holder" is one who has legal possession of a negotiable instrument and is entitled to receive payment on it. See **Garner B. (ed) Black's Law Dictionary, 8 th ed.**
3. "Creditor" means a person or entity with a definite claim against another, esp. a claim that is capable of adjustment and liquidation. **See Garner B. (ed.) Black's Law Dictionary 8 th ed.**
4. "Company" means a company formed and registered under this Act or, as the case may be, formed and registered in Nigeria before and in existence on the commencement of this Act. See **section 567, CAMA C20 LFN 2004**

**Cross Reference**

On liability of members of a company prior to and during winding up, see **section 92 CAMA Cap. C20, LFN 2004**

---

**Cases**

Where shareholders do not give up anything, it only an arrangement and not compromise. ***Yinka Folawiyo & sons Limited v. Hammond Projects Limited (1977) FRCR 143***

A registered holder of shares in a company becomes entitled to certain rights, benefits and privileges. Except as otherwise provided by the Law and the provisions of the memorandum and Articles of Association of the company, he has the right to sell, mortgage or otherwise dispose of the shares. He is entitled to receive dividends on the shares registered in his name and to keep the dividends so received for his own use. In other words, the essence of being registered as an owner or a holder of shares in a company is that one is inter alia, entitled to enjoy in one's right the foregoing rights, benefits and privileges. ***Kotoye vs. Saraki (1994) 7 N.W.L.R (part 357) 414*** .

## 538. Arrangement on sale of company's property during members' voluntary winding up

(1) With a view to effecting any arrangement [1], a company [2] may by special resolution [3] resolve that the company [2] be put into members' voluntary winding up [4] and that the liquidator [5] be authorised to sell the whole or part of its undertaking or assets to another body corporate, whether a company [2] within the meaning of this Act or not (in this section called "the transferee company" [2]) in consideration or part consideration of fully paid shares, [6] and to distribute the same in specie among the members [7] of the company in accordance with their rights in the liquidation.

(2) Any sale or distribution in pursuance of a special resolution [3] under this section shall be binding on the company [2] and all members[7] thereof and each member [7] shall be deemed to have agreed with the transferee company [2] to accept the fully paid shares,[6] debentures,[8] policies, cash or other like interests to which he is entitled under such distribution:

Provided that if-

(a) within one year from the date of the passing of any special resolution[3] as is referred to in subsection (1) of this section, an order is made under sections 310 to 312 of this Act dealing with relief on the grounds of unfairly prejudicial and oppressive conduct or for the winding up [9] of the company[2] under a creditors' voluntary winding up, [10] the arrangement [1] for the sale and distribution shall not be valid unless sanctioned by the court [11];

(b) any member [7] of the company, [2] by writing addressed to the liquidator[5] and left at the registered office or head office of the company, within 30 days after the passing of the resolution[3], dissents therefrom in respect of any of the shares[6] held by him, the liquidator [5] shall either abstain from carrying the specila resolution [3] into effect or shall purchase such shares [6] at a price to be determined in the manner provided by subsection (4) of this section.

(3) Any member [7] who fails to signify his dissent in accordance with subsection (2) of this section shall be deemed to have accepted the resolution. [3]

(4) If the liquidator [5] elects to purchase the shares [6] of any member[7] who has expressed his dissent in accordance with subsection (2) of this section, the price payable therefore shall be

determined by agreement in the case of a private company [12] in which aliens[13] do not participate, and in the case of a public company[14] or a private company [12] in which aliens [13] participate, by the Securities and Exchange Commission:
Provided that in the case of a private company [12] in which no aliens[13] participate-

(a) such price shall be determined by estimating what the member[7] concerned would have received had the whole of the undertaking of the company [2] been sold as a going concern for cash to a willing buyer and the proceeds, less the cost of winding up, [9] been divided amongst the members[7] in accordance with their rights;

(b) the purchase money shall be paid by the company [2] before the company[2] is dissolved and be raised by the liquidator [5] or, in default of any direction in the special resolution [3], in such manner as he may think fit as part of the expenses of the winding up[9].

(5) Nothing contained in this section shall authorise any variation or abrogation of the rights of any creditor [15] of the company.[2]

(6) If any company [2], otherwise than under the foregoing provisions of this section, sells or resolves to sell the whole or part of its undertaking or assets to another body corporate in consideration or part consideration of any shares [6], debentures [8], policies or other like interest in that body corporate, and resolves to distribute the same in specie among members [7] of the company [2] (whether in liquidation or by way of dividend [16]), any member [7] of the company[2] may by notice in writing addressed to the company [2] and left at the registered office or head office of the company [2] within 30 days after the passing of the resolution [3] authorising such distribution, require the company [2] either to abstain from carrying the resolution[3] into effect or to purchase any of his shares [6] at a price to be determined in the manner provided by subsection (4) of this section.

(7) Nothing contained in subsection (6) of this section shall authorize any company [2] to purchase its own shares [6] or make any distributions to its shareholders [17] except in accordance with the provisions of this Act.

**Notes**
**Section 538(1)**

1. "Arrangement" means any change in the rights or liabilities of members, debenture holders or creditors of a company [4] or any class of them or in the regulation of a company, other than a change effected under any other provision of this Act or by the unanimous agreement of all parties affected thereby. **See section 537 CAMA, Cap. C20, LFN 2004**
2. "Company" means a company formed and registered under this Act or, as the case may be, formed and registered in Nigeria before and in existence on the commencement of this Act. See **section 567, CAMA Cap.C20 LFN 2004**
3. "Special resolution" means a resolution passed by not less than three fourths of the votes cast by such members of the company as, being entitled to do so, vote in person or by proxy at a general meeting of which 21 days' notice, specifying the intention to propose the resolution as a special resolution, has been duly given. See **Section 233(2)CAMA Cap. C20, LFN,2004** .
4. "Members voluntary winding up" has the meaning assigned to it by section 462 (4) of this Act. See **Section 567 CAMA, Cap. C20, LFN 2004**
5. "Liquidator" "means a person appointed to wind up business affairs, esp. by selling off its assets. See **Garner B. (ed.) Black's Law Dictionary 8th ed**
6. "Shares" see "share." It means the interests in the company's shares capital of a member who is entitled to share in the capitalor income of such company, and except where a distinction between stock and shares is expressed or implied, includes stock. See **section 567, CAMA Cap. C20 LFN 2004.**
7. "Members" see "member." It includes the heir, executors, administrator or other personal representative, as the case may be of the member. See **section 567 CAMA, Cap. C20, LFN 2004.**
8. Debentures" see"debenture." It means a written acknowledgement of indebtedness by the company, setting out the terms and conditions of the indebtedness, and includes debenture stock, bonds and any other securities of a company whether constituting a charge on the assets of the company or not. See **section 567, CAMA Cap. C20 LFN 2004.**
9. "Winding up" means the process of settling accounts and liquidating assets in anticipation of a partnership or dissolution. See **Garner B. (ed.) Black's Law Dictionary 8 th ed.**
10. "Creditor's voluntary winding up" has the meaning assigned to it by section 462(4) of this Act.See **section 567 CAMA, Cap. C20 , LFN 2004.**
11. "Court" means the Federal High Court, and to the extent to which application may be made to it as; Court also includes the Court of Appeal and the Supreme Court of Nigeria. See **section 567 CAMA, Cap. C20 , LFN 2004**
12. "Private company" has the meaning assigned to it by section 22 (1) of this Act. See section **567 CAMA, Cap. C20, LFN 2004**

13. "Alien" means a person or association, whether corporate or unincorporated, other than a Nigeria citizen or association. section **567 CAMA, Cap. C20, LFN 2004**
14. "Public company" means any company other than a private company and is stated in its memorandum of Association that it is a public company. See **section 24 CAMA Cap. C20, LFN 2004**
15. "Creditor" means a person or entity with a definite claim against another, esp. a claim that is capable of adjustment and liquidation. **See Garner B. (ed.) Black's Law Dictionary 8 th ed.**
16. "Dividend" a proportion of the distributed profits of the company which may be a fixed annual percentage, as in the case of preference shares, or it may be variable according to the prosperity or other circumstances of the company, as in the case of equity shares. See **section. 567 CAMA, Cap. C20 , LFN 2004**

**Cross reference**

On registered offices of company and change therein, see section **35, 547 CAMA**

On procedure for members voluntary winding up see **section 463-470**

On procedure for creditors voluntary winding up see **section 471-478**

On various rights of members of a company **see 81, 300, 385 CAMA**

On distinction between private and public company **see section 21 & 22 CAMA**

On relief on the grounds of unfairly prejudicial and oppressive conduct see generally section 300-312

On payment of dividend

On the establishment and management of the Securities and Exchange Commission, see generally, **Part 1, Investment and Securities Act (ISA) 2007**

---

**For Further Reading**

On sale of company's property on member's voluntary winding up, see, Ola, C.S. **Company Law in Nigeria**, Heinemann Educational Books (Nig), 1999

Adeogun, A. A "Membership of a Company," **Essays on Company Law** Pages 73 – 75.

## 539. Power to compromise with creditors and members

(1) Where a compromise [1] or arrangement [2] is proposed between a company [3] and its creditors [4] or any class of them, the court [5] may, on the application, in a summary way, of the company [3] or any of its creditors [4] or members [6] or, in the case of a company [3] being wound up, [7] of the liquidator, [8] order a meeting [9] of the creditors [4] or class of creditors [4], or of the members [6] of the

company[3], or class of members, [6] as the case may b, to be summoned in such a manner as the court [5] directs.

(2) If a majority representing not less than three quarters in value of the shares[10] of members[6] or class of members, [6] or of the interest of creditors[4] or class of creditors [4], as the case may be, being present and voting either in person or by proxy at the meeting, [9] agree to any compromise[1] or arrangement,[2] the compromise[1] or arrangement[2] may be referred by the court [5] to the Securities and Exchange Commission which shall appoint one or more inspectors to investigate the fairness of the said compromise [1] or arrangement[2] and to make a written report thereon to the court [5] within a time specified by the court. [5]

(3) If the court[5] is satisfied as to the fairness of the compromise[1] or arrangement[2], it shall sanction the same and the compromise[1] or arrangement[2] shall be binding on all the creditors [4] or the class of creditors [4] or on the members [6] or the class of members[6] as the case may be, and also the company [3] or in the case of a company[3] in the course of being wound up, [7] on the liquidator[8] and contributories[11] of the company. [3]

(4) An order made under subsection (3) of this section shall have no effect until a certified true copy of the order has been delivered by the company[3] to the Commission [12] for registration and a copy of every such order shall be annexed to every copy of the memorandum[13] of the company[3] issued after the order has been made.

(5) If a company[3] makes default in complying with subsection (4) of this section, the company [3] and every officer [14] of the company [3]who is in default shall be liable to a fine of N5 for each copy in respect of which default is made.

(6) In this section and section 540 of this Act, "company" means any company liable to be wound up under this Act.

---

**Notes**
**Section 539(1)**

1. "Compromise" means a debtor's partial payment coupled with the creditor's promise not to claim the rest of the amount due or claimed. **See Garner B. (ed.) Black's Law Dictionary 8 th ed.**
2. "Arrangement" means any change in the rights or liabilities of members,[1] debenture holders or creditors of a company or any class of

them or in the regulation of a company, other than a change effected under any other provision of this Act or by the unanimous agreement of all parties affected thereby. See section **567 CAMA, CAP C20, LFN 2004**

3. "Company" means a company formed and registered under this Act or, as the case may be, formed and registered in Nigeria before and in existence on the commencement of this Act. See **section 567, CAMA C20 LFN 2004**

   "Company in this section means any company liable to be wound up under the Act. See **section 539(6)**
4. "Creditors" see "creditor." It means one to whom a debt is owed **. See Garner B. (ed.) Black's Law Dictionary 8 th ed.**
5. "Court" means the Federal High Court, and to the extent to which application may be made to it as; Court also includes the Court of Appeal and the Supreme Court of Nigeria. See **section 567 CAMA, CAP C20, LFN 2004**
6. "Members" see "member." It includes the heir, executors, administrator or other personal representative, as the case may be of the member. See **section 567 CAMA, CAP C20, LFN 2004.**
7. "Wound up" see "winding up." It means the process of settling accounts and liquidating assets in anticipation of a partnership or dissolution. See **Garner B. (ed.) Black's Law Dictionary 8 th ed.**
8. "Liquidator" means a person appointed to carry the winding up of a company. See **Garner B. (ed.) Black's Law Dictionary 8 th ed.**
9. "Meeting" means a coming together of persons, an assembly. Particularly, in law, an assembling of a number of persons for the purpose of discussing and acting upon some matter(s) which they have common interest. **See Garner B. (ed.) Black's Law Dictionary 8 th ed.**
10. "Shares" see "share." It means the interests in a company's share capital of a member who is entitled to share in the capital or income of such company; and except where a distinction between stock and shares is expressed or implied, includes stock. See **section 567 CAMA, CAP C20, LFN 2004**
11. "Contributory" means every person liable to contribute to the assets of a company in the event of its being wound up and for the purposes of all proceedings for determining, and all proceedings prior to the final determination of, the persons who are to be deemed contributories, the expression includes any person alleged to be contributory **. See section 567 CAMA, CAP C20, LFN 2004.**
12. "Commission" means the Corporate Affairs Commission established under section 1 of this Act; See **section 567 CAMA, CAP C20 , LFN 2004**
13. "Memorandum" means the memorandum of association of a company as originally framed or as altered in pursuance of any enactment **. See section 567 CAMA, CAP C20 , LFN 2004**

**Cross Reference**

On the establishment and management of Securities and Exchange commission, see **Part 1, Investment and Securities Act (ISA) 2007.**

On the establishment and management of Securities and Exchange commission, see **Part 1, Investment and Securities Act (ISA) 2007.**

## 540.Information as to compromise with creditors and members

(1) Where a meeting [1] of creditors [2] or any class of creditors [2] or of members [3] or any class of members [3] is summoned under section 539 of this Act, there shall-

(a) with every notice summoning the meeting [1] which is sent to a creditor [2] or member, [3] be sent also a statement explaining the effect of the compromise [4] or arrangement [5] and in particular stating any material interests of the directors [6] of the company, [7] whether as directors [6] or as members [3] or as creditors [2] of the company [7] or otherwise, and the effect thereon of the compromise [4] or arrangement [5] in so far as it is different from the effect on the like interest of other persons; and

(b) in every notice summoning the meeting [1] which is given by advertisement, be included such a statement as aforesaid, or a notification of the place at which and the manner in which creditors [2] or members [3] entitled to attend the meeting [1] may obtain copies of such a statement as aforesaid.

(2) Where the compromise [4] or arrangement [5] affects the rights of debenture holders [8] of the company, [7] the statement shall give the like explanation as respects the trustees [9] of any deed for securing the issue of the debenture [10] as it is required to give as respects the company's [2] directors. [6]

(3) Where a notice given by advertisement includes a notification that copies of a statement explaining the effects of the compromise [4] or arrangement [2] proposed can be obtained by creditors [2] or members [3] entitled to attend the meeting, [1] every such creditor [2] or member [3] shall, on making application in the manner indicated by the notice, be furnished by the company [7] free of charge with a copy of the statement.

(4) Where a company [7] makes default in complying with any requirement of this section, the company [7] and every officer [11] of the company [7] who is in default shall be liable to a fine of N1,500 and for the purpose of this subsection any liquidator [12] of the company [7]

and any trustee[9] of a deed for securing the issue of debentures [10] of the company[7] shall be deemed to be an officer [10] of the company[7]: Provided that a person shall not be liable under this subsection, if that person shows that the default was due to refusal of any other person, being a director [6] or trustee[9] for debenture holders, [8] to supply the necessary particulars as to his interests.

(5) It shall be the duty of any director [6]of the company[7] and of any trustee[9] for debenture holders [8] of the company[7] to give notice to the company[7] of such matters relating to himself as may be necessary for the purpose of this section, and any person who makes default in complying with this subsection shall be liable to a fine of Nl00.

---

**Notes**
**Section 540**

1. "Meeting" means a coming together of persons, an assembly. Particularly, in law, an assembling of a number of persons for the purpose of discussing and acting upon some matter(s) which they have common interest.See **Garner B. (ed.) Black's Law Dictionary 8th ed.**
2. "Creditor" means one to whom a debt is owed. See **Garner B. (ed.) Black's Law Dictionary 8 th ed.**
3. "Members" see "member." It includes the heir, executors, administrator or other personal representative, as the case may be of the member. See **section 567 CAMA, Cap. C20, LFN 2004.**
4. "Compromise" means a debtor's partial payment coupled with the creditor's promise not to claim the rest of the amount due or claimed. **See Garner B. (ed.) Black's Law Dictionary 8 th ed.**
5. "Arrangement" means any change in the rights or liabilities of member, debenture holder or creditor of a compan or any class of them or in the regulation of a company, other than a change effected under any other provision of this Act or by the unanimous agreement of all parties affected thereby. See **section 537 CAMA, Cap. C20 , LFN 2004**
6. "Director" includes any person occupying the position of director by whatever name called; and includes any person in accordance with whose directions or instructions the directors of the company are accustomed to act. See **section 567 CAMA, Cap. C20 , LFN 2004**
7. "Company" means a company formed and registered under this Act or, as the case may be, formed and registered in Nigeria before and in existence on the commencement of this Act. See **section 567, CAMA Cap. C20 LFN 2004**

"Company in this section means any company liable to be wound up under the Act. See **section 539(6) CAMA Cap. C20 LFN 2004**

8. "debenture holder" see "denebture" and "holder." "Debenture" means a written acknowledgement of indebtedness by the company, setting out the terms and conditions of the indebtedness and includes debenture stock, bonds and any other securities of any company whether constituting a charge on the assets of the company or not. **See 567 CAMA Cap. C20, LFN 2004**. "Holder" is one who has legal possession of a negotiable instrument and is entitled to receive payment on it. See **Garner B. (ed) Black's Law Dictionary, 8 th ed.**
9. "Trustee" means person who property in trust. See **Garner B. (ed.) Black's Law Dictionary 8 th ed.**
10. "Debenture" means a written acknowledgement of indebtedness by the company, setting out the terms and conditions of the indebtedness, and includes debenture stock, bonds and any other securities of the company whether constituting a charge on the assets of the company or not. See **Section 567 CAMA, Cap. C20 , LFN 2004**
11. "Officer" in relation to a body corporate, includes a director, manager or secretary. See **section 567 CAMA, Cap. C20, LFN 2004**
12. "Liquidator" means a person appointed to carry the winding up of a company. See **Garner B. (ed.) Black's Law Dictionary 8th ed.**

**Cross Reference**

On arrangement on sale of company's property during members' voluntary winding up, see **section 538 CAMA Cap. C20, LFN 2004**

---

*PART XVII*

*Miscellaneous and supplemental*

*Application of this Part of this Act*

## 541. Application of this Part of this Act

(1) Except as otherwise provided, this Part, that is, Part A of this Act, shall apply to-

(a) all companies[1] formed and registered under this Act;
(b) all existing companies[1];
(c) all companies[1] incorporated, formed or registered under other enactments; and
(d) unregistered companies.[2]

(2) This Act shall not apply to unions [3] of workers or of employers; and registration of any such union [3] whether described as such a union[2] or as trade union shall, if effected under the Companies Act, 1968 before its repeal by this Act, be void.

---

**Notes**
**Section 541**

1. "Companies" see"Company." It means a company formed and registered under this Act or, as the case may be, formed and registered in Nigeria before and in existence on the commencement of this Act. See **section 567, CAMA Cap. C20 LFN 2004.**
2. "Unregistered companies" where used in Part XV of this Act, includes any partnership, association or company with the following exceptions- (a) a company and any existing company registered under this Act; and (b) a partnership, association or company which consists of less than eight members and is not a foreign partnership, association or company. See **Section 567 CAMA, Cap. C20, LFN 2004.**
3. "Union" means an organization of workers, formed for the purpose of negotiating with employers on matters of wages, seniority, working conditions, fringe benefits, and the like. See **Garner B.( ed.) Black's Law Dictionary 8$^{th}$ ed.**

**Cross Reference**

For the provisions relating to the incorporation of companies and incidental matters, see generally **Part II, Chapter 1, CAMA CAP C20 LFN, 2004**

---

[1968 No. 51.]

## 542. Act to over-ride memorandum, articles, etc.

(1) Except as otherwise expressly provided in this Act-

(a) the provisions of this Act shall have effect notwithstanding anything to the contrary contained in the memorandum[1] or articles[2] of a company,[3] or in any agreement executed, by it, or in any resolution [4] passed by the company[3] in general meeting[5] or by its board of directors[6] whether the same be registered, executed or passed, as the case may be, before or after the commencement of this Act; and

(b) any provision contained in the memorandum [1] or articles,[2] agreement or resolution[4] as in paragraph (a) of this subsection shall, to the extent to which it is repugnant to the provisions of this Act, become or be void, as the case may be.

(2) Any provision of this Act overriding or interpreting a company's[3] articles[2] as if are-enacted provision of the Companies Act, 1968 shall, except as provided by this Act, apply in relation to articles[2] in force at the commencement of this Act, as well as to articles[2] coming into force thereafter, and shall apply also in relation to a company's [3] memorandum[1] as it applies in relation to its articles[2].

---

**Notes**
**Section 542**

1. "Memorandum" "means the memorandum of association of a company as originally framed or as altered in pursuance of any enactment **. See section 567 CAMA, Cap. C20, LFN 2004**
2. "Articles" means the articles of association of a company, as originally framed or as altered by special resolution, including so far as they apply to the regulations contained in Table A in the First Schedules of the Companies Act, 1922 or in that Table as altered by any subsequent enactment or reprint of the laws, or in Table A in the First Schedule to this Act. See **567 CAMA, Cap. C20, LFN 2004**
3. "Company" means a company formed and registered under this Act or, as the case may be, formed and registered in Nigeria before and in existence on the commencement of this Act. See **section 567, CAMA Cap.C20 LFN 2004**
4. "Resolution" a formal expression of the opinion or will of an official body or public assembly, adopted by a vote. See **Garner B. (ed.) Black's Law Dictionary 8th ed.**
5. "Meeting" means a coming together of persons, an assembly. Particularly, in law, an assembling of a number of persons for the purpose of discussing and acting upon some matter(s) which they have common interest.See **Garner B. (ed.) Black's Law Dictionary 8 th ed**
6. "Board of directors" means the governing body of a corporation, elected by the shareholders to establish corporate policy, appoint executive officers, and make major business and financial decisions. See **Garner B. (ed.) Black's Law Dictionary 8 th ed.**

**Cross Reference**

On registration of a company's memorandum and articles and effect thereof . see **sec. 36 and 37 CAMA Cap. C20, LFN 2004**

On form and content of the Articles of Association, see **section 34 CAMA Cap. C20 LFN 2004**

---

**Cases**

The Articles of Association is the contract governing the relationship between shareholders and any infraction of such articles may confer on the shareholder adversely affected a right of action See ***Attorney General of Lagos State v Eko Hotel Ltd &Oha Ltd [2001] FWLR page 1996*** *at* ***2000***

**For Further Reading**

On memorandum, articles of Association, see Ephraim Madeueulosi Asomugha, ***Company law in Nigeria under the companies and Allied Matters Act***, (1994) E.M. Asumughai Lagos

[1968 No. 51.]

## 543. Application of Act to companies under former enactments

In the application of this Act to existing companies, [1] it shall apply in the same manner-

(a) in the case of a limited company, [2] other than a company limited by guarantee, [3] as if the company [1] had been formed and registered under this Act as a company limited by shares[4];

(b) in the case of a company limited by guarantee, [3] as if the company[2] has been formed and registered under this Act as a company limited by guarantee [3]; and

(c) in the case of a company, [1] other than a limited company, [2] as if the company [1] had been formed and registered under this Act as an unlimited company: [5]

Provided that reference, express or implied, to the date of registration shall be construed as a reference to the date at which the company[1] was registered under the Companies Act, 1912 as the first Nigerian enactment in respect of companies, or as the case may be, any enactment relating to companies [1] thereafter in force in Nigeria before the commencement of this Act.

**Notes**

**Section 543(a)**

1."Existing company" means a company formed and registered under this Act or, as the case may be, formed and registered in Nigeria before and in existence on the commencement of this Act. See **section 567 CAMA, Cap. C20, LFN 2004**

2. "Company" means a corporation – or, less commonly, an association, partnership, or union – that carries on a commercial or industrial enterprise. **See Garner B. (ed.) Black's Law Dictionary 8 th ed.**

3. "Company Limited by Guarantee" means a company having the liability of its members limited by the memorandum to such amount as the members may respectively thereby undertake to contribute to the assets of the company in the event of its being wound up. **See section 21(1)(b)CAMA, Cap. C20, LFN 2004**

4. "Company limited by shares" "means a company having the liability of its members limited by the memorandum to the amount, if any, unpaid on the shares respectively held by them. See **Section 21(1)(a)CAMA, Cap. C20, LFN 2004**
5. "Unlimited Company" is a company not having any limit on the liability of its members. **See section 21(1)(c) CAMA, Cap. C20, LFN 2004**

Cross Reference

On application of the Act to companies under former enactments, see **section 543 CAMA Cap. C20, LFN 2004**

---

[Vol. VIII of 1912.]

## 544.Application of Act to companies registered but not formed

This Act shall apply to every company [1] registered but not formed under the Companies Act, 1912 referred to in section 543 of this Act or, as the case may be, any enactment relating to companies[1] thereafter in force in Nigeria before the commencement of this Act:

[Vol. VIII of 1912.]

Provided that reference, express or implied, to the date of registration shall be construed as a reference to the date at which the company[1] was registered under the enactment in force in Nigeria at the date when it was registered.

---

**Notes**

**Section 544**

1. "Company" means a company formed and registered under this Act or, as the case may be, formed and registered in Nigeria before and in existence on the commencement of this Act. See **section 567, CAMA Cap. C20 LFN 2004**

Cross Reference

On application of the Act to companies under former enactments, see **section 543 CAMA Cap. C20, LFN 2004**

---

## 545.Application of Act to unlimited companies registered under former enactments

This Act shall apply to every unlimited company [1] registered as a limited company[2] in pursuance of section 52 of the Companies Act, 1968 or of any enactment replaced by that section, as the case may be, in the same manner as it applies to an unlimited company [1] registered in pursuance of this Act as a limited company: [2] Provided that reference, express or implied, to the date of registration shall be construed as a reference to the date at which the company[3] was registered as a limited company [2] under the said section 52 or any enactment replaced by that section, as the case may be.

---

**Notes**
**Section 545**

1. "Unlimited company' has the meaning assigned to it by section 21 (1) of this Act. See **Section 567 CAMA, CAP C20 , LFN 2004.**
2. "Limited company" means a company having the liability of its members limited by the memorandum to the amount, if any, unpaid on the shares respectively held by them. See **Section 21(1)(a)CAMA, CAP C20, LFN 2004**

---

## 546.Restricted application of Act to unregistered companies

(1) The provisions of this Act specified in column 2 of the Thirteenth Schedule to this Act (which respectively related to all bodies corporate, incorporated in and having a principal place of business in Nigeria, other than those mentioned in subsection (2) of this section as if they were companies [1] registered under this Act, but subject to any limitations mentioned in relation to those provisions respectively in the third column of that Schedule and to such adaptation and modifications (if any) as may be specified by order made by the Minister [2] and published in the Gazette [3]

(2) The provisions of subsection (1) of this section shall not apply by virtue of this section to any of the following, that is to say-

(a) any body incorporated under any enactment other than this Act;

(b) any body not formed for the purpose of carrying on a business which has for its objects the acquisition of gain by the body or by the individual members thereof; and

(c) any body for the time being exempted by the direction of the President.

(3) This section shall not repeal or revoke in whole or in part any enactment or other instrument constituting or regulating any body in relation to which the said provisions are applied by virtue of this section; but in relation to any such body, the operation of any such enactment or instrument shall be suspended in so far as it is inconsistent with any of the said provisions as they apply for the time being to that body.

**Notes**
**Section 546**

1. "Companies" see "Company." It means a company formed and registered under this Act or, as the case may be, formed and registered in Nigeria before and in existence on the commencement of this Act. See **section 567, CAMA Cap. C20 LFN 2004.**
2. "Minister" means the Minister charged with responsibility for trade; and "Ministry" shall be constituted accordingly. See **Section 567 CAMA, Cap. C20, LFN 2004.**
3. "Gazette" means the official Gazette of the federation. **See Section 567 CAMA, Cap. C20 , LFN 2004.**

**Cross Reference**

On the appointment of Ministers, See **Section 147 of the Constitution of the Federal Republic of Nigeria 1999 as amended.**

## 547. Registered and head office of company

(1) The address of the registered or head office of a company [1] given to the Commission[2] in accordance with paragraph (e) of subsection (2) of section 35 of this Act or any change in the address made in accordance with the provisions of this section, shall be the office to which all communications and notices to the company [1] may be addressed.

(2) Notice of any change in the address of the registered or head office of the company[1] shall be given within 14 days of the change to the Commission[2] which shall record the same:
Provided that a postal box address or a private mailbag address shall not be accepted by the Commission [2] as the registered or head office.

(3) If a company[1] carries on business without complying with subsection (2) of this section, the company [1] and every officer[3] in default shall be guilty of an offence liable on conviction to a fine of N50 for every day during which the company [1] so carries on business.

(4) The fact that a change in the address of a company [1] is included in its annual return [4] shall not be taken to satisfy the obligation imposed by this section.

(5) Where a company [1] incorporated before the commencement of this Act has provided an address not in accordance with this section or section 35 of this Act, as the case may be, it shall within 14 days after such commencement comply with the requirements of this section and the failure shall be an offence punishable as prescribed by this section.

---

**Notes**
**Section 547**

1. "Company" means a company formed and registered under this Act or, as the case may be, formed and registered in Nigeria before and in existence on the commencement of this Act. See **section 567, CAMA Cap. C20 LFN 2004.**
2. "Commission" means the Corporate Affairs Commission established under section 1 of this Act.See **Section 567 CAMA, Cap. C20, LFN 2004**
3. "Officer" in relation to a body corporate, includes a director, manager or secretary; **Section 567 CAMA, Cap. C20, LFN 2004.**
4. "Annual returns" means the return required to be made, in the case of a company limited by shares under sections 371 and 372 and, in the case of a company limited by guarantee, under **Section 567 CAMA, Cap. C20 , LFN 2004.**

**Cross Reference**

On obligation to provide registered address during process of incorporation see **sec, 35 CAMA**

On meaning of offence, see **section 2, Criminal Code Cap. C38 LFN 2004**

---

**For Further Rreading**

Akaki J. O. **Essays on Company Law,** University of Lagos Press, 1992

Irukwu J. O. **The Company, The Shareholder, The Director and The Law,** Fourth Dimension Publishing Co. Ltd 1994

Ola C. S. **Company Law in Nigeria,** Heunemann Educational Books (Nig), 1999

Adeogun A. A. "Membership of a Company," **Essays on Company Law** Pages 73 - 75

## 548. Publication of name by company

(1) Every company, [1] after incorporation, shall-

(a) paint or affix, and keep painted or affixed, its name and registration number on the outside of every office or place in which its business is carried on, in a conspicuous position, in letters easily legible;

(b) have its name engraved in legible characters on its seals [2]; and

(c) have its name and registration number mentioned in legible characters in all business letters of the company [1] and in all notices, advertisements, and other official publications of the company,[1] and in all bills of exchange,[3] promissory notes, endorsements, cheques, and orders for money or goods purporting to be signed by or on behalf of the company[1], and in all bills or parcels, invoices, receipts, and letters of credit of the company. [1]

(2) If a company [1] fails to paint or affix, and keep painted or affixed its name in the manner directed by this Act, it shall be liable to a fine of N100 for not so painting or affixing its name, and for every day during which its name is not so kept, painted or affixed; and every director [4] and manager[5] of the company[1] who knowingly and willfully authorises or permits the default shall be liable to the like penalty.

(3) If a company [1] fails to comply with the provisions of paragraph (b) or (c) of subsection (1) of this section, the company [1] shall be guilty of an offence and liable to a fine of N500.

(4) If any officer [5] of a company[1] or any person on its behalf-

(a) uses or authorises the use of any seal [2] purporting to be a seal[2] of the company[1] whereon its name is not so engraved as aforesaid; or

(b) issues or authorises the issue of any business letter of the company[1] or any notice, or other official publication of the company,[1] or signs or authorises to be signed on behalf of the company any bill of exchange, [3] promissory note, endorsement, cheque or order for money or goods wherein its name is not mentioned in the manner aforesaid; or

(c) issues or authorises to be issued any bill or parcel, invoice, receipt, or letter of credit of the company, [1] wherein its name is not mentioned in manner aforesaid, he shall be guilty of an offence and on conviction liable to a fine of N500 and shall further be personally liable to the holder of any such bill of exchange, [3] promissory note, cheque, or order for money or goods, for the amount thereof, unless it is duly paid by the company. [1]

---

**Notes**
**Section 548**

1. "Company" means a company formed and registered under this Act or, as the case may be, formed and registered in Nigeria before and in existence on the commencement of this Act. See **section 567, CAMA Cap. C20 LFN 2004.**
2. "Seal" see "Common seal." It means a design embossed or stamped on paper to authenticate, confirm, or attest; an impression or sign that has legal consequence when applied to an instrument. The purpose of a seal is to secure or prove authenticity. See **Garner B. (ed.) Black's Law Dictionary, 8th ed**
3. "Bill of exchange" means an unconditional written order in writing, addressed by one person to another, signed by the person givin it, requiring the person whom it is addressed to pay on demand or at a fixed or determinable future time a sum certain in money or to the order of a specified person, or to bearer. See **section 3, Bills of Exchange Act, Cap. B8, LFN 2004**
4. "Director" includes any person occupying the position of director by whatever name called; and includes any person in accordance with whose directions or instructions the directors of the company are accustomed to act. See **Section 567 CAMA, Cap. C20, LFN 2004**
5. "Manager" means one who is in charge of a corporation and in control of its business, or establishments, division, or departments, and who is vested with a certain amount of discretion and independent jugement. See **Garner B. (ed.) Black's Law Dictionary 8th ed.**
6. "Officer" in relation to a body corporate, includes a director, manager or secretary; **Section 567 CAMA, Cap. C20, LFN 2004.**

**Cross Reference**

On obligation of the company to have and use common seal, see section 74 CAMA, Cap. **C20, LFN 2004**

On meaning of offence, see section 2, Criminal Code Cap. **C38 LFN 2004**

---

## 549. Fees

(1) There shall be paid to the Commission [1] in respect of the several matters mentioned in the Fifteenth Schedule to this Act the fees thereon specified; and where no provision is made for fees in particular cases, the Minister [2] may with the approval of the President by order published in the Gazette [3] prescribe fees and amend the said Schedule to give effect to it.
[Fifteenth Schedule.]

(2) Subject to subsection (3) of this section, any fees paid to the Registrar of Companies before the commencement of this Act shall be deemed to have been validly paid under this Act.

(3) The fees referred to in subsection (2) to this section shall cease to be payable immediately the fees specified in the Fifteenth Schedule of this Act become operative and payable.
[Fifteenth Schedule.]

(4) All fees paid to the Commission [1] and not otherwise directed by this Act for payment into a particular account, shall be paid into the Consolidated Revenue Fund [4] of the Federation.

---

**Notes**
**Section 549**

1. "Commission" means the Corporate Affairs Commission established under section 1 of this Act; **Section 567 CAMA, Cap. C20 , LFN 2004.**
2. "Minister" means the Minister charged with responsibility for trade; and "Ministry" shall be constituted accordingly; **Section 567 CAMA, Cap. C20, LFN 2004.**
3. "Gazette" "means the official Gazette of the Federation; **Section 567 CAMA, Cap. C20, LFN 2004.**
4. "Consolidated Revenue Fund" is a fund where all revenues or other moneys raised or received by the Federation are paid into, but excluding revenues or other moneys payable under the constitution or any Act of the National Assembly into any other public fund of the Federation established for any specific purpose. **See Section 80 Constitution of the Federal Republic of Nigeria as amended**

Cross Reference
On the establishment of the Consolidated Revenue Fund, see **section 80 CAMA CAP C20, LFN 2004**

---

## 550. Form of register, etc.

(1) Any register, record, index, minute book or book of account required by this Act to be made and kept by a company [1] may be made by making entries in bound books or in loose leaves, whether pasted or not, or in a photographic film form, or may be entered or recorded by any information storage device that is capable of reproducing the required information in intelligible written form within a reasonable time, or by recording the matters in question in any other manner in accordance with accepted commercial usage.

(2) Where any such register, record, index, minute book or book of account is not kept by making entries in a bound book, but by some other means, adequate precautions shall be taken for guarding against falsification and for facilitating its discovery and where default is made in complying with the provisions of this subsection, the company [1] and every officer [2] of the company [1] who is in default shall be liable to a fine of N50 and where the offence is a continuing one, shall in addition be liable to a fine of N50 for every day during which the default continues.

(3) Where any such register, index, minute book or accounting record is not kept by making entries in a bound book, but by some other means including electronic means, adequate precautions shall be taken for guarding against falsification and facilitating its discovery.

(4) If default is made in complying with the provisions of subsection (3) of this section, the company [1] and every officer [2] of it who is in default shall be guilty of an offence and liable to a fine of N50 and for continuing contravention, to a daily default fine of N5.

(5) The power conferred on a company [1] by subsection (1) of this section to keep a register, or other record by recording the matters in question otherwise than by making entries in bound books, includes power to keep the register or other record by recording those matters otherwise than in legible form, so long as the recording is capable of being reproduced in a legible form.

(6) Any provisions of an instrument made by a company [1] before 1 October, 1968 which requires a register of holders of the company[1] debentures[3] to be kept in a legible form, shall be read as requiring the register to be kept in a legible or non-legible form.

(7) If any such register or other record of a company as is mentioned in subsection (2) of this section or a register of holders of a company's [1] debentures,[3] is kept by the company [1] by recording the matters in question otherwise than in a legible form, the duty imposed on the company by this Act to allow inspection of or to furnish a copy of the register or other record or any part of it, shall be treated as a duty to allow inspection of, or to furnish a reproduction of the recording or of the relevant part of it in a legible form.

**Notes**
**Section 550**

1. "Company" means a company formed and registered under this Act or, as the case may be, formed and
registered in Nigeria before and in existence on the commencement of this Act. **See section 567, CAMA Cap. C20, LFN 2004**
2. "Officer' in relation to a body corporate, includes a director, manager or secretary. See **section 567 CAMA, Cap. C20, LFN 2004.**
3. "Debenture' means a written acknowledgement of indebtedness by the company, setting out the terms and conditions of the indebtedness, and includes debenture stock, bonds and any other securities of a company whether constituting a charge on the assets of the company or not. See **Section 567 CAMA, Cap. C20, LFN 2004**

**Cross Reference**

On the obligation of a company to maintain a register of debenture holders, see section 193 **CAMA Cap. C20, LFN 2004**

---

## 551. Inspection, etc., of documents kept by the Commission

(1) Any person may, on payment of the fees prescribed in Part III of the Fifteenth Schedule to this Act, inspect documents [1] or obtain certificates of incorporation or copies of or extracts from documents[1] held by the Commission [2] for the purposes of this Act. [Fifteenth Schedule.]

(2) Where a copy or extract from any document [1] registered under this Act is certified by the Commission [2] to be a true copy or extract, it shall in all proceedings be admissible in evidence as of equal validity with the original document, and it shall be unnecessary to prove the official position of the person certifying the copy or extract.

(3) No process for compelling the production of any document[1] kept by the Commission [2] shall issue from any court, [3] except with the leave of that court, [3] and such process, if issued, shall bear thereon a statement that it is issued with the leave of the court. [3]

---

**Notes**
**Section 551**

1. "Document" includes summons, notice, order and other legal process, and register. See **Section 567 CAMA, Cap. C20, LFN 2004.**

2. "Commission" means the Corporate Affairs Commission established under section 1 of this Act. See **Section 567 CAMA, Cap. C20 , LFN 2004.**
3. "Court" used in relation to a company, means the Federal High Court, and to the extent to which application may be made to it as; court includes the Court of Appeal and the Supreme Court of Nigeria. See**Section 567 CAMA, Cap. C20, LFN 2004.**

**Cross Reference**

On the issue of and effect of certificate of incorporation, see **section 36(6) CAMA Cap. C20, LFN 2004**

On the nature of the certified true copy of the entry in any register book issued by the Registrar, **see section 89(f) Evidence Act , 2011**

On Jurisdiction of the Federal High Court, see **section 250 of the Constitution of the Federal Republic of Nigeria, 1999 (as amended)**

---

**Cases**

The only admissible evidence of legal capacity of a body corporate is the certificate of incorporation and no other and not even an admission of incorporation by an adverse partyorally, by document or admission in pleadings would be admitted as proof of legal capacity. See ***Ndoma-Egba v. Chukwugor (2004) 26 NWLR (Pt 869) 32*** **, see also** ***NNPC v. Lutin Investment Ltd (2006) CLRN 1***

## 552. Rules of court for winding-up of companies, etc.

(1) The Chief Judge of the Federal High Court [1] may make rules of court [1] for carrying into effect the objects of this Act so far as they relate to the winding up [2] of companies[3] or generally in respect of other applications to a court [1] under this Act.

(2) For the purpose of this section, it is declared that rules made for the purpose of any enactment passed or made on or before, or to have effect on or after, the commencement of this Act shall, on its commencement, ensure and have effect where they are not inconsistent with rules of court made or deemed to have been made, under this section.

---

**Notes**

**Section 552**

1. "Court" used in relation to a company, means the Federal High Court, and to the extent to which application may be made to it as; court includes the Court of Appeal and the Supreme Court of Nigeria. See **Section 567 CAMA, Cap. C20 , LFN 2004**

2. "Winding up" means the process of settling accounts and liquidating assets in anticipation of a partnership or dissolution.See **Garner B. (ed.) Black's Law Dictionary 8 th ed.**
3. "Companies" see "company." It means a company formed and registered under this Act or, as the case may be, formed and registered in Nigeria before and in existence on the commencement of this Act. See **section 567 CAMA, Cap. C20 LFN, 2004.**

Cross Reference

On the jurisdiction of the Federal High Court, see **section 250, Constitution of the Federal Republic of Nigeria, 1999 Constitution (as amended)**

---

**Cases**

The definition of a company in section 650 of Companies and Allied Matters Act puts the matter beyond doubt. It defines a 'company' or 'existing' to mean....a company formed and registered in Nigeria before and in existence on the commencement of this Act. See ***Agro Allied Dev. Ent. Ltd. v. Reefer* (2009) vol.31 W.R.N 1-185 at pg 7.**

## 553.Certain companies to publish statement in prescribed form

(1) Every banking company [1] or an insurance company [1] or a deposit, provident, or benefit society shall, before it commences business,[2] and also on the first Monday in February and the first Tuesday in August in every year [3] during which it carries on business[2], submit to the Commission [4]a statement in the form in the Fourteenth Schedule to this Act or as near thereto as circumstances may admit.

(2) A copy of the statement shall be put up in a conspicuous place in the registered office of the company, [1] and in every branch office or place where the business [2] of the company [1] is carried on.

(3) Every member [5] and every creditor [6]of the company[1] shall be entitled to a copy of the statement, on payment of a sum not exceeding N1.

(4) If default is made in compliance with this section, the company[1] shall be guilty of an offence and liable to a fine of N100 for every day during which the default continues; and every director[7] and manager[8] of the company who knowingly and willfully authorises or permits the default shall be liable to the like penalty.

(5) For the purposes of this Act, a company [1] that carries on the business[2] of insurance in common with any other business [2] or businesses[2] shall be deemed to be an insurance company [1]

---

**Notes**
**Section 553**

1. "Company" means a company formed and registered under this Act or, as the case may be, formed and registered in Nigeria before and in existence on the commencement of this Act. **See section 567, CAMA Cap. C20 LFN 2004.**
2. "Business" includes any trade, industry and profession and any occupation carried on for profit. See **section 567 CAMA Cap. C20, LFN 2004.**
3. "Year" means period of 12months. See **section 18, Interpretation Act Cap. I23 LFN 2004.**
4. "Commission" means the Corporate Affairs Commission established under section 1 of this Act. See **section 567 CAMA, Cap. C20, LFN 2004.**
5. "Member" includes the heir, executor, administrator or other personal representative, as the case may be, of the member. See **section 567 CAMA, Cap. C20 , LFN 2004.**
6. "Creditor" means one to whom a debt is owed. See **Garner B.(ed.) Black's Law Dictionary 8th ed.**
7. "Director" includes any person occupying the position of director by whatever name called; and includes any person in accordance with whose directions or instructions the directors of the company are accustomed to act. See **section 567 CAMA, Cap. C20 , LFN 2004.**
8. "Manager" means one who is in charge of a corporation and in control of its business, or establishments, division, or departments, and who is vested with a certain amount of discretion and independent jugement. **See Garner B. (ed.) Black's Law Dictionary 8 th ed.**

**Cross Reference**

On laws governing Banking companies, see generally **Banking and other Financial Institutions Act (BOFIA) Cap. B3, LFN 2004.**

On Laws governing Insurance Institutions, **see Insurance Act, Cap. I 17, LFN 2004**

---

*Legal proceedings, etc.*

## 554. Prosecution of offences

(1) All offences under this Act may be tried by a court [1] of competent jurisdiction in the place where the offence is alleged to have been committed.

(2) Where provision is made in this Act for a criminal sanction to be imposed in case of an act, omission or default without reference therein to the default being an offence, or without reference to conviction thereof in a court, [1] as the case may be, the reference to the act, omission or default shall be construed as referable to an offence, and the expression "offences" as used in this section shall have effect in relation to any such act, omission or default.

---

**Notes**
**Section 554**

1. "Court" used in relation to a company, means the Federal High Court, and to the extent to which application may be made to it as; court includes the Court of Appeal and the Supreme Court of Nigeria; **Section. 567 CAMA, Cap. C20, LFN 2004.**

**Cross Reference**

On jurisdiction of the Federal High Court, **see section 251 of the Constitution of the Federal Republic of Nigeria, 1999( as amended).**

On the meaning of offence, see **section 2, Criminal Code, Cap. C 38, LFN 2004.**

---

**Cases**

On a court of competent jurisdiction:

In ***Madukolu v. Nkemdilim (1962)2 NSCC 374 at 379-380*** , this court stated that "a court is properly constituted as regards the number and qualification of its members on the bench , and no member is disqualified for one reason or the other and the subject matter of the case is within the jurisdiction and there is no feature in the case which prevents the court from exercising its jurisdiction and the case coming up before the court was initiated by due process of law and upon fufilment if any condition precedent to the exercise of jurisdiction." See ***SLB Consortium v. Nigerin National Peroleum Corporation (NNPC) SC 180/2008 delivered 15/04/11***

**For Further Reading**

Akaki, J.O, **Essays on Company Law**, University of Lagos Press, 1992

Irukwu, J.O, **The Company, The Shareholder, The Director and The Law**, Fourth Dimension Publishing Co. Ltd 1994

Ola C. S. **Company Law in Nigeria,** Heunemann Educational Books (Nig), 1999

Adeogun A.A. "Membership of a Company," **Essays on Company Law** Pages 73 - 75

## 555. Production, etc. of books where offences suspected

(1) If, on application made to a Judge of the Federal High Court in chambers by the Attorney-General of the Federation, there is shown to be reasonable cause to believe that a person has, while an officer[1] of a company[2], committed an offence in connection with the management of the company's [2] affairs and that evidence of the commission of the offence is to be found in any books or papers of or under the control of the company [2], an order may be made-

(a) authorising any person named therein to inspect the said books or papers or any of them for the purpose of investigating and obtaining evidence of the offence; or

(b) requiring the secretary [3] of the company[2] or any other officer[1] thereof as may be named in the order to produce the said books or papers, to a person and at a place named in the order.

(2) The provisions of subsection (1) of this section shall apply also in relation to any books or papers of a person carrying on the business of banking so far as they relate to the company's [2] affairs, as it applies to any books or papers of or under the control of the company,[2] except that no such order as is referred to in paragraph (b) of that subsection shall be made by virtue of this subsection.

(3) No appeal shall lie from the decision of a Judge of the Federal High Court on any application under this section.

---

**Notes**
**Section 555**

1. "Officer" in relation to a body corporate, includes a director, manager or secretary. See **section 567 CAMA, Cap. C20, LFN 2004.**
2. "Company" means a company formed and registered under this Act or, as the case may be, formed and registered in Nigeria before and in existence on the commencement of this Act. See **section 567, CAMA Cap. C20 LFN 2004.**
3. "Secretary" means an officer charged with the direction and management of that part of the business of the company which is concerned with keeping the records , the official correspondence, with giving and receiving notices, countersigning documents. See **Garner B. (ed.) Black's Law Dictionary 6 th ed.**

**Cross Reference**

On appointment of the Establishment, appointment of Judges and the Jurisdiction of the Federal High Court, see **sections 249-251, Constitution of the Federal Republic of Nigeria, 1999 (as amended)**

On establishment of the office of the Attorney General of the Federation, see **section of the Constitution of the Federal Republic of Nigeria, 1999 (as amended)**

---

## 556. Costs in actions by certain limited companies

Where a limited company [1] is the plaintiff in any action or other legal proceedings, any Judge having jurisdiction [1] in the matter may, if it appears by credible testimony that there is reason to believe that the company[2] may be unable to pay the costs of the defendant if successful in his defence, require sufficient security [3] to be given for those costs, and may stay all proceedings until the security [3] is given.

---

**Notes**
**Section 556.**

1. "Limited company" means a company having the liability of its members limited by the memorandum to the amount, if any, unpaid on the shares respectively held by them. See s **ection 21(1)(a) of CAMA, Cap. C20, LFN 2004.**
2. **"**Company**"** means a company formed and registered under this Act or, as the case may be, formed and registered in Nigeria before and in existence on the commencement of this Act. See **section 567, CAMA Cap. C20 LFN 2004**
3. "Security" see "securities". They are collaterals given or pledged to guarantee the fulfillment of an obligation, especially, the assurance that a creditor will be repaid**. See Garner B. (ed.) Black's Law Dictionary 8th ed.**

   "Securities" includes shares, debentures, debenture stock, bonds, notes (other than promissory notes) and units under a unit trust scheme. See **section 567 CAMA Cap. C20, LFN 2004**

---

**Cases**

On a court of competent jurisdiction:

In ***Madukolu v. Nkemdilim (1962)2 NSCC 374 at 379-380*** **,** this court stated that "a court is properly constituted as regards the number and qualification of its members on the bench, and no member is disqualified for one reason or the other and the subject matter of the case is within the jurisdiction and there is no feature in the case which prevents the court from exercising its jurisdiction and the case coming up before the court was initiated by due process of law and upon fufilment if any condition precedent to the exercise of jurisdiction." See ***SLB Consortium v. Nigerin National Peroleum Corporation (NNPC) SC 180/2008 delivered 15/04/11***

## 557. Saving for privileged communications

Where proceedings are instituted under this Act against any person by the Attorney-General of the Federation, nothing in this Act shall be taken to require any person who has acted as legal practitioner[1] for the defendant to disclose any privileged communication[2] made to him in that capacity.

---

**Notes**
**Section 557**

1. "Legal practitioner" has the meaning assigned to it by the Legal Practitioners Act. See Section **. 567 CAMA, Cap. C20, LFN 2004.**
2. "Privileged communication" means a communication made within a certain protected relationship and legally protected from compelled disclosure in a legal proceeding. See **Garner B. (ed.) Black's Law Dictionary 8th ed.**

Cross Reference

On the appointment of and the powers of the the Attorney General of the Federation, see **section 150 & 174, Constitution of the Federal Republic of Nigeria, 1999 (as amended)**

On meaning of a legal practitioner, see **section 24, Legal Practioners Act, Cap. L11, LFN 2004**

---

**For Further Reading**

Akaki J. O. **Essays on Company Law**, University of Lagos Press, 1992.
Irukwu, J. O. **The Company, The Shareholder, The Director and The Law** , Fourth Dimension Publishing Co. Ltd 1994.
Ola C. S. **Company Law in Nigeria,** Heunemann Educational Books (Nig), 1999.
Adeogun A. A. "Membership of a Company," **Essays on Company Law** Pages 73 – 75.

## 558. Power of court to grant relief in certain cases

(1) If in any proceeding for negligence, default or breach of duty or breach of trust against an officer [1] of a company[2] or a person employed by a company[2] as auditor,[3] it appears to the court [4] hearing the case that the officer [1] or person is or may be liable in respect of the negligence, default, or breach of duty or breach of trust, but that he has acted honestly and reasonably and that, having regard to all the circumstances of the case, including those connected with his appointment he ought fairly to be excused for the negligence, default or breach of duty or breach of trust, that court[4] may relieve him, either wholly or partly, from this liability on such terms as the court [4] may deem fit.

(2) When any such officer [1] or person aforesaid has reason to apprehend that any claim may be made against him in respect of any negligence, default, breach of duty or breach of trust, he may apply to the court [4] for relief, and the court [4] on any such application shall have the same power to relieve him as under this section it would have had if it had been a court [4] before which proceedings against that person for negligence, default, breach of duty or breach of trust had been brought.

---

**Notes**
**Section 558(1)**

1. "Officer" in relation to a body corporate, includes a director, manager or secretary. See s **ection 567 CAMA, Cap. C20, LFN 2004.**
2. "Company" means a company formed and registered under this Act or, as the case may be, formed and registered in Nigeria before and in existence on the commencement of this Act. See **section 567, CAMA Cap. C20 LFN 2004**
3. "Auditor" means one who checks the accuracy, fairness and general acceptability of accounting records and statements and then attests to them. **Garner B. (ed.) Black's Law Dictionary 8 th ed.**
4. "Court" used in relation to a company, means the Federal High Court, and to the extent to which application may be made to it as; court includes the Court of Appeal and the Supreme Court of Nigeria; **Section. 567 CAMA, Cap. C20, LFN 2004**

**Cross Reference**

On appointment of auditors, see **section 357 CAMA Cap. C20, LFN 2004**

---

## 559. Penalty for improper use of certain words

If any person trades or carries on business under any name or title of which the last word or words are "Unlimited," "Limited," "Public Limited Company" [2] or "Limited by Guarantee" [3] or their abbreviations, he shall, unless duly incorporated as an unlimited company,[4] a private company limited by shares, [5] a public company limited by shares,[2] or a company limited by guarantee, [3] respectively, be guilty of an offence and liable to a fine of N50 for every day during which the name or title is used.

---

**Notes**
**Section 559**

1. "Public limited company" means any company other than a private company and states in its memorandum that it is a public company. See **section 24 CAMA, Cap. C20, LFN 2004** .
2. "Limited by guarantee" means a company formed for promoting commerce, art, science, religion, sports, culture, education, research, charity or other similar objects, and the income and property of the company are to be applied solely towards the promotion of its objects and no portion thereof is to be paid or transferred directly or indirectly to the members of the company except as permitted by this Act. Such a company shall not be registered as a company limited by shares, but may be registered as a company limited by guarantee. **See section 26(1) CAMA, Cap. C20 , LFN 2004.**
3. "Unlimited company" has the meaning assigned to it by section 21 (1) of this Act. See **section. 567 CAMA, Cap. C20, LFN 2004.**
4. "Private company limited by shares" means a company having the liability of its members limited by the memorandum to the amount, if any, unpaid on the shares respectively held by them. **See section 21(1)(a) of CAMA, Cap. C20, LFN 2004.**

**Cross Reference**

On the process of incorporation and effect of incorporation, see **section 35, 36 & 37 CAMA Cap. C20, LFN 2004.**

On distinction between private &public company, see **sections 22 & 24 , CAMA Cap. C20, LFN 2004.**

On meaning of offence, see **section 2, Crimnal Code Cap. C38 LFN 2004**

## 560. Penalty for false statements

(1) Where a penalty is not elsewhere prescribed in this Act and subject to the provisions of subsection (2) of this section, if any person in any return, report, certificate, balance sheet, [1] or other document[2] required by or for the purpose of any of the provisions of this Act, wilfully makes a statement which is false in any material particular knowing it to be false, he shall be guilty of an offence and liable-

(a) on conviction in the High Court to imprisonment for a term of two years; or

(b) on conviction in a lower court, to a fine of N1000 or to imprisonment for a term of four months, or to both such fine and imprisonment.

(2) Nothing in this section shall affect the provisions of any enactment imposing penalties in respect of perjury [3] in force in Nigeria.

**Notes**
**Section 560**

1. "Balance sheet" means statement of financial position of any economic unit, disclosing as at a given moment of time, the value of its assets, liabilities and equity of the owners in conformity, with generally accepted accounting principles.See **Garner B. (ed.) Black's Law Dictionary 8th ed.**
2. "Document" includes summons, notice, order and other legal process, and register. See **section. 567 CAMA, Cap. C20 , LFN 2004.**
3. "Perjury" means the act or instance of a person's deliberately making material force or misleading statements while under oath. **See Garner, B.(ed.) Black's Law Dictionary 8 th ed.**

Cross Reference

On meaning of offence, see **section 2 Criminal Code Cap. C38 LFN 2004**
On the Establishment of the High Court and its jurisdiction, see **sections 255 & 270 of the Constitution of the Federal Republic of Nigeria, 1999.**
On the offence of pejury, see **section 117 Criminal Code, Cap. C38, LFN 2004.**

## 561.Extended effect of penalty for offence of fraudulent trading

The provisions of section 506 (3) of this Act (which imposes a penalty for certain offences connected with fraudulent trading discovered on winding up[1] a company[2] shall extend and apply to cases where fraudulent trading is discovered in circumstances other than on winding up[1] a company.[2]

**Notes**
**Section 561**

1. "Winding up" means the process of settling accounts and liquidating assets in anticipation of a partnership or dissolution. See **Garner B. ( ed.) Black's Law Dictionary 8 th ed.**
2. "Company" means a company formed and registered under this Act or, as the case may be, formed and registered in Nigeria before and in existence on the commencement othe Companies and Allied Matters Act. See **section 567 CAMA Cap. C20, LFN 2004.**

Cross Reference

On responsiblility for fraudulent trading, see **section 506(3) CAMA Cap. C20, LFN 2004**
On Winding –up generally, see **Part XV, CAMA Cap. C20, LFN 2004**

## 562. Application of fines

Any court[1] imposing a fine under this Act may direct that the whole or any part thereof be applied in or towards payment of the costs of the proceedings, or in or towards rewarding the person on whose information or at whose suit the fine is recovered and subject to any such direction, all fines under this Act shall, notwithstanding anything in any other enactment, be paid into the appropriate Consolidated Revenue Fund.

---

**Notes**
**Section 562**

1. "Court" means the Federal High Court, and to the extent to which application may be made to it as; court includes the Court of Appeal and the Supreme Court of Nigeria. See **section. 567 CAMA, Cap. C20 , LFN 2004**

Cross Reference

On the establishment and jurisdiction of the Federal High Court, see **section 249 & 251 , Constitution of the Federal Republic of Nigeria, 1999(as amended).**

On Consolidated Revenue Fund, **see section 80,Constitution of the Federal Republic of Nigeria 1999 (as amended).**

---

## 563.Application by the Commission to the court for directions

(1) The Commission[1] may apply to court[2] for directions in respect of any matter concerning its duties, powers and functions under this Act and on any such application, the court [2] may give such directions and make such further order as it thinks fit in the circumstances.

(2) The Commission[1] may conduct enquires with respect to the compliance with the provisions of this Act by any person or company.[3]

---

**Notes**
**Section 563(1)**

1. "Commission" means the Corporate Affairs Commission established under section 1 of this Act. See **section 567 CAMA Cap. C20, LFN 2004.**
2. "Court" means the Federal High Court, and to the extent to which application may be made to it as; court includes the Court of Appeal and the Supreme Court of Nigeria.See **section 567 CAMA, Cap. C20, LFN 2004**
3. "Company" means a company formed and registered under this Act or, as the case may be, formed and registered in Nigeria before and in

existence on the commencement othe Companies and Allied Matters Act. See **section 567 CAMA Cap. C20, LFN 2004**

**Cross Reference**

On the establishment, powers and function of Corporate Affairs Commission, see **sections 1-7 CAMA Cap. C20, LFN 2004.**

On the establishment and Jurisdiction fo the Federal High Court, see **sections 249& 251, Constitution of the Federal Republic of Nigeria, 1999(as amended).**

---


**For Further Reading**

Akanki J.O, **Essays on Company Law**, University of Lagos Press, 1992

Irukwu, J. O. **The Company, The Shareholder, The Director and The Law,** Fourth Dimension Publishing Co. Ltd 1994

Ola, C.S. **Company Law in Nigeria,** Heunemann Educational Books (Nig), 1999

Adeogun A.A, "Membership of a Company," **Essays on Company Law** Pages 73 - 75


*Miscellaneous*

## 564.Schedules, Tables and Forms; alteration and application

(1) The Commission[1] may, with the approval of the President, by regulation or order, published in the Gazette, [2] add to, delete from or otherwise alter the whole or any part of any of the Schedules, Tables or Forms prescribed or in force under this Act.

(2) It is hereby declared that until regulations, rules or orders are made under and for the purposes of this Act prescribing forms for use, the forms in force at the commencement of this Act shall be deemed to have been made under it and shall have effect accordingly.

---

**Notes**

**Section 564(1)**

1. "Commission" means the Corporate Affairs Commission established under section 1 of this Act. See s **ection. 567 CAMA, Cap. C20 , LFN 2004.**
2. "Gazette" means the official Gazette of the Federation. **Section. 567 CAMA, Cap. C20 , LFN 2004**

**Cross Reference**

On the Minister's power to make regulations generally for the purpose of the Companies and Allied Matters Act, see **section 16 CAMA Cap. C20 , LFN 2004**

On the establishment of the office of the President of Nigeria, see **section 147 of the Constitution of the Federal Republic of Nigeria, 1999 Constitution**

---

## 565.Enforcement of duty of company to make returns to Commission

(1) If a company,[1] having made default in complying with any provision of this Act requiring it to file with, deliver or send to the Commission[2] any return, account or other document, [3] or to give notice to it of any matter, fails to make good the default within 14 days after the service of a notice on the company requiring it to do so, the court[4] may, on the application of any member [5] or creditor[6] of the company[1] or of the Commission,[2] order the company[1] and any officer[7] to make good the default within such time as may be specified in the order.

(2) Any order under this section may provide that all costs of or incidental to the application shall be borne by the company [1] or by any officer[7] of the company[1] responsible for the default.

(3) Nothing in this section shall be taken to prejudice the operation of any enactment imposing penalties on a company [1] or its officers[7] in respect of any such default as aforesaid.

---

**Notes**

**Section 565(1)**

1. "Company" means a company formed and registered under this Act or, as the case may be, formed and registered in Nigeria before and in existence on the commencement othe Companies and Allied Matters Act. See **section 567 CAMA Cap. C20, LFN 2004.**
2. "Commission" means the Corporate Affairs Commission established under section 1 of this Act. See **section. 567 CAMA, Cap. C20, LFN 2004.**
3. "Court" means the Federal High Court, and to the extent to which application may be made to it as; court includes the Court of Appeal and the Supreme Court of Nigeria. **See section 567 CAMA, Cap. C20 ,LFN 2004.**
4. "Member" is defined to include the heir, executor, administrator or other personal representative, as the case may be, of the member **. See section 567 CAMA Cap. C20 , LFN 2004.**
5. "Creditor" means one to whom a debt is owed. See **Garner B. (ed.) Black's Law Dictionary 8th ed.**

6. "Officer" in relation to a body corporate, includes a director, manager or secretary. **See section 567 CAMA, Cap. C20 , LFN 2004**

Cross Reference

On the establishment and Jurisdiction of the Federal High Court, see **sections 249& 251, Constitution of the Federal Republic of Nigeria, 1999(as amended).**

---

## 566.Power of company to provide for employees on cessation or transfer of business

(1) The powers of a company [1] include (if they would not otherwise do so apart from this section) power to make the following provisions for the benefit of persons employed or formerly employed by the company [1] or any of its subsidiaries, [2] that is to say, provision in connection with the cessation or the transfer, to any person of the whole or part of the undertaking of the company[1] or subsidiary. [2]

(2) The power conferred by subsection (1) of this section shall be exercisable notwithstanding that its exercise is not in the best interest of the company. [1]

(3) The power which a company [1] may exercise by virtue only of subsection (1) of this section shall only be exercised by the company[1] if sanctioned-

(a) in a case not falling within paragraph (b) or (c) of this subsection, by a resolution [3] of the company [1]; or

(b) if so authorized by the memorandum [4] or articles, [5] a resolution[3] of the directors [6]; or

(c) if the memorandum [4] or articles [5] require the exercise of the power to be sanctioned by a resolution [3] other than a simple resolution[7] of the company, [1] with the sanction of that other resolution. [3]

(4) Any payment which may be made by a company [1] under this section may, if made before the commencement of any winding up[8] of the company [1], be made out of profits of the company [1] which are available for dividend [9].

---

**Notes**

**Section 566**

1. "Company" means a company formed and registered under this Act or, as the case may be, formed and registered in Nigeria before and in

existence on the commencement othe Companies and Allied Matters Act. See **section 567 CAMA Cap. C20, LFN 2004.**

2. "Resolution" means a formal statement of an opinion agreed on by a committee or a council especially by means of a vote See **Oxford Advanced Learners Dictionary. 6 th ed.**
3. "Memorandum" means the memorandum of association of a company as originally framed or as altered in pursuance of any enactment. **See section 567 CAMA, Cap. C20, LFN 2004.**
4. "Articles" means the articles of association of a company, as originally framed or as altered by special resolution, including so far as they apply to the regulations contained in Table A in the First Schedules of the Companies Act, 1922 or in that Table as altered by any subsequent enactment or reprint of the laws, or in Table A in the First Schedule to this Act. See **section 567 CAMA, Cap. C20, LFN 2004.**
5. "Directors" includes any person occupying the position of director by whatever name called; and includes any person in accordance with whose directions or instructions the directors of the company are accustomed to act. See **section. 567 CAMA, Cap. C20, LFN 2004.**
6. "Simple resolution" means resolution passed by a simple majority of votes cast by such members of the company as being entitled to do so, vote in person or by proxy at a general meeting. See **section. 233(1) CAMA, Cap. C20 , LFN 2004.**
7. "Winding up" means the process of settling accounts and liquidating assets in anticipation of a partnership or dissolution. See **Garner B. (ed.) Black's Law Dictionary 8 th ed.**
8. "Dividend" a proportion of the distributed profits of the company which may be a fixed annual percentage, as in the case of preference shares, or it may be variable according to the prosperity or other circumstances of the company, as in the case of equity shares. See **section. 567 CAMA, Cap. C20, LFN 2004.**

**Cross Reference**

On various types of resolution see **section 233 CAMA Cap. C20, LFN 2004**

On the payment of dividend by a company see **section 379 CAMA Cap. C20, LFN 2004**

---

## 567. Interpretation of certain words used in Part A of this Act

(1) In this Part, that is, Part A of this Act, unless the context otherwise requires-

"accounts" includes a company's group accounts, whether prepared in the form of accounts or not;

"agent" does not include a legal practitioner acting as counsel for any person;

"alien" means a person or association, whether corporate or unincorporated, other than a Nigeria citizen or association;
"annual return" means the return required to be made, in the case of a company limited by shares under sections 371 and 372 and, in the case of a company limited by guarantee, under section 373 of this Act;
"the appointed day" means a period of one year from the commencement of this Act;
"arrangement" has the meaning assigned to it under section 537 of this Act;
"articles" means the articles of association of a company, as originally framed or as altered by special resolution, including so far as they apply to the regulations contained in Table A in the First Schedules of the Companies Act, 1922 or in that Table as altered by any subsequent enactment or reprint of the laws, or in Table A in the First Schedule to this Act;
[First Schedule.]
"authorised minimum share capital" means N10,000 in the case of a private company and N500,00 in the case of a public company;
"authorised share capital" means the share capital of a company at any given time;
"book and paper" and "book or paper" include accounts, deeds, writings, and documents;
"circulating capital" means a portion of the subscribed capital of the company intended to be used by being temporarily parted with and circulated in business, in the form of money, goods and other assets, and which, or the proceeds of which, are intended to return to the company with an increment, and are intended to be used again and again, and to always return with some accretion;
"Commission" means the Corporate Affairs Commission established under section 1 of this Act;
"company" or "existing company" means a company formed and registered under this Act or, as the case may be, formed and registered in Nigeria before and in existence on the commencement of this Act;
"company limited by guarantee" and "company limited by shares" have the meanings assigned to them respectively by section 21 of this Act;
"companies liquidation account" means the account kept on behalf of the Commission pursuant to section 428 of this Act;

"contributory" means every person liable to contribute to the assets of a company in the event of its being wound up and for the purposes of all proceedings for determining, and all proceedings prior to the final determination of, the persons who are to be deemed contributories, the expression includes any person alleged to be contributory;

"court" or "the court" used in relation to a company, means the Federal High Court, and to the extent to which application may be made to it as; court includes the Court of Appeal and the Supreme Court of Nigeria;

"creditors voluntary winding up" has the meaning assigned to it by section 462 (4) of this Act;

"debenture" means a written acknowledgement of indebtedness by the company, setting out the terms and conditions of the indebtedness, and includes debenture stock, bonds and any other securities of a company whether constituting a charge on the assets of the company or not;

"director" includes any person occupying the position of director by whatever name called; and includes any person in accordance with whose directions or instructions the directors of the company are accustomed to act;

"dividend" means a proportion of the distributed profits of the company which may be a fixed annual percentage, as in the case of preference shares, or it may be variable according to the prosperity or other circumstances of the company, as in the case of equity shares;

"document" includes summons, notice, order and other legal process, and register;

"equity share" means a share other than a preference share; and "equity capital" shall be construed accordingly;

"fixed capital" means that capital which a company retains in the form of assets upon which the subscribed capital or other sum has been expended, and which assets either themselves produced income, independent of any further action by the company, or being retained by the company are made use of to produce income or gain profits;

"foreign company" means a company incorporated elsewhere than in Nigeria;

"forename" includes a Christian name and a personal name, and "surname" includes a patronymic;

"Gazette" means the official Gazette of the Federation;

"group financial statements" has the meaning assigned to it by section 336 (1) of this Act;

"holding company" means a holding company as defined by section 338 of this Act;

"inability to pay debts" in relation to a company has the meaning assigned by section 409 of this Act;

"insolvent person" where used in this Act means any person in Nigeria who, in respect of any judgment, Act or court order against him, is unable to satisfy execution or other process issued thereon in favour of a creditor, and the execution or other process remains unsatisfied for not less than six weeks;

"issued generally" means, in relation to a prospectus, issued to persons who are not existing members or debenture holders of the company;

"issued share capital" in relation to any reduction has the meaning assigned by section 105 (2) of this Act;

"legal practitioner" has the meaning assigned to it by the Legal Practitioners Act;

[Cap. Lll.]

"member" includes the heir, executor, administrator or other personal representative, as the case may be, of the member;

"members' voluntary winding up" has the meaning assigned to it by section 462 (4) of this Act;

"memorandum" means the memorandum of association of a company as originally framed or as altered in pursuance of any enactment;

"Minister" means the Minister charged with responsibility for trade; and "Ministry" shall be constituted accordingly;

"non-cash asset" means any property or interest in property other than cash and for this purpose, cash includes foreign currency;

"officer" in relation to a body corporate, includes a director, manager or secretary;

"official receiver" means the officer by whatever name called or known charged with control of affairs in bankruptcy and if the appointment is vacant for any reason whatsoever, means the sheriff;

"personal representative" where customary law is applicable, includes successors appointed in respect of deceased contributories;

"preference share" means a share, by whatever name designated, which does not entitle the holder of it to any right to participate beyond a specified amount in any distribution whether by way of dividend or on redemption, in a winding up, or otherwise;

"prescribed" means, as respects the provisions of this Act (other than as to the winding up of companies), prescribed by court or, as the case may be, by other proper authority by regulations or order, and as to winding up, means as prescribed by rules of court, or deemed so to be;

"private company" has the meaning assigned to it by section 22 (1) of this Act;

"prospectus" means any prospectus, notice, circular, advertisement, or other invitation, offering to the public for subscription or purchase any shares or debentures of a company and includes any document which, save to the extent that it offers securities for a consideration other than cash, is a prospectus;

"receiver" includes a manager;

"recognised stock exchange" means any body of persons for the time being recognised by the Securities and Exchange Commission as a stock exchange dealing in shares, debentures and other securities;

"registered company" means a company incorporated or deemed to be incorporated under this Act;

"the Registrar-General" means the Registrar-General appointed under section 8 of this Act;

"resolution for reducing share capital" has the meaning assigned to it by section 106 of this Act;

"resolution for voluntary winding up" has the meaning assigned to it by section 457 of this Act;

"rules" includes rules made by the Chief Judge of the Federal High Court for the purpose of section 453 or 516 of this Act, and includes rules of court made or deemed to have been made under section 552 of this Act and all incidental forms; and also rules made by the Corporate Affairs Commission and the Securities and Exchange Commission under this Act;

"securities" includes shares, debentures, debenture stock, bonds, notes (other than promissory notes) and units under a unit trust scheme;

"share" means the interests in a company's share capital of a member who is entitled to share in the capital or income of such company; and except where a distinction between stock and shares is expressed or implied, includes stock;

"small company" has the meaning assigned to it under section 351 of this Act;
"statutory declaration" means a declaration voluntarily made under the Oaths Act and in Nigeria includes one so made under any other enactment or law providing for the taking of a voluntary declaration;
[Cap. 01.]
"statutory meeting" means the meeting required to be held by section 211 (1) of this Act;
"statutory report" has the meaning assigned to it by section 211 (2) of this Act;
"subsidiary" means, in relation to a body corporate, a subsidiary as defined by section 338 of this Act;
"Table A" means Table A in the First Schedule to this Act;
"unlimited company" has the meaning assigned to it by section 21 (1) of this Act;
"unregistered company" where used in Part XV of this Act, includes any partnership, association or company with the following exceptions-

(a) a company and any existing company registered under this Act; and
(b) a partnership, association or company which consists of less than eight members and is not a foreign partnership, association or company.

(2) References in this Act to bodies corporate or to corporations exclude corporations sole; but unless the context otherwise requires, they shall include references to companies incorporated outside Nigeria.

(3) For the purpose of any provision in this Act which stipulates that an officer of a company who is in default shall be liable to a fine or other penalty, or personally liable to any third party, reference to "officer who is in default" shall be construed as a reference to any officer of the company who knowingly and wilfully authorises or permits or connives at default, refusal or contravention specified in the provision.

## 568. Repeal and savings

(1) Subject to the provisions of this section, the Companies Act 1968 and the Companies (Special Provisions) Act shall, on the commencement of this Act, be repealed.

[1968 No. 51.]

(2) Nothing in this Act shall affect any order, rule, regulation, appointment, conveyance,[1] mortgage,[2] deed[3] or agreement, made, resolution [4] passed, direction given, proceeding taken, instrument issued or thing done under the enactment hereby repealed; but any such order, rule, regulation, appointment, conveyance,[1] mortgage,[2] deed,[3] agreement, resolution,[4] direction, proceeding, instrument or thing if in force immediately before the commencement of this Act shall, on the commencement of this Act, continue in force, and so far as it could have been made, passed, given, taken, issued or done under this Act shall have effect as if so made, passed, given, taken, issued or done.

(3) Nothing in this Act shall be construed so as to prohibit the continuation of an inspection by inspectors appointed under any enactment hereby repealed, begun before the commencement of this Act, and section 325 of this Act shall apply to a report of inspectors appointed under any enactment hereby repealed as it applies to a report of inspectors appointed under section 314 of this Act.

(4) Where, under the provisions of section 261 of the Companies Act 1968 a prosecution by a liquidator [5] has been directed by the court [6] and has not been completed on the commencement of this Act, subsection (2) of that section shall have effect and be construed as if all expenses properly incurred by the liquidator[5] in the prosecution are to be defrayed as directed by the court[6] under section 438 of this Act, and not in accordance with that subsection.

[1968 No. 51.]

(5) Any register kept under the enactment hereby repealed shall be deemed to be kept under the corresponding provisions of this Act.

(6) Funds and accounts constituted under this Act shall be deemed to be in continuation of the corresponding funds and accounts constituted under the enactment hereby repealed.

(7) Nothing in this Act shall affect-

(a) the incorporation of any company [7] registered under any enactment hereby repealed; or

(b) Table A in the First Schedule of the Companies Act in so far as it applies to any company [7] existing at the commencement of this Act, except as otherwise provided in this Act.

[1968 No. 51.]

(8) Where any offence, being an offence for the continuance of which a penalty was provided, has been committed under any enactment hereby repealed, proceedings may be taken under this Act in respect of the continuance of the offence after the commencement of this Act, in the same manner as if the offence had been committed under the corresponding provisions of this Act.

(9) Where by any enactment repealed by this Act a time is fixed for the doing of an act or the performance of a duty and in any particular case that time has expired or but for this Act would have expired between the date of the commencement of this Act and the date of its signing, the time so fixed shall, for the avoidance of doubt, be deemed to have been extended so as to expire not later than 7 days after the date of commencement of this Act, so however that nothing herein shall be construed to authorise any extension of time for the doing or performance, as the case may be, of an act or duty otherwise to be done or performed within a period of time limited by any such repealed enactment.

(10) The provisions of this Act with respect to winding up [8] (other than section 510 which imposes a penalty for corrupt inducement affecting appointment of a liquidator [5], shall not apply to any company[7] of which the winding up [8] commenced before the coming into operation of this Act, but every such company [7] shall be wound up[8] in the same manner and with the same incidents as if this Act (apart from section 510) had not been made and, for the purposes of the winding up, [8] the enactment under which the winding up[8] commenced shall be deemed to remain in force.

(11) A copy of every order staying the proceedings in a winding up[8] commenced as aforesaid shall forthwith be forwarded by the company[7], or otherwise as may be prescribed, to the Commission, which shall make a minute of the order in its books relating to the company. [7]

(12) In this section "enactment hereby repealed" includes any enactment repealed or replaced by the Companies Act 1968, which itself is repealed by this Act.

---

**Notes**
**Section 568**

1. "Conveyance"means the voluntary transfer of a right or of property. See **Garner B. (ed.) Black's Law Dictionary 8 th ed.**

2. "Mortgage" means a conveyance of title to property that is given as security for the payment of a debt or performance according to the stipulated terms. See **Garner B. (ed.) Black's Law Dictionary 8 th ed.**
3. "Deed" means is a written instrument by which land is conveyed.It is usually signed,sealed and delivered. **See Garner B. (ed.) Black's Law Dictionary 8th ed.**
4. "Resolution" means a formal statement of an opinion agreed on by a committee or a council especially by means of a vote.See **Oxford Advanced Learners Dictionary.6th ed.**
5. "Liquidation" means the action of liquidating See **Oxford Advanced Learners Dictionary.6th ed.**
6. "Court" means the Federal High Court, and to the extent to which application may be made to it as; court includes the Court of Appeal and the Supreme Court of Nigeria;. See **section 567 CAMA, Cap. C20, LFN 2004.**
7. "Winding up" " means the process of settling accounts and liquidating assets in anticipation of a partnership or dissolution. See **Garner B. (ed.) Black's Law Dictionary 8 th ed.**
8. "Company" means a company formed and registered under this Act or, as the case may be, formed and registered in Nigeria before and in existence on the commencement othe Companies and Allied Matters Act. See **section 567 CAMA Cap. C20, LFN 2004**
9. "Commission" means the Corporate Affairs Commission established under section 1 of this Act.See **section 567 CAMA, Cap. C20, LFN 2004**

**Cross Reference**

On use of Inspector's report during legal proceedings, see **section 325 CAMA Cap. C20, LFN 2004**

---

*PART B*

*Business names*

## 569. The Commission to administer business names

This Part of this Act and Part C thereof shall be administered by the Corporate Affairs Commission established under Part A of this Act.

---

**Cross Reference**

On the establishment and functions of Corporate Affairs Commission, see **Part 1, sections 1-7 CAMA Cap. C20, LFN 2004**

---

## 570. Establishment of business names' registry in each State

There shall be established in each State of the Federation, a register office of business names [1] where there shall be kept a register in the prescribed form in which shall be entered such matters as are required by this Act or any regulation made there under to be entered in it.

**Notes**
**Section 570**

1. "Business names" means the name or style under which any business is carried on whether in partnership or otherwise. See **section 588(1) CAMA Cap. C20, LFN 2004**

Cross Reference

On the States that make up the Federation of Nigeria, **see section 3 (1) of the Constitution of the Federal Republic of Nigeria, 1999 (as amended).**

## 571. Appointment of Registrar and other officers

(1) The Registrar-General [1] of Companies[2] appointed under section 8 of this Act shall be the Registrar [3] of Business Names.[4]

(2) There may be appointed from time to time fit persons to be Assistant Registrars[5] of Business Names[4] or other officers as may be necessary for the administration of this part of this Act.

**Notes**
**Section 571(1)**

1. "Registrar general" means the Registrar-General appointed under section 8 of this Act. See **section 567 CAMA Cap. C20, LFN 2004**
2. "Companies" **see "Company." It** means a company formed and registered under this Act or, as the case may be, formed and registered in Nigeria before and in existence on the commencement of this Act. See **section 567 CAMA Cap. C20, LFN 2004.**
3. "Registrar "means the Registrar of Business Names . **Section. 567 CAMA, Cap. C20, LFN 2004.**
4. "Assistant Registrar" means an Assistant Registrar of Business Names appointed under section 571 of this Act. **See section. 588(1) CAMA, Cap. C20 , LFN 2004.**

## 572. Functions of Registrar and Assistant Registrars

(1) The Registrar [1] shall cause business names [2] to be registered in accordance with the provisions of this part of this Act.

(2) For the purpose of the registration under this Part of this Act, of the business names [2] of a firm, [3] individual or corporation at any of the register offices of business names, [2] any Assistant Registrar[4] may, subject to any direction that the Commission [5] may give, perform any act or discharge any duty which the Registrar [1] may lawfully perform or discharge or is required by this Act to perform or discharge, and, subject to that, any reference in this Part of this Act to the Registrar, [1] unless the context otherwise admits, shall accordingly be deemed to include a reference to an Assistant Registrar. [4]

(3) Without prejudice to the generality of the foregoing provisions of subsection (1) of this section, an Assistant Registrar [4] may be assigned to the registry of business names [2] in a State for the purpose of registering business names [2] and keeping a register of business names. [2]

---

**Notes**
**Section 572**

1. "Registrar" means the registrar of business names.See **section. 588(1) CAMA, Cap. C20, LFN 2004.**
2. "Business names" means the name or style under which any business is carried on for profit. See **section. 588(1) CAMA, Cap. C20 , LFN 2004.**
3. "Firm" means an unincorporated body of two or more individuals or one or more individual and one or more corporations, or two or more corporations, who or which have entered into partnership with one another with a view to carrying on business for profit **. See section. 588(1) CAMA, Cap. C20 , LFN 2004**
4. "Assistant Registrar" means Assistant Registrar of Business Names appointed under Section 654 of this Act. **See section 588(1) CAMA, Cap. C20 , LFN 2004.**
5. "Commission" means the Corporate Affairs Commission established under section 1 of this Act. See **section 567 CAMA, Cap. C20, LFN 2004.**

**Cross Reference**

On the States that make up the Federation of Nigeria, **see section 3 (1) of the Constitution of the Federal Republic of Nigeria, 1999 (as amended)**

---

## 573. Registration of business names

(1) Every individual, firm [1] or corporation having a place of busines[2] in Nigeria and carrying on business [2] under a business name[3] shall be registered in the manner provided in this Part of this Act if-

(a) in the case of a firm [1], the name does not consist of the true surname of all partners without any addition other than the true forenames [4] of the individual partners or the initials[5] of such forenames [4];

(b) in the case of an individual, the name does not consist of his true surname without any addition other than his true forenames[4] or the initials [5] thereof;

(c) in the case of a corporation whether or not registered under this Act, the name does not consist of its corporate name without any addition.

(2) Notwithstanding subsection (1) of this section where-

(a) the addition merely indicates that the business [2] is carried on in succession to a former owner of the business, [2] that addition shall not of itself render registration necessary;

(b) two or more individual partners have the same surname, the addition of an "s" at the end of that surname shall not of itself render registration necessary; and

(c) the business [2] is carried on by a receiver [6] or manager [7] appointed by any court, [8] registration shall not be necessary.

---

**Notes**
**Section 573**

1. "Firm" means an unincorporated body of two or more individuals or one or more individual and one or more corporations, or two or more corporations, who or which have entered into partnership with one another with a view to carrying on business for profit. See **Section 671(1) CAMA, Cap. C20, LFN 2004.**
2. "Business" includes any trade, industry and profession and any occupation carried on for profit. See **Section 671(1) CAMA, Cap. C20, LFN 2004.**
3. "Business names" means the name or style under which any business is carried on for profit. See **Section. 671(1) CAMA, Cap. C20, LFN 2004.**
4. "Forenames" when used with a surname includes any first names. See **Section 671(1) CAMA, Cap. C20 , LFN 2004.**

5. "Initials" means any recognized abbreviation of a forename. See **Section 671(1) CAMA, Cap. C20 , LFN 2004.**
6. "Receiver" means a disinterested person appointed by a court, or by a corporation or other person, for the protection or collection of property that is subject of diverse claims. See **Garner B. (ed.) Black's Law Dictionary 8th ed.**
   "Receiver" includes a manager; **Section. 567 CAMA, Cap. C20, LFN 2004.**
7. "Manager" one who has charge of corporation and control of its business, or of its branch establishments, divisions, or departments **See Garner B. (ed.) Black's Law Dictionary 8 th ed.**
8. "Court" used in relation to a company, means the Federal High Court, and to the extent to which application may be made to it as; court includes the Court of Appeal and the Supreme Court of Nigeria. See **Section. 567 CAMA, Cap. C20 , LFN 2004.**

Cross Reference

On procedure for appointing receiver or manager by court see **section 389 CAMA Cap. C20, LFN 2004**

---

## 574. Procedure for registration

(1) Every firm [1], individual or corporation required under this Act to be registered shall, within 28 days after the firm [1], individual or corporation commences the business [2] in respect of which registration is required or within three months of the coming into operation of this Act, furnish to the Registrar [3] at the registry in the State in which the principal place of business [2] of the firm, [1] company[4] or individual is situated, a statement in writing in the prescribed form, signed as required by this section and containing the following particulars-

(a) the business name [5] or, if the business [2] is carried on under two or more business names, [5] each of those business names[5];

(b) the general nature of the business [2];

(c) the full postal address of the principal place of business [2];

(d) the full postal address of every other place of business [2];

(e) where the registration to be effected is that of a firm [1]-

(i) the present forenames [6] and surname, any former forenames[6] or surname, the nationality and, if that nationality is not the nationality of origin, the nationality of origin, the age, the sex, the usual residence and any other business [2] occupation of each of the individuals who are partners; and

(ii) the corporate name and registered office of such corporation which is a partner;

(f) where the registration to be effected is that of an individual, the present forenames [6] and surname, any former forenames [6] or surnames, the nationality and, if that nationality is not the nationality of origin, the nationality of origin, the age, the sex, the usual residence and any other business [2] occupation of the individual;

(g) where the registration to be effected is that of a company, [4] the name and registered office of the company [4];

(h) the date of commencement of the business, [2] whether before or after the coming into operation of this Act.

(2) Where the registration to be effected is that of an individual or a firm [1] consisting only of individuals, there shall be submitted to the Registrar [3] copies of the passport photographs of the individual certified in a manner required by the Registrar. [3]

(3) Where the registration to be effected is that of a firm [1] or individual carrying on business [2] on behalf of another individual, firm [1] or corporation whether as nominee or trustee, [7] the statement required by subsection (1) of this section to be furnished shall contain the following particulars in addition to the particulars required by that subsection-

(a) the present forenames [6] and surname, any former forenames [6] or surname, the nationality and, if that nationality is not the nationality of origin, the nationality of origin and the usual residence of each individual on whose behalf the business [2] is carried on;

(b) the name of each firm [1] or corporation in whose behalf the business [2] is carried on.

(4) Where the registration to be effected is that of a firm [1] or individual carrying on business [2] as general agent for any concern carrying on business [2] outside Nigeria and not having a place of business [2] in Nigeria, the statement required by subsection (1) of this section to be furnished shall, in addition to the particulars required by that subsection, state the name and full postal address of each such concern, provided that in the case of a firm [1] or individual carrying on business [2] as general agent for three or more such concerns, it shall be sufficient to state the fact that the business [2] is so carried on and the countries in which the concerns carryon business. [2]

(5) A statement furnished in accordance with subsections (1) to (4) of this section shall-

(a) in the case of a statement furnished by an individual, be signed by him;

(b) in the case of a statement furnished by a firm, [1] be signed by each individual who is a partner and by a director [7] or the secretary[8] of each corporation which is partner;

(c) in the case of a company, be signed by a director [7] or the secretary:[8]

Provided that, if the statement is accompanied by a statutory declaration[9] made by any person to the effect that he is a partner of the firm[1] or is a director [7] or the secretary [8] of a corporation which is a partner of the firm, [1] the statement may be signed by that person alone.

(6) A statement furnished in accordance with subsections (1) to (4) of this section by an individual who is a minor or by a firm [1] of which one of the partners is a minor shall, in addition to the requirements of subsection (1) of this section, be signed by a magistrate, legal practitioner [10] or police officer of or above the rank of Assistant Superintendent of Police.

---

**Notes**
**Section 574**

1. "Firm" means an unincorporated body of two or more individuals or one or more individual and one or more corporations, or two or more corporations, who or which have entered into partnership with one another with a view to carrying on business for profit. **See section 588 (1) CAMA, Cap. C20, LFN 2004.**
2. "Business" means employment, occupation, profession,or commercial activity engaged in for gain or livelihood. **Garner B. (ed.) Black's Law Dictionary 8th ed.**
   "Busines" includes any trade, industry and profession and any occupation carried on for profit. See **section 588 (1) CAMA, Cap. C20 , LFN 2004.**
3. "Registrar" means the registrar of business names. **See section 588 (1) CAMA, Cap. C20, LFN 2004.**
4. "Company" means a company formed and registered under this Act or, as the case may be, formed and registered in Nigeria before and in existence on the commencement of this Act. See **section 567, CAMA Cap. C20 LFN 2004.**

5. **"Business names"** means the name or style under which any business is carried on for profit. See **section 588 (1) CAMA, Cap. C20, LFN 2004.**
6. "Forename" when used with a surname includes any first names. **See section 588 (1) CAMA, Cap. C20 , LFN 2004.**
7. "Director" includes any person occupying the position of director by whatever name called; and includes any person in accordance with whose directions or instructions the directors of the company are accustomed to act. See **section 567 CAMA, Cap. C20, LFN 2004.**
8. "Secretary" means an officer charged with the direction and management of that part of the business of the company which is concerned with keeping the records, the official correspondence, with giving and receiving notices, countersigning documents. See **Garner B. (ed.) Black's Law Dictionary 8 th ed.**
9. "Statutory declaration" means a declaration voluntarily made under the Oaths Act and in Nigeria includes one so made under any other enactment or law providing for the taking of a voluntary declaration. See s**ection 567 CAMA, Cap. C20, LFN 2004.**
10. "Legal practitioner" has the meaning assigned to it by the Legal Practitioners Act. See **section 567 CAMA, Cap. C20, LFN 2004.**

**Cross Reference**

On meaning of Legal Practitioner, **See section 24 of the Legal Practitioners Act, Cap. L11 LFN 2004**

On the States that make up the Federation of Nigeria, **see section 3 (1) of the Constitution of the Federal Republic of Nigeria, 1999** (as amended)

On registered offices of company and change therein, see **section 35& 547 CAMA Cap. C20, LFN 2004**

---

## 575. Entry of business name in the register

(1) On receipt by the Registrar [1] of the statement of particulars required to be furnished under section 574 of this Act, he shall, subject to subsection (2) of this section and to the provisions of any regulations made under this Act, cause to be entered in the register the business name[2] of the individual, company [3] or firm [4] and file the statement.

(2) The Registrar [1] shall add to the business name [2] in the register the identification letters of the State which shall be in brackets at the end of the business name, [2] and these shall form part of the business name. [2]

---

**Notes**

**Section 575**

1. "Registrar" means the registrar of business names. See **section 588(1) CAMA, Cap. C20, LFN 2004.**

2. "Business name" means the name or style under which any business is carried on for profit **Section. 588(1) CAMA, Cap. C20, LFN 2004**
3. "Company" means a company formed and registered under this Act or, as the case may be, formed and registered in Nigeria before and in existence on the commencement of this Act. See **section 567, CAMA Cap. C20 LFN 2004.**
4. "Firm" means an unincorporated body of two or more individuals or one or more individual and one or more corporations, or two or more corporations, who or which have entered into partnership with one another with a view to carrying on business for profit. **See section. 588(1) CAMA, Cap. C20 , LFN 2004**

Cross Reference

On the States that make up the Federation of Nigeria, **see section 3 (1) of the Constitution of the Federal Republic of Nigeria, 1999 (as amended)**

On Power of Minister to make regulations under the Companies and Allied Matters Act, see **section 8, CAMA Cap. C20, LFN 2004.**

On powers of the Minister to make regulations concerning the governance and guidance of the Registrar and Assistant Registrars and of all persons acting under them, see **section 585 CAMA Cap. C20, LFN 2004.**

---

## 576. Certificate of registration

(1) On the registration of any firm, [1] company[2] or individual under this Act, the Registrar [3] shall issue a certificate in the prescribed form containing the business name [4] together with the distinguishing State identification letters in brackets at the end of the name.

(2) On the registration of any change in the particulars registered in respect of any firm, [1] company[2] or individual, the Registrar[3] may in his discretion either amend the certificate previously issued or issue a fresh certificate.

(3) A certificate issued under this section shall be sent by registered post or delivered to the firm, [1] company[2] or individual registering, who shall thereupon exhibit and thereafter maintain the same in a conspicuous position at the principal place of the business[4] so registered:

Provided that-

(a) where a fresh certificate has been issued under subsection (2) of this section, the provisions of this subsection shall apply to such fresh certificate only and not to the certificate originally issued; and

(b) where any certificate has been lost or destroyed or rendered illegible, a copy of such certificate certified by the Registrar[3] may be exhibited in place of the original.

(4) Where a firm [1], company[2] or individual registered under this Act has more than one place of business [4], the original certificate shall be exhibited and maintained as required by subsection (3) of this section at the principal place of business [4] and a copy of the certificate certified by the Registrar [3] shall be exhibited and thereafter maintained in a conspicuous position in each of the other places of business[4].

---

**Notes**
**Section 576**

1. "Firm" means an unincorporated body of two or more individuals or one or more individual and one or more corporations, or two or more corporations, who or which have entered into partnership with one another with a view to carrying on business for profit. **See section 588(1) CAMA, Cap. C20 , LFN 2004.**
2. "Company" means a company formed and registered under this Act or, as the case may be, formed and registered in Nigeria before and in existence on the commencement of this Act. See **section 567, CAMA Cap. C20 LFN 2004.**
3. "Registrar" means the registrar of business names. **See section 588(1) CAMA, Cap. C20, LFN 2004.**
4. "Business name" means the name or style under which any business is carried on for profit. **See section 588(1) CAMA, Cap. C20, LFN 2004.**

**Cross Reference:**

On procedure for registration of business name, see **section 579 CAMA Cap. C20, LFN 2004**

---

## 577. Registration of changes

(1) Whenever a change is made or occurs in the particulars required by section 574 of this Act to be furnished in respect of any firm,[1] company[2] or individual registered under that section, other than particulars as to the age of an individual, the firm [1] or individual shall within 28 days after such change notify the change to the Registrar[3] at the register office at which the firm, [1] company[2] or individual is registered.

(2) The notice required under subsection (1) of this section shall be in writing signed as provided in section 574 of this Act.

**Notes**
**Section 577**

1. "Firm" means an unincorporated body of two or more individuals or one or more individual and one or more corporations, or two or more corporations, who or which have entered into partnership with one another with a view to carrying on business for profit. **See section. 588(1) CAMA, Cap. C20 , LFN 2004.**
2. "Company" means a company formed and registered under this Act or, as the case may be, formed and registered in Nigeria before and in existence on the commencement of this Act. See **section 567, CAMA Cap. C20 LFN 2004.**
3. "Registrar" means the registrar of business names. **See section 588(1) CAMA, Cap. C20, LFN 2004**

**Cross Reference**

On obligation to provide address of principal place of business and other places of business at registration, Section. **574(1) CAMA.**

## 578. Removal of name from register

(1) If any firm, [1] company[2] or individual registered under this Act ceases to carry on business, [3] it shall be the duty of the partner in the firm[1] at the time when it ceased to carry on business [3] or of the individual or if he is dead his personal representative, [4] within three months after the business [3] has ceased to be carried on, to send by post or deliver to the Registrar [5] a notice, stating that the firm [1] or individual has ceased to carryon business. [3]

(2) On receipt of such a notice as mentioned in subsection (1) of this section, the Registrar [5] may remove the firm, [1] company[2] or individual from the register.

(3) Where the Registrar [5] has reasonable cause to believe that any firm,[1] company[2] or individual registered under this Act is not carrying on business,[3] he may send to the firm, [1] company[2] or individual by registered post a notice that, unless an answer is received to such notice within two months from the date thereof, the firm, company[2] or individual may be removed from the register.

(4) If the Registrar [5] either receives an answer from the firm, [1] company[2] or individual to the effect that the firm, company or individual is not carrying on business [3] or does not within two months from the date of the notice receive an answer, he may remove the firm, [1] company[2] or individual from the register.

**Notes**
**Section 578 (1)**

1. "Firm" means an unincorporated body of two or more individuals or one or more individual and one or more corporations, or two or more corporations, who or which have entered into partnership with one another with a view to carrying on business for profit. **See section. 588(1) CAMA, Cap. C20, LFN 2004.**
2. "Company" means a company formed and registered under this Act or, as the case may be, formed and registered in Nigeria before and in existence on the commencement of this Act. See **section 567, CAMA Cap. C20 LFN 2004.**
3. "Business" means employment, occupation, profession,or commercial activity engaged in for gain or livelihood. See **Garner B. (ed.) Black's Law Dictionary 8th ed.**
   "Business" includes any trade, industry and profession and any occupation carried on for profit. See **section 588(1) CAMA, Cap. C20 , LFN 2004**
4. "Personal Representative" where customary law is applicable, includes successors appointed in respect of deceased contributories **. See section 567 CAMA, Cap. C20, LFN 2004**
5. "Registrar" means the registrar of business names. **See section 588(1) CAMA, Cap. C20, LFN 2004**

## 579. Prohibited and restricted names

(1) Where any business name [1] under which the business [2] of a person is carried on or to be carried on-

(a) contains the word "National," "Government," "Municipal", "State," "Federal," or any other word which imports or suggests that the business[2] enjoys the patronage of the Federal, State or Local Government; or

(b) contains the word "co-operative" or its equivalent in any other language or any abbreviation thereof; or

(c) contains the words "Chamber of Commerce", "Building Society" "Guarantee," "Trustee," "Investment," "Bank," "Insurance," or any word of similar connotation; or

(d) is identical with or similar to a name by which any firm, [3] company[4] or individual is registered under this Part of this Act or any company [4] is registered under this Act; or

(e) is similar to any trade mark [5] registered in Nigeria,

and the Registrar[6] is of opinion that registration would likely mislead the public, then the Registrar [6] shall, unless the consent of the Commission[7] has been first obtained by the person, refuse to register the business name [1] or, as the case may be, cancel the registration thereof.

(2) Where any business name [1] under which the business[2] of a person is carried on-

(a) contains any word which, in the opinion of the Registrar, [6] is likely to mislead the public as to the nationality, race or religion of the persons by whom the business [2] is wholly or mainly owned or controlled; or

(b) is, in the opinion of the Registrar, [6] deceptive or objectionable in that it contains a reference direct or otherwise to any personage, practice or institution, or is otherwise unsuitable as a business name, [1]

the Registrar[6] shall refuse to register the business name, [1] or, as the case may be, cancel the registration thereof, but any person aggrieved by a decision of the Registrar [6] under this subsection may, within one month of such refusal or cancellation, appeal to the Commission. [7]

(3) The Registrar[6] may refuse to register an individual or firm[3] under this Part of this Act if the age of the individual or of any individual who is a partner is stated in the statement furnished under section 574 of this Act to be less than 18 years.

(4) Where the Registrar [6] has irrefutable evidence to the effect that an individual, firm [3] or corporation that has previously been involved in fraudulent trade malpractices, either in local or international trade, is submitting an application for the registration of a new business name, [1] the Registrar[6] shall refuse to register such a business name. [1]

---

**Notes**
**Section 579**

1. "Business name" means the name or style under which any business is carried on for profit **See section. 588(1) CAMA, Cap. C20, LFN 2004**
2. "Business" means employment, occupation, profession,or commercial activity engaged in for gain or livelihood. **See Garner B. (ed.) Black's Law Dictionary 8th ed.**

"Business" includes any trade, industry and profession and any occupation carried on for profit. See **section 588(1) CAMA, Cap. C20 , LFN 2004.**

3. "Firm" means an unincorporated body of two or more individuals or one or more individual and one or more corporations, or two or more corporations, who or which have entered into partnership with one another with a view to carrying on business for profit. **See section 588(1) CAMA, Cap. C20 , LFN 2004.**
4. "Company" means a company formed and registered under this Act or, as the case may be, formed and registered in Nigeria before and in existence on the commencement of this Act. See **section 567, CAMA Cap. C20, LFN 2004.**
6. "Trademark" means, except in relation to a certification trade mark, a mark used or proposed to be used in relation to goods for the purpose of indicating, or so as to indicate, a connection in the course of trade between the goods and some person having the right either as proprietor or as registered user to use the mark, whether with or without any indication of the identity of that person. See **section 67, Trade Marks Act, Cap T 13, LFN 2004.**
7. "Registrar" means the registrar of business names. **See section 588(1) CAMA, Cap. C20 , LFN 2004.**
8. "Commission" means the Corporate Affairs Commission established under section 1 of this Act. See section **567 CAMA, Cap. C20, LFN 2004.**

**Cross Reference**

On powers of the Commission to reserve a name or change a name of a company, see **section 32(1) CAMA , Cap. C20, LFN 2004**

On registration of trademarks, see **section 22, Trademarks Act, Cap. T13, LFN 2004**

---

## 580. Searches

The Registrar[1] shall allow searches to be made at all reasonable times in any register book, register or file of registered documents[2] in his possession.

---

**Notes**

**Section 580**

1. "Registrar" means the registrar of business names. **See section 588(1) CAMA, Cap. C20 , LFN 2004.**
2. "Documents" includes summons, notice, order and other legal process, and register. See s **ection 567 CAMA, Cap. C20, LFN 2004**

---

## 581. Copies of entries in registers

(1) The Registrar [1] shall upon request give a certified copy of any entry in any register book, register or filed documents [2] in his possession.

(2) Every such certified copy shall be received in evidence, without any further or other proof, in all legal proceedings, civil or criminal.

---

**Notes**
**Section 581**

1. "Registrar" means the registrar of business names. **See section. 588(1) CAMA, Cap. C20, LFN 2004.**
2. "Documents" includes summons, notice, order and other legal process, and register. See s **ection 567 CAMA, Cap. C20, LFN 2004.**

**Cross Reference**

On the nature of the certified true copy of the entry in any register book issued by the Registrar, **see section 89(f) Evidence Act, 2011**

---

## 582. Publication of true name

(1) Every individual or firm [1] required by this Act to be registered shall in all trade catalogues, trade circulars, show cards [2] and business letters issued or sent by the individual or firm [1] to any person, have mentioned in legible characters-

(a) in the case of an individual, his present forenames [3] or the initials[4] thereof and present surname and any former forenames[3] or surname and his nationality; and

(b) in the case of a firm, the present forenames [3] or the initials[4] thereof and present surname, and any former forenames[3] or surnames and the nationality of all the partners in the firm or in the case of a corporation being a partner, the corporate name; and

(c) the registration number of the business name. [5]

(2) Where the individual referred to in subsection(1) of this section is a minor,the words "a minor" [6] shall be added, in brackets, after his name.

---

**Notes**
**Section 582**

1. "Firm" means an unincorporated body of two or more individuals or one or more individual and one or more corporations, or two or more corporations, who or which have entered into partnership with one

another with a view to carrying on business for profit. **See section 588(1) CAMA, Cap. C20 , LFN 2004.**

2. "Show card" means card showing or exhibiting articles dealt with, or sample or representations thereof. **Section. 671(1) CAMA, Cap. C20 , LFN 2004**
3. "Forename" when used with a surname includes any first names. See **section. 588(1) CAMA, Cap. C20, LFN 2004.**
4. "Initial" means any recognized abbreviation of a forename. See **section 588(1) CAMA, Cap. C20, LFN 2004.**
5. "Business name" means the name or style under which any business is carried on for profit **See section. 588(1) CAMA, Cap. C20, LFN 2004**
6. "Minor" is defined as a person who has not reached full legal age a child or juvenile. See **Garner, B.(ed.) Black's Law Dictionary 8 th ed.**

**Cross Reference**

On nationality and citizenship, **see sections 25 to 32, Constitution of the Federal Republic of Nigeria, 1999 (as amended).**

## 583. Liability of person in default

Where any firm[1] or individual required under this Act to furnish a statement of particulars or of any change in particulars, makes default in so doing, the rights of such defaulter under or arising out of any contract made or entered into by or on behalf of such defaulter in relation to the business[2] in respect of which particulars where required at any time while he is in default, shall not be enforceable by action or other legal proceedings either in the business name[3] or otherwise:

Provided that-

(a) the defaulter may apply to a High Court in which any such contract would otherwise be enforceable for relief against the disability imposed by this section and a High Court in which any such contract would otherwise be enforceable, on being satisfied that the default was accidental, or due to inadvertence, or some other sufficient cause, or that on other grounds it is just and equitable to grant relief, may grant such relief either generally as regards all contracts enforceable by the court or as respect any particular contract and on such conditions as the court may impose;

(b) nothing herein contained shall prejudice the rights of any other parties as against the defaulter in respect of such contract as aforesaid;

(c) if any action or proceeding shall be commenced by any other party against the defaulter to enforce the rights of such party in respect of such contract, nothing herein contained shall preclude the defaulter from enforcing in that action or proceeding by way of counterclaim, [4] set-off[5] or otherwise such rights as he may have against that party in respect of such contract.

---

**Notes**
**Section 583**

1. "Firm' means an unincorporated body of two or more individuals or one or more individual and one or more corporations, or two or more corporations, who or which have entered into partnership with one another with a view to carrying on business for profit. **See section. 671(1) CAMA, Cap. C20, LFN 2004.**
2. "Business" means employment, occupation, profession,or commercial activity engaged in for gain or livelihood. **See Garner B. (ed.) Black's Law Dictionary 8th ed.**
   "Business" includes any trade, industry and profession and any occupation carried on for profit. See **section 588(1) CAMA, Cap. C20 ,LFN 2004.**
3. "Business name" means the name or style under which any business is carried on for profit. See **section 588(1) CAMA, Cap. C20, LFN 2004.**
4. "Counter claim" means a claim for relief asserted against an opposing party after an original claim has been made. See **Garner B. (ed.) Black's Law Dictionary 8th ed.**
5. "Set-off" means a defendant's counter-demand against the plaintiff arising out of a transaction independent of the plaintiff's claim. See **Garner, B.(ed.) Black's Law Dictionary 8 th ed.**

**Cross Reference**

On the establishment of high court in states and Federal Capital Territory, see **section 255&270, Constitution of the Federal Republic of Nigeria, 1999(as amended).**

---

## 584. Offences and penalties

(1) If any firm [1] or individual required under this Act to be registered-

(a) fails to comply with the provisions of section 574 of this Act; or

(b) fails to comply with the provisions of section 577 of this Act; or subsection (4) of section 576 of this Act; or

(c) fails to comply with the provisions of subsection (3) or subsection (4) of section 576 of this Part; or

(d) carries on business [2] under a business name, [3] registration of which has been refused or cancelled under section 579 of this Act, every partner in the firm [1] or the individual shall be guilty of an offence and liable on conviction to a fine of N50 for every day during which the default continues, and the court shall order a statement of the required particulars to be furnished to the Registrar [4] within such time as may be specified in the order.

(2) If any person whose duty it is under subsection (1) of section 578 of this Act to give notice that any firm [1] or individual has ceased to carry on business [2], fails to comply with the provisions of that subsection, he shall be guilty of an offence and liable on conviction to a fine of N520.

(3) If any firm, [1] company[5] or individual in issuing any trade catalogues, trade circular, show card [6] or business letter fails to comply with the provisions of section 582, of this Act, every partner in the firm [1] or the individual shall be guilty of an offence and liable on conviction to a fine of N 250.

(4) If any statement required to be furnished under this Act contains any matter which is false in any material particular to the knowledge of any person [4] signing it, such person [4] shall be guilty of an offence and liable on conviction to a fine of N500 or to imprisonment for six months or to both such fine and imprisonment.

---

**Notes**
**Section 584**

1. "Firm' means an unincorporated body of two or more individuals or one or more individual and one or more corporations, or two or more corporations, who or which have entered into partnership with one another with a view to carrying on business for profit **Section. 671(1) CAMA, Cap. C20, LFN 2004.**
2. "Business" means employment, occupation, profession,or commercial activity engaged in for gain or livelihood. **See Garner B. (ed.) Black's Law Dictionary 8th ed.**
   "Business" includes any trade, industry and profession and any occupation carried on for profit. See **section 588(1) CAMA, Cap. C20 ,LFN 2004.**

3. **"Business name"** means the name or style under which any business is carried on for profit **. See section 671(1) CAMA, Cap. C20, LFN 2004.**
4. "Person" includes a firm, individual or corporation. See **section 588 (1) CAMA, Cap. C20 , LFN 2004**
5. **"Company"** means a company formed and registered under this Act or, as the case may be, formed and registered in Nigeria before and in existence on the commencement of this Act. See **section 567, CAMA Cap. C20, LFN 2004.**
6. "Show card" means card showing or exhibiting articles dealt with, or sample or representations thereof. **See section. 588(1) CAMA, Cap. C20, LFN 2004**

Cross Reference

On meaning of offence, see **section 2, Criminal Code Cap. C38, LFN 2004**

---

## 585. Regulations

The Minister[1] may with the approval of the President, make regulations-

(a) for the governance and guidance of the Registrar [2] and Assistant Registrars[3] and of all persons acting under them;

(b) Prescribing the forms to be used for the purpose of this Part of this Act;

(c) prescribing the fees to be taken by the officers by or before whom the acts for which the fees are payable are done under this Part of this Act;

(d) generally for the conduct and regulation of registration under this Part of this Act and any matters incidental thereto.

---

**Notes**

**Section 585**

1. "Minister" means the Minister charged with responsibility for trade; and "Ministry" shall be constituted accordingly. See **Section.567 CAMA, Cap. C20 , LFN 2004.**
2. "Registrar" means registrar of Business Names. See **section. 588(1) CAMA, Cap. C20, LFN 2004.**
3. "Assistant Registrar" means an Assistant Registrar of Business Names appointed under section 654 of this Act. **See section. 588(1) CAMA, Cap. C20, LFN 2004.**

Cross Reference

On the establishment of the Office of the President of Nigeria, see **section 147, Constitution of the Federal Republic of Nigeria( as amended).**

## 586. Validity of previous registration

Any firm[1] or company[2] or individual who immediately before the coming into operation of this Act was registered under the Registration of Business Names Act 1961, hereby repealed, shall be deemed to be registered under and in accordance with this Act and the provisions of this Act shall apply in respect of such firm, [1] company[2] or individual accordingly, and any statement furnished under the said Act hereby repealed shall be deemed to have been furnished under and in accordance with this Act.
[1961 No. 17.]

**Notes**
**Section 586**

1. "Firm' means an unincorporated body of two or more individuals or one or more individual and one or more corporations, or two or more corporations, who or which have entered into partnership with one another with a view to carrying on business for profit. **See section. 588(1) CAMA, Cap. C20 , LFN 2004.**
2. "Company" means a company formed and registered under this Act or, as the case may be, formed and registered in Nigeria before and in existence on the commencement of this Act. See **section 567, CAMA Cap. C20, LFN 2004.**

## 587. Annual returns

(1) Every firm, [1] company[2] or individual carrying on business [3] under a registered business name [4] shall, not later than the 30th day of June in each year, except the calendar year in which the business name[4] is registered, deliver to the Commission [5] a return in a prescribed form showing the particulars of the firm, [1] company[2] or individuals, the nature of the business [3] carried on and the state of the financial affairs of the business [3] carried on by the firm, [1] company[2] or individual in the business name [4] during the preceding period of January 1 to December 31.

(2) The returns shall be signed, in the case of an individual or firm[1] consisting only of individuals, by the individuals and in the case of a company [2] or a partner who is a company, [2] by a director [6] and the secretary. [7]

(3) Failure to comply with any of the provisions of this section shall be punishable with a fine of N200, and a daily default fine of N25.

---

**Notes**
**Section 587**

1. "Firm" means an unincorporated body of two or more individuals or one or more individual and one or more corporations, or two or more corporations, who or which have entered into partnership with one another with a view to carrying on business for profit. See **section. 588(1) CAMA, Cap. C20, LFN 2004.**
2. "Company" means a company formed and registered under this Act or, as the case may be, formed and registered in Nigeria before and in existence on the commencement of this Act. See **section 567, CAMA Cap. C20, LFN 2004.**
3. "Business" means employment, occupation, profession,or commercial activity engaged in for gain or livelihood. **Garner B. (ed.) Black's Law Dictionary 8th ed.**
   "Business" includes any trade, industry and profession and any occupation carried on for profit. See **section 588(1) CAMA, Cap. C20 ,LFN 2004.**
4. "Business name" means the name or style under which any business is carried on for profit **See section. 588(1) CAMA, Cap. C20, LFN 2004.**
5. "Commission" means the Corporate Affairs Commission established under section 1 of this Act. See **section 567 CAMA, Cap. C20, LFN 2004.**
6. "Director" includes any person occupying the position of director by whatever name called; and includes any person in accordance with whose directions or instructions the directors of the company are accustomed to act. See **Section. 567 CAMA, Cap. C20 , LFN 2004**
7. "Secretary" means an officer charged with the direction and management of that part of the business of the company which is concerned with keeping the records, the official correspondence, with giving and receiving notices, countersigning documents. See **Garner, B.(ed.) Black's Law Dictionary 8 th ed.**

---

## 588. Interpretation of words used in this Part

(1) In this Part of this Act, unless the context otherwise requires-

"Assistant Registrar" means an Assistant Registrar of Business Names appointed under section 571 of this Act;

"business" includes any trade, industry and profession and any occupation carried on for profit;
"business name," means the name or style under which any business is carried on whether in partnership or otherwise;
"firm" means an unincorporated body of two or more individuals or one or more individual and one or more corporations, or two or more corporations, who or which have entered into partnership with one another with a view to carrying on business for profit;
"forename" when used with a surname includes any first name;
"initials" includes any recognised abbreviation of a forename;
"Minister" means the Minister charged with responsibility for matters relating to the registration of business names;
"minor" means a person who has not attained the age of 18 years;
"person" includes a firm, individual or corporation;
"Registrar" means the Registrar of Business Names;
"show cards" means a card containing or exhibiting articles dealt with, or samples or representations thereof.

(2) The Registration of a business name under this Act shall not be construed as authorising the use of that name if, apart from such registration, the use thereof could be prohibited.

589. Repeal of 1961 No. 17
The Registration of Business Names Act 1961 is hereby repealed.
[1961 No. 17.]

*PART C*

*Incorporated trustees*

## 590. Incorporation of trustees of certain communities, bodies and associations

(1) Where one or more trustees [1] are appointed by any community of persons bound together by custom, religion, kinship or nationality or by any body or association of persons established for any religious, educational, literary, scientific, social, development, cultural, sporting or charitable purpose, he or they may, if so authorised by the community, body or association (in this Act referred to as "the association") apply to the Commission [2] in the manner hereafter provided for registration under this Act as a corporate body.

(2) Upon being so registered by the Commission, [2] the trustee[1] or trustees[1] shall become a corporate body [3] in accordance with the provisions of section 679 of this Part of this Act.

---

**Notes**
**Section 590(1)**

1. "Trustee" means one having legal title to property and holds it in trust for the benefit of another and owes a fiduciary duty to that beneficiary. See **Garner B.(ed.) Black's Law Dictionary 8 th ed.**
2. "Commission" means the Corporate Affairs Commission established under section 1 of this Act. **See section 567 CAMA, Cap. C20, LFN 2004**

---

**Cases**
The effect of incorporation or registration of a company,firm, etc is to confer on it legal entity as a person separate and distinct from its members. It is a legal person with personality of its own. It is more than a mere association of individuals. It becomes an artificial legal entity once the formal procedure of registration or incorporation has been complied with. See ***Rufus Iwuajoku Onuekwusi & 8 Ors. v. The Registered Trustees of the Christ Methodist Zion Church (2011) LPELR SC 58/***
In a corporate body, the death of a member or more of that body cannot alter the legal position of a corporate body or deprive it of its power to sue or be sued. See ***Rufus Iwuajoku Onuekwusi & 8 Ors. v. The Registered Trustees of the Christ Methodist Zion Church (2011) LPELR SC 58/***

## 591. Method of application

(1) Application under section 596 of this Act shall be in the form prescribed by the Commission [1] and shall state-

(a) the name of the proposed corporate body which must contain the words "Incorporated Trustees of';

(b) the aims and objects of the association which must be for the advancement of any religious, educational, literary, scientific, social, development, cultural, sporting or charitable purpose, and must be lawful;

(c) the names, addresses and occupations of the secretary [2] of the association, if any.

(2) There shall be attached to the application-

(a) two printed copies of the constitution of the association;

(b) duly signed copies of the minutes of the meeting appointing the trustees[3] and authorising the application, showing the people present and the votes scored;

(c) the impression or drawing of the proposed common seal [4].

(3) The application shall be signed by the person making it.

(4) The Commission[1] may require such declaration or other evidence in verification of the statements and particulars in the application, and such other particulars, information, and evidence, if any, as it may think fit.

(5) If any person knowingly makes any false statement or gives any false information for the purpose of incorporating trustees under this Part of this Act, he shall be guilty of an offence and liable on conviction to imprisonment for one year or to a fine of N100 .

---

**Notes**
**Section 591**

1. "Commission" means the Corporate Affairs Commission established under section 1 of this Act. See **section. 567 CAMA, Cap. C20 , LFN 2004.**
2. "Secretary" means a corporate officer in charge of official correspondence, minutes of board meetings and records of stock ownership and transfer. **See Garner B. (ed) Black's Law Dictionary, 8th ed.**
3. "Trustee" means one having legal title to property and holds it in trust for the benefit of another and owes a fiduciary duty to that beneficiary. **See Garner B. (ed.) Black's Law Dictionary 8 th ed.**
4. "Common seal" means a piece of wax, a wafer, or some other substance affixed to the paper or other material on which a promise or release, or conveyance is written together with recital or expression of intention by which the promisor , releasor, or grantor manifest that a piece of wax, wafer , or other substance is a seal. See **Garner B. (ed.) Black's Law Dictionary 8 th ed.**

Cross Reference

On effect of use of common seal, see **section 604 CAMA Cap. C20, LFN 2004.**

---

**Cases**

Where a company executes a deed, the seal affixed to the document must bear the name of the company. See ***Western Nigeria Finance Corp v. West Coast Builders (1971)1.U.I.L.R.93,*** .

## 592. Qualification of trustees

(1) A person shall not be qualified to be appointed as a trustee[1] if-

(a) he is an infant; or

(b) he is a person of unsound mind having been so found by a court[2];

(c) he is an undischarged bankrupt [3]; or

(d) he has been convicted of an offence involving fraud or dishonesty within five years of his proposed appointment.

(2) If a person disqualified under paragraph (c) or (d) of subsection (1) of this section acts as a trustee [1], he shall be liable to a fine ofN50 for every day during which he so acts.

---

**Notes**
**Section 592**

1. "Trustee" "means one having legal title to property and holds it in trust for the benefit of another and owes a fiduciary duty to that beneficiary. **See Garner B. (ed.) Black's Law Dictionary 8 th ed.**
2. "Court" means the Federal High Court, and to the extent to which application may be made to it as; court includes the Court of Appeal and the Supreme Court of Nigeria. See **section 567 CAMA, Cap. C20 ,LFN 2004.**
3. "Bankrupt" means the state or condition of a person, individual, partnership, corporation, municipality who is unable to pay its debts as they are, or become, due. See **Garner B. (ed.) Black's Law Dictionary 8th ed.**

**Cross Reference**

As to when a debtor commits an act of bankruptcy, see **section 1, Bankruptcy Act Cap. B2 LFN 2004.**

---

## 593. Constitution

The constitution of the association shall in addition to any other matter-

(a) state the name or title of the association which shall not conflict with that of a company, [1] or with a business name [2] or trade mark [3] registered in Nigeria;

(b) the aims and objects of the association; and

(c) make provisions, in respect of the following-

(i) appointment, powers, duties, tenure of office and replacement of the trustees [4];

(ii) the use and custody of the common seal [5];

(iii) the meetings[6] of the association;

(iv) the number of members of the governing body, if any, the procedure for their appointment and removal, and their powers; and

(v) where subscriptions and other contributions are to be collected, the procedure for disbursement of the funds of the association, the keeping of accounts and the auditing of such accounts.

---

**Notes**

**Section 593**

1. "Company" means a company formed and registered under this Act or, as the case may be, formed and registered in Nigeria before and in existence on the commencement of this Act. See **section 567, CAMA Cap. C20, LFN 2004**
2. "Business name" means the name or style under which any business is carried on for profit. See **section. 588(1) CAMA, Cap. C20, LFN 2004**
3. "Trademark" means, except in relation to a certification trade mark, a mark used or proposed to be used in relation to goods for the purpose of indicating, or so as to indicate, a connection in the course of trade between the goods and some person having the right either as proprietor or as registered user to use the mark, whether with or without any indication of the identity of that person. See **section 67, Trade Marks Act, Cap T 13, LFN 2004.**
4. 'Trustees" means one having legal title to property and holds it in trust for the benefit of another and owes a fiduciary duty to that beneficiary. See **Garner B. (ed.) Black's Law Dictionary 8 th ed.**
5. "Common seal" means a piece of wax, a wafer, or some other substance affixed to the paper or other material on which a promise or release, or conveyance is written together with recital or expression of intention by which the promisor, releasor, or grantor manifest that a piece of wax, wafer, or other substance is a seal. See **Garner B. (ed.) Black's Law Dictionary 8th ed.**
6. "Meetings" means an assembling of a number of persons for the purpose of discussing and acting upon some matter or matters in which they have a common interest. **See Garner B. (ed.) Black's Law Dictionary 8th ed.**

**Cross Reference**

On effect of use of common seal, see **section 604 CAMA Cap. C20, LFN 2004.**

On the effect of non- registration of trade marks, see **section 3 Trade marks Act, Cap. T13 LFN 2004.**

---

## 594. Advertisement and objections

(1) If the Commission [1] is satisfied that the application has complied with the provisions of sections 591,592 and 593 of this Act, it shall cause the application to be published in a prescribed form in two daily newspapers circulating in the area where the corporation is to be situated and at least one of the newspaper shall be a national newspaper.

(2) The advertisement shall invite objections, if any, to the registration of the body.

(3) The objection shall state the grounds on which it is made and shall be forwarded to reach the Commission [1] within 28 days of the date of the last of the publications in the newspapers.

(4) If any objections are made, the Commission [1] shall consider them and may require the objections and applicants to furnish further information or explanation, and may uphold or reject the objections as it considers fit and inform the applicant accordingly.

---

**Notes**
**Section 594**

1. "Commission" "means the Corporate Affairs Commission established under section 1 of this Act. See **section. 567 CAMA, Cap. C20, LFN 2004**

---

**Cases**

In the performance of their duties, section 677(1) of CAMA gives the respondents absolute discretion. The community reading of section 32(1) and section 677(1) confirm the absolute discretion given to the Commission in the Registration of proposed names. See **Benard Amasike v. R.G Corporate Affairs Commission & Anor. (2010) LPELR-SC.204/2005**

## 595. Registration and certificate

(1) If, after the advertisement, no objection is received within the period specified in section 596 of this Act or, where any objection is received, and the same is rejected, the Commission [1], having regard to all the circumstances, may assent to the application or withhold its assent.

(2) If the Commission[1] assents to the application, it shall register the trustees[2] and issue a certificate in the prescribed form.

---

**Notes**
**Section 595**

1. "Commission" " means the Corporate Affairs Commission established under section 1 of this Act. See **section 567 CAMA, Cap. C20, LFN 2004.**
2. "Trustee" means one having legal title to property and holds it in trust for the benefit of another and owes a fiduciary duty to that beneficiary. **See Garner B. (d.) Black's Law Dictionary 8 th ed.**

**Cross Reference**

On effect of registration and issue of certificate, **see section 596 CAMA Cap. C20, LFN 2004**

---

## 596. Effect of registration and certificate

(1) From the date of registration, the trustee [1] or trustees[1] shall become a body corporate by the name described in the certificate, and shall have perpetual succession and a common seal, [2] and power to sue and be sued in its corporate name as such trustee [1] or trustees[1] and subject to section 602 of this Part of this Act to hold and acquire, and transfer, assign or otherwise dispose of any property, or interests therein belonging to, or held for the benefit of such association, in such manner and subject to such restrictions and provisions as the trustees might without incorporation, hold or acquire, transfer, assign or otherwise dispose of the same for the purposes of such community, body or association of persons.

(2) The certificate of incorporation shall vest in the body corporate all property and interests of whatever nature or tenure belonging to or held by any person in trust for such community, body or association of persons.

(3) A certificate of incorporation when granted shall be prima facie evidence that all the preliminary requisitions herein contained and required in respect of such incorporation have been complied with, and the date of incorporation mentioned in such certificate shall be deemed to be the date on which incorporation has taken place.

---

**Notes**

**Section 596**

1. "Trustee" means one having legal title to property and holds it in trust for the benefit of another and owes a fiduciary duty to that beneficiary. See **Garner B. (ed.) Black's Law Dictionary 8 th ed.**
2. "Common seal" means a piece of wax, a wafer, or some other substance affixed to the paper or other material on which a promise or release, or conveyance is written together with recital or expression of intention by which the promisor, releasor, or grantor manifest that a piece of wax, wafer, or other substance is a seal. **Garner B. (ed.) Black's Law Dictionary 8th ed.**

Cross Reference

On effect of use of common seal, see **section 604 CAMA Cap. C20, LFN 2004.**

---

**Cases**

The effect of incorporation or registration of a company,firm, etc is to confer on it legal entity as a person separate and distinct from its members. It is a legal person with personality of its own. It is more than a mere association of individuals. It becomes an artificial legal entity once the formal procedure of registration or incorporation has been complied with. See ***Rufus Iwuajoku Onuekwusi & 8 Ors. v. The Registered Trustees of the Christ Methodist Zion Church (2011) LPELR SC 58/***

## 597. Changes of names or objects

(1) Where the association is desirous of changing or altering its name or objects or any of them, the trustees [1] shall apply to the Commission[2] in the prescribed form setting out the alterations desired and attaching a copy of the resolution [3] approving the change and duly certified by the trustees [1].

(2) The Commission[2] on receipt of the application shall consider it and, if satisfied that the change or alteration is prima facie lawful shall-

(a) cause the application to be published in two daily newspapers in the manner specified in subsection (1) of section 593 of this Act; and

(b) direct the corporation to display for at least 28 days a notice of the proposed change or alteration conspicuously mounted at the corporation headquarters, or at any branch offices, or any such places where a majority of the members are likely to see it, as the Commission [2] may require,

(3) The publication and notices shall call for objections which, if any, shall state the grounds of objection and be forwarded to reach the Commission[2] not later than 28 days after the last of the publications in the newspapers.

(4) The provisions of section 593 and of subsection (1) of section 594 of this Part of this Act shall apply to this section as they apply to an application for registration.

(5) If the Commission assents[2] to the application, the alterations shall be made and in the case of a change of name, the Commission[2] shall issue a new certificate in the new name in place of the former certificate.

---

**Notes**
**Section 597**

1. "Trustee" means one having legal title to property and holds it in trust for the benefit of another and owes a fiduciary duty to that beneficiary. See **Garner B. (ed.) Black's Law Dictionary 8 th ed.**
2. "Commission" means the Corporate Affairs Commission established under section 1 of this Act. See **Section. 567 CAMA, Cap. C20, LFN 2004**
3. "Resolution" means a formal expression of the opinion or will of an official body or a public assembly, adopted by vote as a legislative resolution. **Garner B. (ed.) Black's Law Dictionary 8 th ed.**

Cross Reference

On nature of certificate of incorporation when granted see **section 596(3) CAMA Cap. C20, LFN 2004.**

On types of resolutions, see **section 233 CAMA Cap C20, LFN 2004.**

---

**Cases**

The only admissible evidence of legal capacity of a body corporate is the certificate of incorporation and no other and not even an admission of incorporation by an adverse partyorally, by document or admission in pleadings would be admitted as proof of legal capacity. See ***Ndoma-Egba v. Chukwugor (2004) 26 NWLR (Pt 869) 32*** **, see also** ***NNPC v. Lutin Investment Ltd (2006) CLRN 1***

## 598. Alteration of provisions of the Constitution

Subject to sections 593 and 594 of this Part of this Act, an association whose trustees[1] are incorporated under this Part of this

Act may alter its constitution by a resolution [2] passed by a simple majority of its members and approved by the Commission [3]

---

**Notes**
**Section 598**

1. "Trustee" means one having legal title to property and holds it in trust for the benefit of another and owes a fiduciary duty to that beneficiary.See **Garner B. (ed.) Black's Law Dictionary 8 th ed.**
2. "Resolution" means a formal expression of the opinion or will of an official body or a public assembly, adopted by vote as a legislative resolution. **See Garner B. (ed.) Black's Law Dictionary 8 th ed.**
3. "Commission" means the Corporate Affairs Commission established under section 1 of this Act. See **section 567 CAMA, Cap. C20, LFN 2004**

---

## 599. Replacement and appointment of additional trustees

(1) Where a body or association intends to replace some or all its trustees[1] or to appoint additional trustees, [1] it may by resolution[2] at a general meeting [3] do so and apply in the prescribed form for the approval of the Commission. [4]

(2) Upon such application the provision of subsections (2) to (4) of section 597 of this Act shall apply to this section as they apply to the change of name or object.

(3) If the Commission [4] assents to the application, it shall signify its assent in writing to the corporation and the appointment shall become valid as from the date of the resolution [2] appointing the trustees.[1]

---

**Notes**
**Section 599**

1. "Trustee" means one having legal title to property and holds it in trust for the benefit of another and owes a fiduciary duty to that beneficiary.**See Garner B. (ed.) Black's Law Dictionary 8 th ed.**
2. "Resolution" means a formal expression of the opinion or will of an official body or a public assembly, adopted by vote as a legislative resolution. See **Garner B. (ed.) Black's Law Dictionary 8 th ed.**
3. "General meeting" means a meeting of all the stockholders of a corporation, all the creditors of a bankrupt, etc . **See Garner B. (ed.) Black's Law Dictionary 8th ed.**

4. "Commission" means the Corporate Affairs Commission established under section 1 of this Act . See **Section. 567 CAMA, Cap. C20, LFN 2004.**

---

## 600.Changes in contravention of certain provisions of this Part of this Act

Any change or alterations purported to be made in contravention of section 597, 598 or 599 of this Part of this Act shall be void.

---

**Notes**
**Section 600**
Cross Reference

On changes in the name and objects of the association, see **section 597 CAMA Cap. C20, LFN, 2004.**

On changes to the number of trustees of the association, see **section 599 CAMA Cap. C20, LFN 2004.**

---

## 601. Council or governing body

The association may appoint a council, or governing body, which shall include the trustees [1] and may, subject to the provisions of this Part of this Act, assign to it such administrative and management functions as it deems expedient.

---

**Notes**
**Section 601**

1. "Trustee" means one having legal title to property and holds it in trust for the benefit of another and owes a fiduciary duty to that beneficiary.**See Garner B. (ed.) Black's Law Dictionary 8 th ed.**

Cross Reference

On Qualification of trustees, see **section 592 CAMA Cap. C20, LFN 2004**

---

## 602. Exercise of powers of trustee

The powers vested in the trustees [1] by or under this Act shall be exercised subject to the directions of the association, or of the councilor governing body appointed under section 601 of this Part of this Act, as the case may be.

---

**Notes**
**Section 602**

1. "Trustee" means one having legal title to property and holds it in trust for the benefit of another and owes a fiduciary duty to that beneficiary. See **Garner, B.(ed.) Black's Law Dictionary 8 th ed.**

Cross reference

On appointment of a council or governing body, **see section 601 CAMA Cap. C20, LFN 2004**

---

## 603. Application of income and property

(1) The income and property of a body or association whose trustee[1] or trustees[1] are incorporated under this Part of this Act shall be applied solely towards the promotion of the objects of the body as set forth in its constitution and no portion thereof shall be paid or transferred directly or indirectly, by way of dividend,[2] bonus, or otherwise by way of profit to any of the members of the association.

(2) Nothing in subsection (1) of this section shall prevent the payment, in good faith, of reasonable and proper remuneration to an officer or servant of the body in return for any service actually rendered to the body or association:

Provided that-

(a) with the exception of ex-officio members of the governing council, no member of a council of management or governing body shall be appointed to any salaried office of the body, or any office of the body paid by fees; and

(b) no remuneration or other benefit in money or money's worth shall be given by the body to any member of such councilor governing body, except repayment of out-of-pocket expenses or reasonable and proper rent for premises demised, or let to the body or reasonable fee for services rendered.

(3) If any person knowingly acts or joins in acting in contravention of this section, he shall be liable to refund such income or property so misapplied to the association.

---

**Notes**

**Section 603**

1. "Trustee" means one having legal title to property and holds it in trust for the benefit of another and owes a fiduciary duty to that beneficiary. **Garner B. (ed.) Black's Law Dictionary 8 th ed.**
2. "Dividend" means a portion of the distributed profit of the company which may be a fixed annual percentage, as in the case of preference

share, or it may be variable according to the prosperity or other circumstances of the company, as in the case of equity shares . **See section 567 of CAMA, Cap. C20, LFN 2004.**

**Cross Reference**

On declaration of dividend and payments, see **section 379 CAMA Cap. C20, LFN 2004**

---

## 604. Common seal

The common seal[1] of the body corporate shall have such device as may be approved by the Commission[2]; and any instrument to which the common seal[1] of the corporate body has been affixed in apparent compliance with the regulations for the use of the common seal[1] shall be binding on the corporate body, notwithstanding any defect or circumstance affecting the execution of such instrument.

---

**Notes**

**Section 604**

1. "Common seal" means a piece of wax, a wafer, or some other substance affixed to the paper or other material on which a promise or release, or conveyance is written together with recital or expression of intention by which the promisor, releasor, or grantor manifest that a piece of wax, wafer, or other substance is a seal. **See Garner B. (ed.) Black's Law Dictionary 8th ed.**
2. "Commission" means the Corporate Affairs Commission established under section 1 of this Act. See **Section. 567 CAMA, Cap. C20, LFN 2004.**

---

## 605. Contract of corporate body

Subject to the provisions of this Part of this Act and of the constitution of the association, the corporate body may contract in the same form and manner as an individual.

---

**Notes**

**Section 605**

---

**Cases**

The effect of incorporation or registration of a company,firm, etc is to confer on it legal entity as a person separate and distinct from its members. It is a legal person with personality of its own. It is more than a mere association of individuals. It becomes an artificial legal entity once the formal procedure of registration or incorporation has been complied with. See ***Rufus Iwuajoku Onuekwusi & 8 Ors. v. The Registered Trustees of the Christ Methodist Zion Church (2011) LPELR SC 58/***

## 606. Documents and inspection

(1) The Commission[1] shall preserve all documents[2] delivered to it under this Part of this Act.

(2) Any person may on application to the Commission[1] be permitted to inspect the documents[2] kept under subsection (1) of this section on payment of a prescribed fee and may require a copy or extract of any such document[2] to be certified by the Commission[1] on payment of a prescribed fee.

**Notes**
**Section 606**

1. "Commission" means the Corporate Affairs Commission established under section 1 of this Act. See **Section 567 CAMA, Cap. C20, LFN 2004.**
2. "Documents" includes summons, notice, order and other legal process, and register. See **section 567 CAMA, Cap. C20 , LFN 2004.**

## 607. Annual returns

(1) The trustees[1] of the corporation shall not earlier than 30 June or later than 31 December each year (other than the year in which it is incorporated), submit to the Commission[2] a return showing, among other things, the name of the corporation, the names, addresses and occupations of the trustees,[1] and members of the councilor governing body, particulars of any land held by the corporate body during the year, and of any changes which have taken place in the constitution of the association during the preceding year.

(2) If the trustees[1] fail to comply with subsection (1) of this section they shall be liable to a fine of N5 for each day during which the default continues.

**Notes**
**Section 607**

1. "Trustee" "means one having legal title to property and holds it in trust for the benefit of another and owes a fiduciary duty to that beneficiary. See **Garner B. (ed.) Black's Law Dictionary 8[th] ed.**

2. "Commission" means the Corporate Affairs Commission established under section 1 of this Act. See **section. 567 CAMA, Cap. C20, LFN 2004.**

---

**608.Dissolution of a corporate body formed under this Act**

(1) A body corporate formed under this Part of this Act may be dissolved by the court [1] on a Petition [2] brought for that purpose by-

(a) the governing body or council; or
(b) one or more trustees [3]; or
(c) members of the association constituting not less than 50 per cent of the total membership; or
(d) the Commission [4].

(2) The grounds on which the body corporate may be dissolved are-

(a) that the aims and objects for which it was established have been fuly realised and no useful purpose would be served by keeping the corporation alive;
(b) that the body corporate is formed to exist for a specified period and that period has expired and it is not necessary for it to continue to exist;
(c) that all the aims and objects of the association have become illegal or otherwise contrary to public policy; and
(d) that it is just and equitable in all the circumstances that the body corporate be dissolved.

(3) At the hearing of the petition, [2] all persons whose interest or rights may, in the opinion of the court, [1] be affected by the dissolution shall be put on notice.

(4) If in the event of a winding up [5] or dissolution of the corporate body there remains after the satisfaction of all its debts and liabilities, any property whatsoever, the same shall not be paid to or distributed among the members of the association, but shall be given or transferred to some other institutions having objects similar to the objects of the body, such institutions to be determined by the members of the association at or before the time of dissolution.

(5) If effect cannot be given to the provisions of subsection (4) of this section, the remaining property shall be transferred to some charitable object. [8]

**Notes**
**Section 608**

1. "Court" means the Federal High Court, and to the extent to which application may be made to it as; court includes the Court of Appeal and the Supreme Court of Nigeria. See **Section 567 CAMA, Cap. C20, LFN 2004.**
2. "Petition" means a written address, embodying an application or prayer from the person or persons preferring it, to the power, body, or person to whom it is presented, for the exercise of their authorityin the redress of some wrong, or the grant of some favour, privilege or licence. See **Garner B. (ed.) Black's Law Dictionary 8 th ed.**
3. "Trustee" "means one having legal title to property and holds it in trust for the benefit of another and owes a fiduciary duty to that beneficiary. **See Garner, B.(ed.) Black's Law Dictionary 8 th ed.**
4. "Commission" means the Corporate Affairs Commission established under section 1 of this Act. See **section 567 CAMA, Cap. C20, LFN 2004.**
5. "Winding up" means the process of settling accounts and liquidating assets in anticipation of a partnership or dissolution. See **Garner B. (ed.) Black's Law Dictionary 8 th ed.**
6. "Charitable object" means dedicated to a general public purpose for the benefit of the needy people who cannot pay for benefits received. See **Garner B. (ed) Black's Law Dictionary, 8th ed.**

## 609. Regulations

The Minister[1] may, with the approval of the President, make regulations generally for the purpose of this Part of this Act and, in particular, without prejudice to the generality of the foregoing provisions, make regulations-

(a) prescribing the forms and returns and other information required under this Part of this Act;

(b) prescribing the procedure for obtaining any information required under this Part of this Act;

(c) requiring returns to be made within the period specified therein by any body corporate to which this Part of this Act applies.

**Notes**
**Section 609**

1. "Minister" means the Minister charged with responsibility for trade; and "Ministry" shall be constituted accordingly. S **ee section 567 CAMA, Cap. C20, LFN 2004**

Cross Reference

On the establishment of the Office of the President of Nigeria, see **section 147, Constitution of the Federal Republic of Nigeria( as amended)**

## 610. Interpretation of words used in this Part

In this Part of this Act, unless the context otherwise requires-

"Commission" means the Corporate Affairs Commission stablished under section 1 of this Act;

"court" means the Federal High Court;

"Federal Gazette" means the Federal Government Official Gazette; and

"Minister" means the Minister charged with responsibility for matters relating to trade.

## 611. Repeal of Cap. 98 of 1958 Edition

The Land (Perpetual Succession) Act, is hereby repealed. [Cap. 98 of 1958 Edition.]

## 612. Validity of previous registrations

All trustees[1] duly registered as bodies corporate under the Land (Perpetual Succession) Act shall, as from the date of coming into operation of this Act, be deemed to be registered under and in accordance with this Part of this Act and the provisions of this Part of this Act shall apply in respect of such trustees [1] accordingly.

**Notes**

**Section 612**

"Trustees" means one having legal title to property and holds it in trust for the benefit of another and owes a fiduciary duty to that beneficiary. See **Garner B. (ed.) Black's Law Dictionary 8 th ed.**

**General Index**

The use of *"et seq"* indicates that the issue concerned continues on subsequent pages. The use of *"passim"* after a number indicates that the subject is referred to in scattered pages in the script.

www.ingramcontent.com/pod-product-compliance
Lightning Source LLC
Chambersburg PA
CBHW061351240926
51846CB00007B/1368
* 9 7 8 9 7 8 8 4 0 7 9 5 9 *